Eyke Hüllermeier   Rudolf Kruse
Frank Hoffmann (Eds.)

Computational Intelligence for Knowledge-Based Systems Design

13th International Conference
on Information Processing and Management
of Uncertainty, IPMU 2010
Dortmund, Germany, June 28 - July 2, 2010
Proceedings

 Springer

Series Editors

Randy Goebel, University of Alberta, Edmonton, Canada
Jörg Siekmann, University of Saarland, Saarbrücken, Germany
Wolfgang Wahlster, DFKI and University of Saarland, Saarbrücken, Germany

Volume Editors

Eyke Hüllermeier
Philipps-Universität Marburg, Fachbereich Mathematik und Informatik
Hans-Meerwein-Str., 35032 Marburg, Germany
E-mail: eyke@mathematik.uni-marburg.de

Rudolf Kruse
Otto-von-Guericke-Universität Magdeburg, Fakultät Informatik
Universitätsplatz 2, 39106 Magdeburg, Germany
E-mail: kruse@iws.cs.uni-magdeburg.de

Frank Hoffmann
Technische Universität Dortmund
Fakultät für Elektrotechnik und Informationstechnik
Otto-Hahn-Str. 4, 44227 Dortmund, Germany
E-mail: hoffmann@tu-dortmund.de

Library of Congress Control Number: 2010929051

CR Subject Classification (1998): I.2, H.3, F.1, H.4, I.5, I.4

LNCS Sublibrary: SL 7 – Artificial Intelligence

ISSN 0302-9743

ISBN 978-3-642-14048-8   ISBN 978-3-642-14049-5 (eBook)

DOI 10.1007/978-3-642-14049-5

springer.com

© Springer-Verlag Berlin Heidelberg 2010

Typesetting: Camera-ready by author, data conversion by Scientific Publishing Services, Chennai, India
Printed on acid-free paper   06/3180

Lecture Notes in Artificial Intelligence   6178

Edited by R. Goebel, J. Siekmann, and W. Wahlster

Subseries of Lecture Notes in Computer Science

Preface

The International Conference on Information Processing and Management of Uncertainty in Knowledge-Based Systems, IPMU, is organized every two years with the aim of bringing together scientists working on methods for the management of uncertainty and aggregation of information in intelligent systems. Since 1986, this conference has been providing a forum for the exchange of ideas between theoreticians and practitioners working in these areas. The 13th IPMU conference took place in Dortmund, Germany, June 28–July 2, 2010.

This volume contains 77 papers selected through a rigorous reviewing process among 320 submissions from 36 countries. The contributions reflect the richness of research in the field of computational intelligence and represent several important developments, specifically focused on the following subfields:

(a) machine learning, data mining, and pattern recognition,
(b) uncertainty handling,
(c) aggregation and fusion of information,
(d) logic and knowledge processing.

We were delighted that Melanie Mitchell (Portland State University, USA), Nihkil R. Pal (Indian Statistical Institute), Bernhard Schölkopf (Max Planck Institute for Biological Cybernetics, Tübingen, Germany) and Wolfgang Wahlster (German Research Center for Artificial Intelligence, Saarbrücken) accepted our invitations to present keynote lectures. Jim Bezdek received the Kampé de Fériet Award, granted every two years on the occasion of the IPMU conference, in view of his eminent research contributions to the handling of uncertainty in clustering, data analysis and pattern recognition.

Organizing a conference like this one is not possible without the assistance and continuous support of many people and institutions. We are particularly grateful to the organizers of sessions on dedicated topics that took place during the conference—these 'special sessions' have always been a characteristic element of the IPMU conference. Frank Klawonn and Thomas Runkler helped a lot to evaluate and select special session proposals. The special session organizers themselves rendered important assistance in the reviewing process, that was furthermore supported by the Area Chairs and regular members of the Programme Committee. Thomas Fober has been the backbone on several organizational and electronic issues, and also helped with the preparation of the proceedings. In this regard, we would also like to thank Alfred Hofmann and Springer for providing continuous assistance and ready advice whenever needed.

Finally, we gratefully acknowledge the support of several organizations and institutions, notably the German Informatics Society (Gesellschaft für Informatik, GI), the German Research Foundation (DFG), the European Society for Fuzzy Logic and Technology (EUSFLAT), the International Fuzzy Systems Association (IFSA), the North American Fuzzy Information Processing Society (NAFIPS) and the IEEE Computational Intelligence Society.

April 2010   Eyke Hüllermeier
                                                                Rudolf Kruse
                                                               Frank Hoffmann

Organization

Conference Committee

General Chair Eyke Hüllermeier (Philipps-Universität Marburg)
Co-chairs   Frank Hoffmann (Technische Universität Dortmund)
               Rudolf Kruse (Otto-von-Guericke Universität Magdeburg)
               Frank Klawonn (Hochschule Braunschweig-Wolfenbüttel)
               Thomas Runkler (Siemens AG, München)
Web Chair   Thomas Fober (Philipps-Universität Marburg)
Executive
   Directors   Bernadette Bouchon-Meunier (LIP6, Paris, France)
               Ronald R. Yager (Iona College, USA)

International Advisory Board

G. Coletti, Italy	C. Marsala, France	L. Valverde, Spain
M. Delgado, Spain	M. Ojeda-Aciego, Spain	J.L. Verdegay, Spain
L. Foulloy, France	M. Rifqi, France	M.A. Vila, Spain
J. Gutierrez-Rios, Spain	L. Saitta, Italy	L.A. Zadeh, USA
L. Magdalena, Spain	E. Trillas, Spain	

Special Session Organizers

P. Angelov	F. Hoffmann	B. Prados Suárez
A. Antonucci	S. Kaci	M. Preuß
C. Beierle	J. Kacprzyk	A. Ralescu
G. Beliakov	G. Kern-Isberner	D. Ralescu
G. Bordogna	C. Labreuche	E. Reucher
A. Bouchachia	H. Legind Larsen	W. Rödder
H. Bustince	E. William De Luca	S. Romaní
T. Calvo	E. Lughofer	G. Rudolph
P. Carrara	E. Marchioni	G. Ruß
J. Chamorro Martínez	N. Marin	D. Sanchez
D. Coquin	M. Minoh	R. Seising
T. Denoeux	G. Navarro-Arribas	A. Skowron
P. Eklund	H. Son Nguyen	D. Slezak
Z. Elouedi	V. Novak	O. Strauss
M. Fedrizzi	P. Melo Pinto	E. Szmidt
J. Fernandez	E. Miranda	S. Termini
T. Flaminio	V.A. Niskanen	V. Torra
L. Godo	D. Ortiz-Arroyo	L. Valet
M. Grabisch	I. Perfilieva	A. Valls
A.J. Grichnik	O. Pons	R.R. Yager

International Programme Committee

Area Chairs

P. Bosc, France
O. Cordon, Spain
G. De Cooman, Belgium
T. Denoeux, France
R. Felix, Germany

L. Godo, Spain
F. Gomide, Spain
M. Grabisch, France
F. Herrera, Spain
L. Magdalena, Spain

R. Mesiar, Slovenia
D. Sanchez, Spain
R. Seising, Spain
R. Slowinski, Poland

Regular Members

P. Angelov, UK
J.A. Appriou, France
M. Baczynski, Poland
G. Beliakov, Australia
S. Ben Yahia, Tunisia
S. Benferat, France
H. Berenji, USA
J. Bezdek, USA
I. Bloch, France
U. Bodenhofer, Austria
P. P. Bonissone, USA
C. Borgelt, Spain
H. Bustince, Spain
R. Casadio, Italy
Y. Chalco-Cano, Chile
C.A. Coello Coello,
  Mexico
I. Couso, Spain
B. De Baets, Belgium
G. De Tré, Belgium
M. Detyniecki, France
D. Dubois, France
F. Esteva, Spain
M. Fedrizzi, Italy
J. Fodor, Hungary
D. Fogel, USA
K. Fujimoto, Japan
P. Gallinari, France
B. Gerla, Italy
M.A. Gil, Spain
S. Gottwald, Germany
S. Grossberg, USA

P. Hajek,
  Czech Republic
L. Hall, USA
E. Herrera-Viedma,
  Spain
C. Noguera, Spain
K. Hirota, Japan
A. Hunter, UK
H. Ishibuchi, Japan
Y. Jin, Germany
J. Kacprzyk, Poland
A. Kandel, USA
G. Kern-Isberner,
  Germany
E.P. Klement, Austria
L. Koczy, Hungary
V. Kreinovich, USA
T. Kroupa,
  Czech Republic
C. Labreuche, France
J. Lang, France
P. Larranaga, Spain
H. Larsen, Denmark
A. Laurent, France
M.J. Lesot, France
C.J. Liau, Taiwan
W. Lodwick, USA
J.A. Lozano, Spain
T. Lukasiewicz, UK
F. Marcelloni, Italy
J.L. Marichal,
  Luxembourg

N. Marin, Spain
T. Martin, UK
L. Martinez, Spain
J. Medina, Spain
J. Mendel, USA
E. Miranda, Spain
P. Miranda, Spain
J. Montero, Spain
S. Moral, Spain
M. Nachtegael, Belgium
Y. Nojima, Japan
V. Novak,
  Czech Republic
H. Nurmi, Finland
E. Pap, Serbia
W. Pedrycz, Canada
F. Petry, USA
V. Piuri, Italy
O. Pivert, France
P. Poncelet, France
H. Prade, France
A. Ralescu, USA
D. Ralescu, USA
M. Ramdani, Morocco
M. Reformat, Canada
D. Ruan, Belgium
E. Ruspini, USA
R. Scozzafava, Italy
P. Shenoy, USA
G. Simari, Argentina
P. Sobrevilla, Spain
U. Straccia, Italy

Table of Contents

Machine Learning and Data Mining

Similarity and Instinguishability

Clustering and Classification

Statistics with Imprecise Data

Data Analysis

Data Mining Applications

Aggregation and Fusion

Aggregation

Information Fusion

Integrals

Preference Modeling

Uncertainty Handling

Fuzzy Methods

Bayesian Networks

Belief Functions

Logics

Towards a Conscious Choice of a Fuzzy Similarity Measure: A Qualitative Point of View

Bernadette Bouchon-Meunier[1], Giulianella Coletti[2],
Marie-Jeanne Lesot[1], and Maria Rifqi[1]

[1] Université Pierre et Marie Curie - Paris 6, CNRS UMR 7606, LIP6,
104 avenue du Président Kennedy, F-75016 Paris, France
{Bernadette.Bouchon-Meunier,Marie-Jeanne.Lesot,Maria.Rifqi}@lip6.fr
[2] Dipartimento Matematica e Informatica, Università di Perugia,
Via Vanvitelli 1, 06123 Perugia, Italy
coletti@dipmat.unipg.it

Abstract. In this paper, we propose to study similarity measures among fuzzy subsets from the point of view of the ranking relation they induce on object pairs. Using a classic method in measurement theory, introduced by Tversky, we establish necessary and sufficient conditions for the existence of a class of numerical similarity measures, to represent a given ordering relation, depending on the axioms this relation satisfies.

Keywords: Fuzzy similarity, comparison measure, ordering relation, representability, weak independence conditions.

1 Introduction

Similarity is a key concept in artificial intelligence [12] and similarity measures have been extensively studied (see [7,14,2,1], see also the surveys [5,8]). The choice of an appropriate measure when facing a particular problem to solve is a central issue. Now, due to the subjective characteristic of similarity as used by human beings, it is more intuitive to compare measures depending on the order they induce rather than the numerical values they take. Therefore, trying to get closer to the human reasoning, we propose to consider an ordinal view on similarity measures. To that aim, we follow the approach proposed by Tversky [14] and applied later in [3], in the framework of measurement theory: it starts from a *comparative similarity* $\preceq$, defined as a binary relation on object pairs, and studies the conditions under which $\preceq$ can be represented by a numerical similarity measure. It establishes representation theorems that state necessary and sufficient conditions under which a given comparative similarity is represented by a specific form of numerical similarity measures.

Previous works [14,3] considered the crisp case of presence/ absence data, we focus in this paper on fuzzy data: for any object, the presence of an attribute is not binary but measured by a membership degree in [0,1]. Considering such fuzzy data raises several difficulties due to the associated softness and change continuity: in the crisp case, for any object pair and any attribute, only four

E. Hüllermeier, R. Kruse, and F. Hoffmann (Eds.): IPMU 2010, LNAI 6178, pp. 1–10, 2010.

configurations can occur, namely whether the attribute is present in both objects, absent from both, or present in one object but not the other one. Moreover, only two kinds of modifications can occur, changing an attribute presence to an absence or reciprocally. In the fuzzy case, all modifications are continuous, and it is not possible to identify a finite set of distinct configurations. Thus matching the ordinal view of similarity with the numerical one requires the definition of new properties and axioms to characterise the possible behaviors of comparative similarity. Furthermore, in the fuzzy framework, similarity measures cannot be reduced to their general form: they also depend on the choice of a t-norm and a complementation operator, to define the membership degrees to the intersection and the complement of fuzzy sets respectively. Indeed, as illustrated in Section 2, changing the t-norm can lead to very different comparative relations for a given similarity measure form and a given fuzzy measure. This implies that the axioms we introduce to characterise comparative similarities depend on the t-norm choice. We consider the three most common t-norms (min, product and Łukasiewicz t-norm) and characterise the comparative similarities representable by (or agreeing with) a class of similarity measures containing as particular elements Jaccard, Dice, Sorensen, Anderberg and Sokal-Sneath measures.

The paper is organised as follows: in Section 2, we recall the definitions of similarity measure representation and equivalence and we introduce basic axioms, in particular those expressing constraints in terms of attribute uniformity and monotonicity. Section 3 presents the considered independence axiom that is required to establish, in Section 4, the representation theorem.

2   From Numerical Similarity to Comparative Similarity

In this section, after introducing the notations used throughout the paper, we discuss the classic definition of equivalence between numerical similarity measures and establish basic axioms satisfied by comparative similarities induced from given classes of numerical similarities, following the ideas of Tversky to study similarity using the framework of measurement theory [14].

2.1   Preliminaries

We consider that each object is described by p attributes, i.e. by the set of characteristics from the predefined list $\mathcal{A}$, which can be present with different degrees of membership: any object is a fuzzy subset of $\mathcal{A}$. The data set is noted $\mathcal{X} = [0,1]^p$: any $X \in \mathcal{X}$ is written $X = (x_1, ..., x_p)$, $x_i \in [0,1]$, and associated with $s_X = \{i : x_i > 0\}$; $\underline{0}$ denotes the object with $s_X = \emptyset$. We consider a t-norm $\top$ and its dual t-conorm $\bot$ and the complement $X^c = 1 - X$. We define, as usual, $X \cap Y = X \top Y$, $X \setminus Y = X \top Y^c$ and $Y \setminus X = Y \top X^c$. We say that X^* is a *strong $\top$-complement* of X if $s_{X \cap X^*} = \emptyset$, when the intersection is ruled by the t-norm $\top$.

For any $0 \le \delta \le x_i$ and $0 \le \eta \le 1 - x_i$ we denote by $x_i^{-\delta} = x_i - \delta$, by $x_i^{\eta} = x_i + \eta$, and by $X_k^{-\delta} = \{x_1, ..., x_k^{-\delta}, ..., x_p\}$. Lastly, given η such that $0 \le \eta \le \min_i(1 - x_i)$, we note $X^{\eta} = \{x_1^{\eta}, ..., x_p^{\eta}\}$.

We indicate by m a measure of fuzzy sets, only depending on the values of the membership and not on the values of the considered domain, for instance $m(X) = \Sigma_i x_i$ ($m(X) = \int_{s_X} X(t)dt$ in the infinite case). Given $X, Y \in \mathcal{X}$, we note $\mathbf{x} = m(X \cap Y), \mathbf{y}^+ = m(X \setminus Y), \mathbf{y}^- = m(Y \setminus X)$ and $\mathbf{y} = \mathbf{y}^+ + \mathbf{y}^-$.

We then consider a *comparative similarity*, defined as a binary relation $\preceq$ on $\mathcal{X}^2$, with the following meaning: for $X, Y, X', Y' \in \mathcal{X}$, $(X, Y) \preceq (X', Y')$ means that X is similar to Y no more than X' is similar to Y'.

The relations $\sim$ and $\prec$ are then induced by $\preceq$ as: $(X, Y) \sim (X', Y')$ if $(X, Y) \preceq (X', Y')$ and $(X', Y') \preceq (X, Y)$, meaning that X is similar to Y as X' is similar to Y'. Lastly $(X, Y) \prec (X', Y')$ if $(X, Y) \preceq (X', Y')$ holds, but not $(X', Y') \preceq (X, Y)$. If $\preceq$ is complete, then $\sim$ and $\prec$ are the symmetrical and the asymmetrical parts of $\preceq$ respectively.

We now introduce the notion of representability for such a comparative similarity by a numerical similarity measure:

Definition 1. *Given a comparative similarity $\preceq$, a similarity measure $S : \mathcal{X}^2 \to \mathbb{R}$ represents $\preceq$ if and only if $\forall (X, Y), (X', Y') \in \mathcal{X}^2$*

$$(X, Y) \preceq (X', Y') \Leftrightarrow S(X, Y) \leq S(X', Y')$$

It is important to notice that in a fuzzy context, if the similarity measure involves the intersection, union or difference of the fuzzy sets whose similarity is studied, then we need to consider also the particular t-norm and t-conorm we choose: the induced comparative similarity can change for different choices of t-norm and t-conorm, as the following example shows: let us consider $\mathcal{X} = [0, 1]^4$, $X = (0, 0, 2/10, 3/10)$, $Y = (0, 0, 4/10, 1/10)$, $U = (0, 7/10, 0, 2/10)$, $V = (0, 0, 3/10, 9/10)$, $W = (0, 0, 1/10, 3/10)$, $Z = (0, 2/10, 4/10, 0)$. As a fuzzy measure, we choose $m(X) = \Sigma_i x_i$ and as a similarity measure

$$S = S_\rho(X, Y) = \frac{\mathbf{x}}{\mathbf{x} + \rho \mathbf{y}} \tag{1}$$

with $\rho = 1$ and we indicate by S_T the measure S when we choose the t-norm T.

If we adopt min as a t-norm, then we obtain: $S_m(X, Y) - 3/13 > S_m(U, V) - 2/21 > S_m(Z, W) = 1/11$, and so $(Z, W) \prec (U, V) \prec (X, Y)$;

If we adopt Łukasiewicz t-norm, we obtain: $S_L(U, V) = 1/18 > S_L(X, Y) = S_L(Z, W) = 0$, and so $(X, Y) \sim (Z, W) \prec (U, V)$;

If we adopt the product as t-norm, we obtain: $S_p(X, Y) = 11/89 > S_p(U, V) = 3/32 > S_p(Z, W) = 1/24$, and so $(Z, W) \prec (X, Y) \prec (U, V)$.

2.2   Similarity Measure Equivalence

Any similarity measure on $\mathcal{X}^2$ induces a comparative similarity $\preceq$, defined as follows: $(X, Y) \prec (X', Y')$ if $S(X, Y) < S(X', Y')$ and $(X, Y) \sim (X', Y')$ if $S(X, Y) = S(X', Y')$.

Now the same ordering relation is induced by any similarity measure that can be expressed as an increasing transformation of S: any similarity measure

$S' = \varphi(S)$, with $\varphi : \mathbb{R} \to \mathbb{R}$ strictly increasing is also a representation of $\preceq$. Moreover, no other measure represents $\preceq$, as shown in [9,10]. Thus, from a comparative point of view, all functions $\varphi(S)$ are indistinguishable. Formally speaking, the relation r defined on the set of similarity measures as SrS' if and only if S and S' induce the same comparative similarity on $\mathcal{X}$ is an equivalence relation. An equivalent formulation of this concept is given in [9,10].

The similarity measures defined by Equation 1, with $\rho > 0$, are all equivalent, since each of them is an increasing transformation of any other. In particular, the Jaccard ($\rho = 1$), Dice ($\rho = 1/2$), Sorensen ($\rho = 1/4$), Anderberg ($\rho = 1/8$) and Sokal and Sneath ($\rho = 2$) measures are equivalent.

The same class also contains the function $S(X, Y) = \log(\mathbf{x}) - \log(\mathbf{y})$, which is of the kind proposed by Tversky [14]: S is an increasing transformation of $S'(X, Y) = \mathbf{x}/\mathbf{y}$ which is an increasing transformation of S_1.

It is to be noted that the function $S(X, Y) = \alpha \log(\mathbf{x}) - \beta \log(\mathbf{y})$ for $\alpha, \beta > 0$ is not in the same class, but it is equivalent to all measures

$$S_\rho^*(X, Y) = \frac{\mathbf{x}^\alpha}{\mathbf{x}^\alpha + \rho \mathbf{y}^\beta}$$

Obviously all these considerations hold for any particular choice of t-norm.

2.3   Basic Axioms

We are now interested in a different classification of similarity measures: instead of considering the measures that induce the same order, we consider the measures that induce orders satisfying the same class of axioms. In this section, we consider axioms that lead to preliminary results regarding relations between similarity measures and comparative similarity.

The first two axioms we introduce describe basic properties a binary relation has to satisfy to define a comparative similarity: the first one only states the relation must be a weak order and the uncountable set $\mathcal{X}$ has a countable subset thoroughly interspersed.

Axiom S1 [weak order]
    The relation $\preceq$ defined on $\mathcal{X}$ is a weak order, i.e it is complete, reflexive and transitive.
    There exists a countable set $\mathcal{Y} \subseteq \mathcal{X}$ which is dense in $\mathcal{X}$ with respect to $\preceq$.

We recall that any comparative structure representable by a real function satisfies S1 (see for instance [6], Theorem 2). We note that if we require that the membership values are rational (and so in particular in the crisp case), then the second part of S1 is automatically satisfied, since in this case $\mathcal{X}$ itself is countable.

The second axiom expresses boundary conditions.

Axiom S2 [boundary conditions]
    $\forall X, X', Y, Y' \in \mathcal{X}$, with $s_{X \cap X'} = s_{Y \cap Y'} = \emptyset$
    $(X, X') \sim (Y, Y') \preceq (X, Y) \preceq (X, X) \sim (Y, Y)$

Axiom S2 requires that any X differs from any Y no more than from its strong $\top$-complements, and not less than itself and it imposes that X is similar to itself as Y is to itself.

It is obvious that S2 strictly depends on the chosen t-norm: in particular for min and product the class of minimal elements coincides with the class of elements such that $s_X \cap s_{X'} = s_Y \cap s_{Y'} = \emptyset$. For Łukasiewicz t-norm it is larger, since we can obtain 0 also starting from two positive values. The axiom moreover implies that, if the membership of the intersection of two object descriptions is null, then it is indifferent whether the attributes are absent of both objects or present in one of them, with any degree of membership. In particular, if we use Łukasiewicz t-norm, two objects having all attributes in common, but with the sum of involved degrees less than 1, are as similar as two objects having each attribute completely present in one of them and completely absent from the other one. This makes a major difference with the crisp case.

The third axiom imposes a symmetry condition.

Axiom S3 [symmetry]
$\forall X, Y \in \mathcal{X}, (X, Y) \sim (Y, X)$

These properties lead to the following two definitions:

Definition 2. *A binary relation $\preceq$ on $\mathcal{X}^2$ is a comparative fuzzy similarity if and only if it satisfies axioms S1 and S2.*

Definition 3. *A comparative fuzzy similarity is symmetric if and only if it satisfies axiom S3.*

The next axiom, named attribute uniformity, examines the conditions under which the attributes can be considered as having the same role with respect to the comparative similarity, i.e. the conditions under which a modification in one attribute is equivalent to the modification of another attribute. In the crisp case, this axiom only has to consider two kinds of modifications, changing an attribute presence to an absence or reciprocally. Moreover, it only has to examine the four categories the attributes belong to (whether they are present in both objects, absent from both, or present in one object but not the other one). In the fuzzy case, all modifications are continuous and their effects cannot be simply expressed as a transition between such categories. The attribute uniformity axiom depends on the considered t-norm that determines the admissible modifications to be considered. Thus the axiom takes three formulations detailed below.

Axiom $S4_{min}$ [attribute uniformity]
$\forall h, k \in \{1, ..., p\}$, such that $x_h \geq y_h$ and $x_k \geq y_k$, and $x_h \geq 1 - y_h$ and $x_k \geq 1 - y_k$
and for all real numbers $\varepsilon, \eta, \vartheta, \gamma$, with
$0 \leq \varepsilon \leq \min_{i=h,k}\{(x_i - y_i), (y_i + x_i - 1)\}$; $0 \leq \eta \leq \min_{i=h,k}\{(1 - x_i)\}$,
$0 \leq \vartheta \leq \min_{i=h,k}\{(y_i + x_i - 1)\}$; $0 \leq \gamma \leq \min_{i=h,k}\{(x_i - y_i)\}$.
one has:

$$(X_k^{-\varepsilon}, Y) \sim (X_h^{-\varepsilon}, Y), \quad (X_k^{\eta}, Y) \sim (X_h^{\eta}, Y)$$
$$(X, Y_k^{-\vartheta}) \sim (X, Y_h^{-\vartheta}), \quad (X, Y_k^{\gamma}) \sim (X, Y_h^{\gamma})$$

The same condition holds for $x_h \leq 1 - y_h$ and $x_k \leq 1 - y_k$ and
$0 \leq \varepsilon \leq \min_{i=h,k}\{(x_i - y_i)\}$; $0 \leq \eta \leq \min_{i=h,k}\{(1 - y_i - x_i)\}$ $0 \leq \vartheta \leq$ $\min_{i=h,k}\{(y_i)\}$; $0 \leq \gamma \leq \min_{i=h,k}\{(x_i - y_i), (1 - y_i - x_i)\}$.

Moreover for $\alpha \leq (x_k - y_k)$ if $x_h \geq 1 - y_h$ and $x_k \geq 1 - y_k$, and $\alpha \leq \min\{(x_k - y_k), (1 - y_k - x_k)\}$ if $x_h \leq 1 - y_h$ and $x_k \leq 1 - y_k$, one has:

$$(X, Y) \sim (X, (Y_h^{-\alpha})_k^\alpha).$$

Axiom $S4_p$ [attribute uniformity] $\forall h, k \in \{1, ..., p\}$, such that $y_k = y_h$, and for all real numbers ε, η, with $0 \leq \varepsilon \leq \min_{i=h,k}\{x_i\}$, $0 \leq \eta \leq \min_{i=h,k}\{1 - x_i\}$, one has:

$$(X_k^{-\varepsilon}, Y) \sim (X_h^{-\varepsilon}, Y); \quad (X_k^\eta, Y) \sim (X_h^\eta, Y)$$

A symmetric condition holds if $x_k = x_h$.
Moreover $((X_h^{-\varepsilon})_k^\varepsilon, Y) \sim (X, Y)$.

Axiom $S4_L$ [attribute uniformity] $\forall h, k \in \{1, ..., p\}$, such that $y_i < x_i$, $x_i \geq 1 - y_i$ $i = h, k$, and for all real numbers ε, γ, with
$0 \leq \varepsilon \leq \min_{i=h,k}\{(x_i - y_i), (y_i + x_i - 1)\}$; $0 \leq \gamma \leq \min_{i=h,k}\{(x_i - y_i)\}$.
one has

$$(X_k^{-\varepsilon}, Y) \sim (X_h^{-\varepsilon}, Y); \quad (X, Y_k^\gamma) \sim (X, Y_h^\gamma).$$

The same condition holds for $x_i \leq 1 - y_i$ and $x_i \leq 1 - y_i$, $i = h, k$, and
$0 \leq \varepsilon \leq \min_{i=h,k}\{(x_i - y_i)\}$ $0 \leq \gamma \leq \min_{i=h,k}\{(x_i - y_i), (1 - y_i - x_i)\}$.

We can prove the following Proposition:

Proposition 1. *Let us consider on $\mathcal{X}^2$ the t-norm $\top$ ($\top = min, p, L$) and the comparative fuzzy similarity $\preceq$ satisfying Axiom $S4_\top$. If $m : \mathcal{X}^2 \to \mathbb{R}$ is a fuzzy measure such that $m(X) = \varphi(\sum_i x_i)$ with φ an increasing real function, then the following condition holds:*

if for (X, Y, Z) one has $\mathbf{x} = \mathbf{z}$, $\mathbf{x}^- = \mathbf{z}^-$ and $\mathbf{x}^+ = \mathbf{z}^+$ then $(X, Y) \sim (Z, Y)$

Proof: let us consider the case $\top = min$. First we note that, starting from (X, Y), we can obtain (Z, Y) with a sequence of steps as those considered in $S4_{min}$. For each of them, we have equivalent pairs or pairs with the same values for $\mathbf{x}$, $\mathbf{x}^-$ and $\mathbf{x}^+$. We prove this in the case $(X_k^{-\varepsilon}, Y)$ and $(X_h^{-\varepsilon}, Y)$, with $x_h \geq 1 - y_h$ and $x_k \geq 1 - y_k$: we have in fact: $m(X_k^{-\varepsilon} \cap Y) = m(X_h^{-\varepsilon} \cap Y) = m(X \cap Y)$; $m(X_k^{-\varepsilon} \setminus Y) = m(X_h^{-\varepsilon} \setminus Y) = m(X \setminus Y)$; $m(Y \setminus X_k^{-\varepsilon}) = m(Y \setminus X_h^{-\varepsilon}) = m(X \setminus Y) + \varepsilon$. Similar proofs can be obtained for the other cases.

It must be underlined also that this axiom is satisfied by any comparative similarity representable by a similarity measure, only depending on $\mathbf{x} = m(X \cap Y), \mathbf{y}^+ = m(X \setminus Y), \mathbf{y}^- = m(Y \setminus X)$ and $\mathbf{y} = \mathbf{y}^+ + \mathbf{y}^-$, where m is a measure of fuzzy sets, depending on the values of the membership and not on the values of the considered domain. Reciprocally, any comparative similarity satisfying S4 can be represented by a function depending only on $\mathbf{x}, \mathbf{y}^+, \mathbf{y}^-$.

2.4 Monotonicity Axioms

The following three axioms of monotonicity govern the comparative similarity among pairs differing in a different degree of belonging of only one attribute, successively for the three considered t-norms.

Axiom $S5_{min}$ [monotonicity] $\forall X, Y \in \mathcal{X}, X \neq Y$
$\forall k, h, j \in s_X \cap s_Y$, such that $y_r > x_r, (r = k, h), x_j > y_j, 1 - x_s < y_s, (s = k, j), 1 - x_h > y_h$ (so $y_k, x_j > 1/2, x_h < 1/2$).
For any $0 < \varepsilon < \min\{x_h, x_k, y_j, 2(y_h + x_h - 1), (y_k + x_k - 1)/2, (x_j + y_j - 1)\}$, one has:

$$(X_k^{-\varepsilon}, Y_k^{-\varepsilon}) \prec (X, Y_j^{-\varepsilon}) \sim (X_k^{-\varepsilon}, Y) \prec ((X_k^{-\varepsilon/2})_h^{-\varepsilon/2}, Y) \prec (X, Y).$$

This axiom means that if an attribute in the support of both objects, i.e. possessed to a certain extent by both objects, is modified in a way that, for the object in which the attribute is "less present", the degree of belonging is decreased, then the modified objects are less similar one to another than the initial objects were. This corresponds to a strong semantic choice: it implies that the common strong presence of an attribute is preferred to a common light presence. Moreover, the axiom states that modifying both objects degrades the similarity more than changing only one of them. In particular we notice that, for the fuzzy measure $m : \mathcal{X}^2 \to \mathbb{R}$ with $m(X) = (\sum_i x_i)$, we have:
$m(Y \cap X) > m(X_k^{-\varepsilon} \cap Y_k^{-\varepsilon}) = m(X_k^{-\varepsilon} \cap Y) = m(X \cap Y_j^{-\varepsilon}) = m((X_k^{-\varepsilon/2})_h^{-\varepsilon/2} \cap Y) = m(X \cap Y) - \varepsilon;$
and
$m(X_k^{-\varepsilon} \setminus Y_k^{-\varepsilon}) + m(Y_k^{-\varepsilon} \setminus X_k^{-\varepsilon}) = m(X \setminus Y) + m(Y \setminus X) + 2\varepsilon > m(X_k^{-\varepsilon} \setminus Y) + m(Y \setminus X_k^{-\varepsilon}) = m(X \setminus Y_j^{-\varepsilon}) + m(Y_j^{-\varepsilon} \setminus X) = m(X \setminus Y) + m(Y \setminus X) + \varepsilon > m((X_k^{-\varepsilon/2})_h^{-\varepsilon/2} \setminus Y) + m(Y \setminus (X_k^{-\varepsilon/2})_h^{-\varepsilon/2}) = m(X \setminus Y) + m(Y \setminus X)$

Axiom $S5_p$ [monotonicity] $\forall X, Y \in \mathcal{X}, X \neq Y$
$\forall k, j, r \in s_X \cap s_Y$, such that $y_k = x_j \geq 1/2$ $x_r < y_k$ and $\forall \varepsilon, \eta, \gamma$ with $\varepsilon, \eta \leq y_k$, and $\varepsilon y_k = \eta y_k + \gamma x_r$ one has:
$$(X_k^{-\eta}, Y_r^{-\gamma}) \prec (X, Y_j^{-\varepsilon}) \sim (X_k^{-\varepsilon}, Y) \sim (X_k^{-\varepsilon/2}, Y_j^{-\varepsilon/2}) \prec (Y, X)$$

Considerations similar to those made for $S5_{min}$ hold, in particular it is easy to see that in this case: $m(Y \cap X) > m(X_k^{-\eta} \cap Y_r^{-\gamma}) = m(X_k^{-\varepsilon} \cap Y) = m(X \cap Y_j^{-\varepsilon}) = m(X_k^{-\varepsilon/2} \cap Y_j^{-\varepsilon/2}) = m(X \cap Y) - \varepsilon y_k;$
and
$m(X_k^{-\eta} \setminus Y_r^{-\gamma}) + m(Y_r^{-\gamma} \setminus X_k^{-\eta}) = m(Y \setminus X) + m(X \setminus Y) + 2\varepsilon y_k - \eta - \gamma > m(X_k^{-\varepsilon} \setminus Y) + m(Y \setminus X_k^{-\varepsilon}) = m(X \setminus Y_j^{-\varepsilon}) + m(Y_j^{-\varepsilon} \setminus X) = m(X_k^{-\varepsilon/2} \setminus Y_j^{-\varepsilon/2}) + m(Y_j^{-\varepsilon/2} \setminus X_k^{-\varepsilon/2}) = m(Y \setminus X) + m(Y \setminus X) + 2\varepsilon y_k - \varepsilon > m(X \setminus Y) + m(Y \setminus X).$

Axiom $S5_L$ [monotonicity] $\forall X, Y \in \mathcal{X}, X \neq Y$
$\forall k, h, j \in s_X \cap s_Y$, such that $x_k < y_k, x_r > y_r, (r = h, j), y_s + x_s > 1, (s = k, j), y_h + x_h < 1$ and $\forall \varepsilon$, with $\varepsilon < \min\{x_k + y_k - 1, x_h - y_h\}$, one has:

$$(X, Y_j^\varepsilon) \sim (X_k^{-\varepsilon}, Y) \prec ((X_k^{-\varepsilon})_h^{-\varepsilon}, Y) \prec (X, Y)$$

Considerations similar to those regarding $S5_{min}$ hold. In particular we notice that:

$$m(Y \cap X) > m(X \cap Y_j^\varepsilon) = m(X_k^{-\varepsilon} \cap Y) = m((X_k^{-\varepsilon})_h^{-\varepsilon}, Y) = m(X \cap Y) - \varepsilon$$

and

$$m(X \backslash Y_j^{-\varepsilon}) + m(Y_j^{-\varepsilon} \backslash X) = m(X_k^{-\varepsilon} \backslash Y) + m(Y \backslash X_k^{-\varepsilon}) = m(Y \backslash X) + m(X \backslash Y) + \varepsilon >$$
$$m((X_k^{-\varepsilon})_h^{-\varepsilon} \backslash Y) + m(Y \backslash (X_k^{-\varepsilon})_h^{-\varepsilon}) = m(X \backslash Y) + m(Y \backslash X).$$

We notice that if axioms S1–S4 hold and m is any fuzzy measure equal to the sum of membership degrees, by using the above computations and taking into account Proposition 1, it is easy to prove that any comparative similarity $\preceq$ agreeing with a similarity measure $S_{f,g,\rho}$ defined as

$$S_{f,g,\rho}(X, Y) = \frac{f(\mathbf{x})}{f(\mathbf{x}) + \rho g(\mathbf{y})} \tag{2}$$

with $\rho > 0$ and f and g non negative increasing functions (or any strictly increasing transformation of this measure) satisfies Axioms $S5_T$. Thus in particular, it is satisfied by the measures belonging to the class S_ρ defined in Equation (1), in which f and g coincide with the identity function.

On the contrary similarity measures such as Ochiai measure or Kulczynski measure, or more precisely their generalization in the fuzzy environment, do not satisfy the monotonicity axioms. In [3] a weaker form of monotonicity axiom has been introduced for the crisp case. It is one of the conditions useful to characterise comparative similarities representable by a large class of similarity measures containing as particular case the Ochiai measure. It is possible to give a similar generalization of monotonicity axioms also in a fuzzy environment. We focus here on the comparative similarities agreeing with similarity measures of the class defined in Equation (1).

3   Independence Condition

In [14], a strong axiom of independence has been introduced but it is not fulfilled by the comparative (fuzzy) similarities induced by most of the similarity measures present in the literature, in particular by the class considered in this paper (as proved in [3] for the crisp case). We now introduce a weaker form of independence in which we only require that the common characteristics are independent of the totality of the characteristics present in only one element of the pair. Let us consider a fuzzy measure m, only depending on the membership values and express, as usual, $\mathbf{x_i}, \mathbf{y_i}, \mathbf{z_i}, \mathbf{w_i}$ in terms of m.

Axiom WI [weak independence]
   For any 4-tuple (X_1, Y_1), (X_2, Y_2), (Z_1, W_1), (Z_2, W_2), if one of the following conditions holds
   (i) $\mathbf{x_i} = \mathbf{z_i}$ for $(i = 1, 2)$, and $\mathbf{y_1} = \mathbf{y_2}$, $\mathbf{w_1} = \mathbf{w_2}$
   (ii) $\mathbf{y_i} = \mathbf{w_i}$ for $(i = 1, 2)$, and $\mathbf{x_1} = \mathbf{x_2}$, $\mathbf{z_1} = \mathbf{z_2}$
   then $(X_1, Y_1) \preceq (X_2, Y_2) \Leftrightarrow (Z_1, W_1) \preceq (Z_2, W_2)$.

It must be underlined that the comparative similarities representable by a similarity measure S defined by Equation (2) satisfy this axiom, and thus in particular the elements of the class $S_{f,g,\rho}$ defined by Equation (2). We prove this assertion for hypothesis (i): by trivial computation it holds that on one hand $(X_1, Y_1) \preceq (X_2, Y_2)$ iff $f(\mathbf{x_1}) \leq f(\mathbf{x_2})$, and on the other hand $(Z_1, W_1) \preceq (Z_2, W_2)$ iff $f(\mathbf{x_1}) \leq f(\mathbf{x_2})$, leading to the desired equivalence. The proof is similar for condition (ii).

The above WI axiom is formulated independently of the t-norm of reference. Nevertheless the choice of the t-norm determines the pairs which are ruled by WI. In fact it is possible to show by simple examples that, for a specific choice of t-norm, the hypotheses of condition WI are satisfied and they are not for a different choice.

4   Representation Theorem

Now we are able to prove a theorem characterising comparative similarities representable by a class of numerical measures, in the case we adopt different t-norms.

Theorem 1. *Let us consider* $\mathcal{X} = [0,1]^p$, *the set of all possible fuzzy subsets of a set of p characteristics, with a t-norm* $\top \in \{\min, p, L\}$. *Let* $\preceq$ *be a binary relation on* $\mathcal{X}^2 \setminus \{(\underline{0}, \underline{0})\}$. *The following conditions are equivalent:*

(i) $\preceq$ *is a comparative fuzzy similarity satisfying axioms* $S4_\top$ *and* $S5_\top$ *and fulfilling the weak independence property WI*

(ii) for the fuzzy measure m : $\mathcal{X} \to \mathbb{R}^+$ *equal to* $\sum_i x_i$, *there exist two non negative increasing functions f and g, with* $f(0) = g(0) = 0$ *such that the function* $S : \mathcal{X}^2 \to [0,1]$ *defined by Equation (2) represents* $\preceq$.

To prove the theorem, taking into account Proposition 1, we first transform monotonicity and independence axioms in terms of a fuzzy measure of intersection and difference among fuzzy subsets. Then we can prove the theorem, by using essentially the same proof as given in [3] for the crisp case.

5   Conclusion

Considering the framework of measurement theory, we established a relation between comparative similarities, i.e. binary weak order, and numerical similarity measures so that the latter represent the former, in the case of fuzzy data. We highlighted the equivalence between specific properties satisfied by the comparative similarity and a specific form of numerical similarity, containing as particular cases Jaccard, Dice, Sorensen, Anderberg and Sokal-Sneath measures. This characterisation aims at helping users of similarity to make an appropriate choice of a similarity measure when facing a particular problem: the selection should rely on the theoretical desired properties, in terms of monotonicity and independence. The desired behaviors can be expressed in terms of induced rankings, which is more compatible with the subjective view of human beings on similarity than desired behaviors imposed on its possible numerical values.

Future works aim at studying the case of other similarity measure forms, and possibly weakening the independence axiom. Another generalization perspective concerns the study of the results obtained when one replaces the sum of the fuzzy measures of $X \setminus Y$ and $Y \setminus X$ with the fuzzy measure of $(X \setminus Y) \cup (Y \setminus X)$.

References

1. Batagelj, V., Bren, M.: Comparing resemblance measures. Journal of Classification 12, 73–90 (1995)
2. Baulieu, F.B.: A classification of presence/absence based dissimilarity coefficients. Journal of Classification 6, 233–246 (1989)
3. Bouchon-Meunier, B., Coletti, G., Lesot, M.J., Rifqi, M.: Towards a Conscious Choice of a Similarity Measure: A Qualitative Point of View. In: Sossai, C., Chemello, G. (eds.) ECSQARU 2009. LNCS (LNAI), vol. 5590, pp. 542–553. Springer, Heidelberg (2009)
4. Bouchon-Meunier, B., Rifqi, M., Bothorel, S.: Towards general measures of comparison of objects. Fuzzy Sets and Systems 84, 143–153 (1996)
5. Bouchon-Meunier, B., Rifqi, M., Lesot, M.J.: Similarities in fuzzy data mining: from a cognitive view to real-world applications. In: Zurada, J., Yen, G., Wang, J. (eds.) Computational Intelligence: Research Frontiers. LNCS, vol. 5050, pp. 349–367. Springer, Heidelberg (2008)
6. Krantz, D., Luce, R., Suppes, P., Tversky, A.: Foundations of measurement, vol. I. Academic Press, London (1971)
7. Lerman, I.C.: Indice de similarité et préordonnance associée. In: Séminaire sur les ordres totaux finis, Aix-en-Provence, pp. 233–243 (1967)
8. Lesot, M.J., Rifqi, M., Benhadda, H.: Similarity measures for binary and numerical data: a survey. Intern. J. of Knowledge Engineering and Soft Data Paradigms (KESDP) 1, 63–84 (2009)
9. Omhover, J.F., Bouchon-Meunier, B.: Equivalence entre mesures de similarités floues: application à la recherche d'images par le contenu. In: 6eme Congrès Européen de Science des Systèmes (2005)
10. Omhover, J.F., Detyniecki, M., Rifqi, M., Bouchon-Meunier, B.: Image retrieval using fuzzy similarity: Measure of equivalence based on invariance in ranking. In: IEEE Int. Conf. on Fuzzy Systems (2004)
11. Rifqi, M.: Mesures de comparaison, typicalité, et classification d'objets flous: théorie et pratique. PhD thesis, University Paris 6 (1996)
12. Rissland, E.: Ai and similarity. IEEE Intelligent Systems 21, 33–49 (2006)
13. Suppes, P., Krantz, D., Luce, R., Tversky, A.: Foundations of measurement, vol. II. Academic Press, New York (1989)
14. Tversky, A.: Features of similarity. Psychological Review 84, 327–352 (1977)

A Stochastic Treatment of Similarity

Anca Ralescu[1], Sofia Visa[2], and Stefana Popovici[3]

[1] Machine Learning and Computational Intelligence Laboratory
Computer Science Department, University of Cincinnati, ML 0030
Cincinnati, OH 45221-0030, USA
Anca.Ralescu@uc.edu
[2] Department of Computer Science, College of Wooster
Wooster, OH, USA
svisa@wooster.edu
[3] AT&T, 2000 W ATT Center Drive, Hoffman Estates, IL, 60196

Abstract. This study investigates a robust measure of similarity applicable in many domains and across many dimensions of data. Given a distance or discrepancy measure on a domain, the similarity of two values in this domain is defined as the probability that any pair of values from that domain are more different (at a larger distance) than these two values are. We discuss the motivation for this approach, its properties, and the issues that arise from it.

1 Introduction

Evaluating similarity remains one of operations underlying human reasoning, as well as automated information processing. Many approaches are present in the literature a review of which exceeds the scope of this paper. See for the example [RM07] and the references therein for a discussion of similarity measures for heterogeneous data. In this paper we expand on the approach introduced in [Pop08], [RPR08], that defines similarity as the probability of a certain event.

In the following we will refer to data items X in a multidimensional space, $D_1 \times \ldots \times D_n$, where $D_i \subset \Re$ or other space (e.g. space of strings, characters, intervals, etc.). We will further assume that each domain D_i comes endowed with a distance function d_i. Often, for simplicity we will assume $n = 1, 2, 3$. However, the approach presented below can be extended to any dimensions across different spaces.

Often, the similarity is defined as a decreasing function of the distance (or more generally discrepancy) between two data items. For example, assuming $n = 1$, and d a distance on the domain D of X, similarity between values a and b of X can be defined as

$$Sim(a, b) = S(d(a, b))$$

where $S : \Re_+ \to \Re_+$ is such that, $0 \leq Sim(a, b) \leq 1$ for any values a, b, $Sim(a, b) = 1$ whenever $a = b$, $Sim(a, b) = 0$ if $d(a, b)$ is sufficiently large,

E. Hüllermeier, R. Kruse, and F. Hoffmann (Eds.): IPMU 2010, LNAI 6178, pp. 11–18, 2010.

and some form of transitivity (or triangle inequality like) relation holds. For example, S could be defined as

$$S(d) = 1 - \frac{d^2}{M^2} \qquad (1)$$

where $M = max\{d(x,y) \mid x,y \in D\}$. Equation (1) seems reasonable enough and it is indeed often used. However, according to the approach taken in this paper, this equation is suitable only in a special case of the data set D.

2   Similarity as Probability

We start by assuming that the attribute X is a random variable. In particular, in the discrete case X takes values $x_i, i = 1, \ldots, n$ with probability $p_i, i = 1, \ldots, n$. Now, given two values of X, a, and b their similarity is determined by how likely it is to find a pair of values of X, which are more **different** than a and b are. The meaning of different is defined by some discrepancy measure (including a distance measure) in the domain of X. Thus, in the probability based approach similarity is evaluated as a function of relative distances, rather than distance magnitudes. The distribution underlying the data is reflected in this definition of the similarity and affects the final outcome. Indeed, we will see that under different underlying distributions of otherwise identical data the similarity of two fixed values changes. We start by defining the similarity along components. For multidimensional data, we will compute the similarity along each dimension and then aggregate it across dimensions.

2.1   Probability Based Similarity along One Component

Let F denote the distribution function for the random variable X. That is, for $x \in D$, $F(x) = P(X \leq x)$. Further denote by d a distance on D.

Definition 1. *The similarity between values a and b of the random variable X taking into account the underlying distribution F, denoted by S_F, is defined as in equation (2) [RPR08], [RM07],*

$$S_F(a,b) = P_F\left(d(X,Y) \geq d(a,b)\right) \qquad (2)$$

where X, Y is independent identically distributed (iid) according to F.

In general, in order to calculate $S_F(a,b)$ according to (2) we must first find the probability distribution of $d(X,Y)$. For example, if $D = \Re$, and $d(x_i, x_j) = |x_i - x_j|$ the distribution of $|X - Y|$ must be computed. The complexity of this computation depends on the distribution function F. It is easy to see that S_F is a similarity measure on the range of values of the attribute X as the following proposition states:

Proposition 1. *For any distribution function F, $S_F(a,b)$ defined by equation (2) satisfies the following properties:*

1. *For any pair of values a, b, $0 \leq S_F(a, b) \leq 1$;*
2. *$S_F(a, b) = 1$ if and only if $a = b$.*
3. *$S_F(a, b) = S_F(b, a)$;*
4. *$S_F(a, b) \leq \min\{S_F(a, c), S_F(c, b)\}$ for all $c \in [a, b]$;*

Proof

1. Obviously, since S_F is a probability, $0 \leq S_F \leq 1$.
2. Obviously, if $a = b$, $d(a, b) = 0$ and therefore $S_F(a, b) = P(|d(X, Y)| \geq 0) = 1$. Conversely, if $S_F(a, b) = P(|d(X, Y)| \geq d(a, b)) = 1$ if follows that $d(a, b)$ is the lowest value that $d(X, Y)$ can take, that is $d(a, b) = 0$ which means that $a = b$.
3. This property is obvious.
4. To proves this transitivity (or triangle-like inequality) property, let $c \in [a, b]$. Obviously, $|a - c|, |c - b| \leq |a - b|$, and hence, with $d(a, b) = |a - b|$ we have

$$S_F(a, b) = P(|X - Y| \geq |a - b|) \leq P(|X - Y| \geq |a - c|) = S_F(a, c)$$

and

$$S_F(a, b) = P(|X - Y| \geq |a - b|) \leq P(|X - Y| \geq |b - c|) = S_F(b, c)$$

and the inequality follows.

2.2 The Effect of the Distribution on the Similarity

The similarity defined by equation (2) is affected by the underlying distribution as the following examples show:

Example 1. Consider that X is distributed uniformly on $[0, M]$ where $M \in \{3, \ldots, 5\}$. By normalization $U[0, M]$ is mapped into $U[0, 1]$, the uniform distribution on $[0, 1]$ with the cumulative distribution function

$$F_{U[0,1]}(x) = \begin{cases} 0 & \text{if } x \leq 0 \\ x & \text{if } 0 \leq x < 1 \\ 1 & \text{if } x \geq 1 \end{cases}$$

Assume that $d(x, y) = |x - y|$. Then Equation (2) reduces

$$Sim_{U[0,1]}(a, b) = 1 - (F_{U[0,1]}(a) - F_{U[0,1]}(b))^2, \text{ for } a, b \in [0, 1] \tag{3}$$

and the similarity between $a, b \in [0, M]$ becomes:

$$Sim_{U[0,M]}(a, b) = Sim_{U[0,1]}(\frac{a}{M}, \frac{b}{M}) = 1 - (F_{U[0,1]}(\frac{a}{M}) - F_{U[0,1]}(\frac{b}{M}))^2 = 1 - \frac{|a - b|^2}{M^2} \tag{4}$$

where we recognize the similarity defined in equation (1).

We will show later that in fact, (1) is really justified only in the case of the uniform distribution. Before that, let us look at other examples:

Example 2. Here X is $N(\mu, \sigma^2)$ and G_{μ, σ^2} denotes its cumulative distribution function. Then for two values a, b, of X, (2) obtains:

$$Sim_{N(\mu, \sigma^2)}(a, b) = P(|X - Y| \geq |a - b|) = 1 - P(|X - Y| < |a - b|)$$
$$= 1 - P(-|a - b| < X - Y < |a - b|) = 1 - P\left(-\frac{d}{\sigma\sqrt{2}} < Z < \frac{d}{\sigma\sqrt{(2)}}\right) \quad (5)$$
$$= 1 - \left[\Phi(\frac{d}{\sigma\sqrt{2}}) - \Phi(-\frac{d}{\sigma\sqrt{2}})\right] = 2\left(1 - \Phi(\frac{d}{\sigma\sqrt{2}})\right)$$

where X, Y are iid $N(\mu, \sigma^2)$, $Z = \frac{X-Y}{\sigma\sqrt{2}}$ is $N(0, 1)$, Φ is its cumulative distribution function, and $d = |a - b|$. Figure 1 shows the change in $Sim_{N(\mu, \sigma^2)}(a, b)$ when $d = |a - b| \in \{1, \ldots, 10\}$, and $\sigma \in \{1, \ldots, 10\}$.

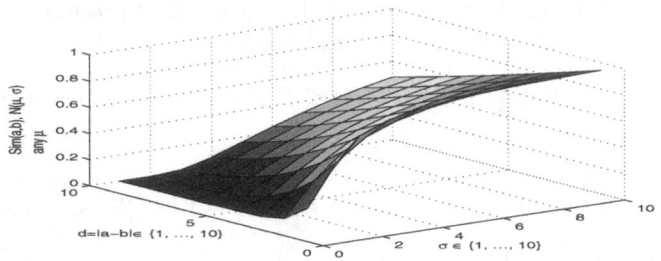

Fig. 1. The similarity between a, b, $d = |a - b| \in \{1, \ldots, 10\}$, under $N(\mu, \sigma)$, for any μ, $\sigma \in \{1, \ldots, 10\}$

Finally, to further compare the similarity under $U[0, M]$ and $N(\mu, \sigma^2)$ consider the following example:

Example 3. In this example we consider the attributes X_M and Y_M following different distributions but having the same mean and variance. More precisely, X_M follows the uniform distribution $U[0, M]$ with $M \in \{3, 4, 5\}$. Its mean and variance are respectively, $E(X_M) = \frac{M}{2}$, and $Var(X_M) = \frac{M^2}{12}$. Next, for each M, we let Y_M be $N(\mu = \frac{M}{2}, \sigma^2 = \frac{M^2}{12})$. Consider a, b, such that $d = |a - b| \in [0, M]$. Table 1 shows the change in the similarity of a, b under uniform and normal distributions respectively. Figure 2 shows these changes and the difference between similarities when the distribution change.

These examples show that the probability based similarity between two values a and b directly depends on the value $d(a, b)$. When the values come from the same family of distributions, for constant $d(a, b)$, this similarity is affected by the parameters of the distribution, and it may be different under different distributions, even when these distributions have the same mean and variance.

2.3   Representations for Similarities

In the previous section we have seen that starting with different distributions, underlying the same set of data, equation (2) leads to different similarity

Table 1. The similarity between the values a, b, for various values $|a - b| = d$, when they come from two different distributions (Uniform, and Normal) with the same mean and variance

M		3			4					5					
$d = |a - b|$	0	1	2	3	0	1	2	3	4	0	1	2	3	4	5
$S_{U[0,M]}(a,b)= 1 - \frac{d^2}{M^2}$	1	0.89	0.56	0	1	0.94	0.75	0.44	0	1	0.96	0.84	0.64	0.36	0
$S_{N(\frac{M}{2}, \frac{M^2}{12})}(a,b) = 2(1 - \Phi(\frac{d\sqrt{6}}{M}))$	1	0.41	0.10	0.01	1	0.54	0.22	0.07	0.01	1	0.62	0.33	0.14	0.05	0.01

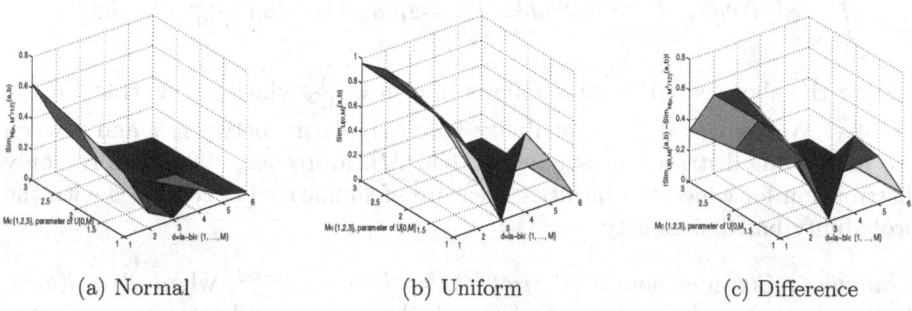

(a) Normal   (b) Uniform   (c) Difference

Fig. 2. Similarity under different distributions with the same mean and variance (a), (b), and the difference between these similarities (c)

values between the same pairs of data points. We now ask when a given similarity measure can be represented as in equation (2). We can prove the following representation result:

Theorem 1. *Let $S(a,b)$ be a similarity between two values a,b of the random variable X, and let $d = d(a,b)$ be the distance (or other discrepancy measure) between a and b. Then S can be represented as in (2) if and only if*

1. *S is differentiable as a function of d, and*
2. *$\int_{-\infty}^{\infty} S'(d)\mathrm{d}d = -1$*

Proof: Assume that as a decreasing function of d, S is represented by (2). The right hand side of this equation can be rewritten as

$$rhs(2) = P(d(X,Y) \geq d(a,b)) = 1 - P(d(X,Y) < d(a,b)) = 1 - F_{d(X,Y)}(d(a,b))$$

Therefore, $S(d)$ must satisfy

$$S(d) = 1 - F_{d(X,Y)}(d).$$

Taking the derivative, we obtain $S'(d) = -F'_{d(X,Y)}(d)$. Since by definition of the distribution function, $F'_{d(X,Y)}$ is a density, it means that

$$\int_{-\infty}^{\infty} F'_{d(X,Y)}(d)\mathrm{d}d = 1, \text{ and therefore, } \int_{-\infty}^{\infty} S'(d)\mathrm{d}d = -1.$$

Let us see what follows from Proposition 3 in the case of various similarity measures.

Example 4. Let $S : \Re^+ \to [0, 1]$, $S(d) = -md^2 + n$ with $m, n > 0$. Obviously $S(d)$ is decreasing in d. We need to determine m and n such that (1) $0 \leq S(d) \leq 1$ and (2) $\int_{-\infty}^{\infty} S'(d) dd = -1$.

Setting $n = 1$, $S(d) \leq 1$ with equality if and only if $d = 0$, that is, $S(d) = 1$ if $d = 0$. Next, m must be such that $S(d) \geq 0$, that is $1 - md^2 \geq 0$, and therefore, $m \leq \frac{1}{d^2}$ for *any value* of the distance d. It follows that $m \leq \frac{1}{\max d^2}$.

Let $M = \max d$. Thus

$$\int_{-\infty}^{\infty} S'(d) \, dd = \int_0^M S'(d) \, dd = \int_0^M -2md \, dd = -2m \frac{d^2}{2} |_0^M = -mM^2$$

Setting the above equal to -1 it follows that $m = \frac{1}{M^2}$ which means that $S(d) = 1 - \frac{d^2}{M^2}$. We recovered the probability based similarity between a and b when the underlying distribution is uniform, $U[0, M]$. Moreover, $U[0, M]$ is the only distribution for which the intuitive measure of similarity (1) coincides with the probability based similarity.

Example 5. Consider now that $Sim(a, b) = S(d) = \beta e^{-\alpha d}$, where $d = d(a, b)$. Again we want to determine α and β such that S is a similarity measure satisfying (2). First, it is obvious that since $S(0) = \beta$, we must have $\beta = 1$. Next, $\int_0^{\infty} S'(d) \, dd = \int_0^{\infty} -\alpha e^{-\alpha d} \, dd = \alpha/\alpha e^{-\alpha d}|_0^{\infty} = -1$ for any α. Thus, $S(d) = e^{-\alpha d}$ is a similarity measure satisfying (2) for any α.

3 Combining the Probability Based Similarity Across Dimensions

A natural way to wish to combine similarities across dimensions, is to define a combination rule which would implement the intuitive rule "*Two data points/vectors are similar across their dimensions if they are similar along each dimension*". Assume that the data points, a, b are $n$dimensional, that is, $a_i \in D_i$, and that $S_i(a, b) = Sim(a_i, b_i)$ computed as above (assuming that the distribution underlying D_i is known). Further, assuming independence of the dimensions, the above rule, can be defined as

$$Sim(a, b) = \prod_{i=1}^n S_i(a, b) \tag{6}$$

A direct computation of $Sim(a, b)$ from equation (2) may be very tedious, as it requires manipulating a multivariate distribution. We now state without proof the following proposition.

Proposition 2. *The combination in equation (6) has desirable properties as follows:*

1. $0 \leq Sim(a, b) \leq 1$.
2. $Sim(a, b) = 1$ if $a = b$.
3. $Sim(a, b)$ is increasing in $S_i(a, b)$.
4. Transitivity: $Sim(a, b) \leq \min\{Sim(a, c), Sim(c, b)\}$.

However, defining $Sim(a, b)$ by equation (6) has also drawbacks: since $S_i \in [0, 1]$, $Sim \leq S_i$ and in fact, it may become very small (for practical purposes 0) as the number of dimensions increases. A common device to avoid this is to consider $-\ln(\prod_{i=1}^{n} S_i) = -\sum_{i=1}^{n} \ln(S_i)$ (the log-likelihood), where the minus sign is used to obtain a result greater than zero. Further, noting that the result does not change qualitatively after multiplication by a constant, we obtain the quantity $X^2 = -2\sum_{i=1}^{n} \ln(S_i)$, widely known as the Fisher Transform [LF71] and used to combine independent probabilities, which, we should note, S_i in fact are. Standard statistical arguments yield that under the hypothesis that each S_i is distributed $U[0, 1]$, the statistics X^2 has a χ^2 distribution with $2n$ degrees of freedom. We define now the similarity of a and b across all their dimensions as shown in equation (7) [LH04], [RPR08].

$$Sim_{all,\chi^2}(a, b) = P(\chi_{2n}^2 \geq X^2) \tag{7}$$

Proposition 3. $Sim_{all,\chi^2}(a, b)$, defined by equation (7), when a, b are n dimensional has the following properties:

1. $0 \leq Sim_{all,\chi^2}(a, b) \leq 1$
2. $Sim_{all,\chi^2}(a, b) = 1$ if and only if $a = b$
3. $Sim_{all,\chi^2}(a, b) = Sim_{all,\chi^2}(b, a)$
4. $Sim_{all,\chi^2}(a, b) \leq \min\{Sim_{all,\chi^2}(a, c), Sim_{all,\chi^2}(c, b)\}$ for any c in the hyper-rectangle determined by the components a_i, b_j with $i, j = 1, \ldots, n$.

Note that only $S_i \neq 0$ can be used in forming X^2. The case when some $S_i = 0$ can be treated by a "fill in" procedure such as used in [Pop08]. Alternatively, we can consider a subset of $\{S_i, i = 1, \ldots, n\}$. We consider two extreme cases, each of which uses the fact that $-2\log S_i$ is distributed $\chi^2(2)$ (or exponential with parameter $\lambda = 1/2$.

1. $X_M^2 = -2\log\max_i S_i$, which can be rewritten as $\min_i\{-2\log S_i\}$. Thus the overall similarity is defined as the tail probability corresponding to the nth order statistic of the exponential distribution with $\lambda = 1/2$:

$$Sim_{M,\chi^2}(a, b) = P(\chi_2^2 \geq X_M^2) \tag{8}$$

2. $X_{Min}^2 = -2\log\min_i S_i$, which can be rewritten as $\max_i\{-2\log S_i\}$. Thus the overall similarity is defined as the tail probability corresponding to the 1st order statistic of the exponential distribution with $\lambda = 1/2$:

$$Sim_{m,\chi^2}(a, b) = P(\chi_2^2 \geq X_m^2) \tag{9}$$

4 Concluding Remarks and Future Work

In the above discussion we made the assumption that the data comes from a known distribution. However, in many applications this may not be the case. In such cases, we can adopt one of the following procedures: (1) Use the available data to obtain an estimate of the underlying distribution. For example, one can use algorithms such as the EM algorithm for approximating the real distribution by mixtures of Gaussian distributions, and then proceed as indicated above, or (2) one can compute directly a histogram distances, of the values $d(x_i, x_j)$, for values x_i of the attribute X. Then, for any values pair (x_i, x_j) we can compute directly their similarity from this histogram. For higher dimensions we discussed the issues that arise when the one dimensional similarities, along individual dimensions must be combined. Many details remain to be addressed in future work, including but not limited to a deeper analysis of the similarities defined, possible relation to other similarities, parametric versus nonparametric measures, adaptability and incremental definitions, and use in concrete applications.

Acknowledgment

Authors are grateful to the anonymous reviewers for their very useful comments which led to a reorganization of the paper. This work was partially supported by ONR Grant N000140710438 for Anca Ralescu and Stefana Popovici, and Howard Hughes Medical Institute Fund for Sofia Visa.

References

[LF71]   Littell, R.C., Folks, J.L.: Asymptotic optimality of fisher's method of combining independent tests. Journal of American Statistical Association 66(336), 802–806 (1971)

[LH04]   Le, S., Hu, T.: Measuring the similarity for heterogenous data: An ordered probability-based approach. In: Suzuki, E., Arikawa, S. (eds.) DS 2004. LNCS (LNAI), vol. 3245, pp. 129–141. Springer, Heidelberg (2004)

[Pop08]   Popovici, S.A.: On evaluating similarity between heterogeneous data (2008)

[RM07]   Ralescu, A., Minoh, M.: Measuring proximity between heterogeneous data. In: Proceedings of FUZZ-IEEE 2007, Imperial College, London, UK, July 23-26 (2007)

[RPR08]   Ralescu, A., Popovici, S., Ralescu, D.: On evaluating the proximity between heterogeneous data. In: Proceedings of the Nineteenth Midwestern Artificial Intelligence and Cognitive Science Conference, MAICS-2008, Cincinnati, Oh, USA, April 12-13 (2008)

Order-Based Equivalence Degrees
for Similarity and Distance Measures

Marie-Jeanne Lesot and Maria Rifqi

Université Pierre et Marie Curie - Paris 6, CNRS, UMR7606, LIP6
104 avenue du President Kennedy, 75016 Paris, France
{marie-jeanne.lesot,maria.rifqi}@lip6.fr

Abstract. In order to help to choose similarity or distance measures
for information retrieval systems, we compare the orders these measures
induce and quantify their agreement by a *degree of equivalence*. We both
consider measures dedicated to binary and numerical data, carrying out
experiments both on artificial and real data sets, and identifying equivalent as well as quasi-equivalent measures that can be considered as
redundant in the information retrieval framework.

Keywords: Similarity, distance, kernel, order-based comparison, equivalence degree, Kendall tau.

1 Introduction

Information retrieval systems provide results in the form of document lists ordered by relevance, usually computed as the similarity between the document
and the user request. The choice of the similarity measure is then a central component of the system. In such applications, the similarity values themselves are
of little importance, only the order they induce matters: two measures leading
to the same document ordering can be considered as equivalent, and it is not
useful to keep them both. Likewise, several machine learning algorithms only
depend on the similarity rankings and not on their values, such as the k-nearest
neighbor classification, hierarchical clustering with complete or single linkage, or
the monotone equivariant cluster analysis [1].

To formalize this notion, several authors introduced the definition of *equivalent*
comparison measures [2,3,4,5], as measures always inducing the same ranking,
and exhibited classes of equivalent measures. To refine the characterization of
non-equivalent measures, *equivalence degrees* were then proposed [6] to quantify
the disagreement between the rankings, considering both the number of inversions and their positions, through the generalised Kendall tau [7,8].

In this paper we propose a systematic study of these equivalence and quasi-
equivalence properties both for measures dedicated to presence/absence and to
numerical data, i.e. data respectively in $\{0, 1\}^p$ and in $\mathbb{R}^p$, taking into account the
main existing similarity, distance and scalar product measures. We compute the
equivalence degrees considering both artificial and real data, the latter consisting
of training data from the 2008 Image CLEF challenge [9].

E. Hüllermeier, R. Kruse, and F. Hoffmann (Eds.): IPMU 2010, LNAI 6178, pp. 19–28, 2010.

As opposed to previous work [6], the protocol we consider here corresponds to the use of an information retrieval system: it consists in comparing to a request data all n points of the data set, ranking them according to their similarity to this request and averaging the result over several requests. This better reflects the application case, whereas the protocol used in [6] considering all $n(n-1)/2$ data pairs simultaneously and ordering them in a single ranking was more focused on a theoretical comparison of similarity measures. Furthermore, in this paper, we extend the comparison framework to the case of numerical data.

The paper is organised as follows: section 2 recalls the definitions of equivalence and equivalence degrees for comparison measures and details the experimental protocol. Sections 3 and 4 respectively analyse the results obtained in the case of binary and numerical data.

2 Order-Based Comparison of Comparison Measures

Denoting $\mathcal{X}$ the data universe, similarity measures are functions $S : \mathcal{X} \times \mathcal{X} \to \mathbb{R}$ quantifying proximity or resemblance: they take as argument object couples and give as a result numerical values that are all the higher as the objects are close. Distance measures $d : \mathcal{X} \times \mathcal{X} \to \mathbb{R}^+$ quantify dissimilarity and return values that are all the smaller as the objects are close. Similarity and distance measures build the set of comparison measures.

2.1 Definitions

Order-based Equivalence. Several authors [2,3,4,5] considered the issue of a theoretical comparison between similarity measures and defined two measures m_1 and m_2 as *equivalent* if they induce the same order when comparing objects: more formally they are equivalent if and only if $\forall x, y, z, t$, it holds that $m_1(x, y) < m_1(z, t) \Leftrightarrow m_2(x, y) < m_2(z, t)$ and $m_1(x, y) = m_1(z, t) \Leftrightarrow m_2(x, y) = m_2(z, t)$.

It has been shown [4,5] that, equivalently, m_1 and m_2 are equivalent if and only if there exists a strictly increasing function $f : Im(m_1) \to Im(m_2)$ such that $m_2 = f \circ m_1$, where $Im(m) = \{s \in [0,1]/\exists(x, y) \in \mathcal{X}^2, s = m(x, y)\}$.

It is to be noted that when a distance is compared to a similarity measure, it is necessary to take into account their opposite sense of variation: the inequalities in the first definition must be the opposite one of the other; the function of the second definition must be strictly decreasing.

Order-based Equivalence Degrees. In order to refine the characterization of non-equivalent measures, it has been proposed to quantify the disagreement between the induced rankings, by *equivalence degrees* [6]: two measures leading to a few inversions can be considered as more equivalent than measures inducing opposite rankings. Furthermore, two measures can be considered as less equivalent if the inversions occur for high similarity values than if they occur for low values: in the framework of information retrieval systems for instance, most often only the first results are taken into account, inversions occurring at the end of the document lists are not even noticed.

The generalized Kendall tau K_{p_t,p_m} [7,8] compares two rankings r_1 and r_2 defined on a set of elements $\mathcal{E}$, taking into account the number of inversions as well as their positions: it associates each element pair $(i,j) \in \mathcal{E}^2$ with a penalty $P(i,j)$ and is defined as the sum of all penalties divided by the number of pairs. Four penalty values are distinguished: if the pair (i,j) is concordant (i.e. r_1 and r_2 agree on the relative position of i and j: formally denoting $\delta_l = r_l(i) - r_l(j)$ the rank difference of i and j in ranking r_l, if $\delta_1 \delta_2 > 0$ or $\delta_1 = \delta_2 = 0$), then $P = 0$; if the pair is discordant (i.e. $\delta_1 \delta_2 < 0$), $P = 1$; if it is tied in one ranking but not in the other one, $P = p_t \in [0,1]$. Lastly if it is present in one ranking but missing from the other one, one distinguishes whether both i and j are missing ($P = p_m \in [0,1]$), or only one is (the pair is then handled as a normal one).

The equivalence degree between two comparison measures m_1 and m_2 is thus computed as follows: given a data set $\mathcal{D}$ and a request $x \in \mathcal{D}$, all points $y \in \mathcal{D}$ are ranked according to their similarity to x, according to m_1 and m_2. The rankings r_1^k and r_2^k induced on $\mathcal{D}$, restricted to their top-k elements, i.e. to the objects with rank smaller than a given k are then compared, leading to:

$$d_{\mathcal{D}}^k(m_1, m_2) = 1 - K_{0.5,1}(r_1^k, r_2^k)$$

It equals 1 for equivalent measures and 0 for measures leading to opposite rankings. We set $p_t = 0.5$ considering that when breaking a tie, there is 1 chance out of 2 to come up with the same order as defined by the second ranking. We set $p_m = 1$ considering that a missing data pair indicates a major difference and can be penalized as a discordant pair. Lastly, for any given k, each data point $x \in \mathcal{D}$ is successively considered as request, and the degrees are averaged over all requests.

2.2 Considered Data Sets

We carry out experiments considering both binary and numerical data, i.e. respectively the universes $\mathcal{X} = \{0,1\}^p$ and $\mathcal{X} = \mathbb{R}^p$, and for each of these two types, artificial and real data set.

For the real data, we consider the ImageClef training corpus [9] that contains 1827 images annotated in a multi-label framework (e.g. indicating whether the image shows buildings or vegetation). On one hand we use the image labels to define binary data, encoding the presence or absence of each label. We suppressed some labels in XOR relation with others (such as night, related to day, or outdoor, related to indoor) as well as subcategory labels (tree, subsumed by vegetation, and sunny, partly cloudy and overcast subsumed by sky). As a result, the binary data set contains $p = 11$ attributes. On the other hand, we encode the images using their histograms in the HSV space (using $p = 6 \times 2 \times 2 = 24$ bins) expressed as percentages, to get a vector description. It is to be noted that this vector description is such that the sum of all attributes is constant.

The artificial data are generated according to the real data, so as to study the effect on equivalence results of potential specific data configurations, e.g. variable density or cluster structures. In the binary case, the artificial data consists of

Table 1. Classic binary data similarity measures, normalised to $[0, 1]$ (the definitions may thus differ from the classic ones)

Similarity measure	Notation	Definition
Jaccard	Jac	$\frac{a}{a+b+c}$
Dice	Dic	$\frac{2a}{2a+b+c}$
Kulczynski 2	Kul	$\frac{1}{2}\left(\frac{a}{a+b} + \frac{a}{a+c}\right)$
Ochiai	Och	$\frac{a}{\sqrt{a+b}\sqrt{a+c}}$
Rogers and Tanimoto	RT	$\frac{a+d}{a+2(b+c)+d}$
Russel and Rao	RR	$\frac{a}{a+b+c+d}$
Simple Matching	SM	$\frac{a+d}{a+b+c+d}$
Sokal and Sneath 1	$SS1$	$\frac{a+d}{a+\frac{1}{2}(b+c)+d}$
Yule Q	YuQ	$\frac{ad}{ad+bc}$
Yule Y	YuY	$\frac{\sqrt{ad}}{\sqrt{ad}+\sqrt{bc}}$

all points in a regular grid in $\{0, 1\}^{11}$, resulting in $2^{11} = 2048$ points. In the numerical case, the artificial data set is randomly generated following a uniform distribution on $[0, 100]^{24}$.

3 Binary Data Similarity Measures

3.1 List of Considered Measures

Formally, similarity measures for binary data are defined as functions $S : \{0, 1\}^p \times \{0, 1\}^p \to \mathbb{R}$ possessing the properties of maximality ($\forall a, y,\ S(x, x) \geq S(x, y)$) and symmetry [10,11], although the latter is not always required [12].

Table 1 recalls the definition of 10 classic similarity measures, using the following notations: for any point $x \in \{0, 1\}^p$, X denotes the set of attributes present in x, i.e. $X = \{i | x_i = 1\}$; for any data pair (x, y), a, b, c, d denote the number of attributes respectively common to both points $a = |X \cap Y|$, present in x but not in y or vice-versa, $b = |X - Y|$ and $c = |Y - X|$, and present in neither x nor y, $d = |\bar{X} \cap \bar{Y}|$. The measures not depending on d (the first 4 in Table 1) are called *type I similarity measures*, the others *type II similarity measures*. As can be seen from the table, the first 2 measures follow the same general scheme proposed by Tversky [12] $Tve_{\alpha,\beta}(x, y) = a/(a + \alpha b + \beta c)$ corresponding to the special case where $\alpha = \beta = 1$ or $1/2$ respectively.

3.2 Analytical Equivalence Results

Several classes of equivalent similarity measures were established, exhibiting their functional dependency [3,4,5]. For the measures defined in Table 1 they are: (i) {Jaccard, Dice, symmetrical Tversky's measures $Tve_{\alpha,\alpha}$}, (ii) {Rogers and Tanimoto, Simple Matching, Sokal and Sneath 1}, (iii) {Yule Q, Yule Y}, (iv) each of the remaining measures forming a class by itself. For the Tversky's measures, it was more generally shown [5] that two measures with parameters (α, β) and (α', β') are equivalent if and only if $\alpha/\beta = \alpha'/\beta'$.

Table 2. Full rank equivalence degrees for artificial binary data

	Jac	Kul2	Och	RT	RR	SM	SS1	YuQ	YuY	Random
Dic	1	0.97	0.99	0.87	0.89	0.87	0.87	0.86	0.86	0.50
Jac		0.97	0.99	0.87	0.89	0.87	0.87	0.86	0.86	0.50
Kul2			0.98	0.88	0.88	0.88	0.88	0.88	0.88	0.50
Och				0.88	0.89	0.88	0.88	0.87	0.87	0.50
RT					0.76	1	1	0.90	0.90	0.50
RR						0.76	0.76	0.77	0.77	0.50
SM							1	0.90	0.90	0.50
SS1								0.90	0.90	0.50
YuQ									1	0.50
YuY										0.50

3.3   Experimental Results

Full Rank Comparison. Table 2 contains the full rank equivalence degrees computed in the case of the artificial data. The top graph of Figure 1 offers a graphical representation of these values, together with their standard deviation.

As a baseline, we include a measure that generates random similarity values so as to have a reference equivalence degree. This measure has an equivalence degree of 0.5 with all measures: on average it ranks differently half of the pairs.

From the equivalence degrees equal to 1, three groups of equivalent measures are numerically identified, accordingly to the theoretical results (see Section 3.2). The non-1 degrees give information on the non equivalent measures. It can first be noted that they all have high equivalence levels: apart from the random measure, the minimal degree equals 0.76, which implies that the proportion of inversions is always lower than 24%. Furthermore, it appears that some measures, although not satisfying the definition of equivalence, have very high equivalence degrees, above 0.97 (Jac/Och, Kul2/Och, and Jac/Kul2): the latter, that actually equals the set of type I measures, lead to very few differences and can actually be considered as quasi-equivalent and thus redundant.

Figure 1 illustrates these degrees with their standard deviation, representing measure pairs in decreasing order of their degrees. To improve the readability, it only represents a single member of each equivalence class, and does not consider further the random measure. Taking into account the standard deviation, it can be observed on the top graph that for full rank comparison there is no significant difference between the degrees computed on the artificial and the real data. Thus all comments on the measures also hold for the real data set.

This graph also highlights the difference between the two measure types, as already mentioned: whereas type I measures appear highly equivalent one to another, the "intra equivalence" of type II measures is smaller. The latter do not resemble each other more than they resemble the type I measures, which makes their category less homogeneous and more diverse.

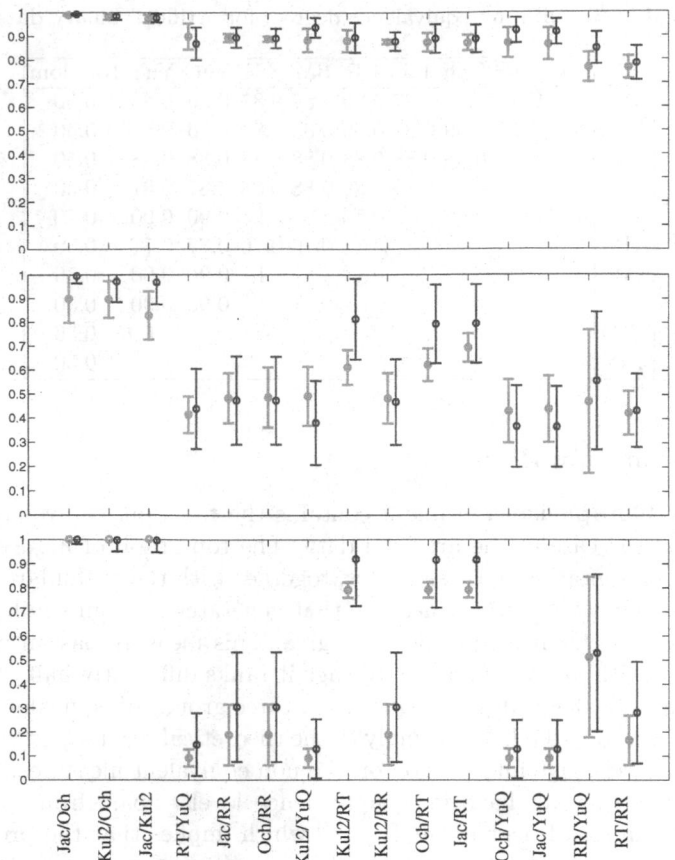

Fig. 1. Equivalence degrees and their standard deviation: (top) full ranking, (middle) top-100 (bottom) top-10. For each measure pair the left (resp. right) bar corresponds to artificial (resp. real) data.

Top-k Comparison. The middle and bottom graphs of figure 1 show the equivalence degrees obtained when considering, respectively, the top-100 and top-10 ranked lists. We keep the same abscisse axis used for the full ranking, to underline the differences occuring when the list is shortened.

It can first be observed that the degrees are globally lower than for the full rank comparison: the minimum is 0.42 for $k = 100$, 0.09 for $k = 10$, indicating major differences in the ranked lists provided by the measures. The equivalence degree of the random measure with any other one (not shown on the graphs) falls down below 0.1: the list it induces has next to nothing in common with the other lists, and almost all data pairs get a missing penalty.

This decrease indicates that the global agreement observed when comparing the full rankings is actually mainly due to the last ranked data. This underlines that a study of the inversion positions, besides their number, is necessary, especially when it comes to selecting non equivalent measures in an informa-tion retrieval framework. Still, this decrease does not occur for all measures: the intra type I pairs as well as those involving a type I measure with Rogers Tanimoto appear to be stable from full ranking to top-100 and top-10. Due to this behaviour, RT, although being a type II measure, is closer to the type I category than to type II. These measures can be considered as equivalent even for restricted rankings, and redundant for information retrieval applications.

Another difference when focusing on the top-k rankings comes from the stan-dard deviations: it appears that their values considerably increase. Furthermore, they globally take higher values on the real data than on the artificial ones. This may be due to the regular distribution of the artificial data, which insures independence with respect to the request data. On the contrary, the real data probably follow a distribution with variable density, and the data request may have different effects, depending on whether it belongs to a dense or to a sparse region. Still, as for the full rank comparison, and except for RT, no significant difference between artificial and real data can be observed.

Lastly, it appears that the Yule Q and Russel Rao measures become the most isolated ones, far from all others: for YuQ, this can be explained by the fact that it very often takes value 1. Indeed, this occurs for all data pairs (x, y) such that $b = 0$ or $c = 0$. Thus, the set of data in its top-k list is much larger than those of the other measures, leading to many missing data pairs. The RR behaviour can be explained similarly: this measure only takes $p + 1 = 12$ different values in a universe of size p. Thus its top-k lists contain the whole data set even for low k values, again leading to many missing pairs when comparing to other measures.

4   Numerical Data Similarity Measures

4.1   List of Considered Measures

Numerical data comparison measures are based on distances or on scalar prod-ucts [11]. The formers possess properties of positivity, symmetry, minimality, equivalently to the binary data similarity measures. Moreover, they satisfy the triangular inequality. The most classic distances are the Minkowski family, and in particular the Euclidean distance, denoted d_e, and the Manhattan distance.

The most common dot products comprise the Euclidean dot product k_e, the gaussian kernel $kg_\sigma = \exp(-d_e(x, y)^2/(2\sigma^2))$ and the polynomial kernel $kp_{\gamma,l} = (\langle x, y \rangle + l)^\gamma$. With the exception of the gaussian kernel, they do not correspond to classic similarity measures because they do not possess the maximality property, as e.g. $k(x, 2x) > k(x, x)$. To obtain it, it is necessary to normalize them, defining $\tilde{k}(x, y) = k(x, y)/\sqrt{k(x, x)k(y, y)}$. The similarity then only depends on the angle between the two vectors.

4.2   Analytical Results

Using the functional definition of equivalence, two equivalence classes can be distinguished. The first one obviously groups the Gaussian kernels with the Eu-clidean distance: $kg_\sigma = f \circ d$ with $f : x \mapsto \exp(-x^2/(2\sigma^2))$ that is decreasing.

Table 3. Full rank equivalence degrees for artificial numerical data

	L2	EDP	NEDP	GK50	GK100	PK3	NPK3	Random
L1	0.90	0.63	0.84	0.90	0.90	0.63	0.89	0.50
L2		0.63	0.87	1	1	0.63	0.97	0.50
EDP			0.76	0.63	0.63	1	0.66	0.50
NEDP				0.87	0.87	0.76	0.90	0.50
GK50					1	0.63	0.97	0.50
GK100						0.63	0.97	0.50
PK3							0.66	0.50
NPK3								0.50

All Gaussian kernels are thus equivalent: in particular, this implies that all σ values always lead to the same ranking.

The second class, grouping the Euclidean dot product and the polynomial kernels, is defined down to a data translation: for even values of γ, the function $g(x) = (x + l)^\gamma$, such that $kp_{\gamma,l} = g \circ k_e$, is increasing only under the condition that $x \geq -l$. Now denoting α the value such that $\forall x \forall i\, x_i + \alpha \geq 0$ and e the vector such that $\forall i\, e_i = \alpha$, after applying the translation by e, one has $\forall x \forall i\, x_i \geq 0$ and thus $\langle x, y \rangle = \sum_i x_i y_i \geq 0 > -l$. It can be underlined that in a classification framework the l value does not matter as it scales the feature space attributes and is counterbalanced by the weighting coefficient learned by the classifier.

In the case where the data are such that $\|x\| = 1$ for all x, these two classes are merged: indeed $d_e = h \circ k_e$ with $h(x) = \sqrt{2(1 - x)}$ that is strictly decreasing.

4.3   Experimental Results

We compare the most common measures namely the Manhattan (denoted L1) and Euclidean (L2) distances, the Euclidean dot product (EDP) and its normalised form (EDPN), the Gaussian kernel for $\sigma = 50$ (GK50) et $\sigma = 100$ (GK100), the polynomial kernel of degree 3 for $l = 2000$ (PK3) and its normalisation (NPK3). The σ and l values for the GK and PK were chosen according to the data properties. We also add a baseline random measure.

Full Rank Comparison. Table 3 contains the full rank equivalence degrees, also illustrated, together with their standard deviation, on the top graph of figure 2.

As in the binary data case, and for the same reason, the random measure has an equivalence degree of 0.5 with all measures. The degrees equaling 1 are concordant with the theoretical results and indicate the two expected equivalence classes. Again, all measures have a high agreement level, as the maximal proportion of inversions is only 37%, obtained when comparing the Gaussian and polynomial kernels. The observed high degree between L2 and NPK3 does not correspond to a theoretically known result. It can be explained by the level lines of these measures (figure omitted for space constraints): even if they locally differ, they have the same global form and the orders they induce globally agree.

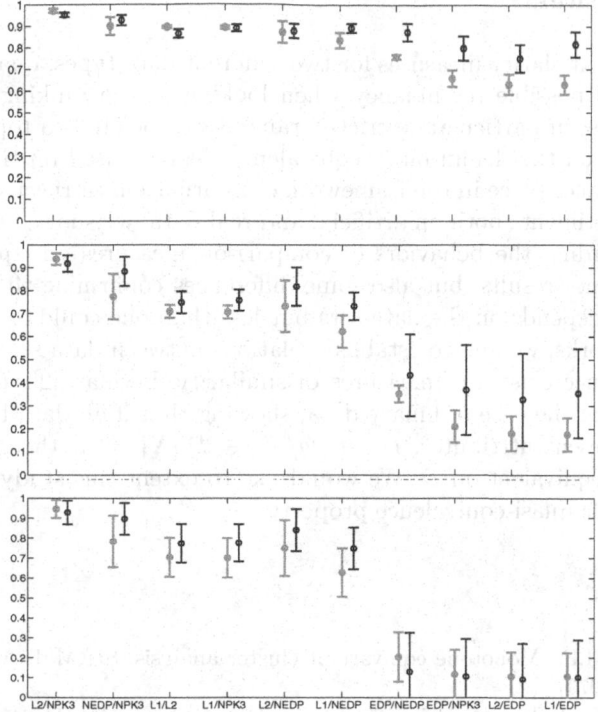

Fig. 2. Equivalence degrees and their standard deviation, for artificial and real numerical data

The top graph of figure 2 highlights a difference between the artificial and real data sets that leads to a slightly different ordering of the measure pairs according to their equivalence degrees. This can be explained by the particularity of the real data: as they correspond to repartition histograms, their L1 norm is constant. This specific structure of the data has consequences on the equivalence degrees.

Top-k Comparison. When focusing on top-k rankings, it can be observed that the difference between the two data types becomes less marked when k decreases. The standard deviations increase, underlying the influence of the request data especially on the beginning of the lists. Besides, although the equivalence degrees significantly decrease, the order of the measure pairs in terms of equivalence degree is not modified. Three equivalence levels can be distinguished in particular for $k = 10$. The highest one is reached by the pair L2/NPK3, meaning that their high agreement holds for the highest similarity values. The lowest values are reached by EDP and any other measures: EDP appears as an isolated measure which has very less in common with the rest of the measures.

5   Conclusion

We compared similarity measures for two different data types, quantifying their proximity and possible redundancy when looking at the ranking they induce, and considering in particular restricted rankings associated to top-k lists. This study, relying on the definition of equivalence degree based on the generalised Kendall tau, takes place in the framework of information retrieval systems. Carrying out experiments both on artificial and real data, we showed some stability property regarding the behaviors of comparison measures on equivalence and quasi-equivalence results, but also some differences confirming that the equivalence degrees depends on the data sets but less than one could expect.

In future works, we aim to establish relations between data set structure and quasi-equivalence classes of measures of similarity. Lerman [2] considered this point of view in the case of binary data, showing that if all data have the same number of present attributes, i.e. if $\exists q / \forall x \in \mathcal{D} \, |X| = q$, then all similarity measures are equivalent on $\mathcal{D}$. We would like to extent this study to numerical data and to the quasi-equivalence property.

References

1. Janowitz, M.F.: Monotone equivariant cluster analysis. SIAM J. Appl. Math. 37, 148–165 (1979)
2. Lerman, I.C.: Indice de similarité et préordonnance associée. In: Séminaire sur les ordres totaux finis, Aix-en-Provence, pp. 233–243 (1967)
3. Baulieu, F.B.: A classification of presence/absence based dissimilarity coefficients. Journal of Classification 6, 233–246 (1989)
4. Batagelj, V., Bren, M.: Comparing resemblance measures. Journal of Classification 12, 73–90 (1995)
5. Omhover, J.-F., Rifqi, M., Detyniecki, M.: Ranking invariance based on similarity measures in document retrieval. In: Detyniecki, M., Jose, J.M., Nürnberger, A., van Rijsbergen, C.J.K. (eds.) AMR 2005. LNCS, vol. 3877, pp. 55–64. Springer, Heidelberg (2006)
6. Rifqi, M., Lesot, M.J., Detyniecki, M.: Fuzzy order-equivalence for similarity measures. In: Proc. of NAFIPS 2008 (2008)
7. Fagin, R., Kumar, R., Sivakumar, D.: Comparing top k lists. SIAM Journal on Discrete Mathematics 17, 134–160 (2003)
8. Fagin, R., Kumar, R., Mahdian, M., Sivakumar, D., Vee, E.: Comparing and aggregating rankings with ties. In: Symp. on Princ. of Database Sys., pp. 47–58 (2004)
9. ImageCLEF challenge (2008), http://www.imageclef.org
10. Bouchon-Meunier, B., Rifqi, M., Bothorel, S.: Towards general measures of comparison of objects. Fuzzy sets and systems 84, 143–153 (1996)
11. Lesot, M.J., Rifqi, M., Benhadda, H.: Similarity measures for binary and numerical data: a survey. Intern. J. of Knowledge Engineering and Soft Data Paradigms (KESDP) 1, 63–84 (2009)
12. Tversky, A.: Features of similarity. Psychological Review 84, 327–352 (1977)

Comparing Partitions by Subset Similarities

Thomas A. Runkler

Siemens Corporate Technology, 81730 Muenchen, Germany
Thomas.Runkler@siemens.com

Abstract. Comparing partitions is an important issue in classification
and clustering when comparing results from different methods, parameters, or initializations. A well–established method for comparing partitions is the Rand index but this index is suitable for crisp partitions
only. Recently, the Hüllermeier–Rifqi index was introduced which is a
generalization of the Rand index to fuzzy partitions. In this paper we
introduce a new approach to comparing partitions based on the similarities of their clusters in the sense of set similarity. All three indices, Rand,
Hüllermeier–Rifqi, and subset similarity, are reflexive, invariant against
row permutations, and invariant against additional empty subsets. The
subset similarity index is not a generalization of the Rand index, but
produces similar values. Subset similarity yields more intuitive similarities than Hüllermeier–Rifqi when comparing crisp and fuzzy partitions,
and yields smoother nonlinear transitions. Finally, the subset similarity
index has a lower computational complexity than the Hüllermeier–Rifqi
index for large numbers of objects.

1 Introduction

A partition of a set $X = \{x_1, \ldots, x_n\}$, $n > 0$, is defined as a tuple of mutually
disjoint subsets $C_1, \ldots, C_c \subseteq X$, $c > 0$, $C_i \cap C_j = \emptyset$, $i, j = 1, \ldots, c$, so that
$C_1 \cup C_2 \cup \ldots \cup C_c = X$. Obviously, for $n = 1$, there is only one partition $C_1 = X$,
and for $n = 2$, there are two partitions $C_1 = X$ and $C_1 = \{x_1\}$, $C_2 = \{x_2\}$. For
arbitrary $n > 0$, the number of partitions is given by the Bell number B_n which
can be recursively computed as

$$B_{n+1} = \sum_{k=0}^{n} \binom{n}{k} B_k, \quad B_1 = 1 \tag{1}$$

For convenience, we represent a c–tuple of partition sets using a partition matrix

$$U = \begin{pmatrix} u_{11} & \cdots & u_{1n} \\ \vdots & \ddots & \vdots \\ u_{c1} & \cdots & u_{cn} \end{pmatrix} \tag{2}$$

$u_{ik} \in \{0, 1\}$, $i = 1, \ldots, c$, $k = 1, \ldots, n$, so $u_{ik} = 1$ if $x_k \in C_i$ and $u_{ik} = 0$ if $x_k \notin C_i$. More generally, we allow that the elements of X may be partially assigned

E. Hüllermeier, R. Kruse, and F. Hoffmann (Eds.): IPMU 2010, LNAI 6178, pp. 29–38, 2010.
© Springer-Verlag Berlin Heidelberg 2010

to several subsets, which become fuzzy subsets then [1], and we obtain fuzzy partitions [2] with $u_{ik} \in [0,1]$, $i = 1, \ldots, c$, $k = 1, \ldots, n$, and the normalization condition

$$\sum_{i=1}^{c} u_{ik} = 1 \tag{3}$$

for all $k = 1, \ldots, n$. Sometimes fuzzy partitions are required to have only non–empty subsets

$$\sum_{k=1}^{n} u_{ik} > 0 \tag{4}$$

but we do not use this restriction in this paper.

Partitions may be learned from data by supervised or unsupervised learning. The supervised variant is called *classification* [3], the unsupervised variant is called *clustering* [4]. Classification uses a set Y of additional objects that are previously assigned to subsets where each subset represents a *class*. Based on similarities between the objects in X and the classified objects in the training set Y classification assigns the objects in X to the respective subsets (classes). Clustering uses the unclassified objects in X and determines a partition in a way that similar objects are assigned to the same subset, and dissimilar objects are assigned to different subsets. So, both classification and clustering are based on object relations (similarities or dissimilarities), and both produce partitions.

Two important problems in classification and clustering are: first, to determine the quality of the resulting partitions, and second, to compare the partitions produced by different methods. To determine the quality of classifiers we (e.g. randomly) divide the set Y into a training set Y_t and a validation set Y_v, ignore the class labels in Y_v, classify the objects in Y_v according to the relations with Y_t, and then compare the resulting class labels of Y_v with the originally given labels. The correspondence of the class labels is then considered as the quality of the obtained partition with respect to its classification perfomance. To determine the quality of (fuzzy) clusterings we use so–called *cluster validity measures* [5,6] which are functions $f(U) \in \mathbb{R}$ that quantify how clearly the objects are assigned to the clusters, e.g. using the *partition coefficient*

$$PC(U) = \frac{1}{n} \sum_{k=1}^{n} \sum_{i=1}^{c} u_{ik}^2 \tag{5}$$

Comparing partitions produced by different methods, parameters, or initializations (obtained by classification, clustering, or in other ways) requires functions $f(U_1, U_2, \ldots, U_j) \in \mathbb{R}$, $j > 1$. Here, we restrict to functions comparing *pairs* of partitions $f(U_1, U_2)$ or $f(U, \tilde{U})$. A popular measure for comparing *crisp* partitions is the *Rand index* [7]. Extensions of the Rand index to *fuzzy* partitions were proposed very recently by Campello [8] and by Hüllermeier and Rifqi [9]. In this paper we present a new approach to comparing both crisp and fuzzy partitions. The underlying idea is that a pair of partitions should be considered similar if their clusters are similar. We compute the similarity of the clusters using subset similarity measures, hence we call this index *subset similarity index*.

This paper is structured as follows: In sections 2 and 3 we will quickly summarize the Rand and Hüllermeier–Rifqi indices. Since Campello's index has some indesirable properties, for example missing reflexivity, $f(U, U) \neq 1$, we will not consider this index here. In section 4 we will present our new approach for comparing partitions using subset similarities. In section 5 we will compare the subset similarity index with the Rand and Hüllermeier–Rifqi indices based on some illustrative experiments. In section 6 we will give our conclusions.

2 The Rand Index

The Rand index [7] measures the similarity of a $c \times n$ partition U and a $\tilde{c} \times n$ partition $\tilde{U}$ (notice that both partitions describe the same number of objects n, but may have a different number of subsets, c and $\tilde{c}$) by considering all pairs of object indices (j, k), $j = 1, \ldots, n$, $k = i + 1, \ldots, n$, and distinguishing the following four cases:

1. Both objects belong to the same subset in U and the same subset in $\tilde{U}$.

$$\forall i = 1, \ldots, c \quad u_{ij} = u_{ik} \tag{6}$$
$$\forall i = 1, \ldots, \tilde{c} \quad \tilde{u}_{ij} = \tilde{u}_{ik} \tag{7}$$

The number of such cases is denoted as n_1.

2. Both objects belong to the same subset in U and different subsets in $\tilde{U}$.

$$\forall i = 1, \ldots, c \quad u_{ij} = u_{ik} \tag{8}$$
$$\exists i = 1, \ldots, \tilde{c} \quad \tilde{u}_{ij} \neq \tilde{u}_{ik} \tag{9}$$

The number of such cases is denoted as n_2.

3. Both objects belong to different subsets in U and the same subset in $\tilde{U}$.

$$\exists i = 1, \ldots, c \quad u_{ij} \neq u_{ik} \tag{10}$$
$$\forall i = 1, \ldots, \tilde{c} \quad \tilde{u}_{ij} = \tilde{u}_{ik} \tag{11}$$

The number of such cases is denoted as n_3.

4. Both objects belong to different subsets in U and different subsets in $\tilde{U}$.

$$\exists i = 1, \ldots, c \quad u_{ij} \neq u_{ik} \tag{12}$$
$$\exists i = 1, \ldots, \tilde{c} \quad \tilde{u}_{ij} \neq \tilde{u}_{ik} \tag{13}$$

The number of such cases is denoted as n_4.

Based on these case counts the Rand index is defined as

$$R(U, \tilde{U}) = \frac{n_1 + n_4}{n_1 + n_2 + n_3 + n_4} \tag{14}$$

3   The Hüllermeier–Rifqi Index

The Hüllermeier–Rifqi index [9] is an extension of the Rand index to fuzzy partitions. Just as the Rand index it computes the similarity between the partitions U and $\tilde{U}$ from the subset assignments of object j $(u_{1j}, \ldots, u_{cj})$, $(\tilde{u}_{1j}, \ldots, \tilde{u}_{\tilde{c}j})$, and the subset assignments of object k $(u_{1k}, \ldots, u_{ck})$, $(\tilde{u}_{1k}, \ldots, \tilde{u}_{\tilde{c}k})$. If both objects belong to the same subset in U, as in case 1 (6) and 2 (8), then $u_{ij} - u_{ik} = 0$ for all $i = 1, \ldots, c$ and therefore

$$E_{jk} = \frac{1}{2} \sum_{i=1}^{c} |u_{ij} - u_{ik}| = 0 \tag{15}$$

If both objects belong to the same subset in $\tilde{U}$, as in case 1 (7) and 3 (11), then $\tilde{u}_{ij} - \tilde{u}_{ik} = 0$ for all $i = 1, \ldots, c$ and therefore

$$\tilde{E}_{jk} = \frac{1}{2} \sum_{i=1}^{\tilde{c}} |\tilde{u}_{ij} - \tilde{u}_{ik}| = 0 \tag{16}$$

If both objects belong to different subsets in U, as in case 3 (10) and 4 (10), then $u_{ij} - u_{ik} = 1$ if object j is in subset i, $u_{ij} - u_{ik} = -1$ if object k is in subset i, and $u_{ij} - u_{ik} = 0$ otherwise, so

$$E_{jk} = \frac{1}{2} \sum_{i=1}^{c} |u_{ij} - u_{ik}| = \frac{1}{2} \cdot 2 = 1 \tag{17}$$

If both objects belong to different subsets in $\tilde{U}$, as in case 2 (9) and 4 (13), then $\tilde{u}_{ij} - \tilde{u}_{ik} = 1$ if object j is in subset i, $\tilde{u}_{ij} - \tilde{u}_{ik} = -1$ if object k is in subset i, and $\tilde{u}_{ij} - \tilde{u}_{ik} = 0$ otherwise, so

$$\tilde{E}_{jk} = \frac{1}{2} \sum_{i=1}^{\tilde{c}} |\tilde{u}_{ij} - \tilde{u}_{ik}| = \frac{1}{2} \cdot 2 = 1 \tag{18}$$

Now the similarity between U and $\tilde{U}$ is low if $E_{jk} = 0$, $\tilde{E}_{jk} = 1$ (case 2) or $E_{jk} = 1$, $\tilde{E}_{jk} = 0$ (case 3), i.e. if $|E_{jk} - \tilde{E}_{jk}| = 1$. And the similarity between U and $\tilde{U}$ is high if both $E_{jk} = \tilde{E}_{jk} = 0$ (case 1) or both $E_{jk} = \tilde{E}_{jk} = 1$ (case 4), i.e. if $|E_{jk} - \tilde{E}_{jk}| = 0$. Averaging and negating this expression finally yields the equation for the Hüllermeier–Rifqi index.

$$H(U, \tilde{U}) = 1 - \frac{1}{n(n-1)} \sum_{j=1}^{n} \sum_{k=j+1}^{n} |E_{jk} - \tilde{E}_{jk}| \tag{19}$$

$$= 1 - \frac{1}{2n(n-1)} \sum_{j=1}^{n} \sum_{k=j+1}^{n} \left| \sum_{i=1}^{c} |u_{ij} - u_{ik}| - \sum_{i=1}^{\tilde{c}} |\tilde{u}_{ij} - \tilde{u}_{ik}| \right| \tag{20}$$

The computational complexity of the Hüllermeier–Rifqi index is $o((c + \tilde{c}) \cdot n^2)$.

4   Comparing Partitions by Subset Similarities

A pair of partition matrices U and $\tilde{U}$ divides a set X into the subsets $C_1, \ldots, C_c$ and $\tilde{C}_1, \ldots, \tilde{C}_{\tilde{c}}$. The set similarity of two subsets C_i and $\tilde{C}_j$, $i \in \{1, \ldots, c\}$, $j \in \{1, \ldots, \tilde{c}\}$ is defined as

$$s_{ij} = \frac{\|C_i \cap \tilde{C}_j\|}{\|C_i \cup \tilde{C}_j\|} \tag{21}$$

If C_i and $\tilde{C}_j$ are fuzzy sets, then the set similarity is defined as

$$s_{ij} = \frac{\sum\limits_{k=1}^{n} T(u_{ik}, \tilde{u}_{jk})}{\sum\limits_{k=1}^{n} C(u_{ik}, \tilde{u}_{jk})} \tag{22}$$

where T is a suitable T norm and C is a suitable T conorm [10]. In this paper, we choose $T = \min$ and $C = \max$, which leads to

$$s_{ij} = \frac{\sum\limits_{k=1}^{n} \min(u_{ik}, \tilde{u}_{jk})}{\sum\limits_{k=1}^{n} \max(u_{ik}, \tilde{u}_{jk})} \tag{23}$$

$i = 1, \ldots, c$, $j = 1, \ldots, \tilde{c}$. The denominator becomes zero if $u_{ik} = \tilde{u}_{jk} = 0$ for all $k = 1, \ldots, n$. In this special case, also the nominator becomes zero, and so we define $s_{ij} = 1$.

The partition subset operator can be defined as follows: $U \subseteq \tilde{U}$ if and only if

$$\begin{aligned} & \left((C_1 = \tilde{C}_1) \vee (C_1 = \tilde{C}_2) \ldots \vee (C_1 = \tilde{C}_{\tilde{c}}) \right) \\ \wedge & \left((C_2 = \tilde{C}_1) \vee (C_2 = \tilde{C}_2) \ldots \vee (C_2 = \tilde{C}_{\tilde{c}}) \right) \\ & \vdots \qquad\qquad\qquad \vdots \\ \wedge & \left((C_c = \tilde{C}_1) \vee (C_c = \tilde{C}_2) \ldots \vee (C_c = \tilde{C}_{\tilde{c}}) \right) \end{aligned} \tag{24}$$

The partition superset operator can be defined accordingly: $U \supseteq \tilde{U}$ if and only if

$$\begin{aligned} & \left((C_1 = \tilde{C}_1) \vee (C_2 = \tilde{C}_1) \ldots \vee (C_c = \tilde{C}_1) \right) \\ \wedge & \left((C_1 = \tilde{C}_2) \vee (C_2 = \tilde{C}_2) \ldots \vee (C_c = \tilde{C}_2) \right) \\ & \vdots \qquad\qquad\qquad \vdots \\ \wedge & \left((C_1 = \tilde{C}_{\tilde{c}}) \vee (C_2 = \tilde{C}_{\tilde{c}}) \ldots \vee (C_c = \tilde{C}_{\tilde{c}}) \right) \end{aligned} \tag{25}$$

We define that U and $\tilde{U}$ are similar if and only if $U \subseteq \tilde{U}$ or $U \supseteq \tilde{U}$. For fuzzy partitions, we define the subset measure

$$\begin{aligned} S_{\subseteq}(U, \tilde{U}) = T\big(& C(s_{11}, s_{12}, \ldots, s_{1\tilde{c}}), \\ & C(s_{21}, s_{22}, \ldots, s_{2\tilde{c}}), \\ & \vdots \\ & C(s_{c1}, s_{c2}, \ldots, s_{c\tilde{c}}) \big) \end{aligned} \tag{26}$$

and the superset measure

$$
\begin{aligned}
S_\supseteq(U,\tilde{U}) = T\big(\; & C(s_{11}, s_{21}, \dots, s_{c1}), \\
& C(s_{12}, s_{22}, \dots, s_{c2}), \\
& \quad\vdots \\
& C(s_{1\tilde{c}}, s_{2\tilde{c}}, \dots, s_{c\tilde{c}}) \; \big)
\end{aligned}
\tag{27}
$$

The similarity measure can then be computed using the subset and superset measures as

$$
S(U,\tilde{U}) = C\big(S_\subseteq(U,\tilde{U}), S_\supseteq(U,\tilde{U}) \big)
\tag{28}
$$

For $T = \min$ and $C = \max$, this can finally be conveniently written as

$$
S = \max\Big(\min_{i=1,\dots,c} \; \max_{j=1,\dots,\tilde{c}} \; s_{ij}, \; \min_{j=1,\dots,\tilde{c}} \; \max_{i=1,\dots,c} \; s_{ij} \Big)
\tag{29}
$$

The computational complexity of the subset similarity index S is $o(c \cdot \tilde{c} \cdot n)$ which is much lower than the complexity of Hüllermeier–Rifqi index for large numbers of objects $n \gg c$, $n \gg \tilde{c}$.

A similar approach has recently been proposed by Beringer and Hüllermeier in chapter 5.2 of [11]. However, Beringer and Hüllermeier suggest to use a T norm T instead of a T conorm C in (28), which yields to much more conservative similarities.

5   Experiments

In this section we present some theoretical considerations and some numerical experiments to compare the properties of the Rand index R, Hüllermeier–Rifqi index H, and the subset similarity index S.

5.1   Reflexivity

As pointed out earlier, we do not consider Campello's index [8] here, because it is not reflexive. For the Rand index, two identical matrices will always yield case 1 or 4 and never case 2 or 3, so $n_1 + n_4 = \frac{n(n-1)}{2}$, $n_2 = n_3 = 0$, which leads to $R = (n_1 + n_4)/(n_1 + n_4) = 1$. For the Hüllermeier–Rifqi index, $U = \tilde{U}$ leads to $E_{jk} = \tilde{E}_{jk}$, $j, k = 1, \dots, n$, and so $H = 1 - 0 = 1$. For the subset similarity index, $U = \tilde{U}$ leads to all ones on the main diagnoal of s, i.e. $s_{ii} = 1$ for all $i = 1, \dots, c$, so $\min_{i=1,\dots,c} \max_{j=1,\dots,c} s_{ij} = 1$, and so $S = \max(1,1) = 1$. So all three considered indices are reflexive.

5.2   Row Permutations

Consider for simplicity an arbitrary matrix U and a matrix $\tilde{U}$ that is equal to U except that two arbitrary rows are exchanged. For the Rand index, exchanging rows will not change the counts n_1, n_2, n_3, and n_4, so we obtain the same result

as with identical matrices, $R = (n_1 + n_4)/(n_1 + n_4) = 1$. For the Hüllermeier–
Rifqi index, exchanging rows will not have any effect either, because for E_{jk}
and $\tilde{E}_{jk}$ we always compute sums over $i = 1, \ldots, c$ which are invariant, so we
obtain the same result as with identical matrices, $H = 1 - 0 = 1$. For the subset
similarity index, exchanging rows in U will change the corresponding rows and
columns in s, but there will still be at least one entry of 1 in each row and
column, so again $\min_{i=1,\ldots,c} \max_{j=1,\ldots,c} s_{ij} = 1$, and so $S = \max(1, 1) = 1$. So
all three considered indices are invariant against row permutations.

5.3   Additional Empty Subsets

We consider adding an empty subset to a partition, i.e. adding a row of zeros to
a partition matrix. For the Rand index, the subset assignments stay the same,
and so will the counts n_1, n_2, n_3, and n_4. Therefore, we obtain the same result
as with identical matrices, $R = (n_1 + n_4)/(n_1 + n_4) = 1$. For the Hüllermeier–
Rifqi index, adding zero entries to $\tilde{u}_{ij}$ and $\tilde{u}_{ik}$ will keep $\tilde{E}_{jk} = E_{jk}$, so we obtain
the same result as with identical matrices, $H = 1 - 0 = 1$. For the subset
similarity index, an additional subset will add a zero row and a zero column to
s which will not change the row and column maxima (except the last), so again
$\min_{i=1,\ldots,c+1} \max_{j=1,\ldots,c+1} s_{ij} = 1$, and so $S = \max(1, 1) = 1$. Notice that up to
here, all indices have shown the same behavior.

5.4   Crisp Binary Partitions

Every crisp binary (i.e. $c = 2$) partition can be represented by a binary number
forming the fist row of the partition. For example, the number $29_{10} = 11101_2$
refers to the partition

$$U = \begin{pmatrix} 1\,1\,1\,0\,1 \\ 0\,0\,0\,1\,0 \end{pmatrix} \tag{30}$$

In this way, for example, all crisp binary 2×5 partitions can be represented
by the numbers $\{0, \ldots, 2^5 - 1\} = \{0, \ldots, 31\}$. The similarities of all pairs of
such crisp binary 2×5 partitions form a 32×32 matrix. Fig. 1 shows the
grey value representations of these matrices for the Rand and Hüllermeier–Rifqi
indices (left) and for the subset similarity index (right). Since we consider here
crisp partitions only, the Rand and Hüllermeier–Rifqi indices always yield the
same results. Light boxes indicate high similarities, and dark boxes indicate
low similarities At the main diagonal and the reverse main diagonal, i.e. for
equal or swapped partitions, all three indices yield maximum similarities, which
corresponds to the findings of sections 5.1 and 5.2. In the other cases the subset
similarity index yields values that are similar (and in some cases even equal) to
the Rand and Hüllermeier–Rifqi indices. Unlike the Hüllermeier–Rifqi index, the
subset similarity index is not a generalization of the Rand index, but it yields
similar values.

   In the following experiments we will focus on fuzzy partitions, so we will not
consider the Rand index any more which is only suitable for crisp partitions.

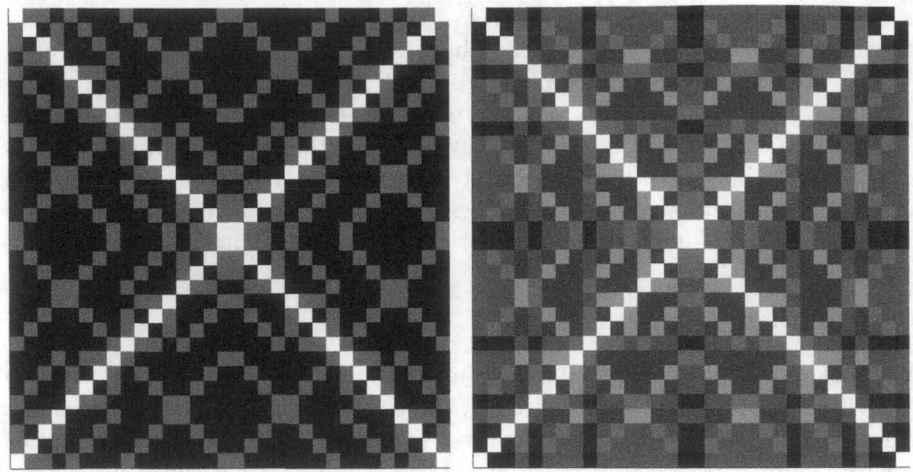

Fig. 1. Similarities between all crisp binary 2×5 partitions. Left: Rand and Hüllermeier–Rifqi indices. Right: Subset similarity index.

5.5   Similarity of 2×2 Crisp and Fuzzy Partitions

Consider the 2×2 crisp unit partition

$$U = \begin{pmatrix} 1 & 0 \\ 0 & 1 \end{pmatrix} \qquad (31)$$

and its similarity with a 2×2 fuzzy partition

$$\tilde{U} = \begin{pmatrix} 1-x & y \\ x & 1-y \end{pmatrix} \qquad (32)$$

For $x, y \in \{0, 0.1, \ldots, 0.5\}$ we compute the Hüllermeier–Rifqi and the subset similarity indices. Fig. 2 shows the corresponding grey value representations (x and y on the horizontal axes, and the similarities on the vertical axis). Again, light boxes indicate high similarities, and dark boxes indicate low similarities. The points at the left corner represent $x = 0$, $y = 0$, i.e. the crisp unit partition. In accordance to section 5.1 both indices yield similarities of one. The points at the right corner represent $x = 0.5$, $y = 0.5$, i.e. the most fuzzy partition

$$\tilde{U} = \begin{pmatrix} 0.5 & 0.5 \\ 0.5 & 0.5 \end{pmatrix} \qquad (33)$$

The Hüllermeier–Rifqi index interprets the crisp unit partition and this fuzzy partition as most dissimilar (similarity zero) which does not match our intuitive expectation. The subset similarity index, in contrast, computes a non-zero similarity of $1/3$ which we consider more intuitive. Inbetween the extremes, the Hüllermeier–Rifqi index is linear in x and y, whereas the subset similarity index has varying slopes allowing smoother transitions.

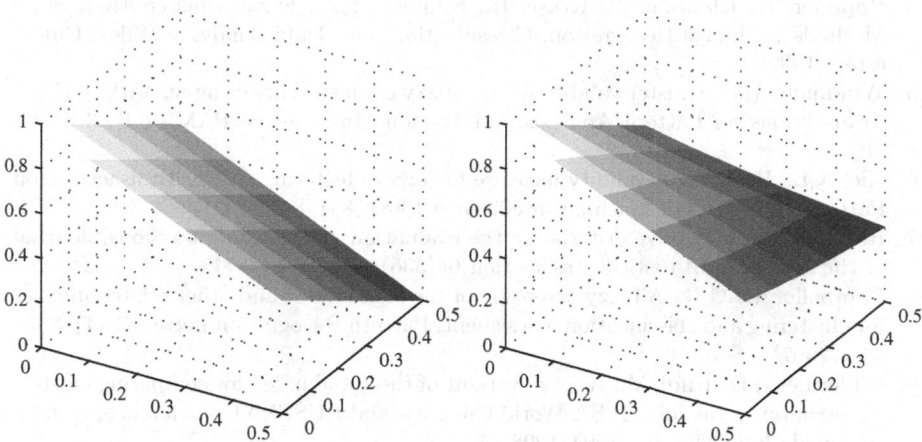

Fig. 2. Similarities between 2×2 Crisp and Fuzzy Partitions. Left: Hüllermeier–Rifqi index. Right: Subset similarity index.

6   Conclusions

We have introduced a new approach to comparing pairs of partitions. The main idea is that partitions should be considered similar if their clusters are similar. We quantify the similarity of the clusters using subset similarity measures, hence we called our new measure *subset similarity index*. Comparisons of this subset similarity index with the Rand and the Hüllermeier–Rifqi indices show that all three indices are reflexive, invariant against row permutations, and invariant against additional empty subsets. Unlike the Hüllermeier–Rifqi index, the subset similarity index is not a generalization of the Rand index, but produces similar values. The Hüllermeier–Rifqi index considers crisp and most fuzzy partitions as completely dissimilar which contradicts our intuitive expectation, while the subset similarity index produces non–zero similarities in this case. The Hüllermeier–Rifqi index is linear with respect to the memberships, while the subset similarity index has varying slopes which allows smoother transitions. The computational complexity of the Hüllermeier–Rifqi index is $o((c + \tilde{c}) \cdot n^2)$, while the subset similarity index has a computational complexity of $o(c \cdot \tilde{c} \cdot n)$, so the subset similarity index is much faster for large numbers of objects $n \gg c$, $n \gg \tilde{c}$.

References

1. Zadeh, L.A.: Fuzzy sets. Information and Control 8, 338–353 (1965)
2. Bezdek, J.C.: Numerical taxonomy with fuzzy sets. Journal of Mathematical Biology 1(1), 57–71 (1974)
3. Schürmann, J.: Pattern Classification — A Unified View of Statistical and Neural Approaches. Wiley, New York (1996)

4. Höppner, F., Klawonn, F., Kruse, R., Runkler, T.A.: Fuzzy Cluster Analysis — Methods for Image Recognition, Classification, and Data Analysis. Wiley, Chichester (1999)
5. Windham, M.P.: Cluster validity for the fuzzy c–means clustering algorithm. IEEE Transactions on Pattern Analysis and Machine Intelligence PAMI-4(4), 357–363 (1982)
6. Xie, X.L., Beni, G.: A validity measure for fuzzy clustering. IEEE Transactions on Pattern Analysis and Machine Intelligence 13(8), 841–847 (1991)
7. Rand, W.M.: Objective criteria for the evaluation of clustering methods. Journal of the American Statistical Association 66(336), 846–850 (1971)
8. Campello, R.J.G.B.: A fuzzy extension of the Rand index and other related indexes for clustering and classification assessment. Pattern Recognition Letters 28(7), 833–841 (2007)
9. Hüllermeier, E., Rifqi, M.: A fuzzy variant of the Rand index for comparing clustering structures. In: Joint IFSA World Congress and EUSFLAT Conference, Lisbon, Portugal, July 2009, pp. 1294–1298 (2009)
10. Schweizer, B., Sklar, A.: Associative functions and statistical triangle inequalities. Publicationes Mathematicae 8, 169–186 (1961)
11. Beringer, J., Hüllermeier, E.: Fuzzy clustering of parallel data streams. In: de Oliveira, J.V., Pedrycz, W. (eds.) Advances in Fuzzy Clustering and its Applications, pp. 333–352. Wiley, Chichester (2007)

Finitely Valued Indistinguishability Operators

Gaspar Mayor[1] and Jordi Recasens[2]

[1] Department of Mathematics and Computer Science, Universitat de les Illes Balears,
07122 Palma de Mallorca, Illes Balears, Spain
gmayor@uib.es
[2] Secció Matemàtiques i Informàtica, ETS Arquitectura del Vallès, Universitat
Politècnica de Catalunya, Pere Serra 1-15, 08190 Sant Cugat del Vallès, Spain
j.recasens@upc.edu

Abstract. Fuzzy equality relations or indistinguishability operators generalize the concepts of crisp equality and equivalence relations in fuzzy systems where inaccuracy and uncertainty is dealt with. They generate fuzzy granularity and are an essential tool in Computing with Words (CWW). Traditionally, the degree of similarity between two objects is a number between 0 and 1, but in many occasions this assignment cannot be done in such a precise way and the use of indistinguishability operators valued on a finite set of linguistic labels such as *small, very much,...* would be advisable. Recent advances in the study of finitely valued t-norms allow us to combine this kind of linguistic labels and makes the development of a theory of finitely valued indistinguishability operators and their application to real problems possible.

Keywords: Representation Theorem, Similarity, T-indistinguishability Operator, finitely valued t-norm.

1 Introduction

1.1 Finitely-Valued t-Norms

In Fuzzy Logic, the logical conjunction is modeled by a t-norm. In this way infinitely valued logics are obtained in which the truth degree of a proposition is a number between 0 and 1. In fuzzy systems, t-norms are also used to model the intersection of fuzzy subsets that are also valued in the unit interval.

In many cases, assigning an exact and precise value between 0 and 1 is not realistic since due to linguistic vagueness or lack of precision in the data this assignment is necessarily imprecise. It would be more reasonable in these cases to consider only a totally ordered finite chain (that can be identified with a finite subset of [0,1]) to valuate the fuzzy concepts.

So the study of operators defined on a finite chain L is of great interest, especially because reasoning is usually done by using linguistic terms or labels that are totally ordered. For instance, the size of an object can be granularized in *very small, small, average, big, very big*. If there is defined an operator T on this set, then we will be able to combine these labels in order to obtain the

E. Hüllermeier, R. Kruse, and F. Hoffmann (Eds.): IPMU 2010, LNAI 6178, pp. 39–48, 2010.

combined one, e.g. $T(average, very\ big)$. In this way of tackling the problem of combining labels, the calculations are very simple since there is no need neither to assign numerical values to them, nor to identify them with an interval or with a fuzzy subset.

Another case when there is useful to use finite chains is when the valued are discrete by nature or by discretization. On a survey of satisfaction of the clients with respect to some service, they may be asked to evaluate it with a natural number between 0 and 5 or with labels going from *not at all satisfied* to *very satisfied*.

In this line, different authors have translated t-norms and t-conorms to finite chains ([5], [6]) obtaining interesting theoretical results.

1.2 Finitely Valued Indistinguishability Operators

In almost all situations the human being categorizes or granularizes the properties or features of the objects in a finite set L of linguistic labels that can be linearly ordered. In these cases, these properties are evaluated on L in a natural way and consequently the fuzzy subsets of the universe of discourse are also valued on L.

In the same way, the degree of similarity, equivalence or indistinguishability between two objects is not a numerical value between 0 and 1, but an element of L that can be interpreted as *rather, very much,*

Indistinguishability operators valued in these finite chains seem to be a very interesting tool that will allow us to study the similarity between objects taking into account the granularity generated by L and will give an interpretation to the calculation on this chain.

The degree of similarity or indistinguishability $E(x, y)$ between two objects x and y will be bounded by the corresponding degrees to $E(x, z)$ and $E(y, z)$.

1.3 Organization of the Paper

After this introductory section a section of preliminary concepts of finitely valued t-norms follows. Section 3 is devoted to some properties of finitely valued indistinguishability operators. In particular, the Representation Theorem [9] is generalized to these operators. Section 4 is devoted to additive generators of finitely valued t-norms. Most of them have additive generators and a new pseudo inverse is defined in order to be able to generate their residuation. The results are applied in section 5 to find the dimension and a basis of finitely valued indistinguishability operators. A section of Concluding Remarks ends the work.

2 Preliminaries

This section contains some definitions and results on finitely valued t-norms that will be needed later on the paper.

Let L be a finite totally ordered set with minimum e and maximum u.

Definition 1. *A binary operation* $T : L \times L \to L$ *is a t-norm if and only if for all* $x, y, z \in L$

1. $T(x, y) = T(y, x)$
2. $T(T(x, y), z) = T(x, T(y, z))$
3. $T(x, y) \leq T(x, z)$ *whenever* $y \leq z$
4. $T(x, u) = x$

The set of t-norms on a finite chain depends only on its cardinality. For this reason we will only consider the chains $L = \{0, 1, ..., n\}$ and $L' = \{0 = \frac{0}{n}, \frac{1}{n}, \frac{2}{n}, ..., \frac{n}{n} = 1\}$.

Example 1

1. The Minimum t-norm T_M on L is defined by $T_M(i, j) = \min\{i, j\}$).
2. The Łukasiewicz t-norm $T_Ł$ on L is defined by $T_Ł(i, j) = \max(i + j - n, 0)$.

Smooth t-norms on finite chains are the equivalent of continuous ones defined on [0,1].

Definition 2. *A map* $f : L \to L$ *is smooth if and only if*

$$0 \leq f(i + 1) - f(i) \leq 1 \text{ for all } i \in L, \ i < n.$$

Definition 3. *A map* $F : L \times L \to L$ *is smooth if and only if it is smooth with respect to both variables.*

Definition 4. *A t-norm* T *on* L *is divisible if and only if for all* $i, j \in L$ *with* $i \leq j$ *there exists* $k \in L$ *such that*

$$i = T(j, k).$$

Smoothness and divisibility are equivalent concepts for t-norms.

Proposition 1. *A t-norm on* L *is smooth if and only if it is divisible.*

The next proposition characterizes all smooth t-norms on L as particular ordinal sums of copies of the t-norm of Łukasiewicz.

Proposition 2. *A t-norm* T *on* L *is smooth if and only if there exists* $J = \{0 = i_0 < i_1 < ... < i_m = n\} \subseteq L$ *such that*

$$T(i, j) = \begin{cases} \max(i_k, i + j - i_k) \text{ if } i, j \in [i_k, i_{k+1}] \text{ for some } i_k \in J \\ \min\{i, j\} \qquad \text{otherwise.} \end{cases}$$

T *is said to be an ordinal sum and can be represented by* $T = < 0 = i_0, i_1, ... i_m = n >$.

3   Finitely Valued Indistinguishability Operators

Indistinguishability operators fuzzify the concepts of crisp equality and crisp equivalence relation. They have been studied under different settings, mainly valued on [0,1] and with respect to a left continuous t-norm, though some generalizations to more general structures like GL-monoids have been carried on.

A very important result is the Representation Theorem that roughly speaking says that every fuzzy set μ on a universe X generates an indistinguishability operator E_μ and that every indistinguishability operator on X can be obtained as the infimum of a family of indistinguishability operators generated in this way. The theorem was first proved by Ovchinnikov for the product t-norm. Then it was generalized to continuous t-norms by Valverde and in [2] it is noticed that it is also true for GL-monoids. Since finitely valued t-norms are such monoids, the Representation Theorem also applies to them.

This section adapts the basic definitions on indistinguishability operators to the finite valued case. In particular, the Representation Theorem and the idea of extensionality are recalled.

Also the concepts of dimension and basis of an indistinguishability operator are considered and the characterization of the set of extensional fuzzy subsets with respect to an indistinguishability operator is adapted to the context of finitely valued t-norms.

Definition 5. *Let T be a t-norm on L. Its residuation $\overrightarrow{T}$ is defined by*

$$\overrightarrow{T}(i|j) = \max\{k \in L \mid T(i,k) \leq j\}.$$

Example 2

1. If $T_{\mathbb{L}}$ is the Łukasiewicz t-norm on L, then $\overrightarrow{T_{\mathbb{L}}}(i|j) = \max(0, n - i + j)$ for all $i, j \in L$.

2. If T_M is the Minimum t-norm on L, then $\overrightarrow{T_M}(i|j) =$
$$\begin{cases} \min\{i,j\} & \text{if } i > j \\ n & \text{otherwise.} \end{cases}$$

Definition 6. *The biresiduation E_T associated to a given t-norm T on L is defined by*
$$E_T(i,j) = T(\overrightarrow{T}(i|j), \overrightarrow{T}(j|i)).$$

Example 3

1. If $T_{\mathbb{L}}$ is the Łukasiewicz t-norm on L, then $E_{T_{\mathbb{L}}}(i,j) = n - |i - j|$ for all $i, j \in L$.

2. If T_M is the Minimum t-norm, then $E_{T_M}(i,j) =$
$$\begin{cases} \min\{i,j\} & \text{if } i \neq j \\ n & \text{otherwise.} \end{cases}$$

Proposition 3. *Let* $T =< 0 = i_0, i_1, ...i_m = n >$ *be a smooth t-norm on* L. *Its residuation* $\overrightarrow{T}$ *is*

$$\overrightarrow{T}(i|j) = \begin{cases} n & \text{if } i \leq j \\ \max(0, i_{k+1} - i + j) & \text{if } i, j \in [i_k, i_{k+1}] \text{ for some } i_k \in J \text{ and } i > j \\ j & \text{otherwise.} \end{cases}$$

Proposition 4. *Let* $T =< 0 = i_0, i_1, ...i_m = n >$ *be a smooth t-norm on* L. *Its biresiduation* E_T *is*

$$E_T(i, j) = \begin{cases} n & \text{if } i = j \\ i_{k+1} - |i + j| & \text{if } i, j \in [i_k, i_{k+1}] \text{ for some } i_k \in J \\ \min\{i, j\} & \text{otherwise.} \end{cases}$$

E_T *is a special kind of* T-*indistinguishability operator.*

Definition 7. *Given a t-norm* T *on* L, *a* T-*indistinguishability operator* E *on a set* X *is a fuzzy relation* $E : X \times X \to L$ *satisfying for all* $x, y, z \in X$

1. $E(x, x) = n$ *(Reflexivity)*
2. $E(x, y) = E(y, x)$ *(Symmetry)*
3. $T(E(x, y), E(y, z)) \leq E(x, z)$ *(T-transitivity).*

Proposition 5. *The biresiduation* E_T *of a t-norm* T *on* L *is a* T-*indistinguishability operator on* L.

Theorem 1. *Representation Theorem for* T-*indistinguishability operators. Let* R *be a fuzzy relation on a set* X *and* T *a t-norm on* L. R *is a* T-*indistinguishability operator if and only if there exists a family* $(\mu_i)_{i \in I}$ *of* L-*fuzzy subsets of* X *(i.e.:* $\mu_i : X \to L$ *for all* $x \in X$*) such that for all* $x, y \in X$

$$R(x, y) = \inf_{i \in I} E_T(\mu_i(x), \mu_i(y)).$$

$(\mu_i)_{i \in I}$ is called a generating family of R and a fuzzy subset that belong to a generating family of R is called a generator of R.

Extensional fuzzy subsets with respect to a T-indistinguishability operator E play a central role since they are the only observable sets taking E into account. In the crisp case, when E is a crisp equivalence relation on a universe X, the only crisp subsets from which something can be said if E is considered are only the union of equivalence classes of E (and intersections if we want to add the empty set). The equivalence classes give the granularity in X. If E is a fuzzy relation, extensional sets play this role and they show the granularity generated by E.

Definition 8. *Let* T *be a t-norm on* L, E *be a* T-*indistinguishability operator on a set* X *and* μ *a fuzzy subset of* X. μ *is extensional with respect to* E *if and only if for all* $x, y \in X$

$$T(E(x, y), \mu(x)) \leq \mu(y).$$

H_E *will denote the set of all extensional fuzzy subsets with respect to* E.

It can be proved that a fuzzy subset is extensional with respect to a T-indistinguishability operator E if and only if it is a generator of E.

The next result is then straightforward.

Proposition 6. *Let T be a t-norm on L, E be a T-indistinguishability operator on a set X and μ a fuzzy subset of X. μ is extensional with respect to E if and only if $E_\mu \geq E$.*

In [2] there is a nice characterization of H_E.

Proposition 7. *Let $F(X)$ be the set of all fuzzy subsets of X and T a t-norm on L. Given a set H of fuzzy subsets of X, there exists a T-indistinguishability operator E on X such that $H = H_E$ if and only if for all fuzzy subsets μ of H and for all $\alpha \in [0,1]$,*

1. $T(\alpha, \mu) \in H$
2. $\overrightarrow{T}(\alpha | \mu) \in H$
3. $\overrightarrow{T}(\mu | \alpha) \in H$
4. $(H, \leq)$ *is a complete sub lattice of $(F(X), \leq)$.*

Going back th the Representation theorem 1, different families of fuzzy subsets can generate the same T-indistinguishability operator E. This gives great interest to the theorem, since if we interpret the elements of the family as degrees of matching between the elements of X and a set of prototypes, we can use different features, giving different interpretations to E.

Among the generating families of a relation, the ones with low cardinality are of special interest, since they have an easy semantical interpretation and also because the information contained in its matrix can be packed in a few fuzzy subsets.

Definition 9. *Let T be a t-norm on L and E a T-indistinguishability operator on X. The dimension of E is the minimum of the cardinalities of the generating families of E in the sense of the Representation Theorem. A generating family with this cardinality is called a basis of E.*

A geometric approach and an algorithm for calculating the dimension and a basis of T-indistinguishability operators with T continuous Archimedean or the Minimum t-norm in [0,1] can be found in [1].

In Section 5 an algorithm to find dimensions and basis of T-indistinguishability operators for an additively generated t-norm T on L will be provided.

4   Additive Generators

Contrarily to the case of t-norms defined on [0,1], many of the t-norms on a finite chain L can be additively generated. In particular, it can be proved that all smooth t-norms on L - including the minimum t-norm and all ordinal sums - have an additive generator. This will provide us of a technique to find the dimension and a basis of a finitely valued T-indistinguishability operator E as well as its set H_E of generators or extensional sets.

Definition 10. *Let $f : L \to [0, \infty)$ be a strictly decreasing function with $f(n) = 0$.*

- *The pseudo inverse $f_+^{(-1)} : [0, \infty) \to L$ is defined by*

$$f_+^{(-1)}(t) = \min\{i \in L; f(i) \le t\} = \min f^{-1}([0, t])$$

- *The pseudo inverse $f_-^{(-1)} : (-\infty, \infty) \to L$ is defined by*

$$f_-^{(-1)}(t) = \begin{cases} \max\{i \in L; f(i) \ge t\} = \max f^{-1}([t, n]) & \text{if } t \ge 0 \\ n & \text{otherwise.} \end{cases}$$

The first pseudo inverse $f_+^{(-1)}$ was first defined in [6]. $f_-^{(-1)}$ is a new pseudo inverse introduced in this paper in order to generate the residuation and biresiduation of a t-norm on L.

Definition 11. *Let T be a t-norm on L. T is generated by a strictly decreasing function $f : L \to [0, \infty)$ with $f(n) = 0$ if and only if*

$$T(i, j) = f_+^{(-1)}(f(i) + f(j)) \text{ for all } i, j \in L.$$

f is called an additive generator of T and we will write $T = \langle f \rangle$.

For an additive generator f, we will indicate $f = (a_0, a_1, a_2, ..., a_n = 0)$ where $a_i = f(i), i \in L$.

Example 4

- An additive generator of the t-norm of Łukasiewicz on L is $(n, n-1, n-2, ..., 1, 0)$.
- An additive generator of the minimum t-norm L is $(2^n - 1, 2^{n-1} - 1, 2^{n-2} - 2, ..., 7, 3, 1, 0)$.

Some results on additive generators are the following ones.

Proposition 8. *Let $f - (a_0, a_1, a_2, ..., a_n = 0)$ and $y = (b_0, b_1, b_2, ..., b_n = 0)$ be strictly decreasing functions on L. Then $\langle f \rangle = \langle g \rangle$ if and only if for all $i, j, k \in L$ with $k \ne 0$,*

1. $a_i + a_j \ge a_0 \Rightarrow b_i + b_j \ge 0$
2. $a_k \le a_i + a_j < a_{k-1} \Rightarrow b_k \le b_i + b_j < b_{k-1}$.

Corollary 1. *If $f : L \to [0, \infty)$ is a strictly decreasing function with $f(n) = 0$ and $\lambda > 0$, then $\langle f \rangle = \langle \lambda f \rangle$.*

Of course, the reciprocal of the corollary is not true.

Proposition 9. *If T is a t-norm on L with additive generator, then we can find an additive generator f of T with $\mathrm{Ran}\, f \in Z^+$.*

Proposition 10. *All smooth t-norms on L have an additive generator.*

For additively generated t-norms we have representations for their residuations and biresiduations.

Proposition 11. *Let T be a t-norm on L with additive generator f. Then*

$$\overrightarrow{T}(i|j) = f_-^{(-1)}\left(f(j) - f(i)\right) \text{ for all } i, j \in L.$$

Proof. Given $i, j \in L$,

$$\begin{aligned}
\overrightarrow{T}(i|j) &= \max\{k \in L \mid T(i, k) \le j\} \\
&= \max\{k \in L \mid f_+^{(-1)}\left(f(i) + f(k)\right) \le j\} \\
&= f_-^{(-1)}\left(f(j) - f(i)\right).
\end{aligned}$$

Proposition 12. *Let T be a t-norm on L with additive generator f. Then*

$$E_T(i, j) = f_-^{(-1)}\left(|f(i) - f(j)|\right) \text{ for all } i, j \in L.$$

Proof

$$\begin{aligned}
E_T(i, j) &= \min\{\overrightarrow{T}(i|j), \overrightarrow{T}(j|i)) \\
&= \min(f_-^{(-1)}\left(f(j) - f(i)\right), f_-^{(-1)}\left(f(i) - f(j)\right)\} \\
&= f_-^{(-1)}\left(|f(i) - f(j)|\right).
\end{aligned}$$

5   Dimension and Basis of an Indistinguishability Operator

In this section we will give a method to calculate the dimension an a basis of a T-indistinguishability operator E on a finite set X when T, a t-norm on L, can be additively generated.

Let μ be a fuzzy subset of a finite set $X = \{r_1, r_2, ..., r_s\}$ of cardinality s. We will write $\mu = (q_1, q_2, ..., q_s)$ when $\mu(r_i) = q_i, i = 1, 2, ..., s$.

A fuzzy subset of X is a generator of E if and only if $E_\mu(r_i, r_j) \ge E(r_i, r_j)$ for all $i, j = 1, 2, ..., s$. If T has f as an additive generator, then this condition can be written as

$$f_-^{(-1)}(|f(\mu(r_i)) - f(\mu(r_j))|) \ge E(r_i, r_j) \text{ for all } i, j = 1, 2, ..., s$$

or

$$|f(\mu(r_i)) - f(\mu(r_j))| \le f(E(r_i, r_j)) \text{ for all } i, j = 1, 2, ..., s.$$

This is equivalent to

$$f(\mu(r_i)) - f(\mu(r_j)) \le f(E(r_i, r_j)) \text{ for all } i, j = 1, 2, ..., s.$$

Proposition 13. *Let T be a t-norm on L with additive generator f and E a T-indistinguishability operator on a finite set X of cardinality s. A fuzzy subset $\mu = (x_1, x_2, ..., x_s)$ is a generator of E if and only if*

$$f(x_i) - f(x_j) \leq f(E(r_i, r_j)) \text{ for all } i, j = 1, 2, ..., s.$$

In other words, H_E is the subset of L^s of solutions of the last system of Diophantine inequalities.

Example 5. If T is the Łukasiewicz t-norm on L, then the last system of inequalities becomes

$$x_i - x_j \leq n - E(r_i, r_j) \text{ for all } i, j = 1, 2, ..., s.$$

Example 6. If T is the minimum t-norm on L, then the last system of inequalities becomes

$$2^{n-x_i} - 2^{n-x_j} \leq 2^{n-E(r_i, r_j)} - 1 \text{ for all } i, j = 1, 2, ..., s.$$

Example 7. The following fuzzy relation E on $X = \{r_1, r_2, r_3, r_4\}$ is a T_M-indistinguishability operator with $L = \{0, 1, 2\}$.

$$E = \begin{pmatrix} 2 & 1 & 0 & 0 \\ 1 & 2 & 0 & 0 \\ 0 & 0 & 2 & 1 \\ 0 & 0 & 1 & 2 \end{pmatrix}.$$

An L-fuzzy subset (x_1, x_2, x_3, x_4) of X is a generator of E if and only if it satisfies the following Diophantine system of inequations.

$$2^{2-x_1} - 2^{2-x_2} \leq 2^{2-1} - 1$$
$$2^{2-x_1} - 2^{2-x_3} \leq 2^2 - 1$$
$$2^{2-x_1} - 2^{2-x_4} \leq 3$$
$$2^{2-x_2} - 2^{2-x_1} \leq 1$$
$$2^{2-x_2} - 2^{2-x_3} \leq 3$$
$$2^{2-x_2} - 2^{2-x_4} \leq 3$$
$$2^{2-x_3} - 2^{2-x_1} \leq 3$$
$$2^{2-x_3} - 2^{2-x_2} \leq 3$$
$$2^{2-x_3} - 2^{2-x_4} \leq 1$$
$$2^{2-x_4} - 2^{2-x_1} \leq 3$$
$$2^{2-x_4} - 2^{2-x_2} \leq 3$$
$$2^{2-x_4} - 2^{2-x_3} \leq 1$$

H_E has 26 elements:

$H_E = \{(2,2,2,2), (2,2,2,1), (2,2,1,2), (2,2,1,1), (2,2,0,0), (2,1,2,2), (2,1,2,1),$
$(2,1,1,2), (2,1,1,1), (2,2,0,0), (2,1,0,0), (1,2,2,2), (1,2,2,1), (1,2,1,2),$
$(1,2,1,1), (1,2,0,0), (1,1,2,2), (1,1,2,1), (1,1,1,2), (1,1,1,1), (1,1,0,0),$
$(0,0,1,2), (0,0,2,1), (0,0,2,2), (0,0,1,1), (0,0,0,0)\}$

E has dimension 2 and $\{(1,2,0,0), (0,0,1,2)\}$ is a basis of E.

6 Concluding Remarks

In this work finitely valued indistinguishability operators have been introduced. The most relevant results are

- A new pseudo inverse has been defined that allow us to generate the residuation of a t-norm.
- A method to find the dimension and a basis of a T-indistinguishability operator solving a Diophantine system of inequalities has been developed.

These results will be related to infinitely valued indistinguishability operators in forthcoming works by the authors.

Acknowledgments. Research partially supported by project numbers TIN2006-14311, TIN2009-07235, MTM2009-10962 and by grant PR2009-0079.

References

1. Boixader, D., Jacas, J., Recasens, J.: Fuzzy Equivalence Relations: Advanced Material. In: Dubois, Prade (eds.) Fundamentals of Fuzzy Sets, pp. 261–290. Kluwer, Dordrecht (2000)
2. Castro, J.L., Klawonn, F.: Similarity in Fuzzy Reasoning. Mathware & Soft Computing (1996)
3. Jacas, J.: Similarity relations - the calculation of minimal generating families. Fuzzy Sets and Systems 35, 151–162 (1990)
4. Ling, C.M.: Representation of associative functions. Publ. Math. Debrecen 12, 189–212 (1965)
5. Mas, M., Monserrat, M., Torrens, J.: QL-Implications on a finite chain. In: Proc. Eusflat 2003, Zittau, pp. 281–284 (2003)
6. Mayor, G., Torrens, J.: Triangular norms on discrete settings. In: Klement, E.P., Mesiar, R. (eds.) Logical, Algebraic, Analytic, and Probabilistic Aspects of Triangular Norms, pp. 189–230. Elsevier BV, Amsterdam
7. Klement, E.P., Mesiar, R., Pap, E.: Triangular norms. Kluwer, Dordrecht (2000)
8. Schweizer, B., Sklar, A.: Probabilistic Metric Spaces. North-Holland, Amsterdam (1983)
9. Valverde, L.: On the structure of F-indistinguishability operators. Fuzzy Sets and Systems 17, 313–328 (1985)
10. Zadeh, L.A.: Similarity relations and fuzzy orderings. Information Science 3, 177–200 (1971)
11. Zadeh, L.A.: Fuzzy logic=Computing with words. IEEE Transactions on Fuzzy Systems 90, 103–111 (1996)
12. Zadeh, L.A.: Towards a theory of fuzzy information granulation and its centrality in human reasoning and fuzzy logic. Fuzzy Sets and Systems 90, 111–127 (1997)

Discovering Rules-Based Similarity in Microarray Data

Andrzej Janusz

Faculty of Mathematics, Informatics, and Mechanics, The University of Warsaw,
Banacha 2, 02-097 Warszawa, Poland
andrzejanusz@gmail.com

Abstract. This paper presents a research on discovering a similarity relation in multidimensional bioinformatic data. In particular, utilization of a Rules-based Similarity model to define a similarity in microarray datasets is discussed. The Rules-based Similarity model is a rough set extension to the feature contrast model proposed by Amos Tversky. Its main aim is to achieve high accuracy in a case-based classification task and at the same time to simulate the human way of perceiving similar objects. The similarity relation derived from the Rules-based Similarity model is suitable for genes expression profiling as the rules naturally indicate the groups of genes whose activation or inactivation is relevant in the considered context. Experiments conducted on several microarray datasets show that this model of similarity is able to capture higher-level dependencies in data and it may be successfully used in cases when the standard distance-based approach turns out to be ineffective.

1 Introduction

In recent years, a lot of attention of researchers from many fields has been put into investigation of DNA microarray data. This growing interest is largely motivated by numerous practical applications of knowledge acquired from such data in medical diagnostics, treatment planning, drugs development and many more. When dealing with microarrays, researchers have to overcome the problem of insufficient availability of data. Due to very high costs of microarray processing, usually the number of examples in datasets is limited to several dozens. This fact, combined with a large number of examined genes, makes many of the classic statistical or machine learning models unreliable and contributes to popularity of case-based models among the microarrays classification methods.

Similarity models play a key role in the case-based classification setting as a notion of similarity is being used in every phase of Case-Based Reasoning cycle (see. [1]). In particular, the decision class of new instances is assigned based on the classes of known examples which were pointed as the most similar to the given case. Numerous a priori given similarity functions have been investigated in the CBR literature but none of them was successful in a wide variety of decision making problems. Especially in domains, such as the bioinformatics, which usually involve working on highly dimensional data, the urge to use the

E. Hüllermeier, R. Kruse, and F. Hoffmann (Eds.): IPMU 2010, LNAI 6178, pp. 49–58, 2010.

similarity learning methods arises. Typically, when exploring microarray data in the case-based fashion, researchers combine distance-based similarity models with genes selection and distance metric learning techniques (e.g. [2], [3], [4]).

The Rules-based Similarity (RBS) model is an alternative approach to the problem of learning a similarity relation from data (see [5], [6]). It may be seen as a rough set extension to the psychologically plausible feature contrast model ([7]). In this model the similarity is expressed in terms of common and distinctive binary features of compared objects. Those features may correspond to higher-level characteristics of examined samples, such as an increased activity (expression level) of a particular group of genes. Due to a large number of genes in a single microarray, the number of such features is also extremely large but with the use of well-established rough set methods it is possible to find those which are the most relevant in the considered context. This approach is different from other rough-set based CBR models (e.g. [8]) as it does not need to consider all pairs of available training samples during the similarity relation learning phase and it does not assume existence of any predefined local similarity measures.

In further sections, an application of RBS model to microarray data will be discussed. First, the basic notation and definitions are given. Section 3 briefly describes the process of discovering the similarity relation from data and Section 4 is an overview of results of experiments in which performance of RBS and some distance-based similarity models were compared on 4 microarray datasets. Finally, the last section concludes the paper and discusses possible directions for the future research.

2   Preliminaries

The problem of learning a similarity relation from data involves working on imprecise concepts and it may be well-handled in a framework provided by the rough set theory ([9]). In this setting available objects are described within an *information system* $I = (U, A)$, where U is a set of objects and A is a set of their attributes. An information system may be seen as a tabular representation of knowledge about a considered universe.

The microarray technology allows to monitor expression levels (activity) of thousands of genes in a single experiment (Fig. 1). Results of multiple microarray experiments can also be arranged in a tabular structure. Unlike in typical information systems, in such a table rows usually correspond to expression levels of particular genes (attributes) and columns represent the samples (objects). However, in order to stay consistent with the standard rough set notation a transposed representation will be used.

Information about a classification of the examined samples may be treated as a special attribute called a *decision*. An information system $T = (U, A, d)$ with a distinguished decision attribute d is called a *decision table*.

The concept of similarity is a relation τ defined over pairs of objects from the set U. If no context is given, it is impossible to determine any features of τ ([7], [10]) and therefore it may be treated as any relation. In such a case,

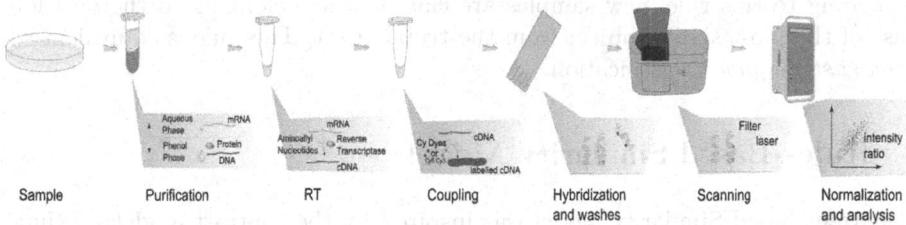

Sample   Purification   RT   Coupling   Hybridization   Scanning   Normalization
                                              and washes   and analysis

Fig. 1. A scheme of a single microarray experiment

approximation of the similarity τ is much more difficult than classification ([11], [12]) because it may be regarded as a problem of assigning binary labels to instances from the set $U' = U \times U$. For this reason, a context of similarity needs to be specified. Since the main scope of this research is the problem of learning the similarity relation for the classification purpose, the context will be narrowed to the decision attribute of given samples.

Definition 1. *Let $T = (U, A, d)$ be a decision table and let τ denote a similarity relation over the set $U' = U \times U$. We will say that τ is a similarity relation in the context of the decision d if the following implication holds for every $u_1, u_2 \in U$:*

$$\forall_{u_1, u_2 \in U} \ (u_1, u_2) \in \tau \Rightarrow d(u_1) = d(u_2) \tag{1}$$

The definition above infers that the similarity relation has to be consistent with the decision classes of d. This feature may be used to guide the relation learning process. Any relation that satisfies the condition (1) may be treated as the similarity relation. It is also worth noting that the definition (1) does not impose any mathematical properties (i.e. reflexivity or symmetry) on τ. However, some similarity models (e.g. distance-based) do that to constrain the searching space of the acceptable *similarity functions*.

Definition 2. *The function $Sim : U \times U \to R$ is a similarity function if*

$$\exists_{\lambda \in R} \forall_{u_1, u_2 \in U} \ Sim(u_1, u_2) \geq \lambda \Leftrightarrow (u_1, u_2) \in \tau \tag{2}$$

for some similarity relation τ defined over $U \times U$.

The function Sim measures a degree of similarity between instances from U. Features of the function Sim depend on a domain of instances. Any similarity function with an appropriate parameter λ define a similarity relation in $U \times U$.

In order to compare the quality of two similarity models it is necessary to introduce a proper quality measure. In the context of the decision attribute it seems natural to check how accurate is the similarity-based classification. In all experiments described in the Section 4 the following classification rule was used:

Definition 3. *If Sim is a similarity function, $x, y \in U$ and the decision value $d(y)$ is unknown, the instance y may be classified using the rule:*

$$\forall_{x' \in U} \ Sim(x, y) \geq Sim(x', y) \wedge d(x) = d_i \Rightarrow d(y) = d_i \tag{3}$$

According to this rule, new samples are classified as belonging to the decision class of the most similar object from the training set. This rule is equivalent to 1-*nearest-neighbor* classification.

3   Rules-Based Similarity Model

The Rules-based Similarity model was inspired by the contrast models of similarity proposed by Amos Tversky in 1977 ([7]). Within this model the similarity is expressed in terms of binary features of compared stimuli. Those features are usually on a higher abstraction level than sensory data available in datasets. For the purpose of gene expression profiling, such features may be interpreted as questions about activity of particular genes or group of genes. Unfortunately in practice it is impossible to verify the value of all $2^{\#genes}$ possible features and only those which are the most relevant in the context of the decision attribute have to be selected. Moreover, it is important to notice that the relevance of a particular feature is strongly dependent on the decision class of compared samples. For instance when examining the *Psorisis* data, different features are important in assessment of the similarity to skin samples taken from patients suffering from skin psoriasis and the samples taken from the healthy controls.

Further in this section, the RBS model for microarray data is briefly described. More insights, general mathematical properties and details regarding its construction are given in [5] and [6].

Selection of Relevant Features
In the RBS model, rough set methods are used to discover the relevant features of investigated objects. First, the expression levels of genes are discretized. For the purpose of this study, a modified version of a discretization algorithm proposed by Hung Son Nguyen in [13] was used. Instead of selecting only one cut at a time, the algorithm was able to choose cuts on several genes that discern most of the samples from different decision classes. Due to the use of the discernibility measure, this method is consistent with the definition of the similarity in the context of the decision attribute (Def. 1) and it turned out to be very effective. It not only discretizes the data but also efficiently decreases its dimensionality. Those genes for which no cut was selected may be removed from the dataset.

For the datasets with more than two decision classes it is necessary to find separate sets of cuts for each of possible decision values. To achieve that, the decision attribute is transformed into a number of binary decision vectors and the discretization is performed for every one of them.

In the second step, the decision and the inhibitory rules[1] are constructed for each of the discretized sets. The decision rules assign a specific decision class to examples which they fit, whereas the inhibitory rules forbid such an assignment. The characteristic function of propositions[2] of those rules define higher-level

---

[1] The inhibitory rules are described in detail in [14].
[2] The left-hand sides.

features. The features extracted in this way are guaranteed to be relevant in the context of the decision attribute, because the rules mining algorithms enforce desired quality on the constructed rules. The features defined by the decision and the inhibitory rules may be treated as arguments for and against the similarity respectively. Those which were defined by the decision rules and match both compared samples form a set of their *common features* and those which were defined by the inhibitory rules and match only to the second sample from the pair will be their *distinctive features*. The sets of common and distinctive features of samples x and y are used to assess a similarity degree of y to x which is denoted by $Sim(x, y)$.

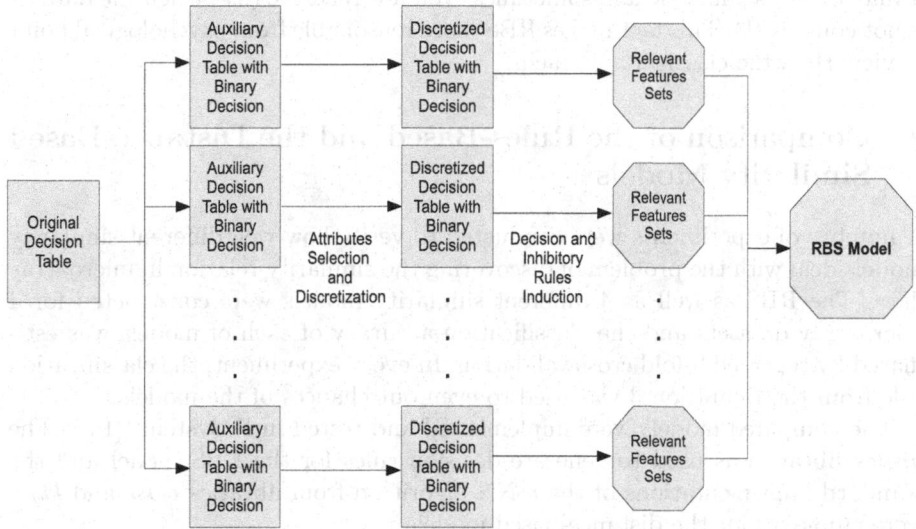

Fig. 2. A scheme showing the process of discovering relevant features in the RBS model. Separate feature sets are constructed for each of the decision classes.

The Similarity Function

The relevant features defined by the rules may be seen as local aspects of the similarity in the context of the decision. To be able to answer the question if a sample y is more similar to sample x_1 than to x_2 it is necessary to aggregate the local similarities and dissimilarities of those samples. The most common way of doing this is to use a special *similarity function* (see Def. 2) which measures a degree of similarity between the samples.

The following similarity function was chosen to aggregate the local similarities in the RBS model:

$$Sim(x, y) = relPower\big(COMM(x, y)\big) - relPower\big(DIST(x, y)\big) \quad (4)$$

In this equation $COMM(x, y)$ and $DIST(x, y)$ are sets of common and distinctive features of x and y. The function $relPower(*)$ approximates the importance of arguments for and against the similarity. Its value is equal to the fraction of training samples from the corresponding decision class which have at least one feature from the set $*$. There are many other similarity functions that can be used with the RBS model. This one was chosen due to its plausible rough set interpretation and effectiveness verified in several benchmarks performed on well-known datasets ([6]). However, in the future more research should be made to establish efficient methods of learning the aggregation function from data.

Unlike in distance-based models, the proposed similarity function does not enforce any properties on the constructed similarity relation. Depending on data, it may be not symmetric and sometimes even not reflexive (e.g. when the dataset is not consistent). This fact makes RBS more reasonable from psychological point of view than the classical approach.

4   Comparison of the Rules-Based and the Distance-Based Similarity Models

A number of experiments were conducted to verify how well different similarity models deal with the problem of discovering the similarity relation in microarray data. The RBS as well as 4 different similarity models were constructed for 4 microarray datasets and the classification accuracy of each of models was estimated by repeated 5-fold cross validation. In every experiment, the classification rule from the Definition 3 was used to even out chances of the models.

The compared models were implemented and tested in R System ([15]). The *arules* library was used to generate decision rules for the RBS model and the standard implementations of the k-NN algorithm from libraries *class* and *kknn* were employed for the distance-based models.

The Competitive Models
The distance-bases similarity models are the most commonly used models in the CBR literature. They were also repeatedly utilized for the classification of microarray data (e.g. [3], [4], [16], [17]). In this approach, the samples are treated as points in a metric space of their attributes and the similarity between them is a non-increasing function of their distance. Due to high dimensionality of microarray data, the distance metric learning techniques usually need to be combined with some genes filtering methods. The distance-based models used in experiments differed in the way they were extracting relevant genes. Their brief description is given below:

1. **1-NN:** This model was based on the classic k-NN algorithm. The similarity function was based on the euclidean distance and no gene selection was made. The results produced by this model were treated as a baseline for other models – it was interesting to observe how much accuracy can be gained with the use of some more sophisticated models.

2. **1-NN+T-test:** In this model one particularly popular filtering algorithm, based on the paired t-test, was used to create a ranking of the genes. For each gene the null hypothesis was tested that its expression levels within different decision classes have equal means. The p-value of the test can be used as a gene relevance measure – the genes with lower p-value are more likely to be important for the classification. The final number of genes used by the model was settled by the *leave-one-out* cross-validation on each training set. It was chosen within the range of 2 to 1000.

3. **1-NN+T-test+ML:** The t-test-based genes selection algorithm was also applied in the third model but this time, in addition to the number of chosen genes, a distance metric was tuned. The Minkowski distance was used in the model and values of the parameter p within the range of 1 to 5 were checked by the *leave-one-out* cross-validation.

4. **1-NN+genetic alg.:** The last distance-based model used in the experiments employed the wrapper approach to genes selection. A genetic algorithm was used to search for an optimal subset of genes. The algorithm was also able to assign weights to selected genes. Each chromosome encoded a subset of genes with their weights. The survival of chromosomes was dependent on the predictive power of the genes reflected by the accuracy of the 1-NN classifier. The weighted euclidean distance was utilized in the algorithm and the classification performance of chromosomes was estimated by the *leave-one-out* cross-validation on the training set.

Datasets and the Results

Four microarray datasets form diverse medical domains were chosen for the experiments. The first one consists of samples taken from patients with papillary thyroid cancer (PTC) and with other non-malignant tumors. The second dataset contains squamous epithelium samples taken from patients suffering from different stages of the reflux disease (Non-Erosive Reflux Disease, Erosive Reflux Disease and Barrett's esophagus). The HepatitisC dataset investigates a role of chronic hepatitis C virus (HCV) in the pathogenesis of HCV-associated hepatocellular carcinoma (HCC). Liver samples from subjects with HCC, liver cirrhosis, HCC developed from liver cirrhosis and normal controls are compared. The fourth dataset is a collection of genetic profiles of skin tissue samples taken from patients examined for skin psoriasis. The tissues are grouped into 3 classes – uninvolved and involved skin from affected individuals and normal skin from healthy controls. Characteristics of those datasets can be found in Table 1.

All datasets were available in processed form and no additional microarray normalization was needed. To increase performance of the distance-based algorithms, data was linearly scaled before the learning phase of those models.

The mean accuracies of compared models are presented in Figure 3. The RBS model achieved the best result on every dataset. The significance of the results was tested with the two-sample t-test[3]. The differences between the RBS

---

[3] The alternative hypothesis in the tests was that the mean accuracy of the RBS model is lower than the accuracies of the compared models.

Table 1. A brief summary of the microarray datasets used in the experiments

Name:	no. samples	no. genes	no. decision classes
PTC	51	16502	2
Barrett	90	22277	3
HepatitisC	124	22277	4
Psoriasis	180	54675	3

and the t-test-based approaches turned out to be statistically meaningful on HepatitisC and Psoriasis data, while the differences between the RBS and the genetic approach was significant on Barrett and Psoriasis data.

The rules-based model outperformed other algorithms in number of utilized genes. The actual number of genes used by the RBS varied for every dataset and cross-validation run but it never exceeded 70, while for the distance-based models (i.e. t-test-based) this number was sometimes as high as several hundreds.

It was also interesting to notice that there was no considerable difference in performance between the two t-test-based models. A possible explanation to this fact is that tuning additional parameters on insufficient number of training examples often causes overfitting.

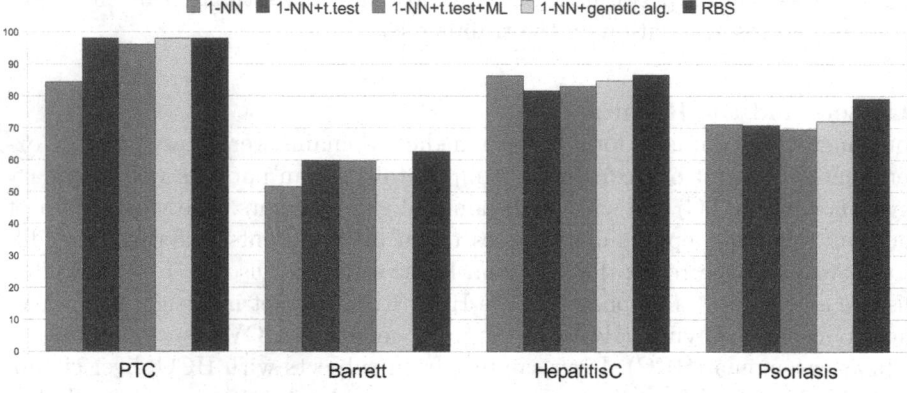

Fig. 3. A performance comparison of several similarity models

5   Conclusions

In this paper a method of discovering a rules-based similarity relation in microarray data was presented. Motivation for this approach comes from works of psychologists who noticed that the human way of perceiving similar objects has different properties than distance-based similarity models. In the model, a decision rules mining algorithm is used to extract features which are relevant in the context of a decision attribute. Such features may correspond to groups of genes whose activation (expression level) is an important argument for or against the similarity of compared samples.

The classification accuracy of the RBS was compared with popular distance-based methods on 4 microarray datasets from different medical domains. The results show that the proposed model is able to outperform other similarity relation learning techniques in both accuracy and the number of utilized genes.

The idea of RBS is a "research in progress" project. Although the early results are encouraging, there are still many areas in which the model may be improved. Currently, one algorithm is used to perform selection of relevant genes and discretization. In the future some other methods should be tried. One promising approach is to employ the idea of dynamic reducts (see [18]). Genes from the dynamic core might be selected and their discretization could be conducted with the use of information about the cuts generated during construction of the reducts. Another idea is to focus on incorporation of domain knowledge into the model. Gene ontologies may be used to reinforce extraction of relevant features. New higher-level features might be constructed from genes which perform similar function and some constrains might be introduced to the rules mining algorithm to merge semantically similar rules. Finally, some specialized indexing algorithms, which would make use of induced rules, may be developed to increase computational performance of the RBS model.

Any progress in the field of learning similarity relation from data would be beneficial to researchers from many fields. It is important, especially in domains as bioinformatics, where efficient and more accurate models could lead to discovering of more effective and safer drugs or better planing of treatments. The classical distance-based approach is sometimes unable to deal with the *few-objects-many-attributes* problem and the Rules-Based Similarity appears to be an interesting alternative.

Acknowledgements. The author would like to thank Michał Grotowski for proofreading this paper. This research was partially supported by the grants N N516 368334 and N N516 077837 from Ministry of Science and Higher Education of the Republic of Poland.

References

1. Aamodt, A., Plaza, E.: Case-based reasoning: Foundational issues, methodological variations, and system approaches. Artificial Intelligence Communications 7(1), 39–59 (1994)
2. Martín-Merino, M., Las Rivas, J.: Improving k-nn for human cancer classification using the gene expression profiles. In: Adams, N.M., Robardet, C., Siebes, A., Boulicaut, J.-F. (eds.) IDA 2009. LNCS, vol. 5772, pp. 107–118. Springer, Heidelberg (2009)
3. Ben-Dor, A., Bruhn, L., Friedman, N., Nachman, I., Schummer, M., Yakhini, Z.: Tissue classification with gene expression profiles. Journal of Computational Biology 7(3-4), 559–583 (2000)
4. Xiong, H., Chen, X.w.: Kernel-based distance metric learning for microarray data classification. BMC Bioinformatics 7(1), 299 (2006)
5. Janusz, A.: Rule-based similarity for classification. In: Proceedings of the WI/IAT 2009 Workshops, September 15-18, pp. 449–452. IEEE Computer Society, Los Alamitos (2009)

6. Janusz, A.: Learning a rule-based similarity: A comparison with the genetic approach. In: Proceedings of the Workshop on Concurrency, Specification and Programming (CS&P 2009), Krakw-Przegorzay, Poland, September 28-30, vol. 1, pp. 241–252 (2009)
7. Tversky, A.: Features of similarity. Psychological Review 84, 327–352 (1977)
8. Greco, S., Matarazzo, B., Slowinski, R.: Dominance-based rough set approach to case-based reasoning. In: Torra, V., Narukawa, Y., Valls, A., Domingo-Ferrer, J. (eds.) MDAI 2006. LNCS (LNAI), vol. 3885, pp. 7–18. Springer, Heidelberg (2006)
9. Pawlak, Z.: Information systems, theoretical foundations. Information systems 3(6), 205–218 (1981)
10. Gati, I., Tversky, A.: Studies of similarity. In: Rosch, E., Lloyd, B. (eds.) Cognition and Categorization, pp. 81–99. L. Erlbaum Associates, Hillsdale (1978)
11. Pawlak, Z.: Rough sets, rough relations and rough functions. Fundamenta Informaticae 27(2-3), 103–108 (1996)
12. Skowron, A., Stepaniuk, J.: Approximation of relations. In: RSKD '93: Proceedings of the International Workshop on Rough Sets and Knowledge Discovery, London, UK, pp. 161–166. Springer, Heidelberg (1994)
13. Nguyen, H.S.: On efficient handling of continuous attributes in large data bases. Fundamenta Informaticae 48(1), 61–81 (2001)
14. Delimata, P., Moshkov, M.J., Skowron, A., Suraj, Z.: Inhibitory Rules in Data Analysis: A Rough Set Approach. Studies in Computational Intelligence, vol. 163. Springer, Heidelberg (2009)
15. R Development Core Team: R: A Language and Environment for Statistical Computing. R Foundation for Statistical Computing, Vienna, Austria (2008)
16. Deutsch, J.M.: Evolutionary algorithms for finding optimal gene sets in microarray prediction. Bioinformatics 19(1), 45–52 (2003)
17. Jirapech-Umpai, T., Aitken, S.: Feature selection and classification for microarray data analysis: Evolutionary methods for identifying predictive genes. BMC Bioinformatics 6(1), 148 (2005)
18. Bazan, J.G., Skowron, A., Synak, P.: Dynamic reducts as a tool for extracting laws from decisions tables. In: Raś, Z.W., Zemankova, M. (eds.) ISMIS 1994. LNCS, vol. 869, pp. 346–355. Springer, Heidelberg (1994)

Fuzzy Clustering of Incomplete Data Based on Cluster Dispersion

Ludmila Himmelspach and Stefan Conrad

Institute of Computer Science
Heinrich-Heine-Universität Düsseldorf
D – 40225 Düsseldorf, Germany
{himmelspach,conrad}@cs.uni-duesseldorf.de

Abstract. Clustering algorithms are used to identify groups of similar data objects within large data sets. Since traditional clustering methods were developed to analyse complete data sets, they cannot be applied to many practical problems, e.g. on incomplete data. Approaches proposed for adapting clustering algorithms for dealing with missing values work well on uniformly distributed data sets. But in real world applications clusters are generally differently sized. In this paper we present an extension for existing fuzzy c-means clustering algorithms for incomplete data, which uses the information about the dispersion of clusters. In experiments on artificial and real data sets we show that our approach outperforms other clustering methods for incomplete data.

Keywords: Fuzzy cluster analysis, incomplete data.

1 Introduction

Clustering is an important technique for automatic knowledge extraction from large amounts of data. Its task is to identify groups or clusters of similar objects within a data set [5]. Data clustering is used in many areas, including database marketing, web analysis, information retrieval, bioinformatics, and others. However, if clustering methods are applied on real data sets, a problem that often arises is that data items are afflicted with missing values. Missing values could be caused for example by problems or failures during the data collection, data transfer, data cleaning or as a result of the data fusion from various sources. Depending on the cause of missingness, missing values can be missing at random or depending on the values of variables in the data set.

The traditional clustering methods were developed to analyse complete data. In cases where the completion of data sets by repeated data collection is undesirable or unpossible e.g. for financial or time reasons, there is a need for analysis methods handling incomplete data. In the literature there are generally three different methods to deal with incomplete data sets [9], [11], [12]. The first one is based on the elimination of data objects or features which comprise missing values. A main drawback of this approach is that a lot of feature values are not taken into account during the analysis and thus much information gets lost. The

E. Hüllermeier, R. Kruse, and F. Hoffmann (Eds.): IPMU 2010, LNAI 6178, pp. 59–68, 2010.
© Springer-Verlag Berlin Heidelberg 2010

most frequently used method is data imputation, where values are estimated
to fill in missing values in a preprocessing step [2]. Afterwards the clustering
methods can be used on compelete data without needing to make any further
modifications. However, in addition to the high computational costs the drawback of this approach is that the results of the data analysis are effected by
imputation techniques, because the observed (real) and the estimated values are
not distinguished during the data analysis. The basic idea of the third method
is to adapt the clustering methods for dealing with missing values. In the literature there are already several proposals for adapting partitioning clustering
algorithms for handling missing values [6], [10], [12], [11]. The experiments conducted in [7] have shown that these methods work well as long as clusters have
similar size. But in real world applications clusters are generally differently sized.
In this paper we present an extension for fuzzy c-means algorithms for incomplete data, which takes the cluster dispersion into account. In experiments on
artificial and real data sets, we demonstrate the capability of our approach and
compare it with other fuzzy c-means clustering algorithms for incomplete data.
We give a particular attention to the analysis of the performance of the methods depending on the different missing-data mechanisms and the percentage of
missing values in the data set.

The remainder of the paper is organized as follows. In Section 2 we give an
overview of the basic fuzzy c-means clustering algorithm and methods for adapting fuzzy c-means algorithm for incomplete data. We introduce our approach to
fuzzy clustering with missing values regarding the dispersion of the clusters in
Section 3. The evaluation results of our method and the comparison with other
existing algorithms are presented in Section 4. We close this paper with a short
summary and discuss future work in Section 5.

2   Fuzzy Clustering of Incomplete Data Sets

2.1   Fuzzy C-Means Algorithm (FCM)

The fuzzy c-means clustering algorithm (FCM) is a partitioning clustering algorithm, which divides a given data set $X = \{x_1, ..., x_n\}$ in d-dimensional metric
data space into c clusters. Unlike the classical partitioning clustering methods,
which assign each data object to exactly one cluster, fuzzy c-means algorithm
assigns data points to clusters with membership degrees [1], [6]. The membership
degree $u_{ik} \in [0, 1]$ expresses the relative degree to which data point x_k belongs
to the cluster C_i and is calculated as follows:

$$u_{ik} = (D_{ik}^{1/(1-m)})/(\sum_{j=1}^{c} D_{jk}^{1/(1-m)}), \tag{1}$$

where $m > 1$ is the fuzzification parameter and $D_{ik} = \| x_k - \mu_{C_i} \|_A^2$.

$$J_m(U, \mu) = \sum_{i=1}^{c} \sum_{k=1}^{n} u_{ik}^m \cdot D_{ik} . \tag{2}$$

Like most partitioning clustering algorithms FCM determines an optimal partitioning by minimizing an objective function given in Equation 2 in an iterative process. The algorithm begins with initialising cluster centers μ_i, which are randomly chosen points in the data space. In the first iteration step the membership degrees of each data point to each cluster are calculated according to Formula 1. In the second iteration step the new cluster prototypes are calculated based on all data points depending on their membership degrees to the cluster:

$$\mu_{ij} = (\sum_{k=1}^{n}(u_{ik})^m x_{kj})/(\sum_{k=1}^{n}(u_{ik})^m), \qquad 1 \leq i \leq c \text{ and } 1 \leq j \leq d . \qquad (3)$$

The iterative process continues as long as cluster centers change up to a value ϵ.

2.2 Fuzzy Clustering of Incomplete Data

The fuzzy c-means algorithm cannot be directly applied to incomplete data sets, because it uses every feature value of each data item. In literature several approaches for adapting FCM for clustering incomplete data are proposed. Some of them such as *whole-data strategy (WDS)* and *partial distance strategy (PDS)* [6] carry out the analysis only on the basis of available values. Other methods estimate and replace the missing feature values or distances in each iteration of the fuzzy c-means algorithm. As examples can be taken the *optimal completion strategy (OCS)*, the *nearest prototype strategy (NPS)* [6] and the *distance estimation strategy (DES)* [10]. The results of object data experiments described in [6], [7] showed that the lowest misclassification errors and the best accuracy are obtained by PDSFCM, OCSFCM and NPSFCM. The results of these three approaches are quite similar in all experiments. As OCSFCM provides a basis for our approach, in the following we focus in on the description of this method.

Optimal Completion Strategy (OCS). The idea of the *Optimal Completion Strategy (OCS)* [6] is to estimate missing values depending on all cluster centers in an additional third iteration step of FCM as follows:

$$x_{kj} = (\sum_{i=1}^{c}(u_{ik})^m \mu_{ij})/(\sum_{i=1}^{c}(u_{ik})^m), \qquad 1 \leq k \leq n \text{ and } 1 \leq j \leq d . \qquad (4)$$

The calculation of membership degrees and the cluster centers in the first two iteration steps works in the same way as in the FCM. The missing values in the data matrix are replaced by random values at the beginning of the algorithm.

The missing values of incomplete data item can be completely substituted by the corresponding values of cluster prototype to which the data point has highest membership degree respectively the minimum partial distance [3]. This modification of OCS is referred to as the *Nearest Prototype Strategy (NPS)* [6].

3   Fuzzy Clustering of Incomplete Data Based on Cluster Dispersion

OCSFCM and NPSFCM estimate missing values of a data point only depending on distances between this data point and cluster centers. These approaches disregard completely the information about the cluster sizes. In real world applications the data objects are generally distributed on differently sized clusters. This way the marginal data objects of a large cluster have a larger distance to their cluster center than marginal objects of a small cluster. If the estimation of missing values and the assignment of a data object are calculated only on the basis of distances between the data point and cluster centers, it is highly possible, that the marginal objects of a large cluster are assigned falsely to the nearest small cluster. Also the experiments described in [7] have shown, that OCSFCM and NPSFCM produce more accurate results on uniformly distributed data sets than on data sets with clusters of different size. In order to avoid such misclassifications we developed a new membership degree u_{ik}^* for estimating missing values, which takes also the cluster dispersion into account.

We divide the data set X into X_{obs}, the set of completely observed data items, and X_{mis}, the set of data items with missing values. Furthermore, we divide the feature set F into F_{obs}, the set of completely observed features, and F_{mis}, the set of features with missing values. Then the membership degree u_{ik}^* of a data point x_k to a cluster C_i is defined as follows:

$$u_{ik}^* = (s_i^{*2} D_{ik}^{1/(1-m)})/(\sum_{j=1}^{c} s_j^{*2} D_{jk}^{1/(1-m)}) . \tag{5}$$

We calculate the squared dispersion s_i^{*2} of a cluster C_i as a squared averaged distance of data points to their cluster centers according to Formula 6.

$$s_i^{*2} = \frac{1}{\mid C_i \cap X_{obs} \mid -1} \sum_{x_j \in C_i \cap X_{obs}} \sum_{f \in F_{obs}} (x_j.f - \mu_{C_i}.f)^2 , \tag{6}$$

where $x_j \in C_i \Leftrightarrow u_{ij} = max\{u_{1j}, ..., u_{cj}\}$ and $\mid C_i \cap X_{obs} \mid \geq 2$. The membership degree u_{ik}^* is the higher the larger the dispersion of the cluster and the smaller the distance between the data point and the cluster center are. If all clusters are uniformly distributed then the membership degree u_{ik}^* depends only on the distances between the data point and cluster centers.

The resulting algorithm is referred to as *Fuzzy C-Means Algorithm for Incomplete Data based on Cluster Dispersion (FCMCD)*. The working principle of FCMCD is adapted from OCSFCM (see Algorithm 1). In the third iteration step the missing values are estimated depending on the cluster prototypes and dispersion of clusters as follows:

$$x_{kj} = (\sum_{i=1}^{c}(u_{ik}^*)^m \mu_{ij}')/(\sum_{i=1}^{c}(u_{ik}^*)^m), \qquad 1 \leq k \leq n \text{ and } 1 \leq j \leq d . \tag{7}$$

Algorithm 1. FCMCD(X, c, m, ϵ)

Require: X is an incompete data set, $1 < c < n$ is a number of clusters, $m > 1$ is a fuzzification parameter, $\epsilon > 0$

1: Initialize the set of data centers $\mu' = \{\mu'_1, ..., \mu'_c\}$
2: Initialize all missing values x_{kj} in X with random values
3: $\mu = \{\}$
4: **repeat**
5:     $\mu = \mu'$
6:     Calculate the membership degrees u_{ik} of each data point x_k to each cluster C_i // *Step 1*
7:     Calculate the set of new cluster centers $\mu' = \{\mu'_1, ..., \mu'_c\}$ // *Step 2*
8:     Estimate and fill in all missing values x_{kj} according to Formula 7 // *Step 3*
9: **until** $\|\mu - \mu'\| > \epsilon$
10: **return** μ'

So far we calculate the cluster dispersion on the basis of completely observed features. Since the values in these features are available for incomplete data points as well, we can also include the data objects with missing values during the calculation of cluster dispersion s_i^*. If the missing values occur in a large number of data objects but in few attributes, this alternative affords to include more available values during the calculation of cluster dispersion than in Formula 6 described. Furthermore, in this way we avoid the restriction that each cluster must consist at least of two completely observed data items. For a distinction from our basic approach, we refer to this alternative method as FCMCD*.

Also NPSFCM can be extended in a straightforward way using the new membership degree. The missing values of incomplete data objects must be substituted by the corresponding values of the cluster prototypes to which the data point shows the highest membership degree u_{ik}^*. For that, the calculation of the numerator of membership degree u_{ik}^* is here sufficient.

4 Data Experiments

We have conducted several experiments on an artificial data set as well as real data. The artificial data set was generated by a composition of three 3-dimensional Gaussian distributions. It consists of 300 data points which are unequally distributed on three differently sized clusters with 52, 101 and 147 data items. The real world data set contains the demographic information about 203 countries. For our experiments we used only the attributes average age, death rate and child mortality. We achieved the best result for the silhouette coefficient [8] of 0.58 for two clusters with 46 and 157 data items using basic FCM. For our experiments we used the range from 0 to 10 for the feature values. As dependent features do not provide additional information for the clustering, we ensured that the values of different features are uncorrelated in both data sets.

To generate incomplete data sets, both data sets are modified by successively removing values in two of three features with different probabilities according to a multivariate pattern [9]. The percentage of missing values was calculated in relation to all values in data set. As missing values can induce a random or conditional reduction of a data set, we deleted the values from test data according to the common missing-data mechanisms MCAR, MAR and NMAR. In this way we want to test whether the performance of algorithms depends on different missing-data mechanisms, which refer the relationship between missingness and the underlying values in the data set [9]. The missing values are called *missing completely at random (MCAR)*, if the missingness does not depend on the data values in the data set independent whether they are missing or observed. The missing values are denoted as *missing at random (MAR)*, if the missingness depends only on values that are observed, and not on the components that are missing. If the missingness of data depends on the missing values themselves then the missing-data mechanism is called *not missing at random (NMAR)*.

In our experiments we proceeded as follows: first we clustered the complete data sets with basic FCM to find out the actual distribution of the data points into clusters. We used these clusterings as baseline for the comparison. Then we clustered the incomplete data with several fuzzy c-means algorithms for incomplete data. To create the test conditions as real as possible, we initialized the cluster prototypes with random values at the beginning. For the stopping criterion $\|\mu - \mu'\| < \epsilon$ we used the Frobenius norm distance. In all our experiments we set the value ϵ on 0.0001. As the experimental results for extension of OCSFCM and NPSFCM are very similar, below we present the results of our experiments on the example of OCSFCM organized according to missing-data mechanisms.

4.1   Test Results for Data with Missing Values MCAR

Figure 1 represents the performance results for OCSFCM, FCMCD and FCMCD* on artificial and real data sets with missing values "missing completely at random". To evaluate performance, we compare the averaged accuracy (percentage of correctly classified data items) obtained over 30 trials in relation to the percentage of missing values in the data sets. For 0% missing values, all approaches reduce to basic FCM, and find the same partitioning of data items as FCM. For 5% or more missing values in the data sets, the performance results of FCMCD and FCMCD* are quite similar. These algorithms produce a lower number of misclassification errors than OCSFCM. The averaged accuracy of these two algorithms exceed 90%, when the percentage of missing values is not greater than 50%. Moreover, FCMCD and FCMCD* are considerably more stable than OCSFCM. With a few exceptions these algorithms produce the same partitioning of data objects independent of initial partitioning. In contrast, OCSFCM produces from trial to trial different partitioning of data items into clusters. Consequently different numbers of misclassification errors are obtained by OCSFCM in every trial. We captured the performance variations of OCSFCM with standard deviation (bars in figures). Furthermore, the standard deviation for OCSFCM significantly increases with increasing number of missing values in data set.

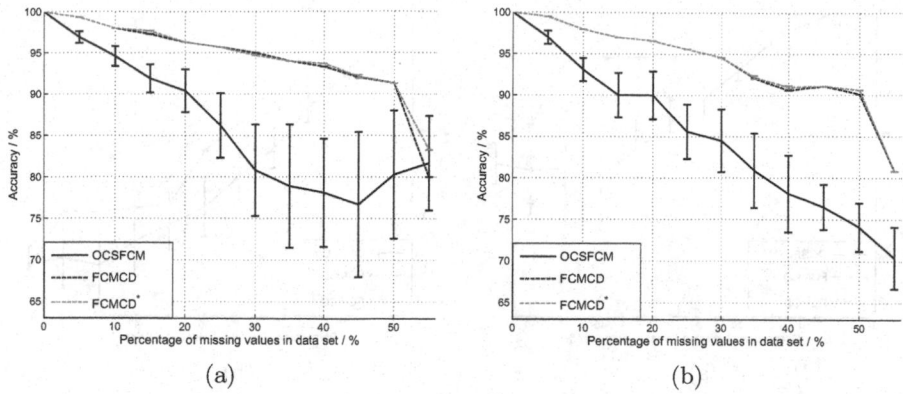

Fig. 1. Averaged results of 30 trials for accuracy on (a) artificial and (b) real data sets with missing values MCAR (bars indicate +/- on standard deviation)

4.2 Test Results for Data with Missing Values MAR

The performance results for OCSFCM, FCMCD and FCMCD* on data with missing values "missing at random" are shown in Figure 2. All algorithms show quite similar performance when the percentage of missing values is relatively low. For 15% or more missing values in the data sets we observe significant differences in the performance of algorithms. In comparison to missing values MCAR, the algorithms perform somewhat worse on data with missing values MAR, especially on real data set. This is due to the fact that missing values MAR occur in data items depending on values of available features and thus, they occur in data objects with particular properties. In this way the completely available data objects do not represent the whole data set anymore. Therefore, the missing values MAR can only be estimated with less accuracy as missing values MCAR. And that leads to more misclassifications with increasing number of missing values in the data set. Also a slightly better performance of FCMCD* compared to FCMCD can be explained by the fact that FCMCD* calculates the dispersion of clusters on the basis of feature values of all data items and FCMCD takes only feature values of completely available data items into account.

4.3 Test Results for Data with Missing Values NMAR

Figure 3 shows the experimental results for OCSFCM, FCMCD and FCMCD* on data with missing values "not missing at random". As in the case of missing values MAR, the performance of the algorithms is worse than on data with missing values MCAR. The reasons behind this are the same as in the case of missing values MAR. Missing values occur in data items with particular properties so that completely available data items do not represent the whole data set. In this way some clusters are more afflicted with missing values than others. Thus, clusters, which contain a lot of data objects with missing values, are not

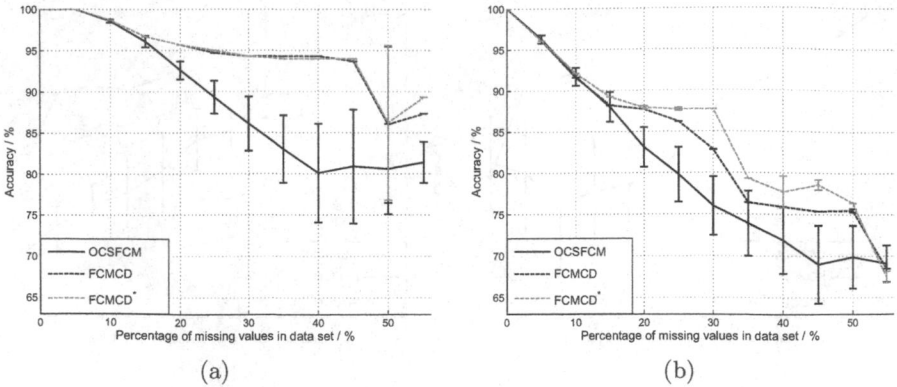

(a)   (b)

Fig. 2. Averaged results of 30 trials for accuracy on (a) artificial and (b) real data sets with missing values MAR (bars indicate +/- on standard deviation)

identified as such by clustering algorithms. Experiments showed, that OCSFCM splits clusters with a low number of incomplete data items in several clusters and disperses data items of clusters with a high number of incomplete data items to other clusters. In contrast, FCMCD and FCMCD* strive to preserve the structure of clustering by estimating missing values with regard to the dispersion of clusters. This is reflected also in the fact that the performance of FCMCD and FCMCD* is better than the performance of OCSFCM on data with missing values NMAR (cf. Figure 3).

4.4 Prototype Error and Runtime

In our experiments we were also interested in comparing the runtime (here: mean number of iterations to termination) of algorithms. Table 1 gives the av-

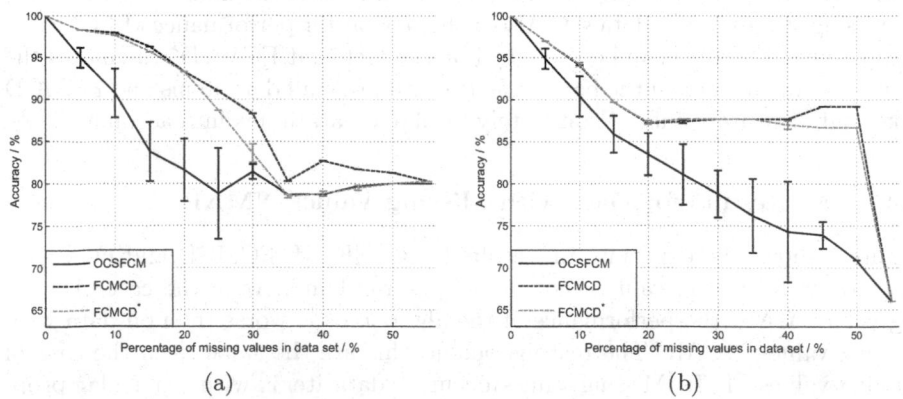

(a)   (b)

Fig. 3. Averaged results of 30 trials for accuracy on (a) artificial and (b) real data sets with missing values NMAR (bars indicate +/- on standard deviation)

Table 1. The average number of iterations to termination

% Missing	Mean Number of Iterations		
	OCSFCM	FCMCD	FCMCD*
5	22.2	17.7	17.8
15	27.8	21.4	19.8
25	35.4	22.7	22.7
35	46.6	26.3	26.5
45	85.5	48.0	49.8
55	143.5	89.6	102.4

Table 2. The average prototype error

% Missing	Mean Prototype Error		
	OCSFCM	FCMCD	FCMCD*
5	0.1756	0.1065	0.1043
15	0.4237	0.1504	0.1504
25	0.5467	0.1585	0.1585
35	0.7468	0.3265	0.3283
45	0.8791	1.0844	1.1387
55	1.1558	2.2040	2.1811

erage number of iterations required to terminate for three approaches obtained over 30 trials on real data set with missing values MCAR. For complete data sets all algorithms require such as basic FCM about 8-12 iterations to termination. With an increasing number of missing values in the data set, the mean number of iterations increases strongly. From 35% of missing values in the data set, OCSFCM requires almost double number of iterations to terminate than the other two algorithms. There are no significant differences in the runtime of FCMCD and FCMCD*.

For some applications the information about the location of clusters is important as well as the information about the partitioning of data objects into clusters. Therefore, we analysed the algorithms regarding the determination of cluster prototypes in presence of missing values in the data set. Table 2 gives the average Frobenius norm distance between the terminal cluster prototypes obtained by FCM on the complete data set and the corresponding terminal cluster prototypes computed by the three algorithms on the real data set with missing values MCAR. When the percentage of missing values is not greater than 40% in the data set, the terminal cluster prototypes obtained by FCMCD and FCMCD* are considerably more accurate than terminal prototypes obtained by OCSFCM. From 45% of missing values in the data set, OCSFCM produces more accurate terminal cluster prototypes than our approach. It is very interesting that the accuracy obtained for FCMCD and FCMCD* is still about 10% higher than for OCSFCM in this range (cf. Figure 1 (b)). This is due to the fact that OCSFCM fills in the missing values by values, which are very close to the corresponding feature values of the nearest cluster prototype. In this way the cluster prototypes are better preserved, but the clustering structure gets lost. In order to preserve the clustering structure, FCMCD takes cluster dispersion into account during the calculation of membership degrees and, consequently, cluster prototypes. In this way FCMCD produces a lower number of misclassification errors than OCSFCM, but terminal prototypes obtained by FCMCD are less accurate in the case of high percentage of missing values in data set.

5   Conclusions and Future Work

The already existing fuzzy c-means algorithms for incomplete data based on missing value estimation leave clustering structure (cluster sizes) out of consideration during the estimation of missing values. For this reason they fail to work on incomplete data with differently sized clusters. Our approach uses a new membership degree for missing value estimation based on cluster dispersion. In experiments on artificial and real data sets with differently sized clusters, we have shown that our approach outperforms other approaches. It produces less misclassification errors, it is more stabil, it requires less iterations to termination, and it produces more accurate terminal cluster prototypes in the cases, where the percentage of missing values in the data set is not greater than 40%.

In all our experiments we assumed the real number of clusters to be known because we calculated it on complete data sets using silhouette coefficient [8]. However, in real world applications the number of clusters is generally not known a priori. Therefore, in our future work, we plan to analyse and compare the clustering methods for incomplete data on several data sets with different numbers of clusters regarding the correct calculation of cluster number. Furthermore, our experiments showed that all clustering methods perform poorer on data sets with missing values MAR and NMAR than in the case of missing values MCAR. In order to improve the performance of our approach on data with missing values MAR and NMAR, we also plan to combine our approach with an approach presented in [11] that uses class specific probabilities for missing values.

References

1. Bezdek, J.C.: Pattern Recognition with Fuzzy Objective Function Algorithms. Kluwer Academic Publishers, Norwell (1981)
2. Dempster, A.P., Laird, N.M., Rubin, D.B.: Maximum Likelihood from Incomplete Data via the EM Algorithm. J. of the Royal Stat. Society Series B 39, 1–38 (1977)
3. Dixon, J.K.: Pattern Recognition with Partly Missing Data. IEEE Transactions on System, Man and Cybernetics 9, 617–621 (1979)
4. Freedman, D., Pisani, R., Purves, R.: Statistics. Norton, New York (1998)
5. Han, J., Kamber, M.: Data Mining: Concepts and Techniques. M. Kaufmann, San Francisco (2000)
6. Hathaway, R.J., Bezdek, J.C.: Fuzzy c-means Clustering of Incomplete Data. IEEE Transactions on Systems, Man, and Cybernetics, Part B, 735–744 (2001)
7. Himmelspach, L.: Clustering with missing values: Analysis and Comparison. Master's thesis, Institut für Informatik, Heinrich-Heine-Universität Düsseldorf (2008)
8. Kaufman, L., Rousseeuw, P.J.: Finding Groups in Data: An Introduction to Cluster Analysis. John Wiley & Sons, Chichester (1990)
9. Little, R.J., Rubin, D.B.: Statistical Analysis with Missing Data. John Wiley & Sons, Chichester (2002)
10. Sarkar, M., Leong, T.-Y.: Fuzzy k-means Clustering with Missing Values. In: Proc. Am. Medical Informatics Association Ann. Fall Symp. (AMIA), pp. 588–592 (2001)
11. Timm, H., Döring, C., Kruse, R.: Different approaches to fuzzy clustering of incomplete datasets. Int. Journal of Approximate Reasoning, 239–249 (2004)
12. Wagstaff, K.: Clustering with Missing Values: No Imputation Required. In: Proc. Meeting of the Int. Federation of Classification Societies, pp. 649–658 (2004)

Automatic Detection of Active Region on EUV Solar Images Using Fuzzy Clustering

M. Carmen Aranda and Carlos Caballero

Department of Languages and Computer Science,
Engineerings School,
University of Malaga,
C/ Doctor Ortiz Ramos s/n, 29071 Málaga, España, Spain
mcarmen@lcc.uma.es, carlos.caballero.gonzalez@uma.es

Abstract. The technique presented in this paper is based on fuzzy clustering in order to achieve robust automatic detection of active regions in solar images. The first part of the detection process is based on seed selection and region growing. After that, the regions obtained are grouped into real active regions using a fuzzy clustering algorithm. The procedure developed has been tested on 400 full-disk solar images (corresponding to 4 days) taken from the satellite SOHO. The results are compared with those manually generated for the same days and a very good correspondence is found, showing the robustness of the method described.

Keywords: Fuzzy clustering, cluster validity measure, active region detection, image processing, region growing.

1 Introduction

The automatic processing of information in Solar Physics is becoming increasingly important due to substantial increase in the size of solar image data archives and also to avoid the subjectivity that carries the manual treatment of this information. The automated detection of solar phenomena such as sunspots, flares, solar filaments, active regions, etc, is important for, among other applications, data mining and the reliable forecast of the solar activity and space weather. Significant efforts have been done to create fully automated Solar Catalogues[1].

In this paper we focus on the automatic detection of active regions on solar Extreme Ultraviolet (EUV) images obtained from the satellite SOHO. Active regions are solar regions with intense magnetic activity which can be detected as bright regions in the bands of $H\alpha$ or EUV. It could be useful to study its evolution and behaviour in the forecast of solar flare activity. Active regions have been manually detected and numbered for dozen of years by the NOAA (National Oceanic and Atmospheric Administration) organization. Some automated detection methods have been developed in order to avoid the inherent subjectivity of manual detections[2,3].

As region growing has proved to be a reliable means to investigate solar features as filaments[3] or active regions, we have based our method on it, improving

E. Hüllermeier, R. Kruse, and F. Hoffmann (Eds.): IPMU 2010, LNAI 6178, pp. 69–78, 2010.

the way seeds and thresholds are chosen. After that, fuzzy clustering is applied to group the candidate regions produced into complete active regions. Fuzzy clustering allows the introduction of fuzziness for the belongingness of each bright region to a concrete active region. Fuzzy clustering has been widely used in image processing for image segmentation or boundary detection, also for solar images[4,5].

The rest of the paper is organized as follows. Section 2 presents the preprocessing stage prior to the region selection. Section 3 introduces the seed selection and region growing procedures which produce a bright regions automatically selected candidates to belong to real active regions. This is followed by the description of the fuzzy clustering procedure in Section 4. A validity measure is also defined to choose the optimal number of clusters in the image. Section 5 shows some experimental results. Finally, Section 6 summarizes the main conclusions of the paper.

2   Image Preprocessing

Prior to any feature recognition, the solar images have to be pre-processed in order to correct them from geometrical or photometric distorsions. The images used for the process are Extreme Ultraviolet (EUV) images of the Sun acquired from the satellite SOHO (Solar and Heliospheric Observatory). They are downloaded in FITS (Flexible Image Transport System) file format. FITS is the most commonly used digital file format in astronomy. It is designed specifically for scientific data and hence includes many descriptions of photometric and spatial calibration information and image origin metadada. The calibrations applied to the images were:

- **Dark current subtraction:** a uniform (identical for all the pixels) zero flux response is subtracted from the raw image.
- **Degridding:** the aluminum filter located close to the focal plane of the instrument casts a shadow on the CCD detector that creates a modulation pattern, or *grid*, in the images. The degridding factors are calculated and stored, and the image is multiplied by the degridding factor for a fairly reasonable correction to the data.
- **Filter normalization:** account is taken for the variable transmittivity of the clear and aluminum filters (Al+1 or Al+2).
- **Exposure time normalization:** the flux is normalized to the exposure time. Binned images are treated properly.
- **Response correction:** due to exposure to EUV flux, the pixel to pixel sensitivity (flat-field) of the CCD detector is highly variable. The flat-fields needed to correct the images are computed regularly from images of visible light calibration lamps.

After the calibration on the image has been made, the background, the halo and the contour of the image are completely erased. The contour is not important because the information received from the satellites about the contour is not

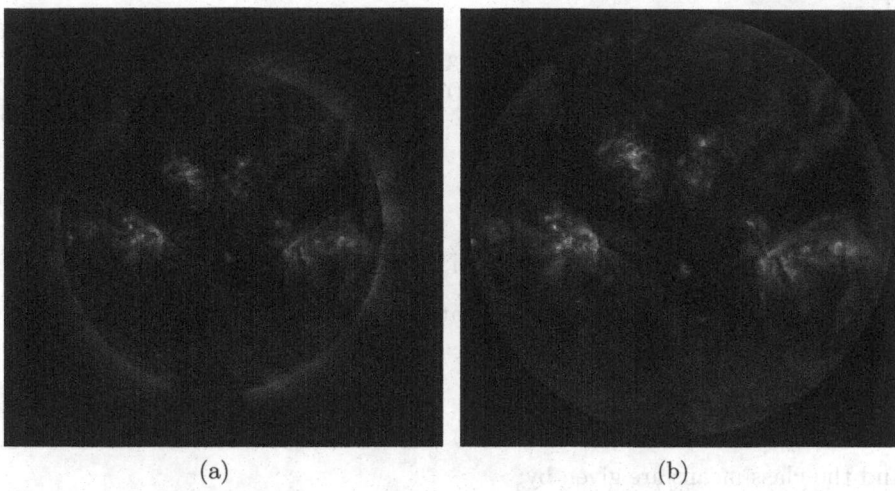

(a)   (b)

Fig. 1. (a) Original image (b) image without background, halo and contour

completely true. This information is not true for problems capturing images of the satellites. The results can be seen in Figure 1, where the image 1 (a) is the original image of the Sun taken on January 15, 2005 and the image 1 (b) is the image without background, halo and contour.

3   Region Detection

Once the image is fully cleaned and pre-processed, we can investigate the active regions using first a region growing method based on the image grey level properties. The principle is to group pixels into large regions if these pixels fall into a predefined intensity range. The procedure is started from a pixel or small region called a seed. This method is more effective than applying a basic automatic threshold as it associates a grey level condition with a connectivity condition. The efficiency of the method will thus depend on the seed selection procedure and on the intensity range definition. The region growing process usually produces a big amount of regions that need to be grouped into real active regions as it will be shown in Section 4.

3.1   Seeds Selection

The seed selection is a major step in the procedure. Firstly, the method calculates the Otsu's optimal value only for the pixels of the Sun area. Let's assume that an image has 2 types of pixels: objects and background. The threshold is obtained minimizing the weighted within-class variance. This turns out to be the same as maximizing the between-class variance.

$$Otsu's\ threshold = \max_{1 \le t \le L} \left\{ \sigma_W^2(t) \right\} \tag{1}$$

where

- An image contains N pixels whose gray levels are between 1 and L.
- $p_i = \frac{f_i}{N}$, f_i is the frequency of occurrence of the value i.
- Pixels are divided into two classes: $C1$, with gray levels $[1, \ldots, t]$ and $C2$, with gray levels $[t+1, \ldots, L]$.

The weighted within-class variance is:

$$\sigma_W^2(t) = q_1(t)\sigma_1^2(t) + q_2(t)\sigma_2^2(t) \tag{2}$$

Where the class probabilities are estimated as:

$$q_1(t) = \sum_{i=1}^{t} P(i) \qquad q_2(t) = \sum_{i=t+1}^{L} P(i) \tag{3}$$

And the class means are given by:

$$\mu_1(t) = \sum_{i=1}^{t} \frac{iP(i)}{q_1(t)} \qquad \mu_2(t) = \sum_{i=t+1}^{L} \frac{iP(i)}{q_2(t)} \tag{4}$$

Finally, the individual class variances are:

$$\sigma_1^2(t) = \sum_{i=1}^{t} [i - \mu_1(t)]^2 \frac{P(i)}{q_1(t)} \qquad \sigma_2^2(t) = \sum_{i=t+1}^{L} [i - \mu_2(t)]^2 \frac{P(i)}{q_2(t)} \tag{5}$$

The optimal value of Otsu will be used to select the seeds. Every pixel which intensity value is less than the value obtained from the Otsu's method will be seed.

$$\forall x, y \in D, seed_{x,y} = Otsu's\ threshold > I(x, y) \tag{6}$$

where

- $D \in [1 \ldots width\_Image, 1 \ldots length\_Image]$.
- $I(x, y)$ is the pixel's value on its coordinates x,y.

3.2 Region Growing

The next step consists in growing the region. The region growing code that has been used in this system was developed by Gonzalez[6]. This method uses three inputs:

- An image.
- A set of seeds (calculated as in the previous section).
- A threshold ($threshold_{limit}$) which set the limit to growth. This limit is in the range: $[seed - threshold_{limit}, seed + threshold_{limit}]$.

$Threshold_{limit}$ is calculated as the average of the values of all pixels in the image. The result obtained after applying these techniques can be seen in Figure 2 (a).

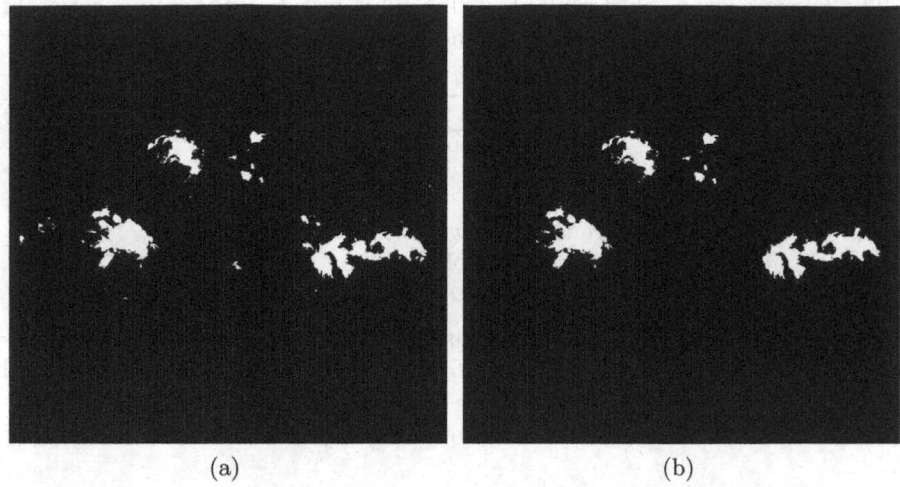

(a)   (b)

Fig. 2. (a) Image after region growing (b) image after selection of candidate regions

3.3 Selection of Candidate Regions

As it can be seen, after making the region growing technique there is too much noise and portions of regions that do not have the importance that they really deserve such as you can see in Figure 2. Thus, it is advisable to make a selection phase of candidate regions. This phase consists of two steps:

1. Removing all regions that do not exceed a minimum value of area. This will eliminate false positives in the selection of seeds.
2. Once large regions have been selected, the next step is to look for regions close to these, regardless of the size of these surrounding regions. Finally we get more compact regions suitable for use in the next step. The result of the segmentation process is positive, as can be seen by comparing 1 (a) and 2 (b).

4   Fuzzy Clustering Algorithm to Identify Active Regions

Once the image has been segmented into independent pieces, a grouping process should be performed for the candidate regions are clustered in real active regions. The algorithm used here is the Gustafson-Kessel fuzzy clustering algorithm[7]. Babuska[8] provided a slight variation of the Gustafson-Kessel algorithm which improved the variance estimation.

This technique has been selected for this problem because it is not known a priori the form or structure of the clusters. Another important point is that the distance measure is the distance of *Mahalanobis*[9]. Gustafson and Kessel extended the standard fuzzy c-means algorithm.

The Fuzzy c-means clustering algorithm[10] is based on the minimization of an objective function called *c-means* functional. It is defined as:

$$J(X;U,V) = \sum_{i=1}^{c} \sum_{k=1}^{M} (\mu_{ik})^m \|x_k - v_i\|_A^2 \tag{7}$$

where

- $X = \{x_1, x_2, \ldots, x_M\}$ are the data which must be classified.
- $U = [\mu_{ik}] \in M_{fc}$, is a fuzzy matrix of X.
- $V = [c_1, c_2, \ldots, c_c]$, is the vector of centroids.

Gustafson and Kessel extended the standard fuzzy c-means algorithm by employing an adaptive distance norm, in order to detect clusters of different geometrical shapes in one data set. Each cluster has its own norm matrix A_i. The matrices A_i are an optimization variable in the following objective function:

$$J(Z,U,V,A) = \sum_{i=1}^{c} \sum_{k=1}^{N} \mu_{i=k}^m (z_k - v_i) A_i (z_k - v_i)^T \tag{8}$$

But the objective function cannot be minimized directly because J depends linearly on A_i. Therefore A_i is constrained by: $det|A_i| = \rho_i, \rho > 0$. Allowing the matrix A_i to vary with its determinant fixed corresponds to optimizing the cluster's shape while its volume is constant. Using the Lagrange multiplier method, the following expression for A_i is obtained:

$$A_i = [\rho_i det(\mathbf{F}_i)]^{1/n} \mathbf{F}_i^{-1} \tag{9}$$

where $\mathbf{F}_i$ is the fuzzy covariance matrix of the *ith* cluster defined by:

$$\mathbf{F}_i = \frac{\sum_{k=1}^{N} (\mu_{ik})^m (\mathbf{x}_k - \mathbf{v}_i)(\mathbf{x}_k - \mathbf{v}_i)^T}{\sum_{k=1}^{N} (\mu_{ik})^m} \tag{10}$$

Clustering algorithm is fuzzy does not mean that a priori information of the number of clusters to be made should not provide. To solve this problem, N iterations with N possible numbers of clusters are made in our system. The value of N is in the range of $[2, M]$. If the number of candidate regions is less than M, the number of possible clusters that exist and therefore iterations will be the number of candidate regions. If the number of candidate regions is greater than M, the number of iterations will be M. This is developed so for several reasons.

- The empirical value of M will be more or less 10. This is because is difficult to find more than ten active regions simultaneously in the Sun.
- The computational cost required to perform clustering is very high and must be optimized.

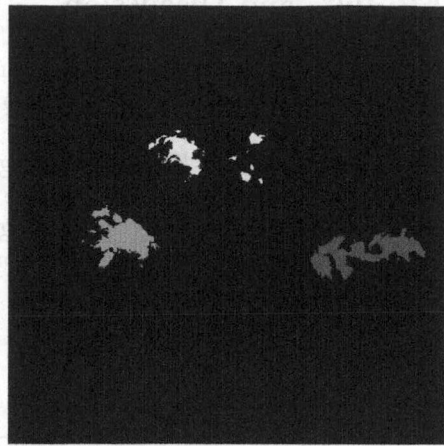

Fig. 3. Three clusters are determined in this image

4.1 Cluster Validation

Once calculated the candidate active regions for different number of clusters, it will be possible to determine the correct number of clusters. To do this we use a modified clustering validation index with different densities developed by Chou, Su and Lai[11]. The index used is defined in the Equation (11) where

- A_i is the set whose elements are the data points assigned to the ith cluster.
- $|A_i|$ is the number of elements in A_i.
- x_j and x_k are the regions' centroids.
- v_i and v_j are the clusters' centroids ith and jth.
- d is a distance function.

$$CS(c) = \frac{\sum_{i=1}^{c} \left\{ \frac{1}{|A_i|} \sum_{x_j \subset A_i} \max_{x_k \in A_i} \{d(x_j, x_k)\} \right\}}{\sum_{i=1}^{c} \left\{ \min_{j \in c, j \neq i} \{d(v_i, v_j)\} \right\}} \tag{11}$$

The correct number of clusters is one that minimizes the value of the index. The main difference between this method and our method is the distance function $d(x_i, x_k)$. In both cases the distance used is the Manhattan distance. In the first case the Manhattan distance is calculated between regions' centroids and in the second case it is calculated between the closest points of two regions. The Gustafson and Kessel algorithm determines which elements belong to each cluster and the index determines the number of clusters. Figure 3 shows the tree clusters finally obtained for the image that appears in Figure 1 (a).

5 Experimental Results and Discussion

The procedure for automatic detection of active regions has been applied to
the period between January 15, 2005 and January 18, 2005, on more than 400
observations.

A summary of the results can be seen in Table 1 showing the percentages of
candidate region detection and the percentage of errors. The errors are classified
in ±1 error, ±2 errors and > 2 errors. For example, if an image has three brilliant
regions and the method detects two or four candidates region it will be an error
classified in the group ±1.

Table 1. Experimental results

Day	Observations	%Candidate region detected	Errors		
			% ±1	% ±2	% > 2
January 15, 2005	95	93.685	6.315	0	0
January 16, 2005	109	89.910	7.339	1.834	0.917
January 17, 2005	94	57.448	29.787	9.574	3.191
January 18, 2005	110	37.275	17.272	18.181	27.272

In this study, it is taken into account that a brilliant region of the Sun is only
manually numbered by the NOAA as an active region when it has high activity
during its life (normally several days). So, it is not possible to determine if a
brilliant region will be numbered or not as an active region considering only
the information of one image. For us, all the brilliant regions will be candidate
active region because they present high activity in that particular moment. The
experimental results show the correspondence of the clustering output with the
candidate active region that there are in each image.

A further processing should be done to analyze which candidate active regions
are real active regions studying its behaviour during a long period of time.

To study the fuzzy clustering algorithm is regarded as being correctly classified
all images correctly detected the active and candidates. Next, the experimental
results will be discussed in detail.

5.1 January 15, 2005 and January 16, 2005

The results obtained on January 15, 2005 using a total of 95 images are:

- 93.685% of automatically detected candidate regions match the manually
  detected ones.
- 6.315% of automatically detected candidate regions don't correspond to manual ones.

On this day there are 2 active regions but the reality is that after the process
of image segmentation we can clearly see three candidate active regions. One of

these images has been developed throughout this paper and the final result can be seen in Figure 3. The result of fuzzy clustering algorithm is quite positive of success getting a value of 93.685%.

The results obtained on January 16, 2005 using a total of 109 images are:

- 89.910% of automatically detected candidate regions match the manually detected ones.
- 7.339% of automatically detected candidate regions has ±1 error.
- 1.834% of automatically detected candidate regions has ±2 errors.
- 0.917% of automatically detected candidate regions has > 2 errors.

On this day the 2 regions of the previous day remain. The results remain very positive being the value of automatic detection 89.910%.

5.2   January 17, 2005

The results for the January 17, 2005 using 94 images are:

- 57.448% of automatically detected candidate regions match the manually detected ones.
- 29.787% of automatically detected candidate regions has ±1 error.
- 9.574% of automatically detected candidate regions has ±2 errors.
- 3.191% of automatically detected candidate regions has > 2 errors.

On this day 2 new active regions appear. So, there exist a total of 4 active regions. The percentage of failing has increased which is a more modest result than those obtained previously. Note that almost 30% of failures belong to the group ±1.

5.3   January 18, 2005

The results for the January 18, 2005 using 110 images are:

- 37.275% of automatically detected candidate regions match the manually detected ones.
- 17.272% of automatically detected candidate regions has ±1 error.
- 18.181% of automatically detected candidate regions has ±2 errors.
- 27.272% of automatically detected candidate regions has > 2 errors.

On this day 6 regions are active but is a day especially complicated. Visually it is imposible to determine whether there are really six active regions because they are very close, even some of them are overlapping. At this point, we can state that the clustering algorithm works well even in these cases. To solve the problem it would be neccesary to combine information from several frequency bands.

6   Conclusions

In this paper some experimental results for the detection of active regions on the Sun have been presented using the Gustafson-Kessel's fuzzy clustering algorithm and the Mu-Chun's index validation. Satisfactory results have been obtained as have been shown in Table 1.

One of the major constraints that have been found in the system is inherent to the algorithm of Gustafson-Kessel, where the density of points per cluster is predetermined.This fact provoke a serious problem in the system because a region of large area is considered equally influential than a small region. A proposal for improving the system could be to modify the parameter input to the Gustafson-Kessel algorithm, as the division of large regions into small regions.

So, the automated techniques developed allow to detect bright regions on the Sun and to group them into real active regions. Further work will be carried out to produce automatic AR detection in other spectral bands or in the magnetogram to combine all the information to obtain more realistic detections.

References

1. Zharkova, V., Abourdarham, J., Zharkov, S., Ipson, S., Benkhalil, A.: Searchable solar feature catalogues. Advances in Space Research 36, 1604–1612 (2005)
2. Benkhalil, A., Zharkova, V., Ipson, S., Zharkov, S.: Active region detection and verification with the solar feature catalogue. Solar Physics 235, 87 (2006)
3. Qahwaji, R., Colak, T.: Automatic detection and verification of solar features. International Journal of Imaging System and technology 15(4), 199–210
4. Banda, J.M., Angryk, R.A.: On the effectiveness of Fuzzy Clustering as a data discretization technique for large-scale classification of solar images. In: IEEE International Conf. on Fuzzy Systems, pp. 2019–2024 (2009)
5. Barra, V., Delouille, V., Hechedez, J.: Segmentation on extreme ultraviolet solar images using a multispectral data fusion process. In: IEEE International Conf. on Fuzzy Systems, pp. 1–6 (2007)
6. Gonzalez, R., Woods, R.: Digital Image Processing Using MATLAB. Pearson Prentice-Hall, New Jersey (2008)
7. Gustafson, E., Kessel, W.: Fuzzy Clustering with a Fuzzy Covariance Matrix. In: IEEE CDC, pp. 761–766. IEEE Press, San Diego (1979)
8. Babuska, R., Van der Venn, P.J., Kaymak, U.: Improved variance estimation for Gustafson-Kessel clustering. In: Proceedings of 2002 IEEE International Conference on Fuzzy Systems, Honolulu, Haway, pp. 1081–1085 (2002)
9. Mahalanobis, P.: On the generalised distance in statistics. Proceedings of the National Institute of Science of India 12, 49–55 (1936)
10. Bezdek, J.C.: Pattern Recognition with Fuzzy Objective Function Algoritms. Plenum Press, New York (1981)
11. Chou, C.H., Su, M.C., Lai, E.: A new cluster validity measure for clusters with different densities. In: IASTED International Conf. on Intelligent Systems and Control, Austria, pp. 276–281 (2003)

On Dynamic Soft Dimension Reduction in Evolving Fuzzy Classifiers*

Edwin Lughofer

Department of Knowledge-Based Mathematical Systems/Fuzzy Logic Laboratorium
Linz-Hagenberg, Johannes Kepler University Linz, Altenbergerstrasse 69, A-4040
Linz, Austria
edwin.lughofer@jku.at

Abstract. This paper deals with the problem of dynamic dimension reduction during the on-line update and evolution of fuzzy classifiers. With 'dynamic' it is meant that the importance of features for discriminating between the classes changes over time when new data is sent into the classifiers' update mechanisms. In order to avoid discontinuity in the incremental learning process, i.e. permanently exchanging some features in the input structure of the fuzzy classifiers, we include feature weights (lying in $[0, 1]$) into the training and update of the fuzzy classifiers, which measure the importance levels of the various features and can be smoothly updated with new incoming samples. In some cases, when the weights become (approximately) 0, an automatic switching off of some features and therefore a (soft) dimension reduction is achieved. The approaches for incrementally updating the feature weights are based on a leave-one-feature-out and on a feature-wise separability criterion. We will describe the integration concept of the feature weights in evolving fuzzy classifiers using single and multi-model architecture. The whole approach will be evaluated based on high-dimensional on-line real-world classification scenarios.

Keywords: Incremental feature weighting, soft dimension reduction, evolving fuzzy classifiers.

1 Motivation and State of the Art

Data-driven fuzzy classifiers are nowadays used in many fields of applications such as decision making [12], fault and novelty detection [8], classification in EEG signals [19], image classification [18]. This is mainly because they are offering a powerful tool which is able to model non-linear dependencies between features and still providing some interpretable insight at the same time.

A significant problem when learning fuzzy classifiers from data is the so-called curse of dimensionality effect, especially when the number of features in a classification problem, compared to the number of available training samples, is quite

---

* This work was funded by the Upper Austrian Technology and Research Promotion. It reflects only the authors' views.

E. Hüllermeier, R. Kruse, and F. Hoffmann (Eds.): IPMU 2010, LNAI 6178, pp. 79–88, 2010.

high: this may deteriorate the predictive performance significantly. Therefore, during the last decade feature selection methods in conjunction with training of fuzzy classifiers for reducing the curse of dimensionality were developed. For instance in [17] features are selected according to the ranking obtained by applying mutual information. Another attempt for reducing dimensionality in fuzzy classifiers is presented in [13], where the best features for a fuzzy integral classifier are elicited by a specific interaction index, comparing the importance of feature pairs with the importance of their sums. An interesting approach for reduction of the feature space is presented in [4], where feature selection is integrated into a multistage genetic learning process, which determines a set of feature subsets by means of the chromosomes in the final population with the best fitness value.

Another important issue in classification scenarios is the usage of incremental updates of classifiers during on-line processes at the systems, ideally in single-pass mode without using any prior data samples (in order to achieve fast updates with low virtual memory demand). An attempt to tackle this issue was made in [2], where two different incremental training methods, *FLEXFIS-Class* [11] and *eClass* [1] are compared with respect to empirical performance and extended to include different classifier architectures (single model, multi model in two variants). Other incremental fuzzy classification approaches are demonstrated in [3] (for generalized fuzzy min-max neural networks) and in [14], using a transformation probability-possibility to construct densities of possibilities.

Now, it is a challenge to apply an adaptive feature selection process during the incremental on-line update of the fuzzy classifiers. This is because at the beginning of the whole learning process specific features may turn out to be much more important than later on. In principle, someone may apply some incremental feature selection techniques synchronously to the update of the fuzzy classifiers. This may serve as a by-information about the most essential features, but the problem remains how to integrate this permanently changing information into the evolving fuzzy classifiers in a smooth way. Smoothness here does not refer to the classifiers' outputs (which are discrete class labels), but to change feature weights step-wise instead of performing any abrupt changes in the input structure (e.g. exchanging features), which may lead to undesired classifiers' behavior resulting in severe performance drops.

2   Our Approach

In this paper, we propose an alternative approach for dynamically reducing curse of dimensionality during the incremental on-line training phase of fuzzy classifiers in a smooth way. Therefore, we exploit the generalization concept of feature selection, called feature weighting, which assigns weights lying in $[0, 1]$ to the features according to their importance level. If the weight of a feature approaches 0, the feature will not have any impact in the learning as well as classification process. Therefore, a (soft) dimension reduction can be achieved through the concept of feature weighting. Soft here means that features with very low weights have little impact and are almost but not completely discarded in the high dimensional feature space. The key point and advantage among a crisp feature selection approach is now that these weights can be updated smoothly during the incremental learning phase with newly loaded data samples in a life-long learning mode (all samples equally weighted): the update with one single sample changes the weights of all features just slightly. In this paper, two novel approaches for incremental feature weighting will be demonstrated, both based on Dy–Brodley's separability criterion [7] (Section 3): a leave-one-feature-out separability criterion by excluding each one of the p features leading to p measures, and a faster feature-wise (single dimension-wise) criterion. We will present update formulas for both criteria (Section 3). Furthermore, we will demonstrate how to integrate the feature weights into the evolving fuzzy classifiers using *FLEXFIS-Class SM* and *FLEXFIS-Class MM* [11] approaches as training engines (Section 4). In Section 5, we will evaluate the impact of including the incrementally updated features weights into the evolving fuzzy classifiers. This will be based on two (noisy and high-dimensional) real-world data sets from surface inspection scenarios.

3   Incremental Feature Weighting - 2 Variants

3.1   Separability Criterion

For assigning weights to the features, we exploit a well-known criterion for measuring the discriminatory power of a feature set in classification problems, the so-called Fisher's interclass separability criterion which is defined as [6]:

$$J = \frac{det(S_b)}{det(S_w)} \tag{1}$$

where S_b denotes the between-class scatter matrix measuring how scattered the cluster means are from the total mean and S_w the within-class matrix measuring how scattered the samples are from their class means. The goal is to maximize this criterion. S_w can be expressed by the sum of the covariance matrices over all classes, i.e. by:

$$S_w = \sum_{j=1}^{K} \Sigma_j \tag{2}$$

with Σ_j the covariance matrix for the jth class:

$$\Sigma_j = \frac{1}{N_j} \sum_{k=1}^{N_j} (X_{k,.} - \bar{X}_j(N_j))^T (X_{k,.} - \bar{X}_j(N_j)) \tag{3}$$

with X the regression matrix containing N_j samples from class j as rows and p features as columns, $\bar{X}_j(N_j)$ the mean value vector of all the features for the N_j samples. The matrix S_b is defined as:

$$S_b = \sum_{j=1}^{K} N_j (\bar{X}_j - \bar{X})^T (\bar{X}_j - \bar{X}) \tag{4}$$

with N_j the number of samples belonging to class j, $\bar{X}_j$ the center of class j and $\bar{X}$ the mean over all data samples.

However, this criterion has the shortcomings [7], that 1.) The determinant of S_b tends to increase with the number of inputs, hence also does the separability criterion (1), preferring higher dimensionality of the input space; and 2.) it is not invariant under any nonsingular linear transformation. This means that once m features are chosen, any nonsingular linear transformation on these features changes the criterion value. Hence, we apply the following criterion (Dy-Brodley's measure) [7]:

$$J = trace(S_w^{-1} S_b) \tag{5}$$

with $trace(A)$ the sum of the diagonal elements in A.

3.2   Incremental Update of Separability Criterion

Regarding incremental capability of this criterion, it is obviously sufficient to update the matrices S_w and S_b and then to compute (5). Both matrices can be updated during incremental mode in single-pass and sample-wise manner. The matrix S_b can be updated by simply updating N_j (the number of samples falling into class j) through counting and $\bar{X}_j$ as well $\bar{X}$ by incrementally calculating the mean $\bar{X}(N+m) = \frac{N\bar{X}(N)+\sum_{k=N}^{N+m} X_{k,\cdot}}{N+m}$. The same update mechanism applies to the mean over samples falling into class j, $\bar{X}_j$.

For S_w, we need to update the covariance matrices of each class, which (leaned on [16]) is given by (for the jth class)

$$\Sigma_j(new) = \frac{1}{N_j + m}(N_j \Sigma_j(old))$$

$$+ m\Sigma_{j;pnew} + \frac{N_j m}{N_j + m}(\bar{X}_j(N_j) - \bar{X}_j(m))^T(\bar{X}_j(N_j) - \bar{X}_j(m)) \tag{6}$$

with $\Sigma_{j;pnew}$ the covariance matrix on the m new samples for class j.

3.3   Variant A: Leave-One-Feature-Out Approach

Now, the question remains how to use this criterion for assigning feature weights. Assuming that the full dimensionality of the data is p, the idea is now to calculate (5) p times, each time one of the p features is discarded $\rightarrow$ leave-one-feature-out approach. In this sense, we obtain p different values for (5), $J_1, ..., J_p$, which can be again updated synchronously and independently in incremental mode. A statement on the relative importance of features can be made, when sorting these values in decreasing order: the maximal value of these indicates that the corresponding discarded feature is the least important one, as the feature was discarded and still a high value is achieved. In the same manner, the minimal value of these indicates that the corresponding discarded feature is the most important one, as dropping the value of the separability criterion (when applied to the remaining $p - 1$ features) more significantly than any of the others. As weights should lie in the full span in $[0, 1]$, we suggest to compute the weights as:

$$\lambda_j = 1 - \frac{J_j - min_{1,\dots,p}(J_j)}{max_{j=1,\dots,p}(J_j) - min_{1,\dots,p}(J_j)} \tag{7}$$

hence the feature with the weakest discriminatory power (and therefore maximal J_j) is assigned a weight value of 0, and the feature with strongest discriminatory power a weight of 1.

3.4 Variant B: Single Feature-Wise Approach

The problem with the leave-one-feature-out approach is that it requires a quite high computation time, as for each single sample falling into class L, the co-variance matrix Σ_L and the between-class scatter matrix for class L need to be updated, which demands an update of the whole S_w resp. S_b by summing up over all classes. The complexity for calculating one J_p is (proof left to the reader) $O((2K + 3)p^2 + 2p^3 + 3p) \approx O((2K + 3)p^2 + 2p^3)$, hence the overall complexity for all J_j's is $O((2K + 3)p^3 + 2p^4)$. For reducing this complexity, we apply a greedy-based approach for approximating Dy-Brodley's separability criterion. This is done by calculating the between-class and within-class scatter for each feature separately. By using the feature-wise approach we obtain scalar values for S_b and S_w, i.e. for the ith feature:

$$S_b(i) = \sum_{j=1}^{K} N_j(\bar{X}_{j;i} - \bar{X}_i)^2 \qquad S_w(i) = \sum_{j=1}^{K} Var_{j;i} \tag{8}$$

with $\bar{X}_i$ the mean value of the ith feature, $\bar{X}_{j;i}$ the mean value of the ith feature over class j samples and $Var_{j;i}$ the variance of the ith feature over class j samples. The single separability criterion for feature i is simply calculated by

$$I_i = \frac{S_b(i)}{S_w(i)} \tag{9}$$

The mean value over features for class j samples can be updated by the incremental mean, the variance of a features x_i is updated in the same manner as the covariance in (6) by setting $x_i = x_1 = x_2$. The update is quite fast as it requires only linear complexity in the number of features $(O(p))$ for each single sample. The final feature weights are obtained by:

$$\lambda_j = \frac{I_j}{max_{j=1,\dots,p}} \tag{10}$$

4 Integrating Feature Weights into EFC

4.1 Integration in FLEXFIS-Class SM

FLEXFIS-Class SM, firstly introduced in [11], extended in [2], exploits the classical fuzzy classifier architectures, which comes with singleton labels in the consequent parts of the rules, see e.g. [15]. The single antecedent parts of the rules contain Gaussian membership functions, which are connected by a product t-norm Hence, during the classification phase feature weights can be simply included when eliciting the rules' activation degrees, that is by:

$$\mu_i(\boldsymbol{x}) = \prod_{j=1}^{p} e^{-\frac{1}{2}\frac{(x_j - c_{ij})^2}{\sigma_{ij}^2}\lambda_j} \quad i = 1, ..., C \tag{11}$$

with p the dimensionality of the feature space, C the number of rules, c_{ij} the center of the jth antecedent part in the ith rule and σ_{ij} the width of the jth antecedent parts in the ith rule. This means that the fuzzy set membership degrees of unimportant features (with feature weights near 0) are 1, hence serving a 'don't care parts' as not influencing the whole rule activation when taking the product over these degrees. For important features (feature weights near 1), the (nearly) actual fuzzy set membership degrees are taken, influencing the rule activation degrees.

The training phase in *FLEXFIS-Class SM* takes place in the cluster space, where an evolving version of vector quantization, eVQ [9] is applied for updating already existing and evolving new clusters on demand based on the characteristics of new incoming samples. Updating of already existing clusters takes place by:

$$c_{win}^{(new)} = c_{win}^{(old)} + \eta_{win}\lambda I(\boldsymbol{x} - c_{win}^{(old)}) \tag{12}$$

with I the identity matrix and η_{win} the decreasing learning. Note the inclusion of the feature weight. Generation of new clusters (=rules) is performed whenever a new sample is lying far away from existing cluster centers. In this case, the inclusion of feature weights in the distance calculation suppresses the generation of superfluous clusters in case when the distance with respect to unimportant features is high. The weighted Euclidean distance measure (used in case of axes-parallel ellipsoidal clusters) between a sample $\boldsymbol{x}$ and a cluster center $\boldsymbol{c}$ is calculated by:

$$dist = \sqrt{\sum_{j=1}^{p} \lambda_j (x_j - c_j)^2} \tag{13}$$

4.2 Integration in FLEXFIS-Class MM

FLEXFIS-Class MM, firstly introduced in [11], extended in [2], exploits a multi model architecture integrating K Takagi-Sugeno fuzzy regression models for K classes. These are trained based on indicator matrices (off-line case) respectively indicator vectors (on-line case), which follows the idea of linear regression by indicator matrix [5]. Opposed to the linear version, the non-linear version triggered by TS fuzzy models with more than one rule is able to circumvent the masking problem in case of $K > 2$. For the TS fuzzy models, it applies Gaussian membership function combined with product t-norm in the rules' antecedent parts. Hence, as in case of *FLEXFIS-Class SM*, during the classification phase feature weights can be simply included when eliciting the rules' activation degrees in the same manner as in (11). This weighting approach is performed when inferencing through each of the K TS fuzzy models and eliciting the final class response by a one-versus-rest classification approach:

$$L = class(\boldsymbol{x}) = \text{argmax}_{m=1,...,K} \hat{f}_m(\boldsymbol{x}) \tag{14}$$

The interpretation of including feature weights in this way during classification is that un-important features do not change the rule activation degrees (low feature weight values triggering high fuzzy set membership values near 1), hence only the important ones are responsible for weighting the consequent hyper-planes in each of the K Takagi-Sugeno fuzzy models.

The training phase of each Takagi-Sugeno fuzzy model is carried out separately and independently. As in case of *FLEXFIS-Class SM*, the rules and their antecedent parts are again generated by an evolving version of quantization eVQ [9]. Hence, the same procedure for including features weights in antecedent part learning as already described in Section 4.1 is applied. When updating the consequent parameters $\hat{w}_{i;m}$ of the ith rule in the mth model from the kth to the $k+1$th sample with $RFWLS = recursive\ fuzzily\ weighted\ least\ squares$ (for local learning using least squares optimization function) — see also [10]: the feature weights are included in $\mu_{i;m}$ as (11) are calculated, affecting the normalized rule membership degree $\Psi_{i;m}$ (appearing in the $RFWLS$ algorithm).

5 Evaluation

This section demonstrates the impact of the incremental feature weighting during incremental on-line evolution of fuzzy classifiers. Thereby, the central aspect will be a comparison of conventional evolving fuzzy classifiers (without using any type of dimensionality reduction method) with included dynamic, incremental feature weighting approach while evolving the fuzzy classifiers. We applied our novel approach to two different application scenarios: 1.) Inspection of CD Imprints where the classification problem is to detect system failures (such as color drift during offset print, a pinhole caused by a dirty sieve, occurrence of colors on dirt, palettes running out of ink) when printing the upper-side of compact discs; and 2.) food production (egg inspection), where the task was to discriminate between dirt (= egg is still ok) and yolk (= egg is broken). We recorded images during the real on-line production process and stored them onto the hard-disc in the same order as recorded. This means that the list of aggregated features extracted from the images appear in the same order in the feature matrix (row-by-row) as the images were recorded on-line. Hence, evolving the classifiers by incrementally sending the samples from the feature matrices into the training algorithms is a one-to-one simulation of the real on-line case. The obtained data sets had the characteristics as shown in Table 1.

Both data sets are divided into a training set and a test set. The first half of the training set is used for an initial training and parameter optimization step (in a CV procedure), eliciting the optimal vigilance parameter ρ (responsible for the sensitivity to allow new rules being evolved in the classifiers), the second half for further adaptation and evolution of the classifiers to simulate the real

Table 1. Data sets from CD imprint, egg inspection and spam recognition and their characteristics

	# Images	# Tr. Samples	# Test Samples	# Feat.	Class D.
CD Imprint	1687	1024 (2x512)	510	74	16.78%/83.22%
Eggs	5341		2895	2302	17+2	79.83%/20.17%

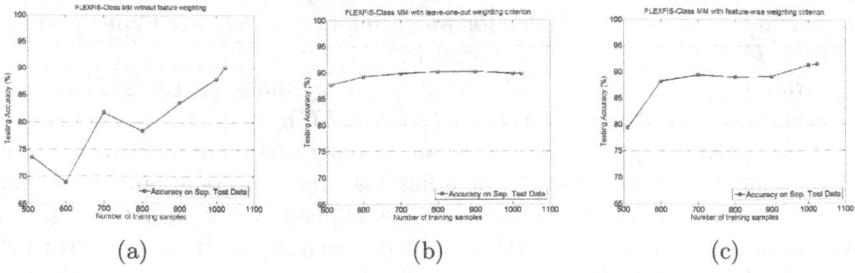

(a)   (b)   (c)

Fig. 1. Progress of accuracies on separate test data set during on-line evolution of fuzzy classifiers with *FLEXFIS-Class MM* for CD imprint data set, (a): without feature weighting, (b): with dynamic (incremental) leave-one-feature-out criterion and (c): with dynamic (incremental) feature-wise separability criterion

on-line case. The test data set denotes the last part of the whole feature matrix, hence is used for calculating the accuracies of the classifiers on new on-line data as an estimation of the generalization performance of the classifiers.

5.1   Results

Figure 1 presents the evolution of the accuracies (on separate on-line test data) during on-line update of the fuzzy classifiers with *FLEXFIS-Class MM* on CD imprint data. The first figure (a) visualizes those obtained without applying any feature weighting strategy implicitly. Here, we can recognize that in fact the accuracy increases with more samples included into the incremental update, however this increase is not as stable as in case when applying dynamic leave-one-feature-out feature weighing (shown in (b)) or dynamic dimension-wise feature weighting (shown in (c)), as showing some down trends, especially for the first part of on-line samples (up to sample #800). Furthermore, the levels of accuracy are significantly higher in both incremental feature weighting variants, especially at the beginning of the whole update process, i.e. from the 512th sample on.

Figure 2 shows a similar behavior between not including feature weights and inclusion of dynamic features weights when *FLEXFIS-Class MM* is applied to egg inspection. The difference is not that big as in case of CD imprint data, but still visible and therefore significant. This can be explained as 1.) the data available for initial training is much larger than in case of CD imprints (1447 versus 512), and 2.) the number of features in both data sets is lower than in CD imprints

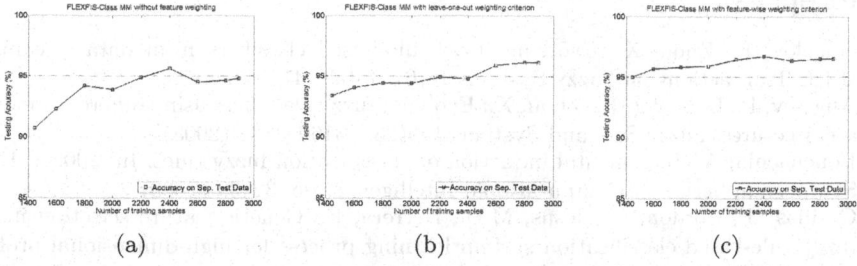

(a)   (b)   (c)

Fig. 2. Progress of accuracies on separate test data set during on-line evolution of fuzzy classifiers with *FLEXFIS-Class MM* for egg inspection data set, (a): without feature weighting, (b): with leave-one-feature-out criterion and (c): with feature-wise separability criterion

(19 versus 74). Therefore, the proportion 'training samples to dimensionality of the feature space' is more beneficial in case of egg data, compared to CD imprint data set, and therefore the impact of a soft dimension reduction step through feature weighting is lower.

Also an interesting and positive observation is that the much faster feature-wise separability criterion is at least as good as the leave-one-feature-out approach in all data sets and for both evolving fuzzy classification variants (in most cases it can even outperform the leave-one-feature-out approach, especially after the whole incremental training procedure is finished). This means the discriminatory power of single features alone are already sufficient to increase accuracies of the evolving fuzzy classifiers.

6   Conclusion

In this paper, we proposed a concept for a dynamic and smooth integration of dimension reduction into evolving fuzzy classifiers in form of an incremental feature weighting algorithm (hence achieving a soft dimension reduction process). For feature weighting, we applied two criteria, one based on a leave-one-feature-out approach, the other based on a feature-wise (single dimension) approach, both exploiting the concept of separability criterion of features (jointly or independently) and both incrementally calculable during on-line phase in a robust manner (in the sense that they converge to the batch version). The feature weights are integrated into the classification phase when using single as well as multi model fuzzy classifier architecture and into the learning phase when using *FLEXFIS-Class SM* as well as *FLEXFIS-Class MM* as evolving fuzzy classifier approaches. Based on the observations when applying evolving fuzzy classifiers to high-dimensional on-line classification scenarios, we can conclude that our incremental feature weighting approaches are able to guide evolving fuzzy classifiers to more predictive power during on-line operation mode than when feature weighting is not included in the training process.

References

1. Angelov, P., Zhou, X.: Evolving fuzzy-rule-based classifiers from data streams. IEEE Transactions on Fuzzy Systems 16(6), 1462–1475 (2008)
2. Angelov, P., Lughofer, E., Zhou, X.: Evolving fuzzy classifiers using different model architectures. Fuzzy Sets and Systems 159(23), 3160–3182 (2008)
3. Bouchachia, A.: Incremental induction of classification fuzzy rules. In: 2009 IEEE Symposium Series on Computational Intelligence, pp. 32–39 (2009)
4. Casillas, J., Cordon, O., Jesus, M.D., Herrera, F.: Genetic feature selection in a fuzzy rule-based classification system learning process for high-dimensional problems. Information Sciences 136, 135–157 (2001)
5. Draper, N., Smith, H.: Applied Regression Analysis. Probability and Mathematical Statistics. John Wiley & Sons, New York (1981)
6. Duda, R., Hart, P., Stork, D.: Pattern Classification, 2nd edn. Wiley-Interscience, Southern Gate (2000)
7. Dy, J., Brodley, C.: Feature selection for unsupervised learning. Journal of Machine Learning Research 5, 845–889 (2004)
8. Filev, D.P., Tseng, F.: Novelty detection based machine health prognostics. In: Proc. of the 2006 International Symposium on Evolving Fuzzy Systems, pp. 193–199. Lake District, UK (2006)
9. Lughofer, E.: Extensions of vector quantization for incremental clustering. Pattern Recognition 41(3), 995–1011 (2008)
10. Lughofer, E.: On-line evolving image classifiers and their application to surface inspection. Image and Vision Computing (in press, 2010) doi: 10.1016/j.imavis.2009.07.002
11. Lughofer, E., Angelov, P., Zhou, X.: Evolving single- and multi-model fuzzy classifiers with FLEXFIS-Class. In: Proceedings of FUZZ-IEEE 2007, London, UK, pp. 363–368 (2007)
12. Maturino-Lozoya, H., Munoz-Rodriguez, D., Jaimes-Romera, F., Tawfik, H.: Hand-off algorithms based on fuzzy classifiers. IEEE Transactions on Vehicular Technology 49(6), 2286–2294 (2000)
13. Mikenina, L., Zimmermann, H.: Improved feature selection and classification by the 2-additive fuzzy measure. Fuzzy Sets and Systems 107, 197–218 (1999)
14. Mouchaweh, M.S., Devillez, A., Lecolier, G., Billaudel, P.: Incremental learning in fuzzy pattern matching. Fuzzy Sets and Systems 132, 49–62 (2002)
15. Nauck, D., Kruse, R.: A neuro-fuzzy method to learn fuzzy classification rules from data. Fuzzy Sets and Systems 89(3), 277–288 (1997)
16. Pang, S., Ozawa, S., Kasabov, N.: Incremental linear discriminant analysis for classification of data streams. IEEE Transaction on Systems, Men and Cybernetics - part B: Cybernetics 35(5), 905–914 (2005)
17. Sanchez, L., Suarez, M., Villar, J., Couso, I.: Mutual information-based feature selection and partition design in fuzzy rule-based classifiers from vague data. International Journal of Approximate Reasoning 49, 607–622 (2008)
18. Sannen, D., Nuttin, M., Smith, J., Tahir, M., Lughofer, E., Eitzinger, C.: An interactive self-adaptive on-line image classification framework. In: Gasteratos, A., Vincze, M., Tsotsos, J. (eds.) ICVS 2008. LNCS, vol. 5008, pp. 173–180. Springer, Heidelberg (2008)
19. Xydeas, C., Angelov, P., Chiao, S., Reoulas, M.: Advances in eeg signals classification via dependant hmm models and evolving fuzzy classifiers. International Journal on Computers in Biology and Medicine, special issue on Intelligent Technologies for Bio-informatics and Medicine 36(10), 1064–1083 (2006)

Multi-class Imbalanced Data-Sets with Linguistic Fuzzy Rule Based Classification Systems Based on Pairwise Learning

Alberto Fernández[1,*], Mara José del Jesus[1], and Francisco Herrera[2]

[1] Dept. of Computer Science, University of Jaén
Tel.:+34-953-212444; Fax:+34-953-212472
{alberto.fernandez,mjjesus}@ujaen.es
[2] Dept. of Computer Science and A.I., University of Granada
herrera@decsai.ugr.es

Abstract. In a classification task, the imbalance class problem is present when the data-set has a very different distribution of examples among their classes. The main handicap of this type of problem is that standard learning algorithms consider a balanced training set and this supposes a bias towards the majority classes.

In order to provide a correct identification of the different classes of the problem, we propose a methodology based on two steps: first we will use the one-vs-one binarization technique for decomposing the original data-set into binary classification problems. Then, whenever each one of these binary subproblems is imbalanced, we will apply an oversampling step, using the SMOTE algorithm, in order to rebalance the data before the pairwise learning process.

For our experimental study we take as basis algorithm a linguistic Fuzzy Rule Based Classification System, and we aim to show not only the improvement in performance achieved with our methodology against the basic approach, but also to show the good synergy of the pairwise learning proposal with the selected oversampling technique.

Keywords: Imbalanced Data-sets, Multi-class Problems, Pairwise Learning, One-vs-One, Oversampling.

1 Introduction

In the research community on imbalanced data-sets [1], recent efforts have been focused on two-class imbalanced problems. However, multi-class imbalanced learning problems appear with high frequency and the correct identification of each kind of concept is equally important for considering different decisions to be taken. In this framework, the solutions proposed for the binary-class problem may not be directly applicable and as a result, there are few works in the specialised literature that cover this issue at present [2].

---

* Corresponding author.

E. Hüllermeier, R. Kruse, and F. Hoffmann (Eds.): IPMU 2010, LNAI 6178, pp. 89–98, 2010.
© Springer-Verlag Berlin Heidelberg 2010

Additionally, learning from multiple classes implies a difficulty for Data Mining algorithms, since the boundaries among the classes can be overlapped, which causes a decrease in performance. In this situation, we can proceed by transforming the original multi-class problem into binary subsets, which are easier to discriminate, via a class binarization technique [3,4].

In this contribution we propose a methodology for the classification of multi-class imbalanced data-sets by combining the pairwise learning or one-vs-one (OVO) approach [3] with the preprocessing of instances via oversampling. The idea is to train a different classifier for each possible pair of classes ignoring the examples that do not belong to the related classes, and to apply a preprocessing technique based on oversampling to those training subsets that have a significant imbalance between their classes. Specifically, in order to rebalance the distribution of training examples in both classes, we will make use of the "Synthetic Minority Over-sampling Technique" (SMOTE) [5], which has shown very good results in our previous works on the topic [6,7].

Our objective is to analyse whether this procedure allows a better discrimination of the different classes of the problem, rather than just applying the basic algorithm, and to study the significance of the preprocessing step by contrasting the performance of our methodology against the simple OVO approach. In order to develop this empirical study, we have chosen a linguistic Fuzzy Rule Based Classification System (FRBCSs), the Fuzzy Hybrid Genetics-Based Machine Learning (FH-GBML) algorithm [8]. Furthermore, we have selected 16 multi-class data-sets from the UCI repository [9] and the measure of performance is based on the Probabilistic AUC [10].

This contribution is organised as follows. First, Section 2 presents the problem of imbalanced data-sets, describing its features and the metric we have employed in the context of multiple classes. Next, Section 3 provides a brief introduction to binarization techniques for dealing with multi-class problems, focusing on the pairwise learning approach. In Section 4 we describe the algorithm selected for the study and we present our classification methodology for multi-class imbalanced data-sets based on pairwise learning and oversampling. In Section 5 the experimental framework for the study is established. The experimental study is carried out in Section 6, where we show the goodness of our model. Finally, Section 7 summarises and concludes the work.

2   Imbalanced Data-Sets in Classification

In the classification problem field, the scenario of imbalanced data-sets appears when the numbers of examples that represent the different classes are very different [2]. The minority classes are usually the most important concepts to be learnt, since they represent rare cases or because the data acquisition of these examples is costly. In this work we use the imbalance ratio (IR) [11], defined as the ratio of the number of instances of the majority class and the minority class, to organise the different data-sets according to their IR.

Most learning algorithms aim to obtain a model with a high prediction accuracy and a good generalisation capability. However, this inductive bias towards such a model poses a serious challenge to the classification of imbalanced data. First, if the search process is guided by the standard accuracy rate, it benefits the covering of the majority examples; second, classification rules that predict the positive class are often highly specialised and thus their coverage is very low, hence they are discarded in favour of more general rules, i.e. those that predict the negative class. Furthermore, it is not easy to distinguish between noise examples and minority class examples and they can be completely ignored by the classifier.

Regarding the empirical measure, instead of using accuracy, a more correct metric is considered. This is due to the fact that accuracy can lead to erroneous conclusions, since it doesn't take into account the proportion of examples for each class. Because of this, in this work we use the AUC metric [12], which can be defined as

$$AUC = \frac{1 + TP_{rate} - FP_{rate}}{2} \tag{1}$$

where TP_{rate} and FP_{rate} are the percentage of correctly and wrongly classified cases belonging to the positive class respectively.

Since this measure has been introduced for binary imbalanced data-sets, we need to extend its definition for multi-class problems. In the specific case of the AUC metric [10], we will compute a single value for each pair of classes, taking one class as positive and the other as negative. Finally we perform the average of the obtained value. The equation for this metric is as follows:

$$PAUC = \frac{1}{C(C-1)} \sum_{j=1}^{C} \sum_{k \neq j}^{C} AUC(j,k) \tag{2}$$

where $AUC(j,k)$ is the AUC (equation (1)) having j as positive class and k as negative class. c also stands for the number of classes. This measure is known as Probabilistic AUC.

3 Reducing Multi-class Problems by Binarization Techniques: One vs. One Approach

Multi-classes imply an additional difficulty for Data Mining algorithms, since the boundaries among the classes can be overlapped, causing a decrease in the performance level. In this situation, we can proceed by transforming the original multi-class problem into binary subsets, which are easier to discriminate, via a class binarization technique [4].

We will make use of the OVO approach [3], which consists of training a classifier for each possible pair of classes ignoring the examples that do not belong to the related classes. At classification time, a query instance is submitted to all binary models, and the predictions of these models are combined into an overall classification [13]. An example of this binarization technique is depicted in Figure 1.

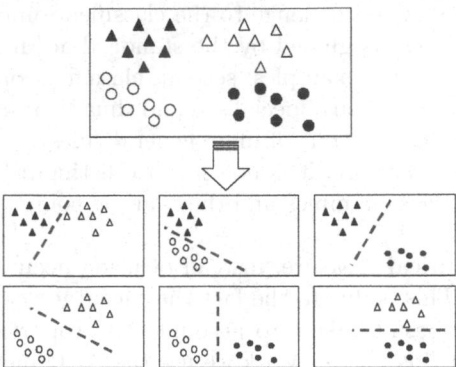

Fig. 1. One-vs-One binarization technique for a 4-class problem

In order to generate the class label, we will use the methodology we have proposed in [14], which considers the classification problem as a decision making problem, defining a fuzzy preference relation with the corresponding outputs of the classifiers. From this fuzzy preference relation, a set of non-dominated alternatives (classes) can be extracted as the solution to the fuzzy decision making problem and thus, the classification output. Specifically, the maximal non-dominated elements of the fuzzy preference relation are calculated by means of the non-dominance criterion proposed by Orlovsky in [15]. In the case of conflict with a given input, i.e. when there are more than one non-dominate value, it remains unclassified due to this ambiguity.

4   Solving Multi-class Imbalanced Data-Sets with Fuzzy Classifiers and Pairwise Learning

In this section we will first describe the FH-GBML algorithm, which will be employed as the base fuzzy model. Then we will present our methodology for dealing with multi-class imbalanced data-sets by means of the combination of multi-classification techniques and preprocessing of instances.

4.1   Fuzzy Hybrid Genetics-Based Machine Learning Rule Generation Algorithm

The FH-GBML method [8] consists of a Pittsburgh approach where each rule set is handled as an individual. It also contains a Genetic Cooperative-Competitive learning (GCCL) approach (an individual represents a unique rule), which is used as a kind of heuristic mutation for partially modifying each rule set.

This method uses standard fuzzy rules with rule weights where each input variable x_i is represented by a linguistic term or label. The system defines 14 possible linguistic terms for each attribute as well as a special "do not care" set.

In the learning process, N_{pop} rule sets are created by randomly selecting N_{rule} training patterns. Then, a fuzzy rule from each of the selected training patterns is generated by probabilistically choosing an antecedent fuzzy set from the 14 candidates $(P(B_k) = \frac{\mu_{B_k}(x_{pi})}{\sum_{j=1}^{14} \mu_{B_j}(x_{pi})})$ and each antecedent fuzzy set of the generated fuzzy rule is replaced with *don't care* using a pre-specified probability.

N_{pop} -1 rule sets are generated by selection, crossover and mutation in the same manner as the Pittsburgh-style algorithm. Next, with a pre-specified probability, a single iteration of the Genetic Cooperative-Competitive-style algorithm is applied to each of the generated rule sets.

Finally, the best rule set is added to the current population in the newly generated (N_{pop} -1) rule sets to form the next population and, if the stopping condition is not satisfied, the genetic process is repeated again.

4.2   Methodology for Dealing with Multi-class Imbalanced Problems with Linguistic Fuzzy Rule Based Classification Systems

Our proposed methodology is defined according to the following two steps:

1. First we will simplify the initial problem into several binary sets, in order to be able to apply those solutions that have been already developed and tested for imbalanced binary-class applications, for example those at data level that change the class size ratio of the two classes via oversampling.

   The advantages of this binarization approach with respect to other techniques, such as confronting one class with the rest ("one-vs-all" [16]), are detailed below:

   - It was shown to be more accurate for rule learning algorithms [17].
   - The computational time required for the learning phase is compensated by the reduction in size for each of the individual problems.
   - The decision boundaries of each binary problem may be considerably simpler than the "one-vs-all" transformation.
   - The selected binarization technique is less biased to obtain imbalanced training-sets which, as we have stated previously in Section 2, may suppose an added difficulty for the identification and discovery of rules covering the positive, and under-represented, samples. Clearly, this last issue is extremely important in our framework.

2. Once we have created all the binary training subsets, we search for those sets that have a significant IR in order to apply the preprocessing step by means of the SMOTE algorithm. According to our previous works on the topic [6], we will consider that the training set is imbalanced if the IR has a value higher than 1.5 (a distribution of 60-40%).

In order to clarify this procedure, the complete process is summarized in Algorithm 1.

Algorithm 1. Procedure for the multi-classifier learning methodology for imbalanced data-sets

---

1. Divide the training set into $C(C-1)/2$ binary subsets for all pairs of classes.
2. For each binary training subset:
   - 2.1. If IR > 1.5
     - Apply SMOTE preprocessing
   - 2.2. Build a classifier generated with any learning procedure
3. For each input test pattern:
   - 3.1. Build a fuzzy preference relation R as:
     - For each class i, $i = 1, \ldots, m$
       - For each class j, $j = 1, \ldots, m$, $j \neq i$
         - The preference degree for $R(i,j)$ is the normalized certainty degree for the classifier associated with classes i and j. $R(j,i) = 1 - R(i,j)$
   - 3.2. Transform R into a fuzzy strict preference relation R'.
   - 3.3. Compute the degree of non-dominance for all classes.
   - 3.4. The input pattern is assigned to the class with maximum non-dominance value.

---

5 Experimental Framework

In this section we first provide details of the real-world multi-class imbalanced problems chosen for the experimentation and the configuration parameters of the methods, and then we present the statistical tests applied to compare the results obtained with the different approaches.

5.1 Data-Sets and Parameters

Table 1 summarizes the properties of the selected data-sets. It shows, for each data-set, the number of examples (#Ex.), the number of attributes (#Atts.), the number of numerical (#Num.) and nominal (#Nom.) features, the number of classes (#Cl.) and the IR. The *penbased*, *page-blocks* and *thyroid* data-sets have been stratified sampled at 10% in order to reduce their size for training. In the case of missing values (*cleveland* and *dermatology*) we have removed those instances from the data-set. Finally, we must point out that the estimates of the performance were obtained by means of a 5-fold cross validation.

The selected configuration for the FH-GBML approach consists of product T-norm as conjunction operator, together with the Penalised Certainty Factor approach for the rule weight and fuzzy reasoning method of the winning rule. Regarding the specific parameters for the genetic process, we have chosen the following values:

- Number of fuzzy rules: $5 \cdot d$ rules (max. 50 rules).
- Number of rule sets: 200 rule sets.
- Crossover probability: 0.9.
- Mutation probability: $1/d$.
- Number of replaced rules: All rules except the best-one (Pittsburgh-part, elitist approach), number of rules / 5 (GCCL-part).

Table 1. Summary Description of the Data-Sets

id	Data-set	#Ex.	#Atts.	#Num.	#Nom.	#Cl.	IR
aut	autos	159	25	15	10	6	16.00
bal	balance scale	625	4	4	0	3	5.88
cle	cleveland	297	13	6	7	5	13.42
con	contraceptive method choice	1,473	9	6	3	3	1.89
der	dermatology	366	33	1	32	6	5.55
eco	ecoli	336	7	7	0	8	71.50
gla	glass identification	214	9	9	0	6	8.44
hay	hayes-roth	132	4	4	0	3	1.70
lym	lymphography	148	18	3	15	4	40.50
new	new-thyroid	215	5	5	0	3	4.84
pag	page-blocks	548	10	10	0	5	164.00
pen	pen-based recognition	1,099	16	16	0	10	1.95
shu	shuttle	2,175	9	9	0	5	853.00
thy	thyroid	720	21	6	15	3	36.94
win	wine	178	13	13	0	3	1.5
yea	yeast	1,484	8	8	0	10	23.15

- Total number of generations: 1,000 generations.
- Don't care probability: 0.5.
- Probability of the application of the GCCL iteration: 0.5.

where d stands for the dimensionality of the problem (number of attributes).

For the use of the SMOTE preprocessing technique, we will consider the 5-nearest neighbour to generate the synthetic samples, and balancing both classes to the 50% distribution. In our preliminary experiments we have tried several percentages for the distribution between the classes and we have obtained the best results with a strictly balanced distribution.

5.2 Statistical Tests for Performance Comparison

In this paper, we use the hypothesis testing techniques to provide statistical support for the analysis of the results. Specifically, we will use non-parametric tests, due to the fact that the initial conditions that guarantee the reliability of the parametric tests may not be satisfied, causing the statistical analysis to lose credibility with these type of tests [18,19].

For performing pairwise comparisons between two algorithms, we will apply the Wilcoxon signed-rank test [20]. Furthermore, we consider the average ranking of the algorithms in order to show graphically how good a method is with respect to its partners. This ranking is obtained by assigning a position to each algorithm depending on its performance for each data-set. The algorithm which achieves the best accuracy in a specific data-set will have the first ranking (value 1); then, the algorithm with the second best accuracy is assigned rank 2, and so forth. This task is carried out for all data-sets and finally an average ranking is computed as the mean value of all rankings.

6   Experimental Study

We show the average results in training and test in Table 2, for the three classification schemes analysed in this study, namely the basic approach (Base), the multiclassification approach (OVO) and the multiclassification scheme with oversampling (OVO+SMOTE).

Table 2. Results for the FH-GBML algorithm with the different classification approaches

Data-set	Base		OVO		OVO+SMOTE	
	AUC_{Tr}	AUC_{Tst}	AUC_{Tr}	AUC_{Tst}	AUC_{Tr}	AUC_{Tst}
aut	.7395	.6591	.8757	**.6910**	.8032	.6829
bal	.7178	.7008	.7307	.7109	.7992	**.7296**
cle	.6395	.5577	.7366	**.5664**	.7949	.5584
con	.5852	.5623	.6468	.6201	.6683	**.6294**
der	.7169	.6862	.9746	**.9084**	.9614	.8716
eco	.7564	.7811	.9269	.8201	.9578	**.8321**
gla	.7426	.6920	.8691	.7444	.9375	**.8207**
lym	.8590	.7626	.9349	.8397	.9284	**.8689**
hay	.7979	**.6954**	.9597	.6656	.9663	.6456
new	.9490	.8861	.9967	**.9564**	.9850	.9457
pag	.7317	.6929	.9472	.7862	.9696	**.8552**
pen	.8460	.8340	.9798	**.9508**	.9740	.9387
shu	.7253	.7709	.9319	.8635	.9950	**.9516**
thy	.5198	.4992	.5304	.4993	.9193	**.8763**
win	.9847	.9501	1.000	**.9710**	.9974	.9519
yea	.6456	.6272	.8042	.7438	.8365	**.7442**
Mean	.7473	.7099	.8653	.7711	.9075	**.8064**

We observe that in most cases the best result in test (which is stressed in boldface) corresponds to the one obtained by our OVO+SMOTE methodology. Nevertheless, in order to support the suggestion that our methodology enables an enhancement of the classification ability of the FH-GBML algorithm for imbalanced problems, we will perform a detailed statistical study.

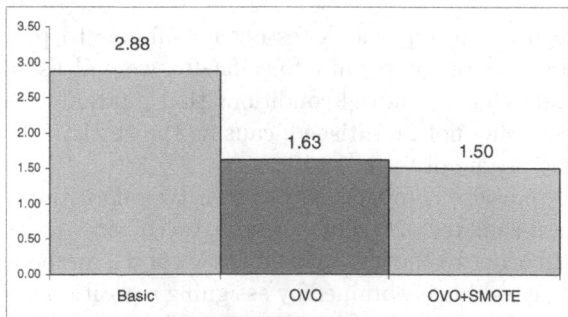

Fig. 2. Average ranking for the FH-GBML method with the different classification schemes

Table 3. Wilcoxon signed-ranks test. R^+ corresponds to the sum of the ranks for the OVO+SMOTE method and R^- to the Basic and OVO classification schemes.

Comparison	R^+	R^-	p-value	Hypothesis ($\alpha = 0.05$)
OVO+SMOTE vs. Basic	131.0	5.0	0.001	Rejected for OVO+SMOTE
OVO+SMOTE vs. OVO	88.0	48.0	0.301	Not Rejected

First, Figure 2 shows the average ranking computed for the different classification schemes, where we can observe that OVO+SMOTE is the best option, whereas the basic FH-GBML approach obtains the worst ranking with a much higher value than the former.

Next, we perform a Wilcoxon test (Table 3) to contrast the different approaches that are being studied. The first conclusion extracted from the result of this test is that our methodology is actually better suited for imbalanced dataset with multiple classes than the basic learning algorithm. Also, we observe that the application of the oversampling step enables the obtention of better results than applying the binarization scheme directly over the original training data, as suggested by both the higher sum of the ranks in favour of our methodology and the average results in Table 2.

The study carried out allow us to discuss several issues as future work:

1. The inclusion of different Machine Learning algorithms to analyse the robustness of our methodology.
2. A comparative study of several preprocessing techniques (oversampling, undersampling and hybrid approaches).
3. A detailed study regarding the IR of the algorithms and the goodness of the application of preprocessing in each case and the definition of a precise threshold in order to rebalance the binary training data.

7   Concluding Remarks

In this paper we have presented a new methodology for the classification of multi-class imbalanced data-sets using a combination of pairwise learning and preprocessing of instances. This methodology divides the original problem into binary-class subsets which are rebalanced using the SMOTE algorithm when the IR between the corresponding classes is higher than a threshold.

We have tested the quality of this approach using the FH-GBML algorithm, a linguistic FRBCSs, for which the experimental results support the goodness of our methodology as it generally outperforms the basic and pairwise learning multi-classifier approach.

Acknowledgment

This work had been supported by the Spanish Ministry of Science and Technology under Projects TIN2008-06681-C06-01 and TIN2008-06681-C06-02, and the Andalusian Research Plan TIC-3928.

References

1. Chawla, N.V., Japkowicz, N., Kolcz, A.: Editorial: special issue on learning from imbalanced data sets. SIGKDD Explorations 6(1), 1–6 (2004)
2. Sun, Y., Wong, A.K.C., Kamel, M.S.: Classification of imbalanced data: A review. International Journal of Pattern Recognition and Artificial Intelligence 23(4), 687–719 (2009)
3. Hastie, T., Tibshirani, R.: Classification by pairwise coupling. The Annals of Statistics 26(2), 451–471 (1998)
4. Allwein, E.L., Schapire, R.E., Singer, Y.: Reducing multiclass to binary: A unifying approach for margin classifiers. Journal of Machine Learning Research 1, 113–141 (2000)
5. Chawla, N.V., Bowyer, K.W., Hall, L.O., Kegelmeyer, W.P.: Smote: Synthetic minority over–sampling technique. Journal of Artificial Intelligent Research 16, 321–357 (2002)
6. Fernández, A., García, S., del Jesus, M.J., Herrera, F.: A study of the behaviour of linguistic fuzzy rule based classification systems in the framework of imbalanced data–sets. Fuzzy Sets and Systems 159(18), 2378–2398 (2008)
7. Fernández, A., del Jesus, M.J., Herrera, F.: On the 2-tuples based genetic tuning performance for fuzzy rule based classification systems in imbalanced data-sets. Information Sciences 180(8), 1268–1291 (2010)
8. Ishibuchi, H., Yamamoto, T., Nakashima, T.: Hybridization of fuzzy GBML approaches for pattern classification problems. IEEE Transactions on System, Man and Cybernetics B 35(2), 359–365 (2005)
9. Asuncion, A., Newman, D.: UCI machine learning repository. University of California, Berkeley (2007), http://www.ics.uci.edu/~mlearn/MLRepository.html
10. Hand, D.J., Till, R.J.: A simple generalisation of the area under the ROC curve for multiple class classification problems. Machine Learning 45(2), 171–186 (2001)
11. Orriols-Puig, A., Bernadó-Mansilla, E.: Evolutionary rule–based systems for imbalanced datasets. Soft Computing 13(3), 213–225 (2009)
12. Huang, J., Ling, C.X.: Using AUC and accuracy in evaluating learning algorithms. IEEE Transactions on Knowledge and Data Engineering 17(3), 299–310 (2005)
13. Hüllermeier, E., Brinker, K.: Learning valued preference structures for solving classification problems. Fuzzy Sets and Systems 159(18), 2337–2352 (2008)
14. Fernández, A., Calderón, M., Barrenechea, E., Bustince, H., Herrera, F.: Enhancing fuzzy rule based systems in multi-classification using pairwise coupling with preference relations. In: EUROFUSE '09 Workshop on Preference Modelling and Decision Analysis (EUROFUSE '09), pp. 39–46 (2009)
15. Orlovsky, S.A.: Decision-making with a fuzzy preference relation. Fuzzy Sets and Systems 1, 155–167 (1978)
16. Rifkin, R., Klautau, A.: In defense of one-vs-all classification. Journal of Machine Learning Research 5, 101–141 (2004)
17. Fürnkranz, J.: Round robin classification. Journal of Machine Learning Research 2, 721–747 (2002)
18. Demšar, J.: Statistical comparisons of classifiers over multiple data sets. Journal of Machine Learning Research 7, 1–30 (2006)
19. García, S., Herrera, F.: An extension on "Statistical comparisons of classifiers over multiple data sets" for all pairwise comparisons. Journal of Machine Learning Research 9, 2677–2694 (2008)
20. Sheskin, D.: Handbook of parametric and nonparametric statistical procedures, 2nd edn. Chapman & Hall/CRC, Boca Raton (2006)

Probabilistic Rough Set Approaches to Ordinal Classification with Monotonicity Constraints

Jerzy Błaszczyński[1], Roman Słowiński[1,2], and Marcin Szeląg[1]

[1] Institute of Computing Science, Poznań University of Technology,
60-965 Poznań, Poland
{jblaszczynski,rslowinski,mszelag}@cs.put.poznan.pl
[2] Institute for Systems Research, Polish Academy of Sciences,
01-447 Warsaw, Poland

Abstract. We present some probabilistic rough set approaches to ordinal classification with monotonicity constraints, where it is required that the class label of an object does not decrease when evaluation of this object on attributes improves. Probabilistic rough set approaches allow to structure the classification data prior to induction of decision rules. We apply sequential covering to induce rules that satisfy consistency constraints. These rules are then used to make predictions on a new set of objects. After discussing some interesting features of this type of reasoning about ordinal data, we perform an extensive computational experiment to show a practical value of this proposal which is compared to other well known methods.

1 Introduction

Rough set analysis of classification data is a useful step preceding the learning of a classifier. It checks the data for possible inconsistencies by calculation of lower approximations of considered sets of objects. Due to this type of data structuring, one may restrict a priori the set of objects on which the classifier is learned to a subset of sufficiently consistent objects belonging to lower approximations. This restriction is motivated by a postulate for learning from consistent data, so that the gained knowledge is relatively certain. Rough set analysis also enables estimation of the attainable training error before learning of the classifier.

The original Rough Set Approach proposed by Pawlak [12] deals with classification data which are not considered to be ordered. In this case, the data structuring is possible using the rough set concept involving an indiscernibility relation. This is why we call the original approach Indiscernibility-based Rough Set Approach (IRSA). *Ordinal classification with monotonicity constraints* considered in this paper requires, however, a structuring tool which would handle the ordered domains of attributes and a monotonic relationship between evaluations of objects on the attributes and the assignment of these objects to ordered decision classes. This tool has been proposed by Greco, Matarazzo and Słowiński [9,14] and called Dominance-based Rough Set Approach (DRSA), since it uses the rough set concept involving a dominance relation. Both in IRSA and in

E. Hüllermeier, R. Kruse, and F. Hoffmann (Eds.): IPMU 2010, LNAI 6178, pp. 99–108, 2010.
© Springer-Verlag Berlin Heidelberg 2010

DRSA, the approximations are built using granules of knowledge, which are either indiscernibility classes (IRSA) or dominance cones (DRSA). In IRSA and DRSA, granules of knowledge have to be consistent, which appears to be too restrictive in practical applications. Therefore, different versions of probabilistic rough set approaches (for IRSA and DRSA) were proposed (see [4] for review). In this paper, we rely on the monotonic Variable Consistency DRSA (VC-DRSA) introduced in [4]. We use various *object consistency measures* to quantify the evidence for membership of an object to a set.

The rule induction algorithm co-operating with VC-DRSA is called VC-DomLEM. It induces a minimal set of *probabilistic decision rules*, by sequential covering [8,10] of training objects structured by VC-DRSA. In other words, it generalizes the description of objects contained in probabilistic lower approximations obtained by variable consistency rough set approaches. To control the quality of the rules, we use three different *rule consistency measures*. They have the same properties as corresponding object consistency measures used for definition of probabilistic lower approximations. Classification of objects by the induced rules is made using the classification scheme described in [2].

This paper is organized as follows. In Section 2, we remind basic definitions of DRSA and VC-DRSA. In Section 3, we describe characteristics and properties of decision rules. In Section 4, we present VC-DomLEM algorithm. Section 5 contains results of an experiment in which we compared classifiers based on VC-DomLEM to other well known classifiers. Section 6 concludes the paper.

2   Basic Definitions of Rough Set Approaches

Data analyzed by Dominance-based Rough Set Approach (DRSA) [9,14] concern a finite universe U of objects described by attributes from a finite set A. It has the form of a decision table, where rows correspond to objects from U and columns correspond to attributes from A. Attributes with preference-ordered value sets are called *criteria*, while attributes whose value sets are not preference-ordered are called *regular attributes*. Moreover, set A is divided into disjoint sets of condition attributes C and decision attributes D. The value set of attribute $q \in C \cup D$ is denoted by V_q, and $V_P = \prod_{q=1}^{|P|} V_q$ is called P-evaluation space, where $P \subseteq C$. For simplicity, we assume that set D is a singleton $D = \{d\}$, and that values of d are ordered class labels. Decision attribute d makes a partition of set U into a finite number of n disjoint sets of objects, called *decision classes*. We denote this partition by $\mathcal{X} = \{X_1, \ldots, X_n\}$.

When among condition attributes from C there is at least one criterion, and there exists a monotonic relationship between evaluation of objects on criteria and their values (class labels) on the decision attribute, then, in order to make a meaningful representation of classification decisions, one has to consider the *dominance relation* in the evaluation space. For each object $y \in U$, two dominance cones are defined with respect to (w.r.t.) $P \subseteq C$. The P-positive dominance cone $D_P^+(y)$ is composed of objects that for each $q_i \in P$ are not worse than

y. The P-negative dominance cone $D_P^-(y)$ is composed of objects that for each $q_i \in P$ are not better than y. The class labels are ordered, such that if $i < j$, then class X_i is considered to be worse than X_j. The approximations concern unions of decision classes: upward unions $X_i^{\geq} = \bigcup_{t \geq i} X_t$, where $i = 2, 3, \ldots, n$, and downward unions $X_i^{\leq} = \bigcup_{t \leq i} X_t$, where $i = 1, 2, \ldots, n - 1$.

In order to simplify notation, we will use symbol X to denote a set of objects belonging to union of classes $X_i^{\geq}$ or $X_i^{\leq}$, unless it would lead to misunderstanding. Moreover, we will use symbol $E_P(y)$ to denote any granule $D_P^+(y)$ or $D_P^-(y)$, $y \in U$. If X and $E_P(y)$ are used in the same equation, then for X representing $X_i^{\geq}$ (resp. $X_i^{\leq}$), $E_P(y)$ stands for dominance cone $D_P^+(y)$ (resp. $D_P^-(y)$).

Probabilistic rough set approaches aim to extend lower approximation of set X by inclusion of objects with sufficient evidence for membership to X. This evidence can be quantified by *object consistency measures*.

Let us give a generic definition of probabilistic P-lower approximation of set X. For $P \subseteq C, X \subseteq U, y \in U$, given a gain-type (resp. cost-type) object consistency measure $\Theta_X^P(y)$ and a gain-threshold (resp. cost-threshold) θ_X, the P-lower approximation of set X is defined as:

$$\underline{P}^{\theta_X}(X) = \{y \in X : \Theta_X^P(y) \propto \theta_X\}, \tag{1}$$

where $\propto$ denotes $\geq$ in case of a gain-type object consistency measure and a gain-threshold, or $\leq$ for a cost-type object consistency measure and a cost-threshold. In the above definition, $\theta_X \in [0, A_X]$ is a technical parameter influencing the degree of consistency of objects belonging to lower approximation of X.

The definition of P-upper approximation, as well as that of P-boundary of set X, given in [4], are not relevant here. In [4], we also introduced and motivated four *monotonicity properties* required from object consistency measures used in definition (1); they were denoted by $(m1)$, $(m2)$, $(m3)$, and $(m4)$.

Let us remind definitions of positive, negative and boundary regions of X in the evaluation space ([3]). First, let us note that each set X has its complement $\neg X = U - X$. P-positive region of X in P-evaluation space is defined as:

$$POS_P^{\theta_X}(X) = \bigcup_{y \in \underline{P}^{\theta_X}(X)} E_P(y), \tag{2}$$

where θ_X comes from (1). Basing on definition (2), we can define P-negative and P-boundary regions of the approximated set as follows:

$$NEG_P^{\theta_X}(X) = POS_P^{\theta_X}(\neg X) - POS_P^{\theta_X}(X), \tag{3}$$

$$BND_P^{\theta_X}(X) = U - POS_P^{\theta_X}(X) - NEG_P^{\theta_X}(X). \tag{4}$$

A classifier learned on P-lower approximations *may* correctly assign object $y \in X_i$ to class X_i if y belongs to the P-positive region of $X_i^{\geq}$ or $X_i^{\leq}$.

Let $P \subseteq C$, $\boldsymbol{\theta}_X = \{\theta_{X_1^{\leq}}, \ldots, \theta_{X_{n-1}^{\leq}}, \theta_{X_2^{\geq}}, \ldots, \theta_{X_n^{\geq}}\}$. The following two measures estimate the attainable training error of the classifier. The first measure estimates the ratio of training objects in the data table that may be learned by the classifier:

$$\lambda_P^{\theta x}(\mathcal{X}) = \frac{|X_1 \cap POS_P^{\theta_{X_{\bar{1}}^{\leq}}}(X_{\bar{1}}^{\leq})|}{|U|} +$$

$$+ \frac{\bigcup_{i=2}^{n-1} |X_i \cap (POS_P^{\theta_{X_{\bar{i}}^{\geq}}}(X_{\bar{i}}^{\geq}) \cup POS_P^{\theta_{X_{\bar{i}}^{\leq}}}(X_{\bar{i}}^{\leq}))|}{|U|} + \frac{|X_n \cap POS_P^{\theta_{X_{\bar{n}}^{\geq}}}(X_{\bar{n}}^{\geq})|}{|U|}. \tag{5}$$

The second measure estimates the average minimal absolute difference between index of the class to which a training object may be assigned and index of the class to which the object belongs. For $i : y_j \in X_i$,

$$\delta_P^{\theta x}(\mathcal{X}) = \frac{1}{|U|} \sum_{j=1}^{|U|} \min_{k \,:\, y_j \in POS_P^{\theta_{X_k^{\geq}}}(X_k^{\geq}) \vee y_j \in POS_P^{\theta_{X_k^{\leq}}}(X_k^{\leq})} |i - k|. \tag{6}$$

Finally, let us recall definitions and monotonicity properties of object consistency measures which will be used in definition (1). The first object consistency measure that we consider is a cost-type measure $\epsilon_X^P(y)$. For $P \subseteq C, X, \neg X \subseteq U$, it is defined as:

$$\epsilon_X^P(y) = \frac{|E_P(y) \cap \neg X|}{|\neg X|}. \tag{7}$$

As proved in [4], this measure has properties $(m1)$, $(m2)$ and $(m4)$.

The second object consistency measure is a cost-type measure $\epsilon_X'^P(y)$. For $P \subseteq C, X, \neg X \subseteq U, y \in U$, it is defined as:

$$\epsilon_X'^P(y) = \frac{|E_P(y) \cap \neg X|}{|X|}. \tag{8}$$

As proved in [4], this measure has all four desirable monotonicity properties.

The third object consistency measure is a gain-type measure $\mu_X'^P(y)$ introduced in [3]. For $P \subseteq C, X_i^{\geq}, X_i^{\leq} \subseteq U, y \in U$, measures $\mu_{X_i^{\geq}}'^P(y)$ and $\mu_{X_i^{\leq}}'^P(y)$ are defined as:

$$\mu_{X_i^{\geq}}'^P(y) = \max_{z \in D_P^-(y) \cap X_i^{\geq}} \mu_{X_i^{\geq}}^P(z), \qquad \mu_{X_i^{\leq}}'^P(y) = \max_{z \in D_P^+(y) \cap X_i^{\leq}} \mu_{X_i^{\leq}}^P(z), \tag{9}$$

where $\mu_X^P(z) = \frac{|E_P(z) \cap X|}{|E_P(z)|}$ denotes rough membership of object $z \in U$ to union of classes $X \subseteq U$, w.r.t. set $P \subseteq C$. Measure $\mu_X^P(y)$ has properties $(m2)$ and $(m3)$, but it lacks properties $(m1)$ and $(m4)$ [4], while measure $\mu_X'^P(y)$, has properties $(m2)$, $(m3)$, and $(m4)$, but it lacks property $(m1)$ [3].

3   Characteristics and Properties of Decision Rules

In VC-DRSA, we consider decision rules of the following type:

$$q_{i_1}(y) \succeq r_{i_1} \wedge \ldots \wedge q_{i_p}(y) \succeq r_{i_p} \wedge q_{i_{p+1}}(y) = r_{i_{p+1}} \wedge \ldots \wedge q_{i_z}(y) = r_{i_z} \Rightarrow y \in X_i^{\geq},$$

$$q_{i_1}(y) \preceq r_{i_1} \wedge \ldots \wedge q_{i_p}(y) \preceq r_{i_p} \wedge q_{i_{p+1}}(y) = r_{i_{p+1}} \wedge \ldots \wedge q_{i_z}(y) = r_{i_z} \Rightarrow y \in X_i^{\leq},$$

where $i \in \{i_1, i_2, \ldots, i_p\}$ is a criterion index, $i \in \{i_{p+1}, i_{p+2}, \ldots, i_z\}$ is a regular attribute index, $r_q \in V_q$, and symbols $\succeq$ and $\preceq$ denote weak preference w.r.t. single criterion and inverse weak preference, respectively.

Let us denote by $r_X^{\hat{\theta}_X} \in R_X^{\hat{\theta}_X}$ a rule with conclusion $y \in X$, and with value of *rule consistency measure* $\hat{\Theta}$ not worse than threshold $\hat{\theta}_X$. The premise of this rule is denoted by $\Phi_{r_X^{\hat{\theta}_X}}$, while its conclusion by $\Psi_{r_X^{\hat{\theta}_X}}$. The set of objects satisfying the premise is denoted by $\|\Phi_{r_X^{\hat{\theta}_X}}\|$. We consider three rule consistency measures:

$$\epsilon\text{-consistency of } r_X^{\hat{\theta}_X} : \epsilon(r_X^{\hat{\theta}_X}) = \frac{|\|\Phi_{r_X^{\hat{\theta}_X}}\| \cap \neg \underline{P}^{\theta_X}(X)|}{|\neg \underline{P}^{\theta_X}(X)|}, \qquad (10)$$

$$\epsilon'\text{-consistency of } r_X^{\hat{\theta}_X} : \epsilon'(r_X^{\hat{\theta}_X}) = \frac{|\|\Phi_{r_X^{\hat{\theta}_X}}\| \cap \neg \underline{P}^{\theta_X}(X)|}{|\underline{P}^{\theta_X}(X)|}, \qquad (11)$$

$$\mu\text{-consistency of } r_X^{\hat{\theta}_X} : \mu(r_X^{\hat{\theta}_X}) = \frac{|\|\Phi_{r_X^{\hat{\theta}_X}}\| \cap \underline{P}^{\theta_X}(X)|}{|\|\Phi_{r_X^{\hat{\theta}_X}}\||}, \qquad (12)$$

where $\hat{\theta}_X = \frac{|\neg X|}{|\neg \underline{P}^{\theta_X}(X)|}\theta_X$ in definition (10), $\hat{\theta}_X = \frac{|X|}{|\underline{P}^{\theta_X}(X)|}\theta_X$ in definition (11), and $\hat{\theta}_X = \theta_X$ in definition (12). ϵ-consistency (ϵ'-consistency) measure is related to cost-type object consistency measure defined by (7) (resp. (8)). μ-consistency measure is related to gain-type rough membership measure used in definition (9). The above rule consistency measures inherit the monotonicity properties from the corresponding object consistency measures.

We expect decision rules to be short and minimal. A rule is *minimal* in set $\mathbf{R}$, if there is no other rule $r' \in \mathbf{R}$ with not less general premise and not less specific conclusion. Moreover, set $R_X^{\hat{\theta}_X}$ of rules with conclusion $y \in X$ has to be *complete*, which in our case means that each object $y \in \underline{P}^{\theta_X}(X)$ has to be covered by at least one rule from $R_X^{\hat{\theta}_X}$. Finally, each rule $r_X^{\hat{\theta}_X} \in R_X^{\hat{\theta}_X}$ should be *non-redundant*, i.e., such that it cannot be removed without breaking the completeness of $R_X^{\hat{\theta}_X}$.

4 Induction of Decision Rules by VC-DomLEM

VC-DomLEM algorithm uses a heuristic strategy called sequential covering [10,8]. It induces a complete set of minimal and non-redundant decision rules $\mathbf{R}$. It operates at two levels. At the first level, in Algorithm 1, unions of classes $X \in \mathbf{X}$ are considered one by one. For each X, set of rules $R_X^{\hat{\theta}_X}$ is induced by the $VC\text{-}SequentialCovering^{mix}$ method (line 4) – Algorithm 2. Each rule $r_X^{\hat{\theta}_X} \in R_X^{\hat{\theta}_X}$ uses elementary conditions constructed for objects from $\underline{P}^{\theta_X}(X)$, on attributes from set P. Value of chosen measure $\hat{\Theta}$, defined by (10), (11) or (12), has to be not worse than given threshold value $\hat{\theta}_X$. Moreover, $r_X^{\hat{\theta}_X}$ is allowed to cover only objects from set $AO_P^{\theta_X}(X)$, calculated according to chosen option

$s \in \{1, 2, 3\}$ (line 3). We consider three options: 1) $AO_P^{\theta_X}(X) = POS_P^{\theta_X}(X)$, 2) $AO_P^{\theta_X}(X) = POS_P^{\theta_X}(X) \cup BND_P^{\theta_X}(X)$, and 3) $AO_P^{\theta_X}(X) = U$.

At the second level, in $VC\text{-}SequentialCovering^{mix}$ method, rules for a given set X are induced. The best elementary condition selected in line 7 is chosen according to the following two quality measures considered lexicographically: 1) rule consistency measure (10), (11) or (12) of $r_X^{\hat{\theta}_X}$ extended by new elementary condition ec, 2) $\left| \left\| \Phi_{r_X^{\hat{\theta}_X} \cup ec} \right\| \cap \underline{P}^{\theta_X}(X) \right|$. It is worth noting that, in general, it is possible to add a new elementary condition on an attribute already present in the rule. However, such condition is always redundant from the viewpoint of ϵ-consistency (10) and ϵ'-consistency (11) measures; this allows to decrease computational complexity by reducing EC in these cases [5]. Moreover, measures (10) and (11) allow for further reduction of EC, since they have property (m4) [5]. Elementary conditions from set EC always come from objects that support the growing rule (line 9). Elementary conditions that are not necessary to satisfy constraints from line 6 are removed from the constructed rule in line 11. Redundant rules are removed in an iterative procedure (line 15), which uses the following measures considered lexicographically: 1) the smallest value of $\left| \left\| \Phi_{r_X^{\hat{\theta}_X}} \right\| \cap \underline{P}^{\theta_X}(X) \right|$, 2) the worst value of $\hat{\Theta}(r_X^{\hat{\theta}_X})$. It can be shown that $VC\text{-}SequentialCovering^{mix}$ method with μ-consistency measure (12) may fail to construct a rule satisfying constraints from line 6 [5]. This is caused by lack of property (m4) of this measure. To overcome this problem, we define P-edge regions of unions of classes $X_i^{\geq}$ and $X_i^{\leq}$ as follows. For $P \subseteq C, X_i^{\geq}, X_i^{\leq} \subseteq U$, $y, z \in U, \theta_{X_i^{\geq}} \in [0, A_{X_i^{\geq}}], \theta_{X_i^{\leq}} \in [0, A_{X_i^{\leq}}]$:

$$EDGE_P^{\theta_{X_i^{\geq}}}(X_i^{\geq}) = \{y \in \underline{P}^{\theta_{X_i^{\geq}}}(X_i^{\geq}) : z \in D_P^-(y) \cap \underline{P}^{\theta_{X_i^{\geq}}}(X_i^{\geq}) \Rightarrow z \in D_P^+(y)\},$$

$$EDGE_P^{\theta_{X_i^{\leq}}}(X_i^{\leq}) = \{y \in \underline{P}^{\theta_{X_i^{\leq}}}(X_i^{\leq}) : z \in D_P^+(y) \cap \underline{P}^{\theta_{X_i^{\leq}}}(X_i^{\leq}) \Rightarrow z \in D_P^-(y)\}.$$

Then, the proposed modification consists in using $EDGE_P^{\theta_X}(X)$ instead of $\underline{P}^{\theta_X}(X)$ in line 1 of $VC\text{-}SequentialCovering^{mix}$.

Algorithm 1. $VC\text{-}DomLEM$

Input : set $\mathbf{X}$ of upward unions of classes $X_i^{\geq} \in U$ or downward unions of classes $X_i^{\leq} \in U$; set of attributes $P \subseteq C$; rule consistency measure $\hat{\Theta}$; set of rule consistency measure thresholds $\{\hat{\theta}_X : X \in \mathbf{X}\}$; object covering option s.

Output: set of rules $\mathbf{R}$.

1 $\mathbf{R} := \emptyset$;
2 **foreach** $X \in \mathbf{X}$ **do**
3    $AO_P^{\theta_X}(X) := AllowedObjects(X, P, \theta_X, s)$;
4    $R_X^{\hat{\theta}_X} := VC\text{-}SequentialCovering^{mix}(\underline{P}^{\theta_X}(X), AO_P^{\theta_X}(X), P, \hat{\Theta}, \hat{\theta}_X)$;
5    $\mathbf{R} := \mathbf{R} \cup R_X^{\hat{\theta}_X}$;
6   RemoveNonMinimalRules($\mathbf{R}$);
7 **end**

Algorithm 2. $VC\text{-}SequentialCovering^{mix}$

Input : set of positive objects $\underline{P}^{\theta X}(X) \subseteq U$; set of objects that can be covered
$AO_P^{\theta X}(X) \subseteq U$, $AO_P^{\theta X}(X) \supseteq \underline{P}^{\theta X}(X)$; set of attributes $P \subseteq C$; rule consistency
measure $\hat{\Theta}$; rule consistency measure threshold $\hat{\theta}_X$.

Output: set of rules $R_X^{\hat{\theta} X}$ assigning objects to X.

1 $B := \underline{P}^{\theta X}(X)$;

2 $R_X^{\hat{\theta} X} := \emptyset$;

3 **while** $B \neq \emptyset$ **do**

4   $\quad r_X^{\hat{\theta} X} := \emptyset$;

5   $\quad EC := \text{ElementaryConditions}(B, P)$;

6   $\quad$ **while** $(\hat{\Theta}(r_X^{\hat{\theta} X})$ *does not satisfy* $\hat{\theta}_X)$ *or* $(\|\Phi_{r_X^{\hat{\theta} X}}\| \nsubseteq AO_P^{\theta X}(X))$ **do**

7   $\quad\quad ec := \text{BestElementaryCondition}(EC, r_X^{\hat{\theta} X}, \hat{\Theta}, \underline{P}^{\theta X}(X))$;

8   $\quad\quad r_X^{\hat{\theta} X} := r_X^{\hat{\theta} X} \cup ec$;

9   $\quad\quad EC := \text{ElementaryConditions}(B \cap support(r_X^{\hat{\theta} X}), P)$;

10 $\quad$ **end**

11 $\quad \text{RemoveRedundantElementaryConditions}(r_X^{\hat{\theta} X}, \hat{\Theta}, \hat{\theta}_X, AO_P^{\theta X}(X))$;

12 $\quad R_X^{\hat{\theta} X} := R_X^{\hat{\theta} X} \cup r_X^{\hat{\theta} X}$;

13 $\quad B := B \setminus supp(r_X^{\hat{\theta} X})$;

14 **end**

15 $\text{RemoveRedundantRules}(R_X^{\hat{\theta} X}, \hat{\Theta}, \underline{P}^{\theta X}(X))$;

---

5   Results of the Computational Experiment

The aim of the experiment was to check what is the predictive accuracy of the rough set approach in classification. To achieve this goal, we measured mean absolute error (MAE) and the percentage of correctly classified objects (PCC) on twelve ordinal data sets listed in Table 1. In this table, we also show the values of λ (5) and δ (6), calculated on the whole data sets. For both measures, we present values for the most restrictive consistency thresholds (i.e., $\epsilon_X^* = 0$, $\mu_X^* = 1$), and values calculated for the consistency thresholds used in the experiment. These values can be compared to MAE and PCC obtained by the classifiers.

We considered VC-DomLEM[1] [5] in two variants: monotonic (i.e., with consistency measure ϵ [4]) and non-monotonic (i.e., with consistency measure μ' [3]). Moreover, we used two ordinal classifiers that preserve monotonicity constraints: Ordinal Learning Model (OLM) [1] and Ordinal Stochastic Dominance Learner (OSDL) [6]. We also used some well known non-ordinal classifiers: Naive Bayes, Support Vector Machine (SVM) with linear kernel [13], decision rule classifier RIPPER, and decision tree classifier C4.5.

The predictive accuracy was calculated by stratified 10-fold cross-validation, which was repeated several times. The results are shown in Tables 2 & 3. Both tables contain values of predictive accuracy together with their standard deviation. Moreover, for each data set we calculated a rank of the result of a classifier when compared to the other classifiers. The rank is presented in brackets (the smaller the rank, the better). Last row of Tables 2 & 3 shows the average rank

---

[1] See http://www.cs.put.poznan.pl/jblaszczynski/Site/jRS.html

Table 1. Characteristics of data sets, values of λ and δ measures for $\theta_X^* = \epsilon_X^* = 0$, $\theta_X^* = \mu_X'^* = 1$, as well as for ϵ_X and μ_X' used to obtain results shown in Tables 2 & 3

Id	Data set	#Obj.	#Attr.	#Class.	$\lambda_C^{\theta_X^*}(\mathcal{X})$	$\delta_C^{\theta_X^*}(\mathcal{X})$	ϵ_X	$\lambda_C^{\epsilon_X}(\mathcal{X})$	$\delta_C^{\epsilon_X}(\mathcal{X})$	μ_X'	$\lambda_C^{\mu_X'}(\mathcal{X})$	$\delta_C^{\mu_X'}(\mathcal{X})$
1	bank-g	1411	16	2	98.02	0.0198	0.001	98.87	0.0113	0.99	98.72	0.0128
2	breast-c	286	8	2	23.78	0.7622	0.45	98.6	0.014	0.55	90.21	0.0979
3	breast-w	699	9	2	97.57	0.0243	0.001	97.57	0.0243	0.95	100	0
4	car	1296	6	4	98.61	0.0162	0.01	99.46	0.0054	0.85	100	0
5	cpu	209	6	4	100	0	0.001	100	0	0.99	100	0
6	denbosch	119	8	2	89.92	0.1008	0.05	99.16	0.0084	0.9	100	0
7	ERA	1000	4	9	11.3	2.826	0.025	80.8	0.28	0.75	87.3	0.129
8	ESL	488	4	9	85.04	0.1578	0.025	100	0	0.95	98.98	0.0102
9	fame	1328	10	5	98.27	0.0211	0.001	99.17	0.0113	0.6	100	0
10	LEV	1000	4	5	41.2	0.801	0.025	97.7	0.023	0.9	88.7	0.113
11	SWD	1000	10	4	48.7	0.68	0.15	100	0	0.85	80.4	0.196
12	windsor	546	10	4	69.6	0.4066	0.05	97.44	0.0256	0.9	80.04	0.1996

Table 2. Mean absolute error (MAE)

Id	monotonic VC-DomLEM	non-monotonic VC-DomLEM	Naive Bayes	SVM	RIPPER	C4.5	OLM	OSDL
1	**0.04536** (1) $\pm$0.001531	0.04867 (2) $\pm$0.000884	0.1146 (6) $\pm$0.01371	0.1280 (7) $\pm$0.001205	0.0489 (3) $\pm$0.00352	0.0515 (4) $\pm$0.005251	0.05528 (5) $\pm$0.001736	0.1545 (8) $\pm$0
2	**0.2331** (1) $\pm$0.003297	0.2436 (3) $\pm$0.007185	0.2564 (4) $\pm$0.005943	0.3217 (7) $\pm$0.01244	0.2960 (5) $\pm$0.01154	0.2424 (2) $\pm$0.003297	0.324 (8) $\pm$0.01835	0.3065 (6) $\pm$0.001648
3	0.03720 (2) $\pm$0.002023	0.04578 (6) $\pm$0.003504	0.03958 (3) $\pm$0.0006744	**0.03243** (1) $\pm$0.0006744	0.04483 (5) $\pm$0.004721	0.05532 (7) $\pm$0.00751	0.1764 (8) $\pm$0.00552	0.04149 (4) $\pm$0.001168
4	**0.03421** (1) $\pm$0.0007275	0.03524 (2) $\pm$0.0009624	0.1757 (7) $\pm$0.002025	0.08668 (4) $\pm$0.002025	0.2029 (8) $\pm$0.01302	0.1168 (6) $\pm$0.003108	0.09156 (5) $\pm$0.005358	0.04141 (3) $\pm$0.0009624
5	**0.08293** (1) $\pm$0.01479	**0.0925** (2) $\pm$0.01579	0.1707 (5) $\pm$0.009832	0.4386 (8) $\pm$0.01579	0.1611 (4) $\pm$0.01372	0.1196 (3) $\pm$0.01790	0.3461 (7) $\pm$0.02744	0.3158 (6) $\pm$0.01034
6	**0.1232** (1) $\pm$0.01048	**0.1289** (2.5) $\pm$0.01428	**0.1289** (2.5) $\pm$0.01428	0.2129 (7) $\pm$0.003961	0.1737 (6) $\pm$0.02598	0.1653 (5) $\pm$0.01048	0.2633 (8) $\pm$0.02206	0.1541 (4) $\pm$0.003961
7	1.307 (2) $\pm$0.002055	1.364 (7) $\pm$0.006018	1.325 (5) $\pm$0.003771	1.318 (3) $\pm$0.007257	1.681 (8) $\pm$0.01558	1.326 (6) $\pm$0.006018	1.321 (4) $\pm$0.01027	**1.280** (1) $\pm$0.00704
8	0.3702 (3) $\pm$0.01352	0.4146 (5) $\pm$0.005112	**0.3456** (2) $\pm$0.003864	0.4262 (6) $\pm$0.01004	0.4296 (7) $\pm$0.01608	0.3736 (4) $\pm$0.01089	0.474 (8) $\pm$0.01114	**0.3422** (1) $\pm$0.005019
9	**0.3406** (1.5) $\pm$0.001878	0.3469 (3) $\pm$0.004	0.4829 (6) $\pm$0.002906	**0.3406** (1.5) $\pm$0.001775	0.3991 (5) $\pm$0.003195	0.3863 (4) $\pm$0.005253	1.577 (7) $\pm$0.03791	1.592 (8) $\pm$0.007555
10	0.4813 (6) $\pm$0.004028	0.5187 (7) $\pm$0.002867	0.475 (5) $\pm$0.004320	0.4457 (4) $\pm$0.003399	0.4277 (3) $\pm$0.00838	0.426 (2) $\pm$0.01476	0.615 (8) $\pm$0.0099	**0.4033** (1) $\pm$0.003091
11	0.454 (4) $\pm$0.004320	0.4857 (7) $\pm$0.005249	0.475 (6) $\pm$0.004320	0.4503 (2) $\pm$0.002867	0.452 (3) $\pm$0.006481	0.4603 (5) $\pm$0.004497	0.5707 (8) $\pm$0.007717	**0.433** (1) $\pm$0.002160
12	**0.5024** (1) $\pm$0.006226	0.5201 (3) $\pm$0.003956	0.5488 (4) $\pm$0.005662	0.5891 (6) $\pm$0.02101	0.6825 (8) $\pm$0.03332	0.652 (7) $\pm$0.03721	0.5757 (5) $\pm$0.006044	0.5153 (2) $\pm$0.006044
	2.04	4.12	4.62	4.71	5.42	4.58	6.75	3.75

obtained by a given classifier. Moreover, for each data set, the best value of the predictive accuracy, as well as values included in the standard deviation of the best one, are marked in bold.

We applied Friedman test to globally compare performance of eight different classifiers on multiple data sets [7]. The null-hypothesis in this test was that all compared classifiers perform equally well. We analyzed the ranks from Tables 2 & 3. The p-values in Friedman test were 0.00017 and 0.00018, respectively.

Table 3. Percentage of correctly classified objects (PCC)

Id	monotonic VC-DomLEM	non-monotonic VC-DomLEM	Naive Bayes	SVM	RIPPER	C4.5	OLM	OSDL
1	**95.46** (1) ±0.1531	95.13 (2) ±0.0884	88.54 (6) ±1.371	87.2 (7) ±0.1205	95.11 (3) ±0.352	94.85 (4) ±0.5251	94.47 (5) ±0.1736	84.55 (8) ±0
2	**76.69** (1) ±0.3297	75.64 (3) ±0.7185	74.36 (4) ±0.5943	67.83 (7) ±1.244	70.4 (5) ±1.154	75.76 (2) ±0.3297	67.6 (8) ±1.835	69.35 (6) ±0.1648
3	96.28 (2) ±0.2023	95.42 (6) ±0.3504	96.04 (3) ±0.06744	**96.76** (1) ±0.06744	95.52 (5) ±0.4721	94.47 (7) ±0.751	82.36 (8) ±0.552	95.85 (4) ±0.1168
4	**97.15** (1) ±0.063	**97.1** (2) ±0.1311	84.72 (7) ±0.1667	92.18 (4) ±0.2025	84.41 (8) ±1.309	89.84 (6) ±0.1819	91.72 (5) ±0.4425	96.53 (3) ±0.063
5	**91.7** (1) ±1.479	**90.75** (2) ±1.579	83.41 (5) ±0.9832	56.62 (8) ±1.579	84.69 (4) ±1.409	88.52 (3) ±1.409	68.58 (7) ±2.772	72.41 (6) ±1.479
6	**87.68** (1) ±1.048	**87.11** (2.5) ±1.428	**87.11** (2.5) ±1.428	78.71 (7) ±0.3961	82.63 (6) ±2.598	83.47 (5) ±1.048	73.67 (8) ±2.206	84.6 (4) ±0.3961
7	26.9 (2) ±0.3742	22.17 (7) ±0.1247	25.03 (3) ±0.2494	24.27 (5) ±0.2494	20 (8) ±0.4243	**27.83** (1) ±0.4028	23.97 (6) ±0.4643	24.7 (4) ±0.8165
8	66.73 (3) ±1.256	62.43 (6) ±1.139	67.49 (2) ±0.3483	62.7 (5) ±0.6693	61.61 (7) ±1.555	66.33 (4) ±0.6966	55.46 (8) ±0.7545	**68.3** (1) ±0.3483
9	**67.55** (1) ±0.4642	67.1 (2.5) ±0.4032	56.22 (6) ±0.2328	**67.1** (2.5) ±0.2217	63.55 (5) ±0.5635	64.33 (4) ±0.5844	27.43 (7) ±0.7179	22.04 (8) ±0.128
10	55.63 (6) ±0.3771	52.73 (7) ±0.17	56.17 (5) ±0.3399	58.87 (4) ±0.3091	60.83 (2) ±0.6128	60.73 (3) ±1.271	45.43 (8) ±0.8179	**63.03** (1) ±0.2625
11	56.43 (6) ±0.4643	52.8 (7) ±0.4320	56.57 (5) ±0.4784	**58.23** (2) ±0.2055	57.63 (3) ±0.66	57.1 (4) ±0.4320	47.83 (8) ±0.411	**58.6** (1) ±0.4243
12	54.58 (2) ±0.7913	53.05 (4) ±1.349	53.6 (3) ±0.2284	51.83 (5) ±1.813	44.08 (8) ±0.8236	47.99 (7) ±2.888	49.15 (6) ±0.7527	**55.37** (1) ±0.3763
	2.25	4.25	4.29	4.79	5.33	4.17	7	3.92

These results and observed differences in average ranks allowed us to conclude that there is a significant difference between compared classifiers.

We checked significance of difference in predictive accuracy for each pair of classifiers. We applied Wilcoxon test [11] with null-hypothesis that the medians of results on all data sets of the two compared classifiers are equal. First, we applied this test to MAE from Table 2. We observed significant difference (p-values lower than 0.05) between monotonic VC-DomLEM and any other classifier except OSDL. The same was true for the following pairs: non-monotonic VC-DomLEM and OLM, Naive Bayes and OLM, C4.5 and RIPPER, C4.5 and OLM, OSDL and OLM. Then, we applied Wilcoxon test to results from Table 3. We observed significant difference between monotonic VC-DomLEM and any other classifier except C4.5 and OSDL. The same was true for following pairs: non-monotonic VC-DomLEM and OLM, Naive Bayes and OLM, RIPPER and OLM, C4.5 and RIPPER, C4.5 and OLM, OSDL and OLM.

Finally, we compared the values from Tables 2 & 3 to the values of δ and λ presented in Table 1. Remember that MAE and PCC were calculated by averaged 10-fold cross validation, while δ and λ were calculated on the whole data sets. Nevertheless, we can observe that these measures are, in general, concordant. Moreover, using δ and λ, we can identify the data sets which are highly inconsistent and thus hard to learn (e.g., ERA). It can also be seen that some classifiers performed better than the values of δ and λ. This means that they overcame inconsistencies in the data.

6   Conclusions

We have shown that variable consistency rough set approaches to ordinal classification with monotonicity constraints enjoy very good properties. The junction of these approaches with induction of decision rules by sequential covering results in classifiers which show usually better predictive accuracy than their competitors. Using twelve benchmark data sets, we have shown that monotonic VC-DomLEM classifier has the best average rank for two predictive accuracy measures used to assess the results.

References

1. Ben-David, A., Sterling, L., Pao, Y.-H.: Learning and classification of monotonic ordinal concepts. Computational Intelligence 5(1), 45–49 (1989)
2. Błaszczyński, J., Greco, S., Słowiński, R.: Multi-criteria classification – a new scheme for application of dominance-based decision rules. European J. Operational Research 181(3), 1030–1044 (2007)
3. Błaszczyński, J., Greco, S., Słowiński, R., Szeląg, M.: On Variable Consistency Dominance-Based Rough Set Approaches. In: Greco, S., Hata, Y., Hirano, S., Inuiguchi, M., Miyamoto, S., Nguyen, H.S., Słowiński, R. (eds.) RSCTC 2006. LNCS (LNAI), vol. 4259, pp. 191–202. Springer, Heidelberg (2006)
4. Błaszczyński, J., Greco, S., Słowiński, R., Szeląg, M.: Monotonic Variable Consistency Rough Set Approaches. Int. J. Approximate Reasoning 50(7), 979–999 (2009)
5. Błaszczyński, J., Słowiński, R., Szeląg, M.: Sequential Covering Rule Induction Algorithm for Variable Consistency Rough Set Approaches, submitted to Information Sciences (2009)
6. Cao-Van, K.: Supervised ranking – from semantics to algorithms, Ph.D. thesis, Ghent University, CS Department (2003)
7. Demsar, J.: Statistical Comparisons of Classifiers over Multiple Data Sets. Journal of Machine Learning Research 7, 1–30 (2006)
8. Fürnkranz, J.: Separate-and-conquer rule learning. Artificial Intelligence Review 13, 3–54 (1999)
9. Greco, S., Matarazzo, B., Słowiński, R.: Rough sets theory for multicriteria decision analysis. J. Operational Research 129(1), 1–47 (2001)
10. Han, J., Kamber, M.: Data Mining: Concepts and Techniques. Morgan Kaufmann, San Francisco (2006)
11. Kononenko, I., Kukar, M.: Machine Learning and Data Mining. Horwood Publishing, Coll House (2007)
12. Pawlak, Z.: Rough Sets: Theoretical Aspects of Reasoning about Data. Kluwer Academic Publishers, Norwell (1991)
13. Platt, J.: Machines using Sequential Minimal Optimization. In: Schoelkopf, B., Burges, C., Smola, A. (eds.) Advances in Kernel Methods – Support Vector Learning. MIT Press, Cambridge (1998)
14. Słowiński, R., Greco, S., Matarazzo, B.: Rough Set Based Decision Support. In: Burke, E., Kendall, G. (eds.) Search Methodologies: Introductory Tutorials in Optimization and Decision Support Techniques, ch. 16, pp. 475–527. Springer, NY (2005)

Web Page Classification: A Probabilistic Model with Relational Uncertainty

Elisabetta Fersini[1], Enza Messina[1], and Francesco Archetti[1,2]

[1] DISCo, Università degli Studi di Milano-Bicocca,
Viale Sarca, 336 - 20126 Milano, Italy
{fersini,messina,archetti}@disco.unimib.it
[2] Consorzio Milano Ricerche,
Via Cicognara 7 - 20129 Milano, Italy
archetti@milanoricerche.it

Abstract. In this paper we propose a web document classification approach based on an extended version of Probabilistic Relational Models (PRMs). In particular PRMs have been augmented in order to include uncertainty over relationships, represented by hyperlinks. Our extension, called PRM with Relational Uncertainty, has been evaluated on real data for web document classification purposes. Experimental results shown the potentiality of the proposed model of capturing the real semantic relevance of hyperlinks and the capacity of embedding this information in the classification process.

Keywords: Probabilistic Relational Models, Relational Uncertainty, Web Page Classification.

1 Introduction

It is well known that web page classification can be improved by exploiting the structural information provided by hyperlinks. However, hyperlinks are usually sparse, noisy and thus in many situations can only provide limited help. Several contextual classification approaches have been proposed in order to opportunely exploite the link structure underlying a set of web documents [8][7] [6]. In [8] the authors provide an approach for automatically identifying those links that are not explicit in the web structure, but can be implicitly inferred by extracting them from the analysis of web query logs. All extracted hyperlinks are then included within the method known as Classification by Linking Neighbors. In [7] a link-based model, based on a logistic regression approach, is introduced for modelling both the link distributions and the attributes of linked documents. In [6] URLs of hyperlinks are segmented into meaningful chunks and, togheter with theri sequential and orthographic features, are added to a Support Vector Machines model.

However, all these approaches assume that all the links have the same importance during the induction of a given inference model. In this paper we propose a contextual classification approach which takes into account the semantic importance of hyperlinks by enhancing a statistical relational approach known as

E. Hüllermeier, R. Kruse, and F. Hoffmann (Eds.): IPMU 2010, LNAI 6178, pp. 109–118, 2010.
© Springer-Verlag Berlin Heidelberg 2010

Probabilistic Relational Model (PRM). Probabilistic Relational Models are a rich representation language, used to combine relational representation with probabilistic directed graphical models. PRMs conceptually extend Bayesian Networks in order to incorporate the relational structure during learning and inference processes. From a high level point of view, PRMs specify a probability model over attributes of interrelated objects rather then over features of propositional samples. Their ability of reasoning in relational domains can be exploited in order to address the web page classification problem.

The simplest form of PRMs was introduced by Friedman in [2]. In order to describe PRMs, we need to introduce their key components: (1) a relational schema S; (2) a dependency structure D_S over attributes, with the corresponding CPDs; (3) a joint probability distribution P.

The relational schema S defines the structure of the relational data, with a set of entities E_i and reference slots r. Two important components can be derived by the relational schema: (a) a relational skeleton σ_S defined as a partial specification of the schema, where objects and reference slots are specified, while attribute values are left unknown and (b) a schema completion I which specifies the objects e_{it} that instantiate entities E_i and the relationships r existing among them. A completion I specifies therefore a value for each attribute $e_{it}.A$ and a value for each reference slot $e_{it}.r$.

The dependency structure D_S over the attributes of the schema, is usually defined by exploiting the same assumption of Bayesian Networks. This means that each variable in a PRM, i.e. attribute $E_i.A$ of an entity belonging to a relational schema S, is directly influenced by only few others. Indeed, PRMs define for each attribute $E_i.A$ a set of parents $Pa(E_i.A)$ that provides direct influences on it. Having a dependency structure that establish causal relationships between entity attributes, a conditional probability distribution (CPD) is associated to each node of the network.

The final key component of PRMs is represented by the joint probability distribution P, defined over the relational model. In particular, given a relational skeleton σ_S the joint probability distribution over all completions of the relational schema S can be computed as:

$$P(I|\sigma_S, D_S) = \prod_{e_{it} \in \sigma_S(E_i)} \prod_{A \in \mathcal{A}(e_{it})} P(e_{it}.A|Pa(e_{it}.A)) \tag{1}$$

The main goal of PRMs is to define a distribution over relational data, i.e. a distribution over possible completions of the relational schema that are consistent with the relational skeleton. This joint probability distribution needs to be computed by considering a given relational skeleton σ_S, which specifies those objects that we have to consider in order to infer a given variable value. In order to explicitly use all the objects which are related to a given variable during the inference process, a PRM induces a Unrolled Bayesian Network. In order to derive a coherent probability distribution the dependency structure on the unrolled Bayesian Network is required to be acyclic [3].

An interesting remark about PRMs is concerned with the relational structure: classical PRMs assume that, for inferring variable distributions, the skeleton σ_S

must be fixed and certain they do not provide a probabilistic model of relationships between objects. This assumption limits the use of PRMs to those domains in which the relationships between objects, i.e. the reference slots, are certain and fixed in advance. These challenges have been addressed in the literature by investigating PRMs with Structural Uncertainty [4]. Two extension of PRMs have been proposed: Reference Uncertainty and Existence Uncertainty.

PRMs with Reference Uncertainty are a form of PRMs able to deal with those domains in which the existence of reference slots are uncertain, but the number of related objects is known. This model specifies a relational skeleton σ_o in which each object that instantiates a entity is given and creates a probabilistic model for the value (true or false) of each reference slot $e_{it}.r \in \sigma_o$. For more details refer to [3]. PRMs with Existence Uncertainty are a form of PRMs where not only the existence of reference slots is uncertain, but also the number of related objects is unknown. In order to manage this kind of uncertainty over the relational structure, all the objects that *potentially* exist into the model are considered. Then a special binary attribute, called *exists variable*, is introduced in order to model the existence of a relationship between two *potential* objects. For more details about PRMs with Existence Uncertainty refer to [5]. Getoor et al. used PRMs with Existence Uncertainty in order to address the classification problem. They assert that while we know the set of web pages, we may be uncertain about which web pages link to each other and thus we have uncertainty over the existence of a link. In their model links may or may not exist, and therefore they are modelled by a binary random variable.

In this paper we want to consider not only the existence of a link, but also if the link is an expression of a semantic coherence between linked pages: in some cases a link can positively contribute to the inference process, while in some other cases a link could only add noise. For example the link from a page speaking about *football* to a page for the *pdf reader download* assumes less importance than a link between two *football* web pages. In this direction, in which a relation between two objects can be represented by a probabilistic connection, we propose a further extension of PRMs named PRM with Relational Uncertainty. In order to consider the semantic value of each link we need to extend PRM in order to account for the relational uncertainty, i.e. relation between documents are modelled as continuos random variables whose value represent the semantic coherence between linked pages.

The outline of the paper is the following. In Section 2 our extension of PRMs, focused on web document classification purposes, is presented in order to model the uncertainty over the relational structure. In Section 3 an experimental evaluation, that includes a comparison with Bayesian Networks and available PRMs, is conducted on a real case-study. Finally, in Section 4 conclusions are derived.

2   Probabilistic Relational Models with Relational Uncertainty

The probability model provided by traditional PRMs, as mentioned above, have a limitation over the relational structure: uncertainty over relationships is not admitted and therefore parent attributes have the same impact on inferring child distribution.

PRMs with Relational Uncertainty, called PRMs/RU, are a form of PRMs able to deal with domains in which the existence of a reference slot is known, but the relationships that they model could assume different degrees of "strength". That is probabilistic relationships are introduced in PRMs in order to model the "strength" of relationships between two related objects.

Consider for instance the inference process for the simplified unrolled citation graph reported in Figure 1. We can state that the attribute $p_7.topic$ depends on its internal parent $p_7.author$ and on its external related parent attribute $p_9.topic$. If we consider the evidence that the cited paper p_9 is about $math$, i.e. $p_9.math$, our expectation in traditional PRM about $p_7.topic$ likely tends to the same topic. However, if we consider the "strength" of this relationship our expectation could change. If we know that p_9 is not cited for related aspects, and therefore there

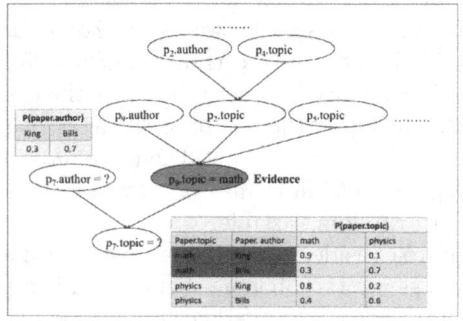

Fig. 1. Toy Example of PRMs/RU

exists a weak relationship, we could smooth our expectation accordingly. The reasoning about the citation graph is applicable also to the web domain: the topic of a web page could be inferred by considering the topic of related pages and by taking into account the "strength" of their relationships.

Thus, we can intuitively think at PRMs with Relational Uncertainty as a probabilistic graphical model in which the local distribution of an attribute is influenced not only by attributes of its related parents but also by the "strength" of their relationships. In order to describe PRMs/RU, we need to provide a new definition of (1) the relational schema, (2) the dependency structure over attributes with the associated set of parameters, (3) the joint probability distribution.

2.1 Relational Schema

In order to model the relational uncertainty we include in the relational schema **Support Entities** that explicitly model probabilistic relationships between couple of related objects. This extended schema is called probabilistic skeleton σ_P

Each support entity contains: two **reference slots** for identifying two linked documents (origin and destination), and one **artificial relationship attribute**, that represents the probabilistic relationship holding between two related objects.

A simple example of probabilistic relational skeleton for the web domain is depicted in Figure 2(a), where objects d_i belong to the standard entity *Document*, objects l_{ij} belong to the support entity *Link* and the uncertain relationship between document is denoted by the *uncRel* attribute.

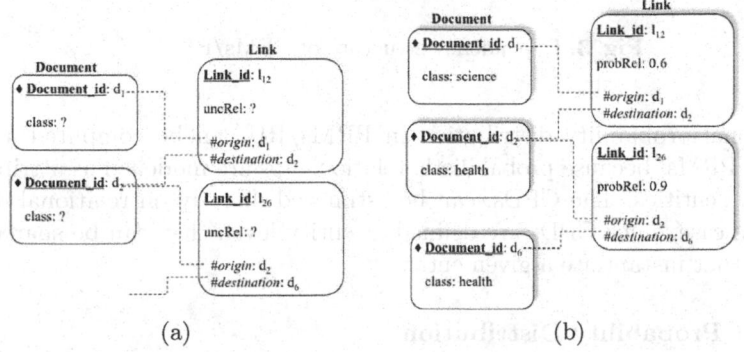

(a)   (b)

Fig. 2. Components of PRM derived from the relational schema

In PRMs/RU a **schema completion** I^* specifies the value for each attribute belonging to standard entity, the value for each attribute belonging to support entity and the two reference slots. In particular, a schema completion I^* for the web domain specifies reference slots $l_{ij}.origin$ and $l_{ij}.destination$, the value of each object attribute, i.e. document category $d_i.class$, and the value of probabilistic relationship $l_{ij}.uncRel$. (See Figure 2(b)). In order to measure the uncertainty over the web we used the procedure proposed in [1]. In particular, we identified those semantic portion of a web page containing a hyperlink and we evaluated its coherence with respect to the origin and the destination pages.

2.2 Dependency Structure and CPDs

In the **dependency structure** D_P of a PRM/RU an edge from each support entity or at least one attribute of its related entities must be ensured. This means that we introduce a node for the descriptive attribute *Document.class*, and a node for the artificial relationship variable *Link.uncRel*. We introduce at entity level an edge from *Document.class* to itself in order to model the dependency between the category label of an origin document and the category label of adjoining destination documents. Moreover, an edge from *Link.uncRel* to *Document.class* is stated in order to take into account, during learning and inference process, probabilistic relationships between related documents. This dependency model is reported in Figure 3. Having a dependency structure that establishes causal relationships between attributes, conditional probability distributions can be estimated for each node of the network.

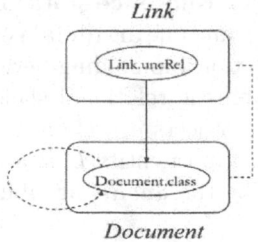

Link

Document

Fig. 3. Dependency structure of PRMs/RU

Conditional probability distribution in PRMs/RU can be computed as for traditional PRMs, because probabilistic relationships are modelled as attributes of (support) entities. The CPDs, can be estimated directly on relational data. Also in this case, since CPDs are defined at entity level, they can be shared by all objects that instantiate a given entity.

2.3   Joint Probability Distribution

A **PRM/RU** Φ^* for a relational schema S is defined as a probabilistic graphical model. In particular, PRMs/RU define, as well as traditional PRMs, a joint probability distribution over all completion of the relational schema σ_P.

In order to explicitly use specific objects during the inference process, PRM/RU induces an Unrolled Bayesian Network. However, to obtain a coherent probability model this Unrolled Bayesian Network must be acyclic and this cannot be always ensured.

For example, in the web domain the acyclicity requirement is not guaranteed. If we state the web dependency model presented in Figure 3, in which the category of a web page depends on the category of its adjoining documents, the corresponding Unrolled Bayesian Network could generate cycles as depicted in Figure 4(a). Moreover, the probabilistic relationship, as pointed out in section 2.1, can be asymmetric. Indeed the link strength from d_i to d_j can have a different value that from d_j to d_i. In order to deal with relational uncertainty and to eliminate graph cycles, a new unrolling procedure based on model decomposition is proposed.

Model Decomposition. The basic idea of dealing with probabilistic relationships and cyclic dependencies is to create a set of unrolled acyclic sub-networks stem from the cyclic one. This model decomposition, that starts from an unrolled Bayesian Network B, remove cycles through the following procedure:

- each attribute $e_{it}.A$ that is involved into a cycle is splitted into $e_{it}.A[in]$ and $e_{it}.A[out]$, which are placed into the set of nodes N_{in} and N_{out} respectively.
- each attribute $e_{it}.A$ (also comprising that ones belonging to support entities) which is not involved into a cycle is mapped into a node $e_{it}.A[ac]$ and placed into a set of nodes N_{ac}

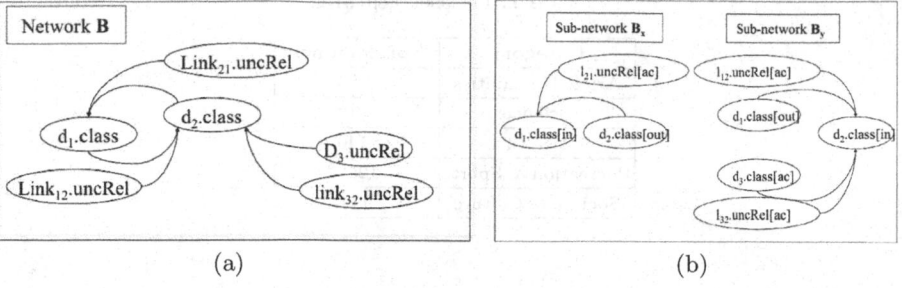

(a)   (b)

Fig. 4. Unrolled PRMs/RU

- an edge from $e_{mp}.A[out]$ to $e_{it}.A[in]$ is established only if there exists an edge in B from $e_{mp}.A$ to $e_{it}.A$
- an edge from $e_{mp}.A[ac]$ to $e_{it}.A[in]$ is established only if there exists an edge in B from $e_{mp}.A$ to $e_{it}.A$
- an edge from $e_{mp}.A[ac]$ to $e_{it}.A[ac]$ is established only if there exists an edge in B from $e_{mp}.A$ to $e_{it}.A$

At the end of this procedure we obtain a set β of N sub-networks B_x that are acyclic by construction. In our web example, from network B shown in Figure 4(a), we derived the sub-networks B_1 and B_2 depicted in Figure 4(b).

Given a relational skeleton σ_P the joint probability distributions for any relational skeleton I^* can be computed over each sub-network B_x as follows:

$$P(I^*|\sigma_P, B_x) = \prod_{e_{it}.A \in B_x} P(e_{it}.A|Pa(e_{it}.A)) \qquad (2)$$

A complete joint probability distribution for the PRM/RU Φ^* is therefore defined as:

$$P(I^*|\sigma_P, \beta) = \sum_{x=1}^{N} \frac{P(I^*|\sigma_P, B_x)}{N}. \qquad (3)$$

3   Experimental Investigation

PRM/RU has been evaluated comparing its accuracy to that one obtained by benchmarks models available in the literature: Bayesian Networks and PRM with Existence Uncertainty. Our experimental investigation starts from a dataset construction step, in which about 10000 web pages from popular sites listed in 5 categories of Yahoo! Directories (http://dir.yahoo.com/) are downloaded. See table 1. The main goal is to infer the class label (topic) of a document d_i by considering the class label of adjoining documents and the "strength" of their

Table 1. Dataset Features

Category	# of document
Art & Humanities	3280
Science	2810
Health	1740
Recreation & Sports	1250
Society & Culture	960

relationships. In particular, the dependency model depicted in Figure 3 and the corresponding acyclic B_x and B_y unrolled networks are constructed.

The Accuracy metric, which estimates the number of elements correctly classified, is used to evaluate the classification performance. Given the documents belonging to the collection reported in Table 1, the accuracy (Acc) is estimated as follows:

$$Acc = \frac{\text{number of documents successfully classified}}{\text{total number of documents}} \qquad (4)$$

Since **Bayesian Networks** are not suitable for relational data, a "flattening" procedure has been performed in order to reduce the document dataset into a propositional form. A propositional representation for relational data could be obtained by fixing the feature space and by mapping multiple feature values into a single one. For our experimental investigation, the feature space is defined by setting *originClass* and *destinationClass* features. Since a destination document d_j could be linked by several origin documents d_i, the value of the *destinationClass* feature could depend on more than one *originClass* value. For this reason, we choose the most frequent *originClass* value with respect to each *destinationClass*. For example if a document is linked by two documents about *Health* and one document about *Science*, the *Health* value is chosen for representing the *originClass*.

The second benchmark predictive model used in this experimental investigation is PRM with Existence Uncertainty. This model, in which the existence or the absence of a relationship is modelled by the *exists* binary variable, will be called **PRM/EU**.

In Figure 5 the classification performance comparison on web relational data is reported: PRMs with relational uncertainty outperforms, in terms of accuracy, the benchmarks algorithms. We can see that PRMs have in general better performance than BNs. Moreover, we can note that the potential of PRMs/RU and PRMs/EU of capturing the real "strength" of a relationship between two linked documents and the capacity of including this "strength" into the probability model can improve the models predictive power. Finally we can see that the continuous version of PRMs/EU, although able to consider the link strength, seem to loose some information: the main limitation is the use of a single variable to model structural uncertainty.

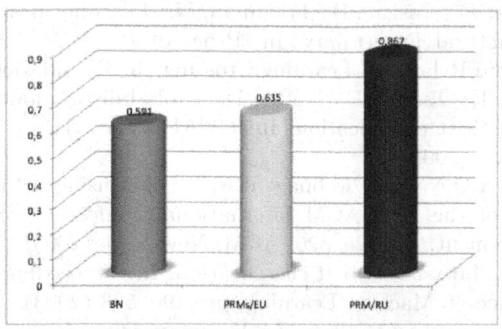

Fig. 5. Performance comparison on web relational data

4   Conclusion

In this paper one of the most promising model able to deal with uncertainty over relational data, known as Probabilistic Relational Model, has been investigated and extended. In particular, Probabilistic Relational Models with Relational Uncertainty have been proposed in order to deal with domains in which the relationships between objects could assume different degrees of "strength". Probabilistic Relational Models with Relational Uncertainty have been experimentally investigated for web document classification purposes. The proposed models have been compared, in terms of classification accuracy, with Bayesian Networks and Probabilistic Relational Models with Existence Uncertainty. The experimental investigation on real data shows that Probabilistic Relational Models with Relational Uncertainty can offer significant improvement with respect to the benchmark models used for prediction in relational domains.

Acknowledgments

This work has been partially supported by Dote ricercatori - FSE, Regione Lombardia.

References

1. Fersini, E., Messina, E., Archetti, F.: Granular modeling of web documents: Impact on information retrieval systems. In: Proc. of the 10th ACM International Workshop on Web Information and Data Management (2008)
2. Friedman, N., Getoor, L., Koller, D., Pfeffer, A.: Learning probabilistic relational models. In: Proc. of the 16th International Joint Conference on Artificial Intelligence, pp. 1300–1309. Morgan Kaufmann Publishers Inc., San Francisco (1999)
3. Getoor, L., Friedman, N., Koller, D., Taskar, B.: Learning probabilistic models of link structure. J. Mach. Learn. Res. 3, 679–707 (2003)

4. Getoor, L., Koller, D., Taskar, B., Friedman, N.: Learning probabilistic relational models with structural uncertainty. In: Proc. of the ICML 2000 Workshop on Attribute-Value and Relational Learning:Crossing the Boundaries, pp. 13–20 (2000)
5. Getoor, L., Segal, E., Taskar, B., Koller, D.: Probabilistic models of text and link structure for hypertext classification. In: IJCAI '01 Workshop on Text Learning: Beyond Supervision (2001)
6. Kan, M.-Y., Thi, H.O.N.: Fast webpage classification using url features. In: CIKM '05: Proceedings of the 14th ACM international conference on Information and knowledge management, pp. 325–326. ACM, New York (2005)
7. Lu, Q., Getoor, L.: Link-based text classification. In: Proceedings of the 12th International Conference on Machine Learning, pp. 496–503 (2003)
8. Shen, D., Sun, J.-T., Yang, Q., Chen, Z.: A comparison of implicit and explicit links for web page classification. In: WWW '06: Proceedings of the 15th international conference on World Wide Web, pp. 643–650. ACM, New York (2006)

Evidential Multi-Label Classification Approach to Learning from Data with Imprecise Labels

Zoulficar Younes, Fahed Abdallah, and Thierry Denœux

UMR CNRS 6599 Heudiasyc,
Université de Technologie de Compiègne, France
{firstname.lastname}@hds.utc.fr

Abstract. Multi-label classification problems arise in many real-world applications. Classically, in order to construct a multi-label classifier, we assume the existence of a labeled training set, where each instance is associated with a set of labels, and the task is to output a label set for each unseen instance. However, it is not always possible to have perfectly labeled data. In many problems, there is no ground truth for assigning unambiguously a label set to each instance, and several experts have to be consulted. Due to conflicts and lack of knowledge, labels might be wrongly assigned to some instances. This paper describes an evidence formalism suitable to study multi-label classification problems where the training datasets are imperfectly labelled. Several applications demonstrate the efficiency of our apporach.

1 Introduction

In multi-label classification problems, each object may belong simultaneously to several classes, contrary to standard single-label problems where objects belong to only one class. Multi-label classification methods have been increasingly required by modern applications where the target classes are not exclusive and an object may belong to an unrestricted set of classes instead of exactly one. For instance, in natural scene classification, each image may belong to several semantic classes, such as sea and sunset [1].

Several methods have been proposed for multi-label learning. These methods can be categorized into two groups. A first group contains the *indirect* methods that transform the multi-label classification problem into a set of binary classification problems (Binary relevance approach (BR): a binary classifier for each class or pairwise classifiers) [12] [11] [6] or into multi-class classification problem (Label powerset approach (LP): each subset of classes is considered as a new class) [9]. A second group consists in extending common learning algorithms and making them able to manipulate multi-label data *directly* [10].

Usually, multi-label classification tasks are based on training datasets where each instance is associated with a perfectly known set of labels. In practice, gathering such high quality information is not always feasible at a reasonable cost. In many problems, however, there is no ground truth for assigning unambiguously a label set to each instance, and the opinions of one or several experts have to be

E. Hüllermeier, R. Kruse, and F. Hoffmann (Eds.): IPMU 2010, LNAI 6178, pp. 119–128, 2010.
© Springer-Verlag Berlin Heidelberg 2010

elicited. Typically, an expert may express lack of confidence for assigning exactly one label set. If several experts are consulted, some conflicts will inevitably arise. This again will introduce some uncertainties in the labeling process.

In [10] and [4], an evidential formalism for handling uncertainty on the classification of multi-labeled data has been presented. This formalism extends all the notions of Dempster-Shafer (D-S) theory [7] to the multi-label case with only a moderate increase in complexity as compared to the classical case. Based on this formalism, an evidence-theoretic k-NN rule for multi-label classification has been presented. The proposed method, called EML-kNN for Evidential Multi-Label k-Nearest Neighbor, generalizes the single-label evidence-theoretic k-NN rule [2] to the multi-label case. Thus, an unseen instance is classified on the basis of its k nearest neighbors under the D-S framework.

In [10], we applied our method on several benchmark datasets where all instances were perfectly labelled. We also noticed that our evidential formalism for set-valued variables allows us to express ambiguities and uncertainties when the available data used to train the multi-label classifier are imprecisely labelled. As far as our knowledge, such imprecise data are not available from real-world problems. Thus, in order to show the performance of EML-kNN in such cases and demonstrate its effectivness, we propose a labeling process to randomly simulate imprecise multi-labelled data.

The remainder of the paper is organized as follows. Section 2 describes the evidence formalism for multi-label case. Section 3 recalls the evidence-theoretic k-NN rule for multi-label classification. Section 4 presents experiments on some real datasets and shows the effectiveness of our approach to handle imprecise data. Finally, Section 5 makes concluding remarks.

2   Evidence Formalism

The Dempster-Shafer (D-S) theory is a formal framework for representing and reasoning with uncertain and imprecise information. Different approaches to single-label classification in the framework of evidence theory have been presented in the literature [3] [2]. This theory is usually applied to handle uncertainty in problems where *only one single hypothesis* is true. However, there exist problems where *more than one hypothesis* are true at the same time, e.g., the multi-label classification task. Let Ω denote the set of all hypotheses in a certain domain, e.g., in classification, Ω is the set of all possible classes. The frame of discernment of the evidence formalism for multi-label case is not Ω, as in the single label classification problem, but its power set $\Theta = 2^{\Omega}$. A mass function m is thus defined as a mapping from the power set of Θ to the interval $[0, 1]$. As proposed in [4], instead of considering the whole power set of Θ, we will focus on the subset $\mathcal{C}(\Omega)$ of 2^{Θ} defined as:

$$\mathcal{C}(\Omega) = \{\varphi(A, B)| \ A \cap B = \emptyset\} \cup \{\emptyset_\Theta\} \tag{1}$$

where $\emptyset_\Theta$ represents the conflict in the frame 2^Θ, and for all A, $B \subseteq \Omega$ with $A \cap B = \emptyset$, $\varphi(A, B)$ is the set of all subsets of Ω that include A and have no intersection with B:

$$\varphi(A, B) = \{C \subseteq \Omega| \ C \supseteq A \text{ and } C \cap B = \emptyset\}. \tag{2}$$

The size of the subset $\mathcal{C}(\Omega)$ of 2^Θ is equal to $3^{|\Omega|} + 1$ and is thus much smaller than the size of 2^Θ ($|2^\Theta| = 2^{2^{|\Omega|}}$). Consequently, this formulation reduces the complexity of multi-label problems, while being rich enough to express evidence in many realistic situations. The chosen subset $\mathcal{C}(\Omega)$ of 2^Θ is closed under intersection, i.e., for all $\varphi(A, B)$, $\varphi(A', B') \in \mathcal{C}(\Omega)$, $\varphi(A, B) \cap \varphi(A', B') \in \mathcal{C}(\Omega)$. Based on the definition of $\varphi(A, B)$, we can deduce that:

$$\varphi(\emptyset, \emptyset) = \Theta, \tag{3}$$

$$\forall A \subseteq \Omega, \ \varphi(A, \bar{A}) = \{A\}, \tag{4}$$

$$\forall A \subseteq \Omega, \ A \neq \emptyset, \ \varphi(A, A) = \emptyset_\Theta. \tag{5}$$

By convention, $\emptyset_\Theta$ will be represented by $\varphi(\Omega, \Omega)$.

For any $\varphi(A, B)$, $\varphi(A', B') \in \mathcal{C}(\Omega)$, the intersection operator over $\mathcal{C}(\Omega)$ is defined as follow:

$$\varphi(A, B) \cap \varphi(A', B') = \begin{cases} \varphi(A \cup A', B \cup B') & if \ A \cap B' = \emptyset \text{ and } A' \cap B = \emptyset \\ \varphi(\Omega, \Omega) & otherwise, \end{cases}$$

$$\tag{6}$$

and the inclusion operator over $\mathcal{C}(\Omega)$ is defined as:

$$\varphi(A, B) \subseteq \varphi(A', B') \iff A \supseteq A' \text{ and } B \supseteq B'. \tag{7}$$

A mass function m on $\mathcal{C}(\Omega)$ can be represented with the following two equations:

$$m : \mathcal{C}(\Omega) \longrightarrow [0, 1] \tag{8}$$

$$\sum_{\varphi(A,B) \in \mathcal{C}(\Omega)} m(\varphi(A, B)) = 1. \tag{9}$$

For convenience of notation, $m(\varphi(A, B))$ will be simplified to $m(A, B)$. For any $\varphi(A, B) \in \mathcal{C}(\Omega)$, the belief and plausibility functions are now defined as:

$$bel(A, B) = \sum_{\varphi(\Omega,\Omega) \neq \varphi(A',B') \subseteq \varphi(A,B)} m(A', B'), \tag{10}$$

and

$$pl(A, B) = \sum_{\varphi(A',B') \cap \varphi(A,B) \neq \varphi(\Omega,\Omega)} m(A', B'). \tag{11}$$

Given two independent bodies of evidence over the same frame of discernment like $\mathcal{C}(\Omega)$, the aggregated mass function, denoted by m_{12}, obtained by combining the mass functions m_1 and m_2 of the two bodies of evidence using the unnormalized Dempster's rule is calculated in the following manner:

$$m_{12}(A, B) = \sum_{\varphi(A',B') \cap \varphi(A'',B'')=\varphi(A,B)} m_1(A', B')m_2(A'', B''). \tag{12}$$

This rule is commutative and associative, and has the vacuous mass function $(m(\emptyset, \emptyset) = 1)$ as neutral element.

3 Evidential Multi-Label k-NN

Problem. Let $\mathcal{X} = R^P$ denote the domain of instances and let $\Omega = \{\omega_1, \ldots, \omega_Q\}$ be the finite set of labels. The multi-label classification problem can now be formulated as follows. Given a set $\mathcal{S} = \{(\mathbf{x}_1, A_1, B_1), \ldots, (\mathbf{x}_M, A_M, B_M)\}$ of M training examples, where $\mathbf{x}_i \in \mathcal{X}$, $A_i \subseteq \Omega$ denotes a set of classes that surely apply to instance i, and $B_i \subseteq \Omega$ is a set of classes that surely do not apply to the same instance. For instance, assume that instances are songs and classes are emotions generated by these songs. Upon hearing a song, an expert may decide that this song certainly evokes happiness and certainly does not evoke sadness, but may be undecided regarding the other emotions (such as quietness, anger, surprise, etc.). In that case, the song cannot be assigned to a single label set, but one can associate to it the set of all label sets containing "happiness" and not containing "sadness". The goal of the learning system is to build a multi-label classifier $\mathcal{H} : \mathcal{X} \rightarrow 2^\Omega$ that associates a label set to each unseen instance.

To determine the multi-label classifier, the evidential multi-label kNN rule introduced in [10] can be used. Hereafter, we recall the principle of this method.

EML-kNN. Let $\mathbf{x}$ be an unseen instance, Y its unknown label set, and $\mathcal{N}_\mathbf{x}$ its k nearest neighbors in $\mathcal{S}$ based on a certain distance function $d(., .)$, usually the Euclidean one. Each element $(\mathbf{x}_i, A_i, B_i)$ in $\mathcal{N}_\mathbf{x}$ constitutes a distinct item of evidence regarding the label set of $\mathbf{x}$.

The mass function m_i over $\mathcal{C}(\Omega)$ induced by the item of evidence $(\mathbf{x}_i, A_i, B_i)$ regarding the label set of $\mathbf{x}$ is defined as:

$$m_i(A_i, B_i) = \alpha \exp(-\gamma d_i) \tag{13}$$
$$m_i(\emptyset, \emptyset) = 1 - \alpha \exp(-\gamma d_i) \tag{14}$$

where $d_i = d(\mathbf{x}, \mathbf{x}_i)$, $0 < \alpha < 1$ and $\gamma > 0$. Parameter α is usually fixed at a value close to 1 such as $\alpha = 0.95$ [2], whereas γ should depend on the scaling of distances and can be fixed by cross-validation [10].

After considering each item of evidence in $\mathcal{N}_\mathbf{x}$, we obtain k mass functions m_i, $i = 1, \ldots, k$ that can be combined using the multi-label extension of the unnormalized Dempster's rule of combination (12) to form the resulting mass function m.

For decision making, different procedures can be used. The following simple and computationally efficient rule was implemented. Let $\widehat{Y}$ be the predicted label set for instance $\mathbf{x}$ to differentiate it from the ground truth label set Y of $\mathbf{x}$. To decide whether to include each class $\omega_q \in \Omega$ or not, we compute the degree of belief $bel(\{\omega_q\}, \emptyset)$ that the true label set Y contains ω_q, and the degree of belief $bel(\emptyset, \{\omega_q\})$ that it does not contain ω_q. We then define $\widehat{Y}$ as

$$\widehat{Y} = \{\omega_q \in \Omega \mid bel(\{\omega_q\}, \emptyset) \geq bel(\emptyset, \{\omega_q\})\}. \tag{15}$$

4   Experiments

4.1   Datasets

Three datasets were used in our experiments: the emotion, scene and yeast datasets[1]. Each one was split into a training set and a test set. Table 1 summarizes the characteristics of the datasets used in the experiments. The label cardinality of a dataset is the average number of labels of the instances, while the label density is the average number of labels of the instances divided by the total number of labels [8].

Table 1. Characteristics of datasets

Dataset	Number of instances	Feature vector dimension	Number of labels	Training instances	Test instances	Label cardinality	Label density	maximum size of a label set
emotion	593	72	6	391	202	1.869	0.311	3
scene	2407	294	6	1211	1196	1.074	0.179	3
yeast	2417	103	14	1500	917	4.237	0.303	11

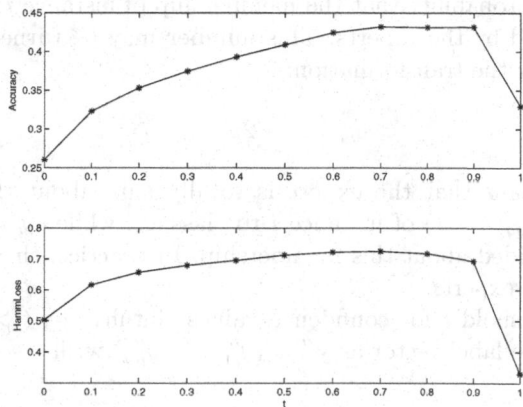

Fig. 1. *Accuracy* and *HammLoss* for EML-kNN on the emotion dataset for different values of the confidence threshold t

4.2   Imprecise Labeling Process

To simulate imprecise labeling by an expert, the following procedure was used. Let Y_i be the true label set for instance i, and let $\mathbf{y}_i = (y_{i1}, \ldots, y_{iQ})$ be the vector of $\{-1, 1\}^Q$ such that $y_{iq} = 1$ if $\omega_q \in Y_i$ and $y_{iq} = -1$ otherwise. For each instance i and each class ω_q, we generated a probability of error $p_{iq} = p'_{iq}/2$, where p'_{iq} was taken from a beta distribution with parameters $a = b = 0.5$ (this consists on a bimodal distribution with modes at 0 and 1), and we changed y_{iq}

---

[1] http://mlkd.csd.auth.gr/multilabel.html

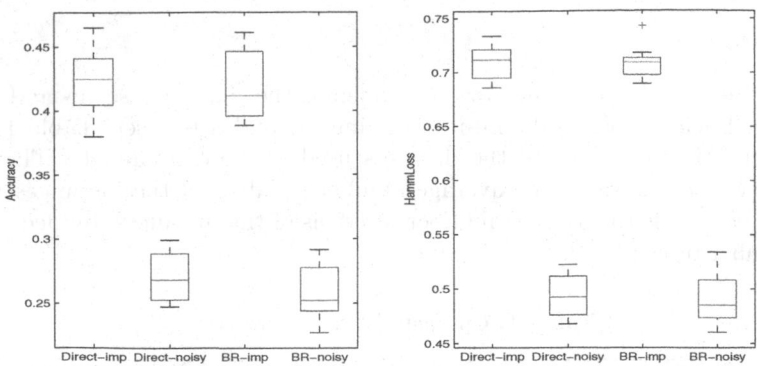

Fig. 2. Comparison between direct and BR versions of EML-kNN over 10 trials on imprecise and noisy labels generated from the emotion dataset

to $-y_{iq}$ with probability p_{iq}, resulting in a *noisy label vector* $\mathbf{y}'_i$. Each number p_{iq} represents the probability that the membership of instance i to class ω_q will be wrongly assessed by the experts. This number may be turned into a degree of confidence c_{iq} by the transformation:

$$c_{iq} = 1 - 2p_{iq}, \tag{16}$$

where $c_{iq} = 1$ means that the expert is totally sure about the membership ($y_{iq} = 1$) or not ($y_{iq} = -1$) of instance i to class ω_q, while $c_{iq} = 0$ means that he is totally undecided about this membership. In practice, these numbers can be provided by the experts.

By fixing a threshold t for confidence values (intuitively, $t > 0.5$), we then define the imprecise label vector as $\mathbf{y}''_i = (y''_{i1}, \ldots, y''_{iQ})$ with

$$y''_{iq} = \begin{cases} y'_{iq} & \text{if } c_{iq} \geq t, \\ 0 & \text{otherwise.} \end{cases} \tag{17}$$

As shown in Section 2, such a vector of $\{-1, 0, 1\}^Q$ can be represented by $\varphi(A_i, B_i)$, the set of subsets of Ω, such that:

$$\begin{cases} A_i = \{\omega_q \in \Omega \mid y''_{iq} = 1\}, \\ B_i = \{\omega_q \in \Omega \mid y''_{iq} = -1\}. \end{cases} \tag{18}$$

The set A_i then contains the classes ω_q that can be definitely assigned to instance i with a high degree of confidence ($c_{iq} \geq t$), while B_i is the set of classes which are definitely *not* assigned to instance i. The remaining set $\Omega \setminus (A_i \cup B_i)$ contains those classes about which the expert is undecided ($c_{iq} < t$). We recall that $\varphi(A_i, B_i)$ contains all the label sets including A_i and non intersecting B_i.

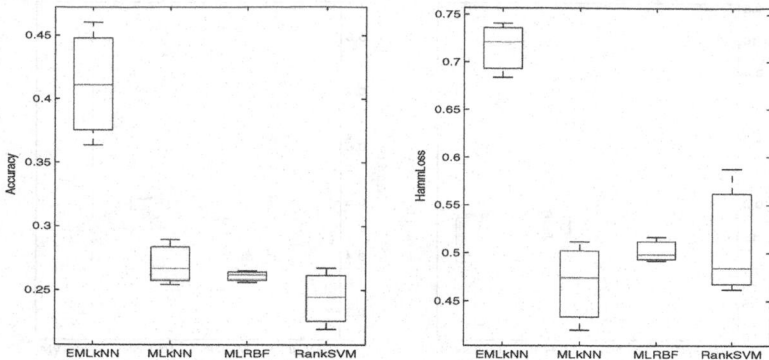

Fig. 3. *Accuracy* and *HammLoss* box plots over 10 trials for the emotion dataset with the following methods: EML-kNN with imprecise labels, ML-kNN, ML-RBF and Rank-SVM with noisy labels

4.3 Evaluation Metrics

Let $\mathcal{D} = \{(\mathbf{x}_1, Y_1), \ldots, (\mathbf{x}_N, Y_N)\}$ be a multi-label evaluation dataset containing N labeled examples. Let $\widehat{Y}_i = \mathcal{H}(\mathbf{x}_i)$ be the predicted label set for the pattern $\mathbf{x}_i$, while Y_i is the ground truth label set for $\mathbf{x}_i$.

A first metric called "Accuracy" gives an average degree of similarity between the predicted and the ground truth label sets of all test examples [8]:

$$Accuracy(\mathcal{H}, \mathcal{D}) = \frac{1}{N} \sum_{i=1}^{N} \frac{|Y_i \cap \widehat{Y}_i|}{|Y_i \cup \widehat{Y}_i|}. \tag{19}$$

A second metric is the "Hamming loss" that counts prediction errors (an incorrect label is predicted) and missing errors (a true label is not predicted). In order to be consistent with the above measure, we report 1-Hamming loss [6]:

$$HamLoss(\mathcal{H}, \mathcal{D}) = 1 - \frac{1}{N} \sum_{i=1}^{N} \frac{1}{Q} |Y_i \triangle \widehat{Y}_i|, \tag{20}$$

where $\triangle$ is an operator to compute the symmetric difference of two sets.

The values of these evaluation criteria are in the interval $[0, 1]$. Larger values of these metrics correspond to higher classification quality.

4.4 Results and Discussions

Figure 1 shows the performance of EML-kNN over the two evaluation criteria *Accuracy* and *HammLoss* for different values of confidence threshold t after 10-fold cross validation on imprecise labels generated from the training emotion dataset. The best results were obtained for $t \in [0.5, 0.9]$. In the following, the

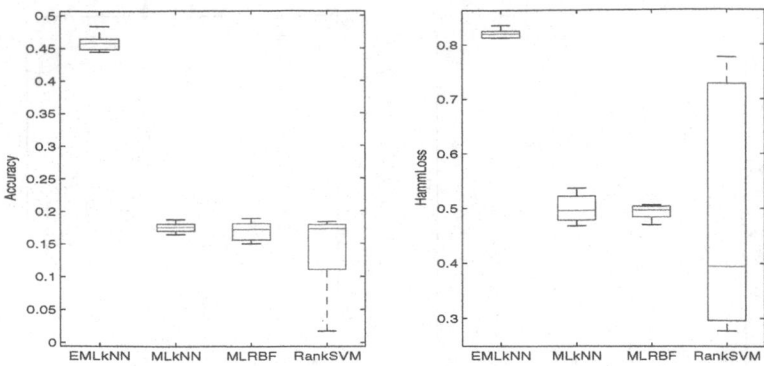

Fig. 4. *Accuracy* and *HammLoss* box plots over 10 trials for the scene dataset with the following methods: EML-*k*NN with imprecise labels, ML-*k*NN, ML-RBF and Rank-SVM with noisy labels

value of t was fixed to 0.6. Note that, for EML-*k*NN, γ was fixed to 0.5 and k to 10. The values of these two parameters can easily be determined by cross validation, but here, they are fixed manually to moderate values.

EML-*k*NN was originally developed in order to construct a multi-label learning system able to handle multi-labeled data directly. However, it can be also used when transforming the multi-label leaning problem into single-label one, which is referred to as indirect approach. To get an idea about the performance of each approach, the original EML-*k*NN (direct version) and the BR version (binary learning for each label) were applied to imprecise and noisy labeled data generated from the emotion dataset. Figure 2 shows the results over 10 trials. First, we notice the improved performances of our leaning system when applied to imprecise labels. This result demonstrates the usefulness of our evidence formalism. Secondly, we remark that the performances of the direct and BR versions of our method are very close, with a slight advantage for the direct approach. Note that, in terms of execution time, the direct approach is much faster. In the next experiments, the originial version (direct) of EML-*k*NN was used.

EML-*k*NN was compared to three existing multi-label classification methods that were shown to exhibit good performances: ML-*k*NN [13] that is the closest to our method as both are based on k-NN rule, ML-RBF [12] derived from radial basis function neural networks, and Rank-SVM [5] that is based on the traditional support vector machine. For ML-*k*NN, k was fixed to 10 as in [13]. As used in [12], the fraction parameter for ML-RBF was set to 0.01 and the scaling factor to 1. For Rank-SVM, the best parameterization reported in [5], i.e. polynomial kernels with degree 8, was used.

After performing the labeling process explained in Section 4.2, noisy labels and imprecise labels were generated for instances from each dataset. EML-*k*NN was applied to imprecise labels ($\mathbf{y}_i''$ corresponding to $\varphi(A_i, B_i)$ in the multi-label

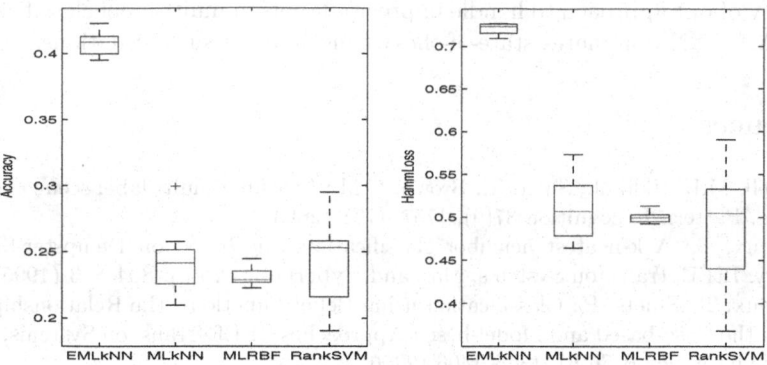

Fig. 5. *Accuracy* and *HammLoss* box plots over 10 trials for the yeast dataset with the following methods: EML-kNN with imprecise labels, ML-kNN, ML-RBF and Rank-SVM with noisy labels

evidence formalism), while the ML-kNN, ML-RBF and Rank-SVM algorithms were applied to noisy labels ($\mathbf{y}'_i$), as it is not clear how imprecise labels could be handled using these methods.

Figures 3, 4 and 5 show the box plots for the *Accuracy* and *HammLoss* measures obtained by the applied methods, over ten generations of imprecise and noisy labels, for the emotion, scene and yeast datasets respectively.

Based on the two evaluation criteria and over the three datasets, EML-kNN clearly dominates the remaining methods. These preliminary results demonstrate the ability of our approach to handle imprecise labels in multi-label classification tasks. In fact, when the available learning data have not a ground truth and have been labeled subjectively by a pool of experts, noisy labels will be inevitably assigned to some instances due to conflicts or lack of knowledge. If an expert gives a degree of confidence about each assigned label, by using EML-kNN method based on the evidence formalism explained in Section 2, we are able to reduce the risk of assigning wrongly some labels to an instance i when the degrees of confidence are not high. That explains the good performances of our method.

5   Conclusion

In this paper, we have used the evidence formalism for multi-label learning and the EML-kNN method introduced in [10] to propose a multi-label learning system able to handle complex learning tasks in which the data are imprecisely labeled. In fact, in many real-world problems, there are no ground truth for assigning unambiguously a label set to each instance, and several experts have to be consulted. Due to lack of confidence and conflicts between experts, uncertainties are introduced when labeling instances. To assess the performances of our approach when learning from data with imprecise labels, we have used an algorithm to randomly simulate such data. Experimental results demonstrate the ability of our approach to handle imprecise labels in multi-label classification tasks. EML-kNN dominates state-of-the-art methods in such situations.

References

1. Boutell, M.R., Luo, J., Shen, X., Brown, C.M.: Learning multi-label scene classification. Pattern Recognition 37(9), 1757–1771 (2004)
2. Denœux, T.: A k-nearest neighbor classification rule based on Dempster-Shafer theory. IEEE Trans. on Systems, Man and Cybernetics 25(5), 804–813 (1995)
3. Denœux, T., Smets, P.: Classification using Belief Functions, the Relationship between the Case-based and Model-based Approaches. IEEE Trans. on Systems, Man and Cybernetics B 36(6), 1395–1406 (2006)
4. Denœux, T., Younes, Z., Abdallah, F.: Representing uncertainty on set-valued variables using belief functions. Artificial Intelligence 174(7-8), 479–499 (2010)
5. Elisseeff, A., Weston, J.: Kernel methods for multi-labelled classification and categorical regression problems. Advances in Neural Information Processing Systems 14, 681–687 (2002)
6. Fürnkranz, J., Hüllermeier, E., Loza Menca, E., Brinker, K.: Multilabel classification via calibrated label ranking. Machine Learning 73(2), 133–153 (2008)
7. Smets, P.: The combination of evidence in the Transferable Belief Model. IEEE Trans. on Pattern Analysis and Machine Intelligence 12(5), 447–458 (1990)
8. Tsoumakas, G., Katakis, I.: Multi-Label Classification: An Overview. International Journal of Data Warehousing and Mining 3(3), 1–13 (2007)
9. Tsoumakas, G., Vlahavas, I.: Random k-Labelsets: An Ensemble Method for Multilabel Classification. In: Kok, J.N., Koronacki, J., Lopez de Mantaras, R., Matwin, S., Mladenič, D., Skowron, A. (eds.) ECML 2007. LNCS (LNAI), vol. 4701, pp. 406–417. Springer, Heidelberg (2007)
10. Younes, Z., Abdallah, F., Denœux, T.: An Evidence-Theoretic k-Nearest Neighbor Rule for Multi-Label Classification. In: Godo, L., Pugliese, A. (eds.) SUM 2009. LNCS (LNAI), vol. 5785, pp. 297–308. Springer, Heidelberg (2009)
11. Younes, Z., Abdallah, F., Denœux, T.: Multi-label classification algorithm derived from k-nearest neighbor rule with label dependencies. In: Proc. of the 16th European Signal Processing Conference, Lausanne, Switzerland, August 25-29 (2008)
12. Zhang, M.-L.: ML-RBF: RBF neural networks for multi-label learning. Neural Processing Letters 29(2), 61–74 (2009)
13. Zhang, M.-L., Zhou, Z.-H.: ML-KNN: A lazy learning approach to multi-label learning. Pattern Recognition 40(7), 2038–3048 (2007)

A K-Nearest Neighbours Method Based on Lower Previsions

Sebastien Destercke

INRA/CIRAD, UMR1208, 2 place P. Viala, F-34060 Montpellier cedex 1, France
sebastien.destercke@supagro.inra.fr

Abstract. K-nearest neighbours algorithms are among the most popular existing classification methods, due to their simplicity and good performances. Over the years, several extensions of the initial method have been proposed. In this paper, we propose a K-nearest neighbours approach that uses the theory of imprecise probabilities, and more specifically lower previsions. This approach handles very generic models when representing imperfect information on the labels of training data, and decision rules developed within this theory allows to deal with issues related to the presence of conflicting information or to the absence of close neighbours. We also show that results of the classical voting K-NN procedures and distance-weighted k-NN procedures can be retrieved.

Keywords: Classification, lower prevision, nearest neighbours.

1 Introduction

The k-nearest neighbours (K-NN) classification procedure is an old rule [1] that uses the notion of similarity and distance with known instances to classify a new one. Given a vector $x \in \mathbb{R}^D$ of input features, a distance $d : \mathbb{R}^D \times \mathbb{R}^D \to \mathbb{R}$ and a data set of training samples composed of N couples (x_i, y_i) where $x_i \in \mathbb{R}^D$ are feature values and $y_i \in \mathcal{Y} = \{\omega_1, \ldots, \omega_M\}$ is the class to which belongs the ith sample, the voting k-NN procedure consists in choosing as the class y of x the one that is in majority in the k nearest neighbours.

One of the main drawback of the original algorithm is that it assumes that the k-nearest neighbors are relatively close to the instance to classify, and can act as reliable instances to estimate some conditional densities. It also assumes that all classes or patterns are well represented in the input feature space, and that the space is well sampled. In practice, this is rarely true, and the distance between a new instance and its nearest neighbour can be large. This makes the way basic k-NN procedure treats the training samples questionable Also, some classes of training samples may only be imperfectly known, and this uncertainty should be taken into account.

To integrate these various features, many extensions of the initial method have been proposed: use of weights to account for distance between neighbours and instance to classification [2]; use of distance and ambiguity rejection, to cope respectively with nearest neighbours whose distance from the instance to classify is too large and with nearest neighbours giving conflicting information [3]; use of uncertainty representations

E. Hüllermeier, R. Kruse, and F. Hoffmann (Eds.): IPMU 2010, LNAI 6178, pp. 129–138, 2010.

such as belief functions to cope with uncertainty [4]. For a detailed survey of the k-NN algorithm and its different extensions, see [5, Chap. 2].

As far as uncertainty representations are concerned, it can be argued that belief functions do not allow to model precisely all kinds of uncertainties. For example, they are unable to model exactly uncertainty given by probability intervals (i.e., lower and upper probabilistic bounds given on each class). Imprecise probability theory and walley's lower previsions [6] are uncertainty models that encompass belief functions as special cases. In this sense, they are more general and allow for a finer modelling of uncertainty.

In this paper, we propose and discuss a k-NN rule based on the use of Walley's lower prevision [6,7], and of the theory underlying them. As for the TBM k-NN procedure (based on evidence theory and on Dempster's rule of combintion), it allows to treat all the issues mentioned above without introducing any other parameters than the weights on nearest neighbours, however it does so with a different approach (being based on different calculus) and allows the use of more general uncertainty models than the TBM. In particular, we argue that using decision rules proper to the lower previsions approach allows to take account of ambiguities and distances without having to include additional parameters. Using these imprecise decision rules, we also introduce a criteria allowing to pick the "best" number k of nearest neighbours, balancing imprecision and accuracy. After recalling the material concerning lower previsions (Section 2) needed in this paper, we details the proposed method and its properties (Section 3), before finishing with some experiments (Section 4).

2 Lower Previsions

This section introduces the very basics about lower previsions and associated tools needed in this paper. We refer to Miranda [7] and Walley [6] for more details.

2.1 Basics of Lower Previsions

In this paper, we consider that information regarding a variable X assuming its values on a (finite) space $\mathcal{X}$ counting N exclusive and disjoint elements is modelled by the means of a so-called coherent lower previsions. We denote by $\mathcal{L}(\mathcal{X})$ the set of real-valued bounded functions on $\mathcal{X}$. A lower prevision $\underline{P} : \mathcal{K} \to \mathbb{R}$ is a real-valued mapping on a subset $\mathcal{K} \subseteq \mathcal{L}(\mathcal{X})$. Given a lower prevision, the dual notion of upper prevision $\overline{P}$ is defined on the set $-\mathcal{K} = \{-f | f \in \mathcal{K}\}$ and is such that $\underline{P}(f) = -\overline{P}(-f)$. As discussed by Walley [6], lower previsions can be used to model information about the variable X. He interprets $\underline{P}(f)$ as the supremum buying price for the uncertain reward f.

Given a set $A \subseteq \mathcal{X}$, its lower probability $\underline{P}(A)$ is the lower prevision of its indicator function $1_{(A)}$, that takes value one on A and zero elsewhere. The upper probability $\overline{P}(A)$ of A is the upper prevision of $1_{(A)}$, and by duality $\underline{P}(A) = 1 - \overline{P}(A^c)$. To a lower prevision $\underline{P}$ can be associated a convex set $\mathcal{P}_{\underline{P}}$ of probabilities, such that

$$\mathcal{P}_{\underline{P}} = \{p \in \mathbb{P}_{\mathcal{X}} | (\forall f \in \mathcal{K})(E_p(f) \geq \underline{P}(f))\}$$

with $\mathbb{P}_{\mathcal{X}}$ the set of all probability mass functions over $\mathbb{P}_{\mathcal{X}}$ and $E_p(f) = \sum_{x \in \mathcal{X}} p(x)f(x)$ the expected value of f given p. As often done, $\mathcal{P}_{\underline{P}}$ will be called the credal set of $\underline{P}$.

A lower prevision is said to avoid sure loss iff $\mathcal{P}_{\underline{P}} \neq \emptyset$ and to be coherent iff it avoids sure loss and $\forall f \in \mathcal{K}$, $\underline{P}(f) = \min\{E_p(f)|p \in \mathcal{P}_{\underline{P}}\}$, i.e. iff $\underline{P}$ is the lower envelope of $\mathcal{P}_{\underline{P}}$. If a lower (upper) prevision is coherent, it corresponds to the lower (upper) expectation of $\mathcal{P}_{\underline{P}}$. If a lower prevision $\underline{P}$ avoids sure loss, its natural extension $\underline{E}(g)$ to a function $g \in \mathcal{L}(\mathcal{X})$ is defined as $\underline{E}(g) = \min\{E_p(g)|p \in \mathcal{P}_{\underline{P}}\}$. Note that $\underline{P}$ and its natural extension $\underline{E}$ coincide on $\mathcal{K}$ only when $\underline{P}$ is coherent, otherwise $\underline{P} \leq \underline{E}$ and $\underline{P}(f) < \underline{E}(f)$ for at least one f.

Lower previsions are very general uncertainty models, in that they encompass (at least from a static viewpoint) most of the other known uncertainty models. In particular both necessity measures of possibility theory [8] and belief measures of evidence theory [9] can be seen as particular lower previsions.

2.2 Vacuous Mixture and Lower Previsions Merging

When multiple sources provide possibly unreliable lower previsions modelling their beliefs, we must provide rules both to take this unreliability into account and to merge the different lower previsions into a single one, representing our final beliefs.

An extreme case of coherent lower prevision is the vacuous prevision $\underline{P}_v$ and its natural extension $\underline{E}_v$, which are such that $\underline{E}_v(g) = \inf_{\omega \in \mathcal{X}} g(\omega)$. It represents a state of total ignorance about the real value of X. Given a coherent lower prevision $\underline{P}$, its natural extension $\underline{E}$ and a scalar $\epsilon \in [0, 1]$, the (coherent) lower prevision $\underline{P}_\epsilon$ that we call vacuous mixture is such that $\underline{P}_\epsilon = \epsilon\underline{P} + (1 - \epsilon)\underline{P}_v$. Its natural extension $\underline{E}_\epsilon$ is such that $\underline{E}_\epsilon(f) = \epsilon\underline{E}(f) + (1 - \epsilon)\inf_{\omega \in \mathcal{X}} f(\omega)$, for any $f \in \mathcal{L}(\mathcal{X})$ and with $\underline{E}$ the natural extension of $\underline{P}$. ϵ can be interpreted as the probability that the information $\underline{P}$ is reliable, $1 - \epsilon$ being the probability of being ignorant. The vacuous mixture is a generalise both the the well-known linear-vacuous mixture and the classical discounting rule of belief functions. In terms of credal sets, it is equivalent to compute $\mathcal{P}_{\underline{P}_\epsilon}$ such that $\mathcal{P}_{\underline{P}_\epsilon} = \{\epsilon p_{\underline{P}} + (1 - \epsilon)p_v | p_{\underline{P}} \in \mathcal{P}_{\underline{P}}, p_v \in \mathbb{P}_\mathcal{X}\}$.

Now, if we consider k coherent lower previsions $\underline{P}_1, \ldots, \underline{P}_k$ and their natural extensions $\underline{E}_1, \ldots, \underline{E}_k$, then we can average them into a natural extension $\underline{E}_\sigma$ by merging them through an arithmetic mean, that is by considering $\underline{E}_\sigma(f) = \frac{1}{k}\sum_{i=1}^{k} \underline{E}_i(f)$ for any $f \in \mathcal{L}(\mathcal{X})$. This rule has been justified and used by different authors to merge coherent lower previsions or, equivalently, convex sets of probabilities [10].

2.3 Decision Rules

Given some beliefs about a (finite) variable X and a set of preferences, the goal of decision rules is here to select the optimal values X can assume, i.e. the class to which X may belong. Here, we assume that preferences are modeled, for each $\omega \in \mathcal{X}$, by cost functions f'_ω, that is $f'_\omega(\omega')$ is the cost of selecting ω' when ω is the true class. When uncertainty over $\mathcal{X}$ is represented by a single probability p, the optimal class is the one whose expected cost is the lowest, i.e. $\hat{\omega} = \arg\min_{\omega \in \mathcal{X}} E_p(f'_\omega)$, thus taking minimal risks. If the beliefs about the value of X are given by a lower prevision $\underline{P}$, the classical expected cost based decision has to be extended [11].

One way to do so is to still require the decision to be a single class. The most well-known decision rule in this category is the maximin rule, for which the final decision is such that

$$\widehat{\omega} = \arg\min_{\omega \in \mathcal{X}} \overline{E}_p(f'_\omega)$$

this amounts to minimising the upper expected cost, i.e., the worst possible consequence, and corresponds to a cautious decision. Other possible rules include minimising the lower expected cost or minimising a value in-between.

The other way to extend expected cost is to give as decision a set (possibly, but not necessarily reduced to a singleton) of classes, reflecting our indecision and the imprecision of our beliefs. This requires to build, among the possible choices (here, the classes), a partial ordering, and then to select only the choices that are not dominated by another one. Two such extensions are the interval ordering $\leq_I$ and the maximality ordering $\leq_M$. Using interval ordering, a choice ω is dominated by a choice ω', denoted by $\omega \leq_I \omega'$, iff $\overline{E}(f'_\omega) \leq \underline{E}(f_\omega)$, that is if the upper expected cost of picking ω' is sure to be lower than the lower expected cost of picking ω. The decision set $\widehat{\Omega}_I$ is then

$$\widehat{\Omega}_I = \{\omega \in \mathcal{X} | \not\exists \omega' \text{s.t.} \omega \leq_I \omega'\}.$$

Using maximality ordering, a choice ω is dominated by a choice ω', denoted by $\omega \leq_M \omega'$, iff $\underline{E}(f_\omega - f_{\omega'}) > 0$. This has the following interpretation: given our beliefs, exchanging ω for ω' would have a strictly positive expected cost, hence we are not ready to do so. The decision set $\widehat{\Omega}_M$ is then

$$\widehat{\Omega}_M = \{\omega \in \mathcal{X} | \not\exists \omega' \text{s.t.} \omega \leq_M \omega'\}.$$

The maximility ordering refines the Interval ordering and is stronger, in the sense that we always have $\widehat{\Omega}_M \subseteq \widehat{\Omega}_I$. Using these decision rules, the more precise and non-conflicting our information is, the smaller is the set of possible classes $\widehat{\Omega}$.

3   The Method

Let $x_1, \ldots, x_N$ be N D-dimensional training samples, $\mathcal{Y} = \{\omega_1, \ldots, \omega_M\}$ the set of possible classes, and $\underline{P}_i : \mathcal{L}(\mathcal{Y}) \to [0, 1]$ be the lower prevision modelling our knowledge about the class to which the sample x_i belongs. Given a new instance x to classify, that is to which we have to assign a class $y \in \mathcal{Y}$, we denote by $x_{(1)}, \ldots, x_{(k)}$ its k ordered nearest neighbours (i.e. $d_{(i)} < d_{(j)}$ if $i \leq j$). For a given nearest neighbour $x_{(i)}$, the knowledge $\underline{P}_{(i)}$ can be regarded as a piece of evidence related to the unknown class of x. However, this piece of knowledge is not 100% reliable, and should be discounted by a value $\epsilon_i \in [0, 1]$ depending of its class, such that, for any $f \in \mathcal{L}(\mathcal{Y})$,

$$\underline{E}_{(i),x}(f) = \epsilon_{(i)}\underline{E}_{(i)} + (1 - \epsilon_{(i)}) \inf_{\omega \in \mathcal{Y}} f(\omega).$$

It seems natural to ask for ϵ be a decreasing function of $d_{(i)}$, since the further away is the neighbour, the less reliable is the information it provides about the unknown class. Similarly to Denoeux proposal, we can consider the general formula

$$\epsilon = \epsilon_0 \phi(d_{(i)}),$$

where ϕ is a non-increasing function that can be depended of the class given by $x_{(i)}$. In addition, the following conditions should hold:

$$0 < \epsilon_0 < 1 \quad ; \quad \phi(0) = 1 \text{ and } \lim_{d \to \infty} \phi(d) = 0.$$

The first condition imply that even if the new instance has the same input as one training data sample, we do not consider it to be 100% reliable, as the relation linking the input feature space and the output classes is not necessarily a function. From $\underline{P}_{(1),x}, \cdots, \underline{P}_{(k),x}$, we then obtain a combined lower prevision $\underline{P}$ such that

$$\underline{P}_x = \frac{1}{k} \sum_{i=1}^{k} \underline{P}_{(i),x}.$$

Using $\underline{P}_x$ as the final uncertainty model for the true class of x, one can predict its final class, either as a single class by using a maximin-like criteria or as a set of possible classes by using maximality or interval dominance. Using maximality or interval dominance is a good way to treat both ambiguity or large distances with the nearest neighbours. Indeed, if all nearest neighbours agree on the output class and are close to the new instance, the obtained lower prevision $\underline{P}_x$ will be precise enough so that the criteria will end up pointing only one possible class (i.e., $\widehat{\Omega}_M$, $\widehat{\Omega}_I$ will be singletons). On the contrary, if nearest neighbours disagree or are far from the new instance, $\underline{P}_x$ will be imprecise or indecisive, and $\widehat{\Omega}_M$, $\widehat{\Omega}_I$ will contain several possible classes.

3.1 Using Lower Previsions to Choose k

A problem when using the k-nearest neighbour procedure is to choose the "best" number k of neighbours to consider. This number is often selected as the one achieving the best performance in a cross-validation procedure, but k-NN rules can display erratic performances if k is slightly increased or decreased, even if it is by one.

We propose here a new approach to guide the choice of k, using the features of lower previsions: we propose to choose the value k achieving the best compromise between imprecision and precision, estimated respectively from the number of optimal classes selected for each test sample, and from the percentage of times where the true class is inside the set of possible ones.

Let $(x_{N+1}, y_{N+1}), \ldots, (x_{N+T}, y_{N+T})$ be the test samples. Given a value k of nearest neighbours, let $\Omega_{M,i}^k$ denote the set of classes retrieved by maximality criteria for x_{N+i}, and $\delta_i^k : 2^{|\mathcal{Y}|} \to \{0, 1\}$ the function such that $\delta_i^k = 1$ if $y_{N+i} \in \Omega_{M,i}^k$ and 0 otherwise. That is, δ_i^k is one if the right answer is in the set of possible classes. Then, we propose to estimate the informativeness Inf_k and the accuracy Acc_k of our k-NN method as:

$$Inf_k = 1 - \frac{\sum_{i=1}^{T} |\Omega_{M,i}^k| - T}{T(M-1)} \quad ; \quad Acc_k = \frac{\sum_{i=1}^{T} \delta_i^k}{T}$$

Note that informativeness has value one iff $|\Omega_{M,i}^k| = 1$ for $i = 1, \ldots, T$, that is decisions are precise, while accuracy measures the number of times the right class is in the set of possible classes. This means that the less informative is a classifier, the more accurate it will be, since the right answer will be in the set of possible classes every time. We then estimate the global performance GP_k as the value $GP_k = \beta Inf_k + (1 - \beta)Acc_k$, that is a weighted average between precision and accuracy, with $\beta \in [0, 1]$ the importance given to informativeness. Letting k vary, we then select the best value k^* as

$$k^* = arg \min_{k=1,...,N} GP_k.$$

The idea of this rule is to choose the value k^* achieving the best compromise between informativeness and accuracy (as some evaluation methods used for experts in classical probabilities).

3.2 Precise Training Samples and Unitary Costs

Let us now consider a particular case, namely the one where all training samples x_i have a single class y_i as output, and where the cost function (called here unitary) f_ω of choosing ω is $f_\omega(\omega') = 1 - \delta_{\omega,\omega'}$ where $\delta_{\omega,\omega'}$ is the classical Kronecker delta ($= 1$ if $\omega = \omega'$, zero otherwise). This assumptions corresponds to the one of classical k-NN procedures. Given these cost functions and a lower prevision $\underline{P}$ on $\mathcal{Y}$, the lower expectation for f_ω is

$$\underline{E}(f_\omega) = \underline{E}(\{\omega\}^c) = 1 - \overline{E}(\{\omega\}),$$

that is one minus the upper probability of the singleton ω. Similarly, the upper expectation of f_ω is one minus the lower probability of the singleton ω.

The lower prevision $\underline{P}_i$ and its natural extension $\underline{E}_i$ modeling our uncertainty about the output of a training sample x_i is simply, for any $f \in \mathcal{L}(\mathcal{Y})$, the value $\underline{E}_i(f) = f(y_i)$ where y_i is the output of x_i. We also have $\underline{E}_i(f) = \overline{E}_i(f)$, and can now show that our method extends classical k-NN

Proposition 1. *Let k be the number of nearest neighbours considered. If training samples are precise, costs unitary and discounting rates $\epsilon_{(1)} = \ldots = \epsilon_{(k)} = \epsilon$, then the method used with a maximin decision criteria gives the same result as a classical k-NN rule.*

Proof. Let us consider a given $\omega \in \mathcal{Y}$ and its unitary cost function f_ω. Let us now compute the upper expectation of f_ω, or equivalently one minus the lower probability of $\{\omega\}$. Given the k nearest neighbour, the lower probability $\underline{E}(\{\omega\})$ of $\{\omega\}$ is

$$\underline{E}(\{\omega\}) = \frac{1}{k} \sum_{i=1}^{k} \epsilon \delta_{\omega,y_{(i)}} + (1 - \epsilon) \inf f_\omega = \frac{\epsilon}{k} \sum_{i=1}^{k} \delta_{\omega,y_{(i)}}.$$

The highest value of $\underline{E}(\{\omega\})$ is reached for the value $\omega \in \mathcal{Y}$ which have the maximal number of representative in the k neighbours, and since the value maximising this lower probability is the same as the one minimising the upper expectation of unitary cost functions, this finishes the proof.

Proposition 2. *Let k be the number of nearest neighbours considered. If training samples are precise, costs unitary and discounting rates $\epsilon_{(i)} = w_i$ are equal to some weights, then the method used with a maximin decision criteria gives the same result as a weighted k-NN rule with the same weights.*

Proof. Similar to the proof of Prop. 1.

The case of precise training samples and unitary costs have another interesting property, namely the one that the set of possible classes obtained by maximality criteria coincide with the one obtained by interval dominance. This avoids any choice and allows using computational procedures used for interval-dominance, which are simpler.

Proposition 3. *Let k be the number of nearest neighbours considered. If training samples are precise and costs unitary, then $\widehat{\Omega}_M = \widehat{\Omega}_I$ for any new instance.*

Proof. To prove this proposition, we will simply show that for ω, ω', the two conditions to have $\omega \geq_I \omega'$ and $\omega \geq_M \omega'$ both coincide in this particular case. First, we have $\omega \geq_M \omega'$ if and only if $\underline{E}(\mathbf{1}_{(\{w\})} - \mathbf{1}_{(\{w'\})}) > 0$. Using Eq. and the particular case that we consider here, we have

$$\underline{E}(\mathbf{1}_{(\{w\})} - \mathbf{1}_{(\{w'\})}) = \frac{1}{k} \left(\sum_{i=1}^{k} \epsilon_{(i)} \delta_{\omega, y_{(i)}} - \sum_{i=1}^{k} \epsilon_{(i)} \delta_{\omega', y_{(i)}} - \sum_{i=1}^{k} (1 - \epsilon_{(i)}) \right).$$

The last part of the equation right-hand side being due to the fact that $\inf_{\omega \in \mathcal{Y}} (\mathbf{1}_{(\{w\})} - \mathbf{1}_{(\{w'\})}) = -1$ if $\omega \neq \omega'$. Hence, $\omega \geq_M \omega'$ iff the number between parenthesis is positive. Now, we have that $\omega \geq_I \omega'$ if and only if $\underline{E}(\mathbf{1}_{(\{w\})}) \geq \overline{E}(\mathbf{1}_{(\{w'\})})$. In our particular case, this becomes

$$\frac{1}{k} \sum_{i=1}^{k} \epsilon_{(i)} \delta_{\omega, y_{(i)}} \geq \frac{1}{k} \left(\sum_{i=1}^{k} \epsilon_{(i)} \delta_{\omega', y_{(i)}} + \sum_{i=1}^{k} (1 - \epsilon_{(i)}) \right).$$

Moving the right hand side to the left finishes the proof.

4 Experiments

Since Proposition 2 indicates that the results of the proposed method can be made equivalent (in terms of prediction accuracy) to those of a weighted k-NN method, we refer to studies comparing the results of different weighted k-NN method to have an idea about the accuracy of the method.

Instead, we have preferred to experiment our method to select the best number k of nearest neighbours on some classical benchmark problems. We used a leave-one-out validation method. The class of each sample is predicted using the $N - 1$ remaining samples. Inf_k, Acc_k and GP_k are averaged over the N obtained results. We also computed the average error rate using a maximin criterion, which gives results equivalent to the weighted k-NN with weights given by the discounting factor.

As discussing and optimising ϕ is not the topic of the paper, we consider the simple heuristic where, for a given training data (x, y), $\phi(d_x) = \exp^{-d/\overline{d_y}}$, with $\overline{d_y}$ the average

Table 1. Experiment data sets

Name	# instances	# input variables	# output classes
Glass	214	9	6
Image segmentation	2100	19	7
Ionosphere	351	9	2
Letter recognition	2500	16	26

distance between elements of the training set having y for class. We fix $\epsilon_0 = 0.99$, in order to not increase too quickly the imprecision.

Four different classification problems taken from the UCI repository [12] are considered. They are summarized in Table 1 . Results obtained for each of them are summarized in Fig 1. In each graphs are displayed, for different values of k nearest neighbours, the informativeness Inf_k, the precision Acc_k, the global score GP_k as well as the precision obtained by using a maximin criterion, equivalent to the one obtained with a weighted k-NN method using the discounting weights.

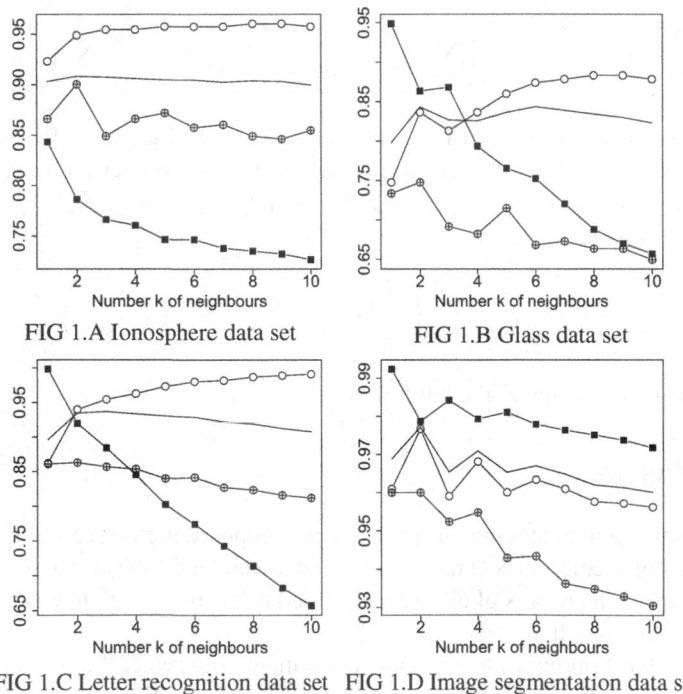

FIG 1.A Ionosphere data set   FIG 1.B Glass data set

FIG 1.C Letter recognition data set   FIG 1.D Image segmentation data set

——■—— : Inf_k —○— : Acc_k —— : GP_k —⊕— : Maximin

Fig. 1. Experiment results

Note that, here, both the choices of β, of ϵ_0 and of $\phi()$ are of importance, for they will directly influence the imprecision of $\underline{P}_x$ and hence the decision imprecision concerning the class of x and the optimal k^*. As could be expected, the informativeness globally decreases with the number k of nearest neighbours, while the number of sample x_i whose true class is in the set of optimal classes $|\Omega^k_{M,i}|$ globally increases. Note that this imprecision is due to two different causes: the presence of conflicting information in (in this case, the different classes to which belongs the neighbours are optimal) and distance of the neighbours to the sample (in this case, $\underline{P}_x$ is very imprecise and no class dominates another, i.e., they are all optimal).

The increase in informativeness that we can see when going from $k = 2$ to $k = 3$ for the Glass and Image segmentation data sets are due to the fact that immediate neighbours provide conflicting information that do not make decisions less informative, but provoke, for some sample, a decision shift from their true class to a false class. Such an increase is then the clue that some classes boundaries may be quite difficult to identify in the input space. A smooth decrease of informativeness is then the clue that there are no significant conflict in the information provided by neighbours, as for the ionosphere and letter recognition data.

The initial number of samples that have imprecise classifications due to the distance with their neighbours can be evaluated from the informativeness for $k = 1$. Indeed, if $k = 1$, there can be no conflict between neighbours, and the imprecise classification can only come from the large distance and the resulting discounting weight. It is therefore also a good way to evaluate the density of the data set, and its representativeness (for example, points in the ionosphere data set seems to have large distances between them, compared to the others).

Although they could probably be improved by optimised choices of the metric, of parameters β, ϵ_0, $\phi()$, our results show that allowing for a small imprecision can improve significantly the resulting classification, and the confidence we have in the classifier answer, without adding additional parameters such as a rejection or distance threshold. They also indicate that, in general, best results are obtained for a small number of neighbours. Finally, if one wants a unique class as answer, it is always possible to come back to the solution of a classical weighted k-NN method. An alternative would be to use another classifier and its answer to precisiate the imprecise answer given by our method.

5   Conclusion and Perspectives

In this paper, we have defined a first K-NN method based on lower previsions (equivalent to convex probability sets). As lower previsions are very generic models of uncertainty, using them allows to handle labels coming from expert opinions expressed in very different ways. Using the theory of lower previsions also allows to settle the problem of ambiguity (conflicting information) and absence of neighbours close to a given instance, without adding additional parameters. This can be done by using decision rules that selects sets of possible (i.e., optimal) classes rather than single ones when information delivered by neighbours is ambiguous or unreliable.

Using this particular feature of lower previsions, we have proposed a simple and new means to select the "best" number k of nearest neighbours to consider. Namely, the number that achieves the best balance between accuracy (good classification) and precision (decision retaining only a small number of classes).

This paper have exposed the basics of a K-NN method using lower previsions. Many surrounding topics remains to be investigated, among which:

- how to distinguish imprecise decisions due to ambiguity from those due to unreliable (i.e. "far away") neighbours ?
- how to optimise (as done in [13]) the whole procedure so that it can give better results for a given problem ?
- how the framework of lower previsions can help in solving the problem of instances having uncertain / missing input values ?
- how does this method compare to other (basic) classification methods using lower previsions, such as the Naive credal classifier [14] ?

References

1. Fix, E., Hodges, J.: Discriminatory analysis, nonparametric discrimination: consistency properties. Technical Report 4, USAF School of Aviation Medicine (1951)
2. Dudani, S.: The distance-weighted k-nearest neighbor rule. IEEE Trans. Syst. Man. Cybern. 6, 325–327 (1976)
3. Dubuisson, B., Masson, M.: A statistical decision rule with incomplete knowledge about classes. Pattern Recognition 26, 155–165 (1993)
4. Denoeux, T.: A k-nearest neighbor classification rule based on dempster-shafer theory. IEEE Trans. Syst. Man. Cybern. 25, 804–813 (1995)
5. Hüllermeier, E.: Case-based approximate reasoning. Theory and decision library, vol. 44. Springer, Heidelberg (2007)
6. Walley, P.: Statistical reasoning with imprecise Probabilities. Chapman and Hall, New York (1991)
7. Miranda, E.: A survey of the theory of coherent lower previsions. Int. J. of Approximate Reasoning 48, 628–658 (2008)
8. Dubois, D., Prade, H.: Possibility Theory: An Approach to Computerized Processing of Uncertainty. Plenum Press, New York (1988)
9. Shafer, G.: A mathematical Theory of Evidence. Princeton University Press, New Jersey (1976)
10. Walley, P.: The elicitation and aggregation of beliefs. Technical report, University of Warwick (1982)
11. Troffaes, M.: Decision making under uncertainty using imprecise probabilities. Int. J. of Approximate Reasoning 45, 17–29 (2007)
12. Asuncion, A., Newman, D.: UCI machine learning repository (2007),
   http://www.ics.uci.edu/~mlearn/MLRepository.html
13. Zouhal, L., Denoeux, T.: An evidence-theoretic k-nn rule with parameter optimization. IEEE Trans. on Syst., Man, and Cybern. 28, 263–271 (1998)
14. Zaffalon, M.: The naive credal classifier. J. Probabilistic Planning and Inference 105, 105–122 (2002)

Fuzzy Probabilities: Tentative Discussions on the Mathematical Concepts

Enric Trillas, Takehiko Nakama, and Itziar García-Honrado

European Center for Soft Computing
Edificio Científico-Technológico
33600 Mieres, Asturias, Spain
enric.trillas@softcomputing.es,
nakama@jhu.edu,
itziar.garcia@softcomputing.es
http://www.softcomputing.es/en/home.php

Abstract. Various forms of probability and probabilistic concepts have been discussed in fuzzy logic since its very inception, but their mathematical foundations have yet to be fully established. In this paper, we investigate theoretical issues concerning (1) probability measures as membership functions, (2) probability measures for fuzzy sets, and (3) fuzzy-valued probabilities.

Keywords: Fuzzy logic, probability measures, conditional probability, independence, fuzzy probability.

1 Introduction

Although the axiomatic foundation of probability theory did not exist until Kolmogorov developed it in the twentieth century, the mathematics of probability has a long history. For instance, the famous correspondence between Pascal and Fermat in the seventeenth century about the "problem of the points" substantially advanced the mathematics of games of chance, and other prominent mathematicians such as James and Jacques Bernoulli, De Moivre, and Laplace established notable limiting results in probability (see, for instance, [8]). Today the importance of probability theory is widely recognized in a variety of fields of research, and probability continues to fascinate the general public because of its relevance to everyday life.

The rigorously established measure-theoretic probability that we have today deals with probabilities of events, which are "crisp" subsets of the sample space. On the other hand, Zadeh [11,13] developed a mathematical system of fuzzy sets and logic, and he introduced what he called "probability measures" on collections of fuzzy sets [12]. He also invented "fuzzy probabilities", which are potential functions (they are fuzzy numbers) highly related to probabilities [14]. Evidently probabilistic concepts have been discussed in fuzzy logic since its very inception, and this is hardly surprising as the importance of probability is ubiquitous both in theory and in practice.

E. Hüllermeier, R. Kruse, and F. Hoffmann (Eds.): IPMU 2010, LNAI 6178, pp. 139–148, 2010.
© Springer-Verlag Berlin Heidelberg 2010

However, there has not been any systematic effort to satisfactorily extend classical probability theory to fuzzy logic. In this paper we attempt to take a first step toward establishing theoretical foundations for several forms of probability in fuzzy logic. We discuss various issues regarding probabilistic concepts developed in fuzzy logic. In Section 3, we examine fuzzy sets whose membership functions are probability measures. We describe some unusual properties of the collection of such fuzzy sets. In Section 4, we investigate probability measures for fuzzy events. Conditional probability and independence have not been thoroughly developed in fuzzy logic, and we attempt to extend these important concepts to probabilities of fuzzy sets. In Section 6, we examine how to theoretically manage the fuzzy numbers that have been described as "fuzzy probabilities". We initiate a discussion on how classical probability theory, which deals only with real-valued probabilities, can be generalized to axiomatically formulate fuzzy-valued probabilities.

2   Preliminaries

First we briefly describe the fundamentals of Kolmogorov's axiomatic probability theory (see, for instance, [1,3]). Let Ω denote the sample space, which is often described as the "set of all possible outcomes". We consider a σ-field $\mathscr{F}$ (also called a σ-algebra or a Borel field) of subsets of Ω: $\mathscr{F}$ is a nonempty collection of subsets of Ω such that it is closed under complementation and countable union. A probability measure P on $\mathscr{F}$ is a numerically valued set function with domain $\mathscr{F}$ that satisfies the following three axioms:

(i) $P(E) \geq 0 \quad \forall E \in \mathscr{F}$.
(ii) $P(\Omega) = 1$.
(iii) If $\{E_i\}$ is a countable collection of (pairwise) disjoint sets in $\mathscr{F}$, then $P\left(\bigcup_i E_i\right) = \sum_i P(E_i)$.

Each set in $\mathscr{F}$ is called an event and considered measurable, and $P(E)$ represents the probability of $E \in \mathscr{F}$. The triple $(\Omega, \mathscr{F}, P)$ is called a probability space, and $(\Omega, \mathscr{F})$ is described as a measurable space.

Axiom (iii) is called "countable additivity", and it can be difficult to check whether a set function satisfies this property. Instead, we consider the following two axioms:

(iii.a) If $\{E_i\}$ is a sequence in $\mathscr{F}$ such that $E_i \downarrow \emptyset$, then $P(E_i) \to 0$.
(iii.b) If $\{E_1, E_2, \ldots, E_n\}$ is a finite collection of (pairwise) disjoint sets in $\mathscr{F}$, then $P\left(\bigcup_{i=1}^{n} E_i\right) = \sum_{i=1}^{n} P(E_i)$.

Axioms (iii.a) and (iii.b) are called the "axiom of continuity" and "finite additivity", respectively. We can prove that these two axioms together are equivalent to (iii), so we will check (iii.a) and (iii.b) to determine whether a set function satisfies the axiom of countable additivity. It is important to note that, by induction on n, P is finitely additive if (iii.b) holds for $n = 2$—if $P(A \cup B) = P(A) + P(B)$ for disjoint sets A and B in $\mathscr{F}$.

Conventional probability theory does not deal with fuzzy sets; each set in $\mathscr{F}$ is a crisp set, and with the set-theoretic operations of union, intersection, and complementation, $\mathscr{F}$ is a boolean algebra with $\emptyset$ its minimum element and Ω its maximum element. Thus probability measures are defined on boolean algebras. For our discussions, it is important to note that in boolean algebras, it follows from the three axioms of probability that $E_1 \subset E_2$ implies $P(E_1) \leq P(E_2)$. In the quantum theory of probability, measurable sets are those in an orthomodular lattice, which is usually the closed vector space of an infinite dimensional Hilbert space [2]. Note that in ortholattices, $a \subset b'$ implies $a \cap b = \emptyset$, but the converse does not hold in general; the two are equivalent only in boolean algebras. In quantum probability theory, if $a \subset b'$, then $P(a \oplus b) = P(a) + P(b)$, where $\oplus$ represents the direct sum, i.e., $a \oplus b$ denotes the space spanned by a and b.

As described in Section 1, we would like to extend axiomatic probability theory to fuzzy sets. If the extension is not possible, then it is desirable to establish an analogous axiomatic theory of probability in fuzzy logic. There exist two main schools of thought in the philosophy of probability: the frequentist school and the Bayesian school. Frequentists view probability as the long-run (limiting) frequency of occurrence, whereas Bayesians view it as the degree of belief. Both positions have advantages and disadvantages, but in either case, we must carefully consider the following two linguistic components of fuzzy sets in order to establish a theory of probability in fuzzy logic. One is the semantic component, which pertains to objects or their information necessary in specifying events that are predicated as probable. Thus this component concerns extending the concept of the measurable space $(\Omega, \mathscr{F})$ to fuzzy logic. The other is the syntactic component, which pertains to a context in which probable events are clearly represented and assigned probabilities. For this, we must establish rules that assign probabilities and specify computations with them. Therefore this component concerns extending the probability measure P to fuzzy logic.

3   Probability Measures as Membership Functions

Any probability measure $P : L \to [0, 1]$ can be used as a membership function of a probabilistic predicate, such as "probable", and thus be considered a fuzzy set. We will describe a membership function that is also a probability measure as a probability membership function. Probability measures in $[0, 1]^L$ form a rather peculiar family of fuzzy sets. First we consider the ordering of such fuzzy sets. Let P_1 and P_2 be two probability measures on L, and suppose that $P_1 \leq P_2$. Then $P_1(a) \leq P_2(a)$ for all $a \in L$. We also have $P_1(a') \leq P_2(a')$, whence $1 - P_1(a) \leq 1 - P_2(a)$ and $P_2(a) \leq P_1(a)$. Therefore two fuzzy sets with probability membership functions are either coincidental or uncomparable.

Let p denote the predicate "probable" acting on a boolean algebra, and suppose that we have two probability membership functions $\mu_p^{(1)}$ and $\mu_p^{(2)}$ for p (they represent two uses of the predicate). Then it follows that either $\mu_p^{(1)} = \mu_p^{(2)}$ or $\mu_p^{(1)} \ NC \ \mu_p^{(2)}$, where NC is used to indicate that they are uncomparable. Hence it appears that the pointwise ordering of such fuzzy sets is not the "right" way to compare them; probability measures seem to be of a different type compared to other fuzzy sets. We are currently investigating various relations that can be effectively used to compare fuzzy sets with probability membership functions.

Compositions of probability measures by the three typical connectives in any algebra $([0,1]^X, \cdot, +,')$ [10] also show some odd properties. Since $P_1 \cdot P_2 \leq P_1$ and $P_1 \cdot P_2 \leq P_2$, it follows that $P_1 \cdot P_2 = P_1 = P_2$. We also have $P_1 + P_2 \geq P_1$ and $P_1 + P_2 \geq P_2$. Hence $P_1 + P_2 = P_1 = P_2$. The negation of a probability measure is not a probability measure, since $N \circ P(0) = N(P(0)) = N(0) = 1$. Thus the collection $\{P | P \text{ is a probability measure}\} \subset [0,1]^L$ is rather peculiar in any algebra of fuzzy sets.

4   Fuzzy-Crisp Probability: Probability Measures for Fuzzy Events

In this section, we consider probabilities of fuzzy events, which we call "fuzzy-crisp probabilities". We should keep in mind that for no algebra of fuzzy sets $([0,1]^X, \cdot, +,')$ does there exist $L \subseteq [0,1]^X$ such that $L \neq \{0,1\}^X$ and such that $(L, \cdot, +,')$ is an ortholattice. A fortiori, $(L, \cdot, +,')$ is not a boolean algebra or an orthomodular lattice. Therefore, neither conventional probability theory nor quantum probability theory is immediately applicable to such L. However, this does not imply that, for any $L \subseteq [0,1]^X$ such that $L \neq \{0,1\}^X$, there is no function $P : L \to [0,1]$ that satisfies the three axioms of probability. Indeed, Zadeh [12] found such functions and described them as probability measures of fuzzy events. We examine his concept of fuzzy-crisp probability.

Let $X := \{x_1, x_2, \ldots, x_n\}$ (thus X is finite). For all $\mu \in [0,1]^X$, $|\mu| := \sum_{i=1}^n \mu(x_i)$ is called the crisp cardinal or sigma-count of μ. Notice that for $\mu \in \{0,1\}^X$ satisfying $\mu^{-1}(1) = A \subseteq X$, we have $|\mu| = Card(A)$, since $\mu(x_i) \in \{0,1\}$ for each i. Clearly $|\mu_0| = 0$ and $|\mu_1| = |X| = n$. Let $L = [0,1]^X$ be a standard algebra of fuzzy sets with (T, S, N) such that

$$N := 1 - id, \tag{1}$$

$$T(a,b) + S(a,b) = a + b. \tag{2}$$

Condition (2) is satisfied by Frank's family, which includes (a) $T = \min, S = \max$; (b) $T = prod, S = prod^*$; and (c) $T = W, S = W^*$. With such an algebra, the mapping $P : L \to [0,1]$ defined by

$$P(\mu) = \frac{|\mu|}{n} \quad \forall\, \mu \in L \tag{3}$$

satisfies the three axioms of probability; it is easy to show that axioms (i)–(ii) and (iii.a)–(iii.b) hold for this P. Also it is easy to verify the identify $P(\mu') = 1 - P(\mu)$. For $\mu, \sigma \in L$, suppose that $\mu \leq \sigma$. Then $\mu(x_i) \leq \sigma(x_i)$ for $1 \leq i \leq n$, so $\sum_{i=1}^n \mu(x_i) \leq \sum_{i=1}^n \sigma(x_i)$. Hence $|\mu| \leq |\sigma|$, and we have $P(\mu) \leq P(\sigma)$, as desired. Due to these properties, we find it agreeable to consider P as a probability measure for the algebra L.

Suppose that $X := [a, b] \subset \mathbb{R}$ $(a \le b)$, and let $[0, 1]^X$ be endowed with (T, S, N) satisfying (1)–(2). Consider

$$L := \{\mu \in [0, 1]^X | \mu \text{ is Riemann-integrable over } [a, b]\}.$$

Clearly L contains all the Riemann-integrable functions in $\{0, 1\}^X$. Notice that L is closed under T, S, and N: $\mu \cdot \sigma$, $\mu + \sigma$, and $1 - \mu$ are all in L for any $\mu, \sigma \in L$. Define $P : L \to [0, 1]$ by

$$P(\mu) := \frac{1}{b-a} \int_a^b \mu(x)\,dx \quad \forall\, \mu \in L. \tag{4}$$

If we have a constant fuzzy set, $\mu_r(x) = r \,\forall\, x \in X$, then clearly $P(\mu_r) = r$. Again, it is easy to verify that P satisfies the three axioms of probability, so it can be considered a probability measure. It is also easy to show that $P(\mu') = 1 - P(\mu)$. Note that we have

$$P(\mu') = \frac{1}{b-a} \int_a^b (1 - \mu(x))\,dx = \frac{b-a}{b-a} - \frac{1}{b-a} \int_a^b \mu(x)\,dx = 1 - P(\mu).$$

The supposition of equipossibility is evident in (3) and (4). However, this supposition is unnecessary, and these measures can be generalized by considering

$$P(\mu) := \int \mu(x)\,d\lambda(x),$$

where λ is a probability measure on the σ-field in X (see [12]). Also notice that, in general, $\mu \le \sigma'$ does not imply $\mu \cdot \sigma = \mu_0$, so it does not imply $P(\mu + \sigma) = P(\mu) + P(\sigma)$. However, if $T = W$, $S = W^*$, and $N = 1 - id$, then $\mu \le \sigma'$ implies $\mu \cdot \sigma = \mu_0$

5   Conditional Probability and Independence for Fuzzy Events

One of the most important concepts in probability theory is conditional probability, and we will examine this concept for fuzzy-crisp probability. Conditioning is a profound concept in measure-theoretic probability, but for simplicity, we will focus on cases where conditioning events have positive measures. Let $(L, \cdot, +, ')$ be a boolean algebra. We let 0 and 1 denote its minimum and maximum, respectively. Let P denote a probability measure on L. For each $a \in L - \{0\}$, $aL := \{a \cdot x | x \in L\}$ is a subalgebra with the restriction of $\cdot$ and $+$ and with a complementation operator $*$ defined by $(a \cdot x)^* = a \cdot x'$. This subalgebra can represent a conditional boolean algebra. The minimum of aL is $0 \cdot a = 0$, and its maximum is $1 \cdot a = a$. Provided that $P(a) \ne 0$, the function $P^* : aL \to [0, 1]$ defined by

$$P^*(a \cdot x) = \frac{P(a \cdot x)}{P(a)} \tag{5}$$

is a probability measure on aL (but not on L), and we use $P(x|a)$ to denote $P^*(a \cdot x)$. Two events $a, b \in L$ are said to be independent if $P(b|a) = P(b)$ [hence $P(a \cdot b) = P(a)P(b)$].

If L is a boolean algebra with 2^n elements resulting from n atoms, then the simplest way of defining P on L is by $P(a) = \frac{Card(a)}{n}$ for all $a \in L$, where $Card(a)$ denotes the number of atoms in a. In this case, for all $x \in aL$, we have $P(x|a) = \frac{Card(a \cdot x)}{Card(a)}$. In general, if $\{a_1, a_2, \ldots, a_n\}$ is the set of n atoms, then we can define a probability measure P by $P(a_i) = \alpha_i \geq 0$ for $1 \leq i \leq n$ such that $\sum_{i=1}^{n} \alpha_i = 1$. In the equipossible case, we have $P(a_i) = 1/n$ for all i.

By the distributive law, we have $a \cdot x + a \cdot y = a \cdot (x + y) \in aL$ for all $a, b, x \in L$. Thus this law is important for aL to be a boolean algebra, and $P(x|a) := P^*(a \cdot x)$ is a probability when L is a boolean algebra. Unfortunately, if L is an orthomodular lattice, then aL is not an orthomodular lattice, so conditional probability cannot be defined in this manner.

We investigate whether the concept of conditional probability for crisp sets can be properly extended to fuzzy sets. We will consider (3) and (4), which satisfy the axioms of probability. First we suppose that X is finite. Thus we let $X := \{x_1, x_2, \ldots, x_n\}$ and examine (3). Consider a fuzzy set $\sigma \in [0,1]^X$ as a conditioning event. We suppose that $P(\sigma) \neq 0$. If we apply (5) to this case, then we obtain

$$P(\mu|\sigma) = \frac{P(\mu \cdot \sigma)}{P(\sigma)} = \frac{1}{|\sigma|} \sum_{i=1}^{n} T(\mu(x_i), \sigma(x_i)). \tag{6}$$

In order for this conditional probability to satisfy

$$P(\sigma|\sigma) = 1, \tag{7}$$

we must have

$$|\sigma| = \sum_{i=1}^{n} T(\sigma(x_i), \sigma(x_i)).$$

This equality is satisfied only by $T = \min$:

$$\sum_{i=1}^{n} \min\{\sigma(x_i), \sigma(x_i)\} = \sum_{i=1}^{n} \sigma(x_i) = |\sigma|.$$

Note that the conditional probability defined by Zadeh [12] is problematic because it does not satisfy (7). (Zadeh uses *prod* for T.) If (T, S) is in Frank's family, then we have $S = \max$ for $T = \min$. In this case, we have

$$P(\mu + \lambda|\sigma) + P(\mu \cdot \lambda|\sigma) = P(\mu|\sigma) + P(\lambda|\sigma),$$

as desired (with crisp sets, $P(\cdot \,|\sigma)$ satisfies the three axioms of probability and is thus a probability measure). Thus by imposing (7), which should be considered rather natural or desirable, we obtain a different definition of conditional probability compared to that of Zadeh [12], who did not provide any rationale for using $T = prod$ instead of $T = \min$ in defining it.

Next we analyze the independence of two fuzzy events. We have

$$P(\mu \cdot \sigma) = \frac{1}{n} \sum_{i=1}^{n} \min\{\mu(x_i), \sigma(x_i)\},$$

$$P(\mu)P(\sigma) = \left(\frac{1}{n} \sum_{i=1}^{n} \mu(x_i)\right) \left(\frac{1}{n} \sum_{i=1}^{n} \sigma(x_i)\right).$$

Thus, for $T = \min$, two fuzzy events are said to be independent if

$$\frac{1}{n} \sum_{i=1}^{n} \min\{\mu(x_i), \sigma(x_i)\} = \left(\frac{1}{n} \sum_{i=1}^{n} \mu(x_i)\right) \left(\frac{1}{n} \sum_{i=1}^{n} \sigma(x_i)\right). \tag{8}$$

This definition of independence is different from Zadeh's [12], because we have chosen $T = \min$ so that the conditional probability (6) satisfies (7). Equation (8) holds for two crisp independent events, and it is also valid when one of the sets is μ_1. (Recall that in classical probability theory, Ω is independent of any event.)

We analyze the case that $X = [a, b] \subset \mathbb{R}$. For $\sigma \in [0, 1]^X$ such that $P(\sigma) \neq 0$, we use the measure P defined at (4) and consider

$$P(\mu|\sigma) = \frac{P(\mu \cdot \sigma)}{P(\sigma)} = \frac{\int_a^b T(\mu(x), \sigma(x))\, dx}{(b - a)P(\sigma)}. \tag{9}$$

In order for (9) to satisfy $P(\sigma|\sigma) = 1$, we again set T to min. In this case, two fuzzy events are said to be independent if

$$\frac{1}{b - a} \int_a^b \min\{\mu(x), \sigma(x)\}\, dx = \left(\frac{1}{b - a} \int_a^b \mu(x)\, dx\right) \left(\frac{1}{b - a} \int_a^b \sigma(x)\, dx\right). \tag{10}$$

There actually exist many pairs of strictly fuzzy (non-crisp) events that satisfy our definition of independence [(8) for the discrete case and (10) for the continuous case]. For instance, $\mu := .75/1 + .75/2 + .25/3 + .25/4$ and $\sigma := .25/1 + .25/2 + .75/3 + .75/4$ are independent according to (8). However, we must thoroughly examine whether our definition (or any other definition of fuzzy independence) makes sense theoretically or practically, and we will do so in our future studies.

6   Fuzzy-Fuzzy Probability: Fuzzy Numbers as Probabilities

In this section we present a tentative discussion on fuzzy numbers as probabilities. We will not present a definitive approach to formulating a rigorous theory for this type of probability. However, we will address issues that appear essential in establishing a theoretical foundation for the concept, and we will describe a possible framework (albeit it has yet to be fully developed) for the formulation of fuzzy probability theory.

Zadeh [14] introduced the idea of using fuzzy numbers to represent probabilities that are derived from imprecise, incomplete, or unreliable sources. We will call these fuzzy numbers "fuzzy-fuzzy probabilities". Jauin and Agogino [6], Dunyak and Wunsch [4], and Halliwell and Shen [5] also presented models of fuzzy-fuzzy probability.

Zadeh's concept of fuzzy-fuzzy probability is as follows. Let X denote a finite universe of discourse $\{x_1, x_2, \ldots, x_n\}$. For each fuzzy set $\mu \in [0,1]^X$, sort the numbers $\mu(x_1), \mu(x_2), \ldots, \mu(x_n)$ in descending order. Without loss of generality, assume that $\mu(x_1) \geq \mu(x_2) \geq \cdots \geq \mu(x_n)$. The fuzzy cardinality $|\mu|_F$ of μ is given by

$$|\mu|_F(i) := \min\{\mu(x_1), \mu(x_2), \ldots, \mu(x_i)\}, \quad 1 \leq i \leq n$$

(thus $|\mu|_F$ is a mapping from $\{1, 2, \ldots, n\}$ to $[0,1]$). Zadeh defines a "fuzzy probability measure" $FP(\mu)$ of μ by the fuzzy number $FP(\mu) := \frac{|\mu|_F}{|X|} = \frac{|\mu|_F}{n}$. For instance, if $X = \{a, b, c, d\}$ and $\mu = 1/a + .8/b + .3/c + .2/d$, then $|\mu|_F = 1/1 + .8/2 + .3/3 + .2/4$, and $FP(\mu) = 1/.25 + .8/.5 + .3/.75 + .2/1$.

Thus for some L and NF satisfying $\{0,1\}^X \neq L \subset [0,1]^X$ and $\{0,1\}^{[0,1]} \subsetneq NF \subset [0,1]^{[0,1]}$, FP is a mapping from L to NF. Can fuzzy-fuzzy probability be considered a form of probability? The answer is clearly no in classical probability theory, where probabilities must be real numbers between 0 and 1 by definition. For this reason, it is probably inappropriate to describe FP as a probability measure, which in classical probability theory is defined as a real-valued set function (see Section 2). Therefore, it seems appropriate to distinguish FP from classical probability measures and to call it, for example, "Zadeh's measure". However, we may be able to extend conventional real-valued probabilities to include "fuzzy-valued" probabilities in a theoretically satisfactory manner.

In order for FP to be considered such an extended probability measure, we must be able to construct an arithmetical structure $(NF, \otimes, \oplus, \ominus, \odot, \leq^*)$ with a unit element $\mathbf{1}$ (this should be the maximum element in NF) and a neutral element $\mathbf{0}$ (this should be the minimum element in NF) so that FP satisfies the three axioms of probability with respect to the operations composing the structure:

(a) $FP(\mu) \geq \mathbf{0} \ \forall \ \mu \in L$.
(b) $FP(\mu_1) = \mathbf{1}$.
(c) If $\{\mu_i | \mu_i \in L\}$ is a countable set so that $\mu_i \cdot \mu_j = \mu_0$ for $i \neq j$, then
$FP(\mu_1 + \mu_2 + \cdots + \mu_n) = FP(\mu_1) \oplus FP(\mu_2) \oplus \cdots \oplus FP(\mu_n)$.

The operations $\otimes, \oplus, \ominus, \odot$ and the relation $\leq^*$ must be carefully specified so that the outcomes of the operations and the ordering resulting from $\leq^*$ are justifiable theoretically or practically. In addition to (a)–(c), we should check whether FP also satisfies the following properties:

(6.1) $FP(\mu') = \mathbf{1} \ominus FP(\mu)$.

(6.2) If $\mu \leq \sigma$, then $FP(\mu) \leq FP(\sigma)$.

(6.3) When restricted to $\{0,1\}^X$, FP takes on elements in $\{0,1\}^{[0,1]}$.

(6.4) For $\sigma \in NF$, $FP(\sigma) \neq \mathbf{0}$, we have a conditional probability $FP(\mu|\sigma) := FP(\mu \cdot \sigma) \odot FP(\sigma)$ with which the independence of μ and σ can be defined by $FP(\mu|\sigma) = FP(\mu)$ or by $FP(\mu \cdot \sigma) = FP(\mu) \otimes FP(\sigma)$.

Regarding (6.1)–(6.2), note that the corresponding properties in classical probability theory follow from the three axioms of probability, but they may not follow from (a)–(c) in $(NF, \otimes, \oplus, \ominus, \odot, \leq^*)$.

Unfortunately, the four existing models of fuzzy-fuzzy probability proposed by [4], [5], [6], and [14] fail to satisfy some of these properties. For instance, using an axiom, Halliwel and Shen [5] ensure only finite subadditivity: If $\mu \cdot \sigma = \mu_0$, then $FP(\mu + \sigma) \leq^* FP(\mu) \oplus FP(\sigma)$. The identity $FP(\mu') = 1 \ominus FP(\mu)$ does not always hold for Zadeh's model [14]. However, consider

$$(\mu \oplus \sigma)(t) := \sup_{t=x+y} \min\{\mu(x), \sigma(y)\}.$$

In words, we add fuzzy numbers according to the extension principle in fuzzy arithmetic. Then Zadeh's model achieves the identity

$$FP(\mu + \sigma) \oplus FP(\mu \cdot \sigma) = FP(\mu) + FP(\sigma).$$

To date, no studies have carefully examined the concept of conditioning or independence for fuzzy-fuzzy probability. The existing models assume that X is finite, and fuzzy-fuzzy probability has yet to be developed in cases where X is countably or uncountably infinite. It is also important to carefully establish the operations $\otimes$, $\oplus$, $\ominus$, $\odot$, and $\leq^*$. They may not be universal (different cases may require different sets of these operations), and we should be able to provide justification for using a particular set of them. The effectiveness of these operations will also depend on what type of fuzzy sets are used in deriving fuzzy-fuzzy probabilities. Therefore, to fully establish a mathematically rigorous foundation for fuzzy-fuzzy probabilities, we must properly design various components of fuzzy systems.

7 Discussion

We have reviewed various forms of probability and probabilistic concepts in fuzzy logic and examined several issues associated with them. Theoretical foundations of fuzzy-crisp or fuzzy-fuzzy probability have yet to be fully established. In particular, the concept of fuzzy-fuzzy probability lacks analytical rigor, and it must be further examined theoretically. We should investigate whether it is possible to properly extend fundamental principles or properties of classical probability theory to fuzzy-fuzzy probability. It is desirable to reinforce the extension principle for fuzzy-fuzzy probability, as we do in extending classical set theory to fuzzy set theory—if we replace fuzzy sets with crisp ones, we must be able to obtain existing results in conventional set theory.

Regarding fuzzy-crisp probability, we should keep in mind that there are other measures of uncertainty for fuzzy events. For instance, Sugeno's λ-measures [9] hold for the algebra $([0,1]^X, W, W^*, 1 - id)$, although they were originally introduced in order to deal with boolean algebras. The value of $\lambda \in (-1, \infty)$ determines the additivity of the measures; they can be sub-additive, super-additive, or additive, and they may not have any of these properties. They have been useful in certain applications [7].

We are currently examining how to establish $(NF, \otimes, \oplus, \ominus, \odot, \leq^*)$, which will form a framework for handling fuzzy numbers as probabilities. We also intend to extend Zadeh's fuzzy-fuzzy probability to cases where the universe of discourse is not finite. Many theoretical issues remain to be resolved in order to develop a rigorous axiomatic theory of probability in fuzzy logic, and we hope that our paper can serve to stimulate studies of fuzzy probability theory.

References

1. Billingsley, P.: Probability and Measure, 3rd edn. Wiley Interscience, New York (1995)
2. Bodiou, G.: Théorie Dialectique des Probabilités (englobant leurs calculs classique et quantique). Gauthier-Villars, Paris (1965)
3. Chung, K.L.: A Course in Probability Theory, 3rd edn. Academic Press, London (2001)
4. Dunyak, J.P., Wunsch, D.: Fuzzy probability for system reliability. In: Proceedings of the 37th IEEE Conference on Decision & Control, vol. 3, pp. 2934–2935 (1998)
5. Halliwell, J., Shen, Q.: Linguistic probabilities: Theory and applications. Soft Computing 13, 169–183 (2009)
6. Jauin, P., Agogino, A.M.: Stochastic sensitive analysis using fuzzy inference diagrams. In: Schachter, M. (ed.) Uncertainty in Artificial Intelligence, pp. 79–92. North-Holland, Amsterdam (1990)
7. Nguyen, H.T., Prasad, N.R. (eds.): Fuzzy Modeling and Control: Selected Works of M. Sugeno. CRC Press, Boca Raton (2000)
8. Ross, S.: A First Course in Probability, 6th edn. Prentice Hall, Upper Saddle River (2002)
9. Sugeno, M.: Fuzzy measures and fuzzy integrals: A survey. In: Fuzzy Automata and Decision Process, pp. 89–102. North-Holland, Amsterdam (1977)
10. Trillas, E., Alsina, C., Pradera, A.: On a class of fuzzy set theories. pp. 1–5 (2007)
11. Zadeh, L.A.: Fuzzy sets. Information and Control 8, 338–353 (1965)
12. Zadeh, L.A.: Probability measures of fuzzy events. Journal of Mathematical Analysis and Applications 23(2), 421–427 (1968)
13. Zadeh, L.A.: Outline of a new approach to the analysis of complex systems and decision processes. IEEE Transactions on Systems, Man and Cybernetics SMC-3, 28–44 (1973)
14. Zadeh, L.A.: Fuzzy probabilities. Information Processing and Management 20(3), 363–372 (1984)

On Dealing with Imprecise Information
in a Content Based Image Retrieval System

Tatiana Jaworska[1], Janusz Kacprzyk[1],
Nicolas Marín[2], and Sławomir Zadrożny[1,3]

[1] Systems Research Institute
Polish Academy of Sciences
ul. Newelska 6, 01-447 Warszawa, Poland
{jaworska,kacprzyk,zadrozny}@ibspan.waw.pl
[2] Department of Computer Science and A.I.
University of Granada
18071 Granada, Spain
nicm@decsai.ugr.es
[3] Warsaw School of Information Technology
ul. Newelska 6, 01-447 Warszawa, Poland
zadrozny@wit.edu.pl

Abstract. In the paper a content-based image retrieval system (CBIR) is considered. We discuss some aspects of image representation and their retrieval when imprecision plays an important role. The sources of imprecision are identified and some ways of dealing with it are proposed. The discussion is illustrated with an example of our pilot implementation of such a CBIR system.

Keywords: Content-based image retrieval, CBIR, imprecision, querying, image comparison, fuzzy logic.

1 Introduction

Content-based image retrieval (CBIR) gains importance due to rapidly growing multimedia collections, notably on the Internet. There are many commercial applications for this technique. However, images exhibit a very complex structure and their advanced automatic processing is difficult. Retrieval in CBIR systems may be seen as inherently fuzzy because of imperfection in the image feature definition, imperfection in query formulation, imperfection in the index structure, etc. [3].

Thus, effective and efficient processing of images requires tools and techniques to deal with a general problem of imperfect information. One of the promising lines of research in this area is based on fuzzy set theory and further efforts to built upon it the computational theory of perceptions [20]. For more information on this topic in the field of image processing, cf. Yager and Petry [19], Prados-Suárez et al. [18] or Chamorro-Martínez et al. [4].

During the last decade some extensions of data models have been proposed in order to allow for the representation and processing of imperfect information.

E. Hüllermeier, R. Kruse, and F. Hoffmann (Eds.): IPMU 2010, LNAI 6178, pp. 149–158, 2010.

Some approaches also concern the CBIR systems [7], [9], [16], [17], or multimedia systems in general – [8].

One of the most challenging tasks consists in grasping the semantic content of an image. Among the most successful attempts the work of Candan and Li [3] should be mentioned. They developed the SEMCOG query processor for retrieving images taking into account their semantic and spatial imperfection.

In this paper we focus on the identification of the sources of imperfect (imprecise) information in a class of the CBIR systems. This imperfection is related to the very representation of images, as discussed above, as well as to the user's preferences expressed directly with the use of natural language elements or, what is more practical, indirectly in the features of an image composed using the query-by-example paradigm.

Images are assumed to be represented by collections of objects extracted from them. These objects are characterized by some low-level visual features and they are assigned to semantically meaningful classes by an automatic procedure. These objects are further characterized by their spatial relationships, which play an important role in determining the matching between the images.

The content of the paper is the following. Section 2 describes various features used to represent images and identifies the imprecision related with the values of these features. Section 3 discusses how to match images while taking into account the imprecision related to their representation.

Our approach is essentially general, but some of its aspects are motivated by a particular CBIR system, whose pilot version has been implemented by Jaworska [11,12]. This system is meant for a specific domain and is customized for the representation of house images. We use its screenshots to illustrate our discussion.

2 Representation of Images in the Database and in the Queries

2.1 The Types of the Features

For an effective and efficient content based retrieval, images have to be represented in a rich format combining purely graphical, structural and semantic features. These features are:

- visual properties of the whole image and of the objects extracted from it (e.g., color, texture, etc.) ,
- spatial or temporal relationships of the above-mentioned objects (the latter relationships are relevant in case of the video data), and the structure of the whole image built upon a set of the objects,
- semantic properties, here corresponding mainly to the classes assigned to the above-mentioned objects, which can also include textual metadata (annotations), which are not considered in this paper, however.

are recorded in a database. Now, we will briefly discuss particular features and possible imprecision of their values. As in our CBIR system queries also take primarily the form of images, then all these considerations apply to them as well. Other forms of queries are discussed too, where appropriate.

In our approach, the objects are extracted from an image using the algorithm presented in detail in [11]. Each object is characterized by some low-level features such as: average color k_{av}, texture parameters T_p, area A, convex area A_c, filled area A_f, centroid $\{x_c, y_c\}$, eccentricity e, orientation a, moments of inertia m_{11}, bounding box $\{b_1(x, y), \ldots, b_w(x, y)\}$ (w number of vertices), major axis length m_{long}, minor axis length m_{short}, solidity s and Euler number E. Some of these features are determined in an obvious way, while the derivation of others is more complex. For example, the average color k_{av} is a triple, computed as the average values of the red, green and blue components intensity over all the pixels of an object. Another complex feature, the texture T_p, is determined using the wavelet transforms.

Thus, at the level of visual properties representation, each object o extracted from an image is represented by a vector $o = [o(k_{av}), o(T_p), o(A), \ldots, o(E)]$. These features are presented in the example window of the interface for a selected object in Fig. 1. Each object is assigned an identifier (a key) and is stored in a separate row of the database.

From the structural point of view, in the simplest approach, an image is treated as a set of objects. A more sophisticated structure may be imposed, e.g. a hierarchy of objects, which is built using a containment relation, and may be exemplified by an object representing the roof containing two other objects representing dormers. For image comparison still other representations may be useful. An image may be treated as a multiset of objects classes, without distinguishing them individually. For example, it may be important to observe that two images of houses contain the same number of objects of a given class, e.g. representing windows, without referring to their individual properties.

For a more advanced comparison of images it may be important to take into account spatial relationships between the objects extracted from each of them. Basically, spatial relationships between objects may be represented by modeling topological relationships or orientation relationships; cf., e.g., [21]. We adopt the latter approach which seems to be more practical for the CBIR systems and, even in its simplest form, is satisfactory for our purposes, in particular for the application domain considered. The way the relative location of particular objects is represented may be best described by the following example.

Let us consider Image 1 in Fig. 2, where object o_2 (a door) is to the left (westward) of object o_3 (a window), which in turn is to the left and below (southwestward) of the object o_4 (a dormer). For four objects extracted from Image 1 in Fig. 2 a matrix of the relative locations is obtained, as shown in Table 1. The information on spatial relationships of the objects is a global feature of the whole image and is stored in the database during the image indexing phase.

Semantic information concerning particular images takes the form of the class assigned to each object extracted from an image. The actual list of the classes under consideration depends on the application domain. In case of our pilot implementation, meant for a real-estate agency, the objects are classified as doors,

Fig. 1. Example of a real graphical object comparison: the extraction and classification of objects (here: window frames) helps to match two images despite the distortion of the low-level visual features

Table 1. Relative locations of the objects extracted from Image 1 in Fig. 2 are as follows: W in a cell means that the object represented by a given column is to the west of an object represented by a given row; similarly for E - to the east, S - to the south, N - to the north, and their combinations, e.g. N-E meaning to the north-east.

	o_1	o_2	o_3	o_4
o_1		S	S-E	E
o_2	N		E	N-E
o_3	S-W	E		S
o_4	W	S-W	S-W	

windows, etc. The classification of the objects is based on a *pattern library* [13]. For each class of objects this library contains a pattern (or a set of patterns) representing a given class in terms of the values of particular low-level image features mentioned above. In our pilot implementation these patterns were constructed

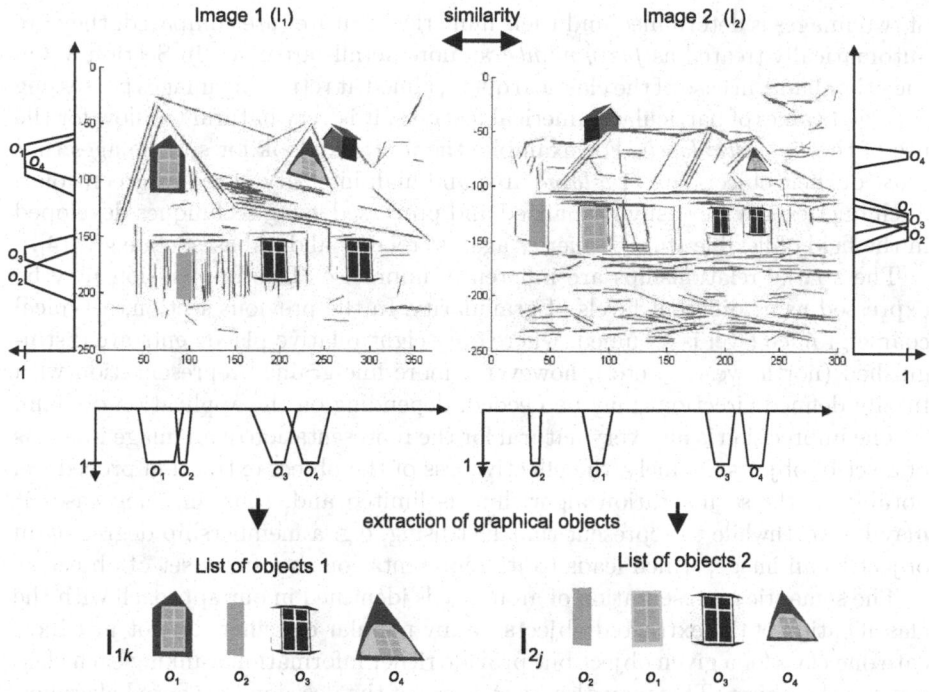

Fig. 2. General scheme of similarity determination between two images compared as two collections of objects. At the bottom, the objects extracted from both images are listed and labeled. The trapezoidal membership functions illustrate the tolerance on the location of the objects' centroids assumed, separately for each coordinate.

in a semi-automatic way. First, a training collection of objects has been manually assigned classes. Then, a decision tree has been created using the MATLAB built-in algorithm. Finally, the resulting tree has been manually tuned, using expert knowledge.

2.2 Imprecision in the Image Representation

All three types of the features mentioned above, i.e. low-level visual features, spatial relationships and structural aspects, as well as semantic features are often difficult to represent in a precise, non-ambiguous way. This imperfection requires special means for the representation and processing of such data, notably during the matching of an image against a query. Due to the complex form of the images and the required rich representation format, various data types are used, admitting various forms of imperfection. In what follows, we briefly discuss the main cases.

The low-level features allow, first of all, for numerical values. In the database they are stored as such. However, obviously some numerical features such as, e.g. the coordinates of the centroid, are inherently imprecise. Thus, when the matching of two images is determined and their numerical features are compared, they are automatically treated as *fuzzy numbers*; more details are given in Section 3. On the other hand, in case of the classical query, aimed at retrieving images possessing specified values of particular numerical features, it is very natural to allow for the use of the *linguistic labels*. For example, the user may look for such images that *most* of their objects are of *a large* area and high intensity of red or green color. Such queries may be easily formalized and processed using techniques developed in the field of flexible (fuzzy) queries against relational databases; cf., e.g., [14].

The spatial relationships are inherently imprecise. This imprecision may be expressed using different levels of granularity. In the previous section, a typical coarse-grained level is assumed, where only eight relative placements are distinguished (north, west,... etc.), however a more fine-grained representation with fuzzily defined directions may be needed, depending on the application domain.

The imprecision is also very natural for the representation of an image in terms of a set of objects. Namely, the effectiveness of the object extraction procedure, notably of the segmentation algorithm, is limited and, thus, in some cases it may be worthwhile to represent that fact using, e.g. a membership degree of an object to an image, which leads to its representation as a fuzzy set of objects.

The semantic representation of an image is identified in our approach with the classification of the extracted objects. Many popular classifiers do not just indicate one class for a given object but provide richer information, ranking each class against the object. This may also be the case of the decision tree based classifier, if there are leaves with a non-zero impurity degree. Thus, some uncertainty is usually related to the output of the classifier and this may be expressed by, e.g. assigning to an object a fuzzy set of classes instead of just one class. This fuzzy set membership function would have the possibilistic, disjunctive interpretation. This should be, of course, reflected in the query matching algorithm (cf. Section 3) as well as in the structural representation of an image as then particular objects may be interpreted as belonging simultaneously to different classes.

3   Matching Images against a Query

The primary way of querying in our CBIR system is via the *graphical query by example* (QBE) interface. The user expresses his or her preferences constructing an image and the system searches the database to find similar images. More advanced users and users with specific preferences may execute a standard query specifying their requirements in terms of the required values of the image features. The features referred to may be of a global character (e.g., concerning an average color intensities in the whole image or its histogram characteristic) or may concern particular objects extracted from an image.

We will now discuss how the imprecision related to different types of features is taken into account while the matching between a query and an image is determined.

First, let us briefly discuss the standard queries where the image sought is characterized by the values of its selected low-level visual features. As mentioned earlier, the techniques developed in the field of flexible (fuzzy) queries against relational databases (cf., e.g., [14]) are here directly applicable. The main idea is to allow queries using linguistic terms instead of numbers to express query conditions. These linguistic terms may be exemplified by:

- the labels of fuzzy numbers, such as "high", "low", etc.,
- fuzzy comparators, such as "much greater than", "more or less equal", etc.,
- linguistic quantifiers, such as "most", "almost all" etc.

The latter class of linguistic terms is especially interesting. They may be used in a query to replace the standard logical connectives of conjunction and disjunction linking query conditions, with the aim to make the aggregation of these conditions more flexible. Namely, instead of requiring an image to satisfy all (conjunction) or just one (disjunction) condition, the user may require that *most* of them are satisfied. The linguistic quantifiers are also very useful in the CBIR systems in a different way, taking into account the representation of an image as a set/multi-set of objects, which is discussed later on.

Imprecision inherent to the values of low-level visual features should be taken into account in a different way when comparing two images, in particular when one of them is composed by the user and represents his or her query. In such a case a comparison of the absolute values of these low-level features is, in general, not reasonable. However, in some scenarios it makes sense: when images are carefully selected and scaled, or when one of the images is manually composed by the user from the objects extracted from the images collected in a database. This latter case is, in particular, assumed in our pilot implementation of the CBIR system for house images. Then, when matching images it is reasonable to compare their feature absolute values. However, it may be advantageous to assume some tolerance for these value differences. For example, it may be reasonable to treat two doors as identical from the point of view of the area feature even if their values differ by, e.g. 10%. Similarly, if the centroids of two objects are taken into account, a slight misplacement should be neglected. Thus, during the matching, the values of these attributes are "fuzzified" and represented by trapezoidal fuzzy numbers. This is illustrated for the centroid feature in Fig. 2, where both coordinates of the centroid are represented by an individual fuzzy number. The actual shape of its membership function depends on the other features of a given object. In case of the centroid feature, the tolerance introduced by the fuzzy number is relative to its size, in particular to the values of the major and minor axes lengths: the higher/wider the object, the higher the tolerance. Then, the values of the low-level features "fuzzified" in such a way are compared using some techniques; cf. [6].

The comparison of low-level feature values determines the similarity between objects belonging to two images under comparison. However, the most important criterion in this comparison is the class assigned to the given objects. If a unique class is assigned to an object, then the result of a comparison is trivially based on the equality relation. If uncertainty in the class assignment is allowed, then some more sophisticated measures are needed. In particular, these assignments may be treated as fuzzy sets and compared using one of the many methods discussed in the literature, cf., e.g. [6]. On the other hand, they may be treated as genuine possibility distributions and compared using, e.g. the approach proposed by Bosc et al. [2]. The results of the comparison of all low-level features are aggregated to yield an overall similarity degree between pairs of objects belonging to the images being compared.

While the whole images are also compared using their global low-level features, the most important is the match between sets/multisets of the objects extracted from them. Thus, we have two sets/multisets, which have to be compared, and additionally a similarity degree between them, computed using their low-level visual features and their class assignments. For such a setting, Hallez et al. [10] have proposed recently a number of indices of similarity, which are thus readily applicable for our CBIR system. On the other hand, the hierarchical structure of some objects makes applicable the methods elaborated by, e.g. Marín et al. [15] and Berzal et al. [1]. See also Chow et al. [5] who proposed a tree-structured image representation in which a root node contains the global features, while the child nodes contain the local region-based ones. This approach hierarchically integrates information on image contents to attain a better retrieval accuracy than the global and regional attributes, individually compared.

Finally, the spatial relationships between objects should be taken into account when deciding on the match between images. Candan and Li [3] analyzed description of the objects' mutual relationships based on different fuzzy operators. In our system [13] spatial relationships of the objects in an image are also used as a global feature; cf. Section 2. Thus, the matching of images is based on the similarities of objects and their spatial relationships. The query image is represented as a vector $Q = \{F_{g_q}, o_{q_1}, \ldots, o_{q_N}\}$, gathering global features of the image F_{g_q} and object feature vectors o_{q_k}, for all objects extracted from the image. For matching the spatial relationships of the objects (cf. Table 1) in two compared images first of all a pairing between the objects is established. This is done during the comparison of whole collections of objects representing both images, when for each object in one image the most similar object in another image is determined. Then, the matrices representing spatial relationships (cf. Table 1) are appropriately arranged so that the rows in the matrix corresponding to a particular image represent the objects paired with the objects represented by the same row in the matrix corresponding to another image. Finally, the cells of two matrices are compared against each other. In the simplest case, the result of the comparison is binary, but it may be worthwhile to adopt a more flexible approach to the comparison by, e.g. declaring the compatibility (matching) between the matrices (to a degree) when most of the cells are identical. In case a more fine-grained representation of spatial relationships is used (cf. Section 2), the need for a more flexible comparison is more evident.

For an in-depth discussion of various related issues, cf. Marín et al. [15].

In order to address some special practical cases the matching procedure should be made even more flexible, concerning both the comparison of the sets of objects and their spatial relationships. For example, if one image matched against another one is a half of it, then the comparison should be based on the inclusion between sets of objects rather than on their identity or similarity. In this case we are able to match the objects location table to a fragment of it. It is worth noticing that then the matrices representing the spatial relationships of the objects in both images, limited only to the paired objects, should still match.

4   Conclusions

In the paper we discuss the sources of imprecision and propose some ways to deal with them in a content-based image retrieval system. The following sources of imprecision have been identified:

- user-defined criteria regarding the values of low-level visual image features while querying the system,
- a need for tolerance when comparing low-level features of two images to be matched against each other,
- the definition of spatial relationships between objects,
- an automatic classification of objects to the predefined semantically meaningful classes.

We have proposed some ways to deal with these kinds of imprecision, mainly via a novel use of some known techniques.

We have also briefly described our pilot implementation of a CBIR system. Further research will focus on an experimental verification of the practical usefulness and effectiveness of the proposed imprecision modeling.

References

1. Berzal, F., Cubero, J.C., Kacprzyk, J., Marín, N., Vila, M.A., Zadrożny, S.: A general framework for computing with words in object-oriented programming. International Journal of Uncertainty, Fuzziness and Knowledge-Based Systems 15(suppl.), 111–131 (2007)
2. Bosc, P., Duval, L., Pivert, O.: Value-based and representation-based querying of possibilistic databases. In: Bordogna, G., Pasi, G. (eds.) Recent Issues on Fuzzy Databases, pp. 3–27. Physica-Verlag, Heidelberg (2000)
3. Candan, K.S., Li, W.S.: On similsrity measures for multimedia database applications. Knowledge and Imformation Systems 3, 30–51 (2001)
4. Chamorro-Martnez, J., Snchez, D., Soto-Hidalgo, J.: A novel histogram definition for fuzzy color spaces. In: IEEE International Conference on Fuzzy Systems, Hong Kong, China, June 2008, pp. 2149–2156 (2008)
5. Chow, T., Rahman, M., Wu, S.: Content-based image retrieval by using tree-structure features and multi-layer self-organizing map. Pattern Analysis and Applications 9(1), 1–20 (2006)
6. Cross, V., Sudkamp, T.: Similarity and Compatibility in Fuzzy Set Theory. Studies in Fuzziness and Soft Computing, vol. 93. Physica–Verlag/Springer, Heidelberg/New York (2002)
7. Deb, S.: Multimedia Systems and Content-Based Image Retrieval. IDEA Group Publishing, Melbourne (2004)

8. Dubois, D., Prade, H., Sedes, F.: Fuzzy logic techniques in multimedia database querying: A preliminary investigation of the potentials. IEEE Trans. Knowl. Data Eng. 13(3), 383–392 (2001)
9. Flickner, M., Sawhney, H., et al.: Query by image and video content: The QBIC system. IEEE Computer 28(9), 23–32 (1995)
10. Hallez, A., Bronselaer, A., De Tré, G.: Comparison of sets and multisets. International Journal of Uncertainty, Fuzziness and Knowledge-Based Systems 17(suppl. 1), 153–172 (2009)
11. Jaworska, T.: Object extraction as a basic process for content-based image retrieval (CBIR) system. Opto-Electronics Review 15, 184–195 (2007)
12. Jaworska, T.: The inner structure of database for the CBIR system. In: Mohammadian, M. (ed.) Proceedings of International Conference on Computational Intelligence for Modelling, Control and Automation - CIMCA '08, Vienna, pp. 30–36 (2008)
13. Jaworska, T.: Multi-criteria object indexing and graphical user query as an aspect of content-based image retrieval system. In: Borzemski, L., Grzech, A. (eds.) Information Systems Architecture and Technology, pp. 103–112. Wyd. Pol. Wroclawskiej, Wroclaw (2009)
14. Kacprzyk, J., Zadrożny, S.: Computing with words in intelligent database querying: standalone and internet-based applications. Information Sciences 134(1-4), 71–109 (2001)
15. Marín, N., Medina, J.M., Pons, O., Sánchez, D., Miranda, M.A.V.: Complex object comparison in a fuzzy context. Information & Software Technology 45(7), 431–444 (2003)
16. Niblack, W., Flickner, M., et al.: The QBIC project: Query image by content using colour, texture and shape. In: SPIE, vol. 1908, pp. 173–187 (1993)
17. Ogle, V., Stonebraker, M.: Chabot: Retrieval from relational database of images. IEEE Computer 28(9), 40–48 (1995)
18. Prados-Suárez, B., Chamorro-Martínez, J., Sánchez, D., Abad, J.: Region-based fit of color homogeneity measures for fuzzy image segmentation. Fuzzy Sets Syst. 158(3), 215–229 (2007)
19. Yager, R., Petry, F.: A framework for linguistic relevance feedback in content-based image retrieval using fuzzy logic. Information Sciences 173(4), 337–352 (2005)
20. Zadeh, L.A., Kacprzyk, J. (eds.): Computing with Words in Information/Intelligent Systems. Foundations. Applications. Studies in Fuzziness and Soft Computing, vol. 1, vol. 2, vol. 33. Physica–Verlag/Springer–Verlag, Heidelberg/New York (1999)
21. Zhou, X.M., Ang, C.H., Ling, T.W.: Image retrieval based on object's orientation spatial relationship. Pattern Recogn. Lett. 22(5), 469–477 (2001)

An Extension of Stochastic Dominance
to Fuzzy Random Variables

Farid Aiche[1] and Didier Dubois[2]

[1] Université de Tizi-ouzou
[2] IRIT-CNRS, Toulouse

Abstract. This paper proposes a joint extension of interval comparison
and random variable comparison methods to the ranking of fuzzy random
variables. First, an extension of stochastic dominance to random intervals
is proposed. It enables to retrieve some previous ranking methods for
belief functions and for fuzzy intervals. On this basis, a direct extension
of stochastic dominance to fuzzy random variables is proposed. This
approach is just one among various possibilities obtained by combining
fuzzy interval and random variable comparison methods.

1 Introduction

Quite often, we are faced with the situation where the values of random variables
are not completely known. When random variables take values that are fuzzy
intervals, it leads to the concept of fuzzy random variables, first introduced
by Kwakernaak [13]. Later, other authors like Kruse and Meyer [12], Puri and
Ralescu [15], among others studied this concept. Puri and Ralescu consider a
fuzzy random variable as a classical one taking values on a metric space of
membership functions. On the contrary, Kwakernaak and Kruse consider a fuzzy
random variable to represent uncertainty about a standard random variable,
i.e. a fuzzy set of random variables. This is the view adopted here. Recently,
Couso and Dubois [4] proposed yet another interpretation of this concept (as a
conditional possibility measure dominating a set of conditional probabilities).

It is of interest to define an extension of stochastic dominance to fuzzy random
variables that would combine dominance between random variable and comparison of fuzzy intervals. The problem of extending the natural ordering of the real
line to fuzzy intervals has produced a large and scattered literature. Wang and
Kerre [17] tried to compare the various methods via the definition of properties
that comparison indices should satisfy. Another point of view consists in noticing
that a fuzzy interval being a generalization of an interval, as well as a special
case of a random set [10], rank-ordering methods for fuzzy intervals should be
somewhat related to interval comparisons as well and dominance indices between
random variables. From this point of view, the comparison of fuzzy and random
variables could be cast into a unified setting.

In this paper, we propose a direct extension of stochastic dominance to fuzzy
random variables whose values are fuzzy intervals of the $L - R$ type. Comparing

E. Hüllermeier, R. Kruse, and F. Hoffmann (Eds.): IPMU 2010, LNAI 6178, pp. 159–168, 2010.

upper and/or lower bounds of intervals of the real line, we first define a direct extension of stochastic dominance to random intervals. We also calculate the probability that a random interval is greater than another in the sense of prescribed relations between intervals. Thereafter, based on these extensions and the valued relations between $L - R$ fuzzy intervals defined by Chanas et al. [1,2], we propose a direct extension of stochastic interval dominance to fuzzy random variables of type $L - R$.

2   Comparison of Random Variables

Let $(\Omega, \mathcal{F}, P)$ be probability space where Ω is a set, $\mathcal{F}$ an algebra of measurable subsets and P a probability measure. The concept of first order stochastic dominance consists in comparing the probability distributions of two random variables a and b as follows: a is said to stochastically dominate b if $F_a(x) = P(\{\omega : a(\omega) \le x\}) \le F_b(x) = P(\{\omega : b(\omega) \le x\}), \forall x \in \mathbb{R}$, where F_a and F_b are the cumulative distribution functions of the random variables a and b respectively. Its importance in decision theory is known. In particular, a random variable a stochastically dominates another random variable b (denoted by $a >^{s.d} b$) if and only if for any increasing function $f : \mathbb{R} \longrightarrow \mathbb{R}$ (a utility function, typically), the expectation of $f(a)$ is greater than the expectation of $f(b)$ (see Chateauneuf et al. [3]). For an early review of stochastic orderings in this vein see Mosler and Scarsini [14].

Apart from stochastic dominance, one can measure the probability that a random variable a is greater than another one b, as $P(a > b) = P(\{(\omega, \omega') : a(\omega) > b(\omega')\})$. One of the two following opposite assumptions is often made:

 - independent random variables with continuous distribution functions p_a and p_b: then $P(a > b) = \int_{x>y} p_a(x)p_b(y)dxdy$.
 - comonotone random variables with a functional link of the form $\omega = \omega'$: then $P(a > b) = P(\{\omega : a(\omega) > b(\omega)\})$.

Then define $a >^P_\alpha b \iff P(a > b) > \alpha$. For $\alpha = 0.5$ one obtain the relation $>^P$: $a >^P b \iff P(a > b) > P(b > a)$ provided that $P(a = b) = 0$ (continuous distributions). Let us note that the relation $>^P$ can have cycles (this is the Condorcet effect). One can eliminate cycles of prescribed length by choosing α sufficiently high (see De Baets et al. [5]). Besides, it is clear that in the case of co-monotonic functional dependence, $P(a > b) = 1$ is generally equivalent to stochastic dominance of a over b.

3   Ranking Real Intervals

Let $A = [\underline{a}, \overline{a}]$ and $B = [\underline{b}, \overline{b}]$ be two real intervals. For ranking them, we have four relations $>_i, i = 1, 2, 3, 4$, defined in [7] as follows:

$$[\underline{a}, \overline{a}] >_1 [\underline{b}, \overline{b}] \Leftrightarrow \underline{a} > \overline{b}; [\underline{a}, \overline{a}] >_2 [\underline{b}, \overline{b}] \Leftrightarrow \underline{a} > \underline{b};$$

$$[\underline{a}, \overline{a}] >_3 [\underline{b}, \overline{b}] \Leftrightarrow \overline{a} > \overline{b}; [\underline{a}, \overline{a}] >_4 [\underline{b}, \overline{b}] \Leftrightarrow \overline{a} > \underline{b}.$$

The relation $>_1$ is the strongest, $>_4$ is the weakest, $>_2$ et $>_3$ are intermediary. Hence the following implications:

$$A >_1 B \Rightarrow A >_2 B \Rightarrow A >_4 B; A >_1 B \Rightarrow A >_3 B \Rightarrow A >_4 B \qquad (1)$$

These relations are known in the literature:

- $A >_1 B \Leftrightarrow \neg(B \geq_4 A)$. The relation $>_1$ is an interval order (Fishburn [11]). In the case of independence between random variables a and b, $P(a > b) = 1$ is generally equivalent to $Support(a) >_1 Support(b)$.
- The simultaneous use of $\geq_2$ and $\geq_3$: $A \succeq B$ if and only if $A \geq_2 B$ and $A \geq_3 B$. This is the canonical order induced by the lattice structure of intervals, equipped with the operations max and min extended to intervals : $A \succeq B \Leftrightarrow \max([\underline{a}, \overline{a}], [\underline{b}, \overline{b}]) = [\underline{a}, \overline{a}] \Longleftrightarrow \min([\underline{a}, \overline{a}], [\underline{b}, \overline{b}]) = [\underline{b}, \overline{b}]$ (we call it *lattice interval* order).

Finally, one way of comparing intervals consists in choosing a number in each interval and to compare these numbers. The selection of representatives of the intervals can be based on some pessimism index $\alpha \in [0, 1]$ reflecting the attitude of a decision-maker. This is the well-known Hurwicz criterion, such that if $A = [\underline{a}, \overline{a}], B = [\underline{b}, \overline{b}], A \succeq_\alpha B$ means $\alpha\underline{a} + (1 - \alpha)\overline{a} \geq \alpha\underline{b} + (1 - \alpha)\overline{b}$. It is obvious that $A \succeq B \Longleftrightarrow A \succeq_\alpha B, \forall \alpha \in [0, 1]$. Note that the Hurwicz order of intervals plays the same role with respect to the lattice interval order as the ranking of random variables by their expected utility with respect to stochastic dominance.

4   Stochastic Dominance for Random Intervals

Let $A(\omega) = [\underline{a}(\omega), \overline{a}(\omega)]$ and $B(\omega') = [\underline{b}(\omega'), \overline{b}(\omega')]$ be two random intervals; where $\underline{a}, \overline{a}, \underline{b}$ et $\overline{b}$ are random variables such that: $P(\overline{a} > \underline{a}) = P(\overline{b} > \underline{b}) = 1$.

Based on the definition of stochastic dominance of random variables and the order relations $>_i, i = 1, 2, 3, 4$, between real intervals, we define a direct extension of stochastic dominance and these four interval orderings to random intervals as follows:

Definition 1. *Let i, j be two integers such that $1 \leq i \leq 4$ and $1 \leq j \leq 4$. A random interval A (i, j)-stochastically dominates a random interval B, if:*

$$P(\{\omega : A(\omega) >_i \{c\}\}) \geq P(\{\omega : B(\omega) >_j \{c\}\}), \forall c \in \mathbb{R} \qquad (2)$$

Remarks

- This definition actually only subsumes 4 definitions of stochastic dominance, not 16. Indeed, $A >_1 \{c\}$ is the same as $A >_2 \{c\}$ (it means $\underline{a} > c$) and $A >_3 \{c\}$ is the same as $A >_4 \{c\}$ (it means $\overline{a} > c$).
- If $\forall \omega \in \Omega, \underline{a}(\omega) = \overline{a}(\omega) = a(\omega)$ and $\underline{b}(\omega) = \overline{b}(\omega) = b(\omega)$, this definition reduces to standard stochastic dominance $a >^{s.d} b$.

- Note that one might have defined stochastic dominance for random intervals as a direct extension, replacing numbers by intervals:

$$P(\{\omega : [\underline{a}(\omega), \overline{a}(\omega)] >_i [\underline{c}, \overline{c}]\}) \geq P(\{\omega : [\underline{b}(\omega), \overline{b}(\omega)] >_j [\underline{c}, \overline{c}]\})$$

for all real numbers $\underline{c}$ and $\overline{c}$ such that, $\underline{c} \leq \overline{c}$. However, such a proposal either comes down to our definition (if $i = j$, as it uses the same bound of $[\underline{c}, \overline{c}]$, or $i = 2, 4, j = 1, 3$ since then $P(\{\omega : A(\omega) >_i \{c\}\}) \geq P(\{\omega : B(\omega) >_j \{c\}\}) \iff P(\{\omega : [\underline{a}(\omega), \overline{a}(\omega)] >_i [\underline{c}, \overline{c}]\}) \geq P(\{\omega : [\underline{b}(\omega), \overline{b}(\omega)] >_j [\underline{c}, \overline{c}]\}), \forall \underline{c} \leq c \leq \overline{c})$, or it is too demanding to make sense (if $i = 1, 3, j = 2, 4$, since it requires $P(\underline{a} > \overline{c}) \geq P(\overline{b} > \underline{c}), \forall \underline{c} \leq \overline{c}$ while in general $lim_{\overline{c} \to +\infty} P(\underline{a} > \overline{c}) = 0$ while $lim_{\underline{c} \to -\infty} P(\overline{b} > \overline{c}) = 1$.

Definition 1 comes down to the following four definitions of stochastic dominance between random intervals:

- If $i = 1, 2, j = 3, 4$: $P(\underline{a} > c) \geq P(\overline{b} > c) \iff \underline{a} \geq^{s.d} \overline{b}$, denoted $A \geq_1^{s.d} B$;
- If $i = 1, 2, j = 1, 2$: $P(\underline{a} > c) \geq P(\underline{b} > c) \iff \underline{a} \geq^{s.d} \underline{b}$, denoted $A \geq_2^{s.d} B$;
- If $i = 3, 4, j = 3, 4$: $P(\overline{a} > c) \geq P(\overline{b} > c) \iff \overline{a} \geq^{s.d} \overline{b}$, denoted $A \geq_3^{s.d} B$;
- If $i = 3, 4, j = 1, 2$: $P(\overline{a} > c) \geq P(\underline{b} > c) \iff \overline{a} \geq^{s.d} \underline{b}$, denoted $A \geq_4^{s.d} B$.

One can connect the concept of random interval to belief functions. A continuous belief function [16] is defined by a density function of mass $m(x, y) \geq 0$ if and only if $x \leq y$, alloted to random interval $A(\omega) = [x, y]$. One can then build the cumulative functions:

$$Bel_A((-\infty, x]) = P(A \subseteq (-\infty, x]) \quad = P(\overline{a} \leq x)$$
$$Pl_A((-\infty, x]) \; = P(A \cap (-\infty, x] \neq \emptyset) = P(\underline{a} \leq x).$$

Our stochastic dominance orderings are then closely related to those proposed by T. Denoeux [6]

- $A \geq_1^{s.d} B$ if and only if $Bel_A((-\infty, x]) \leq Pl_B((-\infty, x])$;
- $A \geq_2^{s.d} B$ if and only if $Bel_A((-\infty, x]) \leq Bel_B((-\infty, x])$;
- $A \geq_3^{s.d} B$ if and only if $Pl_A((-\infty, x]) \leq Pl_B((-\infty, x])$;
- $A \geq_4^{s.d} B$ if and only if $Pl_A((-\infty, x]) \leq Bel_B((-\infty, x])$.

In the general case, based on the implications (1) in section 2, some properties of stochastic dominance of random intervals follow.

Proposition 1. *Let A and B be two random intervals:*

1. $A \leq_1^{s.d} B \Rightarrow A \leq_2^{s.d} B \Rightarrow A \leq_4^{s.d} B$;
2. $A \leq_1^{s.d} B \Rightarrow A \leq_3^{s.d} B \Rightarrow A \leq_4^{s.d} B$.

These results always hold due to the fact that $Bel \leq Pl$.

5   Probabilistic Ordering Relation between Random Intervals

Instead of generalizing stochastic dominance, one can randomize the four order relations between intervals and compute the probability for a random interval A to be greater than a random interval B in the sense of $>_i$, $i = 1, 2, 3, 4$. the corresponding fuzzy relations are then defined by:

1. $\mu_1(A, B) = P(\{(\omega, \omega') : A(\omega) >_1 B(\omega')\} = P(\underline{a}(\omega) > \overline{b}(\omega')).$
2. $\mu_2(A, B) = P(\{(\omega, \omega') : A(\omega) >_2 B(\omega')\} = P(\underline{a}(\omega) > \underline{b}(\omega')).$
3. $\mu_3(A, B) = P(\{(\omega, \omega') : A(\omega) >_3 B(\omega')\} = P(\overline{a}(\omega) > \overline{b}(\omega')).$
4. $\mu_4(A, B) = P(\{(\omega, \omega') : A(\omega) >_4 B(\omega')\} = P(\overline{a}(\omega) > \underline{b}(\omega')).$

The first expression is the natural probabilistic extension of interval order.

Proposition 2. *For continuous distribution functions, one can check the following properties:*

- $\mu_4(A, B) = 1 - \mu_1(B, A)$
- $\mu_1(A, B) \leq \mu_i(A, B) \leq \mu_4(A, B)$ *for* $i \in \{2, 3\}$

One can finally consider a stochastic extension of the lattice interval order:

$$\mu_\succ(A, B) = P(\{(\omega, \omega') : (\underline{a}(\omega) > \underline{b}(\omega')) \wedge (\overline{a}(\omega) > \overline{b}(\omega'))\})$$

By virtue of Frechet inequalities, one easily gets:

$$\mu_2(A, B) + \mu_3(A, B) - 1 \leq \mu_\succ(A, B) \leq \min(\mu_2(A, B), \mu_3(A, B)).$$

6 Valued Relations between $L - R$ Fuzzy Intervals

One can consider a fuzzy interval like a nested random set [10]. One can thus apply the above definitions to the comparison of fuzzy intervals, as done by Chanas and colleagues [1,2]. To simplify, one considers here the comparison of intervals of the same shape up to homothety.

6.1 Fuzzy Intervals of the $L - R$ Type

A fuzzy interval of type L-R is a fuzzy interval whose membership function $\mu_{\widetilde{A}}$ is defined by: (cf [8])

$$\mu_{\widetilde{A}}(x) = \left\{ \begin{array}{ll} 1 & \text{if } x \in [\underline{a}, \overline{a}], \\ L(\frac{\underline{a}-x}{\lambda_A}) & \text{if } x \leq \underline{a}, \\ R(\frac{x-\overline{a}}{\rho_A}) & \text{if } x \geq \overline{a} \end{array} \right\}.$$

The functions L and R are defined on the half real line $[0, \infty)$ such that $L(0) = R(0) = 1$, non-negative, decreasing, continuous on the left. The spreads λ_A and ρ_A are positive real numbers. By convention, if $\lambda_A = 0$ and $\rho_A = 0$, then $\widetilde{A} = [\underline{a}, \overline{a}]$. Let FN($LR$) be the set of fuzzy interval of type L-R. $\widetilde{A} \in FN(L, R)$ is denoted by $\widetilde{A} = (\underline{a}, \overline{a}, \lambda_A, \rho_A)$.

6.2 Probabilistic Relations between Fuzzy Intervals

Let $\alpha \in (0, 1]$, and $\widetilde{A}^\alpha$ the α-cut of $\widetilde{A}$. One can easily see that:

$$\widetilde{A}^\alpha = [\underline{a} - L^{-1}(\alpha)\lambda_A, \overline{a} + R^{-1}(\alpha)\rho_A],$$

where L^{-1} and R^{-1} are the reciprocal functions of L and R respectively. The functions L and R being continuous, α can scan the interval $(0,1]$ in a continuous and uniform way. Let ξ be a uniformly distributed random variable on $(0,1]$ and such that for each $\xi = \alpha$, one obtains the set $\widetilde{A}^\alpha$ as a realization. In this case, $\widetilde{A}$ is considered as a random interval $A(\xi) = [\underline{a} - L^{-1}(\xi)\lambda_A, \overline{a} + R^{-1}(\xi)\rho_A]$ and $1 - \xi$ is the degree of confidence of finding the value described by $\widetilde{A}$ inside $A(\xi)$.

Definition 2. *Let $\widetilde{A} = (\underline{a}, \overline{a}, \lambda_A, \rho_A) \in FN(L,R)$ and $\widetilde{B} = (\underline{b}, \overline{b}, \lambda_B, \rho_B) \in FN(L,R)$ be two $L-R$ fuzzy intervals. For $i = 1,2,3,4$ the membership functions $\mu_i : FN(L,R)^2 \to [0,1]$, are defined by:*
$\mu_1(\widetilde{A}, \widetilde{B}) = P(\{\underline{a} - L^{-1}(\xi)\lambda_A > \overline{b} + R^{-1}(\zeta)\rho_B\})$
$\mu_2(\widetilde{A}, \widetilde{B}) = P(\{\underline{a} - L^{-1}(\xi)\lambda_A > \underline{b} - L^{-1}(\zeta)\lambda_B\})$
$\mu_3(\widetilde{A}, \widetilde{B}) = P(\{\overline{a} + R^{-1}(\xi)\rho_A > \overline{b} + R^{-1}(\zeta)\rho_B\})$
$\mu_4(\widetilde{A}, \widetilde{B}) = P(\{\overline{a} + R^{-1}(\zeta)\rho_A > \underline{b} - L^{-1}(\xi)\lambda_B\})$
where ξ and ζ are uniform random variables on $[0,1]$.

This is just the application of definitions proposed in the previous section for random intervals; ξ and ζ could be independent, comonotonic or coupled by any other copula. The actual form of μ_i is depending on this copula.

Lemma 1. *For two arbitrary fuzzy intervals of type $L - R$, the following condition are fulfilled: $\mu_1(\widetilde{A}, \widetilde{B}) > 0 \Rightarrow \underline{a} > \overline{b}$. And $\mu_4(\widetilde{A}, \widetilde{B}) < 1 \Leftrightarrow \underline{b} \geq \overline{a}$ (or equivalently $\mu_4(\widetilde{A}, \widetilde{B}) = 1 \Leftrightarrow \overline{a} \geq \underline{b}$).*

No assumption of independence between ξ and ζ is needed to obtain this obvious result. For instance, $\mu_1(\widetilde{A}, \widetilde{B}) > 0$ implies $\{(\xi, \zeta) : \underline{a} - L^{-1}(\xi)\lambda_A > \overline{b} + R^{-1}(\zeta)\rho_B\} \neq \emptyset$. Then it must contain the pair $(\xi, \zeta) = (1,1)$.

Proposition 3. *Let $\widetilde{A}$ and $\widetilde{B}$ be two fuzzy intervals of type $L-R$ with underlying continuous random variables.*

1. $\mu_1(\widetilde{A}, \widetilde{B}) = 1 - \mu_4(\widetilde{B}, \widetilde{A})$
2. $\mu_1(\widetilde{A}, \widetilde{B}) \leq \mu_i(\widetilde{A}, \widetilde{B}) \leq \mu_4(\widetilde{A}, \widetilde{B})$ for all $i \in \{2,3\}$
3. $\mu_1(\widetilde{A}, \widetilde{B}) > 0 \Rightarrow \mu_4(\widetilde{A}, \widetilde{B}) = 1$

The two first results are the consequences of Proposition 2. For the last property, it is due to Lemma 1 (it is also an instance of the property $N(F) > 0 \to \Pi(F) = 1$ for events F in possibility theory). These properties and the lemma above will be used in the proof of propositions concerning the stochastic dominance of fuzzy random variables of type $L - R$.

Remark. If $\widetilde{A}$ and $\widetilde{B}$ reduce to intervals $A = [\underline{a}, \overline{a}]$ and $B = [\underline{b}, \overline{b}]$ then, the above indices $\mu_i(\widetilde{A}, \widetilde{B})$ become characteristic functions of relations $>_i$ namely: $A >_i B$ if and only if $\mu_i(A, B) = 1$ for $i = 1,2,3,4$.

    Two assumptions are considered by Chanas et al. in [2]: functionally dependent fuzzy intervals and independent fuzzy intervals.

Functionally Dependent Fuzzy Intervals. One can for example suppose that the fuzzy intervals $\widetilde{A}$ and $\widetilde{B}$ are associated the same random variable ξ on the unit interval. In other words, one must select the same α-cuts of $\widetilde{A}$ and $\widetilde{B}$ (it is the case for two fuzzy numbers provided by the same expert selecting a single degree of confidence). One will speak of fuzzy intervals with *positively related degrees of confidence*. Let us note that this dependence is the one between the sources producing $\widetilde{A}$ and $\widetilde{B}$, and not between the underlying variables. The indices in Definition 2 become (using a superscript D for this case):

$$\mu_1^D(\widetilde{A}, \widetilde{B}) = P(\{\underline{a} - L^{-1}(\xi)\lambda_A > \overline{b} + R^{-1}(\xi)\rho_B\});$$

$$\mu_2^D(\widetilde{A}, \widetilde{B}) = P(\{\underline{a} - L^{-1}(\xi)\lambda_A > \underline{b} - L^{-1}(\xi)\lambda_B\});$$

$$\mu_3^D(\widetilde{A}, \widetilde{B}) = P(\{\overline{a} + R^{-1}(\xi)\rho_A > \overline{b} + R^{-1}(\xi)\rho_B\});$$

$$\mu_4^D(\widetilde{A}, \widetilde{B}) = P(\{\overline{a} + R^{-1}(\xi)\rho_A > \underline{b} - L^{-1}(\xi)\lambda_B\});$$

where ξ is a uniform random variable on $[0,1]$. The use of fuzzy intervals of type $L - R$ allows an explicit calculation of these indices, for instance

- Since L and R are decreasing functions, if $\overline{b} < \underline{a}$ and $\underline{a} - \lambda_A < \overline{b} + \rho_B$ then there is single value $\xi = \alpha_1$ such that $\underline{a} - L^{-1}(\xi)\lambda_A = \overline{b} + R^{-1}(\xi)\rho_B$. If $L = R$, $\alpha_1 = L(\frac{\underline{a}-\overline{b}}{\lambda_A + \rho_B})$. Hence $\mu_1(\widetilde{A}, \widetilde{B}) = 1 - \alpha_1 = 1 - \mu_4(\widetilde{B}, \widetilde{A})$. One thus gets $\mu_1(\widetilde{A}, \widetilde{B}) > \beta$ if and only if $\forall \alpha > 1 - \beta, \widetilde{A}^\alpha >_1 \widetilde{B}^\alpha$.
- If $\underline{a} > \underline{b}$ but $\underline{a} - \lambda_A < \overline{b} + \lambda_B$ one can solve the equation $\underline{a} - L^{-1}(\xi)\lambda_A = \underline{b} - L^{-1}(\xi)\lambda_B$, the single solution of which is $\alpha_2 = L(\frac{\underline{a}-\underline{b}}{\lambda_A - \lambda_B})$. Then, $\mu_2(\widetilde{A}, \widetilde{B}) = 1 - \alpha_2$ and $\mu_2(\widetilde{A}, \widetilde{B}) > \beta$ if and only if $\forall \alpha > 1 - \beta, \widetilde{A}^\alpha >_2 \widetilde{B}^\alpha$.
- In the same way, if $\overline{a} < \overline{b}$ but $\overline{a} - \rho_A > \overline{b} + \rho_B$ one can solve the equation $\overline{a} + R^{-1}(\xi)\rho_A = \overline{b} + R^{-1}(\xi)\rho_B$, the single solution of which is $\alpha_3 = R(\frac{\overline{b}-\overline{a}}{\rho_A - \rho_B})$. Then, $\mu_3(\widetilde{A}, \widetilde{B}) = \alpha_3$ and $\mu_3(\widetilde{A}, \widetilde{B}) > \beta$ if and only if $\forall \alpha > \beta, \widetilde{A}^\alpha >_3 \widetilde{B}^\alpha$.

Consider now the extension of the relation $\succ$ to fuzzy intervals, as

$$\mu_\succ(\widetilde{A}, \widetilde{B}) = P(\{(\underline{a} - L^{-1}(\xi)\lambda_A > \underline{b} - L^{-1}(\xi)\lambda_B) \wedge (\overline{a} + R^{-1}(\zeta)\rho_A > \overline{b} + R^{-1}(\zeta)\rho_B)\}).$$

If $\underline{a} > \underline{b}$ but $\underline{a} - \lambda_A < \overline{b} + \lambda_B$, and $\overline{a} > \overline{b}$ but $\overline{a} - \rho_A < \overline{b} + \rho_B$, one gets $\{\xi : \underline{a} - L^{-1}(\xi)\lambda_A > \underline{b} - L^{-1}(\xi)\lambda_B\} \subseteq \{\xi : \overline{a} + R^{-1}(\xi)\rho_A > \overline{b} + R^{-1}(\xi)\rho_B\}$ or conversely. Thus : $\mu_\succ(\widetilde{A}, \widetilde{B}) = \min(\mu_2(\widetilde{A}, \widetilde{B}), \mu_3(\widetilde{A}, \widetilde{B}))$.

Independent Fuzzy Intervals. The other assumption used by Chanas *et al.* is that the cuts of $\widetilde{A}$ and $\widetilde{B}$ are induced by two independent random variables ξ and ζ on the unit interval. It is the case of two fuzzy intervals supplied by independent sources. One then speaks of fuzzy intervals with independent confidence levels. The explicit calculation of indices can also be carried out. For instance, if $\overline{b} < \underline{a}$ and $\underline{a} - \lambda_A < \overline{b} + \rho_B$ then $\mu_1^I(\widetilde{A}, \widetilde{B})$ (superscript I for independence) is the surface above the line defined by $\underline{a} - \lambda_A L^{-1}(\xi) = \overline{b} + \rho_B R^{-1}(\zeta)$ in the unit square. Namely we must have $\underline{a} - \lambda_A L^{-1}(\xi) < \overline{b} + \rho_B R^{-1}(\zeta)$ to have overlapping cuts. Hence

$$\mu_1^I(\widetilde{A}, \widetilde{B}) = 1 - \int_0^1 R(\min(1, \max(0, \frac{\underline{a} - \overline{b} - \lambda_A L^{-1}(\xi)}{\rho_B})))d\xi.$$

Moreover, the two events $\{\xi : \underline{a} - L^{-1}(\xi)\lambda_A > \underline{b} - L^{-1}(\xi)\lambda_B\}$ and $\{\zeta : \overline{a} + R^{-1}(\zeta)\rho_A > \overline{b} + R^{-1}(\zeta)\rho_B\}$ being independent, the valued relation $\mu_{\succ}^I$ breaks up now as follows:

$$\mu_{\succ}^I(\widetilde{A}, \widetilde{B}) = \mu_2^I(\widetilde{A}, \widetilde{B}) \cdot \mu_3^I(\widetilde{A}, \widetilde{B})$$

7 Stochastic Dominance between Fuzzy Random Variables

Fuzzy random variables were originally introduced by Kwakernaak [13]:

Definition 3. *A fuzzy random variable $\widetilde{X}$ is a function from a probability space $(\Omega, \mathcal{F}, P)$ to the set of fuzzy intervals : $\omega \in \Omega \mapsto \widetilde{X}(\omega) \in \mathcal{F}(R)$.*

If $\mathcal{F}(R)$ is restricted to $FN(LR)$, $\widetilde{X}$ is called fuzzy random variable of type $L - R$ and denoted $\widetilde{X}(\omega) = (\underline{x}(\omega), \overline{x}(\omega), \lambda_X(\omega), \rho_X(\omega))$ such that $\forall \omega \in \Omega, \lambda_X(\omega) \geq 0, \underline{x}(\omega) < \overline{x}(\omega), \rho_X(\omega)) \geq 0.$

We now define stochastic dominance of fuzzy random variables of type $L - R$.

Definition 4. *Let $\widetilde{A}$ and $\widetilde{B}$ be two fuzzy random variables of type $L - R$, and $i, j \in \{1, 2, 3, 4\}$. $\widetilde{A}$ (i, j)-stochastically dominates $\widetilde{B}$ if and only if $\forall \beta \in [0, 1)$, $P(\mu_i(\widetilde{A}, \{c\}) > \beta) \geq P(\mu_j(\widetilde{B}, \{c\}) > \beta), \forall c \in \mathbb{R}.$*

Notice that it again comes down to 4 forms of stochastic dominance. Indeed, denoting by $\mu_{\widetilde{A}(\omega)}$ the membership function of $\widetilde{A}(\omega)$ and by $\widetilde{A}^1(\omega)$ its core:

$$\mu_1(\widetilde{A}, \{c\}) = \mu_2(\widetilde{A}, \{c\}) = 1 - \mu_{\widetilde{A}}(c) \text{ if } c \leq \inf \widetilde{A}^1 \text{ and } 0 \text{ otherwise};$$
$$\mu_4(\widetilde{A}, \{c\}) = \mu_3(\widetilde{A}, \{c\}) = \mu_{\widetilde{A}}(c) \text{ if } c \geq \sup \widetilde{A}^1 \text{ and } 1 \text{ otherwise}.$$

So we can denote $P(\mu_i(\widetilde{A}, \{c\}) > \beta) \leq P(\mu_j(\widetilde{B}, \{c\}) > \beta), \forall c \in \mathbb{R}$ as follows:

- If $i = 1, 2, j = 3, 4 : \widetilde{A} \geq_1^{s.d} \widetilde{B}$; if $i = 1, 2, j = 1, 2 : \widetilde{A} \geq_2^{s.d} \widetilde{B}$;
- If $i = 3, 4, j = 3, 4$: $\widetilde{A} \geq_3^{s.d} \widetilde{B}$; if $i = 3, 4, j = 1, 2 : \widetilde{A} \geq_4^{s.d} \widetilde{B}$.

These relations extend to fuzzy random variables both stochastic dominance and the 4 interval orderings. Moreover we can show:

Proposition 4. *If $\widetilde{A} \leq_1^{s.d} \widetilde{B}$ then $\overline{a} \leq^{s.d} \underline{b}$.*

Proof. $\widetilde{A} \leq_1^{s.d} \widetilde{B}$ if and only if $\forall \beta \in [0, 1)$ and $\forall c \in \mathbb{R}, P(\mu_4(\widetilde{A}, \{c\}) > \beta) \leq P(\mu_1(\widetilde{B}, \{c\}) > \beta)$. From lemma 1, the condition $\mu_1(\widetilde{B}, \{c\}) > \beta$ implies $\underline{b} > c$. Likewise, from lemma 1, the condition $\mu_4(\widetilde{A}, \{c\}) > \beta$ implies $\overline{a} > c$. Now the following inclusions hold: $\{\omega : \overline{a}(\omega) > c\} = \{\omega : \mu_4(\widetilde{A}(\omega), \{c\}) = 1\} \subset \{\omega : \mu_4(\widetilde{A}(\omega), \{c\}) > \beta\}$, and $\{\omega : \underline{b}(\omega) > c\} = \{\omega : \mu_1(\widetilde{B}(\omega), \{c\}) > 0\} \supset \{\omega : \mu_1(\widetilde{B}(\omega), \{c\}) > \beta\}$. Hence:

$$P(\overline{a} > c) \leq P(\mu_4(\widetilde{A}, \{c\}) > \beta) \leq P(\mu_1(\widetilde{B}, \{c\}) > \beta) \leq P(\underline{b} > c).$$

Likewise, we can check that

- If $\widetilde{A} \leq_2^{s.d} \widetilde{B}$ then $\underline{a}$ is stochastically dominated by $\underline{b}$;
- If $\widetilde{A} \leq_3^{s.d} \widetilde{B}$ then $\overline{a}$ is stochastically dominated by $\overline{b}$;
- If $\widetilde{A} \leq_4^{s.d} \widetilde{B}$ then $\overline{a}$ is stochastically dominated by $\underline{b}$.

Relying on the previous definition and properties of probabilistic orderings of fuzzy intervals, the following properties of the stochastic dominance of fuzzy random variables extend the relations between the 4 basic interval orderings:

$$\widetilde{A} \leq_1^{s.d} \widetilde{B} \Rightarrow \widetilde{A} \leq_2^{s.d} \widetilde{B} \Rightarrow \widetilde{A} \leq_4^{s.d} \widetilde{B};$$
$$\widetilde{A} \leq_1^{s.d} \widetilde{B} \Rightarrow \widetilde{A} \leq_3^{s.d} \widetilde{B} \Rightarrow \widetilde{A} \leq_4^{s.d} \widetilde{B}.$$ More properties of these ordering

relations should be studied. Moreover, they should be applied to the extension of linear programming techniques when coefficients are fuzzy random variables, thus jointly extending fuzzy and stochastic programming.

8 Conclusion

An extension of the stochastic dominance to fuzzy random variables of type $L - R$ was proposed in two following successive stages: First, the extension of stochastic dominance from random variables to random intervals by means of the four order relations between bounds of intervals. Then, the extension, to random intervals, and in a second step to fuzzy random variables of type $L - R$, of the probability of dominance between random variables by means of the fuzzy relations defined in [1],[2].

This work is clearly preliminary. There are several ways of comparing intervals. And two basic ways of extending the ordering of reals to random variables: by stochastic dominance (of the first order), or by calculating the probability that a random variable is greater than another. Thus, there are two lines to consider for the comparison of random intervals: by applying the stochastic dominance to each of pair of bounds, or by calculating the probability that one random bound is greater than another. One can also directly generalize stochastic dominance according to a relation between intervals. One can apply these extensions to fuzzy intervals seen as particular cases of random intervals. In the case of the comparison of fuzzy random variables, one is then in front of several possible definitions of stochastic dominance that blend these various ingredients. In this paper we just outlined the direct extension of stochastic dominance. Other relations of dominance between fuzzy random variables $\widetilde{A}$ and $\widetilde{B}$ could be considered, for instance

1. One can apply the indices of interval dominance $>_i, i = 1, 2, 3, 4$ between their α-cuts : $\forall \alpha \in (0, 1], \mu_i^\alpha(\widetilde{A}, \widetilde{B}) = P(\widetilde{A}^\alpha >_i \widetilde{B}^\alpha)$, and define dominance degrees $\mu_i(\widetilde{A}, \widetilde{B})$ as the integral $\int_0^1 \mu_i^\alpha(\widetilde{A}, \widetilde{B}) d\alpha$ w.r.t. α.
2. As $\widetilde{A}^\alpha$ and $\widetilde{B}^\alpha$ are random intervals, one can require stochastic dominance of Def. 1 between these random intervals for each α. One can thus define another form of stochastic dominance for fuzzy random variables:

$$\widetilde{A} \leq_{sd}^{ij} \widetilde{B} \iff P(\widetilde{A}^\alpha >_i \{c\}) \leq P(\widetilde{B}^\alpha >_j \{c\}), \forall \alpha \in (0,1], \forall c \in \mathbb{R}.$$

Yet other combinations are possible. It will be necessary of course to understand the links between these possible definitions, and to find out those that have the best properties (in the light of [17]), and for which the evaluations are easy to calculate in practice. In this work, we considered a particular type of fuzzy random variables. For future works, an extension of stochastic dominance of fuzzy random variables to more general settings could be considered. Moreover, one can also combine the comparison between random variables and the max-min possibilistic approach to the comparison of fuzzy intervals [9].

References

1. Chanas, S., Delgado, M., Verdegay, J.L., Vila, M.A.: Ranking fuzzy real intervals in the setting of random sets. Information Sciences 69, 201–217 (1993)
2. Chanas, S., Zielinski, P.: Ranking fuzzy real intervals in the setting of random sets-further results. Information Sciences 117, 191–200 (1999)
3. Chateauneuf, A., Cohen, M., Tallon, J.-M.: Decision under Risk: The Classical Expected Utility Model. In: Bouyssou, D., Dubois, D., Pirlot, M., Prade, H. (eds.) Decision-Making Process, ch. 8, pp. 363–382. ISTE, London (2009)
4. Couso, I., Dubois, D.: On the variability of the concept of variance for fuzzy random variables. I.E.E.E. Trans. on Fuzzy Systems 17, 1070–1080 (2009)
5. De Baets, B., De Meyer, H.: On the cycle-transitive comparison of artificially coupled random variables. Int. J. Approximate Reasoning 47, 306–322 (2008)
6. Denoeux, T.: Extending stochastic order to belief functions on the real line. Information Sciences 179, 1362–1376 (2009)
7. Dubois, D.: Linear programming with fuzzy data. In: Bezdek, J.C. (ed.) Analysis of Fuzzy Information, vol. III, pp. 241–263. CRC Press, Boca Raton (1987)
8. Dubois, D., Prade, H.: Operations on fuzzy numbers. Int. J. of Systems Science 30, 613–626 (1978)
9. Dubois, D., Prade, H.: Ranking fuzzy numbers in the setting of possibility theory. Information Sciences 30, 183–224 (2003)
10. Dubois, D., Prade, H.: Random sets and fuzzy interval analysis. Fuzzy Sets and Systems 42, 87–101 (1991)
11. Fishburn, P.: Interval Orderings. Wiley, New-York (1987)
12. Kruse, R., Meyer, K.D.: Statistics with Vague Data. D. Reidel Publishing Company, Dordrecht (1987)
13. Kwakernaak, H.: Fuzzy random variables, I. Definitions and theorems, Information Sciences 15, 1–29 (1978)
14. Mosler, K., Scarsini, M.: Stochastic Orders and Decision under Risk. IMS Lecture Notes, pp. 261–284 (1991)
15. Puri, M.L., Ralescu, D.: Fuzzy random variables. J. Math. Anal. and Appl. 114, 409–420 (1986)
16. Smets, P.: Belief functions on real numbers. Int. J. of Approximate Reasoning 40, 181–223 (2005)
17. Wang, X., Kerre, E.: Reasonable properties for the ordering of fuzzy quantities (2 parts). Fuzzy Sets and Systems 118, 375–406 (2001)

Correlation of Intuitionistic Fuzzy Sets

Eulalia Szmidt and Janusz Kacprzyk

Systems Research Institute, Polish Academy of Sciences,
ul. Newelska 6, 01–447 Warsaw, Poland
Warsaw School of Information Technology, ul. Newelska 6, 01-447 Warsaw, Poland
{szmidt,kacprzyk}@ibspan.waw.pl

Abstract. The correlation coefficient (Pearson's r) is one of the most frequently used tools in statistics. In this paper we propose a correlation coefficient of Atanassov's intuitionistic fuzzy sets (A-IFSs). It provides the strength of the relationship between A-IFSs and also shows if the considered sets are positively or negatively correlated. Next, the proposed correlation coefficient takes into account not only the amount of information related to the A-IFS data (expressed by the membership and non-membership values) but also the reliability of the data expressed by a so-called hesitation margin.

1 Introduction

Since Karl Pearson's proposal of the correlation coefficient r (so called Pearson's coefficient) in 1895, it has became one of the most broadly applied indices in statistics [12]. Generally, correlation indicates how well two variables move together in an linear fashion. In other words, correlation reflects a linear relationship between two variables. It is an important measure in data analysis and classification, in particular in decision making, predicting the market behavior, medical diagnosis, pattern recognition, and other real world problems concerning environmental, political, legal, economic, financial, social, educational, artistic, etc. systems.

As many real world data may be fuzzy, the concept has been extended to fuzzy observations (cf. e.g., Chiang and Lin [4], Hong and Hwang [7], Liu and Kao [11]).

A relationship between A-IFSs (representing, e.g., preferences, attributes) seems to be of a vital importance, too, so that there are many papers discussing the correlation of A-IFSs: Gersternkorn and Mańko [5], Bustine and Burillo [3], Hong and Hwang [6], Hung [8], Hung and Wu [9], Zeng and Li [33]. In some of those papers only the strength of relationship is evaluated (cf. Gersternkorn and Mańko [5], Hong and Hwang [6], Zeng and Li [33]). In other papers (cf. Hung [8], Hung and Wu [9]), a positive and negative type of a relationship is reflected but the third term describing an A-IFS, which is important from the point of view of all similarity, distance or entropy measures (cf. Szmidt and Kacprzyk, e.g., [14], [16], [23], [18], [25]), [26]) is not accounted for.

In this paper we discuss a concept of correlation for data represented as A-IFSs adopting the concepts from statistics. We calculate it by showing both a positive and negative relationship of the sets, and showing that it is important to take into account all three terms describing A-IFSs.

E. Hüllermeier, R. Kruse, and F. Hoffmann (Eds.): IPMU 2010, LNAI 6178, pp. 169–177, 2010.
© Springer-Verlag Berlin Heidelberg 2010

2   A Brief Introduction to Intuitionistic Fuzzy Sets

One of the possible generalizations of a fuzzy set in X (Zadeh [32]), given by

$$A' = \{< x, \mu_{A'}(x) > | x \in X\} \tag{1}$$

where $\mu_{A'}(x) \in [0, 1]$ is the membership function of the fuzzy set A', is Atanassov's intuitionistic fuzzy set (Atanassov [2]) A:

$$A = \{< x, \mu_A(x), \nu_A(x) > | x \in X\} \tag{2}$$

where: $\mu_A : X \rightarrow [0, 1]$ and $\nu_A : X \rightarrow [0, 1]$ such that $0 \leq \mu_A(x) + \nu_A(x) \leq 1$, and $\mu_A(x)$, $\nu_A(x) \in [0, 1]$ denote the degree of membership and a degree of non-membership of $x \in A$, respectively, and the *hesitation margin* of $x \in A$ is:

$$\pi_A(x) = 1 - \mu_A(x) - \nu_A(x) \tag{3}$$

The $\pi_A(x)$ expresses a lack of knowledge of whether x belongs to A or not (Atanassov [2]); obviously, $0 \leq \pi_A(x) \leq 1$, for each $x \in X$;

The hesitation margin turns out to be important while considering the distances (Szmidt and Kacprzyk [14], [16], [23], entropy (Szmidt and Kacprzyk [18], [25]), similarity (Szmidt and Kacprzyk [26]) for the A-IFSs, etc. i.e., the measures that play a crucial role in virtually all information processing tasks. The hesitation margin is shown to be indispensable also in the ranking of intuitionistic fuzzy alternatives as it indicates how reliable (sure) information represented by an alternative is (cf. Szmidt and Kacprzyk [27], [28]).

The use of A-IFSs instead of fuzzy sets implies the introduction of additional degrees of freedom (non-memberships and hesitation margins) into the set description. Such a generalization of fuzzy sets gives us an additional possibility to represent imperfect knowledge which may lead to describing many real problems in a more adequate way. This is confirmed by successful applications of A-IFSs to group decision making, negotiations, voting and other situations are presented in Szmidt and Kacprzyk [13], [15], [17], [19], [20], [21], [22], [24], [29], Szmidt and Kukier [30], [31].

2.1   A Geometrical Representation

One of possible geometrical representations of an intuitionistic fuzzy sets is given in Figure 1 (cf. Atanassov [2]). It is worth noticing that although we use a two-dimensional figure (which is more convenient to draw in our further considerations), we still adopt our approach (e.g., Szmidt and Kacprzyk [16], [23], [18], [25]), [26]) taking into account all three terms (membership, non-membership and hesitation margin values) describing an intuitionistic fuzzy set. Any element belonging to an intuitionistic fuzzy set may be represented inside an MNO triangle. In other words, the MNO triangle represents the surface where the coordinates of any element belonging to an A-IFS can be represented. Each point belonging to the MNO triangle is described by the three coordinates: (μ, ν, π). Points M and N represent the crisp elements. Point $M(1, 0, 0)$ represents elements fully belonging to an A-IFS as $\mu = 1$, and may be seen as the

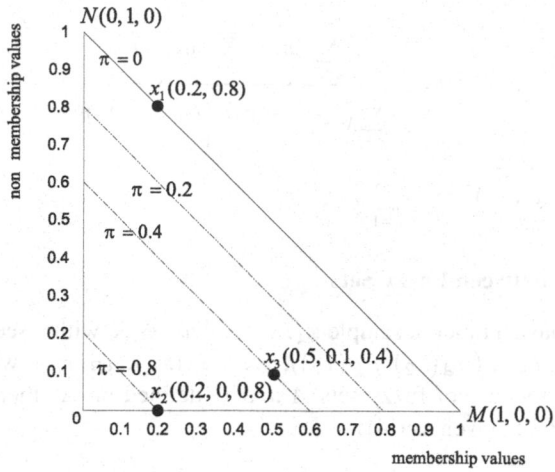

Fig. 1. Geometrical representation

representation of the ideal positive element. Point $N(0, 1, 0)$ represents elements fully not belonging to an A-IFS as $\nu = 1$, i.e. can be viewed as the ideal negative element. Point $O(0, 0, 1)$ represents elements about which we are not able to say if they belong or not belong to an A-IFS (the intuitionistic fuzzy index $\pi = 1$). Such an interpretation is intuitively appealing and provides means for the representation of many aspects of imperfect information. Segment MN (where $\pi = 0$) represents elements belonging to the classic fuzzy sets ($\mu + \nu = 1$). For example, point $x_1(0.2, 0.8, 0)$ (Figure 1), like any element from segment MN represents an element of a fuzzy set. A line parallel to MN describes the elements with the same values of the hesitation margin. In Figure 1 we can see point $x_3(0.5, 0.1, 0.4)$ representing an element with the hesitation margin equal 0.4, and point $x_2(0.2, 0, 0.8)$ representing an element with the hesitation margin equal 0.8. The closer a line that is parallel to MN is to O, the higher the hesitation margin.

3   Correlation

The correlation coefficient (Pearson's r) between two variables is a measure of the linear relationship between them.

The correlation coefficient is 1 in the case of a positive (increasing) linear relationship, -1 in the case of a negative (decreasing) linear relationship, and some value between -1 and 1 in all other cases. The closer the coefficient is to either -1 or 1, the stronger the correlation between the variables.

3.1   Correlation between Crisp Sets

Let (X_1, Y_1), (X_2, Y_2), ..., (X_n, Y_n) be a random sample of size n from a joint probability density function $f_{X,Y}(x, y)$, let $\overline{X}$ and $\overline{Y}$ be the sample means of variables X and Y, respectively, then the sample correlation coefficient $r(X, Y)$ is given as (e.g., [12]):

$$r(A, B) = \frac{\sum\limits_{i=1}^{n}(x_i - \overline{X})(y_i - \overline{Y})}{(\sum\limits_{i=1}^{n}(x_i - \overline{X})^2 \sum\limits_{i=1}^{n}(y_i - \overline{Y})^2)^{0.5}} \tag{4}$$

where: $\overline{X} = \frac{1}{n}\sum\limits_{i=1}^{n} x_i$, $\overline{Y} = \frac{1}{n}\sum\limits_{i=1}^{n} y_i$.

3.2   Correlation between Fuzzy Sets

Suppose that we have a random sample $x_1, x_2, \ldots, x_n \in X$ with a sequence of paired data $(\mu_A(x_1), \mu_B(x_1))$, $(\mu_A(x_2), \mu_B(x_2))$, $\ldots$, $(\mu_A(x_n), \mu_B(x_n))$ which correspond to the membership values of fuzzy sets A and B defined on X, then the correlation coefficient $r_f(A, B)$ is given as ([4]):

$$r_f(A, B) = \frac{\sum\limits_{i=1}^{n}(\mu_A(x_i) - \overline{\mu_A})(\mu_B(x_i) - \overline{\mu_B})}{(\sum\limits_{i=1}^{n}(\mu_A(x_i) - \overline{\mu_A})^2)^{0.5}(\sum\limits_{i=1}^{n}(\mu_B(x_i) - \overline{\mu_B})^2)^{0.5}} \tag{5}$$

where: $\overline{\mu_A} = \frac{1}{n}\sum\limits_{i=1}^{n} \mu_A(x_i)$, $\overline{\mu_B} = \frac{1}{n}\sum\limits_{i=1}^{n} \mu_B(x_i)$.

3.3   Correlation between A-IFSs

We propose a correlation coefficient for two A-IFSs, A and B, so that we could express not only a relative strength but also a positive or negative relationship between A and B. Next, we take into account all three terms describing an A-IFSs (membership, non-membership values and the hesitation margins) because each of them influences the results.

Suppose that we have a random sample $x_1, x_2, \ldots, x_n \in X$ with a sequence of paired data $[(\mu_A(x_1), \nu_A(x_1), \pi_A(x_1)), (\mu_B(x_1), \nu_B(x_1), \pi_B(x_1))]$, $[(\mu_A(x_2), \nu_A(x_2), \pi_A(x_2)), (\mu_B(x_2), \nu_B(x_2), \pi_B(x_2))]$, $\ldots$, $[(\mu_A(x_n), \nu_A(x_n), \pi_A(x_n)), (\mu_B(x_n), \nu_B(x_n), \pi_B(x_n))]$ which correspond to the membership values, non-memberships values and hesitation margins of A-IFSs A and B defined on X, then the correlation coefficient $r_{A-IFS}(A, B)$ is given by Definition 1.

Definition 1. The correlation coefficient $r_{A-IFS}(A, B)$ between two A-IFSs, A and B in X, is:

$$r_{A-IFS}(A, B) = \frac{1}{3}(r_1(A, B) + r_2(A, B) + r_3(A, B)) \tag{6}$$

where

$$r_1(A, B) = \frac{\sum\limits_{i=1}^{n}(\mu_A(x_i) - \overline{\mu_A})(\mu_B(x_i) - \overline{\mu_B})}{(\sum\limits_{i=1}^{n}(\mu_A(x_i) - \overline{\mu_A})^2)^{0.5}(\sum\limits_{i=1}^{n}(\mu_B(x_i) - \overline{\mu_B})^2)^{0.5}} \tag{7}$$

$$r_2(A, B) = \frac{\sum\limits_{i=1}^{n} (\nu_A(x_i) - \overline{\nu_A})(\nu_B(x_i) - \overline{\nu_B})}{(\sum\limits_{i=1}^{n} (\nu_A(x_i) - \overline{\nu_A})^2)^{0.5}(\sum\limits_{i=1}^{n} (\nu_B(x_i) - \overline{\nu_B})^2)^{0.5}} \tag{8}$$

$$r_3(A, B) = \frac{\sum\limits_{i=1}^{n} (\pi_A(x_i) - \overline{\pi_A})(\pi_B(x_i) - \overline{\pi_B})}{(\sum\limits_{i=1}^{n} (\pi_A(x_i) - \overline{\pi_A})^2)^{0.5}(\sum\limits_{i=1}^{n} (\pi_B(x_i) - \overline{\pi_B})^2)^{0.5}} \tag{9}$$

where: $\overline{\mu_A} = \frac{1}{n}\sum\limits_{i=1}^{n}\mu_A(x_i)$, $\overline{\mu_B} = \frac{1}{n}\sum\limits_{i=1}^{n}\mu_B(x_i)$, $\overline{\nu_A} = \frac{1}{n}\sum\limits_{i=1}^{n}\nu_A(x_i)$,

$\overline{\nu_B} = \frac{1}{n}\sum\limits_{i=1}^{n}\nu_B(x_i)$, $\overline{\pi_A} = \frac{1}{n}\sum\limits_{i=1}^{n}\pi_A(x_i)$, $\overline{\pi_B} = \frac{1}{n}\sum\limits_{i=1}^{n}\pi_B(x_i)$,

The proposed correlation coefficient (6) depends on two factors: the amount of information expressed by the membership and non-membership degrees (7)–(8), and the reliability of information expressed by the hesitation margins (9).

Remark: Analogously as for the crisp and fuzzy data, $r_{A-IFS}(A, B)$ makes sense for A-IFS variables whose values vary. If, for instance, the temperature is constant and the amount of ice cream sold is the same, then it is impossible to conclude about their relationship (as, from the mathematical point of view, we avoid zero in the denominator).

The correlation coefficient $r_{A-IFS}(A, B)$ (6) fulfills the following properties:

1. $r_{A-IFS}(A, B) = r_{A-IFS}(B, A)$

2. If $A = B$ then $r_{A-IFS}(A, B) = 1$

3. $|r_{A-IFS}(A, B)| = \leq 1$

The above properties are not only fulfilled by the correlation coefficient $r_{A-IFS}(A, B)$ (6) but also by its every component (7)–(9).

Remark: It is should be emphasized that $r_{A-IFS}(A, B) = 1$ occurs not only for $A = B$ but also in the cases of a perfect linear correlation of the data (cf. Example 2) (the same concerns each component (7)–(9)).

Now we will show some simplified examples. The size of the data set is too small to look at them as for significant samples, but the purpose is just for illustration.

Example 1. Let A and B be A-IFSs in $X = \{x_1, x_2, x_3\}$:

$$A = \{(x_1, 0.1, 0.2, 0.7), (x_2, 0.2, 0.1, 0.7), (x_3, 0.3, 0, 0.7)\}$$

$$B = \{(x_1, 0.3, 0, 0.7), (x_2, 0.2, 0.2, 0.6), (x_3, 0.1, 0.6, 0.3)\}$$

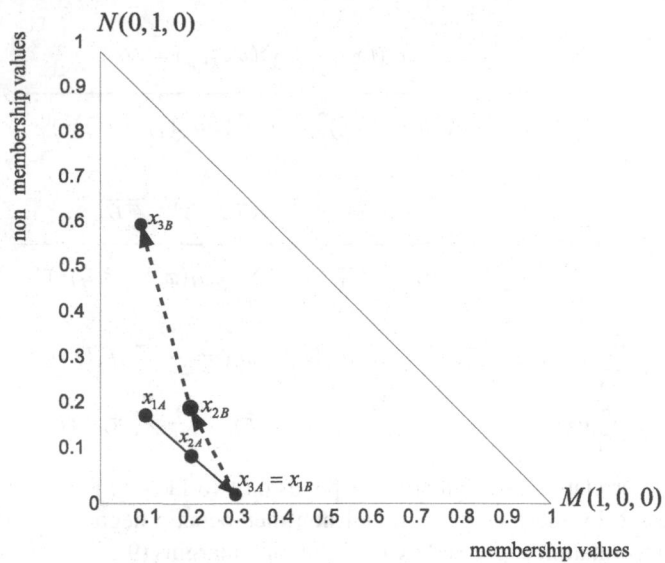

Fig. 2. Data from Example 1: we can see that there is no perfect negative linear relationship among elements from A and B

It is easy to notice that

- the membership values of the elements in A (i.e.: $0.1, 0.2, 0.3$) increase whereas the membership values of the elements in B (i.e.: $0.3, 0.2, 0.1$) decrease. In the result (7) we have $r_1(A, B) = -1$.
- the non-membership values of the elements in A (i.e.: $0.2, 0.1, 0.0$) decrease whereas the non-membership values of the elements in B (i.e.: $0.0, 0.2, 0.6$) increase. In the result (8) we have $r_2(A, B) \approx -1$.
- the hesitation margins of the elements in A (i.e.: $(0.7, 0.7, 0.7)$ do not change while the hesitation margins of the elements in B (i.e.: $0.7, 0.6, 0.2$) decrease. In the result (9) we have $r_3(A, B) = 0$.

Therefore, finally, from (6) we obtain $r_{A-IFS}(A, B) = \frac{1}{3}(-1 - 1 + 0) = -0.67$.

If we exclude from considerations the hesitation margins, and take into account two components (7) and (8) only, we obtain $r_{A-IFS}(A, B) = \frac{1}{2}(-1 - 1) = -1$ which means that there is a perfect negative linear relationship between A and B (which is difficult to agree).

In Figure 2 there is a geometrical interpretation (cf. Section 2.1) of the data from Example 1.

It is worth emphasizing that for practical purposes (e.g., in decision making) it seems rather useful to know correlation (9) concerning lack of knowledge represented by the variables considered. If, for example, the data represent reactions of patients to a new medicine, it seems unavoidable to carefully examine just the part (9) of the correlation coefficient (6) as it may happen that a new treatment/medicine increases unforseen reactions. In such situations it may be important not only to assess all components separately but even to give them different weights in (6).

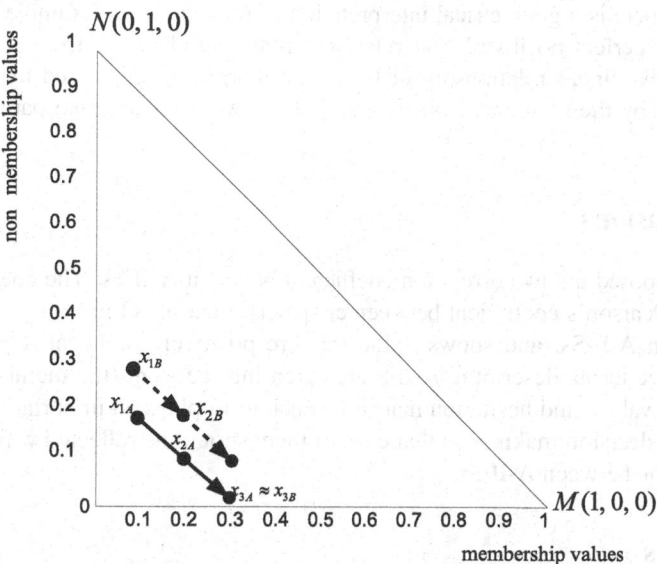

Fig. 3. Data from Example 2 - we can see perfect positive linear relationship among elements from A and B

Certainly, we may find an example when $r_3(A, B)$ does not influence the correlation coefficient $r_{A-IFS}(A, B)$ in a sense of the final result (an obtained number). But such situations are the exceptions, not a rule.

Example 2. Let A and B be A-IFSs in $X = \{x_1, x_2, x_3\}$:

$$A = \{(x_1, 0.1, 0.2, 0.7), (x_2, 0.2, 0.1, 0.7), (x_3, 0.29, 0.0, 0.71)\}$$

$$B = \{(x_1, 0.1, 0.3, 0.6), (x_2, 0.2, 0.2, 0.6), (x_3, 0.29, 0.1, 0.61)\}$$

Now we have

– the membership values of the elements in A (i.e.: $0.1, 0.2, 0.29$) increase and the membership values of the elements in B (i.e.: $0.1, 0.2, 0.29$) are the same, so from (7) we have $r_1(A, B) = 1$.

– the non-membership values of the elements in A (i.e.: $0.2, 0.1, 0.$) decrease and the non-membership values of the elements in B (i.e.: $0.3, 0.2, 0.1$) decrease, and from (8) we have $r_2(A, B) = 1$.

– the hesitation margins of the elements in A, are equal to $(0.7, 0.7, 0.71)$, and the hesitation margins of the elements in B are equal to $(0.6, 0.6, 0.61)$, so from (9) we have $r_3(A, B) = 1$.

So, finally, from (6) we obtain $r_{A-IFS}(A, B) = \frac{1}{3}(1+1+1) = 1$. Now the result is just the same in spite of we take into account $r_3(A, B)$ or not (in the sense of considering (7) and (8) only, and dividing their sum by 2). But in general, $r_3(A, B)$ plays an important role in the correlation coefficient.

In Figure 3 there is a geometrical interpretation of the data from Example 2. It is easy to notice the perfect positive linear relationship among elements from A and B (the perfect positive linear relationship of hesitation margins is expressed by the parallel lines formed by the elements from A and B (the two lines are also parallel to MN segment).

4   Conclusions

We have proposed a new correlation coefficient between A-IFSs. The coefficient proposed, like Pearson's coefficient between crisp sets, measures the strength of relationship between A-IFSs, and shows if the sets are positively or negatively correlated. Next, all three terms describing A-IFS are taken into account (the membership, non-membership values and hesitation margins). Each term plays an important role in data analysis and decision making, so that each of them should be reflected while assessing the correlation between A-IFSs.

References

1. Atanassov, K.: Intuitionistic Fuzzy Sets. VII ITKR Session. Sofia (Centr. Sci.-Techn. Libr. of Bulg. Acad. of Sci., 1697/84) (1983) (in Bulgarian)
2. Atanassov, K.: Intuitionistic Fuzzy Sets: Theory and Applications. Springer, Heidelberg (1999)
3. Bustince, H., Burillo, P.: Correlation of interval-valued intuitionistic fuzzy sets. Fuzzy Sets and Systems 74, 237–244 (1995)
4. Chiang, D.-A., Lin, N.P.: Correlation of fuzzy sets. Fuzzy Sets and Systems 102, 221–226 (1999)
5. Gersternkorn, T., Manko, J.: Correlation of intuitionistic fuzzy sets. Fuzzy Sets and Systems 44, 39–43 (1991)
6. Hong, D.H., Hwang, S.Y.: Correlation of intuitionistic fuzzy sets in probability spaces. Fuzzy Sets and Systems 75, 77–81 (1995)
7. Hong, D.H., Hwang, S.Y.: A note on the correlation of fuzzy numbers. Fuzzy Sets and Systems 79, 401–402 (1996)
8. Hung, W.L.: Using statistical viewpoint in developing correlation of intuitionistic fuzzy sets. Int. Journal of Uncertainty, Fuzziness and Knowledge-Based systems 9(4), 509–516 (2001)
9. Hung, W.L., Wu, J.W.: Correlation of intuitionistic fuzzy sets by centroid method. Information Sciences 144, 219–225 (2002)
10. Kendler, K.S., Parnas, J.: Philosophical Issues in Psychiatry: Explanation, Phenomenology, and Nosology. Johns Hopkins University Press, Baltimore (2008)
11. Liu, S.-T., Kao, C.: Fuzzy measures for correlation coefficient of fuzzy numbers. Fuzzy Sets and Systems 128, 267–275 (2002)
12. Rodgers, J.L., Nicewander, W.A.: Thirteen Ways to Look at the Correlation Coefficient. The American Statistician 42(1), 59–66 (1988)
13. Szmidt, E., Kacprzyk, J.: Remarks on some applications of intuitionistic fuzzy sets in decision making. Notes on IFS 2(3), 22–31 (1996c)
14. Szmidt, E., Kacprzyk, J.: On measuring distances between intuitionistic fuzzy sets. Notes on IFS 3(4), 1–13 (1997)
15. Szmidt, E., Kacprzyk, J.: Group Decision Making under Intuitionistic Fuzzy Preference Relations. In: IPMU '98, pp. 172–178 (1998)

16. Szmidt, E., Kacprzyk, J.: Distances between intuitionistic fuzzy sets. Fuzzy Sets and Systems 114(3), 505–518 (2000)
17. Szmidt, E., Kacprzyk, J.: On Measures on Consensus Under Intuitionistic Fuzzy Relations. In: IPMU 2000, pp. 1454–1461 (2000)
18. Szmidt, E., Kacprzyk, J.: Entropy for intuitionistic fuzzy sets. Fuzzy Sets and Systems 118(3), 467–477 (2001)
19. Szmidt, E., Kacprzyk, J.: Analysis of Consensus under Intuitionistic Fuzzy Preferences. In: Proc. Int. Conf. in Fuzzy Logic and Technology, pp. 79–82. De Montfort Univ. Leicester, UK (2001)
20. Szmidt, E., Kacprzyk, J.: Analysis of Agreement in a Group of Experts via Distances Between Intuitionistic Fuzzy Preferences. In: Proc. 9th Int. Conf. IPMU 2002, pp. 1859–1865 (2002a)
21. Szmidt, E., Kacprzyk, J.: An Intuitionistic Fuzzy Set Based Approach to Intelligent Data Analysis (an application to medical diagnosis). In: Abraham, A., Jain, L., Kacprzyk, J. (eds.) Recent Advances in Intelligent Paradigms and Applications, pp. 57–70. Springer, Heidelberg (2002b)
22. Szmidt, E., Kacprzyk, J.: An Intuitionistic Fuzzy Set Based Approach to Intelligent Data Analysis (an application to medical diagnosis). In: Abraham, A., Jain, L., Kacprzyk, J. (eds.) Recent Advances in Intelligent Paradigms and Applications, pp. 57–70. Springer, Heidelberg (2002c)
23. Szmidt, E., Kacprzyk, J.: Distances Between Intuitionistic Fuzzy Sets: Straightforward Approaches may not work. In: IEEE IS'06, pp. 716–721 (2006)
24. Szmidt, E., Kacprzyk, J.: An Application of Intuitionistic Fuzzy Set Similarity Measures to a Multi-criteria Decision Making Problem. In: Rutkowski, L., Tadeusiewicz, R., Zadeh, L.A., Żurada, J.M. (eds.) ICAISC 2006. LNCS (LNAI), vol. 4029, pp. 314–323. Springer, Heidelberg (2006)
25. Szmidt, E., Kacprzyk, J.: Some problems with entropy measures for the Atanassov intuitionistic fuzzy sets. In: Masulli, F., Mitra, S., Pasi, G. (eds.) WILF 2007. LNCS (LNAI), vol. 4578, pp. 291–297. Springer, Heidelberg (2007)
26. Szmidt, E., Kacprzyk, J.: A New Similarity Measure for Intuitionistic Fuzzy Sets: Straightforward Approaches may not work. In: 2007 IEEE Conf. on Fuzzy Systems, pp. 481–486 (2007a)
27. Szmidt, E., Kacprzyk, J.: A new approach to ranking alternatives expressed via intuitionistic fuzzy sets. In: Ruan, D., et al. (eds.) Computational Intelligence in Decision and Control, pp. 265–270. World Scientific, Singapore (2008)
28. Szmidt, E., Kacprzyk, J.: Amount of information and its reliability in the ranking of Atanassov's intuitionistic fuzzy alternatives. In: Rakus-Andersson, E., Yager, R., Ichalkaranje, N., Jain, L.C. (eds.) Recent Advances in decision Making, SCI 222, pp. 7–19. Springer, Heidelberg (2009)
29. Szmidt, E., Kacprzyk, J.: Ranking of Intuitionistic Fuzzy Alternatives in a Multi-criteria Decision Making Problem. In: Proceedings of the conference: NAFIPS 2009, Cincinnati, USA, June 14-17, IEEE, Los Alamitos (2009)
30. Szmidt, E., Kukier, M.: Classification of Imbalanced and Overlapping Classes using Intuitionistic Fuzzy Sets. In: IEEE IS'06, London, pp. 722–727 (2006)
31. Szmidt, E., Kukier, M.: A New Approach to Classification of Imbalanced Classes via Atanassov's Intuitionistic Fuzzy Sets. In: Wang, H.-F. (ed.) Intelligent Data Analysis: Developing New Methodologies Through Pattern Discovery and Recovery, pp. 85–101. Idea Group, USA (2008)
32. Zadeh, L.A.: Fuzzy sets. Information and Control 8, 338–353 (1965)
33. Zeng, W., Li, H.: Correlation coefficient of intuitionistic fuzzy sets. Journal of Industrial Engineering International 3(5), 33–40 (2007)

A Correlation Ratio for Possibility Distributions

Robert Fullér[1], József Mezei[2], and Péter Várlaki[3,4]

[1] IAMSR, Åbo Akademi University,
Joukahaisenkatu 3-5 A, FIN-20520 Turku
[2] Turku Centre for Computer Science,
Joukahaisenkatu 3-5 B, FIN-20520 Turku
[3] Budapest University of Technology and Economics,
Bertalan L.u. 2, H-1111 Budapest, Hungary
[4] Széchenyi István University,
Egyetem tér 1, H-9026 Győr, Hungary
{robert.fuller,jozsef.mezei}@abo.fi,
varlaki@kme.bme.hu

Abstract. Generalizing the probabilistic correlation ratio we will introduce a correlation ratio for marginal possibility distributions of joint possibility distributions.

Keywords: Correlation ratio, possibility distribution, joint possibility distribution.

1 Introduction

In statistics, the correlation ratio is a measure of the relationship between the statistical dispersion within individual categories and the dispersion across the whole population or sample. The correlation ratio was originally introduced by Karl Pearson [5] as part of analysis of variance and it was extended to random variables by Andrei Nikolaevich Kolmogorov [4] as,

$$\eta^2(X|Y) = \frac{D^2[E(X|Y)]}{D^2(X)},$$

where X and Y are random variables. If X and Y have a joint probability density function, denoted by $f(x,y)$, then we can compute $\eta^2(X|Y)$ using the following formulas

$$E(X|Y=y) = \int_{-\infty}^{\infty} xf(x|y)\mathrm{d}x$$

and

$$D^2[E(X|Y)] = E(E(X|y) - E(X))^2,$$

and where,

$$f(x|y) = \frac{f(x,y)}{f(y)}.$$

E. Hüllermeier, R. Kruse, and F. Hoffmann (Eds.): IPMU 2010, LNAI 6178, pp. 178–187, 2010.
© Springer-Verlag Berlin Heidelberg 2010

Note 1. The correlation ratio measures the functional dependence between X and Y. It takes on values between 0 (no functional dependence) and 1 (purely deterministic dependence). It is worth noting that if $E(X|Y = y)$ is linear function of y (i.e. there is a linear relationship between random variables $E(X|Y)$ and Y) this will give the same result as the square of the correlation coefficient, otherwise the correlation ratio will be larger in magnitude. It can therefore be used for judging non-linear relationships. Also note that the correlation ratio is asymmetrical by nature since the two random variables fundamentally do not play the same role in the functional relationship; in general, $\eta^2(X|Y) \neq \eta^2(Y|X)$.

A *fuzzy number*. A is a fuzzy set $\mathbb{R}$ with a normal, fuzzy convex and continuous membership function of bounded support. The family of fuzzy numbers is denoted by $\mathcal{F}$. Fuzzy numbers can be considered as possibility distributions. A fuzzy set C in $\mathbb{R}^2$ is said to be a joint possibility distribution of fuzzy numbers $A, B \in \mathcal{F}$, if it satisfies the relationships

$$\max\{x \mid C(x,y)\} = B(y) \quad \text{and} \quad \max\{y \mid C(x,y)\} = A(x)$$

for all $x, y \in \mathbb{R}$. Furthermore, A and B are called the marginal possibility distributions of C. A γ-level set (or γ-cut) of a fuzzy number A is a non-fuzzy set denoted by $[A]^\gamma$ and defined by $[A]^\gamma = \{t \in X | A(t) \geq \gamma\}$ if $\gamma > 0$ and $\mathrm{cl}(\mathrm{supp}A)$ if $\gamma = 0$, where $\mathrm{cl}(\mathrm{supp}A)$ denotes the closure of the support of A.

Let $A \in \mathcal{F}$ be fuzzy number with a γ-level set denoted by $[A]^\gamma = [a_1(\gamma), a_2(\gamma)]$, $\gamma \in [0,1]$ and let U_γ denote a uniform probability distribution on $[A]^\gamma$, $\gamma \in [0,1]$.

In possibility theory we can use the principle of *expected value* of functions on fuzzy sets to define variance, covariance and correlation of possibility distributions. Namely, we can equip each level set of a possibility distribution (represented by a fuzzy number) with a uniform probability distribution, then apply their standard probabilistic calculation, and then define measures on possibility distributions by integrating these weighted probabilistic notions over the set of all membership grades [1,2]. These weights (or importances) can be given by weighting functions. A function $g: [0,1] \to \mathbb{R}$ is said to be a weighting function if g is non-negative, monotone increasing and satisfies the following normalization condition $\int_0^1 g(\gamma)d\gamma = 1$. Different weighting functions can give different (case-dependent) importances to level-sets of possibility distributions. In this paper we will introduce a correlation ratio for marginal possibility distributions of joint possibility distributions.

2   A Correlation Ratio for Marginal Possibility Distributions

Definition 1. *Let us denote A and B the marginal possibility distributions of a given joint possibility distribution C. Then the g-weighted possibilistic correlation ratio of marginal possibility distribution A with respect to marginal possibility distribution B is defined by*

$$\eta_f^2(A|B) = \int_0^1 \eta^2(X_\gamma|Y_\gamma)g(\gamma)\mathrm{d}\gamma \tag{1}$$

where X_γ and Y_γ are random variables whose joint distribution is uniform on $[C]^\gamma$ for all $\gamma \in [0,1]$, and $\eta^2(X_\gamma|Y_\gamma)$ denotes their probabilistic correlation ratio.

So the g-weighted possibilistic correlation ratio of the fuzzy number A on B is nothing else, but the g-weighted average of the probabilistic correlation ratios $\eta^2(X_\gamma|Y_\gamma)$ for all $\gamma \in [0,1]$.

3   Computation of Correlation Ratio: Some Examples

In this section we will compute the g-weighted possibilistic correlation ratio for joint possibility distributions $(1 - x - y)$, $(1 - x^2 - y)$, $(1 - \sqrt{x} - y)$, $(1 - x^2 - y^2)$ and $(1 - \sqrt{x} - \sqrt{y})$ defined on proper subsets of the unit square.

3.1   A Linear Relationship

Consider the case, when

$$A(x) = B(x) = (1 - x) \cdot \chi_{[0,1]}(x),$$

for $x \in \mathbb{R}$, that is $[A]^\gamma = [B]^\gamma = [0, 1 - \gamma]$, for $\gamma \in [0,1]$. Suppose that their joint possibility distribution is given by $C(x,y) = (1 - x - y) \cdot \chi_T(x,y)$, where

$$T = \left\{ (x,y) \in \mathbb{R}^2 \mid x \geq 0, y \geq 0, x + y \leq 1 \right\}.$$

Then we have $[C]^\gamma = \left\{ (x,y) \in \mathbb{R}^2 \mid x \geq 0, y \geq 0, x + y \leq 1 - \gamma \right\}$. The density function of a uniform distribution on $[C]^\gamma$ is

$$f(x,y) = \begin{cases} \dfrac{2}{(1-\gamma)^2} & \text{if } (x,y) \in [C]^\gamma \\ 0 & \text{otherwise} \end{cases}$$

The marginal functions are obtained as

$$f_1(x) = \begin{cases} \dfrac{2(1 - \gamma - x)}{(1-\gamma)^2} & \text{if } 0 \leq x \leq 1 - \gamma \\ 0 & \text{otherwise} \end{cases}$$

$$f_2(y) = \begin{cases} \dfrac{2(1 - \gamma - y)}{(1-\gamma)^2} & \text{if } 0 \leq y \leq 1 - \gamma \\ 0 & \text{otherwise} \end{cases}$$

For the correlation ration we need to calculate the conditional probalility distribution:

$$E(X|Y = y) = \int_0^{1-\gamma-y} x f(x|y) \mathrm{d}x = \int_0^{1-\gamma-y} x \frac{f(x,y)}{f_2(y)} \mathrm{d}x = \frac{1 - \gamma - y}{2},$$

where $0 \leq x \leq 1-\gamma$. The next step is to calculate the variation of this distribution:

$$D^2[E(X|Y)] = E(E(X|y) - E(X))^2$$

$$= \int_0^{1-\gamma} (\frac{1-\gamma-y}{2} - \frac{1-\gamma}{3})^2 \frac{2(1-\gamma-y)}{(1-\gamma)^2}$$

$$= \frac{(1-\gamma)^2}{72}.$$

Using the relationship

$$D^2(X_\gamma) = \frac{(1-\gamma)^2}{18},$$

we obtain that the probabilistic correlation of X_γ on Y_γ is

$$\eta^2(X_\gamma|Y_\gamma) = \frac{1}{4}.$$

From this the g-weighted possibilistic correlation ratio of A with respect to B is,

$$\eta_f^2(A|B) = \int_0^1 \frac{1}{4} g(\gamma) d\gamma = \frac{1}{4}.$$

Note 2. The g-weighted normalized measure of interactivity between $A \in \mathcal{F}$ and $B \in \mathcal{F}$ (with respect to their joint distribution C) is defined by [3]

$$\rho_f(A, B) = \int_0^1 \rho(X_\gamma, Y_\gamma) g(\gamma) d\gamma$$

where

$$\rho(X_\gamma, Y_\gamma) = \frac{\text{cov}(X_\gamma, Y_\gamma)}{\sqrt{\text{var}(X_\gamma)}\sqrt{\text{var}(Y_\gamma)}}.$$

and where X_γ and Y_γ are random variables whose joint distribution is uniform on $[C]^\gamma$ for all $\gamma \in [0, 1]$, and $\rho(X_\gamma, Y_\gamma)$ denotes their probabilistic correlation coefficient. In this simple case

$$\eta_f^2(A|B) = \eta_f^2(B|A) = [\rho_f(A, B)]^2,$$

since $E(X_\gamma|Y_\gamma = y)$ is a linear function of y. Really, in this case we have,

$$E(X_\gamma|Y_\gamma = y) = \frac{1-\gamma-y}{2} = \frac{1-\gamma}{3} - \frac{y}{2} + \frac{1-\gamma}{6}$$

$$= \frac{1-\gamma}{3} - \frac{1}{2}y - (-\frac{1}{2}) \times \frac{1-\gamma}{3}$$

$$= \frac{1-\gamma}{3} - \frac{1}{2}(y - \frac{1-\gamma}{3}) = E(X_\gamma) - \rho(X_\gamma, Y_\gamma)(y - E(Y_\gamma)).$$

3.2   A Nonlinear Relationship

Consider the case, when

$$A(x) = (1 - x^2) \cdot \chi_{[0,1]}(x),$$

$$B(x) = (1 - y) \cdot \chi_{[0,1]}(y),$$

for $x \in \mathbb{R}$, that is $[A]^\gamma = [0, \sqrt{1 - \gamma}], [B]^\gamma = [0, 1 - \gamma]$, for $\gamma \in [0, 1]$. Suppose that their joint possibility distribution is given by:

$$C(x, y) = (1 - x^2 - y) \cdot \chi_T(x, y),$$

where

$$T = \left\{ (x, y) \in \mathbb{R}^2 \mid x \geq 0, y \geq 0, x^2 + y \leq 1 \right\}.$$

A γ-level set of C is computed by

$$[C]^\gamma = \left\{ (x, y) \in \mathbb{R}^2 \mid x \geq 0, y \geq 0, x^2 + y \leq 1 - \gamma \right\}.$$

The density function of a uniform distribution on $[C]^\gamma$ can be written as

$$f(x, y) = \begin{cases} \dfrac{1}{\int_{[C]^\gamma} dxdy} & \text{if } (x, y) \in [C]^\gamma \\ 0 & \text{otherwise} \end{cases} = \begin{cases} \dfrac{3}{2(1 - \gamma)^{\frac{3}{2}}} & \text{if } (x, y) \in [C]^\gamma \\ 0 & \text{otherwise} \end{cases}$$

The marginal functions are obtained as

$$f_1(x) = \begin{cases} \dfrac{3(1 - \gamma - x^2)}{2(1 - \gamma)^{\frac{3}{2}}} & \text{if } 0 \leq x \leq \sqrt{1 - \gamma} \\ 0 & \text{otherwise} \end{cases}$$

$$f_2(y) = \begin{cases} \dfrac{3\sqrt{1 - \gamma - y}}{2(1 - \gamma)^{\frac{3}{2}}} & \text{if } 0 \leq y \leq 1 - \gamma \\ 0 & \text{otherwise} \end{cases}$$

For the correlation ration we need to calculate the conditional probability distribution:

$$E(Y|X = x) = \int_0^{1 - \gamma - x^2} y f(y|x) dy = \int_0^{1 - \gamma - x^2} y \frac{f(x, y)}{f_1(x)} dy = \frac{1 - \gamma - x^2}{2},$$

where $0 \leq y \leq 1 - \gamma$. The next step is to calculate the variation of this distribution:

$$D^2[E(Y|X)] = E(E(Y|x) - E(Y))^2$$

$$= \int_0^{\sqrt{1 - \gamma}} \left(\frac{1 - \gamma - x^2}{2} - \frac{2(1 - \gamma)}{5} \right)^2 \frac{3(1 - \gamma - x^2)}{2(1 - \gamma)^{\frac{3}{2}}} dx$$

$$= \frac{2(1 - \gamma)^2}{175}.$$

Using the relationship

$$D^2(Y_\gamma) = \frac{12(1-\gamma)^2}{175},$$

we obtain that the probabilistic correlation ratio of Y_γ with respect to X_γ is

$$\eta^2(Y_\gamma|X_\gamma) = \frac{1}{6}.$$

From this the g-weighted possibilistic correlation ratio of B with respect to A is,

$$\eta_f^2(B|A) = \int_0^1 \frac{1}{6}g(\gamma)\mathrm{d}\gamma = \frac{1}{6}.$$

Similarly, from $D^2[E(X|Y)] = \frac{3(1-\gamma)}{320}$, and from

$$D^2(X_\gamma) = \frac{19(1-\gamma)}{320},$$

we obtain,

$$\eta_f^2(A|B) = \int_0^1 \frac{3}{19}g(\gamma)\mathrm{d}\gamma = \frac{3}{19}.$$

That is $\eta_f^2(B|A) \neq \eta_f^2(A|B)$.

3.3   Joint Distribution: $(1 - \sqrt{x} - y)$

Consider the case, when

$$A(x) = (1 - \sqrt{x}) \cdot \chi_{[0,1]}(x),$$

$$B(x) = (1 - y) \cdot \chi_{[0,1]}(y),$$

for $x \in \mathbb{R}$, that is $[A]^\gamma = [0, (1-\gamma)^2], [B]^\gamma = [0, 1-\gamma]$, for $\gamma \in [0,1]$. Suppose that their joint possibility distribution is given by:

$$C(x,y) = (1 - \sqrt{x} - y) \cdot \chi_T(x,y),$$

where

$$T = \left\{(x,y) \in \mathbb{R}^2 \mid x \geq 0, y \geq 0, \sqrt{x} + y \leq 1\right\}.$$

A γ-level set of C is computed by

$$[C]^\gamma = \left\{(x,y) \in \mathbb{R}^2 \mid x \geq 0, y \geq 0, \sqrt{x} + y \leq 1 - \gamma\right\}.$$

The density function of a uniform distribution on $[C]^\gamma$ can be written as

$$f(x,y) = \begin{cases} \dfrac{1}{\int_{[C]^\gamma} \mathrm{d}x\mathrm{d}y} & \text{if } (x,y) \in [C]^\gamma \\ 0 & \text{otherwise} \end{cases} = \begin{cases} \dfrac{3}{(1-\gamma)^3} & \text{if } (x,y) \in [C]^\gamma \\ 0 & \text{otherwise} \end{cases}$$

The marginal functions are obtained as

$$f_1(x) = \begin{cases} \dfrac{3(1-\gamma-\sqrt{x})}{(1-\gamma)^3} & \text{if } 0 \le x \le (1-\gamma)^2 \\ 0 & \text{otherwise} \end{cases}$$

$$f_2(y) = \begin{cases} \dfrac{3(1-\gamma-y)^2}{(1-\gamma)^3} & \text{if } 0 \le y \le 1-\gamma \\ 0 & \text{otherwise} \end{cases}$$

For the correlation ration we need to calculate the conditional probability distribution:

$$E(Y|X=x) = \int_0^{1-\gamma-\sqrt{x}} yf(y|x)dy = \int_0^{1-\gamma-\sqrt{x}} y\frac{f(x,y)}{f_1(x)}dy = \frac{1-\gamma-\sqrt{x}}{2},$$

where $0 \le y \le 1-\gamma$. The next step is to calculate the variation of this distribution:

$$\begin{aligned} D^2[E(Y|X)] &= E(E(Y|x) - E(Y))^2 \\ &= \int_0^{(1-\gamma)^2} (\frac{1-\gamma-\sqrt{x}}{2} - \frac{1-\gamma}{4})^2 \frac{3(1-\gamma-\sqrt{x})}{(1-\gamma)^3}dx \\ &= \frac{(1-\gamma)^2}{80}. \end{aligned}$$

Using the relationship

$$D^2(Y_\gamma) = \frac{3(1-\gamma)^2}{80},$$

we obtain that the probabilistic correlation ratio of Y_γ with respect to X_γ is

$$\eta^2(Y_\gamma|X_\gamma) = \frac{1}{3}.$$

From this the g-weighted possibilistic correlation ratio of B with respect to A is,

$$\eta_f^2(B|A) = \int_0^1 \frac{1}{3}g(\gamma)d\gamma = \frac{1}{3}.$$

Similarly, from $D^2[E(X|Y)] = \dfrac{3(1-\gamma)^4}{175}$, and from

$$D^2(X_\gamma) = \frac{37(1-\gamma)^4}{700},$$

we obtain:

$$\eta_f^2(A|B) = \int_0^1 \frac{12}{37}g(\gamma)d\gamma = \frac{12}{37}.$$

3.4   A Ball-Shaped Joint Distribution

Consider the case, when

$$A(x) = B(x) = (1 - x^2) \cdot \chi_{[0,1]}(x),$$

for $x \in \mathbb{R}$, that is $[A]^\gamma = [B]^\gamma = [0, \sqrt{1 - \gamma}]$, for $\gamma \in [0, 1]$. Suppose that their joint possibility distribution is ball-shaped, that is,

$$C(x, y) = (1 - x^2 - y^2) \cdot \chi_T(x, y),$$

where

$$T = \left\{ (x, y) \in \mathbb{R}^2 \mid x \geq 0, y \geq 0, x^2 + y^2 \leq 1 \right\}.$$

A γ-level set of C is computed by

$$[C]^\gamma = \left\{ (x, y) \in \mathbb{R}^2 \mid x \geq 0, y \geq 0, x^2 + y^2 \leq 1 - \gamma \right\}.$$

The density function of a uniform distribution on $[C]^\gamma$ can be written as

$$f(x, y) = \begin{cases} \dfrac{1}{\int_{[C]^\gamma} dxdy} & \text{if } (x, y) \in [C]^\gamma \\ 0 & \text{otherwise} \end{cases} = \begin{cases} \dfrac{4}{(1 - \gamma)\pi} & \text{if } (x, y) \in [C]^\gamma \\ 0 & \text{otherwise} \end{cases}$$

The marginal functions are obtained as

$$f_1(x) = \begin{cases} \dfrac{4\sqrt{1 - \gamma - x^2}}{(1 - \gamma)\pi} & \text{if } 0 \leq x \leq 1 - \gamma \\ 0 & \text{otherwise} \end{cases}$$

$$f_2(y) = \begin{cases} \dfrac{4\sqrt{1 - \gamma - y^2}}{(1 - \gamma)\pi} & \text{if } 0 \leq y \leq 1 - \gamma \\ 0 & \text{otherwise} \end{cases}$$

For the correlation ration we need to calculate the conditional probability distribution:

$$E(Y|X = x) = \int_0^{\sqrt{1-\gamma-x^2}} yf(y|x)dy = \int_0^{\sqrt{1-\gamma-x^2}} y\frac{f(x, y)}{f_1(x)}dy = \frac{\sqrt{1 - \gamma - x^2}}{2},$$

where $0 \leq y \leq \sqrt{1 - \gamma}$. The next step is to calculate the variation of this distribution:

$$D^2[E(Y|X)] = E(E(Y|x) - E(Y))^2$$

$$= \int_0^{\sqrt{1-\gamma}} \left(\frac{\sqrt{1 - \gamma - x^2}}{2} - \frac{4\sqrt{1 - \gamma}}{3\pi} \right)^2 \frac{4\sqrt{1 - \gamma - x^2}}{\pi(1 - \gamma)} dx$$

$$= \frac{(1 - \gamma)(27\pi^2 - 256)}{144\pi^2}.$$

Using the relationship

$$D^2(Y_\gamma) = \frac{(1-\gamma)(9\pi^2 - 64)}{36\pi^2},$$

we obtain that the probabilistic correlation ratio of Y_γ with respect to X_γ is

$$\eta^2(Y_\gamma | X_\gamma) = \frac{27\pi^2 - 256}{36\pi^2 - 256}.$$

Finally, we get that the g-weighted possibilistic correlation ratio of B with respect A is,

$$\eta_f^2(B|A) = \int_0^1 \frac{27\pi^2 - 256}{36\pi^2 - 256} g(\gamma) d\gamma = \frac{27\pi^2 - 256}{36\pi^2 - 256}.$$

3.5 Joint Distribution: $(1 - \sqrt{x} - \sqrt{y})$

Consider the case, when $A(x) = B(x) = (1 - \sqrt{x}) \cdot \chi_{[0,1]}(x)$, for $x \in \mathbb{R}$, that is $[A]^\gamma = [B]^\gamma = [0, (1-\gamma)^2]$, for $\gamma \in [0,1]$. Suppose that their joint possibility distribution is given by:

$$C(x,y) = (1 - \sqrt{x} - \sqrt{y}) \cdot \chi_T(x,y),$$

where

$$T = \left\{ (x,y) \in \mathbb{R}^2 \mid x \geq 0, y \geq 0, \sqrt{x} + \sqrt{y} \leq 1 \right\}.$$

A γ-level set of C is computed by

$$[C]^\gamma = \left\{ (x,y) \in \mathbb{R}^2 \mid x \geq 0, y \geq 0, \sqrt{x} + \sqrt{y} \leq 1 - \gamma \right\}.$$

The density function of a uniform distribution on $[C]^\gamma$ can be written as

$$f(x,y) = \begin{cases} \dfrac{1}{\int_{[C]^\gamma} dxdy} & \text{if } (x,y) \in [C]^\gamma \\ 0 & \text{otherwise} \end{cases} = \begin{cases} \dfrac{6}{(1-\gamma)^4} & \text{if } (x,y) \in [C]^\gamma \\ 0 & \text{otherwise} \end{cases}$$

The marginal functions are obtained as

$$f_1(x) = \begin{cases} \dfrac{6(1 - \gamma - \sqrt{x})^2}{(1-\gamma)^4} & \text{if } 0 \leq x \leq (1-\gamma)^2 \\ 0 & \text{otherwise} \end{cases}$$

$$f_2(y) = \begin{cases} \dfrac{6(1 - \gamma - \sqrt{y})^2}{(1-\gamma)^4} & \text{if } 0 \leq y \leq (1-\gamma)^2 \\ 0 & \text{otherwise} \end{cases}$$

For the correlation ration we need to calculate the conditional probability distribution:

$$E(Y|X=x) = \int_0^{(1-\gamma-\sqrt{x})^2} yf(y|x)dy = \int_0^{(1-\gamma-\sqrt{x})^2} y \frac{f(x,y)}{f_1(x)} dy = \frac{(1 - \gamma - \sqrt{x})^2}{2},$$

where $0 \leq y \leq (1 - \gamma)^2$. The next step is to calculate the variation of this distribution:

$$
\begin{aligned}
D^2[E(Y|X)] &= E(E(Y|x) - E(Y))^2 \\
&= \int_0^{(1-\gamma)^2} (\frac{(1 - \gamma - \sqrt{x})^2}{2} - \frac{(1-\gamma)^2}{5})^2 \frac{6(1 - \gamma - \sqrt{x})^2}{(1-\gamma)^4} dx \\
&= \frac{19(1 - \gamma)^4}{1400}.
\end{aligned}
$$

Using the relationship

$$
D^2(Y_\gamma) = \frac{9(1 - \gamma)^4}{350},
$$

we obtain that the probabilistic correlation of Y_γ with respect to X_γ is,

$$
\eta^2(Y_\gamma|X_\gamma) = \frac{19}{36}.
$$

That is, the g-weighted possibilistic correlation ratio of B with respect to A is,

$$
\eta_f^2(B|A) = \int_0^1 \frac{19}{36} g(\gamma) d\gamma = \frac{19}{36}.
$$

4 Summary

In this paper we have introduced a correlation ratio for marginal possibility distributions of joint possibility distributions. We have illustrated this new principle by five examples.

Acknowledgments

We are greatly indebted to Prof. Tamás Móri of Department of Probability Theory and Statistics, Eötvös Loránd University, Budapest, for his long-term help with probability distributions.

References

1. Carlsson, C., Fullér, R., Majlender, P.: On possibilistic correlation. Fuzzy Sets and Systems 155, 425–445 (2005)
2. Fullér, R., Majlender, P.: On interactive fuzzy numbers. Fuzzy Sets and Systems 143, 355–369 (2004)
3. Fullér, R., Mezei, J., Várlaki, P.: An improved index of interactivity for fuzzy numbers. Fuzzy Sets and Systems (submitted)
4. Kolmogorov, A.N.: Grundbegriffe der Wahrscheinlichkeitsrechnung, p. 62. Julius Springer, Berlin (1933)
5. Pearson, K.: On a New Method of Determining Correlation, when One Variable is Given by Alternative and the Other by Multiple Categories. Biometrika 7(3), 248–257 (1910)

On Nonparametric Predictive Inference for Ordinal Data

Frank P.A. Coolen*, Pauline Coolen-Schrijner**, and Tahani A. Maturi

Department of Mathematical Sciences
Durham University, Durham, DH1 3LE, UK
frank.coolen@durham.ac.uk, tahani.maturi@durham.ac.uk
http://npi-statistics.com

Abstract. Nonparametric predictive inference (NPI) is a powerful frequentist statistical framework based only on an exchangeability assumption for future and past observations, made possible by the use of lower and upper probabilities. In this paper, NPI is presented for ordinal data, which are categorical data with an ordering of the categories. The method uses a latent variable representation of the observations and categories on the real line. Lower and upper probabilities for events involving the next observation are presented, and briefly compared to NPI for non-ordered categorical data. As an example application the comparison of two groups of ordinal data is presented.

Keywords: Categorical data; lower and upper probabilities; nonparametric predictive inference; ordinal data; pairwise comparison.

1 Introduction

Nonparametric Predictive Inference (NPI) is a frequentist statistical framework based only on few modelling assumptions, enabled by the use of lower and upper probabilities to quantify uncertainty [2,6]. In NPI, attention is restricted to one or more future observable random quantities, and Hill's assumption $A_{(n)}$ [11] is used to link these random quantities to data, in a way that is closely related to exchangeability [10]. Coolen and Augustin [7,8] presented NPI for categorical data with no known relationship between the categories, as an alternative to the Imprecise Dirichlet Model (IDM) [15]. However, in many practical applications the categories are ordered, in which case such data are also known as ordinal data. It is important that such knowledge about ordering of categories is taken into account, this paper presents the first NPI results for such data. The method uses an assumed underlying latent variable representation, with the categories represented by intervals on the real-line, reflecting the known ordering of the categories and enabling application of the assumption $A_{(n)}$. An excellent recent

---

* Corresponding author.
** This work was started by Pauline Coolen-Schrijner, and completed by the other authors after her death (April 2008).

E. Hüllermeier, R. Kruse, and F. Hoffmann (Eds.): IPMU 2010, LNAI 6178, pp. 188–197, 2010.

overview of established statistical methods for ordinal data was presented by Liu and Agresti [12]. The IDM can be applied to ordinal data, see e.g. Coolen [4] who applied it to grouped lifetime data including right-censored observations, but it does not naturally use the ordering of the categories.

Section 2 provides a brief introduction to NPI. Section 3 presents NPI for ordinal data. For events which are of most practical interest, closed form formulae for the NPI lower and upper probabilities are derived, and some properties of these inferences are discussed. These results are briefly compared to NPI for non-ordered categorical data [8] in Section 4. To illustrate the application of this new method to practical problems, comparison of two groups of ordinal data is briefly presented in Section 5. More general results, including multiple comparisons and inferences for multiple future observations, together with more detailed analyses of properties of such methods, will be presented elsewhere.

2   Nonparametric Predictive Inference

Nonparametric predictive inference [2,6] is based on Hill's assumption $A_{(n)}$ [11]. Let $X_1, \ldots, X_n, X_{n+1}$ be real-valued absolutely continuous and exchangeable random quantities. Let the ordered observed values of $X_1, X_2, \ldots, X_n$ be denoted by $x_1 < x_2 < \ldots < x_n$ and let $x_0 = -\infty$ and $x_{n+1} = \infty$ for ease of notation. We assume that no ties occur; ties can be dealt with in NPI [6] but it is not relevant in this paper. For X_{n+1}, representing a future observation, $A_{(n)}$ [11] partially specifies a probability distribution by $P(X_{n+1} \in I_j = (x_{j-1}, x_j)) = \frac{1}{n+1}$ for $j = 1, \ldots, n+1$. $A_{(n)}$ does not assume anything else, and can be considered to be a post-data assumption related to exchangeability [10]. Inferences based on $A_{(n)}$ are predictive and nonparametric, and can be considered suitable if there is hardly any knowledge about the random quantity of interest, other than the n observations, or if one does not want to use such information. $A_{(n)}$ is not sufficient to derive precise probabilities for many events of interest, but it provides bounds for probabilities via the 'fundamental theorem of probability' [10], which are lower and upper probabilities in interval probability theory [14,16,17].

In NPI, uncertainty about the future observation X_{n+1} is quantified by lower and upper probabilities for events of interest. Lower and upper probabilities generalize classical ('precise') probabilities, and a lower (upper) probability for event A, denoted by $\underline{P}(A)$ ($\overline{P}(A)$), can be interpreted as supremum buying (infimum selling) price for a gamble on the event A [14], or just as the maximum lower (minimum upper) bound for the probability of A that follows from the assumptions made [6]. This latter interpretation is used in NPI, we wish to explore application of $A_{(n)}$ for inference without making further assumptions. So, NPI lower and upper probabilities are the sharpest bounds on a probability for an event of interest when only $A_{(n)}$ is assumed. Informally, $\underline{P}(A)$ ($\overline{P}(A)$) can be considered to reflect the evidence in favour of (against) event A.

Augustin and Coolen [2] proved that NPI has strong consistency properties in the theory of interval probability [14,16,17]. Direct application of $A_{(n)}$ for inferential problems is only possible for real-valued random quantities. However, by using assumed latent variable representations and variations to $A_{(n)}$, NPI has been developed for different situations, including Bernoulli quantities [5]. Defining an assumption related to $A_{(n)}$, but on a circle instead of the real-line, Coolen [6] enabled inference for circular data. This 'circular-$A_{(n)}$' assumption, in combination with a latent variable representation using a probability wheel, enabled NPI for non-ordered categorical data as presented by Coolen and Augustin [8], with as additional attractive feature the possibility to include both defined and undefined new categories in the event of interest [7]. Whilst it is natural to consider inference for a single future observation in many situations, one may also be interested in multiple future observations. This is possible in a sequential way, taking the inter-dependence of the multiple future observations into account. For example in NPI for Bernoulli quantities this was included throughout [5], and dependence of specific inferences on the choice of the number of future observations was explicitly studied in the context of multiple comparisons [9].

3   NPI for Ordinal Data

In situations with ordinal data, there are $k \geq 2$ categories to which observations belong, and these categories have a natural fixed ordering, hence they can be denoted by $C_1 < C_2 < \ldots < C_k$. It is attractive to base NPI for such data on the naturally related latent variable representation with the real-line partitioned into k categories, with the same ordering, and observations per category represented by corresponding values on the real-line and in the specific category. Assuming that multiple observations in a category are represented by different values in this latent variable representation, the assumption $A_{(n)}$ can be applied for the latent variables. This is now explained in detail, and for several important situations closed forms for the NPI lower and upper probabilities are derived. We focus mostly on situations with $k \geq 3$, although the arguments also hold for $k = 2$, in which case the NPI method presented in this paper is identical to NPI for Bernoulli data [5]. We restrict attention to a single future observation, the interesting case of ordinal data with multiple future observations will be presented elsewhere.

We assume that n observations are available, with only the number of observations in each category given. Let $n_l \geq 0$ be the number of observations in category C_l, for $l = 1, \ldots, k$, so $\sum_{l=1}^{k} n_l = n$. Let Y_{n+1} denote the random quantity representing the category a future observation will belong to. We wish to derive the NPI lower and upper probabilities for events $Y_{n+1} \in \bigcup_{l \in L} C_l$ with $L \subset \{1, \ldots, k\}$. These do not follow straightforwardly from the NPI lower and upper probabilities for the events involving single categories as lower (upper) probabilities are super-additive (sub-additive) [14].

Using the latent variable representation, we assume that category C_l is represented by interval IC_l, with the intervals $IC_1, \ldots, IC_k$ forming a partition of the real-line and logically ordered, that is interval IC_l has neighbouring intervals IC_{l-1} to its left and IC_{l+1} to its right on the real-line (or only one of these neighbours if $l = 1$ or $l = k$, of course). We further assume that the n

observations are represented by $x_1 < \ldots < x_n$, of which n_l are in interval IC_l, these are also denoted by x_i^l for $i = 1, \ldots, n_l$. A further latent variable X_{n+1} on the real-line corresponds to the future observation Y_{n+1}, so the event $Y_{n+1} \in C_l$ corresponds to the event $X_{n+1} \in IC_l$. This allows $A_{(n)}$ to be directly applied to X_{n+1}, and then transformed to inference on the categorical random quantity Y_{n+1}. The ordinal data structure for the latent variables is presented in Fig. 1.

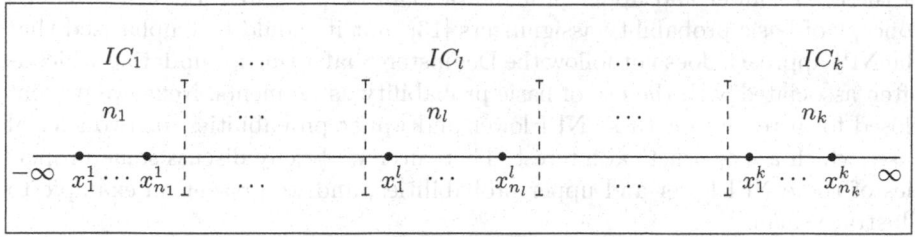

Fig. 1. Ordinal data structure

We now derive the NPI lower and upper probabilities for general events of the form $Y_{n+1} \in C_L$, with $C_L = \bigcup_{l \in L} C_l$ and $L \subset \{1, \ldots, k\}$. We assume that L is a strict subset of $\{1, \ldots, k\}$, as the event that a future observation falls into any of the k categories is necessarily true and has NPI lower and upper probabilities both equal to 1. Assuming $A_{(n)}$ for X_{n+1} in the latent variable representation, each interval I_j has been assigned probability mass $1/(n + 1)$ (see Section 2). Although we do not know exactly the values x_j, since they only exist in the latent variable representation, we do know the number of these x_j values in each interval IC_l.

To derive the NPI lower probability for the event $Y_{n+1} \in C_L$, we derive the NPI lower probability for the corresponding latent variable event $X_{n+1} \in \mathcal{IC}_L$, where $\mathcal{IC}_L = \bigcup_{l \in L} IC_l$ and $L \subset \{1, \ldots, k\}$. This lower probability is derived by summing all probability masses assigned to intervals I_j that are fully within $\mathcal{IC}_L$, so in effect we minimise the total probability mass assigned to $\mathcal{IC}_L$. Hence, these NPI lower probabilities are

$$\underline{P}(Y_{n+1} \in C_L) = \underline{P}(X_{n+1} \in \mathcal{IC}_L) = \frac{1}{n+1} \sum_{j=1}^{n+1} \mathbf{1}\{I_j \subset \mathcal{IC}_L\} \qquad (1)$$

where $\mathbf{1}\{A\}$ is equal to 1 if A is true and equal to 0 else. As we do not know the exact locations of the intervals IC_l, this may appear to be vague, yet the fact that we know the numbers of x_j values within each interval IC_l suffices to get unique values for these NPI lower probabilities.

The corresponding NPI upper probabilities are derived by maximising the total probability mass that can be assigned to $\mathcal{IC}_L$. Without any further assumptions on the way the probability mass $1/(n + 1)$ is spread over an interval I_j, this means that we can include all such probability masses corresponding to intervals I_j that have a non-empty intersection with $\mathcal{IC}_L$. So the NPI upper probabilities are

$$\overline{P}(Y_{n+1} \in \mathcal{C}_L) = \overline{P}(X_{n+1} \in \mathcal{IC}_L) = \frac{1}{n+1} \sum_{j=1}^{n+1} 1\{I_j \cap \mathcal{IC}_L \neq \emptyset\} \qquad (2)$$

These NPI upper probabilities are also uniquely determined. The construction of these NPI lower and upper probabilities can be presented following Shafer's concept of basic probability assignments [13], but it should be emphasized that the NPI approach does not follow the Dempster-Shafer rule for updating which is often associated with the use of basic probability assignments. Next, we present closed form results for these NPI lower and upper probabilities for two special cases which are of practical interest. Thereafter we briefly discuss some properties of these NPI lower and upper probabilities, and we present an example to illustrate them.

3.1   Special Cases

An important special case of these inferences concerns the event $Y_{n+1} \in \mathcal{C}_L$, with $\mathcal{C}_L$ consisting of adjoining categories, so the corresponding union of intervals $\mathcal{IC}_L$ forms a single interval on the real-line in the latent variable representation. For this case simple closed forms for the NPI lower and upper probabilities are available. Let $L = \{s, \ldots, t\}$, with $s, t \in \{1, \ldots, k\}$, $s \leq t$, excluding the case with $s = 1$ and $t = k$ for which both the NPI lower and upper probabilities are equal to 1. Let $\mathcal{C}_{s,t} = \bigcup_{l=s}^{t} \mathcal{C}_l$, $\mathcal{IC}_{s,t} = \bigcup_{l=s}^{t} IC_l$ and let $n_{s,t} = \sum_{l=s}^{t} n_l$. Using the notation $(x)^+ = \max(x, 0)$, the NPI lower and upper probabilities (1) and (2) for such events are

$$\underline{P}(Y_{n+1} \in C_{s,t}) = \underline{P}(X_{n+1} \in \mathcal{IC}_{s,t}) = \begin{cases} \dfrac{(n_{s,t} - 1)^+}{n+1} & \text{if } 1 < s \leq t < k \\[2mm] \dfrac{n_{s,t}}{n+1} & \text{if } s = 1 \text{ or } t = k \end{cases} \qquad (3)$$

$$\overline{P}(Y_{n+1} \in C_{s,t}) = \overline{P}(X_{n+1} \in \mathcal{IC}_{s,t}) = \frac{n_{s,t} + 1}{n+1} \quad \text{for } 1 \leq s \leq t \leq k \qquad (4)$$

Of course, $s = t$ is the event that the next observation belongs to one specific category.

A further special case for which closed form expressions are available for the NPI lower and upper probabilities occurs if $n_l > 0$ for all $l \in \{1, \ldots, k\}$, so there are observations in all k categories. We need to consider if the categories C_1 and C_k are included in $\mathcal{C}_L$ (so IC_1 and IC_k in $\mathcal{IC}_L$) and we need to take account of all pairs of neighbouring categories which are both included in $\mathcal{C}_L$. Let

$$p_L = \sum_{r=1}^{k-1} 1\{r, r+1 \in L\}$$

be the number of neighbouring pairs of categories included in $\mathcal{C}_L$, and let

$$e_L = \mathbf{1}\{1 \in L\} + \mathbf{1}\{k \in L\} + p_L$$

We further introduce the notation s_L for the number of categories in $\mathcal{C}_L$, so $s_L = |L|$, and $n_L = \sum_{l \in L} n_l$. Then the NPI lower probability (1), with L a strict subset of $\{1, \ldots, k\}$, is

$$\underline{P}(Y_{n+1} \in \mathcal{C}_L) = \underline{P}(X_{n+1} \in \mathcal{IC}_L) = \frac{\sum_{l \in L}(n_l - 1) + e_L}{n+1} = \frac{n_L - s_L + e_L}{n+1} \quad (5)$$

and the corresponding NPI upper probability (2) is

$$\overline{P}(Y_{n+1} \in \mathcal{C}_L) = \overline{P}(X_{n+1} \in \mathcal{IC}_L) = \frac{\sum_{l \in L}(n_l + 1) - p_L}{n+1} = \frac{n_L + s_L - p_L}{n+1} \quad (6)$$

These two special cases are likely to cover many situations of practical interest. The problem for deriving a simple general closed form expression for the NPI lower and upper probabilities (1) and (2) results from accounting for one or more consecutive categories without any observations in the event of interest, in which case it is important whether or not there are observations in the neighbouring categories.

3.2 Properties

The NPI lower and upper probabilities (1) and (2) satisfy the conjugacy property $\underline{P}(Y_{n+1} \in \mathcal{C}_L) = 1 - \overline{P}(Y_{n+1} \in \mathcal{C}_{L^c})$ for all $L \subset \{1, \ldots, k\}$ and $L^c = \{1, \ldots, k\}\backslash L$, which follows from $\mathbf{1}\{I_j \subset \mathcal{IC}_L\} + \mathbf{1}\{I_j \cap \mathcal{IC}_L^c \neq \emptyset\} = 1$ for all $j = 1, \ldots, n+1$. Augustin and Coolen [2] prove stronger consistency properties for NPI lower and upper probabilities for real-valued random quantities within the theory of Weichselberger [16,17], in particular that they are F-probability. Their results apply directly to the NPI lower and upper probabilities for X_{n+1} in the latent variable representation in this paper, and hence also imply that the NPI lower and upper probabilities (1) and (2) for the categorical random quantity Y_{n+1} are F-probability. This implies the above mentioned conjugacy property, and also coherence of these lower and upper probabilities in the sense of Walley [14]. However, Walley-coherence goes further by also considering such lower and upper probabilities at different moments in time, that is to say with different numbers of observations as is relevant in case of updating. In NPI, updating is performed by just calculating the relevant lower and upper probabilities using all available data, and is not performed via conditioning on prior sets of probabilities [2]. The NPI lower and upper probabilities (1) and (2) bound the corresponding empirical probability for the event of interest, so

$$\underline{P}(Y_{n+1} \in \mathcal{C}_L) \leq \frac{n_L}{n} \leq \overline{P}(Y_{n+1} \in \mathcal{C}_L) \quad (7)$$

Property (7) can be considered attractive when aiming at 'objective inference', and the possibility to satisfy this property is an important advantage of statistical methods using lower and upper probabilities [6].

3.3   Example

Suppose there are $k = 5$ ordered categories, $C_1 < \ldots < C_5$, and $n = 11$ observations with $n_1 = 1$, $n_2 = 3$, $n_3 = 1$, $n_4 = 4$ and $n_5 = 2$, so equations (5) and (6) can be used. The NPI lower and upper probabilities for several events $Y_{12} \in C_L$ are given in Table 1, together with the corresponding empirical probability n_L/n.

Table 1. NPI lower and upper probabilities

L	$\underline{P}$	$\overline{P}$	n_L/n
$\{1\}$	1/12	2/12	1/11
$\{2\}$	2/12	4/12	3/11
$\{3\}$	0	2/12	1/11
$\{4\}$	3/12	5/12	4/11
$\{5\}$	2/12	3/12	2/11
$\{1,2\}$	4/12	5/12	4/11
$\{1,2,3\}$	5/12	6/12	5/11
$\{2,3,4\}$	7/12	9/12	8/11
$\{1,2,4\}$	7/12	10/12	8/11
$\{1,2,4,5\}$	10/12	1	10/11

These lower and upper probabilities illustrate the relation (7), and they also show that the difference between corresponding upper and lower probabilities is not constant. The lower and upper probabilities for the events with L consisting of a single category or a group of adjoining categories also illustrate the lower and upper probabilities (3) and (4) from the first special case discussed above.

4   Comparison to NPI for Non-ordered Categorical Data

Coolen and Augustin [8] presented NPI for categorical data with a known number of possible categories yet with no ordering or other known relationship between the categories. Their inferences are based on a latent variable representation using a probability wheel, with each category represented by a single segment of the wheel yet without any assumption about the specific configuration of the wheel. Their NPI lower and upper probabilities with regard to the next observation are further based on a circular version of $A_{(n)}$ [6] and optimisation over all possible configurations of the probability wheel that are possible corresponding to the data and this so-called circular-$A_{(n)}$ assumption. Coolen and Augustin [7] illustrated how this model can also be used in case of an unknown number of possible categories, which is less likely to be of relevance in case of ordinal data hence we have not addressed it here. For further details of NPI for non-ordered categorical data we refer to Coolen and Augustin [8], we just wish to emphasize that the inferences can differ substantially if categories are known to be ordered and therefore the inferences presented here are applied.

To illustrate that NPI for non-ordered categorical data and NPI for ordinal data can be very different, consider the following simple example. Suppose we have $k = 6$ ordered categories, $C_1 < \ldots < C_6$, and only $n = 3$ observations, one in each of the first three categories, so $n_1 = n_2 = n_3 = 1$ and $n_4 = n_5 = n_6 = 0$. Following the results presented in this paper, the NPI lower and upper probabilities for the event $Y_4 \in \{C_1, C_2, C_3\}$ are $3/4$ and 1, respectively. If, however, the categories were not assumed to be ordered, then the corresponding NPI lower and upper probabilities for this event would be 0 and 1, respectively [8]. The latter lower probability may be surprising, it results from the possibility that the categories C_1, C_2, C_3 could, in the probability wheel representation, be separated by the other three categories, and from the fact that no single category has been observed more than once. We do not discuss this difference in more detail, but it is important to recognize that the inferences for categorical data can differ substantially if one can use a known ordering of the categories. Due to the different latent variable representations for these two situations, it is not the case that the NPI lower and upper probabilities according to these two models are nested, as could perhaps have been expected. One could consider different structures for the categories and different latent variable representations, this is left as an interesting topic for future research.

5   Comparison of Two Groups

In many applications of statistics, one aims at comparing multiple groups of data. We briefly illustrate how the NPI approach presented in this paper can be used for comparison of two groups of data, detailed justification of these results will be presented elsewhere, together with generalization to comparisons of more than two groups of data. Suppose that, as before, we consider k ordered categories, $C_1 < \ldots < C_k$, but now we have data for two independent groups which we wish to compare. Traditional statistical methods [12] tend to formulate problems of comparison of multiple groups as tests of hypotheses, but in NPI comparisons are necessarily predictive, hence one or more future observations per group are compared. Let us denote the two different groups by A and B, and we add a superscript a or b to our earlier notation to indicate the group. So, the total number of observations for group A (B) is n^a (n^b), of which n_j^a (n_j^b) are in category C_j. To use NPI for the comparison of these two groups, restricting attention to a single future observation per group, we assume $A_{(n^a)}$ for the next observation $Y_{n^a+1}^a$ from group A, and $A_{(n^b)}$ for the next observation $Y_{n^b+1}^b$ from group B, and per group we use the same latent variable representation as before.

Whilst ordinal data do not normally have meaningful associated location summaries (e.g. mean or median), due to the natural ordering of the categories it is meaningful to consider the events $Y_{n^a+1}^a < Y_{n^b+1}^b$ and $Y_{n^a+1}^a \leq Y_{n^b+1}^b$ for comparison of the two groups. For the corresponding underlying latent variables, this then follows NPI comparison of two groups of real-valued data as presented by Coolen [3], with the added complication that no actual observations are available for the latent variables and hence there is no knowledge about the ordering of values of the two groups within a category. Hence, the NPI lower and upper probabilities for these events are derived by minimisation and maximisation, respectively, of corresponding lower and upper probabilities for all possible orderings of the latent variables per category. This leads to the following NPI lower and upper probabilities, with $\gamma = ((n^a + 1)(n^b + 1))^{-1}$,

$$\underline{P}(Y^a_{n^a+1} < Y^b_{n^b+1}) = \gamma \sum_{v=2}^{k} \sum_{w=1}^{v-1} n^a_w n^b_v \tag{8}$$

$$\overline{P}(Y^a_{n^a+1} < Y^b_{n^b+1}) = \gamma \left(\sum_{v=2}^{k} \sum_{w=1}^{v-1} n^a_w n^b_v + n^b - n^b_1 + n^a - n^a_k + 1 \right) \tag{9}$$

and

$$\underline{P}(Y^a_{n^a+1} \leq Y^b_{n^b+1}) = \gamma \left(\sum_{v=1}^{k} \sum_{w=1}^{v} n^a_w n^b_v + n^a_1 + n^b_k \right) \tag{10}$$

$$\overline{P}(Y^a_{n^a+1} \leq Y^b_{n^b+1}) = \gamma \left(\sum_{v=1}^{k} \sum_{w=1}^{v} n^a_w n^b_v + n^a + n^b + 1 \right) \tag{11}$$

We illustrate such comparison of two ordinal data sets, using these NPI lower and upper probabilities, by considering the data presented in Table 2, which were also used by Agresti [1] who provides further references to the origins of this data set. The data consider tonsil size for two groups of children, namely 1326 noncarriers (Group A) and 72 carriers (Group B) of streptococcus pyogenes. An observation in category C_1 implies that tonsils are present but not enlarged, C_2 that tonsils are enlarged and C_3 that tonsils are greatly enlarged.

Table 2. Data: size of tonsils

	C_1	C_2	C_3
Noncarriers (A)	497	560	269
Carriers (B)	19	29	24

The NPI lower and upper probabilities (8)-(11) for these data are $\underline{P}(Y^a_{1327} < Y^b_{73}) = \frac{39781}{1327 \times 73} = 0.4107$, $\overline{P}(Y^a_{1327} < Y^b_{73}) = \frac{40892}{1327 \times 73} = 0.4221$, $\underline{P}(Y^a_{1327} \leq Y^b_{73}) = \frac{72441}{1327 \times 73} = 0.7478$ and $\overline{P}(Y^a_{1327} \leq Y^b_{73}) = \frac{73319}{1327 \times 73} = 0.7569$. Agresti [1] considered all $1326 \times 72 = 95472$ different carrier-noncarrier pairs that can be put together from these children, of which for $19(560 + 269) + 29(269) = 23552$ pairs the noncarrier has larger tonsils than the carrier, hence for 71920 pairs the carrier's tonsils are as least as large as those of the noncarrier, and for 39781 pairs the carrier has the larger tonsils. Notice that the relative frequencies corresponding to these pairs, $\frac{39781}{95472} = 0.4167$ and $\frac{71920}{95472} = 0.7533$ are bounded by the corresponding NPI lower and upper probabilities. In this example, the differences between corresponding NPI upper and lower probabilities are small, due to the large numbers of observations. Clearly, if one considers groups with fewer observations, there will be more imprecision. However, this NPI approach remains valid and keeps its attractive frequentist properties for all sizes of data sets, so inferences are not only valid for large samples as is often the case in more established frequentist statistical methods.

References

1. Agresti, A.: Generalized odds ratios for ordinal data. Biometrics 36, 59–67 (1980)
2. Augustin, T., Coolen, F.P.A.: Nonparametric predictive inference and interval probability. Journal of Statistical Planning and Inference 124, 251–272 (2004)
3. Coolen, F.P.A.: Comparing two populations based on low stochastic structure assumptions. Statistics & Probability Letters 29, 297–305 (1996)
4. Coolen, F.P.A.: An imprecise Dirichlet model for Bayesian analysis of failure data including right-censored observations. Reliability Engineering and System Safety 56, 61–68 (1997)
5. Coolen, F.P.A.: Low structure imprecise predictive inference for Bayes' problem. Statistics & Probability Letters 36, 349–357 (1998)
6. Coolen, F.P.A.: On nonparametric predictive inference and objective Bayesianism. Journal of Logic, Language and Information 15, 21–47 (2006)
7. Coolen, F.P.A., Augustin, T.: Learning from multinomial data: a nonparametric predictive alternative to the imprecise dirichlet model. In: Cozman, F.G., Nau, R., Seidenfeld, T. (eds.) ISIPTA'05: Proceedings of the Fourth International Symposium on Imprecise Probabilities and their Applications, pp. 125–134 (2005)
8. Coolen, F.P.A., Augustin, T.: A nonparametric predictive alternative to the imprecise dirichlet model: the case of a known number of categories. International Journal of Approximate Reasoning 50, 217–230 (2009)
9. Coolen, F.P.A., Coolen-Schrijner, P.: Nonparametric predictive comparison of proportions. Journal of Statistical Planning and Inference 137, 23–33 (2007)
10. De Finetti, B.: Theory of Probability: a Critical Introductory Treatment. Wiley, London (1974)
11. Hill, B.M.: Posterior distribution of percentiles: Bayes' theorem for sampling from a population. Journal of the American Statistical Association 63, 677–691 (1968)
12. Liu, I., Agresti, A.: The analysis of ordered categorical data: an overview and a survey of recent developments (with discussion). TEST 14, 1–73 (2005)
13. Shafer, G.A.: Mathematical Theory of Evidence. Princeton University Press, Princeton (1976)
14. Walley, P.: Statistical Reasoning with Imprecise Probabilities. Chapman & Hall, London (1991)
15. Walley, P.: Inferences from multinomial data: learning about a bag of marbles (with discussion). Journal of the Royal Statistical Society Series B 58, 3–57 (1996)
16. Weichselberger, K.: The theory of interval-probability as a unifying concept for uncertainty. International Journal of Approximate Reasoning 24, 149–170 (2000)
17. Weichselberger, K.: Elementare Grundbegriffe einer allgemeineren Wahrscheinlichkeitsrechnung I. Intervallwahrscheinlichkeit als umfassendes Konzept. Physika, Heidelberg (2001)

Using Cloudy Kernels for Imprecise Linear Filtering

Sebastien Destercke[1] and Olivier Strauss[2]

[1] INRA/CIRAD, UMR1208, 2 place P. Viala, F-34060 Montpellier cedex 1, France
[2] LIRMM (CNRS & Univ. Montpellier II), 161 rue Ada, F-34392 Montpellier cedex 5, France
sebastien.destercke@supagro.inra.fr, olivier.strauss@lirmm.fr

Abstract. Selecting a particular summative (i.e., formally equivalent to a probability distribution) kernel when filtering a digital signal can be a difficult task. To circumvent this difficulty, one can work with maxitive (i.e., formally equivalent to a possibility distribution) kernels. These kernels allow to consider at once sets of summative kernels with upper bounded bandwith. They also allow to perform a robustness analysis without additional computational cost. However, one of the drawbacks of filtering with maxitive kernels is sometimes an overly imprecise output, due to the limited expressiveness of summative kernels. We propose to use a new uncertainty representation, namely cloud, to achieve a compromise between summative and maxitive kernels, avoiding some of their respective shortcomings. The proposal is then experimented on a simulated signal.

Keywords: Signal treatment, interval-valued fuzzy sets, generalised p-boxes.

1 Introduction

Reconstructing a continuous signal from a set of sampled and possibly corrupted observations is a common problem in both digital analysis and signal processing [1]. In this context, kernel-based methods can be used for different purposes: reconstruction, impulse response modelling, interpolation, (non)-linear transformations, filtering, etc.

Most kernels used in signal processing are linear combination of summative kernels, which are positive functions with an integral equal to one. A summative kernel can therefore be associated to a particular probability distribution. Still, how to choose a particular kernel and its parameters to filter a given signal is often a tricky question. Using maxitive kernels [2], that is kernels that are formally equivalent to possibility distributions [3], can overcome this difficulty. This can be done by interpreting maxitive kernels and associated possibility distributions [3] as sets of summative kernels (or sets of probability distributions [4]). The output of a maxitive kernel-based filtering is an interval valued signal that gathers all the outputs of conventional filtering based on the summative kernels belonging to the considered set. This property allows to perform a rosbustness or sensitivity analysis of the filtering during the filtering process itself.

The main interests of maxitive kernels are their simplicity of representation and their computational tractability. The price to pay for such features is a limited expressiveness and the impossibility to exclude unwanted summative kernels from the set represented by maxitive kernels in some applications. For instance, this set always includes a Dirac measure, meaning that the filtered interval-valued signal always includes the original (noisy) signal itself.

E. Hüllermeier, R. Kruse, and F. Hoffmann (Eds.): IPMU 2010, LNAI 6178, pp. 198–207, 2010.

To overcome this shortcoming of maxitive kernel while keeping their interesting features, we propose to use another uncertainty representation, called clouds [5], as a compromise between summative and maxitive kernels. we call the resulting kernels cloudy kernels. The interest of cloudy kernels is two-fold: they are more expressive than maxitive kernels, the latter being a special case of the former [6], and their use only require low computational efforts, an important feature in signal processing.

We first introduce summative and maxitive kernels, before showing how cloudy kernels can act as a compromise between the two (Section 2). The computational aspects of using cloudy kernels are then discussed, and an efficient algorithm to perform signal filtering with them is devised (Section 3). Some experiments on a simulated signal are then performed and their results discussed (Section 4).

2   Between Summative and Maxitive Kernels: Cloudy Kernels

This section recalls the basics of summative and maxitive kernels. It then introduces cloudy kernels and shows how they can model summative kernels with lower-bounded bandwidth . For readability purpose, we will restrict ourselves to representations defined on the real line $\mathbb{R}$ and its discretization $\mathscr{X}$.[1]

2.1   Summative Kernels

A summative kernel κ is formally equivalent to a Lebesgue-measurable probability distribution $\kappa : \mathbb{R} \to \mathbb{R}^+$, and can be interpreted as such. The associated probability measure $P_\kappa : \mathscr{B} \to [0,1]$ defined on the real Borel agebra $\mathscr{B}$ is such that, for any measurable subset $A \subseteq \mathbb{R}$ (also called an event), $P_\kappa(A) = \int_A \kappa(x)dx$.

In this paper, we restrict ourselves to bounded, symmetrical and mono-modal kernels. To shorten notations, we consider that kernels belong to a family of kernels parameterized by their bandwidth Δ and defined on a compact interval $[-\Delta, \Delta] \subseteq \mathbb{R}$ centred around zero. Typical kernels belonging to such families are recalled and represented in Table 1. We denote them by κ_Δ, and they are such that $\kappa_\Delta(x) = \kappa_\Delta(-x)$. To a summative kernel κ_Δ can be associated its cumulative distribution function $F_{\kappa_\Delta} : [-\Delta, \Delta] \to [0,1]$ such that, for any $x \in [-\Delta, \Delta]$, $F_{\kappa_\Delta}(x) = \int_{-\Delta}^x \kappa_\Delta(x)dx$ which is such that $F_{\kappa_\Delta}(0) = 1/2$ and $F_{\kappa_\Delta}(x) + F_{\kappa_\Delta}(-x) = 1$.

2.2   Maxitive Kernels

A maxitive kernel π is a normalised function $\pi : \mathbb{R} \to [0,1]$ with at least one $x \in \mathbb{R}$ such that $\pi(x) = 1$. A maxitive kernel can be associated to a possibility distribution [3], hence inducing two (lower and upper) confidence measures, respectively called necessity and possibility measures. They are such that, for any event $A \subseteq \mathbb{R}$, we have:

$$\Pi(A) = \max_{x \in A} \pi(x) \qquad N(A) = 1 - \Pi(A^c) = \inf_{x \in A^c}(1 - \pi(x)), \qquad (1)$$

---

[1] Extension of presented methods to some product space $\mathbb{R}^p$ is straightforward.

Table 1. Some classical summative kernels

Name	κ	Shape
Triangular	$\kappa(x) = (1 - \lvert\frac{x}{\Delta}\rvert)I_\Delta$	
Uniform	$\kappa(x) = \frac{1}{2\Delta}I_\Delta$	

with A^c the complement of A. A maxitive kernel π can be associated to a set of summative kernels $\mathscr{P}_\pi$ dominated by the possibility measure Π of π, such that $\mathscr{P}_\pi = \{\kappa \in \mathbb{P}_\mathbb{R} \vert \forall A \subseteq \mathbb{R}, P(A) \leq \Pi(A)\}$, with $\mathbb{P}_\mathbb{R}$ the set of all summative kernels over $\mathbb{R}$. If a summative kernel κ is in $\mathscr{P}_\pi$, we say, by a small abuse of language, that π includes κ. This interpretation makes maxitive kernels instrumental tools to filter signal when the identification of a single summative kernel is difficult.

There are many ways to build a maxitive kernel including a given summative kernel [7]. Here, we consider the so-called Dubois-Prade transformation, since it provides the most specific solution. Given a summative kernel κ_Δ, the maxitive kernel π_{κ_Δ} resulting from the Dubois-Prade transformation is such that

$$\pi_{\kappa_\Delta}(x) = \begin{cases} 2 * F_{\kappa_\Delta}(x) & \text{if } x \leq 0 \\ 2 * (1 - F_{\kappa_\Delta}(x)) & \text{if } x > 0 \end{cases}$$

We will denote by $\pi_{\kappa_\Delta}^+, \pi_{\kappa_\Delta}^-$ the following functions

$$\pi_{\kappa_\Delta}^-(x) = \begin{cases} \pi_{\kappa_\Delta}(x) & \text{if } x \leq 0 \\ 1 & \text{if } x > 0 \end{cases} \qquad \pi_{\kappa_\Delta}^+(x) = \begin{cases} 1 & \text{if } x \leq 0 \\ \pi_{\kappa_\Delta}(x) & \text{if } x > 0. \end{cases} \tag{2}$$

The (convex) set $\mathscr{P}_{\pi_{\kappa_\Delta}}$ includes, among others, all summative kernels $\kappa_{\Delta'}$ with $\Delta' \in [0, \Delta]$ [7]. Hence, maxitive kernels allow to consider families of kernels whose bandwidth are upper-bounded, but not lower-bounded, which in some situations may be a shortcoming. For instance, in those cases where it is desirable to smoothen a signal, the interval-valued signal resulting from an imprecise filtering should not envelope the initial signal, i.e., the Dirac measure should be excluded from the set of summative kernels used to filter. It is therefore desirable to dispose of representations allowing to model sets of summative kernels whose bandwidths are both lower- and upper-bounded. Next sections show that the uncertainty representation called clouds can meet such a need.

2.3 Cloudy Kernels

Clouds, the uncertainty representation used to model cloudy kernels, have been introduced by Neumaier [5]. On the real line, they are defined as follows:

Definition 1. *A cloud is a pair of mappings* $[\pi, \eta]$ *from* $\mathbb{R}$ *to the unit interval* $[0,1]$ *such that* $\eta \leq \pi$ *and there is at least one element* $x \in \mathbb{R}$ *such that* $\pi(x) = 1$ *and one element* $y \in \mathbb{R}$ *such that* $\eta(y) = 0$

A cloud $[\pi, \eta]$ induces a probability family $\mathscr{P}_{[\pi, \eta]}$ such that

$$\mathscr{P}_{[\pi, \eta]} = \{\kappa \in \mathbb{P}_{\mathbb{R}} | P_{\kappa}(\{x | \eta(x) \geq \alpha\}) \leq 1 - \alpha \leq P_{\kappa}(\{x | \pi(x) > \alpha\})\}. \tag{3}$$

And $\mathscr{P}_{[\pi, \eta]}$ induces lower and upper confidence measures $\underline{P}_{[\pi, \eta]}, \overline{P}_{[\pi, \eta]}$ such that, for any event $A \subseteq \mathbb{R}$, $\underline{P}_{[\pi, \eta]}(A) = \inf_{\kappa \in \mathscr{P}_{[\pi, \eta]}} P_{\kappa}(A)$ and $\overline{P}_{[\pi, \eta]}(A) = \sup_{\kappa \in \mathscr{P}_{[\pi, \eta]}} P_{\kappa}(A)$. Also note that, formally, clouds are equivalent to interval-valued fuzzy sets having boundary conditions (i.e., $\pi(x) = 1$ and $\eta(y) = 0$ for some $(x, y) \in \mathbb{R}^2$). A family of clouds that will be of particular interest here are the comonotonic clouds [6]. They are defined as follows:

Definition 2. *A cloud is comonotonic if* $\forall x, y \in \mathbb{R}, \pi(x) < \pi(y) \Rightarrow \eta(x) \leq \eta(y)$

A cloudy kernel is simply a pair of functions $[\pi, \eta]$ that satisfies Definition 1. As for maxitive kernels, we can associate $\mathscr{P}_{[\pi, \eta]}$ to the corresponding set of summative kernels. In this paper, we will restrict ourselves to cloudy kernels induced by bounded, symmetric and unimodal comonotonic clouds. Again, to make notations easier, we will consider that they are defined on the interval $[-\Delta, \Delta]$.

Definition 3. *A unimodal symmetric cloudy kernel defined on* $[-\Delta, \Delta]$ *is such that, for any* $x \in [-\Delta, \Delta]$, $\eta(x) = \eta(-x)$, $\pi(x) = \pi(-x)$ *and* η, π *are non-decreasing (non-increasing) in* $[-\Delta, 0]$ $([0, \Delta])$

As for maxitive kernels, given a unimodal symmetric cloudy kernel, we will denote by $\eta^{|}, \eta$ the functions such that

$$\eta^-(x) = \begin{cases} \eta(x) & \text{if } x \leq 0 \\ 1 & \text{if } x > 0 \end{cases} \quad \eta^+(x) = \begin{cases} 1 & \text{if } x \leq 0 \\ \eta(x) & \text{if } x > 0. \end{cases} \tag{4}$$

Two particular cases of comonotonic symmetric cloudy kernel are the so-called thin and fuzzy clouds. A cloudy kernel is said to be thin if $\forall x \in \mathbb{R}, \pi(x) = \eta(x)$, i.e., if the two mappings coincide. A cloudy kernel is said to be fuzzy if $\forall x \in \mathbb{R}, \eta(x) = 0$, i.e. if the lower mapping η conveys no information.

A cloudy kernel is pictured in Figure 1. Note that a fuzzy cloudy kernel $[\pi, \eta]$ induces the same summative kernel set $\mathscr{P}_{[\pi, \eta]}$ as the maxitive kernel π. We now recall some useful properties of clouds and cloudy kernels.

Proposition 1. *A cloudy kernel* $[\pi, \eta]$ *is included in another one* $[\pi', \eta']$ *(in the sense that* $\mathscr{P}_{[\pi, \eta]} \subseteq \mathscr{P}_{[\pi', \eta']}$*) if and only if, for all* $x \in \mathbb{R}$, $[\pi(x), \eta(x)] \subseteq [\pi'(x), \eta'(x)]$.

Hence, given a cloudy kernel $[\pi, \eta]$, any thin cloud $[\pi', \eta']$ such that $\eta \leq \eta' = \pi' \leq \pi$ is included in $[\pi, \eta]$. Inversely, for any thin cloud $[\pi', \eta']$ not satisfying this condition (i.e. $\exists x$ such that $\eta'(x) < \eta(x)$ or $\pi'(x) > \pi(x)$), we have $\mathscr{P}_{[\pi, \eta]} \cap \mathscr{P}_{[\pi', \eta']} = \emptyset$.

Proposition 2. *The convex set* $\mathscr{P}_{[\pi, \eta]}$ *induced by a thin cloud* $[\pi, \eta]$ *includes the two summative kernels having for cumulative distributions* F^-, F^+ *such that, for all* $x \in \mathbb{R}$

$$F^-(x) = \eta^-(x) = \pi^-(x) \quad ; \quad F^+(x) = 1 - \eta^+(x) = 1 - \pi^+(x). \tag{5}$$

$\mathscr{P}_{[\pi, \eta]}$ being a convex set, any convex combination of F^-, F^+ is also in the thin cloud.

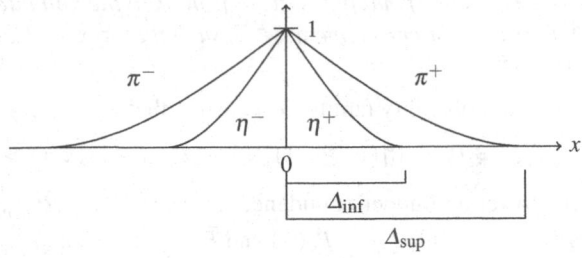

Fig. 1. Example of cloudy kernel

2.4   Summative Kernel Approximation with Cloudy Kernels

Let us show that cloudy kernels can remediate to the main drawback of maxitive kernels, i.e. they can model sets of summative kernels κ_Δ where Δ is lower and upper-bounded. Assume that we want to represent the set of summative kernels κ_Δ such that $\Delta \in [\Delta_{\text{inf}}, \Delta_{\text{sup}}]$. To satisfy this requirement, we propose to consider the cloudy kernel $[\pi, \eta]_{[\Delta_{\text{inf}}, \Delta_{\text{sup}}]}$ such that, for any $x \in \mathbb{R}$:

$$\pi_{\Delta_{\text{sup}}}(x) = \begin{cases} 2 * F_{\Delta_{\text{sup}}}(x) & \text{if } x \leq 0 \\ 2 * (1 - F_{\Delta_{\text{sup}}}(x)) & \text{if } x \geq 0 \end{cases} \; ; \; \eta_{\Delta_{\text{inf}}}(x) = \begin{cases} 2 * F_{\Delta_{\text{inf}}}(x) & \text{if } x \leq 0 \\ 2 * (1 - F_{\Delta_{\text{inf}}}(x)) & \text{if } x \geq 0 \end{cases} \quad (6)$$

Let us first show that this cloud contains all the desired summative kernels, starting with the summative kernels such that $\Delta = \Delta_{\text{inf}}$ and $\Delta = \Delta_{\text{sup}}]$.

Proposition 3. *The cloudy kernel* $[\pi, \eta]_{[\Delta_{\text{inf}}, \Delta_{\text{sup}}]}$ *includes the two summative kernels* $\kappa_{\Delta_{\text{inf}}}$ *and* $\kappa_{\Delta_{\text{sup}}}$ *having for cumulative distributions* $F_{\Delta_{\text{inf}}}, F_{\Delta_{\text{sup}}}$.

Proof. From the definition of our cloudy kernel, we have that the thin cloudy kernels having for distributions $\pi_{\Delta_{\text{sup}}}$ and $\eta_{\Delta_{\text{inf}}}$ are included in $[\pi, \eta]_{[\Delta_{\text{inf}}, \Delta_{\text{sup}}]}$ (Proposition 1).

Let us denote F_π^-, F_π^+ and F_η^-, F_η^+ the cumulative distributions given by Eq. (5) respectively applied to the thin cloudy kernels $\pi_{\Delta_{\text{sup}}}$ and $\eta_{\Delta_{\text{inf}}}$. By Proposition 2, they are included in the cloudy kernel $[\pi, \eta]_{[\Delta_{\text{inf}}, \Delta_{\text{sup}}]}$, and since $\mathscr{P}_{[\pi, \eta]_{[\Delta_{\text{inf}}, \Delta_{\text{sup}}]}}$ is a convex set, $^1/_2 F_\pi^- + {}^1/_2 F_\pi^+$ and $^1/_2 F_\eta^- + {}^1/_2 F_\eta^+$ are also included in the kernel. These two convex mixtures being equals to $F_{\Delta_{\text{inf}}}, F_{\Delta_{\text{sup}}}$, this ends the proof.

Proposition 4. *The cloudy kernel* $[\pi, \eta]_{[\Delta_{\text{inf}}, \Delta_{\text{sup}}]}$ *includes any summative kernel* κ_Δ *having* F_Δ *for cumulative distribution with* $\Delta \in [\Delta_{\text{inf}}, \Delta_{\text{sup}}]$.

Proof. We know, by Proposition 2, that the thin cloudy kernel $[\pi, \eta]_{F_\Delta}$ such that

$$\pi_\Delta(x) = \begin{cases} 2 * F_\Delta & \text{if } x \leq 0 \\ 2 * (1 - F_\Delta) & \text{if } x \geq 0 \end{cases}$$

includes the cumulative distribution $[\pi, \eta]_{F_\Delta}$. Also, we have that $F_{\Delta_{\text{inf}}}(x) \leq F_\Delta(x) \leq F_{\Delta_{\text{sup}}}(x)$ for $x \leq 0$, and $F_{\Delta_{\text{sup}}}(x) \leq F_\Delta(x) \leq F_{\Delta_{\text{inf}}}(x)$ for $x \geq 0$, due to the symmetry of the retained summative kernels. This means that $\pi_{\Delta_{\text{sup}}} \leq \pi_\Delta \leq \eta_{\Delta_{\text{inf}}}$, therefore the thin cloudy kernel $[\pi, \eta]_{F_\Delta}$ is included in $[\pi, \eta]_{[\Delta_{\text{inf}}, \Delta_{\text{sup}}]}$, and this ends the proof.

Let us now show that the proposed cloudy kernels exclude summative kernels with a bandwidth smaller than $\Delta_{\inf}$, among which is the Dirac measure.

Proposition 5. *Any kernel κ_Δ having F_Δ for cumulative distribution with $\Delta \leq \Delta_{\inf}$ or $\Delta \geq \Delta_{\sup}$ is not included in the cloudy kernel $[\pi, \eta]_{[\Delta_{\inf}, \Delta_{\sup}]}$*

Proof. Similar to the one of Proposition 4, considering that the thin cloud induced by F_Δ when $\Delta \leq \Delta_{\inf}$ is not included in the cloudy kernel $[\pi, \eta]_{[\Delta_{\inf}, \Delta_{\sup}]}$.

These proposition show that cloudy kernels are fitted to our purpose, i.e., representing sets of summative kernels with lower- and upper-bounded bandwidth. Still, as for max-itive kernels, other kernels than the summative kernels belonging to the family κ_Δ are included in $\mathscr{P}_{[\pi, \eta]_{[\Delta_{\inf}, \Delta_{\sup}]}}$.

3 Practical Computations

In practice, imprecise filtering is done by extending the expectation operator to representations inducing probability sets, in our case by using Choquet integrals [9]. In this section, we recall what is a Choquet integral and its links with expectation operators. We then propose an efficient algorithm to compute this Choquet integral for cloudy kernels. To shorten notations $[\pi, \eta]_{[\Delta_{\inf}, \Delta_{\sup}]}, \eta_{\Delta_{\inf}}$ and $\pi_{\Delta_{\sup}}$ will be denoted by $[\pi, \eta], \eta$ and π. Since computations are achieved on a discretised space, we consider that we are working on a finite domain $\mathscr{X}$ of N elements. In our case, this space corresponds to a finite sampling of the signal.

3.1 Expectation Operator and Choquet Integral

Consider the domain $\mathscr{X} = \{x_1, \ldots, x_N\}$ with an arbitrary indexing of elements x_i (not necessarily the usual ordering between real numbers) and a real-valued function f (here, the sampled values of the signal) on $\mathscr{X}$, together with a discretized summative kernel $\kappa_i, i = 1, \ldots, N$, where $\kappa_i = \kappa(x_i)$. Classical convolution between the kernel κ and the sampled signal f is equivalent to compute the expectation $\mathbb{E}_\kappa(f) = \sum_{i=1}^N \kappa_i f(x_i)$.

When working with a set $\mathscr{P}$ of summative kernels defined on $\mathscr{X}$, the expectation operator $\mathbb{E}(f)$ becomes inter-valued $[\underline{\mathbb{E}}(f), \overline{\mathbb{E}}(f)]$, with $\underline{\mathbb{E}}(f) = \inf_{\kappa \in \mathscr{P}} \mathbb{E}_\kappa(f)$ and $\overline{\mathbb{E}}(f) = \sup_{\kappa \in \mathscr{P}} \mathbb{E}_\kappa(f)$. These bounds are generally hard to compute, still there are cases where practical tools exist that make their computation more tractable. First recall [10] that lower and upper confidence measures of $\mathscr{P}$ on an event $A \subseteq \mathscr{X}$ are such that $\underline{P}(A) = \inf_{\kappa \in \mathscr{P}} P_\kappa(A)$ and $\overline{P}(A) = \sup_{\kappa \in \mathscr{P}} P_\kappa(A)$ and are dual in the sense that $\underline{P}(A) = 1 - \overline{P}(A^c)$. If $\underline{P}$ satisfy a property of 2-monotonicity, that is if for any pair $\{A, B\} \subseteq \mathscr{X}$ we have $\underline{P}(A \cap B) + \underline{P}(A \cup B) \geq \underline{P}(A) + \underline{P}(B)$, then expectation bounds can be computed by a Choquet Integral.

Consider a positive bounded function[2] f on $\mathscr{X}$. If we denote by $()$ a reordering of elements of $\mathscr{X}$ such that $f(x_{(1)}) \leq \ldots \leq f(x_{(N)})$, the Choquet Integral giving the lower expectation reads

---

[2] Positivity is not constraining here, since if c is a constant $\underline{\mathbb{E}}(f + c) = \underline{\mathbb{E}}(f) + c$ and the same holds for $\overline{\mathbb{E}}$.

$$C_{\underline{P}}(f) = \underline{\mathbb{E}}(f) = \sum_{i=1}^{N} (f(x_{(i)}) - f(x_{(i-1)})\underline{P}(A_{(i)}),\tag{7}$$

with $f(x_{(0)}) = 0$ and $A_{(i)} = \{x_{(i)},\ldots,x_{(N)}\}$. Upper expectation can be computed by replacing the lower measure $\underline{P}$ by the upper one $\overline{P}$. The main difficulty to evaluate Eq. (7) is then to compute the lower (or upper) confidence measure for the N sets A_i.

3.2 Imprecise Expectation with Cloudy Kernels

Cloudy kernels satisfying Definition 2 induce lower confidence measure that are ∞-monotone [8,6], hence Choquet integral can be used to compute lower and upper expectations. Let us now detail how the lower confidence measure value on events can be computed efficiently (upper confidence measure are obtained by duality). Cloudy kernels $[\pi,\eta]$ defined on $\mathscr{X}$ induce a complete pre-order $\leq_{[\pi,\eta]}$ between elements of $\mathscr{X}$, in the sense that $x \leq_{[\pi,\eta]} y$ if and only if $\eta(x) \leq \eta(y)$ and $\pi(x) \leq \pi(y)$. Given a set $A \subseteq \mathscr{X}$, we denote respectively by $\underline{x}_A$ and by $\overline{x}_A$ its lowest and highest elements with respect to $\leq_{[\pi,\eta]}$. We now introduce the concepts of $[\pi,\eta]$-*connected* sets, that are instrumental in the computation of lower confidence measures.

Definition 4. *Given a cloudy kernel* $[\pi,\eta]$ *over* $\mathscr{X}$, *a subset* $C \subseteq \mathscr{X}$ *is* $[\pi,\eta]$-connected *if it contains all elements between* $\underline{x}_C$ *and by* $\overline{x}_C$, *that is* $C = \{x \in \mathscr{X} \mid \underline{x}_C \leq_{[\pi,\eta]} x \leq_{[\pi,\eta]} \overline{x}_C\}$

We denote by $\mathscr{C}$ the set of all $[\pi,\eta]$-*connected* sets of $\mathscr{X}$. Now, any event A can be inner approximated by another event A_* such that $A_* = \bigcup_{C \in \mathscr{C},C \subset A} C$ is the union of all maximal $[\pi,\eta]$-*connected* sets included in A. Due to an additivity property of the lower confidence measure on $[\pi,\eta]$-*connected* sets [11], $\underline{P}(A)$ is then

$$\underline{P}(A) = \underline{P}(A_*) = \sum_{C \in \mathscr{C},C \subset A} \underline{P}(C)\tag{8}$$

We consider that elements of $\mathscr{X}$ are indexed accordingly to $\leq_{[\pi,\eta]}$, i.e., elements $x_1,\ldots,$ x_N are indexed such that $i \leq j$ if and only if $\eta(x_i) \leq \eta(x_j)$ or $\pi(x_i) \leq \pi(x_j)$. Given this ordering, the lower confidence measure of a $[\pi,\eta]$-connected set $C = \{x_i,\ldots,x_j\}$ is given by the simple formula

$$\underline{P}(C) = \max\{0,\eta(x_{j+1}) - \pi(x_{i-1})\},$$

with $\eta(x_{N+1}) = 1$ and $\pi(x_0) = 0$. Note that, as $\leq_{[\pi,\eta]}$ is a pre-order, we have to be cautious about equalities between some elements. Figure 2 illustrates a cloudy kernel with 7 (irregularly) sampled values, its associated indexing and order.

Algorithm 1 describes how to compute lower confidence measures and the incremental summation giving the lower expectation. At each step, the $[\pi,\eta]$-connected sets forming $A_{(i)}$ are extracted and the corresponding lower confidence measure is computed. The value of the Choquet integral is then incremented. To simplify the algorithm, we assume $\leq_{[\pi,\eta]}$ to be an order (i.e., it is asymmetric). Note that two orderings and indexing are used in the algorithm: the one where elements are ordered by values of f, denoted by (), and the other where elements are ordered using $\leq_{[\pi,\eta]}$, without parenthesis. Except if the function f is increasingly monotonic in $\mathbb{R}$, the indexing following the natural order of numbers is never used.

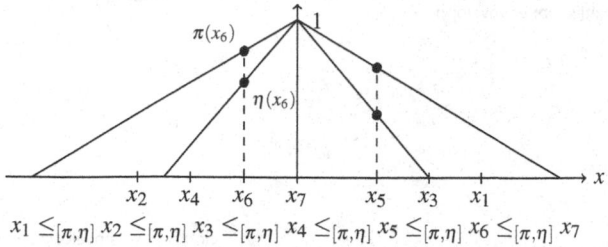

$$x_1 \leq_{[\pi,\eta]} x_2 \leq_{[\pi,\eta]} x_3 \leq_{[\pi,\eta]} x_4 \leq_{[\pi,\eta]} x_5 \leq_{[\pi,\eta]} x_6 \leq_{[\pi,\eta]} x_7$$

Fig. 2. Discretization of cloudy kernels and indexing of elements around x_7 (each x_i corresponds to a sampled value)

Algorithm 1. Algorithm for lower expectations: basic ideas

Input: $f, [\pi, \eta]$, N (number of discretized points)
Output: Lower/upper expectations
$\mathbb{E} = 0$;
for $i = 1, \ldots, N$ **do**
    Compute $f(x_{(i)}) - f(x_{(i-1)})$;
    Extract $[\pi, \eta]$-connected sets such that $A_{(i)} = C_1 \cup \ldots \cup C_{M_i}$;
    With $C_j = \{x_k | \underline{j} \leq k \leq \overline{j}\}$;
    Compute $\underline{P}(A_{(i)}) = \sum_{j=1}^{M_i} \max(0, \eta(x_{\overline{j}+1}) - \pi(x_{\underline{j}-1}))$;
    $\mathbb{E} = \mathbb{E} + [f(x_{(i)}) - f(x_{(i-1)})] \times \underline{P}(A_{(i)})$

---

4 Experiment: Comparison with Summative and Maxitive Kernels

Let us now illustrate the advantage of using cloudy kernels rather than simple maxitive kernels when filtering a noisy signal. Figure 3 shows in cyan a (noisy) signal that has to be filtered by a smoothing kernel. Imprecise kernels (cloudy or maxitive) can be used if one does not know the exact shape of the impulse response of the filter, but can assume that this filter is symmetric, centred and has a lower and upper bounded bandwidth $\Delta \in [\Delta_{\text{inf}}, \Delta_{\text{sup}}]$. The signal pictured in 3 has been obtained by summing nine sine waves with random frequencies and then by adding a normal centered noise with a standard deviation $\sigma = 5$.

Assume that the summative kernels to be considered are the uniform ones bounded by $\Delta \in [0.018, 0.020]$. The most specific maxitive kernel dominating this family is the triangular kernel with a bandwidth equal to 0.02 (see [2]). The bounds obtained by using such a kernel are displayed on Figure 3 (dotted red and blue lines). As expected, the inclusion of the Dirac measure in the maxitive kernel gives very large upper and lower filtered bounds, that encompass the whole signal (i.e. the signal is always in the interval provided by the maxitive kernel). Given our knowledge about the desired bandwidth, it is clearly desirable to also take account of the lower bound 0.018.

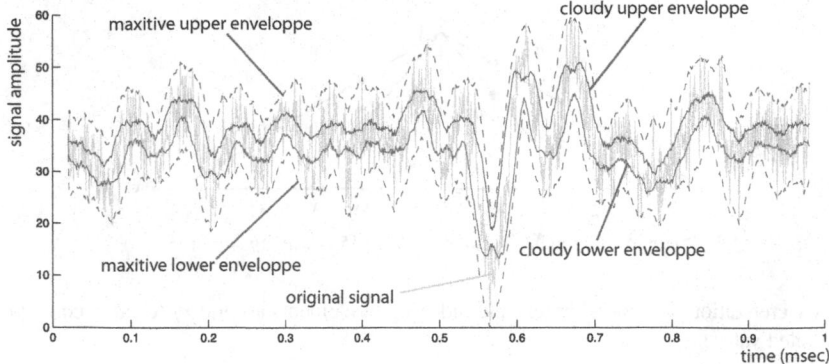

Fig. 3. Superposition of the original signal (cyan), the maxitive imprecise filtering (dotted blue - upper, dotted red - lower) and the cloud based imprecise filtering (blue - upper, red - lower)

Cloudy kernels can model a more specific set of summative kernels, accounting for the lower bound, by using the cloudy kernel composed of two triangular maxitive kernels, the lower kernel having a bandwidth $\Delta_{inf} = 0.018$ and the upper kernel having a bandwidth $\Delta_{sup} = 0.020$, and filtering the signal with Algorithm 1. The result is also pictured in Figure 3 (full red and blue lines). We can see that the lower and upper bounds are now much tighter, as expected. Hence, we now have bounds to whose are associated a good confidence and that are more informative.

To illustrate the capacity of maxitive and cloudy kernels to encompass the desired kernels, we have plotted on 4 ten filtered signals (in cyan) obtained by using different symmetric centered summative kernels whose bandwidth belongs to the interval $[\Delta_{inf}, \Delta_{sup}]$. Every filtered signal belongs to the interval-valued signal obtained by using the cloudy kernel based approach.

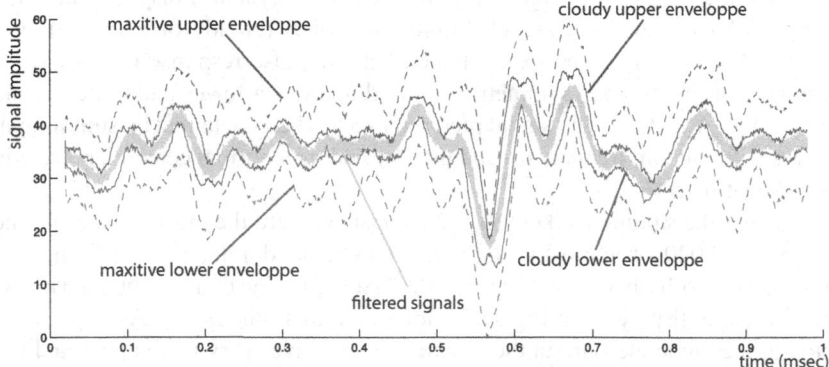

Fig. 4. Superposition of nine filtered signals (cyan), the maxitive imprecise filtering (dotted blue - upper, dotted red - lower) and the cloud based imprecise filtering (blue - upper, red - lower)

5 Conclusion

Both summative and maxitive kernels suffer from some defects when it comes to filter a given signal. The former asks for too much information and the latter is often too imprecise to give tight information. In this paper, we have proposed to use cloudy kernels (using the uncertainty representations called cloud) as a compromis between the two representations to achieve imprecise linear filtering. We have also proposed a simple and efficient (but not necessarily the most efficient) algorithm to compute lower and upper bounds of the filtered signal.

Our experiments show that using cloudy kernels does have the expected properties. Compared to summative and maxitive kernels, they allow to retrieve reliable and informative envelope for the filtered signal. However, it appears that envelopes resulting from the filtering using cloudy kernel are still not so smooth. We suspect that this is due to summative kernels inside the cloudy kernels for which probability masses are concentrated around some particular points (i.e. mixtures of Dirac measures). To avoid this, we could consider the use of technics already proposed [12] to limit the accumulation of such probability masses.

References

1. Jan, J.: Digital Signal Filtering, Analyses and Restoration. IET (2000)
2. Loquin, K., Strauss, O.: On the granularity of summative kernels. Fuzzy Sets and Systems 159(1952-1972) (2008)
3. Dubois, D., Prade, H.: Possibility Theory: An Approach to Computerized Processing of Uncertainty. Plenum Press, New York (1988)
4. Dubois, D., Prade, H.: When upper probabilities are possibility measures. Fuzzy Sets and Systems 49, 65–74 (1992)
5. Neumaier, A.: Clouds, fuzzy sets and probability intervals. Reliable Computing 10, 249–272 (2004)
6. Destercke, S., Dubois, D., Chojnacki, E.: Unifying practical uncertainty representations: II clouds. Int. J. of Approximate Reasoning (in press, 2007)
7. Baudrit, C., Dubois, D.: Practical representations of incomplete probabilistic knowledge. Computational Statistics and Data Analysis 51(1), 86–108 (2006)
8. Destercke, S., Dubois, D., Chojnacki, E.: Unifying practical uncertainty representations: I generalized p-boxes. Int. J. of Approximate Reasoning (in press, 2008)
9. Denneberg, D.: Non-additive measure and integral, basic concepts and their role for applications. In: Fuzzy Measures and Integrals – Theory and Applications, pp. 42–69. Physica Verlag, Heidelberg (2000)
10. Walley, P.: Statistical reasoning with imprecise Probabilities. Chapman and Hall, New York (1991)
11. Destercke, S., Dubois, D.: The role of generalised p-boxes in imprecise probability models. In: Augustin, T., Coolen, F., Moral, S., Troffaes, M.C.M. (eds.) Proc. of the 6th Int. Symp. on Imprecise Probability: Theories and Applications, pp. 179–188 (2009)
12. Kozine, I., Krymsky, V.: Enhancement of natural extension. In: Proc. 5th Int. Symp. on Imprecise Probabilities: Theories and Applications (2007)

Peakedness and Generalized Entropy
for Continuous Density Functions

Inés Couso[1] and Didier Dubois[2]

[1] University of Oviedo, Spain
[2] IRIT-CNRS, Toulouse

Abstract. The theory of majorisation between real vectors with equal sum of components, originated in the beginning of the XXth century, enables a partial ordering between discrete probability distributions to be defined. It corresponds to comparing, via fuzzy set inclusion, possibility distributions that are the most specific transforms of the original probability distributions. This partial ordering compares discrete probability distributions in terms of relative peakedness around their mode, and entropy is monotonic with respect to this partial ordering. In fact, all known variants of entropy share this monotonicity. In this paper, this question is studied in the case of unimodal continuous probability densities on the real line, for which a possibility transform around the mode exists. It corresponds to extracting the family of most precise prediction intervals. Comparing such prediction intervals for two densities yields a variant of relative peakedness in the sense of Birnbaum. We show that a generalized form of continuous entropy is monotonic with respect to this form of relative peakedness of densities.

1 Introduction

Possibility theory, in its quantitative variants, proves to be closely related to various notions in probability theory and statistics. On the one hand, a possibility measure is a coherent upper probability in the sense of Walley [19], i.e. it characterizes some convex sets of probabilities. Moreover, as a possibility measure can be characterized by a family of nested sets equipped with lower probability bounds, a possibility distribution is closely related to so-called probabilistic inequalities (such as Chebyshev, Gauss, etc...) and to prediction or confidence intervals of probability densities, that can be useful for representing measurement uncertainty [14].

On the other hand, the issue of measuring the dispersion of a probability density has been a major concern for a long time. It is well-known that computing variance is not the end of the story. There are many other dispersion indices such as the entropy families, the Gini index and so on. They actually evaluate to what extent a distribution is far from expressing randomness (maximal entropy corresponding to full-fledged randomness, minimal entropy to determinism). In other words, to what extent the probability vector is peaked. Variance, risk aversion measures in decision theory [17,18] are another view for dispersion, where the metric of the space plays a central role.

E. Hüllermeier, R. Kruse, and F. Hoffmann (Eds.): IPMU 2010, LNAI 6178, pp. 208–219, 2010.

The definition of a qualitative relation between probability measures expressing that a probability density is less random than another is a less known question. As there is a constraint on probability weights (they must sum to 1), an equivalent question is to compare probability measures in terms of their relative peakedness, a term coined by Birnbaum [1]. An important remark made by Birnbaum is that peakedness must be defined around some prescribed value. The idea proposed by Birnbaum is to compare the probabilities of a nested family of intervals symmetrically defined around this prescribed value (like the mean, the median or the mode). In the case of entropy, the metric of the set on which the probability density is defined is immaterial, i.e. entropy measures a "vertical" concentration of probability values around the mode.

A bridge between possibility theory, Birnbaum peakedness and entropy-like dispersion indices was pointed out by Dubois and Hüllermeier [6] in the finite case. Namely, on a finite set consider the possibility measure Π that is the most specific one dominating the probability measure P, assuming the probability and the possibility distributions are comonotone. This possibility distribution exists and is unique [7,3,10]. Dubois and Hüllermeier [6] proved that given two probability vectors $\mathbf{p} = (p_1, \ldots, p_n)$ and $\mathbf{q} = (q_1, \ldots, q_n)$ corresponding to the same ordering of elements of Ω, if the possibility distribution $\pi^{\mathbf{p}}$ is less specific than $\pi^{\mathbf{q}}$ (which means that $\mathbf{p}$ is less peaked than $\mathbf{q}$ in the spirit of Birnbaum) then the dispersion of $\mathbf{p}$ is greater than the dispersion of $\mathbf{q}$ for a large class of entropy-like indices.

The aim of this paper is to extend this result to the continuous case. In the next section we recall the historical background of this problem, which has roots in the early XXth century. Then we motivate the continuous extension of the above result. Section 3 states the problem and provides a proof. Finally, we comment on the difference between variance and entropy, and point out the similarity between the obtained result and similar properties existing for risk aversion measures in decision theory.

2   Historical and Mathematical Background in the Finite Case

Let $\mathbf{x}$ and $\mathbf{y}$ be two vectors with n non-negative decreasingly ordered integer components, that satisfy the restriction $\sum_{i=1}^{n} x_i = \sum_{i=1}^{n} y_i$. A Pigou-Dalton transfer on $\mathbf{x}$ consists in adding 1 to some component x_i while subtracting 1 from another component $x_j, j > i$. As cited by Marshall and Olkin [12], in 1903, Muirhead discussed what Dalton called a "transfer" and proved the following result.

Proposition 1. *The following conditions are equivalent:*

(i) $\mathbf{x}$ *can be derived from* $\mathbf{y}$ *by a finite number of transfers;*
(ii) *the sum of the k largest components of $\mathbf{x}$ is less than or equal to the sum of the largest components of $\mathbf{y}$, $k = 1, \ldots, n$, with equality when $k = n$ (this is the "majorization relation").*

The vector obtained by sum of the k largest components of $\mathbf{x}$ for $k = 1$ to n is called the Lorentz curve.

Later on, Hardy, Littlewood and Polya, 1929 (cf. [12], Theorem 2.B.2) proved that a necessary and sufficient condition that a positive real vector $\mathbf{x}$ is majorized by $\mathbf{y}$, the sum of components of each being equal, is that there exists a doubly stochastic matrix A such that $\mathbf{x} = \mathbf{y}A$. We can restrict without loss of generality to positive n-component vectors $\mathbf{x}$ such that $\sum_{i=1}^{n} x_i = 1$, i.e. probability vectors $\mathbf{p} = (p_1, \ldots, p_n)$, and let Δ_n be the set of such probability vectors. Hardy Polya and Littlewood also consider, for any concave function $\phi : \mathbb{R} \to \mathbb{R}$, the mapping $H_\phi : \Delta_n \to \mathbb{R}$ defined as $H_\phi(p_1, \ldots, p_m) = \sum_{i=1}^{m} \phi(p_i)$, which is concave and symmetric. They showed that $\mathbf{p}$ is majorized by $\mathbf{q}$ if and only if $H_\phi(\mathbf{p}) > H_\phi(\mathbf{q}), \forall \phi$ continuous and concave.

As examples of entropy functions, choosing $\phi(x) = -x \log(x)$ yields Shannon entropy, of the form $-\sum_{i=1}^{n} p_i \log(p_i)$. Choosing $\phi(x) = x(1 - x)$ yields the quadratic entropy $1 - \sum_{i=1}^{n} p_i^2$.

A function $H(\mathbf{p})$ mapping probability distributions to reals is said to be Schur-concave [15] if $H(\mathbf{b}A) \geq H(\mathbf{b})$ for all bistochastic matrices A. It is clear that Schur-concavity and functions H_ϕ are very closely related. In fact, any concave and symmetric function is Schur-concave. The converse does not hold [15].

3   Peakedness from the Finite to the Continuous Case

Consider the finite set Ω with n elements. A possibility distribution π on Ω is a mapping from Ω to the unit interval such that $\pi(\omega) = 1$ for some $\omega \in \Omega$. A possibility degree $\pi(\omega)$ evaluates the absence of surprise about ω being the actual state of the world. We may write π_i for $\pi(\omega_i)$, for short. A possibility distribution generates a set function $\Pi(\cdot)$ called a possibility measure such that $\Pi(A) = \max_{\omega \in A} \pi(\omega)$. The degree of necessity (certainty) of an event A is computed from the degree of possibility of the complementary event A^c as $N(A) = 1 - \Pi(A^c)$.

In the following definition, we recall a basic notion from possibility theory (e.g. Dubois *et al.* [9]) already mentioned in the introduction.

Definition 1. *We say that a possibility distribution $\pi(\cdot)$ is* more specific *than a possibility distribution $\rho(\cdot)$ iff $\pi \leq \rho$ pointwisely. It is* strictly more specific *if $\pi \leq \rho$ and $\pi(\omega) < \rho(w)$ for at least one $\omega \in \Omega$.*

Clearly, the more specific $\pi(\cdot)$, the more informative it is. If $\pi(w_i) = 1$ for some ω_i and $\pi(\omega_j) = 0$ for all $j \neq i$, then $\pi(\cdot)$ is maximally specific (full knowledge); if $\pi(\omega_i) = 1$ for all i, then $\pi(\cdot)$ is minimally specific (complete ignorance).

A numerical degree of possibility can be viewed as an upper bound to a probability degree [8]. Namely, with every possibility distribution $\pi(\cdot)$ one can associate a non-empty family of probability measures dominated by the possibility measure:

$$\mathcal{P}(\pi) = \{\, P \mid P(A) \leq \Pi(A) \text{ for all } A \subseteq \Omega \,\}.$$

On such a basis, it is possible to change representation from possibility to probability and conversely [7,3]. Changing a probability distribution into a possibility distribution means losing information as the variability expressed by a probability measure is changed into incomplete knowledge or imprecision. Some principles for this transformation have been suggested in [10]. They come down to selecting a most specific element from the set of possibility measures dominating $P(\cdot)$, that is,

$$\forall A \subseteq \Omega : \Pi(A) \geq P(A)$$

with $\Pi(A) = \max_{\omega \in A} \pi(\omega)$ and $P(A) = \sum_{\omega \in A} p(\omega)$. A minimal consistency between the ordering induced by the probability distribution and the one of the possibility distribution, is also required, namely a form of comonotony: $\pi(\omega) > \pi(\omega')$ whenever $p(\omega) > p(\omega')$. Results concerning tightest probability-possibility transforms in the finite case [3,10] can be summarized by the following proposition.

Proposition 2. *Consider a probability vector* $\mathbf{p} = (p_1, \ldots, p_n)$ *determining a probability measure* P *on a finite universe* $\Omega = \{\omega_1, \ldots, \omega_n\}$ *with the restriction* $p_1 > p_2 \cdots > p_n$ *where* $p(\omega_i) = p_i$ *denotes the probability mass of* $\omega_i \in \Omega$. *Define the nested family* $(A_\alpha)_{\alpha \in [0,1)}$ *such that for each* $\alpha \in [0,1]$, A_α *is a minimal cardinality set satisfying* $P(A_\alpha) \geq 1 - \alpha$. *Build the possibility distribution* $\pi^{\mathbf{P}}$ *with* α-*cuts* $(A_\alpha)_{\alpha \in [0,1)}$, *such that* $\pi^{\mathbf{P}}(x) = \sup\{\alpha : x \in A_\alpha\}$. *Then*

1. *The sets* A_α *are of the form* $N_i = \{\omega_j, p_j \geq p_i\} = \{\omega_1, \ldots, \omega_i\}$
2. *The sets* A_α *are maximizing the probability* $P(A)$ *among all sets* A *with the same cardinality as* A_α.
3. $\pi^{\mathbf{P}}(\omega_i) = 1 - P(N_{i-1})$
4. *The possibility measure* $\Pi^{\mathbf{P}}$ *associated to* $\pi^{\mathbf{P}}$ *is the most specific possibility distribution dominating* P *and comonotonic to it.*

Proof. Consider the nested family of sets $N_i = \{\omega_1, \ldots, \omega_i\}$. *It is of the form* $\{\omega_j, p_j \geq p_i\}$. *It is clear that* $P(N_i) > P(A), \forall A \subset \Omega$ *with cardinality* i, $A \neq N_i$. *Note that* $P(N_i) = \sum_{j=1}^{i} p_j$. *Hence* $N_i = A_\alpha$ *for* $\alpha \in [\sum_{j=i+1}^{n} p_j, \sum_{j=i}^{n} p_j)$. *Define the possibility distribution* $\pi_1^{\mathbf{P}} > \pi_2^{\mathbf{P}} \cdots > \pi_n^{\mathbf{P}}$ *where* $\pi_i^{\mathbf{P}} = \sup\{\alpha : \omega_i \in A_\alpha\}$. *It is clear that* $\pi_i^{\mathbf{P}} = \sum_{j=i}^{n} p_i = 1 - P(N_{i-1})$. *This possibility distribution dominates* $\mathbf{p}$, *i.e. such that* $\Pi^{\mathbf{P}}(A) = \max_{\omega_i \in A} \pi_i^{\mathbf{P}} \geq P(A)$, $\forall A \subseteq \Omega$. *Note that by construction,* $P(N_i^c) = \Pi^{\mathbf{P}}(N_i^c) = \pi_i^{\mathbf{P}}, \forall i = 1, \ldots, n$; *so any possibility measure* Π *dominating* P *must be such that* $\Pi(N_i^c) \geq \Pi^{\mathbf{P}}(N_i^c)$. *As* π *is comonotonic to* p, $\pi(\omega_i) \geq \pi_i^{\mathbf{P}}$. *Hence* $\Pi^{\mathbf{P}}$ *is maximally specific among those which dominate* P. □

When $p_i = p_{i+1}$ for some i the above result still applies to a large extent except that maximally specific possibility distributions dominating $\mathbf{p}$ are no longer unique nor will they be strictly comonotonic to it (e.g. $\pi_i^{\mathbf{P}} > \pi_{i+1}^{\mathbf{P}}$ or conversely). For instance, the most specific possibilistic transform of the uniform probability measure is $\pi_i^{\mathbf{P}} = i/n$ where the ordering of elements is arbitrary.

A probability vector $\mathbf{p}$ is said to be *less peaked* than probability vector $\mathbf{q}$ whenever $\pi^{\mathbf{P}}$ is less specific than $\pi^{\mathbf{q}}$. The main result in [6], which is a consequence of results by Hardy *et al.* as explained in Section 2 reads as follows: let $H_\phi(\mathbf{p}) = \sum_{i=1}^{m} \phi(p_i)$ be a generalized entropy function, where ϕ continuous and concave. Then:

Theorem 1. *If a probability vector* **p** *is less peaked than a vector* **q**, *then* $H_\phi(\mathbf{p})$
$\geq H_\phi(\mathbf{q}), \forall \phi$ *continuous and concave; if* **p** *is strictly less peaked than* **q**, *then*
$H_\phi(\mathbf{p}) > H_\phi(\mathbf{q})$.

On the other hand, possibility transforms of continuous unimodal densities were
studied by Dubois *et al.* [10,5]. The above concept of "minimal cardinality confidence interval" in the finite case extends to the idea of minimal length confidence interval in the continuous case. More specifically, the following result was
established:

Proposition 3. *[5] Consider a probability measure P on the real line with continuous unimodal density p and mode m. Define the nested family $(A_\alpha)_{\alpha \in [0,1)}$
such that for each $\alpha \in [0,1]$, A_α is a minimal length closed interval satisfying
$P(A_\alpha) \geq 1 - \alpha$. Build the possibility distribution π^p with α-cuts $(A_\alpha)_{\alpha \in [0,1)}$, such
that $\pi^p(x) = \sup\{\alpha : x \in A_\alpha\}$. Then*

1. *The sets A_α are of the form $F_c = \{x : p(x) \geq c\}$;*
2. *The sets A_α are maximizing the probability $P(A)$ among all intervals A with
the same length as A_α;*
3. $\pi^p(\inf A_\alpha) = \pi^p(\sup A_\alpha) = 1 - P(A_\alpha)$;
4. π^p *is the most specific possibility distribution dominating P.*

Thus, we see that the possibility distribution constructed this way is the counterpart of the probability-possibility transformation in the discrete case. This result extends to multimodal probability densities (then replacing minimal length
closed intervals by minimal length closed sets formed by finite unions of intervals), and even to multidimensional densities [16].

4   From Peakedness to Entropy in the Continuous Case

Entropy can be defined in the continuous setting. This is the so-called differential
entropy of the form $H(p) = - \int p(y) log(p(y)) dy$ for a continous density p on the
real line. As described in [[11], Section 1.1.2, page 5], this expression is provably
the limit of the Shannon entropy of a discrete probability vector obtained using
a partition of the support of the density p into adjacent intervals of the same
length and making this length vanish. This limit idea can be extended to other
types of entropies, i.e. ϕ-entropies H_ϕ. We aim to check that Theorem 1 given
in [6], connecting the (total) preordering on probability measures defined by
entropies and the (partial) ordering defined by possibilistic specificity, can be
extended to continuous probabilities.

Consider an absolutely continuous probability measure (wrt the Lebesgue
measure) P satisfying the following restrictions:

(i) Its support is contained in a bounded interval $[a, b]$.
(ii) Its density function p is continuous, unimodal (i.e., there exists a unique
$m \in [a, b]$ such that $p(m) = \max\{p(x) : x \in [a, b]\}$), and it is strictly
increasing on the open interval (a, m) and strictly decreasing on (m, b).

(The above conditions include strictly concave functions on $[a, b]$ for instance). We will define a specific possibility measure, Π^p that dominates P. The construction (following [5]) will be as follows: For every $c \in \mathbb{R}^+$, define F_c as the subset of the real line $F_c = \{x : p(x) \geq c\}$. Let us consider the possibility measure Π^p whose possibility distribution π^p is defined as follows:

$$\pi^p(x) = \sup\{\alpha : x \in F_{\kappa(\alpha)}\},$$

where $\kappa : [0, 1] \to \mathbb{R}^+$ is such that $\kappa(\alpha)$ satisfies the condition $P(F_{\kappa(\alpha)}) = 1 - \alpha$. The following theorem will be the main result in this section:

Theorem 2. *Consider two probability measures P and Q satisfying the above restrictions (i) and (ii), and denote by p and q their respective density functions. Let H_ϕ be a ϕ-entropy defined as $H_\phi(p) = \int \phi(p(x))dx$, where ϕ is concave and continuous. Then the following implication holds:*

$$\pi^p(x) \leq \pi^q(x), \ \forall x \in \mathbb{R} \Rightarrow H_\phi(p) \leq H_\phi(q).$$

Before proving the main result, we will check the following auxiliary claims:

Lemma 1. *Suppose that p is a continuous density, unimodal (with mode m) strictly increasing in (a, m) and strictly decreasing in (m, b) and that its support is contained in the interval $[a, b]$. For every $c \in (0, p(m)]$, define F_c as the subset of the real line $F_c = \{x : p(x) \geq c\}$. Then each F_c is a closed interval $F_c = [A(c), B(c)]$. Furthermore the range of the mapping $L : \mathbb{R}^+ \setminus \{0\} \to \mathbb{R}^+$ defined as $L = B - A$ contains the whole interval $(0, b - a)$.*

Proof. By the continuity of p we can easily derive that the set F_c has a maximum, $B(c)$, and a minimum, $A(c)$. Furthermore, we observe that $A(c) \leq m \leq B(c)$ and so, by the respective monotonicity conditions assumed for p on (a, m) and (m, b), F_c is convex. Furthermore, the mappings $A : [0, p(m)] \to \mathbb{R}$ and $B : [0, p(m)] \to \mathbb{R}$ are continuous and so is the mapping $L = B - A$. Hence, by Darboux theorem, we conclude the thesis of this lemma. $\square$

Remark 1. Note that $L(c)$ can be alternatively written as $\lambda(F_c)$, $\forall c$, where λ is the Lebesgue measure.

Lemma 2. *Suppose that the density function, p, associated to the probability measure P is continuous, unimodal (with mode m) strictly increasing in (a, m) and strictly decreasing in (m, b), and that its support is contained in the interval $[a, b]$. Then, there exists a mapping $\kappa : [0, 1] \to \mathbb{R}^+$ satisfying the condition $P(F_{\kappa(\alpha)}) = 1 - \alpha$, for all $\alpha \in [0, 1]$, with $F_c = \{x : p(x) \geq c\}$.*

Proof. Let $\kappa(\alpha)$ be defined as $\kappa(\alpha) = \sup\{c : P(F_c) \geq 1 - \alpha\}$. Then, we can easily check that $P(F_{\kappa(\alpha)}) = 1 - \alpha$. Notice that, under the above hypotheses, $F_{\kappa(\alpha)}$ is a closed interval $[A(\kappa(\alpha)), B(\kappa(\alpha))]$. If, by reductio ad absurdum, we suppose that $P(F_{\kappa(\alpha)}) > 1 - \alpha$ we could find some $\epsilon > 0$ such that $P_f([A(\kappa(\alpha)) + \epsilon, B(\kappa(\alpha) - \epsilon]) \geq 1 - \alpha$. The union of family of intervals $\{[A(\kappa(\alpha)) + \epsilon, B(\kappa(\alpha) - \epsilon], \epsilon \in$

$(0, \min\{m - A(c), B(c) - m\})\}$ *coincides with the open interval* $(A(\kappa(\alpha)), B(\kappa(\alpha)))$, *so their probability tends (as ϵ goes to 0) to the probability of such an open interval, that coincides with the probability of the closed one. Since p is strictly increasing in (a, m) and strictly descreasing in (m, b), there exists some $c > \kappa(\alpha)$ such that $p(x) > \kappa(\alpha)$, $\forall x \in [A(\kappa(\alpha)) + \epsilon, B(\kappa(\alpha)) - \epsilon]$. It contradicts the definition of supremum.* □

Lemma 3. *Consider the possibility distribution π^p:*

$$\pi^p(x) = \sup\{\alpha : x \in F_{\kappa(\alpha)}\}, \; \forall x$$

Denote by π^p_α and $\pi^p_{\overline{\alpha}}$ respectively its weak and its strong α-cut. Then:

$$\pi^p_{\overline{\alpha}} = (A(\kappa(\alpha)), B(\kappa(\alpha))) \; and \; \pi^p_\alpha = [A(\kappa(\alpha)), B(\kappa(\alpha))].$$

Proof. It is immediate, since the union $\cup_{\alpha > \beta}(A(\kappa(\alpha)), B(\kappa(\alpha)))$ coincides with the open interval $(A(C(\beta)), B(C(\beta)))$ and, on the other hand, the intersection $\cap_{\alpha < \beta}[A(\kappa(\alpha)), B(\kappa(\alpha))]$ is the closed interval $[A(C(\beta)), B(C(\beta))]$. □

Now, let us use the last lemmas to prove Theorem 2.

Proof of the main result: Suppose that $\pi^p \leq \pi^q$ and so

$$\pi^p_{\overline{\alpha}} \subseteq \pi^q_{\overline{\alpha}}, \; \forall \alpha \tag{1}$$

1. We will first "discretize" the probability measures associated to p and q, by dividing their support into n subintervals, for each $n \in \mathbb{N}$ (see Figure 1). We will check that the discretized probability associated to p is more peaked than the one associated to q.

   For each $n \in \mathbb{N}$ define the class of subsets of the interval $[a, b]$,

   $$\{A^p_{0,n}, \ldots, A^p_{n,n}\} = \{\emptyset, F_{c(1,n)}, \ldots, F_{c(n,n)}\},$$

   where $c(i, n) \in \mathbb{R}^+$ is such that $L(c(i, n)) = \frac{i(b-a)}{n}$. Such a $c(i, n)$ exists in virtue of Lemma 2. In other words, we define a nested family of $n + 1$ "level-cuts" of p, each one of length $\frac{i(b-a)}{n}$ included in the support $[a, b]$. Based on this family, we can define a partition on $[a, b]$ as follows:

   $$B^p_{0,n} = A^p_{0,n}, \; B^p_{i,n} = A^p_{i,n} \setminus (\cup_{j=1}^{i-1} B^p_{j,n}).$$

   By construction, the Lebesgue measure of each $B^p_{i,n}$ is $\frac{b-a}{n}$. Let us do the same construction for the density q to define the partition $\{B^q_{1,n}, \ldots, B^q_{n,n}\}$. Let us now denote $p^n_i = P(B^p_{i,n})$ and $q^n_i = Q(B^q_{i,n})$, $\forall i = 0, \ldots, n$.

   Let us check that, for any $n \in \mathbb{N}$, the probability $(p^n_1, \ldots, p^n_n)$ is more peaked than $(q^n_1, \ldots, q^n_n)$. Let us pick an arbitrary $n \in \mathbb{N}$ and an arbitrary $r \in \{1, \ldots, n\}$. Let us consider the value of α such that $\pi^q_{\overline{\alpha}}$ coincides with the set $A^q_{r,n}$. There exists some $k \in \{1, \ldots, n\}$ such that $A^p_{k,n} \subset \pi^q_{\overline{\alpha}} \subseteq A^p_{(k+1),n}$. By construction, and according to the above hypotheses we can check that:

   $$\frac{k(b-a)}{n} < \lambda(\pi^q_{\overline{\alpha}}) \leq \frac{(k+1)(b-a)}{n} \; and$$

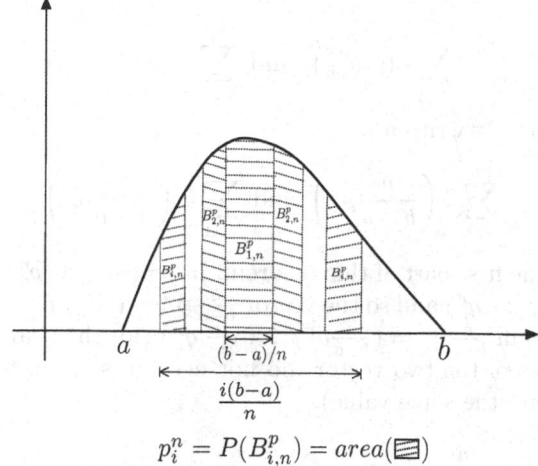

$$p_i^n = P(B_{i,n}^p) = area(\text{▨})$$

Fig. 1. Partitioning the support of a density

$$\frac{r(b-a)}{n} = \lambda(\pi_{\frac{q}{\alpha}}).$$

Furthermore, by hypothesis $\pi_{\frac{p}{\alpha}}$ is included in $\pi_{\frac{q}{\alpha}}$ so, $\lambda(\pi_{\frac{p}{\alpha}}) \leq \lambda(\pi_{\frac{q}{\alpha}})$ and then $k < r$, or, equivalently $k + 1 \leq r$. Moreover, according to Lemma 2, $q_1^n + \ldots + q_r^n = Q(A_{r,n}^q) = Q(\lambda(\pi_{\frac{q}{\alpha}}))$ is $1 - \alpha$ which is less than or equal to $p_1^n + \ldots + p_{k+1}^n = P(A_{k,n}^p)$.

Thus, we conclude that $p_1^n + \ldots + p_r^n \leq q_1^n + \ldots + q_r^n$. Since this has been proved for an arbitrary r, we conclude that $(p_1^n, \ldots, p_n^n)$ is more peaked than $(q_1^n, \ldots, q_n^n)$.

2. Let us now check that the ϕ−entropies $H_\phi(p)$ and $H_\phi(q)$ can be obtained as limits of the valuations on the discretized probabilities.

If we apply the mean-value theorem twice (the set $B_{i,n}^p$ can be written as the union of two intervals) and we take into account the properties of the function p, we have:

$$p_i^n = \int_{B_{i,n}^p} p(x)\,dx = p(b_{i,n}^p)\frac{(b-a)}{n},$$

for some $b_{i,n}^p \in B_{i,n}^p$. Analogously, we see obtain:

$$q_i^n = \int_{B_{i,n}^q} q(x)\,dx = q(b_{i,n}^q)\frac{(b-a)}{n}$$

for some $b_{i,n}^q \in B_{i,n}^q$. Thus, the following equalities hold,

$$\frac{n}{b-a}p_i^n = p(b_{i,n}^p) \text{ and } \frac{n}{b-a}q_i^n = q(b_{i,n}^q),$$

for some $b_{i,n}^p \in B_{i,n}^p$ and some $b_{i,n}^q \in B_{i,n}^q$, and for all $n \in \mathbb{N}$ and all $i \in \{1, \ldots, n\}$.

Hence,

$$\sum_{i=1}^{n} \phi(p(b_{i,n}^p)) \text{ and } \sum_{i=1}^{n} \phi(p(b_{i,n}^q))$$

can be alternatively written as

$$\sum_{i=1}^{n} \phi\left(\frac{n}{b-a}p_i^n\right) \text{ and } \sum_{i=1}^{n} \phi\left(\frac{n}{b-a}q_i^n\right).$$

According to the first part of this theorem, $\mathbf{p}^n = (p_1^n, \ldots, p_n^n)$ is more peaked than $\mathbf{q}^n = (q_1^n, \ldots, q_n^n)$ and so the vector $\frac{n}{b-a}\mathbf{p}^n = (\frac{n}{b-a}p_1^n, \ldots, \frac{n}{b-a}p_n^n)$ is also more peaked than $\frac{n}{b-a}\mathbf{q}^n = (\frac{n}{b-a}q_1^n, \ldots, \frac{n}{b-a}q_n^n)$ (for the peakedness relation, the components of the two vectors do not need to sum up to one, but they just need to sum the same value).

Thus,

$$\sum_{i=1}^{n} \phi\left(\frac{n}{b-a}p_i^n\right) \leq \sum_{i=1}^{n} \phi\left(\frac{n}{b-a}q_i^n\right),$$

and hence also

$$\frac{n}{b-a}\sum_{i=1}^{n} \phi\left(\frac{n}{b-a}p_i^n\right) \leq \frac{n}{b-a}\sum_{i=1}^{n} \phi\left(\frac{n}{b-a}q_i^n\right), \; \forall n.$$

Now, by the definition of the Riemann integral, we have that

$$\sum_{i=1}^{n} \frac{b-a}{n}(\phi \circ p)(b_{i,n}^p) \text{ and } \sum_{i=1}^{n} \frac{b-a}{n}(\phi \circ q)(b_{i,n}^q)$$

respectively converge to the integrals $\int_a^b (\phi \circ p)(x)\,dx$ and $\int_a^b (\phi \circ q)(x)\,dx$, so the result is checked. □

5 Vertical vs. Horizontal Dispersion

The above comparison between probability distributions in terms of their peakedness does not depend on the underlying metric. There are other ways of evaluating the dispersion of probability densities, that look strikingly different. The first one is the variance. It takes into account the metric of the probability space. The empirical variance, for instance, depends on the distance between the observed measurements, while the entropy does not.

In fact, it is possible to relate entropy and a form of variance, provided that we operate a ninety-degree rotation of the usual variance, considering the dispersion of the $p(x)$ values, not the x values. Namely, in the discrete case, the quadratic entropy $1 - \sum_{i=1}^{n} p_i^2$ is basically the opposite of such a vertical variance. Namely, sticking to a finite setting, the variance $\sigma_{\mathbf{p}}^2$ of $\{p_1, \ldots, p_n\}$ takes the following form, based on the fact that the mean value of the p_i's is $1/n$:

$$\sigma_{\mathbf{p}}^2 = \frac{\sum_{i=1}^{n}(p_i - 1/n)^2}{n} = \frac{\sum_{i=1}^{n} p_i^2}{n} - (1/n)^2 = \frac{1}{n}(1 - 1/n - \sum_{i=1}^{n} p_i(1 - p_i)),$$

since $1 - \sum_{i=1}^{n} p_i^2 = \sum_{i=1}^{n} p_i(1 - p_i)$ so that it corresponds, up to an affine rescaling, to the opposite of the quadratic entropy, of the form $\frac{1}{n}(1 - 1/n - H_\phi)$ with $\phi(x) = x(1 - x)$. In other words, the quadratic entropy is a kind of vertical variance.

We can also try to express the generalized entropy as the arithmetic mean $H(p_1, \ldots, p_n) = \sum_{i=1}^{n} p_i f(p_i)$, where f is a decreasing function. It is easy to check that any concave function ϕ satisfying the boundary condition $\phi(0) = 0$ can be written as a product $\phi(x) = x f(x)$, where f is a decreasing mapping. Letting $f(p_i) = p_1 - p_i$, where p_1 is the probability of the mode, any ϕ-entropy with $\phi(0) = 0$ can also be understood as the expectation of (an increasing function of) the vertical distances $p_1 - p_i$ of the probabilities to the mode.

Besides, there is another niche in the literature of decision theory that studies risk-aversion indices. The seminal works in this area are those of Rothschild and Stiglitz in [17,18]. These authors consider the dispersion around the mean, but they question the variance as a legitimate risk aversion measure. They consider a distribution p to be more risky ($=$ more scattered) than another one q if and only if

$$\int_{\mathbb{R}} u(x)p(x)dx \geq \int_{\mathbb{R}} u(x)q(x)dx,$$

for all risk-concave utility functions $u : \mathbb{R} \to \mathbb{R}$, where concave utility functions model risk-averse decision-makers. Interestingly, in their paper they try to approach the intuition by considering transfers similar to Pigou-Dalton ones, albeit keeping the mean value constant. Moreover their idea of p being more risky than q corresponds to adding a zero-mean random variable to the variable x with distribution g. Finally they show that relative risk is checked by second order stochastic dominance, which means comparing cumulative distributions by their Lorentz curve, i.e. $\int_{-\infty}^{y} F_P(x)dx \leq \int_{-\infty}^{y} F_Q(x)dx$, where F_P is the cumulative distribution of measure P. So there is a full-fledged similarity between peakedness and risk in this sense as shown on table 1:

Table 1. Comparison between peakedness around the mode and risk aversion

Notion	Discrete entropy	Risk aversion
definition	majorization for probability vectors	majorization for real vectors
property	$\sum_{i=1}^{n} p_i = 1$	P, Q have equal mean
dominance	$\pi^P(x) \leq \pi^q(x), \ \forall x \in \mathbb{R}$	$\int_{-\infty}^{y} F_P(x)dx \leq \int_{-\infty}^{y} F_Q(x)dx$
transfer	vertical	horizontal
index	$\forall \phi$ concave $H_\phi(\mathbf{p}) \leq H_\phi(\mathbf{q})$	$\int u(x)q(x)dx \geq \int u(x)p(x)dx \ \forall u$ concave
adding noise	$\mathbf{q} = A \circ \mathbf{p}, A =$ bistochastic matrix	$Y = X + \theta, \theta$ has zero mean

This analogy is worth studying further. Marshall and Olkin [12], p. 16-17 also point out the concept of dilation. Q is a dilation of P if the integral of any convex function with respect to P is less than or equal to the integral of the same convex function with respect to Q. It seems to be related to second order stochastic dominance in the infinite case, but it generalizes also the concept of "majorization" in the finite case. However, in relation to entropies, the majorization concerns probability vectors, while in relation to risk measures, it concerns real-valued vectors having the same mean (hence the same sum) value. So, it seems that the comparison of probability measures in terms of risk aversion, using second-order stochastic dominance, is a concept similar but orthogonal to the comparison of probability-possibility transforms, just like variance is orthogonal to quadratic entropy.

6   Conclusion

This paper proposes a rather general way of comparing continuous probability densities on the real line, with respect to their peakedness around the mode, by generalizing differential entropy by means of concave continuous functions. This is equivalent to checking the inclusion of the tightest prediction intervals around the mode, which comes down to comparing the relative specificity of possibility transforms. This result sheds some light on the respective meanings of differential entropy and variance and suggests several possible lines of research:

- First, entropy maximization is a very common technique for justifying the use of some specific probability measures in the presence of incomplete information. For instance, the Gaussian density is obtained by maximizing Shannon entropy under fixed mean and variance [11]. This kind of methodology could be reconsidered in terms of minimizing peakedness, using the possibility (Lorentz curve) ordering as a qualitative criterion.
- Next, one may try to exploit the qualitative peakedness ordering as a substitute to informational distances (such as Kullback-Leibler relative entropy), defining a ternary relation of the form "p_1 is more peaked than p_2 but less peaked than p_3", and finding relative entropies in agreement with this comparison. One could then reconsider probability kinematics problems [4] in a more general setting, not dependent on the choice of a numerical distance-like index.

Acknowledgments. This work has been supported by the FEDER-MEC Grants TIN2007-67418-C03-03, TIN2008-06681-C06-04 and MTM2007-61193.

References

1. Birnbaum, Z.W.: On random variables with comparable peakedness. The Annals of Mathematical Statistics 19, 76–81 (1948)
2. Couso, I., Montes, S., Gil, P.: The necessity of the strong α-cuts of a fuzzy set. International Journal of Uncertainty, Fuzziness and Knowledge-Based Systems 9, 249–262 (2001)
3. Delgado, M.: On the concept of possibility-probability consistency. Fuzzy Sets and Systems 21, 311–318 (1987)
4. Domotor, Z.: Probability kinematics, Conditionals and entropy principles. Synthese 63, 74–115 (1985)

5. Dubois, D., Foulloy, L., Mauris, G., Prade, H.: Probability-Possibility Transformations, Triangular Fuzzy Sets, and Probabilistic Inequalities. Reliable Computing 10, 273–297 (2004)
6. Dubois, D., Hüllermeier, E.: Comparing Probability Measures Using Possibility Theory: A Notion of Relative Peakedness. International Journal of Approximate Reasoning 45, 364–385 (2007)
7. Dubois, D., Prade, H.: On several representations of an uncertain body of evidence. In: Gupta, M.M., Sanchez, E. (eds.) Fuzzy Information and Decision Processes, pp. 167–181. North-Holland, Amsterdam (1982)
8. Dubois, D., Prade, H.: When upper probabilities are possibility measures. Fuzzy Sets and Systems 49, 65–74 (1992)
9. Dubois, D., Nguyen, H.T., Prade, H.: Possibility theory, probability and fuzzy sets: misunderstandings, bridges and gaps. In: Dubois, D., Prade, H. (eds.) Fundamentals of Fuzzy Sets. The Handbooks of Fuzzy Sets Series, pp. 343–438. Kluwer, Boston (2000)
10. Dubois, D., Prade, H., Sandri, S.: On possibility/probability transformations. In: Lowen, R., Roubens, M. (eds.) Fuzzy Logic, State of the Art, pp. 103–112. Kluwer Acad. Publ., Dordrecht (1993)
11. Johnson, O.: Information Theory and the Central Limit Theorem. Imperial College Press, London (2004)
12. Marshall, A.W., Olkin, I.: Inequalities: Theory of majorization and its applications. In: Mathematics in Science and Engineering, vol. 143, Academic Press, New York (1979)
13. Mauris, G.: Possibility distribution: a unified representation for parameter estimation. In: IFSA World Congress-EUSFLAT Conference (2009)
14. Mauris, G., Lasserre, V., Foulloy, L.: A fuzzy approach for the expression of uncertainty in measurement. Int. J. Measurement 29, 165–177 (2001)
15. Morales, D., Pardo, L., Vajda, I.: Uncertainty of Discrete Stochastic Systems: General Theory and Statistical Inference. IEEE Transactions on Systems Man and Cybernetics, Part A 26, 681–697 (1996)
16. Nuñez-Garcia, J., Kutalik, Z., Cho, K.-H., Wolkenhauer, O.: Level sets and minimum volume sets of probability density functions. Int. J. Approximate Reasoning 34, 25–48 (2003)
17. Rothschild, M., Stiglitz, J.E.: Increasing Risk: I. A Definition. Journal of Economic Theory 2, 225–243 (1970)
18. Rothschild, M., Stiglitz, J.E.: Increasing Risk: II. Its Economic Consequences. Journal of Economic Theory 3, 66–84 (1971)
19. Walley, P.: Statistical reasoning with imprecise probabilities. Chapman and Hall, London (1991)

The Most Representative Utility Function for Non-Additive Robust Ordinal Regression

Silvia Angilella, Salvatore Greco, and Benedetto Matarazzo

Department of Economics and Quantitative Methods,
Faculty of Economics, University of Catania,
Corso Italia 55, I-95129 Catania, Italy
angisil@unict.it, salgreco@unict.it, matarazz@unict.it

Abstract. Non-additive robust ordinal regression (NAROR) considers Choquet integral or one of its generalizations to represent preferences of a Decision Maker (DM). More precisely, NAROR takes into account all the fuzzy measures which are compatible with the preference information given by the DM and builds two preference relations: possible preference relation, when there is at least one compatible fuzzy measure for which an alternative is preferred to the other, and necessary preference relation, when an alternative is preferred to the other for all compatible fuzzy measures. Although it is interesting to take into consideration all the compatible fuzzy measures, in some decision problems we need to give a value to every alternative and it results necessary to obtain the *most representative* fuzzy measures among all the compatible ones. The aim of the paper is to propose an algorithm to the DM for selecting the *most representative* utility function expressed as Choquet integral from which a DM's representation of preferences is obtained.

Keywords: Multiple Criteria Decision Analysis; Choquet integral; Non-additive robust ordinal regression; Most representative fuzzy measures.

1 Introduction

1.1 A Multicriteria Problem

In Multiple Criteria Decision Analysis (MCDA), a decision problem is composed of a finite set of m alternatives $A = \{a_1, a_2, \ldots, a_j, \ldots, a_m\}$, evaluated on the basis of a family of n consistent criteria $G = \{g_1, g_2, \ldots, g_i, \ldots, g_n\}$, with $g_i \colon A \to \mathbb{R}$. From here on, we will use the terms criterion g_i or criterion i interchangeably $(i = 1, 2, \cdots, n)$. For the sake of simplicity, but without loss of generality, we suppose that the evaluations with respect to the considered criteria are increasing with respect to preference, *i.e.* "the more the better".

1.2 Multicriteria Methods Based on DM's Indirect Preference Information

In the context of multiple criteria decision analysis, several approaches have been proposed based upon the disaggregation-aggregation paradigm. In such methods

E. Hüllermeier, R. Kruse, and F. Hoffmann (Eds.): IPMU 2010, LNAI 6178, pp. 220–229, 2010.

some holistic judgements on some reference actions $A' \subseteq A$ are elicitated from the Decision Maker (DM) in order to infer the decision parameters (for example, weights and thresholds) compatible with the DM's preference information (disaggregation phase). These parameters, induced using a methodology called *ordinal regression*, are used in the decision model to rank all the alternatives in A (aggregation phase).

The multicriteria methods based on the disaggregation-aggregation paradigm, are interesting since they are less cognitive demanding from the DM's point of view. The most important and applied of such multicriteria approaches are UTA [22] and its variants [26]. In UTA the utility evaluation of every alternative $a \in A$ is the additive one, *i.e.*:

$$U(a) = \sum_{i=1}^{n} u_i(g_i(a)).$$

UTA, after DM's comparisons on some reference alternatives, infers via linear programming the marginal utilities at each break point of the subintervals into which the range of values of every criterion is divided, with the underling hypothesis that the marginal utilities are piecewise linear.

In UTA, the marginal utilities, obtained by a methodology called *additive ordinal regression*, restore the DM's preorder on A'.

The principles of ordinal regression have been applied also to some non-additive decision models. In this case, we shall speak of *non-additive ordinal regression* and in this context we remember some UTA like-methods within the Choquet integral framework (see [1] and [23]) and the DRSA methodology [18].

Usually, among the many sets of parameters of a decision model translating the DM's preference information, only a specific set is considered. For example, only one among the many utility functions representing the DM's holistic preference information is selected, like in the papers of Marichal and Roubens [23] and of Angilella, Greco, Lamantia and Matarazzo [1] where, in case of modelling preference with Choquet integral [7], the authors choose one among many fuzzy measures compatible with the DM's preferences.

Since such choice is arbitrary to some extent, recently *robust ordinal regression* (for a recent survey see [21]) has been proposed with the aim of taking into account all the sets of parameters compatible with the DM's preference information. In literature, the first method based on robust ordinal regression is a recent generalization of UTA, called UTA^{GMS} [19]. The UTA^{GMS} is a multiple criteria method, that instead of considering only one additive utility function compatible with the preference information provided by the DM such as in UTA, takes into consideration the whole set of additive utility functions compatible with the preference information provided by the DM. In particular, the UTA^{GMS} method requires a set of pairwise comparisons on a set of reference alternatives A' as DM's preference information. Then, the model, via linear programming, defines two relations on the set A: the *necessary* weak preference relation, which holds for any two alternatives $a, b \in A$ if all compatible utility functions give to a a value not smaller than the value given to b, and the *possible* weak preference relation, which holds for this pair if at least one compatible utility function gives to a a value not smaller than the value given to b.

Recently an extension of UTA^{GMS} has been proposed: the GRIP method [8], that builds a set of additive value functions, taking into account not only a preorder on a set of alternatives, but also the intensities of preference among alternatives.

Both UTA^{GMS} and GRIP are based on the *additive robust ordinal regression*.

Until now, robust ordinal regression has been implemented to additive utility functions under the assumption of criteria independence. In [4], the authors have proposed a *non-additive robust ordinal regression* (NAROR) on a set of alternatives A, whose utility is evaluated in terms of the Choquet integral which permits to represent the interaction among criteria, modeled by the fuzzy measures, parameterizing their approach.

In [4], besides holistic pairwise preference comparisons of alternatives from a subset of reference alternatives A', the DM is also requested to express the intensity of preference on pairs of alternatives from A', to supply pairwise comparisons on the importance of criteria, and the sign and intensity of interaction among pairs of criteria. More precisely NAROR takes into account all the fuzzy measures which are compatible with the preference information given by the DM and builds two preference relations: possible preference relation, when there is at least one compatible fuzzy measure for which an alternative is preferred to the other, and necessary preference relation, when an alternative is preferred to the other for all compatible fuzzy measures.

Recently, in [3] the NAROR approach has been extended to some generalizations of the Choquet integrals specifically, bipolar Choquet integral (see [13], [14] and [17]), level dependent Choquet integral and bipolar level dependent Choquet integral (see [10].)

Although, considering all compatible fuzzy measures, the possible and necessary preference has a lot of methodological advantages, however, the DM can have some difficulty to interpret the results. In fact, in general, the necessary preference relation is a partial preorder, i.e. a transitive and reflexive binary relation, while the possible preference relation is a strongly complete and negatively transitive binary relation (see [19]). Therefore the necessary preference relation and the possible preference relation are quite different from usual complete preorders supplied by the classical utility functions. The aim of the paper is to propose an utility function that represents in the best way the necessary preference and the possible preference relations, in order to help the DM in better understanding the results of the NAROR methodology. This utility function is obtained maximizing the difference between the values assigned by the Choquet integral to pairs of alternatives for which there is a necessary preference and minimizing the difference in case there is not a necessary preference. This utility function is called the *most representative* utility function, because it represents in the "best way" the difference between the necessary and the possible preference. In this sense, the objective of the most representative utility function, is quite different from the simple choice of one utility functions among some compatible utility functions which is a subject well-known in literature. For example in UTA (see [22]), several algorithms have been presented to explore the set of admissible value functions and to test the stability of the ranking obtained (post-optimality analysis). Instead, within NAROR methodology, the robustness concerns are taken into account through the necessary and possible preference relation on the basis of the whole set of all utility functions, compatible with the preferences expressed by the DM, and the most representative value function is not "the best one" of all those utility function, but simply it is the best to highlight the results obtained by all those compatible utility functions.

The maximization of the difference between the utility values of two alternatives resembles UTAMP1, a variant of the UTA method (see [5] and also one of its recent extensions, the method ACUTA [6]). The same methodology is adopted by [23] with respect to the utility function expressed as Choquet integral. However, our approach differs from those ones, because it does not consider only the preferences given by the DM, but it takes into account first of all the *necessary* and *possible* preference relations built through NAROR.

In the context of *robust ordinal regression*, the idea of the *most representative* value functions among the compatible ones has been already presented for choice and ranking problems in [9] and for sorting problems in [15].

The basic principle of *the most representative value function* approach is *"one for all, all for one"*:

- One for all: one value function is representing all compatible value functions;
- All for one: all compatible value functions contribute to the definition of the most representative value function.

The paper is organized as follows. In Section 2, the *non-additive robust ordinal regression* (NAROR) is described. Section 3 proposes the methodology to obtain the most representative fuzzy measure compatible with the DM's preference information. Section 4 presents a didactic example illustrating the methodology. Section 4 contains conclusions.

2   Non-Additive Robust Ordinal Regression (NAROR)

2.1   Notation and Definitions: Choquet Integral

A *fuzzy discrete measure* (called also capacity) on G with $|G| = n$ is a set function $\mu : 2^G \rightarrow [0,1]$ with $\mu(\emptyset) = 0$, $\mu(G) = 1$ (*boundary conditions*) and $\forall\, R \subseteq S \subseteq G,\ \mu(R) \leq \mu(S)$ (*monotonicity condition*). Let us observe that we will use the terms fuzzy measures or capacities interchangeably.

A fuzzy measure is *additive* if $\mu(R \cup S) = \mu(R) + \mu(S)$, for any $R, S \subseteq G$ such that $R \cap S = \emptyset$. In case of additive fuzzy measures, $\mu(R)$ is simply obtained by $\mu(R) = \sum_{i \in R} \mu(\{i\})$, $\forall\, R \subseteq G$. In the other cases, we have to define a value $\mu(R)$ for every subset R of G, obtaining 2^n coefficients values. Given $a \in A \subseteq \mathbb{R}^n_+$ and μ being a fuzzy measure on G, then the *Choquet integral* [7] is defined by:

$$\mathcal{C}_\mu(a) = \sum_{i=1}^n \left[g_{(i)}(a) - g_{(i-1)}(a)\right] \mu\left(A_i\right) =$$
$$= \sum_{i=1}^n g_{(i)}(a)\left(\mu\left(A_i\right) - \mu\left(A_{i+1}\right)\right)$$

where $_{(\cdot)}$ stands for a permutation of the indices of criteria such that:

$$g_{(1)}(a) \leq g_{(2)}(a) \leq g_{(3)}(a) \leq \cdots \leq g_{(n)}(a), \tag{1}$$

with $A_i = \{(i), \ldots, (n)\}$, $i = 1, \ldots, n$, $g_{(0)} = 0$ and $\mu(A_{n+1}) = \emptyset$.

The *importance index* or *Shapley* value of criterion $i \in G$ [25] with respect to fuzzy measure μ is defined by:

$$\varphi(\{i\}) = \sum_{R \subseteq G\setminus\{i\}} \frac{(|G| - |R| - 1)!|R|!}{|G|!}[\mu(R \cup \{i\}) - \mu(R)],$$

The interaction index between criteria $i, j \in G$ with respect to the value $\mu(R)$ is measured by the *Murofushi-Soneda interaction index* introduced in [24], that is defined by:

$$\varphi(\{i, j\}) =$$

$$\sum_{R \subseteq G\setminus\{i,j\}} \frac{(|G| - |R| - 2)!|R|!}{(|G| - 1)!}\left[\mu(R \cup \{i,j\}) - \mu(R \cup \{i\}) - \mu(R \cup \{j\}) + \mu(R)\right]$$

Note that in the rest of the paper the Choquet integral, the importance and interaction indices will be expressed in terms of Möbius representation with regard to 2-additive measures [12], i.e., in simple words, we take into account only interactions between couples of criteria, for their computational advantages and their easy interpretation from the decisional point of view.

2.2   Description of NAROR

In this section, we recall the binary preference relations on the set of reference alternatives A' defined in [4].

Let us suppose that the preference of the DM is given by a partial pre-order $\succsim$ on $A' \subseteq A$.

The preference relation $\succsim$ can be decomposed into its symmetric part $\sim$ and into its asymmetric part $\succ$, whose semantics are, respectively:

$$a \sim b \;\Leftrightarrow\; a \text{ is indifferent to } b,$$

$$a \succ b \;\Leftrightarrow\; a \text{ is preferred to } b, \text{ with } a, b \in A'.$$

The relation on the intensity of preference on pairs alternatives is represented by a partial pre-order $\succsim^*$ on $A' \times A'$, whose semantics is: for $a, b, c, d \in A'$

$$(a, b) \succsim^* (c, d) \;\Leftrightarrow\; a \text{ is preferred to } b$$

$$\text{at least as much as } c \text{ is preferred to } d;$$

The following system of linear constraints synthesizes the DM's preference information expressed in the approach proposed in [4].

$$E_\varepsilon^{A'} \begin{cases} C_\mu(a) > C_\mu(b) + \varepsilon \text{ if } a \succ b \text{ with } a, b \in A', \\ C_\mu(a) = C_\mu(b) + \varepsilon \text{ if } a \sim b \text{ with } a, b \in A', \\ C_\mu(a) - C_\mu(b) > C_\mu(c) - C_\mu(d) + \varepsilon \text{ if } (a,b) \succ^* (c,d) \text{ with } a,b,c,d \in A', \\ \vdots \\ \text{Constraints on the importance and interaction of criteria} \\ \vdots \\ \text{Boundary, monotonicity conditions} \end{cases}$$

The set of constraints $E_\varepsilon^{A'}$ with ε defines a set of fuzzy measures (capacities) μ compatible with the DM's preference information if the Choquet integral, calculated with respect to it, restores the DM's ranking on A', i.e.

$$a \succsim b \Leftrightarrow C_\mu(a) \geq C_\mu(b) \quad \forall a, b \in A'.$$

Moreover, using linear programming, our decision model establishes two preference relations:

- for any $x, y \in A$, the *necessary* weak preference relation $\succsim^N$, if for all compatible fuzzy measures the utility of x is not smaller than the utility of y, i.e. $x \succsim^N y \Leftrightarrow C_\mu(x) \geq C_\mu(y)$, for all compatible fuzzy measures;
- for any $x, y \in A$, the *possible* weak preference relation $\succsim^P$, if for at least one compatible fuzzy measure the utility of x is not smaller than the utility of y, i.e. $x \succsim^P y \Leftrightarrow C_\mu(x) \geq C_\mu(y)$ for at least one compatible fuzzy measures.

Specifically, the *necessary* preference relation $\succsim^N$ and the *possible* preference relation $\succsim^P$ on A are obtained by solving the two following linear programs, $\forall x, y \in A$:

$$\max \varepsilon \text{ s.t. } \begin{cases} E_\varepsilon^{A'} \\ C_\mu(y) \geq C_\mu(x) + \varepsilon. \end{cases} \tag{2}$$

and

$$\max \varepsilon \text{ s.t. } \begin{cases} E_\varepsilon^{A'} \\ C_\mu(x) \geq C_\mu(y). \end{cases} \tag{3}$$

If the optimization problem (2) is solved by a $\varepsilon \leq 0$, then $C_\mu(x) \geq C_\mu(y)$ for all compatible fuzzy measures μ, that implies $x \succsim^N y$ with $x, y \in A$. On the contrary, if a positive ε solves the linear program (3), then there exists at least one compatible fuzzy measures μ such that $C_\mu(x) \geq C_\mu(y)$, that implies $x \succsim^P y$ with $x, y \in A$.

3   The Most Representative Utility Function

In this section we suggest an algorithm for building the *most representative* utility function expressed as Choquet integral.

The algorithm is composed of the following steps

1. Establish the necessary and possible preference relations on the set A of alternatives, on the basis of the procedure explained in Section 2.
2. Add to the set of constraints $E_\varepsilon^{A'}$ the constraints $C_\mu(x) \geq C_\mu(y) + \gamma$ for all pairs $(x, y) \in A \times A$ such that $x \succsim^N y$ and $y \not\succsim^N x$, i.e. $x \succ^N y$. [1]
3. Compute $\max \gamma$.
4. Let the $\max \gamma$ found in the previous point equal to γ^* and add the constraint $\gamma = \gamma^*$ to the set of constraints of point 2.
5. For all pairs of alternatives $(x, y) \in A \times A$ such that $x \not\succsim^N y$ and $y \not\succsim^N x$, which are the pairs of alternatives such that $x \succsim^P y$ and $y \succsim^P x$, add the constraints $C_\mu(x) \geq C_\mu(y) + \delta$ and $C_\mu(y) \geq C_\mu(x) + \delta$ to the set of constraints of point 4.
6. Compute $\min \delta$.

Let us describe the above procedure in more details. Concerning the pairs of alternatives in relation of necessary preference, i.e. for all $(x, y) \in A \times A$ such that $x \succsim^P y$ and not $y \succsim^P x$, the maximization of γ in the constraints of type $C_\mu(x) \geq C_\mu(y) + \gamma$ aims at maximizing the minimal difference between the utility values of the alternatives.

Concerning the pairs of alternatives $(x, y) \in A \times A$ such that $x \succsim^P y$ and $y \succsim^P x$, the maximization of δ in the constraints of type $C_\mu(x) \geq C_\mu(y) + \delta$ and $C_\mu(y) \geq C_\mu(x) + \delta$ aims at minimizing the maximum difference between the utility values.

At the end of the algorithm, the procedure finds the *most representative* utility function. The corresponding capacities can be considered as the *most representative*. Observe, however, that they may not be unique and therefore a sensitivity analysis can be useful.

4   A Didactic Example

Let us consider a ranking problem of five alternatives $A = \{a_1, a_2, a_3, a_4, a_5\}$ evaluated on the basis of three criteria $G = \{g_1, g_2, g_3\}$. Table 1 presents the evaluation matrix, i.e. the scores of each alternative with respect to the considered criteria on a $[0, 20]$ scale. We suppose that the criteria have to be maximized.

Such evaluation matrix, if the DM chooses $A^* = \{a_1, a_2, a_3\}$ as the reference set of actions, is the same example proposed by Marichal and Roubens [23].

In particular, the DM's preference information considered in [23], can be synthesized as follows:

- $a_1 \succsim a_3$
- $a_3 \succsim a_2$

---

[1] $\succ^N$ denotes the asymmetric part of $\succsim^N$.

Table 1. Evaluation Matrix

	g_1	g_2	g_3
a_1	12	12	19
a_2	16	16	15
a_3	19	19	12
a_4	20	12	16
a_5	16	14	17.5

- $\varphi(\{g_3\}) > \varphi(\{g_1\})$
- $\varphi(\{g_3\}) > \varphi(\{g_2\})$
- $\varphi(\{g_2, g_3\}) < 0$

Adopting the methodology implemented in [23], we obtain a set of fuzzy measures that evaluates the utility of every alternative, in terms of the Choquet integral. The ranking obtained is displayed in the following table on the left (see Table 2).

Table 2. The two rankings obtained with the Marichal-Roubens methodology (on the left) and with NAROR (on the right)

	N. of ranking
a_1	1st
a_2	4th
a_3	3rd
a_4	2nd ex-aequo
a_5	2nd ex-aequo

	N. of ranking
a_1	2nd
a_2	5th
a_3	3rd
a_4	1st
a_5	4th

Then, we apply the methodology NAROR with the same DM's preference information proposed in [23], but enlarging the reference set to $A^* = \{a_1, a_2, a_3, a_4, a_5\}$ and adding a DM's statement on the intensity of preference between pairs of alternatives i.e.: $(a_4, a_5) \succsim^* (a_1, a_2)$.

After computing the necessary and possible relations, we apply the algorithm proposed in Section 3.

The second table on the right shows the results obtained with the most representative fuzzy measures obtained within NAROR where $\gamma^* = 0.096019$ and $\delta = 0$ (see Table 2).

5   Conclusions

In this paper, we have proposed an algorithm to help the DM to better interpret the necessary and the possible preference relations supplied by NAROR methodology with the *most representative* utility function. Let us remark that the most representative utility function has not to be considered as the "best" among the whole set of utility functions compatible with the DM's preferences. It simply can support the DM in the comprehension of the necessary and the possible preference relations. Observe also that differently from other approaches, our methodology does not aim to build a utility function representing the initial input information, being the preference given by the DM, but instead it highlights the final output results being the necessary and the possible preference relations.

The algorithm, illustrated in Section 3, could be enriched including also some statements on the strength of preference among pairs of alternatives, as done in the example, and on the interaction among criteria. In this case, the most representative utility function should highlight also these characteristics of the preference relations supplied by NAROR methodology.

One of the future research directions could be to extend the concept of most *representative* fuzzy measures also for sorting problems. In this case, the most *representative* fuzzy measures will be useful to identify the range of classes to which every alternative could possibly be assigned.

Lastly, let us observe that the most *representative* utility function, that has been proposed here to interpret the results obtained within the methodology NAROR, could be applied for the ranking of the alternatives, as an output of an autonomous multicriteria procedure, independently from NAROR.

References

1. Angilella, S., Greco, S., Lamantia, F., Matarazzo, B.: Assessing non-additive utility for multicriteria decision aid. European Journal of Operational Research 158, 734–744 (2004)
2. Angilella, S., Greco, S., Matarazzo, B.: Sorting decisions with interacting criteria. Presented at A.M.A.S.E.S. Conference, Trento, Italy, September 1-4 (2008)
3. Angilella, S., Greco, S., Matarazzo, B.: Non-additive robust ordinal regression with Choquet integral, bipolar Choquet integral and level dependent Choquet integral. In: IFSA/EUSFLAT, pp. 1194–1199 (2009) ISBN: 978-989-95079-6-8
4. Angilella, S., Greco, S., Matarazzo, B.: Non-additive Robust Ordinal Regression: a multiple criteria decision model based on the Choquet integral. European Journal of Operational Research 201(1), 277–288 (2010)
5. Beuthe, M., Scannella, G.: Comparative analysis of UTA multicriteria methods. European Journal of Operational Research 130, 246–262 (2001)
6. Bous, G., Fortemps, P., Glineur, F., Pirlot, M.: ACUTA: A novel method for eliciting additive value functions on the basis of holistic preferences. European Journal of Operational Research (to appear, 2010)
7. Choquet, G.: Theory of capacities. Annales de l'Institut Fourier 5, 131–295 (1953)
8. Figueira, J., Greco, S., Słowiński, R.: Building a Set of Additive Value Functions Representing a Reference Preorder and Intensities of Preference: GRIP method. European Journal of Operational Research 195(2), 460–486 (2008)
9. Figueira, J., Greco, S., Słowiński, R.: Identifying the "most representative " value function among all compatible value functions in the GRIP method. Presented at 68th Meeting of the European Working Group on Multiple Criteria Decision Aiding, Chania, October 2-3 (2008)
10. Greco, S., Giove, S., Matarazzo, B.: The Choquet integral with respect to a Level Dependent Capacity. Submitted to Fuzzy Sets and Systems (2010)

11. Grabisch, M.: The application of fuzzy integrals in multicriteria decision making. European Journal of Operational Research 89, 445–456 (1996)
12. Grabisch, M.: k-Order additive discrete fuzzy measures and their representation. Fuzzy Sets and Systems 92, 167–189 (1997)
13. Grabisch, M., Labreuche, C.: Bi-capacities–I: definition, Möbius transform and interaction. Fuzzy Sets and Systems 151, 211–236 (2005)
14. Grabisch, M., Labreuche, C.: Bi-capacities–II: the Choquet integral. Fuzzy Sets and Systems 151, 237–259 (2005)
15. Greco, S., Kadziński, M., Słowiński, R.: The most representative value function in robust multiple criteria sorting. Presented at the 69 Meeting of the European Working Group on Multiple Criteria Decision Aiding, Bruxelles, April 2-3 (2009) (submitted to Computers & Operations Research)
16. Greco, S., Giove, S., Matarazzo, B.: The Choquet integral with respect to a Level Dependent Capacity. Submitted to Fuzzy Sets and Systems (2008)
17. Greco, S., Matarazzo, B., Słowiński, R.: Bipolar Sugeno and Choquet integrals. In: De Baets, B., Fodor, J., Pasi, G. (eds.) EUROWorking Group on Fuzzy Sets, Workshop on Informations Systems (EUROFUSE 2002), Varenna, Italy, pp. 191–196 (September 2002)
18. Greco, S., Matarazzo, B., Słowiński, R.: Rough sets theory for multicriteria decision analysis. European Journal of Operational Research 129, 1–47 (2001)
19. Greco, S., Mousseau, V., Słowiński, R.: Ordinal regression revisited: Multiple criteria ranking with a set of additive value functions. European Journal of Operational Research 191(2), 415–435 (2008)
20. Greco, S., Mousseau, V., Słowiński, R.: Multiple criteria sorting with a set of additive value functions. Submitted to European Journal of Operational Research (2009)
21. Greco, S., Słowiński, R., Figueira, J., Mousseau, V.: Robust ordinal regression. In: Ehrgott, M., Greco, S., Figueira, J. (eds.) New Trends in Multiple Criteria Decision Analysis, pp. 273–320. Springer Science + Business Media, Inc., Heidelberg (2010)
22. Jacquet-Lagrèze, E., Siskos, Y.: Assessing a set of additive utility functions for multicriteria decision-making, the UTA method. European Journal of Operational Research 10, 151–164 (1982)
23. Marichal, J.L., Roubens, M.: Determination of weights of interacting criteria from a reference set. European Journal of Operational Research 124, 641–650 (2000)
24. Murofushi, T., Soneda, S.: Techniques for reading fuzzy measures (iii): interaction index. In: Proc. 9th Fuzzy Systems Symposium, Sapporo, Japan, pp. 693–696 (1993)
25. Shapley, L.S.: A value for n-person games. In: Kuhn, H.W., Tucker, A.W. (eds.) Contributions to the Theory of Games II, pp. 307–317. Princeton University Press, Princeton (1953)
26. Siskos, Y., Grigoroudis, E., Matsatsinis, N.: UTA methods. In: Figueira, J., Greco, S., Ehrgott, M. (eds.) Multiple Criteria Decision Analysis: State of the Art Surveys, pp. 298–335. Springer Springer Science + Business Media, Inc., Heidelberg (2005)

Alternative Normalization Schemas
for Bayesian Confirmation Measures

Salvatore Greco[1], Roman Słowiński[2,3], and Izabela Szczęch[2]

[1] Faculty of Economics, University of Catania, Corso Italia, 55, 95129 Catania, Italy
salgreco@unict.it
[2] Institute of Computing Science, Poznan University of Technology,
60-965 Poznan, Poland
{Izabela.Szczech,Roman.Slowinski}@cs.put.poznan.pl
[3] Systems Research Institute, Polish Academy of Sciences, 01-447 Warsaw, Poland

Abstract. Analysis of rule interestingness measures with respect to their properties is an important research area helping to identify groups of measures that are truly meaningful. In this article, we analyze property Ex_1, of preservation of extremes, in a group of confirmation measures. We consider normalization as a mean to transform them so that they would obtain property Ex_1 and we introduce three alternative approaches to the problem: an approach inspired by Nicod, Bayesian, and likelihoodist approach. We analyze the results of the normalizations of seven measures with respect to property Ex_1 and show which approaches lead to the desirable results. Moreover, we extend the group of ordinally non-equivalent measures possessing valuable property Ex_1.

Keywords: Normalization, Bayesian confirmation measures, property Ex_1.

1 Introduction

One of the main objectives of data mining process is to identify "*valid, novel, potentially useful, and ultimately comprehensible knowledge from databases*" [6]. When mining large datasets, the number of knowledge patterns, often expressed in a form of "*if..., then...*" rules, can easily be overwhelming rising an urgent need to identify the most useful ones. Addressing this issue, various quantitative measures of rule interestingness (attractiveness) have been proposed and studied, e.g., *support*, *confidence*, *lift* (for a survey on interestingness measures see [1], [9], [13]). The literature is a rich resource of ordinally non-equivalent measures that reflect different characteristics of rules. There is no agreement which measure is the best. To help to analyze objective measures, some `properties` have been proposed, expressing the user's expectations towards the behavior of measures in particular situations. Properties of measures group the measures according to similarities in their characteristics. Using the measures which satisfy the desirable properties, one can avoid considering unimportant rules. Different properties were surveyed in [5], [9], [10], [19]. In this paper, we focus on two desirable properties: *property of confirmation* quantifying the degree to which the

E. Hüllermeier, R. Kruse, and F. Hoffmann (Eds.): IPMU 2010, LNAI 6178, pp. 230–239, 2010.

premise of the rule provides evidence for or against the conclusion [8], [2], and *property Ex_1* guaranteeing that any conclusively confirmatory rule, for which the premise ϕ entails the conclusion ψ (i.e. such that $\phi \models \psi$), is assigned a higher value of measure than any rule which is not conclusively confirmatory, and that any conclusively disconfirmatory rule, for which ϕ refutes ψ (i.e. such that $\phi \models \neg\psi$), is assigned a lower value than any rule which is not conclusively disconfirmatory [4], [11]. Though property Ex_1 is so intuitively clear and required, it is not satisfied by many popular measures. Looking for a way of transforming seven chosen confirmation measures, so they would fulfill Ex_1, Crupi et al. [4] proposed to normalize them. Their approach, however, is only one of many ways to handle this issue. In this paper, we extend their analysis and propose three other alternative normalization schemas. Moreover, we analyze them with respect to property Ex_1 presenting and commenting the results of application of different normalizations to the chosen measures. Furthermore, as the result of our work, there also emerges a set of interestingness measures (alternative to one of Crupi et al.) that satisfy desirable properties and thus extend the family of valuable measures.

2   Preliminaries

A *rule* induced from a dataset U shall be denoted by $\phi \rightarrow \psi$. It consists of a premise (evidence) ϕ and a conclusion (hypothesis) ψ. A rule is a logical sentence in the sense that elementary conditions on attributes are connected by logical "and", on both sides of the rules. However, on a particular attribute they can concern evaluations expressed on nominal, ordinal or cardinal scales. For each rule we consider the number of objects which satisfy both the premise and the conclusion, only the premise, only the conclusion, neither the premise nor the conclusion. However, this does not mean that in our data each object can assume only values e.g., ψ or $\neg\psi$. It simply means that when we evaluate a rule of the type "if ϕ, then ψ" we take into account set of objects that satisfy ψ and a set of objects that do not satisfy ψ.

In general, by $sup(\gamma)$ we denote the number of objects in the dataset for which γ is true. Thus, $sup(\phi \rightarrow \psi)$ is the number of objects satisfying both the premise and the conclusion of a $\phi \rightarrow \psi$ rule. Moreover, the following notation shall be used throughout the paper: $a = sup(\phi \rightarrow \psi)$, $b = sup(\neg\phi \rightarrow \psi)$, $c = sup(\phi \rightarrow \neg\psi)$, $d = sup(\neg\phi \rightarrow \neg\psi)$. Observe that b can be interpreted as the number of objects that do not satisfy the premise but satisfy the conclusion of the $\phi \rightarrow \psi$ rule. Analogous observations hold for c and d. Moreover, the following relations occur: $a+c = sup(\phi)$, $a+b = sup(\psi)$, $b+d = sup(\neg\phi)$, $c+d = sup(\neg\psi)$, and the cardinality of the dataset U, denoted by $|U|$, is the sum of a, b, c and d.

3   Property of Bayesian Confirmation

Formally, an interestingness measure $c(\phi \rightarrow \psi)$ has the property of Bayesian confirmation (or simply confirmation) iff it satisfies the following conditions:

$$c(\phi \to \psi) \begin{cases} > 0 & if \quad Pr(\psi|\phi) > Pr(\psi), \\ = 0 & if \quad Pr(\psi|\phi) = Pr(\psi), \\ < 0 & if \quad Pr(\psi|\phi) < Pr(\psi). \end{cases} \tag{1}$$

where $Pr(\psi)$ denotes the probability of ψ, and $Pr(\psi|\phi)$ is the conditional probability of ψ given ϕ.

This definition identifies confirmation with an increase in the probability of the conclusion provided by the premise, neutrality with the lack of influence of the premise on the probability of conclusion, and disconfirmation with a decrease of probability of the conclusion imposed by the premise [2]. Under the "closed world assumption" adopted in inductive reasoning, and because U is a finite set, it is legitimate to estimate probabilities in terms of frequencies, e.g., $Pr(\psi) = sup(\psi)/|U| = (a + b)/|U|$. In consequence, we can define the conditional probability as $Pr(\psi|\phi) = Pr(\phi \wedge \psi)/Pr(\phi)$, and it can be regarded as $sup(\phi \to \psi)/sup(\phi)$ (i.e. $a/(a+c)$). Thus, the above condition can be re-written:

$$c(\phi \to \psi) \begin{cases} > 0 & if \quad \dfrac{a}{a+c} > \dfrac{a+b}{|U|}, \\ = 0 & if \quad \dfrac{a}{a+c} = \dfrac{a+b}{|U|}, \\ < 0 & if \quad \dfrac{a}{a+c} < \dfrac{a+b}{|U|}. \end{cases} \tag{2}$$

Measures that possess the property of confirmation are referred to as *confirmation measures* or *measures of confirmation*. They quantify the degree to which the premise ϕ provides "support for or against" the conclusion ψ [8]. By using the attractiveness measures that possess this property one can filter out rules which are misleading and disconfirm the user, and this way, limit the set of induced rules only to those that are meaningful [18]. The only constraints (2) that the property of confirmation puts on a measure are that it assigns positive values in the situation when confirmation occurs, negative values in case of disconfirmation and zero otherwise. As a result, many alternative, non-equivalent measures of confirmation have been proposed. Most commonly used ones are gathered in Table (1) (selection provided in [4]):

4   Property Ex_1 of Preservation of Extremes

To handle the plurality of alternative confirmation measures Crupi et al. [4] have proposed a property (principle) Ex_1 resorting to considering inductive logic as an extrapolation from classical deductive logic. On the basis of classical deductive logic they construct a function v:

$$v(\phi, \psi) = \begin{cases} the \quad same \quad positive \quad value \quad if \quad \phi \models \psi, \\ the \quad same \quad negative \quad value \quad if \quad \phi \models \neg\psi, \\ 0 \quad otherwise. \end{cases} \tag{3}$$

For any argument (ϕ, ψ) v assigns it the same positive value (e.g., +1) if and only if the premise ϕ of the rule entails the conclusion ψ (i.e. $\phi \models \psi$). The same

Table 1. Common confirmation measures

$D(\phi \rightarrow \psi) = Pr(\psi\|\phi) - Pr(\psi) = \dfrac{a}{a+c} - \dfrac{a+b}{\|U\|}$	Carnap [2]
$S(\phi \rightarrow \psi) = Pr(\psi\|\phi) - Pr(\psi\|\neg\phi) = \dfrac{a}{a+c} - \dfrac{b}{b+d}$	Christensen [3]
$M(\phi \rightarrow \psi) = Pr(\phi\|\psi) - Pr(\phi) = \dfrac{a}{a+b} - \dfrac{a+c}{\|U\|}$	Mortimer [14]
$N(\phi \rightarrow \psi) = Pr(\phi\|\psi) - Pr(\phi\|\neg\psi) = \dfrac{a}{a+b} - \dfrac{c}{c+d}$	Nozick [16]
$C(\phi \rightarrow \psi) = Pr(\phi \wedge \psi) - Pr(\phi)Pr(\psi) = \dfrac{a}{\|U\|} - \dfrac{(a+c)(a+b)}{\|U\|^2}$	Carnap [2]
$R(\phi \rightarrow \psi) = \dfrac{Pr(\psi\|\phi)}{Pr(\psi)} - 1 = \dfrac{a\|U\|}{(a+c)(a+b)} - 1$	Finch [7]
$G(\phi \rightarrow \psi) = \dfrac{Pr(\neg\psi\|\phi)}{Pr(\neg\psi)} = 1 - \dfrac{c\|U\|}{(a+c)(c+d)}$	Rips [17]

value but of opposite sign (e.g., -1) is assigned if and only if the premise ϕ refutes the conclusion ψ (i.e. $\phi \models \neg\psi$). In all other cases (i.e. when the premise is not conclusively confirmatory nor conclusively disconfirmatory for the conclusion) function v obtains value 0.

From definition, any confirmation measure $c(\phi \rightarrow \psi)$ agrees with function $v(\phi, \psi)$ in the way that if $v(\phi, \psi)$ is positive then the same is true for $c(\phi \rightarrow \psi)$, and when $v(\phi, \psi)$ is negative, so is $c(\phi \rightarrow \psi)$. According to Crupi et al., the relationship between the logical implication or refutation of ψ by ϕ, and the conditional probability of ψ subject to ϕ should go further and demand fulfillment of the principle Ex_1 [4]:

$$if \quad v(\phi_1, \psi_1) > v(\phi_2, \psi_2), \quad then \quad c(\phi_1 \rightarrow \psi_1) > c(\phi_2 \rightarrow \psi_2). \qquad (4)$$

Property Ex_1 is desirable for any interestingness measure as it guarantees that the measure will assign a greater value to any conclusively confirmatory rule (i.e. such that $\phi \models \psi$, e.g., *if x is seven of spades then x is black*) than to any rule which is not conclusively confirmatory (e.g., *if x is black then x is seven of spades*). Moreover, rules that are conclusively disconfirmatory (i.e. such that $\phi \models \neg\psi$, e.g., *if x is seven of spades then x is red*) will obtain smaller values of interestingness measures than rules which is not conclusively disconfirmatory (e.g., *if x is black then x is seven of spades*).

5   Normalization of Confirmation Measures

Having observed that confirmation measures D, S, M, N, C, R, G (defined earlier on) are contrary to Ex_1, Crupi et al. [4] proposed to normalize them by dividing each of them by the maximum (minimum, respectively) the measure obtains when $\phi \models \psi$, i.e. when the rule's premise entails its conclusion ($\phi \models \neg\psi$, respectively). Determining the maximum or minimum that a confirmation measure obtains in case of confirmation or disconfirmation has, however, no unique interpretation, and the approach applied by Crupi et al. is only one of many ways to handle this issue. We shall now propose and analyze four (including the approach of Crupi et al.) alternative schemas allowing to determine the maximum (or minimum) of any confirmation measure in those two situations. We denote by a', b', c' and d' the values of a, b, c and d, respectively, in case of maximizing or minimizing the confirmation. Each of the analyzed schemas eventually leads to a different normalization, as we divide the original measures by their maximum or minimum calculated using alternative schemas. Therefore next, we will present and discuss results of normalization of measures D, S, M, N, C, R, G using those approaches.

5.1   Approach Inspired by Nicod

The Nicod's criterion presented in [15] says that an evidence confirms a rule $\phi \rightarrow \psi$ if and only if it satisfies both the premise and the conclusion of the rule, and disconfirms it if and only if it satisfies the premise but not the conclusion of the rule. Thus, objects for which the premise and the conclusion is supported are considered as positive examples for the rule and objects satisfying the premise but not the conclusion are counter-examples. Moreover, according to Nicod's criterion, an evidence that does not satisfy the premise is neutral with respect to the rule. It means that objects for which the premise is not satisfied are irrelevant to the rule, no matter whether they support the conclusion or not. Now, let us propose a schema, based on Nicod's criterion, for determination of maximum (or minimum) of a confirmation measure. Following Nicod's directives, the only objects that are relevant to a rule are positive examples and counter-examples. It brings us to an observation that a measure will obtain its maximum when all counter-examples change into positive examples. It means that the number of positive examples should take over all counter-examples (i.e. $a' = a + c$), and the number of counter-examples should drop to 0 (i.e. $c' = 0$). The number of evidence which are irrelevant to the rule should remain unchanged (i.e. $b' = b$ and $d' = d$). The schema for determination of the minimal value is analogous. Putting all the considerations together we obtain the approach, inspired by Nicod, to determine the extremes of any measure (Table 2).

Table 2. Schemas for determination of the extremes of any measure

Nicod's		Bayesian		Likelihoodist		Crupi's et al.	
Max	Min	Max	Min	Max	Min	Max	Min
$a' = a+c$	$a' = 0$	$a' = a+b$	$a' = 0$	$a' = a+c$	$a' = 0$	$a' = a+c$	$a' = 0$
$b' = b$	$b' = b$	$b' = 0$	$b' = a+b$	$b' = 0$	$b' = b+d$	$b' = b-c$	$b' = a+b$
$c' = 0$	$c' = a+c$	$c' = 0$	$c' = c+d$	$c' = 0$	$c' = a+c$	$c' = 0$	$c' = a+c$
$d' = d$	$d' = d$	$d' = c+d$	$d' = 0$	$d' = b+d$	$d' = 0$	$d' = c+d$	$d' = d-a$

5.2   Bayesian Approach

Bayesian approach is related to the idea that the evidence confirms the hypothesis, if the hypothesis is more frequent with the evidence rather than without the evidence. Analogously, the evidence disconfirms the hypothesis, if $\neg$ hypothesis is more frequent with the evidence rather than without the evidence. Thus, determination of measure's extremes based on this approach should consider a rule from the perspective of its conclusion. Following Bayesian approach, let us observe that for a rule *if x is a raven then x is black* [12] a measure will obtain its maximum if *all black non-ravens* change into *black ravens* (i.e. $a' = a + b$ and $b' = 0$), and all *non-black ravens* change into *non-black non-ravens* (i.e. $d' = c + d$ and $c' = 0$). It is due to the fact that when there are no *black non-ravens* (i.e. $b' = 0$), the hypothesis of being *black* is more frequent with the premise of being a *raven* rather than with ¬premise of being a *non raven*, which means that the premise confirms the rule's conclusion. Moreover, when there are no *non-black ravens* (i.e. $c' = 0$), the ¬hypothesis of being *non-black* is disconfirmed as it is more frequent with the ¬premise of being a *non-raven* rather than with the premise of being a *raven*. Disconfirmation of ¬hypothesis is desirable as it results in confirmation of the hypothesis. The considerations about determination of the minimal value are analogous. The Bayesian approach to determination of a measure's maximum or minimum is summarized in Table 2.

5.3 Likelihoodist Approach

The likelihoodist approach is based on the idea that the evidence confirms the hypothesis, if the evidence is more frequent with the hypothesis rather than without the hypothesis, and in this context, analogously, the evidence disconfirms the hypothesis, if the evidence is more frequent without the hypothesis rather than with the hypothesis. Thus, one can informally say that likelihoodists look at the rule from the perspective of its premise. According to likelihoodist approach, for a rule *if x is a raven then x is black* [12] a measure will obtain its maximum if all *non-black ravens* change into *black ravens* (i.e. $a' = a + c$ and $c' = 0$), and all *black non-ravens* change into *non-black non-ravens* (i.e. $d' = b + d$ and $b' = 0$). It results from the fact that when there are no *non-black ravens* (i.e. $c' = 0$), the evidence of being a *raven* is more frequent with the hypothesis of being *black* rather than with ¬hypothesis of being *non black*, which means that the premise confirms the rule's conclusion. Moreover, when there are no *black non-ravens* (i.e. $b' = 0$), the ¬evidence of being a *non-raven* is more frequent with the hypothesis of being *non-black* rather than with the hypothesis of being *black*. Thus, we can conclude that hypothesis is disconfirmed by the ¬premise and as a result of that the hypothesis is confirmed by the premise. Determination of the minimal value of confirmation measure is analogous. The whole likelihoodist approach to calculating the measure's extremes is presented in Table 2.

5.4 Approach of Crupi et al.

Having proved that none of the measures: D, S, M, N, C, R nor G satisfies the desirable property Ex_1, Crupi et al. [4] showed an easy way to transform them into measures that do fulfill Ex_1. They presented formulas to which the considered measures boil down when $\phi \models \psi$ and when $\phi \models \neg\psi$, and proposed to normalize the measures by dividing them by the obtained formulas. Their article, however, does not provide any methodological schema to determine the measure's extremes - only the calculated formulas are given. Since, the approach of Crupi et al. brings such interesting results, we have analyzed it thoroughly in terms of our notation, i.e. a, b, c and d, and came up with a clear schema (see Table 2) that can be used to determine the extremes of any measure.

According to Crupi et al., dividing a measure by the formula obtained when $\phi \models \psi$ produces the normalized measure in case of confirmation (i.e. when $Pr(\psi|\phi) \geq Pr(\psi)$), and the division by absolute value of the formula obtained when $\phi \models \neg\psi$ gives the normalized measure in case of disconfirmation (i.e. when $Pr(\psi|\phi) < Pr(\psi)$). Interestingly, it turned out that the considered measures all gave the same result after that transformation, i.e. $D_{norm} = S_{norm} = M_{norm} = N_{norm} = C_{norm} = R_{norm} = G_{norm}$. Crupi et al. labeled the newly obtained measure of confirmation Z. In case of confirmation $Z = G$ and in case of disconfirmation $Z = R$. Crupi et al. [4] have proved that measure Z and all confirmation measures ordinally equivalent to Z satisfy property Ex_1.

6   Results of Applying Normalization Schemas to Measures

Each of the schemas presented by us to determine the extremes of measures eventually results in a different normalization. Table 3 presents them all. For the sake of the presentation, the definitions of the analyzed measures were simplified by basic mathematical transformations (column 1). The next four columns contain results for different normalization schemas, for each measure there are two rows containing the normalized measure in case of confirmation (the first row) and disconfirmation (the second row). The notation we used assumes that lower indexes signify the applied normalization (N stands for Nicod, B for Bayesian, L for likelihoodist, and C for Crupi et al.), and that the case of confirmation is marked by a "+" and the case of disconfirmation by a "-" (e.g., D_{N+} stands for measure D normalized in case of confirmation, using the approach inspired by Nicod).

Since the normalization of Crupi et al. was introduced as a tool for transforming the measures so they would satisfy the property Ex_1, we have analyzed the results of different normalizations of measures D, S, M, N, C, R, G from the view point of this property. Let us observe, that Ex_1 is satisfied by any confirmation measure that obtains its maximal value when there are no counterexamples to the rule and its minimal value when there are no positive examples to the rule. These two conditions can be regarded as sufficient for proving the possession of Ex_1 by measure $c(\phi \to \psi)$.

Theorem 1. *All confirmation measures D, S, M, N, C, R, G normalized using approach inspired by Nicod or approach of Crupi et al. satisfy property Ex_1. Moreover normalization using Bayesian approach gives measures satisfying Ex_1 only in case of measure D, R and G, whereas using likelihoodist approach, Ex_1 does not hold for any of the considered measures.*

Table 3. Results of alternative normalization approaches

Original measure	Nicod's norm.	Bayesian norm.	Likelihoodist norm.	Crupi et al norm.
$D(\phi \to \psi) = \frac{ad-bc}{|U|(a+c)}$	$D_{N+} = \frac{ad-bc}{d(a+c)}$	G	S	G
	$D_{N-} = \frac{ad-bc}{b(a+c)}$	R	S	R
$S(\phi \to \psi) = \frac{ad-bc}{(a+c)(b+d)}$	D_{N+}	S	S	G
	D_{N-}	S	S	R
$M(\phi \to \psi) = \frac{ad-bc}{|U|(a+b)}$	$M_{N+} = \frac{(ad-bc)(a+b+c)}{d(a+b)(a+c)}$	N	$M_{L+} = \frac{ad-bc}{(a+b)(b+d)}$	G
	R	N	R	R
$N(\phi \to \psi) = \frac{ad-bc}{(a+b)(c+d)}$	$N_{N+} = \frac{(ad-bc)(a+b+c)}{(a+b)(a+c)(c+d)}$	N	N	G
	$N_{N-} = \frac{(ad-bc)(a+c+d)}{(a+b)(a+c)(c+d)}$	N	N	R
$C(\phi \to \psi) = \frac{ad-bc}{|U|^2}$	D_{N+}	N	S	G
	D_{N-}	N	S	R
$R(\phi \to \psi) = \frac{ad-bc}{(a+b)(a+c)}$	M_{N+}	G	M_{L+}	G
	R	R	R	R
$G(\phi \to \psi) = \frac{ad-bc}{(a+c)(c+d)}$	G	G	G	G
	$G_{N-} = \frac{(ad-bc)(a+c+d)}{b(a+c)(c+d)}$	R	$G_{L-} = \frac{ad-bc}{(c+d)(b+d)}$	R

Proof. Possession of property Ex_1 can be verified by putting $c = 0$ and $a = 0$ in the normalized measure and checking whether it's formula boils down to 1 in case $c = 0$ and to -1 in case $a = 0$. The considered measures normalized using approach inspired by Nicod or approach of Crupi et al. are equal to 1 (or -1) when $c = 0$ (or $a = 0$).

The new measures obtained during normalization inspired by Nicod can be regarded as alternative ones with respect to measure Z advocated by Crupi et al. [4]. D_N, S_N, M_N, N_N, C_N, R_N, and G_N are as valuable as Z in terms of possession of Ex_1 and, generally, produce different rankings on rules than Z. It is an important result widening the group of non-equivalent measures satisfying property Ex_1.

Theorem 2. *Measures D_N, S_N, M_N, N_N, C_N, R_N, and G_N (resulting from application of normalization inspired by Nicod) are ordinally non-equivalent to measure Z.*

Proof. Measure f is ordinally equivalent to measure g iff for any rules r_1, r_2:

$$f(r_1) \begin{Bmatrix} > \\ = \\ < \end{Bmatrix} g(r_1) \quad iff \quad f(r_2) \begin{Bmatrix} > \\ = \\ < \end{Bmatrix} g(r_2). \tag{5}$$

The above condition needs to be fulfilled both in case of confirmation and disconfirmation. For Table 3 it is enough to consider measures D_{N+}, M_{N+}, N_{N+} and G_{N-}. The situation in which the number of objects in U is distributed over a, b, c and d is called scenario α. In scenario α, rule $r : \phi \to \psi$ is supported by a objects from U. Table 4 contains a counterexample proving that in two exemplary scenarios α_1 and α_2 measures D_{N+}, and M_{N+} produce rankings different than measure G. Measure G assigns r_2 greater value than to r_1, whereas measures D_{N+}, and M_{N+} rank those rules the other way round. Thus, D_N and M_N are ordinally non-equivalent to measure Z. By the next counterexample in Table 4, let us show that in scenarios α_3 and α_4 measure N_{N+} produces different ranking than measure G. Observe that measure G assigns r_1 greater value, whereas measures N_{N+} favors r_2, thus we can conclude that N_N is ordinally non-equivalent to Z. Finally, scenarios α_1 and α_2 from Table 4 prove that measure G_{N-} produces different ranking than measure R. Here, G_{N-} assigns r_1 greater value, whereas R favors r_2. Thus, G_N is ordinally non-equivalent to Z.

Table 4. Counterexamples showing ordinal non-equivalence of measures D_N, M_N, N_N, G_N and measure Z

Counterexample concerning measures D_{N+} and M_{N+}						
α_1 $a=90$	$b=8$	$c=1$	$d=1$	$\|U\|=100$	$D_{N+}(r_1)$=**0.90** $M_{N+}(r_1)$=**0.91**	$G(r_1)=0.45$
α_2 $a=70$	$b=16$	$c=4$	$d=10$	$\|U\|=100$	$D_{N+}(r_2)=0.86$ $M_{N+}(r_2)=0.90$	$G(r_1)$=**0.61**
Counterexample concerning measure N_{N+}						
α_3 $a=70$	$b=1$	$c=19$	$d=1$	$\|U\|=100$	$N_{N+}(r_1)=0.33$	$G(r_1)$=**0.26**
α_4 $a=55$	$b=2$	$c=26$	$d=17$	$\|U\|=100$	$N_{N+}(r_2)$=**0.37**	$G(r_1)=0.25$
Counterexample concerning measure G_{N-}						
α_1 $a=90$	$b=8$	$c=1$	$d=1$	$\|U\|=100$	$G_{N-}(r_1)$=**5.18**	$R(r_1)=0.009$
α_2 $a=70$	$b=16$	$c=4$	$d=10$	$\|U\|=100$	$G_{N-}(r_2)=3.22$	$R(r_1)$=**0.099**

7 Conclusions

Analysis of interestingness measures with respect to their properties is an important research area helping to identify groups of measures that are truly meaningful. In this article, we have focused on possession of property Ex_1 in a group of popular confirmation measures. Normalization of measures as a way to transform them so that they would obtain property Ex_1 has been considered. A crucial step of such normalization is determination of the extremes of the measures in case of confirmation and disconfirmation. In this article, we have introduced three alternative approaches to this problem, i.e. an approach inspired by Nicod, Bayesian, and likelihoodist approach. All these approaches, as well as that of Crupi et al., lead to different results and normalizations, as they consider the concept of confirmation from different perspectives. A set of seven confirmation measures, earlier analyzed by Crupi et al., has been normalized using those four schemas. We have analyzed the results of the normalizations with respect to property Ex_1. The conclusions that we obtained show that approach inspired by Nicod, as well as approach of Crupi et al., give normalized measures with property Ex_1 in cases of all of the considered measures. Moreover, we have proved that measures obtained through those normalizations are ordinally non-equivalent. Thus, we have extended the group of measures possessing valuable property Ex_1.

References

1. Bramer, M.: Principles of Data Mining. Springer, New York (2007)
2. Carnap, R.: Logical Foundations of Probability, 2nd edn. University of Chicago Press, Chicago (1962)
3. Christensen, D.: Measuring confirmation. Journal of Philosophy 96, 437–461 (1999)
4. Crupi, V., Tentori, K., Gonzalez, M.: On Bayesian measures of evidential support: Theoretical and empirical issues. Philosophy of Science (2007)
5. Eells, E., Fitelson, B.: Symmetries and asymmetries in evidential support. Philosophical Studies 107(2), 129–142 (2002)
6. Fayyad, U., Piatetsky-Shapiro, G., Smyth, P.: From data mining to knowledge discovery: an overview. In: Fayyad, U., Piatetsky-Shapiro, G., Smyth, P., Uthursamy, R. (eds.) Advances in Knowledge Discov. and Data Mining, pp. 1–34. AAAI Press, Menlo Park (1996)
7. Finch, H.A.: Confirming Power of Observations Metricized for Decisions among Hypotheses. Philosophy of Science 27, 293–307, 391–404 (1999)
8. Fitelson, B.: Studies in Bayesian Confirmation Theory. Ph.D. Thesis, University of Wisconsin, Madison (2001)
9. Geng, L., Hamilton, H.J.: Interestingness Measures for Data Mining: A Survey. ACM Computing Surveys, article 9 38(3) (2006)
10. Greco, S., Pawlak, Z., Słowiński, R.: Can Bayesian confirmation measures be useful for rough set decision rules? Eng. Application of Artif. Intelligence 17, 345–361 (2004)
11. Greco, S., Sowiski, R., Szczch, I.: Assessing the quality of rules with a new monotonic interestingness measure Z. In: Rutkowski, L., Tadeusiewicz, R., Zadeh, L.A., Zurada, J.M. (eds.) ICAISC 2008. LNCS (LNAI), vol. 5097, pp. 556–565. Springer, Heidelberg (2008)
12. Hempel, C.G.: Studies in the logic of confirmation (I). Mind 54, 1–26 (1945)
13. McGarry, K.: A survey of interestingness measures for knowledge discovery. The Knowledge Engineering Review 20(1), 39–61 (2005)
14. Mortimer, H.: The Logic of Induction. Paramus/Prentice Hall (1988)
15. Nicod, J.: Le probleme de la logique de l'induction. Alcan, Paris (1923)
16. Nozick, R.: Philosophical Explanations. Clarendon Press, Oxford (1981)
17. Rips, L.J.: Two Kinds of Reasoning. Psychological Science 12, 129–134 (2001)
18. Szczęch, I.: Multicriteria Attractiveness Evaluation of Decision and Association Rules. In: Peters, J.F., Skowron, A., Wolski, M., Chakraborty, M.K., Wu, W.-Z. (eds.) Transactions on Rough Sets X. LNCS, vol. 5656, pp. 197–274. Springer, Heidelberg (2009)
19. Tan, P.-N., Kumar, V., Srivastava, J.: Selecting the right interestingness measure for association patterns. In: Proc. of the 8th international Conf. on Knowledge Discovery and Data Mining (KDD 2002), Edmonton, Canada, pp. 32–41 (2002)

Gender and Age Estimation from Synthetic Face Images

Alberto N. Escalante B. and Laurenz Wiskott

Institut für Neuroinformatik, Ruhr-University of Bochum, Germany
{alberto.escalante,laurenz.wiskott}@ini.rub.de

Abstract. Our ability to recognize the gender and estimate the age of people around us is crucial for our social development and interactions. In this paper, we investigate how to use Slow Feature Analysis (SFA) to estimate gender and age from synthetic face images. SFA is a versatile unsupervised learning algorithm that extracts slowly varying features from a multidimensional signal. To process very high-dimensional data, such as images, SFA can be applied hierarchically. The key idea here is to construct the training signal such that the parameters of interest, namely gender and age, vary slowly. This makes the labelling of the data implicit in the training signal and permits the use of the unsupervised algorithm in a hierarchical fashion. A simple supervised step at the very end is then sufficient to extract gender and age with high reliability. Gender was estimated with a very high accuracy, and age had an RMSE of 3.8 years for test images.

Keywords: Slow feature analysis, human face images, age, gender, hierarchical network, feature extraction, pattern recognition.

1 Introduction

The estimation of gender and age is crucial for many social interactions, and is done everyday consciously or unconsciously. This process happens very quickly and requires relatively little visual information which is usually of dynamic nature, but we are also capable of performing this process with still images.

In this work we investigate how an unsupervised algorithm for signal extraction can be used to automatically extract gender and age information from single frontal images of simulated subjects (random 3D face models). This has applications to man-machine interaction, face recognition, and as an aid in the supervision of age and gender related policies.

In order to learn the gender and age of the subjects, we decided to use a versatile unsupervised algorithm called Slow Feature Analysis (SFA). SFA extracts slowly varying features from a high-dimensional signal. Contrary to other unsupervised learning algorithms, for SFA time plays a key role. In this paper, the high-dimensional signal is a sequence of images (e.g. each image is a $135 \times 135 = 18225$-dimensional vector), and it is enforced that one or more (hidden) parameters involved in image generation change on a relatively slow

E. Hüllermeier, R. Kruse, and F. Hoffmann (Eds.): IPMU 2010, LNAI 6178, pp. 240–249, 2010.

timescale. Although individual signal components (e.g. pixels of an image) might change on a very fast timescale, the algorithm should find a way to combine several signal components at any time step, such that the resulting computed signals vary each as slowly as possible over time, while still containing information about the input.

The trick in using this unsupervised algorithm to learn some particular feature is to create an appropriate training sequence in which the slowest varying parameter is the feature we want to learn. Thus, for instance, for the age estimation problem, the training signal is a sequence of face images in which the age of the subjects increases very slowly. We show that in this case, the slowest learned feature is strongly correlated with the original age of the subject.

1.1 Related Work

Berkes et al. [3] used (a single unit of) quadratic SFA to analyze sequences of image patches from natural images. They studied optimal stimuli yielding the largest and smallest responses from the unit, and showed that SFA is capable of learning receptive fields with properties similar to those found in complex cells in the primary visual cortex.

Later Franzius et al. [4] implemented a hierarchical model of SFA and used it to extract position and view direction in a simulated box environment. They showed that the type of features learned, which resemble certain cells in a rodent's brain, depend solely on the statistics of the sequences of images generated by the movement inside the box.

More recently, Franzius et al. [5] also used the temporal slowness principle and followed an invariant object recognition approach. They estimate the identity and pose of artificial fish and textured spheres from still images. They studied the simultaneous change in one or more slow parameters at different timescales. Contrary to this work, the supervised post-processing used for feature estimation is based on linear regression and they used a much larger number of signals for this step, while we used only three signals.

Some existing methods for gender classification, which can be roughly divided into appearance-based and geometric-based approaches, are briefly described in [8,6] and for age classification in [6].

2 Slow Feature Analysis (SFA)

SFA is a biologically inspired unsupervised learning algorithm [7], that in its linear version is somewhat related to PCA and ICA, but has the essential property that the temporal component of the variables is also considered (i.e., the temporal ordering of the samples matters).

The input is a multidimensional signal $x(t) = (x_1(t), \ldots, x_N(t))^T$. SFA then computes a set of weights $w_i = (w_{i,1}, \ldots, w_{i,N})^T$, such that each output signal $y_i(t) = x(t)^T w_i$ has the slowest possible temporal variation and is uncorrelated to signals y_j for $j < i$.

More formally, the output signals $y_i(t)$, for $0 \leq i < N$ must be optimally slow in the sense that the objective function $\Delta(y_i) \stackrel{\text{def}}{=} \langle \dot{y}_i(t)^2 \rangle$ (i.e., the variance of the time derivative of y_i) is minimal while the following constraints must hold:

- Zero mean: $\langle y_i(t) \rangle = 0$
- Unit variance: $\langle y_i(t)^2 \rangle = 1$
- Decorrelation: $\langle y_i(t) y_j(t) \rangle = 0$ for $j < i$

The SFA problem is to find an optimal set of weights $\{w_i\}$ such that the conditions above are met. Fortunately, it is well known that the optimal solutions to this problem depend only on the covariance matrix $B = \langle xx^T \rangle$ of the training sequence $x(t)$, and the covariance matrix $A = \langle \dot{x}\dot{x}^T \rangle$ of the time derivative of the training sequence $\dot{x}(t)$. In practice, time is discrete and the time derivative is approximated by the difference of consecutive samples in the training sequence.

Moreover, it is possible to state the SFA problem as a generalized eigenvalue problem, and traditional algorithms for solving the latter problem can be used. As a consequence, the algorithm has a similar complexity as PCA and is guaranteed to find an optimal solution.

3 Hierarchical Slow Feature Analysis

To apply even linear SFA on the whole training data would be too expensive, since it would have a computational complexity of $\mathcal{O}(LN^2 + N^3)$ where L is the number of samples and N is the dimensionality. This complexity problem becomes more severe if a non-linear preprocessing step is applied to the images to obtain non-linear SFA. Hierarchical SFA allows us to cope with this problem by dividing the image sequence in smaller dimensionality sequences that are separately processed by SFA units, cf. [4]. Afterwards, the slow signals separately computed by these units can be grouped together and further processed by the SFA units in the next layer. This process can be repeated and organized in a multi-layer hierarchy until global slow features are extracted, where each layer is trained separately from the first to the last.

Although hierarchical networks based on SFA have been successfully tested on different stimuli before, e.g. images of fish, textured spheres [5] and the interior of boxes [4], it is unclear whether this type of network would also succeed at learning from frontal face images, because changes in the slow parameters in the training data only produce subtle changes at the pixel level (compared for example to fish identity or pose, which offer larger variability at the pixel level). We prove that hierarchical SFA is powerful enough to learn these slow parameters.

The hierarchical SFA networks we have developed can be employed unchanged to extract different relevant parameters from image sequences, where the learned parameters are implicit in the training data. Thus, we only need to modify the training set according to the particular parameter to be learned.

A special effort was made to keep the computational cost of the training procedure low because, as in many learning algorithms, training is a relatively expensive procedure. However, once trained the computational and memory cost for SFA are very low, and thus feature extraction from a single image is a fast procedure.

We built several networks and tested several values of the parameters that define its structure and the composition of the layers. In this article, we focus only on one particular linear and a non-linear network. We remark that its structure is not problem-specific, except for the input dimensionality of the networks which should agree with the image size. This is in accordance with the desire of building a flexible architecture capable of tackling different problems without modification.

Linear SFA Network. This is the simplest network we developed. As any linear system, it has well known limitations that reduce the type of relevant features that can be correctly extracted. This limitation is slightly reduced by the use of a Gaussian classifier on top of the linear network (see Section 4.3 on post-processing).

The network has 4 processing layers, which operate one after the other and reduce the dimensionality from 135x135 pixel values in the input images to just 40 signals at the network output. Each layer can be further subdivided into a few elementary sub-layers, which in turn are composed of elementary data processing units arranged in a square array. These units can be, for example, SFA nodes or PCA/whitening nodes. For reasons of space we omit here the details of the network structure. The first layer contains an SFA sub-layer with 27x27 SFA nodes, each one having a non-overlapping fan-in of 5x5x(1 pixel) and a fan-out of 16 signals, thus reducing the data dimensionality by 36%. Similarly, the second layer has a 9x9 grid structure, each unit has a fan-in of 3x3x(16 signals) and a fan-out of 30 signals, which reduces the data dimensions from 27x27x16 to 9x9x30 signals, a further reduction of 79%. In the same way, the third layer has a 3x3 grid structure, each unit has a fan-in of 3x3x(30 signals) and a fan-out of 40 signals. The forth layer has a single SFA node that takes the whole output of the previous layer and outputs only 40 signals. The complete network reduces the amount of signals from 135x135 to just 40 signals, where only 3 of them are given to the classifier.

Non-Linear SFA Network. Our non-linear network has the same architecture as the linear network, with the only difference that non-linear expansion nodes are added in each sub-layer before the SFA nodes. These nodes introduce some amount of non-linearity that depends on the expansion function that was chosen. The more powerful this expansion is, the more capable the network becomes in extracting complex features. Therefore, it is tempting to use a complex expansion, say a 5th degree product expansion, where all products up to degree five on the input signal components appear. However, a large expansion increases the computational cost and the amount of training data needed to avoid overfitting.

Therefore, more conservative non-linearities are typically preferred, such as a quadratic expansion (including all terms of the form x_i and $x_i x_j$ for $0 \leq i, j < N$, where $(x_0, \ldots, x_{N-1})$ is the original signal). In this work, we use modest non-linearities. The expansion function computes all terms $x_i x_{i+1}$ for $0 \leq i < N-1$ in addition to the linear terms x_i. Each non-linear expansion node roughly doubles the number of signals. However, the number of slow signals extracted by the SFA nodes is kept the same as in the linear case to avoid an explosion in the number of signals.

Other expansions that we have tested include the product of pairs of variables with similar slowness values, and sums or differences instead of products combined with other non-linearities such as absolute values and square roots. We did not find any advantage in using these expansions.

4   Training and Test Sequences for Age and Gender Estimation

After having built suitable SFA networks, the next step was to generate an appropriate data set for training and testing. The network learns to estimate gender or age from artificial frontal images based solely on the particular sequence of images used for training. After training we separately test its performance with respect to these images and new images not seen before by the network. All the training and test images were generated in software only once before training took place.

The software used for face model generation is called FaceGen [2], image rendering was done with POV-Ray [1], other tools were used for format conversions, and the process was partially automated with many Perl scripts, and a few Python scripts. The arguably large amount of images is required to reduce overfitting.

4.1   Sequences for Gender Estimation

The first data set was created as follows. A large number of random subjects was needed. In this case, we created 12000 random subjects, each one defined by a unique 3D face model without hair, glasses, earrings or other accessories. These models are generated with several randomized low- and high-level facial parameters that include (at a high-level) age, symmetry, gender and racial composition, and it is possible to change any of these parameters. For example, the gender parameter is a real value, defined by the software for face generation as: -3 = very masculine, -1=masculine, 1=feminine to 3 = very feminine. This allowed us to arbitrarily select the level of masculinity or femininity of the models, and thus create sequences of images of random subjects where the gender value slowly increases from very masculine to very feminine. We selected 60 fixed gender values: $(-3, -2.9, \ldots, 2.9)$ and 200 subjects per gender value, thus requiring 12000 face images. A neutral expression was chosen, random vertical and horizontal translations of +/- 2 pixels were added to each image, and pink-noise like random backgrounds were used. Notice that the addition of a translation and randomized backgrounds makes the problem more difficult and is inspired by more realistic conditions of real photographs. The network should now learn to remain invariant to small translations. It should actually also become invariant to the quickly changing randomized background since it is not a good source of slow signals.

The training sequence (Figure 1) is composed of 180 of the subjects for each gender value accounting for 10800 images, while the test sequence is composed of the remaining 20 subjects per gender value accounting for 1200 images.

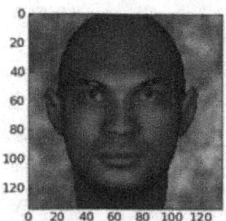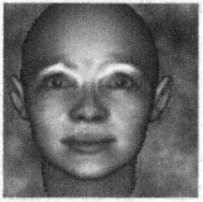

Fig. 1. A few examples of the images of the training sequence used for gender estimation. The gender parameter varies here from -3.0 (left), -1.1, 0.9 to 2.9 (right).

4.2 Sequences for Age Extraction

The face generation software only allows for generating subjects from 15 to 65 years. For efficiency purposes, we selected 23 specific ages non-uniformly, increasing from 15 to 65 years: (15, 16, 18, 20, ..., 55, 60, 65 years). The separation between samples was shorter for smaller ages because we expected a larger variability at the pixel level in young subjects than in older subjects.

We created 200 random subjects for each age value, accounting for 4600 random subjects of different ages. Again, no hair, glasses, earrings or other accessories were present. Also a neutral expression was chosen, pink-noise like random backgrounds were used, and smaller random vertical and horizontal translations of +/- 1 pixel were added to each centered image.

For the training set we took 180 of the generated subjects for each age value accounting for 4140 images, while the test sequence is composed of the remaining 460 images.

4.3 Supervised Post-processing of the Slow Signals

A classifier is taught to relate the output of the network to the known values of the relevant parameters, such as the true age or gender of the input samples (while the network itself is unsupervised, the labels with the known gender or age are used to train the classifier). For the linear network, this constitutes the single non-linear step in the architecture.

Theoretically, we expect that the slow signals extracted by the network should depend on the slow parameter that we want the network to learn. Notice however, that the slowest signal does not have to be linearly related to the slow parameter, so it might not be possible to use it directly to recover the parameter. What

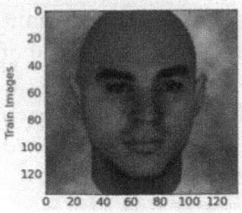

Fig. 2. Examples of the images of the training sequence used for age estimation. The age parameter varies here from left to right from 15, 26, 44 to 65 years.

we need is a way to establish a connection between the domain of the slow signals, and the parameter domain. The classifier takes advantage of the fact that the slow parameter is redundantly coded in the slow signals, as the theory indicates, as the slowest signal and as its harmonics. Additionally, we exploit the fact that the training set is labelled (since we know gender and age during image generation) to estimate the parameter. In theory, images with the same slow parameter cluster in a single point in the output domain. We use a small set of slow signals, here the 3 slowest output signals, to train a classifier. As labels for the classifier we use the real gender or age parameter. If the network generalizes well, then the classifier should be able to output the correct value of the parameter for new images. Moreover, if class probabilities are present, we can improve the estimation of the parameter aiming at minimizing the MSE. Two classifiers were used: a closest center classifier and a Gaussian classifier. A class was defined for each possible value of the labels.

We assumed that the Gaussian Classifier perfectly learned the distribution of the data, and is able to perfectly estimate the class probabilities. Then, we used the class probabilities and the labels to find the value that minimizes the MSE. Let $P(l_i)$ be the probability that a given image actually has label l_i, for $1 \leq i \leq C$, then our estimate of the parameter is $\sum_i l_i P(l_i)$, where i ranges over the C classes.

5   Results

For the gender extraction experiment, the linear SFA network followed by a simple Gaussian classifier on 3-dimensional signals was capable of estimating the gender of new random subjects with a root mean squared error (RMSE) of 0.33 (Table 1). Recall that the gender parameter varies in the interval $(-3, 2.9)$. Thus the standard error from the true parameter is about 5% of the parameter's range.

In Figure 3 we can see the three slowest signals extracted by the linear network from the training sequence of the gender estimation experiment. Notice that the slowest signal (in black) is less noisy than the other signals. The same figure for the test sequence (not shown) is very similar, except that it has fewer data points.

Table 1. Performance of the networks in terms of the root mean squared error (RMSE) using a Gaussian classifier (GC) and a closest center classifier (CCC)

	Linear Network		Non-Linear Network	
	RMSE Gaussian	RMSE CCC	RMSE Gaussian	RMSE CCC
Gender Estimation				
Training Images	0.3084	0.6098	0.2229	0.3119
Test Images	0.3318	0.6857	0.4180	0.5858
Age Estimation (years)				
Training Images	3.2963	5.6461	2.2313	3.3914
Test Images	3.8365	7.0697	5.3618	7.9660

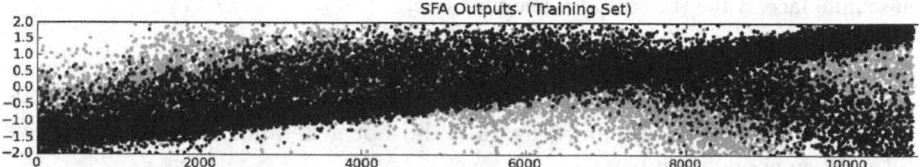

Fig. 3. Linear network: slowest signals for the gender experiment. The black, dark grey and light grey points are the slowest, second slowest and third slowest signals, resp. The horizontal axis indicates the image number, and the vertical axis is the amplitude of the slow signals.

The reported performance was achieved when the classifier was trained with only the 3 slowest signals computed by the network. The precise number of signals given to the classifier has a direct influence on the performance of the system. Its optimal value depends on the combination of the network employed and the training sequence.

Using only one signal degrades the quality of the estimation, because it reduces the available redundancy. Using many signals, however, is not useful because faster varying extracted signals are increasingly noisier than the slowest ones, thus the classifier cannot take much advantage of them. Moreover, if the number of signals is increased, the Gaussian classifier also needs more samples to reliably learn the input distribution.

The non-linear network performs better on the training data than the linear one, as expected, but suffers from more overfitting, which explains why it does not outperform the linear network on new data. The non-linear network will become superior for newer data once enough training samples are used.

The problem of age estimation is more difficult than gender estimation. In informal tests, it was clear that the ability of a human operator at estimating age from the images was limited. Thus we were not expecting a good performance from the system. The linear network had an RMSE of 3.8 years from the true age of the subjects, and 3.3 years for the training samples. The performance of the

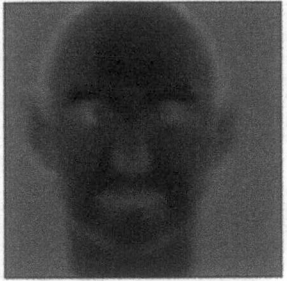 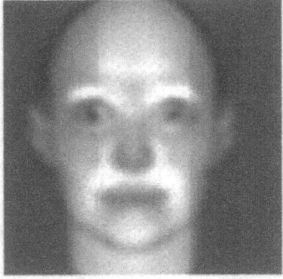

Fig. 4. The linear mask (weights) that encodes the slowest output signal and its negative (normalized for display purposes). Notice how the first image resembles more a masculine face, while the second a feminine one.

non-linear network for the training samples was clearly superior with an RMSE of only 2.2 years. Unfortunately, again it did not generalize as well because we did not use enough samples.

6   Conclusion and Future Work

We developed two very flexible hierarchical networks for slow feature analysis. These networks are application independent, and can be used to learn slow parameters from very different two-dimensional signals. Training was accomplished in less than 30 minutes. Importantly, the output of the network agreed to a large extent with the theoretically predicted properties of SFA on the whole images.

The expansion of the data in a non-linear way, even a small expansion, increases the performance of the network, but has the disadvantage that larger training sequences are required, otherwise the generalization property is diminished. The amount of training data was earlier shown to be related to the number of features that the system must become invariant to. Hence the addition of rotation, translation, scaling, glasses, clothes, etc. require more training data for the network to be able to ignore such features.

It must be underlined that the networks learn slowly varying parameters according to the underlying model used by the face generation software. Learning from real face images is an interesting topic that we are currently studying. For age and gender estimation using normalized real images we expect a small decrease in the performance. The development of a full SFA-based pipeline for face detection, pose estimation and face recognition is also a challenging topic that we would like to address.

As future work, we will develop more complex SFA hierarchies and design methods to reduce the amount of training data and specially labelled data required, which is now the main factor required to handle real images with this architecture.

Acknowledgments

We would like to thank Marco Müller for his support in using the software for face generation, and Michael Brauckmann for inspiring discussions and for his technical support.

References

1. POV-Team, POV-Ray, http://www.povray.org
2. Singular Inversions Inc., FaceGen SDK, http://www.facegen.com
3. Berkes, P., Wiskott, L.: Slow feature analysis yields a rich repertoire of complex cell properties. J. Vis. 5(6), 579–602 (2005)
4. Franzius, M., Sprekeler, H., Wiskott, L.: Slowness and sparseness lead to place, head-direction, and spatial-view cells. PLoS Computational Biology 3(8), e166 (2007)
5. Franzius, M., Wilbert, N., Wiskott, L.: Invariant object recognition with slow feature analysis. In: Kurkov, V., Neruda, R., Koutnik, J. (eds.) ICANN 2008, Part I. LNCS, vol. 5163, pp. 961–970. Springer, Heidelberg (2008)
6. Ramesha, V.K.R., Raja, K.K.B., Patnaik, L.M.: Feature extraction based face recognition, gender and age classification. International Journal on Computer Science and Engineering (IJCSE) 02(01S), 14–23 (2010)
7. Wiskott, L., Sejnowski, T.: Slow feature analysis: Unsupervised learning of invariances. Neural Computation 14(4), 715–770 (2002)
8. Zheng Ji, X.-C.L., Lu, B.-L.: State of the Art in Face Recognition. In: ICONIP 2008. LNCS, vol. 5507, pp. 647–654. Springer, Heidelberg (2009)

Attribute Value Selection Considering the Minimum Description Length Approach and Feature Granularity

Kemal Ince[1] and Frank Klawonn[2]

[1] Volkswagen AG, Komponenten-Werkzeugbau
Gifhornerstr. 180, 38037 Braunschweig, Germany
kemal.ince@volkswagen.de
http://www.volkswagen-braunschweig.de/
[2] Data Analysis and Pattern Recognition Lab
Ostfalia University of Applied Sciences
Salzdahlumer Str. 46/48, 38302 Wolfenbüttel, Germany
f.klawonn@ostfalia.de
http://public.ostfalia.de/~klawonn/

Abstract. In this paper we introduce a new approach to automatic attribute and granularity selection for building optimum regression trees. The method is based on the minimum description length principle (MDL) and aspects of granular computing. The approach is verified by giving an example using a data set which is extracted and preprocessed from an operational information system of the Components Toolshop of Volkswagen AG.

Keywords: Minimum Description Length, Granular Computing, Regression Tree, Decision Support, Intelligent Decision Algorithm.

1 Introduction

The ideas presented in this paper are motivated by an application in the Components Toolshop of Volkswagen AG in Brunswick. This business area is responsible for producing tools in other divisions of Volkswagen AG for the the serial production. The Components Toolshop has approximately 700 members of staff and includes a 30.000m^2 production area so that it can be considered as one of the biggest tool shops in the world. The product range includes forming tools, (like gearbox cases and engine boxes), injection moulds, casting moulds and production lines and other machined tools.

These tools are denoted in this paper as products. In the Components Toolshop a very large data set is available describing the different processes of manufacturing the products. This data set is mainly obtained from operational information systems. A subset of this data set contains the production time of the products. Every product contains an allocated time δ_s and an actual time δ_i which can differ from each other. The subset contains additional information on the manufacturing process which is used later in the analysis phase.

E. Hüllermeier, R. Kruse, and F. Hoffmann (Eds.): IPMU 2010, LNAI 6178, pp. 250–259, 2010.

This paper describes how a regression tree is built to predict the relative deviation between these two time values. By building the model the regression tree must fulfill the following two criteria as good as possible:

- The predicted deviation should deviate as little from the true deviation **and**
- the complexity of the constructed regression tree Δ_K should be as small as possible.

Another aspect which must be considered is that the input values have different granularities. An example is the feature *component* which specifies the automotive part, the feature *component assembly* in which the *components* are aggregated and the feature *component category* in which the *component assemblies* are combined.

It is obvious that identified rules containing features with fine granularity are less general than rules which are composed of features with coarse granularity. The developed algorithm has to decide in favour of the feature which delivers the best result for both criteria described above.

The paper is organised as follows. Section 2 provides a brief overview on the basics of regression trees and the minimum description length principle. In Section 3, the motivation and discussion of the approach is presented in detail. Section 4 describes how the generated model is evaluated and Section 5 concludes with a discussion of the results and an outlook on future work.

2   Theoretical Background of Regression Tree and MDL

This section provides a brief introduction to regression trees and the minimum description length principle. Further details can be found in [1,2].

2.1   The Regression Tree Idea

Regression is besides classification one of the most important problems in predictive statistics [1]. It deals with predicting values of a continuous variable from one or more continuous and/or categorical predictor variables [3]. In general the regression tree method allows input values to be a mixture of numerical and nominal values. The output value has to be numerical. The result of this approach is that a tree is generated where each decision node contains a test on some input values. The terminal nodes of the tree contain the predicted output values [4]. In [5] an example is given how to build a regression tree using the program XMLMiner with an example data set.

The CART algorithm is an example for building classification and regression trees. This algorithm was developed by Leo Breiman in 1984. An important property of this algorithm is that it delivers only binary trees. This means every node of the tree is either a terminal node or followed exactly by two successor nodes [6].

The basic regression tree growing algorithm which is used in the different approaches works in the following way:

1. The starting point is the initial node which contains the whole data set. Here, the values m_c, the regression value for the node and the error S are calculated as defined below.
2. If all the points in the node have the same value for all the independent variables, stop the algorithm. Otherwise, search over all binary splits of all variables for the one which will reduce S as much as possible. If the largest decrease in S is less than some threshold δ, or one of the resulting nodes would contain less than q data objects, stop the algorithm. Otherwise, take that split and create two new nodes.
3. Go back to step 1, in each new node.

In the above described algorithm S is the sum of squared errors for the regression tree R_T measured as follow:

$$S = \sum_{c \in leaves(R_T)} \sum_{i \in c} (y_i - m_c)^2 \tag{1}$$

where $m_c = \frac{1}{n_c} \sum_{i \in c} y_i$ is the prediction for leaf c [7].

2.2   The Minimum Description Length Principle

The minimum description length principle (MDL) is based on the fundamental idea that any regularity in a data set can be used to compress it [2]. Compression means to describe the data set with fewer symbols than the number of symbols which are needed to describe the data set literally. Such a data set can for example be described by a decision tree which has fewer symbols as the initial data set. The more regularities in the data set exist, the more the data set can be compressed. Folowing this idea, it is possible to understand 'learning' as 'finding regularities' in the data.

Therefore the MDL principle can be used in different ways for inductive inference such as to choose a model that trades-off the goodness-of-fit on the observed data set with the complexity of the model (in statistical questions) or in a predictive interpretation where MDL methods can be used to search for a model with good predictive performance on unseen data sets [2].

In the following example, the idea is illustrated that learning can be interpreted as data compression. In the sample below a 2000 bits long sequence S_1 is shown, where just the beginning and the end of it is listed.

$$'01110011100111001110.....01110011100111001110' \tag{2}$$

It seems that S_1 is a 400-fold repetition of '01110'. A decription method which maps descriptions $\overline{D}$ in a unique manner to a data set D is needed to compress S_1. A programming language can be used as description method to carry out the compression of S_1. In the sample below such a computer program is displayed in the programming language $C\#$. It describes the regularity in S_1 and is shorter than S_1 itself.

Example of a computer program in $C\#$ describing the regularity in sequence S_1

```
string sequence = "";
for (int i = 1; i <= 400; i++)
{
    sequence = sequence + "01110";
}
Console.WriteLine("The sequence = " + sequence);
```

The example above is very theoretical, since in practical applications such highly compressible data seldom exist. Usually sequences with lower compressibility such as described in the sample below are given.

$$'00110000001100100001.....11001000000100110010000' \qquad (3)$$

The sequence S_2 has a recognizable regularity because it contains approximately twice as many 0's as 1's. But the regularity S_2 is more of statistical than of deterministic character. So it seems possible to find a description which is able to generate future sequences that is similar to S_2.

If we consider that n is the length of the sequence (in both samples above is $n = 2000$ bits long), S_1 can be compressed to $O(\log n)$ and S_2 can be compressed to αn with $0 < \alpha < 1$. This fact allows to make the following case:

$$\exists\, \overline{D}(s) \text{ where } n(\overline{D}(s)) \leq n(s) \quad \text{with } s \subseteq S \qquad (4)$$

where S is the initial sequence, s is a subsequence of S, $\overline{D}(s)$ is the description of the subsequence s, $n(\overline{D}(s))$ is the length of $\overline{D}(s)$ and $n(s)$ is the length of s.

3   Motivation and Solution

As mentioned initially, in the Components Toolshop of Volkswagen AG different operational information systems are in use, which are required to support the manufacturing process. This means several of these systems are concerned with the manufacturing process directly and some of them, for example organization-ally attached, indirectly. The application of these systems delivers large amounts of data which can contain interesting and hidden coherences. It is suspected that the type of specific events depends on various facts and could not be detected by a manual inspection of the large data set. The cycle time of a product could, for example, depend on the milling machine which is used to manufacture it. Due to this problem data mining approaches were used to detect these coherences in the data.

The considered application area has to deal with data containing divers information like the machine on which the product was manufactured, by whom the product was processed, to which greater category the product belongs etc. These features are the input values for the decision model which has to be generated. Furthermore, information about the real time which was needed to manufacture the product δ_i and the expected time δ_s which is estimated initially by the planner are available. The ratio Δ_r of these two features constitutes the output value, which has to be predicted.

$$\Delta_r = \frac{\delta_i}{\delta_s} \tag{5}$$

Both time values are numerical. Therefore the output value has a continuous character. Table 1 shows a fictitious data set with the following features:

- The *machine* which was planned to be used during manufacturing process: M_s,
- the *machine* which was used in the real manufacturing process: M_i,
- the *machine category* of M_i: MC_i,
- the *component* which has to be manufactured: C,
- the *component assembly* of C: C_a,
- the *component category* of C: C_c and
- the *output value*, the ratio between the two time values: Δ_r

A row (data object) in the data set to be analysed is characterised by the above value and the data set might look as in Table 1. Of course, the real data sets are much larger.

Table 1. A fictitious data set

M_s	M_i	MC_i	C	C_a	C_c	Δ_r
a	b	B	10201	1020	10	0.76
a	a	A	10202	1020	10	0.74
a	b	B	10301	1030	10	0.75
c	d	D	20301	2030	20	0.44
a	c	C	20302	2030	20	0.46

We need an algortihm to build a regression tree which predicts Δ_r. During building the regression tree, it is necessary to decide which granularity for the input values makes sense to predict the output value as good as possible. The simpler the constructed model (regression tree) is and the smaller the errors it delivers in predicting the output value the better it is. In the following section we describe our approach of the implemented algorithm in more detail in the form of pseudo-code.

Pseudo-code of the combined MDL and RegTree algorithm

```
program RegtreeMDL (Output)
  var
     mean; outputValue: double;
     meanList: Dictionary<string, double>;
     ds: DataSet;
     dt1, dt2: DataTable;
     dcc: DataColumnCollection;
     rows: DataRow[];
     colName, colValue, filter: string;
  begin
     ds = GetInitialData();
     for int i = 0 to ds.rows.Count
     step
        outputValue = outputValue +
           ds.rows[i][ds.IndexOf(lastColumn)];
     next
     mean = outputValue / ds.rows.Count;
     meanList.Add("wholeDataSet", mean);
     dcc = ds.dt1.Columns;
     for int i = 1 to dcc.Count - 1
     step
        colName = dcc[i].ColumnName;
        dt2 = SelectDistinct("tbl_AttValue",ds.dt1,colName);
        for int j = 0 to dt.rows.Count
        step
           colValue = dt.rows[j]-ItemArray[0];
           filter = colName + " LIKE " + colValue;
           rows = ds.dt1.Select(filter);
           for  int k = 0 to rows.Count
           step
              outputValue = outputValue +
                 rows[k].ItemArray[rows[k].ItemArray.Length - 1];
           next
           mean = outputValue / rows.Count;
           meanList.Add(colName + " _ " + colValue , mean);
        next
     next
     for int i = 0 to meanList.Count - 1
     step
        if SumOfFailureRegtree(meanList[i]) <=
           SumOfFailureRegtree(meanList[i+1])
        then break;
        else
     next
  end
```

The above pseudo-code describes the functionality of the implemented algorithm. In first step, the *mean* of the initial data set is calculated. First the numbers of *rows* in the data table *dt*1 is identified. For each *row* in *rows* the sum of the *outputValue* is computed. Finally the *mean* of the numeric output value is calculated by using the sum of the output values and dividing it by the number of *rows*. Afterwards, in the second step all other possibilities for splitting are calculated. Therefore, all the *columnNames* of the input values have to be considered. The codomain of the input values are identified by using these *columnNames*. In the following step, these *columnNames* and codomains were used to *filter* the data set and calculate the means for the subset. The last loop of the algorithm deals with the method *SumOfFailureRegtree*() to calculate, in which step the algorithm delivers the 'best' result and has to terminate.

4   Validation with Generated Data

In this section, a brief example is given, how the algorithm handles the data and which results it delivers. Therefore, the input value A with the value set $A = \{a_1, a_2\}$ is defined. The output value Z consists of continuous values. In this fictitious case we define the target value Z as follows:

$$Z = \left\{ +\frac{\Delta}{2} + R(0,1), -\frac{\Delta}{2} + R(0,1) \right\}$$

with $R(0,1)$ constituting a minimal random noise between 0 and 1 and Δ is a constant. Furthermore it is suggested that both values of A occur equally often in the whole data set. In Table 2 such a data set is displayed.

Table 2. Abstract data set containing random noise

A	Z
a_1	$+\frac{\Delta}{2} + R(0,1)$
a_2	$-\frac{\Delta}{2} + R(0,1)$
a_1	$+\frac{\Delta}{2} + R(0,1)$
a_2	$-\frac{\Delta}{2} + R(0,1)$
a_2	$-\frac{\Delta}{2} + R(0,1)$
a_1	$+\frac{\Delta}{2} + R(0,1)$

A regression tree for this simple data set can have the following two forms displayed in Figures 1 and 2. The first tree delivers the arithmetic mean $\bar{x} = 0$. The error F_1 in predicting Z is

$$F_1 = \frac{\Delta}{2} + R_1(0,1) + \frac{\Delta}{2} + R_2(0,1) + \frac{\Delta}{2} + R_3(0,1) + \frac{\Delta}{2} + R_4(0,1) + \frac{\Delta}{2} + R_5(0,1) + \frac{\Delta}{2} + R_6(0,1)$$

$$= 3 * \Delta + \sum_{i=1}^{6} R_i(0,1)$$

Provided that the random noise $R_i(0,1)$ is close to zero, the error F_1 becomes

$$F_1 = 3 * \Delta$$

The length of the regression tree L_1 is 0. It has only one predicting value 0 which is generaly valid for the whole data set. The MDL-value M_1 consists of the sum of F_1 and L_1. The result is that the MDL-value of the first tree is

$$M_1 = F_1 + L_1 = 3 * \Delta.$$

Fig. 1. Regression tree with one node including the whole data set and predicting Z as $\bar{x} = 0$

The second regression tree delivers a model which separates the data set into two subsets. The error in predicting Z in this case is

$$F_2 = R_1(0,1) + R_2(0,1) + R_3(0,1) + R_4(0,1) + R_5(0,1) + R_6(0,1)$$

$$= \sum_{i=1}^{6} R_i(0,1)$$

Provided like above that the statistical noise $R_i(0,1)$ (almost) zero, the error becomes $F_2 = 0$. To get the MDL-value the length of the regression tree L_2 is needed to be calculated.

$$\left| \frac{\Delta}{2} \right| + \left| \frac{-\Delta}{2} \right| = \Delta$$

The MDL-value of the second tree is calculated as followed.

$$M_2 = F_2 + L_2 = \Delta.$$

Because of minimizing the MDL-value a split like described by the second regression tree below makes sense.

The above considerations are only valid when the noise is small compared to the constant Δ. When the noise becomes larger, the more complex decision tree might not be favoured anymore. Let $\frac{\Delta}{2}$ be the predicted value of the model and assume $\Delta = 0.002$ and therefore $\frac{\Delta}{2} = 0.001$

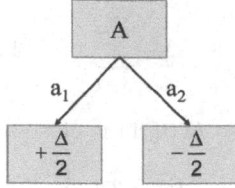

Fig. 2. Regression tree with one root node and two leafs

In binary code this means

$$(0.002)_2 = 0.0000000010000011$$

and

$$(0.001)_2 = 0.0000000001000001$$

If the noise has the value $N = 0.123$

$$N = 0.123 \rightarrow (0.123)_2 = 0.0001111101111100$$

$$0.001 + 0.123 = \underline{0.124}$$

The sum of both binary values is calculated in binary coding as follows:

$$
\begin{array}{r}
0.0000000001000001 \\
+\ 0.0001111101111100 \\
\hline
0.0001111110111101
\end{array}
$$

The error is much higher than the difference between the prediction of the Δ. This means every bit in the predicted value has to be corrected so that the deviation in the predicted Δ is not relevant any more.

5   Conclusion

Decision support is getting more and more important even for industrial application areas such as the Components Toolshop. It has a wide range of topics where the field of building models by generating decision and regression trees is a less but itself established detail. If only the aspect of minimizing the predicting error is considered, the model might exhibit a very high complexity. Additionally considering the fact to reduce the complexity of the model delivers a result, which can be used to answer universally valid questions in decision support. With the described approach the possibility to select automatically the 'best' input values by predicting a continuous output value is accomplished. This approach can be adapted in different analysis problems to resolve decision support problems.

References

1. Wei-Yin, L.: Classification and Regression Tree Methods. In: Encyclopedia of Statistics in Quality and Reliability, pp. 315–323. Wiley-VCH, Chichester (2008)
2. Grünwald, P.: A Tutorial Introduction to the Minimum Description Length Principle.Centrum voor Wiskunde en Informatica, Netherlands
3. Overview Classification and Regression Trees,
   http://www.statsoft.com/textbook/classification-and-regression-trees/
4. Online Help of XMLMiner, http://www.resample.com/xlminer/help/Index.htm
5. Example of a Regression Tree,
   http://www.resample.com/xlminer/help/rtree/rtree_.htm
6. Wikipedia The Free Encyclopedia,
   http://de.wikipedia.org/wiki/CART_Algorithmus
7. Shalizi, C.: Classification and Regression Trees. In: 36-350 Data Mining, Lecture 10 (2009)

Possibility Theory and Formal Concept Analysis: Context Decomposition and Uncertainty Handling

Yassine Djouadi[1,2], Didier Dubois[2], and Henri Prade[2]

[1] University of Tizi-Ouzou,
BP 17, RP, 15000 Tizi-Ouzou, Algeria
[2] IRIT, Université Paul Sabatier,
118 Route de Narbonne, 31062 Toulouse Cedex 09, France
ydjouadi@mail.ummto.dz, dubois@irit.fr, prade@irit.fr

Abstract. Formal Concept Analysis uses a simple representation framework called 'formal context'. In the classical setting, a formal context specifies existing Boolean relationships between a set of objects and their corresponding properties. Formal concepts are then defined as pairs consisting of a set of objects and a set of properties that mutually characterize each other through a Galois connection. Another Galois connection is also introduced in this setting on the basis of operators induced by a recent possibility theory reading of Formal Concept Analysis. It is shown that this second Galois connection enables us to characterize independent sub-contexts inside the formal context. The second part of the paper discusses an extension of Formal Concept Analysis that has not been much studied, namely the situation where one may be uncertain on the fact that an object possesses or not a Boolean property. Uncertainty is here represented in the possibilistic representation framework.

1 Introduction

The main aim of Formal Concept Analysis (FCA for short) is to extract interesting clusters of knowledge, called formal concepts, from a particular representation of data, called formal contexts. The original idea of FCA has been introduced by Wille [23] and is becoming increasingly popular among various methods of conceptual data analysis and knowledge processing.

In the classical setting [18,23], a formal context consists of a (crisp) binary relation between a set of objects and a set of properties. This relation is usually represented as a table with rows corresponding to objects, columns corresponding to properties (or conversely) and table entries containing cross marks or blank marks depending on whether an object possesses the corresponding property or not. During the last years, FCA has been applied in a number of different areas like psychology, sociology, anthropology, medicine, biology, linguistics, etc. [24]. In such cases, FCA unavoidably deals with a Boolean relational information structure (formal context) derived from human investigation (judgement, observation, measure, etc.). It is nevertheless widely agreed that this setting is very

E. Hüllermeier, R. Kruse, and F. Hoffmann (Eds.): IPMU 2010, LNAI 6178, pp. 260–269, 2010.

restrictive: such knowledge may often involve gradual properties, or be pervaded with uncertainty.

In this paper, we exploit basic concepts of possibility theory and possibilistic logic, so as to expand the framework of FCA.

A first line of investigation exploits the fact that that the notion of formal concept relies on the notion of sufficiency operator, which corresponds to one of the four basic set-functions in possibility theory [14]. Three other operators can thus be introduced in FCA, and they lead to a new Galois connection whose role seems to be very different from the usual one.

The second line of investigation consists in handling uncertainty about a Boolean context. Indeed, in the classical setting, it is always assumed that for any object:

i) either it is known (with complete certainty) that the object o satisfies the property p,

ii) or it is known (with complete certainty) that the object o does not satisfy the property p,

iii) only one of the two above cases is true.

In this paper, we shall address the extension of FCA to properties held as uncertain for objects. For instance, one may not be completely certain that a person is married, or being almost certain that another person is single. How to accommodate that kind of information in a formal context? Only the case of total ignorance has been considered by Burmeister and Holzer [6] until now. They have proposed to introduce a third value, denoted "?", in a formal context, that they handle as a third truth value, beside "true" (the property holds for the object) and "false" (the property does not hold for the object).

In the following, uncertainty will be represented by a *pair* of values expressing to what degree it is certain that the property holds for the object and what degree it is certain that it does not hold, in the setting of possibility theory [13]. At the limit, $(1; 0)$ (resp. $(0; 1)$) indicates full certainty of truth (resp. falsity), whereas the pair $(0; 0)$ stands for total ignorance (and corresponds to the question mark "?").

The reason for choosing possibility theory here is that it is basically less information-demanding than a probabilistic approach where one should know with full precision the probability that an object possesses a property. Besides, considering ignorance as a truth-value as done in [6] is also very questionable (Dubois [12]), since it amounts to confusing ill-known Boolean properties and gradual properties. The extension of FCA to fuzzy formal contexts with gradual properties has received much attention [2]. In this case the extent to which an object satisfies a property becomes a matter of degree, and properties are no longer binary but gradual. This situation may be still further extended, when the precise degree to which a property holds for an object is imprecisely known, and only assessed under the form of an interval, which provides the ability to encode partial/total ignorance about the value of a property grade for an object; for instance, one may try to assess in a formal context, to what extent a person masters English, and we may use his/her score at TOEFL (maybe normalized on [0,1]) when available as a grade in the fuzzy formal context relation, while in other cases, on may just know for instance that the person has some practice of English, meaning that the grade is strictly positive but not precisely assessed, see e.g. [8]. Our paper is not along this line, as the notion of context remains Boolean, while degrees are located at the meta-level.

This paper is structured in two sections : the first one exploits the analogy between FCA and possibility theory and studies some properties of the new Galois connexion that decomposes contexts into subcontexts. The next section deals with the possibilistic view of uncertain formal concepts.

2   New Galois Connexions in Formal Concept Analysis

After recalling basic concepts of standard FCA, together with additional operators having their counterpart in possibility theory that have been recently discussed in the FCA setting [14,16], a new Galois connection is considered which enables us to decompose a formal context in independent sub-contexts. Other Galois compositions are also briefly introduced. They provide upper and lower approximations of concepts.

2.1   Formal Concept Analysis: Basic Notions

Formal Concept Analysis [18] provides a theoretical framework for learning hierarchies of knowledge clusters called formal concepts. A basic notion in FCA is the *formal context*. Given a set $\mathcal{O}$ of objects and a set $\mathcal{P}$ of properties, a formal context consists of a triple $\mathcal{K} := (\mathcal{O}, \mathcal{P}, \mathcal{R})$ where $\mathcal{R}$ specifies (Boolean) relationships between objects of $\mathcal{O}$ and properties of $\mathcal{P}$. Usually, formal contexts are given under the form of a table that formalizes these relationships. A table entry indicates whether an object satisfies the property (this is usually denoted by a cross mark), or not (it is often indicated by the absence of mark). We use the following notation $o\mathcal{R}p$ (resp. $o\overline{\mathcal{R}}p$) to indicate that object o satisfies (resp. does not satisfy) property p. Let $\mathcal{R}(o) = \{p \in \mathcal{P} \mid o\mathcal{R}p\}$ be the set of properties satisfied by object o, and let $\mathcal{R}(p) = \{o \in \mathcal{O} \mid o\mathcal{R}p\}$ be the set of objects that satisfy the property p.

By extending singleton operators $\mathcal{R}(.)$ to powerset operators between $2^{\mathcal{O}}$ and $2^{\mathcal{P}}$, we obtain the so-called Galois operator, denoted here $(.)^{\Delta}$, which is at the basis of FCA, and is sometimes named *sufficiency* operator, see e.g. [17]. It is given as follows. For a set of objects X we define the set X^{Δ} of properties that are satisfied by all objects in X.

$$X^{\Delta} = \{p \in \mathcal{P} \mid \forall o \in \mathcal{O}(o \in X \Rightarrow o\mathcal{R}p)\} = \{p \in \mathcal{P} \mid X \subseteq \mathcal{R}(p)\} \qquad (1)$$

Similarly, for a set of properties Y, we define the set Y^{Δ} of objects that satisfy all properties in Y as:

$$Y^{\Delta} = \{o \in \mathcal{O} \mid \forall p \in \mathcal{P}(p \in Y \Rightarrow o\mathcal{R}p)\} = \{o \in \mathcal{O} \mid Y \subseteq \mathcal{R}(o)\} \qquad (2)$$

Given $X \in \mathcal{O}$ and $Y \in \mathcal{P}$, a *formal concept* is a pair $\langle X, Y \rangle$ where $X^{\Delta} = Y$ and $Y^{\Delta} = X$. The set X (resp. Y) is called extent (resp. intent). It is easy to see that

Proposition 1. *The pairs (X, Y) are such that $X^{\Delta} = Y$ and $Y^{\Delta} = X$ if and only if they are maximal in the sense of the inclusion $X \times Y \subseteq \mathcal{R}$.*

The set of all formal concepts equipped with a partial order (denoted $\preceq$) defined as: $\langle X_1, Y_1 \rangle \preceq \langle X_2, Y_2 \rangle$ iff $X_1 \subseteq X_2$ (or, equivalently, $Y_2 \subseteq Y_1$), forms a complete lattice, called the concept lattice of $\mathcal{K}$. Its structure is given by the following theorem.

Theorem 1. Ganter and Wille [18]. *The concept lattice $\mathcal{L}(\mathcal{K})$ is a complete lattice in which infimum and supremum are given by:*

$$\bigwedge_{j \in J}(X_j, Y_j) = \langle \bigcap_{j \in J} X_j, \left(\bigcup_{j \in J} Y_j \right)^{\Delta\Delta} \rangle, \bigvee_{j \in J}(X_j, Y_j) = \langle \left(\bigcup_{j \in J} X_j \right)^{\Delta\Delta}, \bigcap_{j \in J} Y_j \rangle$$

2.2 Alternative Power Set Operators

Taking lesson from the possibility theory setting where four set-valued functions are defined for respectively evaluating the (potential) possibility, the (actual) necessity, the actual (guaranteed) possibility, the potential necessity of an event [15], it is natural to introduce three other powerset operators (among $2^{\mathcal{O}}$ and $2^{\mathcal{P}}$), namely the necessity operator (denoted $(.)^N$), the possibility operator (denoted $(.)^{\Pi}$) and the dual sufficiency operator (denoted $(.)^{\nabla}$), on top of the (classical) sufficiency derivation operator $(.)^{\Delta}$ (which is the counterpart of the actual possibility measure) [14,16]. Note that these four operators are also used in [22] for achieving rough approximations of crisp formal concepts.

– X^{Π} is the set of properties associated with at least one object in X:

$$X^{\Pi} = \{p \in \mathcal{P} \mid X \cap \mathcal{R}(p) \neq \emptyset\} = \{p \in \mathcal{P} \mid \exists o \in X, o\mathcal{R}p\}$$

– X^N is the set of properties s.t. any object that satisfies one of them is necessarily in X:

$$X^N = \{p \in \mathcal{P} \mid \mathcal{R}(p) \subseteq X\} = \{p \in \mathcal{P} \mid \forall o \in \mathcal{O} \, (o\mathcal{R}p \Rightarrow o \in X)\}$$

– X^{∇} is the set of properties that are not satisfied by at least one object in $\overline{X}$:

$$X^{\nabla} = \{p \in \mathcal{P} \mid X \cup \mathcal{R}(p) \neq \mathcal{O}\} = \{p \in \mathcal{P} \mid \exists o \in \overline{X}, o\overline{\mathcal{R}}p\}$$

2.3   Formal Context Decomposition

A new Galois connection can be defined from $(.)^N$ [16] in a similar formal way as when defining formal concepts. Namely consider pairs (X, Y) s.t. $X^N = Y$ and $Y^N = X$. Note that $(.)^\Pi$ induces the same Galois connection as $(.)^N$, while $(.)^\nabla$ gives back the one defined from $(.)^\Delta$.

The pairs (X, Y) s.t. $X^N = Y$ and $Y^N = X$ allow us to characterize independent sub-contexts (i.e. that have no common objects and no common properties), and are thus of interest for the decomposition of a formal context into smaller independent ones. That is expressed through the following property:

Proposition 2. *The following properties of pairs (X, Y) are equivalent*

1. $X^N = Y$ and $Y^N = X$
2. $\overline{X}^N = \overline{Y}$ and $\overline{Y}^N = \overline{X}$
3. $X^\Pi = Y$ and $Y^\Pi = X$
4. $\mathcal{R} \subseteq (X \times Y) \cup (\overline{X} \times \overline{Y})$

Proof. Let us first show that property 1 implies property 4. First it is clear that: $X^N = Y \Leftrightarrow \bigcap_{o \in \overline{X}} \overline{\mathcal{R}(o)} = Y \Leftrightarrow \bigcup_{o \in \overline{X}} \mathcal{R}(o) = \overline{Y}$.

Denoting $X + Y = \overline{\overline{X} \times \overline{Y}}$, it implies $\mathcal{R} \subseteq X + \overline{Y}$.

Likewise due to $Y^N = X$, $\mathcal{R} \subseteq Y + \overline{X}$.

Finally: $\mathcal{R} \subseteq (X + \overline{Y}) \cap (Y + \overline{X}) = (X \times Y) \cup (\overline{X} \times \overline{Y})$.

Conversely assume property 4. Then it is clear that $X^N \subseteq Y$ and $Y^N \subseteq X$ hold since there is no property possessed by any object in X outside Y, and no object outside X that possesses a property outside Y. Suppose $X^N \subset Y$, i.e. $\exists y^* \in Y$ such that property y^* is possessed by objects outside X. But then $\mathcal{R}(x, y*) = 1$ for some $x \in X, y \in \overline{Y}$. So property 4 does not hold. Contradiction.

Property 4 indicates that the choice of (X, Y) versus $(\overline{X}, \overline{Y})$ in property 1 is immaterial. Hence the equivalence with property 2. For property 3, note that $X^N = Y$ is equivalent to $\overline{X}^\Pi = \overline{Y}$.   □

Thus, (X, Y) and $(\overline{X}, \overline{Y})$ are two independent sub-context in $\mathcal{R}$, in the sense that there is no object / property pair (o, p) of the context $\mathcal{R}$ in $X \times \overline{Y}$ nor in $\overline{X} \times Y$. The above proposition does not involve any minimality claim in the inclusion property 4 of the above proposition. In particular, the pair $(\mathcal{O}, \mathcal{P})$ trivially satisfies it. However, this result leads to a decomposition of $\mathcal{R}$ into a disjoint union of *minimal* independent sub-contexts. Indeed, suppose two pairs (X_1, Y_1), (X_2, Y_2) satisfy Proposition 2. It implies that for instance, the pair $(X_1 \cap X_2, Y_1 \cap Y_2)$ satisfies it (it can be checked that $(X_1 \cap X_2)^N = Y_1 \cap Y_2)$, and likewise with any element of the partition refining both partitions $(X_1, \overline{X_1})$ and $(X_2, \overline{X_2})$. Due to point 4 of Proposition 2, it yields

$$\mathcal{R} \subseteq ((X_1 \times Y_1) \cup (\overline{X_1} \times \overline{Y_1})) \cap ((X_2 \times Y_2) \cup (\overline{X_2} \times \overline{Y_2})),$$

where the intersection on the right-hand side comes down to the union of sub-contexts $(X_1 \cap X_2) \times (Y_1 \cap Y_2)$, $(X_1 \cap \overline{X_2}) \times (Y_1 \cap \overline{Y_2})$, $(\overline{X_1} \cap X_2) \times (\overline{Y_1} \cap Y_2)$,

$(\overline{X_1} \cap \overline{X_2}) \times (\overline{Y_1} \cap \overline{Y_2})$. The decomposition of $\mathcal{R}$ into minimal subcontexts is achieved by taking the following intersection

$$\bigcap_{(X,Y):X^N=Y,Y^N=X} (X \times Y) \cup (\overline{X} \times \overline{Y}).$$

Example

Figure 1 presents a formal context. Pairs $(\{6,7,8\}, \{c,d,e\})$, or $(\{5,6,7,8\}, \{d, e\})$, or $(\{2,3,4\}, \{g,h\})$ are examples of formal concepts, while $(\{5,6,7,8\}, \{a,b, c,d,e\})$, $(\{2,3,4\}, (\{f,g,h\})$, $(\{1\}, \{i\})$ are minimal subcontexts.

		objects
p		1 2 3 4 5 6 7 8
r	a	×
o	b	× ×
p	c	× × ×
e	d	× × × ×
r	e	× × × ×
t	f	× ×
i	g	× × ×
e	h	× × ×
s	i	×

Fig. 1. Formal concepts and sub-contexts

2.4 Toward Composite Powerset Operators

Combining the four powerset operators leads to different Galois compositions that differ from a semantic and an algebraic (topological) point of view. Indeed, the composition $(.)^{N \circ \Pi} = ((.)^{\Pi})^{N}$ provides an upper approximation, whereas the composition $(.)^{\Pi \circ N} = ((.)^{N})^{\Pi}$ provides a lower approximation of the set on which these operators are applied. Indeed, we have:

Proposition 3. $(X)^{\Pi \circ N} \subseteq X \subseteq (X)^{N \circ \Pi}$.

Proof. $((X)^{N})^{\Pi} = \{o \in \mathcal{O} \mid \mathcal{R}(o) \cap \{p \in \mathcal{P} \mid \mathcal{R}(p) \subseteq X\} \neq \emptyset\}$, is the set of objects that have properties of which some are among the ones that only elements in X have. Those objects are clearly in X.

$((X)^{\Pi})^{N} = \{o \in \mathcal{O} \mid \mathcal{R}(o) \subseteq X^{\Pi}\}$. Suppose $o \in X$. Then $\{o\}^{\Pi} = \mathcal{R}(o) \subseteq X^{\Pi}$, hence $o \in ((X)^{\Pi})^{N}$.

When $((X)^{\Pi})^{N} = X$, itcorresponds to formal pairs (X,Y) of fixed points such that $X = Y^{N}$ and $Y = X^{\Pi}$, and $((X)^{N})^{\Pi} = X$ to formal pairs of fixed points such that $X = Y^{\Pi}$ and $Y = X^{N}$. The semantic interpretation of such pairs remains to be found, and a systematic investigation of these compositions to be carried out.

3   Uncertainty

Neither the standard FCA approach nor its fuzzy extension are equipped for representing situations of partial or complete ignorance. To this end, in the Boolean case, we need to introduce a proper representation of partial uncertainty including ignorance in the relational table of the formal context. One may think of introducing gradations of uncertainty by changing crosses and blanks in the table into probability degrees, or by possibility or necessity degrees. In the probabilistic case, one number shall assess the probability that a considered property holds for a given object (its complement to 1 corresponding to the probability it does not hold). However, this is assuming precise knowledge on the probability values, which is not really appropriate if we have to model the state of complete ignorance. It is why we investigate the use of the possibilistic setting in the following. In the possibilistic setting, crosses may be replaced by positive degrees of necessity for expressing some certainty that an object satisfies a property. The blanks could be refined by possibility degrees less than 1.

In the possibilistic setting, possibility and necessity functions are related by the duality relation $N(A) = 1 - \Pi(\overline{A})$, that holds for any event A, where $\overline{A}$ denotes the opposite event [13]. Then, for entries (o, p) in the table, we use a representation as a pair of necessity degrees $(\alpha, 1 - \beta)$ where $\alpha = N(o\mathcal{R}p)$ (resp $1 - \beta = N(o\overline{\mathcal{R}}p)$) corresponds to the necessity (certainty) that object o has (resp. does not have) property p. Moreover, we should have $\min(\alpha, 1 - \beta) = 0$, since $\min(N(A), N(\overline{A})) = 0$ in agreement with complete ignorance for which nothing (i.e., neither A nor $\overline{A}$) is even somewhat certain. The pairs (1,0) and (0,1) correspond to the completely informed situations where it is known that object o has, respectively does not have, property p. The pair (0,0) reflects total ignorance, whereas pairs $(\alpha, 1 - \beta)$ s.t. $1 > \max(\alpha, 1 - \beta) > 0$ correspond to partial ignorance.

An uncertain formal context is thus represented by

$$\mathcal{R}^U = \{(\alpha(o, p), 1 - \beta(o, p)) \mid o \in \mathcal{O}, p \in \mathcal{P}\}$$

where $\alpha(o, p) \in [0, 1]$, $\beta(o, p) \in [0, 1]$. A relational database with fuzzily-known attribute values is *theoretically* equivalent to a fuzzy set of all ordinary databases corresponding to the different possible ways of completing the information consistently with the fuzzy restrictions on the attribute values [4]. In the same way, an uncertain formal context may be viewed as a weighted family of all standard formal contexts obtained by changing uncertain entries into sure ones. More precisely, one may consider all the completions of an uncertain formal context. This is done by substituting entries (o, p) that are uncertain, i.e., such that $1 > \max(\alpha(o, p), 1 - \beta(o, p))$ by a pair (1,0), or a pair (0,1). Replacing $(\alpha(o, p), 1 - \beta(o, p))$ by $(1, 0)$ is possible at degree $\beta(o, p)$, the possibility that o has property p. Similarly, replacing $(\alpha(o, p), 1 - \beta(o, p))$ by $(0, 1)$ is possible at degree $1 - \alpha(o, p)$, the possibility that o has *not* the property p. In this way, one may determine to what extent a particular completion (a context $\mathcal{C}$) is possible, by aggregating the possibility degrees associated with each completed entry (using min operator). Formally, one can write

$$\pi(\mathcal{C}) = \min(\min_{(o,p):o\mathcal{C}p}\beta(o,p), \min_{(o,p):o\overline{\mathcal{C}}p}1 - \alpha(o,p)).$$

Likewise the degree of possibility that (X, Y) is a formal context of $\mathcal{R}^U$ is $\pi(X, Y) = \sup\{\pi(\mathcal{C}) : \mathcal{C}$ such that (X, Y) is a formal context of $\mathcal{C}\}$.

Useful completions are those where partial certainty becomes full certainty. Indeed, given an uncertain formal context and a threshold pair (a, b), let us replace all entries of the form $(\alpha, 0)$ such that $\alpha \geqslant a$ with $(1, 0)$ and entries of the form $(0, 1 - \beta)$ such that $1 - \beta \geqslant b$ with $(0, 1)$. All such replacements have possibility 1 according to the above formula. Remaining entries, which are more uncertain, will be *all* systematically substituted either by (1,0), or by (0,1), giving birth to two completions. In this way, two classical (Boolean) formal contexts, denoted $\mathcal{R}^*_{(a,b)}$ and $\mathcal{R}_{*(a,b)}$ are obtained as respective results of the two completions. They allow to determine, for a given threshold (a, b), maximal extensions (resp. minimal intensions) and minimal extensions (resp. maximal intensions) of uncertain formal concepts. It is clear that $\mathcal{R}_{*(a,b)} \subseteq \mathcal{R}^*_{(a,b)}$. Let us illustrate the idea with an example.

Example (continued). Figure 2 exhibits a modified version of the Figure 1, where some entries are now pervaded with uncertainty. Some of the ×'s or blanks of the previous example have been replaced by uncertain entries. Let us examine the situation regarding formal concepts first. Take $a = 0.7, b = 0.5$ for instance. Context $\mathcal{R}_{*(0.7,0.5)}$, is the same as in Figure 1. Namely, pairs $(\{6, 7, 8\}, \{c, d, e\})$, or $(\{5, 6, 7, 8\}, \{d, e\})$, or $(\{2, 3, 4\}, \{g, h\})$ are still examples of formal concepts, although with $a = 0.9$, the last formal concept would reduce to $(\{2, 3\}, \{g, h\})$, i.e. the extent of the concept is smaller.

		objects							
p		1	2	3	4	5	6	7	8
r	*a*							×	
o	*b*					×	×		
p	*c*					(0.5,0)	×	×	×
e	*d*					×	×	×	×
r	*e*					×	×	×	×
t	*f*		(0, 0.8)		×	(0, 0.3)			
i	*g*		×	×	(0.8, 0)				
e	*h*		×	×	(0.8, 0)				
s	*i*	×							

Fig. 2. Uncertain formal concepts and sub-contexts

Now consider $\mathcal{R}^*_{(0.7,0.5)}$, where the entries with low certainty levels (either in favor or against the existence of the link between o and p) are turned into positive links. Then, $(\{2, 3, 4\}, \{g, h\})$ remains unchanged as a formal concept, while a larger concept now emerges, namely $(\{5, 6, 7, 8\}, \{c, d, e\})$. However, one may prefer to consider the results obtained from $\mathcal{R}_{*(0.7,0.5)}$, where only the almost certain information is changed into positive links. In the example, if we move down a to 0.5, and use $\mathcal{R}_{*(0.5,0.5)}$ we still validate the larger former concept $(\{5,6,7,8\},\{c,d,e\})$. This illustrates the fact that becoming less and less demanding on the level of certainty, may enable the fusion of close concepts (here $(\{6,7,8\},\{c,d,e\})$, and $(\{5,6,7,8\},\{d,e\})$, providing a more synthetic view of the formal context.

Let us now examine the situation with respect to sub-contexts. In the example, the situation will remain unchanged with respect to the non-uncertain version of the example: $(\{5,6,7,8\},\{a,b,c,d,e\})$, $(\{2,3,4\},(\{f,g,h\})$, $(\{1\},\{i\})$ are still minimal sub-contexts in $\mathcal{R}_{*(a,b)}$ for any value of a and b. Indeed in Figure 2, $(5,f)$ is the only possible link which would make the first two sub-contexts dependent. However, we are 0.3-certain that $(5,f)$ does not belong to the context.

This small example is intended to illustrate several points. First of all, it should be clear that being uncertain about the existence of a link between an object and a property is not the same as being certain about a gradual link. Second, under uncertainty, there are formal concepts and formal sub-contexts whose boundaries are not affected by uncertainty, while others are. Lastly, regarding certain enough pieces of information as certain may help simplifying the analysis of the formal context. Besides, the proposed setting may also handle inconsistent information by relaxing the constraint $\min(\alpha, 1 - \beta) = 0$. This would amount to introducing paraconsistent links between objects and properties.

4 Concluding Remarks

This paper has shown how the parallel between possibility theory and FCA has fruitfully led to introduce other operators and to define a new Galois connection useful for decomposing a formal context into sub-contexts when possible. Moreover, the possibility theory setting may be also useful to model uncertain formal contexts, which at least when considering the part that is sufficiently certain could be handled as completely certain formal contexts, still keeping track of the uncertainty, as briefly suggested in the final discussion. Relationships with more logic-oriented views [5] would be also worth exploring in connection with possibilistic logic. Note that several other extensions of FCA are worth investigating, apart from the handling of uncertain or gradual properties, such as taking into account the typicality of objects and the importance of properties, See [10,11] for preliminary discussions about these different extensions.

References

1. Belohlavek, R.: Fuzzy Galois connections. Math. Logic Quart. 45, 497–504 (1999)
2. Belohlavek, R.: Fuzzy Relational Systems. Kluwer Acad. Pub., Dordrecht (2002)
3. Belohlavek, R., Vychodil, V.: What is a fuzzy concept lattice. In: Proc. CLAV '05, Olomuc, pp. 34–45. Czech Republic (2005)
4. Bosc, P., Pivert, O.: About projection-selection-join queries addressed to possibilistic relational databases. IEEE Trans. Fuzzy Systems 13(1), 124–139 (2005)

5. Ferré, S., Ridoux, O.: Introduction to logical information systems. Information Processing and Mgmt. 40, 383–419 (2004)
6. Burmeister, P., Holzer, R.: Treating incomplete knowledge in formal concepts analysis. In: Ganter, B., Stumme, G., Wille, R. (eds.) Formal Concept Analysis. LNCS (LNAI), vol. 3626, pp. 11–126. Springer, Heidelberg (2005)
7. Burusco, A., Fuentes-Gonzalez, R.: The study of the L-fuzzy concept lattice. Mathware & Soft Comput. 3, 209–218 (1994)
8. Djouadi, Y., Prade, H.: Interval-valued fuzzy formal concept analysis. In: Rauch, J., Raś, Z.W., Berka, P., Elomaa, T. (eds.) ISMIS 2009. LNCS, vol. 5722, pp. 592–601. Springer, Heidelberg (2009)
9. Djouadi, Y., Prade, H.: Interval-valued fuzzy Galois connections: algebraic requirements and concept lattice construction. Fund. Inform. (to appear)
10. Djouadi, Y., Dubois, D., Prade, H.: On the possible meanings of degrees when making formal concept analysis fuzzy. In: EUROFUSE'09, Preference Modelling and Decision Analysis Workshop, Pamplona, Spain, pp. 253–258 (2009)
11. Djouadi, Y., Dubois, D., Prade, H.: Différentes extensions floues de l'analyse formelle de concepts. Actes Renc. Franc. sur la Logique Floue et ses Applications (LFA 2009) Cépadues edn., Toulouse, pp. 141–148 (2009)
12. Dubois, D.: On ignorance and contradiction considered as truth-values. Logic Journal of the IGPL 16(2), 195–216 (2008)
13. Dubois, D., Prade, H.: Possibility Theory. Plenum Press, New York (1988)
14. Dubois, D., Dupin de Saint Cyr, F., Prade, H.: A possibilty-theoretic view of formal concept analysis. Fundamenta Informaticae 75(1-4), 195–213 (2007)
15. Dubois, D., Prade, H.: Possibility theory: qualitative and quantitative aspects. In: Gabbay, D., Smets, P. (eds.) Quantified Representation of Uncertainty and Imprecision. Handbook of Defeasible Reasoning and Uncertainty Management Systems, vol. 1, pp. 169–226. Kluwer Acad. Publ., Dordrecht (1998)
16. Dubois, D., Prade, H.: Possibility theory and formal concept analysis in information systems. In: Proc. IFSA'09, International Fuzzy Systems Association World Congress, Lisbon, Portugal, pp. 1021–1026 (2009)
17. Düntsch, I., Orlowska, E.: Mixing modal and sufficiency operators. Bulletin of the Section of Logic, Polish Academy of Sciences 28(2), 99–106 (1999)
18. Ganter, B., Wille, R.: Formal Concept Analysis. Springer, Heidelberg (1999)
19. Medina, J., Ojeda-Aciego, M., Ruiz-Calvino, J.: Formal concept analysis via multi-adjoint concept lattices. Fuzzy Sets and Systems 160(2), 130–144 (2009)
20. Messai, N., Devignes, M., Napoli, A., Tabbone, M.: Many-valued concept lattices for conceptual clustering and information retrieval. In: Proc. 18th Europ. Conf. on Artif. Intellig., Patras, pp. 722–727 (2008)
21. Pollandt, S.: Fuzzy Begriffe. Springer, Heidelberg (1997)
22. Yao, Y.Y., Chen, Y.: Rough Set Approximations in Formal Concept Analysis. In: Peters, J.F., Skowron, A. (eds.) Transactions on Rough Sets V. LNCS, vol. 4100, pp. 285–305. Springer, Heidelberg (2006)
23. Wille, R.: Restructuring Lattice Theory: an Approach Based on Hierarchies of Concepts. In: Rival, I. (ed.) Ordered Sets, pp. 445–470. Reidel, Dordrecht (1982)
24. Wolff, K.E.: A first course in Formal Concept Analysis - How to understand line diagrams. In: Faulbaum, F. (ed.) SoftStat'93, Advances in Statistical Software 4, pp. 429–438. Gustav Fischer Verlag, Stuttgart (1994)

A Parallel between Extended Formal Concept Analysis and Bipartite Graphs Analysis

Bruno Gaume[1], Emmanuel Navarro[2], and Henri Prade[2]

[1] CLLE-ERSS, Université de Toulouse II
gaume@univ-tlse2.fr
[2] IRIT, Université de Toulouse III
navarro@irit.fr, prade@irit.fr

Abstract. The paper offers a parallel between two approaches to conceptual clustering, namely formal concept analysis (augmented with the introduction of new operators) and bipartite graph analysis. It is shown that a formal concept (as defined in formal concept analysis) corresponds to the idea of a maximal bi-clique, while a "conceptual world" (defined through a Galois connection associated of the new operators) is a disconnected sub-graph in a bipartite graph. The parallel between formal concept analysis and bipartite graph analysis is further exploited by considering "approximation" methods on both sides. It leads to suggests new ideas for providing simplified views of datasets.

Keywords: Formal concept analysis (FCA), bipartite graph.

1 Introduction

Human mind in order to make sense of a complex set of data usually tries to conceptualize it by some means or other. Roughly speaking, it generally amounts to putting labels on subsets of data that are judged to be similar enough. Formal concept analysis [12,11] offers a theoretical setting for defining the notion of a formal concept as a pair made of (i) the set of objects that constitutes the extension of the concept and of (ii) the set of properties shared by these objects and that characterize these objects as a whaole. This set of proporties defines the intention of the concept. Thus, particular subsets of objects are biunivoquely associated with conjunctions of properties that identify them. This provides a formal basis for data mining algorithms [19]. Formal concept analysis exploits a relation that links objects with properties. Such a relation can be viewed as well as a bi-graph (or bipartite graph) i.e. a graph having two kinds of vertices, and whose links are only between vertices of different kinds.

The recent discovery that real-world complex networks from many different domains (linguistics, biology, sociology, computer science, ...) share some non-trivial characteristics has a considerable raised an interest [25,1,17,13]. These networks are sparse, highly clustered, and the average length of shortest paths is rather small with regard to the graph size [25], hence their name of "small worlds". Moreover, most of parameters, and in particular their vertices degree,

E. Hüllermeier, R. Kruse, and F. Hoffmann (Eds.): IPMU 2010, LNAI 6178, pp. 270–280, 2010.

follow a power-law distribution [2,17]. One of the most active fields of this new *network science* concerns the problem of graph clustering [21,10]. This problem is often called "community detection" in the literature due to its application to social networks. Intuitively a cluster (or community) corresponds to a group of vertices with a high density of internal links and only a few links with external vertices. Nevertheless there is no universally accepted formal definition [10] and making a parallel with formal concept analysis may lead to some relevant way to define graph clusters. Many real-world large networks are bipartite and it has been shown that such networks also share properties similar to the above-mentioned ones [15]. While clustering is usually done on projected graphs, some authors address the problem of community detection directly on bipartite networks [3,16]. Besides, techniques inspired from formal concept analysis have been also used for detecting human communities in social bipartite networks [23].

The purpose of this paper is to start to systematically investigate the parallel between formal concept analysis and graph-based detection of communities. In fact, we consider here not only standard formal concept analysis but also an enlarged setting that includes new operators [8,9]. This is the graph counterpart of this enlarged setting that is discussed here. Moreover, extensions of this setting which allows various forms of approximations of the original setting are then paralleled and compared with methods used in bi-graph clustering. The paper is organized as follows, the basic elements of formal concept analysis are first restated and the other operators are introduced. This leads to the definition of two Galois connections, namely the classical one inducing formal concepts, and another one identifying conceptual worlds. Then after a short background on graphs, it is shown that a formal concept corresponds to a maximal bi-clique in a bi-graph, while conceptual worlds, obtained by the second Galois connection, correspond to disconnected sub-parts in the graph. Then different ways of introducing graduality, uncertainty, or approximation in formal concept analysis [7,6] are summarized, before briefly discussing their counterpart in the bi-graph setting.

2   Extended Formal Concept Analysis

Let R be a *binary relation* between a set $\mathbf{O}$ of objects and a set $\mathbf{P}$ of Boolean properties. We note $\mathcal{R} = (\mathbf{O}, \mathbf{P}, R)$ the tuple formed by these objects and properties sets and the binary relation. It is called a *formal context*. The notation $(x, y) \in R$ means that object x has property y. Let $R(x) = \{y \in \mathbf{P} | (x, y) \in R\}$ be the set of properties of object x. Similarly, $R^{-1}(y) = \{x \in \mathbf{O} | (x, y) \in R\}$ is the set of objects having property y.

Formal concept analysis defines two set operators here denoted $(.)^{\Delta}$, $(.)^{-1\Delta}$, called *intent* and *extent* operators respectively, s.t. $\forall Y \subseteq \mathbf{P}$ and $\forall X \subseteq \mathbf{O}$:

$$X^{\Delta} = \{y \in \mathbf{P} | \forall x \in X, (x, y) \in R\} \tag{1}$$
$$Y^{-1\Delta} = \{x \in \mathbf{P} | \forall y \in Y, (x, y) \in R\} \tag{2}$$

X^{Δ} is the set of properties possessed by all objects in X. $Y^{-1\Delta}$ is the set of objects having all properties in Y.

These two operators induce a Galois connection between 2^O and 2^P : A pair such that $X^\Delta = Y$ and $Y^{-1\Delta} = X$ is called a *formal concept*, X is its extent and Y its intent. In other words, a formal concept is a pair (X, Y) such that X is the set of objects having all properties in Y and Y is the set of properties shared by all objects in X.

A recent parallel between formal concept analysis and possibility theory [8] has led to emphasize the interest of three other remarkable set operators $(.)^\Pi$, $(.)^N$ and $(.)^\nabla$. These three operators and the already defined intent operator can be written as follows, $\forall X \subset \mathbf{O}$:

$$X^\Pi = \{y \in \mathbf{P} | R^{-1}(y) \cap X \neq \emptyset\} \ (3) \qquad X^\Delta = \{y \in \mathbf{P} | R^{-1}(y) \supseteq X\} \qquad (5)$$
$$X^N = \{y \in \mathbf{P} | R^{-1}(y) \subseteq X\} \qquad (4) \qquad X^\nabla = \{y \in \mathbf{P} | R^{-1}(y) \cup X \neq \mathbf{O}\} \ (6)$$

Note that (5) is equivalent to the definition of operator $(.)^\Delta$ in (1). Operators $(.)^{-1\Pi}$, $(.)^{-1N}$, $(.)^{-1\Delta}$ and $(.)^{-1\nabla}$ are defined similarly on a set Y of properties by substituting R^{-1} to R and by inverting $\mathbf{O}$ and $\mathbf{P}$.

These new operators lead to consider the following Galois connections:

- the pairs (X, Y) such that $X^\Pi = Y$ and $Y^{-1\Pi} = X$;
- the pairs (X, Y) such that $X^N = Y$ and $Y^{-1N} = X$;
- the pairs (X, Y) such that $X^\nabla = Y$ and $Y^{-1\nabla} = X$.

In fact only one new type of Galois connection appears, indeed $(.)^N$ and $(.)^\Pi$ as well as $(.)^\nabla$ and $(.)^\Delta$ lead to the same remarkable pairs. But pairs (X, Y) such that $X^\Pi = Y$ and $Y^{-1\Pi} = X$ do not define formal concepts, but rather what may be called *conceptual worlds* (or sub-contexts). Indeed, it has been recently shown [6] that pairs (X, Y) of sets exchanged through the new connection operators, are minimal subsets such that $(X \times Y) \cup (\overline{X} \times \overline{Y}) \supseteq R$, just as formal concepts correspond to maximal pairs (X, Y) such that $X \times Y \subseteq R$. For example in Figure 1, pairs $(\{1, 2, 3, 4\}, \{g, h, i\})$ and $(\{5, 6, 7, 8\}, \{a, b, c, d, e, f\})$ are two conceptual worlds, whereas pairs $(\{1, 2, 3, 4\}, \{g, h\})$, $(\{5, 6\}, \{a, b, c, d, f\})$ and $(\{5, 6, 7, 8\}, \{a, c, d\})$ are -among others- formal concepts.

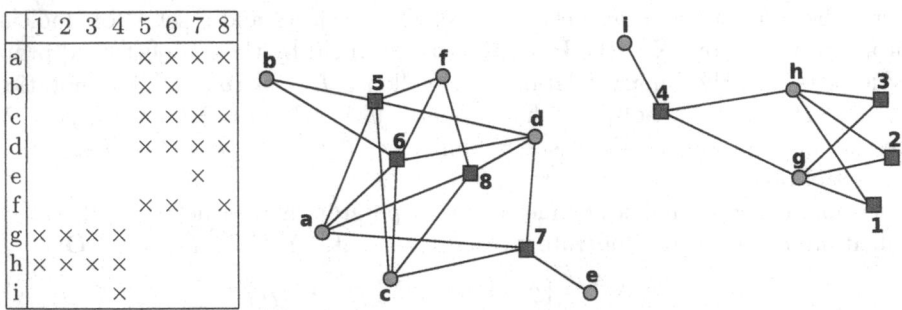

	1	2	3	4	5	6	7	8
a					×	×	×	×
b					×	×		
c					×	×	×	×
d					×	×	×	×
e						×		
f					×	×		×
g	×	×	×	×				
h	×	×	×	×				
i				×				

Fig. 1. A formal context R and the corresponding bi-graph

3 Graph Reading of Formal Concept Analysis

Let us start by restating some graph theory definitions. A *graph* is a pair of sets $\mathcal{G} = (V, E)$, where V is a set of *vertices* and E a set of *edges*. In the paper only *undirected graphs* will be considered, it means that edges are unordered pairs of vertices. A graph is *bipartite* if the vertex set V can be split into two sets A and B such that there is no edge between vertices of the same set (in other words for every edge $\{u, v\}$ either $u \in A$ and $v \in B$ or $u \in B$ and $v \in A$). We note $\mathcal{G} = (A, B, E)$ such a graph where A and B constitute two *classes* of vertices.

A vertex v is a *neighbour* of a vertex u if $\{v, u\} \in E$, we say that u and v are *adjacent*. $\Gamma(u)$ is the set of neighbours of a given vertex u, it is called *neighbourhood* of u. An ordinary graph is *complete* if every couple of vertices from $V \times V$ are adjacent. A bi-graph is *complete* if every couple of vertices from $A \times B$ are adjacent.

An *induced subgraph* on the graph $\mathcal{G}$ by a set of vertices S is a graph composed of a vertex set $S \subseteq V$, and an edge set $E(S)$ that contains all vertices of E that bind vertices of S ($\forall u, v \in S, \{u, v\} \in E \Leftrightarrow \{u, v\} \in E(S)$). A set of vertices S that induces a complete subgraph is called a *clique*. If no vertex could be added to this induced subgraph without loosing the clique property then the clique is *maximal*. It is straightforward that every subgraph of a bi-graph is still bipartite, every vertex keeping the same class. A set of vertices S that induces a complete subgraph (in a bipartite sense) on a bi-graph $\mathcal{G}$ is called a *bi-clique* and if no vertex could be added without loosing this bi-clique property then the bi-clique is *maximal*.

A path from a vertex u to a vertex v is a sequence of vertices starting with u and ending with v and such that from each of its vertices there exists an edge to the next vertex in the sequence. The *length* of a path is the length of this vertices sequence minus one (it is to say the number of edges that run along the path). Two vertices are *connected* if there is a path between them. We note S^k the set of vertices connected to at least one vertex of S with a path of length inferior or equal to k. By definition $S^0 = S$. One can observe that $\forall k, S^k \subseteq S^{k+1}$. S^* is the set of vertices connected to at least one vertex of S with a path of any length, we have $S^* = \bigcup_{k \geq 0} S^k$. Two vertices are *disconnected* if there is no path between them. Two subsets A, B of vertices are disconnected if every vertex of A is disconnected from any vertex of B. A subset of vertices S is *connected* if there is a path between every pair of vertices of S, An induced subgraph that is connected is called a *connected component*. If no vertex could be added to this induced subgraph without loosing the property of connectedness then the connected component is *maximal*. Note that often "connected component" is used for speaking of a "maximal connected component".

3.1 From Formal Context to Bi-graph

For every formal context $\mathcal{R} = (\mathbf{O}, \mathbf{P}, R)$, we can build an undirected bi-graph $\mathcal{G} = (V_o, V_p, E)$ s.t. there is a direct correspondence between: the set of objects $\mathbf{O}$ and a set V_o of "o-vertices", the set of properties $\mathbf{P}$ and a set V_p of "p-vertices", and between the binary relation R and a set of edges E. In other words, there is one o-vertex for each object, one p-vertex for each property, and one edge between an o-vertex and a p-vertex if and only if the corresponding object possesses the corresponding property (according to R).

The four operators $(.)^\Pi$, $(.)^N$, $(.)^\Delta$ and $(.)^\nabla$ can be redefined for a set of vertices in this graph framework by replacing, in equations (3) to (6), $\mathbf{O}$ by V_o, $\mathbf{P}$ by V_p and $R^{-1}(y)$ by $\Gamma(y)$. Operators $(.)^\Pi$ and $(.)^\Delta$ can also be rewritten in the following way:

$$X^\Pi = \cup_{x \in X} \Gamma(x) \qquad (7) \qquad\qquad X^\Delta = \cap_{x \in X} \Gamma(x) \qquad (8)$$

These notations are interesting since only the neighbourhood of vertices of X is involved. It permits to immediately understand operators $(.)^\Pi$ and $(.)^\Delta$ in terms of neighbourhood in the bi-graph : X^Π is the union of neighbours of vertices of X whereas X^Δ is the intersection of these neighbours. Note that with this writing and interpretation there is no difference between $(.)^\Pi$ and $(.)^{-1\Pi}$ neither between $(.)^\Delta$ and $(.)^{-1\Delta}$.

Graph interpretations of $(.)^N$ and $(.)^\nabla$ are less straightforward, nevertheless X^N can be understood as the union of neighbours of vertices of X that have no neighbours outside of X. In other words it is the set of vertices exclusively connected with vertices of X (but not necessarily all). Whereas X^∇ is —if we ignore vertices of X— the set of p-vertices not connected to all o-vertices.

3.2   Galois Connections as Two Views of Graph Clusters

Galois connections induced by $(.)^\Delta$ and $(.)^\Pi$ can also be understood in the graph setting framework. On the bi-graph $\mathcal{G} = (V_o, V_p, E)$, with $X \subseteq V_o$ and $Y \subseteq V_p$:

Proposition 1. $X = Y^{-1\Delta}$ and $Y = X^\Delta$, iff $X \cup Y$ is a maximal bi-clique.

Proof. Let (X, Y) be a pair such that $X = Y^{-1\Delta}$ and $Y = X^\Delta$. For all $x \in X$ and $y \in Y$, as $Y = \cap_{x \in X} \Gamma(x)$ we have $y \in \Gamma(x)$ thus $\{x, y\} \in E$. It means that the subgraph induced by $X \cup Y$ is complete. Moreover there is no vertex that are adjacent to all vertices of X (resp. Y) which are not in X^Δ (resp. $Y^{-1\Delta}$), therefore $X \cup Y$ is a maximal bi-clique.

If $X \cup Y$ is a maximal bi-clique, every vertex of X (resp. Y) is adjacent to any vertex of Y (resp. X) and there exists no vertex that is adjacent to all vertices of X (resp. Y) which are not in Y (resp. X), therefore it's straightforward that $Y = X^\Delta$ (resp. $X = Y^{-1\Delta}$).

Proposition 2. *For a pair (X, Y) the two following propositions are equivalent:*
1. $X = Y^{-1\Pi}$ and $Y = X^\Pi$.
2. $(X \cup Y)^* = (X \cup Y)$ and $\forall v \in (X \cup Y), \Gamma(v) \neq \emptyset$.

Proof. $1 \Rightarrow 2$. By definition $(X \cup Y) \subseteq (X \cup Y)^*$. We show by recurrence that $(X \cup Y)^* \subseteq (X \cup Y)$. $(X \cup Y)^0 \subseteq (X \cup Y)$ is given by definition. We then assume that it exists k such that $(X \cup Y)^k \subseteq (X \cup Y)$. We can notice that $(X \cup Y)^{k+1} \subseteq ((X \cup Y)^k)^1$, by considering that a $k + 1$ long path is a path of length k followed of a one edge setp. So $(X \cup Y)^{k+1} \subseteq (X \cup Y)^1$. But as $X = Y^{-1\Pi}$ and $Y = X^{\Pi}$ all vertices connected to $X \cup Y$ with a path of length 1 are in $X \cup Y$. So $(X \cup Y)^{k+1} \subseteq (X \cup Y)$. This implies by recurrence that $\forall k \geq 0, (X \cup Y)^k \subseteq (X \cup Y)$. Thus $(X \cup Y)^* = \bigcup_{k \geq 0}(X \cup Y)^k \subseteq (X \cup Y)$. We still have to show that any vertex v of $X \cup Y$ has at least one neighbour, which is straightforward if we consider that either $v \in X^{\Pi}$ or $v \in Y^{-1\Pi}$.

2 $\Rightarrow$ 1. We show that $X = Y^{-1\Pi}$, the proof is exactly the same for $Y = X^{\Pi}$. $Y^{-1\Pi}$ is the set of vertices adjacent to one vertex of Y, so $Y^{-1\Pi} \subset Y^*$ and then $Y^{-1\Pi} \subset (X \cup Y)^*$. That means that $Y^{-1\Pi} \subset (X \cup Y)$, but as the graph is bipartite: $Y^{-1\Pi} \subset X$. Let x be a vertex of X, x has at least one neighbour v, v is in X^* and therefore in $(X \cup Y)^*$, so $v \in X \cup Y$, but the graph is bipartite, so $v \in Y$. It's then straightforward that $X \subset Y^{-1\Pi}$ and therefore $X = Y^{-1\Pi}$.

A set S such that $S^* = S$ is not exactly a maximal connected component but it is a set of vertices disconnected from the rest of the graph. So if there is no strict subset S' of S satisfying $S'^* = S'$ it means that there is no subset of S disconnected from other vertices of S. In other words S is connected and then S is a maximal connected component. Therefore, the following property:

Proposition 3. *For a pair (X, Y) the two following propositions are equivalent:*

1. $X = Y^{-1\Pi}$ *and* $Y = X^{\Pi}$ *and there is no strict subset* $X' \subset X$ *and* $Y' \subset Y$ *such that* $X' = Y'^{-1\Pi}, Y' = X'^{\Pi}$.
2. $X \cup Y$ *is a maximal connected component (which counts at least 2 vertices).*

According to Prop. 1-3, it's worthnoting that the two Galois connections correspond to extreme definitions of what a cluster (or a community) could be:

1. a group of vertices with **no link missing inside.**
2. a group of vertices with **no link with outside.**

One the one hand a maximal bi-clique is a maximal subset of vertices with a maximal edge density. Vertices can not be moved closer, and in that sense one can not build a stronger cluster. On the other hand, a set of vertices disconnected from the rest of the graph can not be more clearly separated from other vertices. It corresponds to another type of cluster. In fact, only the smallest of such sets are really interesting, and they are nothing else than maximal connected components. This two extreme definitions were already pointed out by [24] for clusters in unipartite graphs.

4   From Approximate Connections to Flexible Clustering

Formal concepts correspond to maximal bi-cliques, while conceptual worlds correspond to disconnected subparts. These two notions need to be defined in a non-crisp manner in practice, for several reasons. First, the data may be incomplete, a link between an object and a property may be just missing although it exists, or the data may be pervaded with uncertainty when it is unsure if the considered object has or not the considered property. In graph terms, it means that an edge may be missing, or be unsure. Second, one may think of forgetting some "details" in order to summarize the information more easily: thus one may forget an unimportant property or an a-typical object. One may also forget that an edge is present only because it simplifies the view by disconnecting weakly connected parts, or introducing some missing edges in order to reinforce the connectedness inside a potential cluster in order to lay bare a simpler and more general concept. There are some recent lines of research in formal concept analysis that aim at making formal concept analysis more flexible. They are now reviewed, and then the use of random walks in clustered small world graphs is paralleled with these extensions of formal concept analysis.

4.1   Graded Extended Formal Concept Analysis

There are at least three different ways for making formal concept analysis (extended with the new −possibility theory-based− operators) more flexible [7,6]. The first way, which has been the most investigated until now, amounts to consider that objects may have properties only to a degree. Such fuzzy formal concept analysis [4] is based on the operator:

$$X^\Delta(y) = \bigwedge_{x \in \mathbf{O}} (X(x) \rightarrow R(x,y)) \tag{9}$$

where now R is a fuzzy relation, and X and X^Δ are fuzzy sets of objects and properties respectively, and $\bigwedge$ denotes the min conjunction operator and $\rightarrow$ an implication operator. A suitable choice of connective (the residuated Gödel implication: $a \rightarrow b = 1$ if $a \leq b$, and $a \rightarrow b = b$ if $a > b$) still enables us to see a fuzzy formal concept in terms of its level cuts X_α, Y_α such that $(X_\alpha \times Y_\alpha) \subseteq R_\alpha$ where $X_\alpha \times Y_\alpha$ are maximal, with $R_\alpha = \{(x,y)|R(x,y) \geq \alpha\}$, $X_\alpha = \{x \in \mathbf{O}|X(x) \geq \alpha\}$, $Y_\alpha = \{y \in \mathbf{P}|Y(y) \geq \alpha\}$.

Another way [7,6] is related to the idea of uncertainty. The possibilistic manner of representing uncertainty here is to associate with each link (x,y) a pair of number (α, β) such as $\alpha, \beta \in [0,1]$ and $\min(\alpha, \beta) = 0$ expressing respectively to what extent it is certain that the link exist (α) and does not exist (β). A link in a classical formal context corresponds to a pair $(1,0)$, the absence of a link to the pair $(0,1)$ and the pair $(0,0)$ models complete ignorance on the existence or not of a link. On this basis a link may be all the more easily added (resp. deleted) as α (resp. β) is larger.

A third idea [7,6] is to consider that in a formal concept some properties are less important, or that some objects are more typical. Then weights are no longer put on links or edges, but rather on the nodes. Thus forgetting a non compulsory property (e.g. the ability to fly for a bird) may help building a larger concept (e.g. birdness, although typical birds fly). Forgetting an object or a property also suppresses links, which may also help obtaining disconnected subparts.

These three views may provide remedies for building larger formal concepts and smaller conceptual worlds. Indeed a missing link (x_0, y_0) may cause that a pair (X, Y) is not a formal concept even if $\forall x, y \in X \times Y, (x, y) \in R$ except for $(x_0, y_0) \notin R$ (missing links $(1, h)$ and $(5, c)$ for example in Figure 2), while a pair (X, Y) is not a conceptual world just because it exists $(x'_0, y'_0) \in R$ s.t. $(x'_0, y'_0) \in \overline{X} \times Y \cup X \times \overline{Y}$ (for example the link $(4, d)$ in Figure 2). In such situations forgetting the "hole" (x_0, y_0) or the asperity (x'_0, y'_0) might be desirable for simplifying the view of the general context/graph. But the suppression of holes or asperities can not be done in a blind manner.

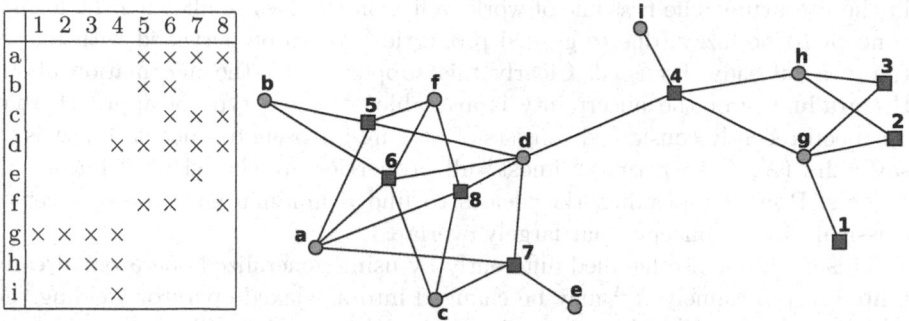

	1 2 3 4 5 6 7 8
a	× × × ×
b	× ×
c	× × ×
d	× × × × ×
e	×
f	× × ×
g	× × × ×
h	× × ×
i	×

Fig. 2. R': Relation R modified and the corresponding bi-graph

4.2 The Random Walk View

A large panel of approaches developed within community detection literature use random walk for identifying communities. The underlying idea is that random walkers tend to be trapped into communities. It may be, for instance, the basis for assessing distances between vertices [13,14]. These distances can then be used with a hierarchical clustering algorithm to compute communities [20]. In another view, measuring "how well" random walkers stay into communities can lead to a relevant quality measure of a given vertices partition [5,22].

We aim in this section to point out the potential benefits that may be expected from the parallel between the "diffusion" operator at the basis of random walk methods and graded extensions of the possibility theory reading of formal concept analysis operators. Let us consider a random walk on a bi-graph, R is now replaced by a probabilistic transition matrix for going from a vertex x to a vertex y, or conversely. The probability is generally equally shared between the edges directly connected to the starting vertex. Let $P_{x \to y}$ be the probability for going from a vertex x to a vertex y. Then when $X(x)$ is the probability for a random walker to be in the vertex $x \in \mathbf{O}$; the probability $X^P(y)$ to reach a vertex y of $\mathbf{P}$ at the next step is given by:

$$X^P(y) = \sum_{x \in \mathbf{O}} X(x).P_{x \to y} \tag{10}$$

Such a formula can formally be paralleled with the formula defining the operator at the basis of the definition of a formal concept:

$$X^\Delta(y) = \min_{x \in \mathbf{O}} X(x) \to R(x, y) \tag{11}$$

and with the formula of the operator inducing a conceptual world:

$$X^{\Pi}(y) = \max_{x \in O} X(x) * R(x, y) \tag{12}$$

where R may now be graded, as well as X, X^{Π} and X^{Δ} and where a usual choice for $*$ is min, and a residuated implication for $\rightarrow$.

Two general ways of relaxing the definition of a formal concept may be found in the literature. The first line of works relies on the idea of allowing the formal concept to be fuzzy (due to graded properties), or to be pervaded with uncertainty as already discussed. Clearly this supposes that the information about the graduality or the uncertainty is available. Another type of approach that has been recently considered consists of looking for pseudo concept [18], it is to say pairs (X, Y) such that "almost" all properties are shared by "almost" all objects. Roughly speaking, the idea is to find a minimal envelope of a set of classical formal concepts that largely overlap.

This could be also handled differently by using generalized operators already hinted in [9]. Namely X^{Δ} may be changed into a relaxed operator yielding the set of properties chaired by *most* objects in X rather than *all*:

$$X_Q^{\Delta}(y) = \min_i \max(R(x_{\sigma(i)}, y), Q(\frac{i-1}{n})) \tag{13}$$

where $R(x_{\sigma(1)}, y) \geq R(x_{\sigma(2)}, y) \geq \cdots \geq R(x_{\sigma(n)}, y)$ and Q is an increasing membership function in $[0, 1]$ modelling some idea of "most".

The parallel between random walks in bi-graph and extended formal concept operators suggests several lines of research worth of interest:

– Random walk methods [13,14] can attach numbers to pairs of vertices (e.g. distance between the two probability distributions to reach any vertex in the graph starting from each of these two vertices). Such number may be renormalised in order to have a "fuzzy" context R'. Note that however these numbers should not be confused with grades representing satisfaction degrees of properties, or uncertainty levels. Indeed they rather accounts for the vicinity of the considered pairs of vertices. Then one may look for fuzzy formal concepts and fuzzy conceptual worlds defined from the fuzzy context R'. Note that this enables us to distinguish between the two views of a cluster either as a set of vertices with no strong links missing inside, or as a set of vertices with only weak links with outside.

– Random walk approaches rely on the idea that good clusters are sets of vertices almost stable in the sense that a random walker that is inside can difficultly escape [5,22]. In formal concept analysis, a formal concept is also a stable set for the Galois connection operator ($X^{\Delta\Delta} = X$ and $Y^{-1\Delta-1\Delta} = Y$). More generally, one may also consider approximate formal concepts s.t. $X_Q^{\Delta} = Y$ and $Y_Q^{-1\Delta} = X$, and similarly approximated conceptual worlds. This raises the questions of possibly adapting graph community detection algorithms for finding approximate formal concepts and approximate conceptual worlds, or to use fuzzy concept lattice machinery for detecting communities.

5 Conclusion

Starting with a view of a formal context as a bi-graph, the paper has shown that formal concepts correspond to the idea of maximal bi-cliques, whereas so-called conceptual worlds, obtained thanks to the introduction of another Galois connection, correspond to disconnected subsets of vertices. Noticeably enough, these two constructs reflect two ideal views of the idea of graph cluster, namely a set of vertices with no link missing inside and a group of vertices with no link with outside. The last section of the paper has outlined different ways of using fuzzy or approximate views of formal concept analysis, making also a parallel with random walks methods. Clearly this is only a preliminary step which suggests several topics worth of investigation.

References

1. Albert, R., Barabási, A.: Statistical mechanics of complex networks (2001)
2. Barabási, A., Albert, R.: Emergence of scaling in random networks. Science 286(5439), 509–512 (1999)
3. Barber, M.J.: Modularity and community detection in bipartite networks. Physical Review E (Statistical, Nonlinear, and Soft Matter Physics) 76(6) (December 2007)
4. Belohlavek, R.: Fuzzy Relational Systems: Foundations and Principles. Kluwer Academic Publishers, Dordrecht (2002)
5. Delvenne, J.-C., Yaliraki, S.N., Barahona, M.: Stability of graph communities across time scales. 0812.1811 (December 2008)
6. Djouadi, Y., Dubois, D., Prade, H.: Differentes extensions floues de l'analyse formelle de concepts. In: Actes Rencontres sur la Logique Floue et ses Applications (LFA'09), Annecy (November 2009)
7. Djouadi, Y., Dubois, D., Prade, H.: On the possible meanings of degrees when making formal concept analysis fuzzy. In: Eurofuse workshop Preference modelling and decision analysis, Pampelune, pp. 253–258 (2009)
8. Dubois, D., Dupin de Saint-Cyr, F., Prade, H.: A possibility theoretic view of formal concept analysis. Fundamenta Informaticae 75(1), 195–213 (2007)
9. Dubois, D., Prade, H.: Possibility theory and formal concept analysis in information systems. In: Proc. 13th International Fuzzy Systems Association World Congress IFSA-EUSFLAT 2009, Lisbon (July 2009)
10. Fortunato, S.: Community detection in graphs. Physics Reports 486(3-5) (2010)
11. Ganter, B., Stumme, G., Wille, R.: Formal Concept Analysis: Foundations and Applications. Springer, Heidelberg (2005)
12. Ganter, B., Wille, R.: Formal Concept Analysis. Springer, Heidelberg (1999)
13. Gaume, B.: Balades aléatoires dans les petits mondes lexicaux. I3 Information Interaction Intelligence 4(2) (2004)
14. Gaume, B., Mathieu, F.: PageRank induced topology for real-world networks. Complex Systems (to appear)
15. Latapy, M., Magnien, C., Del Vecchio, N.: Basic notions for the analysis of large two-mode networks. Social Networks 30(1), 31–48 (2008)
16. Lehmann, S., Schwartz, M., Hansen, L.K.: Biclique communities. Physical Review E (Statistical, Nonlinear, and Soft Matter Physics) 78(1) (2008)
17. Newman, M.E.J.: The structure and function of complex networks. SIAM Review 45, 167–256 (2003)

18. Okubo, Y., Haraguchi, M.: Finding Top-N pseudo formal concepts with core intents. In: Proceedings of the 6th International Conference on Machine Learning and Data Mining in Pattern Recognition, Leipzig, Germany, pp. 479–493 (2009)
19. Pasquier, N., Bastide, Y., Taouil, R., Lakhal, L.: Efficient mining of association rules using closed itemset lattices. Information Systems 24(1), 25–46 (1999)
20. Pons, P., Latapy, M.: Computing communities in large networks using random walks (long version). Journal of Graph Algorithms and Applications (JGAA) 10(2), 191–218 (2006)
21. Porter, M., Onnela, J.P., Mucha, P.J.: J Mucha. Communities in networks. Notices of the American Mathematical Society 56(9), 1082–1097 (2009)
22. Rosvall, M., Bergstrom, C.T.: Maps of random walks on complex networks reveal community structure. Proceedings of the National Academy of Sciences 105(4), 1118–1123 (2008)
23. Roth, C., Bourgine, P.: Epistemic communities: Description and hierarchic categorization. Mathematical Population Studies 12, 107–130 (2005)
24. Schaeffer, S.E.: Graph clustering. Computer Science Review 1(1), 27–64 (2007)
25. Watts, D., Strogatz, S.: Collective dynamics of'small-world' networks. Nature 393, 440–442 (1998)

Negotiation as Creative Social Interaction Using Concept Hierarchies

Frederick E. Petry[1] and Ronald R.Yager[2]

[1] Naval Research Laboratory, Stennis Space Center, MS 39529
fpetry@nrlssc.navy.mil
[2] Machine Intelligence Institute, Iona College, New Rochelle, NY 10801
yager@panix.com

Abstract. Negotiation is a process that ranges from international issues to common society interactions. We present approaches to facilitate the process by exploring alternative spaces for this process. We base the approach on exploring alternative terminology that can resolve conflicts in the negotiation solution. Concept hierarchies can provide higher level concepts that can be used to obtain agreement between parties in the negotiation.

Keywords: Negotiation, Concept Hierarchy, Generalization, Partitions, Consensus.

1 Introduction

In this paper we propose an approach to the negotiation process which views this inexact process as a co-operative societal interaction among concerned parties. Negotiation can be defined as a process in which explicit proposals are put forward for the purpose of reaching agreement on an exchange or on the realization of common interest when conflicting interests are present [1]. Specifically we focus on ways to overcome barriers in negotiations due to differences in the semantics of language and concepts used by the negotiating parties. Since this is a complex issue we can view solutions as representing creative aspects of problem resolution.

A specific mechanism we utilize to assist in this resolution is the use of concept hierarchies to generalize specific terminology that occurred during the negotiations. We will assume that for each party there is a space of concept hierarchies that captures the semantics of terms under discussion in one or more relevant conceptual contexts. Thus when differences arise, some searching of the space of these concept hierarchies could discover common generalizations for the terms in dispute. Such generalizations can then be used to cast the discussions into a broader context that is more acceptable or amenable to both parties avoiding the otherwise contentious implications of the original terminology.

2 Background

In this section we provide an overview of the generalization approach that can be used in exploration of the space of alternative terminology for the negotiation process. Next creativity as related to generalization and the exploration of alternatives is described.

E. Hüllermeier, R. Kruse, and F. Hoffmann (Eds.): IPMU 2010, LNAI 6178, pp. 281–289, 2010.

2.1 Generalization

Generalization is a broad concept that has been used in several contexts. One is the idea of data summarization, a process of grouping of data, enabling transformation of similar item sets, stored originally in a database at the low (primitive) level, into more abstract conceptual representations. Summarization of data is typically performed with utilization of concept hierarchies [2,3], which in ordinary databases are considered to be a part of background knowledge In fuzzy set theory an important consideration is the treatment of data from a linguistic viewpoint. From this an approach has been developed that uses linguistically quantified propositions to summarize the content of a database, by providing a general characterization of the analyzed data [4-7]. There have also been several approaches to the use of fuzzy hierarchies for data generalization [8-10]. Fuzzy gradual rules for data summarization have also been considered [11]. In a previous research effort [12] we developed an approach to data summarization that involves aspects of generalization and compression. The use of concept hierarchies, ontologies, to provide categories to be utilized in this process has been well established [13].

Now consider an example of data generalization letting D= {Oakland, San Jose, ..., Sacramento} be a set of cities. However for a particular application, this data may be at too low a level, i.e. too specific.

Figure 1 illustrates part of a concept hierarchy H_1 for an attribute Location, describing US cities based on the geographical location. This concept hierarchy represents some of the domain background knowledge we have a priori.

By ascending the hierarchy, for the attribute Location in the set D, the values San_Francisco, Santa_Cruz, Oakland, and San_Jose are generalized to the higher level category (also called the hypernym) Bay_Area, while the value (or hyponym) Sacramento is generalized to Sacramento_Metropolitan_Area. Thus $R_1 = G (D, H_1) =$ {Bay_Area, Sacramento_Metropolitan_Area. }.

As we have discussed depending on a semantic context there may be other hierarchy for the data being generalized. These may represent another application for the data or another context that is desired to be related to the original one. For the domain of cities we have discussed, another context might be the classification of the city based on population compared to the geographical context of Figure 1. This is illustrated by H_2 below in Figure 2.

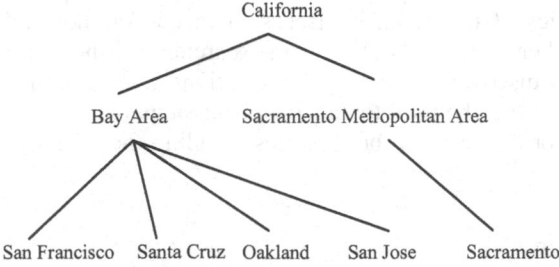

Fig. 1. Example Concept Hierarchy for Cities in California

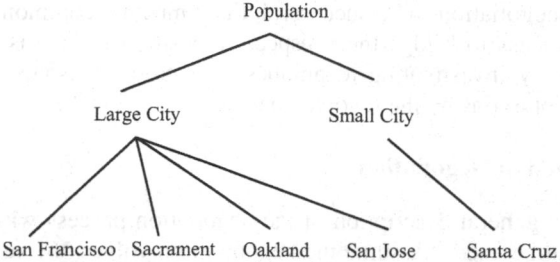

Fig. 2. Concept Hierarchy Based on Population Size

2.2 Creativity

Generalization construed broadly is a central facet of intelligent behavior, an inductive process going from the specific to the general. Here we focus on a data generalization process **G** for which relevant concept hierarchies are used to reduce the specific set of terms T into a small set of general concepts by an induction process.

There have been a number of approaches to evaluating machine creativity and we discuss here some aspects relevant to generalization [14, 15]. Usually it is desired to use domain independent criteria to be as broadly applicable as possible. A creative act can be thought of in two stages – generation and evaluation. The basis for the evaluation of creativity can be viewed as an assessment of the output of a generation process after factoring out the input to the process.

The input to the process can be considered as the implicit and explicit knowledge termed the inspiring set I by Ritchie [16] If we denote by R the results of the generation, then the items to be considered as creative must lie in R/I, i.e. R-I. For the generalization process **G** we are considering that $I = T \cup H_i$, where T is some set of terms and $H_i \in \{H_1, H_2, \ldots H_n\}$ is one hierarchy of the set of hierarchies that may be used for generalization. $R_i = G(I)$ therefore is the result of the generalization process on T using H_i.

Often it may become difficult to exactly specify the input I so strong and weak versions of I have been introduced [15]. I_S contains those values specifically known to the generalization process **G**, so a creative item must be completely new. Often the influence of other information on the process is difficult to quantify so I_W is introduced, containing items that are known to have influenced the generalization. Since this information may be difficult to identify exactly, it may be desirable to consider I_W as a fuzzy set.

3 Negotiation

The process of negotiation is a pervasive activity in human society ranging from negotiations between nations to individual negotiations in everyday life. The importance of negotiation is reflected by article 33, paragraph 1 of the United Nations charter which states that negotiation should be the first method to be used for peaceful settlement of international disputes [17].

In order for a negotiation to be successful, there must be common ground between parties for the process to bridge their respective positions. This is an issue our approach addresses by investigating techniques to explore the space of concepts and terms used in negotiations by the involved parties.

3.1 Formalization of Negotiation

We can provide a general description of the negotiation process with respect to how generalization can be used. Assume the negotiation involves N issues $\{I_1,...,I_N\}$ and these issues encompass a domain X of the terminology involved relative to the issues under consideration. Also let there be two hierarchies over X: H_1 and H_2 for sides 1 and 2 respectively in the negotiation. Each specific issue I_k involves some set of terms $T_k \subseteq X$. So the problem can be described as that in order to negotiate an issue both sides must be in agreement A on a *sufficient* number of terms.

Let an agreement A be a simple one – assume each side has partitioned the terminology space X into two sets – terms with a *positive* import P and terms with a *negative* import N. Then for issue I_k and the term set T_k, side 1 has $T_k = P1_k \cup N1_k$. Similarly for side 2, $T_k = P2_k \cup N2_k$. Obviously if there is not *enough overlap* in positive / negative terms for both sides negotiations will not succeed.

The negotiation process must obtain *sufficient* agreement to succeed. Let us assume in this case a simple agreement A is obtained for the positive terms, $A(P1_k, P2_k)$ and for the negative $A(N1_k, N2_k)$. The objective is that the positive terms agreed upon should *mostly* cover the term set T_k under negotiation and the negative terms agreed upon should *mostly* be avoided in the negotiation issue I_k. This means $A(N1_k, N2_k) \cap T_k$ should be *small*. In order to achieve these agreements the sets of terms in dispute can be generalized by the two sides' hierarchies H_1 and H_2. Then it might be possible that there are more general concepts that the two sides can accept as agreeable. We will illustrate in the next section approaches to find consensus among the possible partitions of term sets induced by the hierarchies.

Clearly much of the inexact negation process involves subjective and soft criteria mentioned above such as "sufficient" agreement or "most" coverage. The representation of such linguistic terms used during the negotiation can be assisted by the concept of linguistic quantifiers. Zadeh [18] noted that human dialogue makes considerable use of terms such as *most, about 50%, some, all* which he referred to as linguistic quantifiers. These terms are used to provide a linguistic explanation of some proportion and can be represented by fuzzy subsets over the unit interval such that the membership measures the satisfaction to the concept. In figure 3 we illustrate a typical graphical representation of the concept "Most".

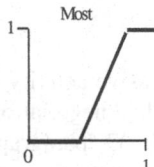

Fig. 3. Example for criterion. "Most"

A specific example of this sort of function is illustrated by the function F1 below:

$$F1(x, a, b) = \begin{cases} 0 & x < a \\ (x\text{-}a)/(b\text{-}a) & a \le x < b \\ 1 & x \ge b \end{cases}$$

where the values of a and b might be 0.75 and 0.85 respectively.

Often the negotiation process involves negotiators who are agents representing the actual parties. If parties are unable to resolve differences by negotiation, a third party may step in to lead the parties to a solution by compromise. This is termed mediation. A mediator may even play an active role in this process and be flexible or innovative enough to obtain some consensus. Such an individual should have psychological understanding to appreciate the way in which the two parties are visualizing the issues between them.

For example labor union representatives must produce a contract that the union members will ratify; lawyers, in a divorce case, must satisfy both wife and husband in the settlement. Often this will concern the varying interpretations of the language in the contract and so a final stage is the actual acceptance by the concerned parties. So as part of the overall process, the negotiation agents may have to explore phrasing that can satisfy the involved parties [19].

Assume there are two negotiators N1 and N2 and that they agree to take an action A1. Next they must explain this to their constituents or audience. Here there are a number of language semantics issues that must be considered. Let the action A1 involve some set of terms in a subset X' of the space X. Then each audience has their own decomposition of X' in the line of positive, negative and indifferent.

D1 – X' = P1∪ N1 ∪ I1; and their own reduction rules
D2 – X' = P2∪ N2 ∪ I2; and their own reduction rules

Can the negotiators explore this space of possibilities to obtain an agreement between D1 and D2? For example consider that there are 3 definite subsets of X, S1, S2 and S3. These are sets that generalize to some specific concept(s) in a given hierarchy H. The remaining elements of X, S0 = X – S1 ∪ S2 ∪ S3. This is a set of undifferentiated elements that the party has no preference for generalization – so they might consider that the domain has positive and negative terms for them but the remaining ones – S0 – are undifferentiated and the person has no preferences relative to them. Note this means that S0 doesn't have specific constraints in the context.

Assume we have two elements of S0 – a and b. These could be generalized to multiple concepts – C and C' – could be included in the generalization to say S2, could generalize independently to different concepts, etc, etc. This leads us to consider the issues of partially generalizing hierarchies and a space of concept hierarchies. – a partially partitioned space. So we consider the process of trying to reach agreements to do negotiations as a search thru this space – an exploration of such a space. This fits into the aspect of creativity – exploration. So we can see that inherently the process of negotiation can be viewed as a creative process.

3.2 Consensus and Partitions

One approach to searching a space of hierarchies can be based on the how different the original data generalized from different hierarchies appears to be. We consider the idea of a consensus of generalized data [20, 21] in terms of the concept of congruence.

One approach is to introduce a measure of similarity, congruence, between two partitions using the underlying equivalence relations. Here we now consider formulating a congruence measure from the perspective of the partitions themselves.

Assume we have two partitions of the set D,

$$P_1 = A_1, ..., A_q$$
$$P_2 = B_1, ..., B_p$$

where $D = \bigcup_{j=1}^{q} A_j$ and $A_i \cap A_j = \emptyset$ for $i \neq j$ and $D = \bigcup_{j=1}^{p} B_j$ and $B_i \cap B_j = \emptyset$ for $i \neq j$.

Without loss of generality we shall assume $q = p$. If $q > p$ we can augment the partition P_2 by adding $q - p$ subsets, $B_{p+1} = B_{p+2} = ... = B_q = \emptyset$. Thus in the following we assume the two partitions have the same number of classes, q.

We now introduce an operation called a pairing of P_1 and P_2, denoted $g(P_1, P_2)$, which associates with each subset A_i of P_1 a unique partner B_j from P_2. Formally if $Q = \{1, 2, ..., q\}$ then a pairing is a mapping $g: Q \rightarrow Q$ that is bijective, one to one and onto. Essentially g is a permutation of Q. We then have that a pairing $g(P_1, P_2)$ is a collection of q pairs, $(A_j, B_{g(j)})$.

We shall now associate with each pairing a score, $Score(g(P_1, P_2))$, defined as follows. Denoting $C_{g,j} = A_j \cap B_{g(j)}$ for $j = 1$ to q we obtain

$$Score(g(P_1, P_2)) = (\sum_{j=1}^{q} Card(C_{g,j})) / Card(D)$$

Example: Now we consider an example of a labor negotiation for a faculty union at a university for which the issues are D = [Medical, Retirement, Raises, Tenure, Intellectual Property}. Based on negotiating positions of the two sides possible partitions might be: P_1 consisting of: A_1 = [Medical, Retirement, Tenure, Raises}, A_2 = { Intellectual Property }; and a partition P_2 is B_1 = [Medical, Retirement, Intellectual Property, Raises }, and B_2 = {Tenure}. In this case there are two pairings.

One pairing is $g(j) = j$ in which case we get the pairs (A_1, B_1), (A_2, B_2). From this

$$C_{g,1} = A_1 \cap B_1 = \{ Medical, Retirement, Holidays \}$$
$$C_{g,2} = A_2 \cap B_2 = \emptyset$$

In this case $Score(g(P_1, P_2)) = 3/5$.

The other pairing is $g(1) = 2$, $g(2) = 1$ and here our pairs are (A_1, B_2), (A_2, B_1). and

$$C_{g,1} = A_1 \cap B_2 = \{Tenure\}$$
$$C_{g,2} = A_2 \cap B_1 = \{ Intellectual Property \}$$

In this case $Score(g(P_1, P_2)) = 2/5$

We now shall use this to obtain a measure of congruence, $Cong_2(P_1, P_2)$. Let G be the set of all pairings, $g \in G$. We define

$$Cong_2(P_1, P_2) = \underset{g \in G}{Max} \; Score(g(P_1, P_2))$$

Thus this measure of congruence is the score of the largest pairing. We see that for

any pairing g, $0 \leq \sum_{j=1}^{q}$ Card $(C_{g,j}) \leq$ Card(D). From this it follows that $0 \leq$

$\text{Cong}_2(P_1, P_2) \leq 1$. More precisely since for any two partitions we can always find a

pairing g in which $\sum_{j=1}^{q}$ Card $(C_{g,j}) \geq 1$ we see that

$$\frac{1}{\text{Card(D)}} \leq \text{Cong}_2(P_1, P_2) \leq 1$$

So this measure allows us to compare partitions produced by generalization using different hierarchies.

Now we can discuss how to apply consensus measures to issues concerning negotiation. Consider the terms that might be part of the dispute in the negotiation. For example one of disagreement on terms is seen in the set

$$D1 = P2 \cap N1$$

By generalizing this set D1 of contentious terms we can, so to speak, cast these into a different phrasing as higher level concepts on which the parties may be able to achieve more agreement. Again recall that negotiation is an inexact process so the degree of agreement on these concepts need not be complete but by mediation the agreement can be phrased as "Mostly" agreed upon. Since it is more likely that agreement can be found on a smaller set of higher level concepts, the search of the space of hierarchies to find a better consensus is the overall objective. Another way of viewing the result of the generalization is that a higher level concept corresponds to (covers) a larger subset of the terms in dispute. Each of the sides in the negotiation may then be able to focus on different aspects or components of such a subset and which they may then find more satisfactory.

Finally if there was not a satisfactory solution obtained, a creative approach could be to consider various combinations of partitions utilizing the sets of terms the parties are indifferent towards. This would mean that the set D1 could be extended prior to generalizations. Let S2 be the set of terms that the second party is indifferent towards. Note not all of these would be indifferent to the other side, indeed some might be viewed as positive, negative, or indifferent. Certainly the subset of S2 viewed negatively (S2 $\cap$ N1) would not be included in an extension. A variety of choices are to include some of the positive and / or indifferent terms of S2 in the extension depending on what negotiators or mediators think would be most beneficial to obtaining a satisfactory resolution.

4 Summary

In this paper we described an approach to the negotiation process which views this inexact process as a co-operative social interaction. Negotiation is a process that ranges from international issues to common society interactions. We presented approaches to facilitate the process by exploring alternative spaces for this process. We based the approach on exploring alternative terminology that can resolve conflicts in the negotiation solution. Concept hierarchies were shown to provide higher level concepts that can be used to obtain agreement between parties in the negotiation

Acknowledgments. We would like to thank the Naval Research Laboratory's Base Program, Program Element No. 0602435N for sponsoring this research. Ronald R. Yager's contribution has been supported in part by ARO MURI grant W911NF-09-1-0392 under Dr. J. Lavery and ONR grant N000141010121.

References

[1] Ikle, F.: How Nations Negotiate. Evanston and London, New York (1964)
[2] Han, J., Cai, Y., Cercone, N.: Knowledge discovery in databases: An attribute-oriented approach. In: Proceedings of 18th VLDB Conf., pp. 547–559 (1992)
[3] Han, J.: Mining Knowledge at Multiple Concept Levels. In: Proc. 4th Int'l Conf. on Information and Knowledge Management, pp. 19–24. ACM Press, New York (1995)
[4] Yager, R.: On linguistic summaries of data. In: Piatesky-Shapiro, G., Frawley (eds.) Knowledge Discovery in Databases, pp. 347–363. MIT Press, Boston (1999)
[5] Kacprzyk, J.: Fuzzy logic for linguistic summarization of databases. In: Proc.8th Int'l Conf. on Fuzzy Systems, Seoul, Korea, pp. 813–818 (1999)
[6] Dubois, D., Prade, H.: Fuzzy sets in data summaries - outline of a new approach. In: Proc. 8th Int'l Conf. on Information Processing and Management of Uncertainty in Knowledge-Based Systems, Madrid, pp. 1035–1040 (2000)
[7] Feng, L., Dillon, T.: Using Fuzzy Linguistic Representations to Provide Explanatory Semantics for Data Warehouses. IEEE Transactions on Knowledge and Data Engineering 15(1), 86–102 (2003)
[8] Lee, D., Kim, M.: Database summarization using fuzzy ISA hierarchies. IEEE Transactions On Systems, Man, and Cybernetics - part B 27(1), 68–78 (1997)
[9] Raschia, G., Mouaddib, N.: SAINTETIQ:a fuzzy set-based approach to database summarization. Fuzzy Sets and Systems 129, 37–162 (2002)
[10] Angryk, R., Petry, F.: Data Mining Fuzzy Databases Using Attribute-Oriented Generalization. In: Proc.IEEE Int. Conf. Data Mining Workshop on Foundations and New Directions in Data Mining, Melbourne, FL, pp. 8–15 (2003)
[11] Cubero, J., Medina, J., Pons, O., Vila, M.: Data Summarization in Relational Databases Through Fuzzy Dependencies. Information Sciences 121(3-4), 233–270 (1999)
[12] Petry, F., Zhao, L.: Data Mining by Attribute Generalization with Fuzzy Hierarchies in Fuzzy Databases. Fuzzy Sets and Systems 160 (#15), 2206–2223 (2009)
[13] Han, J., Kamber, M.: Data Mining: Concepts and Techniques, 2nd edn. Morgan Kaufmann, San Francisco (2006)
[14] Boden, M.: The Creative Mind: Myths and Mechanisma. Weidenfield and Nicholson, London (1990)
[15] Pease, A., Winterstein, D., Colton, S.: Evaluating Machine Creativiity. In: Proc. of ICCBR'01 – Workshop on Creative Systems, Vancouver, CA, pp. 56–61 (2001)
[16] Ritchie, G.: Assessing Creativity. In: Proc. Of AISB '01 Symp. on AI and Creativity in Arts and Science, pp. 3–11 (2001)
[17] Northedge, F., Donelan, M.: International Disputes – the Political Aspects. St. Martin's Press, New York (1971)

[18] Zadeh, L.: Fuzzy logic = computing with words. IEEE Transactions on Fuzzy Systems 4, 103–111 (1996)

[19] Jackson, M.: Industrial Relations, 3rd edn. Croom Helm Ltd., Beckenham (1985)

[20] Yager, R.: Some Measures Relating Partitions Useful for Computatuional Intelligence. Int. Jour. Computational Intelligence Systems 1(#1), 1–18 (2008)

[21] Petry, F., Yager, R.: A Framework for Use of Imprecise Categorization in Developing Intelligent Systems. IEEE Transactions On Fuzzy Systems 18(#2), 348–361 (2010)

Estimating Top-k Destinations in Data Streams

Nuno Homem and Joao Paulo Carvalho

TULisbon – Instituto Superior Técnico, INESC-ID
R. Alves Redol 9, 1000-029 Lisboa, Portugal
nuno_homem@hotmail.com, joao.carvalho@inesc-id.pt

Abstract. One considers the problem of estimating the most frequent values in a data stream. In many cases an approximate answer may be enough. A novel algorithm is presented to approximate the most frequent values using a mixed approach between counter-based techniques and sketch-based ones. The algorithm is then used to find the most frequent destinations of calls by individual customers of telecommunications operators. The use of fast and small footprint algorithms is critical due to the huge number of customers to check and approximate answers are enough in most situations. The problem is that such detection needs to be performed for each individual customer and kept up to date at all times. This paper presents telecommunications customer's behavior to justify the use of approximate algorithms. Although used in this paper on telecommunications this algorithm may well be used in other contexts.

Keywords: Approximate algorithms; estimation; data-stream frequencies; most frequent destinations; telecommunications.

1 Introduction

Classical top-k algorithms require the list of used destinations or products to be checked every time a new transaction or event is processed to see if the value is already in the list and update the counters. Exact top-k algorithms require large amounts of memory as they need to store the complete list of values. Storing 1000 values per customer if only the top-20 are needed seems a complete waste of space. The problem is not just keeping one single list, big or small, is keeping huge numbers of small lists. Telecom operators can range from less than 500 000 customers (a small operator) to more than 25 000 000 customers, and a list of the top-20 services or destinations might be needed for each one. Retail sellers have also similar or even bigger number of customers, in some cases identified by the use of fidelity cards. The number of elements to be stored per customer is usually small as people tend to make frequent calls to a relatively small number of destinations and to buy frequently the same products.

The biggest challenge to the systems that gather this information is accurately identify this in near real time while not allocating huge amount of resources into it. To a company with several million customers making multiple transactions per day, this represents a huge challenge. Optimizing the process is therefore critical.

E. Hüllermeier, R. Kruse, and F. Hoffmann (Eds.): IPMU 2010, LNAI 6178, pp. 290–299, 2010.

This paper proposes a new algorithm for identifying the approximate top-k values designed to be memory efficient. Although the focus is to produce large number of good top-k lists each based on a not that large set of transactions, it can also be used to efficiently produce a single top-k list for a huge number of transactions. The new proposed algorithm is innovative also by merging two distinct approaches commonly used to solve this sort of problems, counter-based and sketch-based techniques. It follows the principles presented by Metwally and al. [13] for Space-Saving algorithm but it tries to narrow down both the number of required counters and the error associated with the frequency estimate by filtering elements using a specially designed sketch. A simple implementation option is discussed to minimize memory foot-print and long term storage needs. A comparison between the Space-Saving algorithm and the new is presented using telecommunications examples.

2 Relation with Previous Work

Exact top-k algorithms require the list of used destinations or products to be checked every time a new element is processed to see if the value is already in the list and update the counters. Exact top-k algorithms also require large amounts of memory as they need to store the complete list of values.

The Space Saving algorithm [13] underlying idea is to monitor only a pre-defined number of m elements and their associated counters. Counters on each element are updated to reflect the maximum possible number of times an element has been observed and the error that might be involved in that estimate. If an element that is already being monitored occurs again, the counter for the frequency estimate is incremented. If the element is not currently monitored it is always added to the list. If the maximum number of elements has been reached, the element with the lower estimate of possible occurrences is dropped. The new estimate error is set to the estimate of frequency of the dropped element. The new element is set with that estimate error and a frequency estimate equal to the error plus 1.

The Space Saving algorithm will keep in the list all the elements that may have occurred at least the new estimate error value (or the last dropped element estimate) of times. This ensures that no false negatives are kept but it allows for false positives. Elements with low frequencies but that have been observed in the end of the stream may still be present at the list.

As the Space Saving algorithm maintains both the frequency estimate and the maximum error this estimate may include, it also maintains implicitly the number of real observations registered while the element was monitored. This allows a check to be performed on the order of the monitored elements that may guarantee that under some cases, the order of the top-k elements is guaranteed to be the correct one. By allowing m, the number of elements in the retrieved list, to be larger than k this provides good results in most cases. In Metwally and al. [13] comparison between several algorithms in this area is provided. Space saving algorithm is already less demanding on counters than other algorithms like Lossy Counting as proposed by [12] or the Probabilistic Lossy Counting proposed by [5].

Sketch-based algorithms are much better at providing estimates of frequencies for all elements by the use of bitmap counters. Each element is hashed into one or more counters and the counters updated. There is an error associated as the hash function will generate collisions. Keeping big enough number of counters to minimize collision probability leads to higher memory footprint than for Space Saving algorithm. Additionally the entire bitmap counter needs to be scanned and elements sorted to answer to the top-k query.

The algorithm proposed in this work uses a filtering approach to improve on Space Saving. It also gets some inspiration on previous work around probabilistic counting and sliding windows statistics [3, 6, 8, 9, 10 and 14]. A bitmap counter is used to filter and minimize updates on the monitored elements list and also to better estimate the error associated with each element. Instead of using a single error estimate value, an error estimate dependent on the hash counter is used. This will allow better estimates by using the maximum possible error for that hash value instead of a global value. Although this requires an additional bitmap counter to be kept, the idea is that this will help reducing the number of extra elements of the list needed to ensure high quality top-k elements. It will also help reducing the number of list updates. As the bitmap counter is used in conjunction with the list of elements, the collision problem of most sketch-based algorithms that forces the bitmap counter to be large will be minimized. This allows the bitmap counter size to be dependent on the number of k elements to be retrieved and not on the number of distinct elements of the stream, which is usually much higher.

3 The Filtered Space-Saving Algorithm

The Filtered Space-Saving (FSS) algorithm uses a bitmap counter with h cells, each containing two values, α_i and c_i, standing for the error and the number of monitored elements in cell i. The hash function needs to be able to transform the input values into a uniformly distributed integer range. The hashed value $h(x)$ is then used to set increment the corresponding counter. Initially all values of α_i and c_i are set to 0.

The second storage element is a list of monitored elements A with size m. The list is initially empty. Each element contains 3 parts; the value itself v_j, the estimate count f_j and the associated error e_j.

The minimum required value to be included in the monitored list is always the minimum of the estimate counts. While there are free elements in the list it is set to 0.

$$min = min \{f_j\}$$

The algorithm is quite simple. When a new value is received, the hash is calculated and the bitmap counter is checked. If there are already monitored elements with that same hash ($c_i > 0$) the list is searched to see if this particular element is already there. If the element is in the list then the estimate count f_j is incremented. If the element is not in the list then it is checked to see if it should be added.

A new element will be inserted into the list if $\alpha_i +1 >= min$. If the elements are not monitored then α_i is just incremented. In fact this α_i stands for the number of elements with hash value i that have not been counted in the monitored list. It is the maximum number of times an element that is not in the list and that has this hash value could have been observed. If the element is included in the monitored list then c_i is incremented and set $f_j = \alpha_i +1$ and $e_j = \alpha_i$.

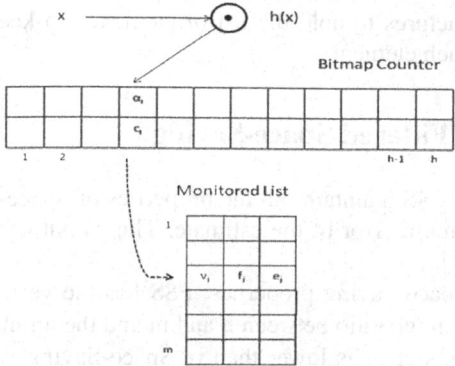

Fig. 1. FSS Algorithm Diagram

If the list has exceeded its maximum allowed size then the element with the lower f_j is selected. If there are several with the same value, the one of those with the larger value of e_j is selected. The selected element is removed from the list and the corresponding bitmap counter cell is updated, c_j is decreased and α_i set with the maximum error incurred for that position in a single element, the estimate for the removed element, $\alpha_i = f_j$.

```
Algorithm: Filtered Space-Saving(h cells, m counters, S stream)
begin
        for each element, x, in S {
            set min to min {f_j}
            let i be the hash(x) mod h
            if c_i is not 0 {
                    if x is monitored {
                            let j be the index of x in the list
                            increment counter fj
                            continue for next x
                    }
            } // will only be executed if x is not monitored

            if α_i +1 >= min {
                    if list size equals m {
                            let m be the index of one element with lower f_j
                                   and for same f_j with higher e_j
                            let k be the hash(x) mod h
                            decrement c_k
                            set α_k = f_i
                            remove v_m
                    }
                    include x in the list in index j
                    set v_j to x
                    set e_j to α_i and f_j to α_i+1
            } else {
                    increment counter α_i
            }
        }// end for
    end
```

When h=1 FSS is exactly the Space-Saving algorithm.

At this stage one will not cover the obvious optimizations to this algorithm, such as the use of better structures to hold the list of elements, to keep up to date min or to speed up access to each element.

4 Properties of Filtered Space-Saving

It can be proved that FSS maintains all the properties of Space-Saving, inclusively the guarantee of a maximum error of the estimate. This is out of the scope of this paper and is detailed in [11].

Additionally to Space-Saving properties, FSS has the very interesting property of the error depending on the ratio between h and m and the number of samples N, and it can be shown that this error is lower than in Space-Saving with a given probability [11]. In fact for high values of N it gives a high probability of being even lower than Space-Saving.

The intuitive justification for this is that by using an error filter to distribute errors throughout a large number of cells h, the estimate error α for each cell can be made lower than a certain value (per example 120%) of N/h for large enough values of N by using more cells in the filter than in the monitored list (in our simple implementation each entry in the monitored list requires space equivalent to 3 counters).

5 Experimental Results

The first set of tests between Space-Saving and FSS try to show performance of both algorithms in a typical telecommunications situation where the top-10 or top-20 destinations are needed per customer. This analysis is based on 962 blocks of calls of distinct customers, each with 500 mobile voice calls (made during a 2 or 3 month period in most cases). Note that 500 calls is not a small number of calls, most of the customers make no more than 15 calls a day. On average, in 500 calls, each customer would call 98.67 distinct numbers (with a standard deviation of 34.99).

Although FSS requires an additional bitmap counter to be kept, the fact that this bitmap counter only requires smaller counters allows a trade-off to be made. By replacing some of the entries in the Space-Saving monitored list by additional cells in this bitmap counter, it is possible to keep the same space but have better expected performance out of the algorithm. In this paper a single entry in the monitored list was exchanged for 6 additional cells in the bitmap counter. This seems to be a reasonable exchange rate specially if one considers the usual counter size (Space-Saving implementations usually use either 16 or 32 bits counters, FSS may use 8 bit or 16 bit counters). This exchange rate coupled to the probabilistic guarantees of FSS (specially for large values of N, the stream size) allows us to achieve better results. In fact FSS exchanges deterministic guarantees for tighter probabilistic ones.

The practical implementation of FSS may include the Stream Summary data structure presented in [13], but depending on the number of elements in the monitored list other options may as well be used. For small number of m, a simple array of m elements can be a viable and fast option. To speed up insertions and replacements, an additional array with the indexes of each element ordered by f_i may be used. This trades some performance by a very compact implementation. This may be the preferred option for telecommunication related implementations where the total number of elements in the list is to be kept near 50 or even less.

Full List Recall is the ratio between the correct top-k elements included in the full monitored list and k; Full List Precision is the ratio between the correct top-k elements included in the full monitored list and its size m.

Top-k Recall (and Top-k Precision) is the ratio between correct top-k elements included in the returned top-k elements and k. This is the main quality indicator of the algorithms as this reflects the number of correct values got when getting a top-k list.

Estimate error is the square root of MSE of the frequency estimate for the top-k elements returned (out of k elements). It does not include incorrect elements or the error of estimate of top-k elements not returned.

The first set of trials uses relatively small blocks of calls per customer and identifies the top-10 or top-20 destinations. Note that for Space-Saving m = 3k is used, so 30 elements are used in the list when finding top-10 elements and 60 when finding top-20 elements. Note that this is a significant size for the list, as an average of 98 distinct numbers in a 500 call block is expected (and 130 in an 800 call block).

Table 1. Comparative performance

		Trial 1.0	Trial 1.1	Trial 2.0	Trial 2.1
Block size		500	800	500	800
Average Distinct		98	130	98	130
Number of Samples		962	715	962	715
Top-k		10	10	20	20
SS m		30	30	60	60
FSS m		15	15	30	30
FSS h		90	90	180	180
FSS	min	9.73	14.8	4.52	6.73
	Full List Recall	0.9758	0.9768	0.9892	0.9893
	Full List Precision	0.6916	0.6748	0.737	0.71
	Top-k Recall	0.9433	0.9409	0.9604	0.9633
	Top-k Precision	0.9433	0.9409	0.9604	0.9633
	Estimate Error	1.27	1.52	0.81	0.95
SS	min	8.96	15.39	2.52	4.70
	Full List Recall	0.9705	0.9631	0.9958	0.9931
	Full List Precision	0.3475	0.3342	0.3856	0.3629
	Top-k Recall	0.9002	0.8858	0.9670	0.9560
	Top-k Precision	0.9002	0.8858	0.9670	0.9560
	Estimate Error	1.35	2.18	0.37	0.64

In these trials it can be observed that Top-k Recall (and Top-k Precision) of FSS to be marginally better than that of Space-Saving for top-10. It's interesting to see that in the top-20 trial the results are much closer. In fact Space-Saving as m = 60 is able to store a large part of the distinct values and therefore the improvement of FSS is not relevant.

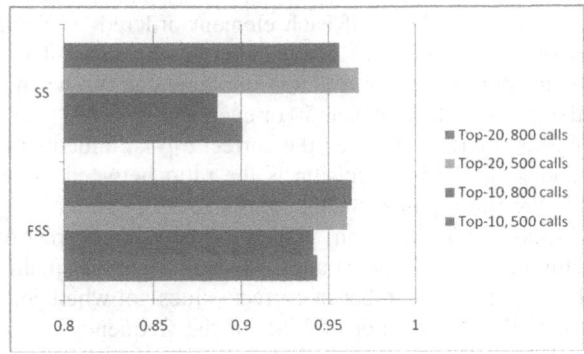

Fig. 2. Top-k Precision for Space-Saving and FSS algorithms

The second block of trials compares Space-Saving (SS) with FSS for larger number of calls made in a consecutive period of time. The number of distinct elements per block of calls is now much higher so the increased m and h proportionally for both algorithms.

Table 2. Top-20 performance for large sets

			Trial 3.0	Trial 3.1	Trial 3.2
Block size			5000	10000	20000
Average Distinct			3130	5322	8774
Number of Samples			166	83	41
FSS	m=100, h=600	min	13.79	25.4	48.41
		Recall and Precision	0.4996	0.4686	0.4439
		Estimate Error	5.57	9.97	18.47
	m=200, h=1200	min	8.04	14.48	27.07
		Recall and Precision	0.7894	0.7734	0.7597
		Estimate Error	2.36	3.37	5.34
	m=400, h=2400	min	5	8.92	15.97
		Recall and Precision	0.9246	0.9265	0.939
		Estimate Error	1.25	1.57	2.019
SS	m=200	min	23.92	48.86	98.8
		Recall and Precision	0.2539	0.1987	0.1585
		Estimate Error	14.87	31.09	63.82
	m=400	min	11.84	23.91	48.87
		Recall and Precision	0.4987	0.4138	0.3402
		Estimate Error	4.71	9.5	18.12
	m=800	min	5	11.42	23.82
		Recall and Precision	0.853	0.7903	0.7329
		Estimate Error	1.25	2.12	4.08

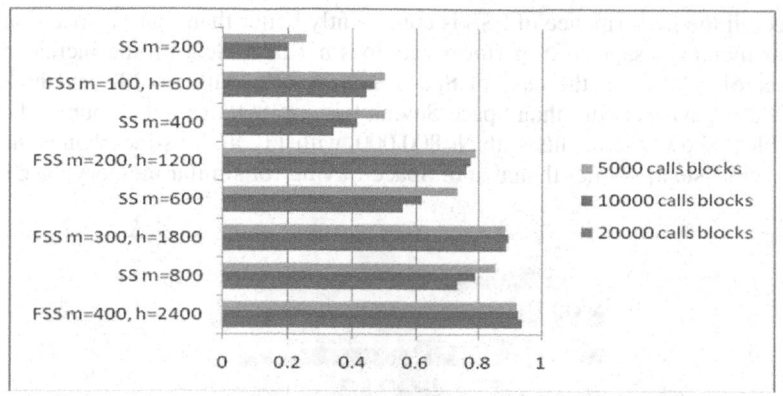

Fig. 3. Top-20 Precision with increasing number of calls

Table 3. Performance with full set of calls

			Trial 4.0	Trial 4.1	Trial 4.2
SS m			2000	4000	8000
FSS m			1000	2000	4000
FSS h			6000	12000	24000
FSS	Top-10	min	207	114	60
		Precision and Recall	0.8	0.9	0.9
		Estimate Error	59.42	36.45	13.06
	Top-20	min	207	114	60
		Precision and Recall	0.85	0.9	0.95
		Estimate Error	59.67	31.27	14.3
	Top-50	min	207	114	60
		Precision and Recall	0.86	0.94	0.96
		Estimate Error	61.69	26.29	11.52
	Top-100	min	207	114	60
		Precision and Recall	0.76	0.89	0.97
		Estimate Error	60.38	25.95	11.39
SS	Top-10	min	388	183	80
		Precision and Recall	0.8	0.8	0.9
		Estimate Error	145.68	66.65	25.5
	Top-20	min	388	183	80
		Precision and Recall	0.7	0.85	0.9
		Estimate Error	170.97	69.87	27.05
	Top-50	min	388	183	80
		Precision and Recall	0.68	0.84	0.92
		Estimate Error	171.95	69.26	26.24
	Top-100	min	388	183	80
		Precision and Recall	0.55	0.74	0.87
		Estimate Error	175.66	67.56	24.85

Overall the performance of FSS is consistently better than that of Space-Saving for similar memory usage. FSS performance does not degrade with the increasing of the number of calls as in the case of Space-Saving. FSS with m=200 and h=1200, for N=20000, behaves better than Space-Saving with m=800 using the double of space.

Table 3 shows the results with N=800 000, with 112 462 distinct values the results. FSS is consistently better than that of Space-Saving for similar memory usage.

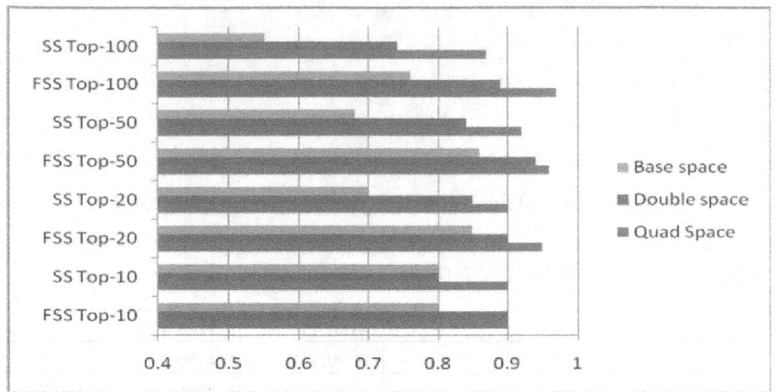

Fig. 4. Top-k Precision with increasing space

6 Conclusions

This paper shows a new algorithm that builds on top of the best existing algorithm for answering the top-k problem and that effectively constitutes a merger of the of two existing and distinct approaches to this problem, the counter-based techniques and sketch-based ones.

The FSS algorithm filters and splits the error of Space-Saving algorithm through the use of a bitmap counter. This helps to minimize the overall error and therefore the error associated with each element. This eliminates the excess of trail elements in the stream that Space-Saving usually includes in the monitored list and that have a very high estimation error.

This paper shows experimental results that detail improvements over Space-Saving algorithm, both in precision and in performance when using similar memory space. Memory consumption was key in the analysis as the practical problem being solved is memory bound. In this regard the use of FSS is envisioned with even less memory than Space-Saving and with better precision.

FSS is a low memory footprint algorithm that can answer not only the top-k problem for large number of transactions but also the problem of answering huge number of top-k problems for relatively small number of transactions. As such its applicability goes much beyond telecommunications or retail applications. It can be used in any other domain as long as the appropriate implementation choices and dimensioning are made.

References

1. Bertsekas, D.P.: Dynamic Programming and Optimal Control, vol. 1. Athena Scientific, Belmont (1995)
2. Cormode, G., Muthukrishnan, S.: What's Hot and What's Not: TrackingMost Frequent Items Dynamically. In: Proceedings of the 22nd ACM PODS Symposium on Principles of Database Systems, pp. 296–306 (2003)
3. Datar, M., Gionis, A., Indyk, P., Motwani, R.: Maintaining Stream Statistics Over Sliding Windows. SIAM Journal on Computing 31(6) (2002)
4. Demaine, E., López-Ortiz, A., Munro, J.: Frequency Estimation of Internet Packet Streams with Limited Space. In: Proceedings of the 10th ESA Annual European Symposium on Algorithms, pp. 348–360 (2002)
5. Dimitropoulos, X., Hurley, P., Kind, A.: Probabilistic Lossy Counting: An efficient algorithm for finding heavy hitters. ACM SIGCOMM Computer Communication Review 38(1) (January 2008)
6. Estan, C., Varghese, G.: New directions in traffic measurement and accounting. In: Proceedings of SIGCOMM 2002. ACM Press, New York (2002); Also: UCSD technical report CS2002-0699 (February 2002); available electronically
7. Estan, C., Varghese, G.: New Directions in Traffic Measurement and Accounting: Focusing on the Elephants, Ignoring the Mice. ACM Trans. Comput. Syst. 21(3), 270–313 (2003)
8. Estan, C., Varghese, G., Fisk, M.: Bitmap algorithms for counting active flows on high speed links. Technical Report CS2003-0738, UCSD (March 2003)
9. Fan, L., Cao, P., Almeida, J., Broder, A.: Summary Cache: A Scalable Wide-Area Web Cache Sharing Protocol. IEEE/ACM Transactions on Networking 8(3), 281–293 (2000), doi:10.1109/90.851975
10. Flajolet, P., Martin, N.: Probabilistic Counting Algorithms for Data Base Applications. Journal of Computer and System Sciences 31(2) (October 1985)
11. Homem, N., Carvalho, J.: Finding top-k destinations in telecommunications, Information Sciences, INS-D-09-158 (under review)
12. Manku, G., Motwani, R.: Approximate Frequency Counts over Data Streams. In: Proceedings of the 28th ACM VLDB International Conference on Very Large Data Bases, pp. 346–357 (2002)
13. Metwally, A., Agrawal, D., Abbadi, A.: Efficient Computation of Frequent and Top- k Elements in Data Streams, Technical Report 2005-23, University of California, Santa Barbara (September 2005)
14. Misra, J., Gries, D.: Finding Repeated Elements. Science of Computer Programming 2, 143–152 (1982)
15. Whang, K., Vander-Zanden, B., Taylor, H.: A Linear-Time Probabilistic Counting Algorithm for Database Applications. ACM Transactions on Database Systems 15(2) (June 1990)

A Data Mining Algorithm for Inducing Temporal Constraint Networks*

Miguel R. Álvarez, Paulo Félix, Purificación Cariñena, and Abraham Otero

Departamento de Electrónica e Computación,
Universidade de Santiago de Compostela,
15782 Santiago de Compostela, Spain
miguel.rodriguez@usc.es

Abstract. A new approach to the problem of temporal knowledge induction from a collection of temporal events is presented. As a result, a set of frequent temporal patterns is obtained, represented following the Simple Temporal Problem (STP) formalism: a set of event types and a set of constraints describing common temporal arrangements between the events. The use of a clustering technique makes it possible to discriminate between the frequent patterns that are found in the collection.

1 Introduction

Temporal Data Mining aims to search for interesting patterns in large collections of temporal data. Every pattern represents a particular temporal arrangement of a set of events, and the number of occurrences is a first measure of its possible interest. Examples of collections susceptible to the application of temporal data mining techniques are those that store event sequences; such as alarms in a telecommunications network, or manifestations in the course of a disease.

In this sense, several techniques have been described in the bibliography, having in common performing the mining procedure by means of the *Apriori* strategy [1], following the premise that if an event sequence is frequent, then all of its subsequences are also frequent. With this idea, frequent sequences of size i are iteratively built from frequent sequences of size $i - 1$.

Agrawal *et al.* present in [2] three algorithms for the obtention of frequent sequences in a set of transactions from several consumers, in the so called *market basket problem*. Every element in a sequence consists of a set of products bought in the same transaction, following a partial order relation between the elements of the sequence. As a result of the mining procedure, the maximal sets of frequent sequences from the data are presented.

The proposal by Mannila *et al.* [3] approaches the mining problem using a technique that allows to obtain two types of episodes, named as parallel and

---

* This work was funded by the Spanish MICINN (TIN2009-14372-C03-03) and by the Xunta de Galicia (08SIN002206PR). M. R. Álvarez is funded by an FPU grant from the Spanish MEC (AP2008-02593).

E. Hüllermeier, R. Kruse, and F. Hoffmann (Eds.): IPMU 2010, LNAI 6178, pp. 300–309, 2010.

sequential. The former allows to know what event types are frequently found in the same temporal proximity, without any further information about their temporal arrangement. The latter allows to obtain an order relation between the event types found in temporal proximity, but provides no further quantitative information about this relation except for its maximum duration.

The proposal by Dousson *et al.* [4] obtains a set of temporal patterns represented as a STP as the result of the mining process. Size-two patterns are found using a heuristic approach that obtains a temporal constraint, represented as an interval, for each pair of event types. Constraints between event types for larger patterns are the result of the union of every constraint between the same pair of event types in previously found frequent patterns. This results in only one pattern for each set of event types.

The aim of our proposal is to provide a technique for temporal data mining that increases the expressiveness of the results of the mining process, bringing them closer to the knowledge representation model that a domain expert would use. From a collection of temporal data, the goal is to discover a set of temporal patterns that frequently appear in the collection, represented as a set of temporal constraint networks, and introducing a clustering technique to make use of the concept of similarity in the pattern induction.

Before describing our temporal data mining algorithm, we will introduce some preliminary concepts and definitions in the following section. Section 3 describes in detail the mining algorithm. Section 4 analyzes the computational complexity of our proposal. Section 5 introduces some experimental results and section 6 presents the conclusions and future work.

2 Definitions

We assume a temporal framework isomorphic to the set of natural numbers $\mathbb{N}$. Every observation procedure locates an observable in time and establishes its attributes by assigning a value to each of them. An event is the result of an observation in a temporal instant.

Definition 1. *An **event** is a tuple $(o, a = v, t)$, where $o \in O$ is an observable, a is an attribute belonging to the observable with value $v \in V(a)$ and $t \in \mathbb{N}$ is a temporal instant.*

An event may be characterized by a set of attributes but we will assume, without loss of generality, that all events have only one attribute represented by its value. From the set of different (o, v) pairs we can define an event type.

Definition 2. *An **event type** is a tuple (o, v, T), where T is a temporal variable corresponding to an instant.*

We call $E = \{E_1, \ldots, E_p\}$ to the set of different event types provided by the observation procedures.

For example, the identification of an *apnea* in the evolution of a patient can be represented by the event *(apnea, central, 02:03:46)*, where *(apnea, central, T)* is the corresponding event type.

Let $<$ be an order relation between two events $e_i = (o_i, v_i, t_i)$ and $e_j = (o_j, v_j, t_j)$ such that $(e_i < e_j) \Leftrightarrow (t_i < t_j) \lor ((t_i = t_j) \land (o_i < o_j))$ assuming a lexicographical order between observable names. This relation allows to define the concept of event sequence.

Definition 3. *An **event sequence** is an ordered set of events $S = \{e_1, \ldots, e_m\}$ where $e_i < e_{i+1}$ for all $i = 1, \ldots, m-1$. The size of the sequence is $|S| = m$. Its beginning is $b_S = t_1$, its ending $e_S = t_m$ and its duration $d_S = t_m - t_1$. Every subset of the sequence is a subsequence.*

It is possible to identify events corresponding to different observables at the same instant, but it is impossible to identify two different events of the same observable at the same instant, that is, no attribute may take different values at the same instant; $\forall e_i, e_j \in S, (o_i = o_j) \land (v_i \neq v_j) \Rightarrow t_i \neq t_j$.

The mining procedure aims to obtain a set of temporal patterns that are frequently found in a sequence S, or in a collection of sequences $\mathcal{S} = \{S_1, \ldots, S_n\}$. Every pattern obtained at the end of the data mining process is represented as a temporal constraint network between a set of event types, according to the STP formalism [5]. A STP defines a temporal constraint L_{ij} between two event types $E_i = (o_i, v_i, T_i)$ and $E_j = (o_j, v_j, T_j)$ as a closed interval $L_{ij} = [a_{ij}, b_{ij}]$ restricting the possible values of the interval duration between both events so that $a_{ij} \leq T_j - T_i \leq b_{ij}$.

Definition 4. *A **temporal pattern** is a directed graph $P = <D, \mathcal{L}>$ where $D = \{E_1, \ldots, E_n\}$ is a subset of E, $E_i \neq E_j$ for all $i \neq j$, and $\mathcal{L} = \{L_{ij}; 1 \leq i, j \leq n\}$ is a set of temporal constraints between the event types in D.*

Definition 5. *An **event occurrence** of an event type $E_i = (o_i, v_i, T_i)$ is an event $e_i = (o_i, v_i, t_i)$ resulting from an observation in $T_i = t_i$.*

Definition 6. *A **pattern occurrence** of a temporal pattern P is a subsequence $X = \{e_1, \ldots, e_n\}$ of S such that, for all $i = 1, \ldots, n$, every e_i is an occurrence of one of the event types in D, satisfying all the temporal constraints in $\mathcal{L}$.*

The user of the mining procedures may be interested in searching for short, mid or long-term relations between the events subject to analysis. His/her knowledge of the domain allows to specify the scope of the search, defining a temporal window of duration ω that scrolls through every sequence $S \in \mathcal{S}$ searching for frequent patterns. This window constrains the search by only considering those subsequences $W \subset S$ where $d_W \leq \omega$, limiting the search space [6] and increasing the efficiency.

Definition 7. *A **temporal window** of size ω in a sequence S is every subsequence $W = \{e_i, \ldots, e_k\}$ of S such that $t_k - t_i \leq \omega$, $e_i, \ldots, e_k \in S$ and $\forall t_j \in [t_i, t_k] \land e_j \in S \Rightarrow e_j \in W$.*

The mining procedure introduced in section 3 uses the concept of temporal association to identify sets of event types frequently found together. The different temporal arrangements of these associations will lead to different temporal patterns. By introducing the order relation $(E_i < E_j \Leftrightarrow (o_i < o_j) \vee ((o_i = o_j) \wedge (v_i < v_j))$ we may represent event types E_i, E_j with capital letters A, B in lexicographical order.

Definition 8. *A* **temporal association** *is an ordered set of event types* $A = \{E_1, \ldots, E_n\}$ *where* $E_i < E_{i+1}$ *for all* $i = 1, \ldots, n-1$, *and there exists a temporal window* $W = \{e_1, \ldots, e_m\}$, *with* $n \leq m$, *containing at least one event occurrence of each* E_i.

Definition 9. *Given two temporal patterns* $P =< D, \mathcal{L} >$ *and* $P' =< D', \mathcal{L}' >$, *we say that* P' *is an* **extension of the pattern** P, $P \preceq P'$, *if* $D \subseteq D'$ *and* $L'_{ij} \subseteq L_{ij}$ *for all* $L_{ij} \in \mathcal{L}$ *and* $L'_{ij} \in \mathcal{L}'$.

A temporal pattern P' usually contains an extended set of the events in P, but its temporal constraints are more restrictive [4]. We can extract an occurrence of P from any occurrence of P'. One of the main operations in the search procedure proposed in section 3 combines two frequent temporal patterns of size $i - 1$ in order to build a candidate temporal pattern of size i.

Definition 10. *Given two temporal patterns* $P =< D_p, \mathcal{L}_p >$ *and* $Q =< D_q, \mathcal{L}_q >$, *we define their* **combination**, $P \bowtie Q$, *as a temporal pattern* $R =< D_r, \mathcal{L}_r >$, *where* $D_r = D_p \cup D_q$ *and* $\mathcal{L}_r = \{L^r_{ij} = L^p_{ij} \cap L^q_{ij} | L^p_{ij} \in \mathcal{L}_p, L^q_{ij} \in \mathcal{L}_q\}$.

The frequency of a temporal arrangement of events in a sequence or collection of sequences is the criteria used to focus the attention of the mining process.

Definition 11. *The* **frequency** *of a temporal pattern* P *in* S *is defined as the number of occurrences of* P *in* S *and is denoted* $f(P)$.

We can further specify the frequency calculation by taking into account the time fraction in which the pattern occurs, as in [3]. The domain usually establishes the minimum frequency that makes a pattern relevant. Given a frequency threshold f_{min}, we say that a temporal pattern P is frequent if $f(P) \geq f_{min}$.

3   Algorithms

We propose a temporal data mining procedure based on the *Apriori* strategy: first we search for event types that are frequently found in the sequence, then we search for patterns comprised by pairs of frequent event types that are frequently found with a distinct temporal arrangement. We continue to increase the size of the patterns until no new frequent pattern is found.

3.1   Main Algorithm

Figure 1 shows the main algorithm for frequent pattern search. Given a collection of event sequences S, a collection of event types E, a window size ω and a frequency threshold f_{min}, the objective is to iteratively search in S for frequent temporal patterns of increasing size where events are, at most, ω time units apart. The algorithm uses three lists: A^i holds frequent temporal associations comprised of i events, C^i stores candidate patterns of i events and P^i represents frequent patterns of i events. The result of the algorithm is a set of frequent temporal patterns represented as STP.

```
procedure PATTERN_SEARCH(S,E,ω,f_min)
begin
    A¹ ← {E_j | E_j ∈ E ∧ f(E_j) ≥ f_min}
    P¹ ← A¹
    while (P^{i-1} ≠ ∅) do begin
        C^i ← CANDIDATE_GENERATION(A^{i-1},P^{i-1})
        P^i ← FREQUENCY_CALCULATION(C^i,ω,f_min)
        A^i ← {D_j | P^i_j = <D_j,L_j>∈P^i}
        i ← i+1
    end;
```

Fig. 1. Main algorithm

The procedure is divided in several steps. The first step searches for event types in E that are frequent in S. Once frequent event types are found, an iterative process searches for increasing patterns until no new patterns are found. Each iteration follows two steps: candidate pattern generation and frequent pattern calculation. These steps are explained in detail in the next sections.

3.2   Candidate Generation

The procedure CANDIDATE_GENERATION receives as arguments the frequent temporal associations and frequent patterns found in the previous iteration, aiming to build the candidate patterns for the iteration in course. Depending on the size of the candidates this procedure presents some differences in execution.

Figure 2 shows the general case $(i > 2)$ for candidate generation following the *Apriori* strategy: from each pair A^{i-1}_j, A^{i-1}_k of frequent temporal associations of size $i - 1$ that share all their event types save one, we generate temporal associations A^i_j of size i by adding the event types that make them different. For the new temporal association to be frequent, the antimonotonicity property [1] states that all temporal associations contained in A^i_j must be frequent. For example, given the set of frequent temporal associations $A^3 = \{$ABC, ABD, ABE, ACD, ACE, BCD, BCE$\}$, the set of candidate associations is $A^4 = \{$ABCD, ABCE$\}$. The association ACDE cannot be frequent because association CDE is not frequent.

```
procedure CANDIDATE_GENERATION(A^{i-1}, P^{i-1})
begin
    C^i ← ∅
    for A_j^{i-1}, A_k^{i-1} ∈ A^{i-1} ∧ E_1^j = E_1^k, ..., E_{i-2}^j = E_{i-2}^k, E_{i-1}^j < E_{i-1}^k do begin
        A_j^i ← A_j^{i-1} ∪ {E_{i-1}^k}
        if all A_h^{i-1} ⊂ A_j^i satisfies A_h^{i-1} ∈ A^{i-1} then
            for all combination of P_{h_k}^{i-1}, P_{h_k}^{i-1} ∈ P^{i-1} ∧ D_h^{i-1} ⊂ A_j^i do
                if ⋈_h P_{h_k}^{i-1} is consistent then
                    C^i ← C^i ∪ (⋈_h P_{h_k}^{i-1})
    end;
    return(C^i)
end;
```

Fig. 2. Candidate generation algorithm

In addition, for each A_j^i it is also necessary to find a consistent combination of frequent temporal patterns $P_{h_k}^{i-1}$ of size $i-1$ with $D_h^{i-1} \subset A_j^i$. This results in a pattern $\bowtie_h P_h$ extension of all of them. For example, a pattern consisting of the event types ABCD is built by combining four patterns, with temporal associations ABC, ABD, ACD and BCD. The constraint propagation and consistency is checked by a Floyd-Warshall algorithm [5]. Consistent patterns of size i obtained by this procedure are the candidate patterns of size i. Figure 3 presents an example of pattern combination to build a larger pattern, extension of all the patterns used in the combination.

According to definition 10, the result of combining two patterns (in figure 3, (a) and (b)) is a new pattern whose constraints are obtained by the intersection of the contraints between common event types in both patterns, assuming there is no constraint when it is not specified. If some of the resulting constraints is given by the empty set, the pattern is inconsistent and any further combination involving it is bound to be inconsistent. If the resulting pattern contains no empty constraints then it is combined with the next pattern (c), and (d), until no further patterns $P_{h_k}^{i-1}$ with different event types $D_h^{i-1} \subset A_j^i$ can be combined.

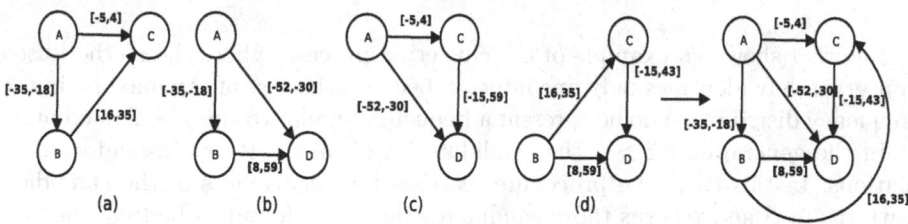

(a)   (b)   (c)   (d)

Fig. 3. Candidate building by combination of frequent patterns

The pattern combination step is not performed when $i = 2$ because there is no information available about the different temporal arrangements at this point. In this case, every candidate C_j^2 is a temporal association of two event types, and the corresponding frequent size-two patterns will be discovered in the frequency calculation step described in the next section.

3.3 Frequent Pattern Calculation

In the particular case $i = 2$ the procedure FREQUENCY_CALCULATION obtains frequent patterns of size two. These patterns are defined as constraints between pairs of event types that will be combined in later iterations to build candidates of greater size. The set C^2 contains temporal associations consisting of two event types. For every occurrence of a temporal association C_j^2 found in S, its temporal arrangement is stored in the frequency distribution δC_j^2, and the frequency of the arrangement in the interval $[-\omega, \omega]$ is increased by one. Then every frequency distribution is subject to a clustering technique in order to obtain a set of non-overlapping intervals $I_1, ..., I_m$ where the occurrences of each association concentrate. These intervals represent different constraints between the event types of C_j^2 and therefore different frequent patterns $P_j^2 = \{P_{j_1}^2, ..., P_{j_m}^2\}$ in P^2.

Any clustering algorithm that can be used for unidimensional domains could be used in this step. In our proposal, we have used an adaptation of the mountain method proposed in [7].

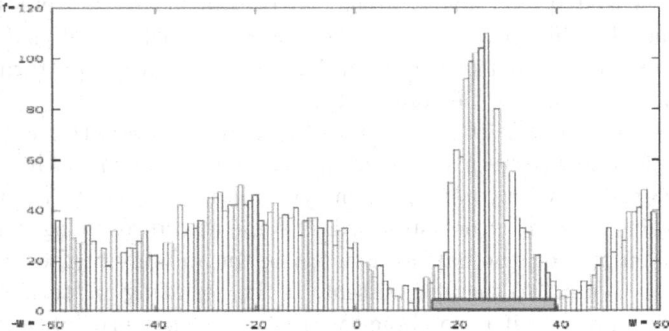

Fig. 4. Clustering of the frequency distribution of a temporal association

Figure 4 shows an example of the clustering process, where the method used conservatively identifies only one interval, because the rest of the maxima in the frequency distribution do not present a frequency similar to the global maximum.

In the general case $i > 2$ the candidates in C^i are patterns instead of associations. In this case, the procedure searches for occurrences of the candidate patterns in S and returns those candidates that were found to be frequent.

4   Computational Complexity Analysis

The computational complexity of these algorithms in every iteration i is calculated as follows:

```
procedure FREQUENCY_CALCULATION(Cⁱ,ω,fₘᵢₙ)
begin
   if i=2 then
      for C²ⱼ ∈C² do
         P² ← P² ∪ CLUSTERING(δC²ⱼ,fₘᵢₙ)
   else
      Pⁱ ← {Cⁱⱼ|Cⁱⱼ ∈Cⁱ ∧ f(Cⁱⱼ)≥fₘᵢₙ}
   return(Pⁱ)
end;
```

Fig. 5. Frequency calculation algorithm

- In the *temporal association generation* step, for a temporal association A^i_j to be frequent, first all of the i temporal associations $A^{i-1}_k \subset A^i_j$ must be frequent. A binary search among these frequent associations has a complexity of $O(log|A^{i-1}|)$. Taking into account the combination step, the complexity of generating all candidate temporal associations is $O(|A^{i-1}|i^2 log|A^{i-1}|)$. This result is slightly better than the approach in [4].
- In the *candidate generation* step, each of the $i(i-1)/2$ constraints of a temporal pattern P^i_{jk} is obtained by combining those patterns $P^{i-1}_{h_k}$ where $D^{i-1}_h \subset A^i_j$. The combination has a complexity of $O(i^2)$, with a maximum number of $\prod_h |P^{i-1}_h|$ possible combinations. Every combination is subject to a consistency check, which has a complexity of $O(i^3)$, resulting in a complexity of $O(|A^i|i^3 \prod_h |P^{i-1}_h|)$ for this step. This result is worse than that found in [4], because our approach is able to find more than just one temporal arrangement amongst a set of event types.
- In the worst case scenario, every time unit may present an occurrence of all p event types with a total of pn events in S. Every time the window is updated, p events enter the window and another p leave. Thus, for every pattern of size i up to $i\omega^{i-1}$ new occurrences may be found in every window update for every pattern. Checking that an occurrence fulfills all the constraints in a pattern has a complexity of $O(i^2)$. Considering that the number of candidate patterns is $|C^i|$, the overall complexity for this step is $O(n\omega^{i-1}i^3|C^i|)$.

5   Experimental Results

We have run several experiments using the algorithms proposed. The purpose of the experiments is to analyze the effect of the window size in the results and the scalability of the algorithms. The database used for our experiments consists of a collection of sequences of events found by inspection of polysomnograms of patients diagnosed with Sleep Apnea-Hypopnea Syndrome. Only the events regarding oxygen saturation decrease and increase, start and stop of an airflow limitation, start and stop of thoracic movement limitation, and start and stop of

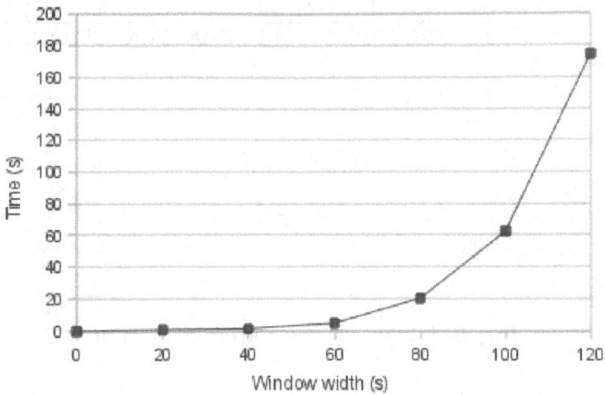

Fig. 6. Processing time required as a function of window width, with a frequency threshold of 30 occurrences

Table 1. Number of possible candidates, candidates generated and frequent patterns in the database; window width 80 s., frequency threshold 30

Pattern size	Possible candidates	Candidates generated	Frequent patterns
1	8	8	8
2	-	-	69
3	768	407	347
4	81543	737	684
5	$4'92 \cdot 10^6$	709	683
6	$1'08 \cdot 10^8$	385	379
7	$7'55 \cdot 10^8$	108	106
8	$8'14 \cdot 10^8$	12	12

abdominal movement limitation are considered, totalling over 18000 events and 34 hours of sleep for the whole collection[1].

Figure 6 shows the effect of the window width in the algorithms: the time required increases rapidly with the window width. It is well known in the domain that an airflow limitation may extend over a period of more than one minute, thus the window size in some of our tests must be higher than 60 seconds.

Table 1 presents the number of candidate and frequent patterns found using a window width of 80 seconds and a frequency threshold of 30 occurrences. The 'Possible candidates' column represents the number of all possible combinations of frequent patterns found in the previous iteration. 'Candidates generated' represents the number of consistent candidates from all 'Possible candidates'. 'Frequent patterns' shows the number of candidate patterns that were found to be frequent in 'Candidates generated'.

It is worth noting that one of the patterns of size 8 found by the algorithm is similar to the notion physicians have of an apnea episode. The episode starts with an airflow limitation, accompanied by the start of thoracic and abodminal movement limitations almost immediatly and, at least ten seconds later, oxygen

---
[1] http://www.gsi.dec.usc.es/datacollections/apnea

saturation decreases. Shortly after, airflow is resumed, as well as the thoracic and abdominal movements, followed by an oxygen saturation increase.

6   Conclusions and Future Work

A new Temporal Data Mining technique that searches for frequent temporal patterns in event sequences is proposed. Patterns found are represented with the STP formalism, as in [4]. The novelty of our proposal lies in the use of a clustering technique to find the constraints in the temporal arrangement between pairs of event types. This increases the expressiveness of the results, because the temporal patterns gather those event types that are commonly found with a similar temporal arrangement. The technique proposed in [4] results in one pattern for each set of event types, which may not fully represent the data analyzed when the same set of event types can be frequently found in several distinct temporal arrangements.

On the other hand, the algorithms proposed are intended to be computationally efficient. The costly computation of a large number of clusters of temporal patterns, involving metric contraints between growing sets of event types is avoided, and clustering is only carried out when searching for patterns of size two. While searching for bigger patterns, it is enough to combine frequent patterns found in the previous iteration, check their temporal consistency with a Floyd-Warshall algorithm, and finally check their frequency in the data.

Our immediate goal is to evaluate our technique in different kinds of databases. Preliminary results with both synthetic and real data are promising. Future work is oriented to introducing previous knowledge of the domain in the form of seed patterns. These patterns are defined by the user and allow him to prune the search process by focusing on the events surrounding the occurrences of the defined patterns.

References

1. Agrawal, R., Srikant, R.: Fast algorithms for mining association rules. In: Proc. 20th Int. Conf. Very Large Data Bases, pp. 487–499. Morgan Kaufmann, San Francisco (1994)
2. Agrawal, R., Srikant, R.: Mining sequential patterns. In: Eleventh International Conference on Data Engineering, pp. 3–14. IEEE Computer Society Press, Los Alamitos (1995)
3. Mannila, H., Toivonen, H., Verkamo, A.: Discovery of frequent episodes in event sequences. Data Mining and Knowledge Discovery 1(3), 259–289 (1997)
4. Dousson, C., Duong, T.: Discovering chronicles with numerical time constraints from alarm logs for monitoring dynamic systems. In: Proceedings of the Sixteenth International Joint Conference on Artificial Intelligence, pp. 620–626 (1999)
5. Dechter, R., Meiri, I., Pearl, J.: Temporal constraint networks. Artificial Intelligence 49, 61–95 (1991)
6. Lu, H., Feng, L., Han, J.: Beyond intratransaction association analysis: mining multidimensional intertransaction association rules. ACM Transaction on Information Systems 18(4), 423–454 (2000)
7. Yager, R., Filev, D.: Approximate clustering via the mountain method. IEEE Transactions on Systems, Man and Cybernetics 24(4), 1279–1284 (1994)

Analysis of the Time Evolution of Scientograms Using the Subdue Graph Mining Algorithm

Arnaud Quirin, Oscar Cordón, Prakash Shelokar, and Carmen Zarco

European Centre for Soft Computing,
Edf. Científico Tecnológico, 33600 Mieres, Spain
{arnaud.quirin,oscar.cordon,prakash.shelokar,carmen.zarco}
@softcomputing.es

Abstract. Scientograms are a kind of graph representations depicting the state of Science in a specific domain. The automatic comparison and analysis of a set of scientograms, to show for instance the evolution of a scientific domain of a given country, is an interesting but challenging task as the handled data is huge and complex. In this paper, we aim to show that graph mining tools are useful to deal with scientogram analysis. We have chosen Subdue, a well-known graph mining algorithm, as a first approach for this purpose. Its operation mode has been customized for the study of the evolution of a scientific domain over time. Our case study clearly shows the potential of graph mining tools in scientogram analysis and it opens the door for a large number of future developments.

1 Introduction

The generation of a map of sciences or *scientogram* has been a persistent idea in the modern ages. For instance, this could be achieved by the drawing of a graph linking together different scientific research fields, topics or categories, using the co-citation rate between the papers of these categories to denote the strength of the links. It has been a persistent idea as the visualization of such information graph has long been used to uncover and divulge the structure of Science [1,2]. However, analyzing scientific data is becoming increasingly difficult due to the vast volumes of data generated nowadays. Up to our knowledge, no previous fully automatic approaches have been designed to support the exploration of large datasets in scientogram mining.

In general, the current scientogram analysis techniques perform a low-level, non-automatic analysis and comparison of the maps [3,4,5]. To do so, they are based on statistical techniques and macro- and micro-structure analysis for the identification of thematic areas and scientific disciplines [6]. However, this approach shows a main limitation: only a single or a very reduced set of maps can be analyzed or compared together. In fact, the field lacks an easy-to-use approach allowing the identification and the comparison of scientific structures within scientograms with a higher degree of automation. In our study, graph mining tools are considered to perform a higher level analysis, allowing the joint comparison of a larger number of maps (i.e., performing *scientogram mining*). Thanks to

E. Hüllermeier, R. Kruse, and F. Hoffmann (Eds.): IPMU 2010, LNAI 6178, pp. 310–319, 2010.

that, the novel high-level analysis methodology introduced in the current contribution and the existing low-level approaches can be used as complementary frameworks for the analysis and comparison of scientograms.

Graph-based data mining (GBDM) [7] involves the automatic extraction of novel and useful knowledge from a graph representation of data. It has been applied for frequent substructure discovery and graph matching in a large number of domains including chemistry and applied biology, classification of chemical compounds, and unsupervised and supervised pattern learning, among many others. In particular, the first proposal in the topic, Subdue [8], based on the use of the minimum description length (MDL) principle [9], has proved to be successful in many different real-world applications. Since the MDL principle allows the discovery of both large and frequent substructures we think that Subdue, as well as any other GBDM technique based on the same idea (i.e., frequent subgraph mining), is well recommended for scientogram analysis.

The structure of the current contribution is as follows. In the second section, we review the current techniques to design and analyze scientograms as well as the current state of the art of GBDM and the particular case of the Subdue algorithm. In the third section we show how a scientogram analysis task, the study of the evolution of a scientific domain over time, can be performed by means of this algorithm. The fourth section presents the obtained results. Finally, some concluding remarks and future works are pointed out in the last section.

2 Preliminaries

In this section we will present a state of the art of the current techniques used to design and analyze scientograms, as well as a review of the GBDM field, describing its scope and the most known techniques.

2.1 Scientogram Design

The generation of a scientogram following a top-down approach based on the existence of a previous document category structure requires the sequential application of several techniques. The scientograms considered in this contribution are built following De Moya-Anegón et al.'s methodology [10,5]. The SCOPUS-SJR co-citation categories are used as units of analysis. Each category agglutinates the journals that were categorized under that name, and likewise the documents that were published in those journals. A co-citation measure is used to compute the relational similarity between two categories i and j. It is defined as $CM(ij) = Cc(ij) + \frac{Cc(ij)}{\sqrt{c(i) \cdot c(j)}}$, where Cc is the co-citation frequency and c is the citation frequency. The Pathfinder algorithm [11,12] is considered to prune the co-citation matrix. As a result, only the salient relationships between categories are kept, capturing the essential underlying intellectual structure of the studied scientific domain. The pruned network is then graphically represented using the Kamada-Kawai's graph drawing algorithm [13], chosen for its ability to represent naturally the most important elements in the center of the representation (called the scientogram *backbone*).

The rough considered data have been extracted from the Scimago Journal & Country Rank portal[1] (SCOPUS-SJR data) [5]. In this contribution, we will deal with the United States and the Ukrainian maps from 1996 to 2005, based on respectively 4 307 536 and 74 248 documents. Overall, the 20 scientograms used have 4991 nodes and 5304 edges.

2.2   Graph-Based Data Mining and the Subdue Algorithm

The need of mining structural data to uncover objects or concepts that relate objects (i.e., subgraphs that represent associations of features) has increased in the past decade, thus creating the area of GBDM [7]. Nowadays, many GBDM algorithms (Apriori-based GM, Frequent Subgraph Discovery, MoFa/MoSS, etc.) have been proposed to deal with problems such as graph matching, graph visualization, frequent substructure discovery, conceptual clustering, and unsupervised and supervised pattern learning [14].

Among them, we can highlight Subdue [8], a graph-based knowledge discovery system that finds structural, relational patterns in data representing entities and relationships. This algorithm was the first proposal in the topic and has been largely extended through the years. It uses the MDL principle [9] to discover interesting and repetitive (frequent) substructures in a structural database (DB), extract them and replace them by a single node in order to compress the DB. These extracted substructures represent structural concepts in the data. Through the years, it has been successfully applied to a large range of real-world problems such as aviation, chemistry, geology, counter-terrorism, bioinformatics, and web structure mining.

Fig. 1 shows the outline of the Subdue GBDM algorithm. It takes as input the original graph DB (comprised by a single graph or a set of graphs) from which the substructures (i.e. subgraphs) have to be extracted and four parameters used to limit the search while reducing the runtime. These parameters (*BeamWidth*, *MaxBest*, *MaxSubSize*, and *Limit*) constrain the number of considered substructures and the total number of iterations of the algorithm. ChildList and BestList are two ordered lists in which the substructures having the best evaluation values appear first which guide the beam search process applied. The algorithm ends up by returning the best substructures found considering the chosen evaluation measure and the constraint parameters.

The evaluation of a substructure (see line 13) can be computed by different measures, but the MDL-measure is the most popular. It measures how well a substructure can compress the entire dataset. Hence, the algorithm aims to maximize the following measure: $value_{MDLi}(S, G) = \frac{I(G)}{I(S) + I(G|S)}$ where G is the input graph, S is the candidate substructure, $I(G)$ and $I(S)$ are the number of bits required to encode G and S, and $I(G|S)$ is the number of bits required to encode the graph obtained by compressing G with S, i.e. substituting each occurrence of S in G by a single node.

---

[1] http://www.scimagojr.com/

```
1.  Subdue(Graph, BeamWidth, MaxBest, MaxSubSize, Limit)
2.      ParentList = {Vertex v | v has a unique label in Graph}
3.      Evaluate each vertex in ParentList
4.      ChildList = {}
5.      BestList = {}
6.      ProcessedSubs = 0
7.      WHILE ProcessedSubs ≤ Limit and ParentList ≠ ∅ DO
8.          WHILE ParentList ≠ ∅ DO
9.              Parent = RemoveHead(ParentList)
10.             CandidateList = ExtendSubstructure(Parent)
11.             FOR EACH Child ∈ CandidateList DO
12.                 IF SizeOf(Child) ≤ MaxSubSize THEN
13.                     Evaluate the Child
14.                     Insert Child in ChildList in order by value
15.                     ChildList = ChildList mod BeamWidth
16.             ProcessedSubs = ProcessedSubs+1
17.             Insert Parent in BestList in order by value
18.             BestList = BestList mod MaxBest
19.         Switch ParentList and ChildList
20.     Return BestList
```

Fig. 1. The Subdue GBDM algorithm (reprinted from [8])

3   Subdue for Scientogram Analysis. Case Study: Evolution of a Scientific Domain over Time

The application of Subdue as a powerful scientogram analysis tool will rely on its frequent subgraph mining activity (i.e., we will perform scientogram mining). Since the underlying scientogram structure is a social network (i.e., a graph), the uncovering of common subgraphs (named *Common Research Categories Substructures* or CRCSs in the following) to different scientograms in an automatic fashion can provide the information analyst with very useful information to explore the characteristics of the scientific domains represented. The latter capability can be applied to many different scientogram analysis and comparison tasks. In the current contribution we have considered the use of Subdue to study the evolution of the scientific domain of a single country over time. The considered Subdue implementation is that made by the original authors, available at http://ailab.wsu.edu/subdue/.

Note that, by maximizing the MDLi measure, the optimization of two criteria is jointly considered within Subdue:

- on the one hand, the measure highlights large substructures as a better compression rate (or better MDLi value) is obtained when a bigger substructure can be extracted and replaced (compressed) by a single node;
- on the other hand, the measure highlights substructures having a large support (the support of a substructure is the number of occurrences of this

substructure in the DB) as a better compression rate is obtained when many substructures are replaced (compressed) by a single node.

In our case, the graph DB G on which Subdue is applied is generally a single set of scientograms. However, the alternative operation mode for Subdue considers two distinct sets, a positive set G_p and a negative set G_n, determined by the user. In this operation mode, the goal of Subdue is to find the largest substructures present in the maximum number of graphs in the positive set, which are not included in the negative set. The MDLi measure is thus computed as follows:

$$value_{MDLi}(S, G_p, G_n) = \frac{I(G_p) + I(G_n)}{I(S) + I(G_p|S) + I(G_n) - I(G_n|S)} \tag{1}$$

The use of negative maps allows the user to consider a given discriminative criterion. For instance, for a given country, we can consider the scientograms of a given (historical) time period as a positive set, and the remaining scientograms as a negative set, to extract relevant information about the substructures appearing or disappearing during this historical transition.

When considering the latter analysis of the evolution of a scientific domain through time, an information science expert would be interested in knowing which substructures appear in the analyzed domain, at which time, how big they are, how many they are, where are they located, and so forth. This will allow him to perform at least two kind of studies. On the one hand, an in-deep analysis of the uncovered substructures themselves, which kind of categories are they linking, etc. On the other hand, the study of some global statistics about the size and the quantity of these substructures to respectively characterize the importance of the evolution of the domain and its dynamics. This could be very helpful to perform domain comparison or domain evolution analysis [5].

To do so, a scientific domain is first chosen. In our study, the scientific production of a whole country is considered. As we want to look for CRCSs which were appearing at a given time, we also need to pick two ranges of years, the positive range and the negative range. The negative range is usually a set of years from the past, in which these substructures (i.e. CRCSs) are not meant to exist. The positive range is usually a set of years dated after the negative range, in which the substructures are meant to be present. Subdue's MDLi evaluation criterion in equation (1) will be considered for this aim. As Subdue will be run to extract the substructures present in the maps of the positive years but not in the maps of the negative years, it will effectively uncover the CRCSs that appeared at least once during the positive years.

4   Experiments and Analysis of Results

Two countries have been selected for this case study, Ukraine and United States. The ten scientograms corresponding to the 1996-2005 period are considered for each country. We have set up the parameters of Subdue so that it finds the best 300 substructures regarding their MDLi-based evaluation, considering a

BeamWidth of 4 to allow small response times. We performed our tests on an Intel Quad-Core 2.40 GHz CPU with 2 GB of memory, obtaining a computation time inferior to 3 seconds. In all the following discussions the substructure support is reported using two values (such as 3:4, for instance), with the first number being the support in the positive set (corresponding to the scientograms in the positive years), and the second number being the support in the negative set (corresponding to the scientograms in the negative years). We consider a substructure having a larger positive support and a smaller negative support as having a better quality. In the same way, substructures having a larger size are preferred over smaller ones as they are more specific.

Table 1. Support and size of the substructures extracted from the Ukrainian dataset

Support (pos:neg)	#subs.	Size (nodes)			Size (edges)		
		min	max	avg	min	max	avg
1:1	10	3	8	5.6	2	7	4.6
2:0	6	1	1	1	0	0	0
2:1	2	1	2	1.5	0	1	0.5
2:2	3	1	1	1	0	0	0
2:4	1	1	1	1	0	0	0
3:0	3	1	1	1	0	0	0
3:1	71	1	23	14.63	0	22	13.63
3:2	7	1	5	2.57	0	4	1.57
3:3	11	1	4	1.55	0	3	0.55
3:4	13	1	1	1	0	0	0
3:5	23	1	2	1.04	0	1	0.04
3:6	32	1	2	1.03	0	1	0.03
3:7	118	1	1	1	0	0	0
TOT.	300			4.45			3.45

First of all, we will look the Ukrainian scientograms domain with 7 negative years (between 1996 and 2002) and 3 positive years (between 2003 and 2005). Table 1 shows the global statistics of the 300 substructures found for this experiment. The substructures have very diverse size, ranging from 1 to 23 nodes and from 0 to 22 edges. Substructures having only one node are the most common (a 70% of the total). Among them, 3 substructures have the optimal support of 3:0. These nodes are respectively *Leadership and Management, Philosophy*, and *Media Technology*, indicating the Ukraine-based researchers developed research in these categories exclusively after 2003. On the other hand, 71 substructures were found with a support of 3:1, among them 5 have the maximal size of 23 nodes. Overall, the most interesting substructures, those having a null negative support as well as the largest ones, are not numerous, thus allowing an expert to quickly browse and analyze all of them.

As an example, Fig. 2 shows one of these substructures comprised by 23 nodes and 22 edges, and its location within the full scientogram of the Ukrainian scientific production in 2005. As can be seen, this substructure is quite large and appears only during the last three years (actually the negative support of 1 comes from the fact that it also appears in the scientogram of 1998). This large substructure has in fact two main clusters, *Biochemistry* and *Physics and Astronomy*, suggesting the research focuses on these topics during the three last years. It occupies the center of the map, where the backbone of the Ukrainian research is concentrated. Note also that, even if *Biochemistry* occupies in general

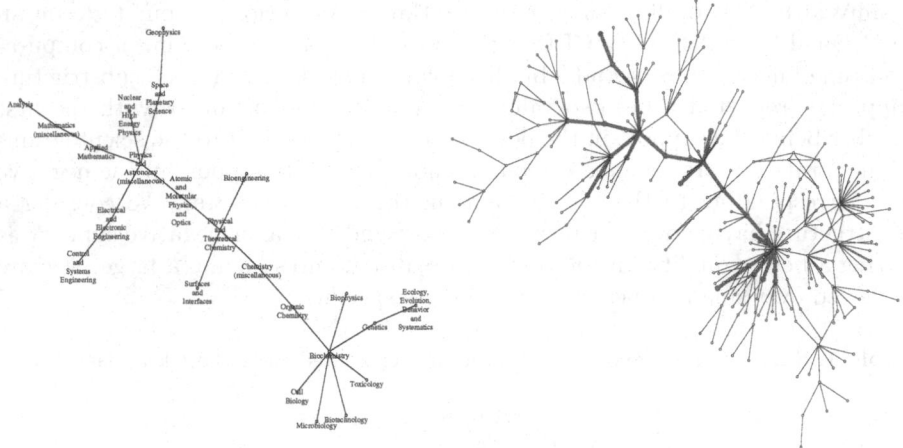

Fig. 2. One of the substructures uncovered in Ukrainian scientograms during period 2003-2005 (on the left), and its location within the 2005 scientogram (on the right)

the central part of the scientograms [5], it could perfectly appear at any location in an extracted substructure, or even not appear at all, depending on how the maps are compared together and if this node is relevant given the chosen criterion.

Table 2. Support and size of the substructures extracted from the USA dataset

Support (pos:neg)	#subs.	Size (nodes)			Size (edges)		
		min	max	avg	min	max	avg
1:2	2	2	3	2.5	1	2	1.5
2:0	8	1	1	1	0	0	0
2:1	32	4	13	9.41	3	12	8.41
3:0	3	1	1	1	0	0	0
3:2	3	1	1	1	0	0	0
3:3	7	4	6	5	3	5	4
3:4	1	1	1	1	0	0	0
3:7	244	1	4	1.05	0	3	0.05
TOT.	**300**			**2.04**			**1.04**

On the other hand, exploring what happens in the United States for the same period shows us that significantly more smallest substructures are highlighted (see Table 2). 300 substructures have been extracted, ranging from 1 to 13 nodes and from 0 to 12 edges, having an average size of 2 nodes instead of 4.5 nodes as in the Ukrainian case. Three substructures were obtained with the best maximum support (that is, 3:0), but they are similar to those observed in the Ukrainian domain, as they only have one node. Fig. 3 shows three more interesting substructures, all of them having a support of 2:1 and a size of only 13 nodes. We interpret that differences in the form of smaller substructures is an evidence of countries having a more stable research infrastructure.

In order to have a deeper insight of the data, we have conducted another study in which the time range is not fixed by the user, but it is defined by moving

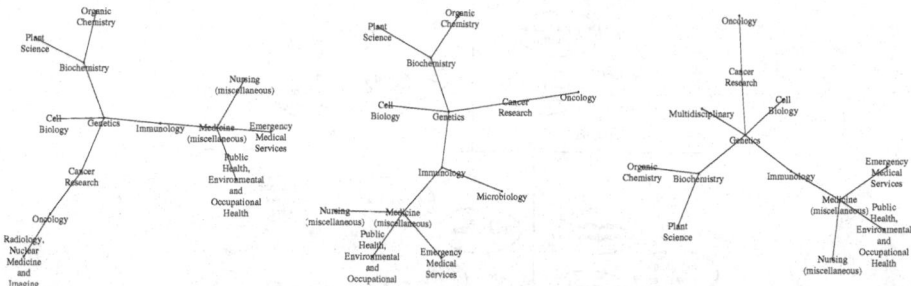

Fig. 3. Some substructures uncovered in the USA scientograms during years 2003-2005

windows. We start with five negative years and two positive years, and we add a new positive year and remove the oldest negative year at each step.

Table 3. Support and size for some substructures extracted from the United States dataset using a moving window of two positive years

Year ranges		Support	#inst.	Size (nodes)		
(negative)	(positive)	(pos:neg)		min	max	avg
1996-1999	2000-2001	2:0	3	1	1	1
1996-1999	2000-2001	2:1	1	1	1	1
1996-2000	2001-2002	2:0	3	1	1	1
1996-2000	2001-2002	2:1	55	3	15	8.82
1996-2001	2002-2003	2:1	3	1	1	1
1996-2002	2003-2004	2:0	3	1	1	1
1996-2003	2004-2005	2:0	8	1	1	1
1996-2003	2004-2005	2:1	32	1	11	8.69

As a matter of comparison with the previous study, we will use the United States dataset to detect smaller changes within the years. Many substructures are extracted following this approach, but we kept only those corresponding to a support of 2:1 or 2:0, i.e. the maximal possible support for this experiment. Table 3 presents some statistics for this experiment. In general, all the uncovered substructures present a small size, ranging from 1 to 15 nodes but being equal to 1 in a 79% of the cases. All the substructures having a support of 2:0 are presented in Fig. 4. These substructures are small as they are composed of only one node. However, even if they are independent, some relationships could be found between them. For instance, during period 2001-2002 research areas focused on care, diagnosis, and emergency are found. During period 2004-2005, more research areas focused on medical specialities (orthodontics, periodontics, oral surgery, pharmacology, etc.) made their apparition.

We should also remark an unusual fact, the high number of instances obtained considering periods 2001-2002 and 2004-2005 with a support of 2:1. We respectively obtained 55 and 32 substructures for those periods, two quite large numbers when compared with the remaining statistics. During these periods, the research in the United States evolved enough to produce a lot of changes in the corresponding maps. These concerned categories mainly belong to the medical domain, such as *Emergency Nursing, Care Planning, Oral Surgery, Orthodontics,*

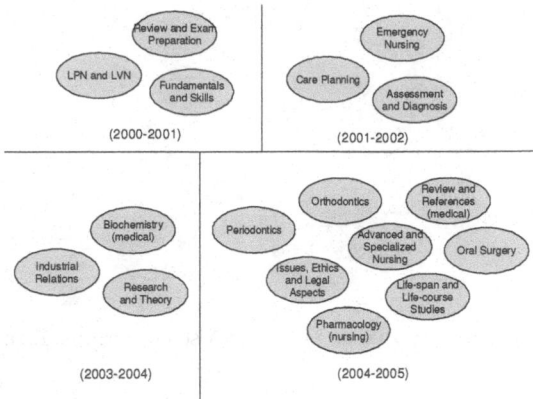

Fig. 4. Some substructures which appear repeatedly between 2000 and 2005 in the USA scientograms

etc. Note also that only an automatic approach can quickly find and highlight those periods with larger changes.

In view of the developed experiments, we can say that Subdue is a useful tool to identify the new CRCSs in a given country and during a given set of years. By looking into the specific research topics developed from one year to another, or even looking at the global statistics, one can figure out some relevant information about the evolution of research in that country. Notice how the extracted substructures are not always located in the scientogram backbone but in other different parts of the map, thus making the use of Subdue become a complementary analysis tool to the existing low-level approaches.

5   Conclusions

In this paper, we showed how a GBDM technique, namely Subdue, can be successfully applied to the complex task of scientogram analysis and comparison. The scientific domains of two countries have been processed to study the evolution of research during time by extracting some interesting substructures as well as some statistical parameters.

This methodology is scalable and it will not suffer if applied to an increased volume of data. It has been shown that the generation of the graph visualizations, graph highlights (see Fig. 2), tables, and histograms is fully automatic. Even if only the Subdue algorithm was used in this proposal, other GBDM algorithms can be considered. For these reasons, GBDM can be viewed as a novel scientogram analysis tool developed in complement to the current state-of-the-art techniques. In the future, we plan to use other GBDM techniques (notably multiobjective-optimization-based ones) and discover other uses of Subdue for the analysis and comparison of scientograms.

Acknowledgments

This work has been supported by the Spanish Ministerio de Ciencia e Innovación under project TIN2009-07727, including EDRF fundings. We would like to thank Elsevier and Drs. Félix De Moya-Anegón and Benjamín Vargas-Quesada for their permission to use the SCOPUS-SJR data to build the scientograms.

References

1. Börner, K., Scharnhorst, A.: Visual conceptualizations and models of science. Journal of Informetrics 3(3), 161–172 (2009)
2. Chen, C.: Information Visualization: Beyond the Horizon. Springer, Berlin (2004)
3. Chen, C., Chen, Y., Horowitz, H., Hou, H., Liu, Z., Pellegrino, D.: Towards an explanatory and computational theory of scientific discovery. Journal of Informetrics 3(3), 191–209 (2009)
4. Leydesdorff, L., Rafols, I.: A global map of science based on the ISI subject categories. Journal of the American Society for Information Science and Technology 60(2), 348–362 (2009)
5. Vargas-Quesada, B., Moya-Anegón, F.D.: Visualizing the Structure of Science. Springer, New York (2007)
6. Wallace, M.L., Gingras, Y., Duhon, R.: A new approach for detecting scientific specialties from raw cocitation networks. Journal of the American Society for Information Science and Technology 60(2), 240–246 (2009)
7. Washio, T., Motoda, H.: State of the art of graph-based data mining. SIGKDD Explorations 5(1), 59–68 (2003)
8. Cook, D.J., Holder, L.B.: Graph-based data mining. IEEE Intelligent Systems 15(2), 32–41 (2000)
9. Rissanen, J.: Stochastic Complexity in Statistical Inquiry Theory. World Scientific Publishing Co., Inc., River Edge (1989)
10. Moya-Anegón, F.D., Vargas-Quesada, B., Herrero-Solana, V., Chinchilla-Rodríguez, Z., Corera-Álvarez, E., Munoz-Fernández, F.J.: A new technique for building maps of large scientific domains based on the cocitation of classes and categories. Scientometrics 61(1), 129–145 (2004)
11. Dearholt, D., Schvaneveldt, R.: Properties of Pathfinder networks. In: Schvaneveldt, R. (ed.) Pathfinder Associative Networks: Studies in Knowledge Organization, pp. 1–30. Ablex Publishing Corporation, Greenwich (1990)
12. Quirin, A., Cordón, O., Guerrero-Bote, V.P., Vargas-Quesada, B., Moya-Anegón, F.D.: A quick MST-based algorithm to obtain Pathfinder networks. Journal of the American Society for Information Science and Technology 59(12), 1912–1924 (2008)
13. Kamada, T., Kawai, S.: An algorithm for drawing general undirected graphs. Information Processing Letters 31(1), 7–15 (1989)
14. Cook, D.J., Holder, L.B. (eds.): Mining Graph Data. Wiley, New Jersey (2006)

Short-Time Prediction Based on Recognition of Fuzzy Time Series Patterns

Gernot Herbst and Steffen F. Bocklisch

Chemnitz University of Technology, D-09107 Chemnitz, Germany
gernot.herbst@etit.tu-chemnitz.de

Abstract. This article proposes knowledge-based short-time prediction methods for multivariate streaming time series, relying on the early recognition of local patterns. A parametric, well-interpretable model for such patterns is presented, along with an online, classification-based recognition procedure. Subsequently, two options are discussed to predict time series employing the fuzzified pattern knowledge, accompanied by an example. Special emphasis is placed on comprehensible models and methods, as well as an easy interface to data mining algorithms.

1 Introduction

Predicting "nasty" time series (instationary, multivariate etc.—stemming from nonlinear dynamic processes) based on a *global* model, such as difference equations, resembles a David-sized answer to a Goliath-like problem, with questionable success in the general case, though. In many real-world time series, however, we may observe patterns that recur not in identical, but similar form according to a regular or irregular scheme, often due to the diversity of loose or strict rhythms and periodicities inherent in the gamut of many natural or social processes. A modest but sound answer to time series prediction might therefore lie in gaining data-based *local* knowledge of a process and employing this for predictions later on. In the following, an approach to the latter shall be outlined which explicitly allows for the fundamental uncertainty attached to this task.

2 Fuzzy Time Series Patterns

2.1 A Multivariate Parametric Fuzzy Set

The elementary approach for modelling time series patterns followed in this paper is a sample-point-wise model using fuzzy sets for each sample. In order to cope with multivariate time series, a suitable multivariate fuzzy set from [1] will be introduced beforehand. A rather unique feature of this set is that it can be derived in parametric form from an intersection of univariate parametric fuzzy sets of the following type:

$$\mu(x) = \frac{1}{1 + \left(\frac{1}{b_{l/r}} - 1\right) \cdot \left|\frac{x - r}{c_{l/r}}\right|^{d_{l/r}}} \quad \text{with} \quad \begin{cases} b_l, c_l, d_l & \text{for} \quad x < r \\ b_r, c_r, d_r & \text{for} \quad x \geq r \end{cases} \quad (1)$$

E. Hüllermeier, R. Kruse, and F. Hoffmann (Eds.): IPMU 2010, LNAI 6178, pp. 320–329, 2010.

The effect of r and the side-specific parameters b and c can be understood from Fig. 1a. While $c_{l/r} > 0$ quantify the uncertainty (as in crisp sets), $b_{l/r} \in (0,1]$ and $d_{l/r} \geq 2$ account for the fuzziness of this uncertain information, where increasing values of $d_{l/r}$ lead to sharper descents of the membership value to zero and $d_{l/r} \to \infty$ result in rectangular (crisp) sets. For the multivariate extension, N fuzzy sets of this type are being combined using a compensatory HAMACHER intersection (2), resulting in an N-dimensional parametric membership function $\mu \colon \mathbb{R}^N \mapsto (0,1]$, cf. (3). Exemplary sets for $N = 2$ are shown in Fig. 1b.

$$\bigcap_{\text{Ham}}^N \mu_i = \left(\frac{1}{N} \sum_{i=1}^N \frac{1}{\mu_i} \right)^{-1} \tag{2}$$

$$\mu(\boldsymbol{x}) = \left(1 + \frac{1}{2N} \sum_{i=1}^N [1 - \operatorname{sgn}(x_i - r_i)] \cdot \left(\frac{1}{b_{li}} - 1 \right) \cdot \left| \frac{x_i - r_i}{c_{li}} \right|^{d_{li}} \right.$$
$$\left. + \frac{1}{2N} \sum_{i=1}^N [1 + \operatorname{sgn}(x_i - r_i)] \cdot \left(\frac{1}{b_{ri}} - 1 \right) \cdot \left| \frac{x_i - r_i}{c_{ri}} \right|^{d_{ri}} \right)^{-1} \tag{3}$$

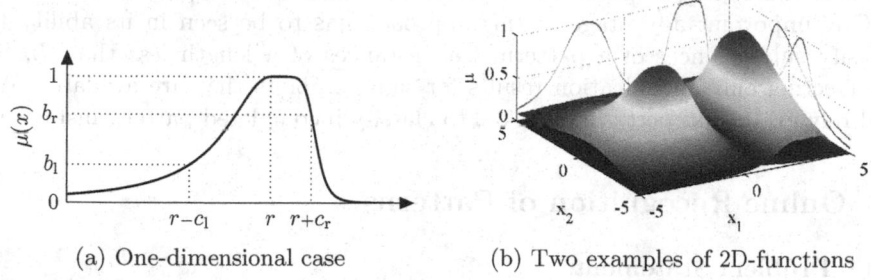

(a) One-dimensional case   (b) Two examples of 2D-functions

Fig. 1. The multivariate parametric membership function (3)

2.2   Modelling and Classification of Time Series Patterns

Equation (3) can now be employed to model equidistantly sampled multivariate time series patterns. For a pattern of length L (sample points), L membership functions are being used and result in a progression of fuzzy sets that can be interpreted and displayed as a fuzzy corridor for instances of the respective pattern, cf. Fig. 2. We will denote the fuzzy set for the t-th sample point of a pattern by $\mu_{P,t}(\boldsymbol{x})$. With (3) being an unimodal function, the mean course of a pattern is therefore being captured along with the uncertainty in its realisations.

The parameters of the fuzzy sets $\mu_{P,t}$ may either be formulated by experts, or—as described in [2]—determined automatically from sets of pattern instances. The latter case is especially suited for joint use with time series motif mining algorithms, e. g. [6], with the sole assumption that instances of one pattern are equal in length and similar in the fuzzy sense of our model.

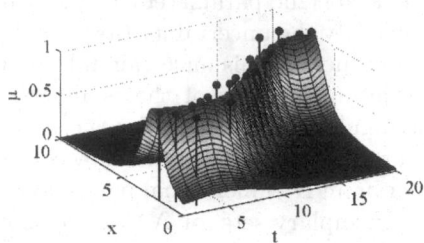

Fig. 2. Fuzzy time series pattern along with a noisy candidate sequence

To classify whole time series $x(1), \ldots, x(L)$ of the same length as the fuzzy model given by $\mu_{P,1}(x), \ldots, \mu_{P,L}(x)$, it is only necessary to combine the individual (elementary) classification results for all samples $x(t)$ in their respective classes $\mu_{P,t}(x)$:

$$\mu = \mu_{P,1}(x(1)) \cap \ldots \cap \mu_{P,L}(x(L)) \tag{4}$$

If (2) is being used for the operator $\cap$ again, we essentially obtain an $(N \cdot L)$-dimensional fuzzy classifier as a natural extension of the multivariate set (3), i. e. with the same parametric structure and mode of operation. Figure 2 gives a visual example of a classifier for a univariate time series sequence.

One important advantage of this approach has to be seen in its ability to classify subsequences of a pattern, i. e. instances of a length less than L, by intersecting only classification results for sample points that are available. We will rely on this property in Sect. 3.2 to classify incompleted pattern instances.

3   Online Recognition of Patterns

3.1   Problem Statement

In a context of streaming time series, with one new datum $x(t)$ being available at each point in time t, we want to be able to recognise previously known local patterns (each of them modelled by the fuzzy means introduced in Sect. 2.2) in an online manner. If we are able to detect a pattern before it is completed (say, at a stage $\tau < L$), a short-time prediction can be derived based upon the knowledge still "left" for the pattern's $(L - \tau)$ remaining sample points.

If we consequently follow a fuzzy approach, however, a recognition system will (and should) recognise every known pattern in every possible stage of development, all at the same time. Although this wealth of information will obviously have to be narrowed down to usable "key" information later on, we will show how to work with and modify the recognition results before. On the other hand, this calls for a recognition approach with computational requirements which are not prohibitive, while still delivering every possible recognition result.

3.2   Motivation for Recursive Equations

At any point in time t, a pattern instance in a streaming time series $x(t)$ may be present and will, due to the fuzzy approach to pattern recognition, be detected in every possible stage $\tau = 1, \ldots, L$. We will denote the classification result for an incompleted pattern at stage τ by $\mu(t, \tau)$, which means that L such results form the complete recognition result for a pattern at one point in time t. For every possible value of τ, $\mu(t, \tau)$ can be computed as given by (5).

$$\mu(t, \tau) = \mu_{P,1}(x(t - \tau + 1)) \cap \ldots \cap \mu_{P,\tau}(x(t)), \quad \tau = 1, \ldots, L \quad (5)$$

Unfortunately, this also means that $\sum_{i=1}^{L} i = \frac{1}{2} L \cdot (L+1)$ elementary classification results $\mu_{P,1\ldots L}$ would have to be computed at every time step. If we compare previous recognition results $\mu(t - 1, \tau)$ against the current results $\mu(t, \tau)$, however, it can be noticed that some of them share almost all elementary classification results, as depicted in Fig. 3a. More precisely, $\mu(t, \tau)$ could be recursively derived from $\mu(t - 1, \tau - 1)$ by incorporating $\mu_{P,\tau}(x(t))$, as shown in (6). As a consequence, only L elementary classification results $\mu_{P,1\ldots L}$ would have to be computed at each point in time to update the recognition results. This equals the computational cost of detecting only completed patterns by using (4), i.e. there is no computational overhead regarding elementary classification steps to obtain recognition results for incompleted patterns at every possible stage.

$$\mu(t, \tau) = \underbrace{[\mu_{P,1}(x(t - \tau + 1)) \cap \ldots \cap \mu_{P,\tau-1}(x(t - 1))]}_{\mu(t-1, \tau-1)} \cap \mu_{P,\tau}(x(t)) \quad (6)$$

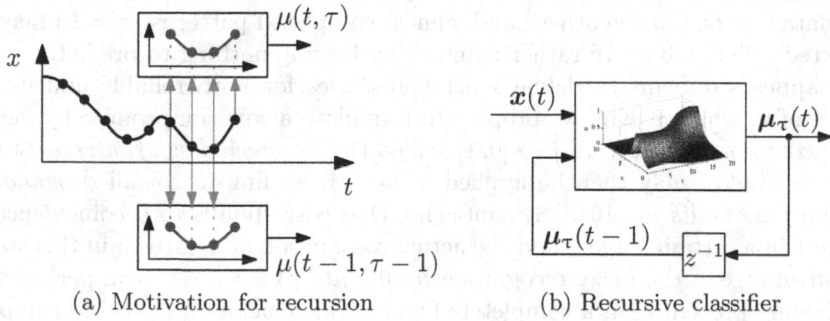

(a) Motivation for recursion   (b) Recursive classifier

Fig. 3. Recursive classification (recognition) of time series patterns

3.3   Update Equations for Recursive Pattern Recognition

In order to derive a recursive equation for $\mu(t, \tau)$ like (6), which must deliver equivalent results compared to the non-recursive equation (5), an intersection operator $\cap$ is needed which preserves the weight of the left- and right-hand side truth values, as $\mu(t - 1, \tau - 1)$ is already the result of the intersection of $(\tau - 1)$ truth values. In [3] we showed how to extend the compensatory HAMACHER intersection (2) to a weighted conjunction (7) preserving given weights as needed here. This allows to reformulate (6) to (8).

$$\mu_a \; {}^{N_a} \cap {}^{N_b} \; \mu_b = \frac{1}{\dfrac{1}{N_a + N_b}\left(\dfrac{N_a}{\mu_a} + \dfrac{N_b}{\mu_b}\right)} \tag{7}$$

$$\mu(t, \tau) = \mu(t-1, \tau-1) \; {}^{(\tau-1)} \cap {}^{1} \; \mu_{P,\tau}(\boldsymbol{x}(t)) \tag{8}$$

If we rearrange the pattern recognition results $\mu(t, \tau) \; \forall \tau$ in a vector $\boldsymbol{\mu}_\tau(t)$, the elementary classification results of $\boldsymbol{x}(t)$ to all classes $\mu_{P,1\ldots L}$ in $\boldsymbol{\mu}_P(\boldsymbol{x}(t))$, and define a vector of weights $\boldsymbol{n}_\tau$,

$$\boldsymbol{\mu}_\tau(t) = \begin{pmatrix} \mu_{\tau,1}(t) \\ \vdots \\ \mu_{\tau,L}(t) \end{pmatrix} = \begin{pmatrix} \mu(t,1) \\ \vdots \\ \mu(t,L) \end{pmatrix}, \; \boldsymbol{\mu}_P(\boldsymbol{x}(t)) = \begin{pmatrix} \mu_{P,1}(\boldsymbol{x}(t)) \\ \vdots \\ \mu_{P,L}(\boldsymbol{x}(t)) \end{pmatrix}, \; \boldsymbol{n}_\tau = \begin{pmatrix} 0 \\ 1 \\ \vdots \\ L-1 \end{pmatrix},$$

we can—as done in [3]—obtain a vectorial update equation for the recursive classifier depicted in Fig. 3b:

$$\boldsymbol{\mu}_\tau(t) = \left(\begin{pmatrix} 1 \\ 0 \end{pmatrix} + \begin{pmatrix} \boldsymbol{0}^T & 0 \\ \boldsymbol{I} & 0 \end{pmatrix} \cdot \boldsymbol{\mu}_\tau(t-1) \right) \; {}^{\boldsymbol{n}_\tau} \cap {}^{1} \; \boldsymbol{\mu}_P(\boldsymbol{x}(t)) \tag{9}$$

3.4 Post-processing of Recognition Results

For prediction purposes, early recognition results $\mu(t, \tau)$ with $\tau \ll L$ promise the largest prediction horizon, but are quite unreliable, as based on only very few data points. On the other hand, almost completed patterns ($\tau \approx L$) may be detected reliably, but are rather pointless by leaving nothing to predict.

It appears difficult to define strict boundaries for both reliable and usable values of τ, which is why we propose to formulate a soft compromise by means of a fuzzy set $\mu_w : \{1, \ldots, L\} \mapsto [0, 1]$, called the *fuzzy window of interest* w.r.t. τ. This window may then be applied to $\mu(t, \tau)$, leading to so-called *windowed recognition results* in (10).[1] Semantically, (10) corresponds to a coincidence of interest in a certain stage τ and the actual recognition of a pattern in this stage. An advantage of the fuzzy recognition results $\mu(t, \tau)$ is that we can perfom this windowing procedure in a completely fuzzy manner before any decision step.

$$\tilde{\mu}(t, \tau) = \mu(t, \tau) \cap \mu_w(\tau) \quad \forall \tau \tag{10}$$

When these results shall serve as a rationale for concrete actions such as predictions, however, crisp values for the similarity and stage of the detected pattern will often be necessary. For the time being, we will employ a first-of-maxima (FOM) approach to the defuzzification of $\tilde{\mu}(t, \tau)$ to obtain crisp results $\tilde{\mu}^*$ and τ^* at every point in time.

---

[1] Non-compensatory intersections (such as all T-norm operators) should be employed for $\cap$ in (10). In this paper, the HAMACHER product will be used.

4   Pattern-Based Short-Time Prediction

As soon as one or more evolving patterns are being detected in a streaming time series (resulting in $\tilde{\mu}^*$ and τ^* as described in the previous section), a short-time prediction of the time series can be provided for a horizon of $(L-\tau^*)$ samples for every detected pattern. While the fuzzy recognition system will be able to detect any pattern at any time, dissimilar pattern instances (with small values of $\tilde{\mu}^*$) will obviously not form a good foundation for predictions and should therefore be neglected, i. e. by requiring $\tilde{\mu}^*$ to pass a certain threshold. Subsequently, two prediction methods will be presented which work with *one* detected pattern; the combination of several of these predictions will be discussed afterwards.

4.1   Prediction Methods

(I) Knowledge-based prediction based on a pattern's mean course. Given the fuzzy time series model of Sect. 2.2 and especially its visual representation in Fig. 2, it almost suggests itself to base a prediction of a detected, but not yet completed pattern (stage τ^*) on its mean course. In the underlying fuzzy sets from Sect. 2.1, this corresponds to the modal parameters r in (3) for each sample point. For a prediction horizon p, $1 \le p \le L-\tau^*$, we can simply use these values for a prediction of the time series x beyond time t:

$$\hat{x}(t+p) = r(\tau^* + p) \tag{11}$$

(II) Extrapolating prediction based on fuzzy implication. While this method from [7] was first and foremost designed for univariate ($N = 1$) global time series and their fuzzy models, it may be used for multivariate ($N > 1$) local time series patterns as well, if applied for every component x_i, $i = 1, \ldots, N$ of the time series according to the following procedure.

In the fuzzy description of the τ^*-th sample point, the position of $x(t)$ in comparison to $r(\tau^*)$ is determined as in (12). For the predicted value of the next time step $\hat{x}(t + 1)$ it is firstly assumed that the qualitative position $\delta(\tau^* + 1)$ in relation to $r(\tau^* + 1)$ will remain the same. Secondly it is implied that if the overall recognition result for the known sample points is $\mu(t, \tau^*)$, the predicted value $\hat{x}(t+1)$ would produce the same value for its future classification result in $\mu_{P,\tau^*+1}(\hat{x}(t + 1))$, cf. (13), similar to the propagation of a truth value from the antecedent part of a fuzzy rule to its consequence.

$$\delta(\tau^*) = \begin{cases} -1 \, , & x(t) < r(\tau^*) \\ +1 \, , & x(t) \ge r(\tau^*) \end{cases} \tag{12}$$

$$\mu_{P,\tau^*+1}(\hat{x}(t+1)) \overset{!}{=} \mu(t, \tau^*) \tag{13}$$

With these premises and $\delta(\tau^*)$ at hand, it is possible to obtain $\hat{x}(t + 1)$ by rearranging the membership function $\mu_{P,\tau+1}$, given in (1), to (14).

$$\hat{x}(t+1) = r(\tau^* + 1) + \tag{14}$$

$$\begin{cases} -\left(\left(\frac{1}{\mu(t,\tau^*)}-1\right)\cdot\left(\frac{b_{\mathrm{l}}(\tau^*+1)}{1-b_{\mathrm{l}}(\tau^*+1)}\right)\right)^{\frac{1}{d_{\mathrm{l}}(\tau^*+1)}} \cdot c_{\mathrm{l}}(\tau^*+1)\,, & \delta(\tau^*) = -1 \\[3mm] +\left(\left(\frac{1}{\mu(t,\tau^*)}-1\right)\cdot\left(\frac{b_{\mathrm{r}}(\tau^*+1)}{1-b_{\mathrm{r}}(\tau^*+1)}\right)\right)^{\frac{1}{d_{\mathrm{r}}(\tau^*+1)}} \cdot c_{\mathrm{r}}(\tau^*+1)\,, & \delta(\tau^*) = +1 \end{cases}$$

For a multi-step prediction, (14) may either be recursively repeated (with $\hat{x}(t+p-1)$ being reclassified for the prediction of $\hat{x}(t+p)$), or the implication of constant relative position $\delta(\tau^*+p)$ and classification results μ_{P,τ^*+p} may be extended to farther sample points $p > 1$. If $\hat{x}(t+p)$ is based on only one detected pattern (cf. Sect. 4.2), both approaches lead to identical results.

4.2   To Combine or Not to Combine

If several (K) patterns are being detected and used for (different) predictions, the latter have to be combined to obtain a compromise that reflects the reliability of the individual recognition results. The center-of-gravity method is one approach to this, resembling the defuzzification step for several active fuzzy rules:

$$\hat{x}(t+1) = \frac{\displaystyle\sum_{k=1}^{K} \tilde{\mu}^{*k} \cdot \hat{x}^k(\tau^{*k}+1)}{\displaystyle\sum_{k=1}^{K} \tilde{\mu}^{*k}} \tag{15}$$

One has, however, to decide application-specifically if such a combination does make sense from a semantic point of view: May different patterns be "active" at the same time? This is especially questionable if the pattern knowledge was gained through motif mining algorithms like [6], which almost always assume only one active pattern at a time. Common sense would probably opt for basing a prediction only on the latest information available. Figure 4 sketches a case were it indeed seems advisable to discard older results and solely use the best and most recently recognised pattern for a local prediction. In other cases, however, (15) may just as well lead to (quantitatively) better results, despite the fact that such a combination might (semantically) not be well justified.

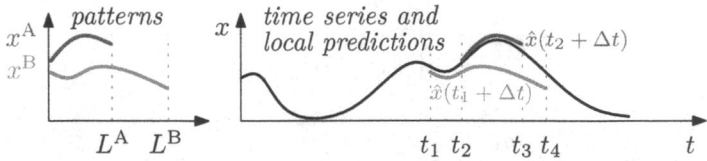

Fig. 4. Pattern-based prediction with varying horizons. From time t_2, a prediction only based on x^{A} would yield better results than a combination of both patterns.

4.3 Selection of a Suitable Method

While the prediction method (I) in Sect. 4.1 may be described as cautious or conservative, only reproducing the knowledge about a pattern's mean course, method (II) is, in principle, able to extrapolate to the entire universe of discourse. When should we select which of these methods?

This question ultimately leads to another, more philosophical question regarding the fuzzy sets describing a pattern: What is the source of the uncertainty and fuzziness represented by the parameters b, c and d in (1)? In time series datasets, we encounter different phenomena that may help answering our initial question. To mention two examples: In Fig. 5a, instances of the pattern and the mean course run mostly in parallel—the instances "breathe". Entirely different is especially the second half of the pattern in Fig. 5b, where the instances exhibit a large amount of high-frequency noise added to the mean course. In the latter case, the cautious prediction method (I) would—on average—deliver better results, whereas method (II) is suited to extrapolate "breathing" instances of the pattern in Fig. 5a.

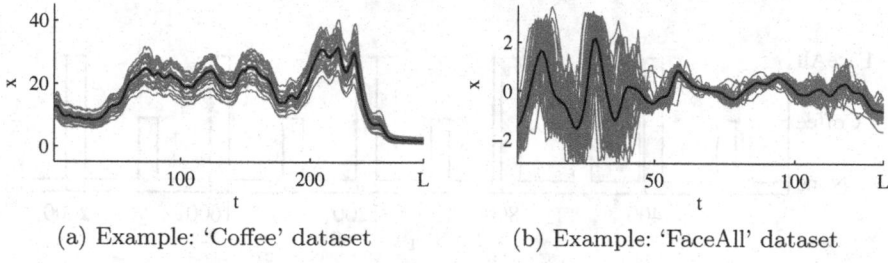

(a) Example: 'Coffee' dataset   (b) Example: 'FaceAll' dataset

Fig. 5. Different reasons for uncertainty in time series patterns (data from [4])

5 Example and Conclusion

In the random time series displayed in Fig. 6a, five randomly chosen instances from each of the two patterns in Fig. 5 were embedded in alternating order, with additional slight noise added. To complicate the recognition process, both pattern ensembles were made more similar by normalisation and resampling to the same mean, variance and length (100 samples). The random parts between the instances were filtered and scaled to closely match the patterns' properties and shapes. For the recognition and prediction, fuzzy models as described in Sect. 2.2 were learned from the datasets, and a fuzzy window of interest formulated such that pattern instances should be at least half-way completed.[2]

The results $\tilde{\mu}^*(t)$ of the decision step based on windowed recognition results $\tilde{\mu}(t, \tau)$ for both patterns are presented in Fig. 6b. Coming to a crisp decision

---

[2] For $\mu_{\mathrm{w}}(\tau)$, the membership function (1) was employed and parameterised with $r = 60$, $c_l = 10$, $c_r = 40$, $b_l = 0.5$, $b_r = 0.7$, $d_l = 4$, $d_r = 2$ to obtain high values μ_{w} for $\tau > 50$ and a rather steep decrease of interest for lower values of τ.

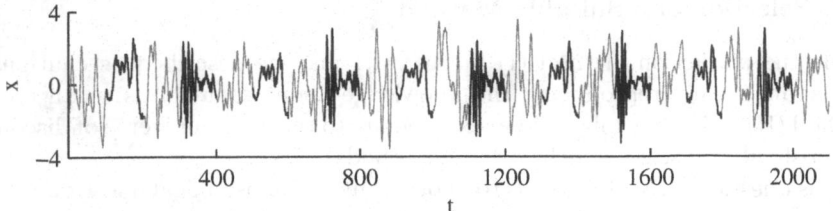

(a) Random time series with embedded pattern instances (marked black)

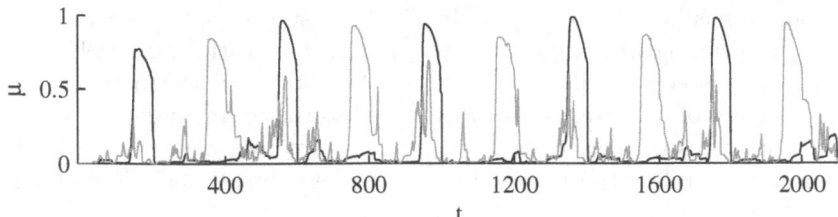

(b) Results $\tilde{\mu}^*(t)$ of the fuzzy decision (black: 'Coffee' pattern, grey: 'FaceAll')

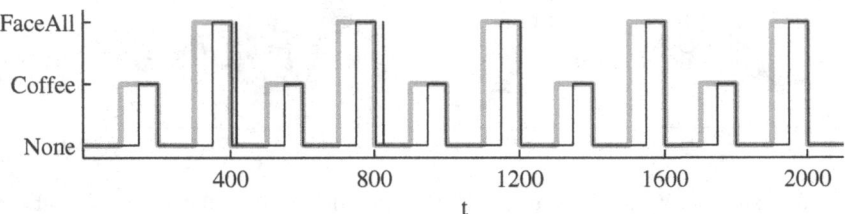

(c) Embedded (grey) and crisp decision on detected patterns (black)

Fig. 6. Example for the recognition of patterns embedded in a random time series

on one active pattern and applying a threshold of $\tilde{\mu}^*(t) \geq 0.5$, we can see from Fig. 6c that the embedded instances are recognised reliably throughout the time series, each—as desired—in its second half of development. Using a more sophisticated decision procedure, which is beyond the scope of this paper, additional short-lived recognition results (the spikes in Fig. 6c) could be filtered out.

To compare the prediction methods qualitatively, two sections of the time series along with different short-time predictions are displayed in Fig. 7 in higher detail. In Fig. 7a, the predictions based on method (II) yield better results, while the simple method (I) outmatches (II) in Fig. 7b. One special property of the prediction approach presented in this paper, which is also visible in Fig. 7, is that a new prediction with a different horizon may be available at each point in time. Due to this fact and that predictions may—depending on the size of the knowledge base—not be available at any time, a quantitive comparison to existing prediction approaches calls for new, suitable performance measures. The comparability with (say: model-based) methods designed for fixed horizons,

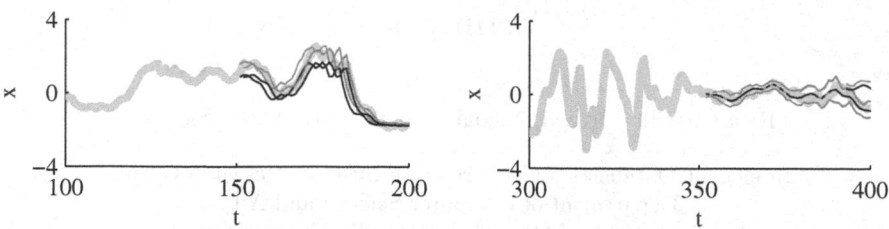

(a) Section with first 'Coffee' instance   (b) Section with first 'FaceAll' instance

Fig. 7. Local predictions of $x(t)$ (light grey) using method (I) (black) and (II) (grey)

however, will always be impaired by the missing flexibility on the one (model-based) side, and the unguaranteed availability on the other (pattern-based).

In contrast to earlier works in similar fields [5,8], the pattern model of this article can directly employ results of motif-oriented data mining algorithms. Besides the possibility of soft windowing, subsequent work should explore further advantageous uses of the fuzzy recognition results, especially a more sophisticated decision strategy.

References

1. Bocklisch, S.F.: Prozeßanalyse mit unscharfen Verfahren. Technik, Berlin (1987)
2. Hempel, A.J., Bocklisch, S.F.: Fuzzy pattern modelling of data inherent structures based on aggregation of data with heterogeneous fuzziness. In: Rey, G.R., Muneta, L.M. (eds.) Modelling Simulation and Optimization, ch. 28, pp. 637–655. INTECH (2010)
3. Herbst, G., Bocklisch, S.F.: Online recognition of fuzzy time series patterns. In: 2009 International Fuzzy Systems Association World Congress and 2009 European Society for Fuzzy Logic and Technology Conference (IFSA-EUSFLAT 2009), pp. 974–979 (2009)
4. Keogh, E., Xi, X., Wei, L., Ratanamahatana, C.A.: The UCR time series classification/clustering homepage, http://www.cs.ucr.edu/~eamonn/time_series_data/
5. Šket Motnikar, B., Pisanski, T., Čepar, D.: Time-series forecasting by pattern imitation. OR Spectrum 18(1), 43–49 (1996)
6. Mueen, A., Keogh, E., Zhu, Q., Cash, S., Westover, B.: Exact discovery of time series motifs. In: Proceedings of the SIAM International Conference on Data Mining (SDM 2009), pp. 473–484. American Statistical Association, ASA (2009)
7. Päßler, M., Bocklisch, S.F.: Fuzzy time series analysis. In: Hampel, R., Wagenknecht, M., Chaker, N. (eds.) Fuzzy Control: Theory and Practice, pp. 331–345. Physica, Heidelberg (2000)
8. Singh, S.: Multiple forecasting using local approximation. Pattern Recognition 34, 443–455 (2001)

Time Series Comparison Using Linguistic Fuzzy Techniques*

Rita Castillo-Ortega, Nicolás Marín, and Daniel Sánchez

Intelligent Databases and Information Systems Research Group,
Department of Computer Science and A.I.,
University of Granada, 18071, Granada, Spain
{rita,nicm,daniel}@decsai.ugr.es

Abstract. In this paper, we face the problem of time series comparison which appears frequently in the Business Intelligence area. Specifically, we provide a linguistic summary of the difference between values of two time series defined on the same time domain. Several kind of summaries with alternative semantics can be obtained depending on the way the difference is calculated.

Keywords: Linguistic Summarization, Time series, Business Intelligence, Fuzzy Logic.

1 Introduction

The process of managing great amounts of information referring to business activities is a current hip topic nowadays. The time dimension is crucial in any activity, either commercial or scientific, or even in daily routine, and, as such, it uses to appear in historical databases. The analysis of this kind of databases allows users to make decision making and forecasting [2]. Researchers within the Information Systems field have focussed a large part of their efforts on searching for this kind of Business Intelligence solutions, and they have found a very useful tool in Data Mining techniques.

Time Series Data Mining is a topic of interest for many authors [1]. A key point in Data Mining is that of understandability of information, to the extent that, in many occasions, simply providing an understandable summary of data is the most valuable contribution. In this process, linguistic summarization techniques are specially helpful because they produce sentences close to natural language for describing data, and this is a very convenient way to provide information to the users.

Due to its well-known capability to fill the gap between understandable and precise data, Fuzzy Set Theory provides us a powerful tool in order to deal with the linguistic summarization problem. An essential part of the research in this

---

* The research reported in this paper was partially supported by the Andalusian Government (Junta de Andalucía) under project P07-TIC03175 and also by the Spanish Government (Science and Innovation Department) under project TIN2009-08296.

E. Hüllermeier, R. Kruse, and F. Hoffmann (Eds.): IPMU 2010, LNAI 6178, pp. 330–339, 2010.

field can be found in R. R. Yager's works, where he uses quantified sentences in the sense of L. A. Zadeh first [15], and OWA operators later [16,17]. Also following Zadeh's footsteps, we can find J. Kacprzyk et al. in [7,9,10,11,12], proposing new quality measures and using the protoform concept. G. Raschia et. al created a model named SaintEtiQ [13], working with hierarchies. From a different point of view, P. Bosc and D. Dubois proposed the use of association rules [3]. In previous work we have also centered our efforts in obtaining linguistic summaries that *briefly* present the *essential* information regarding the evolution of a given variable over time [4,5].

Linguistic description is specially interesting in the comparison of time series as well. In [6] M. Umano et al. carry out a study about the description of time series data using their global trend and local features. In another related work, J. Kacprzyk and A. Wilbik [8] focus on the evaluation of similarity of time series. They propose a fuzzy quantifier based aggregation approach and apply their method to the analysis of investment fund quotations in order to show its usefulness.

The aim of this paper is to present a method for the linguistic comparison of time series. The method is based on the computation of a linguistic summary of a special type of time series that represents the difference between the series being compared. For that purpose we use as basis our previously developed summarization techniques. The possibility of obtaining alternative semantics in the summary is given by the use of several approaches to compute the difference between series. The paper is organized as follows: Section 2 defines the comparison problem; Section 3 presents the proposed approach to obtain the linguistic comparison. Finally, a practical example appears in Section 4 and some conclusions are presented in Section 5.

2 A Linguistic Framework to Describe Time Series

As we have mentioned in the introduction, our intention is to obtain a linguistic summary that describes the difference in value between two series across time. The series are required to be defined over the same variable scale and the same time domain. In order to obtain the linguistic summary we will use a hierarchical fuzzy partition of the time domain and a fuzzy linguistic granulation of the variable domain. In the following, we will present how the data series are described at the start up.

As we can see, Figure 1.a) represents the behavior of a given variable V along *time* in two different series. The y-coordinate displays the domain of the variable V and the x-coordinate shows the time dimension.

We assume that the time dimension is described in its finest grained level of granularity by $T = \{t_1, ..., t_m\}$. Then, we consider a couple of time series defined on this time dimension, namely, TS_1 and TS_2. $TS_i(t_j)$ represents the value of the variable V under study in t_j as given by TS_i.

Once we have the difference time series data, we have to obtain an appropriate linguistic summary of this new series. In order to do that, we will describe the linguistic context [See Figure 1.b)]:

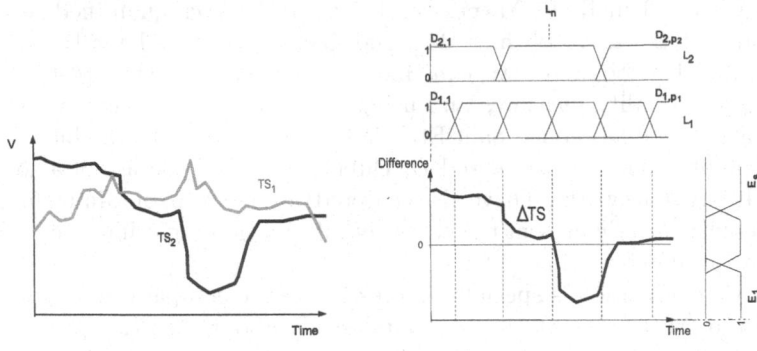

a) Initial time series.   b) General context for the
                                 summarization of a time series.

Fig. 1. TS_1, TS_2, and ΔTS

- The basic domain of variable V is partitioned by a set of linguistic labels $E=\{E_1, ..., E_s\}$.
- The time dimension is hierarchically organized in n levels, namely, $L=L_1, ...,$ L_n. Each level L_i has associated a partition $\{D_{i,1}, ..., D_{i,p_i}\}$ of the basic time domain.

There is no restriction concerning the form of the membership function of a label apart from that it must be normalized. In our approach, we will use trapezoidal functions. When necessary, labels $D_{i,j}$ in time dimension can be the union of a set of trapezoidal functions. In this work, a set of labels $\{X_1, ..., X_r\}$ is a partition on X iff:

1. X_i is normalized $\forall i \in \{1..r\}$.
2. $\forall x \in X, \exists X_i, i \in \{1..r\} | \mu_{X_i}(x) > 0$.
3. $\forall i,j \in \{1..r\}, i \neq j, core(X_i) \cap core(X_j) = \emptyset$.

Conditions 1 and 3 imply $X_i \not\subseteq X_j \ \forall i \neq j$. Additionally, concerning the hierarchy of the time dimension, we add the following constraints:

1. $\forall i,j \in \{1..n\}, i < j, p_i > p_j$ (i.e, as we move upward in the hierarchy, the number of labels of the partition decreases).
2. $\forall i \in \{2..n\}, \forall j \in \{1..p_i\}, \forall k \in \{1..p_{i-1}\} | (D_{i,j} \subseteq D_{i-1,k}) \rightarrow (D_{i,j} = D_{i-1,k})$ (i.e., labels cannot generalize another label of an upper level).

3   Linguistic Comparison of Time Series

The method we proposed is based in two main steps. The first step is the obtention of a new time series as the difference ΔTS between the two series being compared. The second one is the obtention of the linguistic summary of this new series with information regarding the comparison.

3.1   Three Semantics for the ΔTS Time Series

ΔTS time series can be obtained in several different ways. Let us consider the following definition.

Definition 1 *Let TS_1 and TS_2 be two time series defined over the same variable V at a given period of time. Then,*

$$\Delta TS_{abs}(t_i) = TS_1(t_i) - TS_2(t_i) \tag{1}$$

$$\Delta TS_{global}(t_i) = \begin{cases} 0, \text{if } TS_1(t_i) - TS_2(t_i) = 0 \\ \dfrac{TS_1(t_i) - TS_2(t_i)}{M - m}, otherwise \end{cases} \tag{2}$$

$$\Delta TS_{local}(t_i) = \begin{cases} 0, \text{if } TS_1(t_i) - TS_2(t_i) = 0 \\ \dfrac{TS_1(t_i) - TS_2(t_i)}{max(TS_1(t_i), TS_2(t_i)) - m}, otherwise \end{cases} \tag{3}$$

where t_i is a specific point in the time domain, M is the global maximum of TS_1 and TS_2, and m is the global minimum of TS_1 and TS_2.

Each of one of the above defined series proposes a different way to face the computation of the new series that describes the difference between the two initial ones. At a given time point t_i,

- $\Delta TS_{abs}(t_i)$ is the difference, in absolute terms, between the two original series at the point t_i (Equation 1).
- $\Delta TS_{global}(t_i)$ is the difference, in relative terms, between the two original series at the point t_i, according to the scale of values of the two original series (i.e., the difference between the global maximum and minimum of the two series)(Equation 2).
- $\Delta TS_{local}(t_i)$ is the difference, also in relative terms, between the two original series at t_i, but now according to the scale of values of the given time point in the two original series (i.e., the difference between the maximum value at the given time point and the global minimum) (Equation 3).

The choice of the strategy depends on the necessities of the user or the problem in each particular situation. ΔTS_{abs} is the only option if we are interested in the analysis of the difference between the series in absolute terms. Figure 2.a depicts an example of the use of this first alternative. As can be seen, the new series ranges over the same variable domain than the original one.

Nevertheless, if we are interested in the analysis of the difference between the series in relative terms, we have two different alternatives. Figure 2.b shows the ΔTS_{global} and ΔTS_{local} obtained for the previous example. The figure illustrates the difference between the two strategies: while in ΔTS_{global} the same difference between the original series produces always the same value in the new one (see points a and b), in ΔTS_{local} the *lower* the original values the greater the *significance* of the difference (see points c and d). In this sense, ΔTS_{abs} behaves like ΔTS_{global} (see Figure 2.a, points a and b).

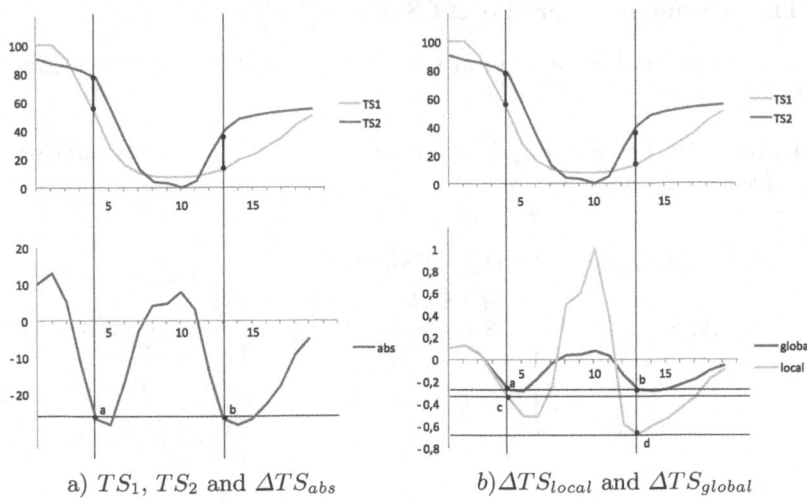

a) TS_1, TS_2 and ΔTS_{abs} b) ΔTS_{local} and ΔTS_{global}

Fig. 2. Time series data

Once we have opted for a given strategy, we have to provide a linguistic description of the domain of the new series. In our method, we use a linguistic variable with the following features (we shall show an example later in this work):

– The linguistic variable covers both positive and negatives values.
– In the case of ΔTS_{abs}, it is defined on the range $[-M, M]$.
– In the case of ΔTS_{global} and ΔTS_{local}, it is defined on the range $[-1, 1]$.

3.2 The Obtention of the Summary

In the previous subsection, we have analyzed how to obtain a new time series that describes the difference between the two time series under study. Now, we have to obtain an appropriate linguistic summary of this new series.

In this work, we are interested in linguistic summaries that take the form of a collection of quantified sentences describing the behavior of a time series. We assume that the basic elements of these summaries are the linguistic labels described in Section 2. That is, our approach will deliver a collection of sentences of the form "Q of $D_{i,j}^{S}$ are A^{S}" where:

– $D_{i,j}$ is a label member of a certain level i of the hierarchy associated to the time dimension and $D_{i,j}^{S}(< t, v >) = D_{i,j}(t)$.
– A is a label or the union of a subset of labels of the partition of the variable V under study (in our case, according to the strategy followed in order to obtain the new series, this partition will be defined on $[-M,+M]$ or $[-1,1]$), and $A^{S}(< t, v >) = A(v)$.

Additionally, the user must provide a collection of quantifiers defining the kind of fuzzy quantities and percentages she is interested in. This can be defined by choosing among a collection of predefined quantifiers. In this work, we consider that the user provides a *totally ordered* subset $\{Q_1, ..., Q_{qmax}\}$ of a coherent family of quantifiers Q [14] to be used in the summarization process. In addition, the user will provide a threshold τ for the minimum accomplishment degree she wishes for the quantified sentences comprising the summaries.

In [5] we presented two different approaches to obtain linguistic summaries. Algorithm 1 represents one of the algorithms. For the sake of brevity in the final summary, we start from the time periods in the top level of the hierarchy. Following that premise, we try to avoid going down in the hierarchy levels: in order to stay in more general levels, the methods try to use groups of labels in the domain or try to use a less strict quantifier. Each level has its own quantifier bound ($Qbound_i$) and grouping bound ($Gbound_i$) that, respectively, indicate the less strict quantifier to be considered and the maximum number of labels E_i to be aggregated in a sentence at this level of the time domain.

The set $ToSummarize$ is the collection of time periods for which a quantified sentence is missing. If it is possible to obtain an accomplishment degree greater than τ for a certain period using a quantifier Q and a single label, then the procedure considers the period is sufficiently described. If it is not possible, the procedure tries with the union of different subsets of labels: couples, trios, quartets, etc, until we obtain an accomplishment degree greater than τ. The size of the subset is given by k being $Gbound$ its maximum value (the second procedure tries with a less strict quantifier being $Qbound_i$ the limit). When a summary is found in a certain time period we say that the period is *covered*. If all the groups were tried without success, the algorithm repeats the grouping process again, but with a less strict quantifier, until $Qbound_i$ is reached (in the second procedure, if all possible quantifiers were tried, the process is repeated with a bigger group of labels, until $Gbound$ is reached). If no result is found for a given period $D_{i,j}$, we try to obtain such sentences with the *corresponding children* $ch(D_{i,j})$ in the next level of the domain (line 21), where where $ch(D_{i,j})$ is defined as follows: $ch(D_{1,j}) = \emptyset$ for all j. Otherwise, $ch(D_{i,j}) = \{D_{i-1,k}, k \in \{1..p_{i-1}\} | D_{i-1,k} \cap D_{i,j} \neq \emptyset$ and $\neg \exists D \in ToSummarize \cup Summarized, (D_{i-1,k} \cap D_{i,j}) \subseteq D\}$, and $C_k = \{\cup_{E_h \in F} E_h \mid F \subseteq E, |F| = k\}$. If $ch(D_{i,j}) = \emptyset$, then a sentence indicating the observed variability is added to the summary ($D_{i,j}$ is *highly variable*[1]). The final set of linguistically quantified sentences comprising the summary is $Summary$.

The second algorithm proposed in [5] is similar to that in Algorithm 1 with the difference that when it is not possible to obtain an accomplishment degree greater than τ for a certain period using a quantifier Q and a single label, the procedure tries with less strict quantifiers before trying with aggregations of labels in E.

In any case, when the summary is obtained, the set of sentences is post-processed in order to produce an easier to read paragraph. The repetitions can

---

[1] Though variability is also analyzed in [9], we refer to this characteristic of the series only when we cannot suitably summarize the values for a given time period.

Algorithm 1 to obtain linguistic summaries.
Input

A time series S, a hierarchical fuzzy partition of the time dimension D, a linguistic variable E, a totally ordered subset $\{Q_1..Q_{qmax}\}$ of a coherent family of quantifiers Q, a threshold τ as minimum accomplishment for quantified sentences, and, for each level i, maximum number of: a) quantifiers to use ($Qbound_i$), and b) labels to group together ($Gbound_i$).

Output

A Summary of S comprised of a set of quantified sentences.

Algorithm
1: $ToSummarize \leftarrow L_n$;
2: $Summary \leftarrow \emptyset$; $Summarized \leftarrow \emptyset$;
3: **while** $ToSummarize \neq \emptyset$ **do**
4:    Take $D_{i,j} \in ToSummarize$
5:    $ToSummarize \leftarrow ToSummarize \backslash \{D_{i,j}\}$;
6:    $p \leftarrow qmax$; $covered \leftarrow false$;
7:    **while** $p \geq Qbound_i$ and *not covered* **do**
8:      $k \leftarrow 1$;
9:      **while** $k \leq Gbound_i$ and *not covered* **do**
10:        Let $A \leftarrow argmax_{B \in C_k} GD_{Q_p}(B^S/D_{i,j}^S)$;
11:        **if** $GD_{Q_p}(B^S/D_{i,j}^S) \geq \tau$ **then**
12:          $Summary \leftarrow Summary \cup \{Q_p$ of $D_{i,j}^S$ are $A^S\}$;
13:          $Summarized \leftarrow Summarized \cup (D_{i,j})$;
14:          $covered \leftarrow true$;
15:        **end if**
16:        $k \leftarrow k + 1$;
17:      **end while**
18:      $p \leftarrow p - 1$;
19:    **end while**
20:    **if** *not covered* and $i > 1$ **then**
21:      $ToSummarize \leftarrow ToSummarize \cup ch(D_{i,j})$;
22:    **else if** $i = 1$ **then**
23:      $Summary \leftarrow Summary \cup \{D_{i,j}^S$ is highly variable$\}$;
24:    **end if**
25: **end while**

---

be removed via merging sentences that cover different time periods but produce the same trend. The merging process takes into account sentences with the same quantifier and trend as well as sentences with the same quantifier. For example, if the summary is *In A, the difference was mostly low or very low. In B, the difference was mostly low or very low*, the function produces the shorter sentence *In A and B, the difference was mostly low or very low*.

4 An Illustrative Example

In this section we will work with an illustrative example in order to apply our process and clarify concepts or procedures introduced in formers sections. Figure 3 contains the time series that shows the patient inflow on two different medical centers during a given year.

Using equations 2 and 3 we obtain the time series data depicted in Figure 4, both relative differences. The y-coordinate represents the relative differences and the x-coordinate represents the time dimension. In Fig. 4, the linguistic

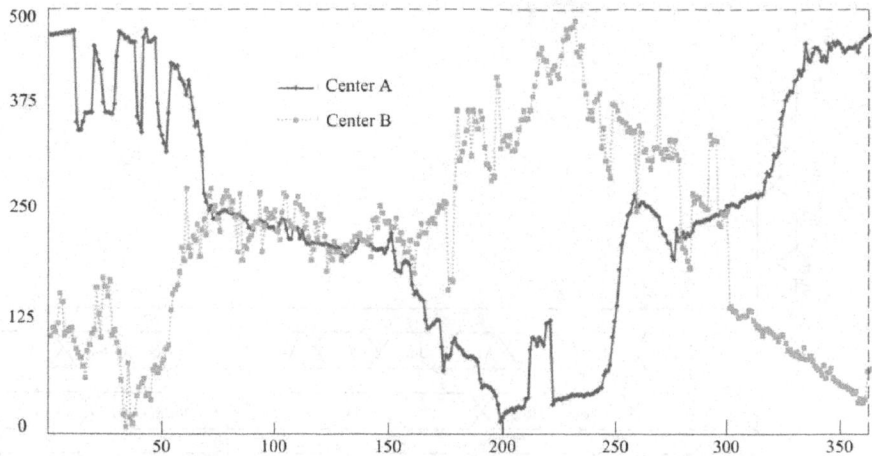

Fig. 3. Patient inflow in two medical centers

labels defined on the domain of the relative differences are depicted on the y-axis as trapezoidal functions with parameters: *much lower*=(-1,-1,-0.8,-0.6), *lower*=(-0.8,-0.6,-0.3,-0.1), *similar*=(-0.3,0,0,0.3), *higher*=(0.1,0.3,0.6,0.8), and *higher*=(0.6,0.8,1,1). As we can see, the time dimension is hierarchically organized following a meteorological criteria thanks to three fuzzy partitions of the time domain, namely: one based on approximate months (in order to avoid a strong dependence of the obtained summaries with respect to the crisp boundaries of conventional months) and two others with different levels of granularity. Fuzziness is specially useful in these two last partitions because transitions between periods are clearly fuzzy.

The example is carried out using a subset of trapezoidal quantifiers $Q = \{Q_1 = (0, 0.4, 0.6, 1), Q_2 = (0, 0.6, 0.8, 1), Q_3 = (0, 0.7, 0.9, 1)\}$ (that we have called *at least half of*, *at least 70% of*, and *most of*, respectively) and a threshold $\tau = 0.7$ and values $Qbound_i = Gbound_i = 2$ $\forall i$ as parameters. For instance, we will use Algorithm 1 with the time data taken from the *local* relative difference (ΔTS_{local}) between patient inflow in centers A and B. The set of quantified sentences obtained is:

- *At least 70% of the time with cold weather, the patient inflow is much higher in center A than in center B*
- *At least 70% of the time with hot weather, the patient inflow is lower or much lower in center A than in center B*
- *At least 70% of the time with cold to hot weather, the patient inflow is higher or similar in center A than in center B*
- *The patient inflow difference between centers A and B in September presents variability*
- *At least 70% of the time in October, the patient inflow is similar or lower in center A than in center B*
- *Most of the time in November, the patient inflow is much higher or higher in center A than in center B.*

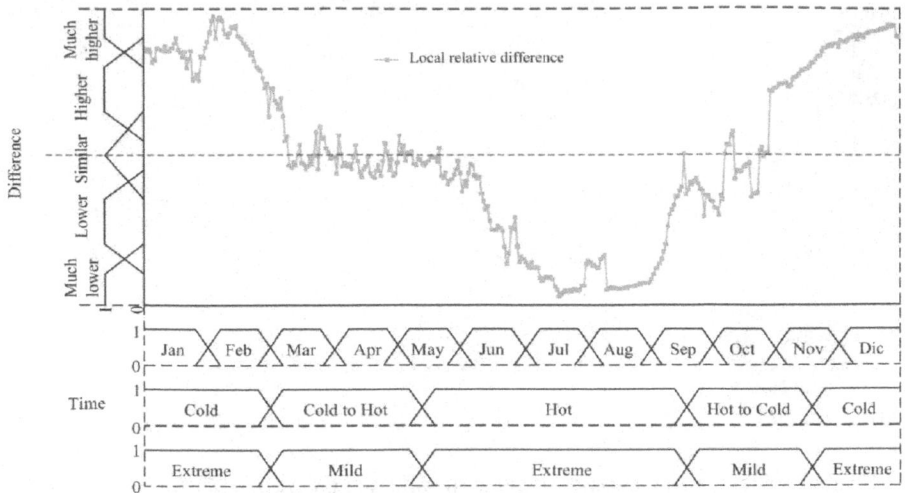

Fig. 4. Local relative difference ΔTS_{local} in the example

5 Conclusions

The approach presented allows us to obtain a linguistic summary about the comparison of two time series. This summary is built using the difference in each time point between the series being compared. Our method provides understandable summaries which help the users in the decision making process. We rely on user-defined features like a hierarchical fuzzy partition of time dimension and a coherent subset of quantifiers to achieve brief and understandable summaries. As future work we plan to perform linguistic comparison on the basis of other features, and to apply new summarization algorithms that are currently being developed.

References

1. Batyrshin, I.Z., Sheremetov, L.: Perception-based approach to time series data mining. Appl. Soft Comput. 8(3), 1211–1221 (2008)
2. Batyrshin, I.Z., Sudkamp, T.: Perception based data mining and decision support systems. International Journal of Approximate Reasoning 48(1), 1–3 (2008)
3. Bosc, P., Dubois, D., Pivert, O., Prade, H., De Calmes, M.: Fuzzy summarization of data using fuzzy cardinalities. In: Int. Conf. Inf. Process. Manag. Uncertainty Knowl. Based Syst., pp. 1553–1559 (2002)
4. Castillo-Ortega, R., Marín, N., Sánchez, D.: Fuzzy quantification-based linguistic summaries in data cubes with hierarchical fuzzy partition of time dimension. In: Yin, H., Corchado, E. (eds.) IDEAL 2009. LNCS, vol. 5788, pp. 578–585. Springer, Heidelberg (2009)
5. Castillo-Ortega, R., Marín, N., Sánchez, D.: Linguistic summary-based query answering on data cubes with time dimension. In: Andreasen, T., Bulskov, H. (eds.) FQAS 2009. LNCS (LNAI), vol. 5822, pp. 560–571. Springer, Heidelberg (2009)

6. Humano, M., Okamura, M., Seta, K.: Improved method for linguistic expression of time series with global trend and local features. In: FUZZ-IEEE 2009, pp. 1169–1174 (2009)
7. Kacprzyk, J.: Fuzzy logic for linguistic summarization of databases. In: IEEE International Fuzzy Systems Conference, pp. 813–818 (1999)
8. Kacprzyk, J., Wilbik, A.: Using fuzzy linguistic summaries for the comparison of time series: an application to the analysis of investment fund quotations. In: Kaymak, U., Carvalho, J.P., Dubois, D., Sousa, J.M.C. (eds.) IFSA-EUSFLAT 2009, pp. 1321–1326 (2009)
9. Kacprzyk, J., Wilbik, A., Zadrozny, S.: Linguistic summarization of time series using a fuzzy quantifier driven aggregation. Fuzzy Sets and Systems 159(12), 1485–1499 (2008)
10. Kacprzyk, J., Yager, R.R.: Linguistic summaries of data using fuzzy logic. International Journal of General Systems 30, 133–154 (2001)
11. Kacprzyk, J., Yager, R.R., Zadrozny, S.: A fuzzy logic based approach to linguistic summaries in databases. International Journal of Applied Mathematical Computer Science 10, 813–834 (2000)
12. Kacprzyk, J., Zadrozny, S.: Linguistic database summaries and their protoforms: towards natural language based knowledge discovery tools. Inf. Sci. Inf. Comput. Sci. 173(4), 281–304 (2005)
13. Raschia, G., Mouaddib, N.: Saintetiq: a fuzzy set-based approach to database summarization. Fuzzy Sets Syst. 129(2), 137–162 (2002)
14. Vila, M.A., Cubero, J.C., Medina, J.M., Pons, O.: The generalized selection: an alternative way for the quotient operations in fuzzy relational databases. In: Bouchon-Meunier, B., Yager, R., Zadeh, L. (eds.) Fuzzy Logic and Soft Computing. World Scientific Press, Singapore (1995)
15. Yager, R.R.: A new approach to the summarization of data. Information Sciences (28), 69–86 (1982)
16. Yager, R.R.: Toward a language for specifying summarizing statistics. IEEE Transactions on Systems, Man, and Cybernetics, Part B 33(2), 177–187 (2003)
17. Yager, R.R.: A human directed approach for data summarization. In: IEEE International Conference on Fuzzy Systems, pp. 707–712 (2006)

Granular Approach for Evolving System Modeling

Daniel Leite[1], Pyramo Costa Jr.[2], and Fernando Gomide[1]

[1] University of Campinas, School of Electrical and Computer Engineering, Brazil
[2] Pontifical Catholic University of Minas Gerais,
Graduate Program in Electrical Engineering, Brazil
danfl7@dca.fee.unicamp.br, pyramo@pucminas.br, gomide@dca.fee.unicamp.br

Abstract. In this paper we introduce a class of granular evolving system modeling approach within the framework of interval analysis. Our aim is to present an interval-based learning algorithm which develops both, granular and singular approximations of nonlinear nonstationary functions using singular data. The algorithm is capable of incrementally creating/adapting both model parameters and structure. These are key features in nonlinear systems modeling. In addition, interval analysis provides rigorous bounds on approximation errors, rounding errors, and on uncertainties in data propagated during computations. The learning algorithm is simple and particularly suited to process stream of data in real time. In this paper we focus on the foundations of the approach and on the details of the learning algorithm. An application concerning economic time series forecasting illustrates the usefulness and efficiency of the approach.

1 Introduction

Recently, systems capable to extract knowledge online from data have been developed [1]-[8]. Approaches, algorithms and systems directed toward this end are known as Evolving Intelligent Systems (EIS).

EIS target nonstationary processes and embody online learning methods and one-pass incremental algorithms that evolve or gradually change individual models to guarantee life-long learning and self-organization of the system structure [9]. According to Zadeh, a model (similarly for a variable and a datum) is granular if it is a carrier of granular information, and it is singular if it is a carrier of singleton information. This paper focuses on evolving granular modeling in the sense of gradual development of granules and associated rules. The emphasis is on the use of singular data to develop interval-type granular models and singular models associated with intervals.

More specifically, the approach we suggest here is an interval-based evolving modeling (IBeM) approach rooted in interval mathematics [10]-[14] and machine learning [15]-[16]. Basically, IBeM is an evolving rule-based modeling scheme that gradually adapts its structure using a stream of data. By structure we mean information granules, the corresponding rules, and their antecedent and consequent

E. Hüllermeier, R. Kruse, and F. Hoffmann (Eds.): IPMU 2010, LNAI 6178, pp. 340–349, 2010.
© Springer-Verlag Berlin Heidelberg 2010

parameters. IBeM develops global models using a one-pass learning algorithm with modest memory requirements. It does not require prior knowledge about learning data (probability distributions, belief intervals, possibility values), and starts learning as soon as data are input.

The framework of interval mathematics supports the learning algorithm, the core of IBeM, and gives simplicity, correctness, totality, closedness, optimality, and efficiency [14]. An application example concerning economic time series forecasting illustrates the usefulness and efficiency of IBeM.

The remainder of this paper is organized as follows. Next section reviews the notions of interval analysis necessary to develop the IBeM learning algorithm. Section 3 details the IBeM approach. Section 4 addresses a stock market forecasting example using actual data. Section 5 concludes the paper and suggests issues for further investigation.

2   Interval Vectors and Functions

Interval analysis is a theory oriented for computational implementation because it supports the development of interval-based algorithms. These algorithms are mainly designed to automatically provide rigorous bounds on approximation errors, rounding errors, and propagated uncertainties in initial data. This is of utmost importance because modeling of complex systems must trade-off complexity and precision. Calculations involving imprecise objects must consider the nature of the imprecision.

The main concern of the interval analysis is to provide a guaranteed approximation of the set of solutions of the underlying problem. Guaranteed in this context means that outer approximations of intervals can always be obtained and, moreover, be made as precise as desired. Intervals acknowledge limited precision by associating with a variable of the model under investigation a set of reals as possible values. For ease of storage and computation, these sets are restricted to intervals [14].

The act of merely enclosing a solution might be seem at first shallower than finding the solution itself. We should reflect that, while this is true, the degree of satisfaction involved in enclosing a solution depends strongly on the tightness of the enclosure obtained. Moreover, when processing exact values we very often have no idea about the error involved. By contrary, if we can compute an interval containing an exact solution to some problem, then we can take e.g. the midpoint of the interval as an approximation. Hence, we obtain both an approximate solution and error bounds on the approximation [11].

2.1   Interval Vectors

An interval I is a closed bounded set of real numbers

$$[l, L] = \{x : l \leq x \leq L\},$$

where l and L denote its endpoints. An n-dimensional interval vector is an ordered n-tuple of intervals $(I_1, ..., I_j, ..., I_n)$. If I is a e.g. two-dimensional interval vector, then $I = (I_1, I_2)$ for some $I_1 = [l_1, L_1]$ and $I_2 = [l_2, L_2]$.

Set-theoretic operations of intersection, $\cap$, and union, $\cup$, are applicable to intervals. The intersection of two intervals, I^1 and I^2, is empty, $I^1 \cap I^2 = \emptyset$, if either $l^1 > L^2$ or $L^1 < l^2$. This indicates that I^1 and I^2 have no common points. Otherwise, the intersection of I^1 and I^2 is again an interval:

$$I^1 \cap I^2 = [max(l^1, l^2), \ min(L^1, L^2)].$$

The intersection of interval vectors is empty if the intersection of any of their components is empty. Otherwise, for $I^1 = (I_1^1, ..., I_j^1, ..., I_n^1)$ and $I^2 = (I_1^2, ..., I_j^2, ..., I_n^2)$ we have:

$$I^1 \cap I^2 = (I_1^1 \cap I_1^2, ..., I_j^1 \cap I_j^2, ..., I_n^1 \cap I_n^2).$$

If two intervals have nonempty intersection, then their union,

$$I^1 \cup I^2 = [min(l^1, l^2), \ max(L^1, L^2)],$$

is an interval. Disconnected sets must not be expressed as a single interval.

The hull of two intervals, I^1 and I^2, namely $\text{ch}(I^1, I^2)$, is the smallest interval containing all their elements. Then,

$$\text{ch}(I^1, I^2) = [min(l^1, l^2), \ max(L^1, L^2)]$$

is always an interval. Hull computations are efficient mechanisms to aggregate and merge sets independently of their connection. It follows that $I^1 \cup I^2 \subseteq \text{ch}(I^1, I^2)$ for any intervals I^1 and I^2.

We denote the width of an interval vector, namely $wdt(I)$, as the length of its largest side:

$$wdt(I) = max(wdt(I_1), ..., wdt(I_j), ..., wdt(I_n)).$$

Finally, it is worth defining the midpoint of an interval I:

$$mp(I) = (l + L)/2.$$

Analogously, if $I = (I_1, ..., I_j, ..., I_n)$ is an interval vector, then:

$$mp(I) = (mp(I_1), ..., mp(I_j), ..., mp(I_n)).$$

2.2   Interval Functions

The image of an interval I under a real mapping f is

$$f(I) = \{f(x) : x \in I\}.$$

More generally, the image of a specified n-dimensional vector I admitting a multivariable real function f is:

$$f(I_1, ..., I_j, ..., I_n) = \{f(x_1, ..., x_j, ..., x_n) : x_j \in I_j \; \forall j\}.$$

Generally, the image of an interval through f is not a box (see Fig. 1) and it may be difficult to obtain in closed form. In practice, $f(I)$ can be approximated by an inclusion function $F(I)$, which is a box in the range of f.

An interval function F from $\mathbb{R}^n$ to $\mathbb{R}^m$ is called inclusion function of f if

$$f(I) \subseteq F(I) \; \forall I \in \mathbb{R}^n.$$

Inclusion functions are not unique and they depend on how we choose F. An inclusion function is optimal if $F(I)$ is the interval hull of $f(I)$. In other words, the optimal inclusion function for $f(I)$ is the smallest box $F^*(I)$ that contains $f(I)$. Fig. 1 illustrates the idea. $F^*(I)$ is unique.

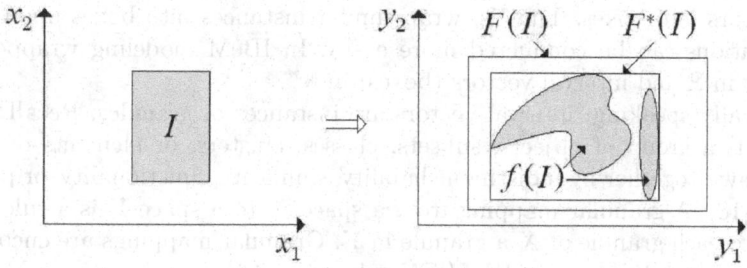

Fig. 1. Image f of box I and inclusion functions F and F^*

Assume f monotonically increasing in $I = [l, L]$. Then we can obtain $f(I)$ using:

$$f(I) = [f(l), f(L)].$$

Consequently,

$$f(x) \subseteq [f(l), f(L)] \; \forall x \in I.$$

With monotonic decreasing functions, we have to order the resulting endpoints correctly. In these cases $f(I) = [f(L), f(l)]$.

An interval function $f(I) \in \mathbb{R}$ is called *thin* when it involves only degenerate interval parameters or, equivalently, singular parameters. For instance, the interval function:

$$f(I) = a_0 + \sum_{j=1}^{n} a_j I_j,$$

is *thin* for $(a_0, ..., a_n)$ degenerated intervals. When an interval function involves at least one interval parameter of nonzero width, it is called *thick*. In this paper we consider *thin* interval functions only.

3   Interval-Based Evolving Modeling

IBeM originated from recent research on how to process nonstationary data in adaptive system modeling. IBeM models process data streams using incremental one-pass-through-the-data learning algorithm. It starts learning from scratch and with no need of prior knowledge about the properties of the data. Models developed by IBeM are transparent and interpretable. IBeM modeling adjusts structures and parameters to learn new concepts; detects concept drift and shift; can cope with uncertainty in the data; develops never-ending lifelong learning using constructive bottom-up and destructive top-down mechanisms; and provides nonlinear approximators/classifiers. Before proceeding with algorithmic details we overview the IBeM working principle in the next section.

3.1   Overview of IBeM

The basic idea behind interval-based evolving modeling (IBeM) is simple: enclose real vectors into boxes. That is, wrap similar instances into boxes upon which computations can be conducted more easily. In IBeM modeling wrappers are intervals in $\mathbb{R}$ and interval vectors (boxes) in $\mathbb{R}^n$.

Generally speaking, interval vectors are instances of granules. Recall that a granule is a group of objects, subsets, classes, clusters, or elements of a universe drawn together by indistinguishability, similarity, functionality, or proximity [17]-[18]. A granular mapping from a space X to a space Y is a rule which assigns to each granule of X a granule in Y. Granular mappings are encoded in IBeM models in the form of IF-THEN rules.

An IBeM granule is a rule. A set of rules, namely the rule base, is a granular mapping that gives a granular approximation of the function which models a system. The granular approximation is an inclusion function P. Moreover, there is, in IBeM, a local function p associated with each rule of P. Each local function p gives a singular local approximation of the function which governs the system behavior. Granular models are created adding rules in the rule base, and are updated merging and revising existing granules and the respective parameters of local functions. The rule base adapts whenever new information is found in the input data.

3.2   Interval-Based Learning Approach

IBeM learns from data streams $(x, y)^{[h]}$, $h = 1, 2, ...$, where the desired output vector $y^{[h]}$ is either known when the corresponding input vector $x^{[h]}$ arrives, or will be known at some latter stage. IBeM encodes new information in input data either creating a new granule, a rule describing the granule, or adapting existing granules and corresponding rules. In both cases, parameters of the local function associated with the corresponding granules are updated.

Figure 2 illustrates the granular model we are interested in this paper. Each segment of the mapping is formed within a scope of the individual information granules occurring in the input-output spaces. The case shown in the figure conveys a collection of three granules γ^i, $i = 1, 2, 3$, constructed in light of the data being available to approximate the process function f. The collection of rules R^i governing the granules γ^i, $i = 1, 2, 3$, is the rule base. Notice that each function p^i approximates f locally in domain of each granule γ^i, $i = 1, 2, 3$.

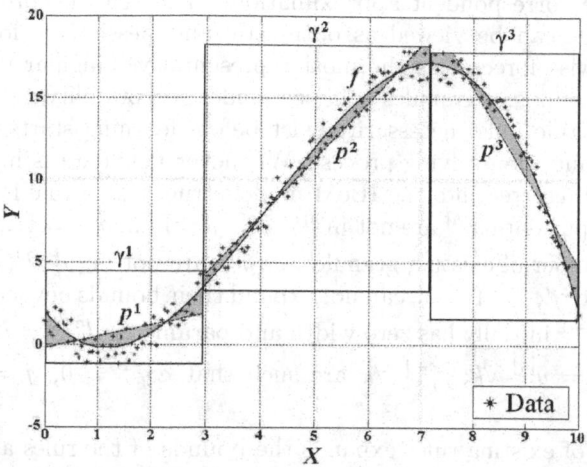

Fig. 2. Approximating a function f using 3 granules and 3 local linear models

More generally, let $\rho \in X \subseteq \mathbb{R}^n$ and $\sigma \in Y \subseteq \mathbb{R}^m$ be the width that a granule can assume in the input and output spaces, respectively. Suitable choices of ρ and σ are very important as they are directly related to the model accuracy. Any granule larger than these values may result in losing some desirable regions. A mechanism to deal with granularity is to learn values for ρ and σ themselves. A simple procedure is as follows. Let β be the number of rules created after a certain number of evolution steps H. If the number of rules grows faster than a threshold rate value η, then ρ and σ are increased by a factor $(1 + \beta/H)$ during the next steps. Otherwise, if the number of rules grows at a rate smaller than η, then ρ and σ are decreased by a factor $(1 - \beta/H)$.

In IBeM models, rules R^i associated with granules γ^i are of the type

R^i: IF $(l_1^i \leq x_1 \leq L_1^i)$ AND $(l_2^i \leq x_2 \leq L_2^i)$ AND ... AND $(l_n^i \leq x_n \leq L_n^i)$
    THEN $(u_1^i \leq y_1 \leq U_1^i)$ AND $p_1^i = a_{01}^i + \sum_{j=1}^n a_{j1}^i x_j$ AND
    $(u_2^i \leq y_2 \leq U_2^i)$ AND $p_2^i = a_{02}^i + \sum_{j=1}^n a_{j2}^i x_j$ AND
    ...
    $(u_m^i \leq y_m \leq U_m^i)$ AND $p_m^i = a_{0m}^i + \sum_{j=1}^n a_{jm}^i x_j$,

where l_j^i, L_j^i are the $j - th$ lower and upper bounds of the antecedent $x \in \mathbb{R}^n$; u_k^i, U_k^i are the $k - th$ lower and upper bounds of the consequent $y \in \mathbb{R}^m$; and p_k^i, $k = 1, ..., m$, are singular local linear functions in this case. In general, each p_k^i, $k = 1, ..., m$, can be of different type and do not need to be linear, but here we adopt linear functions for simplicity. The recursive least mean square (RLMS) algorithm can be used to determine the coefficients of the approximation functions.

It is interesting to notice that outputs for singular inputs enrich IBeM models power because they provide both, an approximate singular output and error bounds for the correspondent approximation. In forecasting problems, for instance, intervals can be viewed as optimistic and pessimistic forecast values, and the pointwise forecast as the most representative singular value. Singular forecasts and bounds of granules enhance model acceptability.

In IBeM no rule must necessarily exist before learning starts. All rules can be created during the evolving process. Whenever new data is input, rules can be created and inserted into the IBeM model structure. A rule is created when either i) the input data $x^{[h]}$ are not in $[l_j^i, L_j^i]$, $j = 1, ..., n$; $i = 1, ..., c$; where c is the current number of existing granules, or $y^{[h]}$ are not in $[u_k^i, U_k^i]$, $k = 1, ..., m$; $i = 1, ..., c$; or ii) γ^i, $i = 1, ..., c$, can not expand their bounds beyond ρ and σ. The new granule γ^{c+1} initially has zero width and parameters $l_j^{c+1} = L_j^{c+1} = x_j^{[h]}$ $\forall j$; $u_k^{c+1} = U_k^{c+1} = y_k^{[h]}$ $\forall k$; p_k^{c+1} $\forall k$ are such that $a_{jk}^{c+1} = 0$, $j = 1, ..., n$, and $a_{0k}^{c+1} = y_k^{[h]}$ $\forall k$.

Adaptation of existing rules expands the bounds of the rules antecedent and consequent to accommodate new data and simultaneously adjusts the coefficients of the local approximation functions. Bounds adaptation can be done as follows. Consider the simplest single input, single output case. Let E_ν^i, $\nu = 1, ..., 4$, be the expansion regions of a generic granule γ^i, such that $E_1^i = [L_j^i - \rho, l_j^i]$; $E_2^i = [L_j^i, l_j^i + \rho]$; $E_3^i = [U_k^i - \sigma, u_k^i]$; $E_4^i = [U_k^i, u_k^i + \sigma]$. If a input data $(x, y)^{[h]}$ is within the current bounds of γ^i for any i, then the endpoints remain at the current values and parameters of the local function p_k^i updated using least squares procedure. If $x_j^{[h]} \in E_1^i$ or $x_j^{[h]} \in E_2^i$, then the bounds of the granule γ^i is updated setting $l_j^i = x_j^{[h]}$ or $L_j^i = x_j^{[h]}$, respectively. Similarly, if $y_k^{[h]} \in E_3^i$ or $y_k^{[h]} \in E_4^i$, then the granule γ^i is updated making $u_k^i = y_k^{[h]}$ or $U_k^i = y_k^{[h]}$, respectively. Otherwise, if either $x_j^{[h]}$ or $y_k^{[h]}$ does not fit the expanded range of any γ^i, then the granule is not updated because they imply granules width beyond allowed values. Clearly, in the multidimensional case, $x_j^{[h]}$, $j = 1, ..., n$, and $y_k^{[h]}$, $k = 1, ..., m$, must be within the allowed expansion range of some γ^i to be accommodated.

New input data may cause revision of a rule R^i if values of the approximand p of f in γ^i change abruptly or gradually. In these cases, a granule can be split into smaller granules. Concept drifts may also cause rules revision. Rules can be deleted when they become inactive during a certain number of steps. This may mean that the process changed and the deletion of granules can be justified to keep the rule base size reasonable.

After a number of evolution steps H_M, two neighbor granules γ^w and γ^z can be close enough to justify their combination into a unique granule formed by their hull $\gamma^\psi = \mathrm{ch}(\gamma^w, \gamma^z)$ whenever the width of γ^ψ remains within the bounds ρ and σ. Clearly, merging granules means reducing the number of rules and contributes to eliminate gaps between close enough granules. If $\gamma^\psi = \mathrm{ch}(\gamma^w, \gamma^z)$ forms a granule whose width is larger than bounds ρ and σ, then gaps can be filled evaluating the endpoints of the neighbor granules. An approach we suggest is to add a new granule γ^{c+1} whose bounds are either $[L^w, l^z]$ or $[L^z, l^w]$, depending on the relative order of the neighbor granules. This approach is simple and particularly useful to extend the current model, to avoid gaps, and to reduce the effect of data input sequence.

The IBeM modeling procedure can be summarized as follows:

BEGIN
Initialize ρ, σ, H_G, η, H_D, H_M, $c = 0$;
Do forever
 Read $(x, y)^{[h]}$, $h = 1, ...$;
 If $(x_j^{[h]} \notin [L_j^i - \rho, l_j^i + \rho] \mid\mid y_k^{[h]} \notin [U_k^i - \sigma, u_k^i + \sigma])$, $i = 1, ..., c$; for any j, k
  Create γ^{c+1} and R^{c+1}; $c = c + 1$;
 Else if $(x_j^{[h]} \notin [l_j^i, L_j^i] \mid\mid y_k^{[h]} \notin [u_k^i, U_k^i])$, $\forall i$; for any j, k
  Update γ^i and R^i to accommodate $(x, y)^{[h]}$;
  Adjust p_k^i, $k = 1, ..., m$;
 Else
  Adjust p_k^i, $\forall k$;
 If $(h = H_G)$
  Update ρ and σ;
 If $(h = H_D)$
  Delete inactive granules and rules;
 If $(h = H_M)$
  If $(\mathrm{ch}(\gamma^w, \gamma^z) \leq \rho, \sigma)$, with γ^w, γ^z neighbor granules
   Merge γ^w and γ^z computing $\gamma^\psi = \mathrm{ch}(\gamma^w, \gamma^z)$;
  Else if $([L^w, l^z] \mid\mid [L^z, l^w] \leq \rho$ & $[U^w, u^z] \mid\mid [U^z, u^w] \leq \sigma)$
   Create γ^{c+1} and R^{c+1} covering the gap between γ^w and γ^z; $c = c + 1$;
 Discard $(x, y)^{[h]}$;
END

---

4 Application Example

In this section we address an economic time series forecasting problem using IBeM. In particular, we deal with daily (end of day) forecast of the Brazil Bovespa BVSP Index. Data from January 2nd, 1998 to December 1st, 2009 were used in the experiments. There are about 500 companies trading at BM&F BOVESPA, the Sao Paulo Stock Market, which is the fourth largest stock exchange in the Americas in terms of market capitalization. The benchmark indicator of BM&F BOVESPA is the Bovespa BVSP index. Forecasts aim at giving information to support investment decisions.

The following parameter values were chosen to evaluate IBeM behavior: $\rho^{[0]}$ $= 0.12$; $\sigma^{[0]} = 0.02$; $H_G = 50$; $\eta = 3$; $H_D = H_M = 200$. Figure 3 summarizes the results. Figures 3(a)-(b) show how the learning algorithm self-adjusts the granules size during evolution and uses more or less granules to capture the non-linearities and novel behaviors occurring in the time series. When the behavior of the time series changes quickly, the IBeM learning algorithm automatically reduces the size of the granules to avoid losing information and the number of rules increases accordingly. Figures 3(c)-(d) show the one-step singular and granular interval forecasts of the BVSP index. We notice that IBeM provides accurate singular forecasts from the point of view of the root mean square error ($RMSE = 0.079$). In addition, IBeM provides interval forecasts (optimistic and pessimistic bounds), an important information which helps to reduce investment risk. The results illustrate the potential of IBeM models to solve forecasting problems that demand online incremental adaptability.

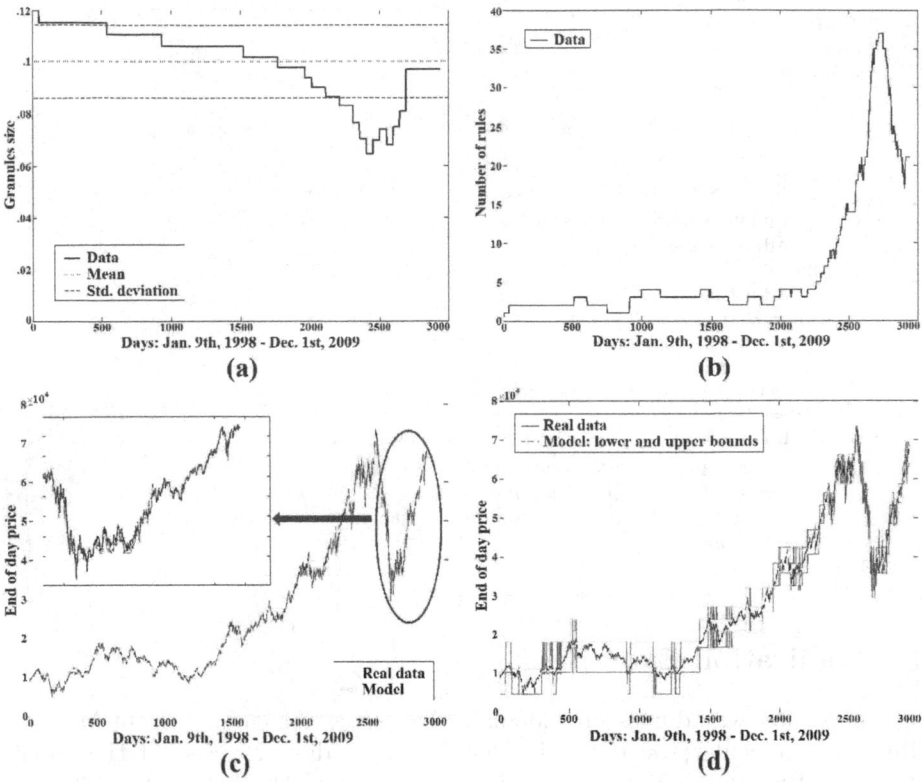

Fig. 3. Evolution of (a) granules size, and (b) number of rules during evolution steps. (c) One-step-ahead forecasts produced by IBeM, and (d) IBeM interval-valued forecasts.

5   Conclusion

This paper has introduced IBeM, a granular evolving approach for system modeling, focusing in intervals. IBeM is a rule-based modeling procedure that gradually reshapes granular model structures using singular data streams. IBeM develops global models using a one-pass learning algorithm, does not require any prior knowledge about learning data and system behavior, and may start learning as soon as data are input. IBeM is able to model nonlinear nonstationary systems and provides singular numerical outputs simultaneously with the bounds of the intervals. Experiments with an actual stock market forecasting problem have shown that IBeM is a feasible and efficient approach. Further work shall consider extensions to handle granular information and models within the framework of interval, fuzzy set, and stochastic evolving modeling.

Acknowledgment

The first author acknowledges CAPES, Brazil, for a fellowship. The second author thanks CEMIG, Brazil, for grant - P&D178. The last author is grateful to CNPq, Brazil, for grant 304596/2009-4.

References

1. Angelov, P., Filev, D.: An approach to online identification of Takagi-Sugeno fuzzy models. IEEE Transactions on SMC - Part B 34(1), 484–498 (2004)
2. Angelov, P., Zhou, X.: Evolving Fuzzy Rule-Based Classifiers from Data Streams. IEEE Transactions on Fuzzy Systems 16(6), 1462–1475 (2008)
3. Gabrys, B., Bargiela, A.: General fuzzy min-max neural network for clustering and classification. IEEE Trans. on Neural Networks 11(3), 769–783 (2000)
4. Kasabov, N.: Evolving Connectionist Systems: The Knowledge Engineering Approach., 2nd edn., 451 p. Springer, Heidelberg (2007)
5. Pedrycz, W., Gomide, F.: Fuzzy systems engineering: Toward human-centric computing, 526 p. Wiley, Hoboken (2007)
6. Leite, D.F., Costa Jr., P., Gomide, F.: Evolving Granular Classification Neural Networks. In: IEEE Int. Joint Conference on Neural Networks, pp. 1736–1743 (2009)
7. Leite, D.F., Costa Jr., P., Gomide, F.: Interval-Based Evolving Modeling. In: IEEE Workshop on Evolving and Self-Developing Intelligent Systems, pp. 1–8 (2009)
8. Bouchachia, A., Gabrys, B., Sahel, Z.: Overview of Some Incremental Learning Algorithms. In: IEEE International Conference on Fuzzy Systems, pp. 1–6 (2007)
9. Angelov, P., Filev, D., Kasabov, N.: Guest ed. Evolving Fuzzy Systems - Preface to the Special Sec. IEEE Trans. on Fuzzy Systems 6(6), 1390–1392 (2008)
10. Hansen, E.R., Walster, G.W.: Global optimization using interval analysis., 2nd edn., 489 p. Marcel Dekker, New York (2004)
11. Jaulin, L.; Keiffer, M.; Didrit, O.; Walter, E.: Applied Interval Analysis. 379 p. Springer-Verlag, London (2001)
12. Moore, R.E.: Interval Analysis, 145 p. Prentice Hall, Englewood Cliffs (1966)
13. Kreinovich, V.: Interval computations and interval-related statistical techniques. In: Adv. in Data Modeling for Meas. in the Metrology, pp. 119–147. Springer, Heidelberg (2008)
14. Hickey, T., Ju, Q., van Emden, M.H.: Interval Arithmetic: From Principles to Implementation. Journal of the ACM 48(5), 1038–1068 (2001)
15. Mitchell, T.: Machine Learning, 1st edn., 414 p. McGraw Hill, New York (1997)
16. Bishop, C.M.: Pattern Recognition and Machine Learning, 738 p. Springer, Heidelberg (2007)
17. Yao, J.T.: A Ten-year Review of Granular Computing. In: IEEE International Conference on Granular Computing, pp. 734–739 (2007)
18. Zadeh, L.A.: Towards a theory of fuzzy information granulation and its centrality in human reasoning and fuzzy logic. Fuzzy Sets Sys. 90(2), 111–127 (1997)

Data Mining in Precision Agriculture: Management of Spatial Information

Georg Ruß[1] and Alexander Brenning[2]

[1] Otto-von-Guericke-Universität Magdeburg, Germany
[2] University of Waterloo, Canada

Abstract. *Precision Agriculture* is the application of state-of-the-art GPS technology in connection with site-specific, sensor-based treatment of the crop. It can also be described as a data-driven approach to agriculture, which is strongly connected with a number of data mining problems. One of those is also an inherently important task in agriculture: yield prediction. The question is: can a field's yield be predicted in-season using available geo-coded data sets?

In the past, a number of approaches have been proposed towards this problem. Often, a broad variety of regression models for non-spatial data have been used, like regression trees, neural networks and support vector machines. But in a cross-validation learning approach, issues with the assumption of the data records' statistical independence keep emerging. Hence, the geographical location of data records should clearly be considered while establishing a regression model and assessing its predictive performance. This paper gives a short overview of the available data, points out in detail the main issue with the classical learning approaches and presents a novel spatial cross-validation technique to overcome the problems with the classical approach towards the aforementioned yield prediction task.

Keywords: Precision Agriculture, Spatial Data Mining, Regression, Spatial Cross-Validation.

1 Introduction

Information technology has become part of our everyday lives. Information-driven management techniques have become necessary and common in industry and services. Improvements in efficiency can be made in almost any part of businesses. This is especially true for agriculture, due to the modernization and better affordability of state-of-the-art GPS technology. Agricultural companies nowadays harvests not only crops but also growing amounts of data. These data are site specific – which is essentially why the combination of GPS, agriculture and data has been termed *site-specific crop management* (SSM). A large amount of information about the soil and crop properties enabling a higher operational efficiency is often contained in these data – appropriate techniques should therefore be applied to find this information. This is a rather common problem for which the term *data mining* has been coined. Data mining techniques aim at finding those patterns in the data that are both valuable and interesting for crop management.

Yield prediction is a specific agricultural problem commonly occurring. As early as possible, a farmer would like to know how much yield he is about to expect. The ability

E. Hüllermeier, R. Kruse, and F. Hoffmann (Eds.): IPMU 2010, LNAI 6178, pp. 350–359, 2010.

to predict yield used to rely on farmers' long-term knowledge of particular fields, crops and climate conditions. However, this knowledge is assumed to be available in the data collected during normal farming operations throughout the season(s) [23]. A multitude of sensor data are nowadays collected, measuring a field's heterogeneity. These data are fine-scale, often highly correlated and carry spatial information which must not be neglected.

The problem of yield prediction encountered can be treated as a problem of data mining and, specifically, multi-variate regression. This article will serve as a reference of how to treat a regression problem on spatial data with a combination of classical regression techniques using a novel data sampling idea. Furthermore, this article will serve as a continuation of [19]: in the previous article, the spatial data were treated with regression models which do not take the spatial relationships into account. In the present work, we will adapt existing approaches for error estimation using spatial cross-validation approaches [4,5] to the context of crop yield prediction and spatial regression more generally. Resampling-based estimation methods (such as cross-validation and the bootstrap) for dependent data in general have been investigated recently in the context of time series data [7] and paired data [6].

1.1 Research Target

The main research target of this work is to improve and further substantiate the validity of *yield prediction* approaches using multi-variate regression modeling techniques. Previous work, mainly the regression work presented in [19,22], will be used as a baseline for this work. Some of the drawbacks of the previous approach will be clearly pointed out in this article. Nevertheless, this work aims to improve upon existing yield prediction models and, furthermore, incorporates a generic, yet novel spatial clustering idea into the process. Therefore, different types of regression techniques will be incorporated into a novel spatial cross-validation framework (compare [4,5]). A comparison of using spatial vs. non-spatial cross-validation will be presented.

1.2 Article Structure

This article will start with a brief introduction into the area of precision agriculture and a more detailed description of the available data in Section 2. This will be followed by an outline of the key techniques and the novel spatial sampling technique described in this work in Section 3. The results obtained from the modeling phase will be presented in Section 4. The article will be completed with a short conclusion in Section 5, which will also point out further lines of research.

2 Data Description

The data available in this work were collected during the growing season of 2007 on two fields south of Köthen, Germany. The data for the two fields, called *F440* and *F611*, respectively, were interpolated using kriging [24] to a grid with 10 by 10 meters grid cell sizes. F440 is geographically located around N51.68, E11.99 and has a size of roughly 95 hectares, whereas F611 has a size of around 50 hectares and is located around N51.68, E11.85. Each grid cell represents a record with all available information. The fields grew winter wheat. Nitrogen fertilizer (N) was applied three times during the growing season. Overall, for each field there are six input attributes, accompanied by the respective current year's yield (2007) as the target attribute. In total, for the F440 field there are 6446 records, for F611 there are 4970 records.

Yield is measured in metric tons per hectare ($\frac{t}{ha}$), along the harvesting lanes (spaced 8 m apart), roughly every ten meters. The yield ranges, as well as those of the remaining attributes, are provided in Table 1. Apparent electrical soil conductivity (EC25) as a measure for a number of soil properties is acquired. Satellite or aerial image processing provides a measure of vegetation called the red edge inflection point (REIP) value, at two points into the growing season (REIP32, REIP49), according to the growing stage defined in [15]. The REIP value may also be used directly for guiding fertilizations [11]. A simplified assumption is that a higher REIP value means more vegetation. Three nitrogen fertilizer dressings are applied (N1, N2, N3, in $\frac{kg}{ha}$). In the available data, due to the fields being experimental agriculture sites, the nitrogen dressings were not temporally autocorrelated. However, this phenomenon may be considered in production sites. EC, REIP and N are measured in 10-m-intervals along the lanes which are spaced 24 meters apart.

Table 1. Statistical summary of data sets

	F440				F611			
	min	mean	median	max	min	mean	median	max
EC25	39.47	50.13	50.22	60.69	38.41	54.44	53.17	81.98
N1	50.00	63.57	70.00	70.00	42.00	65.09	68.00	70.00
N2	2.00	47.60	48.00	80.00	0.00	47.89	50.00	80.00
N3	0.00	37.98	40.00	95.00	0.00	45.61	50.00	68.00
REIP32	721.33	725.11	725.19	728.14	721.41	724.37	724.41	726.09
REIP49	724.50	727.20	727.34	729.82	721.30	727.12	727.23	729.41
YIELD07	0.49	7.37	6.89	13.92	1.32	5.42	5.51	11.88

2.1 Spatial vs. Non-spatial Data Treatment

According to [10], *spatial autocorrelation* is the correlation among values of a single variable strictly attributable to the proximity of those values in geographic space, introducing a deviation from the *independent observations* assumption of classical statistics. Given a spatial data set, spatial autocorrelation can be determined using Moran's I ([16]) or semivariograms. For the data sets used in this article, each of the attributes exhibits spatial autocorrelation. Figure 1 shows two representative experimental omnidirectional semivariograms, while the remaining attributes behave similarly. In practice, it is usually also known from the data origin whether spatial autocorrelation exists. For further information it is referred to, e.g., [8].

In previous articles using the above data, such as [20,19], the main focus was on finding a suitable regression model to predict the current year's yield sufficiently well. However, the used regression models, such as neural networks [20,21] or support vector

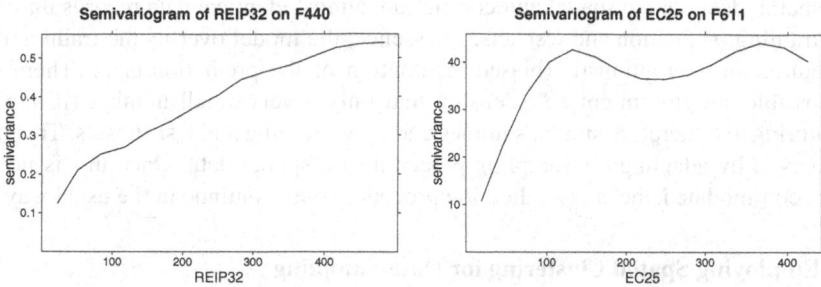

Fig. 1. Semivariograms (omnidirectional, experimental) for REIP32 (F440) and EC25 (F611)

regression [19], among others, generally assume statistical independence of the data records. However, with the given geo-tagged data records at hand, this is clearly not the case, due to (natural) spatial autocorrelation. Therefore, the spatial relationships between data records have to be taken into account, which the following section will deal with.

3 Regression Techniques on Spatial Data

Due to the shortcomings in classical regression and cross-validation learning approaches when using them on spatial data, this section will present a novel regression model for data sets which exhibit spatial autocorrelation. In non-spatial regression models, data records which appear in the training set are not supposed to appear in the test set during a cross-validation learning setup. Classical sampling methods do not take spatial neighborhoods of data records into account. Therefore, the above assumption may be rendered invalid when using non-spatial models on spatial data. This inevitably leads to overfitting and underestimates the true prediction error of the regression model (compare [4,6] for similar observations in a classification context). Therefore, the main issue is to avoid having neighboring or the same samples in training and testing data subsets during a cross-validation learning approach. The basic idea therefore is to apply changes to the resampling method and keep the regression modeling techniques as-is. The resulting procedure can be seen as spatial cross-validation technique.

3.1 From Classical to Spatial Cross-Validation

Traditionally, k-fold cross-validation for regression randomly subdivides a given data set into three parts: a training set, a validation set and a test set. A 10- to 20-fold cross-validation is usually considered appropriate to remove bias [13]. The regression model is trained on the training set until the prediction error on the validation set starts to rise. Once this happens, the training process is stopped and the error on the test set is reported for this fold. This procedure is repeated r times to remove a possible sampling bias. In our case, r has been empirically determined as 100.

In spatial data, due to spatial autocorrelation, almost identical data records may end up in training, validation and test sets. In essence, the model overfits the training data and returns an overoptimistic (biased) estimation of the prediction error. Therefore, one possible solution might be to ensure that only a very small number (if any) of neighboring and therefore similar samples end up in training and test subsets. This may be achieved by adapting the sampling procedure for spatial data. Once this issue has been accommodated, the cross-validation procedure may continue in the usual way.

3.2   Employing Spatial Clustering for Data Sampling

Given the data sets F440 and F611, a regular tessellation using a grid-based approach may be used to subdivide the fields into spatially disjunct areas. However, even though the data have been sampled on a regular grid, there are irregularities in the field. These are due to the fields' outer shape, "holes" in the data (power poles, buildings etc.) or the lanes of machinery, among other reasons. This would lead to some grid cells being much less equally dense populated than others. Therefore, a grid-based approch is rather rigid and would have to be adapted manually for each field. Hence, a more flexible method will be used here.

We assume that a spatial clustering procedure can be employed to subdivide the fields into spatially disjunct clusters or zones. The clustering algorithm can easily be run on the data records' spatial map, using the data records' longitude and latitude. Depending on the clustering algorithm parameters, this results in a tesselation map which does not consider any of the attributes, but only the spatial neighborhood between data records. A depiction of this clustering process can be found in Figure 2(a). As may be seen in the figure, the clustering leads to clusters (spatial areas) covering roughly the same number of points, due to the relatively regular data point density encountered here. In analogy to the non-spatial regression treatment of these data records, now a spatially-aware cross-validation regression problem can be handled using the k resulting zones of the clustering algorithm as an input for k-fold cross-validation. This ensures that the training set has only a small amount of spatial autocorrelation with the test set. Standard models, as described below, can be used straightforwardly, without requiring changes to the models themselves. The experimental setup and the results are presented in the following section.

The training and test sets are selected from the clusters using random sampling. Therefore, a small number of points in neighboring areas are still possibly spatially autocorrelated. This could be avoided by using a sampling method which takes the spatial relationships between the clusters into account. However, when comparing the standard, non-spatial regression setup to the one described here, it is assumed that the difference in the error underestimation is much higher than the one of introducing a space-aware sampling method on the clusters.

The spatial clustering procedure may be considered as a broader definition of the standard cross-validation setup. This can be seen as follows: when refining the clustering further, the spatial zones on the field become smaller. The border case is reached when the field is subdivided into as many clusters as there are data records, i.e. each data record describes its own cluster. In this special case, the advantages of spatial clustering are lost since no spatial neighborhoods are taken into account in this approach.

Therefore, the number of clusters should be seen as a tradeoff between predictive precision and statistical validity of the model. The parameter k for the size of the tessellation has to be determined heuristically.

3.3 Regression Techniques

In previous work ([19,20]), numerous regression modeling techniques have been compared on similar data sets to determine which of those modeling techniques works best. Support vector regression has been determined as the best modeling technique. It has furthermore recently been shown to work rather successfully in spatial classification tasks, albeit without spatial cross-validation, as in [17]. Hence, in this work support vector regression will serve as a benchmark technique against which further models will have to compete. Experiments are conducted in R [18]. It is assumed that the reader is mostly familiar with the regression techniques below. Therefore, the techniques used are described in short. References to further details are given, where appropriate. The performance of the models will be determined using the root mean squared error (RMSE).

Support Vector Regression. Support Vector Machines (SVMs) are a supervised learning method discovered by [1]. They were originally described for the use in classification, but can also be applied to regression tasks, where optimization of a cost function is achieved. The model produced by support vector regression depends only on a subset of the training data – which are essentially the support vectors. Further details can be found in [19]. In the current experiments, the *svm* implementation from the *e1071* R package has been used.

Regression Trees. Regression trees have seen some usage in agriculture [9,12,14]. Essentially, they are a special case of decision trees where the outcome (in the tree leaves) is a continuous function instead of a discrete classification. The *rpart* R package has been used.

Random Forests. According to [3], random forests are a combination of tree predictors such that each tree depends on the values of a random vector sampled independently and with the same distribution for all trees in the forest. In the version used here, the random forest is used as a regression technique. Basically, a random forest is an ensemble method that consists of many regression trees and outputs a combined result of those trees as a prediction for the target variable. Usually, the generalization error for forests converges to a limit as the number of trees in the forest becomes large. The *randomForest* R package has been used.

Bootstrap Aggregating. Bootstrap aggregating (or bagging) has first been described in [2]. It is generally described as a method for generating multiple versions of a predictor and using these for obtaining an aggregate predictor. In the regression case, the prediction outcomes are averaged. Multiple versions of the predictor are constructed by taking bootstrap samples of the learning set and using these as new learning sets. Bagging is generally considered useful in regression setups where small changes in the training data set can cause large perturbations in the predicted target variables. Since random forests are a variant of bagging where regression trees are used as the internal predictor, both random forests and bagging should deliver similar results. Running them on the data sets should therefore deliver similar results as well, since the bagging implementation in the R *ipred* package internally uses regression trees for prediction. Therefore, the main difference between random forests and bagging in this article is that both techniques are implicitly run with different parameters.

4 Results

The main research target of this article is to assess whether existing spatial autocorrelation in the data sets may fail to be captured in standard, non-spatial regression modeling setups. Therefore, the approach consists of a comparison between a non-spatial and a spatial regression with cross-validation setup. The non-spatial setup was described in Section 3.1, the spatial setup has been presented in Section 3.2.

The results in Table 2 confirm that the spatial autocorrelation inherent in the data set leads classical, non-spatial regression modeling setups to a substantial underestimation of the prediction error. This outcome is consistent throughout the results, regardless of the used technique and regardless of the parameters. Furthermore, it can be seen that Random Forests seem to yield better performance in terms of lower prediction error, regardless of the setup used. For an illustrative depiction of the RMSE in the spatial approach see Figure 2(b), which shows the dataset partitioned into 50 spatial clusters with the cross-validation RMSE displayed.

Moreover, the spatial setup can be easily set to emulate the non-spatial setup: set k to be the number of data records in the data set. Therefore the larger the parameter k is set, the smaller the difference between the spatial and the non-spatial setup should be. This assumption also holds true for almost all of the obtained results.

Table 2. Results of running different setups on the data sets F440 and F611; comparison of spatial vs. non-spatial treatment of data sets; root mean squared error is shown, averaged over clusters/folds; k is either the number of clusters in the spatial setup or the number of folds in the non-spatial setup

	k	F440		F611	
		spatial	non-spatial	spatial	non-spatial
Support Vector Regression	10	1.06	0.54	0.73	0.40
	20	1.00	0.54	0.71	0.40
	50	0.91	0.53	0.67	0.38
Regression Tree	10	1.09	0.56	0.69	0.40
	20	0.99	0.56	0.68	0.42
	50	0.91	0.55	0.66	0.40
Random Forest	10	0.99	0.50	0.65	0.41
	20	0.92	0.50	0.64	0.41
	50	0.85	0.48	0.63	0.39
Bagging	10	1.09	0.59	0.66	0.42
	20	1.01	0.59	0.66	0.42
	50	0.94	0.58	0.65	0.41

F440, 20 clusters

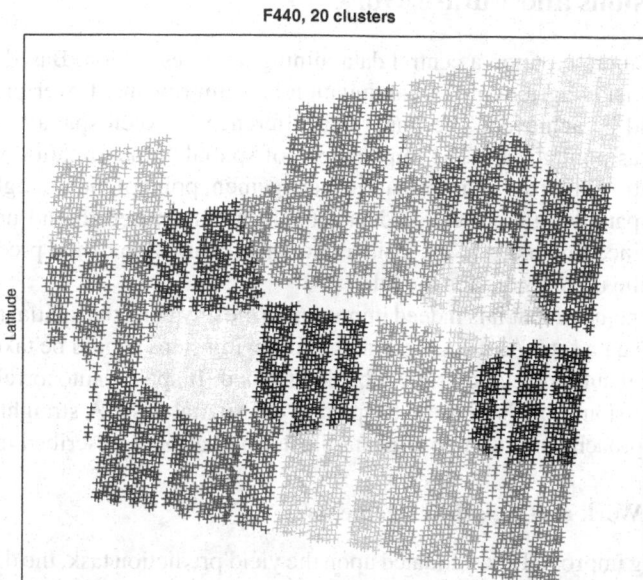

(a) k-means clustering on F440, $k = 20$

F440, 50 clusters, svm.rmse

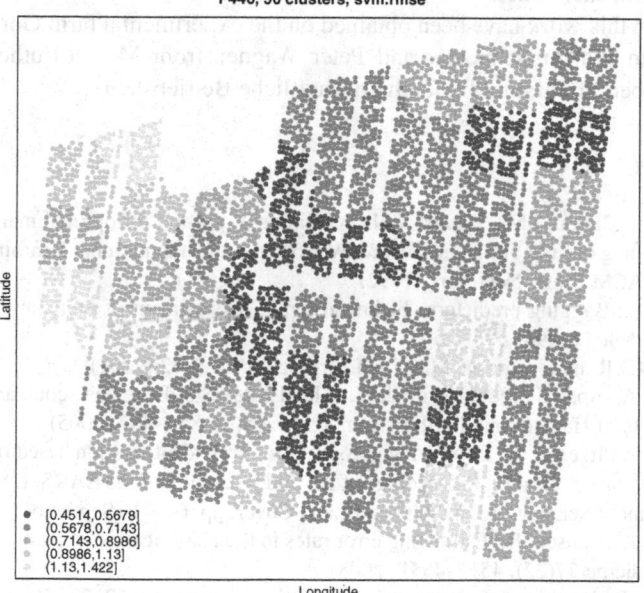

● [0.4514,0.5678]
● [0.5678,0.7143]
● (0.7143,0.8986]
● (0.8986,1.13]
● (1.13,1.422]

(b) spatial cross-validation on field F440, $k = 50$, RMSE is shown

Fig. 2. k-means clustering on F440 and resulting cross-validation RMSE

5   Conclusions and Future Work

This article elaborated upon a central data mining task: regression. Based on two data sets from precision agriculture, a continuation and improvement over previous work ([19,20]) could be achieved. The important difference between spatial data and non-spatial data was pointed out. The implications of spatial autocorrelation in these data sets were mentioned. From an information management point of view, neighboring data records in a spatially autocorrelated data sets are not supposed to end up in training and test sets since this leads to a considerable underestimation of the prediction error, regardless of the used regression model.

It can be concluded that it is indeed important to closely consider spatial relationships inherent in the data sets. As a suggestion, the following steps should be taken: for those data, the spatial autocorrelation should be determined. If spatial autocorrelation exists, standard regression models must be adapted to the spatial case. A straightforward and illustrative approach using simple k-means clustering has been described in this article.

5.1   Future Work and Acknowledgements

Despite having improved and validated upon the yield prediction task, the data sets carry further information. *Variable importance* refers to the question which of the variables is actually contributing most to the yield prediction task. *Management zones* refers to discovering interesting zones on the (heterogeneous) field which should be managed differently from each other.

The data in this work have been obtained on the experimental farm Görzig and were acquired from Martin Schneider and Peter Wagner from Martin-Luther-Universität Halle-Wittenberg, Lehrstuhl für landwirtschaftliche Betriebslehre.

References

1. Boser, B.E., Guyon, I.M., Vapnik, V.N.: A training algorithm for optimal margin classifiers. In: Proceedings of the 5th Annual ACM Workshop on Computational Learning Theory, pp. 144–152. ACM Press, New York (1992)
2. Breiman, L.: Bagging predictors. Technical report, Department of Statistics, Univ. of California, Berkeley (1994)
3. Breiman, L.: Random forests. Machine Learning 45(1), 5–32 (2001)
4. Brenning, A.: Spatial prediction models for landslide hazards: review, comparison and evaluation. Natural Hazards and Earth System Science 5(6), 853–862 (2005)
5. Brenning, A., Itzerott, S.: Comparing classifiers for crop identification based on multitemporal landsat tm/etm data. In: Proceedings of the 2nd workshop of the EARSeL Special Interest Group Remote Sensing of Land Use and Land Cover, pp. 64–71 (September 2006)
6. Brenning, A., Lausen, B.: Estimating error rates in the classification of paired organs. Statistics in Medicine 27(22), 4515–4531 (2008)
7. Bühlmann, P.: Bootstraps for time series. Statistical Science 17, 52–72 (2002)
8. Cressie, N.A.C.: Statistics for Spatial Data. Wiley, New York (1993)
9. Crone, S.F., Lessmann, S., Pietsch, S.: Forecasting with computational intelligence - an evaluation of support vector regression and artificial neural networks for time series prediction. In: International Joint Conference on Neural Networks, 2006. IJCNN '06, pp. 3159–3166 (2006)

10. Griffith, D.A.: Spatial Autocorrelation and Spatial Filtering. In: Advances in Spatial Science, Springer, New York (2003)
11. Heege, H., Reusch, S., Thiessen, E.: Prospects and results for optical systems for site-specific on-the-go control of nitrogen-top-dressing in germany. Precision Agriculture 9(3), 115–131 (2008)
12. Huang, C., Yang, L., Wylie, B., Homer, C.: A strategy for estimating tree canopy density using landsat 7 etm+ and high resolution images over large areas. In: Proceedings of the Third International Conference on Geospatial Information in Agriculture and Forestry (2001)
13. Kohavi, R.: A study of cross-validation and bootstrap for accuracy estimation and model selection. In: Proceedings of International Joint Conference on Artificial Intelligence (1995)
14. Lobell, D.B., Ortiz-Monasterio, J.I., Asner, G.P., Naylor, R.L., Falcon, W.P.: Combining field surveys, remote sensing, and regression trees to understand yield variations in an irrigated wheat landscape. Agronomy Journal 97, 241–249 (2005)
15. Meier, U.: Entwicklungsstadien mono- und dikotyler Pflanzen. In: Biologische Bundesanstalt fünd- und Forstwirtschaft, Braunschweig, Germany (2001)
16. Moran, P.A.P.: Notes on continuous stochastic phenomena. Biometrika 37, 17–33 (1950)
17. Pozdnoukhov, A., Foresti, L., Kanevski, M.: Data-driven topo-climatic mapping with machine learning methods. Natural Hazards 50(3), 497–518 (2009)
18. R Development Core Team: R: A Language and Environment for Statistical Computing. In: R Foundation for Statistical Computing, Vienna, Austria (2009) ISBN 3-900051-07-0
19. Ruß, G.: Data mining of agricultural yield data: A comparison of regression models. In: Perner, P. (ed.) Advances in Data Mining. Applications and Theoretical Aspects. LNCS, vol. 5633, pp. 24–37. Springer, Heidelberg (2009)
20. Ruß, G., Kruse, R., Schneider, M., Wagner, P.: Estimation of neural network parameters for wheat yield prediction. In: Bramer, M. (ed.) AI in Theory and Practice II, July 2008. Proceedings of IFIP 2008, vol. 276, pp. 109–118. Springer, Heidelberg (July 2008)
21. Ruß, G., Kruse, R., Schneider, M., Wagner, P.: Optimizing wheat yield prediction using different topologies of neural networks. In: Verdegay, J., Ojeda-Aciego, M., Magdalena, L. (eds.) Proceedings of IPMU '08, pp. 576–582. University of Málaga (June 2008)
22. Ruß, G., Kruse, R., Wagner, P., Schneider, M.: Data mining with neural networks for wheat yield prediction. In: Perner, P. (ed.) ICDM 2008. LNCS (LNAI), vol. 5077, pp. 47–56. Springer, Heidelberg (2008)
23. Stafford, J.V., Ambler, B., Lark, R.M., Catt, J.: Mapping and interpreting the yield variation in cereal crops. Computers and Electronics in Agriculture 14(2-3), 101–119 (1996), Spatially Variable Field Operations
24. Stein, M.L.: Interpolation of Spatial Data: Some Theory for Kriging. Springer Series in Statistics. Springer, Heidelberg (June 1999)

Fuzzy Multivariable Gaussian Evolving Approach for Fault Detection and Diagnosis

André Lemos[1], Walmir Caminhas[1], and Fernando Gomide[2],*

[1] Department of Electrical Engineering, Federal University of Minas Gerais, MG, Brazil
[2] School of Electrical and Computer Engineering, University of Campinas, SP, Brazil

Abstract. This paper suggests an approach for fault detection and diagnosis capable to detect new operation modes online. The approach relies upon an evolving fuzzy classifier able to incorporate new operational information using an incremental unsupervised clustering procedure. The efficiency of the approach is verified in fault detection and diagnosis of an induction machine. Experimental results suggest that the approach is a promising alternative for fault diagnosis of dynamic systems when there is no a priori information about all failure modes. It is also attractive for incremental learning of diagnosis systems with streams of data.

Keywords: Evolving Fuzzy Systems, Participatory Learning, Adaptive Fault Detection and Diagnosis.

1   Introduction

Fault detection and diagnosis (FDD) of dynamical systems has been systematically pursued by many researchers during the last decade. Basically, this is due to the high importance of FDD in real world applications, specially in industry. Conventional methods for FDD use complete operation information to identify all operation modes, i.e., normal and faulty operation modes [1].

However, in practical situations some operation modes may be unknown and/or may change due to wear off, maintenance, repair or replacement of parts and components. In these situations, conventional fault detection and diagnostics approaches are impractical, but health monitoring approaches can be used to detect abnormal operation modes related to failures. Health monitoring literature emphasizes methods based on statistical process control [2], machine learning approaches [3, 4, 5], and on the notion of novelty detection [6]. These health monitoring approaches can be used for fault detection but normally they lack diagnosis ability because they can detect, but can not classify faults [3].

This paper suggests an online fault detection and diagnosis approach capable to detect faults and to perform adaptive diagnostic. The proposed method uses an evolving

* The authors thank the Brazilian National Research Council, CNPq, for grants 141323/2009-4, 309666/2007-4 and 304857/2006-8, respectively. The second author also acknowledges the support of FAPEMIG, the Research Foundation of the State of Minas Gerais, grant PPM-00252-09.

E. Hüllermeier, R. Kruse, and F. Hoffmann (Eds.): IPMU 2010, LNAI 6178, pp. 360–369, 2010.

fuzzy classifier for fault diagnosis. Evolving fuzzy systems (eFS) are a synergy between fuzzy systems, as a mechanism for information compactation and representation, and recursive methods of machine learning [7, 8].

The evolving fuzzy classifier is a set of linguistic fuzzy rules built using features extracted from data of the monitored process. The classifier uses an incremental unsupervised clustering algorithm and information provided by the process operator. Each cluster created by the clustering algorithm generates a corresponding fuzzy rule with antecedent parameters extracted from the cluster. New clusters may indicate new operation conditions or faults. The process operator is notified whenever a novel operation condition is detected and prompted to identify the corresponding operation mode. The mode identified defines the consequent of the new rule.

The clustering algorithm adopted by the evolving fuzzy classifier is based on the idea of participatory learning [9]. Participatory learning (PL) is a learning paradigm which assumes that learning beliefs about the system depend on what the learning mechanism has already learned. An essential characteristic of this learning mechanism is that a new observation impact in causing learning or belief revision depends on its compatibility with the current system belief. Therefore, clustering algorithms based on participatory learning [10], and hence the classifier suggested herein, tend to be robust to noisy data because outliers are likely to be incompatible with the current system belief and can be either discarded or have their effect smoothed. The evolving clustering procedure developed here is as an extension of the one addressed in [10]. Differently from the algorithm of [10], here the clustering procedure assumes that each cluster can be represented by a multivariable Gaussian distribution and, based on this assumption, statistical tests help to find the cluster structure (number and shape of clusters) at each step of the algorithm.

Different evolving fuzzy fault detection approaches have been developed [11, 12, 13, 14], but none of them is capable to perform online diagnosis of a system. This paper differs from the ones reported in literature because it addresses a fault and diagnosis approach capable to perform online detection of new operation modes using an algorithm robust to noisy data. It also performs model-free adaptive diagnosis with simultaneous update of operation modes, and incorporates information about new operation modes.

The remaining of the paper is organized as follows. Next Sect. 2 details the evolving fuzzy classifier. Section 3 addresses the fault detection and diagnosis approach. Section 4 illustrates an application in online fault detection and diagnosis of induction machines. Conclusions and further developments are summarized in Sect. 5.

2   Gaussian Participatory Evolving Clustering

The clustering algorithm assumes that knowledge about the system to be modeled is a cluster structure, i.e, the number of clusters and the corresponding cluster centers c_i^k for $i = 1, \cdots, nc^k$, where nc^k is the number of clusters at step k. The shape of clusters is encoded in Σ^k. At each step, the learning process may create a new cluster, modify the parameters of an existing one, or merge two similar clusters.

The cluster structure is updated using a compatibility measure $\rho_i^k \in [0, 1]$ and an arousal index, $a_i^k \in [0, 1]$. The compatibility measure shows how much an observation is compatible with the current cluster structure. The arousal index is the output of a arousal device that acts as a critic which prompts the learning mechanism when the current structure should be revised in front of new information.

Thresholds are defined for the compatibility measure (T_ρ) and the arousal index (T_a). At each step, if the compatibility measure of the current observation is smaller than the threshold for all clusters, i.e, $\rho_i^k < T_\rho \ \forall \ i = 1, \cdots, nc^k$, and the arousal index of the cluster with the greatest compatibility is greater than its threshold, i.e, $a_i^k > T_a$ for $i = \arg\max_i \rho_i^k$, then a new cluster is created. Otherwise the cluster with the highest compatibility is adjusted as follows:

$$c_i^{k+1} = c_i^k + G_i^k(x^k - c_i^k) \tag{1}$$

$$G_i^k = \alpha(\rho_i^k)^{1-a_i^k} \tag{2}$$

where $\alpha \in [0, 1]$ is the basic learning rate.

If $a_i^k = 0$, then $G_i^k = \alpha\rho_i^k$ and the PL procedure has no arousal. The basic learning rate is modulated by the compatibility measure.

The arousal index is the output of an arousal device used to measure the confidence about the current knowledge of the system. For example, while a single low value of the compatibility measure causes aversion to learning, a sequence of low values of the compatibility measure should imply on a revision of the current knowledge about the system. The arousal device is a monitoring mechanism of the dynamics of the compatibility measure that monitors the values of the compatibility level. Its output is interpreted as the complement of the confidence about the current knowledge. A low value of a_i^k implies in a high confidence about the system belief, while a high value indicates the necessity to revise the current belief. Analysis of (2) shows that as the arousal index increases the compatibility measure reduces its effect. This means that if a sequence of observations presents low compatibility values, then it is more likely that the current knowledge is incorrect and should be revised. As explained later in this section, the extreme case is when the arousal index exceeds a threshold and a new cluster is generated.

This paper assumes each cluster is modeled by a multivariable Gaussian distribution, similarly as in Gaussian mixture models [15]. In particular, the compatibility measure ρ_i^k suggested herein uses the squared of the normalized distance between the new observation and cluster centers (*M-Distance*):

$$M(x^k, c_i^k) = (x^k - c_i^k)(\Sigma_i^k)^{-1}(x^k - c_i^k)^T \tag{3}$$

To compute the *M-Distance*, the dispersion matrix of each cluster Σ_i^k must be estimated at each step. The recursive estimation of the dispersion matrix proceeds as follows [16]:

$$\Sigma_i^{k+1} = (1 - G_i^k)(\Sigma_i^k - G_i^k(x^k - c_i^k)(x^k - c_i^k)^T) \tag{4}$$

It is interesting to note that, in the particular case when $G_i^k = 1/k = \delta^k$, it can be easily shown that (1) is the recursive estimation of the mean vector for each cluster and (4) is the recursive estimation of the covariance matrix.

The compatibility measure at each step k is computed as follows:

$$\rho_i^k = F(x^k, c_i^k) = \exp\left[-\frac{1}{2}M(x^k, c_i^k)\right] \tag{5}$$

To find a threshold value for the compatibility measure, we notice that, since it is assumed that each cluster is a multivariable Gaussian distribution, $M(x^k, c_i^k)$ can be modeled by a Chi-Square distribution. Thus, given a significance level λ, the threshold can be computed as follows

$$T_\rho = \exp\left[-\frac{1}{2}\chi^2_{m,\lambda}\right] \tag{6}$$

where $\chi^2_{m,\lambda}$ is the λ upper unilateral confidence interval of a Chi-Square distribution with m degrees of freedom (m is the number of inputs).

This paper adopts an arousal mechanism to monitor the compatibility index using a sliding window assembled by the last w values. More specifically, the arousal index is defined as the probability of observing less then v violations of the compatibility threshold on a sequence of w observations. Low values of the arousal index are associated with no or few violations of the compatibility threshold, implying a high confidence about the system knowledge. High values of the arousal index are associated with several threshold violations, which means that the current cluster structure must be revised.

The arousal index for each observation is computed using *occurrence* values o^k

$$o^k = \begin{cases} 0 \text{ for } M(x^k, c_i^k) < \chi^2_{n,\lambda} \\ 1 \text{ otherwise} \end{cases} \tag{7}$$

Assuming that the current observation fits a cluster, the probability of observing $o^k = 1$ is known, i.e., it is equal to the confidence level used to estimate the threshold given by (6). This assumption means that the random variable O^k can be described by a *Bernoulli* distribution with a probability of success λ.

For a sequence assembled by the last w observations, the number of threshold violations ($o^k = 1$), v^k is

$$v^k = \sum_{i=0}^{w-1} o^{k-i} \tag{8}$$

The discrete probability distribution of observing v threshold violations on a window of size w is $p(V^k = v)$, with V^k assuming the values $v = 0, 1, \cdots, w$. Since V^k is the sum of a sequence of i.i.d. random variables drawn from a Bernoulli distribution with the same probability of success λ, $p(V^k = v)$ can be described by a *binomial* distribution. The binomial distribution gives the probability of observing v threshold violations in a sequence of w observations, assuming that the observations used to compute the *M-Distance* fits the multivariable Gaussian distribution of a current cluster. High probability values enforce the assumption that observations can be described by the current cluster structure while low probability values suggests that the observations should be described by a new cluster. The arousal index is the value of the cumulative probability of V^k, $a_i^k = p(V^k < v)$, i.e., the cumulative probability of a binomial distribution.

The threshold value of the arousal index T_a (used to decide creation of new clusters) is defined for a given significance level λ (the same as the one that defines the threshold for the compatibility measure). However, since each observation is in w windows, a multiple-comparison correction must be used to avoid spurious cluster creation. The

Bonferroni correction [17] must be performed dividing the desired significance level by the number of tests. Thus, for a significance level λ, a new cluster is created only if

$$a_i^k > 1 - \frac{\lambda}{w} \tag{9}$$

As discussed later, the clustering algorithm continuously revises the current cluster structure and eventually merges two similar clusters. The compatibility between all pairs of cluster centers is computed at each step. If, for each pair, the compatibility exceeds the threshold T_ρ, then the two clusters are merged.

The clustering process can be started using either a single observation or an initial data set. If an initial data set is available, then an off-line clustering algorithm can be used to estimate an initial number of clusters and their parameters. If the clustering process starts with a single observation, then an initial dispersion matrix Σ_{init} must be chosen, eventually using a priori information.

Whenever a new cluster is created, the new cluster center is set as the current observation and the new dispersion matrix set to an initial value Σ_{init}. When two clusters are merged, the center of the resulting cluster is the average of the corresponding clusters centers and the dispersion matrix the average of the corresponding dispersion matrices.

3   Online Fault Detection and Diagnosis Approach

The online fault detection and diagnosis (FDD) approach proposed in this paper is an evolving fuzzy classifier. The classifier is an adaptive set of linguistic fuzzy rules defined and updated using the incremental unsupervised Gaussian participatory clustering procedure. The classifier inputs are features extracted from data of the monitored process. We assume that the feature extraction procedure selects all features needed to distinguish the different operation modes. Initially, these features are used to estimate the current operation mode using the current rule base. Next, these features are input to

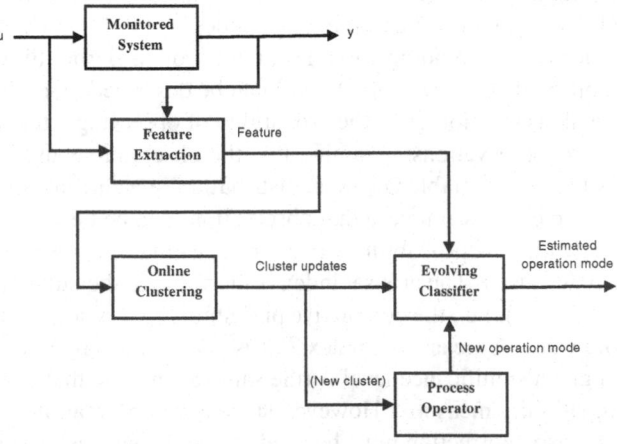

Fig. 1. Online fault detection and diagnosis approach

the online clustering procedure which may update the parameters of the clusters, merge two clusters, or create a new cluster. Clusters update causes adaptation of the fuzzy rules. Figure 1 summarizes the online FDD approach.

Whenever a new cluster is created, if the membership degree of the current operation mode estimation is bellow threshold $T_{\mu_y} \in (0, 1]$, then the operator is notified and he informs if the associated event is either a new operation mode or a mode already identified. If the event is a new operation mode, then the operator must identify it. This information is incorporated in the evolving fuzzy classifier as a new rule whose antecedent parameters are extracted from the cluster found, and the consequent is the operation mode defined by the operator. When a new cluster is created, but the membership degree of the current operation mode estimation is above threshold T_{μ_y}, then a new rule is created. The rule antecedent parameters are extracted from the new cluster, and the rule consequent is the operation mode estimated by the classifier.

Rules merge only when they have the same consequent because, otherwise, they represent distinct operation modes.

Procedure *FDD Algorithm*
Estimate the current operation mode;
$[\hat{y}^k \mu_{\hat{y}^k}] = classifier.classify(x^k)$
Compute ρ_i and a_i for all clusters;
$\rho_i = \exp\left[-\frac{1}{2}M(x^k, c_i)\right] \forall i;$
$a_i = p(V^k < v) \; \forall i;$
$idx = \arg\max_i(\rho);$
if $\rho_i < T_{rho} \; \forall i$ *and* $a_{idx^k} > T_a$ **then**
    Create new rule;
    $c_{new} = x^k;$
    $\Sigma_{new} = \Sigma_{init};$
    if $\mu_{\hat{y}^k} > T_{\mu_y}$ **then**
        Rule consequent defined by classifier;
        $y_{new} = \hat{y}^k$
    else
        Rule consequent defined by operator;
        $y_{new} = operator.classify(x^k)$
    end
else
    Update an existing rule antecedent parameters (eq. (1) and (4));
end
Check for redundant rules;
for $i = 1, num\_rules$ **do**
    for $j = 1, num\_rules$ **do**
        if $\rho_i(c_j, c_i) > T_\rho$ *and* $y_i == y_j$ **then**
            Merge two redundant rules;
            $c_i = mean(c_j, c_i);$
            $\Sigma_i = \Sigma_{init};$
        end
    end
end

Fig. 2. Fault detection and diagnosis algorithm

Clearly, the evolving fuzzy classifier is an adaptive set of fuzzy classification rules. The number of classification rules is the same as the number of clusters found by the clustering algorithm at each step. Rules have antecedents in the form:

$$x^k \text{ IS } A_i \tag{10}$$

where x^k is a $1 \times m$ input vector and A_i is fuzzy set with a multivariable Gaussian membership function:

$$\mu(x) = \exp\left[-\frac{1}{2}(x-c)\Sigma^{-1}(x-c)^T \right] \tag{11}$$

where c is a $1 \times m$ cluster center and Σ is the $m \times m$ dispersion matrix of the corresponding cluster. The dispersion matrix plays the same role of a covariance matrix if we assume that c is the mean.

The classifier is formed by a set of rules of the form:

$$R_i \ : \ \text{IF } x^k \text{ IS } A_i \text{ THEN } y_i \text{ IS } OM_j \tag{12}$$

where $i = 1, \cdots, c^k$, c^k is the number of rules at step k and OM_j is the operation mode defined by the operator when the corresponding cluster is created. More than one rule can be associated with the same operation mode. Therefore, the classifier aggregates rule outputs with the same consequent using a *s-norm*.

The estimated operation mode associated with the current input is the one with the highest membership value.

Figure 2 summarizes the algorithm of the online FDD approach.

4   Experimental Results

This section illustrates the use of the FDD approach to monitor the operation of industrial induction motors. The aim is to evaluate and validate its performance.

Induction motors are commonly used electrical drives because they are rugged, mechanically simple and adaptable to a wide variety of operation conditions. Motors are often exposed to different loading and environmental conditions. Monitoring the motor condition is crucial to detect faults in early stage to eliminate the hazards of severe motor damages [18].

All experiments reported here were performed using data from a dynamic model of an induction motor. The model is based on the classical fourth order transient model for symmetrical induction machines and is able to simulate normal operation and several failure modes. A complete description of the dynamic model is provided in [19]. The experiments consider normal and six failure modes, Table 1. Gaussian random values with zero mean and 1% variance were added to the measured variables to simulate noisy data.

The feature extraction technique used was simply the calculation of the root mean square (RMS) values of the currents and voltages for all three phases, resulting in a set of six features. The set of six inputs is the input of the incremental unsupervised clustering procedure.

To validate the FDD approach developed, the following experiment was done. Initially, a data stream with all seven operation modes was input to the FDD. The data

Table 1. Operation modes

Index	Description
0	Normal Operation
1	Short Circuit on phase A
2	Short Circuit on Phase B
3	Short Circuit on phase C
4	Short Circuit on phase A and B
5	Short Circuit on phase A and C
6	Short Circuit on phase B and C

stream was generated using an integration time of 0.2 ms during approximately 70 seconds. First, 15 seconds of normal operation was simulated followed by all six failure modes to verify the online detection of new operation modes. Next, random failures were simulated to check the adaptive diagnosis. Because all operation modes have been input in the evolving classifier, it should be capable to identify all of them afterwards.

The FDD approach was initialized assuming normal operation after the transient phase. The clustering procedure parameters were set to $\Sigma_{init} = I$, $w = 100$, $\lambda = 0.01$, $\alpha = 0.01$ and the classifier parameter to $T_{\mu_y} = 0.01$. Transient phase data were not used during the experiments.

Figure 3 shows (a) the sequence of operation modes that occurred during simulation, and (b) the operation modes estimated. Time instants marked by '*' represent time instants at which new clusters were created and identified by operator. From the total of 9248 input values, only 17 (0.2%) needed operator intervention. Comparing Fig. 3 (a) and (b) we notice that the FDD is able to detect all failure modes and to identify all of them afterwards. Notice also that as soon as all failure modes were input to the classifier for the first time ($t > 70$ sec), only 3 new clusters needed to be identified by the operator, two related with normal operation condition ($t \approx 140$ sec and $t \approx 150$ sec) and one associated with failure mode 5 ($t \approx 110$ sec).

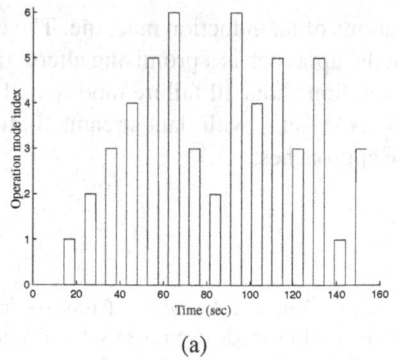

(a)

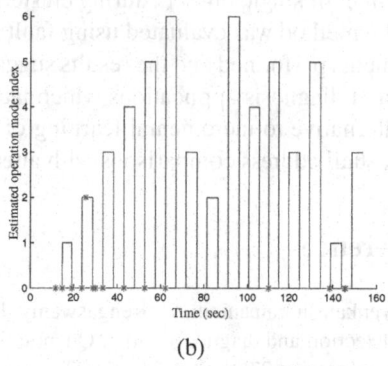

(b)

Fig. 3. Sequence of operation modes simulated (a) and estimated by the online FDD approach (b)

Table 2 summarizes the values of two additional performance indexes: detection delay time (DDT) in seconds, i.e., the time lag between the occurrence of a failure mode and its detection, and the final number of rules (FNR) for each operation mode. Looking at this Table one can note that most failure modes were detected with a DDT ≈ 0.1 sec, with the exception of failure mode 1 (DDT $= 0.63$ sec). However, the next time failure mode 1 was seen by the FDD, it was able to detect and classify it in 0.02 sec. One can also note that the classifier is very compact, containing only 1 or 2 rules for each operation mode.

Table 2. Performance indexes

Index	Description	DDT (sec)	FNR
0	Normal Operation	-	2
1	Short Circuit on phase A	0.63	1
2	Short Circuit on phase B	0.08	2
3	Short Circuit on phase C	0.13	2
4	Short Circuit on phase A and B	0.13	1
5	Short Circuit on phase A and C	0.13	1
6	Short Circuit on phase B and C	0.13	2

5 Conclusion

This paper has introduced a new approach for online fault detection and diagnosis of dynamical systems. The approach is model-free and only uses features extracted from raw data to perform diagnosis. The approach is an evolving fuzzy classifier capable to incorporate information about new operation modes as soon as they are detected, and to perform adaptive fault diagnosis.

The method can be used in both, off-line and on-line, real-time environments. The clustering algorithm used to develop and update the fuzzy rule base of the classifier uses the concept of participatory learning and is robust to noisy data because it filters the effect of single outliers during clustering.

The method was evaluated using fault simulations of an induction machine. The experiments performed and the results suggest that the approach is a promising alternative for fault diagnosis applications which lack information about all failure modes, and as an alternative to incremental learning of diagnosis systems with data streams. Future work shall address comparisons with alternative approaches.

References

1. Venkatasubramanian, V., Rengaswamy, R., Kavuri, S., Yin, K.: A review of process fault detection and diagnosis Part I: Quantitative model-based methods. Computers & Chemical Engineering 27(3), 293–311 (2003)
2. Montgomery, D.: Introduction to Statistical Quality Control, 4th edn. Wiley, Chichester (2001)

3. Dasgupta, D., Forrest, S.: Novelty detection in time series data using ideas from immunology. In: Neural Information Processing Systems (NIPS) Conference (1996)
4. Wong, M., Jack, L., Nandi, A.: Modified self-organising map for automated novelty detection applied to vibration signal monitoring. Mechanical Systems and Signal Processing 20(3), 593–610 (2006)
5. Timusk, M., Lipsett, M., Mechefske, C.K.: Fault detection using transient machine signals. Mechanical Systems and Signal Processing 22(7), 1724–1749 (2008)
6. Markou, M., Singh, S.: Novelty detection: A review part 1: Statistical approaches. Signal Processing 83, 2499–2521 (2003)
7. Angelov, P.P.: Evolving Rule-Based Models: A Tool for Design of Flexible Adaptive Systems. Springer, London (2002)
8. Kasabov, N., Filev, D.: Evolving intelligent systems: Methods, learning, & applications. In: International Symposium on Evolving Fuzzy Systems, pp. 8–18 (2006)
9. Yager, R.: A Model of Participatory Learning. IEEE Transactions on Systems Man and Cybernetics 20(5), 1229–1234 (1990)
10. Silva, L., Gomide, F., Yager, R.: Participatory learning in fuzzy clustering. In: The 14th IEEE International Conference on Fuzzy Systems, pp. 857–861 (2005)
11. Filev, D., Tseng, F.: Novelty detection based machine health prognostics. In: International Symposium on Evolving Fuzzy Systems, pp. 193–199 (2006)
12. Lughofer, E., Guardioler, C.: On-line fault detection with data-driven evolving fuzzy models. Control and Intelligent Systems 36(4), 307–317 (2008)
13. Wang, W., Vrbanek, J.: An evolving fuzzy predictor for industrial applications. IEEE Transactions on Fuzzy Systems 16(6), 1439–1449 (2008)
14. Lughofer, E.: Extensions of vector quantization for incremental clustering. Pattern Recognition 41(3), 995–1011 (2008); Part Special issue: Feature Generation and Machine Learning for Robust Multimodal Biometrics
15. Duda, R.O., Hart, P.E., Stork, D.G.: Pattern Classification, 2nd edn. Wiley-Interscience, Hoboken (2000)
16. Schürmann, J.: Pattern classification: a unified view of statistical and neural approaches. John Wiley & Sons, Inc., New York (1996)
17. Miller, R.: Simultaneous statistical inference. McGraw-Hill, Inc., New York (1966)
18. D'Angelo, M.F., Palhares, R.M., Takahashi, R.H., Loschi, R.H., Baccarini, L.M., Caminhas, W.M.: Incipient fault detection in induction machine stator-winding using a fuzzy-bayesian change point detection approach. Applied Soft Computing (2009) (in Press, Corrected Proof)
19. Baccarini, L.M.R., de Menezes, B.R., Caminhas, W.M.: Fault induction dynamic model, suitable for computer simulation: Simulation results and experimental validation. Mechanical Systems and Signal Processing 24(1), 300–311 (2010)

Dispersion Estimates for Telecommunications Fraud

Nuno Homem and João Paulo Carvalho

TULisbon – Instituto Superior Técnico, INESC-ID
R. Alves Redol 9, 1000-029 Lisboa, Portugal
nuno_homem@hotmail.com, joao.carvalho@inesc-id.pt

Abstract. One considers the problem of estimating the call destination dispersion on telecommunications usage to use in fraud detection. The problem is that such detection needs to be performed for each individual customer and kept up to date at all times. The use of fast and small footprint algorithms is critical due to the huge number of events and customers to verify and since approximate answers are enough in most situations. This paper presents telecommunications customer behavior to justify the use of approximate estimators and then presents multiple options of algorithms to solve the problem. These algorithms present a novel approach to the moving window dispersion problem by the use of a probabilistic time decay mechanism.

Keywords: Approximate estimation, sliding window algorithms, probabilistic counters.

1 Introduction

Estimating the call destination dispersion on telecommunications usage is critical in systems used to detect fraud in Telecom operators. Call destination patterns may point to abnormal uses of services and can help identifying fraud situation. One such situation is the so-called bypass fraud. Telecom operators establish agreements on how traffic between them is handled and how are the costs assigned for each of the operators. An operator may route an international call through several networks to reach a final destination: each operator involved receives a fee for routing the call through its network and pays the next in route a cost for him to deliver the call. Each country regulates who and how can participate in this scheme. Subverting these rules in a manner that avoids these agreed interconnection points is bypass fraud.

Sending voice calls from one country to another through Internet or owned IP networks is easy and cheap. A long distance call can now be routed through VoIP and delivered locally at the destination country without paying the costs of interconnection. Local calls are usually much cheaper than long distance, therefore, the difference easily out pays the increased IP traffic and required equipment.

For a telecom operator, long distance calls may represent a large part of its revenues, in the order of several thousand million Euros per year. Although bypassing the operator is legal in some countries and might be allowed for personal use in others, it is a crime in most. Bypass fraud is therefore a huge threat for operator profitability. The problem is made worse by the fact that not only individuals and small companies

E. Hüllermeier, R. Kruse, and F. Hoffmann (Eds.): IPMU 2010, LNAI 6178, pp. 370–379, 2010.

engage in such fraudulent schemes: global telecommunication operators can also establish local hubs for traffic transfer to avoid interconnection costs.

Classical call dispersion detection algorithms require the list of used destinations to be checked every time a new call is processed to see if the call is already in the list. Even if a time limited window is to be checked (last hour, last day) this may require a large list of destinations to be maintained. Moving time windows require additionally a timestamp to be maintained for each destination. The problem is not just keeping one estimate or an estimate for a large set, is keeping huge number of estimates on medium size sets. Operators range from less than 500 000 customers (a small operator) to more than 25 000 000 customers; for each one a reasonable estimate of dispersion might be needed. The number of destinations for each customer is not a huge number, but the number of customers for which one has to compute individual dispersion is.

The paper introduces new algorithms for counting distinct values over time based on the use of Probabilistic Counters [9] and Bloom filters [2], based on a simple probabilistic time decay process of bitmaps that allow building simple and compact estimators.

2 Typical Behavior of Mobile Users

To better understand bypass fraud is important to analyze typical behavior of individual customers. In this case a set of calls from mobile customers was used as a sample. Mobile telecommunication operators suffer more from bypass fraud as the interconnection fees they charge to deliver calls are higher. This makes them ideal for use as a reference in the analysis.

The following analysis is presented only to illustrate the typical use by mobile users of their service. It is based on 962 blocks of calls of distinct customers, each with 500 mobile voice calls (made during a 2 or 3 month period in most cases).

Note that 500 calls is not a small number of calls, most of the customers make no more than 15 calls a day. However as the average mobile call duration is not very long (119 seconds in this sample) a single SIM Box system (basically a PBX – private branch extension – that includes a mobile phone to connect to a mobile network) is capable of achieving that number in a single day.

For each block the call frequency to distinct numbers (with distinct number ranked per received calls) is presented in the following charts. On average, in 500 calls, each customer would call 98.67 distinct numbers (with a standard deviation of 34,99), the 30 more frequent numbers will include around 80% of the total calls.

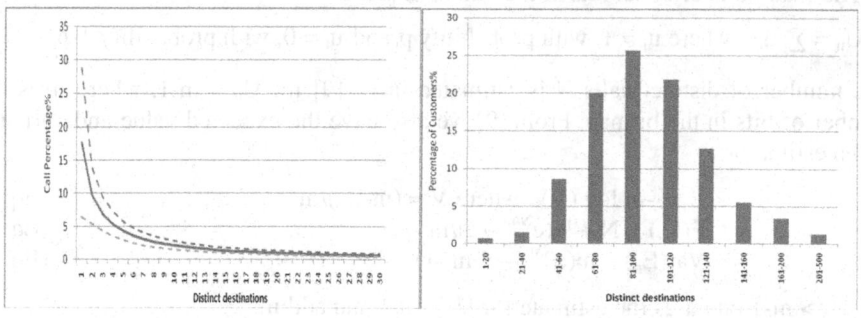

Fig. 1. Percentage of distinct destinations per customer

The highest value in this sample was 262 destinations for a single customer. A 500 call block having 262 distinct destinations is not common in individual customers. In fact this particular case is a SIM Box, a mobile service being used by a company to deliver calls from its fixed network to the operators network. This particular case is not fraud as the telecom operator is aware of its existence and allows it.

3 Using a Probabilistic Counter (PC) as a Dispersion Indicator

As the algorithm for exact counting of the distinct number of destinations is quite demanding on memory (requires each distinct number to be stored for each user) and computational power, a probabilistic counter was used to estimate the number of distinct calls. This follows Whang et al. [9] and subsequent work [5, 6, 7, 8].

This particular implementation uses a bitmap to store pseudo-distinct values. In this process the destination numbers are never stored. It assumes that every destination number will be transformed by the use of a hash function into a position in the bitmap. The hash function needs to be able to transform the destination numbers into a uniformly distributed integer range. The hashed value (the normalized destination number) h(x) is then used to set the corresponding position in the bitmap, by setting the corresponding bit to 1. Since the hash function will probably generate collisions, the distinct number of destinations can be obtained by correcting the number of set bits (cardinality of the bitmap).

In this process, initially all bits are set to 0.

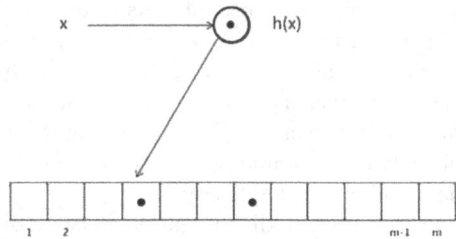

Fig. 2. Probabilistic Counter

The total number of set bits in the bitmap U_n is:

$$U_n = \sum_i u_i \quad \text{where } u_i = 1, \text{ with probability } p_i \text{ and } u_i = 0, \text{ with probability } 1-p_i$$

The number of distinct calls N is estimated in E_n [9] for $U_n \le m-1$, where m is the number of bits in the bitmap. From [9] we also have the expected value and variance of the estimator:

$$E_n = -m \log (V) \quad \text{where } V = (m-U_n)/m \tag{Eq. 1}$$
$$E(E_n) = N + \tfrac{1}{2}(e^{N/m} - N/m - 1) \tag{Eq. 2}$$
$$Var(E_n) = m(e^{N/m} - N/m - 1) \tag{Eq. 3}$$

For $U_n > m-1$ one uses the estimate for $U_n = m-1$ and add m:

$$E_n = m \log(m) + m$$

4 The Need for Sliding Window Indicators

The increase in traffic and specially the sophistication of the fraud schemes has increased the challenge for fraud detection.

Fraud needs to be identified as soon as possible and within the shortest possible time after it has begun. Sophisticated fraudsters are able to use the fixed periods of time the operators may use in fraud detection to their benefit.

There is therefore interest in having the dispersion indicator over a sliding window of time instead of a fixed period. This will allow detection processes to be spread over time instead of being concentrated at specific moments.

Once again the challenge is to provide a relevant indicator without consuming too much memory or computer resources. The objective is to maintain a count of the distinct values of called numbers over the last T period of time ending in the moment of the measure, without the need to keep a list of timed events to process every time.

5 Decaying Probabilistic Counter (PD)

A novel approach to this problem is the use of a decaying mechanism for estimating dispersion on a time sliding window period.

Based on the probabilistic counter used before and on the idea of a time decaying counter with a average time to live of T, one can propose the following algorithm: assuming a probabilistic counter with a bitmap or length m, one will decay one bit (i.e., clear the bit) every t=2T/m in sequence. On average every set bit will take T to be cleared. Clearing the bits in sequence (returning to the start when it reaches the end) will ensure that a bit that is set once, will never take more than 2T to be cleared.

The system can be seen as a continuous time system receiving events during a 2T period and distributing then uniformly over m bits, each with a different time buffer [1].

For the purpose of this analysis, the set of events to be considered can be considered as arriving at a rate of $\lambda = N/T$.

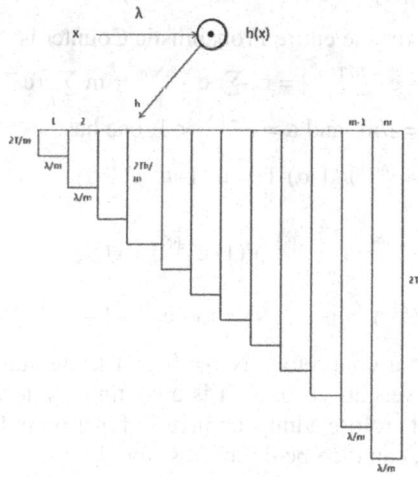

Fig. 3. Decaying Probabilistic Counter

By establishing the bit order as the reverse order in which the bits have been cleared, one can illustrate the algorithm as follows.

To estimate the N number of distinct values received during the period of time T, one assumes that events are received in a Poisson distribution, and that the rate is kept uniformly over the averaging period 2T. Although this assumes something about the behavior of the customer, this is a reasonable assumption as a random uniformly distributed arrival over a period of time will show event Poisson distribution. Consider:

$$\lambda = N/T$$

Note that approximating the real arrival of distinct events by a random variable with Poisson distributed time arrival time introduces an error in the analysis. In fact, although the expected value of this random variable is the same as the considered initial value, the variance is much higher being equal to the expected value. This will translate in introducing a higher variance in the analysis of the algorithm.

One will consider that the hash function $h(x)$ distributes x uniformly over the m bits. The average rate of events falling in bit i can then be calculated at $\lambda_i = \lambda/m$. For simplicity one will inverse time for the following analysis and will consider the time of analysis the final of the 2T period T_f.

$$E(U_n) = E(\sum_i u_i) = \sum_i p_i = \sum_i P_{i1}(u_i|t=T_f) = \sum_i P_{i1}(u_i|t=2T)$$

The probability P_{i0} of bit i receiving 0 events in [0, t] is given by:

$$P_{i0}(t) = e^{-\lambda_i t}$$

The probability of bit i not receiving an event in the time since it was last cleared is:

$$P_{i0}(t=2i\ T/m) = e^{-2i\lambda\ T/m^2}$$

This remains unchanged for t in]2iT/m, 2T].

Therefore, the expected value for this bit to be set ui is:

$$E(u_i|t=2T) = P_{i1}(u_i|t=2T) = 1-P_{i0}(t=2iT/m) = 1 - e^{-2i\lambda T/m^2}$$

and the expected value for the entire Probabilistic Counter is:

$$E(U_n) = \sum_i [1 - e^{-2i\lambda T/m^2}] = m-\sum_i e^{-2iN/m^2} = m-\sum_i (e^{-2N/m^2})^i$$

Considering $N >= 0$, $\beta = 2/m^2$ and $\alpha = e^{-\beta N} < 1$, one has:

$$\sum_{i=1..m} \alpha^i = (1-\alpha^{m+1})/(1-\alpha)-1 = \alpha(1-\alpha^m)/(1-\alpha)$$

$$\sum_i (e^{-\beta N})^i = e^{-\beta N}(1-e^{-\beta m N})/(1-e^{-\beta N}) = g(N)$$

$$E(U_n) = m - g(N) = m - e^{-\beta N}(1-e^{-\beta m N})/(1-e^{-\beta N}) \tag{Eq.4}$$

The function g(N), for a continuous $N >= 0$ is a finite sum of positive decreasing exponentials, each converging to 0, so it is a continuous decreasing function as well and converges to 0. It therefore admits an inverse function in U [0, m[.

The estimator for N, can then be defined as (for $U_n \le m-1$):

$$E_n = f(U_n) = g^{-1}(m - U_n) \tag{Eq. 5}$$

For $U_n > $ m-1 consider:

$$E_n = g^{-1}(1) + m$$

For $U_n \leq$ m-1, one cannot invert g function analytically, but it is possible to construct an inverse table for this function. As U_n can only take integer numbers this is not a complex task.

6 Decaying Averaged Probabilistic Counter (PAD)

To smooth the decay and minimize the impact of a single bit being set to 0 too soon or too late it is possible to devise an alternate algorithm. In this algorithm, from now on designated as Decaying Averaged Probabilistic Counter, one will set 2 bits for each distinct value, the first by mapping the hash value into the bitmap range [0, m/2[and the second by setting another bit with an offset of m/2.

By keeping the same clearing rate of one bit every t_c=2T/m in sequence and using the appropriate function, one can obtain an equivalent estimate. The average time a bit takes to decay is still T. Please note that if one wants to keep the same rate of collisions as for the previous algorithm one should double the m value.

This new approach should lead to better error value when using increased size bitmaps, larger m values. Using the same m may lead to better results as the increase in collision rate may be compensated by the use of a smoother average function, especially for low distinct values as one can observe in typical telecom usages.

To calculate the correction table, one applies the same reasoning as before (as the events $\lambda_i = 2N/Tm$ were doubled).

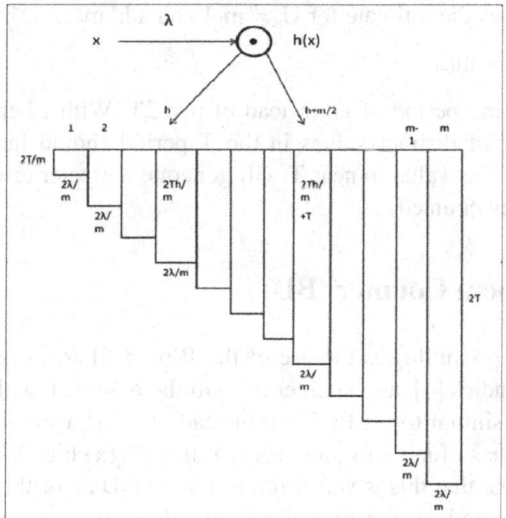

Fig. 4. Decaying Averaged Probabilistic Counter

This allows the determination of the probability of this bit being set in the final time as:

$$P_{i1}(u_i|t=2T) = 1 - P_{i0}(t=2iT/m) = 1 - e^{-2i\lambda_i T/m}$$

The expected value for the entire Probabilistic Counter is:

$$E(U_n) = \sum_i [1 - e^{-4iN/m^2}] = m - \sum_i e^{-4iN/m^2}$$

The main problem with this approach is that it still estimates the number of distinct values in T as an average over a 2T period. A further step to minimize this relies in the correction formula. In fact this allows the estimation of the number of distinct values based on any period of time by changing the clearing rate and the formula. Consider the parameter τ in]0,2] and:

$$t_c = \tau T/m$$

$$t_i = i\, t_c$$

One has:

$$E(U_n) = \sum_i [1 - e^{-i\lambda_i t_c}] = m - \sum_i e^{-2iN\tau/m^2}$$

This can then be resumed into Eq. 4 with $\beta = 2\tau/m^2$.

$$E(U_n) = m - g(N) \tag{Eq. 6}$$

The estimator for PAD for $U_n \leq m-1$ can then be defined as:

$$E_n = f(U_n) = g^{-1}(m - U_n) \tag{Eq. 7}$$

For $U_n > m-1$ one uses the estimate for $U_n = m-1$ and add $m/2$:

$$E_n = g\text{-}1(1) + m/2$$

This allows a sampling period of τT instead of just 2T. With τ below 2 the the accuracy on the number of distinct values in the T period should increase but one can expect that bringing this value to near T will generate a greater error as many bits are cleared without being counted.

7 Decaying Bloom Counter (BD)

Another interesting possibility is the use of the Bloom filter, as presented by Bloom [2] and following studies [4], as a counter in a similar approach with time decay.

The idea is quite similar to the PAD but instead of using a single hash function one uses k independent hash functions and set each of the $h_j(x)$ bits. When k equals 1 one has in fact a PD. Note that this is very similar to the PAD algorithm but with randomized gap between bits to be set instead of a fixed value.

Designing k different independent hash functions can be quite problematic for large k. For a good hash function with a wide output, there should be little if any correlation between different bit-fields of such a hash, so this type of hash can be used to generate multiple different hash functions by slicing its output into multiple bit fields. Alternatively, one can pass k different initial values (such as 0, 1, ..., k-1) to a hash function that takes an initial value.

This algorithm leads to a correction formula similar to the PAD, where the number of bits to be set equals the number of hash functions to be set.

To calculate the correction table one has to apply the same reasoning as before (as one has k events $\lambda_i = kN/Tm$ and $t_c = \tau T/m$).

This allows the determination of the probability of this bit being set in the final time:

$$P_{i1}(u_i|t=\tau T) = 1 - P_{i0}(t=i\tau T/m) = 1 - e^{-i\tau\lambda_i T/m}$$

The expected value for the entire Probabilistic Counter is:

$$E(U_n) = \sum_i [1 - e^{-ik\tau N/m^2}] = m - \sum_i e^{-ik\tau N/m^2}$$

This can then be resumed into Eq. 4 with $\beta = k\tau/m^2$.

$$E(U_n) = m \cdot g(N) \tag{Eq. 8}$$

The estimator for BC for $U_n \leq m-1$ can then be defined as:

$$E_n = f(U_n) = g^{-1}(m - U_n) \tag{Eq. 9}$$

For $U_n > m-1$ one uses the estimate for $U_n = m-1$ and add m/k:

$$E_n = g^{-1}(1) + m/2$$

Better averaging could be achieved by increasing the number of set bits per distinct value (and increasing the bitmap size to avoid excessive collisions).

8 Evaluating Sliding Window Algorithms

To evaluate these algorithms the call blocks presented in section 2 are used with the calls distributed uniformly over a period of 3T, keeping the order of the calls. Each block is processed 3 times with distinct random call times. Measures every T/10 are taken and the error against an exact indicator is computed:

$$e = \text{sqrt}(E\{(x_{est}(t_i)-x(t_i))^2\}), \qquad t_i = \{T/10, 2T/10, 3T/10 \ldots 3T\}$$

Using a relative measure:

$$er = \text{sqrt}(E\{((x_{est}(t_i)-x(t_i))/x(t_i))^2\})$$

The results obtained for 962 blocks are shown in Table 1.

Note that all estimates were rounded to the nearest integer before applying the error formula. Note also that no change in computational load happens when m is changed, only memory requirements double when changing from m=100 to 200, and from m=200 to 400.

Table 1. Algorithm evaluation

			e	er
PD	m=100		4.22	11.5%
	m=200		4.01	12.6%
	m=400		3.85	11.1%
PAD	m=200		3.55	10.6%
	m=400		3.48	10.5%
	m=200	τ=7/8	3.42	9.4%
		τ=3/4	4.09	12.0%
		τ=5/8	5.62	17.1%
BD	m=200	k=2	3.52	9.8%
		k=3	3.41	8.8%
	m=400	k=2	3.48	10.5%
		k=3	3.17	8.6%

9   Conclusions and Discussion

Using 100 bits, it is possible to estimate dispersion with an average error of 4.22, relative error of 11.5%, over time (although only PD results are shown, other algorithms were tested for this m but with higher error results mainly due to the bitmap getting over-crowded). For the intended application, detecting a high dispersion situation, it will generate a good enough indicator of possible fraud situations (it will not be the single indicator). In fact for the presented estimators both the relative error and the average error are more than adequate for the purpose of distinguishing between low and high dispersion values required for this sort of fraud detection algorithms.

Using 200 bits, the relative error is reduced to 3.41, relative error to 8.8%, by using a BD with 3 hash functions. All variants of PD, PAD and BD could not get below this error value even for much higher m values. The increase in accuracy might not justify the double memory needs.

Using 400 bits, the relative error can be reduced to 3.11, relative error 8.6%, by using a BD with 3 hash functions. In fact only BD seems to take advantage of additional bits (and additional hash functions).

In fact for this range of dispersions you get reasonable estimators from 100 bits onwards. Increasing this value does not translate in a much increased performance, 100 bits will be a good compromise between accuracy and memory usage.

References

1. Bertsekas, D.P.: Dynamic Programming and Optimal Control, vol. 1. Athena Scientific, Belmont (1995)
2. Bloom, B.: Space/time trade-offs in hash coding with allowable errors. Communications of the ACM 13(7), 422–426 (1970)
3. Datar, M., Gionis, A., Indyk, P., Motwani, R.: Maintaining Stream Statistics Over Sliding Windows. SIAM Journal on Computing 31(6) (2002)
4. Dillinger, P., Manolios, P.: Bloom Filters in Probabilistic Verification. In: Hu, A.J., Martin, A.K. (eds.) FMCAD 2004. LNCS, vol. 3312, pp. 367–381. Springer, Heidelberg (2004)
5. Estan, C., Varghese, G.: New directions in traffic measurement and accounting. In: Proceedings of SIGCOMM 2002. ACM Press, New York (2002); Also: UCSD technical report CS2002-0699 (February 2002); available electronically
6. Estan, C., Varghese, G., Fisk, M.: Bitmap algorithms for counting active flows on high speed links. Technical Report CS2003-0738, UCSD (March 2003)
7. Flajolet, P.: Approximate counting: A detailed analysis. BIT 25, 113–134 (1985)
8. Flajolet, P., Martin, N.: Probabilistic Counting Algorithms for Data Base Applications. Journal of Computer and System Sciences 31(2) (October 1985)
9. Whang, K., Vander-Zanden, B., Taylor, H.: A Linear-Time Probabilistic Counting Algorithm for Database Applications. ACM Transactions on Database Systems 15(2) (June 1990)

The Link Prediction Problem
in Bipartite Networks

Jérôme Kunegis, Ernesto W. De Luca, and Sahin Albayrak

DAI Lab, Technische Universität Berlin
Ernst-Reuter-Platz 7
D-10587 Berlin, Germany
{jerome.kunegis,ernesto.deluca,sahin.albayrak}@dai-labor.de

Abstract. We define and study the link prediction problem in bipartite networks, specializing general link prediction algorithms to the bipartite case. In a graph, a link prediction function of two vertices denotes the similarity or proximity of the vertices. Common link prediction functions for general graphs are defined using paths of length two between two nodes. Since in a bipartite graph adjacency vertices can only be connected by paths of odd lengths, these functions do not apply to bipartite graphs. Instead, a certain class of graph kernels (spectral transformation kernels) can be generalized to bipartite graphs when the positive-semidefinite kernel constraint is relaxed. This generalization is realized by the odd component of the underlying spectral transformation. This construction leads to several new link prediction pseudokernels such as the matrix hyperbolic sine, which we examine for rating graphs, authorship graphs, folksonomies, document–feature networks and other types of bipartite networks.

1   Introduction

In networks where edges appear over time, the problem of predicting such edges is called *link prediction* [1,2]. Common approaches to link prediction can be described as *local* when only the immediate neighborhood of vertices is considered and *latent* when a latent model of the network is used. An example for local link prediction methods is the triangle closing model, and these models are conceptually very simple. Latent link prediction methods are instead derived using algebraic graph theory: The network's adjacency matrix is decomposed and a transformation is applied to the network's spectrum. This approach is predicted by several graph growth models and results in *graph kernels*, positive-semidefinite functions of the adjacency matrix [3].

Many networks contain edges between two types of entities, for instance item rating graphs, authorship graphs and document–feature networks. These graphs are called bipartite [4], and while they are a special case of general graphs, link prediction methods cannot be generalized to them. As we show in Section 2, this is the case for all link prediction functions based on the triangle closing model, as well as all positive-semidefinite graph kernels. Instead, we will see that

E. Hüllermeier, R. Kruse, and F. Hoffmann (Eds.): IPMU 2010, LNAI 6178, pp. 380–389, 2010.

their odd components can be used, in Section 3. For each positive-semidefinite graph kernel, we derive the corresponding odd pseudokernel. One example is the exponential graph kernel $\exp(\lambda)$. Its odd component is $\sinh(\lambda)$, the hyperbolic sine. We also introduce the bipartite von Neumann pseudokernel, and study the bipartite versions of polynomials with only odd powers. We show experimentally (in Section 4) how these odd pseudokernels perform on the task of link prediction in bipartite networks in comparison to their positive counterparts, and give an overview of their relative performances . We also sketch their usage for detecting near-bipartite graphs.

2   Bipartite Link Prediction

The link prediction problem is usually defined on unipartite graphs, where common link prediction algorithms make several assumptions [5]:

- *Triangle closing*: New edges tend to form triangles.
- *Clustering*: Nodes tend to form well-connected clusters in the graph.

In bipartite graphs these assumptions are not true, since triangles and larger cliques cannot appear. Other assumptions have therefore to be used. While a unipartite link prediction algorithm technically applies to bipartite graphs, it will not perform well. Methods based on common neighbors of two vertices will for instance not be able to predict anything in bipartite graphs, since two vertices that would be connected (from different clusters) do not have any common neighbors.

Several important classes of networks are bipartite: authorship networks, interaction networks, usage logs, ontologies and many more. Many unipartite networks (such as coauthorship networks) can be reinterpreted as bipartite networks when edges or cliques are modeled as vertices. In these cases, special bipartite link prediction algorithms are necessary. The following two sections will review local and algebraic link prediction methods for bipartite graphs. Examples of specific networks of these types will be given in Section 4.

Definitions. Given an undirected graph $G = (V, E)$ with vertex set V and edge set E, its adjacency matrix $A \in \mathbb{R}^{V \times V}$ is defined as $A_{uv} = 1$ when $(u, v) \in E$ and $A_{uv} = 0$ otherwise. For a bipartite graph $G = (V + W, E)$, the adjacency matrix can be written as $A = \begin{bmatrix} 0 \, B; B^T \, 0 \end{bmatrix}$, where $B \in \mathbb{R}^{V \times W}$ is the biadjacency matrix of G.

2.1   Local Link Prediction Functions

Some link prediction functions only depend on the immediate neighborhood of two nodes; we will call these functions local link prediction functions [1].

Let u and v be two nodes in the graph for which a link prediction score is to be computed. Local link prediction functions depend on the common neighbors of u and v. In the bipartite link prediction problem, u and v are in different clusters,

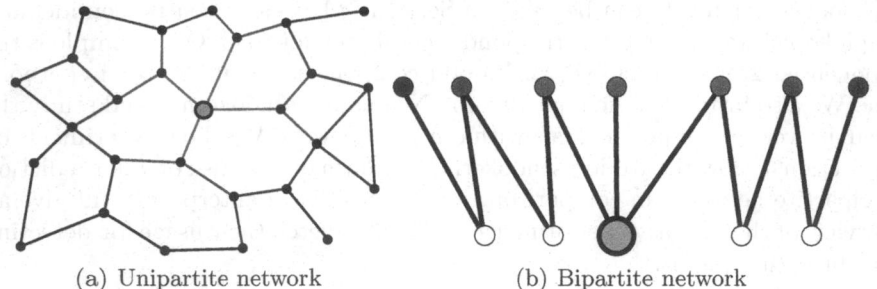

(a) Unipartite network   (b) Bipartite network

Fig. 1. Link prediction by spreading activation in unipartite and bipartite networks. In the unipartite case, all paths are used. In the bipartite case, only paths of odd length need to be considered. In both cases, the weight of paths is weighted in inverse proportion to path length.

and thus have no common neighbors. The following link prediction functions are therefore not applicable to bipartite graphs: The number of common neighbors [1], the measure of Adamic and Adar [6] and the Jaccard coefficient [1]. These methods are all based on the *triangle closing* model, which is not valid for bipartite graphs.

Preferential Attachment. Taking only the degree of u and v into account for link prediction leads to the *preferential attachment* model [7], which can be used as a model for more complex methods such as modularity kernels [8,9].

   If $d(u)$ is the number of neighbors of node u, the preferential attachment models gives a prediction between u and v of $d(u)d(v)/(2|E|)$. The factor $1/(2|E|)$ normalizes the sum of predictions for a vertex to its degree.

3   Algebraic Link Prediction Functions

Link prediction algorithms that not only take into account the immediate neighborhood of two nodes but the complete graph can be formulated using algebraic graph theory, whereby a decomposition of the graph's adjacency matrix is computed [10]. By considering transformations of a graph's adjacency matrix, link prediction methods can be defined and learned. Algebraic link prediction methods are motivated by their scalability and their learnability. They are scalable because they rely on a model that is built once and which makes computation of recommendations fast. These models correspond to decomposed matrices and can usually be updated using iterative algorithms [11]. In contrast, local link prediction algorithms are *memory-based*, meaning they access the adjacency data directly during link prediction. Algebraic link prediction methods are learnable because their parameters can be learned in a unified way [12].

   In this section, we describe how algebraic link prediction methods apply to bipartite networks. Let $G = (V, E)$ be a (not necessarily bipartite) graph. Algebraic link prediction algorithms are based on the eigenvalue decomposition of its adjacency matrix A:

$$A = U \Lambda U^T$$

To predict links, a *spectral transformation* is usually applied:

$$F(A) = U F(\Lambda) U^T$$

where $F(\Lambda)$ applies a real function $f(\lambda)$ to each eigenvalue λ_i. $F(A)$ then contains link prediction scores that, for each node, give a ranking of all other nodes, which is then used for link prediction. If $f(\lambda_i)$ is positive, F is a graph kernel, otherwise, we will call F a pseudokernel.

Several spectral transformations can be written as polynomials of the adjacency matrix in the following way. The matrix power A^i gives, for each vertex pair (u, v), the number of paths of length i between u and v. Therefore, a polynomial of A gives, for a pair (u, v), the sum of all paths between u and v, weighted by the polynomial coefficients. This fact can be exploited to find link prediction functions that fulfill the two following requirements:

- The link prediction score should be higher when two nodes are connected by *many* paths.
- The link prediction score should be higher when paths are *short*.

These requirements suggest the use of polynomials f with decreasing coefficients.

3.1   Odd Pseudokernels

In bipartite networks, only paths of odd length are significant, since an edge can only appear between two vertices if they are already connected by paths of odd lengths. Therefore, only odd powers are relevant, and we can restrict the spectral transformation to odd polynomials, i.e. polynomials with odd powers.

The resulting spectral transformation is then an odd function and except in the trivial and undesired case of a constant zero function, will be negative at some point. Therefore, all spectral transformations described below are only pseudokernels and not kernels.

The Hyperbolic Sine. In unipartite networks, a basic link prediction function is given by the matrix exponential of the adjacency matrix [13,14,15]. The matrix exponential can be derived by considering the sum

$$\exp(\alpha A) = \sum_{i=0}^{\infty} \frac{\alpha^i}{i!} A^i$$

where coefficients are decreasing with path length. Keeping only the odd component, we arrive at the matrix hyperbolic sine [16].

$$\sinh(\alpha A) = \sum_{i=0}^{\infty} \frac{\alpha^{1+2i}}{(1+2i)!} A^{1+2i}$$

Figure 2 shows the hyperbolic sine applied to the (positive) spectrum of the bipartite Slovak Wikipedia user–article edit network.

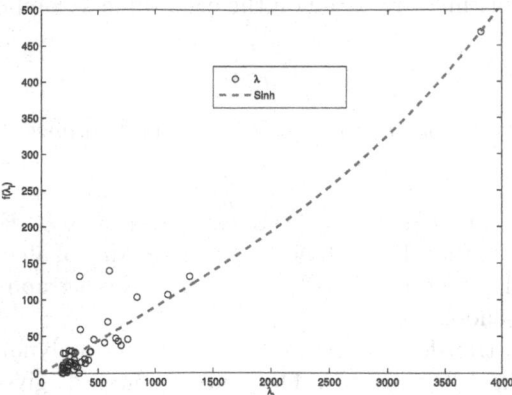

Fig. 2. In this curve fitting plot of the Slovak Wikipedia, the hyperbolic sine is a good match, indicating that the hyperbolic sine pseudokernel performs well

The Odd von Neumann Pseudokernel. The von Neumann kernel for unipartite graphs is given by the following expression [13].

$$K_{\text{NEU}}(A) = (I - \alpha A)^{-1} = \sum_{i=0}^{\infty} \alpha^i A^i$$

We call its odd component the odd von Neumann pseudokernel:

$$K_{\text{NEU}}^{\text{odd}}(A) = \alpha A (I - \alpha^2 A^2)^{-1} = \sum_{i=0}^{\infty} \alpha^{1+2i} A^{1+2i}$$

The hyperbolic sine and von Neumann pseudokernels are compared in Figure 3, based on the path weights they produce.

Rank Reduction. Similarly, rank reduction of the matrix A can be described as a pseudokernel. Let λ_k be the eigenvalue with k-th largest absolute value, then rank reduction is defined by

$$f(\lambda) = \begin{cases} \lambda & \text{if } |\lambda| \geq |\lambda_k| \\ 0 & \text{otherwise} \end{cases}$$

This function is odd, but does not have an (odd) Taylor series expansion.

3.2   Computing Latent Graph Models

Bipartite graphs have adjacency matrices of the form

$$A = \begin{pmatrix} & B \\ B^T & \end{pmatrix}$$

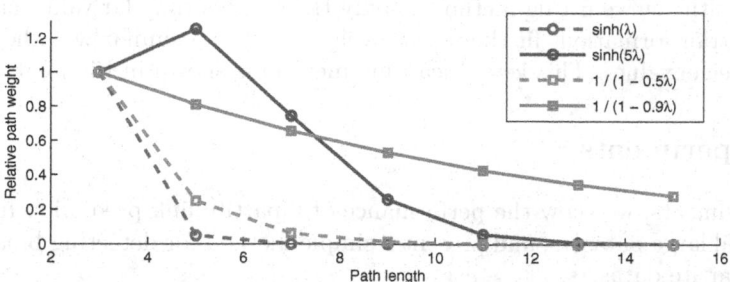

Fig. 3. Comparison of several odd pseudokernels: the hyperbolic sine and the odd von Neumann pseudokernel. The relative path weight is proportional to the corresponding coefficient in the Taylor series expansion of the spectral transformation.

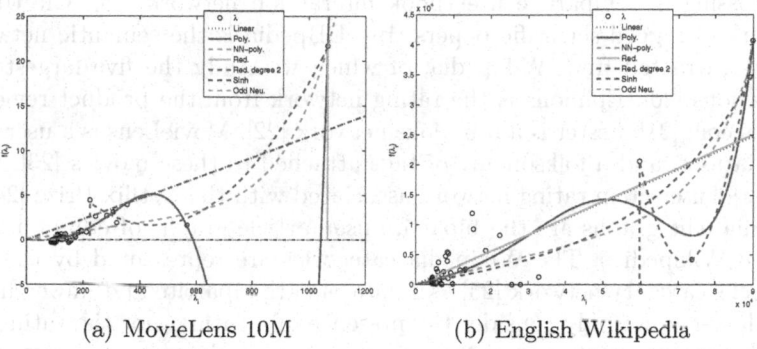

(a) MovieLens 10M   (b) English Wikipedia

Fig. 4. Learning a pseudokernel that matches an observed spectral transformation in the MovieLens 10M rating network and English Wikipedia edit history

where B is the biadjacency matrix of the graph. This form can be exploited to reduce the eigenvalue decomposition of A to the equivalent singular value decomposition $B = \tilde{U}\Sigma\tilde{V}$.

$$A = \begin{pmatrix} U & U \\ V & -V \end{pmatrix} \begin{pmatrix} +\Sigma & \\ & -\Sigma \end{pmatrix} \begin{pmatrix} U & U \\ V & -V \end{pmatrix}^{T}$$

with $U = \tilde{U}/\sqrt{2}$, $V = \tilde{V}/\sqrt{2}$ and each singular value σ corresponds to the eigenvalue pair $\{\pm\sigma\}$.

3.3 Learning Pseudokernels

The hyperbolic sine and the von Neumann pseudokernel are parametrized by α, and rank reduction has the parameter k, or equivalently λ_k. These parameters can be learned by reducing the spectral transformation problem to a one-dimensional curve fitting problem, as described in [12]. In the bipartite case, we can apply the curve fitting method to only the graph's singular value, since odd spectral transformations fit the negative eigenvalue in a similar way they fit the positive eigenvalues. This kernel learning method is shown in Figure 4.

4   Experiments

As experiments, we show the performance of bipartite link prediction functions on several large datasets, and present a simple method for detecting bipartite or near-bipartite datasets.

4.1   Performance on Large Bipartite Networks

We evaluate all bipartite link prediction functions on the following bipartite network datasets. BibSonomy is a folksonomy of scientific publications [17]. BookCrossing is a bipartite user–book interaction network [18]. CiteULike is a network of tagged scientific papers [19]. DBpedia is the semantic network of relations extracted from Wikipedia, of which we study the five largest bipartite relations [20]. Epinions is the rating network from the product review site Epinions.com [21]. Jester is a user–joke network [22]. MovieLens is a user–movie rating dataset, and a folksonomy of tags attached to these movies [23]. Netflix is the large user–item rating network associated with the Netflix Prize [24]. The Wikipedia edit graphs are the bipartite user–article graphs of edits on various language Wikipedias. The Wikipedia categories are represented by the bipartite article–category network [25]. All datasets are bipartite and unweighted. In rating datasets, we only consider the presence of a rating, not the rating itself. Table 1 gives the number of nodes and edges in each dataset.

In the experiments, we withhold 30% of each network's edges as the test set to predict. For datasets in which edges are labeled by timestamps, the test set consists of the newest edges. The remaining training set is used to compute link prediction scores using the preferential attachment model and the pseudokernel learning methods described in the previous sections. For the pseudokernel learning methods, the training set is again split into 70% / 30% subsets for training. Link prediction accuracy is measured by the mean average precision (MAP), averaged over all users present in the test set [26]. The evaluation results are summarized in Table 1.

4.2   Detecting Near-Bipartite Networks

Some networks are not bipartite, but nearly so. An example would be a network of "fan" relationships between persons where there are clear "hubs" and "authorities", i.e. popular persons and persons being fan of many people. While these networks are not strictly bipartite, they are mostly bipartite in a sense that has to be made precise. Measures for the level of bipartivity exist in several forms [4,27], and spectral transformations offer another method. Using the link prediction method described in Section 3.3, nearly bipartite graphs can be recognized by the *odd* shape of the learned curve fitting function.

Table 1. Overview of datasets and experiment results. See the text for a description of the datasets and link prediction methods. Link prediction methods: Poly: odd polynomials, NN-poly: odd nonnegative polynomials, Sinh: hyperbolic sine, Red: rank reduction, Odd Neu: odd von Neumann pseudokernel, Pref: preferential attachment.

Dataset	Nodes	Edges	Poly.	NN-poly.	Sinh	Red.	Odd Neu.	Pref.
BibSonomy tag-item	975,963	2,555,080	0.921	**0.925**	**0.925**	0.782	0.917	0.924
BibSonomy user-item	777,084	2,555,080	0.748	0.771	0.771	0.645	0.750	**0.821**
BibSonomy user-tag	210,467	2,555,080	0.801	0.820	0.820	0.777	0.295	**0.878**
CiteULike tag-item	885,046	2,411,819	0.593	0.608	0.608	0.510	0.635	**0.698**
CiteULike user-item	754,484	2,411,819	0.853	**0.856**	**0.856**	0.735	0.855	0.838
CiteULike user-tag	175,992	2,411,819	0.812	0.836	0.836	0.782	0.202	**0.881**
DBpedia artist-genre	47,293	94,861	0.824	**0.971**	0.833	0.736	0.841	0.961
DBpedia birthplace	191,652	273,695	0.952	0.977	**0.978**	0.733	0.813	0.968
DBpedia football club	41,846	131,084	**0.685**	0.678	0.674	0.505	0.159	0.680
DBpedia starring	83,252	141,942	0.908	0.916	**0.924**	0.731	0.570	0.897
DBpedia work-genre	156,145	222,517	0.879	0.941	0.908	0.746	0.867	**0.966**
Epinions	876,252	13,668,320	0.644	**0.690**	0.546	0.501	0.061	**0.690**
French Wikipedia	3,989,678	41,392,490	0.667	0.744	0.744	0.654	0.108	**0.803**
German Wikipedia	3,357,353	51,830,110	0.673	0.699	0.699	0.651	0.156	**0.799**
Japanese Wikipedia	1,892,869	18,270,562	0.740	0.752	0.755	0.618	0.076	**0.776**
Jester	25,038	616,912	0.575	0.571	**0.581**	0.461	0.579	0.501
MovieLens 100k	2,625	100,000	**0.822**	0.774	0.738	0.718	0.631	0.812
MovieLens 10M	136,700	10,000,054	**0.683**	0.682	0.663	0.500	0.298	0.680
MovieLens 1M	9,746	1,000,209	0.640	**0.662**	0.538	0.500	0.221	**0.662**
MovieLens tag-item	24,129	95,580	0.860	0.860	0.860	0.737	**0.865**	0.863
MovieLens user-item	11,610	95,580	0.755	0.741	0.728	0.659	0.674	**0.812**
MovieLens user-tag	20,537	95,580	0.782	0.798	0.798	0.672	0.663	**0.915**
Netflix	497,959	100,480,507	**0.674**	0.671	0.670	0.500	0.322	0.672
Spanish Wikipedia	2,684,231	23,392,353	0.634	0.750	0.750	0.655	0.094	**0.799**
Wikipedia categories	2,036,440	3,795,796	0.591	0.659	0.663	0.500	0.589	**0.675**

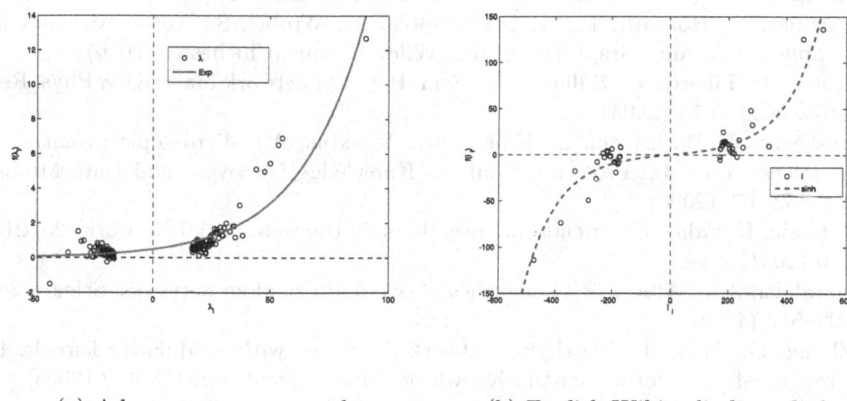

(a) Advogato trust network (b) English Wikipedia hyperlinks

Fig. 5. Detecting near-bipartite and non-bipartite networks: If the hyperbolic sine fits, the network is nearly bipartite; if the exponential fits, the network is not nearly bipartite. (a) the Advogato trust network, (b) the English Wikipedia hyperlink network. These graphs show the learned transformation of a graph's eigenvalues; see the text for a detailed description.

Figure 5 shows the method applied to two unipartite networks: the Advogato trust network [28] and the hyperlink network in the English Wikipedia [25]. The curves indicate that the Advogato trust network is *not* bipartite, while the Wikipedia link network is nearly so.

5   Discussion

While technically the link prediction problem in bipartite graphs is a subproblem of the general link prediction problem, the special structure of bipartite graphs makes common link prediction algorithms ineffective. In particular, all methods based on the triangle closing model cannot work in the bipartite case. Out of the simple local link prediction methods, only the preferential attachment model can be used in bipartite networks.

Algebraic link prediction methods can be used instead, by restricting spectral transformations to odd functions, leading to the matrix hyperbolic sine as a link prediction function, and an odd variant of the von Neumann kernel. As in the unipartite case, no single link prediction method is best for all datasets.

References

1. Liben-Nowell, D., Kleinberg, J.: The link prediction problem for social networks. In: Proc. Int. Conf. on Information and Knowledge Management, pp. 556–559 (2003)
2. Taskar, B., Wong, M.F., Abbeel, P., Koller, D.: Link prediction in relational data. In: Advances in Neural Information Processing Systems (2003)
3. Gärtner, T., Horváth, T., Le, Q.V., Smola, A., Wrobel, S.: Kernel Methods for Graphs. In: Mining Graph Data. John Wiley & Sons, Chichester (2006)
4. Holme, P., Liljeros, F., Edling, C.R., Kim, B.J.: On network bipartivity. Phys. Rev. E 68, 6653–6673 (2003)
5. Leskovec, J., Backstrom, L., Kumar, R., Tomkins, A.: Microscopic evolution of social networks. In: Proc. Int. Conf. on Knowledge Discovery and Data Mining, pp. 462–470 (2008)
6. Adamic, L., Adar, E.: Friends and neighbors on the web. Social Networks 25, 211–230 (2001)
7. Barabási, A.L., Albert, R.: Emergence of scaling in random networks. Science 286, 509–512 (1999)
8. Zhang, D., Mao, R.: Classifying networked entities with modularity kernels. In: Proc. Conf. on Information and Knowledge Management, pp. 113–122 (2008)
9. Newman, M.E.J.: Finding community structure in networks using the eigenvectors of matrices. Phys. Rev. E 74 (2006)
10. Chung, F.: Spectral Graph Theory. American Mathematical Society, Providence (1997)
11. Rendle, S., Schmidt-Thieme, L.: Online-updating regularized kernel matrix factorization models for large-scale recommender systems. In: Proc. Int. Conf. on Recommender Systems, pp. 251–258 (2008)
12. Kunegis, J., Lommatzsch, A.: Learning spectral graph transformations for link prediction. In: Proc. Int. Conf. on Machine Learning, pp. 561–568 (2009)

13. Ito, T., Shimbo, M., Kudo, T., Matsumoto, Y.: Application of kernels to link analysis. In: Proc. Int. Conf. on Knowledge Discovery in Data Mining, pp. 586–592 (2005)
14. Wu, Y., Chang, E.Y.: Distance-function design and fusion for sequence data. In: Proc. Int. Conf. on Information and Knowledge Management, pp. 324–333 (2004)
15. Kandola, J., Shawe-Taylor, J., Cristianini, N.: Learning semantic similarity. In: Advances in Neural Information Processing Systems, pp. 657–664 (2002)
16. Cardoso, J.R., Leite, F.S.: Computing the inverse matrix hyperbolic sine. In: Vulkov, L.G., Waśniewski, J., Yalamov, P. (eds.) NAA 2000. LNCS, vol. 1988, pp. 160–169. Springer, Heidelberg (2001)
17. Hotho, A., Jäschke, R., Schmitz, C., Stumme, G.: BibSonomy: A social bookmark and publication sharing system. In: Proc. Workshop on Conceptual Structure Tool Interoperability, pp. 87–102 (2006)
18. Ziegler, C.N., McNee, S.M., Konstan, J.A., Lausen, G.: Improving recommendation lists through topic diversification. In: Proc. Int. World Wide Web Conf., pp. 22–32 (2005)
19. Emamy, K., Cameron, R.: CiteULike: A researcher's social bookmarking service. Ariadne (51) (2007)
20. Bizer, C., Cyganiak, R., Auer, S., Kobilarov, G.: DBpedia.org–querying Wikipedia like a database. In: Proc. Int. World Wide Web Conf. (2007)
21. Massa, P., Avesani, P.: Controversial users demand local trust metrics: an experimental study on epinions.com community. In: Proc. American Association for Artificial Intelligence Conf., pp. 121–126 (2005)
22. Goldberg, K., Roeder, T., Gupta, D., Perkins, C.: Eigentaste: A constant time collaborative filtering algorithm. Information Retrieval 4(2), 133–151 (2001)
23. GroupLens Research: MovieLens data sets (October 2006), http://www.grouplens.org/node/73
24. Bennett, J., Lanning, S.: The Netflix prize. In: Proc. KDD Cup, pp. 3–6 (2007)
25. Wikimedia Foundation: Wikimedia downloads (January 2010), http://download.wikimedia.org/
26. Manning, C.D., Raghavan, P., Schütze, H.: Introduction to Information Retrieval. Cambridge University Press, Cambridge (2008)
27. Estrada, E., Rodríguez-Velázquez, J.A.: Spectral measures of bipartivity in complex networks. Phys. Rev. E 72 (2005)
28. Stewart, D.: Social status in an open-source community. American Sociological Review 70 (5), 823–842 (2005)

Symmetrization of Modular Aggregation Functions

Radko Mesiar[1,2] and Andrea Mesiarová-Zemánková[3]

[1] Slovak University of Technology, Bratislava, Slovakia
mesiar@math.sk
[2] Institute for Research and Application of Fuzzy Modelling, University of Ostrava,
Czech Republic
[3] Mathematical Institute of SAS, Bratislava, Slovakia
zemankova@mat.savba.sk

Abstract. Ordered modular aggregation functions (OMAF in short) can be seen as symmetrized modular aggregation functions and they are characterized by comonotone modularity. As such, OMAFs generalize OWA operators. We show a one-to-one correspondence between idempotent OMAFs and copula-based integrals with respect to a symmetric capacity.

Keywords: Modularity, Comonotone modularity, Copula, Symmetric capacity, Symmetric fuzzy measure.

1 Introduction

The OWA functions (Ordered Weighted Averages) were introduced in 1988 by Yager [13] and since then they are used in many theoretical papers and several applications. Among generalizations of OWA recall WOWA [12], IOWA [14], GOWA [1], IGOWA [9] functions, etc. For more details see also [15,16]. The OWA functions can be characterized as a symmetrization [6] of a weighted arithmetic mean, i.e., as a symmetrization of an additive aggregation function. In [5,10] it was shown that OWA function is a particular case of the Choquet integral, where the considered capacity (fuzzy measure) is symmetric (see also [7]).

Recall that modularity generalizes additivity. The aim of this contribution is to introduce a symmetrization of modular aggregation functions – OMAF functions and show a relation of this class of functions to a class of non-additive integrals, namely, to the class of copula-based integrals with respect to a symmetric capacity.

2 Ordered Modular Aggregation Functions

Definition 1. *Let $n \in \mathbb{N}$. The mapping $A \colon [0,1]^n \longrightarrow [0,1]$ is called an aggregation function whenever it is non-decreasing and $A(0,\ldots,0) = 0$, $A(1,\ldots,1) = 1$.*

E. Hüllermeier, R. Kruse, and F. Hoffmann (Eds.): IPMU 2010, LNAI 6178, pp. 390–397, 2010.
© Springer-Verlag Berlin Heidelberg 2010

For more details on aggregation functions see [6].

Two classes of aggregation functions that are important for our work are additive and modular aggregation functions. For details see [2,6].

Definition 2. *Let* $A \colon [0,1]^n \longrightarrow [0,1]$ *be an aggregation function. Then*
(i) A is additive whenever

$$A(\mathbf{x} + \mathbf{y}) = A(\mathbf{x}) + A(\mathbf{y}) \tag{1}$$

for all $\mathbf{x}, \mathbf{y}, \mathbf{x} + \mathbf{y} \in [0,1]^n$.

(ii) A is modular whenever

$$A(\mathbf{x} \vee \mathbf{y}) + A(\mathbf{x} \wedge \mathbf{y}) = A(\mathbf{x}) + A(\mathbf{y}). \tag{2}$$

for all $\mathbf{x}, \mathbf{y} \in [0,1]^n$.

Due to the valuation equality $\mathbf{x} \vee \mathbf{y} + \mathbf{x} \wedge \mathbf{y} = \mathbf{x} + \mathbf{y}$, each additive aggregation function is necessarily also modular. For each of these two classes we have the following characterization (see [2,6]).

Proposition 1. *Let* $A \colon [0,1]^n \longrightarrow [0,1]$ *be an aggregation function. Then*
(i) A is additive if and only if

$$A(\mathbf{x}) = \sum_{i=1}^{n} w_i x_i \tag{3}$$

for some weights $(w_1, \ldots, w_n) \in [0,1]^n$, $\sum_{i=1}^{n} w_i = 1$ *(and A is called a weighted arithmetic mean).*

(ii) A is modular if and only if

$$A(\mathbf{x}) = \sum_{i=1}^{n} w_i f_i(x_i). \tag{4}$$

for some weights $(w_1, \ldots, w_n) \in [0,1]^n$, $\sum_{i=1}^{n} w_i = 1$, *where for* $i = 1, \ldots, n$, $f_i \colon [0,1] \longrightarrow [0,1]$ *are 1-dimensional aggregation functions, i.e.,* f_i *is non-decreasing and* $f_i(0) = 0$, $f_i(1) = 1$.

Observe that a modular aggregation function A can be written equivalently in the form

$$A(\mathbf{x}) = \sum_{i=1}^{n} g_i(x_i),$$

where $g_i \colon [0,1] \longrightarrow [0,1]$ are non-decreasing functions satisfying $g_i(0) = 0$ and $\sum_{i=1}^{n} g_i(1) = 1$. In this paper we prefer the form (4) to stress the relationships of modular n-ary aggregation functions with unary aggregation functions.

Evidently, each additive aggregation function is also modular ($f_i = $ id for all $i = 1, \ldots, n$ in this case). On the other hand, for example the function $A \colon [0,1]^2 \longrightarrow [0,1]$ given by

$$A(x, y) = \frac{x^2 + y}{2}$$

is modular but not additive. Hence modularity of aggregation function generalizes the additivity.

Yager [13] has introduced OWA function as a symmetrization of a weighted arithmetic mean (of an additive aggregation function).

Definition 3. *Let $A \colon [0,1]^n \longrightarrow [0,1]$ be an aggregation function. The symmetrized aggregation function $S_A \colon [0,1]^n \longrightarrow [0,1]$ is given by*

$$S_A(\mathbf{x}) = A(x_{\sigma(1)}, \ldots, x_{\sigma(n)}), \tag{5}$$

where σ is a permutation of $(1, \ldots, n)$ such that $x_{\sigma(1)} \geq \cdots \geq x_{\sigma(n)}$. In particular, if A is additive (with weights $w_1, \ldots, w_n$) then $S_A = $ OWA is called an Ordered Weighted Average,

$$S_A(\mathbf{x}) = \mathrm{OWA}(\mathbf{x}) = \sum_{i=1}^{n} w_i x_{\sigma(i)}. \tag{6}$$

Though there may exist more permutations fitting the requirements of Definition 3, both (5) and (6) are well-defined, independently of the choice of such σ. We propose the following extension of the concept of OWA functions – the OMAF functions arising from modular aggregation functions by symmetrization.

Definition 4. *Let $A \colon [0,1]^n \longrightarrow [0,1]$ be a modular aggregation function,*

$$A(\mathbf{x}) = \sum_{i=1}^{n} w_i f_i(x_i).$$

Then its symmetrization S_A is called Ordered Modular Aggregation Function, shortly OMAF, i.e., $S_A = $ OMAF,

$$\mathrm{OMAF}(\mathbf{x}) = \sum_{i=1}^{n} w_i f_i(x_{\sigma(i)}),$$

where the permutation σ satisfies $x_{\sigma(1)} \geq \cdots \geq x_{\sigma(n)}$.

In the following we show that OMAF functions cover the class of ordered weighted maximum functions.

Definition 5. *Let $1 = v_1 \geq v_2 \geq \cdots \geq v_n \geq 0$ be given weights. Then the Ordered Weighted Maximum function OWMax$\colon [0,1]^n \longrightarrow [0,1]$ is given by*

$$\mathrm{OWMax}(\mathbf{x}) = \bigvee_{i=1}^{n} \left(v_i \wedge x_{\sigma(n-i+1)} \right). \tag{7}$$

Proposition 2. *Let OWMax function be given by formula* (7). *Then* OWMax $=$ S_A, *where* $A: [0,1]^n \longrightarrow [0,1]$ *is a modular aggregation function,*

$$A(\mathbf{x}) = \sum_{i=1}^{n} w_i f_i(x_{\sigma(i)}),$$

where $w_i = v_{n-i+1} - v_{n-i+2}$, *for* $i = 1, \ldots, n$, *with convention* $v_{n+1} = 0$, *and* $f_i(x) = \max(0, \min(\frac{x - v_{n-i+2}}{w_i}, 1))$, *for* $i = 1, \ldots, n$.

Example 1. (i) Let $w_1 = \cdots = w_{n-1} = 0$, $w_n = 1$, and

$$f_n(x) = \begin{cases} 0 & \text{if } x \in [0,1[, \\ 1 & \text{if } x = 1, \end{cases}$$

(i.e., f_n is the weakest 1-dimensional aggregation function). Then

$$\text{OMAF}(\mathbf{x}) = \begin{cases} 1 & \text{if } \mathbf{x} = 1 \\ 0 & \text{else,} \end{cases}$$

i.e., we have recovered the weakest n-ary aggregation function on $[0,1]$. Similarly, if $w_1 = 1, w_2 = \cdots = w_n = 0$, and

$$f_1(x) = \begin{cases} 0 & \text{if } x = 0, \\ 1 & \text{else,} \end{cases}$$

i.e., here f_1 is the strongest 1-dimensional function, then the corresponding OMAF is the strongest n-ary aggregation function on $[0,1]$,

$$\text{OMAF}(\mathbf{x}) = \begin{cases} 0 & \text{if } \mathbf{x} = 0 \\ 1 & \text{else.} \end{cases}$$

(ii) for $n = 2$, put $w_1 = w_2 = 0.5$, $f_1(x) = x$ and $f_2(x) = x^2$. Then the corresponding function OMAF: $[0,1]^2 \longrightarrow [0,1]$ is given by

$$\text{OMAF}(x,y) = \frac{1}{2}(\max(x,y) + \min(x,y)^2).$$

If we reverse the order of functions in (ii), i.e., if we put $f_1(x) = x^2$ and $f_2(x) = x$, then

$$\text{OMAF}(x,y) = \frac{1}{2}(\max(x,y)^2 + \min(x,y)).$$

(iii) for $n = 3$, let $w_1 = 0.3$, $w_2 = 0.2$, $w_3 = 0.5$ and $f_1(x) = \min(\frac{x}{0.3}, 1)$, $f_2(x) = \max(0, \min(\frac{x-0.3}{0.2}, 1))$ and $f_3(x) = \max(0, 2x - 1)$. Then $\text{OMAF}(x,y,z)$ $= \text{OWMax}(x,y,z)$, where weights for OWMax operator are $v_1 = 1, v_2 = 0.5, v_3 = 0.3$.

(iv) for $n = 3$, let $w_1 = 0.5$, $w_2 = 0.2$, $w_3 = 0.3$, $f_1(x) = \max(0, 2x - 1)$, $f_2(x) = \max(0, \min(\frac{x - 0.3}{0.2}, 1))$ and $f_3(x) = \min(\frac{x}{0.3}, 1)$. Then $\mathrm{OMAF}(0.7, 0.3, 1) = 1$ and $\mathrm{OMAF}(0.6, 0.2, 0.9) = 0.8$.

An aggregation function A is called a kernel aggregation function [3] (or, equivalently, it has minimal Chebyshev norm) if

$$|A(\mathbf{x}) - A(\mathbf{y})| \leq ||\mathbf{x} - \mathbf{y}||_{L_\infty} = \max_i |x_i - y_i|.$$

Moreover, an aggregation function A is called 1-Lipschitz (with respect to L_1-norm) if

$$|A(\mathbf{x}) - A(\mathbf{y})| \leq ||\mathbf{x} - \mathbf{y}||_{L_1} = \sum_{i=1}^n |x_i - y_i|.$$

OWA's and OWMax's are examples of kernel aggregation functions [4]. Taking the OMAF function from Example 1(iv) we have

$$\mathrm{OMAF}(0.7, 0.3, 1) - \mathrm{OMAF}(0.6, 0.2, 0.9) \nleq 0.1,$$

and thus this OMAF is not a kernel aggregation function. However, it is 1-Lipschitz.

Theorem 1. *Let A be an ordered modular aggregation function given by $A(\mathbf{x}) = \sum_{i=1}^n w_i f_i(x_{\sigma(i)})$, with $x_{\sigma(1)} \geq \cdots \geq x_{\sigma(n)}$. Assume $g_i(x) = \sum_{j=1}^i w_j f_j(x)$ for $x \in [0,1]$, $i = 1, \ldots, n$. Then A is kernel if and only if for all $i \in \{1, \ldots, n\}$ the function g_i is concave, and $g_n = \mathrm{id}$.*

Theorem 2. *Let A be an ordered modular aggregation function given by $A(\mathbf{x}) = \sum_{i=1}^n w_i f_i(x_{\sigma(i)})$, with $x_{\sigma(1)} \geq \cdots \geq x_{\sigma(n)}$. Then A is 1-Lipschitz if and only if each f_i, $i = 1, \ldots, n$, is $\frac{1}{w_i}$-Lipschitz, i.e., $w_i \cdot |f_i(x) - f_i(y)| \leq |x - y|$ for each $x, y \in [0, 1]$.*

Observe that a sufficient condition ensuring the 1-Lipschitz property of an OMAF A is $g_n = \mathrm{id}$, i.e., each idempotent OMAF A is 1-Lipschitz. Note that all OMAFs introduced in Example 1 are 1-Lipschitz. However, only Example 1 (iii) brings a kernel OMAF. $A \colon [0,1]^2 \longrightarrow [0,1]$ given by $A(x, y) = \frac{1}{2}(\max(x, y) + \min(x, y)^4)$ is an OMAF function which is not 1-Lipschitz.

In [5] it was shown that OWA operators are exactly those aggregation functions that are symmetric and comonotone additive. We have a similar result for OMAF operators in the following theorem.

Theorem 3. *An aggregation function $A \colon [0,1]^n \longrightarrow [0,1]$ is an OMAF function if and only if it is symmetric and comonotone modular.*

3   Copula-Based Integrals with Respect to Symmetric Capacities and Idempotent OMAFs

An aggregation function $C\colon [0,1]^2 \longrightarrow [0,1]$ is called a copula whenever 1 is its neutral element, i.e., $C(x,1) = C(1,x) = x$ for all $x \in [0,1]$, and C is supermodular, i.e., for all $\mathbf{x}, \mathbf{y} \in [0,1]^2$, $C(\mathbf{x} \vee \mathbf{y}) + C(\mathbf{x} \wedge \mathbf{y}) \geq C(\mathbf{x}) + C(\mathbf{y})$. Copulas are applied in statistics and probability to model the structure of stochastic dependence of random vectors, and for more details we recommend Nelsen's lecture notes [11]. In [8] Klement et al. introduced the concept of copula-based integrals. In our contribution we will assume these integrals defined on a discrete universe $X = \{1, \ldots, n\}$ for some $n \in \mathbb{N}$. We will use a capacity m on X, i.e., a mapping $m\colon 2^X \longrightarrow [0,1]$ which is non-decreasing, $m(E) \leq m(F)$ whenever $E \subseteq F \subseteq X$, and satisfies the boundary conditions $m(\emptyset) = 0$, $m(X) = 1$.

Definition 6 ([8]). *Let m be a given capacity on X and C a fixed copula. Then a mapping $C_m\colon [0,1]^n \longrightarrow [0,1]$ given by*

$$C_m(x) = \sum_{i=1}^{n}(C(x_{\sigma(i)}, m(\{\sigma(1), \ldots, \sigma(i)\})) - C(x_{\sigma(i)}, m(\{\sigma(1), \ldots, \sigma(i-1)\})))$$

(8)

(with convention $\{\sigma(1), \sigma(0)\} = \emptyset$), where $\sigma\colon X \longrightarrow X$ is a permutation such that $x_{\sigma(1)} \geq \cdots \geq x_{\sigma(n)}$, is called a (C,m)-based integral.

The aggregation function C_m is idempotent and 1-Lipschitz and it is symmetric if and only if m is a symmetric capacity. Recall that if the capacity m is symmetric then it is uniquely given by values $m(\#i)$, where the symbol $\#i$ denotes any set with cardinality i. If we denote $v_{n-i+1} = m(\#i)$ and $w_i = m(\#i) - m(\#i-1)$ we get $\sum_{j=1}^{i} w_j = v_{n-i+1}$. Thus also $m(X) = 1 = \sum_{i=1}^{n} w_i = v_1$, and for such a symmetric capacity m, the formula (8) can be rewritten into

$$C_m(x) = \sum_{i=1}^{n}(C(x_{\sigma(i)}, v_{n-i+1}) - C(x_{\sigma(i)}, v_{n-i+2}))$$

(9)

(with convention $v_{n+1} = 0$).

Example 2.   (i) For copula $C = \Pi$ given by $\Pi(x,y) = xy$ (product is a copula describing the independence of random variables) and for a symmetric capacity m we have

$$\Pi_m(x) = \sum_{i=1}^{n} x_{\sigma(i)} \cdot w_i,$$

i.e., Π_m is just an OWA function.

(ii) For the strongest copula Min, $\text{Min}(x,y) = \min(x,y)$, and a symmetric capacity m, we have

$$\text{Min}_m(x) = \sum_{i=1}^{n} (\min(x_{\sigma(i)}, v_{n-i+1}) - \min(x_{\sigma(i)}, v_{n-i+2}) =$$

$$\bigvee_i \min(x_{\sigma(i)}, v_{n-i+1}) = \bigvee_i \min(v_i, x_{\sigma(n-i+1)}),$$

i.e., Min_m is an OWMax function.

The following results show the one-to-one correspondence between idempotent OMAF functions and copula-based integrals with respect to symmetric capacities.

Theorem 4. *Let C be a copula and m a symmetric capacity on X. Then C_m is an n-ary idempotent OMAF.*

Theorem 5. *Let $A \colon [0,1]^n \longrightarrow [0,1]$ be an idempotent OMAF. Then there is a copula C and a symmetric capacity m on X such that $A = C_m$.*

Observe that additional constraints on idempotent OMAFs relate them to special fuzzy integrals. For example, comonotone additive OMAFs are exactly OWAs, i.e., Choquet integral based on symmetric capacities. Similarly, comonotone maxitivity relates idempotent OMAFs and Sugeno integral.

4   Conclusion

We have introduced and studied some elementary properties of a new class of symmetric aggregation functions – Ordered Modular Aggregation Functions, OMAF in short. These aggregation functions naturally generalize the concept of OWA operators, with striking similarities in integral representation and characterization by comonotone modularity (comonotone additivity). A detailed study of this new type of aggregation functions will be the topic of our further investigations. Moreover, we expect the application of OMAFs in all domains where OWAs have shown their usefulness.

Acknowledgement. This work was supported by grants MSM VZ 619889 8701, APVV-0012-07 and VEGA 1/0080/10.

References

1. Beliakov, G.: Learning Weights in the Generalized OWA Operators. Fuzzy Optimization and Decision Making 4, 119–130 (2005)
2. Beliakov, G., Pradera, A., Calvo, T.: Aggregation functions: a Guide for Practitioners. Springer, Heidelberg (2007)
3. Calvo, T., Mesiar, R.: Stability of aggregation op- erators. In: Proc of Int. Conference in Fuzzy Logic and Technology, Leicester, pp. 475–478 (2001)

4. Calvo, T., Kolesárová, A., Komorníková, M., Mesiar, R.: Aggregation Operators: Properties, Classes and Construction Methods. In: Calvo, T., Mayor, G., Mesiar, R. (eds.) Aggregation Operators, pp. 3–107. Physica-Verlag, Heidelberg (2002)
5. Grabisch, M.: Fuzzy integral in multicriteria decision making. Fuzzy Sets and Systems 69, 279–298 (1995)
6. Grabisch, M., Marichal, J.-L., Mesiar, R., Pap, E.: Aggregation Functions. Cambridge University Press, Cambridge (2009)
7. Grabisch, M.: OWA operators and nonadditive integrals. In: [16] (to appear)
8. Klement, E.P., Mesiar, R., Pap, E.: Measure-based aggregation operators. Fuzzy Sets and Systems 142(1), 3–14 (2004)
9. Merigó, J.M., Gil-Lafuente, A.M.: The induced generalized OWA operator. In: New dimensions in fuzzy logic and related technologies. Proceedings of the 5th EUSFLAT Conference, Ostrava, Czech Republic, pp. 463–470 (2007)
10. Murofushi, T., Sugeno, M.: Some quantities represented by the Choquet integral. Fuzzy Sets and Systems 56, 229–235 (1993)
11. Nelsen, R.B.: An Introduction to Copulas. Springer, New York (1999)
12. Torra, V.: The weighted OWA operator. Int. J. of Intelligent Systems 12, 153–166 (1997)
13. Yager, R.R.: On ordered weighted averaging aggregation operators in multicriteria decision making. IEEE Transactions on Systems, Man and Cybernetics 18, 183–190 (1988)
14. Yager, R.R., Filev, D.P.: Induced Ordered Weighted Averaging Operators. IEEE Transactions on Systems, Man and Cybernetics 29(2), 141–150 (1999)
15. Yager, R.R., Kacprzyk, J.: The Ordered Weighted Averaging Operators: Theory and Applications. Kluwer Academic Publishers, Boston (1997)
16. Yager, R.R., Kacprzyk, J., Beliakov, G.: Recent Developments in the Ordered Weighted Averaging Operators: Theory and Practice. Springer, Heidelberg (to appear)

Smooth Aggregation Functions on Finite Scales

Margalida Mas, Miquel Monserrat, and Joan Torrens

Department of Mathematics and Computer Science
University of the Balearic Islands
07122 Palma de Mallorca, Spain
dmimmg0@uib.es, dmimma0@uib.es, dmijts0@uib.es

Abstract. In this paper smooth aggregation functions on a finite scale are studied and characterized as solutions of a functional equation analogous to the Frank functional equation. The particular cases of quasi-copulas and copulas are also characterized through a similar functional equation. Previous characterizations of these kind of operations through special matrices are used jointly with the new ones to derive some invariant properties on quasi-copulas and copulas on finite scales.

Keywords: Aggregation functions, smoothness, finite scale, quasi-copulas, copulas.

1 Introduction

The fact that the theory of aggregation functions and their applications is a field of increasing interest is clear from the great number of researchers working on this topic and it is corroborated by the different and complementary monographs that have been appeared in last years (see [2], [3] and [7]). On the other hand, the study of operations defined on a finite chain is also in a hight development because in practical situations it is necessary to reduce the range of calculations and reasonings to a finite set of values.

In this direction many different classes of aggregation functions have been considered in the framework of finite scales. Such kind of operations are usually known as discrete operations. In almost all cases, this study is devoted to discrete aggregation operations with the smoothness property (or at least with some kind of smoothness), usually considered as the counterpart of continuity for operations defined on finite chains. For instance, t-norms and t-conorms in [15], weighted ordinal means in [11], uninorms and nullnorms in [12], non-commutative versions of these operations in [5] and [13], idempotent uninorms in [4], copulas in [14] and quasi-copulas in [1]. However, the whole class of smooth aggregation functions has not been considered yet in this framework.

In this paper we want to deal with smooth aggregation functions on a finite scale in general, and we present a characterization theorem for them based on the Frank functional equation in a similar way as it was done in the case of [0,1] (see [10]). Moreover quasi-copulas, as a special kind of smooth aggregation functions, are also characterized as solutions of a similar functional equation and

E. Hüllermeier, R. Kruse, and F. Hoffmann (Eds.): IPMU 2010, LNAI 6178, pp. 398–407, 2010.

the particular case of copulas is adapted. These new characterizations, jointly with previous characterizations based on special kinds of matrices (given in [1] and [14]), are used in deriving some invariant properties for discrete quasi-copulas and copulas.

2   Preliminaries

In this section we recall some definitions and basic facts on discrete aggregation operators. As in this framework any finite chain is equivalent (see for instance [15]) we will deal with the most simple one with $n + 1$ elements:

$$L_n = \{0, 1, 2, \ldots, n\}$$

and we will use also the notation $[a, b]$ to denote the finite subchain given by $[a, b] = \{x \in L \mid a \leq x \leq b\}$. For details on smooth discrete t-norms not included here see for instance [15].

Definition 1. *A (binary) discrete aggregation function is a binary operation* $F : L_n^2 \longrightarrow L_n$ *such that it is non-decreasing in each component,* $F(0, 0) = 0$ *and* $F(n, n) = n$.

Definition 2. *([15]) A function* $f : L_n \rightarrow L_n$ *is said to be smooth if it satisfies:*

$$\mid f(x) - f(x - 1) \mid \leq 1 \text{ for all } x \in L_n \text{ with } x \geq 1.$$

Definition 3. *([15]) A binary operation* F *on* L *is said to be smooth when each one of its vertical and horizontal sections* $(F(x, -)$ *and* $F(-, y)$*, respectively) are smooth.*

The importance of the smoothness condition lies in the fact that it is generally used as a discrete counterpart of continuity and it is equivalent to the Lipschitz condition (see [15]).

Definition 4. *([14]) A discrete copula* C *on* L_n *is a binary operation* $C : L_n^2 \longrightarrow L_n$ *such that*

(C1) $C(x, 0) = C(0, x) = 0$ *for all* $x \in L_n$
(C2) $C(x, n) = C(n, x) = x$ *for all* $x \in L_n$
(C3) $C(x, y) + C(x', y') \geq C(x, y') + C(x', y)$
    for all $x, x', y, y' \in L_n$ *with* $x \leq x', y \leq y'$ (*2-increasing condition*)

Definition 5. *([1]) A discrete quasi-copula* Q *on* L_n *is a binary operation* $Q : L_n^2 \longrightarrow L_n$ *such that*

(Q1) $Q(x, 0) = Q(0, x) = 0$ *and* $Q(x, n) = Q(n, x) = x$ *for all* $x \in L_n$
(Q2) Q *is non-decreasing in each component*
(Q3) Q *is smooth.*

We will call a discrete *dual quasi-copula* to any operation satisfying conditions of quasi-copula but replacing condition (Q1) by the following one

(*D*1) $Q(x,0) = Q(0,x) = x$ and $Q(x,n) = Q(n,x) = n$ for all $x \in L_n$.

In fact operations introduced in Definitions 4 and 5 were called "irreducible" discrete copulas and quasi-copulas in [14] and [1], respectively. For simplicity we will avoid the word irreducible in this paper. Note also that conditions (Q1) and (Q2) in Definition 5 can be derived one of each other because smoothness and so only one of them is necessary in the definition.

Clearly each copula is a quasi-copula but not vice versa. Quasi-copulas which are not copulas are called *proper quasi-copulas*. These classes of operations were characterized through special kinds of matrix representations as follows. Recall that an $n \times n$ permutation matrix A is an $n \times n$ matrix $(a_{i,j})$ such that there exists a permutation σ of $\{1, 2, \ldots, n\}$ such that

$$a_{i,j} = \begin{cases} 1 & \text{if } i = \sigma(j) \\ 0 & \text{otherwise} \end{cases}$$

Note that this is equivalent to say that in each row and each column of A all entries are equal to 0 except one which is 1.

Proposition 1. *([14]) A binary operation C on L_n is a discrete copula if and only if there exists an $n \times n$ permutation matrix $A = (a_{i,j})$ such that*

$$C(r,s) = \begin{cases} 0 & \text{if } r = 0 \text{ or } s = 0 \\ \sum_{\substack{i \leq r \\ j \leq s}} a_{i,j} & \text{otherwise} \end{cases} \tag{1}$$

for all $(r,s) \in L_n^2$. Given the discrete copula C, the matrix A is obtained as

$$a_{i,j} = C(i,j) + C(i-1,j-1) - C(i,j-1) - C(i-1,j) \tag{2}$$

Definition 6. *([1], [16]) An $n \times n$ Alternating-Sign Matrix (ASM matrix) is an $n \times n$ matrix $A = (a_{i,j})$ such that*

1. $a_{i,j} \in \{-1, 0, 1\}$ *for all $i, j \in \{1, \ldots, n\}$*
2. *The first and the last elements $a_{i,j} \neq 0$ of each row and each column are 1.*
3. *All the elements $a_{i,j} \neq 0$ of each row and each column have alternating signs.*

Remark 1. In particular, the sum of each row and each column equals 1 and consequently each ASM with no negative entries is in fact a permutation matrix.

Proposition 2. *([1]) A binary operator $Q : L_n \times L_n \longrightarrow L_n$ is a discrete quasi-copula if and only if there exists an $n \times n$ ASM matrix $A = (a_{i,j})$ such that*

$$Q(r,s) = \begin{cases} 0 & \text{if } r = 0 \text{ or } s = 0 \\ \sum_{\substack{i \leq r \\ j \leq s}} a_{i,j} & \text{otherwise} \end{cases} \tag{3}$$

for all $(r, s) \in L_n^2$. *Given the quasi-copula* Q, *the matrix* A *is obtained as*

$$a_{i,j} = Q(i, j) + Q(i - 1, j - 1) - Q(i, j - 1) - Q(i - 1, j) \tag{4}$$

Finally, let us recall that a smooth t-norm T (t-conorm S) on L_n is Archimedean if and only if $T(x, x) < x$ ($S(x, x) > x$) for all $x \in L_n \setminus \{0, n\}$, and that there is one and only one Archimedean smooth t-norm (t-conorm) on L_n, usually called the Łukasiewicz t-norm (t-conorm), which is given by

$$T_{\mathbf{L}}(x, y) = \max(0, x + y - n) \quad (S_{\mathbf{L}}(x, y) = \min(x + y, n)) \tag{5}$$

3   Smooth Discrete Aggregation Functions

Let us deal in this section with smooth aggregation functions on L. We begin with the characterization of the general case through the well known Frank functional equation (see [6]). We do not include the proof of this result because it is very similar as the one given in the case of $[0, 1]$ (see [10]).

Theorem 1. *Let* F *be a binary aggregation function on* L_n. *Then* F *is smooth if and only if there is a binary aggregation function* F' *such that*

$$F(x, y) + F'(x, y) = x + y \quad \text{for all} \quad x, y \in L_n.$$

Moreover, in this case, the binary aggregation function F' *is also smooth.*

This result implies in particular that for any smooth aggregation function F we have

$$x + y - n \leq x + y - F'(x, y) \leq x + y \quad \text{for all} \quad x, y \in L_n$$

and consequently, $T_{\mathbf{L}} \leq F \leq S_{\mathbf{L}}$. Also, if we denote by $\mathcal{F}$ the set of all binary, smooth aggregation functions on L_n, from the theorem above we can define the function $\Phi : \mathcal{F} \to \mathcal{F}$ given by $\Phi(F) = F'$ leading to a kind of duality of $\mathcal{F}$, because we clearly have $(F')' = F$. Note that this assignation preserves commutativity and moreover, Φ interchanges neutral elements with annihilator elements in the following sense:

If $\alpha \in L_n$ is a neutral element of F, then $F'(x, \alpha) = x + \alpha - F(x, \alpha) = \alpha$ and similarly for $F'(\alpha, x)$. That is, α is an annihilator element of F' and vice versa, if α is an annihilator element of F then α is a neutral element of F'.

Now, we can characterize the particular cases when the smooth aggregation function has an annihilator or a neutral element.

Theorem 2. *Consider* $\alpha \in L_n$ *and let* $F : L_n^2 \to L_n$ *be a discrete binary operation. Then* F *is a smooth discrete aggregation function with annihilator element* α *if and only if there exist a quasi-copula* Q_F *on* $[\alpha, n]$ *and a dual quasi-copula* D_F *on* $[0, \alpha]$ *such that* F *is given by*

$$F(x, y) = \begin{cases} D_F(x, y) & \text{if } x, y \in [0, \alpha] \\ Q_F(x, y) & \text{if } x, y \in [\alpha, n] \\ \alpha & \text{otherwise.} \end{cases} \tag{6}$$

Proof. If F is a smooth aggregation function with annihilator α, the restriction of F to $[\alpha, n]^2$ is a smooth aggregation function on the finite chain $[\alpha, n]$ with the least element α as annihilator and consequently is a quasi-copula on $[\alpha, n]$. Similarly, the restriction of F to $[0, \alpha]^2$ is a dual quasi-copula. Moreover, for all $x, y \in L_n$ such that $x < \alpha < y$ we have

$$\alpha = F(x, \alpha) \le F(x, y) \le F(\alpha, y) = \alpha,$$

that is, $F(x, y) = \alpha$ and the same is true when $y < \alpha < x$.

Conversely, it is clear that functions given by equation (6) are smooth aggregation functions with annihilator α. ∎

Theorem 3. *Consider* $\alpha \in L_n$ *and let* $F : L_n^2 \to L_n$ *be a discrete binary operation. Then* F *is a smooth discrete aggregation function with neutral element* α *if and only if there exist a quasi-copula* Q_F *on* $[0, \alpha]$ *and a dual quasi-copula* D_F *on* $[\alpha, n]$ *such that* F *is given by*

$$F(x, y) = \begin{cases} Q_F(x, y) & \text{if } x, y \in [0, \alpha] \\ D_F(x, y) & \text{if } x, y \in [\alpha, n] \\ x + y - \alpha & \text{otherwise.} \end{cases} \tag{7}$$

Proof. If F is a smooth aggregation function with neutral element α, the restriction of F to $[0, \alpha]^2$ is a smooth aggregation function on the finite chain $[0, \alpha]$ with the greatest element α as neutral element and consequently is a quasi-copula on $[0, \alpha]$. Similarly, the restriction of F to $[\alpha, n]^2$ is a dual quasi-copula. Moreover, from Theorem 1 we have that F' is a smooth aggregation function with annihilator element α and, applying Theorem 2, we can ensure $F'(x, y) = \alpha$ whenever $\min(x, y) < \alpha < \max(x, y)$. Thus, for all these values

$$F(x, y) = x + y - F'(x, y) = x + y - \alpha.$$

Conversely, it is clear that functions given by equation (7) are smooth aggregation functions with neutral element α. ∎

The structure of smooth discrete aggregation functions with annihilator and with neutral element can be viewed in Figure 1.

4   Discrete Quasi-copulas and Copulas

In this section we give a new characterization of discrete quasi-copulas, in this case as the solutions of a functional equation. Let us begin with the commutative case.

Theorem 4. *Let* F *be a commutative discrete aggregation function on* L_n. *Then* F *is a commutative discrete quasi-copula if and only if there is an aggregation function* F^{*1} *such that*

$$F(x, y) + F^{*1}(n - x, y) = y \quad \text{for all} \quad x, y \in L_n. \tag{8}$$

Moreover, in this case, the binary aggregation function F^{*1} *is also a discrete quasi-copula.*

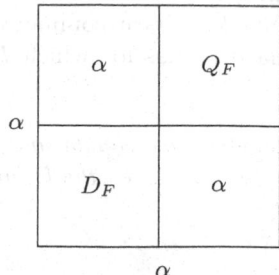
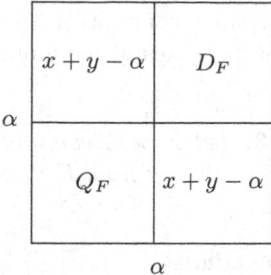

Fig. 1. Structure of smooth discrete aggregation function with annihilator element α (left) and with neutral element α (right)

Proof. If F is a commutative quasi-copula on L_n then defining

$$F^{*1}(x,y) = y - F(n - x, y) \qquad \text{for all} \quad x, y \in L_n \tag{9}$$

we obtain a binary function on L_n with $F^{*1}(0,0) = 0$ and $F^{*1}(n,n) = n$ satisfying equation (8). Moreover, for all $x > 0$ we have

$$F^{*1}(x,y) - F^{*1}(x-1,y) = y - F(n-x,y) - (y - F(n - x + 1, y))$$
$$= F(n - x + 1, y) - F(n - x, y) \geq 0$$

which proves that F^{*1} is non-decreasing in the first component. Since non-decreasingness in the second component can be prove similarly, we have that F^{*1} is an aggregation function. Moreover, the arguments before prove also that $F^{*1}(x,y) - F^{*1}(x-1,y) \leq 1$ and that F^{*1} is smooth. Since it also satisfies

$$F^{*1}(x,n) = n - F(n - x, n) = x \text{ and } F^{*1}(n,x) = x - F(n - n, x) = x$$

we have that F^{*1} is in fact a quasi-copula.

Conversely, if the aggregation function F^{*1} exists let us prove first that F must be smooth. For all $y > 0$ we have

$$F(x,y) - F(x, y - 1) = y - F^{*1}(n - x, y) - (y - 1 - F^{*1}(n - x, y - 1))$$
$$= 1 - (F^{*1}(n - x, y) - F^{*1}(n - x, y - 1)) \leq 1$$

where the inequality holds because F^{*1} is non-decreasing. Since F is commutative we have smoothness in both components. Finally, note that $F(n, 0) = F(0, n) = 0 - F^{*1}(n - n, 0) = 0$ which also implies that F has annihilator element 0 and then is a quasi-copula. ∎

A similar characterization can be done for copulas but then F^{*1} needs to be also a copula, leading to the result: If F is commutative then F is a copula if and only if F^{*1} is a copula. Note that this result for copulas is in fact true also for non-commutative operations and can be proved directly as in the framework of

[0,1] (see for instance [9]). What is not true in general is that the quasi-copula F^{*1} obtained from a commutative quasi-copula F is itself commutative. Next proposition characterizes all commutative quasi-copulas for which F^{*1} is also commutative.

Proposition 3. *Let F be a commutative discrete quasi-copula and let F^{*1} be the quasi-copula obtained from F through equation (9). Then the following items are equivalent.*

(i) F^{*1} is commutative
(ii) F and its dual quasi-copula $F^d(x,y) = n - F(n-x, n-y)$ satisfy the Frank functional equation.

Proof. Note that by equation (9) we obtain that F^{*1} is commutative if and only if $y - F(n-x, y) = x - F(n-y, x)$ for all $x, y \in L_n$. Now, changing $z = n - x$, this is equivalent to $y - F(z, y) = n - z - F(n-y, n-z)$ or also to $F(z,y) + F^d(z,y) = z + y$ for all $z, y \in L_n$, proving the equivalence between (i) and (ii). ∎

For the non-commutative case we have the following result with proof very similar to the one given for the commutative case.

Theorem 5. *Let F be a discrete binary aggregation function on L_n. Then F is a discrete quasi-copula if and only if there exist two aggregation functions F^{*1} and F^{*2} such that*

$$F(x,y) + F^{*1}(n-x, y) = y \quad and \quad F(x,y) + F^{*2}(x, n-y) = x \quad (10)$$

for all $x, y \in L_n$. Moreover, in this case, both binary aggregation functions F^{*1} and F^{*2} are also discrete quasi-copulas.

5   Invariant Quasi-copulas and Copulas

Note that in the framework of copulas on [0,1], operations F^{*1} and F^{*2} are well known transformations of copulas. Characterizations of those copulas that are invariant for these kinds of transformation were studied in [9]. There is another transformation commonly used for copulas on [0,1], which is given by $\hat{C}(x,y) = x + y - n + F(n-x, n-y)$ for all $x, y \in [0, 1]$ and for any copula C. Transformation $\hat{C}$ is known as the *survival* copula (see again [9]), but we can extend this notion to discrete quasi-copulas on L_n in general and we have the following result.

Lemma 1. *Let $Q : L_n^2 \to L_n$ be a binary operation on L_n. Then Q is a discrete quasi-copula if and only if $\hat{Q}$ is a discrete quasi-copula, where $\hat{Q}$ is defined by*

$$\hat{Q}(x,y) = x + y - n + Q(n-x, n-y) \quad for\ all \quad x, y \in L_n.$$

Proof. If Q is a quasi-copula, it is clear that $\hat{Q}(n,x) = x$ for all $x \in L_n$. To see the other conditions note that

$$\hat{Q}(x+1,y) - \hat{Q}(x,y) = 1 - (Q(n-x,n-y) - Q(n-x-1,n-y))$$

and since Q is a quasi-copula we have $0 \leq \hat{Q}(x+1,y) - \hat{Q}(x,y) \leq 1$, proving both, non-decreasingness and smoothness. The converse follows similarly.   ∎

Remark 2. In the framework of $[0,1]$ it is well known that a binary operation C is a copula if and only if $\hat{C}$ is a copula. Of course for discrete copulas on L_n this is also true and it can be proved similarly as in the case of $[0,1]$ or through matrix arguments from the previous lemma and the matrix representation given in Propositions 1 and 2 (see Proposition 4 below).

From this result one can wonder if there exist discrete quasi-copulas $Q : L_n^2 \to L_n$ being invariant for these kinds of transformation, as it was studied in [9]. To answer this question we will use the matrix representations given in Propositions 1 and 2. Recall that any discrete quasi-copula has associated an ASM matrix in such a way that equation (3) holds. Thus, if a quasi-copula Q has associated matrix $A = (a_{i,j})$, then a straightforward computation proves that the associated matrices of the quasi-copulas Q^{*_1}, Q^{*_2} and $\hat{Q}$ are given by $A^{*_1} = b_{i,j}$, $A^{*_2} = b'_{i,j}$ and $\hat{A} = (c_{i,j})$, where

$$b_{i,j} = a_{n+1-i,j} \qquad \text{for all } \ i,j = 1,\ldots,n, \tag{11}$$

$$b'_{i,j} = a_{i,n+1-j} \qquad \text{for all } \ i,j = 1,\ldots,n, \tag{12}$$

$$c_{i,j} = a_{n+1-i,n+1-j} \qquad \text{for all } \ i,j = 1,\ldots,n. \tag{13}$$

That is, the matrix A^{*_1} is obtained from A just by reversing columns, A^{*_2} is obtained similarly by reversing the rows of A, and $\hat{A}$ is obtained by reversing both rows and columns.

Taking into account the previous equations we can easily give characterizations of invariant quasi-copulas and copulas through these transformations.

Proposition 4. *Let Q be a discrete quasi-copula (copula) with associated ASM matrix (permutation matrix) given by $A = (a_{i,j})$. Then the following items are equivalent.*

(i) $Q = \hat{Q}$

(ii) Q and its dual quasi-copula (copula) $Q^d(x,y) = n - Q(n-x,n-y)$ satisfy the Frank functional equation

(iii) A satisfies $a_{i,j} = a_{n+1-i,n+1-j}$ for all $i,j =, 1,\ldots,n$.

Proof. The equivalence between (i) and (ii) is clear from the fact that $\hat{Q}$ can be written as $\hat{Q}(x,y) = x + y - Q^d(x,y)$. Now the equivalences between (i) and (iii) follows from the matrix associated to $\hat{Q}$ given in equation (13). Finally, note that for the case of copulas the reasonings are the same taking into account that if A is a permutation matrix then also $\hat{A}$ is a permutation matrix.   ∎

Remark 3. Note that when Q is a commutative quasi-copula we can obtain the following equivalent property
$$Q = \hat{Q} \text{ if and only if } a_{n+1-i,j} = a_{n+1-j,i} \text{ for all } i, j =, 1, \ldots, n,$$
that directly follows from Proposition 3 and equation (11).

With respect to the other transformations we have the following result.

Proposition 5. *Let Q be a discrete quasi-copula (copula) with associated ASM matrix (permutation matrix) given by $A = (a_{i,j})$. Then*

(i) $Q^{*1} = Q$ if and only if A satisfies $a_{n+1-i,j} = a_{i,j}$ for all $i, j =, 1, \ldots, n$.
(ii) $Q^{*2} = Q$ if and only if A satisfies $a_{i,n+1-j} = a_{i,j}$ for all $i, j =, 1, \ldots, n$.

Proof. Again the result is clear from equations (11) and (12). ∎

Let us illustrate the previous results with some examples.

Example 1. It is clear from Proposition 5 that there are no discrete copulas invariant with respect to the transformations $*_1$ and $*_2$ (each row and/or column must be self-reverse but it has only one entry 1 and all the others 0). The same is true for quasi-copulas on L_n when n is an even number. However, when n is odd, consider for instance the following matrices

$$M_1 = \begin{pmatrix} 0 & 0 & 0 & 1 & 0 \\ 0 & 1 & 0 & 0 & 0 \\ 1 & -1 & 1 & -1 & 1 \\ 0 & 1 & 0 & 0 & 0 \\ 0 & 0 & 0 & 1 & 0 \end{pmatrix} \quad \text{and} \quad M_2 = \begin{pmatrix} 0 & 0 & 1 & 0 & 0 \\ 0 & 1 & -1 & 1 & 0 \\ 0 & 0 & 1 & 0 & 0 \\ 1 & 0 & -1 & 0 & 1 \\ 0 & 0 & 1 & 0 & 0 \end{pmatrix}$$

Both are ASM matrices and if we take Q_1 and Q_2 the quasi-copulas with associated matrices M_1 and M_2 respectively, we have $Q_1 = Q_1^{*1}$ and $Q_2 = Q_2^{*2}$ (because matrices M_1 and M_2 satisfy equations given in Proposition 5 (i) and (ii), respectively).

Example 2. With respect to the survival transformation it is well known (see [15]) that all smooth t-norms on L_n are associative copulas. Moreover, if T is one of them then T and its dual t-conorm T^d satisfy the Frank equation if and only if the set of idempotent of T, $J = \{x \in L_n \mid T(x, x) = x\}$, is self-dual, that is, $N(J) = J$ where $N(J) = \{n - x \mid x \in L_n\}$ (see again [15]). Thus, from Proposition 4 all these t-norms are examples of invariant copulas, $T = \hat{T}$.

On the other hand, if we consider the ASM matrix

$$M = \begin{pmatrix} 1 & 0 & 0 & 0 & 0 \\ 0 & 0 & 1 & 0 & 0 \\ 0 & 1 & -1 & 1 & 0 \\ 0 & 0 & 1 & 0 & 0 \\ 0 & 0 & 0 & 0 & 1 \end{pmatrix}$$

the quasi-copula Q with associated matrix M is also invariant, $Q = \hat{Q}$, because M satisfies equation (13).

Conclusions. In this paper smooth aggregation functions on finite scales are studied, devoting special attention to the particular case of quasi-copulas and copulas. Some characterizations as solutions of functional equations are presented and, in the case of quasi-copulas and copulas, this characterization is used to derive some invariant properties in terms of their associated representation matrices (see [1], [14]).

Acknowledgements. This work has been partially supported by the Spanish Grant MTM2009-10320 with FEDER support.

References

1. Aguiló, I., Suñer, J., Torrens, J.: Matrix representation of discrete quasi-copulas. Fuzzy Sets and Systems 159, 1658–1672 (2008)
2. Beliakov, G., Pradera, A., Calvo, T.: Aggregation Functions: A Guide for Practicioners. Springer, Berlin (2007)
3. Calvo, T., Mayor, G., Mesiar, R. (eds.): Aggregation operators. New trends and applications, Studies in Fuzziness and Soft Computing, vol. 97. Physica-Verlag, Heidelberg (2002)
4. De Baets, B., Fodor, J., Ruiz-Aguilera, D., Torrens, J.: Idempotent uninorms on finite ordinal scales. International Journal of Uncertainty, Fuzziness and Knowledge-Based Systems 17, 1–14 (2009)
5. Fodor, J.C.: Smooth associative operations on finite ordinal scales. IEEE Trans. on Fuzzy Systems 8, 791–795 (2000)
6. Frank, M.J.: On the simultaneous associativity of F(x,y) and x + y - F(x,y). Aequationes Math. 19, 194–226 (1979)
7. Grabisch, M., Marichal, J.L., Mesiar, R., Pap, E.: Aggregation functions. Encyclopedia of Mathematics and its Applications, vol. 127. Cambridge University Press, Cambridge (2009)
8. Klement, E.P., Mesiar, R., Pap, E.: Triangular norms. Kluwer Academic Publishers, London (2000)
9. Klement, E.P., Mesiar, R., Pap, E.: Invariant copulas. Kybernetika 38, 275–285 (2002)
10. Kolesárová, A.: 1-Lipschitz aggregation operators and quasi-copulas. Kybernetika 39, 615–629 (2003)
11. Kolesárová, A., Mayor, G., Mesiar, R.: Weighted ordinal means. Information Sciences 177, 3822–3830 (2007)
12. Mas, M., Mayor, G., Torrens, J.: t-Operators and uninorms on a finite totally ordered set. International Journal of Intelligent Systems 14, 909–922 (1999)
13. Mas, M., Monserrat, M., Torrens, J.: On left and right uninorms on a finite chain. Fuzzy Sets and Systems 146, 3–17 (2004)
14. Mayor, G., Suñer, J., Torrens, J.: Copula-like operations on finite settings. IEEE Transactions on Fuzzy Systems 13, 468–477 (2005)
15. Mayor, G., Torrens, J.: Triangular norms in discrete settings. In: Klement, E.P., Mesiar, R. (eds.) Logical, Algebraic, Analytic, and Probabilistic Aspects of Triangular Norms, pp. 189–230. Elsevier, Amsterdam (2005)
16. Robbins, D.P., Rumsey, H.: Determinants and alternating-sign matrices. Advances in Math. 62, 169–184 (1986)

Dual Representable Aggregation Functions and Their Derived S-Implications

Isabel Aguiló, Marc Carbonell, Jaume Suñer, and Joan Torrens

Department of Mathematics and Computer Science
University of the Balearic Islands
07122 Palma de Mallorca, Spain
isabel.aguilo@uib.es, marc.carbonell@uib.es, jaume.sunyer@uib.es,
dmijts0@uib.es

Abstract. In this paper dual representable aggregation functions (DRAF's) are introduced and studied. After giving a representation theorem for them, it is proved that they can be viewed as a non-associative generalization of nilpotent t-conorms, some basic properties are proved and some examples are given. On the other hand, using DRAF's a new kind of strong implications are derived and some usual properties are studied for this new class of implications. In particular, it is shown that they have an easy structure always divided into three parts depending on the strong negation.

Keywords: Aggregation function, representable aggregation function, duality, nilpotent t-conorm, implication function, strong negation, continuity.

1   Introduction

Aggregation functions are operations that perform the process of merging several inputs (numerical or qualitative) into a single output that must be representative of the initial information. From their nature, aggregation functions become essential in many pure and applied fields, such as mathematics, economics, decision making, image processing, data fusion, etc. Many researchers are currently working on this topic from both, theoretical and applicational point of view. This is corroborated by the different and complementary monographs that have appeared in last years (see [4], [7], [14] and [23]).

Many kinds of aggregation functions have been studied and characterized classifying them usually into four general classes: *conjunctive* when they lie under the minimum, *disjunctive* when they lie over the maximum, *averaging or compensatory* when they lie between the minimum and the maximum, and *mixed* in any other case. In the conjunctive class we obviously find t-norms, t-subnorms, copulas, quasi-copulas and semicopulas (see for instance [4]). On the other hand, representable aggregation functions (RAF's for short, see Definition 2 below) are another kind of conjunctive aggregation functions that appear for the first time in [19] and also recently in [8] introducing residual implications derived

E. Hüllermeier, R. Kruse, and F. Hoffmann (Eds.): IPMU 2010, LNAI 6178, pp. 408–417, 2010.

from them. RAF's admit a representation through a unary increasing function $g : [0, 1] \to [0, g(1)]$ and a strong negation N, generalizing the well known nilpotent t-norms.

On the other hand, implication functions play a crucial role in fuzzy logic and approximate reasoning because they are used to perform conditionals and to manage forward and backward inferences. Moreover, they are also useful in many applications like fuzzy control, mathematical morphology and image processing, fuzzy relational equations, computing with words, fuzzy measures (see for instance [5], [6], [12], [13], [16], [18]). Implication functions are also studied from the theoretical point of view ([1], [2], [18]). In many cases they are derived from t-norms and t-conorms but recently, more general classes of aggregation functions have also been considered in this framework, like uninorms ([9], [17], [20], [21], [22]), conjunctors including copulas and quasi-copulas ([10]) and RAF's ([8]).

In this paper we want to deal with dual (with respect to the strong negation N) representable aggregation functions (DRAF's) that obviously belong to the disjunctive class, and their derived implications. Directly from duality we obtain that DRAF's are representable in the same way as RAF's through a decreasing function $f : [0, 1] \to [0, f(0)]$ and the proper negation N. Some basic properties are proved pointing out that they can be viewed as a non-associative generalization of nilpotent t-conorms. Moreover, some representative examples are studied in detail showing a very simple structure easy to manipulate. On the other hand, strong implications derived from DRAF's are introduced (via the generalization of the classical meaning $p \to q \equiv \neg p \vee q$) and some properties are studied. It is proved that such implications have a very simple structure divided in three parts depending on the negation N and some usual properties are studied for this new class of implications.

2 Preliminaries

We will suppose the reader to be familiar with the basic theory of t-norms, t-conorms, and strong negations (see for instance [15]). We recall here only some facts on aggregation functions and fuzzy implications.

Definition 1. *([7], [10]) A binary function $F : [0, 1] \times [0, 1] \to [0, 1]$ will be called an* aggregation function *when it is non-decreasing in each place, $F(0, 0) = 0$ and $F(1, 1) = 1$.*

Aggregation functions are usually classified in conjunctive (when they are under the minimum), disjunctive (when they lie over the maximum), compensative (when they are between the minimum and the maximum) and mixed (all the others).

The following special kind of aggregation functions was introduced in [19]. Along the paper we will use indistinctly the notation $\min(x, y)$ and $x \wedge y$ to denote the minimum of the numbers x and y. Analogously, we will use $\max(x, y)$ and $x \vee y$ to denote their maximum.

Definition 2. *([19]) A binary function $F : [0,1] \times [0,1] \rightarrow [0,1]$ will be called a representable aggregation function (RAF in short) if there is a continuous strictly increasing function $g : [0,1] \rightarrow [0,+\infty]$ with $g(0) = 0$ and a strong negation N such that F is given by*

$$F(x,y) = g^{-1}\left(\max(0, g(x \wedge y) - g(N(x \vee y)))\right) \quad \text{for all } x,y \in [0,1] \quad (1)$$

The pair (g, N) is called a generating pair of F and we will denote it by $F = <g, N>$.

The importance of representation (1) lies in the fact that it is unique up to a positive multiplicative constant as it is stated in next proposition.

Proposition 1. *([19]) Let $F_1 =<g_1, N_1 >$ and $F_2 =<g_2, N_2 >$ be two RAF's. Then they are equal if and only if $N_1 = N_2$ and there exists a constant $k > 0$ such that $g_2 = kg_1$.*

RAF's are specially interesting because they are conjunctive, continuous, commutative aggregation functions with neutral element 1, and they have the representation theorem stated before. That is, they have the same properties as nilpotent t-norms except associativity. In this sense, we say that RAF's are a non-associative generalizations of nilpotent t-norms, and moreover we have the following result.

Proposition 2. *([19]) Let $F =< g, N >$ be a RAF. Then F is a t-norm if and only if $g(1) < +\infty$ and*

$$N(x) = g^{-1}(g(1) - g(x)) \quad \text{for all } x \in [0,1]$$

Moreover, in this case F is a nilpotent t-norm with additive generator given by the composition gN.

There are two different classes of RAF's depending on whether the value $g(1)$ is finite or not. In the first class, we have all nilpotent t-norms, and also the family of RAF's: $F =< g, N >$ with $g(x) = x$. Functions in this family will be denoted simply by F_N and they are given by

$$F_N(x,y) = \max\left(0, x \wedge y - N(x \vee y)\right) \quad \text{for all } x,y \in [0,1].$$

In the class where $g(1) = +\infty$, we have the family $F =< g, N >$ with $g(x) = -\ln(1-x)$. In this case they will be denoted by F^N and are given by

$$F^N(x,y) = \max\left(0, \frac{x \wedge y - N(x \vee y)}{1 - N(x \vee y)}\right) \quad \text{for all } x,y \in [0,1].$$

Definition 3. *([11], [2]) A binary operator $I : [0,1] \times [0,1] \rightarrow [0,1]$ is said to be an implication operator, or an implication, if it satisfies:*

I1) I is decreasing in the first variable and increasing in the second one.
I2) $I(0,0) = I(1,1) = 1$ and $I(1,0) = 0$.

Note that, from the definition, it follows that $I(0,x) = 1$ and $I(x,1) = 1$ for all $x \in [0,1]$ whereas the symmetrical values $I(x,0)$ and $I(1,x)$ are not derived from the definition.

A special kind of fuzzy implications are strong implications usually derived from a t-conorm and a negation through the expression $I(x,y) = S(N(x),y)$ for all $x,y \in [0,1]$ (see the survey [1]). Recently also other kinds of aggregation functions have been used, specially uninorms (see [3]).

3   Dual Representable Aggregation Functions (DRAF's)

It is well known that, given a fuzzy negation N, the N-dual of a conjunctive aggregation function F is always a disjunctive aggregation function, given by

$$F^*(x,y) = N(F(N(x),N(y))) \quad \text{for all} \quad x,y \in [0,1].$$

In this way, we can dualize any RAF, $F = \langle g,N \rangle$, with respect to the proper strong negation N and we obtain

$$\begin{aligned} F^*(x,y) &= N(g^{-1}(\max(0, g(N(x) \wedge N(y)) - g(N(N(x) \vee N(y)))))) \\ &= N(g^{-1}(\max(0, g(N(x \vee y) - g(x \wedge y))))) \\ &= f^{-1}(\max(0, f(x \vee y) - f(N(x \wedge y)))) \end{aligned}$$

where $f = g \circ N$ is a continuous strictly decreasing function $f : [0,1] \to [0,+\infty]$ with $f(1) = 0$.

Thus, we can give the following definition.

Definition 4. *([19]) A binary function $G : [0,1] \times [0,1] \to [0,1]$ will be called a dual representable aggregation function (DRAF in short) if there is a continuous strictly decreasing function $f : [0,1] \to [0,+\infty]$ with $f(1) = 0$ and a strong negation N such that G is given by*

$$G(x,y) = f^{-1}(\max(0, f(x \vee y) - f(N(x \wedge y)))) \quad \text{for all } x,y \in [0,1] \quad (2)$$

The pair (f,N) will be called a *generating pair* of G (similarly as for RAF's) and we will denote it by $G = < f,N >$. From this definition we can easily prove the following result on duality, (here and from now on gN and fN denote the composition of these functions).

Proposition 3. *Let $F = < g,N >$ a RAF. Then the dual F^* is a DRAF with generating pair $\langle gN,N \rangle$, and reciprocally, the dual of a DRAF $G = < f,N >$ is a RAF with generating pair $\langle fN,N \rangle$.*

The importance of the representation (2) lies in the fact that it is unique up to a positive multiplicative constant.

Proposition 4. *([19]) Let $G_1 = < f_1,N_1 >$ and $G_2 = < f_2,N_2 >$ be two DRAF's. Then they are equal if and only if $N_1 = N_2$ and there exists a constant $k > 0$ such that $f_2 = kf_1$.*

Proof. If $N_1 = N_2$ and there exists a constant $k > 0$ such that $f_2 = kf_1$, it is a straightforward computation to show that $G_1 = G_2$.

Conversely, if $G_1 = G_2$ then their N-duals RAF's $G_1^* = \langle f_1 N_1, N_1 \rangle$ and $G_2^* = \langle f_2 N_2, N_2 \rangle$ are also equal. Thus, by Proposition 1 we necessarily have $N_1 = N_2$ and there must be a positive constant $k > 0$ such that $f_2 N = kf_1 N$. That is,

$$f_2(N(x)) = kf_1(N(x)) \quad \text{for all} \quad x \in [0, 1]$$

and taking $y = N(x)$ we obtain $f_2(y) = kf_1(y)$ for all $y \in [0, 1]$.   ∎

Also we can derive the following properties of DRAF's directly from the duality with RAF's.

Proposition 5. *([19]) Let $G = < f, N >$ be a DRAF. Then*

- *G is a continuous, commutative disjunctive aggregation function with neutral element 0.*
- *The one-region of G, that is, the set of points $(x, y) \in [0, 1]^2$ such that $G(x, y) = 1$, is given by*

$$O(F) = \{(x, y) \mid y \geq N(x)\}.$$

- *G is strictly increasing in each place in the region $\{(x, y) \mid y \leq N(x)\}$.*
- *$G(x, x) > x$ for all $x \in (0, 1)$.*

These properties show the importance of DRAF's because they allow to view them as a non-associative generalization of nilpotent t-conorms. Thus, they could be useful in those fields where nilpotent t-conorms are usually applied although the associative property is not necessary. This fact is reinforced by the following proposition.

Proposition 6. *Let $G = \langle f, N \rangle$ be a DRAF. Then G is a t-conorm if and only if $f(0) < +\infty$ and*

$$N(x) = f^{-1}(f(0) - f(x)) \quad \text{for all } x \in [0, 1]$$

Moreover, in this case G is a nilpotent t-conorm with additive generator given by the composition fN.

Proof. If $G = \langle f, N \rangle$ is such that $f(0) < +\infty$ and

$$N(x) = f^{-1}(f(0) - f(x)),$$

it is a straightforward computation to prove that G is a nilpotent t-conorm with additive generator fN.

Conversely, if $G = \langle f, N \rangle$ is a t-conorm then its N-dual $G^* = \langle fN, N \rangle$ is a t-norm and by Proposition 2, it must be $fN(1) < +\infty$ and $N(x) = (fN)^{-1}(fN(1) - fN(x))$ for all $x \in [0, 1]$. That is, $f(0) < +\infty$ and $x = f^{-1}(f(0) - f(N(x)))$ or, taking $y = N(x)$, $N(y) = f^{-1}(f(0) - f(y))$ for all $y \in [0, 1]$.   ∎

There are two different classes of DRAF's depending on whether the value $f(0)$ is finite or not.

- In the first class, we have all nilpotent t-conorms as we have seen just before. We can also consider the family of DRAF's: $G = < f, N >$ with $f(x) = 1 - x$. Functions in this family will be denoted simply by G_N and they are given by

$$G_N(x, y) = \min(1, 1 - (N(x \wedge y) + x \vee y)) \qquad \text{for all} \quad x, y \in [0, 1].$$

Another particular family in this class, is given by dualizing the family F_N of RAF's. Specifically, we will denote by $F_N^* = \langle N, N \rangle$ the DRAF N-dual of F_N given by

$$F_N^*(x, y) = N(\max(0, N(x \vee y) - x \wedge y)) \quad \text{for all} \quad x, y \in [0, 1].$$

- In the second class, where $f(0) = +\infty$, we can consider also two different families. One is given by DRAF's $G = < f, N >$ with $f(x) = -\ln x$. In this case they will be denoted by G^N and are given by

$$G^N(x, y) = \min\left(1, \frac{x \vee y}{N(x \wedge y)}\right) \qquad \text{for all} \quad x, y \in [0, 1].$$

The other one is obtained again by dualizing the family F^N. Specifically, we will denote by $(F^N)^*$ the DRAF N-dual of F^N. In this case we obtain

$$(F^N)^*(x, y) = N\left(\max\left(0, \frac{N(x \vee y) - x \wedge y}{1 - x \wedge y}\right)\right) \qquad \text{for all} \quad x, y \in [0, 1].$$

4   S-Implications Derived from DRAF's

In this section we want to study S-implications derived from G where $G = \langle f, N \rangle$ is a DRAF, that is,

$$I_G(x, y) = G(N(x), y) \qquad \text{for all} \quad x, y \in [0, 1]. \tag{3}$$

Note that the same strong negation N from the function G is considered in Equation (3). However, any other strong negation N_1 could be used to derive S-implications, but this general case is left for further work.

Since $G(1, 0) = G(0, 1) = 1$, expression (3) always gives an implication in the sense of Definition 3.

Proposition 7. *Let $G = \langle f, N \rangle$ be a DRAF. Then I_G is given by*

$$I_G(x, y) = \begin{cases} 1 & \text{if } x \leq y \\ f^{-1}(f(y) - f(x)) & \text{if } x > y \geq N(x) \\ f^{-1}(f(N(x)) - f(N(y))) & \text{if } \min(x, N(x)) > y \end{cases} \tag{4}$$

Proof. If $x \le y$, then clearly $I_G(x,y) = f^{-1}(0) = 1$. On the other hand, if $x > y$, we have two cases:

a) $N(x) \le y$. In this case, we have

$$I_G(x,y) = f^{-1}\left(\max(0, f(N(x) \vee y) - f(N(N(x) \wedge y)))\right) = f^{-1}(f(y) - f(x))$$

b) $N(x) > y$. In this case, we have

$$\begin{aligned} I_G(x,y) &= f^{-1}\left(\max(0, f(N(x) \vee y) - f(N(N(x) \wedge y)))\right) \\ &= f^{-1}(f(N(x)) - f(N(y))) \end{aligned}$$ ∎

The structure of I_G can be viewed in Figure 1.

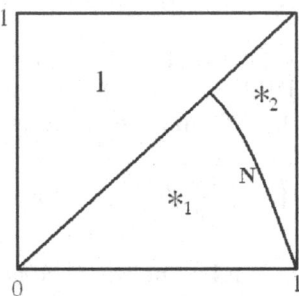

Fig. 1. Structure of the S-implication I_G obtained from the DRAF, $G = \langle f, N \rangle$, where $(*_1) = f^{-1}(f(N(x)) - f(N(y)))$ and $(*_2) = f^{-1}(f(y) - f(x))$

From the definition and the proposition above we can easily derive the following properties.

Proposition 8. *Let $G = \langle f, N \rangle$ be a DRAF and I_G the S-implication derived from G. Then the following properties hold:*

i) I_G satisfies the left neutrality principle: *$I_G(1,y) = y$ for all $y \in [0,1]$.*
ii) $I_G(x,0) = N(x)$ for all $x \in [0,1]$.
iii) I_G satisfies the ordering property:

$$I_G(x,y) = 1 \quad \Longleftrightarrow \quad x \le y, \qquad \text{for all} \quad x,y \in [0,1].$$

iv) I_G is continuous.

Next we present some examples derived from the special families of DRAF's introduced in the previous section.

Example 1.

1) If we take $f(x) = 1 - x$, then we have

$$I_{G_N}(x, y) = \begin{cases} 1 & \text{if } x \le y \\ 1 + y - x & \text{if } x > y \ge N(x) \\ 1 - N(y) + N(x) & \text{if } \min(x, N(x)) > y \end{cases} \tag{5}$$

Note that in the particular case when N is the classical negation $N(x) = 1 - x$, the corresponding G_N is the Łukasiewicz t-conorm and the S-implication is given by the well known Łukasiewicz implication:

$$I_{\mathbf{LK}}(x, y) = \min\{1, 1 - x + y\} \qquad \text{for all} \quad x, y \in [0, 1].$$

2) The S-implication of $F_N^* = \langle N, N \rangle$, the DRAF N-dual of F_N, is given by

$$I_{F_N^*}(x, y) = \begin{cases} 1 & \text{if } x \le y \\ N(N(y) - N(x)) & \text{if } x > y \ge N(x) \\ N(x - y) & \text{if } \min(x, N(x)) > y \end{cases} \tag{6}$$

3) If we take $f(x) = -\ln x$, then

$$I_{G_N}(x, y) = \begin{cases} 1 & \text{if } x \le y \\ \dfrac{y}{x} & \text{if } x > y \ge N(x) \\ \dfrac{N(x)}{N(y)} & \text{if } \min(x, N(x)) > y \end{cases} \tag{7}$$

Moreover, when $N(x) = 1 - x$, let us denote by G^0 the corresponding DRAF and by I_{G^0} the derived S-implication. Then they are respectively given by $G^0(x, y) = \max\{0, \frac{x+y-1}{x \vee y}\}$ and

$$I_{G^0}(x, y) = \begin{cases} 1 & \text{if } x \le y \\ \dfrac{y}{x} & \text{if } x > y \ge 1 - x \\ \dfrac{1-x}{1-y} & \text{if } \min(x, 1 - x) > y \end{cases}$$

4) The S-implication of $(F^N)^* = \langle -\ln(1 - N), N \rangle$, the DRAF N-dual of F^N, is given by

$$I_{F^N}^*(x, y) = \begin{cases} 1 & \text{if } x \le y \\ N\left(\dfrac{N(y) - N(x)}{1 - N(x)}\right) & \text{if } x > y \ge N(x) \\ N\left(\dfrac{x - y}{1 - y}\right) & \text{if } \min(x, N(x)) > y \end{cases} \tag{8}$$

Another important property for fuzzy implications is the contraposition property with respect to a strong negation N, that is,

$$I(N(y), N(x)) = I(x, y) \quad \text{for all} \quad x, y \in [0, 1].$$

Let us investigate now whether the implications derived from DRAF's satisfy this property.

Proposition 9. *Let $G = \langle f, N \rangle$ be a DRAF and I_G the S-implication derived from G. Then I_G satisfies contraposition with respect to a fuzzy negation N' if and only if $N'(x) = N(x)$ for all $x \in [0, 1]$.*

Proof. First of all, it is clear that I_G satisfies contraposition with respect to N due to the commutativity of G. On the other hand, since I_G satisfies the left neutrality principle with N, this is the only possible negation for which I_G can satisfy contraposition (see [2]).   ∎

Conclusions and Future Work

In this paper dual representable aggregation functions (DRAF's) have been introduced. Obtained by duality from representable aggregation functions (RAF, see [8]), these operators have all usual properties of nilpotent t-conorms except associativity. In particular, any DRAF G admits a representation theorem from a continuous and strictly decreasing function $f : [0, 1] \rightarrow [0, +\infty]$ with $f(1) = 0$ and a strong negation N that limits the one-region of $G = \langle f, N \rangle$. We have also studied strong implications derived from DRAF's obtaining their expression from f and N. Some properties of these implications have been analyzed including contraposition with respect to a fuzzy negation N'.

As a future work, we want to deal with many other possible properties of such implications like the exchange principle, the law importation, the modus ponens and modus tollens, some distributive properties with conjunctions and disjunctions, and so on.

Acknowledgements

This work has been partially supported by the Spanish Grant MTM2009-10320 with FEDER support.

References

1. Baczyński, M., Jayaram, B.: (S,N)- and R-implications: A state-of-the-art survey. Fuzzy Sets and Systems 159, 1836–1859 (2008)
2. Baczyński, M., Jayaram, B.: Fuzzy Implications. Studies in Fuzziness and Soft Computing, vol. 231. Springer, Berlin (2008)
3. Baczyński, M., Jayaram, B.: (U,N)-implications and their characterizations. Fuzzy Sets and Systems 160, 2049–2062 (2009)

4. Beliakov, G., Pradera, A., Calvo, T.: Aggregation Functions: A Guide for Practicioners. Springer, Berlin (2007)
5. Bustince, H., Mohedano, V., Barrenechea, E., Pagola, M.: Definition and construction of fuzzy DI-subsethood measures. Information Sciences 176, 3190–3231 (2006)
6. Bustince, H., Pagola, M., Barrenechea, E.: Construction of fuzzy indices from fuzzy DI-subsethood measures: application to the global comparison of images. Information Sciences 177, 906–929 (2007)
7. Calvo, T., Mayor, G., Mesiar, R. (eds.): Aggregation operators. New trends and applications. Studies in Fuzziness and Soft Computing, vol. 97. Physica-Verlag, Heidelberg (2002)
8. Carbonell, M., Torrens, J.: Continuous R-implications generated from representable aggregation functions. Fuzzy Sets and Systems (to appear)
9. De Baets, B., Fodor, J.C.: Residual operators of uninorms. Soft Computing 3, 89–100 (1999)
10. Durante, F., Klement, E.P., Mesiar, R., Sempi, C.: Conjunctors and their residual implicators: Characterizations and construction methods. Mediterranean Journal of Mathematics 4, 343–356 (2007)
11. Fodor, J., Roubens, M.: Fuzzy preference modelling and multicriteria decision support. Kluwer Academic Publishers, Dordrecht (1994)
12. González, M., Mir, A., Ruiz-Aguilera, D., Torrens, J.: Edge-Images using a Uninorm-Based Fuzzy Mathematical Morphology. Opening and Closing. In: Tavares, J., Jorge, N. (eds.) Advances in Computacional Vision and Medical Image Processing, Springer, Heidelberg (2009)
13. Gottwald, S.: A Treatise on Many-Valued Logic. Research Studies Press, Baldock (2001)
14. Grabisch, M., Marichal, J.L., Mesiar, R., Pap, E.: Aggregation functions. Encyclopedia of Mathematics and its Applications, vol. 127. Cambridge University Press, Cambridge (2009)
15. Klement, E.P., Mesiar, R., Pap, E.: Triangular norms. Kluwer Academic Publishers, London (2000)
16. Klir, G.J., Yuan, B.: Fuzzy Sets and Fuzzy Logic. In: Theory and Applications, Prentice Hall, New Jersey (1995)
17. Mas, M., Monserrat, M., Torrens, J.: Two types of implications derived from uninorms. Fuzzy Sets and Systems 158, 2612–2626 (2007)
18. Mas, M., Monserrat, M., Torrens, J., Trillas, E.: A survey on fuzzy implication functions. IEEE Transactions on Fuzzy Systems 15(6), 1107–1121 (2008)
19. Mayor, G., Torrens, J.: On a class of binary operations: Non-strict Archimedean aggregation functions. In: Proceedings of ISMVL '88, pp. 54–59. Palma de Mallorca, Spain (1988)
20. Ruiz, D., Torrens, J.: Residual implications and co-implications from idempotent uninorms. Kybernetika 40, 21–38 (2004)
21. Ruiz-Aguilera, D., Torrens, J.: Distributivity of residual implications over conjunctive and disjunctive uninorms. Fuzzy Sets and Systems 158, 23–37 (2007)
22. Ruiz-Aguilera, D., Torrens, J.: S- and R-implications from uninorms continuous in $]0, 1[^2$ and their distributivity over uninorms. Fuzzy Sets and Systems 160, 832–852 (2009)
23. Torra, V., Narukawa, Y.: Modeling decisiona. Information fusion and aggregation operators. In: Cognitive Technologies. Springer, Heidelberg (2007)

Aggregation Functions with Stronger Types of Monotonicity

Erich Peter Klement[1], Maddalena Manzi[2], and Radko Mesiar[3,4]

[1] Department of Knowledge-Based Mathematical Systems,
Johannes Kepler University, Linz, Austria
ep.klement@jku.at
[2] Department of Pure and Applied Mathematics,
University of Padua, Padova, Italy
mmanzi@math.unipd.it
[3] Department of Mathematics and Descriptive Geometry,
Faculty of Civil Engineering, Slovak University of Technology, Bratislava, Slovakia
mesiar@math.sk
[4] Institute of Theory of Information and Automation,
Czech Academy of Sciences, Prague, Czech Republic

Abstract. Following the ideas of stronger forms of monotonicity for unary real functions and for capacities, k-monotone and strongly k-monotone aggregation functions are introduced and discussed. In the special case $k = 2$ also some applications are given.

1 Introduction

The monotonicity of a real function $f\colon I \to \mathbb{R}$, where $I \subseteq \mathbb{R}$ is some real interval, can be strengthened into the total monotonicity. Recall that a real function f is *totally monotone* if it is smooth and all its derivatives are nonnegative. In particular, a real function $f\colon [0,1] \to [0,1]$ is totally monotone if and only if $f(x) = \sum_{i=0}^{\infty} a_i \cdot x^i$ with $a_i \geq 0$ for all $i \in \mathbb{N} \cup \{0\}$ and $\sum_{i=0}^{\infty} a_i \leq 1$. Observe that if $f(0) = 0$ and $f(1) = 1$ are required then necessarily $a_0 = 0$ and $\sum_{i=0}^{\infty} a_i = 1$. Similarly, the monotonicity of capacities can be strengthened into the k-monotonicity, $k = 2, 3, \ldots, \infty$. Recall that, for a measurable space $(X, \mathcal{A})$, a mapping $m\colon \mathcal{A} \to [0,1]$ is called a *capacity* if $m(\emptyset) = 0$, $m(X) = 1$ and m is monotone, i.e., $m(E) \leq m(F)$ whenever $E \subseteq F$. For a fixed $k \in \mathbb{N} \setminus \{1\}$, m is called k-*monotone* if for all $E_1, \ldots, E_k \in \mathcal{A}$ we have

$$m\left(\bigcup_{i=1}^{k} E_i\right) \geq \sum_{\emptyset \neq J \subseteq \{1,\ldots,k\}} (-1)^{|J|+1} m\left(\bigcap_{j \in J} E_j\right) \tag{1}$$

Moreover, if a capacity m satisfies (1) for all $k \in \mathbb{N} \setminus \{1\}$ then m is called an ∞-*monotone capacity* (or, equivalently, a *belief measure*). For more details see [8,10].

E. Hüllermeier, R. Kruse, and F. Hoffmann (Eds.): IPMU 2010, LNAI 6178, pp. 418–424, 2010.

The k-monotonicity (1) of a capacity m can be formulated in an equivalent way: m is k-monotone if for all $r \in \{2, \ldots, k\}$ and for all pairwise disjoint $E, E_1, \ldots, E_r \in \mathcal{A}$,

$$\sum_{J \subseteq \{1, \ldots, r\}} (-1)^{r-|J|} m \left(E \cup \bigcup_{j \in J} E_j \right) \geq 0. \tag{2}$$

Inequality (2) can be generalized to an arbitrary bounded lattice $(L, \vee, \wedge, \mathbf{0}, \mathbf{1})$. Indeed, let $g \colon L \to \mathbb{R}$ be a non-decreasing mapping, i.e., $g(a) \leq g(b)$ whenever $a \leq b$. Then g is k-monotone, $k \in \mathbb{N} \setminus \{1\}$, if for all $r \in \{2, \ldots, k\}$, for all $a \in L$, and for all pairwise disjoint $a_1, \ldots, a_r \in L$ (i.e., $a_1 \wedge a_2 = \mathbf{0}$, etc.) we have

$$\sum_{J \subseteq \{1, \ldots, r\}} (-1)^{r-|J|} g \left(a \vee \bigvee_{j \in J} a_j \right) \geq 0. \tag{3}$$

If the lattice L under consideration is a sublattice of some vector lattice (and if $\mathbf{0}$ is the neutral element of the addition on that vector space) then another condition equivalent to (3) can be given: a non-decreasing mapping $g \colon L \to \mathbb{R}$ is k-monotone if for all $r \in \{2, \ldots, k\}$ and for all $a, a_1, \ldots, a_r \in L$ with

$$a = a + \bigvee a_i = a + a_1 + \cdots + a_r \in L$$

we have

$$\sum_{J \subseteq \{1, \ldots, r\}} (-1)^{r-|J|} g \left(a + \sum_{j \in J} a_j \right) \geq 0. \tag{4}$$

(observe that $\bigvee a_i = a_1 + \cdots + a_r$ is equivalent to $a_1, \ldots, a_r$ being pairwise disjoint).

Moreover, in this case the following strong k-monotonicity related to (4) can be introduced: a non-decreasing mapping $g \colon L \to \mathbb{R}$ is called *strongly k-monotone* if for all $r \in \{2, \ldots, k\}$ and for all $a, a_1, \ldots, a_r \in L$ with $a + a_1 + \cdots + a_r \in L$ we have

$$\sum_{J \subseteq \{1, \ldots, r\}} (-1)^{r-|J|} g \left(a + \sum_{j \in J} a_j \right) \geq 0. \tag{5}$$

Observe that if $(L, \vee, \wedge, \mathbf{0}, \mathbf{1}) = (\mathcal{A}, \cup, \cap, \emptyset, X)$ then conditions (2) and (3) coincide (if we put $m = g$). Moreover, taking into account that each set $E \in \mathcal{A}$ is represented by the corresponding characteristic function $\mathbf{1}_E$, then $\iota \colon \mathcal{A} \to \mathbb{R}^X$ defined by $\iota(E) = \mathbf{1}_E$ provides an embedding of $(\mathcal{A}, \cup, \cap, \emptyset, X)$ into the vector lattice $(\mathbb{R}^X, \sup, \inf, \mathbf{0}, \mathbf{1})$, where $\mathbf{0}$ and $\mathbf{1}$ are the constant functions assuming only the value 0 and 1, respectively. Then $\iota(\mathcal{A})$ is a bounded sublattice of $\mathbb{R}^X$ (and even a sublattice of $\{0, 1\}^X$). Putting $g(\mathbf{1}_E) = m(E)$, we see the equivalence of (2), (4) and (5).

This contribution aims at discussing aggregation functions $A \colon [0, 1]^n \to [0, 1]$ which are k-monotone or strongly k-monotone. As more details on aggregation functions can be found in the recent monograph [3], here we only recall that, for a fixed $n \in \mathbb{N}$, a real function $A \colon [0, 1]^n \to [0, 1]$ is called an *aggregation function* if it is non-decreasing and satisfies $A(0, \ldots, 0) = 0$ and $A(1, \ldots, 1) = 1$.

The paper is organized as follows. In Section 2, k-monotone and strongly k-monotone aggregation functions are discussed in general, i.e., for $k = 2, 3, \ldots, \infty$. Under some specific requirements, well-known aggregation functions are recovered. Section 3 is devoted to the particular cases $k = 2$ and $k = \infty$, while in Section 4 some possible applications are indicated. Finally, several open problems are posed.

2   (Strongly) k-Monotone Aggregation Functions

Based on (4) and (5), we introduce the following stronger forms of monotonicity for aggregation functions.

Definition 1. Let $A \colon [0,1]^n \to [0,1]$ be an aggregation function and $k \in \mathbb{N} \backslash \{1\}$.

(i) The aggregation function A is called *k-monotone* if for each $r \in \{2, \ldots, k\}$ and for all $\mathbf{x}, \mathbf{x}_1, \ldots, \mathbf{x}_r \in [0,1]^n$ with $\mathbf{x} + \mathbf{x}_1 + \cdots + \mathbf{x}_r = \mathbf{x} + \bigvee \mathbf{x}_i \in [0,1]^n$ we have

$$\sum_{J \subseteq \{1, \ldots, r\}} (-1)^{r - |J|} A\Big(\mathbf{x} + \bigvee_{j \in J} \mathbf{x}_j\Big) \geq 0. \tag{6}$$

(ii) The aggregation function A is said to be *strongly k-monotone* if for each $r \in \{2, \ldots, k\}$ and for all $\mathbf{x}, \mathbf{x}_1, \ldots, \mathbf{x}_r \in [0,1]^n$ with $\mathbf{x} + \mathbf{x}_1 + \cdots + \mathbf{x}_r \in [0,1]^n$ we have

$$\sum_{J \subseteq \{1, \ldots, r\}} (-1)^{r - |J|} A\Big(\mathbf{x} + \sum_{j \in J} \mathbf{x}_j\Big) \geq 0. \tag{7}$$

(iii) The aggregation function A is called *strongly ∞-monotone (totally monotone)* if it is strongly k-monotone for each $k \in \mathbb{N} \setminus \{1\}$.

Note that if $\mathbf{x} + \mathbf{x}_1 + \cdots + \mathbf{x}_r = \mathbf{x} + \bigvee \mathbf{x}_i \in [0,1]^n$ then formulae (6) and (7) coincide (and then $\mathbf{x}_1, \ldots, \mathbf{x}_r$ have pairwise disjoint supports, i.e., $\min(\mathbf{x}_i, \mathbf{x}_j) = \mathbf{0}$ for all $i \neq j$). Clearly, for an n-ary aggregation function A, its k-monotonicity for $k > n$ is equivalent to the n-monotonicity of A, which is not true for strong monotonicity. For example, for a unary aggregation function $f \colon [0,1] \to [0,1]$, k-monotonicity is just the non-decreasingness of f, while strong 2-monotonicity of f is equivalent to its convexity.

The following results can be found in [1].

Proposition 1. *Let $f \colon [0,1] \to [0,1]$ be an aggregation function. Then we have:*

(i) *f is strongly k-monotone for some $k \in \mathbb{N} \setminus \{1\}$ if and only if all derivatives of f of order $1, \ldots, k - 2$ are nonnegative and $f^{(k-2)}$ is a non-decreasing convex function.*

(ii) *f is strongly ∞-monotone if and only if f is a totally monotone real function, i.e., it has non-negative derivatives of all orders on $[0,1[$.*

Proposition 2. *Let $A: [0,1]^n \to [0,1]$ be an aggregation function. Then A is totally monotone if and only if all partial derivatives of A are nonnegative. In particular, this means that*

$$A(u_1,\dots,u_n) = \sum a_{i_1,\dots,i_n} \cdot u_1^{i_1} \cdots u_n^{i_n},$$

where $i_1,\dots,i_n$ run from 0 to ∞, $a_{0,\dots,0} = 0$, all $a_{i_1,\dots,i_n} \geq 0$, and $\sum a_{i_1,\dots,i_n} = 1$.

As a particular consequence of Proposition 2 we see that, for each $n \in \mathbb{N}$, the product $\Pi: [0,1]^n \to [0,1]$ is a totally monotone aggregation function. Also, each weighted arithmetic mean $W: [0,1]^n \to [0,1]$ given by $W(u_1,\dots,u_n) = \sum w_i \cdot u_i$ is totally monotone.

Proposition 3. *Fix $k \in \{2,3,\dots,\infty\}$. Then for all $n,m \in \mathbb{N}$ and for all strongly k-monotone n-ary aggregation functions $A: [0,1]^n \to [0,1]$ and for all strongly k-monotone m-ary aggregation functions $B_1,\dots,B_n: [0,1]^m \to [0,1]$ also the composite function $D: [0,1]^m \to [0,1]$ given by*

$$D(\mathbf{x}) = A(B_1(\mathbf{x}),\dots,B_n(\mathbf{x}))$$

is strongly k-monotone.

It is possible to show that for each fixed $n \in \mathbb{N}$ and $k \in \{2,3,\dots,\infty\}$, the class of all (strongly) k-monotone n-ary aggregation functions is convex and compact (with respect to the topology of pointwise convergence).

For $n \in \mathbb{N} \setminus \{1\}$ and for n-ary aggregation functions $A: [0,1]^n \to [0,1]$, the notion of n-increasingness was introduced in the framework of copulas [7,9]:

Definition 2. *Let $n \geq 2$. An aggregation function $A: [0,1]^n \to [0,1]$ is called n-increasing if for all $\mathbf{x},\mathbf{y} \in [0,1]^n$ with $\mathbf{x} \leq \mathbf{y}$ we have*

$$\sum_{J \subseteq \{1,\dots,n\}} (-1)^{n-|J|} A(\mathbf{z}_J) \geq 0, \tag{8}$$

where $\mathbf{z}_J \in [0,1]^n$ is given by $z_j = y_j$ if $j \in J$, and $z_j = x_j$ otherwise.

It is not difficult to check that, under the hypotheses of Definition 2, formulae (8) and (6) coincide, i.e., n-monotonicity and n increasingness for n-ary aggregation functions mean the same. Hence, k-monotonicity extends the notion of n-increasingness to higher dimensions.

Remark 1

(i) Because of [1], strong k-monotone aggregation functions are important in the theory of non-additive measures: for k-monotone capacities $m_1,\dots,m_n$ acting on a fixed measurable space $(X,\mathcal{A})$ and for a strongly k-monotone n-ary aggregation function A, the set function $A(m_1,\dots,m_n): \mathcal{A} \to [0,1]$ given by

$$A(m_1,\dots,m_n)(E) = A(m_1(E),\dots,m_n(E))$$

is a k-monotone capacity whenever A is strongly k-monotone (if $|X| \geq k$, this is also necessary condition if the claim should be valid for arbitrary k-monotone capacities $m_1,\dots,m_n$).

(ii) k-monotonicity is an axiom for k-dimensional copulas [9].
(iii) Strong 2-monotonicity is known also as *ultramodularity*, and it was discussed in general in [6] (see also [4]). Another name for 2-monotonicity is *super-modularity*, a widely used concept in the theory of non-additive measures and of aggregation functions.

3   (Strongly) 2-Monotone Aggregation Functions

Recall that an aggregation function $C \colon [0,1]^2 \to [0,1]$ which is 2-monotone and satisfies $C(x,1) = C(1,x) = x$ for all $x \in [0,1]$ is called a 2-*copula* (or, shortly, a *copula*). Copulas play a key role in the description of the stochastic dependence of two-dimensional random vectors and they are substantially exploited in several applications in finance, hydrology, etc. The construction of new types of copulas is one of the important theoretical tasks allowing a better modelling of real problems involving stochastic uncertainty. From [2] we have the following representation result:

Proposition 4. *An aggregation function* $A \colon [0,1]^2 \to [0,1]$ *is 2-monotone if and only if there are non-decreasing functions* $g_1, g_2, g_3, g_4 \colon [0,1] \to [0,1]$ *with* $g_i(0) = 0$ *and* $g_i(1) = 1$ *for each* $i \in \{1,2,3,4\}$*, a binary copula* $C \colon [0,1]^2 \to [0,1]$*, and numbers* $a, b, c \in [0,1]$ *with* $a + b + c = 1$ *such that, for all* $(x,y) \in [0,1]^2$*,*

$$A(x,y) = a \cdot g_1(x) + b \cdot g_2(y) + c \cdot C(g_3(x), g_4(y)). \tag{9}$$

If 0 is an annihilator of the aggregation function $A \colon [0,1]^2 \to [0,1]$, i.e., if $A(x,0) = A(0,x) = 0$ for all $x \in [0,1]$, then (9) reduces to

$$A(x,y) = C(f(x), g(y)), \tag{10}$$

where $f, g \colon [0,1] \to [0,1]$ are non-decreasing functions with $f(0) = g(0) = 0$ and $f(1) = g(1) = 1$. Note that then we have $f(x) = A(x,1)$ and $g(x) = A(1,x)$ for all $x \in [0,1]$. The following result can be derived from [6].

Proposition 5. *An aggregation function* $A \colon [0,1]^2 \to [0,1]$ *is strongly 2-monotone if and only if* A *is 2-monotone and each horizontal and each vertical section of* A *is a convex function.*

In the class of copulas, the greatest strongly 2-monotone copula is the product copula Π, while the smallest strongly 2-monotone copula is the Fréchet-Hoeffding lower bound W given by $W(x,y) = \max(x + y - 1, 0)$. Note that the only totally monotone 2-copula is the product copula Π. The following theorem will be helpful in the construction of copulas.

Theorem 1. *Let* $A \colon [0,1]^n \to [0,1]$ *be an aggregation function and* $k \geq 2$*. Then the following are equivalent:*

(i) A *is strongly 2-monotone.*
(ii) *If* $B_1, \ldots, B_n \colon [0,1]^k \to [0,1]$ *are non-decreasing 2-monotone functions then the composite* $D \colon [0,1]^k \to [0,1]$ *given by* $D(\mathbf{x}) = A(B_1(\mathbf{x}), \ldots, B_n(\mathbf{x}))$ *is a 2-monotone function.*

4   Construction of Copulas

Theorem 2. *Let $A: [0,1]^n \to [0,1]$ be a continuous, strongly 2-monotone aggregation function. Let $C_1, \ldots, C_n: [0,1]^2 \to [0,1]$ be copulas and assume that the functions $f_1, \ldots, f_n, g_1, \ldots, g_n: [0,1] \to [0,1]$ satisfy $f_i(1) = g_i(1) = 1$ for each $i \in \{1, \ldots, n\}$ and $A(f_1(0), \ldots, f_n(0)) = A(g_1(0), \ldots, g_n(0)) = 0$. Define $\xi, \eta: [0,1] \to [0,1]$ by*

$$\xi(x) = \sup\{u \in [0,1] \mid A(f_1(u), \ldots, f_n(u)) \leq x\},$$
$$\eta(x) = \sup\{u \in [0,1] \mid A(g_1(u), \ldots, g_n(u)) \leq x\}.$$

Then the function $C: [0,1]^2 \to [0,1]$ given by

$$C(x,y) = A\big(C_1(f_1 \circ \xi(x), g_1 \circ \eta(y)), \ldots, C_n(f_n \circ \xi(x), g_n \circ \eta(y))\big) \qquad (11)$$

is a copula.

For k-monotone aggregation functions we have the following result.

Theorem 3. *Let $A: [0,1]^n \to [0,1]$ be a totally monotone aggregation function, and let $B_1, \ldots, B_n: [0,1]^m \to [0,1]$ be k-monotone aggregation functions. Then the composite function $D: [0,1]^m \to [0,1]$ given by $D(\mathbf{x}) = A(B_1(\mathbf{x}), \ldots, B_n(\mathbf{x}))$ is a k-monotone aggregation function.*

This result can be applied to the construction of k-dimensional copulas (i.e., k-monotone aggregation functions $C: [0,1]^k \to [0,1]$ satisfying

$$C(x, 1, \ldots, 1) = C(1, x, \ldots, 1) = C(1, \ldots, 1, x) = x$$

for all $x \in [0,1]$) in a way similar to Theorem 2.

Example 1

(i) If we put $n = 2$, $A = W$, $C_1 = C_2 = M$ and define the functions f_1, f_2, g_1, g_2 by $f_1(x) = g_2(x) = \frac{x+2}{3}$ and $f_2(x) = g_1(x) = \frac{2x+1}{3}$, then the construction in (11) yields the copula C given by

$$C(x,y) = \frac{1}{3} \cdot \max(\min(x+1, 2y) + \min(2x, y+1) - 1, 0).$$

(ii) Consider the totally monotone aggregation function $A: [0,1]^n \to [0,1]$ given by $A(\mathbf{x}) = x_1^{p_1} \cdots x_n^{p_n}$, where $p_1, \ldots, p_n \in \mathbb{N} \cup \{0\}$ and $p = \sum p_i > 0$. Then for all k-dimensional copulas $C_1, \ldots, C_n: [0,1]^k \to [0,1]$, the aggregation function $C: [0,1]^k \to [0,1]$ given by $C(\mathbf{x}) = A(C_1(\tau(\mathbf{x})), \ldots, C_n(\tau(\mathbf{x})))$, where $\tau: [0,1]^k \to [0,1]^k$ is given by $\tau(\mathbf{x}) = (x_1^{1/p}, \ldots, x_k^{1/p})$, is a k-dimensional copula. This result can be derived also from [5]. For example, for $n = 2$ and $A(x,y) = x \cdot y^2$ (i.e., $p = 3$) and for the ternary copulas $C_1 = M$ (i.e., $M(x,y,z) = \min(x,y,z)$) and $C_2 = \Pi$ (i.e., $\Pi(x,y,z) = xyz$), the composite function $C: [0,1]^3 \to [0,1]$ given by

$$C(x,y,z) = \min\left(x(yz)^{\frac{2}{3}}, y(xz)^{\frac{2}{3}}, z(xy)^{\frac{2}{3}}\right)$$

is a ternary copula.

5   Concluding Remarks

We have introduced two properties which are stronger than the monotonicity of aggregation functions, with some representation results and with an application for constructing copulas. Our proposal opens several new questions for future research. For example, it is not clear whether there are strongly 3-monotone copulas different from the product Π. Also it is still open whether/how the conditions of Theorem 3 can be relaxed yielding still the same result — is the strong k-monotonicity of A sufficient? We also expect applications in the construction of copulas of higher dimensions, and subsequently, in the modeling of stochastic dependence of random vectors with dimension $n \geq 3$ (note that, so far, there are only few methods in this case known in the literature).

Acknowledgment

The first and the third author were supported by a bilateral project Austria-Slovakia (WTZ, Project SK 04/2009), the second and the third author by the grant APVV-0012-07, and the third author also by the grant VEGA 1/0080/10.

References

1. Bronevich, A.G.: On the closure of families of fuzzy measures under eventwise aggregations. Fuzzy Sets and Systems 153, 45–70 (2005)
2. Durante, F., Saminger-Platz, S., Sarkoci, P.: On representations of 2-increasing binary aggregation functions. Inform. Sci. 178, 4534–4541 (2008)
3. Grabisch, M., Marichal, J.-L., Mesiar, R., Pap, E.: Aggregation Functions. Cambridge University Press, Cambridge (2009)
4. Klement, E.P., Manzi, M., Mesiar, R.: Ultramodular aggregation functions and a new construction method for copulas (submitted for publication)
5. Liebscher, E.: Construction of asymmetric multivariate copulas. J. Multivariate Anal. 99, 2234–2250 (2008)
6. Marinacci, M., Montrucchio, L.: Ultramodular functions. Math. Oper. Res. 30, 311–332 (2005)
7. Nelsen, R.B.: An Introduction to Copulas, 2nd edn. Lecture Notes in Statistics, vol. 139. Springer, New York (2006)
8. Pap, E.: Null-Additive Set Functions. Kluwer Academic Publishers, Dordrecht (1995)
9. Sklar, A.: Fonctions de répartition à n dimensions et leurs marges. Publ. Inst. Statist. Univ. Paris 8, 229–231 (1959)
10. Wang, Z., Klir, G.J.: Generalized Measure Theory. Springer, New York (2009)

Some Remarks on the Characterization of Idempotent Uninorms

Daniel Ruiz-Aguilera[1], Joan Torrens[1], Bernard De Baets[2], and Janos Fodor[3]

[1] University of the Balearic Islands
07122 Palma de Mallorca, Spain
daniel.ruiz@uib.es, dmijts0@uib.es
[2] Ghent University
Gent, Belgium
bernard.debaets@ugent.be
[3] Óbuda University
Budapest, Hungary
fodor@uni-obuda.hu

Abstract. In this paper the characterization of idempotent uninorms given in [21] is revisited and some technical aspects are corrected. Examples clarifying the situation are given and the same characterization is translated in terms of symmetrical functions. The particular cases of left-continuity and right-continuity are studied retrieving the results in [7].

Keywords: Uninorm, idempotent uninorm, symmetrical function, left-continuity.

1 Introduction

Uninorms are a special kind of associative and commutative aggregation operators allowing a neutral element in the unit interval. They were introduced in 1996 in [30] and their structure was characterized in 1997 in [14]. Since then, many works on this kind of operators have appeared and many authors have devoted their efforts to this topic. Uninorms are specially interesting from the theoretical point of view because of their structure as a special combination of a t-norm and a t-conorm, but their major significance is due to the great quantity of fields where they have proved to be useful for applications. Some of these application fields are: aggregation in general (see [30], [5]), expert systems ([8]), neural networks ([1]), fuzzy system modelling ([27], [28], [29]), pseudo-analysis and measure theory ([2], [18], [23]), fuzzy DI-subsethood measures and image processing ([3] and [4]) and data mining ([31]).

Taking into account that uninorms are divided into conjunctive and disjunctive ones, they have also used as logical connectives modeling AND and OR operators, implication functions derived from uninorms have been introduced (see [9] and [25]) and so they become interesting and useful also in fuzzy logic (see for instance [15]), approximate reasoning ([26]), mathematical morphology and image processing ([11], [16], [17]) and so on.

E. Hüllermeier, R. Kruse, and F. Hoffmann (Eds.): IPMU 2010, LNAI 6178, pp. 425–434, 2010.
© Springer-Verlag Berlin Heidelberg 2010

Among different classes of uninorms, the class of idempotent uninorms is specially interesting because of its simplicity, any idempotent uninorm is a special combination of minimum and maximum. Thus they have been studied in several papers (see [7], [21], [9], [24], [25]). Moreover, operators defined on finite chains are a topic of increasing interest ([22]) and idempotent uninorms in this context have been also characterized in [10].

Those idempotent uninorms that are left-continuous or right-continuous were characterized in [7] and the whole characterization was given in [21]. From then many papers dealing with idempotent uninorms have appeared using such a characterization.

This paper wants to go deeply into the characterization theorem of idempotent uninorms, to debug some mistakes in its original statement and to present an equivalent characterization in terms of identity-symmetrical functions. Some examples clarifying the situation are given and the particular cases of left-continuity and right-continuity are studied in detail retrieving the results in [7].

2   Idempotent Uninorms

Definition 1. ([14]) *A* uninorm *is a two-place function* $U : [0,1] \times [0,1] \to [0,1]$ *which is associative, commutative, increasing in each place and such that there exists some element* $e \in [0,1]$, *called* neutral element, *such that* $U(e,x) = x$ *for all* $x \in [0,1]$.

It is clear that the function U becomes a t-norm when $e = 1$ and a t-conorm when $e = 0$. For any uninorm we have $U(0,1) \in \{0,1\}$ and a uninorm U is said conjunctive when $U(1,0) = 0$ and disjunctive when $U(1,0) = 1$.

Definition 2. *A binary operator* $U : [0,1] \times [0,1] \to [0,1]$ *is said to be* idempotent *whenever* $U(x,x) = x$ *for all* $x \in [0,1]$.

In [6], the general form of idempotent, associative and increasing binary operators with a neutral element was given. Particular cases of operators with these properties are of course, idempotent uninorms. A detailed characterization for the cases of left-continuous and right-continuous idempotent uninorms is given in the following theorems.

Theorem 1. ([7]) *A binary operator* U *is a left-continuous idempotent uninorm with neutral element* $e \in [0,1]$ *if and only if there exists a decreasing function* $g : [0,1] \to [0,1]$ *with fixed point* e, *satisfying* $g(g(x)) \geq x$ *for all* $x \leq g(0)$ *and* $g(x) = 0$ *for all* $x > g(0)$ *such that, for all* $x,y \in [0,1]$, U *is given by*

$$U(x,y) = \begin{cases} \min(x,y) & \text{if } y \leq g(x) \text{ and } x \leq g(0) \\ \max(x,y) & \text{elsewhere.} \end{cases}$$

Theorem 2. ([7]) *A binary operator* U *is a right-continuous idempotent uninorm with neutral element* $e \in [0,1]$ *if and only if there exists a decreasing function* $g : [0,1] \to [0,1]$ *with fixed point* e *satisfying:* $g(g(x)) \leq x$ *for all* $x \geq g(1)$ *and* $g(x) = 1$ *for all* $x < g(1)$ *such that, for all* $x,y \in [0,1]$, U *is given by*

$$U(x, y) = \begin{cases} \max(x,y) & \text{if } y \geq g(x) \text{ and } x \geq g(1) \\ \min(x,y) & \text{elsewhere.} \end{cases}$$

A complete characterization of idempotent uninorms can be found in [21], as follows.

Theorem 3. ([21]) *Let U be a binary operator on $[0,1]$. U is an idempotent uninorm with neutral element $e \in [0,1]$ if and only if there exists a decreasing function $g : [0,1] \to [0,1]$ with fixed point e, satisfying*

$$\begin{aligned} g(x) &= 0 \quad \text{for all } x > g(0), \\ g(x) &= 1 \quad \text{for all } x < g(1) \end{aligned} \tag{1}$$

and

$$\inf\{y \mid g(y) = g(x)\} \leq g(g(x)) \leq \sup\{y \mid g(y) = g(x)\} \tag{2}$$

for all $x \in [0,1]$, such that

$$U(x,y) = \begin{cases} \min(x,y) & \text{if } y < g(x) \text{ or } y = g(x) \text{ and } x < g(g(x)) \\ \max(x,y) & \text{if } y > g(x) \text{ or } y = g(x) \text{ and } x > g(g(x)) \\ x \text{ or } y & \text{if } y = g(x) \text{ and } x = g(g(x)) \end{cases} \tag{3}$$

in such a way that U is commutative on the set of points (x, y) such that $y = g(x)$ with $x = g(g((x))$. Such function g is usually called the associated function of U.

This is the theorem that we want to study in depth. We will see that conditions required on the function g are in fact not sufficient in order to be U always a uninorm. Note that in [12] (see also [13]) some necessary properties on the function g associated to an idempotent uninorm U are derived from the associativity and commutativity of U. The mistake in the proof of Theorem 3 in [21] lies precisely in the commutativity property which cannot be derived from conditions (1) and (2) as we will see below[1]. Let us begin by recalling what can be actually derived from these two conditions.

Let $g : [0,1] \to [0,1]$ be a decreasing function with $g(e) = e$. Note that condition (2) implies that:

i) If g is strictly decreasing and continuous on an interval $]a, b[\subseteq [0,1]$ and $g(]a, b[) =]c, d[$, then g must be strictly decreasing and continuous also in the interval $]c, d[$ and $g^2(x) = x$ for all $x \in]a, b[\cup]c, d[$. That is, g must be involutive in these points deriving in a commutative behavior of U in the vertical and horizontal regions determined by these subintervals.

ii) If g is constant in an interval $]a, b[$ then $a \leq g(g(x)) \leq b$ for all $x \in]a, b[$.

---

[1] Note that from conditions (1) and (2) neither, associativity nor commutativity can be derived, but when we assume commutativity, then associativity follows (see [21], Proposition 2).

Example 1

i) Function g can be, for instance, a strictly decreasing function. In such case, we obtain $g^2(x) = x$ for all $x \in [0,1]$ and then g is in fact a strong negation. This is the situation for instance of the idempotent uninorm given by

$$U(x,y) = \begin{cases} \max(x,y) & \text{if } y \geq 1 - x \\ \min(x,y) & \text{otherwise.} \end{cases}$$

Note that there are infinitely many different idempotent uninorms U with associated function such a strong negation g, because for each $x \in [0,1]$ the values $U(x, g(x))$ can be the minimum or the maximum independently, just being careful to maintain commutativity in these points.

ii) Other possibility lies in g being stepwise constant. For instance, the following functions g given respectively by:

$$g(x) = \begin{cases} 1 & \text{if } 0 \leq x < e \\ e & \text{if } e \leq x \leq 1 \end{cases}$$

and

$$g(x) = \begin{cases} e & \text{if } 0 \leq x \leq e \\ 0 & \text{if } e < x \leq 1, \end{cases}$$

give respectively the only idempotent uninorm in $\mathcal{U}_{\min}$ and in $\mathcal{U}_{\max}$ with neutral element e.

iii) Note that depending on function g, there can be different idempotent uninorms with the same associated function g and neutral element e (even infinitely many), as in Example (i), or there can be one and only one idempotent uninorm as in Example (ii).

However, some peculiar situations can occur violating commutativity (and associativity) as the following examples show.

Example 2. Consider an element $e \in]0, 1[$ and let $g : [0,1] \rightarrow [0,1]$ be the decreasing function given by:

$$g(x) = \begin{cases} 1 & \text{if } x < e \\ e & \text{if } x = e \\ 0 & \text{if } x > e. \end{cases}$$

For such a function g, let us consider an idempotent aggregation function U given by equation (3). Then function g satisfies conditions (1) and (2), but clearly U is neither commutative nor associative (just take $x, y, z \in [0,1]$ such that $0 < z < x < e < y$).

Example 3. Let $g : [0,1] \rightarrow [0,1]$ be the decreasing function given by:

$$g(x) = \begin{cases} 0.9 & \text{if } x = 0 \\ 0.75 & \text{if } 0 < x < 0.25 \\ 1 - x & \text{if } 0.25 \leq x \leq 0.75 \\ 0.1 & \text{if } 0.75 < x < 0.9 \\ 0 & \text{if } x \geq 0.9. \end{cases}$$

For such a function g, let us consider any idempotent aggregation function U given by equation (3). Then function g satisfies conditions (1) and (2), but again U is neither commutative nor associative. Note for instance that in this case we have for all $x < 0.25 < 0.75 < y < 0.9$,

$$U(x,y) = \max(x,y) \neq \min(x,y) = U(y,x).$$

The functions g used in the Examples 2 and 3, together with the corresponding idempotent aggregation functions U given by (3), can be viewed in Figures 1 and 2 respectively.

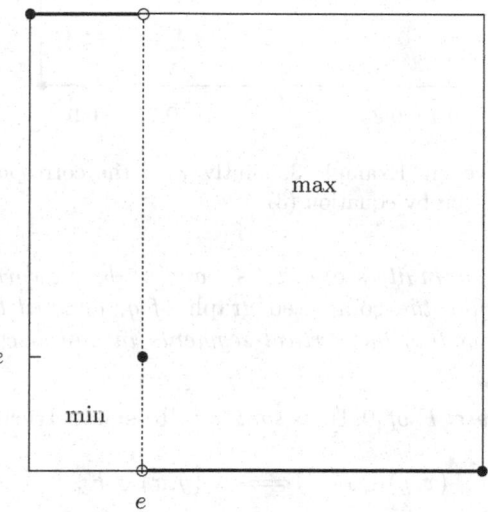

Fig. 1. Function g given in Example 2, jointly with the corresponding idempotent aggregation function given by equation (3)

Thus, from an idempotent uninorm with neutral element $e \in]0,1[$ we obtain a decreasing function g with fixed point e satisfying conditions (1) and (2), but for the converse more conditions on g will be necessary. In fact, in [12] and [13] functions g from idempotent uninorms were studied in detail and it was proved that they must satisfy some additional property related with their possible discontinuity points (see condition (C) below).

On the other hand, idempotent uninorms defined on finite chains were recently characterized very similarly through decreasing functions, but using the terminology of Id-symmetrical functions. Let us recall some definitions about this topic, that can be found in [20].

Definition 3. *Let* $g : [0,1] \to [0,1]$ *be any decreasing function and let G be the graph of g, that is*

$$G = \{(x, g(x)) \mid x \in [0,1]\}.$$

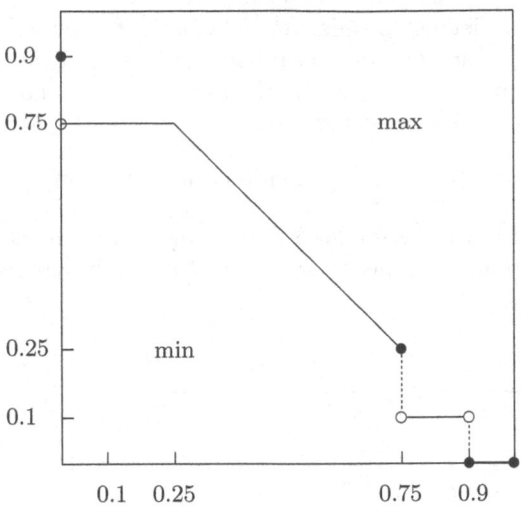

Fig. 2. Function g given in Example 3, jointly with the corresponding idempotent aggregation function given by equation (3)

For any point of discontinuity s of g, let s^- and s^+ be the corresponding lateral limits. Then, we define the completed graph *of g, denoted by F_g, as the set obtained from G by adding the vertical segments in any discontinuity point s, from s^- to s^+.*

Definition 4. *A subset F of $[0,1]^2$ is said to be* Id-symmetrical *if for all $(x,y) \in [0,1]^2$ it holds that*

$$(x,y) \in F \quad \Longleftrightarrow \quad (y,x) \in F.$$

The above definition expresses that a subset F of $[0,1]^2$ is symmetrical w.r.t. the diagonal of the unit square. A similar notion of symmetry is introduced for decreasing functions (see [20]) as follows.

Definition 5. *A decreasing function $g : [0,1] \to [0,1]$ is called* Id-symmetrical *if its completed graph F_g is Id-symmetrical.*

With this notations and to sum up, let us prove a more detailed and correct version of Theorem 3. First, let us introduce the following condition on a decreasing function g:

Condition (C) g is constant, say $g(x) = s$ in the interval $]p,q[$ with $p < q$, where

$$p = \inf\{x \in [0,1] \mid g(x) = s\}$$

and

$$q = \sup\{x \in [0,1] \mid g(x) = s\},$$

if and only if, $s \in]0,1[$ is a point of discontinuity of g or $s = 0,1$ and it is satisfied that

$$p = \begin{cases} s^+ & \text{if } s < 1 \\ 0 & \text{if } s = 1 \end{cases} \quad \text{and} \quad q = \begin{cases} s^- & \text{if } s > 0 \\ 1 & \text{if } s = 0 \end{cases}$$

Theorem 4. *Consider* $e \in]0, 1[$. *The following items are equivalent:*

i) *U is an idempotent uninorm with neutral element e.*

ii) *There exists a decreasing function* $g : [0, 1] \rightarrow [0, 1]$ *with fixed point e, satisfying conditions (2) and (C), such that U is given by equation (3), being commutative on the set of points* $(x, g(x))$ *such that* $x = g^2(x)$.

iii) *There exists a decreasing, Id-symmetrical function* $g : [0, 1] \rightarrow [0, 1]$ *with fixed point e such that U is given by equation (3), being commutative on the set of points* $(x, g(x))$ *such that* $x = g^2(x)$.

Proof. i) $\Rightarrow$ *ii)*. If U is an idempotent uninorm with neutral element e it is proved in [21] that such a decreasing function g with fixed point e exists satisfying condition (2). Moreover, it is proved in [12] that g must also satisfy condition (C) (see Lemma 5 in this reference and note that in the case $s = 0, 1$ it is not necessary to have a discontinuity in such points).

ii) $\Rightarrow$ *iii)*. In this case we only need to prove that a decreasing function g satisfying conditions (2) and (C) must be Id-symmetrical. In order to prove that F_g is Id-symmetrical we distinguish some cases:

- If $(x, y) \in G$ and x is a point where g is strictly decreasing. Then $y = g(x)$ and $g^2(x) = x$. That is, $x = g(y)$ and $(y, x) \in G \subseteq F_g$.
- If $(x, y) \in G$ and g is constant on the interval $]p, q[$ with $p < x < q$, then y is a point of discontinuity with $p = y^-$ and $q = y^+$ and so (y, x) is in the vertical segment from y^- to y^+. That is $(y, x) \in F_g$.
- If $(x, y) \in F_g \setminus G$, then x is a point of discontinuity and we can deduce similarly as above that $(y, x) \in G \subseteq F_g$.

iii) $\Rightarrow$ *i)*. If U is given by equation (3), it is clear that U is increasing in each variable and has neutral element e. The fact that g is Id-symmetrical implies that such U must be commutative and then U must be also associative (see Proposition 2 in [21]). $\qquad\qquad\square$

Remark 1. Note that in particular condition (C) implies that $g(x) = 0$ for all $x < \lim_{x \to 0^+} g(x)$, and similarly $g(x) = 1$ for all $x < \lim_{x \to 1^-} g(x)$. Morcover, this happens whether $0, 1$ are points of discontinuity or whether they are not. (Compare with the initial condition (1) and see also Example 3).

Let us point out that this characterization includes those given in Theorems 1 and 2 for left-continuous and right-continuous idempotent uninorms (see [7]). In fact, we have the following results from Theorem 4:

i) If the idempotent uninorm U is left-continuous (right-continuous) then its associated function g must be also left-continuous (right-continuous).

ii) If the idempotent uninorm U is left-continuous (right-continuous) then its associated function g must satisfy $g(g(x)) \geq x$ for all $x \leq g(0)$ and $g(x) = 0$ for all $x > g(0)$ ($g(g(x)) \leq x$ for all $x \geq g(1)$ and $g(x) = 1$ for all $x < g(1)$).

iii) If the idempotent uninorm U is left-continuous (right-continuous) it must be given by the minimum (maximum) in all points (x, y) such that $y = g(x)$ and $x \leq g(0)$ ($x \geq g(1)$).

432   D. Ruiz-Aguilera et al.

Now, it is clear from the three points before that Theorems 1 and 2 follow easily from the general case.

Note that from condition (i), if we take a function g with no lateral continuity then, among all idempotent uninorms with associated function g, there will be neither any left nor right-continuous one.

Example 4. Let $g : [0, 1] \rightarrow [0, 1]$ be the decreasing function given by:

$$g(x) = \begin{cases} 1 & \text{if } x \leq 0.25 \\ 1.25 - x & \text{if } 0.25 < x < 0.5 \\ 0.75 & \text{if } 0.5 \leq x < 0.6 \\ 0.6 & \text{if } 0.6 \leq x \leq 0.75 \\ 1.25 - x & \text{if } x > 0.75. \end{cases}$$

For such a function g, that is nor left neither right-continuous, there not exists any left-continuous nor right-continuous uninorm U such that U has g as associated function. Function g can be observed in Figure 3.

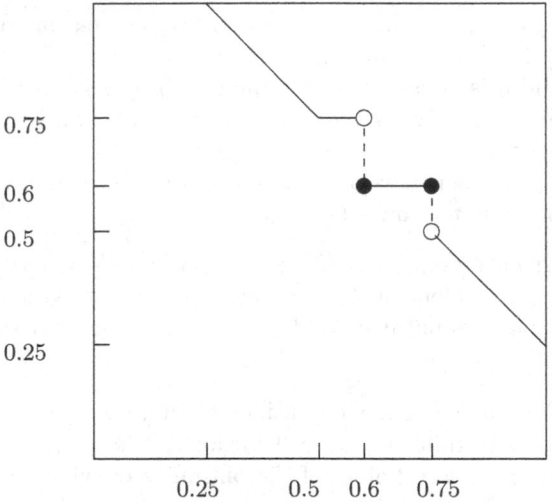

Fig. 3. Function g given in Example 4

3   Conclusion

One part of Theorem 3 published originally in [21] states that binary operations U on $[0, 1]$ defined by (3) using a decreasing function $g : [0, 1] \rightarrow [0, 1]$ with fixed point $e \in [0, 1]$ that satisfies conditions (1) and (2) are uninorms with neutral element e. However, Examples 2 and 3 reveal that such a U is neither commutative nor associative in general. This anomaly can occur if g is not continuous, and it is due to the permissive nature of conditions (1) and (2) at discontinuity points of g. Fortunately, we can guarantee commutativity and associativity of U by adding a new condition (C) to control the behaviour of g at its possible discontinuity points. This is formulated and proved in Theorem 4, providing alternative characterizations of idempotent uninorms.

Acknowledgments. The first two authors have been partially supported by the Spanish grant MTM2009-10320 (with FEDER support).

References

1. Benítez, J.M., Castro, J.L., Requena, I.: Are artificial neural networks black boxes? IEEE Transactions on Neural Networks 8, 1156–1163 (1997)
2. Benvenuti, P., Mesiar, R.: Pseudo-arithmetical operations as a basis for the general measure and integration theory. Information Sciences 160, 1–11 (2004)
3. Bustince, H., Mohedano, V., Barrenechea, E., Pagola, M.: Definition and construction of fuzzy DI-subsethood measures. Information Sciences 176, 3190–3231 (2006)
4. Bustince, H., Pagola, M., Barrenechea, E.: Construction of fuzzy indices from fuzzy DI-subsethood measures: application to the global comparison of images. Information Sciences 177, 906–929 (2007)
5. Calvo, T., Mayor, G., Mesiar, R. (eds.): Aggregation operators. New trends and applications, Studies in Fuzziness and Soft Computing, vol. 97. Physica-Verlag, Heidelberg (2002)
6. Czogala, E., Drewniak, J.: Associative monotonic operations in fuzzy set theory. Fuzzy Sets and Systems 12, 249–269 (1984)
7. De Baets, B.: Idempotent uninorms. European J. Oper. Res. 118, 631–642 (1999)
8. De Baets, B., Fodor, J.: Van Melle's combining function in MYCIN is a representable uninorm: an alternative proof. Fuzzy Sets and Systems 104, 133–136 (1999)
9. De Baets, B., Fodor, J.C.: Residual operators of uninorms. Soft Computing 3, 89–100 (1999)
10. De Baets, B., Fodor, J., Ruiz-Aguilera, D., Torrens, J.: Idempotent uninorms on finite ordinal scales. Int. J. of Uncertainty, Fuzziness and Knowledge-based Systems 17, 1–14 (2009)
11. De Baets, B., Kwasnikowska, N., Kerre, E.: Fuzzy morphology based on uninorms. In: Seventh IFSA World Congress, Prague, pp. 215–220 (1997)
12. Drygaś, P.: Discussion of the structure of uninorms. Kybernetika 41, 213–226 (2005)
13. Drygaś, P.: Remarks about idempotent uninorms. Journal of Electrical Engineering 57, 92–94 (2006)
14. Fodor, J.C., Yager, R.R., Rybalov, A.: Structure of Uninorms. Int. J. Uncertainty, Fuzziness, Knowledge-based Systems 5, 411–427 (1997)
15. Gabbay, D., Metcalfe, G.: Fuzzy logics based on $[0, 1)$-continuous uninorms. Arch. Math. Logic 46, 425–449 (2007)
16. González, M., Mir, A.: Noise Reduction Using Alternate Filters Generated by Fuzzy Mathematical Operators Using Uninorms (ΦMM-U Morphology). In: Proceedings of EUROFUSE 2009, Pamplona, pp. 233–238 (2009)
17. González, M., Mir, A., Ruiz-Aguilera, D., Torrens, J.: Edge-Images using a Uninorm-Based Fuzzy Mathematical Morphology. Opening and Closing. In: Tavares, J., Jorge, N. (eds.) Advances in Computational Vision and Medical Image Processing, pp. 137–157. Springer, Netherlands (2009)

18. Klement, E.P., Mesiar, R., Pap, E.: Integration with respect to decomposable measures, based on a conditionally distributive semiring on the unit interval. Int. J. Uncertainty, Fuzziness, Knowledge-Based Systems 8, 701–717 (2000)
19. Klement, E.P., Mesiar, R., Pap, E.: Triangular norms. Kluwer Academic Publishers, London (2000)
20. Maes, K.C., De Baets, B.: Orthosymmetrical monotone functions. Bulletin of the Belgian Mathematical Society - Simon Stevin 14, 99–116 (2007)
21. Martín, J., Mayor, G., Torrens, J.: On locally internal monotonic operations. Fuzzy Sets and Systems 137, 27–42 (2003)
22. Mayor, G., Torrens, J.: Triangular norms in discrete settings. In: Klement, E.P., Mesiar, R. (eds.) Logical, Algebraic, Analytic, and Probabilistic Aspects of Triangular Norms, pp. 189–230. Elsevier, Amsterdam (2005)
23. Pap, E.: Pseudo-additive measures and their applications. In: Pap, E. (ed.) A Handbook of Measure Theory, pp. 1403–1468. Elsevier, Amsterdam (2002)
24. Ruiz-Aguilera, D., Torrens, J.: Distributive idempotent uninorms. Int. J. Uncertainty, Fuzziness, Knowledge-based Systems 11, 413–428 (2003)
25. Ruiz-Aguilera, D., Torrens, J.: Residual implications and co-implications from idempotent uninorms. Kybernetika 40, 21–38 (2004)
26. Takács, M.: Approximate reasoning in fuzzy systems based on pseudo-analysis and uninorm residuum. Acta Polytechnica Ungarica 1, 49–62 (2004)
27. Yager, R.R.: Uninorms in fuzzy systems modeling. Fuzzy Sets and Systems 122, 167–175 (2001)
28. Yager, R.R., Kreinovich, V.: On the relation between two approaches to combining evidence: Ordered abelian groups and uninorms. J. Intell. Fuzzy Syst. 14, 7–12 (2003)
29. Yager, R.R., Kreinovich, V.: Universal approximation theorem for uninorm-based fuzzy systems modelling. Fuzzy Sets and Systems 140, 331–339 (2003)
30. Yager, R.R., Rybalov, A.: Uninorm aggregation operators. Fuzzy Sets and Systems 80, 111–120 (1996)
31. Yan, P., Chen, G.: Discovering a cover set of ARsi with hierarchy from quantitative databases. Information Sciences 173, 319–336 (2005)

On the Median and Its Extensions

Gleb Beliakov[1], Humberto Bustince[2], and Javier Fernandez[2]

[1] School of Information Technology, Deakin University, Australia
gleb@deakin.edu.au
[2] Departamento de Automática y Computación, Universidad Pública de Navarra,
Pamplona, Spain
bustince@unavarra.es, fcojavier.fernandez@unavarra.es

Abstract. We review various representations of the median and related aggregation functions. An advantage of the median is that it discards extreme values of the inputs, and hence exhibits a better central tendency than the arithmetic mean. However the value of the median depends on only one or two central inputs. Our aim is to design median-like aggregation functions whose value depends on several central inputs. Such functions will preserve the stability of the median against extreme values, but will take more inputs into account. A method based on graduation curves is presented.

Keywords: Median, aggregation functions, means, OWA.

1 Introduction

The median is one of the best known aggregation functions. Along with the arithmetic mean, it plays an important role in statistics, regression analysis, pattern recognition, decision sciences and image processing. Various classes of aggregation functions have been considered in detail in the recent monographs [5, 10, 17].

In statistics, the median of a sample is a number dividing the higher half of a sample, from the lower half. The median of a finite list of numbers can be found by arranging all the numbers in increasing or decreasing order and picking the middle one. If the number of inputs is even, one takes the mean of the two middle values.

The median is a type of average which is more representative of a "typical" value than the mean. It essentially discards very high and very low values (outliers). For example, the median price of houses is often reported in the real estate market, because the mean can be influenced by just one or a few very expensive houses, and will not represent the cost of a "typical" house in the area.

An attractive property of the medians is that they are applicable to inputs on the ordinal scale, i.e., when only the ordering, rather than the numerical values matter. For example, one can use medians for aggregation of inputs like labels of fuzzy sets, such as *very high, high, medium, low* and *very low*.

In this paper we look at various representations of the median and its extensions. We review the existing representations of the median and its relation to

E. Hüllermeier, R. Kruse, and F. Hoffmann (Eds.): IPMU 2010, LNAI 6178, pp. 435–444, 2010.

other aggregation functions. Then we define a new class of median-like aggregation functions by using the process of data approximation, similar to Gini's graduation curves [9]. Our goal is to account for more than one or two inputs, as is the case with the mean, while at the same time discard extreme values.

The paper is organized as follows. We provide definitions and background material in Section 2. We discuss various extensions in Section 3 and conclude in Section 4.

2   Representations of the Median

2.1   First Definitions

Let $X = [a, b] \subseteq \bar{\Re} = [-\infty, \infty]$ be a nonempty closed interval. Unless specified otherwise, we will deal with aggregation functions defined on X^n.

Definition 1. *A function $f : [a, b]^n \to [a, b]$ is called an aggregation function if it is monotone non-decreasing in each variable and satisfies $f(\mathbf{a}) = a$, $f(\mathbf{b}) = b$, with $\mathbf{a} = (a, a, \dots, a), \mathbf{b} = (b, b, \dots, b)$.*

Definition 2. *An aggregation function f is called averaging if it is bounded by the minimum and maximum of its arguments*

$$\min(\mathbf{x}) := \min(x_1, \dots, x_n) \leq f(x_1, \dots, x_n) \leq \max(x_1, \dots, x_n) =: \max(\mathbf{x}).$$

It is immediate that averaging aggregation functions are idempotent (i.e., $\forall t \in X : f(t, t, \dots, t) = t$) and (because of monotonicity) vice versa. Then clearly the boundary conditions $f(\mathbf{a}) = a$, $f(\mathbf{b}) = b$ are satisfied. Often averaging aggregation functions collectively are referred to as means.

Our focus is on the median.

Definition 3. *The median is the function*

$$Med(\mathbf{x}) = \begin{cases} \frac{1}{2}(x_{(k)} + x_{(k+1)}), & \text{if } n = 2k \text{ is even} \\ x_{(k)}, & \text{if } n = 2k - 1 \text{ is odd,} \end{cases}$$

where $x_{(k)}$ is the k-th largest (or smallest) component of $\mathbf{x}$.

Of course, Definition 3 is meaningful only if the arithmetic mean is properly defined, which is not the case if $\mathbf{x} \in D^n$, and D is a discrete chain. In this case one can use the concepts of the lower and upper median, which guarantee that the output of this operation coincides with one of the inputs.

Definition 4. *The lower (upper) median is the function*

$$Med_l(\mathbf{x}) = x_{(k)}$$

where $x_{(k)}$ is the k-th smallest component of $\mathbf{x}$, and $k = \lfloor \frac{n}{2} \rfloor$, the nearest integer smaller or equal to $\frac{n}{2}$, for the lower median, and $k = \lceil \frac{n}{2} \rceil$ for the upper median.

A related notion is the a-median.

Definition 5. *Given a value* $a \in [0,1]$, *the a-median is the function*

$$Med_a(\mathbf{x}) = Med(x_1, \ldots, x_n, \overbrace{a, \ldots, a}^{n-1 \; times}).$$

The concept of the weighted median was treated in detail in [18].

Definition 6. *Let* $\mathbf{w}$ *be a weighting vector with* $w_i \geq 0$, $\sum w_i = 1$, *and let* $\mathbf{u}$ *denote the vector obtained from* $\mathbf{w}$ *by arranging its components in the order induced by the components of the input vector* $\mathbf{x}$, *such that* $u_k = w_i$ *if* $x_i = x_{(k)}$ *is the k-th largest component of* $\mathbf{x}$. *The lower weighted median is the function*

$$Med_{\mathbf{w},l}(\mathbf{x}) = x_{(k)}, \tag{1}$$

where k is the index obtained from the condition

$$\sum_{j=1}^{k-1} u_j < \frac{1}{2} \; and \; \sum_{j=1}^{k} u_j \geq \frac{1}{2}. \tag{2}$$

The upper weighted median is the function $Med_{\mathbf{w},u}$ *defined as in(1) where k is the index obtained from the condition*

$$\sum_{j=1}^{k-1} u_j \leq \frac{1}{2} \; and \; \sum_{j=1}^{k} u_j > \frac{1}{2}.$$

The mean of $Med_{\mathbf{w},l}$ *and* $Med_{\mathbf{w},u}$ *gives the weighted median* $Med_{\mathbf{w}}$.

It is clear that the usual median, the upper and the lower medians are averaging homogeneous symmetric aggregation functions.

The following result allows us to define the concept of quasi-median. To shorten the notation we will use $\mathbf{h}(\mathbf{x}) = (h(x_1), \ldots, h(x_n))$ for any $h : X \to \bar{\Re}$.

Proposition 1. *[6] Let f be an averaging aggregation function on* X^n, *and h be a continuous strictly monotone function* $Y \to X$, *called scaling (or generating) function, and* $X, Y \subseteq \bar{\Re}$. *Then* $f_h(\mathbf{x}) = h^{-1}(f(\mathbf{h}(\mathbf{x}))$ *is also an averaging aggregation function on* Y^n.

By applying scaling functions to the median we obtain

Definition 7. *Let* $Med_{\mathbf{w}}$ *be a weighted median and h be a generating function. The function* $f(\mathbf{x}) = h^{-1}(Med_{\mathbf{w}}(\mathbf{h}(\mathbf{x})))$ *is called a weighted quasi-median with respect to h.*

If h is a power function or a logarithm, the resulting quasi-median is also homogeneous.

2.2   Median as an OWA Function

OWA functions and their generalizations are also well known examples of averaging functions.

Definition 8. *For a given weighting vector* **w**, *the OWA function is given by*

$$OWA_{\mathbf{w}}(x_1, \ldots, x_n) = \sum_{i=1}^{n} w_i x_{(i)},$$

where $x_{(i)}$ *denotes the i-th largest value of* **x**.

The median can be conveniently expressed as an OWA function with a special weighting vector. For an odd n let $w_{\frac{n+1}{2}} = 1$ and all other $w_i = 0$, and for an even n let $w_{\frac{n}{2}} = w_{\frac{n}{2}+1} = \frac{1}{2}$, and all other $w_i = 0$. Then $Med(\mathbf{x}) = OWA_{\mathbf{w}}(\mathbf{x})$.

Based on the weighted median, Yager [18] also defined an ordinal OWA function, using the following construction.

Definition 9. *The ordinal OWA function is*

$$OOWA_{\mathbf{w}}(\mathbf{x}) = Med_{\mathbf{w}}(\mathbf{x}_{\searrow}),$$

where $\mathbf{x}_{\searrow}$ *denotes the vector obtained from* **x** *by arranging its components in non-increasing order.*

Since the components of the argument of the weighted median in Definition 9 are already ordered, calculation of the ordinal OWA is reduced to the formula

$$OOWA_{\mathbf{w}}(\mathbf{x}) = x_{(k)},$$

where k is the index obtained from the condition

$$\sum_{j=1}^{k-1} w_j < \frac{1}{2} \text{ and } \sum_{j=1}^{k} w_j \geq \frac{1}{2}.$$

Note that the ordinal OWA is a symmetric aggregation function, whereas the weighted median is not. A more general class of aggregation functions on an ordinal scale is that of weighted ordinal means, presented in [12].

2.3   Median as a Fuzzy Integral

Since OWA functions are a special case of discrete Choquet integral, it will be worth to look at other fuzzy integrals, and in particular the Sugeno integral, to establish its relation to the median. Fuzzy integrals are defined with respect to a fuzzy measure.

Definition 10. *Let* $\mathcal{N} = \{1, 2, \ldots, n\}$. *A discrete fuzzy measure is a set function* $v : 2^{\mathcal{N}} \to [0, 1]$ *which is monotonic (i.e.* $v(S) \leq v(T)$ *whenever* $S \subseteq T$) *and satisfies* $v(\emptyset) = 0, v(\mathcal{N}) = 1$.

Choquet integral

Definition 11. *The discrete Choquet integral with respect to a fuzzy measure v is given by*

$$C_v(\boldsymbol{x}) = \sum_{i=1}^{n} x_{(i)}[v(H_i) - v(H_{i+1})], \tag{3}$$

where $\boldsymbol{x}_\nearrow = (x_{(1)}, x_{(2)}, \ldots, x_{(n)})$ is a non-decreasing permutation of the input $\boldsymbol{x}$, $x_{(n+1)} = \infty$ by convention, and $H_i = \{(i), \ldots, (n)\}$.

The class of Choquet integrals includes weighted arithmetic means and OWA functions as special cases. As such, it includes the median as a special case.

Sugeno integral

Definition 12. *The Sugeno integral with respect to a fuzzy measure v is given by*

$$S_v(\boldsymbol{x}) = \max_{i=1,\ldots,n} \min\{x_{(i)}, v(H_i)\}, \tag{4}$$

where $\boldsymbol{x}_\nearrow = (x_{(1)}, x_{(2)}, \ldots, x_{(n)})$ is a non-decreasing permutation of the input $\boldsymbol{x}$, and $H_i = \{(i), \ldots, (n)\}$.

Sugeno integrals can be expressed, for arbitrary fuzzy measures, by means of the Median function in the following way:

$$S_v(\boldsymbol{x}) = Med(x_1, \ldots, x_n, v(H_2), v(H_3), \ldots, v(H_n)).$$

In the special case of a symmetric fuzzy measure (i.e., when $v(H_i) = v(|H_i|)$ depends only on the cardinality of the set H_i), Sugeno integral becomes the median $S_v(\boldsymbol{x}) = Med(x_1, \ldots, x_n, 1, v(n-1), v(n-2), \ldots, v(1))$.

The Sugeno integral with respect to a symmetric fuzzy measure given by $v(\mathcal{A}) = v(|\mathcal{A}|)$ is the Median $Med(x_1, \ldots, x_n, v(n-1), v(n-2), \ldots, v(1))$.

Ordered weighted maximum $OWMAX_{\boldsymbol{w}}(\boldsymbol{x}) = \max_{i=1,\ldots,n} \min\{w_i, x_{(i)}\}$ with a non-increasing weighting vector $1 = w_1 \geq w_2 \geq \ldots \geq w_n$ can can be expressed by means of the Median function as $OWMAX_{\boldsymbol{w}}(\boldsymbol{x}) = Med(x_1, \ldots, x_n, w_2, \ldots, w_n)$.

Ordered weighted minimum $OWMIN_{\boldsymbol{w}}(\boldsymbol{x}) = \min_{i=1,\ldots,n} \max\{w_i, x_{(i)}\}$ with a non-increasing weighting vector $w_1 \geq w_2 \geq \ldots \geq w_n = 0$ can can be expressed by means of the Median function as $OWMIN_{\boldsymbol{w}}(\boldsymbol{x}) = Med(x_1, \ldots, x_n, w_1, \ldots, w_{n-1})$.

2.4 Median as a Nullnorm

a-medians can be considered as the limiting cases of idempotent nullnorms. They have absorbing element a and are continuous, symmetric and associative (and, hence, bisymmetric). They can be expressed as

$$Med_a(\boldsymbol{x}) = \begin{cases} \max(\boldsymbol{x}), & \text{if } \boldsymbol{x} \in [0,a]^n, \\ \min(\boldsymbol{x}), & \text{if } \boldsymbol{x} \in [a,1]^n, \\ a & \text{otherwise.} \end{cases}$$

2.5   Median as a Penalty Based Aggregation Function

We can look at the average of n inputs as a representative value for these inputs. A measure of deviation from this value has been studied in various works [17, 20, 8, 11, 2, 9, 7]. It was already known to Laplace (quoted from [17], p.15), see also [9], that the weighted arithmetic and geometric means, the median and the mode are functions that minimize some simple penalty functions. In particular, the weighted arithmetic mean is a solution to the following problem

$$M_{\mathbf{w}}(\mathbf{x}) = \arg\min_{y} \sum_{i=1}^{n} w_i(x_i - y)^2,$$

whereas the median is a solution to

$$Med_{\mathbf{w}}(\mathbf{x}) = \arg\min_{y} \sum_{i=1}^{n} w_i|x_i - y|.$$

Note that the latter equation has multiple solutions for even $n = 2k$, which are values $y^* \in [x_{(k)}, x_{(k+1)}]$. The median takes the midpoint of this interval, whereas the lower and upper medians take the extreme points.

In [7,20,8,13,14] the authors have studied penalty-based aggregation functions from several perspectives. Any averaging aggregation function can be expressed as a penalty-based aggregation function [7]. The authors of [8] studied a special class of penalty functions called "faithful" penalty functions.

Definition 13. *The function $p : X^2 \to \Re_+$ is called faithful penalty function, if it satisfies*
1) $p(t, s) = 0$ if and only if $t = s$, and
2) it can be represented as $p(t, s) = K(h(t), h(s))$, where $h : X \to \Re$ is some continuous monotone function (scaling function) and $K : \Re^2 \to \Re_+$ is convex.

Definition 14. *Let the penalty function P be given by*

$$P(\mathbf{x}, y) = \sum_{i=1}^{n} w_i p(x_i, y),$$

where p is a faithful penalty function. The function

$$f(\mathbf{x}) = \arg\min_{y} P(\mathbf{x}, y)$$

is a faithful penalty based function.

Faithful penalty based function f in Definition 14 is not always monotone, but in a special case of p given by $p(t, s) = K(h(t) - h(s))$ it is, as shown in [13], and therefore it is an aggregation function.

If $p(t, s) = |t - s|$, then the corresponding faithful penalty based aggregation function is a weighted median. Now, let us consider faithful penalty-based functions with $p(t, s) = |t - s|^r, r \geq 1$. Consider the limiting case $r \to 1$. Interestingly, it does not correspond to the median when $n = 2k$ (see [11]), but to a solution of the following equation, called Jackson's equation

$$(y - x_{(1)})(y - x_{(2)}) \ldots (y - x_{(k)}) = (y - x_{(k+1)}) \ldots (y - x_{(n)}).$$

For example, for $n = 4$ we have

$$f(\mathbf{x}) = \frac{x_{(1)}x_{(2)} - x_{(3)}x_{(4)}}{(x_{(1)} + x_{(2)}) - (x_{(3)} + x_{(4)})},$$

whereas the standard definition of median gives $f(\mathbf{x}) = \frac{x_{(2)} + x_{(3)}}{2}$. Weighted medians were considered from this perspective in [2].

What is also remarkable about the Jackson's equation is that the actual value of the median (for even n) is not determined by just two extremes of the interval $[x_{(k)}, x_{(k+1)}]$, but all the components of $\mathbf{x}$. We will return to this issue in the next section.

3 Extensions

One arguably weak point in using the median is that it discards all but one (or two) inputs. On one hand, one wants to preserve its central tendency and insensitivity to the extreme values of the inputs (often considered to be outliers), but on the other hand one wishes to take into account contributions of several central inputs. Jackson's equation provides one solution when n is even. In the following we explore two other constructions which address these issues.

3.1 Centered OWA

We have seen that one can express the median as an OWA function with a special weighting vector $\mathbf{w} = (0, \ldots, 0, 1, 0, \ldots, 0)$ for odd n and $\mathbf{w} = (0, \ldots, 0, \frac{1}{2}, \frac{1}{2}, 0, \ldots, 0)$ for even n. The concept of centered OWA operators was proposed by Yager in [19] and later also investigated in [21]. Here the weights are symmetric ($w_j = w_{n+1-j}$), strongly decaying ($w_i < w_j$ if either $i < j \leq (n+1)/2$ or $i > j \geq (n+1)/2$), and inclusive ($w_j > 0$), although we will relax the latter condition.

We can now take weighting vectors with several non-zero values, for example $\mathbf{w} = (0, \ldots, 0, \frac{1}{6}, \frac{1}{3}, \frac{1}{3}, \frac{1}{6}, 0, \ldots, 0)$, and take into account as many central inputs.

3.2 Means Defined by Using Graduation Curves

The following construction based on graduation curves was inspired by [9]. Consider unweighted means first. Order the inputs in non-decreasing order and take the points $(0, x_{(1)}), (\frac{1}{n-1}, x_{(2)}), \ldots, (\frac{n-2}{n-1}, x_{(n-1)}), (1, x_{(n)})$. We can draw these points in the coordinate plane and obtain a picture presented on Fig. 1.

Now let us interpolate (or approximate) the resulting points with a monotone non-decreasing function g, whose graph is called the graduation curve. To underline its dependence on the data, we will use the notation $g(t; x_1, \ldots, x_n)$ where necessary. The value $M(x_1, \ldots, x_n) = g(\frac{1}{2}; x_1, \ldots, x_n)$ is a mean of the components of $\mathbf{x}$. We can formulate the following general results.

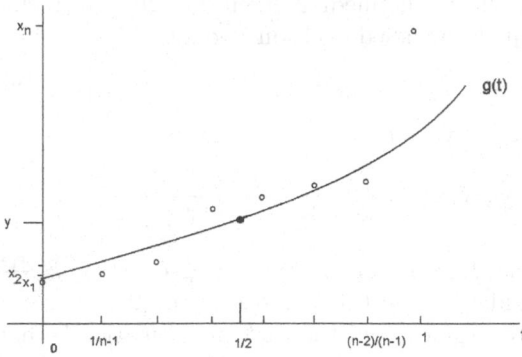

Fig. 1. An example of graduation curve. $g(t)$ approximates the data $(\frac{i-1}{n-1}, x_i)$. The average is the value $y = g(\frac{1}{2})$.

Proposition 2. *If g preserves the range of the data, i.e., $\min(x_1, \ldots, x_n) \le g(t; x_1, \ldots, x_n) \le \max(x_1, \ldots, x_n)$ for all $0 \le t \le 1$, then M is an averaging function.*

Proof. Clearly $x_{(1)} \le g(\frac{1}{2}) = M(\mathbf{x}) \le x_{(n)}$ $\qquad\qquad\qquad\qquad$ $\square$

Corollary 1. *If g interpolates the data and is monotone in t, then M is an averaging function.*

Proposition 3. *If g is monotone non-decreasing in $x_1, \ldots, x_n$, then M is also monotone, and hence an aggregation function.*

Proposition 4. *If g is scale invariant, i.e., when all the data x_i are multiplied by a scalar, the values of g are also multiplied by the same scalar, $\lambda g(t; \mathbf{x}) = g(t; \lambda \mathbf{x})$, then M is homogeneous. If g is shift invariant, i.e. , $g(t; \mathbf{x}) + \lambda = g(t; \mathbf{x} + \lambda)$, then M is shift invariant.*

Not all methods of interpolation or approximation deliver these properties of g. However several known methods do, and below we consider several examples.

Example 1. Let g be a piecewise linear interpolant to the data, also called broken line or linear spline. g is monotone in $\mathbf{x}$, scale invariant and shift invariant. The resulting value of $g(\frac{1}{2}) = Med(\mathbf{x})$.

Example 2. Let g be a constant function fitted to the data in the least squares sense. In this case $g(t) = M(\mathbf{x})$ for all $t \in [0, 1]$, the arithmetic mean.

Example 3. Let g be a linear function fitted to the data, $g(t) = at + b$. From the theory of linear regression we know that if $\hat{t} = \frac{1}{n} \sum t_i$ then $g(\hat{t}) = a\hat{x} + b = \frac{1}{n} \sum x_i$. So we again obtain the arithmetic mean $y = g(\frac{1}{2}) = M(\mathbf{x})$. Note that linear regression function g is monotone in $\mathbf{x}$, scale invariant and shift invariant.

If we use polynomial interpolation, the resulting polynomial g is not always non-decreasing in t, nor in $\mathbf{x}$, hence this method is not suitable. Below we present three advanced monotone approximation techniques which yield suitable graduation curves.

Let us now take monotone interpolating, smoothing or regression splines as g. Splines are piecewise continuous functions joined at the knots $t_i, i = 1, \ldots, n$. In our case $t_i = \frac{i-1}{n-1}$. There are several possibilities here.

Example 4. g is monotone interpolating spline in tension [16, 15] given by

$$g(t) = \frac{h_i^2}{u_i \sinh(u_i)} [c_i \sinh(u_i z) + c_{i+1} \sinh(u_i(1 - z))]$$
$$+(x_i - h_i^2 c_i/u_i^2)z + (x_{i+1} - h_i^2 c_{i+1}/u_i^2)(1 - z),$$

where $t_i \leq t \leq t_{i+1}$, $z = (t_{i+1} - t)/h_i$, $t_i = ph_i$, $h_i = t_{i+1} - t_i$, $p \geq 0$ is tension parameter, and c_i are spline coefficients found by solving a linear system of equations with a tridiagonal matrix. We note that for odd n we obtain $g(1/2) = Med(\mathbf{x})$, because this spline is interpolating and $g(t_i) = x_i$ for all $i = 1, \ldots, n$.

Example 5. g is monotone smoothing spline presented in [1]. The coefficients of the spline are found by solving a convex optimization problem. Here the value $M(\mathbf{x}) = g(1/2)$ is different from the median for both even and odd n.

Example 6. g is monotone regression spline presented in [3, 4]. The coefficients of the spline are found by solving a quadratic optimization problem.

In the three examples above, the value of the spline depends on several data, located just around the central value (the number of such data depends on the order of the spline). Because B-splines have local support, the extreme values are excluded. In these examples g is scale and shift invariant and so is M.

Now we look at weighted averages. In the proposed scheme based on graduation curves, this is achieved by changing the abscissae of the data: given a weighting vector $\mathbf{w}$, we position the data in the following way. Partition the interval $[0, 1]$ into n subintervals, the length of each is u_i, i.e. $t_{i+1} - t_i = u_i, i = 1, \ldots, n$ with $t_1 = 0$ and $t_{n+1} = 1$, and the components of vector $\mathbf{u}$ are a permutation of components of $\mathbf{w}$ induced by $\mathbf{x}$, i.e., $u_k = w_i$ if $x_i = x_{(k)}$, as in Definition 6. The data to be fitted is (ϵ_i, x_i) where the points $\epsilon_i \in [t_i, t_{i+1}]$ are chosen as either the centers or extremes of the respective interval. When ϵ_i is in the center we obtain the usual median-like function, otherwise we obtain the analogues of the lower and upper weighted medians respectively. This coincides with the definition of the lower and upper median when g is a piecewise linear function interpolating the data as in Example 3. All the examples we presented except Example 2 remain valid for weighted averages.

4   Conclusion

We have summarized various representation of the median function, and looked at some of its extensions. Our aim was to design median-like aggregation functions which depend on a few central values of the vector of arguments. The method based on graduation curves provides one such construction, in which extreme values can be discarded.

References

1. Andersson, L.-E., Elfving, T.: Interpolation and approximation by monotone cubic splines. J. Approx. Theory 66, 302–333 (1991)
2. Barral Souto, J.: El modo y otras medias, casos particulares de una misma expresion matematica. Boletin Matematico 11, 29–41 (1938)
3. Beliakov, G.: Shape preserving approximation using least squares splines. Approximation Theory and Applications 16, 80–98 (2000)
4. Beliakov, G.: Monotone approximation of aggregation operators using least squares splines. Int. J. of Uncertainty, Fuzziness and Knowledge-Based Systems 10, 659–676 (2002)
5. Beliakov, G., Pradera, A., Calvo, T.: Aggregation Functions: A Guide for Practitioners. Springer, Heidelberg (2007)
6. Borwein, J.M., Borwein, P.B.: PI and the AGM: A Study in Analytic Number Theory and Computational Complexity. Wiley, New York (1987)
7. Calvo, T., Beliakov, G.: Aggregation functions based on penalties. Fuzzy Sets and Systems 161, 1420–1436 (2010) doi:10.1016/j.fss.2009.05.012
8. Calvo, T., Mesiar, R., Yager, R.: Quantitative weights and aggregation. IEEE Trans. on Fuzzy Systems 12, 62–69 (2004)
9. Gini, C.: Le Medie. Unione Tipografico-Editorial Torinese, Milan (1958); Russian translation, Srednie Velichiny, Statistica, Moscow (1970)
10. Grabisch, M., Marichal, J.-L., Mesiar, R., Pap, E.: Aggregation Functions. Cambridge University press, Cambridge (2009)
11. Jackson, D.: Note on the median of a set of numbers. Bulletin of the Americam Math. Soc. 27, 160–164 (1921)
12. Kolesárová, A., Mesiar, R., Mayor, G.: Weighted ordinal means. Inform. Sci. 177, 3822–3830 (2007)
13. Mesiar, R.: Fuzzy set approach to the utility, preference relations, and aggregation operators. Europ. J. Oper. Res. 176, 414–422 (2007)
14. Mesiar, R., Špirková, J., Vavríková, L.: Weighted aggregation operators based on minimization. Inform. Sci. 178, 1133–1140 (2008)
15. Sapidis, N.S., Kaklis, P.D.: An algorithm for constructing convexity and monotonicity preserving splines in tension. Comp. Aided Geom. Design 5, 127–137 (1988)
16. Schweikert, D.G.: An interpolation curve using a spline in tension. J. Math. Phys. 45, 312–317 (1966)
17. Torra, Y., Narukawa, V.: Modeling Decisions. Information Fusion and Aggregation Operators. Springer, Berlin (2007)
18. Yager, R.: Fusion of ordinal information using weighted median aggregation. Int. J. Approx. Reasoning 18, 35–52 (1998)
19. Yager, R.: Centered owa operators. Soft Computing 11, 631–639 (2007)
20. Yager, R., Rybalov, A.: Understanding the median as a fusion operator. Int. J. General Syst. 26, 239–263 (1997)
21. Zarghami, M., Szidarovszky, F., Ardakanian, R.: Sensitivity analysis of the OWA operator. IEEE Trans. on Syst. Man and Cybernetics Part B 38(2), 547–552 (2008)

Evidential Combination of Multiple HMM Classifiers for Multi-script Handwritting Recognition

Yousri Kessentini[1], Thomas Burger[2], and Thierry Paquet[1]

[1] Université de Rouen, Laboratoire LITIS EA 4108, site du Madrillet,
St Etienne du Rouvray, France
{yousri.kessentini,thierry.paquet}@univ-rouen.fr
http://yousri.kessentini.perso.neuf.fr
[2] Université Européenne de Bretagne, Université de Bretagne-Sud, CNRS,
Lab-STICC, F-56017 Vannes cedex, France
thomas.burger@univ-ubs.fr
http://www-labsticc.univ-ubs.fr/ burger/

Abstract. In this work, we focus on an improvement of a multi-script handwritting recognition system using a HMM based classifiers combination. The improvement relies on the use of Dempster-Shafer theory to combine in a finer way the probabilistic outputs of the HMM classifiers. The experiments are conducted on two public databases written on two different scripts : IFN/ENIT (latin script) and RIMES (arabic script). The obtained results are compared with the classical algorithms of the field and the superiority of the proposed approach is shown.

1 Introduction

Classifier combination is a widely used technique in handwritting recognition to improve the classification rates, or to preserve them when dealing whith more difficult vocabularies or scripts. This is why, several reviews propose an exhaustive description of the state-of-the-art in this field [1,2,3]. Most of them stress the real interest of Dempster-Shafer Theory (DST) [4,5] to combine classifiers in a manner accurate and robust to difficult conditions (set of weak classifiers, degenerated training phase, too specific training sets, large vocabulary, etc.). Nonetheless, to our knowledge, no work precisely follows these conclusions in the field of multiple script handwritting recognition. On the contrary, such DST-based classifiers have largely been used in other fields.

Let us mention a few of them: in [6], the authors present a DST-based combination classifier built on a neural network architecture for speech recognition. In [7,8], different classifiers (resp. SVMs and HMMs) are combined for automatic recognition of gestural languages (resp. Cued Speech and Sign Languages). In [9], the authors merge several modalities for audio-visual speech recognition. The authors of [10] present a model to fuse the decisions of several optical scanners to improve the reading of addresses in postal mails. Finally, in [11] a generic theoretical framework for DST-based ensemble classifier is provided.

E. Hüllermeier, R. Kruse, and F. Hoffmann (Eds.): IPMU 2010, LNAI 6178, pp. 445–454, 2010.
© Springer-Verlag Berlin Heidelberg 2010

We propose the following explanation for the lack of DST-based combination classifiers which deal with handwritting recognition: in the very popular [2], a general method is provided to combine a set of classifiers of type I. Type I is the most general type of classifiers, as the ouput is simply a membership function indicating the class, whithout any additional information, such as an ordered list of the "best" classes (Type II), or a distance to each class (Type III). Now, most of the efficient classification techniques are of Type III, as they provide a posterior probability of belonging to any of the classes (For example Support Vector Machines, HMM classifiers, AdaBoost, Bayesian belief network, neural networks, etc. see [12] for a complete review). The advantages of outputs of Type III are known, but are lost when the method described in [2] is used.

Thus, the first contribution of this paper is to adapt the method described in [2] and to derive a complete handwritten recognition strategy. Then, the second goal is to evaluate the performances of this strategy. Section 2 is a background review on the basis of Dempster-Shafer Theory, and on handwritting recognition. In section 3, we present how to adapt the algorithm of [2] to classifiers with probabilistic outputs, and how to derive a complete recognition algorithm. This algorithm is evaluated and discussed in section 4.

2   Background

First, we rapidly cover the basis of the Dempster-Shafer Theory. Readers interested in a more complete understanding should refer to [4,5]. Then, the most classical procedure to recognize handwritting is summarized, as well as the principle of the DST-based combination classifier of [2].

2.1   Dempster-Shafer Theory

In general, the various pieces of information that must be combined to make a decision (or to perform a classification) may be of rather heterogeneous quality, so that, in case of difficult problems, each evidence may be (1) imprecise (it is not focused enough on which decision to make), (2) uncertain (when modeling random events), (3) incomplete (when representing a partial point of view on the problem), (4) conflictive (the evidences do not concur). Bayesian decision theory does not provide tools to model all these imperfections of data. Nonetheless, it is efficient, as its purpose is to convert imprecision, incompleteness, partiality and conflict into subjective uncertainty. In this set-up, the uncertainty can be used to model not only randomization (in a frequentist interpretation), but also the subjectivity of an agent. On the contrary, the purpose of DST is to provide richer models, so that decision making is more robust to the quality of the data.

The probability of any event B for the realization of a random variable X is noted $\mathbb{P}(X \in B)$. In case of discrete models, B can be a singleton (usually noted x), and if we write $p(x) = \mathbb{P}(X = x), \forall x$, it defines the probability distribution p followed by X. A random set (usually noted S) is more general than a random variable, as its outcomes are not necessarily singleton events, but sets (of random size). Then, to define the distribution m followed by $\mathcal{S}$ (in a discrete setting), we have to consider $m(A) = \mathbb{P}(\mathcal{S} = A)$, $\forall A$. The central idea of the DST is to use the theory of random sets to model problems so that a distinction is made between uncertainty and imprecision at the very definition of the evidence. Intuitively, the random aspect of $\mathcal{S}$ models the uncertainty (as with random variables), whereas the cardinality of the outcome of $\mathcal{S}$ models the imprecision.

Formaly, let $\Omega = \{\omega_1, ..., \omega_K\}$ be a finite set called the **frame** or the **state-space** which is made of exclusive and exhaustive hypotheses. A **mass function** m is defined on the power set of Ω, noted $\mathcal{P}(\Omega)$ and it maps onto $[0, 1]$ so that $\sum_{A \subseteq \Omega} m(A) = 1$ and $m(\emptyset) = 0$.

A subset $F \subseteq \Omega$ such that $m(F) > 0$ is called a **focal set** of m. If the c focal sets of m are nested ($F_1 \subseteq F_2 \subseteq ... \subseteq F_c$), m is said to be **consonant**.

Two mass functions m_1 and m_2, based on the evidences of two independant and reliable sources can be combined into a new mass function $m_\cap$ by the use of the **conjunctive combination**, noted $\bigcirc\!\!\!\!\cap$. It is defined $\forall A \subseteq \Omega$ as:

$$m_\cap(A) = [m_1 \bigcirc\!\!\!\!\cap m_2](A) = \frac{1}{1 - \mathcal{K}_{12}} \sum_{B \cap C = A} m_1(B) \cdot m_2(C) \qquad (1)$$

where $\mathcal{K}_{12} = \sum_{B \cap C = \emptyset} m_1(B) \cdot m_2(C)$ measures the conflict between m_1 and m_2.

When all the evidences have been combined, the problem is summarized by a single mass function which represents all the knowledge of the agent who makes the decision. This mass function is defined on $\mathcal{P}(\Omega)$. Hence, the description of the problem is richer than with a probabilistic expression, as expected.

Most of the time, the final decision is made in the context of the theory of games of chance, as a statistically winning bet is expected. In this setting, the imprecision of the evidence is equivalent to some uncertainty, as stated by the insufficient reason principle [13]. Thus, there is no more interest in working on a mass function rather than on a probability (of course, postponing to the very last step the use of a rougher probabilistic description has prevented early loss of information). There are numerous ways to convert a mass function onto a probability. Here, we use the **pignistic transform** [5]. Intuitively, it is based on the idea that the imprecision encoded in the final mass function should be shared equally, as there is no reason to promote a choice rather than another one. If $|A|$ is the cardinality of the subset $A \subseteq \Omega$, the **pignistic probability** $BetP$ is defined on Ω as:

$$BetP(\omega_i) = \sum_{A \ni \omega_i} \frac{m(A)}{|A|} \qquad \forall \omega_i \in \Omega \qquad (2)$$

2.2 Handwritting Recognition and DST-Based Combination Classifier

One of the most popular technique for automatic handwritting recognition is to use generative classifiers based on Hidden Marov Models (or HMM) [14]. For each word ω_i of a lexicon $\Omega_{lex} = \{\omega_1, ..., \omega_V\}$ of V words, a HMM λ_i is defined, so that λ_i best fits a training set made of several different instances of the word ω_i. Practically, this training phase is conducted by using the Viterbi EM or the Baum-Welch algorithm.

Then, when a new word $\omega*$ is considered, the likelihoods $\mathbb{P}(\omega * | \lambda_i)$, $\forall i \leq V$ are approximated by the likelihoods provided by the Viterbi decoding algorithm (noted $L(\omega_i)$, $\forall i$), and the $\omega*$ is recognized as the word ω_j for which $L(\omega_j) \geq L(\omega_i), \forall i \leq V$. Generally, in the evaluation step, not only the "best" class is given, but an ordered list of the TOP N best classes. Then, for each value of $n \leq N$, a recognition rate is computed as the percentage of words for which the ground truth class is proposed in the first n elements of the TOP N list.

This complete set-up is called a HMM classifier. In order to improve the recognition accuracy, it is possible to define several HMM classifiers, each working on different features (then, the likelihood of the q-th classifier for ω_i is noted $L_q(\omega_i)$). Hence, in [15], it is shown that it is more efficient to define several HMM classifiers and to fuse their results: somes working on directional contours density (upper and lower contours), and somes working on foreground (black) pixel densities. Notice that in order to build the feature vector sequence, the word image is divided into vertical overlapping windows. The sliding window is shifted along the word image from right to left (in case of arabic words) or left to right (in case of latin words) and a feature vector is computed for each frame (see figure 1 and [15]). There are several ways to combine these classifiers in a probabilistic setup. A simple and efficient technique is to multiply their output [16]. As, for computational constraint, the likelihoods are rescaled and converted to log-likelihoods, the outputs of the HMM classifiers are summed to achieve the best results (see Section 4).

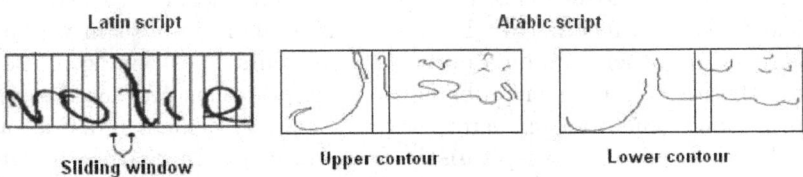

Fig. 1. Features extraction illustration

HMMs are Type III classifiers, whereas the DST-based combination classifier of [2] is based on classifiers of Type I. For the latter, the following procedure is proposed: let us consider Q classifiers. Each classifier q provides the following information: (1) its output is the index of a class, noted $output(q)$. Obviously, $\omega_{output(q)} \in \Omega_{lex} = \{\omega_1, ..., \omega_V\}$. (2) its global accuracy is the rate $r_q \leq 1$ of words it correctly recognizes on its own. The idea is simply to define Q mass functions $m_1, ..., m_Q$ on Ω_{lex}, so that $\forall q \leq Q$:

$$m_q(\{\omega_{output(q)}\}) = r_q, \qquad m_q(\{\Omega_{lex} \setminus \omega_{output(q)}\}) = 1 - r_q$$

and $m_q(.) = 0$ otherwise. Here, $m_q(\omega_{output(q)})$ represents the confidence in the fact that $\omega_{output(q)}$ is the true class, and $m_q(\Omega_{lex} \setminus \omega_{output(q)})$ represents the confidence that the q-th classifier provides a wrong estimation of the class. Then, the Q mass functions are combined, $m_\cap = \bigcirc_{q=1}^{Q} m_q$ and a decision is made by any adapted decision process, such as the pignistic transform. This method is interesting as it allows modeling the reliability of each classifier.

3 The Proposed Strategy

We aim at using Q HMM classifiers on Q different features to perform hand-writting recognition, while improving the naive probabilistic combination of the classifiers (the product of their outputs) by using a DST-based combination classifier. To do so, we have to (1) convert the probabilistic output of each of our Q classifiers into a mass function, (2) modify the mass function associated to each classifier so that it takes into account its reliability, (3) compute the conjunctive combination of the Q mass functions, and (4) make a decision by using the pignistic transform. Nonetheless, at each step, there are several difficulties to overcome, which are described in this section.

3.1 Converting Log-Likelihoods into Mass Functions

The conversion of the probabilistic outputs into mass functions rises two difficulties. First of all, in case of HMM classifiers, the "real" probabilities are not available as output: the probability propagation algorithm underlying HMM implies a very wide range of numerical values that leads to overflows. This is why, instead of a classical likelihood, a log-likelihood is used. Moreover, it is regularly re-scaled during the computation, so that, at the end, $\mathbb{R}$-values are given rather than $[0, 1]$-values.

The second problem is that, a mass function provides a richer description than a probability function. Thus, the conversion from a probability into a mass function requires additional information.

Finally, we have to convert a $\mathbb{R}$-valued set of V scores (the $L_q(\omega_i)$) onto a mass function which is a richer description, as it is defined with 2^V distinct values. Amongst the various methods that have been tested to achieve this conversion [16], we have choosen the following procedure:

1. Convert the set of $L_q(\omega_i)$ onto a new subjective probability distribution p_q. Note that $p_q(\omega_i)$ is supposed to be a fair evaluation of $\mathbb{P}(\omega * |\lambda_i, q)$, in spite of that $\sum_i \mathbb{P}(\omega * |\lambda_i, q) \neq 1$, whereas $\sum_i p_q(\omega_i) = 1$.
2. Convert this subjective probability into a mass function by adding the constraints that (1) the mass function is consonant, (2) the pignistic transform of the mass function corresponds to the subjective probability p_q. Under these two assumptions, it is proven that the mass function is uniquely defined [7].

The choice of this procedure rather than the two others described in [16] is sensible, as it provides the best balance between the accuracy, the robustness to the variation of the parameters, and the computation cost. Moreover, the link with the inverse of the pignistic function ensure that the conversion process is coherent with the decision making process. Finally, it is really interesting to obtain a consonant mass function as output of each classifier: as a matter of fact, the classifiers are assumed independant sources of information conditionnaly to the dataset. Thus, each source, as a whole, is suppose to provide a view on the problem which does not contradict itself. Consonant mass functions are coherent in the meaning that a self conjunctive combination does not provide any conflict. Hence, a model in which the sources provide consonant mass functions is fair. Finally, a consonant output intuitively corresponds to an ordered list (like the TOP N list).

Pratically, the conversion from the $\mathbb{R}$-valued scores $L_q(\omega_i)$, $i \leq V$ to subjective probabilities $p_q(\omega_i)$ is achieved by applying the following sigmoid function that maps $\mathbb{R}$ onto $[0, 1]$:

$$p_q(\omega_i) = \frac{1}{1 + e^{-\lambda(L_q(\omega_i) - \tilde{L}_q)}} \quad \text{with} \quad \lambda = \frac{1}{\max_i |L_q(\omega_i) - \tilde{L}_q|} \tag{3}$$

where $\tilde{L}_q$ is the median of the $L_q(\omega_i)$, $\forall q$. Then, the set of $p_q(\omega_i)$, $i \leq V$ is re-scaled so that it sums up to 1, and the index i is chosen so that, it corresponds to the order $p_q(\omega_1) \geq p_q(\omega_2) \geq \ldots \geq p_q(\omega_V)$. We define m_q as:

$$m_q(\{\omega_1, \omega_2, \ldots, \omega_V\}) = m_q(\Omega) = V \times p_q(\omega_V)$$
$$m_q(\{\omega_1, \omega_2, \ldots, \omega_i\}) = i \times [p_q(\omega_i) - p_q(\omega_{i+1})] \quad \forall\, i < V$$
$$m_q(.) = 0 \quad \text{otherwise}$$

3.2 Dealing with the Computation Cost Involoved by the Powerset

When dealing with a lexicon set of V words, the mass functions involved are defined on 2^V values, which implies a exponential growth of the computation needs. In order to remain efficient on large vocabularies, we propose to control the size of the frame: Instead of working on $\Omega_{lex} = \{\omega_1, \ldots, \omega_V\}$, we use another frame Ω, which is dynamically defined. For each classification task, the TOP N outputs of all the Q classifiers are considered for increasing values of N, until a particular value $N = M$ is reached, and until at minimum m words are in common to all the outputs of the classifiers: if the Q classifiers globally concur, their respective TOP M lists are similar and an important proportion of the M words are likely to be found in common. On the contrary, if the Q classifiers mostly disagree, among the TOP M lists, very few words are in common (less than m), and it is necessary to consider the TOP N for values of $N > M$ in order to find m common words. Consequently, it garantees a frame of size $\geq m$ and $\leq M$. We call that a m/M-sized frame. This method allows controling the size of the frame, as it is independant of V the size of the vocabulary.

3.3 Taking into Account the Reliability of the Classifiers

In [2], each of the Q mass functions is categorical, i.e., the entire mass is associated to the class given by the classifier. Then, the reliability of the classifiers is taken into account: r_q corresponds to the TOP 1 accuracy, and this value is used to decrease the mass associated to the class given by the classifier, and to rise the mass associated to the complement of this class in Ω. This approch can be generalized to situations in which the mass functions are not necessarily categorical, but consonant. Let us call r_q^N the recognition rate of classifier q at TOP N, $N \leq M$, and let us suppose that all the r_q^N, $\forall N, q$ are known. We apply the following modification to the q-th mass function:

$$m_q \left(\{\omega_1\} \right) \leftarrow m_q \left(\{\omega_1\} \right) * r_q^{rank(q,\omega_1)}$$

$$m_q \left(\Omega \setminus \{\omega_1\} \right) \leftarrow m_q \left(\{\omega_1\} \right) * \left(1 - r_q^{rank(q,\omega_1)} \right)$$

$$m_q \left(\{\omega_1,\omega_2\} \right) \leftarrow m_q \left(\{\omega_1,\omega_2\} \right) * r_q^{rank(q,\omega_2)}$$

$$m_q \left(\Omega \setminus \{\omega_1,\omega_2\} \right) \leftarrow m_q \left(\{\omega_1,\omega_2\} \right) * \left(1 - r_q^{rank(q,\omega_2)} \right)$$

$$\vdots$$

$$m_q \left(\{\omega_1,\omega_2,\ldots,\omega_{\mathfrak{M}-1}\} \right) \leftarrow m_q \left(\{\omega_1,\omega_2,\ldots,\omega_{\mathfrak{M}-1}\} \right) * r_q^{rank(q,\omega_{\mathfrak{M}-1})}$$

$$m_q \left(\{\omega_{\mathfrak{M}}\} \right) \leftarrow m_q \left(\{\omega_1,\omega_2,\ldots,\omega_{\mathfrak{M}-1}\} \right) * \left(1 - r_q^{rank(q,\omega_{\mathfrak{M}-1})} \right)$$

where $\mathfrak{M}$ represents the number of element in Ω (thus, $m \leq \mathfrak{M} \leq M$), and where $rank(q,\omega_i)$ is a function which gives the rank of ω_i in the ordered list provided by classifier q (it plays a role similar to the one of the function $output(q)$, in case of a Type I classifier). It is important to notice that if the element of Ω are orderd, ω_i is at the i-th position in the ordered list of the common words. On the contrary, $rank(q,\omega_i)$ gives the position in the list without omiting the words which are not present in the Q lists. Hence, $rank(q,\omega_i) \geq i$. This redistribution of the mass is only possible thanks to the consonancy of the m_q.

4 Evaluations

In this section, we evaluate the performances of the algorithm described above and we compare it to an equivalent technique in a probabilistic setting. Experiments have been conducted on two publicly available databases: IFN/ENIT benchmark database of arabic words and RIMES database for latin words. The IFN/ENIT [17] contains a total of 32,492 handwritten words (arabic symbols) of 946 Tunisian town/villages names written by 411 different writers. Four different sets (a, b, c, d) are predefined in the database for training and one set (e) for testing. The RIMES database [18] is composed of isolated handwritten word snippets extracted form handwritten letters (latin symbols). In our experiments, 36000 snippets of words are used to train the different HMM classifiers and 3000 words are used in the test.

Three classifiers are defined, each working on different feature sets: upper contour, lower contour and density. As it appears latter, the lower contour is really not informative: When using only two of the three classifiers, the performances are better. Nonetheless, we keep it in order to investigate the behaviour of our method in case of the presence of a very weak classifier. The values of m and M are respectively set to 5 and 20. These values are only choosen with respect to computation time constraints. The TOP N performances of each classifier (expressed as a rate of the number of recognized words divised by the total number of words) is computed on a dedicated part of the database for any necessary value of N: These rates are used to modify the masses according to the reliability of the classifiers (section 3.3).

There is no more parameter to set in the algorithm of the DST-based combination classifier. Once the pignistic probability is computed, the results can be interpreted in a probabilistic setting. Thus, we present the result in the classical form of the handwritting recognition community, by using TOP 1 and TOP 2 performance rates. These TOP 1 and TOP 2 performances are compared to the results obtained in a probabilistic setting. As explained in section 2, the most classical way to combine the output of the classifiers in a probabilititistic setting is to multiply the corresponding likelihoods. In [16], we have also tested their sum, as well as the Borda count [19], which is a ranked vote procedure. From our experiments the product of the likelihoods is clearly the most efficient method. Nonetheless, we compare the results of the DST-based combination classifier to these three probabilistic methods.

Table 1 provides the TOP 1 and TOP 2 performances of each of the three HMM classifiers. It clearly shows that the two data sets are of heterogeneous difficulty. Moreover, the lower contour is always the less informative feature, and in the case of the RIMES database, it is really not informative. In Table 2, we present the performance of the combination of these HMM classifiers on the IFN/ENIT database (arabic). We use the DST-based combination classifier presented in the previous sections and we compare it to the sum, the product and the Borda count rules. The results are given for all possible combination of two classifiers among the three, as well as for the three of them. Similarly, we present in Table 3 the results for the RIMES (latin) database.

All these comparaisons show that the DST-based combination classifier is more efficient than the other methods. The improvement in terms of points is not really important, as the original scores are rather hight, and as the combination results mainly depend on the results of the original classifiers. Nontheless,

Table 1. Individual performances of the HMM classifiers

	IFN/ENIT		RIMES	
	Top 1	Top 2	Top 1	Top 2
HMM 1: Upper contour	73.60	79.77	54.10	66.40
HMM 2: Lower contour	65.90	74.03	38.93	51.57
HMM 3: Density	72.97	79.73	53.23	65.83

Table 2. IFN/ENIT recognition performance for different combination rules

	DST		Sum		Product		Borda	
	Top 1	Top 2	Top 1	Top 2	Top 1	Top 2	Top 1	Top 2
1-2	76.50	82.30	76.00	80.53	76.27	80.70	76.27	80.07
1-3	79.40	84.17	76.90	82.13	79.43	83.17	77.77	83.03
2-3	76.97	82.30	72.97	79.47	76.67	80.50	74.63	80.20
1-2-3	80.13	84.00	78.47	82.87	79.53	83.10	79.43	83.20

Table 3. RIMES recognition performance for different combination rules

	DST		Sum		Product		Borda	
	Top 1	Top 2	Top 1	Top 2	Top 1	Top 2	Top 1	Top 2
1-2	59.53	70.47	60.73	70.03	60.83	70.10	54.87	66.63
1-3	65.90	76.33	63.47	73.60	65.27	74.60	63.93	73.87
2-3	59.63	71.07	57.70	68.97	58.13	67.37	54.97	66.27
1-2-3	65.50	74.90	63.03	70.63	63.33	70.83	62.30	70.53

in terms of proportion of mistakes which are avoided, the results are meaningful. Moreover, the DST-based combination is more robust to the presence of a
weak classifier (here, HMM classifier 2, working on the lower contour), which
corresponds to the conclusions of [2].

5   Conclusion

In this paper, we have presented an combination classifier based on Dempster-
Shafer theory, which combines the outputs of several HMM classifiers. This combination classifier is interesting as (1) it can easily be generalized to other classifiers of Type III, as long as they provide a probabilistic output, (2) it generalizes
the DST-based combination classifier of [2] which was restricted to classifiers of
Type I, (3) it improves the results with respect to classical probabilistic combination of HMM classifiers, (4) the complexity is kept under control in spite of
the use of the DST, which is known for its computation cost (due to the ma-
nipulation of the power set). But the main interest of the use of DST is to open
new insights to refine the decision process. For instance, it is possible to consider
the conflict during the conjunctive combination, or the cardinality of the focal
sets of highest masses, or even, the value N to which it has been necessary to
search for the common word of the frame, in order to assess the reliability of
the decision process. In case of lack of reliability, it would be possible to remain
imprecise in the decision process, or on the contrary to decide that the word
does not belong to the database. These refinements of the decision process are
in the scope of our future extensions of this study.

References

1. Kuncheva, L.I.: Combining Pattern Classifiers: Methods and Algorithms. Wiley-Interscience, Hoboken (2004)
2. Xu, L., Krzyzak, A., Suen, C.: Methods of combining multiple classifiers and their applications to handwriting recognition. IEEE Trans. Syst., Man, Cybern. (3) (1992)
3. Arica, N., Yarman-Vural, F.T.: An overview of character recognition focused on off-line handwriting. IEEE Trans. Systems, Man and Cybernetics, Part C: Applications and Reviews (2), 216–232 (2001)
4. Shafer, G.: A Mathematical Theory of Evidence. Princeton University Press, Princeton (1976)
5. Smets, P.: The transferable belief model. Artif. Intell. 66(2), 191–234 (1994)
6. Valente, F., Hermansky, H.: Combination of acoustic classifiers based on dempster-shafer theory of evidence. In: IEEE International Conference on Acoustics, Speech and Signal Processing, ICASSP, vol. 4, pp. 1129–1132 (April 2007)
7. Burger, T., Aran, O., Urankar, A., Akarun, L., Caplier, A.: A dempster-shafer theory based combination of classifiers for hand gesture recognition. In: Computer Vision and Computer Graphics - Theory and Applications. Lecture Notes in Communications in Computer and Information Science (2008)
8. Aran, O., Burger, T., Caplier, A., Akarun, L.: A belief-based sequential fusion approach for fusing manual and non-manual signs. Pattern Recognition 42(5), 812–822 (2009)
9. Gagnon, L., Foucher, S., Laliberte, F., Boulianne, G.: A simplified audiovisual fusion model with application to large-vocabulary recognition of french canadian speech. Canadian Journal of Electrical and Computer Engineering 33(2), 109–119 (Spring 2008)
10. Mercier, D., Cron, G., Denoeux, T., Masson, M.H.: Fusion de décisions postales dans le cadre du modéle des croyances transférables. Traitement du Signal 24(2), 133–151 (2007)
11. Masson, M.H., Denoeux, T.: Belief functions and cluster ensembles. In: Sossai, C., Chemello, G. (eds.) ECSQARU 2009. LNCS, vol. 5590, pp. 323–334. Springer, Heidelberg (2009)
12. Duda, R., Hart, P., Stork, D.: Pattern Classification. Wiley, Chichester (2001)
13. Keynes, J.M.: Fundamental ideas. A Treatise on Probability, ch. 4 (1921)
14. Rabiner, L.R.: A tutorial on hidden markov models and selected applications in speech recognition. Proceedings of the IEEE, 257–286 (1989)
15. Kessentini, Y., Paquet, T., Hamadou, A.B.: Off-line handwritten word recognition using multi-stream hidden markov models. Pattern Recognition Letters 30(1), 60–70 (2010)
16. Kessentini, Y., Paquet, T., Burger, T.: Comparaison des méthodes probabilistes et évidentielles de fusion de classifieurs pour la reconnaissance de mots manuscrits. In: CIFED (to appear, 2010)
17. Pechwitz, M., Maddouri, S., Maergner, V., Ellouze, N., Amiri, H.: Ifn/enit - database of handwritten arabic words. In: Colloque International Francophone sur l'Ecrit et le Doucement, pp. 129–136 (2002)
18. Grosicki, E., Carre, M., Brodin, J., Geoffrois, E.: Results of the rimes evaluation campaign for handwritten mail processing. In: International Conference on Document Analysis and Recognition, pp. 941–945 (2009)
19. Kittler, J., Hatef, M., Duin, R.P., Matas, J.: On combining classifiers. IEEE Transactions on Pattern Analysis and Machine Intelligence 20(3), 226–239 (1998)

Using Uncertainty Information to Combine Soft Classifications

Luisa M.S. Gonçalves[1,2], Cidália C. Fonte[2,3], and Mario Caetano[4,5]

[1] Polytechnic Institute of Leiria, School of Technology and Managment,
Department of Civil Engeneering, Portugal
[2] Institute for Systems and Computers Engineering at Coimbra, Portugal
[3] Department of Mathematics, University of Coimbra, Portugal
[4] Portuguese Geographic Institute (IGP), Remote Sensing Unit (RSU), Lisboa, Portugal
[5] CEGI, Instituto Superior de Estatística e Gestão de Informação, ISEGI,
Universidade Nova de Lisboa, 1070-312 Lisboa, Portugal
luisa.goncalves@ipleiria.pt,
cfonte@mat.uc.pt,
mario.caetano@igeo.pt

Abstract. The classification of remote sensing images performed with different classifiers usually produces different results. The aim of this paper is to investigate whether the outputs of different soft classifications may be combined to increase the classification accuracy, using the uncertainty information to choose the best class to assign to each pixel. If there is disagreement between the outputs obtained with the several classifiers, the proposed method selects the class to assign to the pixel choosing the one that presents less uncertainty. The proposed approach was applied to an IKONOS image, which was classified using two supervised soft classifiers, the Multi-layer Perceptron neural network classifier and a fuzzy classifier based on the underlying logic of the Minimum-Distance-to-Means. The overall accuracy of the classification obtained with the combination of both classifications with the proposed methodology was higher than the overall accuracy of the original classifications, which shows that the methodology is promising and may be used to increase classification accuracy.

Keywords: Soft classifiers, uncertainty information, combining soft classifications.

1 Introduction

A variety of different classification outputs can be obtained applying different classifiers to the same image with the same training sets. The classifiers have different capabilities and their performance depends of the application fields and image characteristics [1]. Through the combination of the outputs of a set of classifiers it is possible to obtain a classification that is often more accurate than the individual classifications ([1], [2], [3], [4]). To this aim several approaches have already been proposed. For example, [5] used an approach in which the class membership values for each class, derived from different methods, were summed and the class with the highest combined

E. Hüllermeier, R. Kruse, and F. Hoffmann (Eds.): IPMU 2010, LNAI 6178, pp. 455–463, 2010.

value is the one assigned to the pixel. In [6], Lu integrated classification results derived from individual classifiers using Dempster-Shafer's theory of evidence. In [1], the authors applied two methods to improve accuracy of hard classifications, one, that he called a consensus builder system, to adjust classification output in the case of disagreement in classification between the maximum likelihood classifier, an expert system classifier and a neural network classifier. The second method integrated a rule-based expert system and a neural network classifier. The output of the expert system classifier was used as an additional new input layer in the neural network classifier. Doan and Foody [4] applied four methods for combining soft classifications. These methods were based on: 1) the selection of the most accurate prediction on a class-specific basis; 2) the average of the outputs of the individual classifications for each case; 3) the direct combination of classifications using reasoning and 4) the adaptation of the outputs to enable the use of a conventional (hard classification) ensemble approach.

Although several approaches have been proposed for combining hard classifications, the development of methods to combine soft classifications is still a field of investigation and the application of uncertainty information in this process is at an early stage.

The use of soft classifiers to perform image classification enables the generation of possibility or probability distributions for each pixel, depending of the classifiers used, where each probability or possibility is associated with a class of the nomenclature. The spatial units are assigned to the class presenting the larger degree of possibility or probability. The additional information provided by these classifiers may be used as indicators of the classifier difficulty to assign only one class to the spatial unit, and, together with the application of uncertainty measures, may provide valuable information that can be used in combined classification methods.

This study tests whether the proposed combining approach, that uses the uncertainty information obtained with two soft classifiers, improves the classification accuracy. The approach developed includes the following steps: 1) pixel-based soft classification; 2) application of an uncertainty measure to the outputs of the previous step to obtain the ambiguity information; 3) evaluation of the accuracy of the classification obtained in the first step; 4) development of rules to combine the soft classifications, that incorporate the information provided by the previous pixel-based classification and the results given by the uncertainty measure; 5) evaluation of the combined classification accuracy.

2 Data

The study was conducted in a rural area with a smooth topographic relief, occupied mainly by agriculture, pastures, forest and agro-forestry areas. The dominant forest species in the region are eucalyptus, coniferous and cork trees. An image obtained by the IKONOS sensor was used, with a spatial resolution of 4m in the multi-spectral mode (XS). The product acquired was the Geo Ortho Kit and the study was performed using the four multi-spectral bands. The geometric correction of the multi-spectral image consisted of its orthorectification. The average quadratic error obtained for the geometric correction was of 1.39m, less than half the pixel size, which guarantees an accurate geo-referencing.

3 Methodology

Two soft classification methods were used in this application: 1) the neural network Multi-Layer Perceptron (MLP); 2) a pixel-based supervised fuzzy soft classifier based on the underlying logic of Minimum-Distance-to-Means (FMDM). Both classifiers were trained using the same sampling protocol that included 100 pixels per-class. The classes used in this study are: Eucalyptus Trees (ET); Cork Trees (CKT), Coniferous Trees (CFT); Shadows (S); Shallow Water (SW), Deep Water (DW), Herbaceous Vegetation (HV), Sparse Herbaceous Vegetation (SHV) and Non-Vegetated Area (NVA). These classification methods assign, to each pixel, different degrees of assignment, in the case of MLP, and different degrees of possibility, in the case of FMDM, to the several classes under consideration. This extra data provide additional information at the pixel level which allows the assessment of the classification uncertainty.

3.1 Classifiers

The MLP is a non-parametric method and is the most commonly used neural network in remote sensing. Details of the MLP can be found in [7] and in [8]. The MLP provides an activation level for every output class of each pixel, and for hard classifications each pixel is allocated to the class with the largest activation level. A soft classification may be derived from this classifier by considering the activation levels of the network output units for each pixel. These activation levels range from 0 to 1, and may be used as the measures of class membership that reflect the class composition of the pixel [9] or indicators of the uncertainty associated with the pixel allocation to the classes. The second interpretation is used in this paper and the output values assigned to the pixels are used to compute classification uncertainty measures.

The second classification method used in this study is a pixel-based supervised fuzzy classifier based on the underlying logic of the Minimum-Distance-to-Means classifier. The underlying logic of this method is that the mean of a given signature represents the ideal point for the class, where fuzzy set membership is one. The fuzzy set membership is calculated based on a standardized Euclidean distance from each pixel reflectance, on each band, to the mean reflectance for each class signature, using a sigmoid membership function ([10]; [11]). When distance increases, fuzzy set membership decreases, until it reaches the user-defined Z-score distance where fuzzy set membership decreases to zero. To determine the value to use for the standard deviation unit, the information of the training data set was used to study the spectral separability of the classes and to determine their average separability.

With this classification methodology, the sum of the degrees of membership of each pixel to each class may sum up to any value between zero and the number of classes. Since fuzzy sets induce possibility distributions [12], a possibility distribution associated to each pixel is obtained.

Unlike traditional hard classifiers, the output obtained with these classifiers is not a single classified map, but rather a set of images (one per class) that expresses the probability, for the first classifier, and the possibility, for the second one, that each pixel belongs to the class in question.

To evaluate the classification accuracy of the two individual soft classifications a stratified random sampling with about 100 pixels per class was selected considering the entire image scene, which also included mixed pixels. The number of pixels was chosen to obtain a standard error of 0.05 for the estimation of the accuracy indexes of each class [13]. Each land cover class was sampled independently and the accuracy assessment was made with an error matrix.

3.2 Combination of Classifiers

The outputs of the two individual soft classifiers were combined through the use of an uncertainty measure. If the output classes for each individual pixel differed, the uncertainty information was compared and the class assigned with the lower value of uncertainty is chosen to be the one assigned to the pixel. In this approach the uncertainty measure E, developed by [14], was used to quantify the uncertainty at each spatial unit. This measure is given by

$$E = 1 - p(x_1) \tag{1}$$

where $p(x_1)$ is the largest degree of possibility or probability of the possibility distributions or probability distributions assigned with the pixel. This measure is also called ambiguity measure [15].

The first phase of the algorithm developed to combine classifications checks whether the same class is assigned to each pixel by both classifiers. If this condition is satisfied the class is accepted. If the two classifiers have different results for a certain pixel, the ambiguity information is used to make a judgement. The class with the lower ambiguity value is taken as the output for the pixel.

To evaluate if the combined classification improves the results, the accuracy assessment was made with the same protocol used with the single classifiers and the results were compared.

4   Results

4.1 Individual Soft Classifications

The accuracy assessment for both classifications was made with an error matrix and was undertaken with the same testing datasets. The error matrixes are generated assigning each pixel to the class with highest degree of possibility or activation level (in the case of the MLP classifier), corresponding to hard versions of the classifiers. The Global Accuracy was computed as well as the Users' Accuracy (UA) and the Producers' Accuracy (PA) for all classes. In terms of the overall accuracy, the classifications were similar. With the FMDM classifier method the overall accuracy was 66% and with the MLP classifier 65%. However, on a per–class basis, differences in accuracy are more evident. The results are shown in Fig.1 and Fig.2. The pixels that are not classified (NC) are also considered.

		Reference Label of the Classification with FMDM									UA
		DW	SW	NVA	ET	S	HV	CKT	CFT	SHV	(%)
M A P L A B E L	NC	4	1	7	1	5	2	1	1	2	
	DW	96	0	0	0	1	0	0	0	0	99.0
	SW	6	92	2	0	0	0	0	0	0	92.0
	NVA	0	0	81	0	0	19	0	1	51	53.3
	ET	0	0	0	39	1	6	11	18	7	47.6
	S	3	0	0	0	87	0	10	1	1	85.3
	HV	0	0	1	0	0	107	0	6	10	86.3
	CKT	0	0	11	14	8	0	54	11	25	43.9
	CFT	0	0	0	8	0	24	6	31	4	42.5
	SHV	0	1	13	2	0	9	11	2	36	48.6
PA (%)		88.1	97.9	70.4	60.9	85.3	64.1	58.1	43.7	26.5	**65.5%**

Fig. 1. Error matrixes of the classifications obtained with the FMDM

		Reference Label of the Classification with MLP									UA
		DW	SW	NVA	ET	S	HV	CKT	CFT	SHV	(%)
M A P L A B E L	NC	0	0	0	0	0	0	0	0	0	
	DW	104	1	2	0	1	0	0	0	0	96.3
	SW	4	92	1	0	0	0	0	0	0	94.8
	NVA	0	0	56	0	0	0	2	0	1	94.9
	ET	0	0	0	8	0	0	0	2	0	80.0
	S	1	0	4	1	83	0	18	0	1	76.9
	HV	0	0	0	2	0	78	0	0	2	95.1
	CKT	0	1	5	18	18	0	40	9	16	37.4
	CFT	0	0	1	32	0	59	22	56	20	29.5
	SHV	0	0	46	3	0	30	11	4	96	50.5
PA (%)		95.4	97.9	48.7	12.5	81.4	46.7	43.0	78.9	70.6	**64.5%**

Fig. 2. Error matrixes of the classifications obtained with the MLP classifiers

Fig. 3 a) and Fig. 3 b) show the classification results when each pixel is assigned to the class with higher degree of possibility with the FMDM classifier, and with the largest activation level with the MLP classifier.

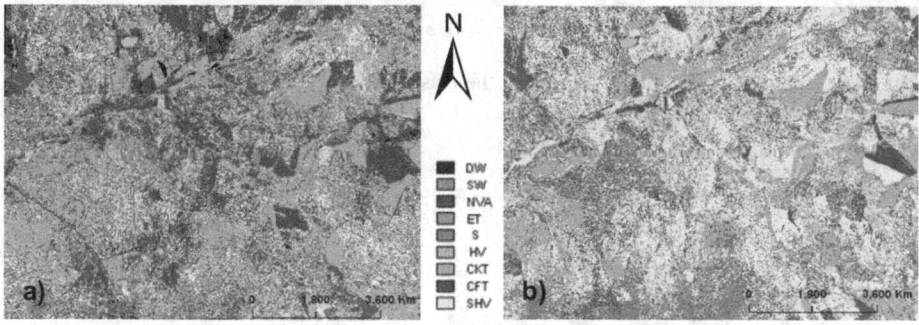

Fig. 3. Hard version of the classification results with a) FMDM and b) MLP

The error matrix shows that water classes (DW and SW) were well identified by both classifiers. Forestry species were often confused between each other and with other classes, such as Sparse Herbaceous Vegetation (SHV) and Herbaceous Vegetation (HV).

With the MLP classifier the class with the smaller value of PA is Eucalyptus Trees (ET) (12.5%), which means it is the class with more omission error. With the FMDM classifier the class with the smaller value of PA is Sparse Herbaceous Vegetation (SHV) (26.5%). The class with smaller UA for both classifiers is Coniferous Trees (CFT). The MLP classification results for the UA was 29.5% and with the FMDM was 42.5%, and therefore it is the class with more commission errors.

The results obtained also shows that different classifications outputs were derived from the application of these two classifiers (Fig. 3). For example, with the MLP classifier the class NVA presents more omission errors then commission error and with the FMDM classifier it's the opposite. With the FMDM classifier a great amount of sites that should have been assigned to other classes, such as SHV and HV, were assigned to NVA, and were therefore absent from those classes, increasing their omission errors. With the MLP classifier a great amount of sites that should have been assigned to the NVA class were assigned to SHV class.

Images shown in Fig. 4 correspond to the spatial distribution of the ambiguity E committed when the pixel is assigned to the class corresponding to the largest degree of assignment. The regions with larger ambiguity (dark zones) are the ones where the assignment degrees were lower.

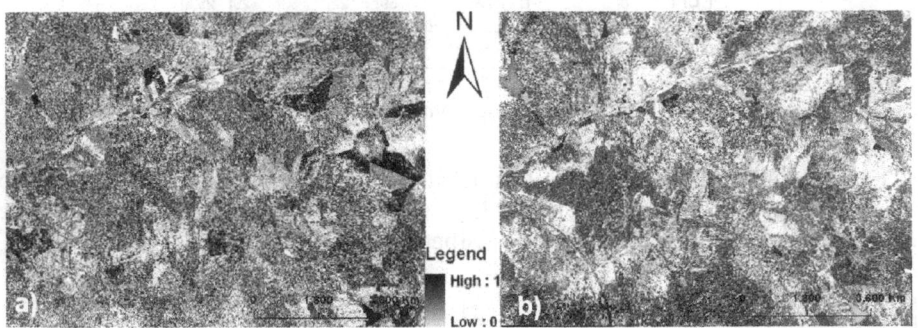

Fig. 4. Spatial distribution of ambiguity for the classifications obtained with: a) FMDM classifier b) MLP classifier

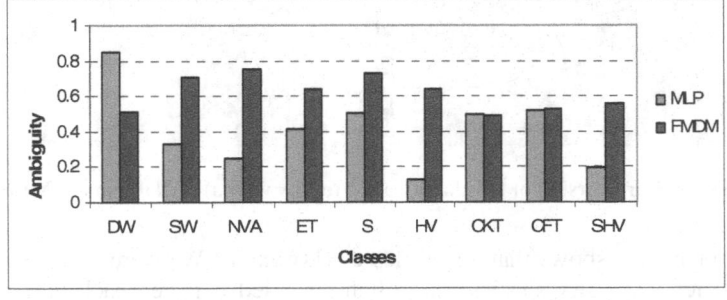

Fig. 5. Mean uncertainty per class

The comparison of the mean ambiguity per class shows that forest species, such as CKT and CFT were assigned to the pixels with similar ambiguity by both classifiers (see Fig. 5). The class DW was assigned to the pixels with lower ambiguity with FMDM classifier, but all the other class presenter higher values of ambiguity with this classifier.

4.2 Combined Classifications

The accuracy assessment of the combined classification was made with the same testing datasets used to evaluate the individual classifications. The overall accuracy of the combined output was 4.5% higher than that of the most accurate individual classification. An improvement in some individual class accuracy was also observed (see Fig. 7 and Fig. 8). For example, the UA of classes SW, NVA, HV, CKT, SHV increased when compared with those of the most accurate individual classification (Fig. 1, Fig. 2, Fig. 6, Fig. 7). However, for some classes, the UA and PA of the combined classification didn't improve when compared to one of the initial classifications, such as the UA of the class ET when compared to the UA obtained with the MLP, or the UA of the class S when compared to the UA obtained with the FMDM. Although, the mean value of the UA and PA of all classes is higher than the mean values obtained for either of the initial classifications.

		Reference Label of Combining Classification									UA
		DW	SW	NVA	ET	S	HV	CKT	CFT	SHV	(%)
M	NC	0	0	0	0	0	0	0	0	0	
A	DW	104	1	1	0	1	0	0	0	0	97.2
P	SW	2	92	2	0	0	0	0	0	0	95.8
	NVA	0	0	56	0	0	0	2	0	0	96.6
L	ET	0	0	0	29	0	2	6	6	2	64.4
A	S	3	0	2	1	91	0	14	0	1	81.3
B	HV	0	0	0	2	0	85	0	0	2	95.5
E	CKT	0	1	7	20	10	0	54	10	15	46.2
L	CFT	0	0	1	10	0	50	10	53	18	37.3
	SHV	0	0	46	2	0	30	7	2	98	53.0
PA (%)		95.4	97.9	48.7	45.3	89.2	50.9	58.1	74.6	72.1	70%

Fig. 6. Error matrix of the combined classification

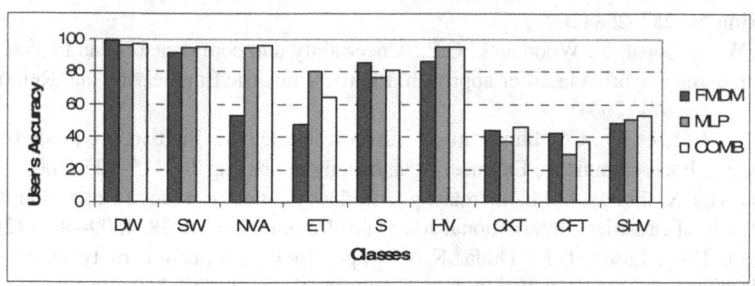

Fig. 7. User's Accuracy of the classes obtained with the FMDM, MLP and combined (COMB) classifications

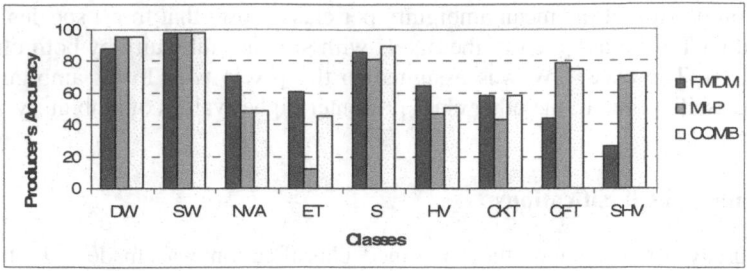

Fig. 8. Producer's Accuracy of the classes obtained with the FMDM, MLP and combined (COMB) classifications

5 Conclusions

The classifiers tested in this study performed differently when applied to the same image, considering the same nomenclature and testing sets, and produced different results. Although the overall accuracy was similar for both individual classifications, on a per–class basis, differences were more evident. The proposed new classification methodology, integrating the results of both individual classifications, improved the overall accuracy of the classification. These results show that the information provided by the uncertainty measure was useful to determine the best class to assign to the pixels. The results achieved in this study indicate that the proposed approach seems to be promising, providing valuable information to the user, and deserves therefore further attention. Additional experiments will have to be made with other classifiers and uncertainty measures as well as the integration, in the combining decision process, of the uncertainty with the individual class accuracy information obtained with each classifier.

References

1. Liu, X.H., Skidmore, A.K., Van Oosten, H.: Integration of classification methods for improvement of land-cover map accuracy. ISPRS Journal of Photogrammetry and Remote Sensing 56, 257–268 (2002)
2. Liu, W.G., Gopal, S., Woodcock, C.E.: Uncertainty and confidence in land cover classification using a hybrid classifier approach. Photogrammetric Engineering and Remote Sensing 70, 963–971 (2004)
3. Huang, Z., Lees, G.: Combining non-parametric models for multisource predictive forest mapping. Photogrammetric Engineering and Remote Sensing 70, 415–425 (2004)
4. Doan, H.T.X., Foody, G.M.: Increasing soft classification accuracy through the use of an ensemble of classifiers. International Journal of Remote Sensing 28, 4609–4623 (2007)
5. Brown, D.G., Lusch, D.P., Duda, K.A.: Supervised classification of types of glaciated landscapes using digital elevation data. Geomorphology 21, 233–250 (1998)
6. Lu, Y.: Knowledge integration in a multiple classifier system. Applied Intelligence 6, 75–86 (1996)
7. Atkinson, P.M., Tatnall, A.R.L.: Neural networks in remote sensing. International Journal of Remote Sensing 18, 699–709 (1997)

8. Brown, K.M., Foody, G.M., Atkinson, P.M.: Estimating per-pixel thematic uncertainty in remote sensing classifications. International Journal of Remote Sensing 30, 209–229 (2009)
9. Zhang, J., Foody, G.M.: Fully-fuzzy supervised classification of sub-urban land cover from remotely sensed imagery: statistical and artificial neural network approaches. International Journal of Remote Sensing 22, 615–628 (2001)
10. Burrough, P.A., McDonnell, R.A.: Principles of geographical information systems. Oxford University Press, Oxford (1998)
11. Kuncheva, I.L.: Fuzzy Classifier Design. Physica-Verlag/Springer-Verlag, Heidelberg (2000)
12. Klir, G.: Generalized information theory: aims, results and open problems. Reliability Engineering and Systems Safety 85, 21–38 (2004)
13. Stehman, S.V.: Statistical rigor and practical utility in thematic map accuracy assessment. Photogrammetric Engineering & Remote Sensing 67, 727–734 (2001)
14. Chow, C.K.: On optimum error and reject tradeoff. IEEE Transactions on Information Theory 16, 41–46 (1970)
15. Le Capitaine, H., Frélicot, C.: Classification with reject options in a logical framework: a fuzzy residual implication approach. In: International Fuzzy Systems Association World Congress 2009 (IFSA 2009) and European Society for Fuzzy Logic and Technology Conference (EUSFLAT 2009), pp. 855–860 (2009)

Performance Evaluation of a Fusion System Devoted to Image Interpretation

Abdellah Lamallem, Lionel Valet, and Didier Coquin

LISTIC - Université de Savoie
Domaine Universitaire - BP 80439
74 944 Annecy le vieux Cedex, France
{abdellah.lamallem,lionel.valet,didier.coquin}@univ-savoie.fr

Abstract. The use of fusion systems has known a wide growth and they now need reliable ways to evaluate their performance. Fusion systems are complex because they involve a complete information treatment chain (from the information extraction to the decision). This paper studies the different approaches used for system evaluation and proposes a local evaluation method for the evaluation of each subpart of the fusion system. The approach is then illustrated on cooperative fusion system devoted to 3D image interpretation.

Keywords: Cooperative fusion system, complex system, performance evaluation.

1   Introduction

This paper presents a means that combines analysis, modeling and evaluation to assess overall as well as detailed system performance compared to the needs of system users. Information fusion systems are more and more complex. They are composed of many subparts which have many parameters. They also require an important computation time. The analysis and the evaluation of such systems are important and not easy to achieve. For complex entities, especially when subjective evaluations are involved, the problem can be difficult so much so that comprehensive assessments are often just not attempted.

The traditional approach to evaluate a complex system is based on a multi-parameter (multi-attribute, multi-criterion) vector-like description of the system. As result, we get a point in a multi-dimensional (multi-parameter) space. After that many approaches can be used to map the point above (i.e., a vector system description) into a quantitative or ordinal scale of system quality (quality metric, effectiveness, productivity, performance, excellence). Many real-world problems involve simultaneous optimization of several incommensurable and often competing objectives. Often, there is no single optimal solution, but rather a set of alternative solutions. These solutions are optimal in the wider sense that no other solutions in the search space are superior to them when all objectives are considered. They are known as Pareto optimal solutions [1].

E. Hüllermeier, R. Kruse, and F. Hoffmann (Eds.): IPMU 2010, LNAI 6178, pp. 464–473, 2010.

Recent years have seen an increase in the use of ROC graphs in the machine learning and pattern recognition communities. One advantage of ROC graphs is that they enable visualizing and organizing classifier performance without regard to class distributions or error costs. Unfortunately, such methods have an inherent limitation. ROC graphs plot true positive rate against false positive rate, treating all errors of a given type to be equivalent [2].

In image analysis, the result evaluation is always a difficult task mainly due to the subjective definition of regions of interest. In the literature, there are a lot of quantitative measurements to quantify the performance of the result [3,4,5,6]. However, in such kind of application in which the experts work in cooperation with the system and in which an entire reference set does not exist, the quantitative measurements are not enough to achieve a relevant evaluation. They must be complete with another kind of subjective information. This paper presents an evaluation method which depends on the variability of the input and on the subpart of the system we want to evaluate.

This paper is organized as follow: section 2 presents the fusion system developed for 3D gray level image interpretation and the classical image analysis system evaluation. Performance evaluation of our fusion system based on local evaluation is explained in section 3. Finally, in section 4 gives an illustration of the proposed approach with synthetic images and real images.

2   A Fusion System for 3D Image Interpretation

Fusion systems are mainly designed to help experts in the analyze of complex phenomena. Its aim is to build a new interesting information from many pieces of information (measures, attributes, partial decisions, ...). Applied to image interpretation, these systems are mainly used for typical region detection to facilitate expert tasks [7].

2.1   Working Environment of a Cooperative Fusion System

To evaluate a fusion system, it is first important to precise the environment in which the system evolved. Figure 1 shows that the working environment of the fusion system is the same than the one of the experts. Input information, noted E, of the fusion system is the same set of data analyzed by the experts. This set is "imposed" to the fusion system generally by the context of the application (tomography images in medical application, video in surveillance application, ...). Output information, noted S, generally corresponds to objects experts are interested by. This set is also imposed to the fusion system and it corresponds to an understandable space for the end-users (regions of interest in medical images, ...). Moreover, experts are able to give some result examples which means that they have their own transfer function noted f_{expert}. The result samples given by experts are generally used as references to evaluate the final output of the information fusion systems.

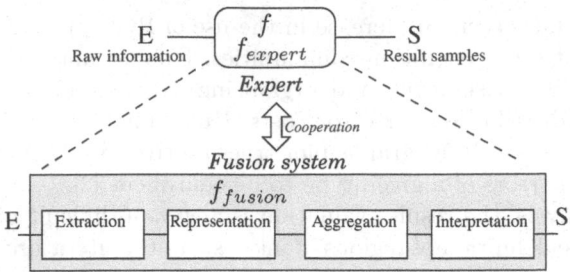

Fig. 1. Cooperative fusion system working environment

The design of an information fusion system consists in finding a computer science based system able to model expert behavior. Fusion system can be divided in four main subparts (illustrated on figure 1) that generally come from the manner experts analyze the input data E: they look at the data and search for typical characteristics (*extraction steps*), then they have some rules (*representation and fusion steps*) based on their experience in order to detect a possible occurring situation. Finally, they decide between the set of possible relevant cases (*interpretation step*).

Conception of a fusion system consists to make several choices for each subpart in order to approach as soon as possible the behavior of the experts. Automatic minimization of $f_{expert} - f_{fusion}$ is obviously not possible for two reasons: Analytic expression of f_{expert} is unknown and f_{fusion} is generally complex (composition of non-linear and non-continuous functions). This specific working environment will influence the performance evaluation of a fusion system.

2.2   The Studied Cooperative Fusion System

The cooperative fusion system concerned in this paper, was designed for 3D gray level image interpretation. In the concerned application, experts introduce their knowledge by pointing references of the regions directly on the input image (i.e. the input space E). The designed system is presented on figure 2. Its efficiency was demonstrated in [7].

First, different image characteristic measurements based on image processing techniques have been implemented to acquire pertinent information on the sought-after regions. The main family measures are based on:

- *local organization measure*: based on voxel intensity gradient analysis.
- *coocurrence matrix evaluation*: useful for texture characterization
- *morphological measurement*: specific form of the object in the images are taken into account.

The representation step consists in building similarity maps for each attribute and for each region. All the information is thus expressed in a common and commensurable space. Then, Choquet integrals are applied to compute a belonging degree for each voxel to the sought-after regions. The main advantage of

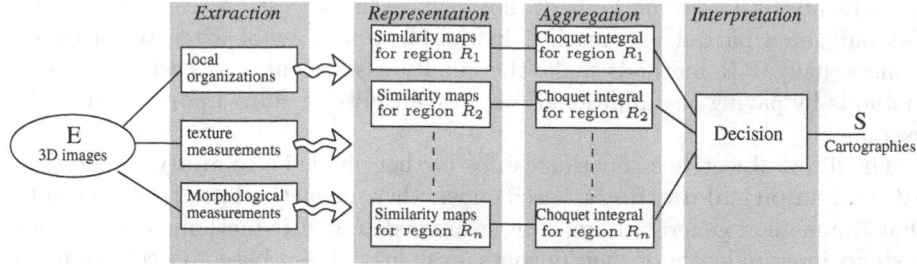

Fig. 2. Fusion system designed for 3D image analysis

this aggregation tool is its capacity to take into account the interaction between attributes [8]. An interpretation stage is then necessary to build the complete mapping of the 3D image.

2.3 Classical Image Analysis System Evaluation

Existing image quality evaluation methods can be divided into subjective and objective evaluations.

- **Subjective evaluation:** subjective or perceptual evaluation methods have been established as a reliable method for general image and video quality assessment with well established experimental procedures and practice. They need *ground truth* for evaluation and validation of objective fusion metrics. These methods are classified as **full reference (FR)** methods.

However, subjective evaluations are inconvenient, time consuming, expensive, and the conditions cannot be guaranteed to be exactly the same. Although widely accepted for their credibility and robustness in evaluating image fusion performance, subjective tests are impractical in many cases due to heavy organizational and equipment requirements and strict test conditions that have to be observed [9].

- **Objective evaluation:** many image quality evaluations in the literature use an ideal fused image as reference for comparison with the image fusion results. However, ideal fusion images are not available to most real world applications. Therefore, objective quality evaluation methods have been developed that do not need a reference image. A mutual information metric was used to evaluate fusion performance by Qu and al [10]. Xydeas and Petrovic [11] evaluated the fusion performance by calculating the relative amount of edge information transferred from the input images to the fused image. Recently, an image quality index based on the structure metric proposed by Wang and Bovik [5] was improved for image fusion assessment by Piella and Heijmans [6] into a pixel by pixel or region by region method, giving weighted averages of the similarities between the fused image and each of the source images. These methods are classified as **no reference (NR)** methods. One interesting development in image quality assessment research is to design **reduce reference (RR)** methods for quality assessment [4]. These methods do not require full access to reference images, but only need partial information, in the form of a set of extracted features. Conceptually, **RR** methods make the quality assessment task easier than **NR** methods by paying the additional cost of transmitting some information to the users.

The direct objective evaluation can be further divided into **analytical methods** and **empirical methods**, based on whether the method itself, or the results that the method generated are being examined. Analytic methods assess fusion systems independently of their outputs, evaluating them based on certain properties of the fusion algorithms, such as processing strategy (parallel, sequential, iterative, or mixed), processing complexity, resource efficiency, and resolution, which are usually not deemed effective for assessing the fusion quality. In other words, analytical methods are only applicable for evaluating algorithms or implementation properties of fusion algorithms. These properties are generally independent of the fused result quality, so these properties are not considered effective at characterizing the performance difference between fusion algorithms [12].

Most fusion systems are evaluated by comparing the similarity between the global result of the fused image and the source image. But here, we want to know the effect of the adjustment of one of the parameters. Possible conflicting impacts on the global result of two adjustments must be kept without more information. So we proposed a local evaluation, which could inform the end-users on which part he must adjust parameters to have a better result.

3   Performance Evaluation of a Fusion System

3.1   Fusion Subpart Evaluation Layout

Let be a system (fig. 1) represented by its transfer function noted f, between an input space E and an output space S. The global evaluation considers implicitly that the input information is *"imposed"* and not questionable. Thus, an evaluation of the result quality is directly correlated to the function f characterizing the system.

Each subpart of a fusion system (noted f_i) cannot be considered as the generic system of figure 1 because their inputs are conditioned by the output of the previous one. In this situation, the evaluation of f_i must be independent to the quality of its inputs. The evaluation consists thus to evaluate the correct role of f_i and not its adequacy to a given type of input.

A layout of subpart evaluation is thus proposed on figure 3. It can be resume by three questions : what's kind of evaluation criteria use? is there reference on the output of the system? and what kind of input the system has? The two first questions correspond to the currently used cases in the literature (see section 2.3). The last one, concerns the type of the input regarding to the system. Two situations are listed : (1) *"raw information"* which is a non questioning information (considered as non editable), (2) *"intermediate information "* (coming from another subpart) considered as a relative information.

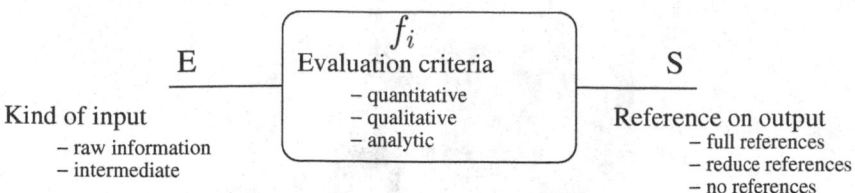

Fig. 3. Complex system evaluation layout

This distinction between the input type has consequences on the evaluation process. In the context of 3D image interpretation, we proposed to define the missions of each subpart f_i and to evaluate their achievement. The evaluation uses only the output when inputs are raw information or it compares the outputs to the inputs when inputs are intermediate information. This idea is now illustrated on the extraction and representation subparts.

3.2 An Example of Local Evaluation

In this example we focuses on the extraction and representation subparts, and we propose a process to evaluate their performance. In the context of the image segmentation, the missions of the two subparts can be expressed by:

- **Extraction subpart:** this block extracts information from the original data. It must bring an efficient separability between the sought-after regions.
- **Representation subpart:** it consists in representing the extracted information in another commensurable space. The objective is to preserve the separability during the transformation.

The evaluation of the separability uses the reference regions initially pointed out by the expert on the original image. It consists in comparing the voxel distribution of the attribute values between points of different sought-after regions. The approach is illustrated on figure 4 : the reference regions pointed out on the original image are reported on the attribute images. It allows to select voxels for which output classes are well-known. Then, the distribution corresponding to a region can be compared to the other one. For example the distribution of region R_1 is compared to the distribution of the region $\overline{R_1}$ ($\overline{R_1} = R_2 \cup R_3$) for a given parameter adjustment of attribute A_j.

The region separability measure is built in comparing the two normalized histograms $\widetilde{H}_{R_i}^{A_j}$ and $\widetilde{H}_{\overline{R_i}}^{A_j}$. Measures between histograms are numerous [13] and the choice was guided by the main objective: the separation between them independently to their forms and stretchness. In this case a simple intersection surface evaluation like the Manhattan distance could be enough, the separability measure is detailed in [14]. Its expression for two histograms is given by:

$$S_{R_i}^{A_j} = d_{Man.}(\widetilde{H}_{R_i}^{A_j}, \widetilde{H}_{\overline{R_i}}^{A_j}) = \frac{1}{2} \sum_{\forall index} |\widetilde{H}_{R_i}^{A_j}(index) - \widetilde{H}_{\overline{R_i}}^{A_j}(index)| \qquad (1)$$

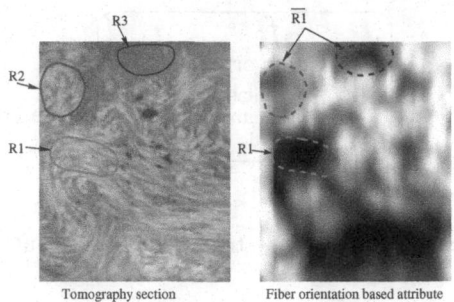

Fig. 4. Utilization of the references given by experts

The obtained distance is equal to 1 when the two histograms have an empty intersection and 0 when they are overlapping. The representation step consists in building similarity maps $C_{A_j}^{R_i}$ for each attribute and for each sought-after region. The evaluation of the representation subpart cannot be based only on the quality of the maps, because this quality depends also of the attributes. The idea is to evaluate the conservation of separability after the representation process. The separability computed on the similarity map is thus compared to the separability obtained on the attribute. We define the loss of separability by $L_{R_i}^{A_j}$ as follows:

$$L_{R_i}^{A_j} = |d_{Man.}(\widetilde{H}_{R_i}^{A_j}, \widetilde{H}_{\overline{R_i}}^{A_j}) - d_{Man.}(\widetilde{H}_{R_i}^{C_{A_j}^{R_i}}, \widetilde{H}_{\overline{R_i}}^{C_{A_j}^{R_i}})| \qquad (2)$$

The representation subpart is efficient when it is able to maintain the separability.

4   Illustration of the Proposed Local Evaluation

The proposed quantitative criteria is illustrated on synthetic images and on tomographic images. In the first illustration, a **full reference (FR)** is available on the output whereas **reduce reference (RR)** characterize the second one.

4.1   Illustration on Synthetic 3D Image

The local evaluation is first illustrated on a synthetic 3D image (presented on figure 5(a)). Image sizes are $245 \times 200 \times 250$ (12 250 000 voxels). Three textured regions are sought-after : R_1 a region with low intensity variance, R_2 is a region with high intensity variance compared to R_1 and R_3 is composed by a succession of two textures that form a kind of *oriented region*.

Attribute A_1 is based on texture measurement and attributes A_2 and A_3 are based on intensity gradient organization. The attributes were adjusted to have an interesting separability of the sought-after regions. The results of the

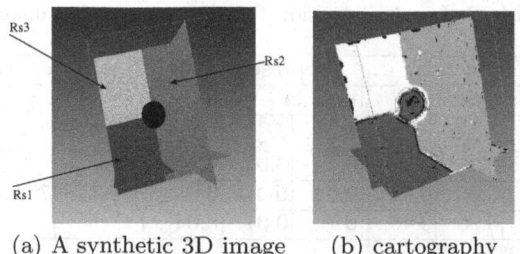

(a) A synthetic 3D image   (b) cartography

Fig. 5. Illustration on a synthetic 3D image

Table 1. Local evaluation for synthetic image

Measure	Extraction			Representation			Global evaluation		
	Separability			Loss of separability			Detection rate		
	$S_{R_1}^{A_j}$	$S_{R_2}^{A_j}$	$S_{R_3}^{A_j}$	$L_{R_1}^{A_j}$	$L_{R_2}^{A_j}$	$L_{R_3}^{A_j}$	T_{R_1}	T_{R_2}	T_{R_3}
A_1	0.95	0.92	0.94	0.02	0.06	0.03			
A_2	0.84	0.82	0.84	0.05	0	0	90.36%	93.88%	94.30%
A_3	0.90	0.88	0.91	0.03	0	0.03			

$T_{Global} = 93.32\%$.

local evaluation are illustrated in Table 1. Detection rates T_{R_i} are obtained by computing a confusion matrix. The global detection rate T_{Global} is satisfactory. A weak loss of separability can be found for region R_1 which can explain the lowest detection rate for this region but the lost is not significant. The classified 3D image is illustrated on figure 5(b) (Dark voxels represent the region R_1, gray level voxel the region R_2 and white voxels the region R_3). In this case, the extraction subpart has an interesting discrimination and the representation subpart achieves well its mission.

4.2   Illustration on 3D Tomographic Image

This application concerns the analysis of electro technical parts manufactured by Schneider Electric Company. Experts try to understand the inside part organization to find the better fabrication process. The method chosen by Schneider Electric to analyze the parts is based on X-ray computed tomography images illustrated on figure 6.

Three regions are also sought-after in this application the *oriented regions* (noted R_1) which have a regular and organized texture with a single preferential orientation. They are made up of long white fibres giving the impression of a flow. The *Disordered regions* (noted R_2) appear as not organized on the images, locally "chaotic", i.e. for which there is not a clearly defined principal orientation. The regions called *Lack of reinforcement* (noted R_3) that only contain resin (or paste) and no glass fibres. They appear in clear and homogeneous gray level on the images. Three attributes are computed: A_1 and A_2 based on texture measurement and A_3 based on intensity gradient organization.

Table 2. Local evaluation for 3D tomographic image

Measure	Extraction Separability			Representation Loss of separability			Global evaluation Detection rate		
	$S^{A_j}_{R_1}$	$S^{A_j}_{R_2}$	$S^{A_j}_{R_3}$	$L^{A_j}_{R_1}$	$L^{A_j}_{R_2}$	$L^{A_j}_{R_3}$	T_{R_1}	T_{R_2}	T_{R_3}
A_1	0.71	0.75	0.98	0	0.05	0			
A_2	0.51	0.27	0.92	0.04	**0.14**	0	79.44%	75.93%	100%
A_3	0.65	0.90	0.46	0	0.01	0.04			

$T_{Global} = 81.93\%$.

In the real case where the images are more complexe (noisy, shape, organization, resolution, ...), it is almost impossible for an attribute to separate all the regions in same time, For this reason, attributes have been chosen so that at least one sought after region is well separate. The results of local evaluation are illustrated in Table 2. Global detection rate T_{Global} remains interesting for this kind of application. The region R_2 is relatively less detected than the two others regions, this is due to the lower separability of this region on the attribute A_2 and to the loss of information in the representation step. To improve the detection, attribute A_2 should be replace by an attribute that bring more separability on regions R_1 and R_2. The results obtained are illustrated in the figure 6.

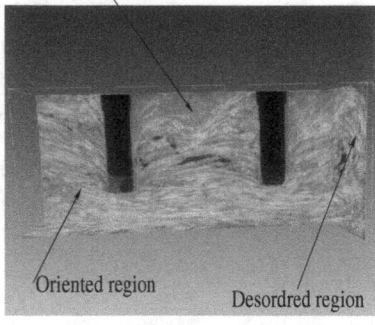

(a) A 3D tomographic image   (b) obtained cartography

(Dark voxels represent the region R_1, gray level voxel the region R_2 and white voxels the region R_3.)

Fig. 6. Input and output of the fusion system for tomographic images

5   Conclusion

This paper expressed the problem of fusion system performance evaluation by a local evaluation of each subpart that composes the system. Subpart evaluation needs to differentiate the kind of input and two situations have been listed. A mission is then proposed for subparts and its achievement is measured thanks to objective functions.

The approach is illustrated on two consecutive subparts of a fusion system devoted to 3D image interpretation. The obtained results are promising for attribute selection and parameter adjustment. They allow a better understanding of the system behavior which is important in a context of cooperation with experts. Work is being done to evaluate the aggregation and representation steps in the same way to finally quantify the global performance of the fusion systems.

References

1. Levin, M.S.: System synthesis with morphological clique problem: fusion of subsystem evaluation decisions. Information Fusion 2, 225–237 (2001)
2. Fawcett, T.: Roc graphs with instance-varying costs. Pattern Recognition Letters 27, 882–891 (2006)
3. Cvejic, N., Loza, A., Bull, D.: A similarity metric for assessment of image fusion algorithms. Journal of Signal Processing 2(3), 178–182 (2005)
4. Wang, Z., Bovik, A.C., Sheikh, H.R., Simoncelli, E.P.: Image quality assessment: from error visibility to structural similarity, vol. 13(4), pp. 600–612 (2004)
5. Wang, Z., Bovik, A.C.: A universal image quality index. International Journal of Signal Processing 9(3), 81–84 (2002)
6. Piella, G., Heijmans, H.: A new quality metric for image fusion. In: Proc. International Conference on Image Processing ICIP 2003, September 14-17, vol. 3, pp. III–173–176 (2003)
7. Jullien, S., Valet, L., Mauris, G., Bolon, P., Teyssier, S.: An attribute fusion system based on the choquet integral to evaluate the quality of composite parts. IEEE Trans. On Instrumentation and Measurement 57(4), 755–762 (2008)
8. Grabisch, M.: The application of fuzzy integrals in multicriteria decision making. European Journal of Operational Research 89, 445–456 (1996)
9. Toet, A., Franken, E.M.: Perceptual evaluation of different image fusion schemes. Displays 24(1), 25–37 (2003)
10. Qu, G., Zhang, D., Yan, P.: Information measure for performance of image fusion. Electronics Letters 38(7), 313–315 (2002)
11. Xydeas, C.S., Petrovic, V.: Objective image fusion performance measure. Electronics Letters 36(4), 308–309 (2000)
12. Cardoso, J.S., Corte-Real, L.: Toward a generic evaluation of image segmentation, vol. 14(11), pp. 1773–1782 (2005)
13. Cha, S.-H., Srihari, S.N.: On measuring distance between histograms. Pattern Recognition 35, 1355–1370 (2002)
14. Lamallem, A., Valet, L., Coquin, D.: Local versus global evaluation of a cooperative fusion system for 3D image interpretation. In: IEEE International Symposium on Optomechatronic Technologies, Istanbul, Turkey, pp. 360–365 (2009)

A New Adaptive Consensus Reaching Process Based on the Experts' Importance

Ignacio J. Pérez[1], F.J. Cabrerizo[2], S. Alonso[3], and Enrique Herrera-Viedma[1]

[1] Dept. of Computer Science and Artificial Intelligence, University of Granada
{ijperez,viedma}@decsai.ugr.es
[2] Dept. of Software Engineering and Computer Systems, Distance Learning
University of Spain, UNED
cabrerizo@issi.uned.es
[3] Dept. of Software Engineering, University of Granada
zerjioi@ugr.es

Abstract. Usually, in a group decision context, the importance level, confidence degree and amount of knowledge are very different among individuals. So, when all the individuals have to reach agreement, is quite important to model these kind of features in order to get more appropriate decisions. Last related works are focussed in the selection process to model the importance of the experts, but such approach, under some circumstances, can behave badly. In this contribution, we present a new adaptive consensus reaching model specifically designed to undertake group decision making situations in which the experts have different importance or confidence levels.

1 Introduction

Group decision making (GDM) consists of multiple individuals interacting to reach a decision. Each decision maker (expert) may have unique motivations or goals and may approach the decision process from a different angle, but have a common interest in reaching eventual agreement on selecting the "best" option(s) [3,16]. To do this, experts have to express their preferences by means of a set of evaluations over a set of alternatives.

There exist different representation formats that experts can use to express their preferences [1,2]. Fuzzy Preference Relations (FPRs) [1,2,3,6,8] have been widely used because they are a very expressive format and also they present good properties that allow to operate with them easily.

Two processes are necessary to solve GDM problems: a consensus process and a selection process. The consensus process is necessary to reach a final solution with a certain level of agreement among the experts. On the other hand, the selection process computes all individual preferences in order to obtain a collective solution. Clearly, it is preferable that the set of experts reach a high degree of consensus before applying the selection process. In order to measure the degree of consensus, different approaches have been proposed [7,9,10,17,18].

E. Hüllermeier, R. Kruse, and F. Hoffmann (Eds.): IPMU 2010, LNAI 6178, pp. 474–483, 2010.

To achieve a good consensus among the experts, it is necessary to provide the whole group of experts with some advice (feedback information) on how far the group is from consensus, what are the most controversial issues (alternatives), whose preferences are in the highest disagreement with the rest of the group, how their change would influence the consensus degree, and so on.

There are some GDM situations defined in homogeneous decision contexts, i.e., all experts' opinions are considered with equal importance, and others in heterogeneous decision contexts, i.e., where the importance levels or confidence degrees experts are quite different. To model such situations, the most of authors suggest to assign weight values in order to compute a weighted aggregation of the preferences [4,5,9,11,19,20]. This approach tries to focus on the discussion on a weighted collective preference and, in such a way, the most considerable experts are the main leaders of the discussion. They try to focuss the negotiation to close the remaining preferences in order to reach agreement. On the other hand, in some situations with many low-important experts, this mechanism could miss the target resulting in the opposite effect to the desired. That is, the moderator could send several recommendations to the high-important experts, who have at their disposal a larger amount of knowledge, in order to change their preferences to narrow them to the remaining experts' opinions. Consequently, the less important experts become the leaders of the discussion.

In this paper we propose a new consensus approach to overcome such problem. We take into account the importance weights not only to aggregate the experts' preferences but also when advising experts to change their preferences. Firstly, the most important experts are advised in order to reach some agreement among them. Then, the remaining experts receive some advice to achieve a high global consensus level. Furthermore, this new approach computes the recommendations in a different way depending on experts' importance in such a way that the experts with lower level of knowledge will need more advice than those experts that previously have at their disposal much more information to make good decisions.

In order to do this, the paper is set out as follows. Some general considerations about GDM and consensus reaching process are presented in Section 2. Section 3 presents the new importance-based consensus reaching process. Finally, Section 4 draws our conclusions.

2 Related Works

2.1 Group Decision Making

A decision making process, consisting in deriving the best option from a feasible set, is present in just about every conceivable human task. It is obvious that the comparison of different actions according to their desirability in decision problems, in many cases, it cannot be done by using a single criterion or an unique person. Thus, we interpret the decision process in the framework of GDM.

In a classical GDM situation there is a problem to solve, a solution set of possible alternatives, $X = \{x_1, x_2, \ldots, x_n\}$, $(n \geq 2)$ and a group of two or more experts, $E = \{e_1, e_2, \ldots, e_m\}$, $(m \geq 2)$ characterized by their own ideas, attitudes, motivations and knowledge, who express their opinions about this set of alternatives to achieve a common solution [12,14,15]. To do this, each expert has to express his preferences on the set of alternatives by means of a fuzzy preference relation, that is defined as $P^k \subset X \mathrm{x} X$, with a membership function, $\mu_{P^k} : X \mathrm{x} X \rightarrow [0,1]$, where $\mu_{P^k}(x_i, x_j) = p_{ij}^k$ denotes the preference degree of the alternative x_i over x_j for the expert e_k.

- $p_{ij}^k > 1/2$ indicates that x_i is preferred to x_j.
- $p_{ij}^k < 1/2$ indicates that x_j is preferred to x_i.
- $p_{ij}^k = 1/2$ indicates indifference between x_i and x_j.

When cardinality of X is small, the preference relation may be conveniently represented by the $n \mathrm{ x } n$ matrix $P^k = (p_{ij}^k)$.

Usual resolution methods for GDM problems are composed by two different processes [3] (see Figure 1):

1. *Consensus process:* Clearly, in any decision process, it is preferable that the experts reach a high degree of consensus on the solution set of alternatives. Thus, this process refers to how to obtain the maximum degree of consensus or agreement among the experts on the solution alternatives.
2. *Selection process:* This process consists in how to obtain the solution set of alternatives from the opinions on the alternatives given by the experts.

2.2 Classical Consensus Reaching Process

A consensus reaching process in a GDM problem is an iterative process composed by several discussion rounds, in which experts are expected to modify their

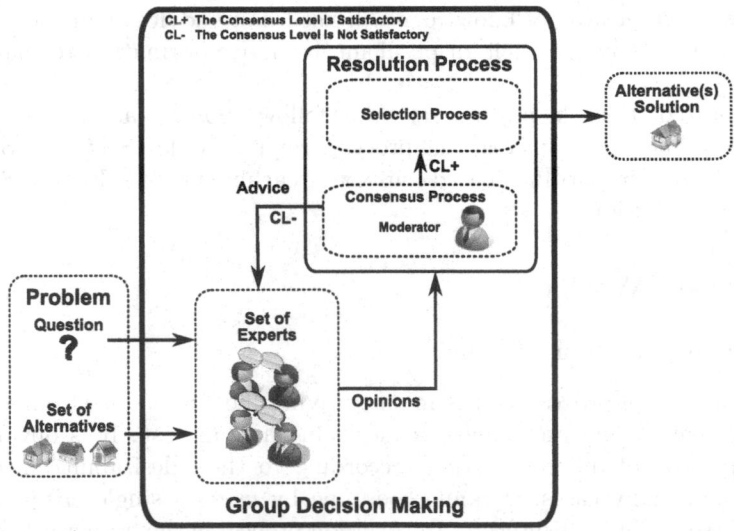

Fig. 1. Resolution process of a GDM

preferences according to the advice given by the moderator. The moderator plays a key role in this process. Normally, the moderator is a person who does not participate in the discussion but knows the preferences of each expert and the level of agreement during the consensus process. He is in charge of supervising and driving the consensus process toward success, i.e., to achieve the maximum possible agreement and reduce the number of experts outside of the consensus in each new consensus round.

Usually, the moderator carries out three main tasks: (i) to compute the consensus measures, (ii) to check the level of agreement and (iii) to produce some advice for those experts that should change their minds. (See Figure 2)

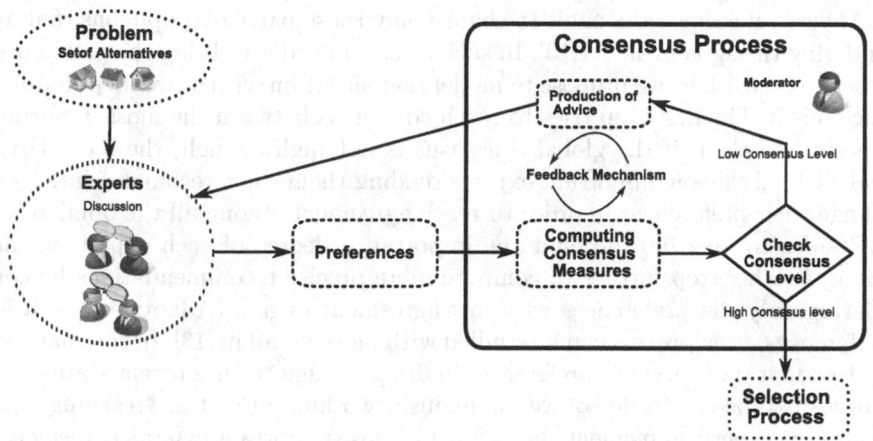

Fig. 2. Classical consensus reaching process

In order to evaluate the agreement, it is required to compute similarity measures among the experts [3,7,17,18]. Two types of measurements to guide the consensus reaching process were proposed in [3]:

1. *Consensus degrees* to evaluate the level of agreement among all the experts. They will be used to identify the preference values where the agreement is not sufficient.
2. *Proximity measures* to evaluate the distance among the experts individual preferences and the group or collective one. They will be used to identify the experts who should change their preferences in the next rounds.

These measurements are computed at the three different levels of representation of a preference relation: pairs of alternatives, alternatives, and relation.

3   Importance-Based Consensus Reaching Process

In heterogeneous GDM scenarios that include a large number of experts with different levels and kind of knowledge, could be necessary to take into account the importance degree of each expert in order to compute the global consensus degree in

a more appropriate and realistic way. Usually, these situations have been modeled
by some authors by including the weights in the computation of the global preferences [4,5,9,11,19,20]. In this contribution, we use the experts' importance on
the discussion phase to generate importance based recommendations and present
a new importance based feedback mechanism that sends different recommendations to the experts according to their own importance degrees.

When the agreement among all experts is low, we can notice one of the following two different reasons. The first one is that the opinions of a few important
experts were far away from each other. The second possibility is that, being
agreement among all the important experts, there exists many low-important
experts in disagreement [11].

Anyway, it seems reasonable to change only those particular opinions that are
hindering the agreement [11,13]. In such a case, in order to bring the preferences
closer to each other, we propose to model that situation with a two-step feedback
mechanism. The first step tries to reach consensus between the most important
experts and then, if the global consensus is not high enough, the second step
deal with all the low-important experts sending them some recommendations to
change their preferences in order to reach agreement among all the opinions.

Besides to take into account the importance degree of each expert, we are
taking another step further to compute more precise recommendations by considering only the preferences with low agreement degree (Adaptive Search for
Preferences), this process can be studied with more detail in [13]. In summary, we
try to adapt the search for preferences in disagreement to the current state of the
consensus process. To do so, we distinguish two kind of states, "reaching high-
important experts agreement" and "reaching low-important experts agreement".
When we are dealing with hight-important experts, it is obvious that their opinions belong to a wider knowledge than the remaining ones. In such a case, only
a few number of changes of opinions might lead to consensus. Similarly, when
the experts have low-importance, a high number of changes of opinions might
be necessary to achieve consensus. Thus, two different methods to identify the
preferences that each expert should modify, in order to increase the consensus
level in the next consensus round, are defined.

Then, we present an importance-based consensus reaching process in order to
compute more suitable advice composed of three stages (see Figure 3).

1. *Computing Consensus Degrees and Control the Consensus Process.*
2. *Importance-Based Search for Preferences.*
3. *Production of advice.*

3.1 Computing Consensus Degree and Control the Consensus Process

Once the preferences have been given, we can compute the level of agreement
achieved in the current round. To do so, we firstly define for each pair of experts
(e^k, e^l) $(k < l)$ a similarity matrix $SM^{kl} = (sm_{ij}^{kl})$ where

$$sm_{ij}^{kl} = (1 - |p_{ij}^k - p_{ij}^l|)$$

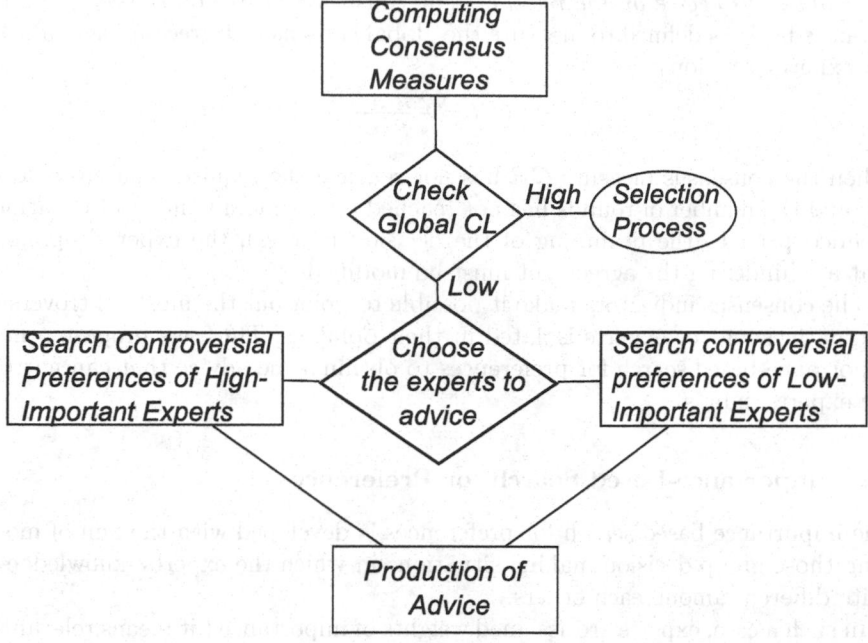

Fig. 3. Importance-based consensus reaching process

Then, a consensus matrix, CM, is calculated by aggregating all the similarity matrices using the arithmetic mean as the aggregation function ϕ:

$$cm_{ij} = \phi(sm_{ij}^{12}, sm_{ij}^{13}, \ldots, sm_{ij}^{1m}, sm_{ij}^{23}, \ldots, sm_{ij}^{(m-1)m}).$$

Once the similarity and consensus matrices are computed we proceed to obtain the consensus degrees at the three different levels to obtain a global consensus degree, called consensus on the relation:

1. *Consensus degree on pairs of alternatives.* The consensus degree on a pair of alternatives (x_i, x_j), denoted cop_{ij}, is defined to measure the consensus degree amongst all the experts on that pair of alternatives:

$$cop_{ij} = cm_{ij}$$

2. *Consensus degree on alternatives.* The consensus degree on alternative x_i, denoted ca_i, is defined to measure the consensus degree amongst all the experts on that alternative:

$$ca_i = \frac{\sum_{j=1;j\neq i}^{n}(cop_{ij} + cop_{ji})}{2(n-1)}$$

3. *Consensus degree on the relation.* The consensus degree on the relation, denoted CR, is defined to measure the global consensus degree amongst all the
   experts' opinions:

$$CR = \frac{\sum_{i=1}^{n} ca_i}{n}$$

When the consensus measure CR has not reached the required consensus level
CL and the number of rounds has not reached a maximum number of iterations
(defined prior to the beginning of the decision process), the experts' opinions
that are hindering the agreement must be modified.

The consensus indicators make it possible to point out the most controversial
alternatives and/or experts isolated in their opinions. Thus, we propose a new
importance-based search for preferences to obtain some advice that can narrow
the experts' minds.

3.2   Importance-Based Search for Preferences

The importance-based search for preferences is developed with the aim of modeling those group decision making situations in which the experts' knowledge is
quite different among each others.

In such a case, experts are assigned weights of importance (it means relevance,
competence, confidence,...) modeled as a fuzzy subset I where the membership
function $\mu_I(e_k) \in [0, 1]$ denotes a degree of importance of the expert e_k.

The preferred method for some authors [4,5,9,19,20] is to use the weight values
like an aggregation operator's parameter and, in this way, to obtain a weighted
collective opinion. However, in this contribution, we are modeling the importance
in a different way [11].

To do so, the experts are included by their own importance degree into two
different subsets E_{High} and E_{Low} in the following way:

– if $\mu_I(e_k) > \lambda_1 \rightarrow e_k \in E_{High}$, and
– if $\mu_I(e_k) < \lambda_2 \rightarrow e_k \in E_{Low}$.

Where λ_1 and λ_2 are two threshold parameters whose values depend on the
problem dealt with.

At first, the process is focused on reaching consensus between the experts
in E_{High}. Then, the second step tries to narrow the opinions of the experts
in E_{Low} to the global opinion. Consequently, if the consensus degree among
experts in E_{High} is not high enough, we should identify the preferences of the
high-important experts to be changed in order to reach agreement between them.
Otherwise, if that agreement has been already reached, we should identify the
preferences of the low-important experts to be changed in order to reach a global
agreement.

1. **Identify High-Important Experts' Controversial Preferences**
   In this situation, we are only dealing with experts whose knowledge level
   is so high that does not need to be strongly modified in order to get a

good solution. Therefore, the agreement can be improved by suggesting a few changes, that is, we only need to change the mind of those experts who have proximity values on the pairs of alternatives identified in disagreement smaller than an specific proximity threshold at level of pairs of alternatives.

2. **Identify Low-Important Experts' Controversial Preferences**
   In the last consensus rounds, the system advises experts with low knowledge or confidence level. It seems reasonable that, a priori, these experts can make more mistakes. Thus, the agreement should be improved by suggesting more changes that in the previous case. To do this, the procedure tries to modify the preference values on all the pairs of alternatives where the agreement is not high enough.

It is worth noting that both searching methods have been previously used to solve a different adaptive reaching consensus model based on the current consensus level. It can be studied with more detail in [13].

3.3 Production of Advice

Once that the system has identified the preferences to be changed depending on the importance degree of the experts, the model shows the right direction of the changes in order to achieve the agreement. For each preference value to be changed, the model will suggest increasing or decreasing the current assessment.

In this contribution, we use a mechanism based on a set of direction rules to identify and suggest the changes [13]. These rules compare the central values of the individual and collective preference assessments $cv(p_{ij}^k)$ and $cv(p_{ij}^c)$. The central value represents the center of gravity of the information contained in the set [13].

As there are two different consensus levels to be reached, at first, in order to reach agreement between high-important experts, the collective preference refers the aggregated preferences from experts in E_{High} and is noted as $p_{ij}^{\sim c}$.

The direction rules in this case are as follows.

- if $(cv(p_{ij}^k) - cv(p_{ij}^{\sim c})) < 0$, then the expert e_k should increase the assessments associated with the pair of alternatives (x_i, x_j).
- if $(cv(p_{ij}^k) - cv(p_{ij}^{\sim c})) > 0$, then the expert e_k should decrease the assessments associated with the pair of alternatives (x_i, x_j).
- if $(cv(p_{ij}^k) - cv(p_{ij}^{\sim c})) = 0$, then the expert e_k should not modify the assessments associated with the pair of alternatives (x_i, x_j).

Once the first objective has been achieved, the next one is to close the preferences of the remaining experts. So, the direction rules are similar, the only change is that the collective preference refers the aggregated preferences from all the experts instead of only the important ones.

- if $(cv(p_{ij}^k) - cv(p_{ij}^c)) < 0$, then the expert e_k should increase the assessments associated with the pair of alternatives (x_i, x_j).
- if $(cv(p_{ij}^k) - cv(p_{ij}^c)) > 0$, then the expert e_k should decrease the assessments associated with the pair of alternatives (x_i, x_j).

- if $(cv(p_{ij}^k) - cv(p_{ij}^c) = 0)$, then the expert e_k should not modify the assessments associated with the pair of alternatives (x_i, x_j).

Finally, it is worth noting that the changes suggested are only recommendations presented for consideration to the experts and they decide if and how to take them into account.

4   Concluding Remarks

In this contribution we have presented a novel consensus approach which has been specially designed to model heterogeneous decision contexts. Assuming fuzzy preference relations to express experts' preferences and different levels of importance in their preferences we present a consensus model in which the more important experts lead the discussion of the consensus reaching process. Moreover, the feedback mechanism computes different kind of recommendations according to the expert importance levels.

Acknowledgements

This paper has been developed with the financing of FEDER funds in FUZZYLING project (TIN2007-61079), PETRI project (PET2007-0460), project of Ministry of Public Works (90/07) and Excellence Andalusian Project (TIC5299).

References

1. Chiclana, F., Herrera, F., Herrera-Viedma, E.: Integrating three representation models in fuzzy multipurpose decision making based on fuzzy preference relations. Fuzzy Sets and Systems 97(1), 33–48 (1998)
2. Chiclana, F., Herrera, F., Herrera-Viedma, E.: Integrating multiplicative preference relations in a multiplicative decision making model based on fuzzy preference relations. Fuzzy Sets and Systems 122(2), 277–291 (2001)
3. Herrera, F., Herrera-Viedma, E., Verdegay, J.L.: A model of consensus in group decision making under linguistic assessments. Fuzzy Sets and Systems 78(1), 73–87 (1996)
4. Herrera, F., Herrera-Viedma, E., Verdegay, J.L.: Direct approach processes in group decision making using linguistic owa operators. Fuzzy Sets and Systems 79, 175–190 (1996)
5. Herrera, F., Herrera-Viedma, E.: Aggregation operators for linguistic weighted information. IEEE Transactions on Systems, Man, and Cybernetics. Part A: Systems and Humans 27, 646–656 (1997)
6. Kacprzyk, J.: Group decision making with a fuzzy linguistic majority. Fuzzy Sets and Systems 18, 105–118 (1986)
7. Kacprzyk, J., Fedrizzi, M.: A soft measure of consensus in the setting of partial (fuzzy) preferences. Eur. J. Oper. Res. 34, 316–323 (1988)
8. Kacprzyk, J., Fedrizzi, M.: Multiperson decision making models using fuzzy sets and possibility theory. Kluwer Academic Publishers, Dordrecht (1990)
9. Kacprzyk, J., Fedrizzi, M., Nurmi, H.: Group decision making and consensus under fuzzy preferences and fuzzy majority. Fuzzy Sets and Systems 49, 21–31 (1992)

10. Kacprzyk, J., Nurmi, H., Fedrizzi, M.: Consensus under fuzziness. Kluwer Academic Publishers, Boston (1997)
11. Kacprzyk, J., Zadrozny, S., Ras, Z.W.: Action Rules in Consensus Reaching Process Support. In: 9th International Conference on Intelligent Systems Design and Applications (ISDA '09), Pisa (Italy), November 30 - December 2, pp. 809–814 (2009)
12. Lu, J., Zhang, G., Ruan, D.: Intelligent multi-criteria fuzzy group decision-making for situation assessments. Soft Computing 12, 289–299 (2008)
13. Mata, F., Martinez, L., Herrera-Viedma, E.: An Adaptive Consensus Support Model for Group Decision Making Problems in a Multi-Granular Fuzzy Linguistic Context. IEEE Transactions on Fuzzy Systems 17(2), 279–290 (2009)
14. Montero, J.: The impact of fuzziness in social choice paradoxes. Soft Computing 12, 177–182 (2008)
15. Nurmi, H.: Fuzzy social choice: a selective retrospect. Soft Computing 12, 281–288 (2008)
16. Roubens, M.: Fuzzy sets and decision analysis. Fuzzy Sets and Systems 90(2), 199–206 (1997)
17. Herrera-Viedma, E., Herrera, F., Chiclana, F.: A consensus model for multiperson decision making with different preference structures. IEEE Trans. Syst. Man Cybern., Part A: Syst. Hum. 32, 394–402 (2002)
18. Herrera-Viedma, E., Martinez, L., Mata, F., Chiclana, F.: A consensus support system model for group decision-making problems with multi-granular linguistic preference relations. IEEE Trans. Fuzzy Syst. 13, 644–658 (2005)
19. Yager, R.: On ordered weighted averaging aggregation operators in multicriteria decision making. IEEE Transactions on Systems, Man, and Cybernetics 18(1), 183–190 (1988)
20. Yager, R.: Weighted maximum entropy owa aggregation with applications to decision making under risk. IEEE Transactions on Systems, Man, and Cybernetics part A-Systems and Humans 39(3), 555–564 (2009)

On the Robustness for the Choquet Integral*

Christophe Labreuche

Thales Research & Technology
Campus de Polytechnique
1 avenue Augustin Fresnel
91767 Palaiseau Cedex, France

Abstract. Preference modeling consists in constructing a preference relation from initial preferences given by a decision maker. We are interested in the preference relation obtained from the use of the Choquet integral. We give some properties related to the completeness of the necessary preference relation and its comparison with the traditional approach where the preference obtained from a unique fuzzy measure. Moreover, an axiomatization of the necessary and possibility preference relations is proposed.

1 Introduction

Multi-Criteria Decision Aid (MCDA) aims at representing the preferences of a Decision Maker (DM) over some options described by a finite set $N = \{1, \ldots, n\}$ of points of view or attributes. Attribute $i \in N$ is described by a set X_i, and the set of potential options is the Cartesian product $X = X_1 \times \cdots \times X_n$. We are interested in this paper in the case where the preference relation can be described by an overall utility in which the aggregation of the criteria is obtained with the Choquet integral. The preference model is then thoroughly constructed once the parameters of the Choquet integral - namely the fuzzy measure - are determined. The DM is usually not interested in all options in X. We denote by $Y \subseteq X$ the set of alternatives of interest for the DM. The goal of decision aid is to propose a recommendation regarding the options in Y.

To this end, the DM provides some preferential information. Unfortunately, there does not usually exist one single fuzzy measure that fulfills this preferential information. Up to recently, most of the elicitation methods based on the Choquet integral consisted in selecting the fuzzy measure that fulfills the preferential information, and that maximizes some functional [1,2,3]. Then the recommendation on Y was made on the basis of the preference relation obtained by the Choquet integral w.r.t. this unique fuzzy measure. This will be referred to as the *traditional approach* in this paper. This preference relation has been extensively studied in the literature. There are several axiomatic characterizations of this representation [4,5].

---

* The work has been sponsored by the MOVIDA project funded by the ANR (French National Research Agency).

E. Hüllermeier, R. Kruse, and F. Hoffmann (Eds.): IPMU 2010, LNAI 6178, pp. 484–493, 2010.

However, the recommendation made by this unique fuzzy measure infers much more than what the DM originally said. The concepts of *necessity* and *possibility* preference relations have been recently introduced to overcome this limitation by providing robust recommendations [6,7]. It has been applied to the Choquet integral in [8]. An option is *necessarily* preferred to another option according to the necessity preference relation, if the first option is preferred to the second one according to all models that fulfill the preferential information provided by the DM. This necessity preference relation can thus be incomplete.

The DM usually has two requirements on the recommendation: the recommendations on Y shall be (i) sure (the recommendation shall be a deduction of the preferential information) and (ii) complete (i.e. a comparison is proposed for each pair of options in Y). Generally speaking, the robust preference relations satisfy (i) but not (ii), and the opposite for the traditional approach. Since the concept of robust preference relations is new, one may wonder whether the recommendations prior to the introduction of this concept were meaningless. Actually, it depends on the subset Y.

The aim of this paper is twofold.

First, we are interested in the special case when $Y = X$ (see Section 4). In the literature, the set Y of the options of interest for the DM is often assumed to be finite and of small cardinality. The situation where $Y = X$ occurs when the options of interest for the DM are not known during the construction of the multi-criteria model. We show that, when $Y = X$, these two requirements (i) and (ii) are satisfied if and only if the preferential information is sufficient to uniquely fix the values of the fuzzy measure. This is the only case when the use of the traditional approach and the robust one yield the same recommendation. However, the DM must provide a large amount of data to uniquely fix the fuzzy measure and one cannot expect this from the DM. When the preferential information is significant (but not sufficient to uniquely specify the fuzzy measure), we show that the necessary preference relation is almost complete. Moreover, we provide an a priori estimate of the worse error in the computation of the overall utility when using the traditional approaches. This gives a justification of the traditional approach when $Y = X$.

When $Y \neq X$, one feels that it is sufficient that the DM provides less infor mation (compare to when $Y = X$). This cannot be easily exploited with the traditional approach, and the necessity and possibility preference relations are very useful tools in an interactive approach with the DM to construct sure preferences over Y. However, unlike the preference obtained from a unique fuzzy measure (traditional approach), very little is known about the robust preference relations. Although a few properties have been identified [6,7], there is still no axiomatic characterization. The behavior of the necessary preference relation was studied on several particular cases of preferential information [9]. These examples show that the completion produced by the necessity preference relation is quite natural. It is crucial for applications to better understand the behavior of the robust preference relations. We propose in Section 5 an axiomatic characterization of the necessary and possibility preference relations.

2 Background

2.1 Choquet Integral

A *fuzzy measure* (also called *capacity*) on a set $N = \{1, \ldots, n\}$ of criteria is a set function $\mu : 2^N \to [0, 1]$ such that [10]

- $\mu(\emptyset) = 0$, $\mu(N) = 1$ (boundary conditions),
- $\forall A \subseteq B \subseteq N$, $\mu(A) \leq \mu(B)$ (monotonicity).

Let $\mathcal{M}$ be the set of all fuzzy measures. The *Choquet integral* of $a = (a_1, \ldots, a_n) \in \mathbb{R}^n$ defined w.r.t. a capacity μ has the following expression [11] :

$$C_\mu(a_1, \ldots, a_n) = \sum_{i=1}^{n} \left(a_{\sigma_a(i)} - a_{\sigma_a(i-1)} \right) \times \mu\left(\{\sigma_a(i), \cdots, \sigma_a(n)\} \right),$$

where σ_a is a permutation on N such that $a_{\sigma_a(1)} \leq a_{\sigma_a(2)} \leq \cdots \leq a_{\sigma_a(n)}$, and $a_{\sigma_a(0)} := 0$. The Choquet integral has been proved to be able to model both the importance of criteria and the interaction between criteria.

2.2 k-Additive Capacities

We introduce a useful linear transformation of fuzzy measures. The *Möbius transform* m of a fuzzy measure μ is the unique solution of the equation

$$\forall A \subseteq N \qquad \mu(A) = \sum_{B \subseteq A} m(B), \tag{1}$$

and is given by $m^\mu(A) := \sum_{B \subseteq A} (-1)^{|A|-|B|} \mu(B)$.

A fuzzy measure is defined by 2^n coefficients, which is much more than a weighted sum. The concept of *k-additive* fuzzy measure has a complexity in-between a fuzzy measure and a weighted sum. More precisely, a fuzzy measure μ is said to be *k-additive* [12] if $m^\mu(A) = 0$ whenever $|A| > k$ and there exists A with $|A| = k$ such that $m^\mu(A) \neq 0$. We denote by $\mathcal{M}^k$ the set of fuzzy measures that are at most k-additive (i.e. 1, or 2, or ..., or k additive). Note that $\mathcal{M} = \mathcal{M}^n$. For the rest of the paper, we fix $k \in \{1, \ldots, n\}$ and we will consider only k-additive capacities, unless explicitly specified.

3 Robust Preference Relations

We focus in this paper on the aggregation part of the multi-criteria model. The utility functions which maps the attributes onto a commensurate scale $\mathbb{R}$ are not our concern here. Hence, we assume that the attributes are directly given in the commensurate scale – i.e. $X_i = \mathbb{R}$ – and thus that $X = \mathbb{R}^N$.

In order to give a recommendation to the DM on the options in Y, some preferential information is asked to the DM. Many types of preferential information are considered in the literature [1,2,3,8]. In practice, it turns out that the most meaningful preferential information for the DM is composed of comparisons of options in X. For the sake of simplicity, we assume thus that the preferential information is composed of a partial order $\unrhd$ over X. For $x, y \in X$, relation $x \unrhd y$ means that the DM finds x at least as good as y. $\unrhd$ is seen as a subset of $X \times X$. This type of preferential information is the most widely used one. Incorporating other types of preferential information would not change the results that are shown in this paper.

We denote by $\mathcal{M}^k(\unrhd)$ the set of fuzzy measures in $\mathcal{M}^k$ that satisfy the preferential information $\unrhd$:

$$\mathcal{M}^k(\unrhd) = \left\{ \mu \in \mathcal{M}^k \ : \forall a, b \in X \quad a \unrhd b \ \Rightarrow \ C_\mu(a) \geq C_\mu(b) \right\}$$

We can show the following results.

Lemma 1. *We have for all* $\unrhd, \unrhd' \subseteq X \times X$

(i) $\unrhd \subseteq \unrhd' \implies \mathcal{M}^k(\unrhd) \supseteq \mathcal{M}^k(\unrhd')$
(ii) $\mathcal{M}^k(\unrhd \cup \unrhd') = \mathcal{M}^k(\unrhd) \cap \mathcal{M}^k(\unrhd')$
(iii) $\mathcal{M}^k(\unrhd \cap \unrhd') \supseteq \mathcal{M}^k(\unrhd) \cup \mathcal{M}^k(\unrhd')$

Our aim is to construct a preference relation denoted by $\succsim_\unrhd$ depending on $\unrhd$. In order to produce a precise recommendation on Y, $\succsim_\unrhd$ should be a total preorder (i.e. reflexive, transitive and complete) over Y. We now describe several ways to obtain $\succsim_\unrhd$.

As said in the introduction, the traditional approach to construct a recommendation on the set Y of options of interest consists in selecting a particular fuzzy measure in $\mathcal{M}^k(\unrhd)$. It is chosen as a (the) solution to an optimization problem

$$\max_{\mu \in \mathcal{M}^k(\unrhd)} F_\unrhd(\mu)$$

where $F_\unrhd$ is a function depending on $\unrhd$ to be maximized. Given a solution μ of the previous problem, the recommendation provided to the DM over the options in Y is then based on $\succsim_\mu$, where $\succsim_\mu$ is the preference relation derived from C_μ:

$$\forall a, b \in X \qquad a \succsim_\mu b \iff C_\mu(a) > C_\mu(b). \tag{2}$$

A preference relation $\succsim_\unrhd$ is said to be *representable by a Choquet integral* if there exists a fuzzy measure $\mu \in \mathcal{M}^k$ such that $\succsim_\unrhd = \succsim_\mu$.

The *necessity preference relation* (*NPR* in short) on X is a cautious way to take into account the fact that the aggregation model is not uniquely determined from $\unrhd$, and is defined by [8,6,7]:

$$\forall a, b \in X \quad , \quad a \succsim_{N,\unrhd} b \iff [\forall \mu \in \mathcal{M}^k(\unrhd) \quad C_\mu(a) \geq C_\mu(b)] \ .$$

It is easy to see that $\succsim_{N,\unrhd}$ is usually incomplete, but is transitive and reflexive. One can also define [9]

$$\forall a, b \in X \quad , \quad a \sim_{N,\unrhd} b \iff [\forall \mu \in \mathcal{M}^k(\unrhd) \quad C_\mu(a) = C_\mu(b)]$$
$$\forall a, b \in X \quad , \quad a \succ_{N,\unrhd} b \iff [\forall \mu \in \mathcal{M}^k(\unrhd) \quad C_\mu(a) > C_\mu(b)]$$

Another interesting order relation derived from $\trianglerighteq$ is the so-called *possibility preference relation* (*PPR* in short) defined as follows [8,6,7]:

$$\forall a, b \in X \quad , \quad a \succsim_{\Pi,\trianglerighteq} b \iff [\exists \mu \in \mathcal{M}^k(\trianglerighteq) \; C_\mu(a) \geq C_\mu(b)] .$$

4   The Particular Case of $Y = X$

Let us first give some motivating examples of the case when $Y = X$. The decision model can be implemented in a decision support system. There are many applications in which a decision has to be taken repetitively. One may think of a training system that assesses trainees. Another example of this situation is the multi-criteria decision function that recommends the assignment of priorities to the radar tasks in radar management [13]. A third example is the design of complex systems in which A last example is the call for tenders in which, for transparency reasons, the multi-criteria evaluation model must be made before the proposals are sent [14]. In these examples, at the time when the decision support system is designed, one does not know the options that will be evaluated. One acts as if all potential options could later be assessed with the model. This means that the multi-criteria model shall produce relevant and precise recommendations for all elements of X.

4.1   Completeness of the Robust Preference Relation

Let us denote by $\succsim_{\mathcal{P}a}$ the Pareto dominance order:

$$\succsim_{\mathcal{P}a} := \{(a, b) \in \mathbb{R}^n \; , \; \forall i \in N \; a_i \geq b_i\} .$$

The comparisons obtained from the Pareto order are clearly satisfied for every possible fuzzy measure. Hence these comparisons are also obtained by the NPR and PPR:

$$\forall \trianglerighteq \subseteq X \times X \quad \succsim_{N,\trianglerighteq} \supseteq \succsim_{\mathcal{P}a} \quad \text{and} \quad \succsim_{\Pi,\trianglerighteq} \supseteq \succsim_{\mathcal{P}a} . \tag{3}$$

The following result shows that when $Y = X$, robust preference relations provide the same recommendations as traditional preference relation (2). It requires to completely specify the fuzzy measure from $\trianglerighteq$.

Proposition 1. *Let $\trianglerighteq \subseteq X \times X$. The following statements are equivalent*

(i) $\succsim_{N,\trianglerighteq} = \succsim_{\Pi,\trianglerighteq}$,
(ii) $\succsim_{N,\trianglerighteq}$ *is complete in* X,
(iii) $\succsim_{N,\trianglerighteq}$ *is representable by a Choquet integral,*
(iv) $\mathcal{M}^k(\trianglerighteq)$ *is reduced to a singleton.*

4.2   Case When $\mathcal{M}^k(\trianglerighteq)$ Is Small

We wish to know how a variation in a fuzzy measure induces a variation in the associated preference relation. It would be desirable that a small difference between two fuzzy measures implies a small difference between their preference relations. If we are able to quantify these differences and to relate them, we will have a way to quantify the completeness of the NPR when $\mathcal{M}^k(\unrhd)$ is reduced to a singleton. In order to achieve that, we are going to define distances in both the set of admissible fuzzy measures (i.e., the set of fuzzy measures satisfying the preferential information) and the set of preference relations.

Definition 1. *We define the* distance *between two fuzzy measures* μ_1, μ_2 *as*

$$d_{\text{fm}}(\mu_1, \mu_2) := \max_{A \subseteq N} |\mu_1(A) - \mu_2(A)| \quad \forall \mu_1, \mu_2 \in \mathcal{M}^k.$$

We define the diameter *of* $M \subseteq \mathcal{M}^k$ *as*

$$\text{diam}(M) = \max_{\mu_1, \mu_2 \in M} d_{\text{fm}}(\mu_1, \mu_2).$$

The diameter of $\mathcal{M}^k(\unrhd)$ measures the maximum distance between two admissible fuzzy measures.

Definition 2. *We define the* distance *between two preference relations representable by a Choquet integral by*

$$d_{\text{pr}}(\succeq_{\mu_1}, \succeq_{\mu_2}) = \max_{a \in X \,:\, \|a\| \neq 0} \frac{|C_{\mu_1}(a) - C_{\mu_2}(a)|}{\|a\|} \quad \forall \mu_1, \mu_2 \in M$$

where $\|a\| = \max_{i \in N} a_i - \min_{i \in N} a_i$.

As in the case of the fuzzy measures, d_{pr} is distance. The following lemma shows that the distance on the fuzzy measures is strongly related to the distance on the preference relations.

Lemma 2. *Let* $M \subseteq \mathcal{M}^k$. *We have*

$$d_{\text{pr}}(\succeq_{\mu_1}, \succeq_{\mu_2}) = d_{\text{fm}}(\mu_1, \mu_2)$$
$$\max_{\mu_1, \mu_2 \in M} d_{\text{pr}}(\succeq_{\mu_1}, \succeq_{\mu_2}) = \text{diam}(M) \,.$$

This lemma is very important. In order to make sure that all possible preference relations within $\mathcal{M}^k(\unrhd)$ are close enough one another, one shall check that $\max_{\mu_1, \mu_2 \in \mathcal{M}^k(\unrhd)} d_{\text{pr}}(\succeq_{C_{\mu_1}}, \succeq_{C_{\mu_2}})$ is small enough. This quantity is not quite easy to compute. Lemma 2 states that it is sufficient to compute $\text{diam}(\mathcal{M}^k(\unrhd))$, which is easy to obtain. Indeed, let us define $\underline{\mu_\unrhd}$ and $\overline{\mu_\unrhd}$ by

$$\forall A \subseteq N \quad \underline{\mu_\unrhd}(A) := \min_{\mu \in \mathcal{M}^k(\unrhd)} \mu(A) \text{ and } \overline{\mu_\unrhd}(A) := \max_{\mu \in \mathcal{M}^k(\unrhd)} \mu(A) \,.$$

These two values are computed with the help of a linear programming solver. Then the diameter of $\mathcal{M}^k(\unrhd)$ is computed from the formulae

$$\text{diam}(\mathcal{M}^k(\unrhd)) = \max_{A \subseteq N} \left(\overline{\mu_\unrhd}(A) - \underline{\mu_\unrhd}(A) \right) \,.$$

Since the DM is not able to provide sufficiently many preferential information to uniquely specify the preference relation, one cannot expect for instance that indifference corresponds to a strict equality. Then indifference is no longer transitive, which yields to a semi-order. Semi-orders are defined by a threshold $\lambda \in \mathbb{R}_+$ where the strict preference holds when the difference of scores is larger than the threshold λ. Applying this for the PPR, we define $\succsim^{\lambda}_{\Pi,\unrhd}$ by

$$\forall a, b \in X \qquad a \succsim^{\lambda}_{\Pi,\unrhd} b \iff [\exists \mu \in \mathcal{M}^k(\unrhd) \;\; C_\mu(a) \geq C_\mu(b) + \lambda].$$

When a is preferred to b, we have a margin λ.

Proposition 2. *Let $\varepsilon > 0$, $r > 0$ and $s \in \mathbb{R}$. Assume that $\mathrm{diam}(\mathcal{M}^k(\unrhd)) \leq \varepsilon$. Then*

$$\succsim^{2r\varepsilon}_{\Pi,\unrhd} \cap [s, s+r]^N \subseteq \succsim_{N,\unrhd} \cap [s, s+r]^N.$$

If ε is small and $r = 1$ (considering the standard $[0,1]$ scale), $\succsim^{2\varepsilon}_{\Pi,\unrhd}$ is almost complete (since $\succsim_{\Pi,\unrhd}$ is complete) and so is $\succsim_{N,\unrhd}$. A preorder $\succsim$ is said to be *almost complete* in $[s, s+r]^N$ if the set of pairs (a, b) in $[s, s+r]^N$ for which we have neither $a \succsim b$ nor $b \succsim a$ has a small measure compare to the measure r^N of $[s, s+r]^N$. This shows that the NPR is almost complete when ε is small. Moreover, we see that the larger the evaluation scale (i.e. the larger r), the worse the estimate becomes.

5   An Axiomatization of the Robust Preference Relations

The NPR and the PPR are both useful in an interactive decision aid process [9]. The NPR is used to provide the (final) recommendations to the DM over the options in Y. If the DM finds that the recommendation made is not sufficient, he may add new preferential information to $\unrhd$. In this case, these new preferential information shall belong to the PPR.

In this section, we are interested in an axiomatic characterization of the NPR and the PPR. The problem is stated as follows:

Given the preferential information $\unrhd$ provided by the DM, what is the preference relation over X that extends $\unrhd$?

This statement has some similarities with decision making under risk (DMUR). In DMUR, the elements of N are the states representing the possible situations, $X_1 = \cdots = X_n =: C$ is the set of possible consequences, and an alternative (also called act) is a mapping from N to C, that is $X = C^N$. The consequence of selecting a particular alternative depends on which state of nature will occur. Moreover the attitude of the DM towards risk influences his choice strategy [15]. In DMUR, a specification of the uncertainty over the states of nature is known. This is quite close to the preferential information $\unrhd$. In DMUR, one aims at constructing a preference relation over X from the specification of the uncertainty over the states of nature. However, the parallel cannot go further since the preference relation in DMUR is always complete, which is not the case for us.

We suppose that $\trianglerighteq$ is given. We denote by $\succsim_{\trianglerighteq}$ the wished preference model.

5.1   General Properties

First of all, the preferential information $\trianglerighteq$ shall be satisfied by the preference model $\succsim_{\trianglerighteq}$, which yields the following property.

A1. $\trianglerighteq \,\subseteq\, \succsim_{\trianglerighteq}$.

As we have already said in the introduction, the preference relation $\succsim_{\trianglerighteq}$ has been axiomatized by Schmeidler [4]. This preference relation is a total preorder. We wish to subsume into this situation the case where $\succsim_{\trianglerighteq}$ turns out to be a total preorder. When $\succsim_{\trianglerighteq}$ is complete, we are in the situation of Section 4.1. Since we are interested in the Choquet integral, we assume that this complete order is representable by a Choquet integral. Following Proposition 1, we propose the following property on $\succsim_{\trianglerighteq}$.

A2. If $\succsim_{\trianglerighteq}$ is complete, then $\succsim_{\trianglerighteq}$ is representable by a Choquet integral.

The NPR and PPR satisfy the two above properties.

5.2   Case of the NPR

The mapping $\trianglerighteq \,\mapsto\, \succsim_{\trianglerighteq}$ is isotone. With the NPR, the larger preferential information (i.e. the larger $\trianglerighteq$ in the sense of the set inclusion), the more recommendations one can make.

A3^N. If $\trianglerighteq \,\subseteq\, \trianglerighteq'$, then $\succsim_{\trianglerighteq}\,\subseteq\,\succsim_{\trianglerighteq'}$.

The following result provides a characterization of the NPR.

Theorem 1. $\succsim_{N,\trianglerighteq}$ *is the largest (in the sense of $\subseteq$) order relation $\succsim_{\trianglerighteq}$ satisfying* **A2** *and* **A3^N.**

We consider other axioms satisfied by the NPR.

A4^N. $\succsim_{\trianglerighteq} \cup \succsim_{\trianglerighteq'}\,\subseteq\,\succsim_{\trianglerighteq\cup\trianglerighteq'}$.

A5^N. If $\trianglerighteq = \emptyset$, then $\succsim_{\trianglerighteq}=\succsim_{Pa}$.

This property, which can be found in [9], extends [6, Remark 4.1] to the case of the Choquet integral. It is related to (3).

5.3   Case of the PPR

A first property of the PPR is that there are complete (unlike the NPR).

The mapping $\unrhd \mapsto \succsim_{\unrhd}$ is anti-isotone. With the PPR, the larger preferential information (i.e. the larger $\unrhd$ in the sense of the set inclusion), the less comparisons are possible.

A3$^{\Pi}$. If $\unrhd \subseteq \unrhd'$, then $\succsim_{\unrhd} \supset \succsim_{\unrhd'}$.

The following result provides a characterization of the PPR.

Theorem 2. $\succsim_{\Pi,\unrhd}$ is the smallest (in the sense of $\subseteq$) order relation $\succsim_{\unrhd}$ satisfying **A2** and **A3$^{\Pi}$**.

We consider other axioms satisfied by the PPR.

A4$^{\Pi}$. $\succsim_{\unrhd \cup \unrhd'} \subseteq \succsim_{\unrhd} \cap \succsim_{\unrhd'}$.

Let us denote by $\succ_{\mathcal{P}a}$ the strict Pareto dominance order:

$$\succ_{\mathcal{P}a} := \{(a,b) \in X \ , \ \forall i \in N \ \ a_i \geq b_i \quad \text{and} \quad \exists i \in N \ \ a_i > b_i\} \ .$$

A5$^{\Pi}$. If $\unrhd = \emptyset$, then $\succsim_{\unrhd} = X \times X \setminus \succ_{\mathcal{P}a}^{-1}$.

5.4   Discussion

We can make a connection between the NPR and PPR, and the necessity and possibility distributions.

Assume that a variable V ranging on a domain U can be described by a possibility distribution $\pi_V : U \to [0,1]$, where $\pi_V(u)$ is the degree of possibility that V is equal to u [16]. A possibility distribution aims at discarding the elements of the set U that are inconsistent with the knowledge. In particular, two pieces of information "V is A_1" and "V is A_2" (where A_1 and A_2 are fuzzy sets on U represented by the membership functions π_{A_1} and π_{A_2} respectively) are represented by the inequality $\pi_V(u) \leq \min(\pi_{A_1}(u), \pi_{A_2}(u))$ for all $u \in U$. It is easy to see that **A4$^{\Pi}$** is the counterpart of this inequality. Indeed $\unrhd$ and $\unrhd'$ play the role of the two pieces of information, $\succsim_{\unrhd \cup \unrhd'}$ plays the role of the distribution of the variable V (i.e. what is sought), the $\subseteq$ and $\cap$ operators becomes the $\leq$ and min operators respectively. Hence property **A4$^{\Pi}$** is similar to the usual fusion operator for possibility distributions.

With the necessity distributions, two pieces of information "V is A_1" and "V is A_2" are represented by the inequality $\pi_V(u) \geq \max(\pi_{A_1}(u), \pi_{A_2}(u))$ for all $u \in U$. It is easy to see that **A4^N** is the counterpart of this inequality.

From Theorem 1, the NPR appears to be the largest order relation satisfying two properties. It shows that $\succsim_{\unrhd}$ cannot provide more information than the NPR, if one wishes to remain cautious and accurate with respect to $\unrhd$.

The PPR relation is the smallest order relation satisfying two relations (see Theorem 2). It shows that $\succsim_{\unrhd}$ cannot less information than the PPR, if one wishes to tell all what is contained in $\unrhd$.

References

1. Grabisch, M., Kojadinovic, I., Meyer, P.: A review of capacity identification methods for Choquet integral based multi-attribute utility theory — applications of the Kappalab R package. Eur. J. of Operational Research 186, 766–785 (2008)
2. Kojadinovic, I.: Minimum variance capacity identification. Quaterly J. of Operations Research (4OR) 12, 23–36 (2006)
3. Labreuche, C.: Identification of a fuzzy measure with an l^1 entropy. In: Int. Conf. on Information Processing and Management of Uncertainty in Knowledge-Based Systems (IPMU), Malaga, Spain, June 22-27 (2008)
4. Schmeidler, D.: Integral representation without additivity. Proc. of the Amer. Math. Soc. 97(2), 255–261 (1986)
5. Marichal, J.L.: An axiomatic approach of the discrete Choquet integral as a tool to aggregate interacting criteria. IEEE Tr. on Fuzzy Systems 8(6), 800–807 (2000)
6. Greco, S., Matarazzo, B., Słowinski, R.: Ordinal regression revisited: Multiple criteria ranking with a set of additive value functions. European Journal of Operational Research 191, 416–436 (2008)
7. Greco, S., Słowinski, R., Figueira, J., Mousseau, V.: Robust ordinal regression. In: Figueira, J., Greco, S., Ehrgott, M. (eds.) New Trends in Multiple Criteria Decision Analysis. Springer, Heidelberg (to appear)
8. Angilella, S., Greco, S., Matarazzo, B.: Non-additive robust ordinal regression: a multiple criteria decision model based on the choquet integral. European Journal of Operational Research 201, 277–288 (2010)
9. Labreuche, C.: On the completion mechanism produced by the choquet integral on some decision strategies. In: Int. Conf. Of the Euro Society for Fuzzy Logic and Technology (EUSFLAT), Lisbon, Portugal, July 20-24 (2009)
10. Grabisch, M., Murofushi, T., Sugeno, M.: Fuzzy Measures and Integrals. Theory and Applications (edited volume). Studies in Fuzziness. Physica Verlag, Heidelberg (2000)
11. Choquet, G.: Theory of capacities. Annales de l'Institut Fourier 5, 131–295 (1953)
12. Grabisch, M.: Alternative representations of discrete fuzzy measures for decision making. Int. J. of Uncertainty, Fuzziness, and Knowledge Based Systems 5, 587–607 (1997)
13. Barbaresco, F., Deltour, J., Desodt, G., Durand, B., Guenais, T., Labreuche, C.: Intelligent M3R radar time resources management: Advanced cognition, agility & autonomy capabilities. In: International Radar Conference, Bordeaux, France, October 12-16 (2009)
14. Bana e Costa, C.A., Correa, E.C., Corte, J.M.D., Vansnick, J.C.: Facilitating bid evaluation in public call for tenders: A socio-technical approach. Omega 30, 227–242 (2002)
15. Savage, L.J.: The Foundations of Statistics, 2nd edn. Dover, New York (1972)
16. Zadeh, L.A.: Fuzzy sets. Information and Control 8, 338–353 (1965)

Explicit Descriptions of Bisymmetric Sugeno Integrals

Miguel Couceiro[1] and Erkko Lehtonen[2]

[1] University of Luxembourg, Mathematics Research Unit
6, rue Richard Coudenhove-Kalergi
L–1359 Luxembourg, Luxembourg
miguel.couceiro@uni.lu
[2] University of Luxembourg, Computer Science and Communications Research Unit
6, rue Richard Coudenhove-Kalergi
L–1359 Luxembourg, Luxembourg
erkko.lehtonen@uni.lu

Abstract. We provide sufficient conditions for a Sugeno integral to be bisymmetric. We explicitly describe bisymmetric Sugeno integrals over chains.

Keywords: Aggregation, Sugeno integral, functional equation, bisymmetry.

1   Introduction

Aggregation functions essentially model the process of merging a set of values into a single representative one. The need to aggregate values in a meaningful way has become more and more present in an increasing number of areas in mathematics and physics, and especially in applied fields such as engineering, computer science, and economical and social sciences. For recent references, see [2,14,15].

In this paper, we are interested in aggregation functions $f: A^n \to A$ satisfying the following identity

$$f\big(f(a_{11}, \ldots, a_{1n}), \ldots, f(a_{n1}, \ldots, a_{nn})\big) =$$
$$f\big(f(a_{11}, \ldots, a_{n1}), \ldots, f(a_{1n}, \ldots, a_{nn})\big),$$

for all $a_{ij} \in A$ $(1 \leq i, j \leq n)$. The relevance of this property is made apparent in works pertinent to different areas of mathematical research. In functional equation theory, and in particular in aggregation function theory, this property is referred to as *bisymmetry* and it is naturally interpreted when reading off data provided by square matrices: essentially, it expresses the fact that aggregating the data by rows and then aggregating the resulting column outputs the same value as that of aggregating the data by columns and then aggregating the resulting row. For motivations and general background, see [1,14]. In the algebraic setting, bisymmetry appears as the natural generalization of the notion of "mediality". It

E. Hüllermeier, R. Kruse, and F. Hoffmann (Eds.): IPMU 2010, LNAI 6178, pp. 494–501, 2010.

is also called self-commutation and it is tightly related to the notions of entropic algebras and centralizer clones.

Among noteworthy aggregation functions are the (discrete) Sugeno integrals, which were introduced by Sugeno [21,22] as a way to compute the average of a function with respect to a nonadditive measure. Since their introduction, Sugeno integrals have been thoroughly investigated and are now considered as one of the most relevant families of aggregation functions in the qualitative setting of ordinal information (e.g., when the values to be aggregated are simply defined on a chain without further structure). This is partially due to the fact that, unlike other aggregation functions, Sugeno integrals can be defined over ordered structures where the usual arithmetic operations are not necessarily available. For general background, see [2,14].

A convenient way to introduce the discrete Sugeno integral is via the concept of (lattice) polynomial functions, i.e., functions which can be expressed as combinations of variables and constants using the lattice operations $\wedge$ and $\vee$. As it was observed in [17], Sugeno integrals can be regarded as polynomial functions $f\colon X^n \to X$ which are idempotent, that is, satisfying $f(x, \ldots, x) = x$.

In this paper, we address the question of characterizing those Sugeno integrals fulfilling the bisymmetry property. This question is answered for discrete Sugeno integrals over bounded chains. In Sect. 2, we recall basic notions in the universal-algebraic setting and settle the terminology used throughout the paper. Moreover, by showing that bisymmetry is preserved under several operations (e.g., permutation of variables, identification of variables and addition of dummy variables), we develop general tools for tackling the question of describing bisymmetric functions.

In Sect. 3, we survey well-known results concerning normal form representations of lattice functions which we then use to specify those Sugeno integrals on bounded chains which are bisymmetric. This explicit description is obtained by providing sufficient conditions for a Sugeno integral to be bisymmetric, and by showing that these conditions are also necessary in the particular case of Sugeno integrals over bounded chains. In Sect. 4 we point out problems which are left unsettled, and motivate directions of future research.

2   Preliminaries

In this section, we introduce some notions and terminology as well as establish some preliminary results that will be used in the sequel. For an integer $n \geq 1$, set $[n] := \{1, 2, \ldots, n\}$. With no danger of ambiguity, we denote the tuple $(x_1, \ldots, x_n)$ of any length by $\mathbf{x}$.

Let A be an arbitrary nonempty set. An *operation* on A (or *function*) is a map $f\colon A^n \to A$ for some integer $n \geq 1$, called the *arity* of f. We denote by $\mathcal{O}_A^{(n)}$ the set of all n-ary operations on A, and we denote by $\mathcal{O}_A$ the set of all finitary operations on A, i.e., $\mathcal{O}_A := \bigcup_{n \geq 1} \mathcal{O}_A^{(n)}$. We assume some familiarity with basic notions of universal algebra and lattice theory, and we refer the reader to [3,4,10,11,12,16,20] for general background.

2.1   Simple Minors

Let $f \in \mathcal{O}_A^{(n)}$, $g \in \mathcal{O}_A^{(m)}$. We say that f is obtained from g by *simple variable substitution*, or f is a *simple minor* of g, if there is a mapping $\sigma\colon [m] \to [n]$ such that

$$f(x_1, \ldots, x_n) = g(x_{\sigma(1)}, x_{\sigma(2)}, \ldots, x_{\sigma(m)}).$$

If σ is not injective, then we speak of *identification of variables*. If σ is not surjective, then we speak of *addition of inessential variables*. If σ is bijective, then we speak of *permutation of variables*. For distinct indices $i, j \in [n]$, the function $f_{i \leftarrow j}\colon A^n \to A$ obtained from f by the simple variable substitution

$$f_{i \leftarrow j}(x_1, \ldots, x_n) := f(x_1, \ldots, x_{i-1}, x_j, x_{i+1}, \ldots, x_n)$$

is called a *variable identification minor* of f, obtained by identifying x_i with x_j.

   For studies of classes of operations that are closed under taking simple minors, see, e.g., [5,19].

2.2   Bisymmetry

Recall that $f \in \mathcal{O}_A^{(n)}$ is *bisymmetric* if

$$f\big(f(a_{11}, \ldots, a_{1n}), \ldots, f(a_{n1}, \ldots, a_{nn})\big) =$$
$$f\big(f(a_{11}, \ldots, a_{n1}), \ldots, f(a_{1n}, \ldots, a_{nn})\big),$$

for all $a_{ij} \in A$ ($1 \leq i, j \leq n$).

   The following proposition asserts that the class of bisymmetric operations on A is minor closed.

Proposition 1. *If $f \in \mathcal{O}_A$ is bisymmetric, then every simple minor of f is bisymmetric.*

   In the particular case when A is finite, Corollary 1 translates into saying that the class of bisymmetric operations on A is definable by functional equations in the sense of [6].

   The set of bisymmetric functions is also closed under special type of substitutions of constants for variables, as described by the following lemma. Let $f\colon A^n \to A$ and $c \in A$. For $i \in [n]$, we define $f_c^i\colon A^{n-1} \to A$ to be the function

$$f_c^i(a_1, \ldots, a_{n-1}) = f(a_1, \ldots, a_{i-1}, c, a_i, \ldots, a_{n-1}).$$

Lemma 2. *Assume that $f\colon A^n \to A$ preserves $c \in A$, i.e., $f(c, \ldots, c) = c$. If f is bisymmetric, then for every $i \in [n]$, f_c^i is bisymmetric.*

3   Bisymmetric Sugeno Integrals

Let $(L; \wedge, \vee)$ be a lattice. With no danger of ambiguity, we denote lattices by their universes. In this section we study bisymmetry on Sugeno integrals. As mentioned, Sugeno integrals can be regarded as certain lattice polynomial functions, i.e., mappings $f: L^n \to L$ which can be obtained as compositions of the lattice operations and applied to variables (projections) and constants. This view has several appealing aspects, in particular, concerning normal form representations of Sugeno integrals. Indeed, as shown by Goodstein [13], polynomial functions on bounded distributive lattices coincide exactly with those functions which are representable in disjunctive normal form (DNF). Thus, in what follows we assume that L is a bounded distributive lattice with least and greatest elements 0 and 1, respectively.

We recall the necessary results concerning the representation of lattice polynomials as well as introduce some related concepts and terminology in Subsect. 3.1. Then, we consider the property of bisymmetry on Sugeno integrals. In Subsect. 3.1, we present explicit descriptions of bisymmetric Sugeno integrals on chains as a corollary of Theorem 3.6 in [8].

3.1   Preliminary Results: Representations of Lattice Polynomials

An n-ary (lattice) polynomial function from L^n to L is defined recursively as follows:

(i) For each $i \in [n]$ and each $c \in L$, the projection $\mathbf{x} \mapsto x_i$ and the constant function $\mathbf{x} \mapsto c$ are polynomial functions from L^n to L.
(ii) If f and g are polynomial functions from L^n to L, then $f \vee g$ and $f \wedge g$ are polynomial functions from L^n to L.
(iii) Any polynomial function from L^n to L is obtained by finitely many applications of the rules (i) and (ii).

If rule (i) is only applied for projections, then the resulting polynomial functions are called (lattice) term functions [4,16,11]. Idempotent polynomial functions are referred to as (discrete) Sugeno integrals [9,14]. In the case of bounded distributive lattices, Goodstein [13] showed that polynomial functions are exactly those which allow representations in disjunctive normal form (see Proposition 3 below, first appearing in [13, Lemma 2.2]; see also Rudeanu [20, Chapter 3, §3] for a later reference).

Proposition 3. *Let L be a bounded distributive lattice. A function $f: L^n \to L$ is a polynomial function if and only if there exist $a_I \in L$, $I \subseteq [n]$, such that, for every $\mathbf{x} \in L^n$,*

$$f(\mathbf{x}) = \bigvee_{I \subseteq [n]} (a_I \wedge \bigwedge_{i \in I} x_i). \tag{1}$$

In particular, a function $f: L^n \to L$ is a Sugeno integral if and only if it can be represented by a formula (1) where $\bigwedge_{I \subseteq [n]} a_I = 0$ and $\bigvee_{I \subseteq [n]} a_I = 1$.

The expression given in (1) is usually referred to as the *disjunctive normal form* (DNF) representation of the polynomial function f.

The following corollaries belong to the folklore of lattice theory and are immediate consequences of Theorems D and E in [13].

Corollary 4. *Every polynomial function is completely determined by its restriction to $\{0,1\}^n$.*

Corollary 5. *A function $g\colon \{0,1\}^n \to L$ can be extended to a polynomial function $f\colon L^n \to L$ if and only if it is nondecreasing. In this case, the extension is unique.*

It is easy to see that the DNF representations of a polynomial function $f\colon L^n \to L$ are not necessarily unique. For instance, in Proposition 3, if for some $I \subseteq [n]$ we have $a_I = \bigvee_{J \subset I} a_J$, then for every $\mathbf{x} \in L^n$,

$$f(\mathbf{x}) = \bigvee_{I \neq J \subseteq [n]} \left(a_J \wedge \bigwedge_{i \in J} x_i \right).$$

However, using Corollaries 4 and 5, one can easily set canonical ways of constructing these normal form representations of polynomial functions. (For a discussion on the uniqueness of DNF representations of lattice polynomial functions see [9].)

Let $2^{[n]}$ denote the set of all subsets of $[n]$. For $I \subseteq [n]$, let $\mathbf{e}_I$ be the *characteristic vector* of I, i.e., the n-tuple in L^n whose i-th component is 1 if $i \in I$, and 0 otherwise. Note that the mapping $\alpha\colon 2^{[n]} \to \{0,1\}^n$ given by $\alpha(I) = \mathbf{e}_I$, for every $I \in 2^{[n]}$, is an order-isomorphism.

Proposition 6 (Goodstein [13]). *Let L be a bounded distributive lattice. A function $f\colon L^n \to L$ is a polynomial function if and only if for every $\mathbf{x} \in L^n$,*

$$f(\mathbf{x}) = \bigvee_{I \subseteq [n]} \left(f(\mathbf{e}_I) \wedge \bigwedge_{i \in I} x_i \right).$$

Moreover, if f is a Sugeno integral, then $f(\mathbf{e}_\emptyset) = 0$ and $f(\mathbf{e}_{[n]}) = 1$.

It is noteworthy that Proposition 6 leads to the following characterization of the essential arguments of polynomial functions in terms of necessary and sufficient conditions [7]. Here, x_i is said to be *essential* in $f\colon L^n \to L$ if there are $a_1, \ldots, a_n, b_i \in L$, $a_i \neq b_i$, such that

$$f(a_1, \ldots, a_{i-1}, a_i, a_{i+1}, \ldots, a_n) \neq f(a_1, \ldots, a_{i-1}, b_i, a_{i+1}, \ldots, a_n).$$

Proposition 7. *Let L be a bounded distributive lattice and let $f\colon L^n \to L$ be a polynomial function. Then for each $j \in [n]$, x_j is essential in f if and only if there exists a set $J \subseteq [n] \setminus \{j\}$ such that $f(\mathbf{e}_J) < f(\mathbf{e}_{J \cup \{j\}})$.*

Remark 8. The assumption that the lattice L is bounded is not very crucial. Let L' be the lattice obtained from L by adjoining new top and bottom elements $\top$ and $\bot$, if necessary. Then, if f is a polynomial function over L induced by a polynomial p, then p induces a polynomial function f' on L', and it holds that the restriction of f' to L coincides with f. Similarly, if L' is a distributive lattice and f' is a polynomial function on L' represented by the DNF

$$\bigvee_{I \subseteq [n]} \left(a_I \wedge \bigwedge_{i \in I} x_i \right),$$

then by omitting each term $a_I \wedge \bigwedge_{i \in I} x_i$ where $a_I = \bot$ and replacing each term $a_I \wedge \bigwedge_{i \in I} x_i$ where $a_I = \top$ by $\bigwedge_{i \in I} x_i$, we obtain an equivalent polynomial representation for f'. Unless f' is a constant function that takes value $\top$ or $\bot$ and this element is not in L, the function f on L induced by this new polynomial coincides with the restriction of f' to L.

3.2 Bisymmetric Sugeno Integrals on Chains

A Sugeno integral $f \colon L^n \to L$ is said to be a *weighted disjunction* if it is of the form

$$f(x_1, x_2, \ldots, x_n) = \bigvee_{i \in [n]} (a_i \wedge x_i) \tag{2}$$

for some elements a_i $(i \in [n])$ of L such that $\bigvee_{i \in [n]} a_i = 1$. Observe that every weighted disjunction (2) is idempotent since for every $x \in L$,

$$f(x, \ldots, x) = \bigvee_{i \in [n]} (a_i \wedge x) = \left(\bigvee_{i \in [n]} a_i \right) \wedge x = 1 \wedge x = x.$$

Thus every weighted disjunction is a Sugeno integral.

We say that f has *chain form* if

$$f(x_1, x_2, \ldots, x_n) = \bigvee_{i \in [n]} (a_i \wedge x_i) \vee \bigvee_{1 \leq \ell \leq r} \left(a_{S_\ell} \wedge \bigwedge_{i \in S_\ell} x_i \right), \tag{3}$$

for a chain of subsets $S_1 \subseteq S_2 \subseteq \cdots \subseteq S_r \subseteq [n]$, $r \geq 1$, $|S_1| \geq 2$, and some elements a_i $(i \in [n])$, a_{S_ℓ} $(1 \leq \ell \leq r)$ of L such that $a_{S_l} \leq a_{S_t}$ whenever $l \leq t$, $\bigvee_{i \in [n]} a_i \vee \bigvee_{\ell \in [r]} a_{S_\ell} = 1$, and for all $i \notin S_1$, there is a $j \in S_1$ such that $a_i \leq a_j$. As in the case of weighted disjunctions, it is easy to verify that every function which has chain form is a Sugeno integral.

Theorem 9. *Let L be a bounded chain. A Sugeno integral $f \colon L^n \to L$ is bisymmetric if and only if it is a weighted disjunction or it has chain form.*

Theorem 9 is a consequence of the following two results proved in [8]. The first provides sufficient conditions for a Sugeno integral to be bisymmetric in the general case of distributive lattices. Its proof was achieved by case analysis.

Lemma 10. *Let L be a distributive lattice. Assume that a function $f \colon L^n \to L$ is a weighted disjunction or has chain form. Then f is bisymmetric.*

The necessity of the conditions in Theorem 9 followed from the lemma below, which can be verified by induction on the arity of functions.

Lemma 11. *Let L be a bounded chain. If a Sugeno integral $f \colon L^n \to L$ is bisymmetric, then it is a weighted disjunction or it has chain form.*

Observe that every binary Sugeno integral is bisymmetric. This is not the case for $n \geq 3$. For instance, let $f \colon [0, 1]^3 \to [0, 1]$ be given by $f(x_1, x_2, x_3) = (0.5 \wedge x_3) \vee (x_1 \wedge x_2)$. Then

$$f\big(f(1, 0, 1), f(1, 1, 0), f(0, 0, 0)\big) = 0.5 \neq 0 = f\big(f(1, 1, 0), f(0, 1, 0), f(1, 0, 0)\big).$$

Clearly, this function is not a weighted disjunction and it does not have chain form because the condition "for all $i \notin S_1$, there is a $j \in S_1$ such that $a_i \leq a_j$" is not fulfilled. However, a minor modification of f yields a function that has chain form (and is hence bisymmetric): $f'(x_1, x_2, x_3) = (0.5 \wedge x_1) \vee (0.5 \wedge x_3) \vee (x_1 \wedge x_2)$.

4   Concluding Remarks and Future Work

We have obtained an explicit form of bisymmetric Sugeno integrals on chains. However, we do not know whether Theorem 9 still holds in the general case of Sugeno integrals over distributive lattices. This constitutes a topic of ongoing research.

Another problem which was not addressed concerns the following generalization of bisymmetry. Two operations $f \colon A^n \to A$ and $g \colon A^m \to A$ are said to commute, denoted $f \perp g$, if for all $a_{ij} \in A$ ($1 \leq i \leq n$, $1 \leq j \leq m$), the following identity holds

$$f\big(g(a_{11}, a_{12}, \dots, a_{1m}), g(a_{21}, a_{22}, \dots, a_{2m}), \dots, g(a_{n1}, a_{n2}, \dots, a_{nm})\big) =$$
$$g\big(f(a_{11}, a_{21}, \dots, a_{n1}), f(a_{12}, a_{22}, \dots, a_{n2}), \dots, f(a_{1m}, a_{2m}, \dots, a_{nm})\big).$$

Commutation has been considered in the realm of aggregation function theory. In this context, functions are often regarded as mappings $f \colon \bigcup_{n \geq 1} A^n \to A$, and bisymmetry is naturally generalized to what is referred to as strong bisymmetry. Denoting by f_n the restriction of f to A^n, the map f is said to be *strongly bisymmetric* if for any $n, m \geq 1$, we have $f_n \perp f_m$. This generalization is both natural and useful from the application point of view. To illustrate this, suppose one is given data in tabular form, say an $n \times m$ matrix, to be meaningfully fused into a single representative value. One could first aggregate the data by rows and then aggregate the resulting column; or one could first aggregate the columns and then the resulting row. What is expressed by the property of strong bisymmetry is that the final outcome is the same under both procedures. Extending the notion of Sugeno integral (as a polynomial function) to such families, we are thus left with the problem of describing those families of Sugeno integrals which are strongly bisymmetric.

Acknowledgments

We would like to thank Jean-Luc Marichal for introducing us to the topic and for helpful discussions.

References

1. Aczél, J., Dhombres, J.: Functional Equations in Several Variables. Encyclopedia of Mathematics and Its Applications, vol. 31. Cambridge University Press, Cambridge (1989)

2. Beliakov, G., Pradera, A., Calvo, T.: Aggregation Functions: A Guide for Practitioners. Studies in Fuzziness and Soft Computing. Springer, Berlin (2007)
3. Birkhoff, G.: Lattice Theory. Amer. Math. Soc. Colloq. Publ. 25 (1967)
4. Burris, S., Sankappanavar, H.P.: A Course in Universal Algebra. Springer, Heidelberg (1981)
5. Couceiro, M., Foldes, S.: On Closed Sets of Relational Constraints and Classes of Functions Closed under Variable Substitution. Algebra Universalis 54, 149–165 (2005)
6. Couceiro, M., Foldes, S.: Functional Equations, Constraints, Definability of Function Classes, and Functions of Boolean Variables. Acta Cybernet. 18, 61–75 (2007)
7. Couceiro, M., Lehtonen, E.: The Arity Gap of Polynomial Functions over Bounded Distributive Lattices. arXiv:0910.5131
8. Couceiro, M., Lehtonen, E.: Self-Commuting Lattice Polynomial Functions. arXiv:0912.0478
9. Couceiro, M., Marichal, J.-L.: Characterizations of Discrete Sugeno Integrals as Polynomial Functions over Distributive Lattices. Fuzzy Sets and Systems 161, 694–707 (2009)
10. Davey, B., Priestley, H.A.: Introduction to Lattices and Order. Cambridge University Press, Cambridge (2002)
11. Denecke, K., Wismath, S.L.: Universal Algebra and Applications in Theoretical Computer Science. Chapman & Hall/CRC, Boca Raton (2002)
12. Denecke, K., Wismath, S.L.: Universal Algebra and Coalgebra. World Scientific, Singapore (2009)
13. Goodstein, R.L.: The Solution of Equations in a Lattice. Proc. Roy. Soc. Edinburgh Sect. A 67, 231–242 ((1965/1967)
14. Grabisch, M., Marichal, J.-L., Mesiar, R., Pap, E.: Aggregation Functions. Encyclopedia of Mathematics and Its Applications, vol. 127. Cambridge University Press, Cambridge (2009)
15. Grabisch, M., Murofushi, T., Sugeno, M. (eds.): Fuzzy Measures and Integrals – Theory and Applications. Studies in Fuzziness and Soft Computing, vol. 40. Physica-Verlag, Heidelberg (2000)
16. Grätzer, G.: Universal Algebra. Springer, Heidelberg (1979)
17. Marichal, J.-L.: An Axiomatic Approach of the Discrete Sugeno Integral as a Tool to Aggregate Interacting Criteria in a Qualitative Framework. IEEE Trans. Fuzzy Syst. 9(1), 164–172 (2001)
18. Marichal, J.-L., Mathonet, P., Tousset, E.: Characterization of Some Aggregation Functions Stable for Positive Linear Transformations. Fuzzy Sets and Systems 102, 293–314 (1999)
19. Pippenger, N.: Galois Theory for Minors of Finite Functions. Discrete Math. 254, 405–419 (2002)
20. Rudeanu, S.: Lattice Functions and Equations. Discrete Mathematics and Theoretical Computer Science Series. Springer, London (2001)
21. Sugeno, M.: Theory of Fuzzy Integrals and Its Applications. Ph.D. thesis, Tokyo Institute of Technology, Tokyo (1974)
22. Sugeno, M.: Fuzzy Measures and Fuzzy Integrals – a Survey. In: Gupta, M.M., Saridis, G.N., Gaines, B.R. (eds.) Fuzzy Automata and Decision Processes, pp. 89–102. North-Holland, New York (1977)

Learning Fuzzy-Valued Fuzzy Measures for the Fuzzy-Valued Sugeno Fuzzy Integral

Derek T. Anderson, James M. Keller, and Timothy C. Havens

Electrical and Computer Engineering Department, University of Missouri
Columbia, MO, 65211, USA
dtaxtd@mail.missouri.edu, kellerj@missouri.edu,
havenst@gmail.com

Abstract. Fuzzy integrals are very useful for fusing confidence or opinions from a variety of sources. These integrals are non-linear combinations of the support functions with the (possibly subjective) worth of subsets of the sources, realized by a fuzzy measure. There have been many applications and extensions of fuzzy integrals and this paper deals with a Sugeno integral where both the integrand and the measure take on fuzzy number values. A crucial aspect of using fuzzy integrals for fusion is determining or learning the measures. Here, we propose a genetic algorithm with novel cross-over and mutation operators to learn fuzzy-valued fuzzy measures for a fuzzy-valued Sugeno integral.

Keywords: Fuzzy-valued fuzzy measure, Fuzzy-valued Sugeno integral, Learning fuzzy measures, Genetic algorithms.

1 Introduction

The fusion of information using the fuzzy integral (Sugeno or Choquet) has a rich history. Much of the theory and several applications can be found in [1,2]. With respect to this problem, we consider a finite set of sources of information, $X = \{x_1, x_2, \cdots, x_E\}$ and a function that maps X into some domain (initially [0,1]) that represents the partial support of a hypothesis from the standpoint of each source of information. Depending on the problem domain, X can be a set of experts, sensors, features, pattern recognition algorithms, etc. The hypothesis is usually thought of as an alternative in a decision process or a class label in pattern recognition. Both Sugeno and Choquet integrals take partial support for the hypothesis from the standpoint of each source of information and fuse it with the (perhaps subjective) worth of each subset of X in a non-linear fashion. This worth is encoded into a fuzzy measure [1]. Initially, the function $h : X \rightarrow [0,1]$, and the measure $g : 2^X \rightarrow [0,1]$ took real number values in [0,1]. Certainly, the output range for both function and measure can be (and have been) defined more generally, but it is convenient to think of them in the unit interval for confidence fusion.

More formally, for a finite set X, a (numeric) fuzzy measure is a function $g : 2^X \rightarrow [0,1]$, (a real valued set function) such that

E. Hüllermeier, R. Kruse, and F. Hoffmann (Eds.): IPMU 2010, LNAI 6178, pp. 502–511, 2010.

1. $g(\phi) = 0$ and $g(X) = 1$;

2. If $A, B \subseteq X$ with $A \subseteq B$, then $g(A) \leq g(B)$.

Note that if X is an infinite set, a third condition guaranteeing continuity is required, but it is a moot point for finite X.   Given a finite set X, a fuzzy measure $g : 2^X \rightarrow [0,1]$ and a function $h : X \rightarrow [0,1]$, the (numeric) Sugeno integral of h with respect to g is given by

$$\int h \circ g = \bigvee_{i=1}^{E} \left(h(x_{(i)}) \wedge g(\{x_{(1)}, \cdots, x_{(i)}\}) \right) \tag{1}$$

where $X = \{x_{(1)}, \cdots, x_{(E)}\}$ has been sorted so that $h(x_{(1)}) \geq h(x_{(2)}) \geq \cdots \geq h(x_{(E)})$. This finite realization of the actual definition [1,2] highlights the fact that the Sugeno integral represents the best pessimistic agreement between the objective evidence in support of a hypothesis (the h function) and the subjective worth of the supporting evidence (the fuzzy measure g).

The Choquet integral is a direct extension of the Lebesque integral and has a similar finite set formulation. This paper deals only with Sugeno integrals and so, the Choquet formulae are not given.

Sometimes numbers are not sufficient to represent the uncertainty in a situation. With respect to fusion by fuzzy integration, this uncertainty can exist in the partial support function and/or in the fuzzy measure.   Extensions of both Sugeno and Choquet integrals to the case where the partial support function outputs are fuzzy numbers (normal convex fuzzy subsets of the reals, $\Re$, called $FN(\Re)$) are direct results of the Extension Principle [3]. They are computable from level set representations using the Decomposition Theorem and results from [1]. Interval logic and arithmetic operations make the extension possible in a practical sense. In this case, we denote the partial support function as $H : X \rightarrow FN(\Re)$. While not actually necessary, we will restrict ourselves to fuzzy numbers over the unit interval, $FN([0,1])$. Applications of these generalized integrals to real world data sets are given in [4]. This works because the theory that shows that the level sets of the generalized fuzzy integral reduce to the fuzzy integrals of the endpoints of the intervals of reals that form the level cuts of fuzzy numbers.

2 Fuzzy-Valued Fuzzy Measures and Fuzzy-Valued Sugeno Fuzzy Integral

It is just as likely that uncertainty exists in the assessment of the worth of various subsets of sources of information. With respect to this case, a general theory of fuzzy number-valued fuzzy measures and a fuzzy number valued Sugeno integral was developed in [5]. That paper represents extensions of [6-9], all of which dealt with the mathematics in a general manner. Much of the theory concerned itself with the situation where the base domain is infinite, in which case convergence theory of infinite sequences plays a major role. Our goal is to examine the practicality of implementing this generalization for the purposes of information fusion.

For completeness, and to establish our notation, we briefly reproduce a few of the results in [5] for the finite set case. To define fuzzy number-valued measures, we first need to describe appropriate interval operations and then base fuzzy number definitions on them. Let $I(\mathfrak{R}^+) = \left\{ \overleftarrow{u} \subset \mathfrak{R}^+ \middle| \overline{u} = [u^l, u^r], u^l \le u^r \right\}$ be the set of all closed intervals over the positive reals. The usual interval-based definitions of min, max, scalar multiplication hold. Because ordering is important for fuzzy measures, $\overline{u} \le \overline{v}$ iff $u^l \le v^l$ and $u^r \le v^r$. Let A be a fuzzy number over $\mathfrak{R}^+$, then for $\alpha \in [0,1]$, the level cut, $^{\alpha}A = [^{\alpha}a^l, {}^{\alpha}a^r]$ is a closed interval. For two fuzzy numbers, A, B over $\mathfrak{R}^+$, we define $A \le B$ iff $^{\alpha}A \le {}^{\alpha}B$ for all $\alpha \in [0,1]$.

A fuzzy-valued fuzzy measure is defined (adapted from [5]) as follows. Let $X = \{x_1, x_2, \cdots, x_E\}$ be a finite set and let $G: 2^X \to FN([0,1])$ be a fuzzy number-valued set function satisfying:

1. $G(\phi) = Z$ (Z stands for Zero) where $Z(y) = \begin{cases} 1, & y = 0 \\ 0, & y \ne 0 \end{cases}$

2. If $A, B \subset X$ with $A \subseteq B$, then $G(A) \le G(B)$. Note here, both G(A) and G(B) are fuzzy numbers.

The corresponding definition holds for the restriction to an interval-valued measure, $\overline{G}$.

Let $\overline{H}$ (respectively H) be a partial support function $\overline{H}: X \to I([0,1])$ (respectively, $H: X \to FN([0,1])$) with respect to some hypothesis under consideration. Then the generalized interval Sugeno integral is defined as $\int \overline{H} \circ \overline{G} = \left[\int \overline{H}^l \circ \overline{G}^l, \int \overline{H}^r \circ \overline{G}^r \right]$, whereas the full generalized fuzzy-number Sugeno integral is defined as $\left(\int H \circ G \right)(u) = \sup \left\{ \alpha \in [0,1] \middle| u \in \int^{\alpha} H \circ {}^{\alpha} G \right\}$. The following Theorem (4.1 of [5]) provides the mechanism to perform efficient computation of this extended Sugeno integral.

Theorem. Let $X = \{x_1, x_2, \cdots, x_E\}$, $H: X \to FN([0,1])$ and $G: 2^X \to FN([0,1])$. Then

$$^{\alpha} \left(\int H \circ G \right) = \int^{\alpha} H \circ {}^{\alpha} G \cdot \tag{2}$$

Hence, just as with the other forms of generalizing numeric fuzzy integrals, this theorem shows that the realization ultimately reduces to interval-based operations. In the next section we demonstrate these calculations on two examples of fuzzy-valued Sugeno fuzzy integrals. In the cases we consider, the fuzzy numbers are all symmetric triangles, but in general, the fuzzy numbers only have the restriction that we can enumerate their level cuts.

3 Fuzzy-Valued Sugeno Fuzzy Integral Examples

We model fuzzy sets as symmetric triangles, which are characterized according to three ordered numbers $\{a,b,c\}$, where $b=(a+c)/2$. The ground truth fuzzy-valued fuzzy measure, G, is shown in Table 1 for a set $X=\{x_1,x_2,x_3,x_4\}$ of sources of information. It is easy to see that these fuzzy numbers satisfy the properties of a fuzzy-valued fuzzy measure.

Table 1. Fuzzy set parameters for this papers fuzzy-valued fuzzy measure ground truth

Evidence sets	Triangle Parameters	Evidence sets	Triangle Parameters
$\varnothing$	$\{0,0,0\}$	$\{x_2,x_3\}$	$\{0.45,0.55,0.65\}$
$\{x_1\}$	$\{0.1,0.2,0.3\}$	$\{x_2,x_4\}$	$\{0.65,0.75,0.85\}$
$\{x_2\}$	$\{0.2,0.3,0.4\}$	$\{x_3,x_4\}$	$\{0.68,0.78,0.88\}$
$\{x_3\}$	$\{0.4,0.5,0.6\}$	$\{x_1,x_2,x_3\}$	$\{0.8,0.85,0.9\}$
$\{x_4\}$	$\{0.6,0.7,0.8\}$	$\{x_1,x_2,x_4\}$	$\{0.82,0.87,0.92\}$
$\{x_1,x_2\}$	$\{0.22,0.32,0.42\}$	$\{x_2,x_3,x_4\}$	$\{0.84,0.9,0.96\}$
$\{x_1,x_3\}$	$\{0.42,0.52,0.62\}$	$\{x_1,x_3,x_4\}$	$\{0.86,0.92,0.98\}$
$\{x_1,x_4\}$	$\{0.62,0.72,0.82\}$	$\{x_1,x_2,x_3,x_4\}$	$\{1,1,1\}$

Now consider the partial support functions H_1 and H_2 given by $H_1(x_1)=\{0.3,0.5,0.7\}$, $H_1(x_2)=\{0.5,0.7,0.9\}$, $H_1(x_3)=\{0.8,0.9,1.0\}$, $H_1(x_4)=\{0.6,0.8,1.0\}$, $H_2(x_1)=\{0.2,0.5,0.8\}$, $H_2(x_2)=\{0.1,0.5,0.9\}$, $H_2(x_3)=\{0.1,0.3,0.5\}$, and $H_2(x_4)=\{0.5,0.75,1.0\}$. Fig. 1(a) shows the function values for H_1 along with its fuzzy-valued fuzzy Sugeno integral with respect to the fuzzy-valued fuzzy measure G in Table 1, and Fig. 1(b) depicts the corresponding information for H_2. Here, 201 evenly spaced alpha cuts are used for representation.

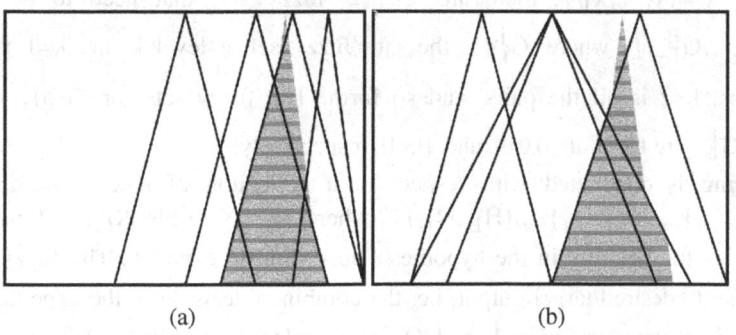

(a)   (b)

Fig. 1. Two example computations of the fuzzy-valued fuzzy Sugeno integral. (a), H_1 and $\int H_1 \circ G$; (b), H_2 and $\int H_2 \circ G$ for the measure G reported in Table 1.

4 Genetic Algorithm for Learning Fuzzy-Valued Fuzzy Measures

The "secret" to using fuzzy integration (whether it be Sugeno or Choquet integrals) in a real application is an ability to learn the fuzzy measures from training data. There are many optimization approaches that have found success for numeric fuzzy integrals, some of which can be found in [2, 10]. For fuzzy-valued fuzzy Sugeno fuzzy integrals, the problem is more complex, though decomposable. We chose to use a genetic algorithm approach to learn the fuzzy triangular number fuzzy measures for a particular problem. Genetic algorithms (GA) are an optimization procedure inspired by evolution. The general format of a GA is as follows [11].

General Structure of a Genetic Algorithm

1. Set generation counter $q = 1$
2. Create the initial generation $P_1 = \{C_1,...,C_N\}$
3. Do until convergence (e.g. maximum number of iterations)
   a. Evaluate the fitness of each chromosome
   b. Increment the generation counter $q = q + 1$
   c. Select parents from P_{q-1}
   d. Recombine selected parents through cross-over to form P_q'
   e. Mutate offspring P_q'
   f. Select the new generation P_q from the previous generation P_{q-1} and the offspring P_q'

The optimization task must first be encoded into a chromosome representation. Herein, chromosome $C_i, 0 < i \leq N$, is a fuzzy-valued fuzzy measure. For E different experts, $X = \{x_1,...,x_E\}$, there are $2^E - 2$ fuzzy sets that need to be learned, $\{G_1^1, G_1^2,...,G_{E-1}^E\}$, where G_k^j is the jth fuzzy set at level k, i.e. k=1 is all the singletons, k=2 is all the pairs, and so forth. The fuzzy sets for $G(\phi)$, G_0^1, and $G(X)$, G_E^1, are fixed at {0,0,0} and {1,1,1} respectively.

Learning is conducted with respect to a collection of labeled training data, $I = \{\{H_1,O_1\},...,\{H_d,O_d\},...,\{H_D,O_D\}\}$, where $H_d : X \rightarrow FN(\Re)$ is a function and $H_d(x_k)$ is the strength in the hypothesis according to expert k. The fuzzy number O_d is the dth desired/target output, i.e. the combined decision of the experts. Herein, $H_d(x_k)$ is a symmetric triangle and O_d is an ordered set of intervals (e.g. a discrete number of α-cuts). The fitness (quality) of C_i, given the training data I, is

$$f(C_i, I) = \left(\left(\sum_{d=1}^{D} s(\int H_d \circ C_i, O_d) \right) / D \right)^P ,$$ (3)

where $\int H_d \circ C_i$ is the fuzzy-valued Sugeno fuzzy integral with respect to C_i, s is a similarity measure, and P is a parameter for changing the weighting/importance of the average score. The similarity measure used is

$$s(B, C) = \frac{\sum_{m=1}^{M} \max \left(\min((^{m/M}B)^r, (^{m/M}C)^r) - \max((^{m/M}B)^l, (^{m/M}C)^l), 0 \right)}{\sum_{m=1}^{M} \max \left(\max((^{m/M}B)^r, (^{m/M}C)^r) - \min((^{m/M}B)^l, (^{m/M}C)^l), 0 \right)} ,$$ (4)

where B and C are fuzzy numbers and $[(^{m/M}B)^l, (^{m/M}B)^r]$ and $[(^{m/M}C)^l, (^{m/M}C)^r]$ are their respective intervals at level cut $\alpha = m/M$.

Learning is not a trivial task. The Sugeno fuzzy integral does not have a well-behaved continuous error space (calculation involves maximums and minimums), as with the case of the Choquet fuzzy integral. In addition, random selection of fuzzy set parameters for all fuzzy subsets in a fuzzy-valued fuzzy measure is not possible. As discussed in the prior section, a fuzzy measure has a set of constraints. Thus, the initialization and the crossover and mutation operations must guarantee that each chromosome is a valid fuzzy-valued fuzzy measure. Initialization of G_k^j, for $0 < k < E$, in C_i is performed pseudo-randomly,

$$a = U(0,1)'$$ (5a)

$$c = (1-a)U(0,1) + a'$$ (5b)

$$b = (c-a)/2 + a'$$ (5c)

where $U(0,1)$ represents a random number generated from a uniform probability distribution over $[0,1]$ and the sequence of calculations is (5a), (5b), then (5c). After pseudo-random parameter initialization, C_i is not guaranteed to be a fuzzy-valued fuzzy measure. The individual G_1^j sets are valid; however, in order for C_i to be a fuzzy-valued fuzzy measure, each G_k^j, for $1 < k < E$, needs to be checked for validity in the context of C_i. This check is performed in the order $k = 2, ..., E-1$. Because symmetric triangles are used here, only parameters a and c (for an α-cut of 0) need be checked. A fuzzy set G_k^j is invalid (thus C_i is not a fuzzy-valued fuzzy measure) if there exists an l such that $G_k^j < G_{k-1}^l$, where l is an index corresponding to one of the fuzzy sets at k-1 involving k-1 sources included in G_k^j (e.g.

$\{G(\{x_1, x_2\}), G(\{x_1, x_3\}), G(\{x_2, x_3\})\}$ for $G(\{x_1, x_2, x_3\})$). If G_k^j is invalid, i.e. one or both of its interval endpoints of the 0 α-cut are invalid, then the invalid interval endpoint is set to the largest value from the corresponding respective set at G_{k-1}^j.

At each generation, a population undergoes recombination (crossover) with a probability of $\lambda_1 \in [0,1]$. Two chromosomes (candidate fuzzy-valued fuzzy measures), C_n and C_m are pseudo-randomly selected. In the order $k = 1,...,E-1$, a fuzzy set is pseudo-randomly selected from C_n (at level k) and another fuzzy set is pseudo-randomly selected from C_m (at level k). These sets are swapped based on a probability of $\lambda_2 \in [0,1]$ and constraints are then verified up the chain, $\{k,...,E-1\}$.

While crossover explores an already opened subset of the search space, mutation helps preserve and introduce diversity. Three different mutation operators have been identified in this work. The first mutation operator is shrinking. Shrinking is performed with a probability of $\lambda_3 \in [0,1]$. Shrinking is an attempt at narrowing the fuzzy sets and making them more certain. A chromosome is pseudo-randomly selected and each individual fuzzy set in that chromosome is potentially shrunk based on another probability of $\lambda_4 \in [0,1]$. If fuzzy set G_k^j is selected for shrinking, then its new parameters are calculated as

$$\beta = U(0,1), \qquad (6a)$$

$$a = b - (b-a)\beta, \qquad (6b)$$

$$c = b + (b-a)\beta, \qquad (6c)$$

$$b = (c-a)/2 + a, \qquad (6d)$$

in the order (6a), (6b), (6c), followed by (6d). Again, after all sets are mutated at level k, levels $\{k+1,...,E-1\}$ are verified.

The second mutation operator, with probability $\lambda_5 \in [0,1]$, is shifting. In the order $k = 1,...,E-1$, each G_k^j is potentially translated with probability $\lambda_6 \in [0,1]$. If G_k^j passes, then it is translated by $\lambda_7 U(-1,1)$, $\lambda_7 \in [0,1]$. The purpose of this operator is to explore the area around the set while keeping its size (or certainty) fixed. Again, when any set is modified, verification up the chain, $\{k,...,E-1\}$, is performed to ensure that the chromosome represents a valid fuzzy-valued measure.

The last mutation operator, with probability $\lambda_8 \in [0,1]$, is pseudo-random exploration. In this work, $\{\lambda_3, \lambda_5, \lambda_8\}$ are selected such that their sum equals 1. If a chromosome is selected for this type of mutation, then each G_k^j, in the order $k = 1,...,E-1$, is potentially mutated with probability $\lambda_9 \in [0,1]$. If G_k^j is chosen, then its parameters are modified according to

$$a = (b-\theta)U(0,1) + \theta, \qquad (7a)$$

$$c = (1-a)U(0,1) + a, \tag{7b}$$

$$b = (c-a)/2 + a, \tag{7c}$$

where θ is the maximum a value from all respective corresponding G_{k-1}^l subsets. The operations are performed in the order (7a), (7b), then (7c), and after all mutations are performed at level k, levels $\{k,...,E-1\}$ are checked for validity.

At each generation, a proportion of the existing population is selected to breed a new generation. First, the fitness of each chromosome is calculated. Next, the best (highest fitness) $\lfloor \lambda_{10}N \rfloor$, $\lambda_{10} \in [0,1]$, chromosomes are included in roulette wheel selection. The best chromosome is always selected for inclusion in the next generation. Additionally, $\lambda_{11} \in \{0,1,...\infty\}$ randomly initialized chromosomes are added at each generation to encourage additional exploration.

5 Experiments

The measure G, in Table 1, and 50 randomly generated H_d are used to demonstrate the proposed learning procedure. Algorithm parameters, $E = 4$, $M = 51$, $N = 50$, $D = 50$, $\lambda_1 = 0.3$, $\lambda_2 = 0.5$, $\lambda_3 = 0.1$, $\lambda_4 = 0.5$, $\lambda_5 = 0.2$, $\lambda_6 = 0.5$, $\lambda_7 = 0.2$, $\lambda_8 = 0.7$, $\lambda_9 = 0.25$, $\lambda_{10} = 0.5$, and $\lambda_{11} = 5$, were empirically selected. The only

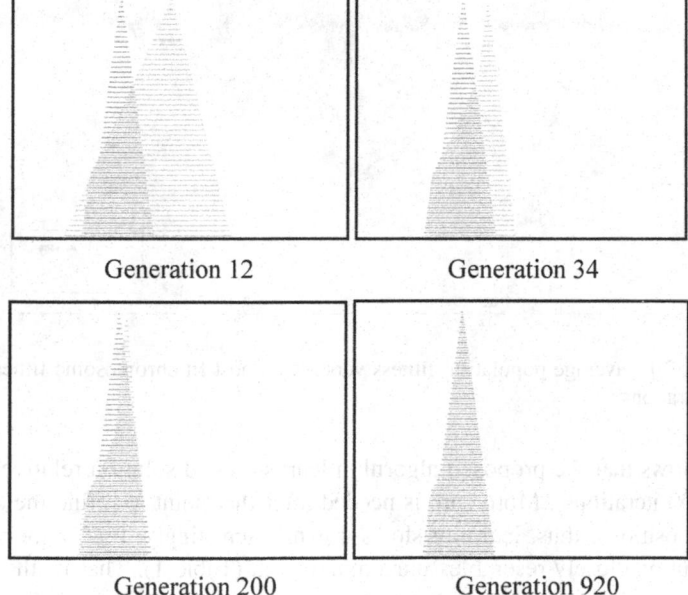

Generation 12   Generation 34

Generation 200   Generation 920

Fig. 2. Fuzzy-valued Sugeno fuzzy integral intervals at different generations for the proposed genetic algorithm for one of the target outputs. Green intervals are the learned results and blue intervals are for the ground truth.

sensitive parameters appear to be $\{\lambda_3, \lambda_5, \lambda_8\}$. In particular, the value λ_8 needed to be large for reasonable convergence properties; it encourages exploration of the search space. Fig. 2 is the result of learning at four different generations, Fig. 3 is the learned fuzzy-valued fuzzy measures in relation to the target output, and Fig. 4 is the plot of the average population fitness versus the fitness of the best chromosome at each generation.

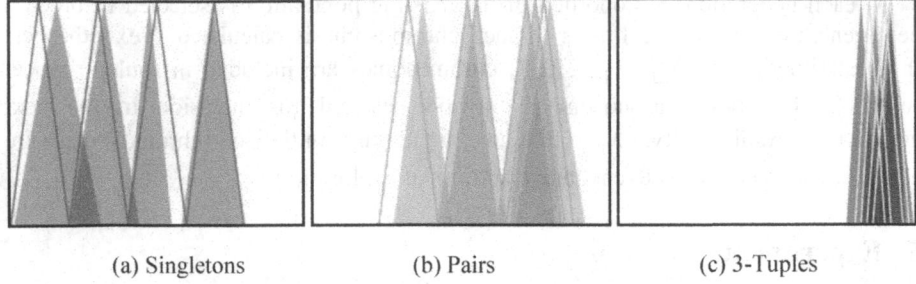

(a) Singletons   (b) Pairs   (c) 3-Tuples

Fig. 3. Visualization of the best chromosome (fuzzy-valued fuzzy measure) after convergence along with the ground truth fuzzy measure. Solid triangles are the learned fuzzy sets and lines depict the fuzzy sets from the ground truth measure (Table 1).

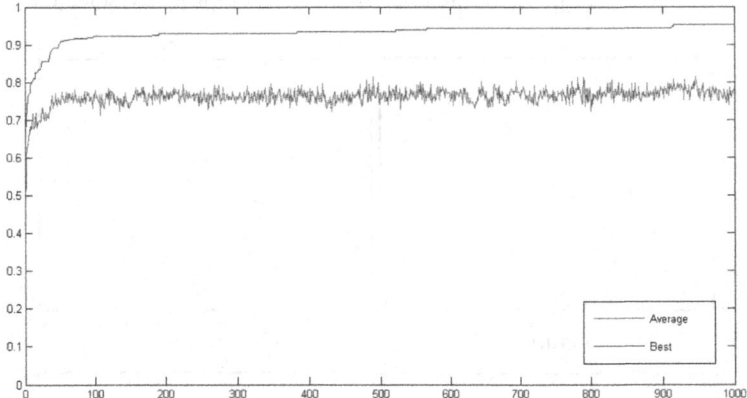

Fig. 4. Plot of the average population fitness versus the most fit chromosome fitness for 1000 algorithm iterations

Fig. 4 shows that the proposed algorithm learns a good solution relatively quickly (the first 100 iterations). More care is needed after that point to refine the exact final parameter positions; thus, learning slows down. Interestingly, Fig. 3 shows that the learned solution closely resembles our ground truth (Table 1). That is, the technique did not just acquire any solution, but one that is highly similar to our desired fuzzy-valued fuzzy measure.

6 Conclusions and Future Work

We demonstrated techniques for computing the generalized Sugeno integral for fuzzy-valued integrands with respect to a fuzzy-valued measure in an information fusion framework with a finite number of sources of information. We introduced a genetic algorithm approach to learn the fuzzy-valued measures from a set of training data and demonstrated the technique with synthetic data.

Future work includes extending the theoretical foundation of this research to a fuzzy-valued fuzzy measures for the fuzzy-valued Choquet integral, exploring this information fusion approach in the context of *computing with words*, further exploring the learning algorithm and attempting to speed up learning in later generations, analyzing a larger set of test data, and attempting learning for measures with greater number of information sources.

Acknowledgments

Derek Anderson is a pre-doctoral biomedical informatics research fellow funded by the National Library of Medicine (T15 LM07089). James Keller and Timothy Havens were partially supported by Leonard Wood Institute grant LWI 181-222 and Army Research Office grant number 48343-EV in support of the U. S. Army RDECOM CERDEC NVESD.

References

1. Grabisch, M., Nguyen, H., Walker, E.: Fundamentals of Uncertainty Calculi with Applications to Fuzzy Inference. Kluwer Academic Publishers, London (1994)
2. Grabisch, M., Murofushi, T., Sugeno, M. (eds.): Fuzzy Measures and Integrals: Theory and Applications. Physica-Verlag, Heidelberg (2000)
3. Klir, G., Yuan, B.: Fuzzy Sets and Fuzzy Logic: Theory and Applications. Prentice-Hall, New Jersey (1995)
4. Auephanwiriyakul, S., Keller, J., Gader, P.: Generalized Choquet Fuzzy Integral Fusion. Information Fusion 3, 69–85 (2002)
5. Guo, C., Zhang, D., Wu, C.: Fuzzy-valued measures and generalized fuzzy integrals. Fuzzy Sets and Systems 97, 255–260 (1998)
6. Wu, C., Wang, S., Ma, M.: Generalized fuzzy integrals I. Fuzzy Sets and Systems 57, 219–226 (1993)
7. Wu, C., Wang, S., Ma, M.: Generalized fuzzy integrals II. Fuzzy Sets and Systems 70, 75–87 (1995)
8. Zhang, D., Wang, Z.: Fuzzy integrals of fuzzy-valued functions. Fuzzy Sets and Systems 54, 63–67 (1993)
9. Zhang, D., Guo, C.: Generalized fuzzy integrals of set-valued functions. Fuzzy Sets and Systems 76, 365–373 (1995)
10. Bezdek, J.C., Keller, J.M., Krishnapuram, R., Pal, N.R.: Fuzzy Models and Algorithms for Pattern Recognition and Image Processing. Kluwer, Norwell (1999)
11. Engelbrecht, A.: Computational Intelligence: An Introduction, 2nd edn. John Wiley, Chichester (2007)

Choquet Integration on Set Systems

U. Faigle[1], M. Grabisch[2], and M. Heyne[1]

[1] Mathematisches Institut/ZAIK, Universität zu Köln, 50931 Köln, Germany
{faigle,heyne}@zpr.uni-koeln.de
[2] Université Paris I Panthéon-Sorbonne
Centre d'Economie de la Sorbonne, 106-112 Bd de l'Hôpital, 75013 Paris, France
michel.grabisch@univ-paris1.fr

Abstract. We present a framework for a general Choquet integral on systems $\mathcal{F}$ of *measurable sets* relative to a finite universe N that do not necessarily include all nonempty subsets. In this context, many functions become nonmeasurable, and the classical Choquet integral does not apply. By considering a lower approximation by step functions, we arrive at a natural notion of an integral which generalizes the classical Choquet integral and is meaningful for any function. We observe that the Choquet integral of a measurable function can be computed by a Monge-type algorithm and we characterize so-called weakly union-closed systems as those set systems that allow the Monge algorithm to compute the general Choquet integral. In addition, we characterize the superadditivity of the Choquet integral on these systems.

1 Introduction

The Choquet integral and the notion of capacity [3] have become popular tools in decision making since they permit to compute expectation w.r.t. nonadditive probabilities that represent the preference of the decision maker.

While the classical approach almost always assumes the family of measurable subsets of N to form an algebra, many practical situations (*e.g.*, cooperative games, multicriteria decision making) require a more general setting with only the members of a certain subfamily $\mathcal{F} \subseteq 2^N$ being feasible and no particular "nice" algebraic structure apparent. In this case, many functions are nonmeasurable because their level sets may not belong to the family $\mathcal{F}$, which makes the use of the Choquet integral difficult.

It is the purpose of the present paper, to extend the notion of a Choquet integral to arbitrary families $\mathcal{F}$ of subsets in such a way that any function can be integrated with respect to general set functions (and capacities being a particular case). This study was initiated in [5], although our present approach, established in [4], is considerably different from the former model.

Our approach to discrete integration is similar to the idea of Riemannian sums in the classical theory. We consider the approximation of functions by step functions from below, focussing on belief functions as integration measures first. We then extend our definition to any set function through its decomposition in belief functions (Sections 2 and 3). Then we present a Monge-type algorithm for integrals of measurable functions. We furthermore prove that it computes our general Choquet integral correctly if and

E. Hüllermeier, R. Kruse, and F. Hoffmann (Eds.): IPMU 2010, LNAI 6178, pp. 512–520, 2010.

only if the underlying set system is weakly union-closed (Section 3.2). Finally, in Section 4 we study the issue of superadditivity of the integral and arrive at a generalization of a result of Lovász [8] for the classical Choquet integral. We establish the equivalence between superadditivity and the supermodularity of the capacity in the wide model of weakly union-closed systems.

2 Preliminaries

Let $f \in \mathbb{R}^N$ be a real-valued function on the finite set N. For any $\alpha \in \mathbb{R}$, set $\{f \geq \alpha\} := \{i \in N \mid f_i \geq \alpha\}$. Let $\alpha_1 < \ldots < \alpha_k$ be the distinct values of f. Then the nonempty *level sets* of f are:

$$N = \{f \geq \alpha_1\} \supset \{f \geq \alpha_2\} \supset \ldots \supset \{f \geq \alpha_k\}.$$

Let $\mathcal{F}$ be a family of m nonempty subsets of N and call f $\mathcal{F}$-*measurable* if every nonempty level set of f belongs to $\mathcal{F}$. Note that every $f \in \mathbb{R}^N$ is measurable if (and only if) $\mathcal{F}$ includes all nonempty subsets of N.

W.l.o.g., we assume $N \in \mathcal{F}$ in the sequel. We furthermore let $\mathbf{1}_X \in \{0,1\}^{\mathcal{F}}$ be the incidence function of a subset $X \subseteq N$. So $\mathbf{1}_F$ is $\mathcal{F}$-measurable for any $F \in \mathcal{F}$.

We set $\langle x, x' \rangle := \sum_{i \in N} x_i x_i'$ for any $x, x' \in \mathbb{R}^N$. Similarly, $\langle y, y' \rangle$ denotes the inner product of arbitrary vectors $y, y' \in \mathbb{R}^{\mathcal{F}}$.

2.1 Games, Capacities and Möbius Representation

A *game* on $\mathcal{F}$ is any mapping $v : \mathcal{F} \to \mathbb{R}$. We let $\mathcal{F}_0 := \mathcal{F} \cup \{\emptyset\}$ and extend v by setting $v(\emptyset) := 0$. A *capacity* c is a nonnegative game which is monotone, that is, if $F \subseteq G$, $F, G \in \mathcal{F}$, then $c(F) \leq c(G)$.

For any $F \in \mathcal{F}$ we introduce the *unanimity game* $\zeta^F : \mathcal{F} \to \{0,1\}$ defined by $\zeta^F(G) = 1$ if and only if $G \supseteq F$.

The m unanimity games ζ^F are linearly independent and form the so-called *incidence basis* of the vector space $\mathcal{V}$ of all games. To see the basis property, choose an arrangement $\mathcal{F} = (F_1, \ldots, F_m)$ so that for all $1 \leq i, j \leq m$,

$$F_i \supseteq F_j \implies i \leq j, \tag{1}$$

and observe that the $(0, 1)$-matrix $Z = [z_{i,j}]$ with $z_{ij} = 1$ if and only if $F_i \supseteq F_j$ is upper triangular and of full rank. Therefore, any game can be written uniquely as

$$v = \sum_{F \in \mathcal{F}} m_F \zeta^F.$$

The above equation is known as the *Möbius representation* of v, and the mapping $F \mapsto m_F$ is the *Möbius transform* or *Möbius inverse* of v. Note that for any $F \in \mathcal{F}$

$$v(F) = \sum_{G \subseteq F} m_G.$$

Games with a nonnegative Möbius transform are necessarily monotone (and hence capacities), and are often called *positive games*. If in addition $v(N) = 1$ holds, we call v a *belief function* (following the terminology of Shafer [12] in the classical case $\mathcal{F}_0 = 2^N$). We denote by

$$\mathcal{V}^+ := \{v = \sum_{F \in \mathcal{F}} m_F \zeta^F \mid m_F \geq 0\}$$

the convex cone of positive games in $\mathbb{R}^m$.

3 Integrals

Let β be a belief function. An *integral* (relative to β) is a real-valued functional $[\beta]$ on $\mathbb{R}^N$ such that for all $f, g \in \mathbb{R}^N$, $\lambda \in \mathbb{R}_+$ and $F \in \mathcal{F}$ one has:

(i) $[\beta](\lambda f) = \lambda[\beta](f)$ (positive homogeneity).
(ii) $[\beta](f + g) \geq [\beta](f) + [\beta](g)$ (superadditivity).
(iii) $[\beta](\mathbf{1}_F) = \beta(F)$ (β-extension).

Let $\Delta_N := \{x \in \mathbb{R}_+^N \mid \langle \mathbf{1}_N, x \rangle = 1\}$ be the simplex of all probability distributions on N.

Lemma 1. *There is a unique integral β^* such that*

$$\beta^*(f) \leq [\beta](f) \quad \text{holds for all belief functions } \beta.$$

Moreover, one has

$$\begin{aligned}
\beta^*(f) &= \min\{\langle f, x \rangle \mid x \in \Delta_N, \langle \mathbf{1}_F, x \rangle \geq \beta(F), \forall F \in \mathcal{F}\} \\
&= \max\left\{\langle \beta, y \rangle \mid \sum_{F \in \mathcal{F}} y_F \mathbf{1}_F \leq f, y_F \geq 0, \forall F \neq N\right\}.
\end{aligned} \tag{2}$$

Remark 1. Formula (2) exhibits $\beta^*(f)$ as the minimal expected value of f relative to the probability distributions x on N that dominate the belief function β.

Lemma 1 may be proved similarly to [4, Lemma 1], by establishing

$$[\beta](f) = \min_{x \in \ker(\beta)} \langle f, x \rangle,$$

where $\ker[\beta] := \{x \in \Delta_N \mid \langle f, x \rangle \geq [\beta](f), \forall f \in \mathbb{R}^N\}$, which follows with arguments from convex analysis (see *e.g.* [10]), since $[\beta](f)$ is concave. We thus define the *Choquet integral* (on $\mathcal{F}$) with respect to the belief function β as

$$\int_{\mathcal{F}} f \, d\beta := \beta^*(f) \quad \text{for all } f \in \mathbb{R}^N. \tag{3}$$

Example 1. An *algebra* is a family $\mathcal{A}$ of subsets of N that is union and complementation closed. Given a probability measure π on $\mathcal{A}$, Lehrer [7] (see also [13]) defines an integral

$$\int_{\mathcal{A}} f \, d\pi := \sup\left\{\langle \pi, y \rangle \mid \sum_{A \in \mathcal{A}} y_A \mathbf{1}_A \leq f y_A \geq 0, \forall A \in \mathcal{A}\right\}, \tag{4}$$

for nonnegative functions $f \in \mathbb{R}^N_+$. It is not difficult to see that a probability measure π is a belief function relative to $\mathcal{A}$. The Monge algorithm below and formula (2) of Lemma 1 exhibit Lehrer's integral as a special case of the Choquet integral.

Lemma 2. *For every unanimity game ζ^F, one has*

$$\int_{\mathcal{F}} f \, d\zeta^F = \min_{i \in F} f_i \quad \text{for all } f \in \mathbb{R}^N.$$

Proof. Let $p \in F$ satisfy $f_p = \min_{i \in F} f_i$ and choose $x^p \in \Delta_N$ as the pth unit vector, i.e., $x^p_i = 1$ if and only if $i = p$. Define $y^F \in \mathbb{R}^{\mathcal{F}}$ by

$$y^F_N := \min_{j \in N} f_j, y^F_F := f_p - y^F_N \quad \text{and } y^F_G := 0 \text{ otherwise.}$$

Then one finds

$$\min\{\langle f, x \rangle \mid x \in \Delta_N, \langle \mathbf{1}_G, x \rangle \geq \zeta^F(G), \; \forall G \in \mathcal{F}\}$$
$$\leq \langle f, x^p \rangle = \langle \zeta^F, y^F \rangle$$
$$\leq \max \Big\{ \langle \zeta^F, y \rangle \mid \sum_{G \in \mathcal{F}} y_G \mathbf{1}_G \leq f, y_G \geq 0, \; \forall G \neq N \Big\}.$$

So the claim follows from Lemma 1.

3.1   The General Choquet Integral

For the game 0 (identically zero everywhere), we define

$$\int_{\mathcal{F}} f \, d0 := 0.$$

If $v \in \mathcal{V}^+ \setminus \{0\}$ is a non-trivial positive game, then $v' := v/v(N)$ is a belief function and we set

$$\int_{\mathcal{F}} f \, dv := v(N) \cdot \int_{\mathcal{F}} f \, dv'$$

and note that Lemma 1, in fact, holds for all positive games in $\mathcal{V}^+$. For a general game $v \in \mathcal{V}$, we group the Möbius coefficients m_F according to their sign and thus obtain the representation

$$v = v^+ - v^- \quad \text{for unique positive functions } v^+, v^- \in \mathcal{V}^+,$$

which motivates the definition

$$\int_{\mathcal{F}} f \, dv := \int_{\mathcal{F}} f \, dv^+ - \int_{\mathcal{F}} f \, dv^-.$$

Theorem 1. *The general Choquet integral functional $f \mapsto \int_{\mathcal{F}} f \, dv$ on $\mathbb{R}^N$ is positively homogeneous and continuous for every fixed game $v \in \mathcal{V}$, and enjoys the extension property*

$$\int_{\mathcal{F}} \mathbf{1}_F = v(F) \quad \text{for all } F \in \mathcal{F}.$$

Proof. The Choquet functional relative to a belief function is a concave $\mathbb{R}$-valued function on $\mathbb{R}^N$ and hence continuous. Its extension to general games preserves continuity, positive homogeneity and the extension property.

3.2 Computation of the Choquet Integral

Consider the following algorithm relative to a given $f \in \mathbb{R}^N$, where we have indexed $\mathcal{F} = \{F_1, \ldots, F_m\}$ as in (1), and write

$$\mathcal{F}(X) := \{F \in \mathcal{F} \mid F \subseteq X\} \quad \text{for any } X \subseteq N.$$

MONGE ALGORITHM (MA):

(M0) Initialize: $X \leftarrow N, c \leftarrow f, y \leftarrow 0$;
(M1) Let $M = F_i \in \mathcal{F}(X)$ be the set with minimal index i and choose an element $p \in M$ of minimal weight $c_p = \min_{j \in M} c_j$;
(M2) Update: $X \leftarrow X \setminus \{p\}, y_M \leftarrow c_p, c \leftarrow (c - c_p \mathbf{1}_M)$;
(M3) If $\mathcal{F}(X) = \emptyset$, Stop and output y. Else goto (M1);

Employing a tie-breaking rule for the selection of p in step (M1), if necessary, we can assume w.l.o.g. that the output y is uniquely determined by the input f. So we obtain the linear *Monge functional*

$$v \mapsto [f](v) := \langle v, y \rangle$$

on the game space $\mathcal{V}$ and observe:

Theorem 2. *(a)* $\int_{\mathcal{F}} f \, dv = [f](v)$ *holds for all $\mathcal{F}$-measurable $f \in \mathbb{R}^N$ and all $v \in \mathcal{V}$.*

(b) $\int_{\mathcal{F}} f \, dv = [f](v)$ *holds for* all $f \in \mathbb{R}^N$ *and all $v \in \mathcal{V}$*
$$\Longleftrightarrow \quad [\forall F, G \in \mathcal{F} : F \cap G \neq \emptyset \implies F \cup G \in \mathcal{F}].$$

Proof. One shows that the equalities hold for v if (and only if) they hold for all unanimity games ζ^F, $F \in \mathcal{F}$, by using the linearity of the Monge functional (*cf.* [4, Theorem 1]). Then one checks that the Theorem is true for these unanimity games.

The set-theoretic condition in (b) defines *weakly union-closed systems* (see Section 4.2).

Corollary 1. *(i) Take an arbitrary family $\mathcal{F}$ and assume that $f \in \mathbb{R}^N$ is $\mathcal{F}$-measurable. Then*

$$\int_{\mathcal{F}} f \, dv = \sum_{F \in \mathcal{F}} m_F \min_{i \in F} f_i \quad \text{for all } v = \sum_{F \in \mathcal{F}} m_F \zeta^F \in \mathcal{V}. \tag{5}$$

(ii) Take an arbitrary function $f \in \mathbb{R}^N$ and a weakly union-closed family $\mathcal{F}$. Then again (5) holds.

Remark 2. Since an algebra $\mathcal{A}$ is union-closed, formula (2) of Lemma 1 and Theorem 2 (b) imply that Lehrer's integral (4) can be computed by the Monge algorithm.

The classical Choquet integral. Assume $\mathcal{F}_0 = 2^N$ and recall Choquet's [3] classical integral

$$\int f \, dv := \sum_{i=1}^{k} (\alpha_i - \alpha_{i-1}) v\{f \geq \alpha_i\} = \sum_{F \in \mathcal{F}} m_F \min_{i \in F} f_i, \tag{6}$$

where $\alpha_1 < \ldots < \alpha_k$ are the distinct values of f and $\alpha_0 := 0$. (The second equality results from the Möbius representation of v and is well-known for the classical Choquet integral (cf. [2]).

Every function $f \in \mathbb{R}^N$ is measurable in the classical context, where the underlying family $\mathcal{F} = 2^N \setminus \{\emptyset\}$ is union-closed. So Corollary 1 exhibits the classical Choquet integral (6) as a special case of our Choquet integral.

3.3 Extension of v

The classical Choquet integral (i.e., $\mathcal{F}_0 = 2^N$) with respect to a capacity was characterized by Schmeidler [11], essentially using the *comonotonic additivity* property. Two functions $f, f' \in \mathbb{R}^N$ are *comonotonic* if there are no $i, j \in N$ such that $f_i > f_j$ and $f_i' < f_j'$ (equivalently, if the combined level sets $\{i \in N \mid f_i \geq \alpha\}$, $\{j \in N \mid g_j \geq \alpha\}$ form a chain). A functional $I : \mathbb{R}^n \to \mathbb{R}$ is *comonotonic additive* if $I(f + f') = I(f) + I(f')$ is true for any two comonotonic $f, f' \in \mathbb{R}^n$.

The next result is a direct consequence of Theorem 4.2 in [9] and generalizes Schmeidler's result.

Proposition 1 (Characterization w.r.t. a Game). *The functional* $I : \mathbb{R}^n \to \mathbb{R}$ *is the Choquet integral w.r.t. a game* v *on* 2^N *if and only if* I *is positively homogeneous, comonotonic additive, and* $I(0) = 0$. v *is then uniquely determined by the extension property* $v(F) = I(\mathbf{1}_F)$.

We can show the next fundamental result.

Proposition 2. *Let* $\mathcal{F}$ *be weakly union-closed* (i.e., for all $F, G \in \mathcal{F}$, $F \cup G \in \mathcal{F}$ holds provided $F \cap G \neq \emptyset$). *Then the Choquet integral is comonotonic additive.*

Proof. From Corollary 1 we know that the Choquet integral satisfies (5), from which it is easy to show comonotonic additivity.

From Proposition 1 we therefore deduce the following important observation [4].

Theorem 3. *Let* $v : \mathcal{F} \to \mathbb{R}$ *be a game on the weakly union-closed system* $\mathcal{F}$. *Then there exists a unique game* $\hat{v} : 2^N \to \mathbb{R}$ *such that*

$$\int_{\mathcal{F}} f \, dv = \int_{2^N} f \, d\hat{v}, \quad \forall f \in \mathbb{R}^N,$$

where the right-hand side integral is the classical Choquet integral. Moreover, $\hat{v}$ *is determined by*

$$\hat{v}(A) = \int_{\mathcal{F}} \mathbf{1}_A \, dv = \sum_{B \text{ maximal in } \mathcal{F}(A)} v(B), \quad \forall A \in 2^N.$$

The last equality is implied by the Monge algorithm.

Clearly $v = \hat{v}$ on $\mathcal{F}$. This shows that $\hat{v}$ is an extension of v on 2^N.

Remark 3. Even if v is monotone relative to $\mathcal{F}$, $\hat{v}$ is not necessarily monotone relative to 2^N. Of course, there are many other extensions of v possible, each of them leading to a different integral with specific properties.

Another natural extension of v is the following v_*, given by

$$v_*(A) := \max_{B \text{ maximal in } \mathcal{F}(A)} v(B), \quad \forall A \in 2^N. \tag{7}$$

The extensions $\hat{v}$ and v_* always coincide if and only if for any $A \subseteq N$, $\mathcal{F}(A)$ contains a unique maximal element, which is equivalent to saying that $\mathcal{F}$ is closed under union. If v is a capacity, then v_* is the smallest extension of v being a capacity. Therefore, by monotonicity of the Choquet integral w.r.t. the set function and the characterization theorem of Schmeidler, $\int f \, dv_*$ is the smallest functional I being nondecreasing w.r.t. the integrand, comonotonic additive and such that $I(\mathbf{1}_F) = v(F)$ for each $F \in \mathcal{F}$.

4   Superadditivity

4.1   Monge Extensions

As in ([6]), we associate with any game $v \in \mathcal{V}$ its *Monge extension*

$$f \mapsto \hat{v}(f) = \langle v, y \rangle,$$

where y is the output of the Monge algorithm on input $f \in \mathbb{R}^N$. It is an extension of v since for every $F \in \mathcal{F}$, $\hat{v}(\mathbf{1}_F) = v(F)$ holds by Theorems 1 and 2. Moreover, we define the *core* of v as the convex set

$$\text{core}(v) := \{x \in \mathbb{R}^N \mid \langle f, x \rangle \geq \hat{v}(f), \ \forall f \in \mathbb{R}^N\}.$$

As in ([6], Theorem 4.1) one can now show

Lemma 3. *Let $v : \mathcal{F} \to \mathbb{R}_+$ be a nonnegative game. Then*

$$\text{core}(v) = \{x \in \mathbb{R}_+^N \mid \langle \mathbf{1}_N, x \rangle = v(N), \langle \mathbf{1}_F, x \rangle \geq v(F), \forall F \in \mathcal{F}\}.$$

As in the discussion of Lemma 1, we thus find

Theorem 4. *Let v be a nonnegative game on $\mathcal{F}$. Then the functional $f \mapsto \hat{v}(f)$ is superadditive if and only if for all $f \in \mathbb{R}^N$,*

$$\begin{aligned} \hat{v}(f) &= \min\{\langle f, x \rangle \mid x \in \text{core}(v)\} \\ &= \max\left\{\langle v, y \rangle \mid \sum_{F \in \mathcal{F}} y_F \mathbf{1}_F \leq f, y_F \geq 0, \ \forall F \neq N\right\}. \end{aligned} \tag{8}$$

Moreover, if $f \mapsto \hat{v}(f)$ is superadditive, then v is necessarily a capacity.

4.2   Weakly Union-Closed Systems

Assume now that $\mathcal{F}$ is *weakly union-closed* in the sense that it satisfies the condition in Theorem 2 (b) (*i.e.*, $F \cap G \neq \emptyset \implies F \cup G \in \mathcal{F}$).

Remark 4. Weakly union-closed systems have been studied by Algaba et al. [1] as *union-stable systems* with respect to games on communication graphs.

For weakly union-closed families, the Monge extension is identical with the Choquet functional for any game v on $\mathcal{F}$. Theorem 4 thus characterizes superadditive Choquet integrals relative to nonnegative games.

Given a nonnegative game v, we will refine this observation. We extend $\mathcal{F}$ to the family $\tilde{\mathcal{F}}$ of all those subsets $\tilde{F} \subseteq N$ with the property (*) $\tilde{F} = F^1 \cup \ldots \cup F^k$ for some suitable pairwise disjoint sets $F^t \in \mathcal{F}$ and define $\tilde{v}(\tilde{F}) := v(F^1) + \cdots + v(F^k)$ accordingly. Then one can verify:

Lemma 4. $\tilde{\mathcal{F}}$ *is union-closed and* $\tilde{v}$ *is a nonnegative game on* $\tilde{\mathcal{F}}$. *Moreover, one has*

$$\text{core}(\tilde{v}) = \text{core}(v).$$

Using the arguments in the proof of [4, Corollary 4], we now arrive at a generalization of Lovász' [8] characterization of superadditivity of the classical Choquet integral, which complements the characterization of supermodularity given in [6] and extends [4, Corollary 4]. We recall that a game v on 2^N is supermodular if

$$v(F \cup G) + v(F \cap G) \geq v(F) + v(G)$$

for every $F, G \subseteq N$.

Theorem 5. *Assume that* $\mathcal{F}$ *is weakly union-closed. Then the following statements are equivalent for every capacity* $v : \mathcal{F} \to \mathbb{R}_+$:

(a) *The functional* $f \mapsto \int_{\mathcal{F}} f \, dv$ *is superadditive on* $\mathbb{R}^N$.
(b) *There exists a supermodular function* $\overline{v} : 2^N \to \mathbb{R}_+$ *with* $v(\emptyset) = 0$ *such that* $\overline{v}(F) = v(F)$ *holds for all* $F \in \mathcal{F}$.

References

1. Algaba, E., Bilbao, J.M., Borm, P., López, J.J.: The Myerson value for union stable structures. Math. Meth. Oper. Res. 54, 359–371 (2001)
2. Chateauneuf, A., Jaffray, J.-Y.: Some characterizations of lower probabilities and other monotone capacities through the use of Möbius inversion. Mathematical Social Sciences 17, 263–283 (1989)
3. Choquet, G.: Theory of capacities. Annales de l'Institut Fourier 5, 131–295 (1953)
4. Faigle, U., Grabisch, M.: A discrete Choquet integral on ordered systems. working paper, University of Paris I (2009)
5. Faigle, U., Grabisch, M.: A Monge algorithm for computing the Choquet integral on set systems. In: Int. Fuzzy Systems Assoc. (IFSA) World Congress and Eur. Soc. for Fuzzy Logic and Technology (EUSFLAT) 2009, Lisbon, Portugal (2009)
6. Faigle, U., Grabisch, M., Heyne, M.: Monge extensions of cooperation and communication structures. European J. of Operational Research 206, 104–110 (2010)
7. Lehrer, E.: A new integral for capacities. Economic Theory (to appear)
8. Lovász, L.: Submodular functions and convexity. In: Bachem, A., Grötschel, M., Korte, B. (eds.) Mathematical programming. The state of the art, pp. 235–257. Springer, Heidelberg (1983)

 9. Murofushi, T., Sugeno, M., Machida, M.: Non-monotonic fuzzy measures and the choquet integral. Fuzzy Sets and Systems 64, 73–86 (1994)
10. Rockafellar, R.T.: Convex Analysis. Princeton University Press, Princeton (1970)
11. Schmeidler, D.: Integral representation without additivity. Proc. of the Amer. Math. Soc. 97(2), 255–261 (1986)
12. Shafer, G.: A Mathematical Theory of Evidence. Princeton Univ. Press, Princeton (1976)
13. Teper, R.: On the continuity of the concave integral. Fuzzy Sets and Systems 160, 1318–1326 (2009)

Necessity-Based Choquet Integrals for Sequential Decision Making under Uncertainty

Nahla Ben Amor[1], Hélène Fargier[2], and Wided Guezguez[1]

[1] LARODEC, Institut Superieur de Gestion Tunis, Tunisie
[2] IRIT-CNRS, UMR 5505 Université de Toulouse, France
nahla.benamor@gmx.fr, fargier@irit.fr, widedguezguez@gmail.com

Abstract. Possibilistic decision theory is a natural one to consider when information about uncertainty cannot be quantified in probabilistic way. Different qualitative criteria based on possibility theory have been proposed the definition of which requires a finite ordinal, non compensatory, scale for evaluating both utility and plausibility. In presence of heterogeneous information, i.e. when the knowledge about the state of the world is modeled by a possibility distribution while the utility degrees are numerical and compensatory, one should rather evaluate each decision on the basis of its Necessity-based Choquet value. In the present paper, we study the use of this criterion in the context of sequential decision trees. We show that it does not satisfy the monotonicity property on which rely the dynamic programming algorithms classically associated to decision trees. Then, we propose a Branch and Bound algorithm based on an optimistic evaluation of the Choquet value.

1 Introduction

Decision under uncertainty is one of the main fields of research in decision theory, due to its numerous applications (e.g. medicine, robot control, strategic decision, games...). In such problems, the consequence of a decision depends on uncertain events. In decision under risk, it is assumed that a precise probability is known for each event. A decision can thus be characterized by a lottery over possible consequences. In multistage decision making, one studies problems where one has to make a sequence of decisions conditionally to observable states. The problem is to choose a strategy assigning a decision (i.e. a lottery) to each state.

A popular criterion to compare lotteries and therefore strategies is the expected utility (*EU*) model axiomatized by von Neumann and Morgenstern [9]. This model relies on a probabilistic representation of uncertainty, while the preferences of the decision maker are supposed to be captured by a utility function assigning a numerical value to each outcome. The evaluation of a lottery is then performed via the computation of its expected utility (the greater, the better). Since strategies can be viewed as compound lotteries, they can also be compared on the basis of their expected utility. When the decision problem is sequential, the number of possible strategies grows exponentially. Hopefully, the EU model satisfies a *monotonicity property* that guarantees completeness of a polytime algorithm of dynamic programming.

E. Hüllermeier, R. Kruse, and F. Hoffmann (Eds.): IPMU 2010, LNAI 6178, pp. 521–531, 2010.

When the information about uncertainty cannot be quantified in a simple, probabilistic way the topic of possibilistic decision theory is often a natural one to consider [2] [4] [6]. Giving up the probabilistic quantification of uncertainty has led to give up the EU criterion as well. In [4], two qualitative criteria based on possibility theory, are proposed and axiomatized whose definitions only require a finite ordinal, non compensatory scale for evaluating both utility and plausibility. This yielded the development of sophisticated qualitative models for sequential decision making, e.g. possibilistic markov decision processes [13] [12], possibilistic ordinal decision trees [5] and possibilistic ordinal influence diagrams [5].

In presence of heterogeneous information, i.e. when the knowledge about the state of the world is possibilistic while the utility degrees are numerical and compensatory the previous models do not apply anymore. Following [14] and [7], Choquet integrals [1] appear as a right way to extend expected utility to non Bayesian models. Like the EU model, this model is a numerical, compensatory, way of aggregating uncertain utilities. But it does not necessarily resort on a Bayesian modeling of uncertain knowledge. Indeed, this approach allows the use of any monotonic set function [1], and thus of a necessity measure (integrals based on a possibility measure are generally given up since too adventurous). Unfortunately, the use of Necessity-based Choquet integrals in sequential decision making is not straightforward: Choquets integrals do not satisfy the principle of monotony in the general case. As a consequence, the optimality of the solution provided by dynamic programming is not granted. Hence a question arises: *do the Necessity-based Choquet integral satisfy the monotony principle and if not, which algorithm should we use to compute an optimal strategy?*

In the present paper, we show that the Necessity-based Choquet integral does not satisfy the monotonicity property and propose a Branch and Bound algorithm based on an optimistic evaluation of the Choquet value of possibilistic decision trees. This paper is organized as follows: the background notions are recalled in Section 2. Possibilistic decision trees are developed in Section 3. Section 4 is devoted to the algorithmic issues.

2   Background on Possibility Theory and Possibilistic Decision Making under Uncertainty

The basic building block in possibility theory is the notion of *possibility distribution* [3]. Let x be a variable whose value is ill-known and denote Ω the domain of x. The agent's knowledge about the value of x can be encoded by a possibility distribution $\pi : \Omega \rightarrow [0,1]$; $\pi(\omega) = 1$ means that value ω is totally possible for variable x and $\pi(\omega) = 0$ means that $x = \omega$ is impossible. From π, one can compute the possibility $\Pi(A)$ and necessity $N(A)$ of an event "$x \in A$":

$$\Pi(A) = sup_{v \in A}\pi(v) \tag{1}$$

$$N(A) = 1 - \Pi(\bar{A}) = 1 - sup_{v \notin A}\pi(v) \tag{2}$$

---

[1] This kind of set function is often called capacity or fuzzy measure.

Measure $\Pi(A)$ evaluates at which level A is *consistent* with the knowledge represented by π while $N(A)$ corresponds to the extent to which $\neg A$ is impossible and thus evaluates at which level A is certainly implied by the knowledge.

Given n non interactive (independent) possibilistic variables $x_1,...,x_n$ respectively restricted by $\pi_1,...,\pi_n$, the joint possibility distribution π on $\Omega_1,...,\Omega_n$ is a combination of $\pi_1,...,\pi_n$:

$$\pi(\omega_1, ..., \omega_n) = \pi_1(\omega_1) \otimes ... \otimes \pi_n(\omega_n). \tag{3}$$

The particularity of the possibilistic scale is that it can be interpreted in twofold: when the possibilistic scale is interpreted in an *ordinal* manner, i.e. when the possibility degree reflect only an ordering between the possible values, the *minimum* operator is used to combine different distributions ($\otimes = \min$). In a *numerical* interpretation, possibility distributions are related to upper bounds of imprecise probability distributions - $\otimes$ then corresponds to *product* operator ($\otimes = *$).

Following [4][2]'s possibilistic approach of decision making under uncertainty a decision can be seen as a possibility distribution over a finite set of states. In a single stage decision making problem, a utility function maps each state to a utility value in a set $U = \{u_1, ..., u_n\} \subseteq \mathbb{R}$ (we assume without loss of generality that $u_1 \leq \cdots \leq u_n$). This function models the attractiveness of each state for the decision maker. An act can then be represented by a possibility distribution on U, also called a (simple) *possibilistic lottery*, and denoted by $(\lambda_1/u_1, ..., \lambda_n/u_n)$: λ_i is the possibility that the decision leads to a state of utility u_i.

In the following, $\mathcal{L}$ denotes the set of simple lotteries (i.e. the set of possibility distributions over U). We shall also distinguish the set $\mathcal{L}_c \subseteq \mathcal{L}$ of constant lotteries over $\mathcal{L}$. Namely, $\mathcal{L}_c = \{\pi \text{ s.t. } \exists u_i, \pi(u_i) = 1 \text{ and } \forall u_j \neq u_i, \pi(u_j) = 0\}$. A possibilistic lottery $L \in \mathcal{L}$ is said to *overcome* a lottery $L' \in \mathcal{L}$ iff:

$$\forall u_i, N(L \geq u_i) \geq N(L' \geq u_i) \tag{4}$$

A *possibilistic compound lottery* $(\lambda_1/L^1, ..., \lambda_m/L^m)$ is a possibility distribution over $\mathcal{L}$. The possibility $\pi_{i,j}$ of getting a utility degree $u_j \in U$ from one of its sub-lotteries L^i depends on the possibility λ_i of getting L^i and on the possibility λ_j^i of getting u_j from L^i i.e. $\pi_{i,j} = \lambda_j \otimes \lambda_j^i$. More generally, the possibility of getting u_j from a compound lottery $(\lambda_1/L^1, ..., \lambda_m/L^m)$ is simply the *max*, over all L^i, of $\pi_{i,j}$. Thus, [4][2] have proposed to reduce $(\lambda_1/L^1, ..., \lambda_m/L^m)$ into a simple lottery defined by:

$$\lambda_1 \otimes L^1 \oplus ... \oplus \lambda_m \otimes L^m = (max_{j=1,m}\lambda_1^j \otimes \lambda_j/u_1, ..., max_{j=1,m}\lambda_n^j \otimes \lambda_j/u_n) \tag{5}$$

where $\otimes = \min$ (resp. $\otimes = *$) if the possibilistic scale is interpreted in an ordinal (resp. numerical) way. $\lambda_1 \otimes L^1 \oplus ... \oplus \lambda_m \otimes L^m$ is considered as equivalent to $(\lambda_1/L^1, ..., \lambda_m/L^m)$ and is called the *reduction* of the compound lottery.

Under the assumption that the utility scale and the possibility scale are commensurate and *purely ordinal*, [4] have proposed the following qualitative pessimistic and optimistic utility degrees for evaluating any simple lottery $L = (\lambda_1/u_1, ..., \lambda_n/u_n)$ (possibly issued from the reduction of a compound lottery):

$U_{pes}(L) = max_{i=1,n} \min(u_i, N(L \geq u_i))$ and $U_{opt}(L) = max_{i=1,n} \min(u_i, \Pi(L \geq u_i))$

$$(6)$$

where $\Pi(L \geq u_i) = max_{j=i,n}\lambda_j$ and $N(L \geq u_i) = 1 - \Pi(L < u_i) = 1 - max_{j=1,i-1}\lambda_j$ are the possibility and necessity degree that L reaches at least the utility value u_i. The U_{pes} degree estimates to what extend it is certain (i.e. necessary according to measure N) that L reaches a good utility. Its optimistic counterpart, U_{opt}, estimates to what extend it is possible that L reaches a good utility. Both are instances of the Sugeno integral [15] expressed as follows:

$$S_\mu(L) = max_{i=1,n} \min(u_i, \mu(L \geq u_i)) \qquad (7)$$

where μ is any capacity function, i.e. any set function s.t. $\mu(\emptyset) = 0, \mu(\Omega) = 1, A \subseteq B \Rightarrow \mu(A) \leq \mu(B)$. U_{pes} is recovered when μ is a necessity measure.

Under the same assumption of commensurability, but assuming that the utility degrees have a richer, cardinal interpretation, one shall synthesize the utility of L by a Choquet integral:

$$Ch_\mu(L) = \Sigma_{i=n,1}(u_i - u_{i-1}) \cdot \mu(L \geq u_i) \qquad (8)$$

If μ is a probability measure then $Ch_\mu(L)$ is simply the expected utility of L. In the present paper, we are interested by studying Choquet decision criterion in the possibilistic framework - this lead to let the capacity μ be a necessity measure N (integrals based on a possibility measure are generally given up since too adventurous). In this case, Equation (8) is expressed by $Ch_N(L) = \Sigma_{i=n,1}(u_i - u_{i-1}) \cdot N(L \geq u_i)$.

3   Possibilisitic Decision Trees

Decision trees [11] are graphical representations of sequential decision problems under the assumption of full observability (i.e. once a decision has been executed, its outcome is known and observed). A decision tree (see e.g. Figure 1) is a tree $GT = (\mathcal{N}, \mathcal{E})$. The set of nodes $\mathcal{N}$ contains three kinds of nodes:

- $\mathcal{D} = \{D_0, \ldots, D_m\}$ is the set of decision nodes (represented by rectangles). The labeling of the nodes is supposed to be in accordance with the temporal order i.e. if D_i is a descendant of D_j, then $i > j$. The root node of the tree is necessarily a decision node, denoted by D_0.
- $\mathcal{LN} = \{LN_1, \ldots, LN_k\}$ is the set of leaves, also called utility leaves: $\forall LN_i \in \mathcal{LN}$, $u(LN_i)$ is the utility of being eventually in node LN_i.
- $\mathcal{C} = \{C_1, \ldots, C_n\}$ is the set of chance nodes represented by circles. Chance nodes represent the possible action outcomes.

For any $X_i \in \mathcal{N}$, $Succ(X_i) \subseteq \mathcal{N}$ denotes the set of its children. Moreover, for any $D_i \in \mathcal{D}, Succ(D_i) \subseteq \mathcal{C}$: $Succ(D_i)$ is the set of actions that can be decided when D_i is observed. For any $C_i \in \mathcal{C}, Succ(C_i) \subseteq \mathcal{LN} \cup \mathcal{D}$: $Succ(C_i)$ is indeed the set of outcomes of action C_i - either a leaf node is observed, or a decision node is observed (and then a new action should be executed).

In classical, probabilistic, decision trees the uncertainty pertaining to the more or less possible outcomes of each C_i is represented by a probability distribution on $Succ(C_i)$. Here, we obviously use a possibilistic labeling, i.e. for any $C_i \in \mathcal{C}$, the uncertainty pertaining to the more or less possible outcomes of each C_i is represented by a *possibility degree* $\pi_i(X), \forall X \in Succ(C_i)$.

Solving the decision tree amounts to building a *strategy* that selects an action (i.e. a chance node) for each reachable decision node. Formally, we define a strategy as a function δ from $\mathcal{D}$ to $\mathcal{C} \cup \{\bot\}$. $\delta(D_i)$ is the action to be executed when a decision node D_i is observed. $\delta(D_i) = \bot$ means that no action has been selected for D_i (because either D_i cannot be reached or the strategy is partially defined). Admissible strategies must be:

– *sound*: $\forall D_i, \delta(D_i) \in Succ(D_i) \cup \{\bot\}$
– *complete*: (i) $\delta(D_0) \neq \bot$ and (ii) $\forall D_i$ s.t. $\delta(D_i) \neq \bot, \forall X_j \in Succ(\delta(D_i))$, either $\delta(X_j) \neq \bot$ or $X_j \in \mathcal{LN}$

Let Δ be the set of sound and complete strategies that can be built from the decision tree. Any strategy in Δ can be viewed as a connected subtree of the decision tree whose arcs are of the form $(D_i, \delta(D_i))$.

In the present paper, we interpret utility degrees in a numerical, compensatory, way and we are interested in strategies in Δ that maximize the Necessity-based Choquet criterion. The Choquet value of a (sound and complete) strategy can be determined thanks to the notion of lottery reduction. Recall indeed that leaf nodes ln in $\mathcal{LN}$ are labeled with utility degrees, or equivalently constant lotteries in $\mathcal{L}_c$. Then a chance node can be seen as either a lottery in $\mathcal{L}$, or as a compound lottery. The principle of the evaluation of a strategy is to reduce it in order to get an equivalent simple lottery, the Choquet value of which can then be computed. Formally, the composition of lotteries will be applied from the leafs of the strategy to its root, according to the following recursive definition:

$$\forall X_i \in \mathcal{N}, \quad L(X_i, \delta) = \begin{cases} < 1/u(X_i) > & if \ X_i \in \mathcal{LN} \\ L(\delta(X_i), \delta) & if \ X_i \in \mathcal{D} \\ Max_{X_j \in Succ(X_i)}\pi_i(X_j) \otimes L(X_j, \delta) & if \ X_i \in \mathcal{C} \end{cases} \quad (9)$$

Depending on the interpretation of the possibility degrees labeling the arcs of the tree, we can distinguish between ordinal, min-based possibilistic decision trees (for which $\otimes$ = min) and numerical, product-based possibilistic decision trees (for which $\otimes$ = *). Equation 9 is simply the adaptation to strategies of lottery reduction (Equation 5). We can then compute $L(\delta) = L(D_0, \delta) : L(\delta)(u_i)$ is simply the possibility of getting utility u_i when δ is applied from D_0. The Choquet value of δ can then be computed:

$$Ch_N(\delta) = Ch_N(L(D_0, \delta)) \quad (10)$$

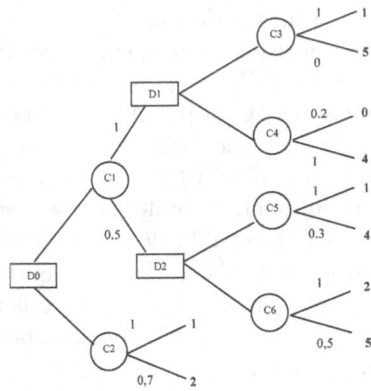

Fig. 1. Example of possibilistic decision tree with $\mathcal{C} = \{C_1, C_2, C_3, C_4, C_5, C_6\}$, $\mathcal{D} = \{D_0, D_1, D_2\}$ and $\mathcal{LN} = U = \{0, 1, 2, 3, 4, 5\}$

4 Finding the Choquet Optimal Strategy in Possibilistic Decision Trees

Given a possibilistic decision tree encoding a set of admissible strategies $\Delta = \{\delta_1 \dots \delta_n\}$, we are looking for a strategy δ^* such that $\forall \delta \in \Delta$, $Ch_N(\delta^*) \geq Ch_N(\delta)$. Unfortunately, finding optimal strategies via an exhaustive enumeration of Δ is a highly computational task. For instance, in a decision tree with n binary decision nodes, the number of potential strategies is in $O(2^{\sqrt{n}})$.

For standard probabilistic decision trees, where the goal is to maximize expected utility [11], an optimal strategy can be computed in polytime (with respect to the size of the tree) thanks to an algorithm of dynamic programming which builds the best strategy backwards, optimizing the decisions from the leaves of the tree to its root. Regarding possibilistic decision trees, Garcia and Sabbadin [5] have shown that such a method can also be used to get a strategy maximizing U_{pes}. The reason is that like EU, U_{pes} satisfies the following key property of monotonicity:

Definition 1. *Let V be a decision criterion. V is said to be monotonic iff whatever L, L' and $L"$, whatever the normalized distribution (α, β):*

$$V(L) \geq V(L') \quad \Rightarrow \quad V((\alpha \otimes L) \oplus (\beta \otimes L")) \geq V((\alpha \otimes L') \oplus (\beta \otimes L")). \quad (11)$$

This property states that the combination of L (resp. L') with a third one, $L"$, does not change the order induced by V between L and L' - this allows dynamic programming to decide in favor of L before considering the compound decision.

Unfortunately monotonicity is not satisfied by any criterion. Some Choquet integrals, e.g. the one encoding the Rank Dependent Utility model, may fail to fulfill this condition (see e.g. [8]). We show in the following counter examples that this can also be the case when using Necessity-based Choquet integrals:

Counter Example 1 (Numerical Setting). *Let* $L =< 0.1/1, 1/2, 0/3 >$, L' $=< 0.9/1, 0/2, 1/3 >$ *and* $L" =< 1/1, 0.1/2, 0/3 >$; *let* $L_1 = (\alpha \otimes L) \oplus (\beta \otimes L")$ *and* $L_2 = (\alpha \otimes L') \oplus (\beta \otimes L")$, *with* $\alpha = 1$ *and* $\beta = 0.9$.
Using equation (5) with $\otimes = *$ *we have:* $L_1 =< 0.9/1, 1/2, 0/3 >$
and $L_2 =< 0.9/1, 0.09/2, 1/3 >$
It is easy to show that $Ch_N(L) = 1.9$ *and* $Ch_N(L') = 1.2$, *then* $L \succ L'$. *But* $Ch_N(L_1) = 1.1 < Ch_N(L_2) = 1.2$: *this contradicts the monotonicity property.*

Counter Example 2 (Ordinal Setting). *Let* $L =< 0.2/0, 0.5/0.51, 1/1 >$, $L' =< 0.1/0, 0.6/0.5, 1/1 >$ *and* $L" =< 0.01/0, 1/1 >$; ; *let* $L_1 = (\alpha \otimes L) \oplus (\beta \otimes$ $L") $ *and* $L_2 = (\alpha \otimes L') \oplus (\beta \otimes L")$, *with* $\alpha = 0.55$ *and* $\beta = 1$.
Using equation (5) with $\otimes = min$ *we have:* $L_1 =< 0.2/0, 0.5/0.51, 1/1 >$ *and* $L_2 =< 0.1/0, 0.55/0.5, 1/1 >$.
Computing $Ch_N(L) = 0.653$ *and* $Ch_N(L') = 0.650$ *we get* $L \succ L'$. *But* $Ch_N(L_1)$ $= 0.653 < Ch_N(L_2) = 0.675$: *this contradicts the monotonicity property.*

As a consequence, the application of dynamic programming to the case of the Necessity-based Choquet integral may lead to a suboptimal strategy. As an alternative, we have chosen to proceed by implicit enumeration via a Branch and Bound algorithm, following [8] for the case of another (non possibilistic) Choquet integral, namely the one encoding the Rank Dependent Utility criterion. The fact that implicit enumeration performs better for RDU than the resolute choice approach proposed in [10] encourages us to adapt it to our case.

The Branch and Bound algorithm (outlined by Algorithm 1.1) takes as argument a partial strategy δ and an upper bound of the best Choquet value it can reach. It returns the value Ch_N^{opt} of the best strategy found so far, δ^{opt}. As initial value for δ we will choose the empty strategy ($\delta(D_i) = \bot, \forall D_i$). For δ^{opt}, we can choose the one provided by the dynamic programming algorithm. Indeed, even not necessarily providing an optimal strategy, this algorithm may provide a good one, at least from a consequentialist point of view.

At each step, the current partial strategy, δ, is developed by the choice of an action for some unassigned decision node. When several decision nodes need to be developed, the one with the minimal rank (i.e. the former one according to the temporal order) is developed first. The recursive procedure stops when either the current strategy is complete (then δ^{opt} and Ch_N^{opt} may be updated) or proves to be worst than δ^{opt} in any case. To this extent, we call a function that computes a lottery $Lottery(\delta)$ that overcomes all those associated with the complete strategies compatible with δ and use $Ch_N(Lottery(\delta))$ as an upper bound of the Choquet value of the best strategy compatible with δ - the evaluation is sound, because whatever L, L', if L overcomes L', then $Ch_N(L) \geq Ch_N(L')$. Whenever $Ch_N(Lottery(\delta)) \leq Ch_N^{opt}$, the algorithms backtracks, yielding the choice of another action for the last decision nodes considered. Moreover when δ is complete, $Lottery(\delta)$ returns $L(D_0, \delta)$; the upper bound is equal to the Choquet value when computed for a complete strategy.

Function $Lottery$ (see algorithm 1.2) inputs a partial strategy. It proceeds backwards, assigning a simple lottery $< 1/u(NL_i) >$ to each terminal.

Algorithm 1. BB

Data: A (possibly partial) strategy δ, the evaluation its Choquet value, Ch_N^δ

Result: Ch_N^{opt} % also memorizes the best strategy found so far, δ^{opt}

begin

if $\delta = \emptyset$ then $\mathcal{D}_{pend} = \{D_1\}$ else

$$D_{pend} = \{D_i \in \mathcal{D} \text{ s.t. } \begin{array}{l} \delta(D_i) = \perp \text{ and} \\ \exists D_j, \delta(D_j) \neq \perp \text{ and } D_i \in Succ(\delta(D_j)) \end{array} \}$$

if $\mathcal{D}_{pend} = \emptyset$ (% δ is a complete strategy) then

if $Ch_N^\delta > Ch_N^{opt}$ then

$\delta^{opt} \leftarrow \delta$

return Ch_N^δ

else

$D_{next} \leftarrow arg\ min_{D_i \in D_{pend}}\ i$

foreach $C_i \in Succ(D_{next})$ **do**

$\delta(D_{next}) \leftarrow C_i$

$Eval \leftarrow Ch_N(Lottery(D_0, \delta))$

if $Eval > Ch_N^{opt}$ then

$Ch_N^{opt} \leftarrow \max(Ch_N^{opt}, \delta, Eval)$

return Ch_N^{opt}

end

Algorithm 2. Lottery

Data: a node X, a (possibly partial) strategy δ

Result: L^X % $L^X[u_i]$ is the possibility degree to have the utility u_i

begin

for $i \in \{1, .., n\}$ **do** $L^X[u_i] \leftarrow 0$

if $X \in \mathcal{LN}$ then $L^X[u(X)] \leftarrow 1$

if $X \in \mathcal{C}$ then

foreach $Y \in Succ(X)$ **do**

$L^Y \leftarrow Lottery(Y, \delta)$

for $i \in \{1, .., n\}$ **do** $L^X[u_i] \leftarrow \max(L^X[u_i], \pi_X(Y) \otimes L^Y[u_i])$

% $\otimes = \min$ in the ordinal setting ; $\otimes = *$ in the numerical setting

if $X \in \mathcal{D}$ then

if $\delta(X) \neq \perp$ then $L^X = Lottery(\delta(X), \delta)$ else

if $|Succ(X)| = 1$ then

$L^X = Lottery(\delta(Succ(X)), \delta)$

else

foreach $Y \in Succ(X) \cap N_\delta$ **do**

$L^Y \leftarrow Lottery(Y, \delta)$

for $i \in \{1, .., n\}$ **do** $G_Y^c[u_i] \leftarrow 1 - max_{u_j < u_i} L^Y[u_j]$

% Compute the upper envelop of the cumulative functions)

for $i \in \{1, .., n\}$ **do** $G^c[u_i] \leftarrow \max_{Y \in Succ(X) \cap N_\delta} G_Y^c[u_i]$

% Compute $Rev(G^c)$

$L^X[u_n] \leftarrow 1$

for $i \in \{n-1, .., 1\}$ **do** $L^X[u_i] \leftarrow 1 - G^c[u_{i+1}]$

return L^X

end

node LN_i . At each chance node C_i, we perform a composition of the lotteries in $Succ(C_i)$ according to Equation (9). At each decision node D_i we ascend a lottery that overcomes all those in $Succ(D_i)$. To this end, let us use the following notations and definitions:

- Given a simple lottery $L \in \mathcal{L}$, G_L^c is the *possibilistic decumulative* function of L: $\forall u \in U, G_L^c(u) = N(L \geq u)$
- Given a set $\mathcal{G} = \{G_{L_1}^c, \ldots, G_{L_k}^c\}$ of decumulative functions, the *upper envelop* of $\mathcal{G}$ is the decumulative function $G_{\mathcal{G}}^c$ defined by:
  $\forall u \in U, G_{\mathcal{G}}^c(u) = max_{G_{L_i}^c \in \mathcal{G}} G_{L_i}^c(u)$
- Given a decumulative function G^c on U, $Rev(G^c)$ is the lottery defined by:
  $$Rev(G^c)(u_i) = \begin{cases} 1 & if \; i = n \\ 1 - G^c(u_{i+1}) & if \; i \in \{1, \ldots, n-1\} \end{cases}$$

Now it is easy to show that the possibilistic decumulative function associated to a lottery $Rev(G^c)$ is equal to G^c. As a consequence:

Proposition 1. [2] *Given a set $\{L_1, \ldots, L_k\} \subseteq \mathcal{L}$ of simple lotteries over U, $\mathcal{G} = \{G_{L_1}^c, \ldots, G_{L_k}^c\}$ the set of their decumulative functions, we have: $Rev(G_{\mathcal{G}}^c)$ overcomes any lottery $L_i \in \{L_1, \ldots, L_k\}$.*

Hence, the Choquet value of $Lottery(D_0, \delta)$ is an upper bound of the Choquet value of the best complete strategy compatible with δ, which proofs the correctness of our algorithm.

Example 1. The major steps executed by the BB algorithm on the min-based possibilistic decision tree of Figure 1 can be summarized as follows (we suppose that δ^{opt} has been initialized with $((D_0, C_2))$, the Choquet value of which is 1).

- $\delta = \emptyset$ and $Ch_N^{opt} = 1$. BB calls $Ch_N(Lottery(D_0, (D_0, C_1)))$
  $L^{D_2} = (0/0, 0.2/1, 0.2/2, 1/4, 1/5)$, $L^{D_3} = (0/0, 0/1, 1/2, 1/4, 1/5)$.
  So, $Lottery(D_0, (D_0, C_1)) = (0/0, 0.2/1, 0.5/2, 0.5/3, 1/4, 1/5)$
  and $Eval = Ch_N(Lottery(D_0, (D_0, C_1))) = 2.8 > 1$.
- $\delta = (D_0, C_1)$ and $Ch_N^{opt} = 1$. BB calls $Ch_N(Lottery(D_0, ((D_0, C_1), (D_2, C_3))))$.
  $Lottery(D_0, ((D_0, C_1), (D_2, C_3))) = (0/0, 1/1, 0.5/2, 0.5/3, 0.5/4, 0.5/5)$
  and $Eval = Ch_N(Lottery(D_0, ((D_0, C_1), (D_2, C_3)))) = 1 = 1$.
  $\delta = (D_0, C_1)$ and $Ch_N^{opt} = 1$. BB calls $Ch_N(Lottery(D_0, ((D_0, C_1), (D_2, C_4))))$
  $Lottery(D_0, ((D_0, C_1), (D_2, C_4))) = (0.2/0, 0/1, 0.5/2, 0.5/3, 1/4, 0.5/5)$
  and $Eval = Ch_N(Lottery(D_0, ((D_0, C_1), (D_2, C_4)))) = 2.6 > 1$.
- $\delta = ((D_0, C_1), (D_2, C_4))$ and $Ch_N^{opt} = 1$. BB calls $Ch_N(Lottery(D_0, ((D_0, C_1), (D_2, C_4), (D_3, C_5))))$,
  $Lottery(D_0, ((D_0, C_1), (D_2, C_4), (D_3, C_5))) = (0.2/0, 0.5/1, 0/2, 0/3, 1/4, 0/5)$
  and $Eval = Ch_N(Lottery(D_0, ((D_0, C_1), (D_2, C_4), (D_3, C_5)))) = 2.3 > 1$.
- $\delta = ((D_0, C_1), (D_2, C_4), (D_3, C_5))$ and $Ch_N^{opt} = 1$.
  There is no more pending decision node. $\delta^{opt} \leftarrow ((D_0, C_1), (D_2, C_4), (D_3, C_5))$, $Ch_N^{opt} \leftarrow 2.3$
- $\delta = ((D_0, C_1), (D_2, C_4))$ and $Ch_N^{opt} = 2.3$. BB calls $Ch_N(Lottery(D_0, ((D_0, C_1), (D_2, C_4), (D_3, C_6))))$,
  $Lottery(D_0, ((D_0, C_1), (D_2, C_4), (D_3, C_6))) = (0.2/0, 0/1, 0.5/2, 0/3, 1/4, 0.5/5)$
  and $Eval = Ch_N(Lottery(D_0, ((D_0, C_1), (D_2, C_4), (D_3, C_6)))) = 2.6 > 2.3$.

---

[2] Obviously, $G_{Rev(G^c)}^c(u_1) = 1 = G^c(u_1)$. Note that $\forall i = 2, n, Rev(G^c)(u_i) \geq Rev(G^c)(u_{i-1})$. Hence $G_{Rev(G^c)}^c(u_i) = 1 - max_{j=1, i-1} Rev(G^c)(u_j) = 1 - Rev(G^c)(u_{i-1})$. Since $Rev(G^c)u_{i-1} = 1 - G^c(u_i)$, we get $G_{Rev(G^c)}^c(u_i) = G^c(u_i)$. Thus $G_{Rev(G^c)}^c = G^c$.

- $\delta = ((D_0, C_1), (D_2, C_4), (D_3, C_5))$ and $Ch_N^{opt} = 2.3$.
  There is no more pending decision node. $\delta^{opt} \leftarrow ((D_0, C_1), (D_2, C_4), (D_3, C_6))$, $Ch_N^{opt} \leftarrow 2.6$
- etc.

The algorithm eventually terminates with $\delta^{opt} = ((D_0, C_1), (D_2, C_4), (D_3, C_6))$ and $Ch_N^{opt} = 2.6$.

5   Conclusion

In this paper, we have proposed to use the Necessity-based Choquet Integral to optimize decision in *heterogeneous* possibilistic decision trees, where the utility levels of consequences are numerical in essence. We have shown that dynamic programming cannot be applied to find optimal strategies since the monotonicity property on which this algorithm relies is not satisfied by this criterion. As an alternative solution, we have developed a Branch and Bound algorithm based on an optimistic evaluation of the Choquet value (namely by taking the upper envelop of the decumulative functions of the concurrent possible actions). The implementation of this approach is under progress.

The further development of this work deals with the optimization of Necessity-based Choquet integrals and Sugeno Integrals in heterogeneous possibilistic influence diagrams, considering, again, both the numerical and the purely ordinal interpretation of possibility degrees.

References

1. Choquet, G.: Théorie des capacités. Technical report, Annales de l'institut Fourier, Grenoble (1953)
2. Dubois, D., Gogo, L., Prade, H., Zapico, A.: Making decision in a qualitative setting: from decision under uncertainty to case-based decision. In: Proceedings of KR'98, Juin 1998, pp. 594–607 (1998)
3. Dubois, D., Prade, H.: Possibility theory, an approach to computerized processing of uncertainty. Plenum Press, New York (1988)
4. Dubois, D., Prade, H.: Possibility theory as a basis for qualitative decision theory. In: Proceedings of IJCAI'95, Montreal, pp. 1924–1930 (1995)
5. Garcia, L., Sabbadin, R.: Possibilistic influence diagrams. In: Brewka, G., et al. (eds.) Proceedings of ECAI'06, Riva del Garda, pp. 372–376 (2006)
6. Giang, P.H., Shenoy, P.P.: Two axiomatic approaches to decision making using possibility theory. EJOR 162(2), 450–467 (2005)
7. Gilboa, I.: Maxmin expected utility with non unique prior. Journal of mathematical economics 18, 141–153 (1988)
8. Jeantet, G., Spanjaard, O.: Rank-dependent probability weighting in sequential decision problems under uncertainty. In: Proceedings of ICAPS'08, pp. 148–155 (2008)
9. Neumann, J.V., Morgenstern, O.: Theory of games and economic behavior. Princeton University Press, Princeton (1948)
10. Nielson, D.N., Jaffray, J.Y.: Dynamic decision making without expected utility: an operationnal approach. EJOR 169, 226–246 (2004)

11. Raiffa, H.: Decision Analysis: Introductory lectures on choices under uncertainty. Addison-Wesley, Reading (1968)
12. Sabbadin, R.: A possibilistic model for qualitative sequential decision problems under uncertainty in partially observable environments. In: Proceedings of UAI'99, pp. 567–574 (1999)
13. Sabbadin, R., Fargier, H.: Towards qualitative approaches to multi-stage decision making. IJAR 19 (1998)
14. Schmeidler, D.: Subjective probability and expected utility without additivity. Econometrica 57, 517–587 (1989)
15. Sugeno, M.: Theory of fuzzy integral and its applications. PhD thesis, Institute of technology, Tokyo (1974)

A Fuzzy-Rule-Based Approach
to Contextual Preference Queries

Allel Hadjali, Amine Mokhtari, and Olivier Pivert

Irisa/Enssat, University of Rennes 1
Technopole Anticipa 22305 Lannion Cedex France
{hadjali,mokhtari,pivert}@enssat.fr

Abstract. In this paper, we propose a fuzzy-rule-based model for the
representation of contextual preferences in a database querying framework. We discuss the augmentation of a query with preferences deduced
from information regarding the current context of the user. To this end,
we present an approach based on generalized modus ponens pattern.

Keywords: Preferences, Context, Fuzzy rules, Query augmentation.

1   Introduction

Personalization systems exploit user preferences for selecting the most relevant
data from a potentially huge amount of information. According to his/her context or situation, a user may have different preferences. For instance, a tourist
visiting Paris may prefer to visit *La Tour Eiffel* on a nice sunny day and *Le
Louvre* museum on a rainy day. In other words, the result of a preference query
may depend on the context.

Context is a term which captures any information that can be used to characterize the situation of an entity [1], i.e. of a person, place or object considered
relevant to the interaction between a user and an application. Common context
types involve the *user context* (e.g., profile, location), the *physical context* (e.g.,
noise levels, temperature), and *time*. A system is said to be context-aware if it
uses context to provide relevant information and/or services to its users.

Contextual preferences have recently attracted considerable attention in many
research fields [2,3]. In the approach to contextual preferences proposed in [4], a
context state is represented as a situation. Situations are uniquely linked through
an n:m relationship with qualitative preferences. A knowledge-based context-
aware preference model for database querying is proposed in [5] where preferences
and associated applicable contexts are treated uniformly through description
logic concept expressions. Context as a set of dimensions is also considered in
[6] where the problem of representing context-dependent semi-structured data
is studied. Context has also been used in information filtering to define filters
which have attributes whose values change frequently [7].

In the approach by Stefanidis *et al.* [8], the context is represented as a set
of multidimensional parameters. Each one takes values from a hierarchical domain which enhances the expressiveness of the model. The objective is to find

E. Hüllermeier, R. Kruse, and F. Hoffmann (Eds.): IPMU 2010, LNAI 6178, pp. 532–541, 2010.
© Springer-Verlag Berlin Heidelberg 2010

the most interesting data items based on user preferences which are enriched with contextual information. However, this approach does not deal with gradual contextual parameters. Moreover, it uses a numeric score (called *interest score*, whose purpose is to rank tuples) without a clear semantics and which is managed in an *ad hoc* way (e.g., when aggregating preferences).

In this paper, we propose a fuzzy-rule-based model for the representation of user preferences and context-related information. This approach allows to capture gradual concepts and to describe the context in a flexible way, thus offering more user-friendliness and robustness. In particular, we show how user queries can be augmented with preferences deduced from rules which describe the current context of the user.

The rest of the paper is structured as follows. Section 2 provides a critical review of Stefanidis *et al.*'s approach that constitutes a starting point of our work. Section 3 presents a fuzzy-rule-based context modeling approach. In Section 4, we address the issue of augmenting user query by inferring new preferences regarding context information. Section 5 deals with algorithmic aspects of the query augmentation process and provides a detailed example to illustrate the approach. Section 6 concludes the paper with a summary of its contributions and outlines some perspectives for future work.

2   Stefanidis *et al.*'s Approach to Contextual Preferences

We take as a starting point the approach by Stefanidis *et al.* [8,9] whose principle is recalled hereafter.

2.1   Context Modeling

In [8,9], the context is modeled as a finite set $\{C_1, C_2, \ldots, C_n\}$ of multidimensional parameters, for instance, $\{location, weather, accompanying\_people\}$. Each parameter C_i takes its values from a hierarchical domain, called *extended domain*, $edom(C_i)$. For example, a weather context parameter can be defined on three levels (see Figure 1): the detailed level $Conditions(L_1)$ whose domain includes *freezing, cold, mild, warm* and *hot* ; the level *weather characterization* (L_2) which just refers to whether the weather is *good* (grouping *mild, warm,* and *hot*) or *bad* (grouping *freezing* and *cold*) ; and the level ALL (L_3) that groups all values into a single value *"all"*. Thus, each context parameter can be viewed from

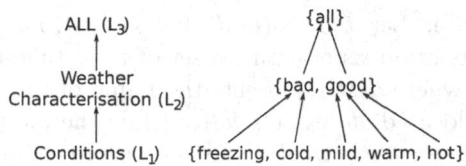

Fig. 1. Extended domain of weather parameter

different levels of detail. An instantiation of the context, called *context state*, is a tuple $\omega = (c_1, c_2, \ldots, c_n)$ where, $c_i \in edom(C_i), 1 \leq i \leq n$. For instance, ω may be (*Athens, warm, friends*) for the example above.

A contextual preference is modeled as a triple *(cod, attributes_clauses, interest_score)* where *cod* is a context descriptor representing a set of context states, the *attributes_clauses* $\{A_1\,\theta_1\,a_1, \ldots, A_n\,\theta_n\,a_n\}$ specify a set of attributes (which represent non-contextual parameters) and their values $a_1, \ldots, a_n$ with $a_i \in dom(A_i)$ — the domain of attribute A_i —, $\theta \in \{=, \neq, \leq, \geq, <, >\}$ and *interest_score* is a real number between 0 and 1. The meaning is that in the set of context states specified by *cod*, all tuples for which the attributes $A_1, A_2, \ldots, A_n$ satisfy the conditions $A_i\,\theta\,a_i, i = 1, n$ get the interest score *interest_score*.

2.2   Context Resolution

Let P be a user *profile tree* representing a set of contextual preferences and Q a contextual query, i.e., a query enhanced with an extended context descriptor (a set of context states with each state having a specific value for each context parameter). The problem addressed by Stefanidis *et al.* is to identify the contextual preferences that are the most relevant to the context states of the query Q. To this end, for every context state s of Q, a *context resolution* technique is used to locate in the profile tree P, the paths which exactly or approximately matches s. In particular, distance-based measures are used to express similarity between two context states.

The main advantages of Stefanidis *et al.*'s approach are its simplicity and its ability to capture the context at different levels of abstraction. Moreover, when a contextual query does not match any of the given preferences, possible relaxations of the query context can be considered by replacing the value of a context parameter by a more general one. However, some major limitations can be noticed, notably in the ability of the approach to make profit of the profile tree, from which no additional preference can be inferred. Only the preferences explicitly defined by the user are used to enhance the query. Besides, the approach fails to capture gradual concepts when describing the context (as for instance, the weather is *fairly cold*) and forces the user to manually set the values of the scores and specify the functions to aggregate these scores.

3   Fuzzy Model to Contextual Preferences

In this section, we show how fuzzy rules can be used for modeling contextual preferences. For the sake of illustration, the following reference example is used.

Reference example: Let $travAg(id\_dest, dest, cost, date_b, date_e, animation, calm, charm)$ be a relation representing a set of trips (flight + hotel) proposed by a travel agency, where *dest* represents the name of the destination and the country where it is located, $date_b$ and $date_e$ define the interval of time wherein the trip is available, *animation, calm* and *charm* are criteria used for describing the destination's surroundings. We assume that a rating score in [0, 100] is assigned to each criterion (defined, e.g., on the basis of user's experiences).

3.1   Fuzzy Context Modeling

We use a finite set of parameters to represent a context that we call *context parameters*. For a given application X, we define its context environment CE_X as a set of n context parameters $\{C_1, C_2, \ldots, C_n\}$. An instantiation of the context, called *context state*, writes:

$$\omega = (C_1 \text{ is } E'_1 \wedge C_2 \text{ is } E'_2 \wedge \ldots \wedge C_k \text{ is } E'_k), k \leq n$$

where each $C_i \in CE_X$, $1 \leq i \leq k$ and $E'_i \subseteq dom(C_i)$ stands for a fuzzy set describing the parameter C_i. In our example, four context parameters may be considered: accompanying people $acc\_people = \{nobody, family, wife, friends\}$, professional status $status = \{student, unemployed, executive, employee, retired person\}$, age of the traveler and $period$ when the traveler wishes to leave. As it will be seen, age and $period$ may be described either in a crisp or a fuzzy way.

An example of a context state is $(acc\_people$ is $\{friends\}$, age is $young$, $period$ is $begin\_summer)$ where $young$ (resp. $begin\_summer$) is a fuzzy set whose trapezoidal membership function[1] (t.m.f.) is $(17, 19, 25, 27, 0)$ (resp. $(Jun.\ 21, Jun.\ 21, Jul.\ 7, Jul.\ 31, 0)$).

3.2   Contextual Preferences

Definition 1 (Contextual Preference). *A contextual preference CP is a fuzzy rule of the form: **if** C_1 is E_1 $\wedge$ $\ldots$ $\wedge$ C_m is E_m **then** A is F, where $E_i, 1 \leq i \leq m \leq n$, represents a crisp or fuzzy value of the context parameter C_i and F is a fuzzy set describing the preference related to attribute A.*

The meaning of CP is that in the context state specified by the left part of the rule, the preference A *is* F is inferred. Roughly speaking, the premise of the rule describes the context wherein the preference contained in the conclusion part of the rule is relevant to the user.

Example 1. *Young* travelers generally prefer *inexpensive* trips. This may be expressed as (CP_1): **if** *age is young* **then** *cost is inexpensive.*

Example 2. A *young* traveler accompanying his/her *friends* usually prefers *animated destinations*, i.e., trips having a *high* animation score. This yields (CP_2): **if** *age is young* **and** *acc_people is {friends}* **then** *animation is high.*

Without loss of generality, only rules with a single conclusion are considered. Let us also emphasize that it is not necessary for a contextual preference to depend on all contextual parameters. In Example 1, contextual preference CP_1 means that a *young* traveler prefers an inexpensive trip independently from other contextual parameters. From a formal viewpoint, contextual preferences are faithfully represented by *gradual rules* [10]. Such rules are of the form "if x is A then y is B" and express "the more x is A, the more y is B".

---

[1] We use t.m.fs of the form (a, b, c, d, Δ) where $[a, d]$ and $[b, c]$ are the support and the core resp., and Δ is an indetermination level which will be explained further.

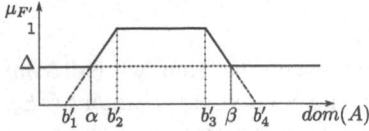

Fig. 2. t.m.f of F'

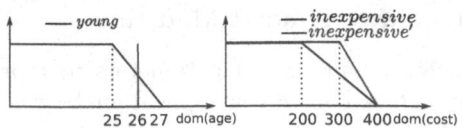

Fig. 3. t.m.f of *young*, *inexpensive* and *inexpensive'*

4   Selection of Relevant Preferences

In this section, we focus on the first step of the query augmentation process that consists in identifying the set of relevant preferences and their semantics regarding the user context. Let $B^{CP} = \{CP_1, \ldots, CP_m\}$ be a fuzzy rule base modeling a set of contextual preferences and Q a user query formulated in a given context ω. We refer to the set of contextual parameters present in ω (resp. $CP_i, i = 1, m$) by $context(\omega) \subseteq CE_X$ (resp. $context(CP_i)$).

4.1   Principle of the Approach

The goal is to infer a set of relevant preferences from the fuzzy rules base B^{CP} regarding the context ω. To achieve this, we make use of the *generalized modus ponens* as an inference pattern. In its simplest form, it reads:

> from the rule: **if** C is E **then** A is F
> and the fact: C is E'

the following preference A *is* F' can be inferred, where F' is computed using E', E and F. For $v \in dom(A)$, $\mu_{F'}(v)$ is computed by means of the combination/projection principle [10]:

$$\mu_{F'}(v) = sup_{u \in dom(C)} \top (\mu_{E'}(u), \mu_E(u) \to \mu_F(v)))$$

where $\top$ stands for a triangular norm and $\to$ a fuzzy implication. Assuming that the operator $\to$ represents Gödel's implication, i.e., $a \to b = 1$ if $a \leq b$ and b otherwise, and $\top$ the *min* operator, we write $F' = [E' \circ (E \to F)]$ where $\circ$ is the sup-min composition operator. In practice, if E, E' and F are represented by $(a_1, a_2, a_3, a_4, 0)$, $(a'_1, a'_2, a'_3, a'_4, 0)$ and $(b_1, b_2, b_3, b_4, 0)$ respectively, the t.m.f. $(b'_1, b'_2, b'_3, b'_4, \Delta)$ (where Δ expresses a global indetermination level) associated with F' is computed in the following way (see [11] for more details):

$$\Delta = sup_{\{u \in dom(C) \mid \mu_E(u)=0\}} \mu_{E'}(u), \qquad b'_1 = b_1 \text{ and } b'_4 = b_4$$
$$b'_2 = b_2 - (1 - H)(b_2 - b_1), \qquad b'_3 = b_3 + (1 - H)(b_4 - b_3),$$

with $H = min(\mu_E(a'_2), \mu_E(a'_3))$. H is the smallest degree of an element belonging to the core of E' in E. As we can see in Figure 2, in the case where $\Delta > 0$, any value outside $[\alpha, \beta]$ is considered acceptable with a degree Δ. In particular, if $\Delta = 1$ (i.e., $core(E') \not\subseteq support(E)$), $\mu_{F'}(v) = 1, \forall v \in dom(A)$. This means that no preference about attribute A is inferred regarding the current context. As a consequence, the smaller Δ, the more certain the inferred preference is.

Obviously, one can choose other fuzzy implication operators. However, the major advantage of Gödel implication is the fact that it is the least sensitive to the mismatching between E and E'. Indeed, the global indetermination level is non-zero only in the case where the support of E' is not included in the support of E. Approximate matching between two context states is then naturally supported by our approach. For a precise input, i.e., $E' = \{e'\}$, the t.m.f of F' is such that: $\Delta = 1$ and $H = 0$ if $e' \notin E$, $\Delta = 0$ and $H = \mu_E(e')$ otherwise.

Example 3. Let CP_1 be a contextual preference defined by **if** *age* is *young* **then** *cost* is *inexpensive*, where *young* and *inexpensive* are fuzzy sets represented by $(0, 0, 25, 27, 0)$ $(0, 0, 200, 400, 0)$ respectively, see Figure 3. For a person with 26 years old (which also writes as $(26, 26, 26, 26, 0)$ in terms of t.m.f.), his/her preference inferred about the attribute *cost* is: *cost* is *inexpensive'* where the fuzzy predicate *inexpensive'* is represented by $(0, 0, 300, 400, 0)$, see Figure 3.

When a context state involves several contextual parameters, we have:

$$\text{Rule } CP: \textbf{if } C_1 \text{ is } E_1 \wedge \ldots \wedge C_q \text{ is } E_q \textbf{ then } A \text{ is } F$$
$$\text{Fact } \omega: C_1 \text{ is } E'_1 \wedge \ldots \wedge C_q \text{ is } E'_q,$$

Where the t.m.f. associated with E_i (resp. E'_i) is $(a_{1i}, a_{2i}, a_{3i}, a_{4i})$ (resp. $(a'_{1i}, a'_{2i}, a'_{3i}, a'_{4i})$, for $i = 1, q$. In this case, the t.m.f. of the conclusion F' is computed in the same way as previously, except for Δ and H which are given by $\Delta = max_{i=1,q}\Delta_i$ and $H = min_{i=1,q}H_i$, with $\Delta_i = sup_{\{u \in dom(C_i), \mu_{E_i}(u)=0\}}\mu_{E'_i}(u)$ and $H_i = min(\mu_{E_i}(a'_{2i}), \mu_{E_i}(a'_{3i}))$.

4.2   Aggregating Preferences

It is usual in practice to have different contextual preferences pertaining to a same attribute A. A same context state can (approximately) match such contextual preferences. Let us consider two rules with a single premise to illustrate this case. We assume also that the coherence of each rule as well as the coherence of the set of rules are fulfilled (see [10] for more details about this issue).

Case 1: CP_1: If C_1 is E_1 then A is F_1
    CP_2: If C_1 is E_2 then A is F_2

For a context $\omega = C_1$ is E' and under the assumption $E' \cap E_i \neq \emptyset, i = 1, 2$, both CP_1 and CP_2 are triggered. To obtain a single overall preference on attribute A, two methods can be applied [10,11]. The first one, called FITA (First Infer Then Aggregate), consists in triggering the rules separately, then combining conjunctively the partial preferences inferred. Let "A is F'_1" and "A is F'_2" be the preferences deduced respectively from CP_1 and CP_2. The overall preference on A is computed as follows (conjunctive aggregation is adopted due to the implication-based modeling of rules) : $F' = \bigcap_{i=1,2} F'_i = \bigcap_{i=1,2}[E' \circ (E_i \to F_i)]$.

Example 4. Let CP_1 and CP_2 be two contextual preferences defined as follows:
    CP_1: **if** *period is begin_summer* **then** *cost is attractive_1*
    CP_2: **if** *period is middle_summer* **then** *cost is attractive_2*

where the t.m.f of *begin_summer, middle_summer, attractive₁* and *attractive₂* are respectively: (Jun.21, Jun.21, Jul.10, Jul.31, 0), (Jun.25, Jul.10, Jul.25, Aug.10, 0), (0, 0, 350, 600, 0) and (0, 0, 600, 700, 0). Predicates *attractive₁* and *attractive₂* describe the concept "good price" for two different periods. For a user wishing to travel between Jul. 02 and Jul. 21 with 10 days of margin[2], CP_1 and CP_2 are triggered and we respectively obtain the following preferences: $attractive'_1 = (0, 0, 420.5, 500, 0)$ and $attractive'_2 = (0, 0, 655, 700, 0)$.

Now, since $attractive'_1 \subseteq attractive'_2$, the final preference about "cost" is $attractive'_1$. This method may result in a non-trapezoidal function, and then a trapezoidal approximation technique from the literature [11,12] must be used.

The second method, called FATI, first combines the rules, then infers. The semantics of F' is then computed as follows: $F' = E' \circ [\bigcap_{i=1,2}(E_i \rightarrow F_i)]$. It has been shown in [10] that: $E' \circ [\bigcap_{i=1,2}(E_i \rightarrow F_i)] \subseteq \bigcap_{i=1,2}[E' \circ (E_i \rightarrow F_i)]$. This means that the FATI method leads to a preference which is more informative than the one obtained with FITA. However, building a t.m.f thanks to FATI is not an easy task as shown in [11,12]. It is worth noticing that for a precise input, both methods yield the same result.

Case 2: CP_1: If C_1 is E_1 then A is F_1
　　　　　CP_2: If C_2 is E_2 then A is F_2

This second case can be seen as a variant of the first one where the premises of the contextual preferences concern different context parameters, but the conclusion is still over the same attribute. Thus, for a context state $\{C_1$ is $E'_1 \wedge C_2$ is $E'_2\}$ such that $E'_1 \cap E_1 \neq \emptyset$ and $E'_2 \cap E_2 \neq \emptyset$, we get in the same situation that in the first case and, in a similar way, we aggregate the partial preferences inferred.

5   Query Augmentation Algorithm

We now show how a fuzzy query [13] can be enhanced with contextual preferences. Let Q be a query formulated in a context $\omega = (C_1$ is $E_1, \ldots, C_k$ is $E_k), k \leq n$. Let A_Q be the set of attributes on which there exists at least one preference in Q. The augmentation process (see Algorithm 1) can be divided into four main steps. The first step (line 1.3) aims to identify the subset $CP_Q \subseteq B^{CP}$ of contextual preferences matching wholly or partially ω. Only contextual preferences: *i)* about attributes which are not present in A_Q[3] (line 2.6); *ii)* whose context parameters are present in ω (line 2.8); and *iii)* that result in an indetermination level $\Delta <$ *threshold*, are added to CP_Q. The second step (lines 1.4-1.7) builds the set of candidate preferences P by inferring a new preference from each $cp \in CP_Q$ using function *GMP* (see line 1.5). In the third step (line 1.8), the set P is reduced into a set P' where the preferences about the same attribute A are aggregated into one preference p'_A. The final step (lines 1.9-1.12) adds each preference $p \in P'$ to Q, then processes the augmented query Q'.

---

[2] It corresponds to the period represented by the t.m.f: (Jun.26, Jul.02, Jul.21, Jul.-31).
[3] We assume that a preference specified by the user is more prioritary than one deduced

---

Algorithm 1. Query Augmentation Algorithm.

Input: rule base $B^{CP} = \{CP_1, CP_2, \ldots, CP_m\}$, the query Q and the set of attributes
        $A_Q = \{A_1, A_2, \ldots, A_l\}$, the user context ω.
Output: An augmented version of Q, denoted by Q'.
1.1   **Variables:** $CP_Q \leftarrow \emptyset$, $P \leftarrow \emptyset$, $P' \leftarrow \emptyset$, $Q' \leftarrow Q$.
1.2   **begin**
1.3 $CP_Q \leftarrow load\_cp(CP, A_Q, \omega)$;
1.4   **foreach** cp **in** CP_Q **do**
1.5   /*GMP: Generalized Modus Ponens function*/
1.6 $P \leftarrow P \cup GMP(cp, \omega)$;
1.7   **end**
1.8 $P' \leftarrow agg\_pref(P)$;
1.9   **foreach** $p \in P'$ **do**
1.10 $Q' \leftarrow Q' \wedge \{p\}$;
1.11   **end**
1.12   **return** Q';
1.13 **end**

Algorithm 2. Function $load\_cp$.

Input: B^{CP}, A_Q and ω.
Output: CP_Q, set of contextual preferences matching the context ω.
2.1   **Variables:** $CP_Q \leftarrow \emptyset$;
2.2   **Constants:** $threshold \leftarrow 1$; /* constraint: $threshold \in [0,1]$*/
2.3   **begin**
2.4   **foreach** cp **in** B^{CP} **do**
2.5   /* function $attribute$ returns the attribute over which cp is defined*/
2.6   **if** $attribute(cp) \notin A_Q$ **then**
2.7   /* function $context$ returns the context parameters present in a cp (resp.
              ω)*/
2.8   **if** $context(cp) \subseteq context(\omega)$ **then**
2.9   **if** $Delta(cp, \omega) < threshold$ **then**
2.10 $CP_Q \leftarrow CP_Q \cup \{cp\}$;
2.11   **end**
2.12   **end**
2.13   **end**
2.14   **end**
2.15   **return** CP_Q;
2.16 **end**

5.1   A Detailed Example

Let $itravAg$ (see Table 1) be an instance of the relation $travAg$ defined in Subsection 3, and B^{CP} be a set of contextual preferences represented by the rules:

CP_1: **if** *age is young* **then** *cost is attractive$_1$*
CP_2: **if** *age is young* $\wedge$ *acc_people is $\{wife\}$* **then** *charm is good$_1$*
CP_3: **if** *age is young* $\wedge$ *acc_people is $\{friends\}$* **then** *animation is good$_2$*
CP_4: **if** *status is $\{executive\}$* **then** *cost is attractive$_2$*
CP_5: **if** *status is $\{retired\}$* $\wedge$ *acc_people is $\{wife\}$* $\wedge$ *period is summer*
         then *calm is good$_1$*

Assume that the fuzzy predicates in B^{CP} are defined as follows: $young = (18, 20, 25, 27, 0)$, $attractive_1 = (0, 0, 200, 500, 0)$, $attractive_2 = (0, 0, 400, 700, 0)$, $good_1 = (50, 80, 100, 100, 0)$, $good_2 = (30, 50, 100, 100, 0)$, $summer = (15/06/2010, 21/06/2010, 22/09/2010, 30/09/2010, 0)$; $wife = \{1/\text{wife}\}$, $friends = \{1/\text{friend}\}$ and $executive = \{1/\text{executive}\}$ are crisp predicates.

Table 1. An instance of *travAg* relation

tuple	id_dest	dest	cost (€)	date_b	date_e	animation	calm	charm
t_1	1	Spain-malaga	527	01/09/09	01/09/10	90	60	67
t_2	2	Spain-malaga	540	01/09/09	01/09/10	10	66	60
t_3	3	Spain-malaga	629	01/09/09	01/10/10	76	70	80
t_4	4	Spain-malaga	400	01/10/09	01/02/10	43	50	30
t_5	5	Spain-malaga	525	01/09/09	01/01/10	23	80	56

Let us consider a *young executive* who would like to visit Malaga (Spain) in *springtime* with his *wife* and formulates the following query:

Q: SELECT * FROM itravAg WHERE
    dest = 'Spain-malaga' AND $date_b$ ≤ '1/04/10' AND $date_e$ ≥ '10/04/10'

The context state wherein Q is formulated writes $\omega = (age$ is *around_26*, *status* is *executive*, *acc_people* is *wife*) with *around_26* $= (24, 26, 26, 28, 0)$. Then, it is easy to see that $A_Q = \{dest, date_b, date_e\}$.

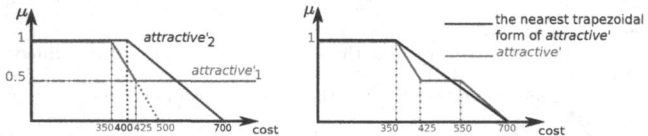

Fig. 4. t.m.fs of *attractive'_1*, *attractive'_2* and *attractive'*

Algorithm 1 yields $CP_Q = \{CP_1, CP_2, CP_4\}$. Indeed, CP_5 is quickly eliminated since it does not match the context state ω. CP_3 results in an indetermination level greater than the *threshold* defined in *load_cp* (see Algorithm 2) is also ruled out. Then, the preferences inferred from CP_Q are P={p_1: *cost* is *attractive'_1*, p_2: *charm* is *good'_1*, p_4: *cost* is *attractive'_2*} with the following semantics $(0, 0, 350, 500, 0.5)$, $(50, 65, 100, 100, 0.5)$, $(0, 0, 400, 700, 0)$ respectively (see Figure 4). Now, by aggregating the preferences p'_1 and p'_4, which concern the same attribute *cost*, we obtain a reduced set of preferences $P' = \{p'_1$: *cost* is *attractive'*, p_2: *charm* is *good'_1$\}$ with $(0, 0, 350, 700, 0)$ as the semantics of *attractive'*. Finally, the query Q' obtained after augmenting Q with P' writes:
SELECT * FROM itravAg WHERE dest = 'Spain-malaga' AND $date_b$ ≤ '1/04/10'
AND $date_e$ ≥ '10/04/10' AND *cost* is *attractive'* AND *charm* is *good'_1*.
    The evaluation of Q' against the instance *itravAg* leads to the following results: $\{0.5/t_5, 0.5/t_4, 0.49/t_1, 0.45/t_2, 0.2/t_3\}$, where the score of each tuple t is computed using the formula: $\mu_{Q'}(t) = min_{i=1,4} \, max(\Delta_i, \mu_{p*_i}(t \cdot v_i))$ where each $p*_i$ represents a preference present in Q'.

6 Conclusion

In this paper, we have proposed a fuzzy-rule-based model for representing context and contextual preferences. We have also shown how an initial user query can be enhanced with new inferred preferences regarding contextual information. An algorithm for query augmentation has been presented and illustrated on a small practical example. Our approach deals with gradual contextual features and offers a natural and user-friendly way to describe contextual parameters. As for future work, it would be interesting to study the different ways to interpret the preferences inferred (for instance, as wishes or constraints with low-priority) when augmenting the query at hand. We also plan to extend this work for handling potential conflictual preferences resulting from an inconsistent rule base.

References

1. Dey, A.: Understanding and using context. Personal and Ubiquitous, Special Issue on Situated Interaction and Ubiquitous Computing 5(1) (2001)
2. Strang, T., Linnhoff-Popien, C.: A context modelling survey. In: Workshop on Advanced Context Modelling, Reasoning and Management (2004)
3. van Bunningen, A.H.: Context aware querying – challenges for data management in ambient intelligence. Technical report, Enschede (December 2004)
4. Holland, S., Kiessling, W.: Situated preferences and preference repositories for personalized database applications. In: Atzeni, P., Chu, W., Lu, H., Zhou, S., Ling, T.-W. (eds.) ER 2004. LNCS, vol. 3288, pp. 511–523. Springer, Heidelberg (2004)
5. van Bunningen, A., Feng, L., Apers, P.: A context aware preference model for database querying in an ambient intelligent environment. In: Bressan, S., Küng, J., Wagner, R. (eds.) DEXA 2006. LNCS, vol. 4080, pp. 33–43. Springer, Heidelberg (2006)
6. Stavrakas, Y., Gergatsoulis, M.: Multidimensional semistructured data: representing context-dependent information on the web. In: Pidduck, A.B., Mylopoulos, J., Woo, C.C., Ozsu, M.T. (eds.) CAiSE 2002. LNCS, vol. 2348, pp. 183–199. Springer, Heidelberg (2002)
7. Dittrich, J., Fisher, P., Kossmann, D.: Agile: Adaptive indexing for context-aware information filters. In: SIGMOD, pp. 215–226 (2005)
8. Stefanidis, K., Pitoura, E., Vassiliadis, P.: Adding context to preferences. In: Proc. of ICDE'07, pp. 846–855 (2007)
9. Stefanidis, K., Pitoura, E., Vassiliadis, P.: On relaxing contextual preference queries. In: Proc. of Int. Conf. on Mobile Data Management, pp. 289–293 (2007)
10. Bouchon-Meunier, B., Dubois, D., Godo, L., Prade, H.: Fuzzy sets and possibility theory in approximate and plausible reasoning. In: Dubois, D., Prade, H., Bezdek, J. (eds.) Fuzzy sets in approximate reasoning and inf. systems, pp. 15–162 (1999)
11. Hadjali, A.: Study of fuzzy sets and possibility theory with a view to their application in knowledge-based systems. Magister Thesis, University of Tizi-Ouzou, Algeria (1991)
12. Martin-Clouaire, R.: Semantics and computation of the generalized modus ponens: the long paper. Int. J. Approx. Reasoning 3(2), 195–217 (1989)
13. Bosc, P., Pivert, O.: SQLf: a relational database language for fuzzy querying. IEEE Transactions on Fuzzy Systems (1995)

Extracting and Modelling Preferences from Dialogue

Nicholas Asher[1], Elise Bonzon[2], and Alex Lascarides[3]

[1] IRIT, CNRS, Université Paul Sabatier, 118 route de Narbonne,
F-31062 Toulouse Cedex 4, France
asher@irit.fr
[2] LIPADE, Université Paris Descartes, 45 rue des Saints Pères, 75006 Paris, France
elise.bonzon@parisdescartes.fr
[3] School of Informatics, University of Edinburgh, 10 Crichton Street, Edinburgh,
EH8 9AB, Scotland, UK
alex@inf.ed.ac.uk

Abstract. Dialogue moves influence and are influenced by the agents' preferences. We propose a method for modelling this interaction. We motivate and describe a recursive method for calculating the preferences that are expressed, sometimes indirectly, through the speech acts performed. These yield partial *CP-nets*, which provide a compact and efficient method for computing how preferences influence each other. Our study of 100 dialogues in the Verbmobil corpus can be seen as a partial vindication of using CP-nets to represent preferences.

1 Introduction

It is well accepted that dialogues are structured by various moves that the participants make—e.g., answering questions, asking follow-up questions, elaborating and defending prior claims, and so on. Such moves often affect the way interlocutors view a speaker's preferences and consequently influence how they respond. Dialogue (1) from the Verbmobil corpus [13] illustrates this.

(1) π_1 A: Shall we meet sometime in the next week?

  π_2 A: What days are good for you?

  π_3 B: Well, I have some free time on almost every day except Fridays.

  π_4 B: Fridays are bad.

  π_5 B: In fact, I'm busy on Thursday too.

  π_6 A: Well next week I am out of town Tuesday, Wednesday and Thursday.

  π_7 A: So perhaps Monday?

Intuitively, A's question π_1 reveals his preference for meeting next week but it does so indirectly: the preference is not asserted and accordingly responding with *I do too* (meaning "I want to meet next week too") would be highly anomalous. Nevertheless, B's response π_3 to π_5 to A's elaborating question π_2 reveals that he has adopted A's preference. This follows his answer π_2 which specifies a non-empty extension for *what days*. Semantically, inferring π_3 to π_5 answers A's question and inferring that the temporal expressions refer to next week are logically dependent.

E. Hüllermeier, R. Kruse, and F. Hoffmann (Eds.): IPMU 2010, LNAI 6178, pp. 542–553, 2010.

Inferences about B's preferences evolve as he gives his extended answer: from π_3 alone one would infer a preference for meeting any day next week other than Friday and its explanation π_4 would maintain this. But the continuation π_5 compels A to revise his inferences about B's preference for meeting on Thursday. These inferences about preferences arise from both the content of B's utterances and the semantic relations that connect them together. A's response π_6 reveals he disprefers Tuesday, Wednesday and Thursday, thereby refining the preferences that he revealed last time he spoke. A's follow-up proposal π_7 then reinforces the inference from π_6 that among Monday, Tuesday and Wednesday—the days that B prefers—A prefers Monday. This may not match his preferred day when the dialogue started: perhaps that was Friday. Further dialogue may compel agents to revise their preferences as they learn about the domain and each other.

The dialogue moves exhibited in (1) are typical of the Verbmobil corpus, and we suspect typical also of task-oriented dialogues generally. [3] annotated 100 randomly chosen dialogues from the Verbmobil corpus with their discourse structure according to Segmented Discourse Representation Theory (SDRT, [2,1])—these structures represent the types of (relational) speech acts that the agents perform. According to this labelled corpus, 40% of the discourse units are either questions or assertions that help to elaborate a plan to achieve the preferences revealed by a prior part of the dialogue—these are marked respectively with the discourse relations *Q-Elab* and *Plan-Elab* in SDRT, and the interpretations of utterances π_2, π_6 and π_7 and the segment π_3–π_5 in dialogue (1) invoke these relations (see Section 2)). Moreover, 10% of the moves revise or correct preferences from the context (like π_5 in (1)); and 15% of them explain prior content or prior moves (like π_4 in (1)). The remaining 35% are not pertinent to our modeling of preferences.

Inferring an agents' preferences from the speeh acts they perform is an important task because preferences are crucial for planning appropriate conversational moves, ensuring that responses in dialogue remain relevant and natural. We will model the interaction between dialogue content in dialogues of the Verbmobil corpus and preferences using (partial) CP-nets. These allow us to exploit dependencies between dialogue moves and mental states in a compact and intuitive way. But we start by motivating and describing the semantic representation of dialogue from which CP-nets will be constructed.

2   The Logical Form of Dialogue

Agents express *commitments* to beliefs and preferences through the speech acts they perform [7]. It is these commitments that concern us here, but in what follows we shall treat a commitment to a preference (or a belief) as an actual preference (or belief).

Our starting point is the aforementioned theory of discourse interpretation SDRT [1]. Like many theories [8,10], it structures discourse into units that are linked together with *rhetorical relations* such as *Explanation, Question Answer Pair (QAP), Q-Elab, Plan-Elab*, and so on. Logical forms in SDRT consist of *Segmented Discourse Representation Structures* (SDRSs). As shown in Def. 1, an SDRS is a set of labels each representing a unit of discourse, and a mapping from each label to an SDRS-formula representing its content—these formulas are based on those for representing clauses or elementary discourse units (EDUs) plus rhetorical relation symbols between labels:

Table 1. The DSDRS for Dialogue (1)

Turn	A's SDRS	B's SDRS
1	$\pi_{1A} : Q\text{-}Elab(\pi_1,\pi_2)$	$\emptyset$
2	$\pi_{1A} : Q\text{-}Elab(\pi_1,\pi_2)$	$\pi_{2B} : Q\text{-}Elab(\pi_1,\pi_2) \wedge QAP(\pi_2,\pi) \wedge Plan\text{-}Elab(\pi_2,\pi)$
		$\pi : Plan\text{-}Correction(\pi',\pi_5)$
		$\pi' : Explanation(\pi_3,\pi_4)$
3	$\pi_{3A} : Q\text{-}Elab(\pi_1,\pi_2) \wedge QAP(\pi_2,\pi) \wedge$	$\pi_{2B} : Q\text{-}Elab(\pi_1,\pi_2) \wedge QAP(\pi_2,\pi) \wedge Plan\text{-}Elab(\pi_2,\pi)$
	$Plan\text{-}Elab(\pi_2,\pi) \wedge Plan\text{-}Elab(\pi_1,\pi_6) \wedge$	$\pi : Plan\text{-}Correction(\pi',\pi_5)$
	$Plan\text{-}Elab(\pi_1,\pi_7) \wedge Plan\text{-}Elab(\pi_6,\pi_7)$	$\pi' : Explanation(\pi_3,\pi_4)$

Def. 1: *An* SDRS *is a pair* $\langle \Pi, \mathcal{F} \rangle$,[1] *where* Π *is a set of labels; and* $\mathcal{F} : \Pi \longrightarrow$ SDRS-*formulas, where:*

- *If* ϕ *is an* EDU-*formula, then* ϕ *is an* SDRS-*formula.*
- *If* $\pi_1,\ldots,\pi_n$ *are labels and R is an n-ary rhetorical relation, then* $R(\pi_1,\ldots,\pi_n)$ *is an* SDRS-*formula.*
- *If* ϕ, ϕ' *are* SDRS-*formulas, then so are* $(\phi \wedge \phi')$, $\neg\phi$.

[9] represent a dialogue turn (where turn boundaries occur whenever the speaker changes) as a set of SDRSs—one for each agent representing all his current commitments, from the beginning of the dialogue to the end of that turn. The representation of the dialogue overall—a Dialogue SDRS or DSDRS—is that of each of its turns. Each agent constructs the SDRSs for all other agents as well as his own. For instance, (1) is assigned the DS-DRS in Table 1, with the content of the EDUs omitted for reasons of space.[2] We adopt a convention of indexing the root label of the nth turn, spoken by agent d, as nd; and $\pi : \phi$ means $\mathcal{F}(\pi) = \phi$.

A's SDRS for turn 1 in Table 1 commits him to 'caring' about the answer to the two questions π_1 and π_2 (because *Q-Elab* is veridical). We take π_1 to commit A to the implicature that he prefers to meet next week. And $Q\text{-}Elab(\pi_1,\pi_2)$ entails that any answer to π_2 must elaborate a plan to achieve the preference revealed by π_1; this makes π_2 paraphrasable as "What days next week are good for you?", which doesn't add new preferences. B's contribution in the second turn attaches to π_2 with *QAP*; also *Plan-Elab* because of its non-empty extension for *what days*. [9] argue that this means that B is also committed to the illocutionary contribution of π_2, as shown in Table 1 by the addition of $Q\text{-}Elab(\pi_1,\pi_2)$ to B's SDRS. This addition commits B also to the preference of meeting next week, with his answer making the preference more precise: π_3 and π_4 reveal that B prefers any day except Friday; but with π_5 he retracts the preference for Thursday. A's third turn exploits B's answer to identify a time to meet: his *Plan-Elab* move π_6 reveals he disprefers Tuesday through Friday; and the suggestion π_7 is a solution to the constraints imposed by his preferences, which have evolved through the dialogue.

---

[1] We omit the distinguished label Last from [1] as it plays no role here.

[2] We also ignore here how to construct this DSDRS from linguistic form and context; see [9] for details.

3 CP-Nets

We saw earlier that dialogue reveals information about preferences. These preferences influence subsequent utterances—people plan strategically so as to achieve outcomes that are most preferred. So in addition to a method for computing preferences from dialogue, we also need a method for computing which of all possible outcomes is the most preferred. We will use CP-nets [4,5] for this.

A CP-net offers a compact representation of preferences. This graphical model exploits conditional preferential independence so as to structure the decision maker's preferences under a *ceteris paribus* assumption. Representing dependencies among preferences while also exploiting their independence when appropriate is a major motivation for using CP-nets in our framework. As we shall demonstrate in Section 5, CP-nets have a major advantage for us in that it is relatively straightforward to build a CP-net *compositionally* from a DSDRS, exploiting recursion over SDRSs.

Although CP-nets generally consider variables with a finite range of values, for simplicity we consider here only propositional variables with binary values (think of each variable as the description of an action that an agent can choose to perform, or not). Moreover, we also introduce indifference relations in these CP-nets, that is the possibility to be indifferent between both values of a variable. More formally, let V be a finite set of propositional variables and L_V the language built from V via Boolean connectives and the constants $\top$ *(true)* and $\bot$ *(false)*. Formulas of L_V are denoted by ϕ, ψ, etc. 2^V is the set of interpretations for V, and as usual for $M \in 2^V$ and $x \in V$, M gives the value *true* to x if $x \in M$ and *false* otherwise. Let $X \subseteq V$. 2^X is the set of X-*interpretations*. X-interpretations are denoted by listing all variables of X, with a $^-$ symbol when the variable is set to false: e.g., where $X = \{a,b,d\}$, the X-interpretation $M = \{a,d\}$ is denoted $a\bar{b}d$.

A *preference relation* $\succeq$ is a reflexive and transitive binary relation (not necessarily complete) on 2^V. Where $M, M' \in 2^V$, as usual, strict preference $M \succ M'$ holds iff $M \succeq M'$ and not $M' \succeq M$.

As we stated earlier, CP-nets exploit conditional preferential independence to compute a preferential ranking over outcomes:

Def. 2: *Let V be a set of propositional variables and $\{X,Y,Z\}$ a partition of V. X is conditionally preferentially independent of Y given Z if and only if $\forall z \in 2^Z$, $\forall x_1, x_2 \in 2^X$ and $\forall y_1, y_2 \in 2^Y$ we have: $x_1 y_1 z \succeq x_2 y_1 z$ iff $x_1 y_2 z \succeq x_2 y_2 z$.*

For each variable X, the agent specifies a set of *parent variables* $Pa(X)$ that can affect his preferences over the values of X. Formally, X is conditionally preferentially independent of $V \setminus (\{X\} \cup Pa(X))$. This is then used to create the CP-net:

Def. 3: *Let V be a set of propositional variables. $\mathcal{N} = \langle \mathcal{G}, \mathcal{T} \rangle$ is a CP-net on V, where $\mathcal{G}$ is a directed graph over V, and $\mathcal{T}$ is a set of conditional preference tables with indifference $CPT(X_j)$ for each $X_j \in V$. $CPT(X_j)$ specifies for each instantiation $p \in 2^{Pa(X_j)}$ either $x_j \succ_p \bar{x}_j$, $\bar{x}_j \succ_p x_j$ or $x_j \sim_p \bar{x}_j$.*

Exploiting the CP-net formalism and semantics enables us to "flip" the value of a variable X within an outcome to obtain a different outcome, which the agent may prefer, disprefer or be indifferent to. An outcome o is better than another outcome o' iff there is a chain of flips from o' to o which yield either preferred or indifferent outcomes, and there is at least one *improving flip*. This definition induces a partial order over the outcomes.

Despite their many virtues, classical CP-nets won't do for representing the preferences expressed in dialogue. Suppose an agent says "I want to go to the mall to eat something". We can infer from this that he prefers to go to the mall given that he wants to eat, but we do not know his preferences over "go to the mall" if he does not want to eat. We thus need *partial* CP-nets. A partial CP-net, as introduced by [11], is a CP-net in which some features may not be ranked. Partiality forces us to relax the semantics:

- An *improving flip* in a partial CP-net changes the value of a variable X such that: if X is ranked, the flip is improving with respect to (wrt) the CPT of X; and if X is not ranked, it is improving wrt the CPT of all features that depend on X.
- An *indifferent flip* changes the value of a variable X such that: if X is ranked, the flip is indifferent in $CPT(X)$; otherwise wrt all CPT, the change in the value of X leaves the outcome in the same position.
- *Incomparable flips* are all those flips which are neither worsening, nor improving, nor indifferent.

As before, an outcome o is preferred to outcome o' ($o \succ o'$) iff there is a chain of flips from o' to o which are all improving or indifferent, with at least one improving one. An outcome o is indifferent wrt o' ($o \sim o'$) iff at least one chain of flips between them consists only of indifferent flips. o is incomparable to o' iff none of $o \succ o'$, $o' \succ o$ or $o \sim o'$ hold.

Unlike classical CP-nets, partial CP-nets with indifference can have more than one optimal outcome even if their dependency graph is acyclic. However, we can still easily determine a best outcome, using the *forward sweep* procedure [4] for outcome optimization (this procedure consists in instantiating variables following an order compatible with the graph, choosing for each variable (one of) its preferred value given the value of the parents).

Partial CP-nets are expressive enough for the examples we have studied in the Verbmobil corpus. Section 5 will show how discourse structure typically leads to a dependence among preferences that is similar to the one exploited in CP-nets.

4   From EDUs to Preferences

Speech acts are relations between sets of commitments, just as factual statements in dynamic semantics are relations between information states. While some speech acts, like greetings, don't affect preference commitments, many speech acts do affect them, as we have seen. We must therefore extract (commitments to) preferences from speech acts. We will compute preferences in two stages: we extract them from EDUs; and modify them recursively via the discourse structure (see Section 5).

EDUs include what we call *atomic* preference statements (e.g., *I want X* or *We need X*). They can be complex, expressing boolean combinations of preferences (e.g. *I want X and Y*); they can also express preferences in an indirect way (e.g., interrogatives like

Shouldn't we go home now? or expressions of sentiment or politeness). We regiment such complexities via a function P that recursively exploits the logical structure of an EDU's logical form to produce a *boolean preference representation* (BPR), expressed as a propositional formula. For the purposes of this paper, we define the BPR output of P manually, although in principle it is possible to learn this mapping from labelled corpus data. This BPR will then affect preferences expressed as partial CP-nets (see Section 5).

SDRT's description logic (*glue logic* or GL) is designed to express statements about the logical structure of SDRS-formulae, and so we use it here to define the function P. Formulae in GL partially describe DSDRSs in general, and the formulae associated with EDUs in particular. For instance, $\pi : \mathrm{Not}(\pi_1)$ means that the label π in the DSDRS being described is associated with a formula $\neg\phi_{\pi_1}$, where $\neg$ is the constructor from the SDRS language that's denoted by Not, and ϕ_{π_1} is the SDRS-formula associated with π_1. We define P recursively over these GL-formulae.

We treat disjunction non-exclusively: i.e., *I want X or Y* means I prefer one of the literals or both. If the preference is exclusive, we rely on model constraints to rule out states where X and Y are satisfied. Conjunctions are ambiguous with respect to preferences, but in certain cases we can resolve the ambiguity. *I want X and Y* can mean that my most preferred state is one where both X and Y are satisfied, but I would still prefer to satisfy one of them to neither being satisfied. This disambiguation for *and* will be represented with the GL predicate &. On the other hand, this EDU could mean that I prefer the "fusion" of X and Y while not preferring either X or Y separately; we mark this in GL with $\wedge$. A final case has to do with questions. Although not all questions entail that their author commits to a preference, in many cases they do. That is, if A asks *can we meet next week?* he implicates a preference for meeting. For negative and *wh*-interrogatives, the implication is even stronger. This yields the following axioms in GL for mapping EDUs to a BPR:

1. $P(\pi) = X_\pi$ for atomic π
2. $\pi : \mathrm{Not}(\pi_1) \rightarrow P(\pi) = \neg P(\pi_1)$
3. $\pi : \mathrm{Or}(\pi_1,\pi_2) \rightarrow P(\pi) = P(\pi_1) \vee P(\pi_2)$
4. $\pi : \&(\pi_1,\pi_2) \rightarrow P(\pi) = P(\pi_1)\&P(\pi_2)$
5. $\pi : \wedge(\pi_1,\pi_2) \rightarrow P(\pi) = P(\pi_1) \wedge F(\pi_2)$
6. $\pi :?(\pi_1) \rightarrow P(\pi) = P(\pi_1)$
7. $\pi :?(\neg\pi_1) \rightarrow P(\pi) = P(\pi_1)$

5   From Discourse Structure to Preferences

We now define how to update CP-nets representing an agent's preferences with the BPRs of EDUs and by discourse structure. More formally, we define a function *Commit* from a label π or discourse relation $R(\pi_1,\pi_2)$ and a contextually given CP-net $\mathcal{N}$ to an updated CP-net. We focus here on the relations that are prevalent in the Verbmobil corpus (see Section 1).

Below, X denotes a propositional variable and ϕ a propositional formula from BPR. $Var(\phi)$ are the variables in ϕ, and $\succ_X$ the preference relation associated with $CPT(X)$. $Sat(\phi)$ is a conjunction of literals from $Var(\phi)$ that satisfy ϕ, while *non-Sat*(ϕ) is a conjunction of literals from $Var(\phi)$ that do not satisfy ϕ. $Sat(\phi) - X$ is the formula that results from removing the conjunct with X from $Sat(\phi)$.

1. Where $P(\pi) = X$ (e.g., *I want X*), $Commit(\pi, \mathcal{N})$ updates $\mathcal{N}$ by adding $X \succ \overline{X}$.
2. Where $P(\pi) = \phi \wedge \psi$ (the agent prefers both ϕ and ψ, but is indifferent if he can't have both), $Commit(\pi, \mathcal{N})$ updates $\mathcal{N}$ as follows:
   - For each $X \in Var(\phi)$, add $Var(\psi)$ to $Pa(X)$ and modify $CPT(X)$ as follows:
     a. If $Sat_i(\psi)$, $Sat_j(\phi) \vdash X$ (resp. $\overline{X}$), then $Sat_i(\psi), Sat_j(\phi) - X: X \succ \overline{X}$ (resp. $\overline{X} \succ X$), for all satisfiers i and j.
     b. If $Sat_i(\psi)$, $Sat_j(\phi) \not\vdash X$ and $\not\vdash \overline{X}$, then $Sat_i(\psi), Sat_j(\phi) - X: X \sim \overline{X}$, for all satisfiers i and j
     c. $non\text{-}Sat_i(\psi)$, $Sat_j(\phi) - X: X \sim \overline{X}$ and $Sat_i(\psi), non\text{-}Sat_j(\phi) - X: X \sim \overline{X}$ for all satisfiers i and j
   - Similarly for each $Y \in Var(\psi)$.

   Where ϕ and ψ are literals X and Y, this rule yields the following: $X : Y \succ \overline{Y}$, $\overline{X} : Y \sim \overline{Y}. Y : X \succ \overline{X}, \overline{Y} : X \sim \overline{X}$.

   And we obtain the following preference relation:

   $$\overline{XY} \longleftrightarrow \begin{array}{c} XY \\ \downarrow \\ X\overline{Y} \end{array} \longleftrightarrow \overline{X}Y$$

   Even though the dependencies are cyclic here, the use of indifference allows us to find the best outcome XY easily.
3. $P(\pi) = \phi \& \psi$ (the agent prefers to have both ϕ and ψ and prefers either one if he can't have both). We use a similar definition to that for $\wedge$, where if ϕ and ψ are literals X and Y we get $Y \succ \overline{Y}$ and $X \succ \overline{X}$.

   We obtain the following preference relation:

   $$\overline{XY} \underset{\overline{X}Y}{\overset{X\overline{Y}}{\rightleftarrows}} X\overline{Y}$$
4. $P(\pi) = \phi \vee \psi$ (the agent prefers to have at least one of ϕ and ψ satisfied). The definition is similar to that for $\wedge$, where if ϕ and ψ are X and Y, we get:
   - $Var(X) \in Pa(Var(Y))$ and $X : Y \sim \overline{Y}, \overline{X} : Y \succ \overline{Y}$.
   - $Var(Y) \in Pa(Var(X))$ and $Y : X \sim \overline{X}, \overline{Y} : X \succ \overline{X}$.

   $$\overline{XY} \longleftrightarrow \begin{array}{c} X\overline{Y} \\ \downarrow \\ XY \end{array} \longleftrightarrow \overline{X}Y$$

   We have the following preference relation:

As before, the use of indifference allows us to find the best outcomes (XY, $X\overline{Y}$ and $\overline{X}Y$) easily.

Due to lack of space, we won't describe rule for $P(\pi) = \neg\phi$.

Iexplanation. $Iexplanation(\pi_1, \pi_2)$, as illustrated with example (2), means that $P(\pi_1)$ (here, going to the mall) is causally dependent upon $P(\pi_2)$ (eating something).

(2) π_1 I want to go to the mall
     π_2 to eat something

Being a veridical relation (and assuming that a commitment to content implies a commitment also to the preferences expressed by it), $Commit(Iexplanation(\pi_1, \pi_2), \mathcal{N})$ starts by applying $Commit(\pi_2, Commit(\pi_1, \mathcal{N}))$ to the contextually given CP-net $\mathcal{N}$. Then, the preferences arising from the illocutionary effects of $Iexplanation$, given its semantics, must ensure that CPTs are modified so that each variable in $P(\pi_1)$ depends on each variable in $P(\pi_2)$: i.e., $\forall X \in Var(P(\pi_1)), \forall Y \in Var(P(\pi_2)), Y \in Pa(X)$. So, $\forall X \in Var(P(\pi_1)), CPT(X)$ is constructed by simply adding all conjunctions $Sat(P(\pi_2))$ to the conditional part of $CPT(X)$. On the other hand, $\succ_X$ when the condition includes $non\text{-}Sat(P(\pi_2))$ is undefined (i.e., we don't know preferences on X if $P(\pi_2)$ is false).

For example, let $P(\pi_1) = X \vee Z$ and $P(\pi_2) = Y$. That is, the agent explains his preferences on $X \vee Z$ by Y: he wants either X or Z if Y is satisfied. We first apply $Commit(Y, Commit(X \vee Z, \langle \emptyset, \emptyset \rangle))$. By rules 4 and 1, we obtain:

- $X \in Pa(Z)$ and $X: Z \sim \overline{Z}, \overline{X}: Z \succ \overline{Z}$.
- $Z \in Pa(X)$ and $Z: X \sim \overline{X}, \overline{Z}: X \succ \overline{X}$.
- $Y \succ \overline{Y}$.

Then, the rule for *Iexplanation* modifies $CPT(X)$ and $CPT(Z)$:

- $Y \in Pa(X)$ and $Z \wedge Y: X \sim \overline{X}, \overline{Z} \wedge Y: X \succ \overline{X}$.
- $Y \in Pa(Z)$ and $X \wedge Y: Z \sim \overline{Z}, \overline{X} \wedge Y: Z \succ \overline{Z}$.

This yields the following, partial, preference relation. As we do not have any information on the preference on X and Z if Y is false, the states in which Y is false are incomparable, as required.

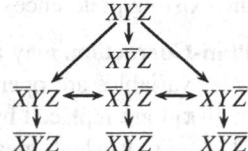

The causal dependence in *Iexplanation* is very close to the logical dependence exhibited in an *Elab*:

(3) π_1 I want wine
     π_2 I want white wine

That is, a preference for white wine depends on a preference for wine. This leads us to the following **Elab** rule: $Commit(Elab(\pi_1, \pi_2), \mathcal{N}) = Commit(Iexplanation(\pi_2, \pi_1), \mathcal{N})$ when π_1 and π_2 express a preference (i.e., $P(\pi_1)$ and $P(\pi_2)$ are defined); otherwise there is no modification of the given CP-net.

Plan-Elab. Marks those cases where the second term of the relation details a plan to achieve the preferences expressed in the first term (see Table 1). So $Commit(Plan-Elab (\pi_1, \pi_2), \mathcal{N}) = Commit(Elab(\pi_1, \pi_2), \mathcal{N})$.
   We now turn to questions.

Q-Elab. $Q\text{-}Elab_A(\pi_1, \pi_2)$ implies that the speaker A who utters the question π_2 takes over the preferences expressed in π_1 (in future, we may often identify the agent who's committed to the speech act as a subscript on the relation, as done here). More formally, $Q\text{-}Elab_A(\pi_1, \pi_2)$ implies that we update A's CP-net $\mathcal{N}$ by applying the rule for $Elab(\pi_1, \pi_2)$, where if π_2 expresses no preferences on their own, we simply set $P(\pi_2) = P(\pi_1)$. Note that this means that A's CP-net is updated with the preferences expressed by utterance π_1, regardless of who said π_1.

QAP. Answers to questions affect preferences in complex ways. The first case concerns yes/no questions and there are two cases, depending on whether B replies *yes* or *no*:

Yes $QAP_B(\pi_1, \pi_2)$ where π_2 is *yes*. B's preferences $\mathcal{N}$ are updated by applying $Commit (Elab_B(\pi_1, \pi_2), \mathcal{N})$ (and so B's preferences include those expressed by π_1 and π_2).
No $QAP_B(\pi_1, \pi_2)$ where π_2 is *no*. If $P(\pi_1)$ and $P(\pi_2)$ are consistent, then B's preferences $\mathcal{N}$ are updated by applying $Commit_B(Elab_B(\pi_1, \pi_2), \mathcal{N})$; if they are not consistent, B's preferences are updated by applying $Commit(Plan-Correction(\pi_1, \pi_2), \mathcal{N})$ (see below).

Now consider $QAP_B(\pi_1, \pi_2)$, where π_1 is a *wh*-question. Then B's preferences over variables in π_1 and π_2 are exactly the same as the ones defined for a yes/no question where the answer is *yes*: variables in π_2 will refine preferences over variables in π_1. So, B's preferences $\mathcal{N}$ are updated by applying $Commit_B(Elab_B(\pi_1, \pi_2), \mathcal{N})$.

Alternatives. The last and most complex sort of question and answer pair involves so called *alternative* questions such as *would you like fish or pizza?* Suppose agent A asks B an alternative question π_1 involving n variables. Then B's answer $QAP_B(\pi_1, \pi_2)$ provides information about B's preferences. Suppose $\pi_2 : \&(X_i, \ldots X_n)$. Intuitively, this response provides several answers as good as any other: for $i \leq j \leq n$, B wants to satisfy the literal X_j. Therefore, we add the following preferences for each X_j, or we change the existing preferences if appropriate: $Pa(X_j) = \emptyset$ and $X_j \succ \overline{X_j}$.

Plan-Correction. may affect preferences in several ways. For example, it can correct what variables are operative. That is, given $Plan\text{-}Correction(\pi_1, \pi_2)$, some variables in $P(\pi_1)$ are replaced by variables in $P(\pi_2)$. We have a set of rules of the form $X \leftarrow \{Y_1, \ldots, Y_m\}$, which means that the variable $X \in Var(P(\pi_1))$ is replaced by the set of variables $\{Y_1, \ldots, Y_m\} \subseteq Var(P(\pi_2))$. We assume that X cannot depend on $\{Y_1, \ldots, Y_m\}$ before the *Plan-Correction* is performed. Then replacement proceeds as follows:

6. If $Pa(X) = \emptyset$, we add $Y_k \succ \overline{Y_k}$ for all $k \in \{1, \ldots, m\}$ and remove $X \succ \overline{X}$ (or $\overline{X} \succ X$). Otherwise, we replace every preference statement in $CPT(X)$ with an equivalent statement using Y_k (to create $CPT(Y_k)$), for all $k \in \{1, \ldots m\}$.
7. For all W such that $Var(X) \in Pa(W)$, we re-define $CPT(W)$ so that every occurrence of X and $\overline{X}$ is replaced by a set of k statements where each statement replaces replaces X with $\overline{X}$ respectively with $\bigwedge_{1 \leq k \leq m} Y_k$ and $\bigvee_{1 \leq k \leq m} \overline{Y_k}$.

Plan-Corrections, like the one in (1), can also remove certain options from consideration in realizing a particular plan or it can put certain options into play that were previously excluded. In particular, suppose, π_1 countenances k options $X_1, \ldots, X_k$ and rules out n options $Y_1, \ldots, Y_n$; thus, $P(\pi_i) = \bigvee_{1 \leq i \leq k} X_i \wedge \bigwedge_{1 \leq r \leq n} \neg Y_r$. Suppose π_2 removes an option X_m from π_1. Then we must replace $P(\pi_1)$ with $\bigvee_{\{1 \leq i \leq k\} \setminus \{m\}} X_i \wedge (\bigwedge_{1 \leq r \leq n} \neg Y_r) \wedge \neg X_m$. The rule for putting an option into play that was previously excluded is similar; one removes one of the conjuncts in $P(\pi_i)$ and adds to the disjunction. It seems impossible to state the effects of *Plan-Correction* without the level of boolean preference representations afforded by the function P; we have not found a way to modify CP-nets directly.

6   Treatment of Our Example

Dialogue (1) illustrates how our rules work to refine preferences as conversation proceeds. While this dialogue doesn't feature all of our rules, other examples in the Verbmobil corpus verify the other rules.

π_1 A: Shall we meet sometime in the next week?
    $Commit_A(\pi_1, \langle \emptyset, \emptyset \rangle) = P(\pi_1) = M$, where M means Meet.

Fig. 1. A's preferences

π_2 *A*: What days are good for you?

Q-Elab(π_1, π_2). *A* continues to commit to *M* on π_2 and no new preferences are introduced by π_2 (i.e. $P(\pi_2) = P(\pi_1)$).

π_3 *B*: Well, I have some free time on almost every day except Fridays.

π_4 *B*: Fridays are bad.

π_4 is linked to π_3 with explanation, but this has no effect on preferences. In π_3, *B* says he has some free time on Monday, Tuesday, Wednesday and Thursday (and so can meet on these days); he does not want to meet on Friday. So, we update *B*'s CP-net $\langle \emptyset, \emptyset \rangle$ with Q-Elab(π_1, π_2) and then $QAP(\pi_2, \pi_3)$, where $P(\pi_3) = (J_1 \lor J_2 \lor J_3 \lor J_4) \land \neg J_5$, with J_1 being Monday, J_2 Tuesday, J_3 Wednesday, J_4 Thursday and J_5 Friday. Where $I = \{1,2,3,4,5\}$ this update yields:

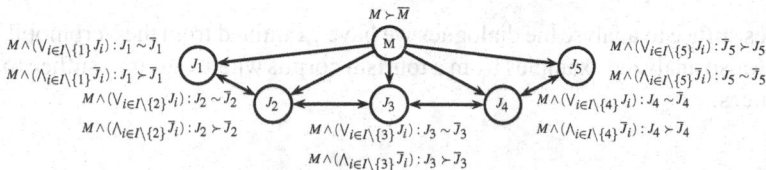

Fig. 2. *B*'s preferences

π_5 *B*: In fact, I'm busy on Thursday too.

This is a *Plan-Correction* with $P(\pi_5) = \neg J_4$, and thus $J_4 \leftarrow \neg J_4$. Thus J_4 is no longer an option. The above rule for updating a CP-net $\mathcal{N}$ with this dialogue move *Plan-Correction*(π, π_5) (where π outscopes π_3 and π_4) therefore removes the disjunct J_4 from the BPR for the first argument π, and adds the conjunct $\neg J_4$. The effect of the resulting BPR is this update to *B*'s CP-net:

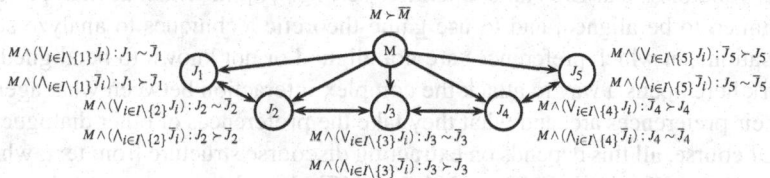

Fig. 3. *B*'s preferences

π_6 *A*: Well next week I am out of town Tuesday, Wednesday and Thursday.

The above rule for updating *A*'s prior CP-net (see Figure 1) with *Plan-Elab*(π_1, π_6), where $P(\pi_6) = \neg J_2 \land \neg J_3 \land \neg J_4$, yields the following CP-net.

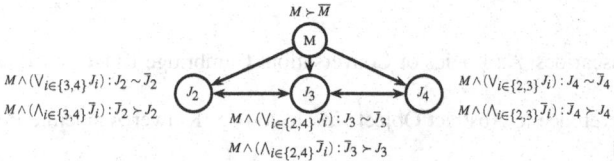

Fig. 4. *A*'s preferences

π_7 A: So perhaps Monday?

Commit updates the CP-net in Figure 4 with the move $Q\text{-}Elab(\pi_1, \pi_7)$, where $P(\pi_7)$ $= J_1$. Using the same rules as before this yields:

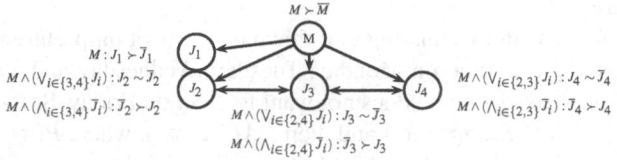

Fig. 5. A's preferences

Our rules suffice to analyse the dialogues we have examined from the Verbmobil corpus. We have also analyzed examples from a tourism corpus where our rules suffice to extract preferences.

7 Conclusion

Computing preferences expressed in texts is important for many NLP applications. We have shown how to use CP-nets and models of discourse structure, together with the intermetiate level BPR, to investigate this task formally. Our rules for preference modelling are straightforward, intuitive and of low complexity. While CP-nets can loose their polynomial time complexity for computing best outcomes, if conjunctive ($\wedge$) or disjunctive ($\vee$) preferences occur, on the whole the formalism remains tractable. Once we can extract preferences, we are in a position to broaden current analyses of dialogue beyond the usual Gricean cooperative settings [6], in which agents' preferences are assumed to be aligned, and to use game-theoretic techniques to analyze strategic conversations, in which preferences are not aligned or not known to be aligned. Thus, our work here opens a way to attack the complex interaction between what agents say, what their preferences are, and what they take the preferences of other dialogue agents to be. Of course, all this depends on extracting discourse structure from text, which has proved to be a difficult task. Nevertheless [3,12] show how one can begin to extract discourse structure automatically from texts like those found in the Verbmobil corpus. So we hope that our proposal will eventually find its way into automatic systems. In any case, our formal approach serves as a model for what such systems should aim to accomplish with respect to preference modeling.

References

1. Asher, N., Lascarides, A.: Logics of Conversation. Cambridge University Press, Cambridge (2003)
2. Asher, N.: Reference to Abstract Objects in Discourse. Kluwer Academic Publishers, Dordrecht (1993)
3. Baldridge, J., Lascarides, A.: Probabilistic head-driven parsing for discourse structure. In: CoNLL'05 (2005)

4. Boutilier, C., Brafman, R., Domshlak, C., Hoos, H., Poole, D.: CP-nets: A Tool for Representing and Reasoning with Conditional *Ceteris Paribus* Preference Statements. Journal of Artificial Intelligence Research 21, 135–191 (2004)

5. Boutilier, C., Brafman, R., Domshlak, C., Hoos, H., Poole, D.: Preference-Based Constrained Optimization with CP-nets. Computational Intelligence 20(2), 137–157 (2004)

6. Grice, H.P.: Logic and conversation. In: Sytnax and Semantics. Speech Acts, vol. 3, pp. 41–58 (1975)

7. Hamblin, C.: Imperatives. Blackwells, Oxford (1987)

8. Hobbs, J.R., Stickel, M., Appelt, D., Martin, P.: Interpretation as abduction. Artificial Intelligence 63(1-2), 69–142 (1993)

9. Lascarides, A., Asher, N.: Grounding and correcting commitments in dialogue. In: Proceedings to SIGDIAL, pp. 29–36 (2008)

10. Mann, W.C., Thompson, S.A.: Rhetorical structure theory: A framework for the analysis of texts. International Pragmatics Association Papers in Pragmatics 1, 79–105 (1987)

11. Rossi, F., Venable, B., Walsh, T.: mCP nets: representing and reasoning with preferences of multiple agents. In: AAAI'04, pp. 729–734 (2004)

12. Schlangen, D., Lascarides, A.: Resolving fragments using discourse information. In: Edilog'02 (2002)

13. Wahlster, W. (ed.): Verbmobil: Foundations of Speech-to-Speech Translation. Springer, Heidelberg (2000)

Argumentation Framework with Fuzzy Preference Relations

Souhila Kaci[1,2] and Christophe Labreuche[3]

[1] Université Lille-Nord de France, Artois
CRIL, CNRS UMR 8188
IUT de Lens F-62307, France
[2] CLLE-LTC, CNRS UMR 5263
5 Allées Machado
31058 Toulouse Cedex 9, France
[3] Thales Research & Technology
1 avenue Augustin Fresnel
91767 Palaiseau Cedex, France

Abstract. Dung's argumentation developed in Artificial Intelligence is based on a binary attack relation. An important particular case arises when there is a Boolean preference relation between the arguments. We propose to extend this argumentation framework to a fuzzy preference relation. This implies that an argument can attack another one to a certain degree. It turns out that the acceptability semantics in this new framework can be obtained in two ways: either from the concept of fuzzy kernel defined in fuzzy preference modeling, or from the acceptability semantics defined on weighted attack relations. Finally, we obtain some requirements on the fuzzy preference relation in the case when it shall be constructed from weights assigned to the arguments.

1 Introduction

Argumentation as developed in Artificial Intelligence is a model for reasoning about an inconsistent knowledge. It consists first in constructing arguments, determining conflicts between them, identifying acceptable ones and finally drawing conclusions. Argumentation can be used in many fields such as autonomous agent, decision making and non-monotonic reasoning. Dung has proposed an abstract argumentation framework that is composed of a set of arguments and a binary relation which is interpreted as an attack relation between arguments [4]. Dung's argumentation framework relies on two principles to define sets of acceptable arguments called acceptable extensions. An extension should be conflict-free, i.e., there are no arguments in the extension related by the attack relation. An extension should also defend each of its arguments, i.e., if an argument in the extension is attacked then there is an argument in the extension that attacks the attacker argument. This framework has been instantiated to take into account the importance of the arguments, yielding several preference-based argumentation frameworks [10,1,2,7].

E. Hüllermeier, R. Kruse, and F. Hoffmann (Eds.): IPMU 2010, LNAI 6178, pp. 554–563, 2010.

In the previous frameworks, the preference relation is Boolean. We are interested in this paper to extend these frameworks to fuzzy preference relations. This implies that the attack between arguments becomes fuzzy. Dung's framework has already been extended to weighted attack relations [9,5]. We instantiate this to the case where a fuzzy preference relation exists. In Section 4, we wish to define acceptable arguments from a fuzzy attack relation. We investigate two alternative ways. The idea behind the first one is to exploit the similarity between argumentation framework and preference modeling (see Section 4.1). The stable extensions in argumentation are similar to the kernels in preference modeling [3]. The stable extensions of a fuzzy argumentation framework can be defined as the fuzzy kernels of an associated fuzzy preference framework. The idea of the second way comes from [9] namely a subset A defends an argument a against the attack of an argument b if the intensity of the attack of A over b is larger than that of b over a. Once this central concept is re-defined, the acceptability semantics is defined as in the standard case.

In practice, the arguments are often constructed from a set of propositional logic formulas [10], and the preference relation on the arguments is then usually derived from some weights associated to these formulas. Section 5 focuses on this particular situation. We compare the notion of defense in the crisp and the fuzzy preference-based argumentation frameworks. From this comparison, we show that some requirements on the construction of the fuzzy preference relation from the weights on the arguments can be derived.

2 Background

2.1 Preference Modeling

A preference framework is a tuple $\langle D, \succ \rangle$, where D is a finite set of alternatives and $\succ$ is a binary relation over D. Relation $x \succ y$ (with $x, y \in D$) means that x is strictly preferred to y. The binary relation $\succ$ is usually supposed to be an *order*, i.e. it is antisymmetric and transitive. One of the leading approaches to identify the best alternatives given $\langle D, \succ \rangle$ comes from cooperative game theory and is called the *stable set* (also named *kernel* in preference modeling) [11].

Definition 1. $A \subseteq D$ *is a kernel of* $\langle D, \succ \rangle$ *if conditions (i) and (ii) hold:*
(i) internal stability: $\nexists a, b \in A : a \succ b$,
(ii) external stability: $\forall a \in D \setminus A, \exists b \in A : b \succ a$.

2.2 Dung's Argumentation Theory

Argumentation is a reasoning model based on constructing arguments, determining potential conflicts between them and selecting acceptable arguments. In Dung's framework [4], arguments are supposed to be given, and conflicts between arguments are represented by a binary *attack* relation.

Definition 2. *An* argumentation framework *(AF) is a tuple* $\langle A, \twoheadrightarrow \rangle$ *where* A *is a finite set (of arguments) and* $\twoheadrightarrow$ *is a binary (attack) relation defined on* $A \times A$.

One then wishes to predict what would be the *winning* arguments in a controversy dialogue based on exchanging and attacking arguments only from $\langle \mathcal{A}, \rightarrow \rangle$. The outcome is sets of arguments, called *extensions*, that are robust against attacks. We say that A *defends* a if $\forall b \in \mathcal{A}$ such that $b \rightarrow a$, $\exists c \in A$ such that $c \rightarrow b$. We say that $A \subseteq \mathcal{A}$ is *conflict-free* if there are no $a, b \in A$ such that $a \rightarrow b$. A subset $A \subseteq \mathcal{A}$ is a *stable extension* iff it is conflict-free, it defends all elements in A, and it attacks any argument in $\mathcal{A} \setminus A$. The set of stable extensions is denoted by $\mathrm{Acc}^{\mathrm{sta}}(\rightarrow)$. Other semantics of extensions can be found in the literature [4].

2.3 Preference-Based Argumentation Framework

Preference-based argumentation framework [1] is an instantiation of Dung's framework that is based on a binary attack relation between arguments and a preference relation over the set of arguments.

Definition 3. *A preference-based argumentation framework (PAF) is a 3-tuple* $\langle \mathcal{A}, \rightsquigarrow, \succ \rangle$ *where* $\mathcal{A}$ *is a set of arguments,* $\rightsquigarrow$ *is a binary attack relation defined on* $\mathcal{A} \times \mathcal{A}$ *and* $\succ$ *is a complete or partial order on* $\mathcal{A} \times \mathcal{A}$.

A PAF $\langle \mathcal{A}, \rightsquigarrow, \succ \rangle$ is said to *represent* $\langle \mathcal{A}, \rightarrow \rangle$ ($\rightarrow$ is then called a *defeat*) if

$$\forall a, b \in \mathcal{A} \; : \quad a \rightarrow b \iff [a \rightsquigarrow b \text{ and } \neg(b \succ a)]. \tag{1}$$

A defeat is an attack that succeeds thanks to the support of the preference relation. The stable extensions of a PAF are simply the stable extensions of the AF it represents.

The most usual way to construct a PAF is to start from a set K of weighted propositional logic formulas [10]. An argument is a pair $\langle H, h \rangle$ where (1) h is a formula of the language, (2) H is a consistent subset of K, (3) H entails h and (4) H is minimal (i.e., no strict subset of H satisfies (1), (2) and (3)). Then for two arguments a, b, we have $a \succ b$ iff $w(a) > w(b)$, where w is a function of the weights of formulas involved in the support of the argument (H is the support of an argument $\langle H, h \rangle$).

3 Argumentation Framework with Fuzzy Attack Relation

Dung's framework has been extended to weighted attack relations in [9,5]. We propose the following definition that is closer to the spirit of fuzzy sets.

Definition 4. *A fuzzy argumentation framework (FAF) is a tuple* $\langle \mathcal{A}, Att \rangle$ *where* $\mathcal{A}$ *is the set of arguments and* $Att : \mathcal{A} \times \mathcal{A} \rightarrow [0, 1]$ *is called a* fuzzy attack relation.

In [5], a *weighted argumentation system* is a triplet $\langle \mathcal{A}, \rightarrow, W \rangle$, where $\rightarrow$ is binary attack relation and $W : \mathcal{A} \times \mathcal{A} \rightarrow (0, 1]$ is a weight of the attacks. It is similar to our framework with the correspondence: $Att(a, b) = W(a, b)$ if $a \rightarrow b$, and $Att(a, b) = 0$ otherwise.

We now extend FAF to accommodate a preference over the arguments. An attack fails in PAF as soon as the attacked argument is strictly preferred to the attacker one (see (1)). However this is no longer sufficient when preferences over arguments ar graded. Rather we should state that the defeat of a over b exists but it is somehow weak. The degree to which the defeat holds shall be based on the intensity of preference among the arguments.

A *fuzzy preference-based argumentation framework* (FPAF) is a 3-tuple $\langle \mathcal{A}, \rightsquigarrow, P \rangle$ where $\mathcal{A}$ is the set of arguments, $\rightsquigarrow$ is a binary attack relation defined on $\mathcal{A} \times \mathcal{A}$ and P is a fuzzy strict preference relation. The fuzzy strict preference relation $P : \mathcal{A} \times \mathcal{A} \to [0, 1]$ is defined from a De Morgan triple (T, S, n) where T is a t-norm, S is a t-conorm and n is a negation [6]. P is usually assumed to be T-antisymmetric and T-transitive [6]. In this paper, the standard negation $n(x) = 1 - x$ will be used. $P(a, b)$ is the degree of credibility of the statement "a *is strictly preferred to* b". Value $P(a, b) = 1$ means that the previous statement is certainly validated, $P(a, b) = 0$ means that the previous statement is certainly non-validated, and $P(a, b) = \frac{1}{2}$ means that it is unknown whether the previous assertion is validated or not.

The simplest way to derive a Boolean relation $\succ_P$ from P is to use a cut [3]:

$$\forall a, b \in \mathcal{A} \ , \quad a \succ_P b \ \text{iff} \ P(a, b) > \frac{1}{2}. \tag{2}$$

Given an order $\succ$, a fuzzy preference relation denoted by $P_\succ$ can be defined:

$$P_\succ(a, b) = 1 \ \text{if} \ a \succ b \ \text{and} \ P_\succ(a, b) = 0 \ \text{otherwise}. \tag{3}$$

Note that this definition is consistent with (2) since we have that $\succ_{P_\succ} = \succ$.

Relation (1) can be easily fuzzyfied: A FPAF $\langle \mathcal{A}, \rightsquigarrow, P \rangle$ represents a FAF $\langle \mathcal{A}, Def \rangle$ iff

$$Def(a, b) = \begin{cases} 0 & \text{if } not(a \rightsquigarrow b) \\ 1 - P(b, a) & \text{if } a \rightsquigarrow b \end{cases} \tag{4}$$

$Def(a, b)$ is the degree of credibility of the statement "a defeats b". The larger $Def(a, b)$, the larger the defeat of a on b.

4 Acceptability Semantics in FAF

Given a FAF, we now need to define ways to compute acceptability semantics.

Starting from a FPAF $\langle \mathcal{A}, \rightsquigarrow, P \rangle$ and the corresponding defeat relation Def (see (4)), let us define a binary attack relation $\rightarrow_{Def}$ from the Boolean order $\succ_P$ (see (2)) in such a way that $\langle \mathcal{A}, \rightsquigarrow, \succ_P \rangle$ represents $\langle \mathcal{A}, \rightarrow_{Def} \rangle$. Then for $a, b \in \mathcal{A}$, $a \rightarrow_{Def} b$ iff $[a \rightsquigarrow b$ and $\neg(b \succ_P a)]$ iff $[a \rightsquigarrow b$ and $P(b, a) \leq \frac{1}{2}]$ iff $[a \rightsquigarrow b$ and $1 - P(b, a) \geq \frac{1}{2}]$ iff $Def(a, b) \geq \frac{1}{2}$. Hence

$$\forall a, b \in \mathcal{A}, a \rightarrow_{Def} b \ \text{iff} \ Def(a, b) \geq \frac{1}{2}. \tag{5}$$

4.1   FAF vs. Fuzzy Preference Modeling

Dung [4] has shown a strong relationship between AF and preference framework in the crisp case. This relationship mainly relies on the correspondences between internal (resp. external) stability in preference modeling and conflict-free (resp. attack of external elements) in AF. See Table 1 for a complete picture of these correspondences. The assumptions made on the attack relation and the binary preference relation are different. But this is minor. On the other hand, we know that internal and external stability are also defined in fuzzy preference modeling [3]. They define to which degree a set is a kernel. Thus the extensions of FAF can be defined by translating the notions of internal, external stability and kernel from fuzzy preference modeling to FAF. Let us establish such a translation.

Table 1. Correspondences between Dung's AF and crisp preference modeling

Argumentation	Preference Modeling
Argument	Alternative/choice
Attack relation	binary preference relation
Conflict-free	Internal stability
Attack all external elements	External stability
Stable extension	Stable sets / Kernel

Let P be a fuzzy strict preference relation over a set D. In fuzzy preference modeling [3], the degree to which a set A is a kernel combines the internal stability index

$$\Delta_{D,P}^{\text{int}}(A) = \min_{b \in A} \min_{a \in A \setminus \{b\}} (1 - P(a,b)), \tag{6}$$

and the external stability index

$$\Delta_{D,P}^{\text{ext}}(A) = \min_{a \in D \setminus A} \max_{b \in A} P(b,a). \tag{7}$$

These two degrees clearly extend the concepts of internal and external stability given in Definition 1. The degree to which the subset A is a kernel is $\Delta_{D,P}(A) = \min(\Delta_{D,P}^{\text{int}}(A), \Delta_{D,P}^{\text{ext}}(A))$. The kernels of $\langle D, P \rangle$ are

$$\mathbb{K}(\langle D, P \rangle) = \{A \subseteq D \mid \Delta_{D,P}(A) > \frac{1}{2}\}. \tag{8}$$

Translating the above notions to FAF consists in replacing P in equations (6) and (7) by Att. Therefore $\Delta_{\mathcal{A},Att}^{int}(A)$ (resp. $\Delta_{\mathcal{A},Att}^{ext}(A)$) corresponds to the degree to which A is conflict-free (resp. attacks external elements). Then, stable extensions in a FAF $\langle \mathcal{A}, Att \rangle$ are

$$\mathbb{K}(\langle \mathcal{A}, Att \rangle) = \{A \subseteq \mathcal{A} \mid \Delta_{\mathcal{A},Att}(A) > \frac{1}{2}\}. \tag{9}$$

From [8], we have the following result:

Proposition 1. *Let* $\langle \mathcal{A}, Att \rangle$ *be a FAF. Let* $\langle \mathcal{A}, \rightharpoonup_{Att} \rangle$ *be Dung's AF, where* $\rightharpoonup_{Att}$ *is defined from* $\langle \mathcal{A}, Att \rangle$ *following equation (5). Let* $\mathbb{K}(\langle \mathcal{A}, Att \rangle)$ *be the stable extensions of* $\langle \mathcal{A}, Att \rangle$ *following equation (9). Then,*

$$\mathbb{K}(\langle \mathcal{A}, Att \rangle) \subseteq Acc^{sta}(\rightharpoonup_{Att}).$$

It is important to notice that when the fuzzy relation Att never takes the indeterminate value $\frac{1}{2}$ (i.e. $Att(a, b) \neq \frac{1}{2}$ for all $a, b \in \mathcal{A}$), then we have $\mathbb{K}(\langle \mathcal{A}, Att \rangle) = Acc^{sta}(\rightharpoonup_{Att})$ in Proposition 1 [3]. However this is rather an undesirable result since it means that the use of a fuzzy attack relation brings nothing. Moreover, it is easy to see that the elements of $Acc^{sta}(\rightharpoonup_{Att})$ that are not in $\mathbb{K}(\langle \mathcal{A}, Att \rangle)$ are the subsets $A \in Acc^{sta}(\rightharpoonup_{Att})$ for which there exists $a, b \in \mathcal{A}$, $a \neq b$ such that $[a \in A$ or $b \in A]$ and $Att(a, b) = \frac{1}{2}$. There is no intuitive reason to remove these particular elements from $Acc^{sta}(\rightharpoonup_{Att})$. As shown in the following result, a slight modification in the definition of $\mathbb{K}(\langle \mathcal{A}, Att \rangle)$ suffices to obtain an equality with $Acc^{sta}(\rightharpoonup_{Att})$. Indeed, $Acc^{sta}(\rightharpoonup_{Att})$ is equal to the set of subsets $A \subseteq \mathcal{A}$ such that $\Delta^{int}_{\mathcal{A}, Att}(A) > \frac{1}{2}$ and $\Delta^{ext}_{\mathcal{A}, Att}(A) \geq \frac{1}{2}$.

Proposition 2. *A set* $A \subseteq \mathcal{A}$ *is conflict free w.r.t.* $\rightharpoonup_{Att}$ *iff* $\Delta^{int}_{\mathcal{A}, Att}(A) > \frac{1}{2}$. *Moreover, a set* A *attacks all external elements w.r.t.* $\rightharpoonup_{Att}$ *iff* $\Delta^{ext}_{\mathcal{A}, Att}(A) \geq \frac{1}{2}$.

In the light of the above facts, we conclude that the kernel of $\langle \mathcal{A}, Att \rangle$ or its extension is not suitable since it does not use the richness of information contained in Att. For these reasons, we do not want to continue in this direction to compute acceptability semantics of a FAF.

4.2 Extension of the Concept of a Defense

In [9], the concept of a defense has been extended to weighted attacks. The idea is to say that the defense provided by A in favor of a is successful if the defeat of c on b is stronger than the defeat of b on a.

Definition 5. *Let* $\langle \mathcal{A}, Att \rangle$ *be a FAF. The set* $A \subseteq \mathcal{A}$ *defends* $a \in \mathcal{A}$ *w.r.t. Att iff*

$$\forall b \in \mathcal{A} \; \exists c \in A \; : \; Att(c, b) \geq Att(b, a).$$

A subset $A \subseteq \mathcal{A}$ is *conflict-free* w.r.t. Att in the FAF $\langle \mathcal{A}, Att \rangle$ if A is conflict-free w.r.t. $\rightharpoonup_{Att}$ (see (5)) in the AF $\langle \mathcal{A}, \rightharpoonup_{Att} \rangle$. From the concepts of defense and conflict-free defined above, we can define in a similar way as for the Boolean case the stable extensions. The stable extensions of a FPAF are stable extensions of the FAF it represents.

Note that the definition of defense and conflict-free in FAF is faithful with the crisp case. Starting from a PAF $\langle \mathcal{A}, \rightsquigarrow, \succ \rangle$, we define the associated AF $\langle \mathcal{A}, \rightharpoonup \rangle$. We can also define the FPAF $\langle \mathcal{A}, \rightsquigarrow, P_{\succ} \rangle$ where $P_{\succ}$ is constructed from $\succ$ following equation (3), and the associated FAF $\langle \mathcal{A}, Def \rangle$. Then $\langle \mathcal{A}, \rightharpoonup \rangle$ and $\langle \mathcal{A}, Def \rangle$ have the same stable extensions.

5 Existence of a Valuation of the Arguments

We assume here that a weight $w : \mathcal{A} \to [0,1]$ is obtained as depicted in Section 2.3, and that an attack relation $\rightsquigarrow$ is also given. From w and $\rightsquigarrow$, we can construct a PAF $\langle \mathcal{A}, \rightsquigarrow, \succ \rangle$ (see Section 2.3 for the relation between $\succ$ and w). Another possibility is to construct a FPAF $\langle \mathcal{A}, \rightsquigarrow, P \rangle$, where P is defined from w. We refer to the former (resp. the latter) as the crisp (resp. fuzzy) case. In this section we compare the notion of defense in both frameworks. From this comparison, some requirements on the construction of P from w will be derived.

5.1 A Case Study

We assume in this section that P is defined from w in the following way:

$$P_N(a, b) = \begin{cases} 1 & \text{if } w(a) > w(b) \\ w(a) - w(b) + 1 & \text{if } w(a) \leq w(b) \end{cases} \tag{10}$$

The N in underscore means that P_N is not constant when $w(a) - w(b)$ is negative. According to P_N, the strict preference between two arguments a and b is certain as soon as $w(a) > w(b)$. Hence by Definition 4 we have

$$Def(a, b) = \begin{cases} 0 & \text{if } w(a) < w(b) \text{ or } not(a \rightsquigarrow b) \\ w(a) - w(b) & \text{if } w(a) \geq w(b) \text{ and } a \rightsquigarrow b \end{cases}$$

Let a, b and c be three arguments such that $c \rightsquigarrow b$ and $b \rightsquigarrow a$. Then we have the following five situations:

- **Situation α:** $w(c) < w(b) < w(a)$. Then $Def(c, b) = Def(b, a) = 0$. We also have neither $b \twoheadrightarrow a$ nor $c \twoheadrightarrow b$ since $a \succ b$ and $b \succ c$. The crisp and fuzzy cases yield the same conclusion: there is no defeat of b on a.
- **Situation β:** $w(a) < w(b)$ and $w(c) < w(b)$ (written in a compact way as $\{w(a), w(c)\} < w(b)$). Then $Def(c, b) = 0$ and $Def(b, a) > 0$. We also have $b \twoheadrightarrow a$ but $not(c \twoheadrightarrow b)$. The defense of c fails both in the crisp and the fuzzy cases.
- **Situation γ:** $w(b) < \{w(a), w(c)\}$ with the compact notation. We have $Def(c, b) > 0$ and $Def(b, a) = 0$. We also have $not(b \twoheadrightarrow a)$ but $c \twoheadrightarrow b$. Hence c defeats b and b does not defeat a in both the crisp and the fuzzy cases.
- **Situation $\delta 1$:** $w(a) < w(b) \ll w(c)$ which means that $w(b) - w(a) < w(c) - w(b)$. Hence $Def(c, b) = w(c) - w(b) > Def(b, a) = w(b) - w(a)$. We also have $b \twoheadrightarrow a$ and $c \twoheadrightarrow b$. Indeed c defends a both in the crisp and the fuzzy cases.
- **Situation $\delta 2$:** $w(a) \ll w(b) < w(c)$, which means that $w(b) - w(a) > w(c) - w(b)$. Hence, $Def(c, b) = w(c) - w(b) < Def(b, a) = w(b) - w(a)$. On the other hand, we have $b \twoheadrightarrow a$ and $c \twoheadrightarrow b$. Indeed the crisp and the fuzzy cases yield different conclusions: c defends a in the crisp case but not in the fuzzy case.

In sum, the crisp and the fuzzy cases yield the same conclusion, except in the fifth situation in which the defeat of b on a is large whereas the defeat of c on b is weak. However, the intuition of the crisp case is valid: c is stronger than both b and a, and, because of that, c deserves to defend a against the attack of b (even if c is just slightly stronger than b). Consequently, we conclude that the expression P_N is not suitable with Definition 5. In the next subsection, we propose a strict preference relation compatible with Definition 5.

5.2   Strict Preference P Compatible with Definition 5

In order to determine which expressions of P are compatible with Definition 5, we assume that the strict preference relation can be written as $P(a,b) = p(w(a), w(b))$ where $p : [0,1]^2 \rightarrow [0,1]$. Function p shall be continuous, non-decreasing in the first argument and non-increasing in the second argument. Moreover, we have the boundary conditions:

$$p(0,1) = 0 \quad \text{and} \quad p(1,0) = 1.$$

Replacing $P(b,a)$ by $p(w(b), w(a))$ in Definition 4, we get:

$$Def(a,b) = \begin{cases} 0 & \text{if } not(a \rightsquigarrow b) \\ 1 - p(w(b), w(a)) & \text{if } a \rightsquigarrow b \end{cases}$$

The situation $p(t,t)$ for $t \in [0,1]$ corresponds to two arguments a and b having the same weight t. The degree of preference of a over b shall not depend on t. Hence, for symmetry reasons, we assume the following condition:

$$\forall t, v \in [0,1] \ , \quad p(t,t) = p(v,v). \tag{11}$$

We assume that p satisfies all previous requirements.

The condition raised by the situation 5 described in Section 5.1 can be formalized in the following way.

Unrestricted positive defense (UPD): Let $A \subseteq \mathcal{A}$, $a, b \in \mathcal{A}$ and $c \in A$. If $c \rightsquigarrow b$, $b \rightsquigarrow a$ and $w(c) \geq w(b) \geq w(a)$ then c defends a against b.

One can easily show the following result.

Proposition 3. *Under* **UPD**, *$P(a,b) = 0$ whenever $w(a) \leq w(b)$.*

Proposition 3 shows that axiom **UPD** implies that the strict preference relation P is unipolar in the sense that P takes the saturation value 0 whenever $w(a) \leq w(b)$. Expression (10) is ruled out by Proposition 3. From Proposition 3, there is no way the statement "a is strictly preferred to b" is validated when $w(a) < w(b)$. By continuity, when $w(a)$ is slightly larger than $w(b)$, then the credibility of the previous statement is still low. One is sure about the credibility of this assertion only when $w(a)$ is significantly larger than $w(b)$. The simplest expression of P is the following one

$$P_P(a,b) = \begin{cases} 0 & \text{if } w(a) < w(b) \\ w(a) - w(b) & \text{if } w(a) \geq w(b) \end{cases}$$

The P in underscore means that P_P has non-constant values only when $w(a) - w(b)$ is positive. Hence

$$Def(a,b) = \begin{cases} 1 & \text{if } w(a) > w(b) \text{ and } a \rightsquigarrow b \\ 1 + w(a) - w(b) & \text{if } w(a) \leq w(b) \text{ and } a \rightsquigarrow b \\ 0 & \text{if } not(a \rightsquigarrow b) \end{cases}$$

Let us assume that $c \rightsquigarrow b$ and $b \rightsquigarrow a$. Then we have the following five situations:

- **Situation $\alpha 1$:** $w(c) \ll w(b) < w(a)$ (i.e. $w(b) - w(c) > w(a) - w(b)$). Then we have $Def(c,b) = 1 + w(c) - w(b) < Def(b,a) = 1 + w(b) - w(a)$. We also have neither $b \rightarrowtail a$ nor $c \rightarrowtail b$. Hence the crisp and the fuzzy cases yield different conclusions: c defends a in the crisp case but not in the fuzzy case.
- **Situation $\alpha 2$:** $w(c) < w(b) \ll w(a)$ (i.e. $w(b) - w(c) < w(a) - w(b)$). Hence $Def(c,b) = 1 + w(c) - w(b) > Def(b,a) = 1 + w(b) - w(a)$. We also have neither $b \rightarrowtail a$ nor $c \rightarrowtail b$. Hence c defends a both in the crisp and the fuzzy cases.
- **Situation β:** $\{w(a), w(c)\} < w(b)$. We have $Def(c,b) < 1$ and $Def(b,a) = 1$. We also have $b \rightarrowtail a$ but $not(c \rightarrowtail b)$. The defense of c fails both in the crisp and the fuzzy cases.
- **Situation γ:** $w(b) < \{w(a), w(c)\}$. We have $Def(c,b) > 0$ and $Def(b,a) = 0$. We also have $not(b \rightarrowtail a)$ but $c \rightarrowtail b$. Hence c defeats b and b does not defeat a in both the crisp and the fuzzy cases.
- **Situation δ:** $w(a) < w(b) < w(c)$. Hence $Def(c,b) = 1$ and $Def(b,a) = 1$. We also have $b \rightarrowtail a$ and $c \rightarrowtail b$. Indeed c defends a both in the crisp and the fuzzy cases.

The situation α in Section 5.1 is decomposed in the two situations $\alpha 1$ and $\alpha 2$ in Section 5.2. The situation δ in Section 5.2 is decomposed in the two situations $\delta 1$ and $\delta 2$ in Section 5.1. Having these correspondences in mind, we obtain different results with P_N and P_P. Situation δ actually follows from **UPD**. In situations $\alpha 1$ and $\alpha 2$, c is weaker than b, and b is weaker than a. Hence the defeats of c over b, and of b over a are weak. In situation $\alpha 1$, $w(c) \ll w(b) < w(a)$ means that c, that is supposed to defend a, is much weaker than a and b. It is thus reasonable that the defense of a by c fails in this case. In situation $\alpha 2$, condition $w(c) < w(b) \ll w(a)$ means that the weight of c is not too far from that of b compared to a. One then may admit that c is sufficiently strong to defend a against b. Hence the results obtained with P_P are natural.

6   Conclusion

We have extended the preference-based argumentation frameworks to deal with fuzzy preference relation. We have shown that this new framework requires to extend the basic notions of conflict-freeness and defense in the fuzzy framework. The intensity in the preference relation is propagated to the defeat relation: the larger the preference between two arguments, the larger the defeat.

The acceptability semantics in this new framework can be obtained in two ways: either from the concept of fuzzy kernel defined in fuzzy preference modeling [3], or from the acceptability semantics defined on weighted attack relations [9]. We have seen that the first way is not satisfactory since it does not basically differentiate between the crisp and the fuzzy cases.

When the fuzzy preference relation is constructed from a weight function w defined on the set $\mathcal{A}$ of arguments, a natural property, called **UPD**, comes up. It says that the defense of an argument a by an argument b against the attack of c shall holds whenever $w(c) \geq w(b) \geq w(a)$. Then we showed that, for every a, b, a is clearly not strictly preferred to b (i.e. $P(a, b) = 0$) if $w(a) \leq w(b)$.

References

1. Amgoud, L., Cayrol, C.: Inferring from inconsistency in preference-based argumentation frameworks. IJAR 29(2), 125–169 (2002)
2. Bench-Capon, T.J.M.: Persuasion in practical argument using value-based argumentation frameworks. Journal of Logic and Computation 13(3), 429–448 (2003)
3. Bisdorff, R., Pirlot, M., Roubens, M.: Choices and kernels from bipolar valued digraphs. EJOR 175, 155–170 (2006)
4. Dung, P.M.: On the acceptability of arguments and its fundamental role in non-monotonic reasoning, logic programming and n-person games. Art. Int. 77, 321–357 (1995)
5. Dunne, P., Parsons, S., Hunter, A., McBurney, P., Wooldridge, M.: Inconsistency tolerance in weighted argumentation systems. In: International Conference on Autonomous Agent and Multiagents Systems (AAMAS), Budapest, Hungary, May 10-15 (2009)
6. Fodor, J., Roubens, M.: Fuzzy preference modelling and multi-criteria decision aid. Kluwer Academic Publisher, Dordrecht (1994)
7. Kaci, S., van der Torre, L.: Preference-based argumentation: Arguments supporting multiple values. International Journal of Approximate Reasoning 48, 730–751 (2008)
8. Kitainik, L.: Fuzzy decision procedures with binary relations: towards a unified theory. Kluwer Academic Publishers, Boston (1993)
9. Martinez, D., Garcia, A., Simari, G.: An abstract argumentation framework with varied weights. In: Eleventh International Conference on Principles of Knowledge Representation and Reasoning (KR), Sydney, Australia, September 16-19 2008, pp. 135–143 (2008)
10. Simari, G.R., Loui, R.P.: A mathematical treatment of defeasible reasoning and its implementation. Artificial Intelligence 53, 125–157 (1992)
11. von Neumann, J., Morgenstern, O.: Game theory and economic behavior. Princeton University Press, Princeton (1953)

An Algorithm for Generating Consistent and Transitive Approximations of Reciprocal Preference Relations

Steven Freson[1], Hans De Meyer[1], and Bernard De Baets[2]

[1] Department of Applied Mathematics and Computer Science
Ghent University, Krijgslaan 281 (S9), B-9000 Gent, Belgium
[2] Department of Applied Mathematics, Biometrics and Process Control
Ghent University, Coupure links 653, B-9000 Gent, Belgium
{steven.freson,hans.demeyer,bernard.debaets}@ugent.be

Abstract. We establish an iterative algorithm to generate for any given reciprocal relation and any given type of transitivity fitting into the framework of cycle-transitivity, a unique reciprocal relation that approximates the given reciprocal relation and possesses the given transitivity property. In the context of decision making, the algorithm can be used to generate a consistent approximation of a non-consistent reciprocal preference relation.

Keywords: Consistency, cycle-transitivity, iterative algorithm, reciprocal relation, stochastic transitivity.

1 Introduction

Often, a decision maker is asked to express his/her preferences on a set of alternatives in a pairwise manner. Preference relations are used to model this information in decision problems of various fields, such as politics, psychology, engineering, managment, business and economics. In the last two decades, preference relations have received increasing attention in the literature (see e.g. [14,21] and references therein).

Consistency is a serious challenge when dealing with decision making problems. It refers to the capability of experts to express their preferences without contradiction. To deal with consistency, it is important to characterize what consistency properties the preferences should comply with. In a crisp context, the concept of consistency has traditionally been defined in terms of acyclicity. This condition is closely related to the transitivity of the corresponding preference relation. In a graded context, the consistency properties that have been proposed for reciprocal preference relations attempt to extend the Boolean notion of transitivity of preferences. Most widespread is the property of additive consistency [16], sometimes abusively called additive transitivity, but many alternative proposals have been formulated [3,11,15,16], among which different types of stochastic transitivity.

E. Hüllermeier, R. Kruse, and F. Hoffmann (Eds.): IPMU 2010, LNAI 6178, pp. 564–573, 2010.

Once the decision analyst has made his/her choice of consistency property, he/she often encounters the following problems: how to repair the inconsistency of preference relations and how to estimate missing values? The first problem has been primordially dealt with in the context of additive consistency [17,22]. However, the proposed algorithms usually generate consistent preference relations far from the given preference relation. Much more research has been devoted to the second problem, mostly again in the context of additive consistency [1,2,12,13,23].

In the present paper, we contribute to the algorithmic solution of the first problem, where we broaden the context from additive consistency to a wide variety of transitivity types. We can cover such different types of transitivity by making use of the unifying cycle-transitivity framework, tailor-made for describing transitivity properties of reciprocal relations [7,9].

The outline of the paper is as follows. In Section 2 we briefly review the concepts of transitivity and consistency of reciprocal preference relations, whereas Section 3 contains an introduction to the cycle-transitivity framework. In Section 4, the problem of repairing inconsistency is analyzed. In Section 5, we describe our new iterative algorithm for generating a transitive approximation of reciprocal relations. Finally, Section 6 reports the numerical experiments we have performed.

2   Transitivity and Consistency of Reciprocal Preference Relations

Reciprocal preference relations have been widely used to model preferences in decision-making problems. In that case, the scale $[0, 1]$ is used to measure the intensity of preference of one alternative over another [1]. A reciprocal preference relation P on a finite set of n alternatives $A = \{a_1, \ldots a_n\}$ is represented by means of a comparison matrix $P = [p_{ij}]$, where every value p_{ij} represents the preference degree or intensity of preference of alternative a_i over alternative a_j: $p_{ij} = 1/2$ indicates indifference between a_i and a_j, whereas $a_{ij} > 1/2$ indicates that a_i is reather preferred to a_j. Furthermore, it holds that $p_{ij} + p_{ji} = 1$, for all i, j. In this paper we deal with reciprocal preference relations only.

The degree of consistency of a reciprocal preference relation is defined as the degree to which it is not contradictory. Consistency is usually characterized by a type of transitivity, which represents the idea that the degree of preference obtained by directly comparing two alternatives should be greater than or equal to the degree of preference between those two alternatives obtained using an indirect chain of alternatives. In literature, different properties to model the concept of transitivity have been suggested. We mention two types of fuzzy transitivity, three types of stochastic transitivity and additive consistency.

(i) $T_{\mathbf{L}}$-*transitivity*: $p_{ik} \geq T_{\mathbf{L}}(p_{ij}, p_{jk})$, where $T_{\mathbf{L}}$ denotes the Łukasiewicz t-norm, i.e. $T_{\mathbf{L}}(x, y) = \max(x+y-1, 0)$ for all $(x, y) \in [0, 1]^2$. This transitivity condition is equivalent with $p_{ij} + p_{jk} \geq p_{ik}$, also known as *the triangle condition*.

(ii) $T_{\mathbf{M}}$-*transitivity:* $p_{ik} \geq \min(p_{ij}, p_{jk})$, where $T_{\mathbf{M}}$ denotes the minimum operator, i.e. $T_{\mathbf{M}}(x, y) = \min(x, y)$ for all $(x, y) \in [0, 1]^2$. This type of transitivity is also called *max-min transitivity*.

(iii) *Weak stochastic transitivity:* $\min(p_{ij}, p_{jk}) \geq 1/2 \Rightarrow p_{ik} \geq 1/2$.

(iv) *Moderate stochastic transitivity:* $\min(p_{ij}, p_{jk}) \geq 1/2 \Rightarrow p_{ik} \geq \min(p_{ij}, p_{jk})$. This type of transitivity is also known as *restricted max-min transitivity*.

(v) *Strong stochastic transitivity:* $\min(p_{ij}, p_{jk}) \geq 1/2 \Rightarrow p_{ik} \geq \max(p_{ij}, p_{jk})$. This type of transitivity is also known as *restricted max-max transitivity*.

(vi) *Additive consistency:* $(p_{ij} - 1/2) + (p_{jk} - 1/2) = (p_{ik} - 1/2)$. Further on we will argue that, strictly speaking, this property cannot be regarded as a type of transitivity.

3   The Cycle-Transitivity Framework

There is lack of uniformity in the mathematical description of the types of transitivity summed up in Section 2. In view of constructing widely applicable algorithms for generating transitive reciprocal preference relations, it is advantageous to reformulate these types within a general transitivity framework. The so-called FG-transitivity framework, established by Switalski [20], is such a framework that has the property of yielding simple descriptions of the stochastic transitivity types. Two of the present authors have developed a more expressive alternative, called cycle-transitivity framework, that is tailor-made for decribing in a uniform manner the various types of transitivity of reciprocal relations encountered in various domains of application. We briefly recall the fundamentals of the cycle-transitivity framework [7,9].

For a reciprocal relation $Q : A^2 \rightarrow [0, 1]$ with matrix representation $[q_{ij}]$ we define the quantities

$$\alpha_{ijk} = \min(q_{ij}, q_{jk}, q_{ki}) , \beta_{ijk} = \mathrm{med}(q_{ij}, q_{jk}, q_{ki}) , \gamma_{ijk} = \max(q_{ij}, q_{jk}, q_{ki}) . \quad (1)$$

Obviously, it holds that $\alpha_{ijk} \leq \beta_{ijk} \leq \gamma_{ijk}$. We introduce the notation $\Delta_n = \{(x_1, x_2, \ldots, x_n) \in [0, 1]^n \mid x_1 \leq x_2 \leq \cdots \leq x_n\}$.

A function $U : \Delta_3 \rightarrow \mathbb{R}$ is called an upper bound function if it satisfies:

(i) $U(0, 0, 1) \geq 0$ and $U(0, 1, 1) \geq 1$;

(ii) for any $(\alpha, \beta, \gamma) \in \Delta_3$:

$$U(\alpha, \beta, \gamma) + U(1 - \gamma, 1 - \beta, 1 - \alpha) \geq 1 . \quad (2)$$

The function $L : \Delta_3 \rightarrow \mathbb{R}$ defined by

$$L(\alpha, \beta, \gamma) = 1 - U(1 - \gamma, 1 - \beta, 1 - \alpha) \quad (3)$$

is called the dual lower bound function of a given upper bound function U. Inequality (2) simply expresses that $L \leq U$.

A reciprocal relation $Q : A^2 \rightarrow [0, 1]$ with matrix representation $[q_{ij}]$ is called cycle-transitive w.r.t. an upper bound function U if for any i, j, k it holds that

$$L(\alpha_{ijk}, \beta_{ijk}, \gamma_{ijk}) \leq \alpha_{ijk} + \beta_{ijk} + \gamma_{ijk} - 1 \leq U(\alpha_{ijk}, \beta_{ijk}, \gamma_{ijk}) , \quad (4)$$

where L is the dual lower bound function of U.

Note that condition (i) ensures that the reciprocal 3-valued representation $Q(a, b) = (1 + R(a, b) - R(b, a))/2$ of any transitive complete $\{0, 1\}$-valued relation R is cycle-transitive w.r.t. any upper bound function.

Due to the built-in duality, it holds that if (4) is true for some (i, j, k), then this is also the case for any permutation of (i, j, k). In practice, it is therefore sufficient to check (4) for a single permutation of any (i, j, k). Alternatively, due to the same duality, it is also sufficient to verify the right-hand inequality (or equivalently, the left-hand inequality) for two permutations of any (i, j, k) not being cyclic permutations of one another, e.g., (i, j, k) and (k, j, i).

Hence, the double inequality (4) can be replaced by

$$\alpha_{ijk} + \beta_{ijk} + \gamma_{ijk} - 1 \leq U(\alpha_{ijk}, \beta_{ijk}, \gamma_{ijk}). \tag{5}$$

Note that a value of $U(\alpha, \beta, \gamma)$ equal to 2 will often be used to express that for the given arguments there is no restriction at all. Indeed, $\alpha + \beta + \gamma - 1$ is always upper bounded by 2.

We now convert the types of transitivity given in Section 2 into the cycle-transitive framework.

(i) A reciprocal relation satisfies the triangle inequality (is T_L-transitive), iff it is cycle-transitive w.r.t. the upper bound function U_L defined by U_L $(\alpha, \beta, \gamma) = 1$.

(ii) A reciprocal relation is T_M-transitive, iff it is cycle-transitive w.r.t. the upper bound function U_M defined by $U_M(\alpha, \beta, \gamma) = \beta$.

(iii) A reciprocal relation is weak stochastic transitive iff it is cycle-transitive w.r.t. the upper bound function U_g, defined by

$$U_g(\alpha, \beta, \gamma) = \begin{cases} \beta + \gamma - g(\beta, \gamma) & \text{, if } \alpha < 1/2 \leq \beta, \\ 1/2 & \text{, if } \alpha \geq 1/2, \\ 2 & \text{, if } \beta < 1/2, \end{cases} \tag{6}$$

where the $[0, 1]^2 \to [0, 1]$ function g is the constant function $g - 1/2$.

(iv) A reciprocal relation is moderate stochastic transitive iff it is cycle-transitive w.r.t. the upper bound function U_g, formally defined by (6) where the function g is given by $g(\beta, \gamma) = \min(\beta, \gamma) = \beta$.

(v) A reciprocal relation is strong stochastic transitive if it is cycle-transitive w.r.t. the upper bound function U_g, formally defined by (6), where the function g is given by $g(\beta, \gamma) = \max(\beta, \gamma) = \gamma$.

(vi) The function $U(\alpha, \beta, \gamma) = 1/2$ is not suitable as an upper bound function as the condition $U(0, 1, 1) \geq 1$ is not satisfied. Reciprocal relations satisfying the condition $\alpha_{ijk} + \beta_{ijk} + \gamma_{ijk} = 3/2$, i.e. condition (4) for this specific U, are called (additive) consistent in the literature [16]. Although it is often presented as a type of transitivity, it does not deserve to be called so, as it is even in general not satisfied by the reciprocal 3-valued representation of a transitive complete $\{0, 1\}$-valued relation [8].

4 Generating Transitive Approximations

Consider a reciprocal relation without missing entries and assume that the decision analyst requires, for the sake of consistency, the reciprocal relation to exhibit a prescribed type of transitivity. If the reciprocal relation does not have this transitivity, he/she accepts to minimally modify the preference degrees w.r.t. some loss function, such that the newly obtained reciprocal relation, regarded as an approximation or update of the given one, has the desired transitivity. The problem of finding an optimal transitive reciprocal approximation of a given reciprocal relation is our main concern in this paper.

Let Q denote the given reciprocal relation and Q^a a reciprocal relation that approximates Q. As Q and Q^a are reciprocal relations on a set of $n > 2$ alternatives, we define the distance between $Q = [q_{ij}]$ and $Q^a = [q_{ij}^a]$ as

$$d(Q, Q^a) = \sqrt{\frac{2}{n(n-1)} \sum_{i<j} (q_{ij} - q_{ij}^a)^2} \, .$$

Note that other definitions of a distance could be used as well.

Let $\mathcal{Q}_n$ denote the class of all reciprocal relations on a set of n alternatives and $\mathcal{Q}_n^t$ the class of all transitive reciprocal relations on the same set, where t refers to a fixed type of transitivity. Then the basic optimization problem of interest is:

$$\text{for given } Q \in \mathcal{Q}_n \text{ find } \min_{Q^a \in \mathcal{Q}_n} d(Q, Q^a) \text{ s.t. } Q^a \in \mathcal{Q}_n^t \, .$$

For $n = 3$, the optimization problem can be solved exactly for each type of transitivity. Also, in the context of additive consistency, the problem can be solved for any $n > 3$ by means of standard techniques. Indeed, the transitivity conditions are linear, i.e. $q_{ij} + q_{jk} + q_{ki} = 3/2$ and $0 \leq q_{ij} \leq 1$, and the solution is obtained from the Karush-Kuhn-Tucker conditions [18]. For the other types of transitivity and for $n > 4$, the optimization problem becomes practically intractable and the need emerges for constructing algorithms that generate suboptimal transitive approximations.

With the aim of finding such an algorithm, we have put forward the following criteria:

1. The algorithm should be an iterative algorithm applicable for any value of n.
2. The approximation generated by the algorithm should be independent of the order in which the data are provided, i.e. changing rows and columns in the matrix representation of the reciprocal relation should not have an influence on the resulting approximation.
3. Reciprocity should be guaranteed at any intermediate step of the iteration process.
4. The algorithm should converge sufficiently fast towards a suboptimal approximation.

Note that the elements of the approximation relation can be smaller or greater than the corresponding elements of the given reciprocal relation. Even reversion of preferences is not excluded. This is in contrast with many algorithms for generating transitive symmetric approximations of symmetric fuzzy relations which either lead to the transitive closure or a transitive opening of the given relation (in this context one usually requires T-transitivity for some t-norm T) [4,5,6,10,19].

On $\mathcal{Q}_n$ we can define a partial order $\leq$ by means of

$$\forall Q, Q' \in \mathcal{Q}_n : \ Q \geq Q' \Leftrightarrow \begin{cases} q'_{ij} \geq q_{ij} & \text{, if } q_{ij} \geq 1/2, \\ q'_{ij} \leq q_{ij} & \text{, if } q_{ij} \leq 1/2. \end{cases}$$

According to this order, the greatest reciprocal relation $Q_{1/2}$ is represented by a matrix with all its elements equal to $1/2$. It is easily verified that $Q_{1/2}$ is transitive, irrespective of the transitivity type considered. Note that the expected distance $d(Q, Q_{1/2})$ from a reciprocal relation Q selected at random in $\mathcal{Q}_n$ to $Q_{1/2}$ is 0.5. It therefore would make sense to look for transitive reciprocal closures of a reciprocal relation, i.e. transitive approximations that are greater than the given relation. However, in the context of decision making, forcing preferences to move systematically in the direction of indifference entails serious loss of information; one should therefore allow for strenghtening of preferences as well.

5   Description of the Algorithm

Assume a transitivity type has been selected, which in the cycle-transitivity framework is characterized by an upper bound function U. Given a reciprocal relation $Q \in \mathcal{Q}_n$ ($n > 2$), a transitive reciprocal approximation of Q is obtained by the application of the algorithm **TRA** given below. As it is an iterative numerical algorithm, a stopping criterion must be provided. To that aim, define the degree of non-transitivity $\sigma(Q, U)$ as

$$\sigma(Q, U) = \max_{i,j,k} (q_{ij} + q_{jk} + q_{ki} - 1 - U(\alpha_{ijk}, \beta_{ijk}, \gamma_{ijk})).$$

and stop the iteration as soon as Q^a satisfies $\sigma(Q^a, U) < \epsilon$ for some given tolerance ϵ.

In each iteration step of algorithm **TRA**, i.e. in each pass of the outer `repeat` loop, two (multiple `for`) loops are consecutively executed. The first loop extends over all couples (i, j). For each fixed couple (i, j) all the triplets (i, j, k) for k running from 1 to n are considered and for each it is checked whether inequality (5) is violated. In that case $\alpha_{ijk} + \beta_{ijk} + \gamma_{ijk} - 1 - U(\alpha_{ijk}, \beta_{ijk}, \gamma_{ijk})$, called the excess in the triplet (i, j, k), is strictly positive. If the generic transitivity condition $\alpha + \beta + \gamma - 1 \leq U(\alpha, \beta, \gamma)$ can be simplified into an inequality in which one or two of the variables α, β, γ have disappeared, and if q_{ij} matches with a missing variable, then q_{ij} is called inactive. Only when q_{ij} is active, it is meaningful to lower its value in order to restore transitivity. Finally, the minimum excess over all triplets (i, j, k) in which q_{ij} is active, is stored in e_{ij}. If in all the triplets (i, j, k) there is either no excess or q_{ij} is inactive, then e_{ij} keeps its initial value 1. When the first loop has been completely executed, all e_{ij} have been computed.

Algorithm TRA
Input: reciprocal relation $Q \in \mathcal{Q}_n$, upper bound function U,
        tolerance ϵ, fraction parameter λ_U

repeat
  for $i := 1$ **to** n **do for** $j := 1$ **to** n **do**
    $e_{ij} := 1$
    for $k := 1$ **to** n **do**
      $\alpha := \min(q_{ij}, q_{jk}, q_{ki})$, $\beta := \mathrm{med}(q_{ij}, q_{jk}, q_{ki})$, $\gamma := \max(q_{ij}, q_{jk}, q_{ki})$
      $d := \alpha + \beta + \gamma - 1 - U(\alpha, \beta, \gamma)$
      if $(d > \epsilon)$ **and** (q_{ij} is active) **and** $(d < e_{ij})$ **then** $e_{ij} = d$ **endif**
    endfor k
  endfor j **endfor** i
  for $i := 1$ **to** n **do for** $j := 1$ **to** n **do**
    if $e_{ij} < e_{ji}$ **then** $q_{ij} := \max(q_{ij} - \lambda_U \, e_{ij}, 0)$, $q_{ji} := 1 - q_{ij}$ **endif**
  endfor j **endfor** i
until $\sigma(Q, U) \leq \epsilon$

The second loop also extends over all couples (i, j). For each (i, j), it is first decided whether q_{ij} should be lowered or not. If $e_{ij} < e_{ji} \leq 1$, the answer is affirmative. Indeed, it is necessary that $e_{ij} < 1$, so that in at least one (i, j, k) the transitivity is violated while q_{ij} is active. Two subcases can be distinguished. Either $e_{ji} = 1$ and there is no necessity to lower q_{ji}, or $e_{ij} < 1$ and both q_{ij} and q_{ji} should be lowered, which are conflicting requirements. Here it is opted to lower q_{ij} when the associated minimal excess e_{ij} is strictly lower than the minimal excess e_{ji}. Note that by lowering q_{ij} then the increase of q_{ji} can strenghten the violation of transitivity in some triplets (j, i, k). Note also that if $e_{ij} = e_{ji}$ then q_{ij} and q_{ji} remain unchanged, an option that might cause a slowing effect on the rate of convergence. On the other hand, allowing for a random choice would no longer make the algorithm satisfy criterion 2 put forward in Section 4.

Finally, in case q_{ij} must be lowered, a fraction of the minimal excess e_{ij} is subtracted. This fraction depends on the type of transitivity. If in the generic transitivity condition none of the variables α, β, γ is explicitly absent (e.g. for transitivity types (i) and (vi)), then q_{ij} is lowered by $e_{ij}/3$ ($\lambda = 1/3$); if one variable is missing (e.g. for transitivity types (ii), (iv) and (v)), then q_{ij} is lowered by $e_{ij}/2$ ($\lambda_U = 1/2$); if just one variable remains (e.g. for transitivity type (iii)), then q_{ij} is lowered by e_{ij} ($\lambda_U = 1$). For the transitivity types (i)–(v) it always holds that $q_{ij} - \lambda_U \, e_{ij} \geq 0$. For additive consistency, being not a true type of transitivity, the difference can become negative, in which case q_{ij} is set equal to 0.

6 Numerical Experiments

For all types of transitivity (i)–(vi) and for $n \le 4$, algorithm **TRA** generates the optimal transitive reciprocal approximation. However, we found counterexamples showing that, in general, this is no longer true for $n > 4$.

Note that for weak stochastic transitivity, algorithm **TRA** only needs one iteration step to converge to the smallest solution that is greater than the given reciprocal relation. For the other types of transitivity, a rigorous proof that the iterative algorithm **TRA** always converges, has not been found so far. But neither counterexamples have been found. In practice, a stopping criterion is added to the algorithm that puts an upper bound on the number of iteration steps.

Table 1. Average number of iteration steps and average distance to input matrix obtained with algorithm **TRA** from 1000 experiments with random input matrices of dimension n and elements rounded off to input precision 0.5, 0.1 and 0.001, respectively. Property: T_L-transitivity. Tolerance: $\epsilon = 10^{-4}$. Fraction parameter: $\lambda_U = 1/3$.

input precision	$n = 5$ average		$n = 10$ average		$n = 15$ average	
	steps	distance	steps	distance	steps	distance
0.5	1.63	0.072	2.00	0.127	2.00	0.141
0.1	3.18	0.090	11.0	0.151	21.4	0.174
0.001	3.71	0.090	14.0	0.156	27.8	0.182

Table 2. Same as in Table 1 but matrix elements rounded off to input precision 0.5, 0.1 and 0.01, respectively. Property: additive consistency. Tolerance: $\epsilon = 1.0^{-3}$. Fraction parameter: $\lambda_U = 1/3$.

input precision	$n = 5$ average		$n = 10$ average		$n = 15$ average	
	steps	distance	steps	distance	steps	distance
0.5	8.36	0.231	358	0.264	1635	0.275
0.1	11.7	0.237	485	0.276	2030	0.278
0.01	12.6	0.239	533	0.276	2060	0.279

We have conducted a number of numerical experiments with four types of transitivity, of which the results are listed in Tables 1–4. The average number of iteration steps for obtaining a transitive approximation with ϵ-accuracy gives insight in the rate of convergence of the algorithm, whereas the average distance from the approximation to the given matrix yields an indication of the strenght of the transitivity condition. Averages have each time been computed on 1000 cases. We have done tests with matrices of dimension 5, 10 and 15. Input matrices have been generated at random, whereafter matrix elements have been rounded off to different decimal positions. Input precision 0.5, for instance, means that matrix elements are in $\{0, 0.5, 1\}$.

Table 3. Same as in Table 1. Property: moderate stochastic transitivity. Tolerance: $\epsilon = 10^{-4}$. Fraction parameter: $\lambda_U = 1/2$.

input	$n = 5$ average		$n = 10$ average		$n = 15$ average	
precision	steps	distance	steps	distance	steps	distance
0.5	1.71	0.113	2.52	0.194	2.83	0.216
0.1	4.26	0.151	20.3	0.216	46.3	0.234
0.001	5.30	0.140	24.9	0.207	56.0	0.224

Table 4. Same as in Table 1. Property: T_M-transitivity. Tolerance: $\epsilon = 10^{-4}$. Fraction parameter: $\lambda_U = 1/2$.

input	$n = 5$ average		$n = 10$ average		$n = 15$ average	
precision	steps	distance	steps	distance	steps	distance
0.5	2.81	0.235	3.26	0.248	2.47	0.250
0.1	9.55	0.218	49.3	0.329	128	0.373
0.001	10.5	0.224	54.1	0.347	144	0.408

The results from Tables 1,3,4 illustrate the fact that T_M-transitivity is stronger than moderate stochastic transitivity, and that in turn T_M-transitivity is stronger than T_L-transitivity. However, somewhat surprisingly, for large matrices it seems more difficult to impose T_M-transitivity than additive consistency.

Especially for the strong properties (such as T_M-transitivity and additive consistency), the rate of convergence is poor. We could accelerate convergence without significant loss of the quality of the approximation by letting the value of λ vary during execution of the algorithm (i.e. letting λ tend to 1 as the number of iteration steps increases). Details of this interesting modification will be reported on elsewhere.

References

1. Alonso, S., Chiclana, F., Herrera, F., Herrera-Viedma, E.: A Consistency-Based Procedure to Estimate Missing Pairwise Preference Values. International Journal of Intelligent Systems 23, 155–175 (2008)
2. Chiclana, F., Herrera-Viedma, E., Alonso, S., Herrera, F.: A Note on the Estimation of Missing Pairwise Preference Values: A Uninorm Consistency Based Method. International Journal of Uncertainty, Fuzziness and Knowledge-Based Systems 16, 19–32 (2008)
3. Chiclana, F., Herrera-Viedma, E., Alonso, S., Herrera, F.: Cardinal Consistency of Reciprocal Preference Relations: A Characterization of Muliplicative Transitivity. IEEE Transactions on Fuzzy Systems 17, 14–23 (2009)
4. Dawyndt, P., De Meyer, H., De Baets, B.: The Complete Linkage Clustering Algorithm Revisited. Soft Computing 9, 385–392 (2005)
5. Dawyndt, P., De Meyer, H., De Baets, B.: UPGMA Clustering Revisited: A Weight-Driven Approach to Transitive Approximation. International Journal of Approximate Reasoning 42, 174–191 (2006)

6. De Baets, B., De Meyer, H.: Transitive Approximation of Fuzzy Relations by Alternating Closures and Openings. Soft Computing 7, 210–219 (2003)
7. De Baets, B., De Meyer, H.: Transitivity Frameworks for Reciprocal Relations: Cycle-Transitivity versus FG-Transitivity. Fuzzy Sets and Systems 152, 249–270 (2005)
8. De Baets, B., De Meyer, H., De Loof, K.: On the Cycle-transitivity of the Mutual Rank Probability Relation of a Poset. Fuzzy Sets and Systems (2010) (under revision)
9. De Baets, B., De Meyer, H., De Schuymer, B., Jenei, S.: Cyclic Evaluation of Transitivity of Reciprocal Relations. Social Choice and Welfare 26, 217–238 (2006)
10. De Meyer, H., Naessens, H., De Baets, B.: Algorithms for Computing the Min-Transitive Closure and Associated Partition Tree of a Symmetric Fuzzy Relation. European Journal of Operational Research 155, 226–238 (2004)
11. Diaz, S., Montes, S., De Baets, B.: Transitivity Bounds in Additive Fuzzy Preference Structures. IEEE Transactions on Fuzzy Systems 15, 275–286 (2007)
12. Fedrizzi, M., Brunelli, M.: On the Normalisation of a Priority Vector Associated with a Reciprocal Relation. International Journal of General Systems 38, 579–586 (2009)
13. Fedrizzi, M., Giove, S.: Incomplete Pairwise Comparison and Consistency Optimization. European Journal of Operational Research 183, 303–313 (2007)
14. Gass, S.I.: Transitivity and Pairwise Comparison Matrices. The Journal of the Operational Research Society 49, 616–624 (1998)
15. Gogus, O., Boucher, T.O.: Strong Transitivity, Rationality and Weak Monotonicity in Fuzzy Pairwise Comparisons. Fuzzy Sets and Systems 94, 133–144 (1998)
16. Herrera-Viedma, E., Herrera, F., Chiclana, F., Luque, M.: Some Issues on Consistency of Fuzzy Preference Relations. European Journal of Operational Research 154, 98–109 (2004)
17. Ma, J., Fan, Z.-P., Jiang, Y.-P., Mao, J.-Y., Ma, L.: A Method for Repairing the Inconsistency of Fuzzy Preference Relations. Fuzzy Sets and Systems 157, 20–30 (2006)
18. Mordecai, A.: Nonlinear Programming: Analysis and Methods. Dover Publishing, New York (2003)
19. Naessens, H., De Meyer, H., De Baets, B.: Algorithms for the Computation of T-transitive Closures. IEEE Transactions on Fuzzy Systems 10, 541–551 (2002)
20. Switalski, Z.: General Transitivity Conditions for Fuzzy Reciprocal Preference Matrices. Fuzzy Sets and Systems 137, 85–100 (2003)
21. Xu, Z.S.: A Survey of Fuzzy Preference Relations. International Journal of General Systems 36, 179–203 (2007)
22. Xu, Z., Da, Q.: An Approach to Improving Consistency of Fuzzy Preference Matrix. Fuzzy Optimization and Decision Making 2, 3–13 (2003)
23. Xu, Z.S.: Goal Programming Models for Obtaining the Priority Vector of Incomplete Fuzzy Preference Relation. International Journal of Approximate Reasoning 36, 261–270 (2004)

Preference Modeling and Model Management for Interactive Multi-objective Evolutionary Optimization

Johannes Krettek, Jan Braun, Frank Hoffmann, and Torsten Bertram

Institute of Control Theory and Systems Engineering
Technische Universität Dortmund, 44221 Dortmund
johannes.krettek@tu-dortmund.de

Abstract. Multiobjective optimization and decision making are strongly inter-related. This paper presents an interactive approach for the integration of expert preferences into multi-objective evolutionary optimization. The experts underlying preference is modeled only based on comparative queries that are designed to distinguish among the non-dominant solutions with minimal burden on the decision maker. The preference based approach constitutes a compromise between global approximation of a Pareto front and aggregation of objectives into a scalar utility function. The model captures relevant aspects of multi-objective decision making, such as preference handling, ambiguity and incommensurability. The efficiency of the approach in terms of number of expert decisions and convergence to the optimal solution are analyzed on the basis of an artificial decision behavior with respect to optimization benchmarks.

Keywords: Multi-objective evolutionary algorithms, optimization, preferences, interaction, instance based learning.

1 Introduction

Decision making is a task inherently intertwined with multi-objective optimization [1]. A decision is made with respect to the optimization objectives either a priori to the optimization, or a posterior by selecting the best solution from the set of Pareto optimal compromise solutions or during optimization as proposed by Branke et al. [2]. Many research activities focus either on the evolutionary multiobjective optimization (EMO) to achieve a good approximation of the Pareto optimal set or on the multicriteria decision making (MCDM) which selects a single optimal solution from a set of Pareto optimal compromises. However the progressive consideration of decision making during optimization offers some advantages. The search within a preferred local region is more efficient than the exploration of the entire Pareto front, in particular in high dimensional spaces. Assuming a limited number of evolutionary fitness evaluations, the final decision for a optimal compromise gets easier and more precise on the basis of a preferred subset due to the focused exploration in this region. An interesting approach of systematically including several decision making techniques into

E. Hüllermeier, R. Kruse, and F. Hoffmann (Eds.): IPMU 2010, LNAI 6178, pp. 574–583, 2010.

multiobjective optimization is presented by Chaudhuri and Deb in [3]. Our approach for interactive integration of preferences into a multi-objective evolution strategy is based on learning a preference model from interactive decisions of an expert. Utilization of expert preferences improves the convergence of optimization in the context of complex and high dimensional problems without the limitations of a priori or a posteriori decision approaches. The preference relation among arbitrary solutions is inferred from training solution pairs for which the decision maker explicitly states his preferences. Our scheme also accounts for the incommensurability of solutions, a concept that is not captured by ordinary comparison of solution pairs. Only comparable solutions are subject to competition in the multi-objective selection step, whereas incommensurable subsets of solutions evolve independently. In case of complete comparability among solutions, the evolutionary search converges to the single best solution according to the experts preferences. In case of complete incommensurability, the selection only differentiates among dominated and non-dominated solutions and approximates the entire Pareto front. The preference modeling is basically integrated as a selection method that complements the non dominated sorting approach of the NSGA-II [4] that constitutes the basis of the algorithm, similar to the approach of the outranking mechanism proposed by Fernandez et al. in [5]. In real world interactive optimization scenarios the effective runtime of the interactive evolutionary algorithm is largely determined by the periods of waiting for an expert response. The time for evolutionary search and in most cases even the time for the fitness evaluation is small compared with the effort that a comparison of candidate solutions demands from the expert. What is proposed here is a preference model that is build incrementally at runtime by querying the expert with comparisons that provide the most discriminative information for selection. This model management decreases the burden of decisions on the expert without sacrificing convergence.

2   Interactive Preference Articulation

It is difficult for an expert to quantify preferences and trade-offs among multiple objectives in particular when lacking knowledge about feasible alternative solutions. It is much easier for a decision maker to articulate his preferences during the optimization in cognizance of alternative solutions. Interactive preference articulation raises a number of questions, that have been previously addressed in numerous publications on decision making in multi-objective evolutionary optimization [6,7]:

1. When and which prototype solutions are presented to the decision maker?
2. Which decision does the expert take?
3. How does the expert decision effect the selection in future evolutionary optimization?

Ideally the expert states his mutual preference or ranking among all solutions of the current population. In this case selection exactly mimics the experts true utility function rather than an approximation of that function. However, complete interaction exceeds the human capability of data processing even in modest optimization problems. The set of non-dominated solutions typically contains many more alternatives than the expert is willing to evaluate and compare against each other.

2.1   Pairwise Solution Comparison Scheme

Our approach for modeling preferences based on an interactive integration of decision making on pairwise comparison is initially presented in [8]. In our scheme a hierarchical clustering algorithm identifies N clusters that best represent the set of n solutions, of which each is associated to its nearest cluster center. The expert expresses his preferences by pairwise comparison of the cluster prototypes in terms of mutual quality and comparability. The number of clusters N burdens the decision maker with $N \times (N-1)/2$ pairwise comparisons. Solutions $S_i = \{x_i, f(x_i)\}$ are represented by their parameter vector x_i and their criteria vector $f(x_i)$. The expert compares two solutions S_i, S_j in terms of their mutual preference $\sigma(S_i, S_j) \in [-1, 1]$. In the extreme cases $\sigma(S_i, S_j) = 1$ and $\sigma(S_i, S_j) = -1$ either S_i is totally preferred over S_j and vice versa. The expert deems two solutions as equal for $\sigma(S_i, S_j) = 0$, whereas any rating in between indicates weaker preference for either of the solutions. In addition the expert classifies the degree of comparability $\rho \in [0, 1]$ of two solutions. In case $\rho = 1$ the two solutions are fully comparable. The set D_σ of pairwise evaluations of prototype solutions $\{S_i, S_j\}$ are stored in a database and provide the training instances.

2.2   Preference Estimation Based on Pairwise Similarity

The preference relationship among all individuals in the current generation is imposed from the preference model set D_σ based on the similarity with the training instances. The similarity of the query pair $\{P_k, P_l\}$ with an instance $\{S_i, S_j\}$ in D_σ is computed based on their distance in the normalized objective space. The similarity weight $w(\{P_k, P_l\}, \{S_i, S_j\})$ of a training pair is determined by a distance based Gaussian kernel scaled with the mean minimal distance of the current population in objective space. The estimated preference of the query pair is computed by the similarity weighted average preference relation of training pairs

$$\hat{\sigma}(P_k, P_l) = \frac{\sum_{i,j} \sigma(S_i, S_j) w(\{P_k, P_l\}, \{S_i, S_j\})}{\sum_{i,j} w(\{P_k, P_l\}, \{S_i, S_j\})}. \tag{1}$$

The comparability $\hat{\rho}$ for each pair is estimated in the same manner.

2.3   Preference Controlled Selection Mechanism

The instance based preference model predicts the pairwise preference and comparability of each solution with the $n-1$ other members of the set of non-dominated solutions. The solutions are ranked according to their estimated preference and comparability based on a relative performance index γ_σ that captures the average preference of a solution in the context of its comparable competitors. Rather than to strive for a global preference order, the comparability $\hat\rho$ restricts competition to more or less disjunct subsets of similar solutions. A comparability index γ_ρ captures the relative density of solutions in the preference space. The objective is to simultaneously maximize the preference γ_σ and minimize the density of comparable solutions γ_ρ in order to balance exploration and exploitation. The μ best solutions with respect to preference and comparability are selected according to the dominance ranking scheme proposed by Fonseca [9].

2.4   Benchmarking with a Decision Model

It would be problematic to rely on a human decision maker for a thorough evaluation and analysis of the proposed interactive optimization algorithm. The burden of interaction would be substantial and it is questionable that a human is able to take consistent and reproducible decisions over a long time span. In order to overcome this limitation, the expert is replaced with an artificial, transparent expert decision model for this purpose. This allows the evaluation of the method in reproducible scenarios. The decision model captures the proximity of a solution to either a single or multiple hypothetical optimal targets in the normalized objective space. The hypothetical targets R lie close to the Pareto front albeit in the unfeasible region of the objective space. The mutual preference for a solution pair $\{S_i, S_j\}$ is

$$\sigma_M(S_i, S_j) = \frac{||f(x_j) - R|| - ||f(x_i) - R||}{||f(x_i) - R|| + ||f(x_j) - R||}. \tag{2}$$

The relative preference depends on the relative distance of the two candidate solutions to the target R, such that the solution closer to the target R is preferred over the remote one. In case of multiple targets, only solution pair of solutions with the same nearest target obtain a mutual preference according to equation 2, whereas pairs belonging to different targets are deemed incommensurable ($\rho = 0$). For a set of uniformly distributed solutions with either one and or two reference solutions, the corresponding expert model results in a preference and comparability model shown in figure 1. The figure shows the true (model based) preference and comparability as well as those approximated based on different numbers of uniformly distributed sample solution instances. The left figure shows the preferences for a single reference solution, the right figure shows preference and comparability for two incommensurable goals. Both figures show that, apart from a smoothing caused by the Gaussian kernel, the preference model converges to the true preference function with increasing number of instances. The comparability, mainly influenced by the number of incommensurable solution pairs, changes in magnitude but always leads to a clear separation of the two local maxima in the preference model. By selecting solutions that are Pareto optimal with respect to these two indices, a focus on the desired references is combined with a diversification to all regions of interest.

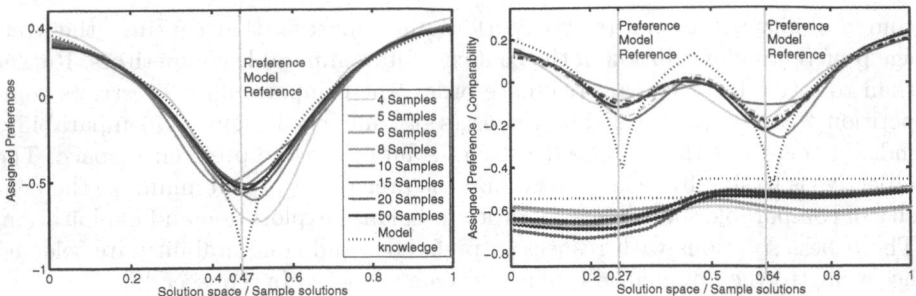

Fig. 1. Quality of preference and comparability approximation for different numbers of sample solutions

3   Selection of Interaction Candidates

The main burden for the expert, which is the number of queries, is further reduced by focusing on those queries that provide the largest information gain. Similar to the concept of active learning in machine learning, in which the learner decides about the next query, those solution pairs are presented to the decision maker which explicit preference evaluation causes potentially the most significant impact on the induced ranking. That way the two relevant aspects of optimization effort, namely the number of interactions as well as the number of overall fitness evaluations are reduced. The most informative queries are those for which either positive or negative hypothetical preference articulation most drastically changes the induced ranking of solutions according to the preference index γ_σ compared to the current model without knowledge of the answer to the additional query. Practically speaking, one should pose those queries for which the answer might change the future course of evolution and avoid queries for which the expert decision is either predictable or irrelevant for the selection. For a potential comparison $\{S_i, S_j\}$ the preference decision $\hat{\sigma}$ for the current model is estimated. The true expert decision is likely to be similar with the decision predicted by the current, but usually differs such that it influences the overall preference model which in turn effects the selection. This deviation is emulated by two prototype hypothetical decisions, $\hat{\sigma}\{S_i, S_j\} + \epsilon$ and $\hat{\sigma}\{S_i, S_j\} - \epsilon$. For both alternative answers the induced selection decision $(R_{+\epsilon}, R_{-\epsilon})$ is computed based on the modified preference estimation. The amount of deviation between estimated and actual preference articulation is assumed to be constant $\epsilon = 0.2$. The first μ potentially selected individuals from both selection rankings are compared to the original selection ranking in ignorance of the new additional comparative information R_0. The sensitivity is measured as the sum of permutations in the ranking of the first μ best solutions. The quantity Δ in the selection decision is the gradient of hypothetical information gain.

$$\Delta_{(+)} = \sum_{i=1}^{\mu} (R_{+\varepsilon}(i) - R_0(i)) \qquad \Delta_{(-)} = \sum_{i=1}^{\mu} (R_{-\varepsilon}(i) - R_0(i)) \qquad (3)$$

Assuming that the larger deviation is caused by a decision that is directed against the local trend, the smaller of both possible changes $\Delta = \min\left(\Delta_{(+)}, \Delta_{(-)}\right)$ describes the potential information gain of this comparison. For N prototypes out of the $N \times (N-1)$ potential comparisons only those with the largest smaller potential of information gain in the selection are selected as queries to be presented to the expert. The interactive evolution leads to a faster and better approximation of the preference compared to the purely dominance based selection scheme. The selection of prototypes based on their potential information profit increases the convergence speed of the algorithm due to an improved preference model.

An incorrect preference model results in convergence of the evolutionary algorithm to suboptimal solutions. Thus it is important to monitor the quality of the preference model. A model error is attributed to the uncertainty inherent in modeling from a limited set of examples in which case more frequent queries help to refine the model. Ambiguity or inconsistency of expert decisions is a second cause for an incorrect model. Inconsistent decisions often emerge as the expert preferences are non-static but change over the course of optimization in light of novel alternatives or stronger focus on exploitation. In general more recent expert decisions bear more relevance than decisions from the past. In the later case preference model management resolves the conflicting answers, either by removing inconsistent answers based on their age or by explicit re-querying. In addition since queries are generated according to information gain, but not absolute preference the presented solution pairs might mislead the expert about the actual progress of optimization. This misinformation is overcome by visualizing the currently best solution with respect to the preference model irrespective of the queries. The model quality index Q_i measures the absolute difference between the preference values for the expert evaluated pairs in the current generation i and the answer predicted by the model. The following experiments are based on the optimization of the Kursawe test-function [10] with 8 parameters. The left plot of figure 2 (left) shows the influence of the interaction rate on the evolution of the model quality index. In general, the prediction error is reduced significantly faster with a higher rate of queries. The comparison of the development for one and two decisions per generation shows the limitation of this

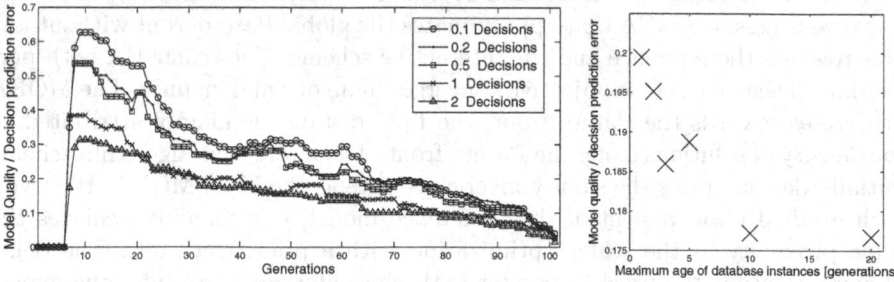

Fig. 2. Evolution of the decision prediction error for changing interaction rates (left), dependency between decision prediction error and age of databse instances (right)

observation as the model quality does not increase significantly due to the ongoing convergence of the optimization. To eliminate such misleading instances and to reduce the size of the database, an aging-mechanism is introduced that limits the training set to those examples evaluated within the recent past. Figure 2 (right) shows the relation of the maximum database age to the mean prediction error during an optimization run. It compares the same decision model based interactive optimization with a single preference decision each generation and different subsets of instances of different maximum age. The compromise is supposed to balance the effort for preference estimation with additional queries and the prediction error.

4   Results

The interactive scheme is compared with the global approximation of the Pareto front without preference model and the optimal a priori decision in terms of a scalar aggregated objective. The efficiency of the optimization is evaluated in terms of proximity of the population to an artificial reference solution in the unfeasible part of objective space. Figure 3 shows the convergence of the interactive MOEA on a Kursawe benchmark function [10]. For the sake of illustration, the graph shows the evolution of a population of ten solutions over the course of ten generations. The black line in the left plot represents the true Pareto front, the cross marks the reference of the artificial expert preference model. The dots indicate the propagation of solutions, in which earlier generations are marked by a lighter shade. The initial generations evolve similar to a standard MOEA, selection is merely based on dominance alone. With progress of optimization the ratio of non-dominated solutions increases such that preference based selection becomes more relevant. This biases the evolution of population towards the region of the Pareto front closest to the reference point. In addition, the preference model becomes more accurate with increasing number of examples further promoting progress towards the reference goal. The right plot in figure 3 shows the convergence with respect to expert preferences in terms of the minimal distance between the current population and the unfeasible reference goal. This performance is visualized for a scalar evolutionary algorithm utilizing this exact distance fitness, a MOEA that approximates the global Pareto front without any bias towards the reference and the interactive scheme. The scalar EA with perfect knowledge of the true objective converges in an optimal manner. The MOEA progresses towards the Pareto front, the final distance is mainly attributed to the density of solutions along the Pareto front. The interactive algorithm scheme initially demonstrates the same convergence rate as the blind MOEA. However, with gradual improvement of the preference model, it ultimately achieves the same proximity as the scalar optimization with a priori trade-offs. The delay in convergence is the price to pay for gathering information to infer the expert preferences during the optimization.

The rate of interaction, and thereby the number of preference model samples, affects the accuracy of the preference model and thereby directly relates to the

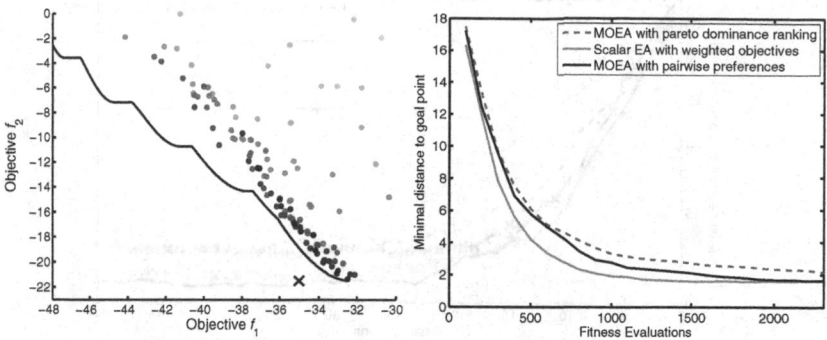

Fig. 3. Convergence of the interactive MOEA in the objective space (left), compared with a scalar EA and a MOEA (right)

convergence of the optimization. The analysis of the selection error is based on an evolution strategy with $\mu = 25$ parents and $\lambda = 100$ offspring evolved over the course of 50 generations on the eight parameter Kursawe function with an artificial expert decision model. The selection error is defined as the discrepancy between the true expert ranking and the ranking induced by the preference model. The difference of the two rankings is computed by the number of permutations required to match both rankings. Ranking errors for solutions closer to the reference goal are weighted more strongly than distant solutions. All plots show the average of the ranking error over ten runs. The plots in figure 4 show the influence of the model size or quality on the selection error. The two plots with crosses reveal the advantage of controlled, informative queries over random queries on the selection error. Selection with the controlled query model results in improved model quality not only in the initial generations but even more so towards the final stages of optimization. With convergence of the population towards the Pareto front solutions become more similar, thus it requires targeted queries to distinguish among these similar solutions. The remaining plots compare different rates of queries and a purely dominance based selection without preference consideration. There is a direct relationship between selection error and query rate, even though the selection error does not only depend on model quality but also on the convergence of the optimization itself. In practical problems the query rate is largely determined by the effort to be imposed on the expert. Beyond more than one query per generation on average, the improvement in convergence does not outweigh the extra burden on the expert. On the other hand too few queries might result in misleading preference model which performs worse than pure dominance based selection.

The advantages of the interactive preference modeling in the context of evolutionary optimization become increasingly important for a large number of objectives. Dominance based selection provides slow progress with large number of objectives as after some optimization almost all solutions are non-dominated and thus indistinguishable on the basis of dominance alone. A preference model

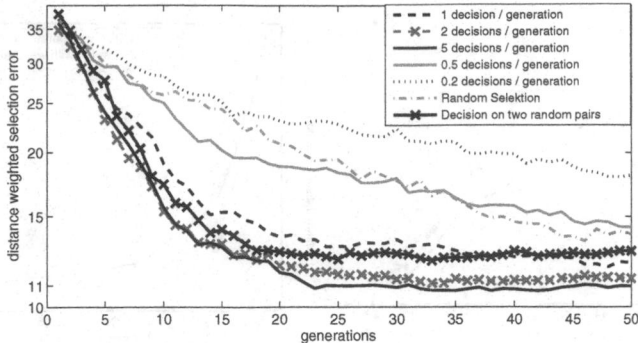

Fig. 4. Distance weighted selection error for different interaction rates

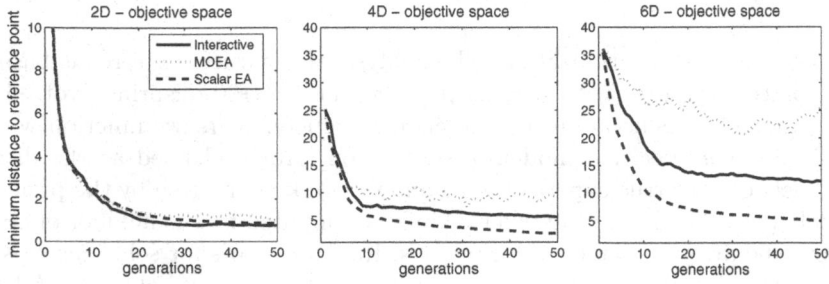

Fig. 5. Influence of the problem dimension to the convergence

focuses optimization on regions of interest to the expert, thus effectively increasing the local density of solutions. Figure 5 illustrates the convergence in terms of distance to the reference goal for different number of objectives generated by duplicating the original binary objective problem. The comparison reveals that the advantage of the interactive algorithm with respect to the MOEA is more pronounced with increasing number of objectives. The left plot shows, that the preference guided optimization even outperforms a scalar EA with weighted objective aggregation, in case the fitness landscape exhibits a local minima in the vicinity of the reference goal.

5   Conclusion

This contribution presents a novel scheme for expert preference incorporation in multi-objective evolutionary algorithms. The main advantages of our scheme are its general applicability and the tight integration of decision making and optimization. The instance based preference model makes no prior assumption about the structure of preferences and allows multiple incommensurable targets. The comparison with global purely dominance based selection and a priori aggregation of objectives reveals that the proposed scheme combines the advantages of both conventional approaches, namely efficient optimization with flexible, unbiased and intuitive decision making. Even though sampling queries to generate model delays optimization, the scheme eventually achieves the same optimization results compared to an omniscient decision maker. The analysis shows that even with a low query rate of only one expert comparison per generation the model quality suffices to find optimal solutions efficiently. The utility of a preference model for faster convergence increases with increasing number of objectives. Future work is concerned to deal with ambiguous expert decision in case the expert preferences change over the course evolution. Non static preferences require a model management in which conflicts among contradictory expert decision are resolved either by re-querying or based on actuality of decisions.

References

1. Coello, C.A.C.: Handling preferences in evolutionary multiobjective optimization: A survey. In: Proceedings of the CEC 2000, pp. 30–37 (2000)
2. Branke, J., Kaußler, T., Schmeck, H.: Guidance in evolutionary multi-objective optimization. Advances in Engineering Software 32(6), 499–507 (2001)
3. Chaudhuri, S., Deb, K.: An interactive evolutionary multi-objective optimization and decision making procedure. Applied Soft Computing 10(2), 496–511 (2010)
4. Deb, K., Agrawal, S., Pratap, A., Meyarivan, T.: A fast elitist non-dominated sorting genetic algorithm for multi-objective optimization: NSGA-II. LNCS, pp. 849–858. Springer, Heidelberg (2000)
5. Fernandez, E., Lopez, E., Bernal, S., Coello Coello, C.A., Navarro, J.: Evolutionary multiobjective optimization using an outranking-based dominance generalization. Comput. Oper. Res. 37(2), 390–395 (2010)
6. Parmee, I.C., Cvetkovic, D., Watson, A., Bonham, C.: Multiobjective satisfaction within an interactive evolutionary design environment. Evolutionary Computation 8(2), 197–222 (2000)
7. Takagi, H.: Interactive evolutionary computation: fusion of the capabilities of ec optimization and human evaluation. Proc. of the IEEE 89(9), 1275–1296 (2001)
8. Krettek, J., Braun, J., Hoffmann, F., Bertram, T.: Interactive incorporation of user preferences in multiobjective evolutionary algorithms. Applications of Soft Computing 58, 379–388
9. Fonseca, C., Fleming, P.: Genetic algorithms for multiobjective optimization: Formulation, discussion and generalization. In: Proceedings of the 5th International Conference on Genetic Algorithms, January 1993, pp. 416–423 (1993)
10. Kursawe, F.: A variant of evolution strategies for vector optimization. In: Schwefel, H.-P., Männer, R. (eds.) PPSN 1990. LNCS, vol. 496, pp. 193–197. Springer, Heidelberg (1991)

Dominance-Based Rough Set Approach to Preference Learning from Pairwise Comparisons in Case of Decision under Uncertainty

Salvatore Greco[1], Benedetto Matarazzo[1], and Roman Słowiński[2]

[1] Faculty of Economics, University of Catania,
Corso Italia, 55, 95129 Catania, Italy
[2] Institute of Computing Science, Poznań University of Technology,
60-965 Poznań, and Institute for Systems Research,
Polish Academy of Sciences, 01-447 Warsaw, Poland

Abstract. We deal with preference learning from pairwise comparisons, in case of decision under uncertainty, using a new rough set model based on stochastic dominance applied to a pairwise comparison table. For the sake of simplicity we consider the case of traditional additive probability distribution over the set of states of the world; however, the model is rich enough to handle non-additive probability distributions, and even qualitative ordinal distributions. The rough set approach leads to a representation of decision maker's preferences under uncertainty in terms of "*if...*, *then...*" decision rules induced from rough approximations of sets of exemplary decisions. An example of such decision rule is "if act a is at least strongly preferred to act a' with probability at least 30%, and a is at least weakly preferred to act a' with probability at least 60%, then act a is at least as good as act a'.

Keywords: Decision under uncertainty, Dominance-based Rough Set Approach, Pairwise Comparison Table, Decision rules, Preference learning.

1 Introduction

Decision under uncertainty has been intensively investigated by many researchers (for a comprehensive review see, e.g., [7]). In this field, the basic model is the expected utility, which has been axiomatized by von Neumann and Morgenstern [27] in case of objective probability, and by Savage [22] in case of subjective probability. Much experimental work uncovered, however, systematic violation of expected utility hypotheses (see, e.g., [1], [4] and [17]). For this reason, many alternative models weakening some of the original axioms have been proposed (for a survey, see [26]). In this context, it is relevant to refer to the literature on ambiguity (see [18], [10], [23], [5],[9],[20]). Another approach to decision under uncertainty has been based on the concept of coherent measure of risk ([2]) applied to financial management problems (see, e.g., [3]).

E. Hüllermeier, R. Kruse, and F. Hoffmann (Eds.): IPMU 2010, LNAI 6178, pp. 584–594, 2010.

In this paper, we propose yet another way of preference modeling for decision under uncertainty, with the aim of weakening the underlying assumptions as much as possible. We assume that the preference information elicited by a Decision Maker (DM) is available in terms of pairwise comparisons of acts described by probabilistic distributions of gains, and we employ for the analysis of this information a stochastic dominance relation. We approach this problem using rough set theory [21]. Since the decisions we are considering, and, in general, all decision problems, involve data expressed on preference-ordered scales (larger outcomes are preferable to smaller outcomes), we use the **Dominance-based Rough Set Approach** (DRSA) [12,14,15,25] that explicitly takes into account also this important feature of data. DRSA to decision under uncertainty has been already proposed in [13,16]. In this paper, we propose rough approximation of a non-transitive preference relation over uncertain acts, using DRSA applied to Pairwise Comparison Table (PCT) [12,11]. Let us remember that non-transitive preference relation over acts have been considered in the literature on decision under uncertainty in the expected regret theory [19], in the skew symmetric additive theory [8], and in the skew symmetric bilinear theory [6].

The paper has the following plan. Section 2 recalls basics of DRSA applied to PCT. Section 3 introduces DRSA to decision under uncertainty for PCT. Section 4 contains conclusions.

2 The Pairwise Comparison Table (PCT) as Preference Information and as a Learning Sample

2.1 Basic Concepts

We consider a set of reference objects (acts) A on which a DM can express his/her own preferences by pairwise comparisons. More precisely, we take into consideration a weak preference relation $\succeq$ on A and a negative weak preference relation $x \succeq^c y$ on A such that, for a pair of objects $(x,y) \in A \times A$, $x \succeq y$ means that x is at least as good as y and $x \succeq^c y$ means that it is not true that x is at least as good as y. The only assumptions with respect to (wrt) these relations are that $\succeq$ is reflexive and $\succeq^c$ is irreflexive, and they are incompatible in the sense that, for all $x, y \in A$, it is not possible that $x \succeq y$ and $x \succeq^c y$.

For each pair of reference objects $(x,y) \in A \times A$, the DM can select one of the three following possibilities:

1. Object x is as good as y, i.e., $x \succeq y$.
2. Object x is not as good as y, i.e., $x \succeq^c y$.
3. The two objects are incomparable at the present stage, in the sense that neither $x \succeq y$ nor $x \succeq^c y$ can be asserted.

Let $\succeq \cup \succeq^c = B$, with $card(B) = m$. We also suppose that objects from A are described by a finite set of criteria $C = \{g_1, \ldots, g_n\}$. Without loss of generality, for each $g_i \in C$ we suppose that $g_i : A \to \Re$, such that, for each $x, y \in A$, $g_i(x) \geq g_i(y)$ means that x is at least as good as y wrt criterion g_i, which is denoted by $x \succeq_i y$. For each criterion $g_i \in C$, we also suppose that there exists a quaternary relation $\succeq_i^*$ defined on A, such that, for each $x, y, w, z \in A$, $(x, y) \succeq_i^* (w, z)$ means that, wrt g_i, x is preferred to y at least as strongly as w is preferred to z. We assume that, for each $g_i \in C$, the quaternary relation $\succeq_i^*$ is monotonic wrt to evaluations on criterion g_i, such that, for all $x, y, w, z \in A$,

$$g_i(x) \geq g_i(w) \text{ and } g_i(y) \leq g_i(z) \Rightarrow (x, y) \succeq_i^* (w, z).$$

We shall denote by $\succ_i^*$ and $\sim_i^*$ the asymmetric and the symmetric part of $\succeq_i^*$, respectively, i.e., $(x, y) \succ_i^* (w, z)$ if $(x, y) \succeq_i^* (w, z)$ and not $(w, z) \succeq_i^* (x, y)$, and $(x, y) \sim_i^* (w, z)$ if $(x, y) \succeq_i^* (w, z)$ and $(w, z) \succeq_i^* (x, y)$. The quaternary relation $\succeq_i^*, g_i \in C$, is supposed to be a complete preorder on $A \times A$. For each $(x, y) \in A \times A$, $C_i(x, y) = \{(w, z) \in A \times A : (w, z) \sim_i^* (x, y)\}$, is the equivalence class of (x, y) wrt $\sim_i^*$. Intuitively, for each $(x, y), (w, z) \in A \times A$, $(w, z) \in C_i(x, y)$ means that w is preferred to z with the same strength as x is preferred to y. We suppose also that, for each $x, y \in A$ and $g_i \in C$, $(x, x) \sim_i^* (y, y)$ and, consequently, $(y, y) \in C_i(x, x)$. Assuming that they are finite, we denote the equivalence classes of $\sim_i^*$ by $\succ_i^{\alpha_i}, \succ_i^{\alpha_i+1}, \ldots, \succ_i^{-1}, \succ_i^0, \succ_i^1, \ldots, \succ_i^{\beta_i-1}, \succ_i^{\beta_i}$, such that

- for all $x, y, w, z \in A$, $x \succ_i^h y$, $w \succ_i^k z$, and $h \geq k$ implies $(x, y) \succeq_i^* (w, z)$,
- for all $x \in A$, $x \succ_i^0 x$.

We call *strength of preference* of x over y the equivalence class of $\succeq_i^*$ to which pair (x, y) belongs. For each $g_i \in C$, we denote by H_i the set of indices (grades) of the equivalence classes of $\succeq_i^*$, i.e.

$$H_i = \{\alpha_i, \alpha_i + 1, \ldots, -1, 0, 1, \ldots, \beta_i - 1, \beta_i\}.$$

Therefore, there exists a function $f : A \times A \times C \to H_i$, such that, for all $x, y \in A, x \succ_i^{f(x,y,g_i)} y$, i.e., for all $x, y \in A$ and $g_i \in C$, function f gives the strength of preference of x over y wrt g_i. Taking into account the dependence of $\succeq_i^*$ on evaluations by criterion $g_i \in C$, there also exists a function $f^* : \Re \times \Re \times C \to H_i$, such that $f(x, y, g_i) = f^*(g_i(x), g_i(y), g_i)$ and, consequently, $x \succ_i^{f^*(g_i(x), g_i(y), g_i)} y$. Due to monotonicity of $\succeq_i^*$ wrt to evaluations on g_i, we have that $f^*(g_i(x), g_i(y), g_i)$ is non-decreasing wrt $g_i(x)$ and non-increasing wrt $g_i(y)$. Moreover, for each $x \in A$, $f^*(g_i(x), g_i(x), g_i) = 0$.

An $m \times (n+1)$ Pairwise Comparison Table (PCT) is then built up on the basis of this information. The first n columns correspond to the criteria from set C, while the m rows correspond to the pairs from B, such that, if the DM judges that two objects are incomparable, then the corresponding pair does not appear in PCT. The last, i.e. the $(n + 1)$-th, column represents the comprehensive binary preference relation $\succeq$ or $\succeq^c$. For each pair $(x, y) \in B$, and for each criterion $g_i \in C$, the respective strength of preference $f^*(g_i(x), g_i(y), g_i)$ is put in the corresponding column.

In terms of rough set theory, the *pairwise comparison table* is defined as a data table $PCT = \langle B, C \cup \{d\}, H_C \cup \{\succeq, \succeq^c\}, f \rangle$, where $B \subseteq A \times A$ is a non-empty set of exemplary pairwise comparisons of reference objects, $H_C = \bigcup_{g_i \in C} H_i$, d is a decision corresponding to the comprehensive pairwise comparison resulting in $\succeq$ or $\succeq^c$, and $f : B \times (C \cup \{d\}) \to H_C \cup \{\succeq, \succeq^c\}$ is a total function, such that $f(x, y, g_i) = f^*(g_i(x), g_i(y), g_i) \in H_i$ for every $(x, y) \in B$ and for each $g_i \in C$, and $f(x, y, g_i) \in \{\succeq, \succeq^c\}$ for every $(x,y) \in B$. Thus, binary relations $\succeq$ and $\succeq^c$ induce a partition of B. In fact, PCT can be seen as a decision table, since the set of considered criteria C and the decision d are distinguished.

On the basis of preference relations $\succ_i^h, h \in H_i, g_i \in C$, upward cumulated preference relations $\succ_i^{\geq h}$, and downward cumulated preference relations $\succ_i^{\leq h}$, can be defined as follows: for all $x, y \in A$,

$$x \succ_i^{\geq h} y \Leftrightarrow x \succ_i^k y \text{ with } k \geq h,$$

$$x \succ_i^{\leq h} y \Leftrightarrow x \succ_i^k y \text{ with } k \leq h.$$

Given $P \subseteq C$ ($P \neq \emptyset$), $(x,y),(w,z) \in A \times A$, the pair of objects (x,y) is said to dominate (w,z) wrt criteria from P (denoted by $(x,y)D_P(w,z)$), if x is preferred to y at least as strongly as w is preferred to z wrt each $g_i \in P$, i.e.,

$$(x, y)D_P(w, z) \Leftrightarrow (x, y) \succeq_i^* (w, z) \text{ for all } g_i \in P,$$

or, equivalently,

$$(x, y)D_P(w, z) \Leftrightarrow f(x, y, g_i) \geq f(w, z, g_i) \text{ for all } g_i \in P.$$

Since $\succeq_i^*$ is a complete preorder for each $g_i \in C$, the intersection of complete preorders is a partial preorder, and $D_P = \bigcap_{g_i \in P} \succeq_i^*$, $P \subseteq C$, then the dominance relation D_P is a partial preorder on $A \times A$.

Let $R \subseteq P \subseteq C$ and $(x,y),(w,z) \in A \times A$; then the following implication holds:

$$(x, y)D_P(w, z) \Rightarrow (x, y)D_R(w, z).$$

Given $P \subseteq C$ and $(x,y) \in B$, the P-dominating set, denoted by $D_P^+(x, y)$, and the P-dominated set, denoted by $D_P^-(x, y)$, are defined as follows:

$$D_P^+(x, y) = \{(w, z) \in B : (w, z)D_P(x, y)\},$$

$$D_P^-(x, y) = \{(w, z) \in B : (x, y)D_P(w, z)\}.$$

The P-dominating sets and the P-dominated sets are "granules of knowledge" that can be used to express P-lower and P-upper approximations of the comprehensive weak preference relations $\succeq$ and $\succeq^c$, respectively:

$$\underline{P}(\succeq) = \{(x, y) \in B : D_P^+(x, y) \subseteq \succeq \},$$

$$\overline{P}(\succeq) = \{(x, y) \in B : D_P^-(x, y) \cap \succeq \neq \emptyset\},$$

$$\underline{P}(\succeq^c) = \{(x, y) \in B : D_P^-(x, y) \subseteq \succeq^c \},$$

$$\overline{P}(\succeq^c) = \{(x, y) \in B : D_P^+(x, y) \cap \succeq^c \neq \emptyset\},$$

The following properties hold [12]:

$$\underline{P}(\succeq) \subseteq \succeq \subseteq \overline{P}(\succeq), \quad \underline{P}(\succeq^c) \subseteq \succeq^c \subseteq \overline{P}(\succeq^c).$$

Furthermore, the following complementarity properties hold:

$$\underline{P}(\succeq) = B - \overline{P}(\succeq^c), \quad \overline{P}(\succeq) = B - \underline{P}(\succeq^c),$$

$$\underline{P}(\succeq^c) = B - \overline{P}(\succeq), \quad \overline{P}(\succeq^c) = B - \underline{P}(\succeq).$$

The P-boundaries (P-doubtful regions) of $\succeq$ and $\succeq^c$ are defined as

$$Bn_P(\succeq) = \overline{P}(\succeq) - \underline{P}(\succeq), \quad Bn_P(\succeq^c) = \overline{P}(\succeq^c) - \underline{P}(\succeq^c).$$

From the above, it follows that $Bn_P(\succeq) = Bn_P(\succeq^c)$.

The rough set theory concepts of the quality of approximation, reducts and core can be extended to the considered approximations of the weak preference relations.

In particular, the coefficient

$$\gamma_P = \frac{|\underline{P}(\succeq) \cup \underline{P}(\succeq^c)|}{|B|}$$

defines the *quality of approximation of* $\succeq$ and $\succeq^c$ by $P \subseteq C$. It expresses the ratio of all pairs of reference objects $(x,y) \in B$ correctly assigned to $\succeq$ and $\succeq^c$ by the set P of criteria to all the pairs of objects contained in B. Each minimal (wrt inclusion) subset $P \subseteq C$, such that $\gamma_P = \gamma_C$, is called a *reduct* of C (denoted by RED_{PCT}). Note that PCT can have more than one reduct. The intersection of all B-reducts is called the *core* (denoted by $CORE_{PCT}$).

It is also possible to use the Variable Consistency Model on PCT [24], being aware that some of the pairs in P-dominating or P-dominated sets belong to the opposite relation, but at least $l*100\%$ of pairs belong to the correct one. Then, the definition of the lower approximations of $\succeq$ and $\succeq^c$ boils down to:

$$\underline{P}^l(\succeq) = \left\{ (x,y) \in B : \frac{|D_P^+(x,y) \cap \succeq|}{|D_P^+(x,y)|} \geq l \right\},$$

$$\underline{P}^l(\succeq^c) = \left\{ (x,y) \in B : \frac{|D_P^-(x,y) \cap \succeq^c|}{|D_P^-(x,y)|} \geq l \right\}.$$

2.2   Induction of Decision Rules from Rough Approximations of Weak Preference Relations

Using the rough approximations of $\succeq$ and $\succeq^c$, it is possible to induce a generalized description of the preference information contained in PCT in terms of suitable decision rules, having the following syntax:

1. **D$_\geq$-*decision rules*:**

$$\text{If } x \succ_{i1}^{\geq h(i1)} y, \text{ and, ..., and } x \succ_{ip}^{\geq h(ip)} y, \text{ then } x \succeq y,$$

where $P=\{g_{i1},...,g_{ip}\}\subseteq C$ and $(h(i1),...,h(ip))\in H_{i1}\times...\times H_{ip}$. These rules are supported by pairs of objects from the P-lower approximation of $\succeq$ only.

2. $\mathbf{D_{\leq}}$-*decision rules*:

$$\text{If } x \succ_{i1}^{\leq h(i1)} y, \text{ and, } ..., \text{ and } x \succ_{ip}^{\leq h(ip)} y, \text{ then } x \succeq^c y,$$

where $P=\{g_{i1},...,g_{ip}\}\subseteq C$ and $(h(i1),...,h(ip))\in H_{i1}\times...\times H_{ip}$. These rules are supported by pairs of objects from the P-lower approximation of $\succeq^c$ only.

3. $\mathbf{D_{\geq\leq}}$-*decision rules*:

$$\text{If } x \succ_{i1}^{\geq h(i1)} y, \text{ and, } ..., \text{ and } x \succ_{ie}^{\geq h(ie)} y,$$
$$\text{and } x \succ_{ie+1}^{\leq h(ie+1)} y, \text{ }..., \text{ and } x \succ_{ip}^{\leq h(ip)} y, \text{ then } x \succeq y \text{ or } x \succeq^c y,$$

where $P=\{g_{i1},\ldots,g_{ie},g_{ie+1},\ldots,g_{ip}\}\subseteq C$ and $(h(i1),\ldots,h_{ie},h_{ie+1},$ $\ldots,h(ip))\in H_{i1}\times\ldots\times H_{ie},H_{ie+1}\times\ldots\times H_{ip}$. These rules are supported by pairs of objects from the P-boundary of $\succeq$ and $\succeq^c$ only.

3 DRSA for Decision under Uncertainty

3.1 Basic Concepts

To perform rough set analysis of PCT data in case of decision under uncertainty, we consider the following basic elements:

- a set $S=\{s_1, s_2, \ldots, s_u\}$ of states of the world, or simply *states*, which are supposed to be mutually exclusive and collectively exhaustive,
- an a priori *probability distribution* P over the states of the world; more precisely, the probabilities of states $s_1, s_2, \ldots, s_u$ are $p_1, p_2, \ldots, p_u$, respectively, $(p_1 + p_2+\ldots+p_u=1, p_i \geq 0, i=1,\ldots,u)$,
- a set $A=\{a_1, a_2, \ldots, a_o\}$ of *acts*,
- a set $X=\{x_1, x_2, \ldots, x_r\}$ of *consequences*,
- function $g: A \times S \to X$ assigning to each pair act-state $(a_i,s_j) \in A \times S$ an outcome $x_k \in X$,
- a quaternary relation $\succeq^*$ on X being a complete preoder on $X \times X$ with $\succ^{\alpha}, \succ^{\alpha+1}, \ldots, \succ^0, \ldots, \succ^{\beta-1}, \succ^{\beta}$ being the equivalence classes of $\sim^*$, $\mathcal{H} = \{\alpha, \alpha + 1, \ldots, 0, \ldots, \beta - 1, \beta\}$, such that for all $x \in A, x \succ^0 x$,
- a function $z: X \times X \to \mathcal{H}$, such that, for any $(x_{i_1}, x_{i_2}) \in X \times X, x_{i_1} \succ^{z(x_{i_1}, x_{i_2})} x_{i_2}$, i.e. $z(x_{i_1}, x_{i_2})$ assigns to each pair (x_{i_1}, x_{i_2}) some strength of the preference relation of x_{i_1} over x_{i_2},
- a weak preference relation $\succeq$ and a negative weak preference relation $\succeq^c$ on A, such that $\succeq \cap \succeq^c= \emptyset$ (i.e. $\succeq$ and $\succeq^c$ are incompatible because for any $a,b \in A$ it is not possible that $a \succeq b$ and $a \succeq^c b$) and $\succeq \cup \succeq^c= B \subseteq A \times A$ (i.e. $\succeq$ and $\succeq^c$ are not necessarily exhaustive, because we can have pairs of actions $(a,b) \in A \times A$ for which not $a \succeq b$ and not $a \succeq^c b$).

On the basis of preference relations $\succ^h, h \in \mathcal{H}$, upward cumulated preference relations $\succ^{\geq h}$ and downward cumulated preference relations $\succ^{\leq h}$ can be defined as follows: for all $x, y \in X$,

$$x \succ^{\geq h} y \Leftrightarrow x \succ^k y \text{ with } k \geq h, \text{ and } x \succ^{\leq h} y \Leftrightarrow x \succ^k y \text{ with } k \leq h.$$

On the basis of the quaternary relation $\succeq^*$ on X, for each $s \in S$ one can define a quaternary relation $\succeq_s^*$ on A as follows: for all $a, b, c, d \in A$,

$$(a, b) \succeq_s^* (c, d) \Leftrightarrow (g(a, s), g(b, s)) \succeq (g(c, s), g(d, s)).$$

Analogously, for each $s \in S$ and for each $a, b \in A$, the strength of preference of $g(a, s)$ over $g(b, s)$ can be extended to the strength of preference of a over b wrt state of nature s, i.e.,

$$a \succ_s^h b \Leftrightarrow g(a, s) \succ^h g(b, s).$$

In the same way, upward and downward cumulated preference relations defined above on X can be extended to A: for any $a, b \in A$, $s \in S$ and $h \in \mathcal{H}$,

$$a \succ_s^{\geq h} b \Leftrightarrow g(a, s) \succ^{\geq h} g(b, s),$$

$$a \succ_s^{\leq h} b \Leftrightarrow g(a, s) \succ^{\leq h} g(b, s).$$

For each $a, b \in A, h \in \mathcal{H}$ and $s \in S$, it is possible to calculate the probability $\rho^{\geq}(a, b, h)$ that a is preferred to b with a strength at least h, and the probability $\rho^{\leq}(a, b, h)$ that a is preferred to b with a strength at most h:

$$\rho^{\geq}(a, b, h) = \sum_{s \in S:\, a \succ_s^{\geq h} b} p_s, \qquad \rho^{\leq}(a, b, h) = \sum_{s \in S:\, a \succ_s^{\leq h} b} p_s.$$

Given $a, b, c, d \in A$, (a, b) *stochastically dominates* (c, d) if, for each $h \in \mathcal{H}$, the probability that a is preferred to b with a strength at least h is not smaller than the probability that c is preferred to d with a strength at least h, i.e., for all $h \in \mathcal{H}$, $\rho^{\geq}(a, b, h) \geq \rho^{\geq}(c, d, h)$.

The stochastic dominance of (a, b) over (c, d) can be equivalently expressed in terms of downward cumulated preference $\rho^{\leq}(a, b, h)$ and $\rho^{\leq}(c, d, h)$ as follows: given $a, b, c, d \in A$, (a, b) stochastically dominates (c, d) if, for each $h \in \mathcal{H}$, the probability that a is preferred to b with a strength at most h is not greater than the probability that c is preferred to d with a strength at most h, i.e., for all $h \in \mathcal{H}$, $\rho^{\leq}(a, b, h) \leq \rho^{\leq}(c, d, h)$.

It is natural to expect that for any $a, b, c, d \in A$, if (a, b) stochastically dominates (c, d), then

- if $c \succeq d$, then also $a \succeq b$,
- if $a \succeq^c b$, then also $c \succeq^c d$.

Considering 2^S, the power set of the set of states of nature S, one can define the set

$$Prob = \left\{ \sum_{s \in T} p_s, \ T \subseteq S \right\}.$$

For any $q \in Prob$ and $a, b \in A$, let

$$f^+(a, b, q) = max\{h \in \mathcal{H} : \rho^{\geq}(a, b, h) \geq q\}$$

and

$$f^-(a, b, q) = min\{h \in \mathcal{H} : \rho^{\leq}(a, b, h) \geq q\}.$$

The above definitions can be interpreted as follows: for any $q \in Prob$ and $a, b \in A$,

- there is a probability at least q that a is preferred to b with a strength not smaller than $f^+(a, b, q)$,
- there is a probability at least q that a is preferred to b with a strength not greater than $f^-(a, b, q)$.

Observe that for any $a, b \in A$,

$$f^+(a, b, q_{\pi(i)}) = f^-(a, b, 1 - q_{\pi(i+1)}), \tag{1}$$

where π is a permutation of the probabilities from $Prob$, such that

$$0 = \pi(1) < \pi(2) < \ldots < \pi(k) = 1, \quad k = card(Prob).$$

Using values $f^+(a, b, q)$ and $f^-(a, b, q)$, we can give an equivalent definition of stochastic dominance of (a, b) over (c, d), for any $a, b, c, d \in A$: (a, b) stochastically dominates (c, d) if, for any $q \in Prob$, $f^+(a, b, q) \geq f^+(c, d, q)$, or, equivalently, $f^-(a, b, q) \leq f^-(c, d, q)$.

In this context, setting $m = card(B)$ and $n = card(Prob)$, an $m \times (n+1)$, Pairwise Comparison Table (PCT) can be set up as follows. The first n columns correspond to the probabilities $q \in Prob$, while the m rows correspond to the pairs from B. The last $(n+1)$-th column represents the comprehensive binary preference relation $\succeq$ or $\succeq^c$. For each pair $(a, b) \in B$, and for each probability $q \in Prob$, the respective value $f^+(a, b, q)$ is put in the corresponding column.

In terms of rough set theory, the *Pairwise Comparison Table* is defined as a data table $PCT = \langle B, Prob \cup \{d\}, \mathcal{H} \cup \{\succeq, \succeq^c\}, f \rangle$, i.e. we can apply the DRSA in this context, considering as set of exemplary pairwise comparisons of reference objects the set of pairs of acts $B \subseteq A \times A$, as set of attributes (criteria) the set $Prob \cup \{d\}$, where to each $q \in Prob$ corresponds a condition attribute assigning some strength of preference $h \in \mathcal{H}$ to each pair $(a, b) \in B$ through function $f^+(a, b, q)$, and d is a decision attribute representing the assignments of pairs of acts $(a, b) \in B$ to classes of weak preference $(a \succeq b)$ or negative weak preference $(a \succeq^c b)$, as set V the set $\mathcal{H} \cup \{\succeq, \succeq^c\}$, and as information function a function f, such that, for all $q \in Prob$, $f(a, b, q) = f^+(a, b, q)$, and $f(a, b, d) = \succeq$ if $a \succeq b$, and $f(a, b, d) = \succeq^c$ if $a \succeq^c b$. A similar PCT can be defined in terms of $f^-(a, b, q)$ replacing $f^+(a, b, q)$.

3.2   Decision Rules

The aim of the rough set approach to decision under uncertainty is to explain the preferences of the DM on the pairs of acts from B in terms of stochastic dominance on values given by functions $f^+(a, b, q)$ and $f^-(a, b, q)$. The resulting preference model is a set of decision rules induced from rough set approximations of weak preference relations. The syntax of decision rules is as follows:

1. **D$_\geq$-*decision rules***:
   If $f^+(a, b, q_{\gamma_1}) \geq h_1$, and,..., and $f^+(a, b, q_{\gamma_z}) \geq h_z$, then $a \succeq b$,
   (i.e. "if with a probability at least q_{γ_1} act a is preferred to act b with a strength at least h_1, and,..., with a probability at least q_{γ_z} act a is preferred to act b with a strength at least h_z, then $a \succeq b$"),
   where $q_{\gamma_1}, \ldots, q_{\gamma_z} \in Prob$, $h_{\gamma_1}, \ldots, h_{\gamma_z} \in \mathcal{H}$;

2. **D$_\leq$-*decision rules***:
   If $f^-(a, b, q_{\gamma_1}) \leq h_1$, and,..., and $f^-(a, b, q_{\gamma_z}) \leq h_z$, then $a \succeq^c b$,
   (i.e. "if with a probability at least q_{γ_1} act a is preferred to act b with a strength at most h_1, and,..., with a probability at least q_{γ_z} act a is preferred to act b with a strength at most h_z, then $a \succeq^c b$"),
   where $q_{\gamma_1}, \ldots, q_{\gamma_z} \in Prob$, $h_{\gamma_1}, \ldots, h_{\gamma_z} \in \mathcal{H}$;

3. **D$_{\geq \leq}$-*decision rules***:
   If $f^+(a, b, q_{\gamma_1}) \geq h_1$, and,..., and $f^+(a, b, q_{\gamma_e}) \geq h_e$, and
   $f^-(a, b, q_{\gamma_{e+1}}) \leq h_{e+1}$, and,..., and $f^-(a, b, q_{\gamma_z}) \leq h_z$ then $a \succeq b$ or $a \succeq^c b$,
   (i.e. "if with a probability at least q_{γ_1} act a is preferred to act b with a strength at least h_1, and,..., with a probability at least q_{γ_e} act a is preferred to act b with a strength at least h_e, and if with a probability at least $q_{\gamma_{e+1}}$ act a is preferred to act b with a strength at most h_{e+1}, and,..., with a probability at least q_{γ_z} act a is preferred to act b with a strength at most h_z, then $a \succeq b$ or $a \succeq^c b$"),
   where $q_{\gamma_1}, \ldots, q_{\gamma_e}, q_{\gamma_{e+1}}, \ldots, q_{\gamma_z} \in Prob$, $h_{\gamma_1}, \ldots, h_{\gamma_e}, h_{\gamma_{e+1}}, \ldots, h_{\gamma_z} \in \mathcal{H}$.

4   Conclusions

We applied the Dominance-based Rough Set Approach (DRSA) to *PCT* in order to learn a rule preference model for decision under uncertainty. Preference information provided by the DM is a set of pairwise comparisons of some representative acts. The resulting preference model expressed in terms of "*if..., then...*" decision rules is much more intelligible than any utility function. Moreover, it permits to handle inconsistent preference information. Let us observe that the approach handles an additive probability distribution as well as a nonadditive probability, and even a qualitative ordinal probability. If the elements of sets *Prob* were very numerous (like in real life applications), it would be enough to consider a subset *Prob'* $\subset$ *Prob* of the most significant probability values (e.g., 0, 0.1, 0.2,..., 0.9, 1).

In the future, we plan to extend this approach to deal not only with uncertain consequences but also with consequences distributed over time. Moreover, we envisage taking into account also non-cardinal criteria, i.e. criteria for which it is not possible to define a set of graded preference relations. Finally, instead of distinguishing only two comprehensive preference relations ($\succeq$ and $\succeq^c$), we will also consider a graded preference relation $\succeq^h$, with $h \in \{-r, -r+1, ..., -1, 0, 1, ..., r-1, r\}$.

Acknowledgement. The third author wishes to acknowledge financial support from the Polish Ministry of Science and Higher Education, grant N N519 314435.

References

1. Allais, M.: Le comportement de l'homme rationnel devant le risque; critique des postulats et axioms de l'école américaine. Econometrica 21, 503–546 (1953)
2. Artzner, P., Delbaen, F., Eber, J., Heath, D.: Coherent measures of risk. Mathematical Finance 9, 203–228 (1999)
3. Borgonovo, E., Peccati, L.: Financial management in inventory problems: risk averse vs risk neutral policies. International Journal of Production Economics 118, 233–242 (2009)
4. Ellsberg, D.: Risk, ambiguity, and the Savage axioms. Quarterly Journal of Economics 75, 643–669 (1961)
5. Epstein, L., Marinacci, M., Seo, K.: Coarse contingencies and ambiguity. Theoretical Economics 2, 355–394 (2007)
6. Fishburn, P.: SSB utility theory and decision-making under uncertainty. Mathematical Social Sciences 8, 253–285 (1984)
7. Fishburn, P.: Nonlinear Preferences and Utility Theory. The John Hopkins University Press, Baltimore (1988)
8. Fishburn, P.: Non-transitive measurable utility for decision under uncertainty. Journal of Mathematical Economics 18(2), 187–207 (1989)
9. Ghirardato, P., Marinacci, M., Maccheroni, F.: Differentiating ambiguity and ambiguity attitude. Journal of Economic Theory 118, 133–173 (2004)
10. Gilboa, I., Schmeidler, D.: Maxmin expected utility with a non-unique prior. Journal of Mathematical Economics 18, 141–153 (1989)
11. Greco, S., Matarazzo, B., Słowiński, R.: Rough approximation of a preference relation by dominance relations. European Journal of Operational Research 117, 63–83 (1999)
12. Greco, S., Matarazzo, B., Słowiński, R.: The use of rough sets and fuzzy sets in MCDM. In: Gal, T., Stewart, T., Hanne, T. (eds.) Advances in Multiple Criteria Decision Making, ch. 14, pp. 14.1–14.59. Kluwer Academic Publishers, Boston (1999)
13. Greco, S., Matarazzo, B., Słowiński, R.: Rough set approach to decisions under risk. In: Ziarko, W.P., Yao, Y. (eds.) RSCTC 2000. LNCS (LNAI), vol. 2005, pp. 160–169. Springer, Heidelberg (2001)
14. Greco, S., Matarazzo, B., Słowiński, R.: Rough sets theory for multicriteria decision analysis. European Journal of Operational Research 129, 1–47 (2001)

15. Greco, S., Matarazzo, B., Słowiński, R.: Decision rule approach. In: Figueira, J., Greco, S., Ehrgott, M. (eds.) Multiple Criteria Decision Analysis: State of the Art Surveys, ch. 13, pp. 507–562. Springer, Berlin (2005)

16. Greco, S., Matarazzo, B., Słowiński, R.: Dominance-based rough set approach to decision under uncertainty and time preference. Annals of Operations Research 176, 41–75 (2010)

17. Kahnemann, D., Tversky, A.: Prospect theory: an analysis of decision under risk. Econometrica 47, 263–291 (1979)

18. Kreps, D.M.: A representation theorem for "preference for flexibility". Econometrica 47, 565–577 (1979)

19. Loomes, G., Sudgen, R.: Regret theory: an alternative theory of rational choice under uncertainty. Economic Journal 92, 805–824 (1982)

20. Marinacci, M., Montrucchio, L.: Introduction to the mathematics of ambiguity. In: Gilboa, I. (ed.) Uncertainty in Economic Theory: a collection of essays in honor of David Schmeidlers 65th birthday, pp. 46–107. Routledge, New York (2004)

21. Pawlak, Z.: Rough Sets. Theoretical Aspects of Reasoning about Data. Kluwer Academic Publishers, Dordrecht (1991)

22. Savage, L.: The Foundations of Statistics. Wiley, New York (1954)

23. Schmeidler, D.: Subjective probability and expected utility without additivity. Econometrica 57, 571–587 (1989)

24. Słowiński, R., Greco, S., Matarazzo, B.: Mining decision-rule preference model from rough approximation of preference relation. In: Proc. 26th IEEE Annual Int. Conference on Computer Software & Applications (COMPSAC 2002), Oxford, pp. 1129–1134 (2002)

25. Słowiński, R., Greco, S., Matarazzo, B.: Rough set based decision support. In: Burke, E., Kendall, G. (eds.) Search Methodologies: Introductory Tutorials in Optimization and Decision Support Techniques, ch. 16, pp. 475–527. Springer, New York (2005)

26. Starmer, C.: Developments in nonexpected utility theory: the hunt for a descriptive theory of choice under risk. Journal of Economic Literature 38, 332–382 (2000)

27. von Neumann, J., Morgenstern, O.: The Theory of Games and Economic Behaviour, 2nd edn. Princeton Univ. Press, Princeton (1947)

Trimming Plethoric Answers to Fuzzy Queries: An Approach Based on Predicate Correlation

Patrick Bosc[1], Allel Hadjali[1], Olivier Pivert[1], and Grégory Smits[2]

[1] Irisa ENSSAT
Univ. Rennes 1 Lannion France
{bosc,hadjali,pivert}@enssat.fr
[2] Irisa IUT Lannion
Univ. Rennes 1 Lannion France
gregory.smits@univ-rennes1.fr

Abstract. Retrieving data from large-scale databases often leads to plethoric answers. To overcome this problem, we propose an approach which selects a set of predicates that the user may use for intensifying his/her query. These predicates are selected among predefined ones according principally to their degree of semantic correlation with the initial query in order to avoid a deep modification of its semantic scope.

Keywords: Plethoric answers, query intensification, correlation.

1 Introduction

The practical need for endowing intelligent information systems with the ability to exhibit cooperative behavior has been recognized since the early '90s. As pointed out in [7], the main intent of cooperative systems is to provide correct, non-misleading and useful answers, rather than literal answers to user queries.

Two antagonist problems are addressed in this field. The first one is known as the "Empty Answer" (EA) problem, that is, the problem of providing the user with some alternative data when there is no item fitting his/her query. The second one is the "Plethoric Answers" (PA) problem which occurs when the amount of returned data is too large to be manageable. Then, users have to go through this large set of answers to examine them and keep only the most relevant ones, which is a tedious and time-consuming task. This paper focuses on this second problem in the context of fuzzy queries. The fuzzy counterpart of the plethoric answers problem can be stated as follows: there are too many data in the database that satisfy a fuzzy query Q with a highest degree h.

The PA problem has been intensively addressed by the information systems community and two main approaches have been proposed. The first one, that may be called data-oriented, aims at ranking the answers in order to return the best k ones to the user. However, this strategy is often faced with the difficulty of comparing and distinguishing between tuples that entirely satisfy the initial query. In this data-oriented approach, we can also mention works which aim at summarizing the set of answers to a query [13].

E. Hüllermeier, R. Kruse, and F. Hoffmann (Eds.): IPMU 2010, LNAI 6178, pp. 595–604, 2010.

The second type of approach may be called query-oriented as it performs a modification of the initial query in order to propose a more selective query. For instance, a strategy consists in intensifying the specified predicates (as an example a predicate $A \in [a_1, a_2]$ becomes $A \in [a_1 + \gamma, a_2 - \gamma]$) [3]. However, for some predicates, this intensification leads to a deep modification of the initial predicate's sense. For example, if we consider a query looking for fast-food restaurants located in a certain district delimited by geographical coordinates, an intensification of the condition related to the location could lead to the selection of restaurants in a very small area (like a block of houses), and the final answers would not necessarily fit the user's need. Another type of approach advocates the use of user-defined preferences on attributes which are not involved in the initial query [8,6,2]. Such a subjective knowledge can then be used to select the most preferred items among the initial set of answers.

Still another category of query-oriented approaches aims at automatically completing the initial query with additional predicates to make it more demanding. Our work belongs to this last family of approaches but its specificity concerns the way additional predicates are selected. Indeed, we consider that the predicates added to the query must respect two properties: i) they must reduce the size of the initial set of answers, ii) they must modify the scope of the initial query as little as possible. To reach this latter goal, we propose to identify the predicates which are the most correlated to the initial query. Such correlation relations are inferred from the data and express semantic links between possible additional predicates and those present in the initial query.

The remainder of the paper is structured as follows. Section 2 introduces the basic underlying notions: fuzzy queries and the PA problem. In Section 3, we discuss related work, in particular the approach proposed by Ozawa et al. [9]. The principle of our approach is then described in Sections 4 and 5. Before concluding and drawing some perspectives, Section 6 illustrates our approach on a concrete example.

2   Preliminaries

2.1   Plethoric Answers to Fuzzy Queries

We consider a database fuzzy querying framework such as the SQLf language introduced in [4].

A typical example of a fuzzy query is: "retrieve the recent and low-mi leage cars", where recent and low-mileage are gradual predicates which could be represented by means of fuzzy sets as illustrated in Figure 1.

Let Q be a fuzzy query. We denote by Σ_Q the set of answers to Q when addressed to a regular relational database D. Σ_Q contains the items of the database that *somewhat* satisfy the fuzzy requirements involved in D. Formally,

$$\Sigma_Q = \{t \in D / \mu_Q(t) > 0\},$$

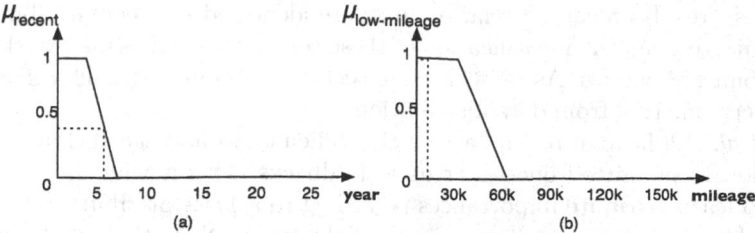

Fig. 1. Fuzzy predicates (a) *recent* and (b) *low-mileage* (where 30K means 30.000 km)

where t stands for a database tuple. Let h, $h \in \,]0,1]$ be the height of Σ_Q, i.e. the highest membership degree assigned to an item of Σ_Q. Let now Σ_Q^* ($\subseteq \Sigma_Q$) denote the set of answers that satisfy Q with a degree h.

$$\Sigma_Q^* = \{t \in D/\mu_Q(t) = h\}$$

Definition 1. Let Q be a fuzzy query, we say that Q leads to a PA problem if the set Σ_Q^* is too large.[1]

To reduce the set Σ_Q^*, we propose an approach aiming at integrating additional predicates as new conjuncts to Q. By doing so, we obtain a more restrictive query Q' which may lead to a reduced set of answers $\Sigma_{Q'}^* \subset \Sigma_Q^*$.

2.2   Correlation Notion

In the approach we propose, predicates added to the initial query as new conjuncts are chosen among a set of possible predicates pertaining to the attributes of the schema of the database queried (see Section 4.1). This choice is made according to their relative correlation with the initial query. The notion of correlation is used to qualify and quantify the extent to which two fuzzy sets (one associated with a predefined predicate P_i^p, the other corresponding to Σ_Q^*) are semantically related. This degree of correlation is denoted by $\mu_{cor}(P_i^p, Q)$. Roughly speaking, we consider that a predicate P_i^p is somewhat correlated with a query if they characterize similar groups of items. For instance, one may notice that a fuzzy predicate "high powerful engine" is more correlated with the predicate "fast cars" than with "low consumption". Adding predefined predicates that are semantically correlated with the user-specified ones makes it possible to comply with the scope of the query (i.e., the user's intent) while making it more demanding. It is worth mentioning that the term *correlation* used in this approach means a mutual semantic relationship between two concepts, and does not have the meaning it has in statistics where it represents similarities between series variations.

3   Related Work

In their probabilistic ranking model, Chaudhuri *et al.* [5] propose to use such a correlation relation between attributes and to take it into account when computing

---

[1] Obviously, the notion "too large" depends on the user and the applicative context.

ranking scores. However, correlation links are identified between attributes and not predicates, and the identification of these correlations relies on a workload of past submitted queries. As we will see in section 4, in our approach correlations are directly inferred from data distributions.

Su *et al.* [12] have also emphasized the difficulty to manage such a workload of previously submitted queries or users feedbacks. This is why they have proposed to learn attribute importances regarding to a *price* attribute and to rank retrieved items according to their commercial interest. Nevertheless, this method is domain-dependent and can only be applied for e-commerce databases.

The approach advocated by Ozawa *et al.* [9,10] is also based on the analysis of the database itself, and aims at providing the user with information about the data distributions and the most efficient constraints to add to the initial query in order to reduce the initial set of answers. The approach we propose in this paper is somewhat close to that introduced in [9], but instead of suggesting an attribute on which the user should specify a new constraint, our method directly suggests a set of fuzzy predicates along with some information about their relative interest for the user needs. The main limit of the approach advocated in [9] is that the attribute chosen is that which maximises the dispersion of the initial set of answers, whereas most of the time, it does not have any semantic link with the predicates that the user specified in his/her initial query. To illustrate this, let us consider a relation *Cars* of schema *(id, model, brand, price, hPower, mileage, year, type, secLevel, comfortLevel, maxSpeed)*. Let Q be a fuzzy query on *Cars*: *"select estate cars which are recent"* resulting in a PA problem. In such a situation, Ozawa *et al.* [9] first apply a fuzzy c-means algorithm [1] to classify the data, and each fuzzy cluster is associated with a predefined linguistic label. After having attributed a weight to each cluster according to its representativity of the initial set of answers, a global dispersion degree is computed for each attribute. The user is then asked to add new predicates on the attribute for which the dispersion of the initial answers is maximal. In this example, this approach may have suggested that the user should add a condition on the attributes *mileage* or *brand*, on which the recent estate cars are probably the most dispersed. We claim that it is more relevant to reduce the initial set of answers with additional conditions which are in the semantic scope of the initial query. Here for instance, it would be more judicious to focus on cars with a high level of security and comfort as well as a low mileage, which are features usually related to recent estate cars.

The problem of plethoric answers to fuzzy queries has been addressed in [3] where a query intensifying mechanism is proposed. Let us consider a fuzzy set $F = (A, B, a, b)$ representing a fuzzy query Q. Bosc *et al.* [3] define a fuzzy tolerance relation E which can be parameterized by a tolerance indicator $\overline{Z}$, where $\overline{Z}$ is a fuzzy interval centered in 0 that can be represented in terms of a trapezoidal membership function by the quadruplet $\overline{Z} = (-z, z, \delta, \delta)$. From a fuzzy set $F = (A, B, a, b)$ and a tolerance relation $E(\overline{Z})$, the erosion operator builds a set $F_{\overline{Z}}$ such that $F_{\overline{Z}} \subseteq F$ and $F_{\overline{Z}} = F \ominus \overline{Z} = (A + z, B - z, a - \delta, b - \delta)$.

As it as been mentioned in Section 1, such an erosion-based approach can lead to a deep modification of the meaning of the user-defined predicate and thus may drift too far away from the initial user's intent.

4   Predicate Correlation

4.1   A Priori Knowledge

Let us consider a relation R containing w tuples $\{t_1, t_2, \ldots, t_w\}$ defined on a set Z of q categorical or numerical attributes $\{Z_1, Z_2, \ldots, Z_q\}$. Let $Q = \{P_{i_1,1}^s, P_{i_2,2}^s, \ldots, P_{i_n,n}^s\}$, $i_k \in [1..q]$ $\forall k$ be a fuzzy query submitted to R. If Q leads to a plethoric answer set, we propose to intensify Q in order to obtain a more restrictive query Q' such that $\Sigma_{Q'}^* \subset \Sigma_Q^*$. Query Q' is obtained through the integration of an additional predefined fuzzy predicate P_i^p defined on an attribute Z_i, $i = 1..q$, $i \neq i_k$ $for\ k = 1..n$.

As mentioned before, background knowledge is obtained in [10] by means of a fuzzy classification process. In our approach, it is defined *a priori* by means of a Ruspini partition of each attribute domain. These partitions are specified by an expert during the database design step and represent "common sense partitions" of the domains instead of the result of an automatic process which may be difficult to interpret.

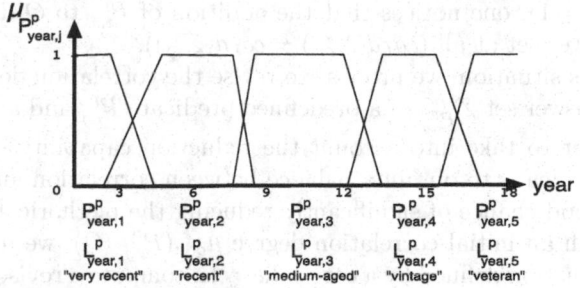

Fig. 2. A partition of the domain of attribute **year** from relation **Cars**

Thus, a partition $\mathscr{P}_i$ associated with an attribute Z_i is composed of a set of m fuzzy predicates $\{P_{i,1}^p, P_{i,2}^p, ..., P_{i,m}^p\}$, such that $\forall z_i \in \mathscr{D}(Z_i)$, $\sum_{j=1}^m \mu_{P_{ij}^p}(z_i) = 1$. Each $\mathscr{P}_i$ is associated with a set of linguistic labels $\{L_{i,1}^p, L_{i,2}^p, \ldots, L_{i,m}^p\}$, each of them corresponding to an adjective which translates the meaning of the fuzzy predicate. For example, if we consider the relation **Cars** again, a common sense partition and labelling of attribute *year* is illustrated in Fig. 2.

4.2   Correlation between a Predefined Predicate and a User Query

In this approach, we consider that a predefined predicate $P_{i,j}^p$ (Section 4.1) is correlated to a query Q, if the sets of tuples contained respectively in $\Sigma_{P_{i,j}^p}^*$ and

Σ_Q^* are somewhat close. The quantification of the semantic link between $P_{i,j}^p$ and Q relies on a correlation measure defined on $[0, 1]$ and denoted by $\mu_{cor}(P_{i,j}^p, Q)$.

Among the measures that can be used to quantify the similarity between two sets or fuzzy sets [11], we choose the well-known Jaccard indice because of its simplicity. However, other similarity mesures should be considered in future work, so as to experimentally assess which is the most appropriate in general.

$$\mu_{cor}(P_{i,j}^p, Q) = \frac{card(\Sigma_{P_{i,j}^p}^* \cap \Sigma_Q^*)}{card(\Sigma_{P_{i,j}^p}^* \cup \Sigma_Q^*)}.$$

It is trivial to check that this measure is reflexive $(\mu_{cor}(P, P) = 1)$ and symmetric $(\mu_{cor}(P, P') = \mu_{cor}(P', P))$.

4.3   Balancing Correlation and Reduction

As it has been pointed out in Section 1, besides being correlated to the query, the predicates used for the intensification must reduce the initial set of results. This is why the intensification process can not only be based on the maximization of this measure as, in some (rare) circumstances, it could lead to the selection of a predefined predicate that does not greatly reduce the initial fuzzy set of answers. For example, if we consider the extreme case of a predicate $P_{i,j}^p$, whose answer set $(\Sigma_{P_{i,j}^p}^*)$ is completely correlated to the answer set of a query Σ_Q^* $(\mu_{cor}(P_{i,j}^p, Q) = 1)$, one notices that the addition of $P_{i,j}^p$ to Q does not reduce the initial answer set at all $(card(\Sigma_{Q'}^*) = card(\Sigma_Q^*))$.

To avoid this situation, we propose to revise the correlation degree computed between the answer set $\Sigma_{P_{i,j}^p}^*$ of a predefined predicate $P_{i,j}^p$ and an initial answer set Σ_Q^* in order to take into account the reduction capability of a predefined predicate. The idea is to obtain a balance between correlation and reduction so as to have a good chance of significantly reducing the plethoric set of answers.

Starting with an initial correlation degree $\mu_{cor}(P_{i,j}^p, Q)$, we use a triangular membership function defined by a core value γ to compute a revised degree noted $\mu_{corRed}(P_{i,j}^p, Q)$. As it is illustrated in Fig. 3, parameter γ represents a degree of balance between correlation and reduction.

One can remark that the closer γ is to 1 the higher the priority given to correlation over the reduction capability of the chosen predefined predicate. In the current version of our approach, this technical parameter is set to a default value $\gamma = 0.7$. Obviously, it should be adapted to fit the particularities of the query (more precisely, the size of the initial result as well as the number of answers desired by the user). This nontrivial issue is left for future work.

5   Query Intensification

5.1   Table of Correlation Degrees

Let us consider an initial query Q resulting in a plethoric answer set. It would be inefficient to dynamically compute correlation degrees between Q and all

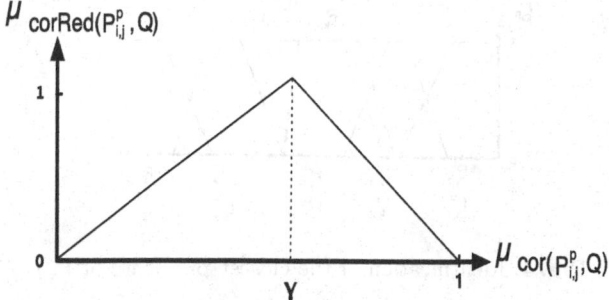

Fig. 3. Balancing correlation and reduction for a predicate $P_{i,j}^p$ and a query Q

the predefined predicates to identify those which are the most correlated to Q. So, we propose to compute and maintain a correlation table containing the degree of correlation $\mu_{cor}(P_{i,j}^p, P_{k,l}^p)$ between each pair of predefined predicates $(P_{i,j}^p, P_{k,l}^p), j, l = 1..q$. To improve the efficiency of the intensification process, we also store for each predefined predicate an ordered list of its κ most correlated predefined predicates, where κ has been initially set to 5. This restriction to the five most correlated predicates is motivated by the fact that an intensification process involving too many predicates would significantly alter the semantic scope of the initial query. Since the correlation degrees needed for establishing these rankings are available in the correlation table, this limit can easily be adapted to the applicative context.

The table stores correlation degrees between each pair of *predefined* predicates. When faced with a PA problem, the first step is thus to identify, for each user-specified predicate $P_{k,l}^s$ involved in the query, its closest predefined predicate $P_{k,j}^p$ among those belonging to the partition $\mathscr{P}(Z_k)$ of the domain of attribute Z_k. In order to evaluate how close a user-specified fuzzy predicate is to a predefined one, we use the same measure as for correlation. However, in this case, the calculus is based on the *membership functions* of the predicates, not on the number of elements in the database which somewhat satisfy these predicates. This closeness measure between two fuzzy predicates $P_{k,l}^s$ and $P_{k,j}^p$ is denoted by $close(P_{k,l}^s, P_{k,j}^p)$ and is defined as follows:

$$close(P_{k,l}^s, P_{k,j}^p) = \frac{\sum_{x \in domain(Z_k)} min(\mu_{P_{k,l}^s}(x), \mu_{P_{k,j}^p}(x))}{\sum_{x \in domain(Z_k)} max(\mu_{P_{k,l}^s}(x), \mu_{P_{k,j}^p}(x))}.$$

As illustrated in Fig. 4, the predefined predicate $P_{k,j}^{s'}$ the closest to a user-specified predicate $P_{k,l}^s$ is that which maximizes the closeness measure wrt $P_{k,l}^s$:

$$P_{k,j}^{s'} = P_{k,j_0}^p, \text{ such that } close(P_{k,l}^s, P_{k,j_0}^p) = sup_{j=1..m}(close(P_{k,l}^s, P_{k,j_0}^p)),$$

where m is the number of elements of the fuzzy partition associated with Z_k.

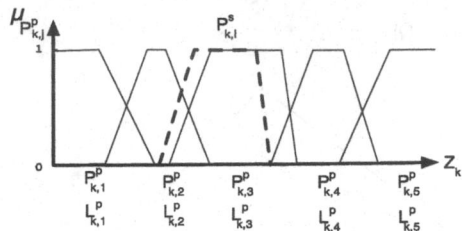

Fig. 4. Identification of the closest predicate of $P_{k,l}^s$

5.2 Atomic Queries

When faced with an atomic fuzzy query $Q = P_{k,l}^s$ resulting in a PA problem, the intensification is straightforward. $P_{k,l}^s$ is first compared with the predefined predicates $P_{k,j}^p$, $j = 1..m$ belonging to the partition $\mathscr{P}_k$ of the attribute Z_k in order to identify its closest predefined predicate $P_{k,l}^{s'}$. From the correlation table, we can then retrieve the κ predefined predicates the most correlated to $P_{k,l}^{s'}$ denoted by $\{P_{P_{k,l}^{s'}}^{c_1}, P_{P_{k,l}^{s'}}^{c_2}, ..., P_{P_{k,l}^{s'}}^{c_\kappa}\}$.

These κ predefined predicates are re-ranked according to their corrected correlation degree, which is calculated using γ. This ranking is then suggested to the user for the intensification of the initial query. The selected additional predicate is then added as a new conjunct to the initial query and the new answer set is computed w.r.t. the set of tuples Σ_Q^*. If the new answer set is still plethoric, the user can integrate another correlated predicate from the list and so on.

5.3 Conjunctive Queries

In case of conjunctive fuzzy queries, which are of the form $Q = P_{k_1,1}^s \wedge P_{k_2,2}^s \wedge ... \wedge P_{k_n,n}^s$, $k_i \in [1..q]$ $\forall i$ where $\wedge$ stands for the connector *and* (interpreted by *min*), the process is slightly revisited. For each user predicate $P_{k_l,l}^s$, $k_l \in [1..q]$, $l \in [1..n]$ we still retrieve the κ predicates $\{P_{P_{k_l,l}^{s'}}^{c_1}, P_{P_{k_l,l}^{s'}}^{c_2}, ..., P_{P_{k_l,l}^{s'}}^{c_\kappa}\}$ the most correlated with $P_{k_l,l}^{s'}$ (i.e., with the predefined predicate the closest to $P_{k_l,l}^s$). The corrected degree of correlation associated with each of these κ predicates is then computed.

Finally, the average corrected degree of correlation associated with each of these predefined predicates $P_{P_{k_l,l}^{s'}}^{c_i}$ is computed:

$$\mu_{corRed}(P_{P_{k_l,l}^{s'}}^{c_i}, Q) = \frac{1}{n} \cdot \sum_{h \in E_l} \mu_{corRed}(P_{P_{k_l,l}^{s'}}^{c_i}, P_{k_l,h}^s)$$

where E_l is the set of predicates from Q which concern attribute Z_l. This ranked set of predicates and their associated degrees are suggested to the user for the intensification of his/her query as described in Section 5.2.

6   Example

Let us consider relation *Cars* from Section 2, which is assumed to describe 936 cars. Let Q be the fuzzy query looking for the 30 best *recent family cars* where the predicate *recent* is defined by the trapezoidal membership function $(0, 3, 0, 2)$ and *family car* as $\{minivan/1, estate/0.9, 4 \times 4/0.7, sedan/0.5, SUV/0.2\}$. The result of Q may be considered plethoric since $|\Sigma_Q^*| = 61$. To reduce this set of answers, we first identify the closest predefined predicates, which are respectively $P^p_{year,1}$ associated with the label "very recent" (see Fig. 2) and the predicate $P^p_{type,2}$ with label *family* defined as $\{estate/1, minivan/1, sedan/0.6\}$.

For the attributes *hPower, price, mileage, secLevel* and *comfortLevel*, Table 1 gives the correlation degrees between the elements of their partitions and the two predefined predicates $P^p_{year,1}$ and $P^p_{type,2}$. The cardinality of the core of each predefined predicate is mentioned in brackets next to its linguistic label and the cardinality of its intersection with $P^p_{year,1}$ and $P^p_{type,2}$ is given after the correlation degree. It is assumed that $|P^p_{year,1}| = 309$ and $|P^p_{type,2}| = 98|$.

Table 1. Extract of the correlation table for $P^p_{year,1}$ and $P^p_{type,2}$

$L_{hPower,i}$	hPower		
	low(279)	medium(482)	high(175)
$P^p_{year,1}$	0.19 (92)	0.2 (131)	0.22 (86)
$P^p_{type,2}$	0.03 (11)	0.09 (48)	**0.17 (39)**

$L_{price,i}$	price				
	veryCheap(102)	cheap(227)	acceptable(301)	expensive(204)	veryExpensive(102)
$P^p_{year,1}$	0.02(9)	0.02(11)	0.08(43)	**0.49(168)**	0.23(78)
$P^p_{type,2}$	0.02(3)	0.02(9)	0.07(25)	**0.17(43)**	0.1(18)

$L_{mileage,i}$	mileage				
	veryLow(109)	low(290)	medium(296)	high(161)	veryHigh(80)
$P^p_{year,1}$	**0.51(142)**	0.25(120)	0.07(39)	0.02(8)	0(0)
$P^p_{type,2}$	0.1(18)	0.07(26)	0.08(29)	0.06(15)	0.05(8)

$L_{secLevel,i}$	secLevel			
	low(120)	medium(340)	high(296)	veryHigh(180)
$P^p_{year,1}$	0.02(8)	0.07(41)	0.26(125)	**0.38(135)**
$P^p_{type,2}$	0.02(3)	0.04(18)	0.1(33)	**0.19(44)**

$L_{comfortLevel,i}$	comfortLevel			
	low(120)	medium(361)	high(305)	veryHigh(150)
$P^p_{year,1}$	0.02(9)	0.16(92)	**0.45(190)**	**0.35(118)**
$P^p_{type,2}$	0.01(2)	0.03(12)	**0.12(43)**	**0.2(41)**

The five predicates most correlated to $P^p_{year,1}$ are {veryLow mileage/0.51, expensive price/0.49, high comfortLevel/0.45, veryHigh secLevel/0.38, veryHigh comfortLevel/0.35} ; for $P^p_{type,2}$, we get {veryHigh comfortLevel/0.2, veryHigh secLevel/0.19, expensive price/0.17, high hPower/0.17, high comfortLevel/0.12}. These correlation degrees are then corrected using $\gamma = 0.7$ and the following ranked candidates are presented to the user:

{veryHigh secLevel/0.41, high comfortLevel/0.41, veryHigh comfortLevel/0.39, veryLow mileage/0.37, expensive price/0.24, high horsePower/0.12}

As expected, these predicates fit well with the semantics of the initial query.

7   Conclusion

The approach presented in this paper deals with the plethoric answers problem by identifying relevant predicates that can be used to intensify the initial query. These predicates are selected among a set of predefined fuzzy terms and are ranked according to their degree of semantic correlation with the initial query. As shown, this is achieved without requiring much information from the end-user. What makes the approach tractable is the fact that it uses a table which stores the correlation degrees between the predefined predicates.

This work opens many perspectives for future research. For instance, we are currently working on a method to infer the "best" value for parameter γ, taking into account the number of results expected by the user. Another important aspect concerns the experimental assessment of the approach. We are currently implementing a prototype which will use imdb (http://www.imdb.com) as a test database.

References

1. Bezdek, J.: Pattern recognition with fuzzy objective function algorithm. Plenum Press, New York (1981)
2. Bodenhofer, U., Küng, J.: Fuzzy ordering in flexible query answering systems. Soft Computing 8, 512–522 (2003)
3. Bosc, P., Hadjali, A., Pivert, O.: Empty versus overabundant answers to flexible relational queries. Fuzzy sets and systems 159(12), 1450–1467 (2008)
4. Bosc, P., Pivert, O.: SQLf: a relational database language for fuzzy querying. IEEE Transactions on Fuzzy Systems 3(1), 1–17 (1995)
5. Chaudhuri, S., Das, G., Hristidis, V., Weikum, G.: Probabilistic ranking of database query results. In: Proc. of VLDB'04, pp. 888–899 (2004)
6. Chomicki, J.: Querying with intrinsic preferences. In: Jensen, C.S., Jeffery, K., Pokorný, J., Šaltenis, S., Bertino, E., Böhm, K., Jarke, M. (eds.) EDBT 2002. LNCS, vol. 2287, pp. 34–51. Springer, Heidelberg (2002)
7. Gaasterland, T.: Relaxation as a platform for cooperative answering. Journal of Intelligent Information Systems 1(3-4), 296–321 (1992)
8. Kiessling, W.: Foundations of preferences in database systems. In: Proc. of VLDB'02 (2002)
9. Ozawa, J., Yamada, K.: Cooperative answering with macro expression of a database. In: Bouchon-Meunier, B., Yager, R.R., Zadeh, L.A. (eds.) IPMU 1994. LNCS, vol. 945, pp. 17–22. Springer, Heidelberg (1995)
10. Ozawa, J., Yamada, K.: Discovery of global knowledge in database for cooperative answering. In: Proc. of Fuzz-IEEE'95. pp. 849–852 (1995)
11. Pappis, C., Karacapilidis, N.: A comparative assessment of measures of similarity of fuzzy values. In: Fuzzy sets and systems (1993)
12. Su, W., Wang, J., Huang, Q., Lochovsky, F.: Query result ranking over e-commerce web databases. In: Proc. of CIKM'06 (2006)
13. Ughetto, L., Voglozin, W.A., Mouaddib, N.: Database querying with personalized vocabulary using data summaries. Fuzzy Sets and Systems 159(15), 2030–2046 (2008)

Searching Aligned Groups of Objects with Fuzzy Criteria

Maria Carolina Vanegas[1,2], Isabelle Bloch[1], and Jordi Inglada[2]

[1] Institut Telecom, Télécom ParisTech , CNRS-LTCI UMR 5141, Paris, France
[2] CNES, Toulouse, France
carolina.vanegas@telecom-paristech.fr,
isabelle.bloch@telecom-paristech.fr, jordi.inglada@cnes.fr

Abstract. The detection of aligned groups of objects is important for satellite image interpretation. This task can be challenging when objects have different sizes. In this paper, we propose a method for extracting aligned objects from a labeled image. In this method we construct a neighborhood graph of the objects of the image, and its dual graph where we incorporate information about the relative direction of the objects, evaluated using fuzzy measures of relative position. The groups of objects satisfying the fuzzy criterion of being locally aligned are extracted from the dual graph. These groups are the candidates for being (globally) aligned. The method was tested on synthetic images, and on objects extracted from real images demonstrating that the method extracts the aligned groups of objects even if the objects have different sizes.

1 Alignment and Related Work

Alignment can be defined as the spatial property possessed by a group of objects arranged in a straight line[1]. Determining the groups of aligned objects is crucial for image interpretation. According to the Gestalt theory, the human perceptual vision system groups objects together using certain rules. Among these rules there is one called continuity of direction which groups together objects in the same direction, and one particular case is the constancy of direction that refers to alignments [5]. An aligned group of objects has the characteristic that it should be seen as a whole, since if its elements are observed in an independent manner then the alignment property is lost. Having to look it as a whole makes alignment detection a difficult task.

Identifying the aligned groups of objects in satellite images is important for several applications. Satellite images provide a huge amount of geographical information, and aligned groups of objects can be seen as a way to reduce this information in a pertinent way. For example in cartography, it is necessary to find groups of aligned buildings for map generalization [12]. Observing if a group of buildings is aligned can give information about the structure of their arrangement, and whether they belong to a urban, rural or residential area [6]. In object detection, complex semantic classes such as parking areas (car parkings,

---

[1] Definition taken from ThinkMap Visual Thesaurus
http://www.visualthesaurus.com/

E. Hüllermeier, R. Kruse, and F. Hoffmann (Eds.): IPMU 2010, LNAI 6178, pp. 605–613, 2010.
© Springer-Verlag Berlin Heidelberg 2010

ports, truck parkings or airports) comprise aligned groups of transport vehicles. Therefore, the identification of aligned groups of transport vehicles can be useful for detecting instantiations of these complex classes, and is meaningful for the description of this kind of scenes.

Alignment extraction has been studied in image processing as a low level feature. For instance methods relying on the Hough transform [5] or the Radon transform [7] are used to find groups of points in digital images which fall into a line. Other examples are the identification of aligned segments which have the same orientations as the alignment [5,10,11,8]. However, alignment extraction as a high level feature has been less studied. One example is the work of [4], where an algorithm to detect aligned groups of buildings in maps is presented. In this algorithm buildings with aligned barycenters are extracted, and the quality of the alignments is evaluated based on the criteria of proximity and similarity laws of Gestalt theory. Nevertheless, when the groups are composed of objects of different sizes, it is not possible to detect the alignment by observing just their barycenters (see Fig. 1). Thus, when considering extended objects and not only points the notion of "falling into a line" becomes imprecise. Therefore it is necessary to consider a degree of satisfaction of the relation of alignment.

In this work we propose a novel method to detect alignments of objects that can be applied to objects of different sizes, or to fuzzy objects. In our approach, we use the direction orientation between any two elements of the group to determine their degree of alignment. To measure the orientation between two objects we make use of what we call orientation histogram which is based on the angle histogram introduced by Mijama and Ralescu in [9] (Sec. 2). Our strategy consists in first determining the *locally* aligned groups which are the candidates to form an aligned group of objects. Then we measure the degree of alignment of each candidate group (Sec. 3) and solve conflicts. The results of the method are shown on synthetic and real images in Sec. 5.

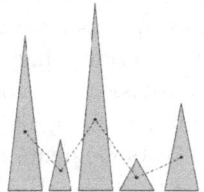

Fig. 1. Problems encountered when the group has objects of different sizes: an aligned group of objects with not aligned barycenters

2   Angle and Orientation Histograms

Angle histograms have proved to be an adequate way for evaluating the directional spatial relation between two objects, since they take into account the shape of the regions [9]. They can be interpreted as a function that captures the directional position between two objects. Let a and b be two objects defined by two regions in the image space $\mathfrak{I}$, that we denote by a and b. The angle histogram from a to b is obtained by computing for each pair of points $p_a \in a$ and $p_b \in b$ the angle between the segment joining them and the horizontal axis, denoted by $\angle(p_a, p_b)$. Angles are organized in a histogram, normalized by the largest frequency:

$$H^a(b)(\theta) = \frac{\sum_{p_a \in a, p_b \in b | \angle(p_a, p_b) = \theta} 1}{\max_{\phi \in [0, 2\pi)} \sum_{p_a \in a, p_b \in b | \angle(p_a, p_b) = \phi} 1}. \tag{1}$$

To determine if an object a is in a given direction with respect to an object b (for example "right of"), we can compute the angle histogram $H^a(b)$ and compare it with a template for the relation "right of" by using for instance a conjunctive operator or the compatibility between the computed histogram and the template [9]. Angle histograms are easily extended to fuzzy objects. In addition, they are invariant to simultaneous translation, scaling and rotation of both objects. They are not symmetrical, but they satisfy: $H^a(b)(\theta) = H^b(a)(\theta + \pi)$.

Since we are interested in the orientation of two objects with respect to the horizontal axis, we introduce the notion of orientation histogram, which is simply an angle histogram where the angles are computed modulus π and its support has a length equal to π. For the case where a and b are fuzzy objects with membership function $\mu_a : \mathfrak{I} \rightarrow [0,1]$ and $\mu_b : \mathfrak{I} \rightarrow [0,1]$, respectively, the orientation histogram is given by:

$$O(a, b)(\theta) = \frac{\sum_{p_a, p_b \in \mathfrak{I} | mod(\angle(p_a, p_b), \pi) = \theta} \mu_a(p_a) \wedge \mu_b(p_b)}{\max_{\phi \in [0, \pi)} \sum_{p_a, p_b \in \mathfrak{I} | mod(\angle(p_a, p_b), \pi) = \phi} \mu_a(p_a) \wedge \mu_b(p_b)}, \tag{2}$$

where $\wedge$ is a t-norm. The orientation histogram is a fuzzy subset of $[0, \pi[$ that represents the orientation between two objects with respect to the horizontal axis, it preserves the same properties as the angle histogram, and in addition it is symmetrical.

To compare if two orientation histograms are similar, it is important to consider the imprecision that is linked to the comparison of two angles that are approximately the same. When a fuzzy morphological dilation [3] is performed on an orientation histogram using a structuring element ν_0, then the high values of the histogram will be propagated to the similar angle values according to ν_0. The structuring element ν_0 is designed such that $\nu_0(\theta - \tilde{\theta})$ represents the degree to which $\tilde{\theta}$ and θ are "approximately" equal (modeled by a trapezoid function in our experiments). Then the similarity degree between two orientation histograms can be given by the maximum height of the intersection of the dilated histograms:

$$sim(O(a, b), O(c, d)) = \max_{\theta \in [0, \pi)} [D_{\nu_0}(O(a, b)) \wedge D_{\nu_0}(O(c, d))](\theta), \tag{3}$$

where $\wedge$ is a t norm, and the fuzzy morphological dilation is given by $D_{\nu_0}(\mu)(\theta) = \sup_{\tilde{\theta} \in [0, \pi[} \min(\mu(\tilde{\theta}), \nu_0(\theta - \tilde{\theta}))$ [3].

This degree of similarity can be extended to evaluate the similarity degree between several orientation histograms. Let $\{O(a_i, b_i)\}_{i=0}^{N}$ be a set of orientation histograms. Then the degree of similarity between them is given by:

$$sim\left(O(a_0, b_0), \ldots, O(a_N, b_N)\right) = \max_{\theta \in [0,\pi[} \bigwedge_{i=0}^{N} D_{\nu_0}(O(a_i, b_i))(\theta). \qquad (4)$$

3   Alignment Detection

In this section we propose the definitions of *globally* aligned and *locally* aligned, both relations depend on a neighborhood relation. Let a, b be two objects. We define $N_d(a)$ as the Voronoi neighborhood of a constrained by a distance d, and the binary relation $Neigh(a, b)$ is satisfied if $b \cap N_d(a) \neq \emptyset$.

A group S is said to be *globally* aligned if all its members are connected by the $Neigh$ relation, and if there exists an angle θ such that every member of the group is able to see the other members of the group in a direction θ or $\theta + \pi$ with respect to the horizontal axis. Thus, it is possible to define the degree of *global* alignment as follows:

Definition 1. *Let $S = \{a_0, \ldots, a_N\}$, with $N \geq 3$, be a group of objects in $\mathfrak{I}$, connected by the Neigh relation. The degree of global alignment of S is given by:*

$$\mu_{ALIG}(S) = sim\left(O(a_0, S \setminus \{a_0\}), \ldots, O(a_N, S \setminus \{a_N\})\right). \qquad (5)$$

A group S with $\mu_{ALIG}(S) = \beta$ is called a *globally* aligned group to a degree β. A group $S = \{a_0, \ldots, a_N\}$ is said to be *locally* aligned to a degree β, if for every two pairs of neighboring objects, having one object in common, the orientations between the objects of each pair are similar to a degree β, and also if the group is connected by the neighbor relation. The latter can be summarized by saying that a group S with $|S| \geq 3$ is *locally* aligned to a degree β if it satisfies the following relations:

$R1 : \forall x, y, z \ (Neigh(x, y) \wedge Neigh(y, z)) \Rightarrow (sim(O(x, y), O(y, z)) \geq \beta)$

$R2 : \forall a, b \ \exists x_0, \ldots, x_m$ for $m > 1$ such that $x_0 = a, x_m = b$ and $\bigwedge_{i=0}^{m-1} Neigh(x_i, x_{i+1})$

Extracting Locally Aligned Groups of Objects: To extract the locally aligned groups, first we construct a neighborhood graph G_N to obtain the information of which objects are connected via the $Neigh$ relation. In a neighborhood graph $G_N = (V, E)$ the vertices represent the objects of the group, and there is an edge between two vertices if and only if the corresponding objects are neighbors. Notice that only the connected subsets of three vertices x, y and z in G_N which share a common vertex, for example y, satisfy $Neigh(x, y) \wedge Neigh(y, z)$. These connected subsets are called *triplets*. According to $R1$, only the *triplets* $\{x, y, z\}$ for which $sim(O(x, y), O(y, z)) \geq \beta$ can belong to a *locally* aligned group. *Triplets* can be easily identified as the edges of the dual graph, when the dual graph is constructed in the following manner. The dual graph is denoted by $\tilde{G}_N = \{\tilde{V}, \tilde{E}\}$ where each vertex $\tilde{v}_i$ represents an edge in the graph G_N. An edge exists between two vertices $\tilde{v}_i$ and $\tilde{v}_j$ of $\tilde{G}_N$ if the two corresponding edges of the graph G_N have a common vertex. If, additionally, we attribute to each edge (i, j) the similarity degree between the orientation histograms of $\tilde{v}_i$ and $\tilde{v}_j$ that we denote by $\tilde{s}_{ij}$, then it will be possible to verify whether the relation $R1$ holds for its corresponding *triplet*. Figure 2 shows an example of neighborhood graph and its dual graph. Notice that the edges of $\tilde{G}_N$ with a high value represent the *triplets* of objects with a similar orientation histogram. For instance, in the dual graph the edge between the nodes (1 - 2) and (2 - 3) has a similarity value of 1, this edge corresponding to the objects labeled 1, 2 and 3 of Fig. 2(a). In a similar way, edges with a low value represent objects which are not aligned, for example in the dual graph the edge between the nodes (1 - 2) and (6 - 2) has a similarity value of 0.11 and corresponds to the objects labeled 1, 2 and 6, which do not form a *globally* aligned *triplet*.

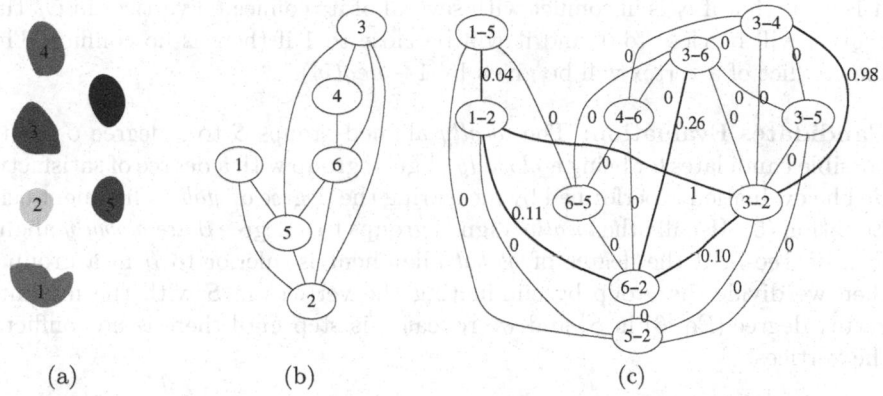

Fig. 2. (a) Labeled image (b) Neighborhood graph (c) Dual graph of (b)

Returning to the conditions expressed by the relations $R1$ and $R2$ of *locally* alignment, the first one states that *triplets* should be *globally* aligned, and the second one that the group should be formed by connected objects according to the *Neigh* relation. Then a group S satisfies these relations if and only if the subset $\tilde{S} \subseteq \tilde{V}$ which represents the dual of S satisfies the following relations:

$\tilde{R}1 : \forall \tilde{v}_i, \tilde{v}_j \; Conn(\tilde{v}_i, \tilde{v}_j) \Rightarrow (\tilde{s}_{ij} \geq \beta)$

$\tilde{R}2 : \forall \tilde{v}_i, \tilde{v}_j \; \exists \tilde{u}_0, \ldots \tilde{u}_K$ for $K > 1$ such that $\tilde{u}_0 = \tilde{v}_i, \tilde{u}_N = \tilde{v}_j$ and $\bigwedge\limits_{k=0}^{K-1} Conn(\tilde{u}_0, \tilde{u}_k)$,

where $Conn(\tilde{u}, \tilde{v})$ is true if there exists an edge between $\tilde{u}$ and $\tilde{v}$. Condition $\tilde{R}2$ expresses that $\tilde{S}$ should be connected, since if $\tilde{S}$ is not connected then S is not connected. Therefore, a *locally* aligned group is a subset $S \subseteq V$ for which its dual set $\tilde{S} \subseteq \tilde{V}$ is connected in $\tilde{G}$ and the value of all the edges joining the vertices within $\tilde{S}$ is greater than or equal to β.

To extract the $\tilde{S}_i \subseteq \tilde{V}$ corresponding to the dual sets of the *locally* aligned sets $S_i \subseteq V$, first we extract the connected components $\{C_k\}$ of $\tilde{V}$ which are connected by an edge value greater that β. Then for each C_k we obtain the minimum value of its edges denoted by $cons(C_k)$:

$$cons(C_k) = \min\{\tilde{s}_{ij}|\tilde{v}_i, \tilde{v}_j \in C_k\}$$

If $cons(C_k) < \beta$ then C_k does not satisfy $\tilde{R}1$, thus vertices are removed until $cons(C_k) \geq \beta$. The vertices which are removed are the ones having more conflict with their neighbors in C_k. We say that two connected vertices $\tilde{u}_i$ and $\tilde{v}_j$ are in conflict if $\tilde{s}_{ij}$ is close to zero, that is if the corresponding orientation histograms of both vertices are not similar. We measure the conflict of a vertex $\tilde{v}_t$ with its neighbors in C_k by using what we call the degree of the vertex in C_k given by:

$$deg(\tilde{v}_t) = \frac{\sum_{\tilde{v}_j \in C_k} \tilde{s}_{tj}}{|\{(i,j)|\tilde{v}_j \in C_k\}|}. \tag{6}$$

It is clear that if $\tilde{v}_t$ is in conflict with several of its connected vertices in C_k then $deg(\tilde{v}_t)$ will be close to 0, and it will be close to 1 if there is no conflict. Then the conflict of a vertex will be given by $1 - deg(\tilde{v}_t)$.

Candidates Evaluation: The *locally* aligned groups S to a degree β are the possible candidates for being a *globally* aligned group with a degree of satisfaction β. The evaluation is performed by measuring the degree of *global* alignment using Equation (5). Usually the *locally* aligned groups to a degree β are *globally* aligned to a degree β. If the degree of *global* alignment is inferior to β in a group S, then we divide the group by eliminating the vertices in $\tilde{S}$ with the minimum vertex degree (Eq. 6) in $\tilde{S}$, and we repeat this step until there is no conflict in the vertices.

Adding More Elements to the Group: Once the *globally* aligned groups of objects are identified, it is possible to add new objects to the group or fusion two *globally* aligned groups to obtain a larger *globally* aligned group. For each group S_i we perform two morphological directional dilations of the group in the directions θ and $\theta + \pi$, where θ is the orientation of the alignment (the angle which maximizes the conjunction of the orientation histograms $O(a_i, S \setminus \{a_i\})$). These dilations will be denoted by $D_{\nu_\theta}(S_i)$ and $D_{\nu_{\theta+\pi}}(S_i)$. An object a which satisfies the $Neigh$ relation with one of the members of S_i and which is seen by S_i to a degree greater than or equal to β (that is $\mu_{include}(a, D_{\nu_\theta}(S_i) \cup D_{\nu_{\theta+\pi}}(S_i)) \geq \beta$, where $\mu_{include}$ denotes a degree of inclusion [2]) is added to S_i. If a whole group S_j is seen by S_i and one of the elements of S_i is connected to one of the members S_j and both groups have similar orientation, then both groups are fused into one.

4   Complexity Analysis

In this section we deal with the cost of the basic operations of the algorithm for extracting *locally* aligned groups and *globally* aligned groups.

First, we consider the complexity of extracting *locally* aligned groups. Consider we have N objects each with at most n_o points. The complexity of the algorithm is $O(N^2)$ since most of steps of the algorithm deal with operations over the graph or its dual. It should be noticed that the step which corresponds to the construction of the orientation histograms has a complexity of $O(N^2 n_o^2)$, since at maximum there are $N(N-1)$ edges on the graph and for each edge an orientation histogram is constructed and the construction of an orientation histogram has a complexity of $O(n_o^2)$.

The complexity of finding a *globally* aligned group from a *locally* aligned group with N_A elements each having at most n_o points lies on the following steps. The first step consists in evaluating the degree of *global* alignment and division of the group in the case where it is not aligned, and this step has a complexity of $O(N_A^2 n_o^2)$. The second step consists in performing the morphological directional dilations of the group in the directions of alignment θ and $\theta + \pi$, and has a complexity of $O(N_I)$ [1], where N_I is the number of points in the image (see [1] for the implementation of the directional morphological dilation using a propagation method). And finally, the complexity of the step of evaluating the degree of inclusion of each object not belonging to the group into the directional dilations of the group is $O((N - N_A)n_o^2)$, where N is the total number of objects. Hence, summing the three steps we obtain that the total complexity is $O(N_A^2 n_o^2 + N_I)$.

5 Results

We applied the method to the objects of the synthetic image of Fig. 3. The method obtains the *locally* aligned group shown in Fig. 3(b) with degree 0.9, and this group is also *globally* aligned with degree 0.85. The group is then extended to add new objects: Fig. 3(c) shows the degree to which each pixel is observed by the group, and finally Fig. 3(d) shows the aligned group after adding the elements. The degree of *global* alignment of the whole group is 0.8. In this example we used objects of different sizes and the method was able to extract the *globally* aligned group. This example highlights the flexibility of the method, since the green and orange objects fall into the line but the orientation between them is different from the one of the *global* alignment.

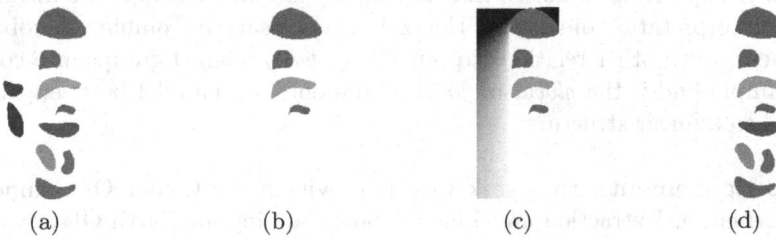

(a)   (b)   (c)   (d)

Fig. 3. (a) Labeled image (b) Locally aligned group (c) The region seen by the group of (b) in the direction of the alignment (white = high value of visibility) (d) Group obtained after adding new elements

We also applied the method to the houses extracted from the satellite image of urban area objects in Fig. 4(b). Figure 4(c) shows some of the *globally* aligned subsets of houses obtained. It is not possible to show all the *globally* aligned groups found by the algorithm since there are objects which belong to more than one group. We can observe that the algorithm obtains the most distinctive groups of the image (pink, orange, white, red and blue sets). However, not all the obtained groups are meaningful for the description of the scene (purple and light green sets), since these are subsets which are *globally* aligned but do not give any information about the arrangement of the houses. Finally, note that all the obtained groups satisfy the notion of *global* alignment discussed in Sec. 3.

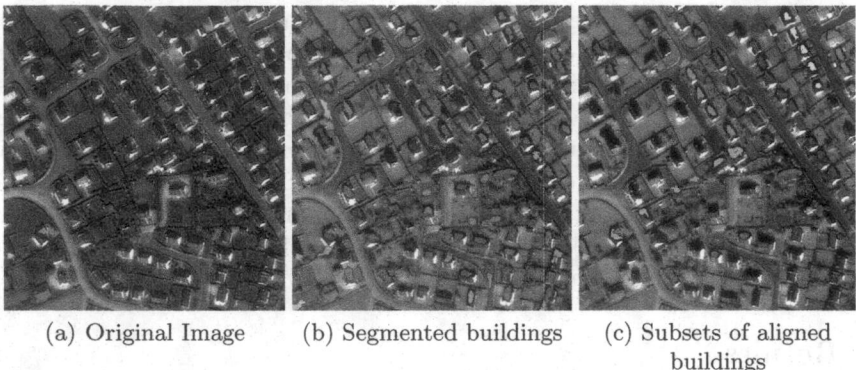

(a) Original Image   (b) Segmented buildings   (c) Subsets of aligned buildings

Fig. 4. Some of the *globally* aligned subsets found by the algorithm with a degree greater than 0.9

6   Conclusions

In this work we have introduced the definitions of *globally* and *locally* aligned groups as fuzzy relations, and gave a method to extract them from an image of labeled objects. Both definitions are appropriate to determine alignments of objects of different sizes. The methods and the definitions were tested on objects extracted from real images, giving satisfactory results. In the obtained results, it is possible to notice that not all the obtained groups are meaningful for the interpretation of a scene. Hence it is necessary to combine the obtained alignments with other relations to put the *globally* aligned groups into context, for example find if the *global* or *local* alignments are parallel between them or parallel to a linear structure.

Acknowledgement. This work was done within the Center Of Competence on Information Extraction and Image Understanding for Earth Observation of CNES-DLR-Telecom ParisTech.

References

1. Bloch, I.: Fuzzy Relative Position between Objects in Image Processing: a Morphological Approach. IEEE Transactions on Pattern Analysis and Machine Intelligence 21(7), 657–664 (1999)
2. Bloch, I.: Fuzzy spatial relationships for image processing and interpretation: a review. Image and Vision Computing 23, 89–110 (2005)
3. Bloch, I., Maître, H.: Fuzzy Mathematical Morphologies: A Comparative Study. Pattern Recognition 28(9), 1341–1387 (1995)
4. Christophe, S., Ruas, A.: Detecting building alignments for generalisation purposes. In: Richardson, D., van Oosterom, P. (eds.) Advances in Spatial Data Handling (Proceedings of 10th International Symposium on Spatial Data Handling), pp. 419–432 (2002)
5. Desolneux, A., Moisan, L., Morel, J.M.: From Gestalt Theory to Image Analysis: A Probabilistic Approach. Interdisciplinary Applied Mathematics, vol. 34. Springer, Heidelberg (2008)
6. Dogrusoz, E., Aksoy, S.: Modeling urban structures using graph-based spatial patterns. In: IEEE International Geoscience and Remote Sensing Symposium, IGARSS 2007, pp. 4826–4829 (2007)
7. Likforman-Sulem, L., Faure, C.: Extracting lines on handwritten documents by perceptual grouping. In: Faure, C., Keuss, P., Lorette, G., Winter, A. (eds.) Advances in Handwriting and Drawing: a multidisciplinary approach, pp. 21–38 (1994)
8. Lowe, D.G.: Three-dimensional object recognition from single two-dimensional images. Artif. Intell. 31(3), 355–395 (1987)
9. Miyajima, K., Ralescu, A.: Spatial organization in 2D segmented images: Representation and recognition of primitive spatial relations. Fuzzy Sets and Systems 65, 225–236 (1994)
10. Ortner, M., Descombes, X., Zerubia, J.: Building outline extraction from digital elevation models using marked point processes. International Journal of Computer Vision 72(2), 107–132 (2007)
11. Ralescu, A.L., Shanahan, J.G.: Perceptual organization for inferring object boundaries in an image. Pattern Recognition 32(11), 1923–1933 (1999)
12. Steiniger, S., Weibel, R.: Relations among map objects in cartographic generalization. Cartography and Geographic Information Science 34(3), 175–197 (2007)

How to Translate Words into Numbers?
A Fuzzy Approach for the Numerical Translation of
Verbal Probabilities

Franziska Bocklisch[1], Steffen F. Bocklisch[2], and Josef F. Krems[1]

Chemnitz University of Technology,
[1] Cognitive and Engineering Psychology, 09107 Chemnitz, Germany
[2] Systems Theory, 09107 Chemnitz, Germany
franziska.bocklisch@psychologie.tu-chemnitz.de,
steffen.bocklisch@etit.tu-chemnitz.de,
josef.krems@psychologie.tu-chemnitz.de

Abstract. The paper describes a general two-step procedure for the numerical translation of linguistic terms using parametric fuzzy potential membership functions. In an empirical study 121 participants estimated numerical values that correspond to 13 verbal probability expressions. Among the estimates are the most typical numerical equivalent and the minimal and maximal values that just correspond to the given linguistic terms. These values serve as foundation for the proposed fuzzy approach. Positions and shapes of the resulting membership functions suggest that the verbal probability expressions are not distributed equidistantly along the probability scale and vary considerably in symmetry, vagueness and overlap. Therefore we recommend the proposed empirical procedure and fuzzy approach for future investigations and applications in the area of decision support.

Keywords: Linguistic terms, fuzzy potential membership functions, probability expressions, probabilistic reasoning, decision making.

1 Introduction

Since the 1960s up to the present time researchers of different scientific areas have sustained an interest in studying the relationship between verbal and numerical probability expressions [1, 2 and 3]. Among these are cognitive psychologists that inquire about the influence of uncertainty expressions on basic cognitive processes such as reasoning and decision making [4] as well as engineers, computer scientists and others that focus on the characterization [5] or on the treatment of uncertainty in applications such as medical decision support systems [6]. This broad interdisciplinary interest may be motivated by the essential role language plays in our daily life. Verbal probability terms, such as *probably* or *thinkable* are very widely used to express uncertainty about the occurrence of future events or about the degree of belief in hypotheses. A typical statement that illustrates the use of linguistic terms in the conversation of market traders exemplarily is: "It is *very unlikely* that there will be a

E. Hüllermeier, R. Kruse, and F. Hoffmann (Eds.): IPMU 2010, LNAI 6178, pp. 614–623, 2010.
© Springer-Verlag Berlin Heidelberg 2010

significant increase in the price of oil in the next month." [7] (p.233). Several studies consistently show that people prefer words over numbers to express uncertainty [8, 9]. This preference may be explained by the possibility of saying something about two different kinds of subjective uncertainty by using only one word. First, the stochastic uncertainty about the occurrence of an event (e.g. the probability of an increase of the oil price) and second, the vagueness of the event or the speakers opinion (e.g. what is meant by "a significant increase" and the speakers subjective belief is only vaguely defined).

The understanding of these kinds of uncertainty, their relations to each other and the way in which they influence human reasoning and decision making is crucial for any application that aims to support decision makers for example in medicine, business, risk management, marketing or politics. In our view, in order to contribute to the understanding of uncertainty, it is essential to first uncover the underlying relationship between word meaning and mathematical concepts such as subjective probability or fuzzy membership. Therefore we propose a general two-step procedure for the numerical translation of verbal probability expressions based on (1) empirical estimates modelled by (2) fuzzy membership functions [10, 11].

At first we compare verbal and numerical probability expressions and discuss existing translation approaches. Then we present our proposal that goes beyond existing methodical issues and the results of an empirical investigation. The contribution to the basic understanding of uncertainty for decision processes is highlighted and consequences, e.g. in the construction of questionnaires and for practical applications in decision support systems, are discussed.

1.1 Verbal and Numerical Probabilities

There is broad agreement concerning the different features of verbal and numerical expressions (see [2] for an overview). Numerical probabilities are commonly described as precise, unambiguous and especially useful for calculations. Additionally, the quality of numerical expressions can be evaluated and compared to predictions of normative models such as Bayes nets. Currently many researchers in the area of cognitive psychology utilize subjective probabilities for the modelling of human reasoning (e.g. Bayes nets in inductive learning and reasoning [12]). This enables the formulation of precise predictions of human behaviour and facilitates the falsification of hypotheses but at the same time it focuses only on the probabilistic understanding of uncertainty. Generally, vagueness is another facet of people's subjective uncertainty and should not be neglected. Zadeh [10] proposed the fuzzy framework for the handling of vagueness and pointed out that probability theory and fuzzy approaches are complementary rather than competitive [13]. Hence, it is possible to combine probability and fuzzy accounts and develop a broad understanding of cognitive uncertainty. The advantages of bridging the gaps have been discussed recently in the cognitive sciences [14, 15].

In contrast to numerical probabilities, probability words are vague, with ambiguous meaning. They cannot easily be used for calculations and their meaning is often only clarified by means of a context (such as domain, speakers' prior knowledge and experience, reference point or prior probabilities and base rates of events). But nevertheless, most people in most everyday situations use words rather than numbers when describing their own uncertainty. Words are perceived as more natural, easier to understand and communicate and they are useful in situations when uncertainty can not at all be verbalized exactly [16]. An example of an approach that deals with words from natural language is computing with words (CW) methodology. It is applied in decision making (see [17] for a review).

Numerical and verbal expressions are closely associated and refer to the underlying concept of probability and there is evidence that people can use numbers and words interchangeably [18] but at the same time they do not mean exactly the same thing. Furthermore it can be assumed from various experimental studies in cognitive psychology that the use of numbers versus words affects human reasoning processes. Windschitl and Wells [4] show that numeric measures of uncertainty tend to sway people toward rule-based, deliberate thinking, whereas verbal expressions tend to elicit more associative and intuitive reasoning. These findings are of particular importance for reasoning situations that create conflicts between logical reasoning and intuitive beliefs (e.g. the belief-bias effect [19]). In belief updating processes, such as customers product evaluation, there is evidence for the influence of information format (verbal vs. numerical) on order effects. An order effect is a judgmental bias that occurs, when the order of information influences opinions in such a way that decisions after A – B differ from those after B – A [20]. There are two types of order effects: a primacy effect appears when the first information is overestimated and a recency effect when the last one is weighted stronger. Order effects can be predicted by situational and individual variables (e.g. length of information series or individual sensitivity to positive/negative information) and they are known to have severe consequences for real-world decisions (e.g. in medical diagnostic reasoning [21] or tactical military decision making [22]). Shen and Hue [23] report that the use of numerical information leads to order effects whereas the use of verbal expressions do not. Generally, it can be assumed that the utilization of numerical vs. verbal expression formats result in different cognitive processes that in turn have different consequences for decisions.

1.2 Translating Words into Numbers

In order to investigate the impact of verbal versus numerical probability expressions on order effects, decision making and the communication of uncertainty means have to be developed for the "translation" of verbal into numerical expressions. There are already a number of translation studies that utilized different estimation and translation procedures. Among these are empirical approaches using direct estimation techniques for instance on a scale from 0 to 100 [24] or pair comparison methods [25] as well as expert consultations for example to create knowledge bases for expert systems [6]. A summary and discussion of different estimation approaches, that map verbal probabilities onto the numerical probability scale, is provided in [2, 11 and 25].

Recurrent findings in the studies using empirical estimations [2] are that the mean estimates of the verbal probability expressions are reasonably similar supporting the idea that words are translatable. But, at the same time, there is a large variability between different individuals indicating inconsistency in word understanding which may lead to communication problems. Although there are different views on whether verbal probability expressions are quantifiable or not [2], we agree with Budescu et al.

[11]. They propose to treat probability words as fuzzy sets and use fuzzy membership functions (MFs) over the probability scale to represent their vague meanings. They elicited judgments of membership by using a multiple stimuli estimation method in which probability values (0, 0.1, ..., 0.9, 1) are presented simultaneously with a verbal probability expression. Their results show that the peak value and skew of the MF describing a probability expression depends on the words meaning. Therefore, they conclude that properties of the MF can predict for example the directionality (positive vs. negative verbal expressions, such as probable vs. improbable) of probability words.

1.3 Objective of the Paper

The present paper has the goal to present a general two-step procedure for the numerical translation of linguistic terms. It is composed of (1) a direct empirical estimation method that yields numerical data participants assigned to presented words and (2) a fuzzy approach for the analysis of the data resulting in parametric membership functions (MFs) of the potential type [26]. We outline this method for verbal probability expressions (e.g. *possible*) but the proposed procedure can also be applied for other linguistic terms such as expressions of frequency (e.g. *occasionally*), strength (e.g. *strong*) or others and is therefore of potential interest for many broad research areas and applications. Furthermore, our method goes beyond existing approaches [e.g. 11] for two reasons: at first, the presented direct estimation method is frugal, efficient and easy to use to yield data from human decision makers. Therefore, it is especially suitable for applications where expert knowledge is crucial but also rare or expensive. Secondly, the proposed parametric MFs of the potential type bring along advantages compared to other MFs [10, 11]. For instance, they are able to account for asymmetric probability terms and are defined continuously over the numerical probability scale. Hence, linguistic terms can be modelled very realistically. In addition, the MFs can be implemented directly in applications (e.g. in fuzzy decision support systems).

In contrast to Boegl et al. [6] we do not expect that the MFs of the probability words are distributed equidistantly along the numerical probability scale and just like Budescu et al. [11] we predict the functions to be skewed and asymmetric in shape.

2 Two-Step Translation Procedure

In this section we present the details of the two-step translation procedure for the numerical translation of verbal probability expressions. At first, the estimation technique and the method of the empirical study is outlined. Thereafter, the fuzzy analysis and the MFs are specified.

2.1 Empirical Investigation

Participants. 121 participants (19 males) took part in the study mainly for exchange of credits. The majority were undergraduate students of the Universities of Chemnitz, Göttingen and Zürich with an average age of 23 years ($SD=4.6$).

Materials and Procedure. Participants read a short contextual story from the area of medical decision making and they were requested to see things from the perspective of a physician. Then they assigned three numerical values to each of 13 exemplars of probability words (see Table 1) that were chosen from previous studies [11, 24 and 25]. Among the three numerical values that had to be estimated were (1) the one that represents the given probability word best and the (2) minimal and (3) maximal values that just correspond. The estimations can be interpreted according to the semantic meaning of the words: the first value characterizes the most typical numerical equivalent for the word whereas the other values indicate the lower and upper border of the verbal probability expression. Participants were instructed to give their estimates in the frequency format (e.g. "In how many of 100 cases a certain diagnosis is correct if it is for instance *improbable*?"). This frequency format of estimation was proved to be better than for instance the estimation of percentages [27]. Participants used a PDF online questionnaire to provide their estimations.

2.2 Fuzzy Analysis

Fuzzy Membership Functions. Membership functions are truth value functions. The membership value (μ) represents the value of truth that an object belongs to a specific class (e.g. that the numerical probability value 0.25 belongs to the word *doubtful*). For the analysis of the empirical data provided by the 121 participants a parametric membership function of the potential type [26, 28] was used.

This function (see Figure 1) is based on a set of eight parameters: r marks the position of the mean value, a is representing the maximum value of the membership function. Regarding a class structure, a expresses the "weight" of the class in the given structure (we use a normalized $a = 1$). The parameters b_l and b_r assign left and right-sided membership values at the borders of the function. Hence, they represent the border memberships whereas c_l and c_r characterize the left and right-sided expansions of the class and therefore mark the range of the class (in a crisp sense). The parameters d_l and d_r specify the continuous decline of the membership function starting from the class centre, being denoted as representative of a class. They determine the shape of the function and hence the fuzziness of the class.

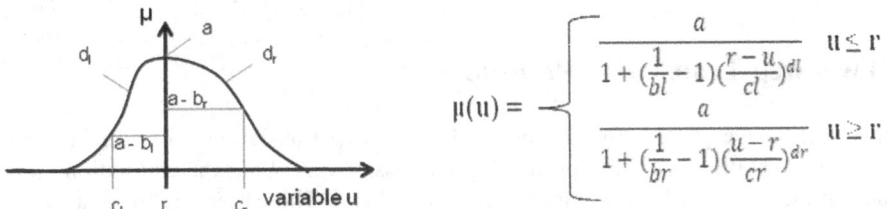

$$\mu(u) = \begin{cases} \dfrac{a}{1 + (\frac{1}{bl} - 1)(\frac{r-u}{cl})^{dl}} & u \leq r \\[3mm] \dfrac{a}{1 + (\frac{1}{br} - 1)(\frac{u-r}{cr})^{dr}} & u \geq r \end{cases}$$

Fig. 1. Parameters of the membership function (for r=0)

A continuous range of membership functions, varying from a high degree of fuzziness to crisp, is available. This function type allows considering asymmetry in fuzzy classes by individual parameters for the left and right hand branches of the function. As we expect the MFs for the probability expressions to be asymmetric, this feature is especially important for the present study.

3   Results

In this paragraph we present the results of the statistical and fuzzy analysis of the present study. The descriptive statistics were calculated with the help of SPSS software. For the fuzzy analysis and the modelling of the MFs a software package (Fuzzy Toolbox) was used [30].

3.1   Descriptive Statistics

Table 1 shows the descriptive statistics for the empirical estimates of the most typical values that correspond to the presented words. The minimal and maximal estimates, that indicate the borders of the semantic meaning of the linguistic terms, were necessary for the modelling of the MFs and so further details are not reported here.

Table 1. Descriptive statistics for the estimates (most typical values)

probability words	Mean	SDev	Skewness	Kurtosis
impossible	1.44	3.009	3.250	13.388
very improbable	5.53	5.477	1.709	2.717
quite improbable	9.99	7.937	1.415	2.200
improbable	11.68	9.027	1.429	1.820
hardly probable	17.01	11.045	1.145	1.023
sparsely probable	18.57	12.185	1.115	.889
doubtful	21.34	13.610	.721	.320
thinkable	49.33	20.241	.347	.100
possible	51.49	21.602	.544	.527
probable	67.68	12.491	-.005	-.850
quite probable	75.07	12.889	-1.012	1.015
very probable	83.95	9.081	-1.023	1.195
certain	96.28	6.453	-2.864	9.987

Results show that the probability words are distributed all over the numerical probability scale with variable distance to each other. The standard deviation and kurtosis show a systematic pattern: probability words near to the borders of the numerical probability scale (e.g. *impossible* and *certain*) have small standard deviations but high values of kurtosis and probability words in the middle (e.g. *thinkable* and *possible*) offer a larger spread but smaller kurtosis values. There are also systematic differences for the skewness indicating that probability expressions with means smaller than $P=0.5$ are skewed to the right whereas words with means higher than $P=0.5$ are asymmetric to the left. These findings are consistent with the results reported by Budescu et al. [11].

3.2   Fuzzy Analysis

Figure 2 shows the MFs for the 13 verbal probability expressions. The representative values (r) indicating the highest memberships are identical to the reported means in table 1.

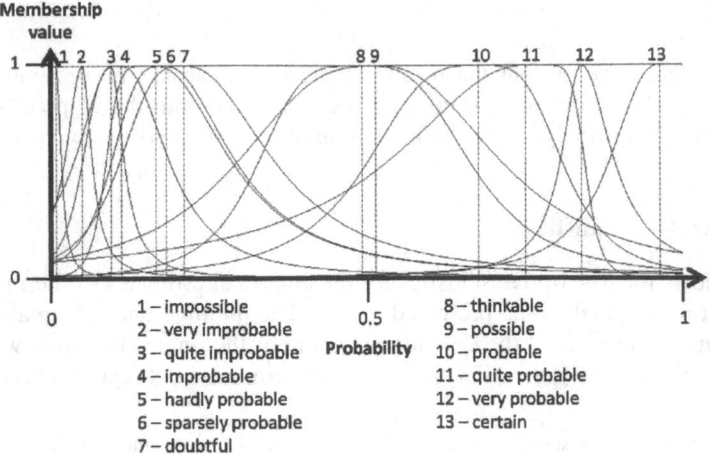

Fig. 2. Membership functions of the 13 verbal probability expressions

Obviously, the functions differ considerably in shape, symmetry, overlap and vagueness. Functions at the borders (e.g. *impossible*) are narrower than those in the middle (e.g. *thinkable*) which is consistent with the observed standard deviations and kurtosis values. Most functions are asymmetric and are not distributed equidistantly along the probability scale. From the functions' positions, three clusters arise, that may be described by (1) *low* (MFs 1-7), (2) *medium* (MFs 8 and 9) and (3) *high* (MFs 10 - 13) probability ranges. The 13 MFs overlap in large part and especially when they belong to the same cluster. To test whether the probability expressions are distinct or not, the participants' estimates were reclassified. Table 2 shows the results of the reclassification.

Table 2. Percentages correct reclassification

probability words	Scale (13)	Scale (5)
impossible	80.0	95.0
very improbable	33.1	
quite improbable	24.8	
improbable	2.5	
hardly probable	15.1	
sparsely probable	2.5	
doubtful	42.4	77.1
thinkable	41.2	61.3
possible	6.6	
probable	44.2	72.5
quite probable	33.9	
very probable	18.4	
certain	93.5	93.5

The second column of the table shows the percentages of the corresponding estimation data that was reclassified correctly. According to these results, some of the probability words are unambiguous and the reclassification was very successful (e.g. *certain*; 93.5% reclassified correctly). Others are inconclusive and almost no estimation data point that was used to describe the MF was reclassified correctly (e.g. *improbable*; 2.5 % classified correctly). Instead, the data was classified as belonging to the neighbor functions.

For a verbal probability scale that could be employed in psychological research or application, a scale with 13 probability words would not be useful because the words are too indifferent according to their meanings. But if a few words with small overlaps are selected, it is possible to create a scale that differentiates very well (see reclassification rate in column three of Table 2). Figure 3 shows an example scale with five probability words described by their MFs.

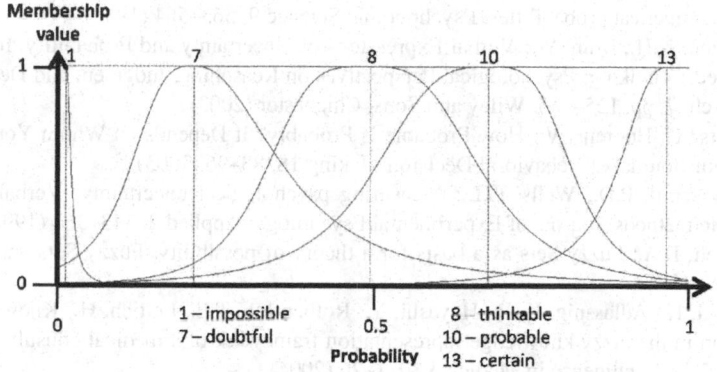

Fig. 3. Membership functions of 5 selected verbal probability expressions

4 Discussion

This paper aims to present a two-step procedure for the numerical translation of linguistic terms that goes beyond existing approaches. First of all, the estimation of three numerical values for each linguistic term (the most typical, minimal and maximal corresponding values) is very frugal and data can be gained very efficiently whereas most alternative procedures are more costly [11]. The resulting estimation data can be analyzed using the proposed parametric MFs of the potential type. Results show, that the functions are able to model the data in a very efficient way, creating averaged membership functions that describe the linguistic terms continuously over the numerical probability scale.

Because of the eight parameters, the functions take into account asymmetry, which was indeed found in the empirical data. Parametric MFs with fewer parameters would model the data without considering asymmetry and would therefore be less accurate and suitable for the reported data. Another advantage of the proposed function type is that the parameters can be interpreted in terms of content on a meta level and illustrate the vague meaning of probability words very realistically.

Large overlaps of the functions (see Figure 2) indicate that the words are very similar in their meanings. Despite the imprecision of natural language, the MFs allow to identify words that are more distinct in their meaning than others. This is especially useful for the creation of verbal probability scales for purposes of research and application that should include unambiguous words when possible.

Finally, the presented translation procedure serves as foundation for future investigations concerning the influence of contexts on word understanding and communication. For instance, it is probable that some of the ambiguous probability words are clarified by the context in which they are used and therefore will become less vague which can be observed in the MFs.

References

1. Lichtenstein, S., Newman, J.R.: Empirical scaling of common verbal phrases associated with numerical probabilities. Psychonomic Science 9, 563–564 (1967)
2. Teigen, K.H., Brun, W.: Verbal Expressions of Uncertainty and Probability. In: Hardman, D. (ed.) Thinking: Psychological Perspectives on Reasoning, Judgment and Decision Making, ch. 7, pp. 125–145. Wiley and Sons, Chichester (2003)
3. Smits, T., Hoorens, V.: How Probable is Probably? It Depends on Whom You're Talking About. Journal of Behavioral Decision Making 18, 83–96 (2005)
4. Windschitl, P.D., Wells, G.L.: Measuring psychological uncertainty: Verbal versus numeric methods. Journal of Experimental Psychology: Applied 2, 343–364 (1996)
5. Zadeh, L.A.: Fuzzy Sets as a basis for a theory of possibility. Fuzzy Sets and Systems 1, 3–28 (1978)
6. Boegl, K., Adlassnig, K.-P., Hayashi, Y., Rothenfluh, T.E., Leitich, H.: Knowledge acquisition in the fuzzy knowledge representation framework of a medical consultation system. Artificial Intelligence in Medicine 30, 1–26 (2004)
7. Zadeh, L.: Toward a perception-based theory of probabilistic reasoning with imprecise probabilities. Journal of statistical planning and inference 105, 233–264 (2002)
8. Erev, E., Cohen, B.L.: Verbal versus numerical probabilities: Efficiency, biases, and the preference paradox. Organizational Behaviour and Human Decision Processes 45, 1–18 (1990)
9. Wallsten, T.S., Budescu, D.V., Zwick, R., Kemp, S.M.: Preferences and reasons for communicating probabilistic information in numerical or verbal terms. Bullet of the Psychonomic Society 31, 135–138 (1993b)
10. Zadeh, L.A.: Fuzzy sets. Information and Control 8, 338–353 (1965)
11. Budescu, D.V., Karelitz, T.M., Wallsten, T.S.: Predicting the Directionality of Probability Words from Their Membership Functions. Journal of Behavioral Decision Making 16, 159–180 (2003)
12. Tenenbaum, J.B., Griffiths, T.L., Kemp, C.: Theory-based Bayesian models of inductive learning and reasoning. Trends in Cognitive Sciences 10(7), 309–318 (2006)
13. Zadeh, L.A.: Discussion: Probability Theory and Fuzzy Logic Are Complementary Rather Than Competitive. Technometrics 37, 271–276 (1995)
14. Dubois, D., Prade, H.: Fuzzy sets and probability: mis-understandings, bridges and gaps. In: Proceedings of the 2nd IEEE International Conference on Fuzzy Systems (FUZZ-IEEE'93), pp. 1059–1068 (1993)
15. Singpurwalla, N.D., Booker, J.M.: Membership Functions and Probability Measures of Fuzzy Sets. Journal of the American Statistical Association 99(467), 867–877 (2004)

16. Wallsten, T.S., Budescu, D.V., Zwick, R.: Comparing the Calibration and Coherence of Numerical and Verbal Probability Judgments. Management Science 39(2), 176–190 (1993)
17. Herrera, E., Alfonso, S., Chiclana, F., Herrera-Viedma, E.: Computing with words in decision making: foundations, trends and prospects. Fuzzy Optimization and Decision Making (8), 337–364 (2009)
18. Jaffe-Katz, A., Budescu, D.V., Wallsten, T.S.: Timed magnitude comparisons of numerical and nonnumerical expressions of uncertainty. Memory & Cognition 17, 249–264 (1989)
19. Evans, J.S.B.T.: In two minds: dual-process accounts of reasoning. Trends in Cognitive Sciences 7(10), 454–459 (2003)
20. Hogarth, R.M., Einhorn, H.J.: Order Effects in Belief Updating: The Belief-Adjustment Model. Cognitive Psychology 24, 1–55 (1992)
21. Chapman, G.B., Bergus, G.R., Elstein, A.S.: Order of Information Affects Clinical Judgment. Journal of Behavioral Decision Making 9, 201–211 (1996)
22. Zhang, J., Johnson, T.R., Whang, H.: The Relation Between Order Effects and Frequency Learning in Tactical Decision Making. Thinking & Reasoning 4(2), 123–145 (1998)
23. Shen, Y.-C., Hue, C.-W.: The role of information presentation formats in belief-updating. International Journal of Psychology 42(3), 189–199 (2007)
24. Beyth-Marom, R.: How Probable is Probable? A Numerical Translation of Verbal Probability Expressions. Journal of Forecasting 1, 257–269 (1982)
25. Wallsten, T.S., Budescu, D.V., Rapoport, A., Zwick, R., Forsyth, B.: Measuring the Vague Meanings of Probability Terms. Journal of Experimental Psychology: General 115, 348–365 (1986)
26. Bocklisch, S.F., Bitterlich, N.: Fuzzy pattern classification – methodology and application. In: Kruse, R., Gebhardt, J., Palm, R. (eds.) Fuzzy Systems in Computer Science, pp. 295–301. Vieweg (1994)
27. Gigerenzer, G., Hoffrage, U.: Using Natural Frequencies to Improve Diagnostic Inferences. Academic Medicine 73(5), 538–540 (1998)
28. Hempel, A.-J., Bocklisch, S.F.: Parametric Fuzzy Modelling for Complex Data-Inherent Structures. In: Proceedings of the Joint 2009 International Fuzzy Systems Association World Congress and 2009 European Society of Fuzzy Logic and Technology Conference (IFSA-EUSFLAT 2009), pp. 885–890 (2009)
29. Bocklisch, S.F.: Handbook Fuzzy Toolbox. GWT-TUDmbH (2004)

Plateau Regions: An Implementation Concept for Fuzzy Regions in Spatial Databases and GIS

Virupaksha Kanjilal, Hechen Liu, and Markus Schneider*

University of Florida, Gainesville, FL 32611, USA
{vk4,heliu,mschneid}@cise.ufl.edu

Abstract. Many geographical applications need to model spatial phenomena with vague or indeterminate boundaries and interiors. A popular paradigm adopted by the GIS community for this task at the modeling level is fuzzy set theory. A spatial object is fuzzy if locations exist that cannot be assigned completely to the object or to its complement. In previous work, we have proposed an abstract data model of *fuzzy spatial data types* for *fuzzy points*, *fuzzy lines*, and *fuzzy regions* to represent the indeterminacy of spatial data. This paper focuses on the problem of finding an appropriate implementation approach to fuzzy regions. The idea is to approximate a fuzzy region by a so-called *plateau region* consisting of a finite number of crisp regions that are all adjacent or disjoint to each other and associated with different membership values determining the degree of belonging to the fuzzy region. *Geometric union, geometric intersection*, and *geometric difference* on fuzzy regions are expressed by corresponding operations on the underlying crisp regions. We leverage that several implementations are already available for crisp regions.

1 Introduction

Spatial databases as the data management foundation of Geographical Information Systems (GIS) represent point, line, and region objects by special data types called *spatial data types* [7]. These data types can be used in the same way as attribute data types as integers, floats, or characters. Their objects have the fundamental feature that they are crisp, that is, they have a definite extent, boundary and shape. However, many spatial objects cannot be described by crisp concepts since they are fuzzy, vague, or indeterminate. A spatial object is fuzzy if locations exist that cannot be assigned completely to the object or to its complement. Hence, spatial fuzziness captures the property of objects that do not have sharp boundaries but rather vague or indeterminate boundaries and interiors. Examples are natural, social, or cultural phenomena like oceans, pollution areas, and English speaking regions. It is impossible to say with precision where the Indian Ocean ends and the Arabian Sea begins. So far, indeterminate spatial objects cannot be represented by available spatial database systems and GIS.

* This work was partially supported by the National Science Foundation under grant number NSF-CAREER-IIS-0347574.

E. Hüllermeier, R. Kruse, and F. Hoffmann (Eds.): IPMU 2010, LNAI 6178, pp. 624–633, 2010.

From a modeling standpoint, especially the GIS field has proposed *fuzzy set theory* to characterize and describe indeterminate spatial data. The spatial database field has provided a few proposals to conceptually model such data through *fuzzy spatial data types*. *Fuzzy points*, *fuzzy lines*, and *fuzzy regions* have been defined by appropriately assigning a membership value ranging from 0 to 1 to each point of such an object. A membership value indicates here how strongly or weakly a point belongs to an object. While conceptually some progress has been made, adequate implementation approaches to representing fuzzy spatial data types in spatial database systems are lacking. The main reason is that the sole approximation of the boundary of a fuzzy region is insufficient; the challenge consists in representing its interior with its varying membership values.

The goal of this paper is to provide discrete representations of fuzzy region objects and to specify geometric set operations like union, intersection, and difference on these representations. The idea is to approximate a fuzzy region by a so-called *plateau region* consisting of a finite number of crisp regions that are all adjacent or disjoint to each other and associated with different membership values determining the degree of belonging to the fuzzy region. The benefit of this approach is that we can leverage widely available concepts and implementations of well known crisp region objects. Geometric set operations on plateau regions are expressed by corresponding operations on the underlying crisp regions.

Section 2 discusses related work on approaches to fuzzy spatial data handling. Section 3 reviews our abstract definition of fuzzy regions, describes our approach to representing them by means of plateau regions, and provides a formal definition of plateau regions. Section 4 focuses on the plateau versions of the geometric set operations *fuzzy union*, *fuzzy intersection*, and *fuzzy difference*. These versions are named *plateau union*, *plateau intersection*, and *plateau difference*. Section 5 draws some conclusions and considers future work.

2   Related Work

The geoscience and GIS communities have proposed a large number of conceptual approaches to handling spatial vagueness that are based on fuzzy set theory [10]. Unfortunately, all these approaches have not been devised for a use in a spatial database context and thus do not enable fuzzy spatial data representation, handling, and querying in databases. The work in [1] has been the first approach in this direction. It presents fuzzy set theoretic approaches for handling imprecision in spatial analysis and introduces *fuzzy regions* as a binary relation on the domain of $\mathbb{N}^2$ ($\mathbb{N}$ denotes the set of natural numbers). The authors themselves have designed an abstract model of *fuzzy spatial data types* [8] based on fuzzy point set topology. This model provides data types for *fuzzy points*, *fuzzy lines*, and *fuzzy regions* as special fuzzy sets from $\mathbb{R}^2$ and also includes important operations on these types like *fuzzy geometric union*, *fuzzy geometric intersection*, and *fuzzy geometric difference*. These concepts have been deliberately developed as a specification for a possible implementation in spatial database systems. A similar type system of so-called *vague spatial data types* is introduced in [5]. Instead of the term "fuzzy", the authors use the term "vague". They distinguish vague points, vague lines, and vague regions with single and multiple components. The operations are similar to our approach described above. All approaches do not provide an implementation of these data types in a spatial database system.

Implementation approaches are only available for a limited class of indeterminate spatial objects. The approaches in [3,4] and our own approach, the *Vague Spatial Algebra* (*VASA*) [6], leverage a three-valued logic with the truth values *true*, *false*, and *maybe*. They approximate a fuzzy region by identifying parts which *definitely* belong to the object, parts which do *definitely not* belong to the object and parts which *maybe* belong to the object. The attractiveness and benefit of these approaches rest on the fact that their conceptual and implementation framework is based on well known, general, and exact models of crisp spatial data types and thus on a wide range of existing definitions, techniques, data structures, and algorithms for crisp spatial objects that need not be redeveloped but only modified and extended, or simply used. However, these approaches are not general enough to represent fuzzy region objects due to their restriction to three truth values and thus three membership values (0, 0.5, 1). On the other hand, plateau region objects with their n-valued logic extend these approaches and preserve their benefits. They provide a better approximation of fuzzy regions as there is no restriction on the number of approximation levels.

3   Plateau Regions

In this section, we propose so-called *plateau regions* as an implementation concept for the fuzzy spatial data type *fregion* for fuzzy regions. We first informally review our earlier abstract definition of fuzzy regions from [8] in Section 3.1. Section 3.2 informally introduces plateau regions for their implementation. In Section 3.3, we give a formal definition of plateau regions.

3.1   Fuzzy Regions

Spatial data handling in available GIS and spatial database systems rests on the assumption that spatial objects like region objects are precisely determined, that each interior point fully belongs to that object, and that the object is delimited by a precisely specified boundary. Many spatial objects, especially those describing natural, social, and cultural phenomena, do not follow this pattern. They are characterized by the feature of *spatial vagueness*. For indeterminate regions this means that the interior may be vague and that the boundary may be blurred.

Figure 1a illustrates an air-polluted area around a chemical factory located at position A. The exhaust fumes emitted by the factory spread around in the region surrounding the factory at A and create a pollution cloud. The shaded region shows the area which has been affected by the pollution particles. The density of pollution particles around the factory is not uniform but varies. The central zone indicated by a darker gray shading has a higher pollution density, and the surrounding zone shown by a lighter gray shading has a lower density.

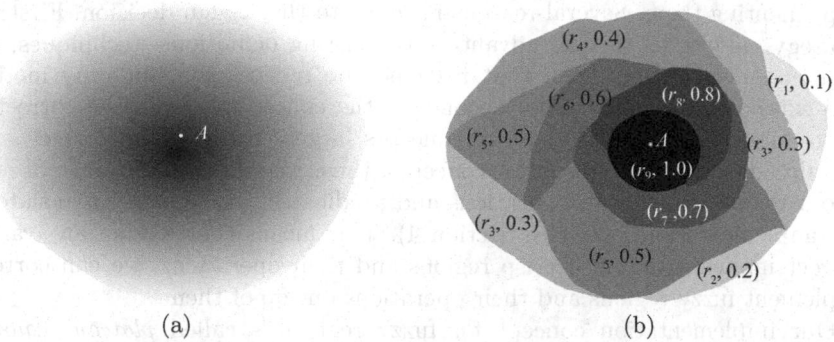

Fig. 1. An example of a fuzzy region modeling an air-polluted area (a) and its representation as a plateau region (b)

There is no clear boundary of this region. We model such a spatial phenomenon by a *fuzzy region*.

Fuzzy set theory [10] has been a popular approach to modeling vague spatial objects and resulted in a concept of fuzzy regions [5,8]. A crisp region object is conceptually modeled as a particular point set of the Euclidean plane [7,9]. Each of its points belongs definitely and completely to it. Let *region* be the spatial data type for crisp region objects. In contrast, a fuzzy region object is conceptually modeled as a particular point set of the Euclidean plane such that each of its points may completely, partially, or not at all belong to it. This especially means that a point can belong to multiple fuzzy spatial objects. Let *fregion* be the spatial data type for fuzzy region objects. If $\tilde{A} \in$ *fregion*, this means that each point of $\mathbb{R}^2$ is mapped to a value of the real interval $[0, 1]$ that represents the degree of its membership in $\tilde{A}$. Hence, for a fuzzy region $\tilde{A}$, $\mu_{\tilde{A}} : \mathbb{R}^2 \to [0, 1]$ is its *membership function*, and $\tilde{A} = \{(p, \mu_{\tilde{A}}(p)) \mid p \in \mathbb{R}^2\}$ describes all its points in $\mathbb{R}^2$ with their membership values. The distribution of membership values within a fuzzy region may be smooth, continuous, or piecewise continuous.

3.2 Plateau Regions as a Representation of Fuzzy Regions

To the authors' best knowledge, implementations of fuzzy regions are not available, especially not in a spatial database and GIS context. A crisp, curvilinear region is usually approximated by well known polygonal structures for outer cycles and holes cycles of its components with the assumption that the enclosed interior belongs completely to the region. However, such an approximation is not so easy to obtain for fuzzy regions since first, they usually have an indeterminate boundary and a blurred interior, second, they have infinitely many interior points but only finitely many representations can be kept in a computer, and third, each point can have a different membership value.

In this paper, the fundamental idea for representing and approximating fuzzy regions is to leverage available crisp spatial data types [7] and software packages implementing them. Several reasons have led to this design decision. First, this strategy enables us to take advantage of existing definitions, techniques, data structures, algorithms, etc., that need not be redeveloped but only modified and extended, or simply used. Second, at the conceptual level, the correctness of the definitions of fuzzy spatial concepts largely rests on the correctness of the already defined crisp spatial concepts; thus, we reduce the chance of errors in our definitions. Third, operations and predicates can be easily translated to the implementation level (see Section 4). This means that having an available correct implementation of crisp regions and their operations, we can correctly implement fuzzy regions and their operations on top of them.

Our implementation concept for fuzzy regions is called *plateau region*. A plateau region is a finite collection of crisp regions where each region is associated with a membership value and thus forms a "plateau" consisting of a conceptually infinite number of points of equal membership. Figure 1b illustrates the concept and shows a representation of the fuzzy region in Figure 1a as a plateau region with the nine crisp regions $r_1, \ldots, r_9$ and their associated membership values. All membership values are different, and any pair of crisp regions is either disjoint (e.g., r_1 and r_9) or adjacent (e.g., r_2 and r_5). A single crisp region can consist of several components (e.g., r_3) that all have the same membership value. Any two crisp regions of a plateau region must be either disjoint or adjacent since otherwise two crisp regions would share interior points with different membership values. While this can be avoided for interior points, this is not the case for the boundaries of two or more adjacent crisp regions since they have common points with different membership values. In Figure 1b, e.g., r_3 and r_5 have the membership values 0.3 and 0.5, respectively, and r_4, r_6, and r_8 have the membership values 0.4, 0.6, and 0.8 respectively. We solve this inconsistency by assigning the highest membership value to all common boundary points of two or more adjacent crisp regions (e.g., in Figure 1b, this is 0.5 for r_3 and r_5, and 0.8 for r_4, r_6, and r_8). The reason is that a boundary point shared by n crisp regions ($n \geq 2$) is guaranteed to belong to the fuzzy region with the highest membership value among the membership values of the n regions.

3.3   Formal Definition of Plateau Regions

We are now able to give a formal definition of the spatial data type *fregion* for fuzzy regions based on the concept of plateau regions.

$fregion = \{pr_1, \ldots, pr_k \mid$
(i) $k \in \mathbb{N}$
(ii) $\forall 1 \leq i \leq k : pr_i = \langle (r_{i,1}, m_{i,1}), \ldots, (r_{i,n_i}, m_{i,n_i}) \rangle$
(iii) $\forall 1 \leq i \leq k : n_i \in \mathbb{N} \cup \{0\}$
(iv) $\forall 1 \leq i \leq k \; \forall 1 \leq j \leq n_i : r_{i,j} \in region$
(v) $\forall 1 \leq i \leq k \; \forall 1 \leq j \leq n_i : m_{i,j} \in \,]0,1]$
(vi) $\forall 1 \leq i \leq k \; \forall 1 \leq j < l \leq n_i : r_{i,j} \; disjoint \; r_{i,l} \; \lor \; r_{i,j} \; meets \; r_{i,l}$
(vii) $\forall 1 \leq i \leq k \; \forall 1 \leq j < l \leq n_i : m_{i,j} < m_{i,l}$
(viii) $\forall 1 \leq i \leq k \; \forall 1 \leq j \leq n_i \; \forall p \in r_{i,j}^\circ : \mu(p) = m_{i,j}$
(ix) $\forall 1 \leq i \leq k \; \forall p \in \bigcup_{j=1}^{n_i} \partial r_{i,j} : \mu(p) = \max\{m_{i,j} \mid 1 \leq j \leq n_i, p \in \partial r_{i,j}\}\}$

Each plateau region is represented as a finite sequence of pairs (condition (ii)) consisting of an object of the well known *spatial data type region* [7] for complex crisp regions (condition (iv)) and a membership value (condition (v)) indicating the degree of belonging of the crisp region to the fuzzy region. We call such a crisp region a *subregion* of the plateau region. The number of pairs, and hence regions, depends on each plateau region and can thus be different for different plateau regions (condition (iii)). If the number of pairs is equal to zero, we obtain the *empty plateau region*. Condition (vi) states that any two crisp regions associated with a plateau region are topologically either disjoint or adjacent to each other. This is expressed by the well known *topological predicates disjoint* and *meet* on complex regions [9]. Condition (vii) requires that all membership values are different and that all pairs of the sequence are ordered by their membership values. This caters for a unique representation of a plateau region. Conditions (viii) and (ix) take care of a precise assignment of membership values to the points of a plateau region. The $^\circ$ operator and the ∂ operator used in the conditions are point-set topological operators which determine all interior points and boundary points, respectively, of a point set. All interior points of a crisp subregion obtain the membership value associated with the region in a corresponding pair of the sequence (condition (viii)) of a plateau region. Each boundary point obtains the highest membership value of all crisp subregions of a plateau region to which the point belongs (condition (ix), compare to Section 3.2). Note that we do not explicitly represent and store single boundary points or linear boundary parts that have a different membership value than the interior of a pertaining subregion.

4   Geometric Set Operations on Plateau Regions

Geometric set operations belong to the most important operations on spatial objects. In the fuzzy region case, the operations fuzzy intersection, fuzzy union, and fuzzy difference all have the signature *fregion* × *fregion* → *fregion* and are supposed to be represented by corresponding operations on plateau regions. These operations are defined on the basis of the already existing geometric set operations *intersection* ($\otimes$), *union* ($\oplus$), and *difference* ($\ominus$) on crisp regions.

Their formal definition requires an auxiliary construction operator $\odot$ that enables us to insert a pair $(r, m) \in region \times [0, 1]$ into the ordered representation of a plateau region $pr = \langle (r_1, m_1), \ldots, (r_n, m_n) \rangle$ for some $n \in \mathbb{N}$. We define:

$$pr \odot (r, m) =$$
$$\begin{cases} pr & \text{if } r = \varnothing \text{ or } m = 0 \\ \langle (r, m) \rangle & \text{if } pr = \langle \rangle \text{ and } r \neq \varnothing \\ \langle (r_1, m_1), \ldots, (r_i \oplus r, m_i), \ldots, (r_n, m_n) \rangle \\ \qquad \text{if } r \neq \varnothing \text{ and } n \geq 1 \text{ and } \exists i \in \{1, \ldots, n\} : m_i = m \\ \langle (r_1, m_1), \ldots, (r_i, m_i), (r, m), (r_{i+1}, m_{i+1}), \ldots, (r_n, m_n) \rangle \\ \qquad \text{if } r \neq \varnothing \text{ and } n \geq 2 \text{ and } \exists i \in \{1, \ldots, n-1\} : m_i < m < m_{i+1} \\ \langle (r, m), (r_1, m_1), \ldots, (r_n, m_n) \rangle \text{ if } r \neq \varnothing \text{ and } n \geq 1 \text{ and } m < m_1 \\ \langle (r_1, m_1), \ldots, (r_n, m_n), (r, m) \rangle \text{ if } r \neq \varnothing \text{ and } n \geq 1 \text{ and } m > m_n \end{cases}$$

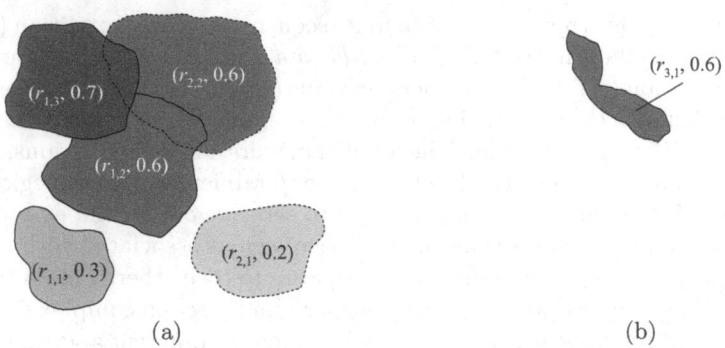

(a)   (b)

Fig. 2. A scenario of two fuzzy regions modeled as plateau regions pr_1 and pr_2 (a) and their geometric intersection $pr_3 = fintersection(pr_1, pr_2)$ (b)

Note that $\odot$ is left-associative, i.e., $pr \odot (r_1, m_1) \odot (r_2, m_2) = (pr \odot (r_1, m_1)) \odot (r_2, m_2)$. For $pr \odot (r_1, m_1) \odot \ldots \odot (r_n, m_n)$ we also write $pr \odot \bigodot_{i=1}^{n}(r_i, m_i)$.

As an illustrating example for demonstrating the geometric set operations, we use the spatial scenario of two plateau regions $pr_1 = \langle(r_{1,1}, 0.3), (r_{1,2}, 0.6), (r_{1,3}, 0.7)\rangle$ and $pr_2 = \langle(r_{2,1}, 0.2), (r_{2,2}, 0.6)\rangle$ given in Figure 2a. Note that each subregion in our example is a simple region but might be a complex region that includes multiple components labeled with the same membership value and that contains holes in the general case.

4.1 Plateau Intersection

Intersecting two plateau regions pr_1 and pr_2 means that each subregion of pr_1 must be geometrically intersected with each subregion of pr_2 and that their smaller membership value is assigned to the resulting non-empty subregion [8]. In our example in Figure 2a, we obtain $3 \cdot 2$ subregion pairs that have to be intersected since pr_1 contains three components and pr_2 contains two components. If the geometric intersection of two subregions is empty, we discard this result. Otherwise, the found subregion is part of the resulting plateau region, and we assign the smaller membership value of both operand subregions to it. The reason is that only the smaller membership value guarantees that the points of the intersection belong to both subregions. For example, in Figure 2a, the intersection of the subregions $r_{1,3}$ and $r_{2,2}$ leads to a non-empty subregion that is assigned the membership value 0.6.

Since the creation of subregion pairs and their intersection is a local operation, it can happen that different resulting subregions are labeled with the same membership value. For example, in Figure 2a, the intersection of $r_{1,3}$ and $r_{2,2}$ will obtain the membership value 0.6. Similarly, the intersection of $r_{1,2}$ and $r_{2,2}$ will obtain the same membership value. Since according to the plateau region definition in Section 3.3 all subregions of a plateau region must have different membership values, we have to compute the geometric union of both subregions obtained so far and assign the common membership value 0.6 to it. Figure 2b shows the result of the plateau intersection for our example. It is a plateau region $pr_3 = \langle (r_{3,1}, 0.6) \rangle$.

The formal definition of the plateau intersection operation leverages the $\odot$ operator that takes care of all the aforementioned particular situations when constructing the resulting plateau region.

Let $pr_1, pr_2 \in fregion$ with $pr_k = \langle (r_{k,1}, m_{k,1}), \ldots, (r_{k,n_k}, m_{k,n_k}) \rangle$ for $k \in \{1, 2\}$. Then

$$fintersection(pr_1, pr_2) = \langle \rangle \odot \bigodot_{\substack{1 \le i \le n_1 \\ 1 \le j \le n_2}} (r_{1,i} \otimes r_{2,j}, \min(m_{1,i}, m_{2,j}))$$

This definition uses an incremental strategy by starting with the empty plateau region $\langle \rangle$ and incrementally adding local results from intersections of subregion pairs.

4.2 Plateau Union

Forming the union of two plateau regions pr_1 and pr_2 means that each subregion of pr_1 must be geometrically merged with each subregion of pr_2 and that their larger membership value is assigned to the resulting non-empty subregion [8]. Two main spatial configurations can arise. If the intersection of the two subregions is empty, both subregions are copied with their respective (equal or unequal) membership values into the resulting plateau region. In Figure 2a, this is the case for the subregions $r_{1,1}$ and $r_{2,1}$. Otherwise, if the two subregions intersect, three new subregions are stored in the resulting plateau region, namely the subregion that is the result of the intersection and that is labeled with the larger membership value, and the two subregions from which we subtract the intersection and which we label with their original membership values. A subregion obtained as an intersection of two subregions gets their larger membership value since at least one of them can guarantee the higher extent of belonging. In Figure 2a, the intersections of $r_{1,3}$ and $r_{2,2}$ as well as of $r_{1,2}$ and $r_{2,2}$ are non-empty. In the first case, we obtain a subregion as an intersection with the membership value 0.7, the subregion of $r_{1,3}$ from which we subtract the intersection with the membership value 0.7, and the subregion of $r_{2,2}$ from which we subtract the intersection with the membership value 0.6. In the second case, the same strategy leads to three subregions that all have the membership value 0.6. Subregions with the same membership value have always to be merged in the resulting plateau region. Figure 3a shows the result of the plateau union for our example. It is a plateau region $pr_4 = \langle (r_{4,1}, 0.2), (r_{4,2}, 0.3), (r_{4,3}, 0.6), (r_{4,4}, 0.7) \rangle$.

For the formal definition of the plateau union operation we assume again two plateau regions $pr_1, pr_2 \in fregion$ with $pr_k = \langle (r_{k,1}, m_{k,1}), \ldots, (r_{k,n_k}, m_{k,n_k}) \rangle$ for $k \in \{1, 2\}$. Then

$$funion(pr_1, pr_2) = \langle \rangle \odot \bigodot_{\substack{1 \le i \le n_1 \\ 1 \le j \le n_2}} \begin{array}{l} ((r_{1,i} \otimes r_{2,j}, \max(m_{1,i}, m_{2,j})) \\ \odot \, (r_{1,i} \ominus r_{2,j}, m_{1,i}) \\ \odot \, (r_{2,j} \ominus r_{1,i}, m_{2,j})) \end{array}$$

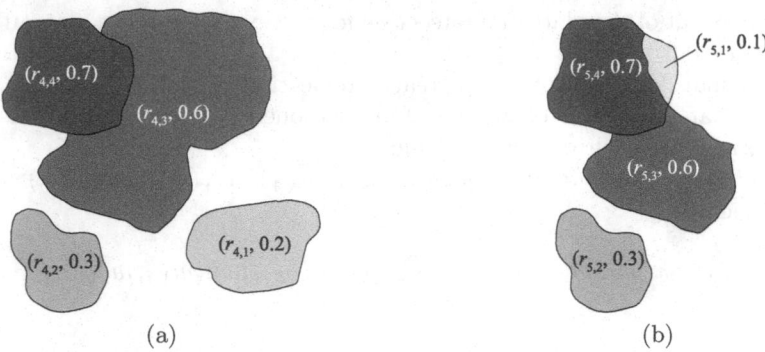

(a)   (b)

Fig. 3. The geometric union $pr_4 = funion(pr_1, pr_2)$ (a) and the geometric difference $pr_5 = fdifference(pr_1, pr_2)$ (b) of the two plateau regions pr_1 and pr_2 in Figure 2a

Again, the $\odot$ operator merges different subregions with equal membership values and orders the resulting subregions with respect to increasing membership values.

4.3 Plateau Difference

Forming the difference of two plateau regions pr_1 and pr_2 means that each subregion of pr_2 must be geometrically subtracted from each subregion of pr_1 and that the membership value of the latter subregion is diminished by the membership value of the former subregion [8]. Two main spatial configurations can arise. If the two subregions do not intersect, then the subregion of pr_1 is copied with its membership value into the resulting plateau region. In Figure 2a, this is the case for the subregion pairs $r_{1,1}$ and $r_{2,1}$, $r_{1,1}$ and $r_{2,2}$, $r_{1,2}$ and $r_{2,1}$, and $r_{1,3}$ and $r_{2,1}$. Otherwise, if the two subregions intersect, we first add the geometric difference of the subregion of pr_1 and the subregion of pr_2 with the membership value of the former subregion to the resulting plateau region. Finally, we add the intersection of both subregions with the difference of both membership values to the resulting plateau region. Figure 2a shows two such scenarios. First, the subregions of $r_{1,3}$ and $r_{2,2}$ intersect. The geometric difference of both subregions is added with the membership value 0.7 to the resulting plateau region. Then the intersection of both subregions is added with the membership value $0.7 - 0.6 = 0.1$ to the new plateau region. Hence, the second subregion "weakens" the first subregion. Second, the subregions of $r_{1,2}$ and $r_{2,2}$ intersect. Again the geometric difference is added in a similar way as before. For the intersection of both subregions we obtain a subregion with membership value 0. This corresponds to an empty region. The $\odot$ operator prevents such a region from being inserted into the resulting plateau region. Figure 3b shows the result of the plateau difference for our example. It is a plateau region $pr_5 = \langle (r_{5,1}, 0.1), (r_{5,2}, 0.3), (r_{5,3}, 0.6), (r_{5,4}, 0.7) \rangle$.

For the formal definition of the plateau difference operation let $pr_1, pr_2 \in$ *fregion* with $pr_k = \langle (r_{k,1}, m_{k,1}), \ldots, (r_{k,n_k}, m_{k,n_k}) \rangle$ for $k \in \{1, 2\}$. For $a, b \in \mathbb{R}$, we define further that $a \doteq b = a - b$ if $a > b$, and $a \doteq b = 0$ otherwise. Then

$$fdifference(pr_1, pr_2) = \langle\rangle \odot \bigodot_{\substack{1 \leq i \leq n_1 \\ 1 \leq j \leq n_2}} ((r_{1,i} \ominus r_{2,j}, m_{1,i})$$
$$\odot (r_{1,i} \otimes r_{2,j}, m_{1,i} \dot{-} m_{2,j}))$$

5 Conclusions and Future Work

This paper introduces plateau regions as an implementation concept of fuzzy regions in the context of spatial databases and GIS. A special characteristic of our approach is that plateau regions rest on well known concepts, data structures, algorithms, and implementations of crisp regions. Since crisp regions are designed and implemented as abstract data types, all structural details are hidden, and all crisp concepts only have to be called and applied.

This paper is the beginning of a larger effort to design and implement a so-called *Spatial Plateau Algebra* that is supposed to offer a type system including *plateau points*, *plateau lines*, and *plateau regions* together with a comprehensive collection of plateau operations and predicates as implementations of their fuzzy counterparts. As to operations, our particular interest relates to metric operations and to topological predicates for fuzzy spatial objects.

References

1. Altman, D.: Fuzzy Set Theoretic Approaches for Handling Imprecision in Spatial Analysis. Int. Journal of Geographical Information Systems 8(3), 271–289 (1994)
2. Burrough, P.A., Frank, A.U. (eds.): Geographic Objects with Indeterminate Boundaries. GISDATA Series, vol. 2. Taylor & Francis, Abington (1996)
3. Clementini, E., Felice, P.: A Spatial Model for Complex Objects with a Broad Boundary Supporting Queries on Uncertain Data. Data & Knowledge Engineering 37, 285–305 (2001)
4. Cohn, A.G., Gotts, N.M.: The 'Egg-Yolk' Representation of Regions with Indeterminate Boundaries. In: Burrough and Frank [2] (1996)
5. Dilo, A., By, R., Stein, A.: A System of Types and Operators for Handling Vague Spatial Objects. Int. Journal of Geographical Information Science 21(4), 397–426 (2007)
6. Pauly, A., Schneider, M.: VASA: An Algebra for Vague Spatial Data in Databases. Information Systems 35(1), 111–138 (2010)
7. Schneider, M.: Spatial Data Types for Database Systems. LNCS, vol. 1288. Springer, Heidelberg (1997)
8. Schneider, M.: Uncertainty Management for Spatial Data in Databases: Fuzzy Spatial Data Types. In: Güting, R.H., Papadias, D., Lochovsky, F.H. (eds.) SSD 1999. LNCS, vol. 1651, pp. 330–351. Springer, Heidelberg (1999)
9. Schneider, M., Behr, T.: Topological Relationships between Complex Spatial Objects. ACM Trans. on Database Systems 31(1), 39–81 (2006)
10. Zadeh, L.A.: Fuzzy Sets. Information and Control 8, 338–353 (1965)

Genuine Linguistic Fuzzy Logic Control: Powerful and Successful Control Method

Vilém Novák*

University of Ostrava
Institute for Research and Applications of Fuzzy Modeling
30. dubna 22, 701 03 Ostrava 1, Czech Republic
Vilem.Novak@osu.cz
http://irafm.osu.cz

Abstract. This paper is devoted to the original idea of fuzzy control — to apply genuine linguistic description of a control strategy. We present the concept of fuzzy logic control which differs from the generally used techniques (based on Mamdani-Assilian or Takagi-Sugeno rules). The leading idea is to *"teach" computer to "understand" genuine linguistic description of a control strategy and follow it analogously as people do*. Our technique applies mathematical theory of the meaning of special expressions of natural language and mathematical theory of formal logical deduction on the basis of (vague) linguistic descriptions. The result is a specific control technique which has several advantages, namely intelligibility, robustness, generality, and also adaptation and learning. We present several examples and mention practical applications.

Keywords: Fuzzy control, evaluative expressions, fuzzy/linguistic IF-THEN rules, linguistic description.

1 Introduction

Fuzzy control is now the standard control method which is a constituent of many industrial systems and companies advertise it no more. The used technique is mostly based on application of fuzzy IF-THEN rules; either of the form first used by Mamdani [1], or by Takagi and Sugeno [2]. Surprisingly, this technique has been theoretically explained and justified only a couple of years ago (cf., e.g., [3, 4, 5, 6, 7, 8, 9, 10, 11, 12]).

The success of fuzzy control is based on the fact that description of real systems is quite often imprecise. The imprecision raises from several factors — too large complexity of the controlled system, insufficient precise information, presence of human factor, necessity to spare time or money, etc. Very often, combination of more such factors is present.

It should be stressed, however, that despite the authors' proclaim that fuzzy control is based on expert knowledge expressed in natural language, the reality is different. Though the rule base of a fuzzy controller is sometimes initially formed on the basis of such knowledge, the used fuzzy sets have in most cases triangular shape and they are further modified to obtain the best control. Consequently, the resulting rule base

---

* The research was supported by the project 1M0572 of the MŠMT ČR.

E. Hüllermeier, R. Kruse, and F. Hoffmann (Eds.): IPMU 2010, LNAI 6178, pp. 634–644, 2010.

comprises of fuzzy sets which have minimal, if any, relation to the original meaning of the words used by experts when presenting their knowledge. Explanation of this fact is easy — the control engineers use, in fact, a system which provides efficient, mathematically well justified *approximation of a control function*. This is the reason why modification of shapes of fuzzy sets is usually necessary. However, it is *not linguistic* control.

In this paper we will demonstrate that the original idea of fuzzy control — to apply genuine linguistic description of a control strategy — can be realized and that it is sufficiently powerful. We will present the concept of fuzzy logic implementation which differs from the above discussed fuzzy control technique. Two specific aspects make it distinguished from the common fuzzy control:

(i) application of a mathematical theory of the meaning of special expressions of natural language. The computer then behaves as if "understanding" them.
(ii) application a mathematical theory of formal derivation (genuine logical deduction) of a conclusion on the basis of (vague) linguistic description.

At present, item (i) requires to limit our use of natural language to narrow but very important part of natural language, namely to the, so called, *evaluative linguistic expressions*, and to *simple conditional statements* formed of the latter. Below, we will speak about fuzzy/linguistic IF-THEN rules. A set of such rules is called *linguistic description*.

Using linguistic description we can characterize the control strategy. Each rule in the description has its own local meaning which is respected during derivation of the conclusion. Furthermore, it is necessary to specify a *linguistic context* of each included variable. The control can be then improved by modifying either the linguistic context, or by modifying (changing) linguistic expressions forming the rule. It should be emphasized that the membership functions are not modified; they are even hidden to the user. This is natural with respect to the main goal of this approach since people also do not specify membership functions to each other when talking.

The conclusion is derived using a special inference rule called *perception-based logical deduction*. This is essentially logical modus ponens realized in fuzzy logic with specific features. The whole concept and the corresponding technique is called *Linguistic Fuzzy Logic Controller* (LFL Controller) and it was implemented in the University of Ostrava in the Czech Republic.

Let us emphasize that the linguistic control realized by means of LFL Control technique is very powerful and general. It enables us to control many kinds of processes with quite different characteristics. The control has a lot of nice properties, namely it is intelligible (the description of the control strategy is well understandable even after years), robust with respect to disturbances and change of conditions, very general, and it can be automatically adapted and it has also good learning abilities. We will discuss them in this paper.

2 Perception-Based Logical Deduction

2.1 Linguistic Descriptions — The Knowledge of Control Strategy

The Linguistic Fuzzy Logic Controller (LFL Controller) is the result of application of the formal theory of the *fuzzy logic in broader sense* (FLb) ([13]). The fundamental concepts of FLb are *evaluative linguistic expressions* and *linguistic description*.

Evaluative (linguistic) expressions are natural language expressions such as *small, medium, big, about twenty five, roughly one hundred, very short, more or less deep, not very tall, roughly warm or medium hot, roughly strong, roughly medium important,* and many others. They form a small, but very important constituent of natural language since we use them in commonsense speech because to be able to evaluate phenomena around. Evaluative expressions have important role in our life because they help us to determine our decisions, help us in learning and understanding, and in many other activities. Let us stress that the evaluative adjectives *small, medium, big* are canonical and, of course, they can be replaced by other proper adjectives depending on the context, for example *deep, shallow, nice, intelligent, beautiful, ugly, weak,* etc. All the details of the theory of evaluative expressions, i.e., their definition, syntactic structure, logical analysis and formal theory of their meaning can be found in the paper [14].

Simple *evaluative linguistic expressions* (possibly with signs) have the general form

$$\langle \text{linguistic modifier} \rangle \langle \text{TE-adjective} \rangle \tag{1}$$

where ⟨TE-adjective⟩ is one of the adjectives (also called gradable) "small, medium, big" (and possibly other specific adjectives), or "zero" (possibly also arbitrary symmetric fuzzy number). The ⟨linguistic modifier⟩ is an intensifying adverb such as "very, roughly, approximately, significantly", etc. Simple evaluative expressions of the form (1) can be combined using logical connectives (usually "and" and "or") to obtain *compound* ones.

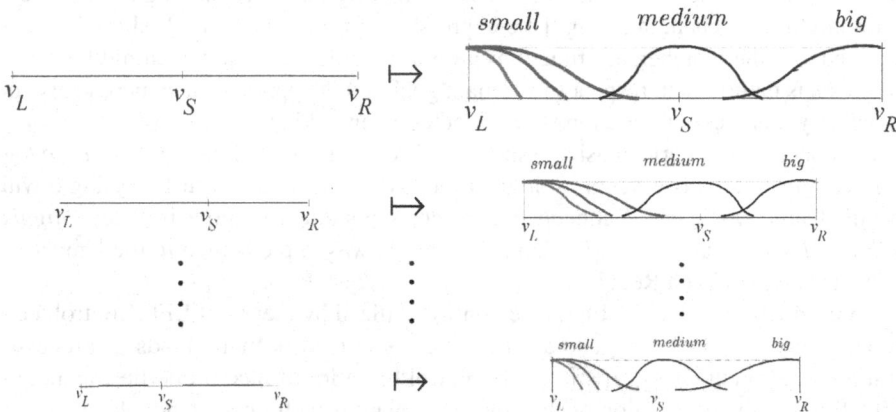

Fig. 1. A general scheme of intension of evaluative expressions (extremely small, very small, small, medium, big) as a function assigning to each context $w \in W$ a specific fuzzy set. The position of the central point v_S can vary and so, shapes of the fuzzy corresponding fuzzy set vary as well.

Two basic kinds of linguistic modifiers can be distinguished in (1), namely those with narrowing and extending effect. *Narrowing* modifiers are, for example, "extremely, significantly, very" and *widening* ones are "more or less, roughly, quite roughly, very roughly". We will take these modifiers as canonical. Note that narrowing modifiers make the meaning of the whole expression more precise while widening ones do the opposite. Thus, "very small" is more precise than "small", which, on the other hand, is more precise (more specific) than "roughly small". The case when ⟨linguistic hedge⟩ is not present is dealt with as a presence of *empty linguistic hedge*. Thus, all the simple evaluative expressions have the same form (1).

We distinguish *evaluative expressions* introduced above from *evaluative predications*, which are expressions of natural language of the form '*X* is *A*'. The *A* is an evaluative expression and *X* is a variable which stands for objects, for example "degrees of temperature, height, length, speed", etc. Examples are "temperature is high", "speed is extremely low", "quality is very high", etc. In control, values of *X* will usually be real numbers.

The semantic model of evaluative expressions in FLb makes distinction between their *intension* (a property) and *extension* in a given *context* of use. This follows the generally accepted idea that intension can be modeled as a function which assigns to each context an extension[1] where the latter is, in our case, a specific fuzzy set. The concepts of intension and extension formalize typical real situations. For example, the expressions *high temperature, high pressure, high tree*, etc. contain the same word "high". In various situations, however, "high temperature" may mean 100°C at home but 1000°C in metal melting process; similarly in the other cases. No satisfactory formalization of such situation without the mentioned concepts is not possible. Thus, the *meaning* of each evaluative expression is identified with its intension. The scheme of intension is in Fig. 1.

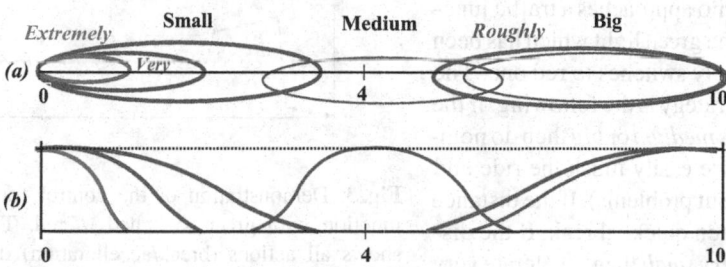

Fig. 2. A scheme of extensions of basic evaluative expressions. Part (a) depicts an intuitive meaning of extensions of the expressions "small, medium", and "big" in a given context ⟨0, 4, 10⟩. Part (b) characterizes them by fuzzy sets.

As can be seen from this example, the meaning of evaluative expressions as well as predications relates always to some *linguistic context*. We will model it by an ordered triple of real numbers ⟨v_L, v_S, v_R⟩ where $v_L < v_S < v_R$. The number v_L is a left bound so that all small values fall between v_L and v_S. Similarly, v_R is a right bound and all big values fall between v_S and v_R. Finally, all values around v_S are "medium". Thus, intension in a given context gives rise to *extension* (cf. Fig. 2). We can thus construct the meaning of expressions in various situations and, at the same time, still keep their essential properties.

---

[1] This idea has been formulated by R. Carnap but roots already to W. Leibniz.

By *linguistic description* we will understand a finite set of fuzzy/linguistic IF-THEN rules

$$\mathcal{R}_1 = \text{IF } X \text{ is } \mathcal{A}_1 \text{ THEN } Y \text{ is } \mathcal{B}_1,$$
$$\mathcal{R}_2 = \text{IF } X \text{ is } \mathcal{A}_2 \text{ THEN } Y \text{ is } \mathcal{B}_2,$$

$$\cdots\cdots\cdots\cdots\cdots\cdots\cdots\cdots\cdots$$

$$\mathcal{R}_m = \text{IF } X \text{ is } \mathcal{A}_m \text{ THEN } Y \text{ is } \mathcal{B}_m$$

where "X is $\mathcal{A}_j$", "$\mathcal{B}_j$ is Y", $j = 1, \ldots, m$ are evaluative linguistic predications. Linguistic description can be understood as a specific kind of a (structured) text which can be used for description of various situations or processes, or for effective description of a *control or decision strategy*. Therefore, elaboration of linguistic descriptions has many interesting applications in various areas. In this paper, we will focus on control.

Perception-Based Logical Deduction (PbLD). This is the main technique of finding a conclusion on the basis of linguistic description. It should be emphasized that the standard Mamdani–Assilian technique [1] widely used in fuzzy control is a *fuzzy approximation* technique. Using it we can effectively approximate continuous functions (cf. [9, 4]). PbLD, on the other hand, is a logical method developed in the frame of FLb, which enables us to mimic the way how people make their decision on the basic of expert information. The detailed mathematical explanation of PbLD can be found in [15, 16]. In this paper, we will illustrate its behavior on a simple example.

Let us consider control strategy of a driver who approaches a traffic junction and the green light which has been on, suddenly switches to red one. The driver's strategy is the following: if the distance is *medium* or *big* then do nothing (i.e., we easily finish the ride and stop without problems). If the distance is *small* then quickly break. If the distance is *very small* then accelerate very much because this is safer than rapid brake. This strategy can be described using the following linguistic description:

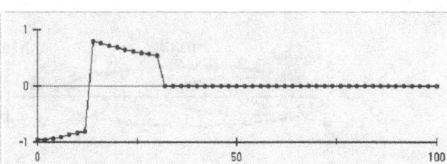

Fig. 3. Demonstration of the control for a traffic junction with green switched to red. The figure shows all actions (break/accelleration) depending on the distance from the junction: first acceleration for very small distance and then break for small one. Otherwise no action.

$$\mathcal{R}_1 := \text{IF Distance is very small THEN } Break \text{ is -very big}$$

$$\mathcal{R}_2 := \text{IF Distance is small THEN } Break \text{ is big}$$

$$\mathcal{R}_3 := \text{IF Distance is medium or big THEN } Break \text{ is zero}$$

where "break is $-$very big" means "acceleration is very big". Note that such linguistic description *characterizes general driver's behavior independently on the concrete place and so, people are able to apply it in a junction of arbitrary size.*

Let the linguistic context of *Distance* be the triple $\langle 0, 40, 100 \rangle$ (in metres) and linguistic context of *Break* force be the triple $\langle 0, 0.4, 1 \rangle$ (relative position of the break/acceleration pedal). If one sees that the distance from the junction is around 10–15 m (and smaller) then his/her *perception* is is that the junction is *very near* (the "distance is very small"). Therefore, it is necessary to "accelerate very much" which might correspond to values about 0.8–0.9. On the other hand, if the distance is around 20–28 m then the perception of the distance of the junction is *near* and so, it is necessary to break strongly. The result of PbLD on the basis of the linguistic description above is depicted in Fig. 3. Note that PbLD can distinguish among the rules and though vague, the result corresponds to the knowledge obtained in this linguistic description.

The basic kind of PbLD leads to monotonous but not continuous behavior. We have also developed a *smooth PbLD* which is monotonous and continuous (see [16]). It is a combination of logical deduction with a special soft computing technique called *fuzzy transform* introduced by I. Perfilieva in [17].

Comparison of PbLD with Mamdani-Assilian Technique. The latter is a a technique providing approximation of a function which is known imprecisely but we have an idea about its course. It works very well with fuzzy sets of triangular (trapezoidal) shape using which a certain imprecise area is characterized. Such fuzzy sets, however, cannot be considered as extensions of evaluative expressions since the latter require the shapes depicted in Figure 2 (for the detailed justification, see [14]). Since they essentially overlap, the Mamdani-Assilian technique cannot cope with linguistic descriptions of the above described form. For example, we can demonstrate that the the driver's behavior would be "break" at any case, but break only "a little" when being very near the junction which would probably lead to car accident. This does not mean, however, that this technique is wrong. It interpolates among the rules and therefore, it cannot distinguish properly the specific rules themselves as is the case of PbLD. The latter, on the other hand, is worse when approximation of a specific function is the main goal. This raises the question which kind of control technique should be used in a specific case.

The Mamdani-Assilian technique is convenient for fuzzy control if the linguistic character of the expert knowledge on the basis of which the control strategy is derived is unimportant and the control engineer thinks mainly in terms of a proper control function. The LFL Controller technique is more general in the sense that it can be used not only for control problems but also for decision-making. It effectively utilizes expert knowledge specified in natural language and, because of that, it can be reconsidered for various kinds of modification even after years because the user (control engineer) can very easily capture meaning of the linguistic description.

3   LFL Controller

3.1   Characteristics of Linguistic Control

The LFL Controller is a special mechanism which applies the above described PbLD method to control. Because of its abilities, the control engineer can focus only on the control strategy which is described in natural language and needs not care about shapes of fuzzy sets; these can even be hidden to him. Instead, the control engineer modifies the used evaluative expressions.

Let us now consider the following variables: *error* E_t, its *derivative/change* dE_t, its *second derivative/change* d^2E_t, *control action* U_t and its *derivative* dU_t. Then the following linguistic descriptions can be used for process control:

(i) *PD-controller*

$$\text{IF } E_t \text{ is } \mathcal{A} \text{ AND } dE_t \text{ is } \mathcal{B} \text{ THEN } U_t \text{ is } \mathcal{C}.$$

(ii) *PI-controller*

$$\text{IF } E_t \text{ is } \mathcal{A} \text{ AND } dE_t \text{ is } \mathcal{B} \text{ THEN } dU_t \text{ is } \mathcal{C}.$$

(iii) *PID-controller*

$$\text{IF } E_t \text{ is } \mathcal{A} \text{ AND } dE_t \text{ is } \mathcal{B} \text{ AND } d^2E_t \text{ is } \mathcal{B} \text{ THEN } dU_t \text{ is } \mathcal{D}$$

where $\mathcal{A}, \mathcal{B}, \mathcal{C}, \mathcal{D}$ are specific evaluative expressions. Of course, any other kinds of variables can also be considered.

The LFL Control control shares nice properties of classical fuzzy control (cf. [8]) but has several additional nice properties:

(a) The linguistic description is written in genuine linguistic form which is well understandable to people, even after years. Therefore, it is easy to modify the description any time without big effort, if necessary.
(b) The linguistic description characterizes a *general control strategy* which is often common to many kinds of processes. Therefore, the same description can be used for control of various kinds of processes with no, or with only little modifications.
(c) The control is very robust and does not require modifications even if the conditions are varying a lot and/or the control is subject to many random disturbances.
(d) The concept of linguistic context turned out to be quite powerful since not only it is possible to learn it partially, but also it can be continuously modified to obtain precise control comparable with classical controllers.

4 Learning

The LFL Control technique has powerful learning abilities. Special algorithms for the following learning problems have been developed:

1. Learning of the linguistic description, i.e. finding a set of linguistic IF-THEN rules.
2. Partial learning of the linguistic context.

4.1 Learning of the Linguistic Description

Let us consider a dynamic process controlled manually by a human operator. The only known general characteristics of the process is that it is a stable process. Our task is to monitor the course of the manual control and to learn the linguistic description on the basis of the obtained data in such a way that LFL Control technique will be similar to that done by the operator. Furthermore, we suppose that the control has proceeded on the basis of errors and their derivations using one of the above considered types of fuzzy PI, PD, or PID control.

The learning procedure has the following steps:

1. Specify a corresponding context for each variable.
2. Find a suitable evaluative predication to each data item. The result is a fuzzy/linguistic rule.
3. Repeat 2. for all the data and generate the linguistic description $\mathcal{R}_1, \ldots, \mathcal{R}_n$.
4. Reduce the generated linguistic description as follows.
   (a) Replace all the identical rules by one only.
   (b) Let $\mathcal{R}_i$ and $\mathcal{R}_j$ be two generated rules such that all terms have the same sign and their succedents be identical. Let the meaning of the antecedent of $\mathcal{R}_i$ be wider than that of $\mathcal{R}_j$. Then exclude the latter rule.
   (c) Let $\mathcal{R}_i$ and $\mathcal{R}_j$ be two generated rules such that all terms have the same sign and their antecedents be identical. Let the meaning of succedent of $\mathcal{R}_i$ be narrower than that of $\mathcal{R}_j$. Then exclude the latter rule.

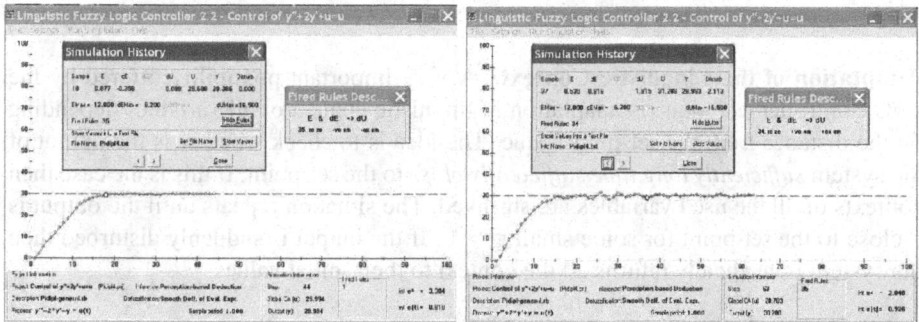

Fig. 4. Comparison of linguistic control using LFLC-technique without and with disturbance which was randomly generated in the input in the range of 20% of the control action. The controller is fuzzy-PI and the controlled proces has the transfer function $\frac{1}{(s+1)^2}$.

4.2 Learning and Adaptation of the Linguistic Context

Learning of the Linguistic Context. By this we mean to find optimal values of the right bound v_R for all the variables. Let us first consider the case of the context of the error c and its change Δe. The idea behind learning of e and Δe is very simple. We start with the assumption that *any non-zero error* in the beginning is *big*. Hence, the context is defined according to the value of the initial error $e(0) = v - y(0)$ where $y(0)$ is the initial process output and v is the required value. Experiments show that this works quite well if we put $V^- = [-k_e e(0), 0]$, $V^+ = [0, k_e e(0)]$ and $W^- = [-k_{\Delta e} e(0), 0]$, $W^+ = [0, k_{\Delta e} e(0)]$ where k_e and $k_{\Delta e}$ are suitable constants (for example, by experiments we have found the values $k_e = 0.7$ and $k_{\Delta e} = 2.4$).

Concerning the context for control action, the situation is more complicated for the context depends on the nature of the controlled process, and also on the technical device used for the control. Therefore, the context must be set by an expert. To set the context for the (change of) control action, we can employ two approaches. First, the context is given by the maximal technically possible position of the "control cap". The other possibility proposed in [18] is based finding optimal values on the basis of two initial values given by expert.

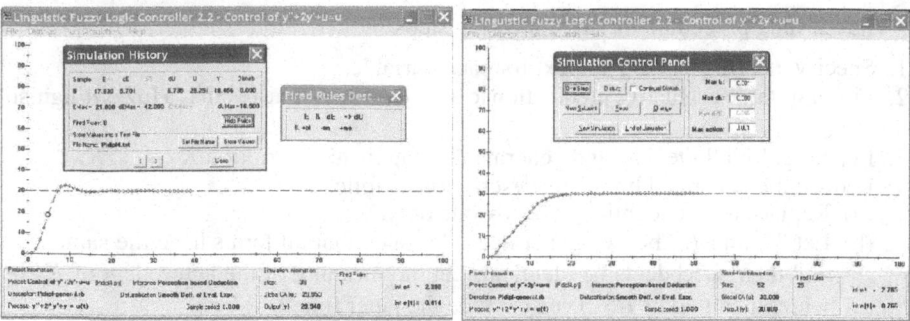

Fig. 5. Linguistic control using LFL Controller technique when the context of error and change of error are learned (left) and when the context is adapted depending on the distance from the set-point (right). The controller is fuzzy-PI and the controlled proces has the transfer function $\frac{1}{(s+1)^2}$.

Adaptation of the Linguistic Context. A very important possibility offered by the LFL Controller technique is adaptation of linguistic context of all variables depending on the distance from the set-point value. The idea is to check whether is the output of the system *sufficiently long time sufficiently close* to the set-point. If this is the case then contexts of all the used variables are shrinked. The situation repeats until the output is ε-close to the set-point for some small $\varepsilon > 0$. If the output is suddenly disturbed then the system immediately returns all the context to their initial values.

5 Practical Applications

There are many various kinds of applications of the LFL Control technique. For example, control of plaster kiln, control system of hydraulic transition water–oil, control of massive 100t steam generator, and few other ones. The most successful application is control of 5 smelting furnaces TLP9 in Al Invest company in a small village Břidličná in the Czech Republic. The applications has been in detail described in [19].

Example of the fuzzy/linguistic rules is the following:

IF E_1 is +Extremely Big AND ΔE_1 is ignored AND E_2 is +Extremely Big

THEN U is Extremely Big

IF E_1 is +Big AND ΔE_1 is +Extremely Big AND E_2 is +Big THEN U is Small

where $E_1 = w - T_1$ is the error of the temperature above the melted metal level, ΔE_1 is its derivative, $E_2 = w - T_2$ is the error of the temperature inside the melted metal, and U is the control action (the amount of the gas brought to the jet). Measuring of the temperature of the metal on two places has been chosen to represent behavior of the metal temperature in two different stages of its melting (melting begins from the top to down, so that some parts may be already fully melted while the others not yet).

The form of rules corresponds to the PD-fuzzy controller. Their number is 155. Though fairly high, we decided not to reduce it. First of all, it was not too difficult to prepare all of them. Moreover, tuning of the whole linguistic description was quite simple because of their linguistic nature (recall that tuning means only replacing less suitable expressions inside the rules by more suitable ones according to their linguistic meaning). Furthermore, the systems turned out to be able to react correctly also in the emergency situations, such as the work of only one sensor instead of two ones. Of course, the control in such a case is worse, but still acceptable.

Because of lack of space, we cannot demonstrate other features of LFL Controller, for example, that just one kind of linguistic description can be used for control of processes with quite different dynamical characteristics. The only thing that must be changed is the linguistic context.

6 Conclusion

This paper is devoted to the original idea of fuzzy control — to apply a genuine linguistic description of a control strategy. We have presented the concept of fuzzy logic implementation (LFL Controller) which differs from the classical fuzzy control technique. Its leading idea is to *teach computer to understand genuine linguistic description of the control strategy in a way to be able to follow it analogously as people do.* Our technique applies mathematical theory of the meaning of special expressions of natural language so that the computer behaves as if "understanding" them. To accomplish the latter, we apply mathematical theory of formal logical deduction. There are hundreds of successful simulations as well as several real working applications of our technique.

The LFL Controler technique has been continuously improved, namely its methodology, adaptation, learning and also improvement in understanding natural language. Let us recall that tuning of our controller means modification of the linguistic description (i.e., changing the words to more suitable ones) or, occasionally modification of the context (but not touching the fuzzy sets which the user may not be aware of). One of the theoretical problems of our technique is proving stability of the proposed controller. This is a conceptual problem because our technique has been proposed for the situations in which the knowledge of the controlled process is very limited and imprecise. Assuring stability in this case is impossible in principle. We can only demonstrate that the PbLD method mimics the way of human reasoning so that if expert control is successful (and stable) then our control accomplishes the same. Mathematical proof of the latter, however, is again impossible in principle.

References

[1] Mamdani, E., Assilian, S.: An experiment in linguistic synthesis with a fuzzy logic controller. Int. J. of Man-Machine Studies 7, 1–13 (1975)
[2] Takagi, T., Sugeno, M.: Fuzzy identification of systems and its applications to modeling and control. IEEE Trans. on Systems, Man, and Cybern. 15, 116–132 (1985)
[3] Buckley, J.J., Hayashi, Y.: Fuzzy input-output controllers are universal approximators. Fuzzy Sets and Systems 58, 273–278 (1993)
[4] Castro, J.: Fuzzy logic controllers are universal approximators. IEEE Transactions on Systems, Man, and Cybernetics 25, 629–635 (1995)
[5] Hájek, P.: Metamathematics of Fuzzy Logic. Kluwer, Dordrecht (1998)

[6] Klawonn, F., Kruse, R.: Equality relations as a basis for fuzzy control. Fuzzy Sets and Systems 54, 147–156 (1993)

[7] Klawonn, F., Novák, V.: The relation between inference and interpolation in the framework of fuzzy systems. Fuzzy Sets and Systems 81(3), 331–354 (1996)

[8] Michels, K., Klawonn, F., Kruse, R., Nürnberger, A.: Fuzzy Control: Fundamentals, Stability and Design of Fuzzy Controllers. Springer, Berlin (2006)

[9] Novák, V., Perfilieva, I., Močkoř, J.: Mathematical Principles of Fuzzy Logic. Kluwer, Boston (1999)

[10] Novák, V., Lehmke, S.: Logical structure of fuzzy IF-THEN rules. Fuzzy Sets and Systems 157, 2003–2029 (2006)

[11] Perfilieva, I., Novák, V.: System of fuzzy relation equations as a continuous model of IF-THEN rules. Information Sciences 177, 3218–3227 (2007)

[12] Perfilieva, I.: Fuzzy function as an approximate solution to a system of fuzzy relation equations. Fuzzy Sets and Systems 147, 363–383 (2004)

[13] Novák, V.: Mathematical fuzzy logic in modeling of natural language semantics. In: Wang, P., Ruan, D., Kerre, E. (eds.) Fuzzy Logic – A Spectrum of Theoretical & Practical Issues, pp. 145–182. Elsevier, Berlin (2007)

[14] Novák, V.: A comprehensive theory of trichotomous evaluative linguistic expressions. Fuzzy Sets and Systems 159(22), 2939–2969 (2008)

[15] Novák, V.: Perception-based logical deduction. In: Reusch, B. (ed.) Computational Intelligence, Theory and Applications, pp. 237–250. Springer, Berlin (2005)

[16] Novák, V., Perfilieva, I.: On the semantics of perception-based fuzzy logic deduction. International Journal of Intelligent Systems 19, 1007–1031 (2004)

[17] Perfilieva, I.: Fuzzy transforms: theory and applications. Fuzzy Sets and Systems 157, 993–1023 (2006)

[18] Bělohlávek, R., Novák, V.: Learning rule base of the linguistic expert systems. Soft Computing 7, 79–88 (2002)

[19] Novák, V., Kovář, J.: Linguistic IF-THEN rules in large scale application of fuzzy control. In: Da, R., Kerre, E. (eds.) Fuzzy If-Then Rules in Computational Intelligence: Theory and Applications, pp. 223–241. Kluwer Academic Publishers, Boston (2000)

Cytoplasm Contour Approximation Based on Color Fuzzy Sets and Color Gradient

Santiago Romaní[1], Belen Prados-Suárez[2], Pilar Sobrevilla[3], and Eduard Montseny[4]

[1] Dpt. Informatics and Mathematics Engineering, Universitat Rovira i Virgili, Spain
[2] Dpt. Software Engineering, University of Granada, Spain
[3] Dpt. Applied Mathematics II, Technical University of Catalonia, Spain
[4] Dpt. Engineering Systems, Automation and Industrial Informatics, UPC, Spain
santiago.romani@urv.net, belenps@ugr.es,
{pilar.sobrevilla,eduard.montseny}@upc.edu

Abstract. Here we propose a method for contour detection of cells on medical images. The problem that arises in such images is that cells' color is very similar to the background, because the cytoplasm is translucent and sometimes overlapped with other cells, making it difficult to properly segment the cells. To cope with these drawbacks, given a cell center, we use hue and saturation histograms for defining the fuzzy sets associated with cells relevant colors, and compute the membership degree of the pixels around the center to these fuzzy sets. Then we approach the color gradient (module and argument) of pixels near the contour points, and use both the membership degrees and the gradient information to drive the deformation of the region borders towards the contour of the cell, so obtaining the cell region segmentation.

Keywords: Color image segmentation, fuzzy characterization, cell contour, color histograms, color gradient.

1 Introduction

Everyday more doctors count on a huge variety of images from which they must extract information, usually in a manual, time consuming and subjective way. Image segmentation, the task of splitting image into homogeneous regions, plays a crucial role in medical areas, since these techniques assist them in diagnosis tasks [1].

Compared with common image segmentation algorithms, the ones used for medical images need more specific background and must satisfy complex and practical requirements. It is due to the partial volume effect, the inhomogeneity of detective fields, the noise and excessive exposition of images at the capture, the focusing problems, the resemblance between the target elements and the background, the presence of translucent objects or the overlapping of elements (like cells), which make medical images imprecise, blurred, and difficult to model and treat [2,13].

The main categories usually distinguished in image segmentation proposals [3] are *clustering methods*, that only consider resemblance in color and require a post processing to incorporate spatial information to get regions; *region based* algorithms that search

E. Hüllermeier, R. Kruse, and F. Hoffmann (Eds.): IPMU 2010, LNAI 6178, pp. 645–654, 2010.

for homogeneous areas, taking into account resemblance in color and spatial information; and *contour based* techniques where great changes and discontinuities in the intensity or color define the borders and limits of the regions, used later to define the regions.

More recent methods specifically developed for medical imaging, such as deformable models, aim to incorporate both the advantages of edge-based and region-based approaches. These methods start with a shape surrounding the target area and define a set of energy functions or force vectors that push the borders of the shape to the contours of the regions. To perform the contour deformation process some methods use edge-functions [1, 2, 4, 5] that stop the curve evolution, but usually only detect objects with edges defined by gradient, and are likely to yield undesirable local minima. To solve this problem other proposals [1, 2, 4, 5] use statistics inside and outside the contour, in addition to the information near the evolving contour. Some improvements on these methods Chan and Vese [6] can handle objects with boundaries not necessarily defined by gradient, but assume highly constrained models for pixel intensities within each region having high computational cost. To overcome this problem some proposals simply use the k-means algorithm [8], or directly calculate the energy alterations [7]. However they usually are quite sensitive to noise and cannot handle objects with ill defined boundaries. In addition soft or imprecise contours, as well as overlapping objects can not be dealt with these proposals.

This is why the latter proposals in the literature are based on fuzzy sets theory. Concretely Krinidis and Chatzis proposed in [9] an algorithm based on an energy minimization where the energy function, based on fuzzy logic, can be seen as a particular case of a minimal partition problem. It is used as the model motivation power evolving the active contour until reaching the desired object boundary, by the fuzzy energy alterations. The stopping term is related to the image color and spatial segments, instead to the gradient. Incorporating fuzziness the method acquires strong robustness to noise and great ability to reject "weak" local minima, as well as independence from the initial position of the model (not necessarily surrounding the target area). Though this proposal remarks the usefulness of incorporating fuzzy logic, it has the main inconvenience that only uses intensity information, which makes that objects without intensity variation are not properly detected.

In [10] Vélez et al. also use, in gray scale images, fuzzy logic and snake models. The snake models are used as energy-minimizing splines, to be applied as shape memory models for biometric identification (signature, palm-print,...). In this case the main objective is fitting the whole contour as much as possible, without loosing it at any point, so the snake can later be used, by comparison, for identification tasks. To do this a new external energy term is introduced: the difference between the angle of the tangent to the snake in a control point and the angle of the tangent to a specific stroke point (for all the strokes of the test pattern).

Our aim here is to incorporate both the advantages of fuzzy logic and contour angle information to the segmentation of medical cells. This way we solve the topology problem of snake methods, and we can adapt and model imprecise contours and overlapping translucent areas, fitting the borders better. Even more, our proposal incorporates the use of the chromatic information, and is applied to medical cell images to show its capabilities.

The majority of the segmentation methods are focused on the RGB space. However, its lack of distinction between chromatic and achromatic information makes it unsuitable for obtaining color edges in an image [11]. This is why we have chosen the HIS color space. In particular, the Smith's HSV model [12] is our preferred transformation since it shows high independence between the three components.

The rest of the paper is structured as follows: first, in section 2, the main structure of our proposal is outlined. Section 3 reviews the computation of the image gradient. Section 4 describes how to obtain the fuzzy sets representing color patterns of cells. Section 5 explains the evolution of contours based on the profiles of image gradient and color fuzzy sets. Finally, sections 6 and 7 show the results and conclusions.

2 General Structure

The algorithm we propose here can be summarized in the following stages.

- Approach the color gradient of the input image (module and argument)
- Load a file with the central position (x, y) of each cell. The centers can be manually given or obtained following proposals in the literature.
- For each cell, define the fuzzy sets for the relevant colors of the cytoplasm, based on hue and saturation histograms of a set of sampling pixels around the cell center.
- Define a set of contour points around each cell center.
- Move the contour points inwards or outwards following its normal direction, according to membership degree and color gradient of the neighboring areas.
- Evolve contour points until their change is less than a certain minimum threshold. The whole process is depicted in Fig. 1 and detailed in next sections.

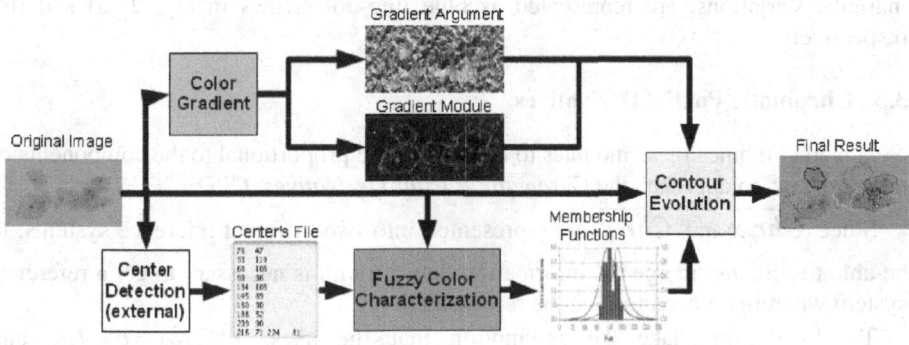

Fig. 1. Workflow of the proposed method

3 Color Gradient Approach

Our proposal to obtain the gradient information is based on the combination of the module and the argument of the *chromatic gradient vector* (CGV). To obtain this module and angle we first combine the chromatic information and later the directional variation, approaching so the two components of the *chromatic gradient vector* (CGV). More information can be found in [14].

3.1 Hue and Saturation First Order Derivatives

Given a pixel p_{ij} of the source image I, we approach the Saturation partial derivatives, $\partial S_{ij}/\partial x$ and $\partial S_{ij}/\partial y$, by taking the saturation plane of the image, and convolving 3x3 kernels of Sobel operator with a window centered on that pixel. We have chosen this operator because of its slightly superior noise-suppression characteristics [13] regarding other similar operators, and its allowance to convolve separately the Hue and Saturation channels of the image.

We perform the same process to approach the *hue partial derivatives* $\partial H_{ij}/\partial x$ and $\partial H_{ij}/\partial y$, but using the circular distance measure defined in [14].

3.2 Directional Chromaticity Variations

In this step we combine the chromatic information obtained in the previous step into one value for each direction.

Here we consider two reference systems, one for the x direction, RS_x, and other for the y direction, RS_y, whose axes are the partial derivatives of H and S in the corresponding directions. These systems are painted as black lines in Fig. 2 (a) and (b). On these systems, we represent the vectors given by $\overrightarrow{Chr_{ij}x} = \left(\partial H_{ij}/\partial x, \partial S_{ij}/\partial x\right)$ and $\overrightarrow{Chr_{ij}y} = \left(\partial H_{ij}/\partial y, \partial S_{ij}/\partial y\right)$ respectively. These vectors, called the Directional Chromaticity Variations, are represented as blue line-dot arrows in Fig. 2 (a) and (b), respectively.

3.3 Chromatic Partial Derivatives

Next step combines these modules to obtain a value proportional to the components of the CGV, i.e. to approach the *Chromatic Partial Derivatives, CPDs*.

Since $\overrightarrow{Chr_{ij}x}$ and $\overrightarrow{Chr_{ij}y}$ are represented into two different reference systems, to be able to mix and merge the information they contain is necessary to get a reference system wherein both vectors can be represented.

To do it, we make the assumption that the axes, $\partial H_{ij}/\partial x = \partial S_{ij}/\partial x$ and $\partial H_{ij}/\partial y = \partial S_{ij}/\partial y$, point to the higher potentials of H and S, and that both components grow equally within these axes. Hence we propose to project the chromaticity vectors into them, approaching the above mentioned CPDs as $\overrightarrow{\partial C_{ij}/\partial x} = proj_{\vec{u}}\overrightarrow{\partial Chr_{ij}x}$ and $\overrightarrow{\partial C_{ij}/\partial y} = proj_{\vec{u}}\overrightarrow{\partial Chr_{ij}y}$, with $\vec{u} = \left(\cos(45°), \sin(45°)\right)$. These new vectors appear as dotted arrows in Fig. 2 (a) and 2 (b).

3.4   Approach to Obtain the Module and Argument of the CGV

Translating the modules of these vectors to the coordinate system of axes $\partial C_{ij}/\partial x$ and $\partial C_{ij}/\partial y$, as indicated in Fig. 2 (c), we get the approach to the module and argument of the Chromatic Gradient Vector as $\left\|\nabla C_{ij}\right\| = \sqrt{\left(\partial C_{ij}/\partial x\right)^2 + \left(\partial C_{ij}/\partial y\right)^2}$ and $\alpha C_{ij} = arctg\left(\dfrac{\partial C_{ij}/\partial y}{\partial C_{ij}/\partial x}\right)$ respectively.

This argument provides us with a direction that is perpendicular to the contour and so it is 0 for a vertical edge and increases for edges moving anti-clockwise of it.

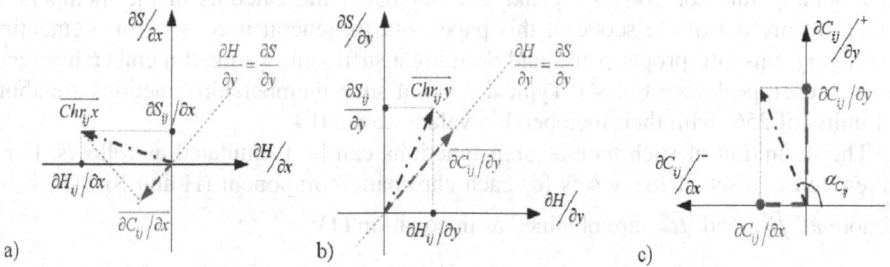

a)   b)   c)

Fig. 2. Coordinate systems to obtain the chromaticity variations in the horizontal (a) and vertical (b) directions; and approach to the chromatic partial derivatives (c)

4   Fuzzy Color Characterization

Our method starts by selecting some sampling pixels around each nucleus position, provided by an external procedure (see Fig. 3.a). We use several concentric circles (e.g. 3) and pick pixels at a certain number of angles (e.g. 8, as in Fig 3.b).

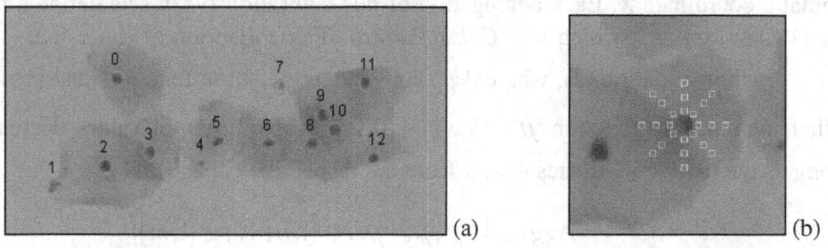

(a)   (b)

Fig. 3. (a) Cell centers on the test image. (b) Sampling points at Cell 3.

The hue and saturation histograms for cell number 3 are represented in Fig. 4. The range of coordinates has been discretized to 32 bins, since we use a low number of sampling pixels (e.g. 24). The final histograms roughly approximate the shape of more detailed histograms, and also imply a certain degree of smoothing.

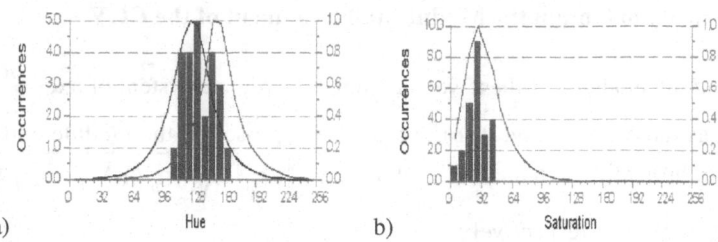

Fig. 4. Hue and Saturation histograms *(bars)* and their membership functions *(lines)*

Thereafter, our method segments the main peaks of each histogram, and builds a membership function for each peak. The details of the calculus of the membership functions are out of the scope of this paper, but in general it consists in segmenting the histograms into proper peaks and defining a sufficiently spread membership function on each peak (see Fig. 4). Typical sizes of such membership functions are about 64 units (of 256) with their membership values above 0.4.

The definition of such membership functions can be formulated as follows. For a given cell c, a set of fuzzy sets for each chromatic component (H and S), which we denote as $\widehat{\mu}_H^c$ and $\widehat{\mu}_S^c$, are obtained as in equation (1):

$$\widehat{\mu}_H^c = \left\{ \mu_H^{c,i} = F\left(SHisto^i\left(\left\{\frac{Hue^{sampling\,pixels(c)}}{binsize}\right\}\right)\right)\right\}_{i=1}^n,$$
$$\widehat{\mu}_S^c = \left\{ \mu_S^{c,j} = F\left(SHisto^j\left(\left\{\frac{Saturation^{sampling\,pixels(c)}}{binsize}\right\}\right)\right)\right\}_{j=0}^m$$

$$(1)$$

where *sampling pixels(c)* are the set of sampling pixels around the center of cell c, *binsize* is the selected size for histogram bins (e.g. 8), *Hue* and *Saturation* are the chromatic values of the selected pixels, $SHisto^i$ represents a segmented part of the histogram collecting the corresponding bins around peak i, and F is a generic function that provides a membership function $\mu_X^{c,i}(x) \rightarrow [0,1] \in \Re$, with output values decreasing monotonically as long as the input coordinate x gets far from the peak i in the chromatic coordinate X. Each aggregation of hue-saturation fuzzy sets define a more general fuzzy set $\mu^{c,k}$, which is a *Color Pattern*. The collection of those fuzzy sets, $\widehat{\mu}^c$, is given in equation (2), where *Aggreg* is the aggregation function, that provides another membership function $\mu^{c,k}(h,s) \rightarrow [0,1] \in \Re$, with output values decreasing as long as the input coordinates get far from the respective peaks i and j.

$$\widehat{\mu}^c = \left\{ \mu^{c,k} = Aggreg\left(\mu_H^{c,i}, \mu_S^{c,j}\right), \forall i \in [1,n] \times \forall j \in [1,m]\right\}_{k=1}^l$$

$$(2)$$

The chosen aggregation function is the minimum, since we only want high membership degree on the general fuzzy set if both components have high degrees.

Since some of the aggregated fuzzy sets may not correspond to a real color of the cell, we suggest to get rid of fuzzy sets with support below a given threshold, i.e. less than 10% of sampling points with maximum membership degree on the candidate fuzzy set.

Once the method has found the most significant color fuzzy sets, we can show the area of influence of those patterns visually as in Fig. 5, where pixels within a radius of 40 pixels have been shaded according to its membership degree, i.e. lighter shades mean higher membership degrees (pixels with less than 0.10 are not shaded). This is what we call the *Membership Field*.

Figures 5.a and 5.b show two membership fields around cell 3, for two significant color patterns. In Fig. 5.a, one can appreciate high membership degrees inside cell 3 and also inside cell 2, because their colors are similar. In Fig. 5.b, pixels with high membership degree roughly correspond to the intersection between cells 2 and 3. This means that the method has correctly detected two color patterns for two complimentary cytoplasm areas (double and single cytoplasm).

5   Contour Evolution

The final process starts by positioning a number of *Contour Points* (e.g. 8) at equally distributed angles and at a fixed distance to the center. Centered on each contour point there is a straight line of a certain number of pixels (e.g. 11), following the normal direction to the contour, which we name as *Normal Segments* (Fig. 5.c).

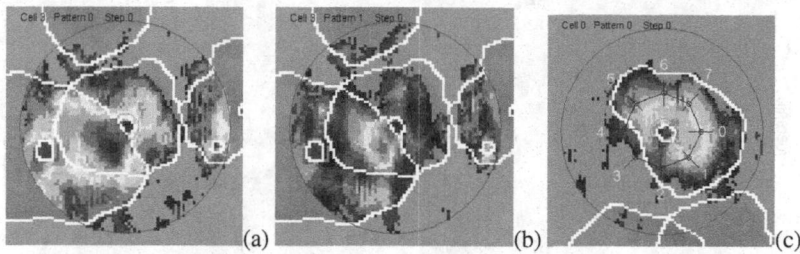

Fig. 5. (a, b) Membership fields of the chromatic patterns of cell 3. (c) Eight contour points and their normal segments around cell number 0.

5.1   Profiles of Membership Degree and Gradient Relevance

For each normal segment NS_j, the method computes the membership degrees of its pixels $p_{NS_j}^i$ to each color pattern of the cell (i.e. each $\mu^{c,k}$), as well as their *Gradient Relevance*, which is defined as the product of the gradient module at the target pixel $\left\| \nabla CGV(p_{NS_j}^i) \right\|$ by the degree of coincidence between its gradient argument $\alpha CGV(p_{NS_j}^i)$ and the normal direction of the contour point, noted as $\perp_j$ in next equation.

$$GR\left(p_{NS_j}^i\right) = \left\| \nabla CGV(p_{NS_j}^i)/Max(\nabla CGV) \right\| \cdot \left(1 - \left| \alpha CGV(p_{NS_j}^i) - \perp_j \right| / \frac{\pi}{2}\right). \tag{3}$$

Both module and argument information are normalized so as to provide values between 0 and 1. Fig. 6 shows the profiles of membership degrees and gradient relevance of three normal segments of cell 0.

5.2 Motion Forces of the Contour Points

The motion of each contour point is obtained from the corresponding profiles. For membership profiles, we suggest to add the membership degrees of the normal pixels with positive offsets (outside the contour), and to subtract the complimentary of membership degrees of the normal pixels with negative offsets (inside the contour).

$$MMotion\left(\{p_{NS_j}\}\right)= \sum_{i=0}^{i=np/2}\mu^c\left(p_{NS_j}^i\right)- \sum_{i=-1}^{i=-np/2}\left(1-\mu^c\left(p_{NS_j}^i\right)\right) \cdot \tag{4}$$

In previous equation, *MMotion* means the motion due to the membership degrees, $\{p_{NS_j}\}$ is the set of normal pixels, $\mu^c\left(p_{NS_j}^i\right)$ is the membership degree of a given pixel, and *np* is the total number of normal pixels, so indices *i* indicate normal positions.

The gradient motion *GMotion* is computed as the difference between gradient relevance at positive and negative parts of the profile, multiplied by a constant K_{GR} that scales the gradient motion to ranges similar to the ones obtained with membership motion (usually $K_{GR} = 3$).

$$GMotion\left(\{p_{NS_j}\}\right)= K_{GR}\cdot\left[\sum_{i=0}^{i=np/2}GR\left(p_{NS_j}^i\right)- \sum_{i=-1}^{i=-np/2}GR\left(p_{NS_j}^i\right)\right] \cdot \tag{5}$$

This motion "forces" are exemplified, for cell 0 in the plots of Fig. 6.

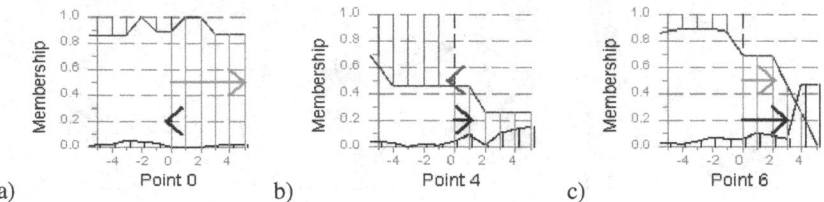

Fig. 6. Membership degree profiles (*high*) and gradient relevance (*low*) for contour points 0 (a), 4 (b) and 6 (c) of cell 0; negative values in *x* correspond to normal pixels inside the contour

The final motion is computed as the sum of *MMotion* and *GMotion*, multiplied by a decay factor that decreases exponentially as the number of the evolution steps *s* increases, modulated by a constant K_d (e.g. 10):

$$Motion\left(\{p_{NS_j}\}\right)= \left[MMotion\left(\{p_{NS_j}\}\right)+ GMotion\left(\{p_{NS_j}\}\right)\right]\cdot\exp\left(- s/K_d\right) \cdot \tag{6}$$

Thus, at each step of the contour evolution process, the total motion value is added to the distance of the contour point to the cell's center. Therefore, the contour points move inward or outward following its normal direction. The profiles and motion values are recomputed on the new position of contour points. The iteration continues until the contour points move less than a certain small threshold. The next figure shows three snapshots of the contour evolution of cell number 0.

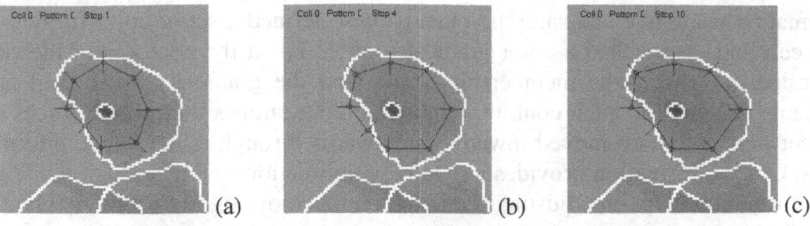

Fig. 7. Motion of the contour of cell number 0 at steps 1 (a), 4 (b) and 10 (c)

As can be seen, the contour quickly converges to a stationary position, which roughly corresponds to the real border of the cytoplasm. We have verified that the contour approaches the limits of the membership field in a robust manner, and that the nearby gradient information attracts the contour points to more precise positions.

6 Results

In Fig. 8 the result of our cytoplasm detection (Fig. 8.a) can be compared with the one obtained with a hybrid snake method proposed in [15] (Fig. 8.b). The snake method wrongly joined cells into three blobs. It is due to the very low brightness contrast between touching cytoplasm.

This problem is solved with our proposal, where all the cells are distinguished. We have set 16 contour points. As can be seen, most of the contour points approach to real cell borders, although some points get far from neighboring points because of local minima on membership fields and gradient relevance. Moreover, some contours get inside neighboring cells, which is a first step in detecting overlapping cytoplasm.

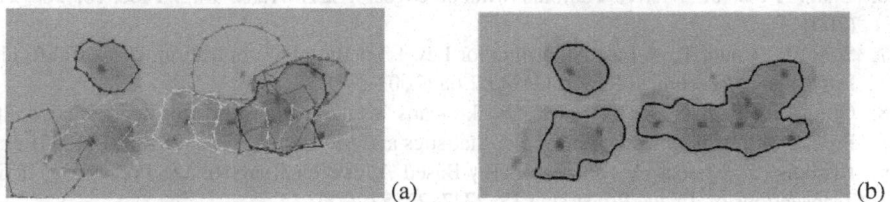

Fig. 8. Comparison of cytoplasm detection: our proposal (a) and the proposal in [15] (b)

As future lines, we will improve the method by including the neighbor point's distance as another motion force, and we will perform a quantitative comparison with other methods. Finally, we want to remark that our method is really fast, since it converges in few steps (20) and in fractions of a second.

7 Conclusions

We have proposed a method to approximate the contour of cells with imprecise borders and overlapping translucent areas. To this purpose we incorporated chromatic information using hue and saturation histograms, defined a set of color fuzzy sets for each cell and approached a color gradient profile. To fit the contours of the cell we suggested computing the membership degree and the gradient relevance of normal segments centered on each contour point, which determines the motion forces of the contour points that are moved inwards or outwards through rather vague information fields. Color information provides a rough approximation to the contour, while gradient information helps in adjusting the final contour more tightly to the real border of the cell.

Acknowledgments. This work has been partially supported by the projects TIN2007-68063 of the Spanish CICYT, P07-TIC-03175 of the Junta de Andalucía, and TIN2009-08296 of the Spanish MCYT.

References

1. He, L., Peng, Z., Everding, B., et al.: A comparative study of deformable contour methods on medical image segmentation. Image and Vision Computing 26, 141–163 (2008)
2. Ma, Z., Tavares, J.M.R.S., Jorge, R.N.: Segmentation of Structures in Medical Images: Review and a New Computational Framework. In: Proc. Int. Symp. CMBBE 2008 (2008)
3. Lucchese, L., Mitra, S.K.: Color image segmentation: A state-of-art survey. Proc. Indian Natural Sciences Academy (INSA-A) 67-A, 207–221 (2001)
4. Cremers, D., Rousson, M., Deriche, R.: A Review of Statistical Approaches to Level Set Segmentation: Integrating Color, Texture, Motion and Shape. Int. Journal of Computer Vision 72, 195–215 (2007)
5. Campadelli, P., Casiraghi, E., Esposito, A.: Liver segmentation from computed tomography scans: A survey and a new algorithm. Artificial Intelligence in Medicine, Computational Intelligence and Machine Learning in Bioinformatics 45, 185–196 (2009)
6. Chan, T., et al.: Active contours without edges. IEEE Trans. Img. Proc. 10, 266–277 (2001)
7. Song, B., Chan, T.: A Fast Algorithm for Level Set Based Optimization, Univ. California, Los Angeles, Technical Report CAM 02-68 (2002)
8. Gibou, F., Fedkiw, R.: A fast hybrid k-means level set algorithm for segmentation. In: Proc. of 4th Annual Hawaii Int. Conf. Statistics and Mathematics, pp. 281–291 (2005)
9. Krinidis, S., Chatzis, V.: Fuzzy Energy-Based Active Contours Image Processing. IEEE Transactions on Image Processing 18, 2747–2755 (2009)
10. Velez, J., Sanchez, A., Fernandez, F.: Improved Fuzzy Snakes Applied to Biometric Verification Problems. In: Intelligent Systems Design and Applications, pp. 158–163 (2009)
11. Wesolkowski, S., Jernigan, M., Dony, R.: Comparison of color image edge detectors in multiple color spaces. In: Int. Conf. on Image Processing, vol. 2, pp. 796–799 (2000)
12. Smith, A.R.: Color gamut transform pairs. Computer Graphics 12, 12–19 (1978)
13. Sobrevilla, P., Keller, J., Montseny, E.: White Blood Cell Detection in Bone Marrow. In: Proc. of 18th North American Fuzzy Information Processing Society, pp. 403–407 (1999)
14. Prados-Suárez, B., Sobrevilla, P., Montseny, E., Romaní, S.: On the reliability of the color gradient vector argument approach. In: Proc. IFSA-EUSFLAT, pp. 1863–1868 (2009)
15. Lankton, S., Nain, D., Yezzi, A., Tannenbaum, A.: Hybrid geodesic region-based curve evolutions for image segmentations. In: Proc. of SPIE Medical Imaging, vol. 6510 (2007)

Keeping Secrets in Possibilistic Knowledge Bases with Necessity-Valued Privacy Policies

Lena Wiese

Technische Universität Dortmund, Germany
wiese@ls6.cs.tu-dortmund.de
http://ls6-www.cs.tu-dortmund.de

Abstract. Controlled Query Evaluation (CQE) is a logical framework for the protection of secrets in databases. In this article, we extend the CQE framework to possibilistic logic: knowledge base, a priori knowledge and privacy policy are expressed with necessity-valued formulas that represent several degrees of certainty. We present a formal security definition and analyze an appropriate controlled evaluation algorithm for this possibilistic case.

1 Introduction

A major security goal for databases is keeping secret entries in a database instance confidential. Two general mechanisms for the enforcement of confidentiality are *modification* of data (like perturbation, noise generation, cover stories, or "lied" answers) and *restriction* (refusal, denial of access, blocking, cell suppression, generalization, data upgrading etc).

The framework of Controlled Query Evaluation (CQE; see for example [1–3]) uses both mechanisms (in the form of lying and refusal) in a logic-based framework. In this article, we extend the CQE framework to possibilistic logic such that degrees of certainty can be specified and attached to logical formulae. This offers the following advantages:

- Certainty degrees can express confidence in some information in a finer-grained way than just returning the values *true*, *false* or *undefined* in incomplete databases (as used in [1]).
- In the same sense, "weakening" of some degrees as a means to restrict access to information is a more cooperative way of communication than denying access to information altogether.
- Certainty degrees are intuitively understood by users as a means to rank confidence in some information.
- Possibilistic logic is well-suited for inferential reasoning as argued in [4, 5].

We consider a client-server architecture where a user issues queries to a knowledge base system. The knowledge base *kb* contains public as well as private data; to achieve confidentiality of the private data, the system maintains a personalized privacy policy *policy* and a user history *log* for each particular user

E. Hüllermeier, R. Kruse, and F. Hoffmann (Eds.): IPMU 2010, LNAI 6178, pp. 655–664, 2010.
© Springer-Verlag Berlin Heidelberg 2010

registered at the system. Based on *policy* and *log*, queries are then evaluated in the knowledge base in a controlled way by the evaluation function *cqe* that makes use of a subroutine called *censor*. The censor module takes care of the modifications and restrictions of data that are necessary to keep entries of the privacy policy confidential.

As the syntactical basis we consider a propositional logic $\mathscr{L}$ that involves a finite alphabet $\mathcal{P}$ of propositional variables and the connectives negation $\neg$, conjunction $\wedge$, and disjunction $\vee$; on occasion, material implication $\rightarrow$ is used as an abbreviation (for a negation and a disjunction).

If to a formula p of $\mathscr{L}$ a weight $\alpha \in (0, 1]$ is attached, we get the "standard possibilistic logic" (SPL; see [6]). As usual, we write possibilistic formulas as (p, α). The weight α denotes a *lower bound* for a "necessity degree" N of p. A necessity degree specifies the certainty of formulas: it "evaluates to what extent p is entailed by the available knowledge" [4]. In other words, with (p, α) we express that $N(p) \geq \alpha$: the certainty of p is at least α. A high certainty for p denotes that a countermodel of p (that is a model of $\neg p$) is relatively impossible to be the "real" world; we will give a precise definition below. In this reading, it is natural that 0 is excluded as a weight: $N(p) \geq 0$ (denoting that the certainty of p is somewhere between 0 and 1) always holds for any formula p.

We now recall how a necessity measure can be induced by a possibilistic knowledge base. A possibilistic knowledge base can be defined as a set of n possibilistic formulas (p_i, α_i). In this article, we let *kb* denote such a knowledge base. The formulas in *kb* have as possible interpretations all $2^{card(\mathcal{P})}$ classical interpretations ("worlds") of the propositional variables $\mathcal{P}$. On these possible worlds, *kb* induces a **possibility distribution** π_{kb}. This possibility distribution assigns to each world u a value from the interval $[0, 1]$. This value specifies how possible it is for u to be the real world – that is, the right one of all the possible interpretations for *kb*. $\pi_{kb}(u) = 0$ means that it is totally impossible for u to be the real world. Hence, worlds that violate formulas in *kb* have a lower value than worlds that propositionally satisfy all formulas in *kb*. The worlds with possibility value 1 are "models" (denoted $\models$) of the propositional formulas in *kb*:

$$\pi_{kb}(u) := \begin{cases} 1 & \text{iff } u \models p_1 \wedge \ldots \wedge p_n \\ 1 - \max\{\alpha_i \mid (p_i, \alpha_i) \in kb \text{ and } u \models \neg p_i\} & \text{otherwise} \end{cases}$$

There need not exist a world with possibility 1 (that is, not all formulas p_i can be satisfied at the same time); in this case, π_{kb} is called *subnormalized*. Otherwise, it is called *normal* if there is at least one world with possibility 1. However, there may also exist more than one world with possibility 1 for a given *kb*. Knowledge bases with a subnormalized possibility distribution have an **inconsistency level** *Inc(kb)* above 0; it is defined as follows:

$$Inc(kb) := 1 - \max_u \{\pi_{kb}(u)\}$$

Based on the possibility distribution, we can compute the **possibility degree** for any formula p':

$$\Pi_{kb}(p') := \max\{\pi_{kb}(u) \mid u \models p'\}$$

That is, the possibility degree identifies the world with maximal possibility that satisfies p: it "it evaluates to what extent p is consistent with the available knowledge" [4].

Then we are interested in the **necessity degree** of a formula p'' induced by Π_{kb} by subtracting from 1 the possibility degree of $\neg p''$ (that is, the maximal possibility of a countermodel of p''):

$$N_{kb}(p'') := 1 - \Pi_{kb}(\neg p'')$$

Note that we could also skip computation of the possibility degree ($\Pi_{kb}(\neg p'')$) by letting $N_{kb}(p'') = \min\{1 - \pi_{kb}(u) \mid u \text{ is model of } \neg p''\}$.

Lastly, **implication** in SPL is defined. We say that kb implies p with maximal necessity degree α (written $kb \models_{SPL} (p, \alpha)$) if $N_{kb}(p) = \alpha$.[1] It has been shown in [6] that this implication can (soundly and completely) be implemented with a set of syntactic inference rules (where $\vdash$ denotes syntactic entailment). This set of rules includes the following:

- **resolution:** $(\neg p \vee q, \alpha); (p \vee r, \beta) \vdash (q \vee r, \min\{\alpha, \beta\})$
- **weight fusion:** $(p, \alpha); (p, \beta) \vdash (p, \max\{\alpha, \beta\})$
- **weight weakening:** for $\beta \leq \alpha$, $(p, \alpha) \vdash (p, \beta)$

With such rules, the implication $kb \models_{SPL} (p, \alpha)$ can be decided by the refutation $kb \cup \{(\neg p, 1)\} \vdash (\bot, \alpha)$. Alternatively, entailment of (p, α) can also be expressed as the inconsistency level $\alpha = Inc(kb \cup \{(\neg p, 1)\})$. Moreover, algorithmically entailment takes only a bounded number propositional satisfiability checks: the bound is the logarithm of the number of certainty degrees occurring in the knowledge base. We refer to [4–6] for further details.

The remainder of this article is organized as follows: Section 2 describes the system settings. Section 3 formally defines "confidentiality-preservation" and Section 4 presents a CQE algorithm for possibilistic knowledge bases. The article concludes in Section 5 with a discussion of our approach and related work.

2 System Components

In this article, we transfer the CQE framework to a possibilistic setting where the knowledge base consists of formulas at differing degrees of certainty and the privacy policy and the user history are maintained in possibilistic logic, too.

The possibilistic **knowledge base** kb is a finite set of possibilistic formulas (p_i, α_i) for $i = 1 \ldots n$; hence $p_i \in \mathcal{P}$ is a propositional formula and each $\alpha_i \in (0, 1]$ is the necessity degree of p_i. For the time being, we assume here that kb is a consistent set of formulas – although possibilistic logic has the ability to cope with inconsistencies in the knowledge base. That is, we assume that the set of the *propositional* formulas occurring in kb (denoted $Prop_{kb}$) form a propositionally consistent set and as such do not lead to a contradiction. In

---

[1] We say "maximal necessity degree" because it also holds that for all $\alpha' \in (0, \alpha]$ that $kb \models_{SPL} (p, \alpha')$.

other words, the *inconsistency level* of kb is 0. To illustrate the settings, we give a small example of a medical knowledge base that contains information about some medical treatment (med) and some diagnoses (aids and cancer):

$$kb = \{(\text{med}, 0.9), (\text{aids}, 0.8), (\text{cancer}, 0.7)\}$$

The knowledge base is able to answer queries based on the necessity degree induced by kb, and hence on implication $\models_{SPL}$ in SPL. That is, the input is a propositional query formula p and **evaluation** of this query outputs the possibilistic formula (p, α) such that α is $N_{kb}(p)$ (that is, the maximal degree of necessity for p in the knowledge base kb) and hence $kb \models_{SPL} (p, \alpha)$:

$$eval_{kb}(p) := (p, \alpha) \text{ where } \alpha = N_{kb}(p)$$

For example, the necessity degree for query aids $\vee$ cancer is $N_{kb}(\text{aids} \vee \text{cancer})$ $= 1 - \Pi_{kb}(\neg\text{aids} \wedge \neg\text{cancer}) = 0.8$ and hence $eval_{kb}(\text{aids} \vee \text{cancer}) = (\text{aids} \vee \text{cancer}, 0.8)$. For the query aids $\wedge$ cancer we have $N_{kb}(\text{aids} \wedge \text{cancer}) = 1 - \Pi_{kb}(\neg\text{aids} \vee \neg\text{cancer}) = 0.7$ and hence $eval_{kb}(\text{aids} \wedge \text{cancer}) = (\text{aids} \wedge \text{cancer}, 0.7)$.

The **privacy policy** *policy* is a finite set of possibilistic formulas. Semantically, a policy entry (q, β) specifies that the user is never allowed to know that q is certain in kb at a necessity degree above β. He may however learn that q is certain at least with degree β. For example the following policy states that a user may know aids with a lower bound of certainty of 0.3 (that is, $N_{kb}(\text{aids}) \geq 0.3$) and cancer with a lower bound of certainty of 0.2 (that is, $N_{kb}(\text{cancer}) \geq 0.2$); he must however never learn greater lower bound values for $N_{kb}(\text{aids})$ and $N_{kb}(\text{cancer})$:

$$policy = \{(\text{aids}, 0.3), (\text{cancer}, 0.2)\}$$

As an exceptional value, we explicitly allow entries with necessity degree 0 in *policy*: an entry $(q, 0) \in policy$ denotes that we do not want to reveal any information on the state of p in kb, that is, we do not give the user any certainty about p.

The **user history** *log* records all answers (as possibilistic formulas) that were given by the knowledge base to a sequence of user queries $Q = \langle q_1, q_2, \ldots q_m \rangle$ for propositional formulas q_j; that is, we have a sequence of history logs where log_j denotes the state of the history after the j-th answer was given. In particular log_0 may contain additional **a priori knowledge** that the user has before starting the query sequence. For example the a priori knowledge may state that a treatment with some medicine implies both diagnoses but at different levels of certainty:

$$log_0 = \{(\text{med} \rightarrow \text{aids}, 0.6), (\text{med} \rightarrow \text{cancer}, 0.5)\}$$

It may occur, that some answer with necessity degree 0 is returned to the user – either because the necessity degree in kb is 0 indeed or because the privacy policy prohibits any more specific return value; yet, in this case while the answer $(q_j, 0)$

is given to the user to acknowledge his query, it is not added to the user history log_j because from a reasoning point of view it has no effect.

In the following we will devise a **controlled query evaluation** function $cqe(Q, kb, log_0, policy)$ that shields the $eval_{kb}$-function from direct access by the user. The cqe-function will – whenever necessary – modify the $eval_{kb}$-answers; that is, the cqe-function will answer the query sequence Q in such a way that the sequence of history files log_j will reveal an entry of the privacy policy at most at the level of certainty specified in the policy. For example, for the query sequence $Q = \langle \texttt{aids}, \texttt{cancer} \rangle$ (and kb, log_0 and $policy$ as in the examples above) we will have the answer sequence $A = cqe(Q, kb, log_0, policy) = \langle (\texttt{aids}, 0.3), (\texttt{cancer}, 0.2) \rangle$; hence the only knowledge that the user receives is that $N_{kb}(\texttt{aids}) \geq 0.3$ and $N_{kb}(\texttt{cancer}) \geq 0.2$. Without controlling the evaluation, the normal evaluation would be $eval_{kb}(\texttt{aids}) = (\texttt{aids}, 0.8)$ (revealing $N_{kb}(\texttt{aids}) \geq 0.8$) and $eval_{kb}(\texttt{cancer}) = (\texttt{cancer}, 0.7)$ (revealing $N_{kb}(\texttt{cancer}) \geq 0.7$); and hence both truthful answers would violate $policy$.

3 A Formal Security Definition

In this section, we adapt the formal definition of confidentiality preservation of a controlled query evaluation function to the possibilistic case. Appropriate definitions were already established for complete databases [2] and incomplete databases with policies in modal logic [1, 3].

Confidentiality preservation of a controlled query evaluation function cqe is ensured by the following Definition 1. It demands that there exists an alternative knowledge base that is compatible with the a priori knowledge log_0 and for which the cqe-function returns the same answers (Item *1*); that is, from the observable behavior (via the cqe-function) kb and kb' are indistinguishable. However the alternative knowledge base does not violate the privacy policy when queries are evaluated without control (Item *2*).

Definition 1 (Confidentiality Preservation). *A controlled query evaluation function cqe is* confidentiality-preserving *iff for all admissible inputs Q, kb, log_0 and policy there is an alternative knowledge base kb' such that $kb' \cup log_0$ is consistent, and the following two properties hold:*

1. [**same controlled answers**]
   $cqe(Q, kb, log_0, policy) = cqe(Q, kb', log_0, policy)$
2. [**alternative knowledge base is secure**]
   there is no policy entry $(q, \beta) \in policy$ such that $eval_{kb'}(q) = (q, \beta')$ with $\beta' > \beta$.

Preconditions for Q, kb, log_0 and $policy$ can be defined to specify what inputs are "admissible" in Definition 1. More precisely, we allow inputs with the following properties:

1. As already mentioned in Section 2, kb is assumed to be a consistent possibilistic knowledge base; that is, $Inc(kb) = 0$.

2. The a priori knowledge log_0 is consistent: $Inc(log_0) = 0$.
3. Moreover, kb and log_0 must be compatible; that is, when combined they are also consistent: $Inc(kb \cup log_0) = 0$.
4. Lastly, the user does not know a policy entry a priori and hence log_0 must be compatible with *policy*: there is no policy entry $(q, \beta) \in$ *policy* such that $log_0 \models_{SPL} (q, \beta')$ with $\beta' > \beta$.

4 A Censor for Possibilistic Knowledge Bases

As a subroutine of a controlled query evaluation function *cqe*, the *censor* is responsible to decide whether a modification or restriction of a database answer is necessary and if so, compute the modified or restricted answer. We list a censor that is appropriate for controlled query evaluation in possibilistic knowledge bases in Figure 1. This censor proceeds as follows: given the current query q_j, it checks whether there are any violated policy entries when adding the correct evaluation $eval_{kb}(q_j)$ to the current user history log_{j-1}. The set of the necessity degrees of all those violated entries is determined. If there are no violated entries, this set is empty and the correct evaluation can be returned without modification. If however there are violated entries, the minimal necessity degree γ is determined and as the modified answer the query with necessity degree γ is returned.

$censor(log_{j-1}, q_j)$:

> $S := \{\beta \mid (q, \beta) \in$ *policy* such that $log_{j-1} \cup eval_{kb}(q_j) \models_{SPL} (q, \beta')$ with $\beta' > \beta\}$
> if $S = \emptyset$
>   return $eval_{kb}(q_j)$
> else
> $\gamma := \min S$
>   return (q_j, γ)

Fig. 1. Possibilistic censor

Note that if the policy is ordered in ascending order of the necessity degrees, the violation check could start with policy entries at the least degree and move on to greater degrees until a violation is encountered. In this manner, the minimum of S can easily be determined without checking all policy entries in the optimal case.

A complete implementation of the *cqe*-function can be made by calling the censor for every query q_j in the query sequence, constructing and returning the answer sequence A and updating the user history log_j; see Figure 2. When updating the user history, answers with necessity degree 0 are filtered out: the fact that $N_{kb}(q_j) \geq 0$ does not carry any information and need not be recorded.

We continue our example with the query sequence $Q = \langle \text{aids}, \text{cancer}, \text{med} \rangle$. Obviously, with the correct answer $eval_{kb}(\text{aids}) = (\text{aids}, 0.8)$ the first policy entry $(\text{aids}, 0.3)$ is violated; the censor thus modifies the first answer to $(\text{aids}, 0.3)$.

$cqe(Q, kb, log_0, policy)$:

```
    A = ⟨a₁, ..., aₘ⟩
    for j = 1 ... m
        aⱼ := censor(log_{j-1}, qⱼ)
        if aⱼ = (qⱼ, γ) with γ > 0
            logⱼ := log_{j-1} ∪ {(qⱼ, γ)}
        else
            logⱼ := log_{j-1}
    return A
```

Fig. 2. cqe implementation

Equivalently, the second answer is modified to $(\text{cancer}, 0.2)$. As for the third query, $log_2 = log_0 \cup \{(\text{aids}, 0.3), (\text{cancer}, 0.2)\}$ combined with $eval_{kb}(\text{med}) = (\text{med}, 0.9)$ violates both policy entries, because $log_2 \cup \{(\text{med}, 0.9)\} \models_{SPL} (\text{aids}, 0.6)$ and $log_2 \cup \{(\text{med}, 0.9)\} \models_{SPL} (\text{cancer}, 0.5)$. That is, we have $S = \{0.3, 0.2\}$ (due to the policy entries). We take its minimum and return $(\text{med}, 0.2)$. The complete answer sequence is thus $A = \langle (\text{aids}, 0.3), (\text{cancer}, 0.2), (\text{med}, 0.2) \rangle$. The resulting user history is $log_m = log_0 \cup \{(\text{aids}, 0.3), (\text{cancer}, 0.2), (\text{med}, 0.2)\}$.

On our way to show that the above cqe-function is compliant with Definition 1, we need the following two lemmas and then move on to the main theorem:

Lemma 1 (User History is Consistent). *For $j = 1 \ldots m$ the user history log_j is consistent; that is, $Inc(log_j) = 0$.*

Proof. By assumption, kb is consistent in itself and with the a priori knowledge log_0 (see the preconditions at the end of Section 3). But then also the set of database answers $eval_{kb}(q_k)$ with necessity degree above 0 for $k = 1 \ldots j$ is consistent. Reducing the correct necessity degree of q_j to a lower value (but still above 0) with the $censor$-function does not influence consistency. As all answers with necessity degree 0 are left out of the user history and the a priori knowledge log_0 is consistent by assumption, each log_j is consistent.

Lemma 2 (User History is Secure). *For each user history log_j it holds that there is no policy entry $(q, \beta) \in policy$ such that $log_j \models_{SPL} (q, \beta')$ with $\beta' > \beta$.*

Proof. By assumption, the security property holds for log_0. Inductively, we argue that if log_{j-1} is secure, then also log_j is. In the $censor$-function there are two cases: if upon adding the correct answer to the history the policy is not violated ($S = \emptyset$), log_j is obviously secure. However, when adding the correct answer violates some policy entries ($S \neq \emptyset$), taking the minimal necessity degree $\min S$ avoids the violation. This is due to the fact that in possibilistic logic a logical consequence is only supported up to the necessity degree of the "weakest link" in its proof chain for the entailment; see [6] for details. For example, the possibilistic resolution rule in Section 1 also takes the minimum of the degrees of the input formulas. In other words, because log_{j-1} is secure, addition of the current answer enables the entailment of a violation in a proof chain; we thus weaken the necessity degree of the answer such that no harmful inference is possible anymore.

Theorem 1 (Possibilistic *cqe* Preserves Confidentiality). *The cqe-function presented in Figure 2 is confidentiality-preserving.*

Proof. We have to identify an alternative knowledge base kb', such that $kb' \cup log_0$ is consistent and the two properties of Definition 1 hold. Let $kb' := log_m$. Clearly, $log_0 \subseteq log_m$ and kb' is consistent by Lemma 1.

Indistinguishability of kb and kb' (Item *1*) can be established by induction on the query sequence and the user history. Base case: Both *cqe*-answer sequences, for kb and kb', start with the same log_0 by definition of the *cqe*-function. Inductive case: Assume that calling the *cqe*-function on kb and kb' led to the same log_{j-1}. We show that for query q_j, the same answer is generated (for kb and kb') and hence both *cqe* answer sequences lead to the same log_j. Assume to the contrary that q_j is answered differently: *cqe* on kb returns (q_j, β_j) and *cqe* on kb' returns (q_j, β'_j) with $\beta_j \neq \beta'_j$. We consider two cases:

- Case 1 ($\beta_j > \beta'_j$): Then, $(q_j, \beta_j) \in log_j$ (because it is returned by *cqe* on kb and $\beta_j > 0$). By definition of kb', $log_j \subseteq kb'$; by Lemma 2 and the rule of weight fusion (see Section 1) $kb' \models_{SPL} (q_j, \beta_j)$ and (q_j, β_j) will also be returned as the answer of kb'. Hence the assumption that $\beta_j > \beta'_j$ leads to a contradiction.
- Case 2 ($\beta_j < \beta'_j$): It holds that $(q_j, \beta_j) \in log_j$ if $\beta_j > 0$; otherwise $\beta_j = 0$ and $log_j = log_{j-1}$. To deduce (q_j, β'_j) in kb', all formulas in the proof chain for (q_j, β'_j) must have necessity degree β'_j or above (see Proposition 9 in [6]). But such formulas cannot exist in kb' because formulas in kb' have same or lower degrees than formulas in kb and log_{j-1}; indeed, for every (r, γ) such that $kb \cup log_{j-1} \models_{SPL} (r, \gamma)$ it holds that $kb' \models_{SPL} (r, \gamma')$ with $\gamma \leq \gamma'$ due to weight minimization in the *cqe*-function. Hence again we have a contradiction.

We conclude that $\beta_j = \beta'_j$ and thus the same answer and history sequence is generated both from *cqe* calls on kb as well as kb'. Security of kb' (Item *2*) follows directly from Lemma 2, because $eval_{kb}$ is based on implication $\models_{SPL}$.

Lastly, we argue that the runtime complexity of the *cqe*-function is dominated by the complexity of solving the satisfiability (SAT) problem for propositional formulas. In particular for fixed sizes of the query sequence Q and privacy policy *policy*, a number of SAT checks that is bounded by the logarithm of the number of necessity degrees occurring in the inputs kb and log_0 and *policy* suffices.

Theorem 2 (Complexity of Possibilistic *cqe*). *For fixed-sized Q and policy, the number of SAT checks used in the cqe-function is logarithmically bounded by the number of necessity degrees occurring in the inputs kb, log_0 and policy.*

Proof. For one single query q_j, the *censor*-function determines $eval_{kb}(q_j)$. This can be done with $\lceil \log d_{kb} \rceil$ SAT checks (with $Prop_{kb}$ and q_j as inputs to the SAT solver) where d_{kb} is the number of necessity degrees occurring in kb; see [6]. Next, for each of the $card(policy)$ many policy entries, the censor determines $log_{j-1} \cup eval_{kb}(q_j) \models_{SPL} (q, \beta')$; this takes accordingly $\lceil \log(d_{log_{j-1}} + 1) \rceil$ SAT checks (with $Prop_{log_{j-1}}$, q_j and q as inputs) where $d_{log_{j-1}}$ is the number of necessity degrees occurring in log_{j-1}. In the worst case, in log_{j-1} all necessity degrees mentioned in kb and log_0 and $policy$ occur. Hence let d be the number of necessity degrees mentioned in kb and log_0 and $policy$. Then the combined runtime of the *cqe*-function for the whole query sequence $Q = \langle q_1, \ldots, q_m \rangle$ is bounded by

$$m \cdot [\lceil \log d \rceil \cdot SAT + (card(policy) \cdot \lceil \log(d+1) \rceil \cdot SAT)]$$

By taking m and $card(policy)$ as constants, the result follows.

Note that although the propositional SAT problem is the classical NP-complete problem, several highly efficient SAT solving programs exist. In the context of CQE, such SAT solvers have been used to preprocess a secure ("inference-proof") view of an input database (see [7]). Hence, it appears to be the case that also possibilistic CQE is efficiently implementable.

5   Related Work and Conclusion

In summary, we presented a security definition and a Controlled Query Evaluation function that avoids harmful inferences which would disclose confidential information in a possibilistic database. Hence this work adds another application of possibilistic logic to information systems to the ones listed in [5]. We used weakening of necessity degrees to achieve compliance with a personalized privacy policy. This can be seen as a form of data restriction: the query formulas are not modified, instead less specific answers are returned to the user where – as a last resort – answers with necessity degree 0 are the most general (and least informative) answers that can be given. However all returned answers are optimal in the sense that the highest possible necessity degree is determined that can safely be given to the user without violating confidentiality.

The presented possibilistic *cqe*-function is akin to generalization techniques for k-anonymity [8] or minimal upgrading of attributes in multilevel secure databases [9]. Yet, in contrast to these, we apply weakening of necessity degrees in an interactive setting with respect to query sequences. A security definition similar to ours (Definition 1) is the one in [10] for retroactive detection of disclosures: they consider gaining confidence in confidential information harmful (but not losing confidence). Previous approaches for CQE in incomplete databases (see [1, 3]) and approaches that detect inferences in ontological knowledge bases [11] handle the case that a query can have one of the three values *true*, *false* or *undefined*. In comparison to these, weakening of necessity degrees offers a finer-grained way to protect secret information while still returning useful answers. [12] analyze secrecy in multi-agent systems in the "runs and systems" framework and provide several formal secrecy definitions including a setting with plausibility measures to represent uncertainty. It would be worthwhile to study the connection of CQE to this setting in more detail.

Further open questions for the possibilistic CQE setting include whether a loss of utility of the weakened answers can be measured or heuristics can be applied to the weakening process to avoid a high loss of utility; for example, if $\alpha > \alpha'$ prefer weakening (p', α') to weakening (p, α). Possibly other preferences on the possible worlds (like Φ- or Δ-based preferences; see [4]) or other base logics (like fragments of first-order logic) can be included. Lastly, the possibilistic CQE approach could be extended to handle inconsistent knowledge bases or knowledge bases with updates or it could be used in a preprocessing approach that computes a secure ("inference-proof"; see [7]) view of the knowledge base.

References

1. Biskup, J., Weibert, T.: Keeping secrets in incomplete databases. International Journal of Information Security 7(3), 199–217 (2008)
2. Biskup, J., Bonatti, P.: Controlled query evaluation for enforcing confidentiality in complete information systems. International Journal of Information Security 3, 14–27 (2004)
3. Biskup, J., Tadros, C., Wiese, L.: Towards controlled query evaluation for incomplete first-order databases. In: Link, S. (ed.) FoIKS 2010. LNCS, vol. 5956, pp. 230–247. Springer, Heidelberg (2010)
4. Benferhat, S., Dubois, D., Prade, H.: Towards a possibilistic logic handling of preferences. Applied Intelligence 14(3), 303–317 (2001)
5. Dubois, D., Prade, H.: Possibilistic logic: a retrospective and prospective view. Fuzzy Sets and Systems 144(1), 3–23 (2004)
6. Lang, J.: Possibilistic logic: complexity and algorithms. In: Lang, J. (ed.) Handbook of Defeasible Reasoning and Uncertainty Management Systems, vol. 5, pp. 179–200. Kluwer Academic Publishers, Dordrecht (2000)
7. Tadros, C., Wiese, L.: Using SAT-solvers to compute inference-proof database instances. In: Garcia-Alfaro, J. (ed.) DPM 2009 and SETOP 2009. LNCS, vol. 5939, pp. 65–77. Springer, Heidelberg (2009)
8. Ciriani, V., di Vimercati, S.D.C., Foresti, S., Samarati, P.: k-anonymity. In: Secure Data Management in Decentralized Systems. Advances in Information Security, vol. 33, pp. 323–353. Springer, Heidelberg (2007)
9. Dawson, S., di Vimercati, S.D.C., Lincoln, P., Samarati, P.: Minimal data upgrading to prevent inference and association. In: Symposium on Principles of Database Systems (PODS 1999), pp. 114–125. ACM Press, New York (1999)
10. Evfimievski, A.V., Fagin, R., Woodruff, D.P.: Epistemic privacy. In: Symposium on Principles of Database Systems (PODS 2008), pp. 171–180. ACM, New York (2008)
11. Stouppa, P., Studer, T.: Data privacy for knowledge bases. In: Artemov, S., Nerode, A. (eds.) LFCS 2009. LNCS, vol. 5407, pp. 409–421. Springer, Heidelberg (2008)
12. Halpern, J.Y., O'Neill, K.R.: Secrecy in multiagent systems. ACM Transactions on Information and System Security (TISSEC) 12(1) (2008)

Inference with
Fuzzy and Probabilistic Information

Giulianella Coletti[1] and Barbara Vantaggi[2]

[1] Dept. Matematica e Informatica, Univ. di Perugia
via Vanvitelli 1, Perugia, Italy
[2] Dept. Metodi e Modelli Matematici, Univ. "La Sapienza"
via Scarpa 16, Roma, Italy
coletti@dipmat.unipg.it, vantaggi@dmmm.uniroma1.it

Abstract. In the paper we deal with fuzzy sets under the interpretation given in a coherent probabilistic setting. We provide a general Bayesian inference process involving fuzzy and partial probabilistic information by showing its peculiarities.

Keywords: Coherence, Fuzzy sets, Inference, Choquet integral, Lower probabilities.

1   Introduction

Randomness and fuzziness may act jointly [15, 16], then this opens new problems in probability and statistics. Many methods and technics have been proposed, which combine probability, statical and fuzzy methods (for recent results see e.g. the following volumes [6, 9, 11–13]).

This paper deals with the specific problem of finding the most probable element among those of a database, when we dispose of a probability assessment and a fuzzy information expressed by a membership function.

We refer to the interpretation, given in [2], of a membership as a coherent conditional probability, regarded as a function of the conditional events, which coincides with a likelihood, from a syntactic point of view. In this frame the problem is amenable to a Bayesian updating of an initial probability, also if the Bayes formula is applied in an unusual semantic way: the distribution, which plays the role of "prior" probability, is here usually obtained by statistical procedure based on data, whereas the membership function, which plays the role of "likelihood" is a subjective evaluation. Starting from this simple case, we analyze the problem in more general situations, in which both the available "prior probability" and "likelihood" are related to sets of events different from those of interest. This reduces to a problem of joint propagation of fuzzy and probabilistic information, maintaining the consistency with a model of reference (in this case that of coherent conditional probabilities). In order to obtain this goal, first of all we need to check whether probabilistic and fuzzy information is globally coherent: they can in fact be separately coherent, but not globally coherent

E. Hüllermeier, R. Kruse, and F. Hoffmann (Eds.): IPMU 2010, LNAI 6178, pp. 665–674, 2010.

(see Example 1). When the global assessment is coherent we need to coherently extend it to the new events of interest. In particular, we need to update the probability of the relevant variable, given a fuzzy event. In general this (posterior) probability is not unique (in fact many coherent extensions can exist), so we can compute its upper and lower envelope.

In this paper we study the general case and moreover we analyze some specific situations in which the lower envelope of the coherent extensions (posterior probabilities) can be directly computed, by means of a the lower envelope of the coherent extensions of the prior, as a Choquet integral.

2   Conditional Probability

What is usually emphasized in the literature – when a conditional probability $P(E|H)$ is taken into account – is only the fact that $P(\cdot|H)$ *is a probability for any given* H: this is a very restrictive (and misleading) view of conditional probability, corresponding trivially to just a modification of the "world" Ω. It is instead essential to regard the conditioning event H as a "variable", i.e. the "status" of H in $E|H$ is not just that of something representing a given *fact*, but that of an (uncertain) *event* (like E) for which the knowledge of its truth value is not required.

We start from the direct definition of a conditional probability, by using the classic set of axioms introduced by de Finetti [7], which is equivalent to that introduced by Popper [14].

Definition 1. *Given a set* $\mathcal{C} = \mathcal{G} \times \mathcal{B}^o$ *of conditional events* $E|H$, *with* $\mathcal{G}$ *Boolean algebra,* $\mathcal{B} \subseteq \mathcal{G}$ *closed with respect to (finite) logical sums, and* $\mathcal{B}^o = \mathcal{B} \setminus \{\emptyset\}$, *a function* $P : \mathcal{C} \to [0,1]$ *is a conditional probability if satisfies the following conditions:*

  (i) $P(H|H) = 1$, *for every* $H \in \mathcal{B}^o$,
  (ii) $P(\cdot|H)$ *is a (finitely additive) probability on* $\mathcal{G}$ *for any given* $H \in \mathcal{B}^o$,
  (iii) $P\big((E \wedge A)|H\big) = P(E|H) \cdot P\big(A|(E \wedge H)\big)$, *for every* $E, A \in \mathcal{G}$ *and* E, $E \wedge H \in \mathcal{B}^o$.

A conditional probability P is defined on $\mathcal{G} \times \mathcal{B}^o$: however it is possible, through the concept of *coherence*, to handle also those situations where we need to assess P on an arbitrary set $\mathcal{C} = \{E_i|H_i\}_{i \in J}$ of conditional events.

Definition 2. *The assessment* $P(\cdot|\cdot)$ *on an arbitrary set of conditional events* $\mathcal{C} = \{E_i|H_i\}$ *is a coherent conditional probability assessment if there is a conditional probability* P' *on* $\mathcal{C}' = \mathcal{G} \times \mathcal{B}^o$ *(where* $\mathcal{G}$ *is the Boolean algebra spanned by the events* $\{E_i, H_i\}$ *and* $\mathcal{B}^o$ *the additive set, spanned by the events* $\{H_i\}$*), extending* P.

There are in the literature many characterizations of coherent conditional probability assessments, we recall the following one proposed in [1].

Theorem 1. *Let C be an arbitrary family of conditional events. For a real function P on C the following statements are equivalent:*

(a) P is a coherent conditional probability on C;

(b) For every finite subfamily $\mathcal{F} \subseteq C$ all systems of the following sequence, with non-negative unknowns x_r^β for $A_r \in \mathcal{A}_\beta$ for $\beta = 0, 1, 2, \ldots, k \le n$ ($\mathcal{A}_0 = \mathcal{A}_o^{\mathcal{F}}$, $\mathcal{A}_\beta = \{E \in \mathcal{A}_{\beta-1} : \sum_{A_r \subseteq E} \mathbf{x}^{\beta-1} = 0\}$), are compatible:

$$(S_\beta) \quad \begin{cases} \displaystyle\sum_{A_r \subseteq E_{j_i} \wedge H_{j_i}} x_r^\beta = P(E_{j_i}|H_{j_i}) \sum_{A_r \subseteq H_{j_i}} x_r^\beta, \\[2mm] \left[\text{for all } E_{j_i}|H_{j_i} \in C \text{ such that } \sum_{A_r \subseteq H_{j_i}} x_r^{\beta-1} = 0 \right] \\[2mm] \displaystyle\sum_{A_r \subseteq H_o^\beta} x_r^\beta = 1, \end{cases}$$

(put, for all H_{j_i}'s, $\sum_{A_r \subseteq H_{j_i}} \mathbf{x}_r^{-1} = 0$), where $H_o^o = H_o = H_1 \vee \ldots \vee H_n$, and $\mathbf{x}_r^{\beta-1}$ denotes a solution of $(S_{\beta-1})$ and H_o^β is, for $\beta \ge 1$, the union of the H_{j_i}'s such that $\sum_{A_r \subseteq H_{j_i}} \mathbf{x}_r^{\beta-1} = 0$.

Coherence of an assessment $P(\cdot|\cdot)$ on an *infinite* set C of conditional events is equivalent to coherence on *any finite* subset $\mathcal{F}$ of C. This is absolutely convenient for proving coherence in particular sets of events, such as that considered in the following Corollary 1, given in [2], which provides the syntactic basis for the interpretation of fuzzy sets as coherent conditional probability, recalled in the following session.

Corollary 1. *Let C be a family of conditional events $\{E_i|H_i\}_{i \in I}$, where $card(I)$ is arbitrary and the events H_i's are a partition of Ω. Any function $f : C \to [0,1]$ such that $f(E_i|H_i) = 0$ if $E_i \wedge H_i = \emptyset$ and $f(E_i|H_i) = 1$ if $H_i \subseteq E_i$ is a coherent conditional probability.*

Moreover if the only coherent assessment on C take values in $\{0,1\}$, then it is $H_i \wedge E = \emptyset$ for every $H_i \in \mathcal{H}_o$, and it is $H_i \subseteq E$ for every $H_i \in \mathcal{H}_1$, where $\mathcal{H}_r = \{H_i : P(E|H_i) = r\}$, $r = 0, 1$.

We recall a fundamental result [7] showing that any coherent conditional probability can be extended by preserving coherence.

Theorem 2. *Let $\mathcal{K}$ be any family of conditional events, and take an arbitrary family $C \subseteq \mathcal{K}$. Let P be an assessment on C; then there exists a (possibly not unique) coherent extension of P to $\mathcal{K}$ if and only if P is coherent on C.*

3 Coherent Conditional Probability and Fuzzy Sets

We adopt the interpretation of fuzzy sets in terms of coherent conditional probabilities, introduced in [2, 3]. We briefly recall here the main concepts.

Let Z be a (not necessarily numerical) random variable, with range $\mathcal{C}_Z$, let A_z be, for any $z \in \mathcal{C}_Z$, the event $\{Z = z\}$. The family $\{A_z\}_{z \in \mathcal{C}_Z}$ is obviously a *partition* of the certain event Ω. Let φ be any *property* related to the random variable Z.

Let us refer to the state of information of a real (or fictitious) person that will be denoted by "You". It is natural to think that You have some information about possible values of Z, which allows You to refer to a suitable *membership function* of the fuzzy subset of "elements of $\mathcal{C}_Z$ with the property φ".

For example, if Z is the numerical quantity expressing the diameter of balls in a box in cm and φ is the property "large", then the interest is in fact directed toward *conditional events* such as $E_\varphi | A_z$, where z ranges over the possible value of the diameters, with

$$E_\varphi = \{\text{You claim that } Z \text{ is } \varphi\}\,, \quad A_z = \{\text{the value of } Z \text{ is } z\}.$$

It follows that You may assign to each of these conditional events a degree of belief (subjective probability) $P(E_\varphi | A_z)$, without any restriction (see Corollary 1). Note that this conditional probability $P(E_\varphi | A_z)$ is directly introduced as a function on the set of conditional events (and without assuming any given algebraic structure).

Thus, it seems sensible to purpose the coherent conditional probability $P(E_\varphi | A_z)$ as a good interpretation of the membership function $\mu_\varphi(z)$. More precisely it is possible to put, for any random variable Z with range $\mathcal{C}_Z$ and a related property φ, *fuzzy subset* E_φ^* of $\mathcal{C}_Z$ as the pair

$$E_\varphi^* = \{E_\varphi\,, \mu_{E_\varphi}\},$$

with $\mu_{E_\varphi}(z) = P(E_\varphi | A_z)$ for every $z \in \mathcal{C}_Z$.

So a membership function $\mu_{E_\varphi}(z)$ is a measure of how much is probable that You claim that Z is φ, when Z assumes the different values of its range.

Given two fuzzy subsets E_φ^*, E_ψ^*, with E_φ and E_ψ logically independent, the definitions of the binary operations of union and intersection related to (archimedean t-norms and t-conorms) and that of complementation are obtained directly by using the rules of coherent conditional probability [2].

3.1   Updating Membership Functions

The above interpretation of fuzzy set as a coherent conditional probability obviously provides a very natural method for choosing the most probable element of $\mathcal{C}_Z$ by using both statistical information and fuzzy information.

Suppose now to extract one ball from the box containing balls with different diameters, we are interested on the most probable diameter of the ball under the hypothesis that You claim that the ball is large.

More in general, if P is a probability distribution on the elements of $\mathcal{C}_Z$ and fuzzy information is expressed by a membership function $\mu_\varphi(\cdot) = P(E_\varphi|\cdot)$, then we can find the most probable element $z \in C_Z$ under the hypothesis E_φ. By using Bayes theorem we can compute, for every $z \in C_Z$, the value $P(A_z|E_\varphi)$ as

$$P(A_z|E_\varphi) = \alpha P(A_z)\mu_\varphi(z)$$

where $\alpha = \sum_z \mu_\varphi(z)P(A_z)$.

So, to get our goal it is sufficient to compute

$$max_z\{P(A_z)\mu_\varphi(z)\} \tag{1}$$

In the following we have the same aim in a more general context, in which both "probability" and "membership" can be partial or/and imprecise. For that some problems must be taken into account. First of all we recall that, when a probability is defined on all the events A_i of a partition, this probability is coherent also with μ whenever μ is defined on the same partition. In this case the extension of the membership is uniquely defined on all the events with positive probability and it is obtained by disintegration rule, as remarked above.

Some time however our data base consists on a probability assessed on a different set of events: for instance, considering again the example of balls, let B_1 ="diameter d_i is less than x", B_2 = "diameter d_i is greater than y", B_2 ="diameter d_i is in the interval $[z, z']$".

Nevertheless, the global coherence of a coherent probability assessment P and of a membership μ is already preserved under a suitable condition, as the next result shows:

Theorem 3. *Let $\mu(\cdot) = p(E_\varphi|\cdot)$ be a membership function on C_Z and let $\mathcal{H}$ the algebra generated by C_Z. Consider a coherent probability P on a set $\mathcal{D} \subseteq \mathcal{H}$, then μ and P are globally coherent.*

Proof: Any probability on $\mathcal{H}$ is globally coherent with μ on C_Z. Then, in particular, any coherent extension of P on $\mathcal{H}$ is globally coherent with μ on C_Z. Therefore μ is globally coherent also with its restriction P.

Hence, by using Theorem 2, the coherent assessment P, μ can be extended.

However, we need to stress that if $\mathcal{D} \not\subseteq \mathcal{H}$, then, also in the case the events of $\mathcal{D}$ are incompatible, the coherence of the assessments P and μ does not imply the global coherence of $\{P, \mu\}$, as the following example shows.

Example 1. *Consider the probability distribution $P(A_1) = \frac{3}{40}$, $P(A_2) = \frac{17}{40}$, $P(A_3) = \frac{1}{8}$, $P(A_4) = \frac{15}{40}$; and let Z be a binary random variable and φ a related property, consider the membership function $\mu_\varphi(z_1) = \frac{2}{5}$ and $\mu_\varphi(z_2) = \frac{1}{8}$.*

Note that $\mu_\varphi(\cdot) = P(E_\varphi|\cdot)$ on C_Z is a coherent conditional probability as well as P on $A_1, ..., A_4$.

Suppose now that $E_\varphi \wedge A_3 = \emptyset$ and $(Z = z_1) = A_1 \vee A_3$, $(Z = z_2) = A_2 \vee A_4$. We need to check whether the assessment $\{\mu, P\}$ is globally coherent, then we consider the atoms generated by A_i and E_φ: $A_i' = A_i \wedge E_\varphi$ for $i = 1, 2, 4$ and $A_3' = A_3 \wedge E_\varphi^c$, moreover $A_{j+4}' = A_j \wedge E_\varphi^c$ for $j = 1, 2$ and $A_7' = A_4 \wedge E_\varphi^c$.

The relevant system to check the coherence is

$$\begin{cases} x_1 + x_5 = \frac{3}{40} \\ x_2 + x_6 = \frac{17}{40} \\ x_3 = \frac{1}{8} \\ x_4 + x_7 = \frac{15}{40} \\ x_1 = \frac{2}{5}(x_1 + x_3 + x_5) \\ x_2 + x_5 = \frac{1}{8}(x_2 + x_4 + x_6 + x_7) \\ \sum_i x_i + 1 \\ x_i \geq 0 \end{cases}$$

From the first, the third and the fifth equation we have $x_1 = \frac{2}{5}(\frac{3}{40} + \frac{1}{8}) = \frac{7}{20} > \frac{3}{40}$, *which contradicts equation 1.*

Then, the above system admits no solution and so the assessment $\{\mu, P\}$ *is not globally coherent even if P is defined on a partition finer than that generated by Z.*

When the assessment $\{\mu, P\}$ is globally coherent, we are interested on the lower and upper envelope of the possible extensions, which are described through the following result:

Theorem 4. *Let $\mathcal{D} = \{K_1, ..., K_m\}$ be a set of incompatible events of the algebra $\mathcal{H}$, generated by the partition $\mathcal{P} = \{z_1, ..., z_n\}$. Let μ be a membership function on $\mathcal{P}$ and P a coherent probability on $\mathcal{D}$. Let $P(K_{m+1}) = 1 - \sum_{j=1}^m K_j$ where $K_{m+1} = (\vee_{j=1}^m K_j)^c$.*

Then, the lower envelope ϕ_* and the upper envelope ϕ^* of the extensions of μ on the algebra $\mathcal{H}$ is such that for any $H \in \mathcal{H}^0$

$$\phi_*(H) \sum_{K_j \subseteq H} P(K_j) = \sum_{K_j \subseteq H} (\inf_{z_i \subseteq K_j} \mu(z_i)) P(K_j),$$

$$\phi^*(H) \sum_{K_j \wedge H \neq \emptyset} P(K_j) = \sum_{K_j \wedge H \neq \emptyset} (\sup_{z_i \subseteq K_j \wedge H} \mu(z_i)) P(K_j).$$

Proof: Since $\mu(\cdot) = P(E_\varphi|\cdot)$ and P on $\mathcal{D}$ are globally coherent, from Theorem 2 there is (at least) an extension on $E \times \mathcal{H}^0$, then for any $H \in \mathcal{H}^0$ we can compute $\phi_*(H) = \inf P'(E_\varphi|H)$ where the infimum is computed over the possible extensions P' of P.

For every $H \in \mathcal{H}$, there is an extension $\mu(\cdot) = P(E_\varphi|\cdot)$ (among the possible ones) such that for any $K_j \subseteq H$

$$P_*(E_\varphi|K_j) = \inf_{z_i \subseteq K_j} \mu(z_i).$$

This follows from Theorem 4 in [5] by giving to atom A_{j_i} probability equal to $P(K_j)$ for j_i such that

$$\inf_{z_s \subseteq K_j} \mu(z_s) = \mu(z_{j_i})$$

for any $j = 1, ..., m, m + 1$ such that $K_j \subseteq H$, while for j such that $K_j \wedge H \neq \emptyset \neq K_j \wedge H^c$, j_i is chosen among z_r such that $z_r \subseteq K_j \wedge H^c$ and 0 to the other ones. Then, ϕ_* is an extension of μ obtained through the above assignment on the atoms.

Analogously, ϕ^* can be obtained by considering the supremum of the likelihood over any K_j with $K_j \wedge H \neq \emptyset$ and it is obtained by giving to the atom A_{j_i} probability equal to $P(K_j)$ if

$$\sup_{z_r \subseteq K_j \wedge H} \mu(z_r) = \mu(z_{j_i})$$

and 0 to the others.

The previous result includes the case in which $\mathcal{D}$ coincides with the set of atoms $\{z_r\}$, where the classic disintegration rule can be applied.

The situation in Theorem 4 is the simplest one. In fact, the lower envelope $\underline{P}$ of the extensions of the coherent probability on $\mathcal{D}$ is infinitely monotone (see e.g. [10]), and so 2-monotone (convex), that is for any $H, K \in \mathcal{H}$:

$$\underline{P}(H \vee K) \geq \underline{P}(H) + \underline{P}(K) - \underline{P}(H \wedge K)$$

Actually, when $\mathcal{D}$ is an arbitrary subset of $\mathcal{H}^0$, we can have different situations.

In general, the lower envelope $\underline{P}$ of the coherent extensions of P on $\mathcal{H}$ is a lower probability $\underline{P}$, i.e. the lower envelope of extensions $\mathcal{P} = \{P_i\}$ to the algebra $\mathcal{H}$, spanned by $\mathcal{D}$, of the coherent probability P on $\mathcal{D}$. More precisely, for any $H \in \mathcal{H}$

$$\underline{P}(H) = \inf_{P_i \in \mathcal{P}} P_i(H).$$

When the set of events $\mathcal{D}$ is finite the above infimum is a minimum (see e.g. [3]), in the sense that there is a finite family of $P_j \in \mathcal{P}$ such that $\underline{P}(H) = \min_{P_j} P_j(H)$ for any $H \in \mathcal{H}$.

In the following we deal with the coherent extensions of the membership and the coherent probability. We first study the general case and then the particular case when the lower probability is convex (2-monotone).

In the general case μ and P can be extended on $H \in \mathcal{H}^0$, first of all, by looking for the minimum of $\sum_{A_r \subseteq H} x_r$ under

$$\mathcal{S} = \begin{cases} \sum_{A_r \subseteq A_i} x_r = P(A_i) \text{ for } A_i \in \mathcal{D} \\ \sum_{A_r} x_r = 1 \\ x_r \geq 0 \qquad\qquad \text{ for } z_r \in \mathcal{C}_Z \end{cases}$$

If the minimum is positive, then the extension is obtained by looking for

$$\min / \max \frac{\sum_{A_r \subseteq H} \mu(z_r) x_r}{\sum_{A_r \subseteq H} x_r} \qquad (2)$$

under the system $\mathcal{S}$. This is a fractional optimization problem, which can be reformulated in terms of a liner problem by finding

$$\min/\max \sum_{A_r \subseteq H} \mu(z_r) y_r \tag{3}$$

under the following system

$$\mathcal{S}^* = \begin{cases} \sum_{A_r \subseteq A_i} y_r = P(A_i) \sum_{A_r} y_r \text{ for } A_i \in \mathcal{D} \\ \sum_{A_r \subseteq H} y_r = 1 \\ y_r \geq 0 \qquad\qquad\qquad \text{for } A_r \in \mathcal{C}_Z \end{cases}$$

Note that the solutions $\{\mathbf{x}_r\}_r$ of the system $\mathcal{S}$ coincide, unless of a normalization constant, with the solutions $\{\mathbf{y}_r\}_r$ of the system $\mathcal{S}^*$, i.e.

$$\mathbf{x}_r = \frac{\mathbf{y}_r}{\sum_{A_r \in \mathcal{C}_Z} \mathbf{y}_r}.$$

Otherwise, if the minimum of $\sum_{A_r \subseteq H} x_r$, under the system $\mathcal{S}$, is 0, the coherent extension of $\{\mu, P\}$ on $H \in \mathcal{H}$ are in the interval $[p_*, p^*]$ with

$$p_* = \min_{A_r \subseteq H} \mu(z_r) \quad \text{and} \quad p^* = \max_{A_r \subseteq H} \mu(z_r).$$

Then, we show that in both cases the extension of $\{\mu, P\}$ on $H \in \mathcal{H}$ is an interval and the extreme values can be found by solving an optimization linear problem. However, we cannot find the extension, in the general case, directly by resorting to the lower envelope of the extensions of P. In fact we need to refer to the solutions of the linear systems $\mathcal{S}^*$.

Notice that, according to equation (3), we are interested on the unconditional lower probability rather than to the conditional one.

Actually, for those events $H \in \mathcal{H}^0$, such that the conditional lower probability $\underline{P}_H(\cdot) = \underline{P}(\cdot|H)$, obtained as the lower envelope of the extensions of P, is 2-monotone we can compute the extension of $\{P, \mu\}$ directly by means of $\underline{P}_H$ as a Choquet integral since μ is upper $\mathcal{H}$-measurable (see [8]). More precisely, being μ a function with values in $[0,1]$

$$\oint \mu d\underline{P}_H = \int_0^1 \underline{P}_H(s : \mu(s) \geq x) dx$$

which, in the discrete case, reduces to:

$$\oint \mu d\underline{P}_H = \sum_{i=1}^n \mu(s_{(j)})(\underline{P}_H(A(s_{(j)})) - \underline{P}_H(A(s_{(j+1)}))),$$

where $(s_{(j)})$'s are such that

$$0 \leq \mu(s_{(1)}) \leq \mu(s_{(2)}) \leq \dots \leq \mu(s_{(n)})$$

and $A(s_{(j)}) = ((s_{(j)}), (s_{(j+1)}), \dots, (s_{(n)}))$ with $A(s_{(n+1)}) = \emptyset$.

Notice that, if $\underline{P}(H) = 0$, then $\underline{P}_H$ is 2-monotone, and, as noted before, the above Choquet integral reduces to the minimum of the function μ on H.

For the maximum we are interested in the conditional upper probability, and the computation of the maximum extensions follows analogously.

Now, in order to choose the most probable element of $\mathcal{C}_Z$, under the hypothesis E_φ, by using both statistical information and fuzzy information, we need to compute the coherent extensions of $(A_i|E_\varphi)$. In this general setting, they are an interval and so we need to find the bounds of such interval by looking for the lower conditional probability and the upper conditional probability of that conditional event. When $\underline{P}(E_\varphi)$ is equal to 0, the interval is [0,1], but this case is not so interesting because it implies that the membership function is greater than 0 only on an event of 0 lower probability.

Then, we examine the interesting case, which is $\underline{P}(E_\varphi) > 0$, in that case

$$\underline{P}(A_i|E_\varphi) = \min \frac{x_i \mu(z_i)}{\sum_j x_j \mu(z_j)}$$

under the system $\mathcal{S}$. Analogously what done before, this problem can be reformulated by finding $\underline{P}(A_i|E_\varphi)$ as

$$\min y_i \mu(z_i)$$

under the following system

$$\begin{cases} \sum_{A_r \subseteq A_i} y_r = P(A_i) \sum_{A_r} y_r \text{ for } A_i \in \mathcal{D} \\ \sum_j y_j \mu(z_j) = 1 \\ y_r \geq 0 \qquad\qquad\qquad \text{for } z_r \in \mathcal{C}_Z \end{cases}$$

Then also in this case the value is found through an optimization linear problem.

4   Conclusion

In this paper we deal with the problem of updating a probability assessment on the basis of a fuzzy information, by using a generalized Bayesian inference. For this aim we start from an interpretation of fuzzy set in terms of coherent conditional probability assessment given in [2]. In particular we study this problem when either prior probability assessment and membership are defined on sets of events different from those directly involved in the inferential process. This fact requires to make inference starting from a set of probabilities (and so their lower and upper envelops). In the paper we study the most general case and some particular cases. The study of the relevant cases is not exhaustive, for instance we need to face the case where logical relations among the events of the initial probability P and the domain $\mathcal{D}$ of the available membership give rise to an upper envelope of the coherent extensions of P to $\mathcal{D}$, which is a possibility (see [4]).

References

1. Coletti, G., Scozzafava, R.: Characterization of Coherent Conditional Probabilities as a Tool for their Assessment and Extension. International Journal of Uncertainty, Fuzziness and Knowledge-Based Systems 4, 103–127 (1996)
2. Coletti, G., Scozzafava, R.: Conditional probability, fuzzy sets and possibility: a unifying view. Fuzzy Sets and Systems 144, 227–249 (2004)
3. Coletti, G., Scozzafava, R.: Probabilistic Logic in a Coherent Setting. Trends in Logic, vol. 15. Kluwer, Dordrecht (2002)
4. Coletti, G., Scozzafava, R., Vantaggi, B.: Possibility measures in probabilistic inference. In: Soft Methodology for Handling Variability and Imprecision, pp. 51–58 (2008)
5. Coletti, G., Scozzafava, R., Vantaggi, B.: Integrated Likelihood in a Finitely Additive Setting. In: Sossai, C., Chemello, G. (eds.) ECSQARU 2009. LNCS (LNAI), vol. 5590, pp. 554–565. Springer, Heidelberg (2009)
6. Coppi, R., Gil, M.A., Kiers, H.A.L. (eds.): The Fuzzy Approach to Statistical Analysis. Computational Statistics & Data Analysis 51, 1–452 (2006)
7. de Finetti, B.: Sull'impostazione assiomatica del calcolo delle probabilitá. Annali Univ. di Trieste 19, 29–81 (1949); English translation in: Probability, Induction, Statistics, ch. 5. Wiley, London
8. Denneberg, D.: Non-Additive Measure and Integral. Kluwer, Dordrecht (1994)
9. Dubois, D., Lubiano, M.A., Prade, H., Gil, M.A., Grzegorzewski, P., Hryniewicz, O. (eds.): Soft Methods for Handling Variability and Imprecision Series. Advances in Intelligent and Soft Computing, vol. 48. Springer, Heidelberg
10. Fagin, R., Halpern, J.: Uncertainty, belief and probability. Computational Intelligence 7, 160–173 (1991)
11. Grzegorzewski, P., Hryniewicz, O., Gil, M.A. (eds.): Soft Methods in Probability, Statistics and Data Analysis. Advances in Intelligent and Soft Computing, vol. 16. Springer, Heidelberg (2002)
12. Lawry, J., Miranda, E., Bugarin, A., Li, S., Gil, M.A., Grzegorzewski, P., Hryniewicz, O. (eds.): Soft Methods for Integrated Uncertainty Modelling. Advances in Soft Computing. Springer, Heidelberg (2006)
13. Lopez-Diaz, M.C., Gil, M.A., Grzegorzewski, P., Hryniewicz, O., Lawry, J.: Soft Methodology and Random Information Systems Series. Advances in Intelligent and Soft Computing, vol. 26. Springer, Heidelberg (2004)
14. Popper, K.R.: The Logic of Scientific Discovery. Routledge, London (1959)
15. Zadeh, L.A.: Fuzzy sets. Information and Control 8, 338–353 (1965)
16. Zadeh, L.A.: Discussion: Probability theory and fuzzy logic are complementary rather than competitive. Technometrics 37, 271–276 (1995)

Modelling Patterns of Evidence in Bayesian Networks: A Case-Study in Classical Swine Fever

Linda C. van der Gaag[1], Janneke Bolt[1],
Willie Loeffen[2], and Armin Elbers[2]

[1] Department of Information and Computing Sciences, Utrecht University,
P.O. Box 80.089, 3508 TB Utrecht, The Netherlands
{linda,janneke}@cs.uu.nl
[2] Central Veterinary Institute, Wageningen UR,
P.O. Box 65, 8200 AB Lelystad, The Netherlands
{armin.elbers,willie.loeffen}@wur.nl

Abstract. Upon engineering a Bayesian network for the early detection of Classical Swine Fever in pigs, we found that the commonly used approach of separately modelling the relevant observable variables would not suffice to arrive at satisfactory performance of the network: explicit modelling of combinations of observations was required to allow identifying and reasoning about patterns of evidence. In this paper, we outline a general approach to modelling relevant patterns of evidence in a Bayesian network. We demonstrate its application for our problem domain and show that it served to significantly improve our network's performance.

1 Introduction

Over the last decades, researchers developed Bayesian networks to support medical and veterinary practitioners in their diagnostic reasoning processes for a variety of biomedical domains. Examples from our own engineering experiences include a Bayesian network for establishing the stage of oesophageal cancer in patients who have been diagnosed with the disease [1], naive Bayesian networks for deciding upon the most likely causal pathogen of clinical mastitis in dairy cows [2], and a dynamic Bayesian network for diagnosing ventilator-associated pneumonia in critically ill patients in an intensive care unit [3]. Our most recent engineering efforts concern a network for the early detection of an infection with the Classical Swine Fever (CSF) virus in individual pigs.

Upon constructing our Bayesian network for the early detection of Classical Swine Fever, we found that the commonly used engineering approach of separately modelling the clinical signs found with the disease, would not suffice to arrive at satisfactory performance of the network. In-depth interviews with researchers and veterinary practitioners across the European Union showed that the aspecificity of especially the early signs of the disease makes a clinical diagnosis highly uncertain and that satisfactory diagnostic performance can only be reached by reasoning about the presence or absence of specific combinations

E. Hüllermeier, R. Kruse, and F. Hoffmann (Eds.): IPMU 2010, LNAI 6178, pp. 675–684, 2010.

of observations hidden in the presented evidence. These combinations of observations are associated with the successive phases of the disease, which cannot be observed in practice yet may or may not be evidenced by clinical signs. To show satisfactory diagnostic performance, therefore, our Bayesian network for the early detection of CSF should reason not just about separate clinical signs but also about relevant patterns in the evidence presented by an animal.

In this paper we present a generally applicable approach to modelling relevant patterns of evidence in a Bayesian network. The basic idea of our approach is to distinguish combinations of observations which are relevant for reasoning in the application domain and to model these by means of hidden variables. The hidden variables then are used to organise the variables which describe the observations themselves. By capturing not just the observations but also their important combinations, the resulting network is able to identify and reason about the synergistic information hidden in the entered evidence. We illustrate how the approach is used to describe combinations of observations commonly seen in the successive phases of a disease. We further show that its application significantly improved the detection abilities of our network for Classical Swine Fever.

The idea of introducing hidden variables in a Bayesian network was described before for the Hailfinder model [4]. In that model, a single hidden variable was introduced as an approach to managing the complexity of the set of observations: the hidden variable was used to abstract from the details hidden in the evidence. In the current paper, we introduce a collection of hidden variables modelling an unobservable disease process, not with the aim of summarising information but for the purpose of identifying significant additional information from the set of observations. The idea of introducing hidden variables thus is taken a step further. Although motivated by our specific application in veterinary science, we feel that the approach of modelling patterns of evidence is more generally applicable. In fact, we expect the approach to be advantageous also for other applications which require identifying and reasoning about the presence or absence of specific combinations of observations, be they related to the separate phases of a disease process or otherwise of relevance for the domain at hand.

The paper is organised as follows. In Section 2, we introduce the problem of early detection of Classical Swine Fever in individual pigs and describe the Bayesian network initially constructed for the problem; in this section we also elaborate on the need to explicitly capture patterns of evidence in the network. In Section 3, we outline our approach to modelling combinations of observations in a Bayesian network in general and demonstrate its application in the CSF network. In Section 4, we compare the performances of the initially constructed and enhanced CSF networks on a variety of pig cases. We end in Section 5 with our conclusions and directions for further research.

2   A Bayesian Network for Classical Swine Fever

We provide some background information on Classical Swine Fever and briefly describe our initial Bayesian network for early detection of the disease.

2.1   Classical Swine Fever

Classical Swine Fever is a highly infectious pig disease with a potential for rapid spread. When a pig is first infected with the CSF virus, it will show an increased body temperature and a sense of malaise, associated with such signs as a lack of appetite and lethargy. Later in the infection, the animal is likely to suffer from abnormal faeces, mostly diarrhoea, as a result of an inflammation of the intestinal tract. Further on, problems of the respiratory tract will be revealed through such signs as a conjunctivitis, nasal secretion, and coughing. The final phases of the disease are associated with circulatory problems, causing cyanotic colouring and pin-point skin haemorrhages, and with a paralysis of the hind legs, respectively. Ultimately, as a result of the accumulating failure of body systems, the pig will die [5]. The disease can be caused by a variety of strains differing in virulence. While highly virulent strains cause the disease to develop aggressively over a short time with a large proportion of affected animals dying, less virulent ones cause the disease to develop more slowly and less prominently.

Classical Swine Fever is a notifiable disease: any suspicion of its presence should be reported immediately to the agricultural authorities and control measures, involving for example closure of the farm, should be installed. The longer a CSF infection remains undetected, the longer the virus can circulate without hindrance, not just within a herd but also between herds. Because of the major socio-economical consequences that an outbreak may have, reducing the high-risk period of time between first infection of a herd and first detection is of major importance. Improving early detection based upon clinical signs is a first step towards reduction of this period. The aspecificity of especially the early signs of the disease causes the clinical diagnosis of CSF to remain highly uncertain for a relatively long period after the infection occurred, however [6].

2.2   The CSF Network

In collaboration with an experimental CSF expert and a senior epidemiologist from the Central Veterinary Institute of the Netherlands, we designed a Bayesian network for the early detection of Classical Swine Fever. An investigation of current practices showed that a veterinarian visits a pig farm with disease problems when called for by the farmer. After investigating a limited number of diseased animals, the veterinarian has to formulate a differential diagnosis for the problems at hand, without having information available about the disease history of the individual pigs. During the visit, the veterinarian also has to decide about whether or not to report a CSF suspicion to the agricultural authorities. Since our Bayesian network was aimed at supporting veterinarians in their current practices, we decided to focus engineering efforts on the clinical signs which are typically associated with a CSF infection and can be observed in an individual animal at a single moment in time without reference to disease history.

For the construction of the network, in-depth interviews were held with the two participating experts; in addition, case reviews were conducted with Dutch swine practitioners, both with and without clinical CSF experience, and with

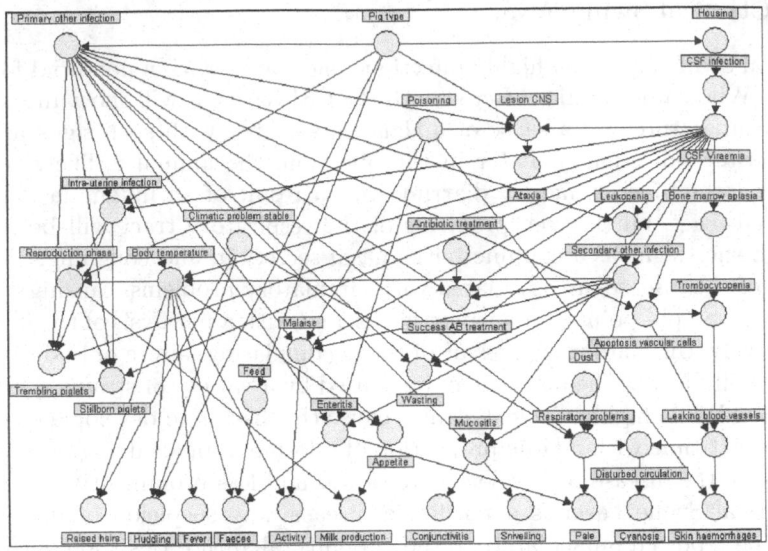

Fig. 1. The graphical structure of the initial network for the early detection of CSF

pig experts in six other countries within the European Union. The graphical structure of the resulting network is shown in Figure 1. It includes 42 stochastic variables. Half of these variables describe clinical signs relevant for confirming or ruling out CSF; the remaining variables capture internal effects of the presence of the virus, risk factors for contracting the virus, and alternative explanations for observed signs. The dependencies among the variables are captured by 84 arcs, which are quantified by some 1500 (conditional) probabilities. The network takes for its input the clinical signs observed in an individual pig and returns the posterior probability of these signs being caused by a CSF infection.

2.3   A Preliminary Evaluation

The performance of the initially constructed network for the early detection of Classical Swine Fever was evaluated informally, using a small number of negative cases from veterinary practice, that is, of pigs without CSF. The findings suggested, unfortunately, that our network would result in an unacceptably large number of false CSF warnings when used in practice; in fact, it performed inadequately in attributing negative cases to primary infections other than CSF.

The pig cases used for the informal evaluation of the CSF network were reviewed by veterinary practitioners from across the European Union. The reviews showed that veterinarians could relatively easily dismiss a diagnosis of CSF for these cases. Subsequent elicitation revealed that the practitioners used their knowledge of the course of a CSF infection in an individual animal for reasoning about the cases. More specifically, we found that a veterinarian would consider not so much the separate signs associated with a CSF infection but would look for the typical combinations of signs associated with the successive phases of the disease. For example, a pattern of cyanosis and paralysis of the hind legs, which are typical late signs of CSF, would not very likely incite them to issue a CSF warning in the absence of diarrhoea and respiratory problems, simply because an animal in which the disease had progressed into the final phases would also show the clinical signs from the earlier phases of the disease.

The initially constructed network described above clearly was able to relate the clinical signs observed in a pig to CSF, but could not reason about the significance of the presence and/or absence of specific combinations of signs. To arrive at a better performance, therefore, the network should be able to identify and reason about relevant combinations of signs hidden in the observed evidence.

3   Modelling Patterns of Evidence in a Bayesian Network

Motivated by our experiences, we designed a generally applicable approach to modelling relevant patterns of evidence in a Bayesian network. The basic idea of the approach is to introduce hidden variables in the network to describe combinations of observations which are relevant for reasoning about the uncertainties in a domain at hand. These hidden variables are subsequently used to organise the stochastic variables which describe the observations themselves. By capturing not just the observations but also their important combinations, the resulting network is able to take the synergistic information hidden in entered evidence into consideration. We describe the basic idea of our approach and outline its application for our network for the early detection of Classical Swine Fever.

3.1   The Basic Idea

Our approach to modelling patterns of evidence in a Bayesian network is to introduce hidden, so-called pattern variables for relevant combinations of observations and to organise the observable variables as contributing evidence to these pattern variables. More formally, we consider $n \geq 1$ combinations of observations which are relevant for reasoning in the domain at hand. For each such combination i, we introduce a pattern variable Φ_i, $i = 1, \ldots, n$, modelling whether or not the combination is present in the entered evidence. Dependent upon the role and meaning of the patterns of evidence in the domain, the newly introduced variables may or may not be (conditionally) dependent. The pattern variables are subsequently used to organise the observable variables, by linking each pattern variable Φ_i to the $m_i \geq 1$ observable variables X_{j_i}, $j_i = 1, \ldots, m_i$, from which the presence or absence of the pattern is established. The direction of the arcs linking the pattern variable to the observable variables, that is, pointing from or to the hidden variable, is again dependent upon the role and meaning of the patterns in the domain of application.

3.2   Enhancing the CSF Network

The basic idea of modelling patterns of evidence was used to enhance the previously constructed Bayesian network for the early detection of Classical Swine

Fever. In the domain of application, the patterns to be modelled are related to the phases of the course of a CSF infection in an individual animal. For each of the five disease phases, therefore, an intermediate phase variable Φ_i was introduced. Since a CSF infection progresses linearly through the various phases, the newly introduced variables could not be considered mutually independent. To describe the progression of the infection, therefore, the phase variables Φ_i were interrelated by means of arcs $\Phi_i \to \Phi_{i+1}$, $i = 1, \ldots, n - 1$; an arc between two successive phase variables thus describes the transition relation between the modelled disease phases. The conditional probability tables associated with the phase variables capture the likelihood that the infection progressed to a specific phase. The probability table for the first phase variable ϕ_1 essentially expresses the prior probability $\Pr(\phi_1 = \text{yes})$ of the animal having been infected. The conditional probability table for the phase variable ϕ_i, $i = 2, \ldots, n$, describes the probability of the disease having entered into the i-th phase given that phase $i - 1$ had, or had not, been entered; the table thus specifies the transition probabilities

$$\Pr(\phi_i = \text{yes} \mid \phi_{i-1} = \text{yes})$$
$$\Pr(\phi_i = \text{yes} \mid \phi_{i-1} = \text{no})$$

The latter probability was set to 0 since a CSF infection is known to progress linearly through the separate phases without skipping any of them. Moreover, since the likelihood of progression of the disease to the next phase is known to depend upon some predisposing factors, the actual transition probabilities for the network were further conditioned on these variables. All transition probabilities were assessed by one of our experts. He was requested to consider a group of 100 pigs in the first phase of the disease. For each phase, he was asked to distribute the group of remaining animals over three subgroups: the group of animals that would enter the next phase, the group that would die, and the group of animals that would successfully fight the infection and be cured. From the estimated group sizes, the transitional probabilities were readily established.

We would like to note that modelling the relevant patterns of evidence in our CSF network by introducing phase variables and their transitional relations bears a strong resemblance to the modelling of stochastic processes in hidden Markov models and their extensions [7,8]. A major difference between our approach and these types of model, however, is that the arcs between our phase variables are not associated with a time interval; also the transition probabilities describing the relationships between the phases do not involve any reference to time. The enhanced CSF network still captures just snapshots of the disease process and thereby allows establishing the current phase of the process, yet does not provide for predicting further evolution of the disease over time.

The five phase variables introduced to capture knowledge of the course of a CSF infection were embedded in the originally constructed CSF network, along with their transitional relations. While the disease phases themselves are not observable in practice, they are evidenced by clinical signs which may, or may not, be seen in an individual animal. The initial network already included various observable variables X_{j_i} to describe these signs. These variables were now linked to the appropriate phase variable Φ_i, essentially by means of arcs $\Phi_i \to X_{j_i}$.

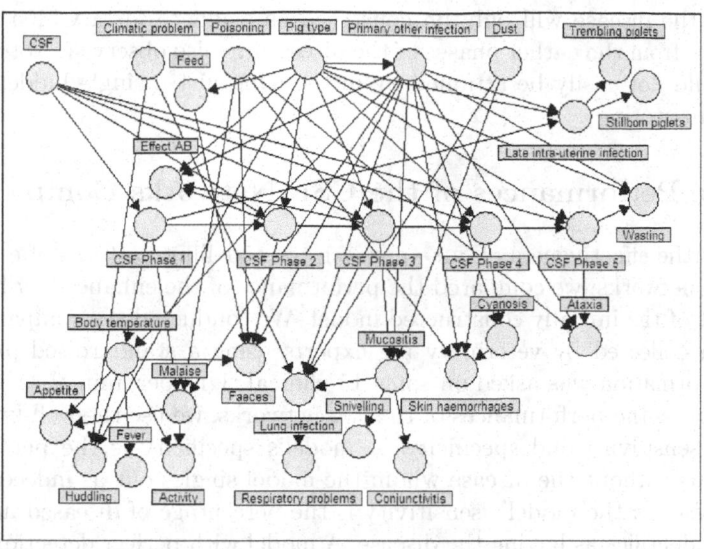

Fig. 2. The graphical structure of the enhanced network for the early detection of CSF

The conditional probability tables for the variables X_{j_i} describe the probability of seeing the associated clinical sign in an animal suffering from the disease in phase i; the tables thus in essence specify the conditional probabilities

$$\Pr(X_{j_i} = \text{yes} \mid \Phi_i = \text{yes})$$
$$\Pr(X_{j_i} = \text{yes} \mid \Phi_i = \text{no})$$

Since a disease phase sometimes is known to induce a hidden process which in turn may cause the associated clinical signs to arise, some phase variables were linked to variables modelling hidden processes rather than to the observable variables themselves. Elicitation had further shown that a pig's body systems are mostly irreversibly affected in the course of a CSF infection. Clinical signs arising in a specific phase would therefore most likely persist throughout subsequent phases of the disease. This knowledge was incorporated implicitly in the network's graphical structure by not including any links from later disease phases to earlier signs. Figure 2 shows the graphical structure of the thus constructed network for the early detection of Classical Swine Fever; we would like to note that the enhanced CSF network includes fewer variables than the originally constructed one, because we decided to not just include the phase variables but to also remove some variables which had proved to not contribute, either positively or negatively, to the network's performance.

The enhanced network for Classical Swine Fever now captures the information that, for example, the first phase of a CSF infection is associated with an elevated body temperature and a sense of malaise. Through the transition probabilities for Phase 2, these signs are modelled as being equally likely in an animal in the second phase of the disease. One of the effects of the introduction of the disease phases into our network thus is that the presence of clinical signs from a later phase of the disease will only be construed as evidence for a CSF infection if most signs from the earlier phases of the disease are also observed. Note that this effect could not easily be attained by introducing just a single hidden variable into the network.

4   The Performances of the CSF Networks Compared

To study the effectiveness of our approach to modelling patterns of evidence in Bayesian networks, we compared the performance of the enhanced CSF network with that of the initially constructed model. We conducted the comparison with real data collected by veterinary pig experts using a standardised protocol in which information was asked on some 15 clinical signs per animal.

To express the performances of the two networks, we use the well-known concepts of sensitivity and specificity. A model's specificity is the percentage of individuals without the disease whom the model singles out as indeed not having the disease; the model's sensitivity is the percentage of diseased individuals whom it identifies as having the disease. A model with perfect detection abilities would thus have both a sensitivity and a specificity of 100%. The concepts of sensitivity and specificity cannot be used directly for a Bayesian network, since its ouput is a probability distribution rather than a determinate diagnosis. For establishing the sensitivity and specificity characteristics of the two CSF networks, therefore, all computed probabilities were compared against a threshold probability α: if the posterior probability of CSF computed for a pig exceeded this threshold probability, we assumed that the diagnosis of CSF was sufficiently confirmed and that a warning was issued for the pig. Small values of α were used to account for the currently small prior probability of Classical Swine Fever.

For comparing the specificities of the two CSF networks, data from pigs without Classical Swine Fever were used; these data were collected by 11 pig veterinarians in the Netherlands and amounted to a total of 375 cases. For each of these cases, the posterior probability of the clinical signs being caused by a CSF infection was computed from both networks and subsequently compared with a threshold probability α as described above. From the numbers of issued warnings, the specificities of the networks were calculated; Table 1 records these specificities for various realistic values of α.

Table 1. The specificities of the initial CSF network and of the enhanced network, given different realistic values of the threshold probability α for issuing a CSF warning

threshold α	specificity initial network	specificity enhanced network
0.05	92%	99%
0.01	86%	98%
0.005	83%	96%
0.001	71%	89%
0.0005	58%	84%

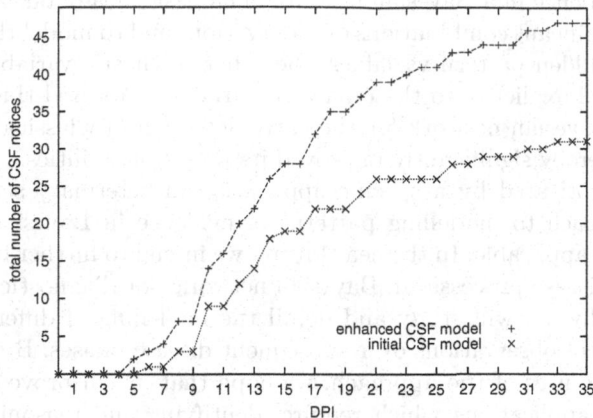

Fig. 3. The cumulative number of CSF warnings issued by the two CSF networks, at $\alpha = 0.001$, for 91 pigs, as a function of the number of days post infection (DPI)

Since commercial pig farms in the European Union have been free from Classical Swine Fever for a long time, the collected field data pertained to animals without the disease only and could not be used to gain insight in the sensitivities of the two CSF networks. For that purpose, experimental data were used. These data were collected from experiments within three countries in the European Union, involving small groups of pigs in which some individuals were inoculated with the CSF virus. A total of 91 animals were followed over a period of 35 days; data were recorded at least every two or three days. For each recording day, for each pig, the posterior probability of the observed clinical signs being caused by a CSF infection was computed from both networks and subsequently compared against a threshold probability α as before. Figure 3 shows, for the two networks, the cumulative number of animals which would receive a CSF warning, as a function of the number of days post infection using the threshold probability $\alpha = 0.001$; similar results were found for other realistic values of α.

Table 1 and Figure 3 show that the enhanced CSF network outperforms the initially constructed network with respect to both its sensitivity and its specificity. The inclusion of patterns of evidence clearly served to improve the detection abilities of the network for our domain of application.

5   Conclusions and Future Research

Engineering Bayesian networks is a creative process in which an engineer is guided by best practices and experiences. While for many diagnostic applications the common approach of separately modelling the relevant observable variables suffices to arrive at satisfactory performance of a network, we found that for our application in veterinary medicine explicit modelling of combinations of observations was required for reasoning about patterns hidden in the evidence. Motivated by this consideration, we presented in this paper an approach to modelling patterns of evidence in a Bayesian network. The basic idea of our approach is to distinguish significant combinations of observations and to model these explicitly by means of hidden pattern variables; the other stochastic variables of interest then are related explicitly to these pattern variables. We used this approach to enhance our Bayesian network for the early detection of Classical Swine Fever in pigs and thereby significantly improved its detection abilities.

Although motivated by a specific application in veterinary science, we feel that our approach to modelling patterns of evidence in Bayesian networks is more generally applicable. In the near future, we intend to further investigate the modelling of disease processes in Bayesian networks for diagnostic applications; more specifically, we will study and detail the modelling of different scenarios for persistence of observations over subsequent disease phases. By investigating further possible uses of the approach, we hope that it will prove advantageous also for other applications which require identifying and reasoning about the presence or absence of specific combinations of observations.

Acknowledgment. The research in this paper was supported by the Netherlands Organisation for Scientific Research.

References

1. van der Gaag, L.C., Renooij, S., Aleman, B.M.P., Taal, B.G.: Evaluation of a probabilistic model for staging of oesophageal carcinoma. In: Medical Infobahn for Europe: Proceedings of MIE 2000 and GMDS 2000, pp. 772–776. IOS Press, Amsterdam (2000)
2. Steeneveld, W., van der Gaag, L.C., Barkema, H.W., Hogeveen, H.: Providing probability distributions for the causal pathogen of clinical mastitis using naive Bayesian networks. Journal of Dairy Science 92, 2598–2609 (2009)
3. Charitos, T., van der Gaag, L.C., Visscher, S., Schurink, K., Lucas, P.: A dynamic Bayesian network for diagnosing ventilator-associated pneumonia in ICU patients. In: Holmes, J.H., Peek, N. (eds.) Proceedings of the 10th Intelligent Data Analysis in Medicine and Pharmacology Workshop, Aberdeen, pp. 32–37 (2005)
4. Abramson, B., Brown, J., Edwards, W., Murphy, A., Winkler, R.L.: Hailfinder: A Bayesian system for forecasting severe weather. International Journal of Forecasting 12, 57–71 (1996)
5. Elbers, A.R.W., Stegeman, A., Moser, H., Ekker, H.M., Smak, J.A., Pluimers, F.H.: The classical swine fever epidemic 1997-1998 in the Netherlands: descriptive epidemiology. Preventive Veterinary Medicine 42, 157–184 (1999)
6. Elbers, A.R.W., Bouma, A., Stegeman, J.A.: Quantitative assessment of clinical signs for the detection of classical swine fever outbreaks during an epidemic. Veterinary Microbiology 85, 323–332 (2002)
7. Ephraim, Y., Merhav, N.: Hidden Markov processes. IEEE Transactions on Information Theory 48, 1518–1569 (2002)
8. Ghahramani, Z., Jordan, M.: Factorial hidden Markov models. Machine Learning 29, 245–273 (1997)

An Importance Sampling Approach to Integrate Expert Knowledge When Learning Bayesian Networks From Data*

Andrés Cano, Andrés R. Masegosa, and Serafín Moral

Department of Computer Science and A.I.
University of Granada, Spain
{acu,andrew,smc}@decsai.ugr.es

Abstract. The introduction of expert knowledge when learning Bayesian Networks from data is known to be an excellent approach to boost the performance of automatic learning methods, specially when the data is scarce. Previous approaches for this problem based on Bayesian statistics introduce the expert knowledge modifying the prior probability distributions. In this study, we propose a new methodology based on Monte Carlo simulation which starts with non-informative priors and requires knowledge from the expert *a posteriori*, when the simulation ends. We also explore a new Importance Sampling method for Monte Carlo simulation and the definition of new non-informative priors for the structure of the network. All these approaches are experimentally validated with five standard Bayesian networks.

1 Introduction

Bayesian networks [1] allow to represent graphically a multivariate joint probability distribution exploiting the dependency structure among the variables. This property together with the graphical nature of BNs make them excellent models to display the complex probabilistic relationships which appear in many real problems. This is one of the main reasons why the problem of automatic discovering of the structure of a BN from data has attracted a great deal of research [2,3,4]. Most of these approaches recovers the model (or its Markov equivalence class) which best explains the data. However, it is well known that if the size of the problem domain is relatively high and there is a limited data sample, there usually are several models that explain the data reasonably well.

The introduction of expert knowledge has been proposed in many studies as an excellent approach to help automatic learning methods to extract more reliable and accurate BN models and to deal with arbitrariness in model selection [2,5,6]. The graphical nature of BNs greatly eases the required interaction with the expert for this purpose.

---

* This work has been jointly supported by Spanish Ministry of Education and Science under project TIN2007-67418-C03-03, by FEDER and by the Spanish research programme Consolider Ingenio 2010: MIPRCV (CSD2007-00018).

E. Hüllermeier, R. Kruse, and F. Hoffmann (Eds.): IPMU 2010, LNAI 6178, pp. 685–695, 2010.

The Bayesian learning framework has been successfully applied to infer BN models because it allows to integrate expert knowledge and deals with several plausible models [2,3,4,5]. The main device explored so far to integrate the expert knowledge within this framework is the elicitation of informative priors. If an expert consider that the presence of an edge is very likely, this knowledge would be represented giving higher prior probabilities to those BN structures containing that edge, as it is proposed in [2,5].

However, we find that there are severe limitations when asking to an expert to provide *a priori* knowledge about any feature of a BN. The main disadvantages we find in this approach are the followings:

- The expert would be requested to submit *a priori* knowledge for each one of the possible edges of the graph. What makes unfeasible the elicitation of the prior distribution for the structure of the graph in large problem domains.
- The expert could be biased to provide the most "easy" or clear knowledge, that is to say, the most strong direct probabilistic dependencies among variables, which happen to be the easiest ones to be discovered.
- The learning algorithm does not help to the user to introduce information about the BN structure.

In this paper we propose a different methodology to take advantage of expert knowledge. We consider the absence of *a priori* knowledge and we will ask to the expert to provide *a posteriori* knowledge, once the learning algorithm has been run in order to refine the output model. The motivation of this approach is to mitigate the above mentioned flaws, so our approach aims: to limit the number of questions that are submitted to the expert; to ask to the expert only the most uncertain structural features; and, finally, to help to the expert to submit his/her knowledge showing him/her the information found in the data. This approach employs a new Importance Sampling (IS) method [7] to sample from the posterior distribution of the space model given the learning data. We also explore some of the possibilities that there are to define non-informative priors about the structure of the BN apart from the common uniform prior.

In that sense, our approach is close to the NPC learning algorithm [8] implemented in *Hugin* [9] which allows the interaction with an expert to solve, when found, conflicts in the independence statements or arc directions after the learning of the graph structure. However, we employ a full Bayesian framework which considers all plausible BN models. In this way, in the NPC approach the expert interaction is restricted to solve, if found, some conflictive specific parts of the model, while in our approach the expert interaction could range from non interaction at all to a full assessment by the expert of each one of the edges.

This approach will assume that a total causal order of the variables (it could be provided by the expert) is known. We impose this strong requirement to limit the super-exponential model space of the BNs and, also, because we have not yet developed an extension of the IS method without this restriction.

In Section 2, we give details about the notation and the Bayesian Learning framework. After that, in Section 3, we present our IS approach [7] to compute marginal probabilities. The methodology to introduce expert knowledge is presented in Section 4. All these approaches are experimentally evaluated in Section 5. Finally, in Section 6, we give the main conclusions and future works.

2   Previous Knowledge

2.1   Notation

We consider the problem of inferring a BN defined over a set of n variables $\mathbf{X} = (X_1, ..., X_n)$ each of which takes values in some finite domain $Val(X_i)$. We are also given a fully observed data set D.

The description of a BN model, $\mathcal{B}$, consists in two parts: the directed acyclic graph G and an associated numerical parameter vector Θ_G. In the graph structure each node corresponds to a random variable and has a set of parents denoted as $Pa_G(X_i)$ (the subindex G will be omitted when is clear from the context), which is a subset of $\mathbf{X}$. At the same time, the parameters Θ_G corresponds to numeric values of the conditional probability tables of that network structure.

As we commented before, throughout this paper we will assume it is given a total causal order of the variables $\mathbf{X} = \{X_1, ..., X_n\}$ in such a way that the graph G is consistent with this order if $X_j \in Pa(X_i)$ then $j < i$. We also define $\mathcal{U}_i$ as a random variable taking values in the space of all possible parent sets of X_i, $Val(\mathcal{U}_i) = \{\mathbf{U} : \mathbf{U} \subset \{X_1, ..., X_{i-1}\}\}$. So, a graph G can be decomposed as a vector of parent sets $G = (Pa(X_1), ..., Pa(X_n))$ where each parent set $Pa(X_i) \in Val(\mathcal{U}_i)$. We will denoted as $\mathcal{G}$ to the random variable taking values in the set of all possible graph structures consistent with the total order.

2.2   The Bayesian Learning Framework

The Bayesian learning framework [7] of BNs has been previously presented in several papers [5,2,4]. Within this framework it is defined a prior probability over all candidate BNs, $P(\mathcal{B})$, and this prior probability is updated in the light of the data, $P(\mathcal{B}|D)$, the posterior probability of the models. The maximum *a posteriori* (MAP) model is returned as the model that the best explain the data.

Due to space reasons and that the basic settings of this approach are clearly detailed in the literature [4], we only show the equations than lead us to the computation of the posterior probability of some structural features of the BN:

The posterior probability of a graph: This posterior probability can be factorized and, then, efficiently computed employing the *Bayesian Dirichlet equivalent* score, *BDe* score [2], which assumes *parameter modularity*, *parameter independence* and a modular structure prior, $P(G) = \prod_i P_i(Pa_G(X_i))$, where $P_i(\mathcal{U}_i)$ is the prior probability over the parent sets of X_i. We get the following expression:

$$P(\mathcal{G} = G|D) = P(G|D) \propto P(G)P(D|G) = \prod_i score(X_i, Pa_G(X_i)|D) \quad (1)$$

So, the posterior is decomposed as a product of local score functions: $score(X_i, Pa_G(X_i)|D)$. This score function has a simple closed form [2] and it is easily computed knowing the prior $P_i(Pa_G(X_i))$ and certain *sufficient statistics* of the data. We implemented the $BDeu$ version, which assumes uniform Dirichlet prior over the parameters Θ_G, with a equivalent sample size equal to 1.

Factorization of $P(\mathcal{G}|D)$: The main advantage of the assumption of a total order is that the posterior probabilities of the parent sets for the variables X_i, $P(\mathcal{U}_i|D)$, become independent among them. So we have the following equality:

$$P(\mathcal{G}|D) = \prod_i P(\mathcal{U}_i|D) \tag{2}$$

So, the problem of approximating this posterior probability $P(\mathcal{G}|D)$ can be decomposed in n independent problems, which are much simpler to compute.

Marginal Probability of an edge: Under the Bayesian framework, we can compute the marginal probability of a feature f of a graph, i.e, the presence of an edge, summing the posterior probabilities of all graph structures consistent with that feature. Because we can use the decomposition of Equation 2, the marginal probability of an edge $X_j \rightarrow X_i$ or of a parent set $\mathbf{U} \in Val(\mathcal{U}_i)$ for X_i are equally computed as the following expected value:

$$P(X_j \rightarrow X_i|D) = E_{P(\mathcal{U}_i|D)}(I_\rightarrow(\mathbf{U})) = \sum_{\mathbf{U} \in Val(\mathcal{U}_i)} I_\rightarrow(\mathbf{U})P(\mathbf{U}|D) \tag{3}$$

where $I_\rightarrow(\mathbf{U})$ is the indicator function and is equals to 1 if $X_j \in \mathbf{U}$, and 0 otherwise. The same expression is employed to compute $P(\mathcal{U}_i = \mathbf{U}|D)$ using the indicator function $I_\mathbf{U}$.

2.3   Monte Carlo Simulation

A natural approach to estimate Equation 3 is the employment of Monte Carlo simulation techniques. Madigan et al. [10] proposed a method based on Markov Chain Monte Carlo (MCMC) simulation for the structural learning of BNs. This MCMC method can be easily adapted to our problem considering $\mathcal{U}_i$ as the space model of the Markov Chain. Using the operations of arc adding, deleting or switch, we could move through this chain and guarantee that it converges to the stationary distribution $P(\mathcal{U}_i|D)$.

However it is well known [3,10] that MCMC simulations usually shows poor mixing rates when the data sample is limited and the space model is high. In our case although the space model is strongly reduced, informal experiments with this approach showed us that these problems are still present, specially when the number of samples is low (less than 500). This fact motivates us to explore other Monte Carlo integration techniques such as Importance Sampling to face this problem.

3 Importance Sampling

Importance sampling (IS) [7] is based on the use of an auxiliary distribution q which roughly approximates the target distribution p which is easier to sample from. Under mild regularity conditions [7], we get that:

$$E_p(f(x)) = \int \frac{p(x)}{q(x)} f(x)q(x)dx = E_q(w(x)f(x)) \tag{4}$$

where $w(x) = \frac{p(x)}{q(x)}$ acts as a weight function. It could also happen that p and q are only known up to a multiplicative constant, as in our problem. In that way, a set of T samples $x^1, ..., x^T$ are generated form q and, then, it is computed $w^t = \frac{p(x^t)}{q(x^t)}$. The estimator $\hat{\mu}$ of $E_p(f(x))$ is finally computed as follows:

$$\hat{\mu} = \frac{\sum_{t=1}^T w(x^t)f(t)}{\sum_{t=1}^T w(x^t)} \tag{5}$$

In our case the sample space model is $\mathcal{U}_i$, the target distribution is $P(Pa(X_i)|D)$ $\propto score(D|Pa(X_i))$. Sampling directly from this distribution is not feasible because the space model is exponential. So, we try to approximate it defining an importance sampling distribution that samples full parent sets by sampling, independently, every single parent node with a probability that tries to approximate the real one. The exact description of this distribution q is as follows:

Algorithm 1. *Importance Sampling Distribution*

Let $\{X_{\sigma(1)}, ..., X_{\sigma(i-1)}\}$ be a random permutation of variables X_j preceding X_i, $j < i$.
$\mathbf{U}^t = \emptyset, q = 1;$
For each $j = 1$ to $i - 1$:

- ***Compute:*** $v = \frac{score(X_i, \mathbf{U}^t \bigcup \{X_{\sigma(j)}\}|D)}{score(X_i, \mathbf{U}^t \bigcup \{X_{\sigma(j)}\}|D) + score(X_i, \mathbf{U}^t|D)}$

- ***Accepts*** $X_{\sigma(j)}$ *as parent of X_i with probability v.*
  Then: $\mathbf{U}^t = \mathbf{U}^t \bigcup \{X_{\sigma(j)}\}$ *and* $q = q * v;$

  Otherwise: $q = q * (1 - v);$
return U^t *as a sampled parent set for X_i with probability q;*

With this algorithm we generate T candidate parent sets for X_i and proceed to estimate $E_{P(\mathcal{U}_i|D)}(f(\mathcal{U}))$ using Equation 5. So, fixing f to the corresponding indicator function, we can compute the posterior probability of given parent set and the posterior probability of an edge using Equation 3.

4 Integrating Expert Knowledge

4.1 Non-informative Structure Priors

As in [5], let us assume that the prior probability of any edge is independent of any other and equals to $P(y \to x) = \rho$. In [11] it is justified the employment of this assumption. With the previous settings, a model with r edges out of s candidate edges would have a prior probability determined by a Binomial distribution with probability of success ρ. To avoid the explicit definition of ρ, it is proposed a Beta prior distribution over ρ. So the prior distribution over a set of parents would be as follows:

$$P_i(Pa_G(X_i)) = \frac{B(r + \alpha, (i-1) - r + \alpha)}{B(\alpha, \alpha)}$$

where r is the cardinality of the set $Pa_G(X_i)$ and $B(\cdot, \cdot)$ is the two parameter Beta function. We also fix $s = i - 1$ because assuming a total order the variable X_i can have up most $i - 1$ candidate parents nodes.

Two possible α values are proposed: $\alpha = 0.5$ to resemble the non-informative Jeffrey's prior for the Beta-Binomial model; and $\alpha = 1$, which would lead to the prior $P(Pa_G(X_i)) = ((s+1)\binom{s}{r})^{-1}$, which were also previously proposed in [3]. As can be easily seen in this last combinatorial formulation, these priors penalize those parent sets which belong to subsets with higher cardinality.

We also point out that both structure prior distributions are modular and score equivalent [2]. Throughout the rest of the paper, we will refer to them as Beta structure priors (β-prior).

4.2 *A Posteriori* Expert Knowledge

In this study we propose the employment of the posterior probability $P(\mathcal{U}_i|D)$, approximated by means of any MC method, as an excellent source of information to carry out an efficient and effective interaction with the expert in order to allow him/her to introduce his/her experience to refine the set of plausible models. Let us denote by E this information provided by the expert about the presence/absence of edges. At the beginning E is empty. We then define a methodology to ask a minimum number of queries to the expert in order to let $P(\mathcal{U}_i|E, D)$ concentrates around one single model.

The methodology we propose for this purpose is quite simple and intuitive. It resembles widely known recursive conditioning method for entropy reduction applied for learning decision trees [12]. It can be describe as follows:

Step 1: Compute the information gain measure [12] of $\mathcal{U}_i$ respect to each possible edge e, that is to say, find the edge e that if known most would reduce the entropy of $P(\mathcal{U}_i|E, D)$. It is easy to check that this edge is the one with probability closest to 0.5.

Step 2: Ask to the expert about the presence or the absence of this edge e with the highest information gain ($E = E \cup e$). It would be also displayed the posterior probability of this edge to help her/him in the decision.

Step 3: We then update the posterior probability $P(\mathcal{U}_i|E, D)$ and we start again from **Step 1** until a stop condition is met.

The stop point could be also provided by the expert. Here we propose a simple stop condition that can be tuned with two parameters. The system stops to ask to the expert when either the ratio between the posterior probability of the MAP (most probable *a posteriori*) model and the second best model is higher than a factor K; or the level of the number of queries submitted for a single variable, $|E|$, is higher than a given threshold L. The K parameter is somehow a measure of confidence in the MAP model (how much the posterior concentrates around it); and L is a parameter that prevents against excessive number of queries.

5   Experiments

5.1   Experimental Set Up

To evaluate this approach we have employed 5 standard BNs usually employed for these evaluations [4]: Alarm network with 37 variables; boblo network with 23 variables; boerlage92 network with 23 variables; hailfinder network with 56 variables; and insurance network with 27 variables. For each of these networks we randomly generate 10 data samples with the same size and we considered different sample sizes: 50, 100, 500 and 1000 cases (there will be displayed on the X-axes of Figures 1 and 2). To measure the effectiveness of each learning method, we recover some the usual measures: number of structural errors (missing plus extra links), Kullback-Leibler (KL) distance w.r.t the true model and number of links. Due to space limitations, we do not detail the error measures for each one of the 5 evaluated BNs, we only show average values across these 5 networks. We recognized the problems of considering the average value, but we think that the main conclusions can be perfectly understood with this evaluation.

The number of samples T generated by the $MCMC$, see Section 2.3, when learning the parent sets of the variable X_i was set to $1000 \cdot ln(i)$. The first $100 \cdot ln(i)$ samples were discarded (the burn-in phase). MCMC was also initialized with the configuration recovered by a simple greedy search with the same Bayesian settings, see Section 2.2 (the initialization with an empty structure was also evaluated and the results were almost identical in all the evaluated measures). We also generated the same number of samples with the Importance sampling method. In both cases, the MAP model was returned as the optimal estimated model.

5.2   Structure Prior Evaluation

In the first subsection we analyze the impact of the employment of different structure prior distributions. We evaluate the impact of the structure prior on both Monte Carlo approaches: MCMC (lines with triangle markers) and IS (lines with square markers). Each one of them is run with the classic uniform prior over the different structures (lines with light grey color) and with the Beta structure prior (lines in black color). For the last prior, we evaluate the two proposed α values (0.5 and 1.0) and we hardly found differences between them. Only results for $\alpha = 0.5$ are reported here. The different evaluation metrics for this four BN learning configurations are displayed in Figure 1.

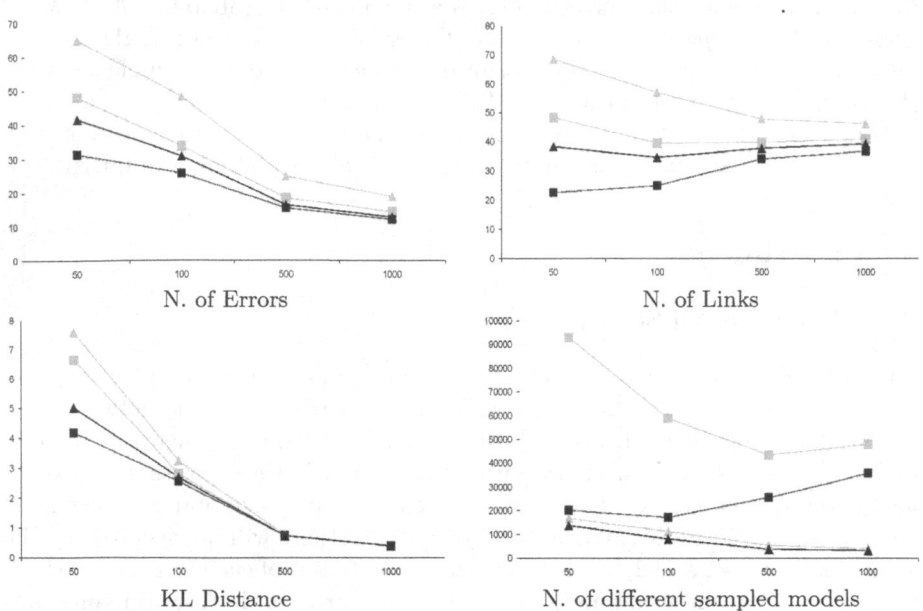

N. of Errors

N. of Links

KL Distance

N. of different sampled models

Fig. 1. Structure Prior Evaluation: Lines with triangle markers are the MCMC results; while square markers corresponds to the IS results. The light grey lines are the results with U-prior while the black lines corresponds to the β-prior($\alpha = 0.5$).

As can be seen, with low sample sizes the employment of the β-prior supposes relevant improvements in the number of structural errors and the KL distance in both approaches MCMC and IS. When the sample size is high (1000 cases), as expected, the impact of the prior decreases in both KL and Number of structural errors. However, β-prior always returns BN models with a low number of links even when there is a higher number of samples. In fact, if we looked at the extra and missing links errors (no depicted in this paper due to space limitations), we would see as the introduction of β-prior strongly reduces the number of extra links. So, this prior reduces the number of false positives structural errors with the help of its new combinatorial penalization (see Section 5.2).

When comparing MCMC and IS, we can see as IS gets better results in terms of number of structural errors and KL distance when the sample size is low, although the differences diminish when the number of available samples grows. Moreover, IS with the β-prior is the only approach where the number of links of the retrieved models constantly grows with the size of the data set and always recover the most simple models (with a lower number of links) and with the best prediction capacity (lower KL distance).

Other interesting evaluation is the comparison of the number of different sampled models in the IS and MCMCM simulations. As can be seen in Figure 1, IS always samples a high number of different models than MCMC, specially when

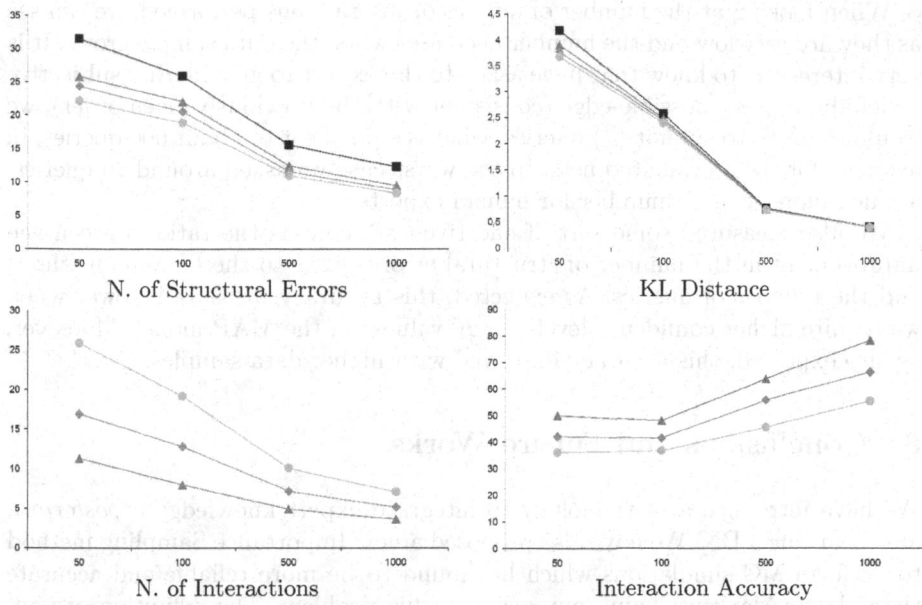

N. of Structural Errors

KL Distance

N. of Interactions

Interaction Accuracy

Fig. 2. Expert Interaction Evaluation: Black line with the square markers corresponds to the baseline method (no interaction); Grey lines with triangle ($K = 3$), diamonds ($K = 5$) and circles ($K = 5$) markers (lighter grey colors are also employed) corresponds to methods which interacts with the expert

the number of data samples grows. This indicates that IS has a lower trend to get trapped in local maxima (but deeper analysis are of course needed).

5.3 Query Evaluation

To evaluate the effectiveness of the proposed approach to integrate posterior expert knowledge, see Section 4, we simulate the interaction with an expert by asking to the true BN model about the presence/absence of any edge. We fix the limit of questions $L = 3$ and we evaluate different confidence factors $K = 3, 5, 10$. We employed the IS learning method with the β-prior ($\alpha = 0.5$). The results are displayed in Figure 2. The black line with the square markers are the baseline results: no interaction with the expert. The results with interaction with the expert for the three evaluated K values are displayed by the lines with triangle, diamonds and circles respectively (lighter grey colors are also employed).

As can be seen in Figure 2, the number of structural errors and the KL distance is reduced by the interaction with the expert. Moreover, as higher the confidence in the MAP model (higher K values), the most the structural errors are reduced. However, when the data sample is high, there hardly is any improvement in the KL distance. That means that the IS approach is recovering the most relevant links and although the interaction could recover some lost links, those do not significantly improve the prediction capacity of the model.

When looking at the number of queries or interactions performed, we can see as they are very low and the number decreases when the data sample grows. It is very interesting to know that if we asked to the expert to give his/her subjective belief about every possible edge (consistent with the previously given order), we would required to submit $\binom{n}{2}$ queries, what is equivalent to about 600 queries, in average, for the 5 evaluated nets. In the worst case we asked around 26 queries, a much more realistic number for human experts.

We also measured some sort of effectiveness score as the ratio between the improvement in the number of structural errors (w.r.t to the baseline method) and the number of queries. As expected, this accuracy measure is lower when we require higher confidence levels (or K values) in the MAP model. Moreover, as also expected, this accuracy improved with higher data samples.

6   Conclusions and Future Works

We have introduce a methodology to integrate expert knowledge *a posteriori*, after learning a BN. We have also proposed a new Importance Sampling method to perform MC simulations which has found to be more reliable and accurate than classic Markov Chain approaches in this problem. The definition of non-informative structure priors was also analyzed here and a new structure prior, the β-prior, was introduced. We found that this prior helps to find simpler (less number of links) and accurate models (lower KL distance).

The requirement of the total order could be overcome using any of the Monte Carlo approaches for learning BNs [3,10] without causal order assumptions. Thus, our methodology will have be extended to ask about the causal order of two variables. We also plan to consider the case in which experts might submit wrong decisions about the structure of the true model.

References

1. Pearl, J.: Probabilistic Reasoning with Intelligent Systems. Morgan & Kaufman, San Mateo (1988)
2. Heckerman, D., Geiger, D., Chickering, D.: Learning Bayesian networks: The combination of knowledge and statistical data. Machine learning 20(3), 197–243 (1995)
3. Friedman, N., Koller, D.: Being Bayesian about Bayesian network structure: A Bayesian approach to structure discovery in Bayesian networks. Machine Learning 50(1-2), 95–125 (2003)
4. Neapolitan, R.E.: Learning Bayesian Networks. Prentice Hall, Englewood Cliffs (2004)
5. Buntine, W.: Theory refinement on bayesian networks. In: Proc. 7th Conf. on Uncertainty in Artificial Intelligence, San Francisco, CA, USA, pp. 52–60 (1991)
6. de Campos, L.M., Castellano, J.G.: Bayesian network learning algorithms using structural restrictions. Int. J. Approx. Reasoning 45(2), 233–254 (2007)
7. Bernardo, J.M., Smith, A.: Bayesian Theory. John Wiley & Sons, New York (1994)
8. Steck, H., Tresp, V.: Bayesian belief networks for data mining, pp. 145–154. University of Magdeburg (1996)

9. Madsen, A.L., Lang, M., Kjrulff, U.B., Jensen, F.: The hugin tool for learning bayesian networks. In: Nielsen, T.D., Zhang, N.L. (eds.) ECSQARU 2003. LNCS (LNAI), vol. 2711, pp. 594–605. Springer, Heidelberg (2003)
10. Madigan, D., Jerrmy, Y.: Bayesian graphical models for discrete data. International Statistical Review 63, 215–332 (1995)
11. Berger, J.O., Bernardo, J., Sun, D.: Reference priors for discrete parameter spaces. Technical report, Universidad de Valencia, Spain (2009)
12. Quinlan, J.R.: Induction of decision trees. Mach. Learn. 1(1), 81–106 (1986)

Conflicts within and between Belief Functions

Milan Daniel*

Institute of Computer Science, Academy of Sciences of the Czech Republic
Pod vodárenskou věží 2, CZ - 182 07, Prague 8, Czech Republic
milan.daniel@cs.cas.cz
http://www.cs.cas.cz

Abstract. This contribution deals with conflicts of belief functions. Internal conflicts of belief functions and conflicts between belief functions are described and analyzed here. Differences between belief functions are distinguished from conflicts between them. Three new different approaches to conflicts are presented: combinational, plausibility, and comparative. The presented approaches to conflicts are compared to Liu's interpretation of conflicts.

Belief functions, Dempster-Shafer theory, internal conflict, conflict between belief functions, combinational conflict, plausibility conflict, comparative conflict.

1 Introduction

When combining belief functions (BFs) by the conjunctive rules of combination, conflicts often appear which are assigned to $\emptyset$ by non-normalized conjunctive rule $\odot$ or normalized by Dempster's rule of combination $\oplus$. Combination of conflicting BFs and interpretation of conflicts is often questionable in real applications, thus a series of alternative combination rules was suggested and a series of papers on conflicting belief functions was published, e.g. [2,5,8,12].

This contribution introduces new ideas to the interpretation, definition and measurements of conflicts of BFs. Three new approaches to interpretation and computation of conflicts are presented here.

The first one, the combinational approach, is a modification of commonly used interpretation of conflict of BFs. An internal conflict within individual BFs is distinguished from a conflict between two BFs which are combined (Section 3).

The second one, the plausibility approach also distinguishes internal conflict and conflict between BFs. This approach uses the normalized plausibility transformation and is based on support / opposition of elements of Ω by the BFs in question. Differences of BFs are distinguished from conflicts between them in this approach; as relatively highly different BFs are not necessarily mutually conflicting (Section 4).

---

* This work was supported by the grant 1ET100300419 GA AV ČR, and in part by the Institutional Research Plan AV0Z10300504 "Computer Science for the Information Society: Models, Algorithms, Applications".

E. Hüllermeier, R. Kruse, and F. Hoffmann (Eds.): IPMU 2010, LNAI 6178, pp. 696–705, 2010.
© Springer-Verlag Berlin Heidelberg 2010

The third approach, the comparative one, is based on a specification of bbms of some focal elements to smaller focal elements and on measuring difference between such more specified BFs (Section 5).

After the presentation of new ideas, the presented approaches are compared and a series of open problems is suggested.

2   Preliminaries

Let us assume an exhaustive finite *frame of discernment* $\Omega = \{\omega_1, ..., \omega_n\}$, whose elements are mutually exclusive.

A *basic belief assignment (bba)* is a mapping $m : \mathcal{P}(\Omega) \longrightarrow [0,1]$, such that $\sum_{A \subseteq \Omega} m(A) = 1$, $m(\emptyset) = 0$; the values of bba are called *basic belief masses (bbm)*.[1] A *belief function (BF)* is a mapping $Bel : \mathcal{P}(\Omega) \longrightarrow [0,1]$, $Bel(A) = \sum_{\emptyset \neq X \subseteq A} m(X)$; let us further recall a *plausibility function* $Pl(A) = \sum_{\emptyset \neq A \cap X} m(X)$; bba m, belief function Bel and plausibility Pl uniquely correspond each to others.

A *focal element* is a subset X of the frame of discernment, such that $m(X) > 0$. If all focal elements are *singletons* (i.e. one-element subsets of Ω), then we speak about a *Bayesian belief function* (BBF), it is a probability distribution on Ω in fact. Let us denote U_n the *uniform Bayesian belief function* on n-element frame $\Omega_n = \{\omega_1, ..., \omega_n\}$, i.e. the uniform probability distribution on Ω_n. The belief function with the only focal element $m(\Omega) = 1$ is called the *vacuous belief function (VBF)*; a belief function with the only focal element $m(A) = 1$ is called *categorical* (or logical [1]) *belief function*; a belief function with two focal elements $m(A) = A$ and $m(\Omega) = 1 - A$ is called a *simple support (belief function*; a belief function which focal elements are nested is called a *consonant belief function*.

The *normalized plausibility of Bel* is the BBF (a probability distribution) $(Pl\_P(m))(\omega_i) = \frac{Pl(\{\omega_i\})}{\sum_{\omega \in \Omega} Pl(\{\omega\})}$. The *pignistic probability of Bel* is the following probability distribution $BetP(\omega_i) = \sum_{\omega_i \in X \subseteq \Omega} \frac{m(X)}{|X|}$.

Any BF on $\Omega_2 = \{\omega_1, \omega_2\}$ is uniquely specified by two bbms $m(\{\omega_1\}), m(\{\omega_2\})$ as $m(\{\omega_1, \omega_2\}) = 1 - (m(\{\omega_1\}) + m(\{\omega_2\}))$. We can represent it as $m = (a, b)$.

Dempster's (conjunctive) rule of combination $\oplus$ is given as $(m_1 \oplus m_2)(A) = \sum_{X \cap Y = A} K m_1(X) m_2(Y)$ for $A \neq \emptyset$, where $K = \frac{1}{1-\kappa}$, $\kappa = \sum_{X \cap Y = \emptyset} m_1(X) m_2(Y)$, and $(m_1 \oplus m_2)(\emptyset) = 0$, see [10]; putting $K = 1$ and $(m_1 \oplus m_2)(\emptyset) = \kappa$ we obtain the *non-normalized conjunctive rule of combination* $\odot$, see e. g. [11].

3   Combinational Conflicts of Belief Functions

3.1   Internal Conflict of Belief Functions

When combining two belief functions Bel_1, Bel_2 given by bbms m_1 and m_2 conflicting masses $m_1(X) > 0$, $m_2(Y) > 0$ for $X \cap Y = \emptyset$ often appear. The

---

[1] $m(\emptyset) = 0$ is often assumed in accordance with Shafer's definition [10]. A classical counter example is Smets' Transferable Belief Model (TBM) which admits $m(\emptyset) \geq 0$.

sum of all pair-wise products of such belief masses corresponds to $m(\emptyset)$ when non-normalized conjunctive rule of combination is applied and $m = m_1 \textcircled{\tiny{$\cap$}} m_2$. This sum is called *weight of conflict between belief functions* Bel_1 *and* Bel_2 in [10], and it is commonly used when dealing with conflicting belief functions. Unfortunately, the name and the interpretation of this notion does not correctly correspond to reality in general. We often obtain positive sum of conflicting belief masses even if two numerically same independent belief functions are combined, see e.g. Example 1 [1], analogical example for $n = 5$ is discussed in [8]. For a generalization to uniform BBFs on Ω_n see [7], for general BFs see Example 2.

Example 1. Let us assume two BFs expressing that a six-sided die is fair. $\Omega_6 = \{\omega_1, ..., \omega_6\} = \{1, 2, 3, 4, 5, 6\}$, $m_j(\{\omega_i\}) = 1/6$ for $i = 1, ..., 6$, $j = 1, 2$, $m_j(X) = 0$ otherwise. Let $m = m_1 \textcircled{\tiny{$\cap$}} m_2$. We obtain $m(\{\omega_i\}) = 1/36$ for $i = 1, ..., 6$, $m(\emptyset) = 5/6$, $m(X) = 0$ otherwise.

Example 2. Let us suppose for simplicity $\Omega_2 = \{\omega_1, \omega_2\}$ now. Let $m_j(\{\omega_1\}) = 0.5$, $m_j(\{\omega_2\}) = 0.4$, $m_j(\{\omega_1, \omega_2\}) = 0.1$ for $j = 5, 6$, $m_j(X) = 0$ otherwise. Let $m = m_5 \textcircled{\tiny{$\cap$}} m_6$ now. We obtain $m(\{\omega_1\}) = 0.35$, $m(\{\omega_2\}) = 0.24$, $m(\{\omega_1, \omega_2\}) = 0.01$, $m(\{\omega_1\}) = 0.4$ $m(\emptyset) = 0.4$, $m(X) = 0$ otherwise.

Almond mentions that $m(\emptyset)$ is hardly interpretable as conflict between BFs in such cases [1]. Liu correctly says in [8], that $m(\emptyset)$ cannot be always interpreted as a degree of conflict between belief functions. On the other hand, many of particular couples of belief masses are really in conflict with each other. From this we can see that the sum of all products of conflicting belief masses, what we call *total combinational conflict*, somehow includes also a conflict which is included within the individual combined belief functions. We will call this *internal conflict*[2]. It is not known whether the internal conflicts are included in total conflict partially or entirely. On the other hand, a source of total combinational conflict $TotC$ arises either from internal combinational conflicts of individual BFs or from their mutual conflicting interrelations. Thus, we can describe this as

$$TotC(m_1, m_2) \leq IntC(m_1) + IntC(m_2) + C(m_1, m_2).$$

In the special case when two identical belief functions are combined, we obtain $TotC(m, m) \leq IntC(m) + IntC(m)$, as we expect no conflict between two same pieces of evidence because they fully agree with each other thus, they are not in any mutual conflict. We further suppose $IntC(m) \leq TotC(m, m)$ thus, we have

$$IntC(m) \leq TotC(m, m) \leq IntC(m) + IntC(m)$$

and $\frac{1}{2} TotC(m, m)) \leq IntC(m) \leq TotC(m, m)$.

---

[2] We have to note, that Smets uses the name 'internal conflict' for $m(\emptyset)$ within individual non-normalized BFs [2]; nevertheless, there are also other interpretations of $m(\emptyset)$ in non-normalized BFs. However, in our situation internal conflicts appear in classic BFs each satisfying $m(\emptyset) = 0$, see Examples 1, 2 and other examples in this contribution.

Unfortunately, we have no precise formula how to precisely compute conflict $C(m_1, m_2)$ between BFs m_1 and m_2. Nevertheless, we assume that it is less than total conflict $TotC(m_1, m_2)$ and the above inequality. We can summarize this as it follows:

$$TotC(m_1, m_2) - (IntC(m_1) + IntC(m_2)) \leq C(m_1, m_2) \leq TotC(m_1, m_2).$$

3.2   Belief Functions with and without Internal Conflict

There are many BFs without any internal conflicts: all categorical and all simple support BFs have no internal conflict, further all consonant BFs, finally all BFs, whose all focal elements have non-empty intersection, have no internal conflict, i.e., all BFs such that there exist $X \subseteq \Omega$, $Pl(X) = 1$.

Example 3. Let us suppose $\Omega_6 = \{\omega_1, ..., \omega_6\}$ and the following simple internally non-conflicting BFs: $m_7(\{\omega_1, \omega_2, \omega_3, \omega_4\}) = 0.4$, $m_7(\{\omega_2, \omega_3, \omega_4\}) = 0.3$, $m_7(\Omega_6) = 0.3$; $m_8(\{\omega_2, \omega_3, \omega_5\}) = 0.6$, $m_8(\{\omega_2, \omega_3, \omega_6\}) = 0.1$, $m_8(\{\omega_2, \omega_3, \omega_4, \omega_5, \omega_6\}) = 0.2$, $m_8(\Omega_6) = 0.1$.

As an example of BFs with internal conflict we can refer BFs from both Examples 1, 2. U_n is the BF with the greatest internal conflict on $\Omega_n (= \{\omega_1, ..., \omega_n\})$. For detail and other examples see [7].

3.3   Couples of Totally Non-conflicting Belief Functions

We say that m_i and m_j form a pair of *totally non-conflicting BFs* if there is no internal conflict within these BFs, and simultaneously there is no conflict between them. This happens whenever all focal elements of both BFs have common non-empty intersection, i.e. whenever both BFs have non-empty intersections $I = \bigcap_{m_i(X)>0} X \neq \emptyset$, $J = \bigcap_{m_j(X)>0} X \neq \emptyset$ and $I \cap J \neq \emptyset$.

As an example we can mention m_7 and m_8 from the Example 3 because the following holds true: $I = \bigcap_{m_7(X)>0} X = \{\omega_2, \omega_3, \omega_4\}$, $J = \bigcap_{m_8(X)>0} X = \{\omega_2, \omega_3\}$ and $I \cap J = \{\omega_2, \omega_3\} \neq \emptyset$ and $(m_7 \odot m_8)(\emptyset) = 0$.

3.4   Combination of Belief Functions with the Uniform BBF U_n

For mutual non-conflictness of Uniform BBF U_n with any general BF (see [7]). Note also that $m \oplus U_n = Pl\_P(m)$ holds true for any BF m (see [6,7]).

4   Plausibility Conflicts of Belief Functions

As in the previous section, we will further distinguish internal conflicts of individual BFs from a mutual conflict between them. Let us first discuss what should belief functions really mean.

There is an unknown element $\omega_0 \in \Omega$ and we have only a partial uncertain evidence about the fact which one is it. This evidence is represented by a BF or by its corresponding bba. If all pieces of our evidence are correct and fully compatible with the situation, all focal elements should contain the unknown element ω_0 and there is now conflict within the corresponding BF. The more precise our evidence is the smaller should be the focal elements. In the extreme limit case of correct complete certain evidence there is the only focal element $\{\omega_0\}$, such that $m(\{\omega_0\}) = 1$. When obtaining new correct fully compatible pieces of evidence represented by BFs, their focal elements should also contain ω_0 and new BFs should be both internally and mutually non-conflicting. When combining such BFs their focal elements are decreasing keeping ω_0 as their element. Unfortunately real pieces of evidence often contain some conflicts or they are mutually conflicting or the situation itself may be (internally) conflicting. Hence we obtain internally and/or mutually conflicting BFs.

How is it possible that uniform BBFs m_1, m_2 from Example 1 (both of them equal to uniform BBF U_6) have the high internal conflict? Let us notice that BF U_6, which was used in the example for description of behaviour of a fair die, does not express any belief about the fact which side of the die is up. It expresses a meta-information about the die, the information which is necessary within a decision making for redistribution of bbms of focal elements among their singletons. It does not express anything about an uncertain case of the die. It is rather related to the betting/pignistic level than to the credal level of beliefs.

4.1   Internal Plausibility Conflict of Belief Functions

Element ω_0 should be element of all focal elements in correct non-conflicting cases, thus $Pl(\{\omega_0\})$ should be equal to 1. When $Pl(\{\omega_0\}) < 1$ there is some focal element X which does not include ω_0, thus $m(X)$ cannot be simply transferred to any $Y \subseteq X$ which includes ω_0. Such a BF is conflicting and it is often mutually conflicting with other BFs. On the other hand there can be more focal elements with plausibility 1 in less informative cases.

Let us define *internal plausibility conflict of belief function Bel* as

$$Pl\text{-}IntC(Bel) = 1 - max_{\omega \in \Omega} Pl(\{\omega\}),$$

where Pl is the plausibility equivalent to Bel. This definition is in accordance with the assumption from Section 3 that a BF is internally non-conflicting (BF has no internal conflict) whenever there exist $X \subseteq \Omega$, $Pl(X) = 1$. Maximal internal (plausibility) conflict has U_n: $Pl\text{-}IntC(U_n) = 1 - \frac{1}{n} = \frac{n-1}{n}$ as all elements ω_i have the same plausibility $\frac{1}{n}$ in the case of U_n and any change of belief masses increases plausibility of some $\omega \in \Omega$, hence internal plausibility conflict is decreased.

4.2   Plausibility Conflict between Belief Functions on Two-Element Frame of Discernment Ω_2

For simplicity, first let us suppose two-element frame of discernment $\Omega_2 = \{\omega_1, \omega_2\}$ in this subsection.

Let us assume BBFs $m_1 = (0.6, 0.4)$, $m_2 = (0.8, 0.2)$, $m_3 = (0.45, 0.55)$ and $m_4 = (0.40, 0.45)$. There is a relatively high difference between m_1 and m_2, and $(m_1 \ominus m_2)(\emptyset) = 0.44$, but both BBFs support ω_1 thus m_1 and m_2 should not be in mutual conflict. m_1 and m_2 are different but non-conflicting. There is a less difference between m_1 and m_3, and $(m_1 \ominus m_3)(\emptyset) = 0.51$ is higher. m_1 and m_3 support different ω_i thus they should be in a mutual conflict. Finally, there is less difference between m_1 and m_4, than between m_1 and m_2, and $(m_1 \ominus m_4)(\emptyset) = 0.43$ is also smaller. However, m_1 and m_4 support different ω_i thus they should be in mutual conflict, despite of mutually non-conflicting m_1 and m_2 which have both greater difference and greater mutual $m(\emptyset)$.

Similarly, all BFs which support ω_1 (i.e., all bbas (a, b) such that $a > b$, i.e., $Pl\_P((a, b))(\omega_1) > \frac{1}{2} > Pl\_P((a, b))(\omega_2)$, i.e. $(a, b) > 0'$) should not be in mutual conflict. On the other hand, there is a conflict between any two BFs which support different ω_i (i.e., $(a, b), (c, d)$ such that $a > b, c < d$ or $a < b, c > d$).

Hence, we have to distinguish conflict from difference of belief functions:

Let us define *difference between two BFs* Bel_1, Bel_2 on Ω represented by m_1, m_2 as $Diff(m_1, m_2) = \sum_{X \subset \Omega} \frac{1}{2}|m_1(X) - m_2(X)|$, i.e., $Diff((a, b), (c, d)) = \frac{1}{2}(|a - c| + |b - d|)$.

Let us further define *Pl-difference between two BFs* Bel_1, Bel_2:
$Pl\text{-}Diff(m_1, m_2) = Diff(Pl\_P(m_1), Pl\_P(m_2))$ which is more related to a support/opposition of elements ω_i by m_i and to their plausibility conflictness.

Example 4. $m_1 = (0.4, 0.4)$, $m_2 = (0.9, 0.1)$, $Diff(m_1, m_2) = Pl\text{-}Diff(m_1, m_2) = 0.4$.

For more detail motivation, more examples, and for definition of the plausibility conflict on Ω_2 see [7].

4.3 Plausibility Conflict between Belief Functions on General Ω_n

Plausibility conflict between belief functions is based on normalized plausibility of elements of Ω. It is computed separately for all elements of the frame of discernment Ω. VBF is usually assumed to be neutral when belief functions are combined. Normalized plausibility masses (see e.g. [3,6]) of all $\omega \in \Omega$ are $Pl\_P(VBF)(\omega) = \frac{1}{n}$ in the case of VBF. Entire normalized plausibility of VBF is $Pl\_P(VBF) = U_n$ (which is idempotent and neutral w.r.t. combination $\oplus$ of BBFs).

Let us suppose a decision with respect to a given BF Bel: Whenever normalized plausibility $Pl\_P(Bel)(\omega)$ is greater than $\frac{1}{n}$, ω is *supported* by the BF in question. On the other hand, ω is *opposed* when $Pl\_P(Bel)(\omega) < \frac{1}{n}$. ω is fully opposed (rejected) when $Pl\_P(Bel)(\omega) = 0$ as bbms of all X ($\omega \in X$) are zeros and all positive bbms are assigned only to focal elements Y such that $\omega \notin Y$.

If *normalized plausibility masses* $Pl\_P(Bel_1)(\omega)$, $Pl\_P(Bel_2)(\omega)$ are both $\geq \frac{1}{n}$ or both $\leq \frac{1}{n}$ we wil say that they *are non-conflicting*. It seems that these normalized plausibility masses are conflicting whenever one of them is $> \frac{1}{n}$ and the other $< \frac{1}{n}$. Let us denote the set of all elements which have not non-conflicting normalized plausibility masses by $\Omega_{PlC}(Bel_1, Bel_2) = \{\omega \in \Omega \mid (Pl\_P(Bel_1)(\omega) - 1/n)(Pl\_P(Bel_2)(\omega) - 1/n) < 0\}$.

We want to define *plausibility conflict between belief functions* Bel_1, Bel_2 (represented by bbas m_1 and m_2) as the sum of differences of conflicting normalized plausibility masses by the following formula

$$Pl\text{-}C_0(Bel_1, Bel_2) = \sum_{\omega \in \Omega_{PlC}(Bel_1, Bel_2)} \frac{1}{2} \mid Pl\_P(Bel_1)(\omega) - Pl\_P(Bel_2)(\omega) \mid$$

Unfortunately this expression produces/classifies conflicts even in some cases of simple intuitively non-conflicting BFs, see Example 5. $Pl\text{-}C_0(Bel_1, Bel_2)$ is usually less than $m(\emptyset)$ in general examples, nevertheless in the case similar to those from Example 5 we have to use the following modified definition:

$$Pl\text{-}C(Bel_1, Bel_2) = min(Pl\text{-}C_0(Bel_1, Bel_2), (m_1 \oslash m_2)(\emptyset)).$$

Example 5. Let us suppose Ω_6 and intuitively non-conflicting bbas m_1, m_2, now, such that $m_1(\{\omega_1\}) = 1$, $m_2(\{\omega_1, \omega_2, \omega_3, \omega_4\} = 1$. We obtain $Pl\_P(m_1)(\omega_1) = 1 > \frac{1}{6}$, $Pl\_P(m_1)(\omega_i) = 0 < \frac{1}{6}$ for $i > 1$; $Pl\_P(m_2)(\omega_i) = \frac{1}{4} > \frac{1}{6}$ for $i = 1, 2, 3, 4$, $Pl\_P(m_2)(\omega_i) = 0 < \frac{1}{6}$ for $i = 5, 6$; normalized plausibility masses are conflicting for $\omega_2, \omega_3, \omega_4$, thus $Pl\text{-}C_0(m_1, m_2) = \frac{1}{2}(\frac{1}{4} + \frac{1}{4} + \frac{1}{4}) = \frac{3}{8}$. But this is not a conflict.

5   Comparative Conflict between Belief Functions

Thirdly, let us suggest another idea of conflictness/non-conflictness between belief functions, which is motivated by interpretation of BFs and their corresponding bbas. We know that our belief on a specific situation can be usually specified by obtaining new evidence tending to decrease size of focal elements. The idea of comparative conflictness/non-conflictness is a specification of bbms to smaller focal elements such that they fit to focal elements of the other BF as much as possible. *The comparative conflict between BFs Bel_1 and Bel_2 is defined as the least difference of these more specified bbms derived from the input m_1 and m_2.*

Example 6. Let us start with a simple example on Ω_2. Let $m_1 = (0.4, 0)$, $m_2 = (0, 0.4)$, $m_3 = (0.6, 0)$, $m_4 = (0, 0.6)$.

All considered BFs are simple support functions thus, they have no internal conflicts either combinational or plausibility one. On the other hand, BFs m_1 and m_2 are mutually conflicting in the previous sense, there are both combinational and plausibility conflicts between them, similarly for BFs m_3 and m_4. $(m_1 \oslash m_2)(\emptyset) = 0.16$, $(m_3 \oslash m_4)(\emptyset) = 0.36$, $Pl\_P(m_1) = (\frac{10}{16}, \frac{6}{16})$, $Pl\_P(m_2) = (\frac{6}{16}, \frac{10}{16})$, $Pl\_P(m_3) = (\frac{10}{14}, \frac{4}{14})$, $Pl\_P(m_4) = (\frac{4}{14}, \frac{10}{14})$, and $Pl\text{-}C(m_1, m_2) = \frac{6}{16} = 0.375$, $Pl\text{-}C(m_3, m_4) = \frac{6}{14} = 0.42857$.

In the first case (of m_1 and m_2) we can specify part of bbms $m_i(\Omega)$ to singletons to obtain numerically same, thus mutually non-conflicting BFs; in the second case (of m_3 and m_4) none of the specifications of the entire $m_i(\Omega)$ produces non-conflicting BFs: $m'_1 = (0.4, 0.4)$, $m'_2 = (0.4, 0.4)$, $m'_3 = (0.6, 0.4)$, $m'_4 =$

$(0.4, 0.6)$, and $cp\text{-}C(m_1, m_2) = 0$, $cp\text{-}C(m_3, m_4) = 0.2$. Thus m_1 and m_2 are comparatively non-conflicting, and there is a comparative conflict $cp\text{-}C(m_3, m_4) = 0.2$ between m_3 and m_4. The result for the later couple of BFs m_3, m_4 is not qualitatively different from combinational and plausibility approaches, however also both combinational and plausibility mutual conflicts between these BFs are greater than those between comparatively non-conflicting m_1 and m_2.

Example 7. Let us assume more general example on Ω_3 now. Let $m_5(\{\omega_1\}) = 0.3$, $m_5(\{\omega_1, \omega_2\}) = 0.6$, $m_5(\{\omega_1, \omega_2, \omega_3\}) = 0.1$, $m_6(\{\omega_2\}) = 0.3$, $m_6(\{\omega_3\}) = 0.1$, $m_6(\{\omega_1, \omega_3\}) = 0.5$, $m_6(\{\omega_2, \omega_3\}) = 0.1$. There is neither combinational nor plausibility internal conflict in m_5, there is $0.18 \leq IntC(m_6) \leq 0.36$, $Pl\text{-}IntC(m_6) = 0.3$, $(m_5 \odot m_6)(\emptyset) = 0.21$, there are the following normalized plausibilities $Pl\_P(m_5) = (\frac{10}{18} > \frac{1}{3}, \frac{7}{18} > \frac{1}{3}, \frac{1}{18} < \frac{1}{3})$, $Pl\_P(m_6) = (\frac{5}{16} < \frac{1}{3}, \frac{4}{16} < \frac{1}{3}, \frac{7}{16} > \frac{1}{3})$, all the elements ω_i supported by m_5 are opposed by m_6 and vice versa, thus there is both combinational and plausibility conflict between m_5 and m_6.

We can specify bbms of focal element to smaller ones (uniquely to singletons in this case) as it follows: $m_5'(\{\omega_1\}) = 0.5$, $m_5'(\{\omega_2\}) = 0.4$, $m_5'(\{\omega_3\}) = 0.1$, $m_6'(\{\omega_1\}) = 0.5$, $m_6'(\{\omega_2\}) = 0.4$, $m_6'(\{\omega_3\}) = 0.1$. We have obtained the numerically same BFs thus m_5 and m_6 are comparatively non-conflicting.

The comparative approach to conflicts classifies less conflicting BFs than the previous two approaches do. Unfortunately, no algorithm for specification of bbms to smaller focal elements has been yet created. Thus, this new approach can be applied only to simple illuminative examples now. An elaboration of this approach remains an open problem for the future.

6   Comparison of the Presented Approaches

Let us compare the presented approaches and Liu's two-dimensional measure of conflict $cf(m_i, m_j) = (m_\oplus(\emptyset), difBetP_{m_i}^{m_j})^3$ on the following example.

Example 8. Let us suppose $\Omega_3 = \{\omega_1, \omega_2, \omega_3\}$ now.
$m_1(\{\omega_1\}) = 0.2$, $m_1(\{\omega_2\}) = 0.1$, $m_1(\{\omega_1, \omega_2\}) = 0.3$, $m_1(\{\omega_1, \omega_3\}) = 0.1$,
$m_2(\{\omega_1\}) = 0.3$, $m_2(\{\omega_2\}) = 0.1$, $m_2(\{\omega_1, \omega_2\}) = 0.1$, $m_2(\{\omega_2, \omega_3\}) = 0.1$,
$m_3(\{\omega_2\}) = 0.1$, $m_3(\{\omega_3\}) = 0.3$, $m_3(\{\omega_1, \omega_2\}) = 0.1$, $m_3(\{\omega_2, \omega_3\}) = 0.1$,
$m_1(\Omega_3) = 0.3$, $m_2(\Omega_3) = 0.4$, $m_3(\Omega_3) = 0.4$,
$Pl\_P(m_1)(\omega_1) = 0.45$, $Pl\_P(m_1)(\omega_2) = 0.35$, $Pl\_P(m_1)(\omega_3) = 0.20$,
$BetP_1(\omega_1) = 0.50$, $BetP_1(\omega_2) = 0.35$, $BetP_1(\omega_3) = 0.15$,
$Diff(m_1, m_2) = 0.25$, $Pl\text{-}Diff(m_1, m_2) = 0.05$, $Diff(BetP_1, BetP_2) = 0.033$,
$Diff(m_1, m_3) = 0.45$, $Pl\text{-}Diff(m_1, m_3) = 0.2$, $Diff(BetP_1, BetP_3) = 0.333$,
$(m_1 \odot m_1)(\emptyset) = 0.06$, $(m_2 \odot m_2)(\emptyset) = 0.12$, $(m_1 \odot m_2)(\emptyset) = 0.08$,
$0.03 \leq IntC(m_1) \leq 0.06$, $0.06 \leq IntC(m_2) \leq 0.12$, $0 \leq C(m_1, m_2) \leq 0.08$,
$TotC(m_1, m_2) = 0.08$, $cf(m_1, m_2) = (m_\oplus(\emptyset), difBetP_{m_1}^{m_2}) = (0.08, 0.033)$,

---

3 This is Liu's notation from [8], $m_\oplus(\emptyset)$ should be rather $m_\ominus(\emptyset)$ in fact (more precisely $(m_i \odot m_j)(\emptyset)$); $difBetP_{m_i}^{m_j} = max_{A \subseteq \Omega}(|BetP_{m_i}(A) - BetP_{m_j}(A)|)$ what is $Diff(BetP_{m_i}, BetP_{m_j})$, see[7].

$Pl\text{-}IntC(m_1) = 0.1$, $Pl\text{-}IntC(m_2) = 0.2$, $Pl\text{-}C(m_1, m_2) = 0$, $cp\text{-}C(m_1, m_2) = 0$, $0.03 \leq IntC(m_1) \leq 0.06$, $0.06 \leq IntC(m_3) \leq 0.12$, $0.14 \leq C(m_1, m_3) \leq 0.23$, $TotC(m_1, m_3) = 0.23$, $cf(m_1, m_3) = (m_\oplus(\emptyset), difBetP_{m_1}^{m_3}) = (0.23, 0.333)$, $Pl\text{-}IntC(m_1) = 0.1$, $Pl\text{-}IntC(m_3) = 0.2$, $Pl\text{-}C(m_1, m_3) = 0.2$, $cp\text{-}C(m_1, m_3) = 0$.

We can notice that all of the approaches agree with the high conflictness of the Zadeh's example (see [7]), the common for these results (incl. Zadeh's ex.) is that the commonly used $m(\emptyset) = TotC$ is the most conflicting and that combinational conflict between m_is is not precise (as its precise definition is missing).

All of the approaches have similar results when comparing the least conflicting case m_1 and m_2 (see Ex. 8). The most important difference in this case is the fact, that there is no plausibility or comparative conflict between m_1, m_2.

The greatest differences among the results are in the most general case of m_1 and m_3. There is again no comparative conflict between the bbas (as there exist non-conflicting common specification of both bbas), but there is the plausibility conflict between them. If we assume that combinational conflict is somewhere close to the middle of its interval, the highest conflict is classified by the common $m(\emptyset)$ and Liu's approaches. It reflects that there are no internal conflicts considered in these approaches. There is also none internal conflict in the comparative approach, but this approach more reflects the individual input bbms and usually produces the least conflict.

Both Liu's and plausibility approaches use a probabilistic transformation for computation of conflict, pignistic and normalized plausibility. Thus Liu's conflict is more related to decisional pignistic level, while the plausibility conflict is more related to credal combinational level (especially when Dempster's rule or the non-normalized conjunctive rule is used), because normalized plausibility transformation commutes with Dempster's rule [3,6]. Nevertheless the main difference between these two approaches is not in different pignistic transformations but in the fact that Liu does not distinguish differences from conflicts. Hence any two different BFs supporting and opposing the same element(s) of Ω are conflicting in Liu's interpretation, but such BFs are never mutually conflicting in the plausibility approach; this speaks in favour of the plausibility approach.

7   Future Research

The ideas presented in this contribution are brand new, thus they open a lot of questions and open problems. The principal ones are the following:

- to find more precise specification of combinational conflict $C(Bel_1, Bel_2)$;
- elaboration of plausibility approach to conflicts;
- to create algorithms for belief mass specification needed for comparative conflict managing;
- to study mathematical properties of defined measures of conflicts;
- to make a detail comparison of the presented combinational, plausibility and comparative approaches; including classic $m(\emptyset)$ and Liu's approach [8];
- to analyze a relation of internal plausibility conflict and Liu's degree of inconsistency of possibility distribution in possibility theory [9].

8   Conclusion

In this theoretical contribution we introduce three new approaches to conflicts of belief functions: new approach to combinational conflicts, plausibility approach and comparative approach. Further, internal conflict of individual belief functions from their mutual conflict between them are distinguished, and important distinctness of differences of belief functions from their mutual conflicts is introduced and underlined. On the other hand, the important role of $m(\emptyset)$ for conflict measurement was strenghtened (see combinational and plausibility conflicts).

The presented ideas enable new, deeper understanding of conflicts of belief functions. They can be applied to studies of belief combination and fusion of beliefs. The series of open problems may be challenging for a future research. The ideas presented in this paper are here to open new scientific discussions about this interesting and complex topic.

References

1. Almond, R.G.: Graphical Belief Modeling. Chapman & Hall, London (1995)
2. Ayoun, A., Smets, P.: Data association in multi-target detection using the transferable belief model. International Journal of Intelligent Systems 16(10), 1167–1182 (2001)
3. Cobb, B.R., Shenoy, P.P.: A Comparison of Methods for Transforming Belief Functions Models to Probability Models. In: Nielsen, T.D., Zhang, N.L. (eds.) ECSQARU 2003. LNCS (LNAI), vol. 2711, pp. 255–266. Springer, Heidelberg (2003)
4. Daniel, M.: Algebraic structures related to Dempster-Shafer theory. In: Bouchon-Meunier, B., Yager, R.R., Zadeh, L.A. (eds.) IPMU 1994. LNCS, vol. 945, pp. 51–61. Springer, Heidelberg (1995)
5. Daniel, M.: Distribution of Contradictive Belief Masses in Combination of Belief Functions. In: Bouchon-Meunier, B., Yager, R.R., Zadeh, L.A. (eds.) Information, Uncertainty and Fusion, pp. 431–446. Kluwer Acad. Publ., Boston (2000)
6. Daniel, M.: Probabilistic Transformations of Belief Functions. In: Godo, L. (ed.) ECSQARU 2005. LNCS (LNAI), vol. 3571, pp. 539–551. Springer, Heidelberg (2005)
7. Daniel, M.: New Approach to Conflicts within and between Belief Functions. Technical report V-1062, ICS AS CR, Prague (2009)
8. Liu, W.: Analysing the degree of conflict among belief functions. Artificial Intelligence 170, 909–924 (2006)
9. Liu, W.: Conflict Analysis and Merging Operators Selection in Possibility Theory. In: Mellouli, K. (ed.) ECSQARU 2007. LNCS (LNAI), vol. 4724, pp. 816–827. Springer, Heidelberg (2007)
10. Shafer, G.: A Mathematical Theory of Evidence. Princeton University Press, Princeton (1976)
11. Smets, P.: The combination of evidence in the transferable belief model. IEEE-Pattern analysis and Machine Intelligence 12, 447–458 (1990)
12. Smets, P.: Analyzing the combination of conflicting belief functions. Information Fusion 8, 387–412 (2007)

Consonant Continuous Belief Functions Conflicts Calculation

Jean-Marc Vannobel

LAGIS
Université Lille1, Sciences et Technologies
59655 Villeneuve d'Ascq Cedex, France
jean-marc.vannobel@univ-lille1.fr

Abstract. Much information sources model imprecision by the way of unimodal, consonant and continuous probability density functions (pdfs). We consider here in the framework of belief functions on real numbers, agents of evidence deduced from such pdfs. First are singletons plausibilities in conjunctive and disjunctive combinations proposed to basically merge agents of evidence with consonant focal elements. Second are partial and global conflict calculation methods provided. An application shows the plausibility curves and conflict values obtained in case of combination operations done on Gaussian based agents and at last, an example of conflict management based on an RCR-S adaptive rule of combination is given.

Keywords: Continuous belief functions, Conjunctive and disjunctive combination, Partial and global conflict calculation.

1 Introduction

The focal elements of agents of evidence obtained from consonant pdfs can be ordered and thus labeled by a continuous index. Under the assumption of cognitive independence between agents, this is useful to simplify expressions of the conjunctive [1] and disjunctive rule of combination [2]. As we will see, this also helps to calculate the partial and global conflict weights when much pieces of evidence are merged.

2 Characteristics of Focal Intervals

2.1 Focal Intervals

Let f be a continuous unimodal and consonant pdf of mode μ and support $\Omega = [\Omega^-, \Omega^+]$ with bounds in $\mathcal{R}$, the extended set of real numbers [1]. Focal elements of the piece of evidence $\mathcal{E}$ based on f are nested intervals that we label according to their fitting order by an continuous index called z. These intervals correspond to $A^z = [A^{z-}, A^{z+}], A^{z-} \in [\Omega^-, \mu], A^{z+} \in [\mu, \Omega^+]$ and are deduced from the pdf by horizontal cuts such that $f(A^{z-}) = f(A^{z+})$ in case of 'bell shaped' pdfs [1].

E. Hüllermeier, R. Kruse, and F. Hoffmann (Eds.): IPMU 2010, LNAI 6178, pp. 706–715, 2010.

2.2   The z Index

Suppose that the focal elements bounds A^{z-} and A^{z+} are defined according to the distances to the pdf's mode $\Delta^-(z)z$ and $\Delta^+(z)z$ such that:

$$A^z = [\mu - \Delta^-(z)z, \mu + \Delta^+(z)z], \ z \in [0, \infty] . \tag{1}$$

When Δ^- and Δ^+ differ from 0, the focal elements bounds are linked by a bijective function called γ [1]. This happens in case of symmetrical pdfs as illustrated in figure 1 or for some triangular distributions for instance [2].

When possible, z has to be expressed by a linear relation depending on the r.v $x \in \Omega$ and the pdf's parameters, giving thus constant values for Δ^- and Δ^+ in some occasions. Defining z using the pdfs parameters provides in most cases single belief functions expressions for a same family of pdfs [2]. For Gaussian or Laplace pdfs for instance, Δ equals to the standard deviation σ if the z index is expressed by the absolute value of the standard score:

$$z = \frac{|x - \mu|}{\sigma}, \ z \in \mathcal{R}^+ = [0, \infty] . \tag{2}$$

Focal intervals A^z correspond in that case to:

$$A^z = [\mu - \sigma z, \mu + \sigma z], \ z \in [0, \infty] . \tag{3}$$

2.3   Focal Set Graphical Representation

The Grey area in figure 1 illustrates the domain representing the focal intervals set $\mathcal{F}_i$ corresponding to a pdf $Betf_i$ with intervals ordered according to their z label value. For a Gaussian pdf and when z is defined as in (2) like done by Ristic et al. [3], $\mathcal{F}_i$ has a triangular shape.

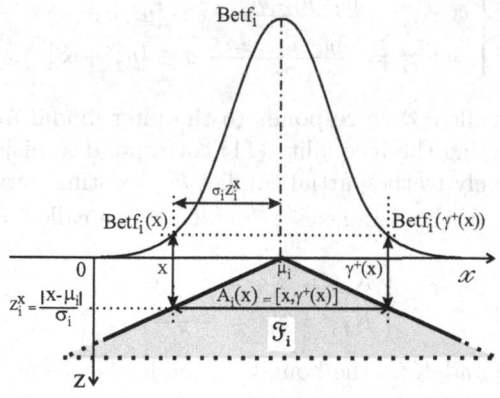

Fig. 1. Focal intervals domain $\mathcal{F}_i$ resulting from a Gaussian pdf

3   Singleton Plausibilities in Combination Operations of Independent Consonant Basic Belief Densities

3.1   Introduction

We propose to construct the plausibility curve resulting of the combination of cognitively independent consonant pieces of evidence.

Suppose two such pieces of evidence $\mathcal{E}_i$ and $\mathcal{E}_j$ related to unimodal ($\mu_i \leq \mu_j$) and consonant basic belief densities (bbd) m_i and m_j and at last a r.v x on $\Omega = [-\infty, \infty]$. Focal sets are called $\mathcal{F}_i$ and $\mathcal{F}_j$. According to x, ordering indexes are z_i^x and z_j^x. We note $\mathcal{F}_i^x$ and $\mathcal{F}_j^x$ the subsets of $\mathcal{F}_i$ and $\mathcal{F}_j$ that intersect with x, $\overline{\mathcal{F}_i^x}$ and $\overline{\mathcal{F}_j^x}$ their complements such that:

$$\begin{cases} \mathcal{F}_i = \mathcal{F}_i^x \cup \overline{\mathcal{F}_i^x}, \ \mathcal{F}_i^x = \{A \in \mathcal{F}_i, x \in \Omega, A \cap x \neq \emptyset\}, \\ \mathcal{F}_j = \mathcal{F}_j^x \cup \overline{\mathcal{F}_j^x}, \ \mathcal{F}_j^x = \{A \in \mathcal{F}_j, x \in \Omega, A \cap x \neq \emptyset\} \end{cases} \quad (4)$$

3.2   Graphical Representation of Combined Focal Sets

Figure 2 illustrates a Venn diagram of the intervals of $\mathcal{F}_i \mathrm{x} \mathcal{F}_j$ concerned in a combination operation of $\mathcal{E}_i$ and $\mathcal{E}_j$ relatively to x. The whole domain represents $\mathcal{F}_i \mathrm{x} \mathcal{F}_j$ into a Cartesian coordinate system that becomes a n-dimensional space when n agents have to be combined. Axes correspond to the focal sets $\mathcal{F}_i$ and $\mathcal{F}_j$, ordered in accordance to their respective z labels. $\mathcal{F}_i^x$, $\mathcal{F}_j^x$ sets and their complements $\overline{\mathcal{F}_i^x}$ and $\overline{\mathcal{F}_j^x}$ are thus separated on axes at locations z_i^x and z_j^x.

When focal domains have a triangular shape as illustrated in figure 1, linear relations link pairs $(z_i^x, z_j^x), x \in \Omega$ and draw the lines ①, ② and ③ shown in figure 2. According to z_i^x and z_j^x expressions given for Gaussian pdfs by relation (2) and the inter-modal distance $|\mu_i - \mu_j|$, these line relations correspond to:

$$\begin{cases} ① : z_j^x = \frac{|\mu_i - \mu_j| + \sigma_i z_i^x}{\sigma_j}, x \in [-\infty, \mu_i], \\ ② : z_j^x = \frac{|\mu_i - \mu_j| - \sigma_i z_i^x}{\sigma_j}, x \in [\mu_i, \mu_j], \\ ③ : z_j^x = \frac{-|\mu_i - \mu_j| + \sigma_i z_i^x}{\sigma_j}, x \in [\mu_j, +\infty] \end{cases} \quad (5)$$

The line segment called ② corresponds to the inter-modal interval $[\mu_i, \mu_j]$ and pairs (z_i^x, z_j^x) satisfying the inequality (11) correspond to disjoint focal intervals A_i^z and A_j^z. Relatively to the partial conflict $k_{i,j}$ existing between the agents $\mathcal{E}_i$ and $\mathcal{E}_j$, the values of the z indexes $z_i^{\mu_j}$ and $z_j^{\mu_i}$ are called $K_{i,j}$ and $K_{j,i}$ such as:

$$\begin{cases} K_{i,j} = z_i^{\mu_j} = \frac{|\mu_j - \mu_i|}{\sigma_i}, \\ K_{j,i} = z_j^{\mu_i} = \frac{|\mu_j - \mu_i|}{\sigma_j} \end{cases} \quad (6)$$

And we note Ki, j and Kj, i the bounds of the line segment ② such as:

$$\begin{cases} Ki, j = (K_{i,j}, 0), \\ Kj, i = (0, K_{j,i}) \end{cases} \quad (7)$$

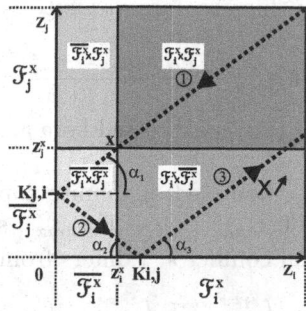

Fig. 2. Venn diagram of two Gaussian pdfs combination ($\mu_i < \mu_j$)

At last, as we can see in figure 2, each pair (z_i^x, z_j^x) separates the domain $\mathcal{F}_i \times \mathcal{F}_j$ in four subsets of interest as in a Karnaugh map. These subsets correspond to $\overline{\mathcal{F}_i^x} \times \overline{\mathcal{F}_j^x}$, $\overline{\mathcal{F}_i^x} \times \mathcal{F}_j^x$, $\mathcal{F}_i^x \times \overline{\mathcal{F}_j^x}$, $\mathcal{F}_i^x \times \mathcal{F}_j^x$.

3.3 Singleton's Plausibility in Conjunctive and Disjunctive Combination of Consonant Bbds

The plausibility of a singleton relatively to a piece of evidence $\mathcal{E}$ with focal elements indexed by z based on a consonant and unimodal pdf is:

$$Pl(x) = Pl(z^x) = \int_{z=z^x}^{z=z^{x max}} m(z)dz = 1 - M(z^x) \tag{8}$$

with M the integral of the bbd m and $z^{x max}$ the upper bound of z's domain.

The singletons plausibility after conjunctive combination of $\mathcal{E}_i$ and $\mathcal{E}_j$ ($\mathcal{E}_i \perp \mathcal{E}_j$) corresponds to:

$$Pl_{i \textcircled{\tiny $\cap$} j}(x) = Pl_i(z_i^x)Pl_j(z_j^x) \ . \tag{9}$$

In case of the disjunctive combination of $\mathcal{E}_i$ and $\mathcal{E}_j$ [2] and as for Smets Disjunctive Rule of Combination (DRC) [5], the plausibility $Pl_{i \textcircled{\tiny $\cup$} j}(x)$ is given by:

$$\begin{aligned} Pl_{i \textcircled{\tiny $\cup$} j}(x) &= 1 - (1 - Pl_i(z_i^x))(1 - Pl_j(z_j^x)), \\ &= 1 - M_i(z_i^x)M_j(z_j^x) \ . \end{aligned} \tag{10}$$

Relations (9) and (10) can be generalized to merge n agents [2].

4   Conflict Calculation in Case of Consonant Bbds

4.1   Partial Conflict

The domain of the partial conflict $k_{i,j}$ existing between two cognitively independent pieces of evidence $\mathcal{E}_i$ and $\mathcal{E}_j$ based on unimodal and consonant pdfs can be observed graphically. It corresponds in figure 2 to the triangle $(0; Ki, j; Kj, i)$.

The intervals concerned by this area are disjoint and in case of Gaussian pdfs for instance, satisfy:

$$0 \le z_j^x \le \frac{|\mu_i - \mu_j| - \sigma_i z_i^x}{\sigma_j} . \tag{11}$$

Calculation of $k_{i,j}$ following this is expressed here according to the z labels and the inter-modal distance.

Consider modes $\mu_i < \mu_j$, bounded or infinite supports $\Omega_i = [\Omega_i^-, \Omega_i^+]$ and $\Omega_j = [\Omega_j^-, \Omega_j^+]$, labels $z_i \in [0, z_{max_i}]$, $z_j \in [0, z_{max_j}]$ satisfying (1).

If $\Omega_i \cap \Omega_j \ne \emptyset$, the partial conflict $k_{i,j}$ differs from 1 and corresponds to:

$$k_{i,j} = m_{i \odot j}(\emptyset) = \int_{z_i=0}^{z_i = zMax_i} \int_{z_j=0}^{z_j = zMax_j} m_i(z_i) m_j(z_j) dz_j dz_i \tag{12}$$

where:

$$\begin{cases} zMax_i = \min(\frac{|\mu_i - \mu_j|}{\Delta_i^+}, z_{max_i}), \\ zMax_j = \min(\frac{|\mu_i - \mu_j| - \Delta_i^+ z_i}{\Delta_j^-}, z_{max_j}) \end{cases} \tag{13}$$

Partial conflict $k_{j,i} = k_{i,j}$ can also be calculated from the variable z_j.
Note that in case of pdfs with infinite support, relations (13) reduce to:

$$\begin{cases} zMax_i = \frac{|\mu_i - \mu_j|}{\Delta_i^+}, \\ zMax_j = \frac{|\mu_i - \mu_j| - \Delta_i^+ z_i}{\Delta_j^-} \end{cases} \tag{14}$$

For symmetrical pdfs as Gaussian or Laplace ones, relations (13) become:

$$\begin{cases} zMax_i = \frac{|\mu_i - \mu_j|}{\sigma_i}, \\ zMax_j = \frac{|\mu_i - \mu_j| - \sigma_i z_i}{\sigma_j} \end{cases} \tag{15}$$

Relation (12) can be reduced to a single integral by using the bbd's cumulative expression M (or equivalently $1 - Pl$) [2]. The weight of conflict becomes thus:

$$k_{i,j} = m_{i \odot j}(\emptyset) = \int_{z_i=0}^{z_i = zMax_i} m_i(z_i) M_j(zMax_j) dz_i . \tag{16}$$

Since bbds resulting from pdfs are normalized, it is possible to calculate the partial conflict from intersecting intervals instead of those that do not. When $\mu_i \le \mu_j$, $k_{i,j}$ corresponds to:

$$\begin{aligned} k_{i,j} &= 1 - \int_{z_i=0}^{z_i=z_{max_i}} \int_{z_j=zMin_j}^{z_j=zMax_j} m_i(z_i) m_j(z_j) dz_j dz_i \\ &= 1 - \int_{z_i=0}^{z_i=z_{max_i}} m_i(z_i)(Pl_j(zMin_j) - Pl_j(zMax_j)) dz_i \end{aligned} \tag{17}$$

with:

$$\begin{cases} zMin_j = \max(0, \frac{|\mu_i - \mu_j| - \Delta_i^+ z_i}{\Delta_j^-}), \\ zMax_j = \max(z_{max_j}, \frac{|\mu_i - \mu_j| - \Delta_i^+ z_i}{\Delta_j^-}) \end{cases} \tag{18}$$

Relations (18) are justified for $zMin_j$ by the fact that $\frac{|\mu_i - \mu_j| - \Delta_i^+ z_i}{\Delta_j^-} < 0$ when $A^{z_i+} > \mu_j$ and means in that case, that all the focal elements of $\mathcal{E}_j$ have to be

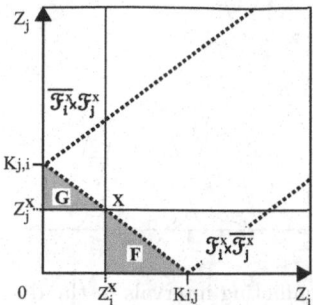

Fig. 3. Conflicting domains F and G included in the $\mathcal{F}_i^x \mathrm{x} \overline{\mathcal{F}_j^x}$ and $\overline{\mathcal{F}_i^x} \mathrm{x} \mathcal{F}_j^x$ sets

considered ($z_{Min_j} = 0$). z_{Max_j}'s relation takes into account the case of a bounded support pdf for $\mathcal{E}_j$ leading to a total conflicting situation when $A_i^{z_i} \cap \Omega_j = \emptyset$, corresponding thus to $z_{Min_j} = z_{Max_j}$.

Relations (17) and (18) can be simplified in case of infinite supports and symmetrical pdfs.

4.2 Conflict Abacus for Least Committed Bbds Based on Gaussian Pdfs

Figure 4 presents an abacus of the partial conflict for bbds deduced from two Gaussian pdfs ($\mathcal{N}_1(x; \mu_1, \sigma_1^2)$, $\mathcal{N}_2(x; \mu_2, \sigma_2^2)$). Parameters Ki, j and Kj, i are defined using relations (6) and correspond to the bounds of the line segment ② showed in figure 2.

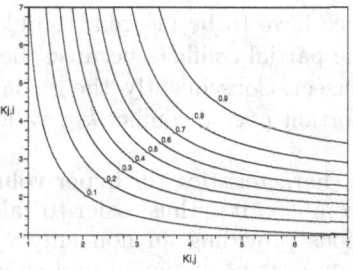

Fig. 4. Conflict's map in case of two Gaussian based agents of evidence combination

4.3 Conflict's Part in Disjunctive Combination

The disjunctive combination of two agents includes the XOR combination of sets $\mathcal{F}_i^x$ and $\mathcal{F}_j^x$. This may take into account non convex focal intervals located in the partial conflict's domain as we can see in figures 2 and 3. Singletons x concerned take values in $[\mu_i - \frac{\Delta_i^-}{\Delta_i^+} |\mu_i - \mu_j|, \mu_j + \frac{\Delta_j^+}{\Delta_j^-} |\mu_i - \mu_j|]$ when $\mu_i \leq \mu_j$ and figure 3

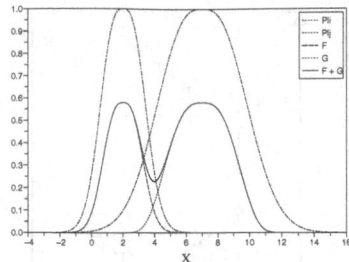

Fig. 5. Weight of conflicting intervals in the disjunctive combination

illustrates this for $x \in [\mu_i, \mu_j]$ with the grey areas F and G. In case of infinite support pdfs, F and G are defined as:

$$
\begin{cases}
F(x) = \int_{z_i=z_i^x}^{z_i=K_{i,j}} M_i(z_i) m_j(\frac{|\mu_i-\mu_j|-\Delta_i^+ z_i}{\Delta_j^-}) dz_i & \text{if } 0 \le z_i^x \le K_{i,j} \\
\quad = 0 & \text{otherwise,} \\
G(x) = \int_{z_j=z_j^x}^{z_j=K_{j,i}} M_j(z_j) m_i(\frac{|\mu_i-\mu_j|-\Delta_j^- z_j}{\Delta_i^+}) dz_j & \text{if } 0 \le z_j^x \le K_{j,i} \\
\quad = 0 & \text{otherwise} \quad .
\end{cases}
\tag{19}
$$

Figure 5 shows the degrees of conflict F and G taken into account in disjunctive combination of two bbds based on Gaussian pdfs. The maximum conflicting situations correspond as an evidence to singletons μ_i and μ_j and thus respectively to index pairs (z_i, z_j) equal to $(0, K_{j,i})$ and $(K_{i,j}, 0)$.

4.4 Global Conflict

When n pieces of evidence have to be merged, the global conflict do not correspond to the sum of the partial conflicts because the domains of intervals on which they are based intersect. Consequently, the global conflict K can never be lower than the most important partial conflict $k_{i,j}$ value existing between the n pieces of evidence.

Depending on the pdfs characteristics, the hyper-volume's shape of conflicting elements $(z_1, \ldots, z_n)$ is complex. It is thus easier to calculate the global conflict from intervals combinations providing an non empty intersection as done in relation (17). When all supports of unimodal and consonant pdfs related to n agents of evidence intersect, and if we consider $\mu_i \le \mu_j, \forall i, j \in \{1, \ldots, n\}, i \le j$ and to simplify, integrals infinite upper bounds assuming that $m_i(z_i) = 0$ if $z_i > z_{max_i}$, the global conflict K existing between these agents corresponds thus to:

$$
K = 1 - \int_{z_1=0}^{z_1=\infty} \int_{z_2=zMin_2}^{z_2=\infty} \ldots \int_{z_n=zMin_n}^{z_n=\infty} m_1(z_1) m_2(z_2) \ldots m_n(z_n) dz_n \ldots dz_2 dz_1 \tag{20}
$$

with:

$$
zMin_j = \max(0, \frac{|\mu_j - \mu_i| - \Delta_i^+ z_i}{\Delta_j^-} \ \forall i \in \{1, \ldots, j-1\}) \ \forall j \in \{2, \ldots, n\} . \tag{21}
$$

Relatively to the bounds of the considered intervals, relation (20) is equivalent to:

$$A_j^{zMinj^-} \leq (min(A_1^{z_1+}, \ldots, A_i^{z_i+}) \; \forall i \in \{1, \ldots, j-1\}) \; \forall j \in \{2, \ldots, n\} \; . \qquad (22)$$

5 Applications

5.1 Conjunctive and Disjunction Combinations of Gaussian Based Agents of Evidence

Under the assumption of cognitive independence, we consider three agents of evidence $\mathcal{E}_1, \mathcal{E}_2$ and $\mathcal{E}_3$ based on Gaussian pdfs $\mathcal{N}_1(x; \mu_1 = 8, \sigma_1^2 = 4), \mathcal{N}_2(x; \mu_2, \sigma_2^2 = 0.5)$ and $\mathcal{N}_3(x; \mu_3, \sigma_3^2 = 1)$. μ_3 and μ_2 are supposed to decrease until to reach μ_1's value. Partial and global conflicts calculations are given in table 1 when figure 6 illustrates the plausibility curves resulting of the conjunctive and disjunctive combination of these three agents of evidence.

As suggested by the plausibility curves of the conjunctive combination in figure 6 and the corresponding values of K, there is no linear relation between the maximum of the plausibility of this combination and the conflict. Examples illustrated in figures 6(c), 6(d) and 6(e) show also the sensitivity of the conjunctive combination to the agreement of precise sources of information.

Table 1. Partial and global conflicts amounts

	μ_1	μ_2	μ_3	$k_{1,2}$	$k_{1,3}$	$k_{2,3}$	K
a)	8	10.5	14.5	0.092	0.867	0.929	0.976
b)	8	10.5	12.5	0.092	0.451	0.195	0.522
c)	8	10.5	10.5	0.092	0.050	0	0.109
d)	8	10.5	8.5	0.092	0.000	0.195	0.257
e)	8	10.5	8	0.092	0	0.415	0.454
f)	8	8	8	0	0	0	0

5.2 Conflict Management by RCR-S Adaptive Combination

Many authors propose adaptive combination rules weighting conjunctive and disjunctive rules of combination. Florea *et al.* [6] give a general formulation of most of them and propose robust combination rules referred as RCR. To illustrate our work, we apply our relations to a RCR-S combination rule defined as:

$$Pl_{RCR-S_{1\ldots n}}(x) = \frac{K}{1-K+K^2} Pl_{1\text{\scriptsize ©}\ldots\text{\scriptsize ©}n}(x) + \frac{1-K}{1-K+K^2} Pl_{1\text{\scriptsize ©}\ldots\text{\scriptsize ©}n}(x) \quad . \qquad (23)$$

Figure 7 illustrates from left to right, the RCR-S plausibility curves obtained for the examples shown in respectively figures 6(b) and 6(c). We observe that the trend in conjunctive combination is preserved even if $K > 0.5$. When applied in a very high conflicting situation as illustrated in figure 6(a) ($K = 0.976$), the RCR-S combination operation is equivalent to the disjunctive one as expected.

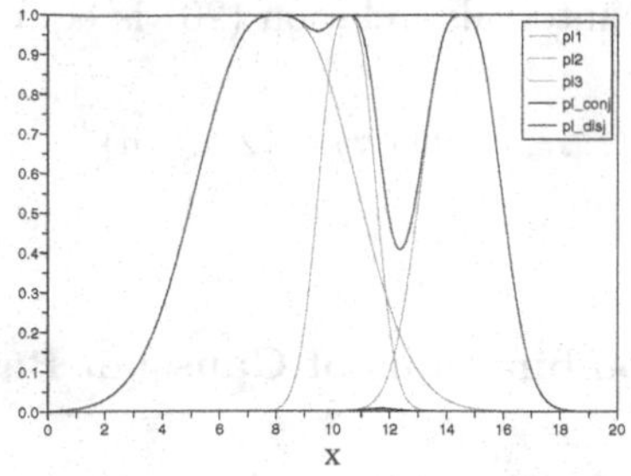

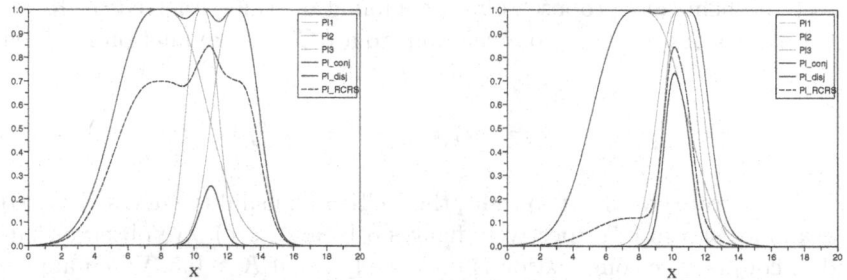

(a) $K = 0.976$

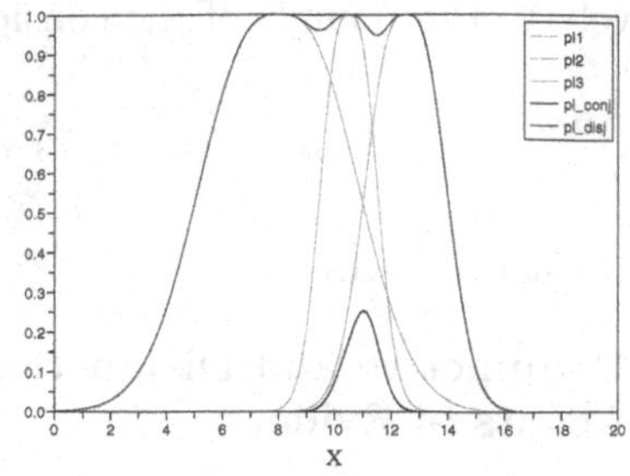

(b) $K = 0.522$

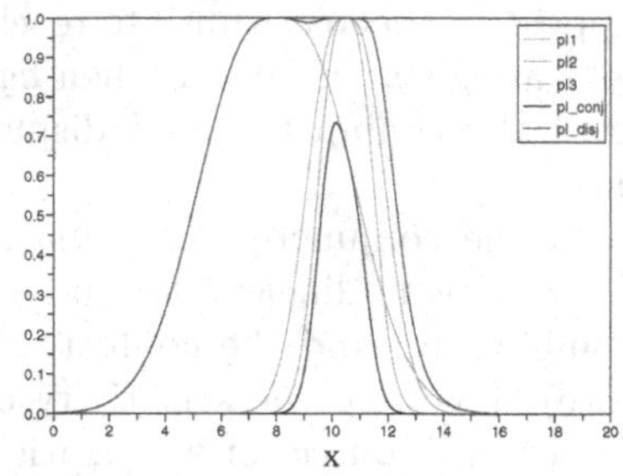

(c) $K = 0.109$

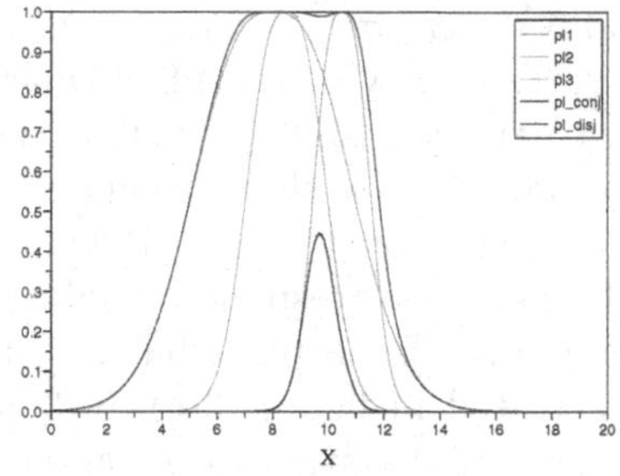

(d) $K = 0.257$

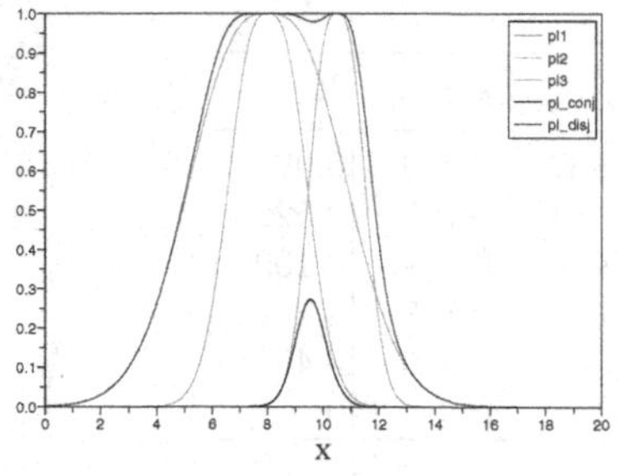

(e) $K = 0.454$

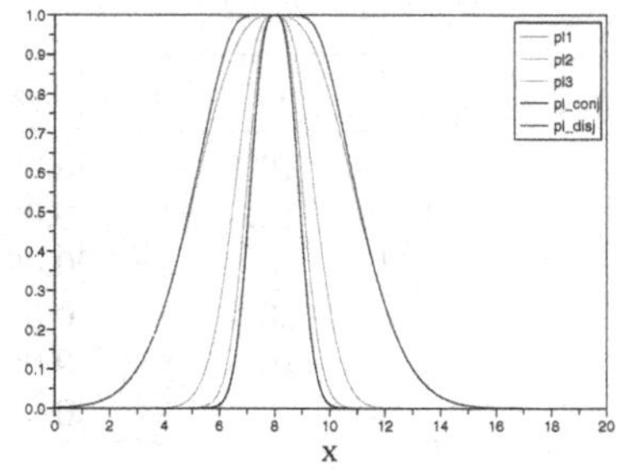

(f) $K = 0$

Fig. 6. Basic combinations of 3 Gaussian based agents of evidence (plausibility curves)

Fig. 7. Plausibilities of Conjunctive, disjunctive and RCR-S combinations

6   Conclusions

Much existing adaptive combination rules can be applied on the plausibilities of conjunctive and disjunctive combinations presented here, mixed according to the global conflict value. But such a conflict's management is inefficient when one source of information is in total conflict with the other ones. Coherent sets of information sources could then be defined using partial conflicts values to perform more accurate combinations.

References

1. Smets, P.: Belief functions on real numbers. International Journal of approximate reasoning 40(3), 181–223 (2005)
2. Vannobel, J.-M.: Continuous belief functions: singletons plausibility function in conjunctive and disjunctive combination operations of consonant bbds. In: Belief 2010, p. 6, Brest (Fr) (2010), http://www.ensieta.fr/belief2010/
3. Ristic, B., Smets, P.: Belief function theory on the continuous space with an application to model based classification. In: IPMU'04, Information Processing and Management of Uncertainty in Knowledge Based Systems, pp. 1119–1126, Paris (Fr) (2004)
4. Caron, F., Ristic, B., Duflos, E., Vanheeghe, P.: Least committed basic belief density induced by a multivariate gaussian: formulation with applications. International Journal on Approximate Reasoning 48(2), 419–436 (2008)
5. Smets, P.: Belief functions: the disjunctive rule of combination and the generalized Bayesian theorem. International Journal of approximate reasoning 9(1), 1–35 (1993)
6. Florea, M.C., Jousselme, A.L., Bosse, E., Grenier, D.: Robust combination rules for evidence theory. Information Fusion 10(2), 183–197 (2009)

Credal Sets Approximation by Lower Probabilities: Application to Credal Networks

Alessandro Antonucci[1] and Fabio Cuzzolin[2]

[1] Istituto Dalle Molle di Studi sull'Intelligenza Artificiale
Galleria 2, Via Cantonale, Manno-Lugano, Switzerland
alessandro@idsia.ch
[2] Department of Computing, Oxford Brookes University
Wheatley Campus, Wheatley, Oxford, United Kingdom
fabio.cuzzolin@brookes.ac.uk

Abstract. *Credal sets* are closed convex sets of probability mass functions. The *lower probabilities* specified by a credal set for each element of the power set can be used as constraints defining a second credal set. This simple procedure produces an outer approximation, with a bounded number of extreme points, for general credal sets. The approximation is optimal in the sense that no other lower probabilities can specify smaller supersets of the original credal set. Notably, in order to be computed, the approximation does not need the extreme points of the credal set, but only its lower probabilities. This makes the approximation particularly suited for *credal networks*, which are a generalization of Bayesian networks based on credal sets. Although most of the algorithms for credal networks updating only return lower posterior probabilities, the suggested approximation can be used to evaluate (as an outer approximation of) the *posterior credal set*. This makes it possible to adopt more sophisticated decision making criteria, without having to replace existing algorithms. The quality of the approximation is investigated by numerical tests.

Keywords: Imprecise probability, lower probabilities, credal sets, credal networks, interval dominance, maximality.

1 Introduction

Consider the problem of modelling a condition of uncertainty about the state of a categorical variable. In the Bayesian framework, this problem is faced by assessing the probability of each possible outcome, thus specifying a (single) probability mass function. Yet, there are situations where the assessment of a precise probabilistic value for each outcome can be difficult. In such cases, multiple assessments (e.g., through intervals) can be considered, leading to the specification of sets of, instead of single, probability mass functions. These sets, which are required to be convex by compelling rationality criteria related to the behavioural interpretation of probability, are called *credal sets* (CS, [1]) and represent a very general class of uncertainty models [2].

E. Hüllermeier, R. Kruse, and F. Hoffmann (Eds.): IPMU 2010, LNAI 6178, pp. 716–725, 2010.

A (partial) characterization of a CS can be obtained by considering its *lower probabilities*, i.e., the infima over all the probability mass functions in the CS, of the probabilities assigned to the elements of the power set.[1] These bounds correspond to a number of constraints satisfied by the original CS. Yet, this is only a partial characterization, as the set of probability mass functions consistent with these constraints is in general a proper superset of the original CS.

This simple procedure is intended in this paper as an outer approximation for CSs. The approximation is proved to be optimal, in the sense that no other outer approximation based on lower probabilities can specify more informative CSs. Furthermore, the number of extreme points[2] of the approximating CS is bounded by the factorial of the number of possible values of the variable.

Notably, in order to achieve this approximation, only the lower probabilities of the CS are needed, while an explicit enumeration of its extreme points is not necessary. This makes the approximation particularly suited for *credal networks* [3], which are a generalization of Bayesian networks based on CSs. In fact, most of the algorithms for credal networks updating only return the lower posterior probabilities, and not the posterior CS. We show that the outer approximation of this posterior CS, as returned by the transformation we consider, can be computed by means of these standard algorithms. This makes it possible to adopt more refined criteria for making decisions on a credal network, without the need to replace existing algorithms. Although the outer approximation can eventually lead to over-cautious decisions, we show by extensive numerical simulations that this happens only in a minority of cases.

The paper is organized as follows. First, we review some background information about CSs (Section 2.1), lower probabilities (Section 2.2), and credal networks (Section 2.3). Then, in Section 3, we provide a characterization of the class of CSs associated to lower probabilities and we detail the transformation to obtain an outer approximation of a CS by means of its lower probabilities. Also some theoretical results characterizing the proposed technique are reported. The transformation is applied to credal networks in Section 4. Numerical tests to investigate the quality of the approximation are in Section 5. Conclusions and future outlooks are finally in Section 6, while the proofs of the theorems can be found in the Appendix.

2 Background

2.1 Credal Sets

Let X denote a generic variable, taking values in a finite set $\mathcal{X} := \{x^{(1)}, \ldots, x^{(n)}\}$. A probability mass function over X, which is a nonnegative real map over $\mathcal{X}$ normalized to one, will be denoted by $P(X)$. A *credal set* (CS) over X, which is a convex set of probability mass functions over X, will be be denoted by $K(X)$.

---

[1] The power set of a variable is made by all the subsets of its set of possible values.

[2] A point in a convex set is *extreme* if it cannot be obtained as a convex combination of other points in this set.

The *extreme points* of $K(X)$ (see Footnote 2) are denoted as $\mathrm{ext}[K(X)]$. Here we only consider CSs with a finite number of extreme points, i.e., such that $|\mathrm{ext}[K(X)]| < +\infty$.[3] Geometrically, a CS is therefore a polytope in the probability simplex, and can be equivalently specified through an explicit enumeration of its extreme points (V-representation) and a finite set of linear constraints (H-representation). Unlike the V-representation, which is clearly uniquely defined, different H-representations can specify the same CS. The notation $\overline{K}(X)$ is used for the vacuous CS, i.e., the (convex) set of all the probability mass functions over X. It is easy to note that $|\mathrm{ext}[\overline{K}(X)]| = |\mathcal{X}|$.

2.2 Lower Probabilities

A conjugate pair of *lower/upper probability* operators [1] is defined as a pair $(\underline{P}, \overline{P})$ of nonnegative real maps over the power set $2^{\mathcal{X}}$, such that: (i) $\underline{P}(\emptyset) = 0$; (ii) the operators are respectively super- and sub-additive, i.e.,

$$\underline{P}(A \cup B) \geq \underline{P}(A) + \underline{P}(B)$$

$$\overline{P}(A \cup B) \leq \overline{P}(A) + \overline{P}(B),$$

for each $A, B \in 2^{\mathcal{X}}$; (iii) the following conjugacy relation holds for each $A \in 2^{\mathcal{X}}$

$$\overline{P}(A) = 1 - \underline{P}(\mathcal{X} \setminus A). \tag{1}$$

According to (1), the operator $\overline{P}$ is completely determined by its conjugate $\underline{P}$ (and vice versa). In this paper, we only consider lower probability operators.

2.3 Credal Networks

Consider a collection of categorical variables $X_1, \ldots, X_v$.[4] Let these variables be in one-to-one correspondence with the nodes of a directed acyclic graph, and assume that this graph depicts conditional independence relations among the variables according to the Markov condition. In the Bayesian framework, this implies the following factorization for the joint probability $P(x_1, \ldots, x_v) = \prod_{i=1}^{v} P(x_i | \mathrm{pa}(X_i))$, where $\mathrm{Pa}(X_i)$ is the joint variable made of the *parents* of X_i according to the graph. This implicitly defines a *Bayesian network* over X.

In order to define a *credal network* [3] over the same variables and the same graph, we simply leave each conditional probability mass function $P(X_i | \mathrm{pa}(X_i))$ free to vary in a conditional CS $K(X_i | \mathrm{pa}(X_i))$. This defines a set of joint probability mass functions, whose convexification is a joint CS $K(X_1, \ldots, X_v)$, to be called the *strong extension* of the credal network. Each extreme point of the strong extension factorizes as the joint probability mass function of a Bayesian network, and its conditional probability mass functions are extreme points of the conditional CSs $K(X_i | \mathrm{pa}(X_i))$.

---

[3] The notation $|S|$ is used for the cardinality of the set S.
[4] The background information in this section is particularly brief for sake of space. More insights on credal networks can be found in [3] or [4].

A typical inference problem to be addressed in a credal network is *updating*, i.e., given some evidence x_E about a set of variables X_E, evaluate the lower probability $\underline{P}(x|x_E)$ (with respect to the strong extension) for each possible value $x \in \mathcal{X}$ of a variable of interest X. Despite its hardness [5], various algorithms for this particular problem have been developed (see [6] for a survey and [7,8] for recent advances).

3   Credal Sets Associated to Lower Probabilities

Given a lower probability operator $\underline{P}$, let us consider the CS of its consistent probability mass functions, i.e.,

$$K_{\underline{P}}(X) := \left\{ P(X) \in \overline{K}(X) \middle| \sum_{x \in A} P(x) \geq \underline{P}(A), \forall A \in 2^{\mathcal{X}} \right\}. \tag{2}$$

The following result (conjectured by Weichselberger and proved by Wallner in [9]) provides a characterization of the the maximum number of extreme points of the CS in (2):

$$|\text{ext}[K_{\underline{P}}(X)]| \leq |\mathcal{X}|!, \tag{3}$$

this being true for each lower probability operator $\underline{P}$ defined as in Section 2.2. Note that, in the case of belief functions, stronger results on the form of the extreme points can be proven [10].

Example 1. *Given a ternary variable X, consider the following CS*

$$K(X) = \text{CH} \left\{ \begin{bmatrix} .90 \\ .05 \\ .05 \end{bmatrix}, \begin{bmatrix} .10 \\ .40 \\ .50 \end{bmatrix}, \begin{bmatrix} .20 \\ .20 \\ .60 \end{bmatrix}, \begin{bmatrix} .20 \\ .70 \\ .10 \end{bmatrix}, \begin{bmatrix} .80 \\ .05 \\ .15 \end{bmatrix}, \begin{bmatrix} .45 \\ .25 \\ .30 \end{bmatrix}, \begin{bmatrix} .05 \\ .80 \\ .15 \end{bmatrix} \right\},$$

where CH denotes the convex hull operator, while probability mass functions are denoted as vertical arrays. Standard techniques (e.g., [11]) can be used to verify that none of these seven probability mass functions is a convex combination of the remaining six, and hence $|\text{ext}[K(X)]| = 7$.

Example 1 violates (3). This simply proves that not any CS can be obtained from a lower probability operator as in (2). The class of CSs associated with lower probability operators should be therefore regarded as a special class of CSs.[5] The idea of this paper is that this class is sufficiently large to provide a reasonable approximation of general CSs (at least from the point of view of decision making based on them, see Section 5).

In fact, the lower probabilities of a CS define a lower probability operator, which can be employed indeed to define a (new) CS. The whole procedure is formalized as follows.

---

[5] The only exception is the case of CSs over binary variables. If general CSs can have an arbitrary number of extreme points, a CS over a binary variable has at most two extreme points. In fact, for binary variables, any CS can be associated with a lower probability operator.

Transformation 1. *Given a CS $K(X)$, consider its extreme points $\text{ext}[K(X)]$ (i.e., its unique, V-representation). Then, for each $A \in 2^{\mathcal{X}}$, compute the lower probability:*[6]

$$\underline{P}_K(A) := \min_{P(X) \in \text{ext}[K(X)]} \sum_{x \in A} P(x). \tag{4}$$

Finally, consider the CS $\tilde{K}(X)$ associated as in (2) with the lower probability operator in (4).[7]

It is straightforward to verify that (4) specifies a lower probability operator as in Section 2.2. Thus, given a generic non-empty CS $K(X)$, Transformation 1 always returns a non-empty CS $\tilde{K}(X)$. The following is an example of the application of this transformation.

Example 2. *The application of Transformation 1 to the CS $K(X)$ in Example 1 returns a CS $\tilde{K}(X)$ whose H-representation, according to (2), is:*

$$\begin{cases} P(\{x^{(1)}\}) \geq .05 \\ P(\{x^{(2)}\}) \geq .05 \\ P(\{x^{(3)}\}) \geq .05 \\ P(\{x^{(1)}\} \cup \{x^{(2)}\}) \geq .40 \\ P(\{x^{(1)}\} \cup \{x^{(3)}\}) \geq .20 \\ P(\{x^{(2)}\} \cup \{x^{(3)}\}) \geq .10. \end{cases}$$

from which (e.g., see [11]) the following V-representation follows:

$$\tilde{K}(X) = \text{CH} \left\{ \begin{bmatrix} .05 \\ .35 \\ .60 \end{bmatrix}, \begin{bmatrix} .05 \\ .80 \\ .15 \end{bmatrix}, \begin{bmatrix} .15 \\ .80 \\ .05 \end{bmatrix}, \begin{bmatrix} .35 \\ .05 \\ .60 \end{bmatrix}, \begin{bmatrix} .90 \\ .05 \\ .05 \end{bmatrix} \right\}.$$

Thus, as expected, (3) is now satisfied. Fig. 1 depicts the polytopes associated with $K(X)$ and $\tilde{K}(X)$ on the same probability simplex.

A characterization of this transformation is provided by the following result.

Theorem 1. *Consider a CS $K(X)$. Let $\underline{P}_K$ denote the corresponding lower probability operator as in (4), and $\tilde{K}(X)$ the output of Transformation 1. Then:*

(i) $K(X) \subseteq \tilde{K}(X)$;

(ii) $K(X) = \tilde{K}(X)$ if and only if a lower probability operator $\underline{P}'$ such that $K_{P'}(X) = K(X)$ exists;

(iii) A lower probability operator $\underline{P}' \neq \underline{P}_K$ such that $K(X) \subseteq K_{\underline{P}'}(X) \subseteq \tilde{K}(X)$ cannot exist.

It is worth noting that, for its application, Transformation 1 does not need the extreme points of the CS, but only its lower probabilities. This feature suggests a possible application to credal networks, which is detailed in the next section.

---

[6] The minimum in (4) is the same we obtain by minimizing over the whole CS [12].

[7] We prefer to avoid the somehow heavy notation $K_{\underline{P}_K}(X)$.

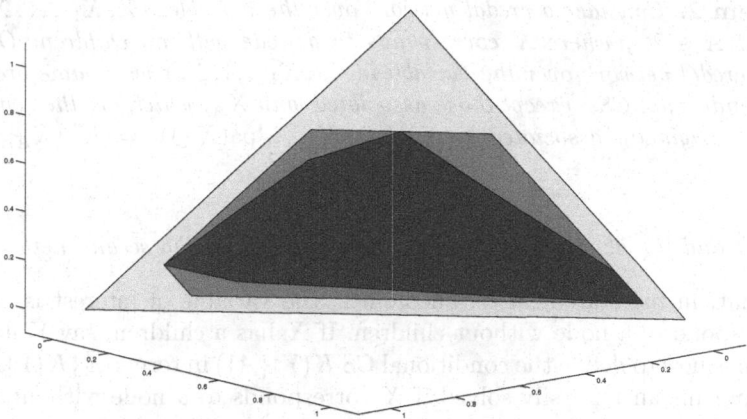

Fig. 1. The CS $K(X)$ as in Example 1 (dark gray), and the output $\tilde{K}(X)$ of Transformation 1 as in Example 2 (medium gray) on the same simplex (light gray)

4 Computing Posterior Credal Sets in a Credal Network

As noted in Section 2.3, a typical inference task to be discussed on a credal network is *updating* knowledge about a variable of interest, after the observation of some evidence x_E about X_E. This is generally intended as the computation of the posterior probability $\underline{P}(x|x_E)$ (with respect to the strong extension) for each $x \in \mathcal{X}$, and this is what most of the updating algorithms for credal networks do. Yet, in the imprecise-probabilistic framework, the proper model of the posterior knowledge about X should be better identified with the posterior CS $K(X|x_E)$. In order to estimate this CS, Transformation 1 can be used to obtain an outer approximation (thus, in a sense, an over-cautious model) of $\tilde{K}(X|x_E)$.

To this aim, the lower probabilities $\underline{P}(A|x_E)$ for each $A \in 2^{\mathcal{X}}$ are needed, while standard updating algorithms only return the lower probabilities of the singletons. To overcome this limitation, we introduce the notion of *coarsening*.[8]

Given a variable X and an element of its power set $A \in 2^{\mathcal{X}}$, the coarsening of X based on A, is a variable X_A such that $\mathcal{X}_A := \{A\} \cup \mathcal{X} \setminus A$. In other words, the coarsening of a variable shrinks the set of possible values by clustering all the elements of A into a single value (denoted as $\{A\}$). The coarsening over A of a probability mass function $P(X)$ is indeed defined as a probability mass function $P_A(X_A)$ such that $P_A(\{A\}) := \sum_{x \in A} P(x)$ and $P_A(x) := P(x)$ for each $x \in \mathcal{X} \setminus A$. Finally, the coarsening over A of a CS $K(X)$ is a CS $K_A(X_A)$ obtained as the convex hull of the coarsening of the extreme points of $K(X)$, i.e,

$$K_A(X_A) := \text{CH}\{P_A(X_A)\}_{P(X) \in \text{ext}[K(X)]}.$$

The following result holds.

---

[8] This is based on a development of the ideas introduced in [13, Transformation 2].

Theorem 2. *Consider a credal network over the variables $(X, X_1, \ldots, X_v)$ and a subset $A \in 2^{\mathcal{X}}$, where X corresponds to a node with no children. Obtain a second credal network over the variables $(X_A, X_1, \ldots, X_v)$ with same graph and same conditional CSs, except those associated with X_A, which are the coarsening of those originally associated to X, i.e., $K(X_A|\mathrm{pa}(X_A)) := K_A(X_A|\mathrm{pa}(X))$. Then:*

$$\underline{P}(A|x_E) = \underline{P}_A(\{A\}|x_E), \tag{5}$$

where $\underline{P}$ and $\underline{P}_A$ denote inferences on the first and on the second network.

Note that, in the statement of Theorem 2, the variable of interest is assumed to correspond to a node without children. If X has a children, say Y, the only problem is how to define the conditional CS $K(Y|\{A\})$ in terms of $\{K(Y|x)\}_{x \in A}$. The problem can be easily solved if X corresponds to a node without parents (see the extension of Theorem 2 in the Appendix), while in more general cases, further inferences on the network should be computed.

According to Theorem 2, we can therefore regard the lower probabilities for non-singletons in a credal network as lower probabilities of singletons in a "coarsened" network. Thus, $\tilde{K}(X|x_E)$ can be obtained through standard updating algorithms, by simply iterating the computation in (5) for each $A \in 2^{\mathcal{X}}$.

This result is important in order to make decisions based on the posterior state of X after the observation of x_E. In fact, as only lower posterior probabilities of the singletons are typically available, decision are based on the *interval dominance* criterion, i.e., we reject the states of X whose upper probability is smaller than the lower probability of some other state. The set of unrejected states is therefore:

$$\mathcal{X}_{\underline{P}}^{\mathrm{ID}} := \left\{ x \in \mathcal{X} \mid \nexists x' \in \mathcal{X} \text{ s.t. } \underline{P}(x') > \overline{P}(x) \right\},$$

and it is regarded as the set of optimal states according to this criterion.[9]

Other, more informative, decision criteria (see [14]) cannot be adopted unless the posterior CS is available. As an example, if decisions are based on the *maximality* criterion, a state is rejected if, for each point (or equivalently extreme point) of the CS, there is another state with higher probability, i.e.,

$$\mathcal{X}_K^{\mathrm{MAX}} := \{ x \in \mathcal{X} \mid \nexists x' \in \mathcal{X} \text{ s.t. } P(x') > P(x), \forall P(X) \in K(X) \}. \tag{6}$$

This clearly requires that the (extreme) points of the posterior CS are available. Yet, by exploiting the result in Theorem 2, we can use Transformation 1 to compute the outer approximation $\tilde{K}(X|x_E)$ of $K(X|x_E)$, and make decisions on the basis of the maximality criterion (or any other criterion) with the CS $\tilde{K}(X|x_E)$. As the CS we work with is an outer approximation of the *true* CS, this can eventually lead to over-cautious decisions, i.e., we can include in the set of optimal decisions some states which in fact are not. Nevertheless, the numerical simulations in the next section show that this tends to happen only in a minority of cases.

---

[9] We can similarly proceed if a linear utility function has been defined.

5   Numerical Tests

Different techniques can be adopted to evaluate the quality of the outer approximation associated with Transformation 1. As an example, a geometrical approach would consist in comparing the area of the polytopes associated with the two CSs. Yet, as CSs model uncertain knowledge to be used for decision-making, it seems more reasonable to compare *decisions* based on the two CSs.

In order to do that, we consider randomly generated CSs over variables with an increasing number of possible values and extreme points, and we compare the number of optimal states according to maximality in the original CS and in its outer approximation. As an obvious consequence of (i) in Theorem 1 and (6), we have that $\mathcal{X}_K^{\mathrm{MAX}} \subseteq \mathcal{X}_{\tilde{K}}^{\mathrm{MAX}}$. Thus, the difference between the two sets can be simply characterized by the difference between the cardinality of the corresponding sets of optimal states. This is shown in the following table.

Table 1. Numerical evaluation of the quality of the approximation associated with Transformation 1. The third column reports the average of the difference between the number of states recognized as optimal by using the outer approximation and those associated with the original CS. For each row, 10000 randomly generated CSs over a variable with $|\mathcal{X}|$ states and $|\mathrm{ext}[K(X)]|$ extreme points have been generated.

$|\mathcal{X}|$	$|\mathrm{ext}[K(X)]|$	$|\mathcal{X}_{\tilde{K}}^{\mathrm{MAX}}| - |\mathcal{X}_K^{\mathrm{MAX}}|$
3	3	0.235
4	4	0.317
5	5	0.353
6	6	0.359
7	7	0.255

As a comment, we note that, on average, the approximation introduces a non-optimal state once every three or four CSs. These values might be regarded as a reasonable approximation, especially for variables with many states.

6   Conclusions

An outer approximation for CSs based on lower probabilities, together with some theoretical and numerical characterizations, has been presented. The approximation is particularly suited for applications to decision making on credal networks, and makes it possible to adopt more sophisticated decision criteria, without the need of newer inference algorithms. As a future work, we want to investigate possible analytical characterizations of the quality of the approximation, and identify an inner approximation with similar features.

Acknowledgments

The work reported in this paper has benefitted from discussions with Sébastien Destercke and Enrique Miranda.

724   A. Antonucci and F. Cuzzolin

References

1. Levi, I.: The Enterprise of Knowledge. MIT Press, London (1980)
2. Walley, P.: Measures of uncertainty in expert systems. Artificial Intelligence 83(1), 1–58 (1996)
3. Cozman, F.G.: Credal networks. Artificial Intelligence 120, 199–233 (2000)
4. Antonucci, A., Zaffalon, M.: Decision-theoretic specification of credal networks: A unified language for uncertain modeling with sets of Bayesian networks. International Journal of Approximate Reasoning 49(2), 345–361 (2008)
5. de Campos, C.P., Cozman, F.G.: The inferential complexity of Bayesian and credal networks. In: Proceedings of the International Joint Conference on Artificial Intelligence, Edinburgh, pp. 1313–1318 (2005)
6. Cozman, F.G.: Graphical models for imprecise probabilities. International Journal of Approximate Reasoning 39(2-3), 167–184 (2005)
7. de Campos, C.P., Cozman, F.G.: Inference in credal networks through integer programming. In: Proceedings of the Fifth International Symposium on Imprecise Probability: Theories and Applications, Prague, Action M Agency, pp. 145–154 (2007)
8. Antonucci, A., Sun, Y., de Campos, C.P., Zaffalon, M.: Generalized loopy 2U: a new algorithm for approximate inference in credal networks. International Journal of Approximate Reasoning (to appear, 2010)
9. Wallner, A.: Maximal number of vertices of polytopes defined by f-probabilities. In: Proceedings of the Fourth International Symposium on Imprecise Probabilities and Their Applications, SIPTA, pp. 126–139 (2005)
10. Cuzzolin, F.: On the credal structure of consistent probabilities. In: Hölldobler, S., Lutz, C., Wansing, H. (eds.) JELIA 2008. LNCS (LNAI), vol. 5293, pp. 126–139. Springer, Heidelberg (2008)
11. Avis, D., Fukuda, K.: A pivoting algorithm for convex hulls and vertex enumeration of arrangements and polyhedra. Discrete and Computational Geometry 8, 295–313 (1992)
12. Walley, P.: Statistical Reasoning with Imprecise Probabilities. Chapman and Hall, London (1991)
13. Antonucci, A., Piatti, A.: Modeling unreliable observations in Bayesian networks by credal networks. In: Proceedings of the 3rd International Conference on Scalable Uncertainty Management table of contents, pp. 28–39. Springer, Heidelberg (2009)
14. Troffaes, M.C.M.: Decision making under uncertainty using imprecise probabilities. International Journal of Approximate Reasoning 45(1), 17–29 (2007)

Appendix

Proof (Theorem 1). As an obvious consequence of (4), for each $P(X) \in K(X)$,

$$\sum_{x \in A} P(x) \geq \underline{P}_K(A).$$

Thus, according to (2), we have that $P(X) \in \tilde{K}(X)$, and hence (i). Now we prove (ii). The *if* implication is trivial, as we simply have $\underline{P}' = \underline{P}_K$. To prove the *only if* implication, note that the existence of $\underline{P}'$ implies that $\underline{P}_K = \underline{P}'$, and hence $\tilde{K}(X) = K_{\underline{P}'}(X) = K(X)$. In order to prove (iii), let us follow an *ad absurdum* scheme. Accordingly, let $\underline{P}' \neq \underline{P}_K$ be the lower probability operator such that $K(X) \subseteq K_{\underline{P}'}(X) \subseteq \tilde{K}(X)$. Thus, for each $A \in 2^{\mathcal{X}}$:

$$\underline{P}'(A) = \min_{P'(X) \in K_{\underline{P}'}(X)} \sum_{x \in A} P'(X) \leq \min_{P(X) \in \tilde{K}(X)} \sum_{x \in A} P(X) = \min_{P(X) \in K(X)} \sum_{x \in A} P(X),$$

where the inequality holds because of the set inclusion and the last equality is because of the definition of Transformation 1. But, as $K_{\underline{P}}(X) \supseteq K(X)$, the inequality should be an equality, this contradicting the assumption $\underline{P}' \neq \underline{P}_K$. □

Proof (Theorem 2). Let us first assume $A := \{x^{(1)}\} \cup \{x^{(2)}\}$ and the network Bayesian. Consider the joint states $(x^{(1)}, x_1, \ldots, x_v)$ and $(x^{(2)}, x_1, \ldots, x_v)$ in the original network, and the joint state $(\{A\}, x_1, \ldots, x_v)$ in the "coarsened" network. By exploiting the factorization described in Section 2.3, we have:

$$P(\{x^{(1)}\} \cup \{x^{(2)}\}, x_1, \ldots) = P(x^{(1)}, x_1, \ldots) + P(x^{(2)}, x_1, \ldots) = P_A(\{A\}, x_1, \ldots),$$

from which the thesis follows by simple marginalization and application of Bayes' rule. The same result holds for credal networks, because of the notion of strong extension and by simply observing that coarsening for CSs consist in the *Bayesian* coarsening of each extreme point.

Extension (of Theorem 2) to the case where X correspond to a parentless node. Let Y be a children of X, and set $A = \{x^{(1)}\} \cup \{x^{(2)}\}$. In the Bayesian case:

$$P(y|\{x^{(1)}\} \cup \{x^{(2)}\}) = \frac{P(y, \{x^{(1)}\} \cup \{x^{(2)}\})}{P(\{x^{(1)}\} \cup \{x^{(2)}\})} = \frac{P(y|x^{(1)})P(x^{(1)}) + P(y|x^{(2)})P(x^{(2)})}{P(x^{(1)}) + P(x^{(2)})}.$$

Thus, in the credal case:

$$K(Y|x^{(1)} \cup x^{(2)}) = \mathrm{CH}\left\{ \frac{P_i(Y|x^{(1)})P_k(x^{(1)}) + P_j(Y|x^{(2)})P_k(x^{(2)})}{P_k(x^{(1)}) + P_k(x^{(2)})} \right\}_{\substack{P_i(Y|x^{(1)}) \in K(Y|x^{(1)}) \\ P_j(Y|x^{(2)}) \in K(Y|x^{(2)}) \\ P_k(X) \in K(X)}}.$$

We similarly proceed if A has cardinality greater than two.

Rule Discovery Process Based on Rough Sets under the Belief Function Framework

Salsabil Trabelsi[1], Zied Elouedi[1], and Pawan Lingras[2]

[1] Larodec, Institut Superieur de Gestion de Tunis, Tunisia
[2] Saint Mary's University Halifax, Canada

Abstract. In this paper, we deal with the problem of rule discovery process based on rough sets from partially uncertain data. The uncertainty exists only in decision attribute values and is handled by the *Transferable Belief Model* (TBM), one interpretation of the belief function theory. To solve this problem, we propose in this uncertain environment, a new method based on a soft hybrid induction system for discovering classification rules called GDT-RS which is a hybridization of the *Generalization Distribution Table* and the *Rough Set* methodology.

Keywords: Rough sets, generalization distribution table, uncertainty, belief function theory, classification.

1 Introduction

The Knowledge Discovery from Databases (KDD) is usually a multi-phase process consisting of numerous steps, including attribute selection, discretization of real-valued attributes, and rule induction. Rough set theory constitutes a sound basis for KDD. It offers useful tools for discovering patterns hidden in data [10,12]. It can be used in different phases of the knowledge discovery process, like feature selection, data reduction, decision rule generation and pattern extraction. Techniques based on standard rough sets do not perform their tasks in an environment characterized by uncertain or incomplete data. Many researchers have adapted rough sets to this kind of environment [8,9]. These extensions deal with incomplete decision tables which may be characterized by missing condition attribute values and not with partially uncertain decision attribute. This kind of uncertainty exists in many real-world applications such as marketing, finance, management and medicine. For the latter, the diseases (classes) of some patients may be totally or partially uncertain. This kind of uncertainty can be represented by belief functions as in the Transferable Belief Model, one interpretation of the belief function theory [14]. In fact, this theory is considered as a useful tool for representing and managing totally or partially uncertain knowledge because of its relative flexibility [11]. The belief function theory is widely applied in machine learning and also in real life problems related to decision making and classification.

E. Hüllermeier, R. Kruse, and F. Hoffmann (Eds.): IPMU 2010, LNAI 6178, pp. 726–736, 2010.

In this paper, we deal with the problem of rule discovery process based on rough sets from partially uncertain data. The uncertainty exists only in decision attribute values and is represented by belief functions. To solve this problem, we propose under the belief function framework a new approach based on a soft hybrid induction system called GDT-RS. The GDT-RS system, presented originally in [4,19], is a combination of *Generalization Distribution Table* [20] and the *Rough Set* methodology [10]. It should be noted that our approach is complementary to the previous study of the relationship between rough sets and belief functions by Busse and Skowron [13]. Busse and Skowron's work can be used to enhance practical application of the proposed approach. The standard version of GDT-RS system deals with certain decision tables (known condition and decision attribute values) or incomplete decision tables (missing condition attribute values and known decision attribute). The advantage of our new approach named belief GDT-RS is that it can generate in an automatic way from decision table characterized by uncertain decision attribute a set of rules with the minimal description length, having large strength and covering all instances. There are some classification techniques such as Belief Decision Tree (BDT) [3,5,18] that can generate classification decision rules from this kind of databases. However to perform this task well, we need at first to build the decision tree and then prune it [16].

This paper is organized as follows: Section 2 provides an overview of the *Generalization Distribution Table* and *Rough Set* methodology (GDT-RS). Section 3 introduces the belief function theory as understood in the TBM. In Section 4, we propose a belief GDT-RS approach for discovering classification rules from partially uncertain data under the belief function framework. Finally, in Section 5, we carry experiments on real databases, based on two evaluation criteria: accuracy and time complexity. To evaluate our belief GDT-RS, we compare the results with those obtained from BDT after pruning.

2 Generalization Distribution Table and Rough Set System (GDT-RS)

GDT-RS is a soft hybrid induction system for discovering classification rules from databases with noisy data [4,19]. The system is based on a hybridization of the *Generalization Distribution Table* (GDT) and the *Rough Set* methodology (RS). The GDT-RS system can generate a set of rules with the minimal description length, having large strength and covering all instances.

2.1 Generalization Distribution Table (GDT)

Any GDT [20] consists of three components: possible instances, possible generalizations of instances, and probabilistic relationships between possible instances and possible generalizations. Possible instances, represented at the top row of *GDT*, are defined by all possible combinations of attribute values from a database. Possible generalizations of instances, represented by the left column of a GDT, are all possible cases of generalization for all possible instances. A wild card '*' denotes the generalization for instances. The probabilistic relationships between possible instances and possible generalizations, represented by entries G_{ij} of a given GDT. The prior distribution is assumed to be uniform if background knowledge is not available. Thus, it is defined by:

$$G_{ij} = p(PI_j|PG_i) = \begin{cases} \frac{1}{N_{PG_i}} & \text{if } PG_i \text{ is a generalization of } PI_j \\ 0 & \text{otherwise.} \end{cases} \tag{1}$$

where PI_j is the j-th possible instance, PG_i is the i-th possible generalization, and N_{PG_i} is the number of the possible instances satisfying the i-th possible generalization,

$$N_{PG_i} = \prod_{k \in \{l|PG_i[l]=*\}} n_k \tag{2}$$

where $PG_i[l]$ is the value of the l-th attribute in the possible generalization PG_i, and n_k is the number of values of the k-th attribute.

2.2 Rough Sets (RS)

Let us recall some basic notions regarding rough sets and rule discovery from databases represented by decision tables [10]. A decision table (DT) is defined as A= (U, C, {d}), where $U = \{o_1, o_2, ...o_n\}$ is a nonempty finite set of n objects called *the universe*, $C = \{c_1, c_2, ...c_k\}$ is a finite set of k *condition* attributes and $d \notin C$ is a distinguished attribute called *decision*. The value set of d is called $\Theta = \{d_1, d_2, ...d_s\}$. By $IND(B)$ we denote the indiscernibility relation defined by $B \subseteq C$, $[o_j]_B$ denotes the indiscernibility (equivalence) class defined by o_j, and U/B is the set of all indiscernibility classes of $IND(B)$.

2.3 Hybrid System GDT-RS

From the decision table (DT), we can generate decision rules expressed in the following form:
$$P \rightarrow Q \text{ with } S,$$

'if P then Q with strength S', where P is a conjunction of descriptors over C, Q denotes a concept that the rule describes, and S is a 'measure of the strength' of the rule. According to the GDT-RS, the strength S [4,19] is equal to:

$$S(P \rightarrow Q) = s(P) * (1 - r(P \rightarrow Q)) \tag{3}$$

where $s(P)$ is the strength of the generalization P (the condition of the rule) and r is the noise rate function. The strength of a given rule reflects incompleteness and noise. On the assumption that the prior distribution is uniform, the strength of the generalization $P = PG$ is given by:

$$s(P) = \sum_l p(PI_l|P) = \frac{1}{N_P} card([P]_{DT}) \tag{4}$$

where $[P]_{DT}$ is the set of all the objects in DT satisfying the generalization P and N_P is the number of the possible instances satisfying the generalization P which is computed using eqn. (2). The strength of the generalization P represents explicitly the prediction for unseen instances. On the other hand, the noise rate is given by:

$$r(P \to Q) = 1 - \frac{card([P]_{DT} \cap [Q]_{DT})}{card([P]_{DT})} \tag{5}$$

It shows the quality of classification measured by the number of the instances satisfying the generalization P which cannot be classified into class Q.

3   Belief Function Theory

In this Section, we briefly review the main concepts underlying the belief function theory as interpreted in the TBM [14]. Let Θ be a finite set of elementary events to a given problem, called the frame of discernment. All the subsets of Θ belong to the power set of Θ, denoted by 2^{Θ}. The impact of a piece of evidence on the subsets of the frame of discernment Θ is represented by a basic belief assignment (bba). The bba is a function $m : 2^{\Theta} \to [0,1]$ such that:

$$\sum_{E \subseteq \Theta} m(E) = 1 \tag{6}$$

The value $m(E)$, called a basic belief mass (bbm), represents the portion of belief committed exactly to the event E. The bba's induced from distinct pieces of evidence are combined by the rule of combination [14]:

$$(m_1 \textcircled{\cap} m_2)(E) = \sum_{F,G \subseteq \Theta : F \cap G = E} m_1(F) \times m_2(G) \tag{7}$$

4   Rule Discovery Process from Partially Uncertain Data

In this Section, we propose our method for discovering a set of classification rules from partially uncertain data. The uncertainty exists in decision attribute values and is represented by the TBM. This method is based on the hybrid system GDT-RS developed originally in [4,19]. Our solution, so-called belief GDT-RS can generate from partially uncertain databases a set of rules with the minimal description length, having large strength and covering all instances.

4.1   Uncertain Decision Table

Our uncertain decision table is given by $A = (U, C \cup \{ud\})$, where $U = \{o_j : 1 \le j \le n\}$ is characterized by a set of certain condition attributes $C = \{c_1, c_2, ..., c_k\}$, and an uncertain decision attribute ud. We represent the uncertainty of each object o_j by a bba m_j expressing beliefs on decisions defined on the frame of discernment $\Theta = \{ud_1, ud_2, ..., ud_s\}$ representing the possible values of *ud*. These bba's are generally given by an expert (or several experts) and in addition to partial uncertainty, they can also present the two extreme cases of total knowledge and total ignorance.

Example: To illustrate this idea by a simple example, let us use Table 1 to describe our uncertain decision table. It contains eight objects, three certain condition attributes $C=\{a, b, c\}$ and an uncertain decision attribute ud with two values $\{yes, no\}$ representing Θ.

Table 1. An example of uncertain decision table

U	a	b	c	ud
o_1	0	0	1	$m_1(\{yes\}) = 0.95 \quad m_1(\{no\}) = 0.05$
o_2	0	1	1	$m_2(\{yes\}) = 1$
o_3	0	0	1	$m_3(\{yes\}) = 0.5 \quad m_3(\Theta) = 0.5$
o_4	1	1	0	$m_4(\{no\}) = 0.9 \quad m_4(\Theta) = 0.1$
o_5	1	1	0	$m_5(\{no\}) = 1$
o_6	0	0	1	$m_6(\{no\}) = 0.9 \quad m_6(\Theta) = 0.1$
o_7	0	2	1	$m_7(\{no\}) = 1$
o_8	1	1	1	$m_8(\{yes\}) = 1$

4.2 Belief GDT-RS Method

In this subsection, we detail the main steps of our belief GDT-RS method allowing to discover of classification rules from partially uncertain decision table under the belief function framework based on the hybrid system GDT-RS.

Step 1. Creation of the GDT: Since the GDT depends only on condition attributes, and not in decision attribute values, our GDT will have the same structure as in [20]. In fact, this step can be omitted because the prior distribution of a generalization can be calculated using eqns. (1) and (2).

Step 2. Definition of the compound objects: Consider the indiscernibility classes with respect to the condition attribute set C as one object, called the compound object o'_j . For objects composing each compound object, combine their bba's using the mean operator as follows:

$$m'_j(E) = \frac{1}{card(o'_j)} \sum_{o_j \in o'_j} m_j(E), \forall E \subseteq \Theta \qquad (8)$$

In our case, the mean operator is more suitable to combine these bba's than the rule of combination in eqn. (7) which is proposed especially to combine different beliefs on decision for one object and not different bba's for different objects.

Let us continue with the same example. By applying *the step 2*, we obtain the following table:

Table 2. The compound objects

U	a	b	c	ud
$o_1'(o_1, o_3, o_6)$	0	0	1	$m_1'(\{yes\}) = 0.48\ \ m_1'(\{no\}) = 0.31\ \ m_1'(\{\Theta\}) = 0.21$
o_2'	0	1	1	$m_2'(\{yes\}) = 1$
$o_4'(o_4, o_5)$	1	1	0	$m_4'(\{no\}) = 0.95\ \ m_4'(\{\Theta\}) = 0.05$
o_7'	0	2	1	$m_7'(\{no\}) = 1$
o_8'	1	1	1	$m_8'(\{yes\}) = 1$

Step 3. Elimination of the contradictory compound objects: For any compound object o_j' from U and for each decision value ud_i, compute $r_{ud_i}(o_j')$ representing a noise rate. If there exists a ud_i such that $r_{ud_i}(o_j') = min\,\{r_{ud_{i'}}(o_j')$ $|ud_{i'} \in \Theta\} < T_{noise}$ (threshold value), then we assign the decision class corresponding to ud_i to the object o_j. If there is no $ud_i \in \Theta$ such that $r_{ud_i}(o_j') < T_{noise}$, we treat the compound object o_j' as a contradictory one, and set the decision class of o_j' to $\perp$(uncertain). The noise rate is calculated originally using eqn. (5). The latter is not appropriate in our uncertain context since the decision value is represented by a bba. So, we propose to compute the noise rate based on a distance measure as follows:

$$r_{ud_i}(o_j') = dist(m_j', m), \text{such that } m(\{ud_i\}) = 1 \tag{9}$$

Where $dist$ is a distance measure between two bba's.

$$dist(m_1, m_2) = \sqrt{\frac{1}{2}(\parallel \overrightarrow{m_1} \parallel^2 + \parallel \overrightarrow{m_2} \parallel^2 - 2 < \overrightarrow{m_1}, \overrightarrow{m_2} >)} \tag{10}$$

$$0 \le dist(m_1, m_2) \le 1 \tag{11}$$

Where $< \overrightarrow{m_1}, \overrightarrow{m_2} >$ is the scalar product defined by:

$$< \overrightarrow{m_1}, \overrightarrow{m_2} > = \sum_{i=1}^{|2^{\Theta}|} \sum_{j=1}^{|2^{\Theta}|} m_1(A_i) m_2(A_j) \frac{|A_i \cap A_j|}{|A_i \cup A_j|} \tag{12}$$

with $A_i, A_j \in 2^{\Theta}$ for $i, j = 1, 2, \cdots, |2^{\Theta}|$. $\parallel \overrightarrow{m_1} \parallel^2$ is then the square norm of $\overrightarrow{m_1}$. The idea is to use the distance between two bba's m_j' and a certain bba m (such that $m(\{ud_i\}) = 1$). With this manner, we can check that the decisions of all instances belong to the compound object are near from a certain case. So, it is considered as a not contradictory object. Many distance measures between two bba's were developed. Some of them are based on pignistic transformation [1,6,15,21]. For these distances, one unavoidable step is the pignistic transformation of the bba's. This kind of distances may lose information given by the initial bba's. However, the distance measures developed in [2,7] are directly defined on bba's. In our case, we choose the distance measure proposed in [2] which satisfies more properties such as non-negativity, non-degeneracy and symmetry.

By applying the *step* 3 to the Table 2, we obtain the Table 3:

Table 3. Contradictory and not contradictory compound objects

U	a	b	c	ud
$o'_1 (o_1, o_3, o_6)$	0	0	1	$\perp$
o'_2	0	1	1	yes
$o'_4 (o_4, o_5)$	1	1	0	no
o'_7	0	2	1	no
o'_8	1	1	1	yes

Step 4. Minimal description length of decision rule: Let U' be the set of all the compound object except the contradictory ones. Select one compound object o'_j from U', create a discernibility vector (the row or the column with respect to o'_j in the discernibility matrix) for o'_j. The discernibility matrix of A is a symmetric n*n matrix with entries a_{ij} as given below. Each entry thus consists of the set of attributes upon which objects o_i and o_j differ.

$$a_{ij} = \{c \in C | c(o_i) \neq c(o_j)\} \; for \; i, j = 1, ..., n \tag{13}$$

Next, we compute all the so-called local relative reducts for the compound object o'_j by using the discernibility function $f_A(o_j)$. It is a boolean function of k boolean variables corresponding to the k condition attributes defined as below:

$$f_A(o_j) = \bigwedge \{\bigvee a_{ij} | 1 \leq i \leq n, a_{ij} \neq \emptyset\} \tag{14}$$

The set of all prime implicants of $f_A(o_j)$ determines the sets of all reducts of o_j. According to the Table 3, the discernibility vector for the compound object o'_2 $(a_0 b_1 c_1)$ is as follows: We obtain two reducts, {a, b} and {b, c} by applying the indiscernibility function : $f_A(o'_2) = (b) \wedge (a \vee c) \wedge (b) = (a \wedge b) \vee (b \wedge c)$

Table 4. Discernibility vector for o'_2

U'	$o'_1(\perp)$	$o'_2(yes)$	$o'_4(no)$	$o'_7(no)$	$o'_8(yes)$
$o'_2(yes)$	b	$\emptyset$	a,c	b	$\emptyset$

Step 5. Selection of the best rules: Construct rules from the local reducts for object o'_j, and revise the strength of each rule using eqn. (3). Select the best rules from the rules for o'_j having the best strength.

According to the same example, the following rules are acquired for object o'_2: $\{a_0 b_1\} \rightarrow yes$ with S $= (\frac{1}{2}*1)*(1) = 0.5$ and $\{b_1 c_1\} \rightarrow yes$ with S $= (\frac{1}{2}*2)*(1) = 1$. The rule $\{b_1 c_1\} \rightarrow yes$ is selected for the compound object o'_2 due to its strength.

Let $U' = U' - \{o'_j\}$. *If* $U' \neq \emptyset$, *then go back to Step 4. Otherwise, STOP.*

As a result, we obtain a set of decision rules able to classify unseen objects shown in the Table 5.

Table 5. Decision rules

U	rules	strengths
o_2', o_8'	$b_1 \wedge c_1 \rightarrow yes$	1
o_4'	$c_0 \rightarrow no$	0.167
o_7'	$b_2 \rightarrow no$	0.25

Note that the time complexity of the algorithm is $O(mn^2 Nr_{max})$, where n is the number of instances in a given database, m stands for the number of attributes, Nr_{max} is the maximal number of reducts for instances. We can apply a method for attribute selection [17] in pre-processing stage before using our belief GDT-RS to avoid the costly calculation.

5 Experimentation

In our experiments, we have performed several tests on real databases obtained from the U.C.I. repository[1] to evaluate our proposed classifier based on our belief GDT-RS. A brief description of these databases is presented in Table 6. These databases were artificially modified in order to include uncertainty in decision attribute. We took different degrees of uncertainty (Low, Middle and High) based on increasing values of probabilities P used to transform the actual decision value d_i of each object o_j to a bba $m_j(\{d_i\}) = 1 - P$ and $m_j(\Theta) = P$. A larger P gives a larger degree of uncertainty.

- Low degree of uncertainty: we take $0 < P \leq 0.3$
- Middle degree of uncertainty: we take $0.3 < P \leq 0.6$
- High degree of uncertainty: we take $0.6 < P \leq 1$

Table 6. Description of databases

Database	#instances	#attributes	#decision values
W. Breast Cancer	690	8	2
Balance Scale	625	4	3
C. Voting records	497	16	2
Zoo	101	17	7
Nursery	12960	8	3
Solar Flares	1389	10	2
Lung Cancer	32	56	3
Hyes-Roth	160	5	3
Car Evaluation	1728	6	4
Lymphography	148	18	4
Spect Heart	267	22	2
Tic-Tac-Toe Endgame	958	9	2

---

[1] http://www.ics.uci.edu/~mlearn/MLRepository.html

The relevant criteria used to judge the performance of our new method are the accuracy of the model (PCC[2]) and the time complexity (seconds). To more evaluate our belief GDT-RS, we compared its results[3] with those obtained from the BDT after pruning in averaging and conjunctive approaches [5,16]. We taked best results between the two approaches related to BDT. Table 7 summarizes the different results relative to our belief GDT-RS and to the BDT for all chosen databases using different degrees of uncertainty (Low, Middle, High) and according to two evaluation criteria: accuracy and time complexity. The latter is almost the same for the different uncertain cases. From the Table 7, we can conclude that belief GDT-RS gives better PCC's than the pruned BDT for all databases and for all degrees of uncertainty. Besides, we can also conclude that our new method is faster than the construction of the BDT after pruning. On the other hand, we note that the PCC slightly increases when the uncertainty decreases.

Table 7. The experimentation results relative to belief GDT-RS and BDT

Database	Belief GDT-RS PCC (%)			Pruned BDT PCC (%)			Belief GDT-RS Time complexity (seconds)	Pruned BDT Time complexity (seconds)
	Low	Middle	High	Low	Middle	High		
W. Breast Cancer	83.77	83.48	83.05	83.46	83.01	82.17	65	156
Balance Scale	81.46	80.21	80.03	78.15	77.83	77.76	42	139
C. Voting records	98.44	98.16	97.92	98.28	97.76	97.71	69	117
Zoo	93.52	93.47	92.87	91.94	91.36	91.41	34	103
Nursery	96.06	95.81	95.27	95.84	95.13	95.11	198	386
Solar Flares	89.67	89.61	89.56	85.78	85.61	85.46	123	160
Lung Cancer	75.50	75.50	66.33	66.33	66.33	66.33	21	56
Hyes-Roth	97.46	97.11	96.75	83.66	83.31	82.14	34	93
Car Evaluation	81.46	81.01	81.17	73.49	73.11	72.97	135	189
Lymphography	84.24	84.03	83.67	79.25	78.97	78.94	66	108
Spect Heart	87.34	87.28	87.07	83.46	83.01	82.17	72	111
Tic-Tac-Toe Endgame	86.26	86.21	86.18	83.91	83.75	83.42	106	149

6   Conclusion and Future Work

In this paper, we have proposed a method called belief GDT-RS of rule discovery process based on the hybrid system called GDT-RS, in order to generate a subset of classification rules from partially uncertain databases. Our belief GDT-RS allows dealing with uncertainty in decision attributes that may characterize objects of a decision table and where uncertainty is represented through the belief function theory. Experimentations done on real databases show interesting results, based on accuracy and time complexity, comparing with those obtained from BDT after pruning. Busse and Skowron [13] suggested the use of rough set theory to develop belief functions. We will explore the use of Busse and Skowron's proposal to compute the bba's in the uncertain decision attributes in the future applications.

---

[2] Percent of correct classification.

[3] A 10-fold cross validation process has been used for making all experimentations.

References

1. Bauer, M.: Approximations algorithm and decision making in the Dempster-Shafer theory of evidence - an empirical study. IJAR 17(2-3), 217–237 (1997)
2. Bosse, E., Jousseleme, A.L., Grenier, D.: A new distance between two bodies of evidence. Information Fusion 2, 91–101 (2001)
3. Denoeux, T., Skarstien-Bajanger, M.: Induction of decision trees form partially classified data using belief functions. In: Proceedings of the IEEE International Conference on Systems, Nashiville, USA, vol. 4, pp. 2923–2928 (2000)
4. Dong, J.Z., Zhong, N., Ohsuga, S.: Probabilistic rough induction: The GDS-RS methodology and algorithms. In: Raś, Z.W., Skowron, A. (eds.) ISMIS 1999. LNCS, vol. 1609, pp. 621–629. Springer, Heidelberg (1999)
5. Elouedi, Z., Mellouli, K., Smets, P.: Belief decision trees: Theoretical foundations. International Journal of Approximate Reasoning, Vol 28(2-3), 91–124 (2001)
6. Elouedi, Z., Mellouli, K., Smets, P.: Assessing sensor reliability for multisensor data fusion within the transferable belief model. IEEE Trans. Syst. Man cyben. 34(1), 782–787 (2004)
7. Fixen, D., Mahler, R.P.S.: The modified Dempster-Shafer approach to classification. IEEE Trans. Syst. Man Cybern. 27(1), 96–104 (1997)
8. Grzymala-Busse, J.W.: Rough set strategies to data with missing attribute values. In: Workshop Notes, Foundations and New Directions of Data Mining, the 3rd International Conference on Data Mining, Melbourne, Florida, 56–63 (2003)
9. Grzymala-Busse, J.W., Siddhaye, S.: Rough Set Approaches to Rule Induction from Incomplete Data. In: Proceedings of the IPMU 2004, Perugia, Italy, July 4-9, vol. 2, pp. 923–930 (2004)
10. Pawlak, Z.: Rough Sets: Theoretical Aspects of Reasoning About Data. Kluwer Academic Publishing, Dordrecht (1991)
11. Shafer, G.: A mathematical theory of evidence. Princeton University Press, Princeton (1976)
12. Skowron, A., Rauszer, C.: The discernibility matrices and functions in information systems. In: Slowinski, R. (ed.) Intelligent Decision Support, pp. 331–362. Kluwer Academic Publishers, Boston (1992)
13. Skowron, A., Grzymala-Busse, J.W.: From rough set theory to evidence theory. In: Advances in the Dempster-Shafer Theory of Evidence, New York, pp. 193–236 (1994)
14. Smets, P., Kennes, R.: The transferable belief model. Artificial Intelligence 66(2), 191–234 (1994)
15. Tessem, B.: Approximations for efficient computation in the theory of evidence. Artif. Intell. 61(2), 315–329 (1993)
16. Trabelsi, S., Elouedi, Z., Mellouli, K.: Pruning belief decision tree methods in averaging and conjunctive approaches. International Journal of Approximate Reasoning 46, 91–124 (2007)
17. Trabelsi, S., Elouedi, Z., Lingras, P.: Dynamic Reduct from Partially Uncertain Data Using Rough Sets. In: Sakai, H., Chakraborty, M.K., Hassanien, A.E., Ślęzak, D., Zhu, W. (eds.) RSFDGrC 2009. LNCS (LNAI), vol. 5908, pp. 160–167. Springer, Heidelberg (2009)
18. Vannoorenberghe, P.: On aggregating belief decision trees. Information Fusion 5(2), 179–188 (2004)

19. Zhong, N., Dong, J.Z., Ohsuga, S.: Data mining: A probabilistic rough set approach. Rough Sets in Knowledge Discovery 2, 127–146 (1998)
20. Zhong, N., Dong, J.Z., Ohsuga, S.: Using generalization distribution tables as a hypotheses search space for generalization. In: Proceedings of fourth International Workshop on Rough Sets, Fuzzy Sets, and Machine Discovery (RSFD-96), pp. 396–403 (1996)
21. Zouhal, L.M., Denoeux, T.: An evidence-theory k-NN rule with parameter optimization. IEEE Trans. Syst. Man Cybern. C 28(2), 263–271 (1998)

Independent Natural Extension

Gert de Cooman[1], Enrique Miranda[2], and Marco Zaffalon[3]

[1] SYSTeMS, Ghent University, Belgium
gert.decooman@ugent.be
[2] University of Oviedo, Spain
mirandaenrique@uniovi.es
[3] IDSIA, Manno (Lugano), Switzerland
zaffalon@idsia.ch

Abstract. We introduce a general definition for the independence of a number of finite-valued variables, based on coherent lower previsions. Our definition has an epistemic flavour: it arises from personal judgements that a number of variables are irrelevant to one another. We show that a number of already existing notions, such as strong independence, satisfy our definition. Moreover, there always is a least-committal independent model, for which we provide an explicit formula: the *independent natural extension*. Our central result is that the independent natural extension satisfies so-called marginalisation, associativity and *strong factorisation* properties. These allow us to relate our research to more traditional ways of defining independence based on factorisation.

Keywords: Epistemic irrelevance, epistemic independence, independent natural extension, strong product, factorisation.

1 Motivation

In the literature on probability we can recognise two major approaches to defining independence. In the Kolmogorovian tradition, independence is defined by requiring a probability model to satisfy a factorisation property. We call this the *formalist approach*. It views independence as a mathematical property of the model under consideration. On the other hand, the tradition of subjective probability follows an alternative route by regarding independence as an assessment: it is a subject who for instance regards two events as independent, because he judges that learning about the occurrence of one of them will not affect his beliefs about the other. We call this the *epistemic approach*.

We investigate the relationships between the formalist and epistemic approaches to independence in a generalised setting that allows probabilities to be imprecisely specified. We consider a finite number of logically independent variables X_n assuming values in respective finite sets $\mathscr{X}_n$, $n \in N$. We want to express that these variables are independent, in the sense that learning the values of some of them will not affect the beliefs about the remaining ones. We base our analysis on *coherent lower previsions*, which are lower expectation functionals equivalent to closed convex sets of probability mass functions. In the case of precise probability, we refer to an expectation functional as a *linear prevision*.

E. Hüllermeier, R. Kruse, and F. Hoffmann (Eds.): IPMU 2010, LNAI 6178, pp. 737–746, 2010.

After discussing the basic notational set-up in Sec. 2, we introduce the formalist approach in Sec. 3. We define three factorisation properties with increasing strength: *productivity*, *factorisation*, and *strong factorisation*. For the product of linear previsions —the classical independence notion—all these properties coincide. For lower previsions, the *strong product* is a straightforward generalisation obtained by taking a lower envelope of products of linear previsions. We show that the strong product is strongly factorising.

In Sec. 4 we move on to the epistemic approach. We introduce two notions: *many-to-many independence*, where a subjects judges that knowing the value of any subset of the variables $\{X_n : n \in N\}$ is irrelevant to any other subset; and the weaker notion of *many-to-one independence*, where any subset of the variables of $\{X_n : n \in N\}$ is judged to be irrelevant to any other single variable. We show that the strong product is a many-to-many (and hence a many-to-one) independent product of its marginals, and that it is uniquely so in the case of linear previsions.

There is no such uniqueness for lower previsions: the strong product is only one of the generally infinitely many possible independent products. In Sec. 5, we focus on the point-wise smallest ones: the least-committal many-to-many, and the least-committal many-to-one, independent products of given marginals. It is an important result of our analysis that these two independent products turn out to be the same object. We call it the *independent natural extension*. The independent natural extension generalises to any finite number of variables a definition given by Walley for two variables [7, Sec. 9.3]. Observe that in the case of two variables, there is no need to distinguish between many-to-one and many-to-many independence.

The relation with the formalist approach comes to the fore in our next result: the independent natural extension is strongly factorising. We go somewhat further in Sec. 6, where we show that a factorising lower prevision must be a many-to-one independent product. Under some conditions, we also show that a strongly factorising lower prevision must be a many-to-many independent product. And since we already know that the smallest many-to-one independent product is the independent natural extension, we deduce that when looking for least-committal models, it is equivalent whether we focus on factorisation or on being an independent product. This allows us to establish a solid bridge between the formalist and epistemic approaches.

In a number of other results we provide useful properties of assorted independent products. Most notably, we show that each independent product (strong, many-to-many, many-to-one, and the independent natural extension) is in some sense associative, and that the operation of marginalisation preserves the type of independent product. We also give an explicit formula for the independent natural extension, as well as simplified expressions in a number of interesting particular cases.

In order to keep this paper reasonably short, we have to assume that the reader has a good working knowledge of the basics of Walley's theory of coherent lower previsions [7]. For a fairly detailed discussion of the coherence notions and results needed in the context of this paper, we refer to [4,5]. An interesting study of some of the notions considered here was done by Vicig [6] for coherent lower *probabilities*.

2   Set-Up and Basic Notation

Consider a finite number of variables X_n assuming values in the finite sets $\mathscr{X}_n$, $n \in N$. We assume that for each of these variables X_n, we have an uncertainty model for the values that it assumes in $\mathscr{X}_n$, in the form of a coherent lower prevision $\underline{P}_n$ on the set $\mathscr{L}(\mathscr{X}_n)$ of all gambles (real-valued maps) on $\mathscr{X}_n$.

For a coherent lower prevision $\underline{P}$ on $\mathscr{L}(\mathscr{X})$, there is a corresponding closed convex set of dominating linear previsions, or credal set, $\mathscr{M}(\underline{P})$, and a corresponding set of extreme points $\mathrm{ext}(\mathscr{M}(\underline{P}))$. Then $\underline{P}$ is the lower envelope of both $\mathscr{M}(\underline{P})$ and $\mathrm{ext}(\mathscr{M}(\underline{P}))$:

$$\underline{P}(f) = \min\{P(f)\colon P \in \mathscr{M}(\underline{P})\} = \min\{P(f)\colon P \in \mathrm{ext}(\mathscr{M}(\underline{P}))\} \text{ for all } f \in \mathscr{L}(\mathscr{X}).$$

For any linear prevision P on $\mathscr{L}(\mathscr{X})$, the corresponding mass function p is defined by $p(x) := P(\mathbb{I}_{\{x\}})$, $x \in \mathscr{X}$, and then of course $P(f) = \sum_{x \in \mathscr{X}} f(x)p(x)$.

If I is any subset of N, then denote by X_I the tuple of variables whose components are the X_i, $i \in I$. We denote by $\mathscr{X}_I := \times_{i \in I} \mathscr{X}_i$ the Cartesian product of the sets $\mathscr{X}_i$, which is the set of all maps x_I from I to $\bigcup_{i \in I} \mathscr{X}_i$ such that $x_I(i) \in \mathscr{X}_i$ for all $i \in I$. The elements of $\mathscr{X}_I$ are generically denoted by x_I or z_I, with corresponding components $x_i := x_I(i)$ or $z_i := z_I(i)$, $i \in I$. We will assume that the variables X_i are logically independent, which means that for each non-empty subset I of N, X_I may assume all values in $\mathscr{X}_I$. We can then consider X_I to be a variable on $\mathscr{X}_I$.

We will frequently use the simplifying device of identifying a gamble on $\mathscr{X}_I$ with a gamble on $\mathscr{X}_N$, namely its cylindrical extension. To give an example, if $\mathscr{K} \subseteq \mathscr{L}(\mathscr{X}_N)$, this trick allows us to consider $\mathscr{K} \cap \mathscr{L}(\mathscr{X}_I)$ as the set of those gambles in $\mathscr{K}$ that depend only on the variable X_I. As another example, this device allows us to identify the indicator gambles $\mathbb{I}_{\{x_R\}}$ and $\mathbb{I}_{\{x_R\} \times \mathscr{X}_{N \setminus R}}$, and therefore also the events $\{x_R\}$ and $\{x_R\} \times \mathscr{X}_{N \setminus R}$. More generally, for any event $A \subseteq \mathscr{X}_R$, we can identify the gambles $\mathbb{I}_A$ and $\mathbb{I}_{A \times \mathscr{X}_{N \setminus R}}$, and therefore also the events A and $A \times \mathscr{X}_{N \setminus R}$. In the same spirit, a lower prevision on all gambles in $\mathscr{L}(\mathscr{X}_I)$ can be identified with a lower prevision defined on the set of corresponding gambles on $\mathscr{X}_N$ (those that depend on X_I only), a subset of $\mathscr{L}(\mathscr{X}_N)$.

If $\underline{P}_N$ is a coherent lower prevision on $\mathscr{L}(\mathscr{X}_N)$, then for any non-empty subset I of N we can consider its $\mathscr{X}_I$-marginal $\underline{P}_I$ as the coherent lower prevision on $\mathscr{L}(\mathscr{X}_I)$ defined by $\underline{P}_I(f) := \underline{P}_N(f)$ for all gambles f on $\mathscr{X}_I$.

3   The Formal Approach

3.1   Basic Definitions

We begin our discussion of independence by following the formalist route: we introduce interesting generalisations of the notion of an independent product of linear previsions.

The first is a stronger, symmetrised version of the notion of 'forward factorisation' introduced elsewhere [3].

Definition 1 (Productivity). *Consider a coherent lower prevision $\underline{P}_N$ on $\mathscr{L}(\mathscr{X}_N)$. We call this lower prevision productive if for all proper disjoint subsets I and O of N, all $g \in \mathscr{L}(\mathscr{X}_O)$ and all non-negative $f \in \mathscr{L}(\mathscr{X}_I)$, $\underline{P}_N(f[g - \underline{P}_N(g)]) \geq 0$.*

In a paper [3] on laws of large numbers for coherent lower previsions, which generalises and subsumes most known versions in the literature, we prove that the condition of forward factorisation (which is implied by the present productivity condition) is sufficient for a law of large numbers to hold.

Theorem 1 (Weak law of large numbers). *Let the coherent lower prevision $\underline{P}_N$ on $\mathscr{L}(\mathscr{X}_N)$ be productive. Let $\varepsilon > 0$ and consider arbitrary gambles h_n on $\mathscr{X}_n$, $n \in N$. Let B be a common bound for the ranges of these gambles and let $\min h_n \leq m_n \leq \underline{P}_N(h_n) \leq \overline{P}_N(h_n) \leq M_n \leq \max h_n$ for all $n \in N$. Then*

$$\overline{P}_N\left(\left\{x_N \in \mathscr{X}_N : \sum_{n \in N} \frac{h_n(x_n)}{|N|} \notin \left[\sum_{n \in N} \frac{m_n}{|N|} - \varepsilon, \sum_{n \in N} \frac{M_n}{|N|} + \varepsilon\right]\right\}\right) \leq 2\exp\left(-\frac{|N|\varepsilon^2}{4B^2}\right).$$

Next comes a generalisation of the linear independence condition that was inspired by, and found to be quite useful in the context of, our research on credal networks [2].

Definition 2 (Factorisation). *Consider a coherent lower prevision $\underline{P}_N$ on $\mathscr{L}(\mathscr{X}_N)$. We call this lower prevision (i) factorising if for all $o \in N$ and all non-empty $I \subseteq N \setminus \{o\}$, all $g \in \mathscr{L}(\mathscr{X}_o)$ and all non-negative $f_i \in \mathscr{L}(\mathscr{X}_i)$, $i \in I$, $\underline{P}_N(f_I g) = \underline{P}_N(f_I \underline{P}_N(g))$, where $f_I := \prod_{i \in I} f_i$; and (ii) strongly factorising if $\underline{P}_N(fg) = \underline{P}_N(f\underline{P}_N(g))$ for all $g \in \mathscr{L}(\mathscr{X}_O)$ and non-negative $f \in \mathscr{L}(\mathscr{X}_I)$, where I and O are any disjoint proper subsets of N.*

Consider a real interval $\overline{a} := [\underline{a}, \overline{a}]$ and a real number b, then we define $\overline{a} \odot b$ to be equal to $\underline{a}b$ if $b \geq 0$, and equal to $\overline{a}b$ if $b \leq 0$. It then follows from the coherence of $\underline{P}_N$ that we also get $\underline{P}_N(f_I \underline{P}_N(g)) = \underline{P}_N(f_I) \odot \underline{P}_N(g)$ and $\underline{P}_N(f\underline{P}_N(g)) = \overline{P}_N(f) \odot \underline{P}_N(g)$ in Definition 2.

In general, the following relationships hold between these properties. It can be shown by means of counterexamples that the implications are strict.

Proposition 1. *Consider a coherent lower prevision $\underline{P}_N$ on $\mathscr{L}(\mathscr{X}_N)$. If $\underline{P}_N$ is strongly factorising, then it is factorising, and if $\underline{P}_N$ is factorising, then it is productive.*

We now look at a number of special cases.

3.2 The Product of Linear Previsions

If we have linear previsions P_n on $\mathscr{L}(\mathscr{X}_n)$ with corresponding mass functions p_n, then their *product* $S_N := \times_{n \in N} P_n$ is defined as the linear prevision on $\mathscr{L}(\mathscr{X}_N)$ with mass function p_N defined by $p_N(x_N) := \prod_{n \in N} p_n(x_n)$ for all $x_N \in \mathscr{X}_N$, so

$$S_N(f) = \sum_{x_N \in \mathscr{X}_N} f(x_N) \prod_{n \in N} p_n(x_n) \text{ for all } f \in \mathscr{L}(\mathscr{X}_N).$$

One of the very useful properties of the product of linear previsions, is that it is associative in the following sense.

Proposition 2. *Consider arbitrary linear previsions P_n on $\mathscr{L}(\mathscr{X}_n)$, $n \in N$.*

  (i) *For any non-empty subset R of N, S_R is the $\mathscr{X}_R$-marginal of S_N: $S_N(g) = S_R(g)$ for all gambles g on $\mathscr{X}_R$;*

  (ii) *For any partition N_1 and N_2 of N, $\times_{n \in N_1 \cup N_2} P_n = (\times_{n \in N_1} P_n) \times (\times_{n \in N_2} P_n)$, or in other words, $S_N = S_{N_1} \times S_{N_2}$.*

Importantly, for linear previsions, all the properties introduced in Sec. 3.1 coincide.

Proposition 3. *Consider any linear prevision P_N on $\mathscr{L}(\mathscr{X}_N)$. Then the following statements are equivalent:* (i) *$P_N = \times_{n \in N} P_n$ is the product of its marginals P_n, $n \in N$;* (ii) *P_N $(\prod_{n \in N} f_n) = \prod_{n \in N} P_N(f_n)$ for all f_n in $\mathscr{L}(\mathscr{X}_n)$, $n \in N$;* (iii) *P_N is strongly factorising;* (iv) *P_N is factorising; and* (v) *P_N is productive.*

3.3 The Strong Product of Coherent Lower Previsions

In a similar vein, if we have coherent lower previsions $\underline{P}_n$ on $\mathscr{L}(\mathscr{X}_n)$, then [1,7] their *strong product* $\underline{S}_N := \times_{n \in N} \underline{P}_n$ is defined as the coherent lower prevision on $\mathscr{L}(\mathscr{X}_N)$ that is the lower envelope of the set of independent products:

$$\{\times_{n \in N} P_n \colon (\forall n \in N) P_n \in \text{ext}(\mathscr{M}(\underline{P}_n))\} .$$

So for every $f \in \mathscr{L}(\mathscr{X}_N)$:

$$\underline{S}_N(f) = \inf\{\times_{n \in N} P_n(f) \colon (\forall n \in N) P_n \in \text{ext}(\mathscr{M}(\underline{P}_n))\} .$$

The set $\text{ext}(\mathscr{M}(\underline{S}_N))$ has the following nice characterisation, which guarantees that the infimum in the equation above is actually a minimum:

$$\text{ext}(\mathscr{M}(\underline{S}_N)) = \{\times_{n \in N} P_n \colon (\forall n \in N) P_n \in \text{ext}(\mathscr{M}(\underline{P}_n))\} .$$

Like the product of linear previsions, the strong product of lower previsions satisfies the following very interesting marginalisation and associativity properties:

Proposition 4. *Consider arbitrary coherent lower previsions $\underline{P}_n$ on $\mathscr{L}(\mathscr{X}_n)$, $n \in N$.*

  (i) *For any non-empty subset R of N, $\underline{S}_R$ is the $\mathscr{X}_R$-marginal of $\underline{S}_N$: $\underline{S}_N(g) = \underline{S}_R(g)$ for all gambles g on $\mathscr{X}_R$;*

  (ii) *For any partition N_1 and N_2 of N, $\times_{n \in N_1 \cup N_2} \underline{P}_n = (\times_{n \in N_1} \underline{P}_n) \times (\times_{n \in N_2} \underline{P}_n)$, or in other words, $\underline{S}_N = \underline{S}_{N_1} \times \underline{S}_{N_2}$.*

This readily leads to the conclusion that the strong product of lower previsions shares many of the interesting properties of the product of linear previsions:

Proposition 5. *The strong product $\underline{S}_N$ is strongly factorising, and therefore factorising and productive. As a consequence, it satisfies the weak law of large numbers of Thm. 1.*

This ends our discussion of the formalist approach to independence for coherent lower previsions. We next turn to the treatment of independence following an epistemic approach, where independence is considered to be an assessment a subject makes.

4   Epistemic Irrelevance and Independence

Consider two disjoint proper subsets I and O of N. We say that a subject judges that X_I is *epistemically irrelevant* to X_O when he assumes that learning which value X_I assumes in $\mathscr{X}_I$ will not affect his beliefs about X_O.

Now assume that our subject has a joint lower prevision $\underline{P}_N$ on $\mathscr{L}(\mathscr{X}_N)$. If a subject assesses that X_I is epistemically irrelevant to X_O, this implies that he can infer from his joint $\underline{P}_N$ a conditional model $\underline{P}_{O \cup I}(\cdot | X_I)$ on the set $\mathscr{L}(\mathscr{X}_{O \cup I})$ that satisfies

$$\underline{P}_{O \cup I}(h|x_I) := \underline{P}_N(h(\cdot, x_I)) \text{ for all gambles } h \text{ on } \mathscr{X}_{O \cup I} . \tag{1}$$

4.1   Epistemic Many-to-Many Independence

We say that a subject judges the variables X_n, $n \in N$ to be *epistemically many-to-many independent* when he assumes that learning the value of any number of these variables will not affect his beliefs about the others. In other words, if he judges for any disjoint proper subsets I and O of N that X_I is epistemically irrelevant to X_O.

Again, if our subject has a joint lower prevision $\underline{P}_N$ on $\mathscr{L}(\mathscr{X}_N)$, and he assesses that the variables X_n, $n \in N$ to be *epistemically many-to-many independent*, then he can infer from his joint $\underline{P}_N$ a family of conditional models

$$\mathscr{I}(\underline{P}_N) := \{ \underline{P}_{O \cup I}(\cdot | X_I) : I \text{ and } O \text{ disjoint proper subsets of } N \} ,$$

where $\underline{P}_{O \cup I}(\cdot | X_I)$ is the conditional lower prevision on $\mathscr{L}(\mathscr{X}_{O \cup I})$ given by Eq. (1).

Definition 3. *A coherent lower prevision $\underline{P}_N$ on $\mathscr{L}(\mathscr{X}_N)$ is called* many-to-many *independent if it is coherent with the family $\mathscr{I}(\underline{P}_N)$. For a collection of coherent lower previsions $\underline{P}_n$ on $\mathscr{L}(\mathscr{X}_n)$, $n \in N$, any many-to-many independent coherent lower prevision $\underline{P}_N$ on $\mathscr{L}(\mathscr{X}_N)$ that coincides with the $\underline{P}_n$ on their domains $\mathscr{L}(\mathscr{X}_n), n \in N$ is called a* many-to-many *independent product of these marginals.*

4.2   Epistemic Many-to-One Independence

There is weaker notion of independence that we will consider here. We say that a subject judges the variables X_n, $n \in N$ to be *epistemically many-to-one independent* when he assumes that learning the value of any number of these variables will not affect his beliefs about any *single* other. In other words, if he judges for any $o \in N$ and any nonempty subset I of $N \setminus \{o\}$ that X_I is epistemically irrelevant to X_o.

Once again, if our subject has a joint lower prevision $\underline{P}_N$ on $\mathscr{L}(\mathscr{X}_N)$, and he assesses the variables X_n, $n \in N$ to be *epistemically many-to-one independent*, then he can infer from his joint $\underline{P}_N$ a family of conditional models

$$\mathscr{N}(\underline{P}_N) := \left\{ \underline{P}_{\{o\} \cup I}(\cdot | X_I) : o \in N \text{ and } I \subseteq N \setminus \{o\} \right\} ,$$

where $\underline{P}_{\{o\} \cup I}(\cdot | X_I)$ is a coherent lower prevision on $\mathscr{L}(\mathscr{X}_{\{o\} \cup I})$ that is given by:

$$\underline{P}_{\{o\} \cup I}(h|x_I) := \underline{P}_N(h(\cdot, x_I)) = \underline{P}_o(h(\cdot, x_I)) \text{ for all gambles } h \text{ on } \mathscr{X}_{\{o\} \cup I} ,$$

where of course $\underline{P}_o$ is the $\mathscr{X}_o$-marginal lower prevision of $\underline{P}_N$. So we see that the family of conditional lower previsions $\mathscr{N}(\underline{P}_N)$ only depends on the joint $\underline{P}_N$ through its $\mathscr{X}_n$-marginals $\underline{P}_n$, $n \in N$. This, of course, explains our notation for it.

Definition 4. *A coherent lower prevision $\underline{P}_N$ on $\mathscr{L}(\mathscr{X}_N)$ is called* many-to-one inde-pendent *if it is coherent with the family $\mathscr{N}(\underline{P}_N)$. For a collection of coherent lower previsions $\underline{P}_n$ on $\mathscr{L}(\mathscr{X}_n)$, $n \in N$, any coherent lower prevision $\underline{P}_N$ on $\mathscr{L}(\mathscr{X}_N)$ that is coherent with the family $\mathscr{N}(\underline{P}_N)$ is called a* many-to-one independent product *of these marginals.*

Obviously, if a joint lower prevision $\underline{P}_N$ is many-to-many independent, then it is also many-to-one independent. Another immediate property is that any independent product of a number of lower previsions must have these lower previsions as its marginals:

Proposition 6. *If the coherent lower prevision $\underline{P}_N$ on $\mathscr{L}(\mathscr{X}_N)$ is a many-to-one inde-pendent product of coherent lower previsions $\underline{P}_n$ on $\mathscr{L}(\mathscr{X}_n)$, $n \in N$, then $\underline{P}_N(g) = \underline{P}_n(g)$ for all $g \in \mathscr{L}(\mathscr{X}_n)$ and for all $n \in N$.*

Moreover, independent products satisfy a number of basic marginalisation and associa-tivity properties.

Proposition 7. *Consider arbitrary coherent lower previsions $\underline{P}_n$, $n \in N$. Let $\underline{P}_N$ be any many-to-one independent product and $\underline{Q}_N$ any many-to-many independent product of the marginals $\underline{P}_n$, $n \in N$. Let R and S be any proper subsets of N.*

(i) *The $\mathscr{X}_R$-marginal of $\underline{P}_N$ is a many-to-one independent product of its marginals $\underline{P}_r$, $r \in R$;*

(ii) *The $\mathscr{X}_R$-marginal of $\underline{Q}_N$ is a many-to-many independent product of its marginals $\underline{P}_r$, $r \in R$;*

(iii) *If R and S constitute a partition of N, then $\underline{Q}_N$ is a many-to-many independent product of its $\mathscr{X}_R$-marginal and its $\mathscr{X}_S$-marginal.*

A basic coherence result [7, Thm. 7.1.6] states that taking lower envelopes of a fam-ily of coherent conditional lower previsions again produces coherent conditional lower previsions. This implies that many-to-many independence and many-to-one indepen-dence are preserved by taking lower envelopes. There is also another interesting way of concluding that a given coherent lower prevision is a many-to-one independent product.

Proposition 8. *Consider arbitrary coherent lower previsions $\underline{P}_n$ on $\mathscr{L}(\mathscr{X}_n)$, $n \in N$, and let $\underline{Q}_1$ and $\underline{Q}_2$ be coherent lower previsions on $\mathscr{L}(\mathscr{X}_N)$ with these marginals $\underline{P}_n$. Let $\underline{Q}_3$ be any coherent lower prevision on $\mathscr{L}(\mathscr{X}_N)$ such that $\underline{Q}_1 \leq \underline{Q}_3 \leq \underline{Q}_2$. Then (i) if $\underline{Q}_1$ and $\underline{Q}_2$ are many-to-one independent products, then so is $\underline{Q}_3$; and (ii) if $\underline{Q}_1$ and $\underline{Q}_2$ are factorising, then so is $\underline{Q}_3$.*

We deduce that a convex combination of many-to-one independent products of the same given marginals is again a many-to-one independent product of these marginals.

5 Independent Natural Extension

The (strong) product turns out to be the central notion when we want to take independent products of linear previsions, as the following proposition makes clear.

Proposition 9. *Any collection of linear previsions P_n, $n \in N$ has a unique many-to-many independent product and a unique many-to-one independent product, and both of these are equal to their strong product $S_N = \times_{n \in N} P_n$.*

However, when the marginals we want to combine are lower rather than linear previsions, the situation is decidedly more complex, as we intend to show in the rest of this section. We begin by showing that there always is at least one many-to-many (and therefore also many-to-one) independent product:

Proposition 10. *Consider arbitrary coherent lower previsions $\underline{P}_n$ on $\mathscr{L}(\mathscr{X}_n)$, $n \in N$. Then their strong product $\times_{n \in N} \underline{P}_n$ is a many-to-many and many-to-one independent product of its marginals $\underline{P}_n$. As a consequence, the collection $\mathscr{N}(\underline{P}_N)$ of conditional lower previsions $\underline{P}_{\{o\} \cup I}(\cdot | X_I)$ is coherent.*

Because all the sets $\mathscr{X}_n$ are finite, we can invoke Walley's Finite Extension Theorem [7, Thm. 8.1.9] to conclude that there always is a *point-wise smallest* joint lower prevision $\underline{E}_N$ that is coherent with the coherent family $\mathscr{N}(\underline{P}_N)$. So there always is a smallest many-to-one independent product. Interestingly, this coherent lower prevision $\underline{E}_N$ can be proved to be also a many-to-many independent product. Summarising:

Theorem 2 (Independent natural extension). *Consider arbitrary coherent lower previsions $\underline{P}_n$ on $\mathscr{L}(\mathscr{X}_n)$, $n \in N$. They always have a point-wise smallest many-to-one independent product, and a point-wise smallest many-to-many independent product, and these products coincide. We call this smallest independent product the* independent natural extension *of the marginals $\underline{P}_n$, and denote it by $\underline{E}_N := \otimes_{n \in N} \underline{P}_n$.*

Since the strong product $\times_{n \in N} \underline{P}_n$ is a many-to-one independent product of the marginals $\underline{P}_n$, $n \in N$ by Prop. 10, it has to dominate the independent natural extension $\otimes_{n \in N} \underline{P}_n$: i.e., we have $\times_{n \in N} \underline{P}_n \geq \otimes_{n \in N} \underline{P}_n$. But these products do not coincide in general: Walley [7, Sect. 9.3.4] discusses an example where the many-to-one independent natural extension is not a lower envelope of independent linear products, and as a consequence does not coincide with the strong product.

The independent natural extension can be derived from the marginals constructively. The following theorem establishes a workable expression for it.

Theorem 3. *Consider arbitrary coherent lower previsions $\underline{P}_n$ on $\mathscr{L}(\mathscr{X}_n)$, $n \in N$. Then for all gambles f on $\mathscr{X}_N$:*

$$\underline{E}_N(f) = \sup_{\substack{h_n \in \mathscr{L}(\mathscr{X}_N) \\ n \in N}} \inf_{z_N \in \mathscr{X}_N} \left[f(z_N) - \sum_{n \in N} [h_n(z_N) - \underline{P}_n(h_n(\cdot, z_{N \setminus \{n\}}))] \right] . \quad (2)$$

The special independent products introduced so far satisfy a monotonicity property:

Proposition 11. *Let $\underline{P}_n$ and $\underline{Q}_n$ be coherent lower previsions on $\mathscr{L}(\mathscr{X}_n)$ such that $\underline{P}_n \leq \underline{Q}_n$, $n \in N$. Then $\otimes_{n \in N} \underline{P}_n \leq \otimes_{n \in N} \underline{Q}_n$ and $\times_{n \in N} \underline{P}_n \leq \times_{n \in N} \underline{Q}_n$.*

Like the strong product, the independent natural extension satisfies very useful marginalisation and associativity properties.

Theorem 4. *Consider arbitrary coherent lower previsions $\underline{P}_n$ on $\mathscr{L}(\mathscr{X}_n)$, $n \in N$.*

(i) *For any non-empty subset R of N, $\underline{E}_R$ is the $\mathscr{X}_R$-marginal of $\underline{E}_N$: $\underline{E}_N(f) = \underline{E}_R(f)$ for all gambles f on $\mathscr{X}_R$;*

(ii) *For any partition N_1 and N_2 of N, $\otimes_{n \in N_1 \cup N_2} \underline{P}_n = (\otimes_{n \in N_1} \underline{P}_n) \otimes (\otimes_{n \in N_2} \underline{P}_n)$.*

Using the associativity of the independent natural extension, and the factorising character of the strong product, we are led to the following practically important conclusion:

Theorem 5. *Consider arbitrary coherent marginal lower previsions $\underline{P}_n$ on $\mathscr{L}(\mathscr{X}_n)$, $n \in N$. Then their independent natural extension $\otimes_{n \in N} \underline{P}_n$ is strongly factorising, and therefore factorising and productive.*

Amongst other things, this implies that, like the strong product, the independent natural extension satisfies the weak law of large numbers of Thm. 1, and as a consequence also any many-to-one independent product.

When some of the marginals are linear or vacuous previsions, the expression for the independent natural extension in Eq. (2) simplifies. Because of the associativity result in Thm. 4, it suffices to consider the case of two variables X_1 and X_2, so $N = \{1, 2\}$.

Proposition 12. *Let P_1 be any linear prevision on $\mathscr{L}(\mathscr{X}_1)$, and let $\underline{P}_2$ be any coherent lower prevision on $\mathscr{L}(\mathscr{X}_2)$. Let $\underline{P}_{\{1,2\}}$ be any (many-to-many) independent product of P_1 and $\underline{P}_2$. Then for all gambles f on $\mathscr{X}_1 \times \mathscr{X}_2$:*

$$\underline{P}_{\{1,2\}}(f) = (P_1 \times \underline{P}_2)(f) = (P_1 \otimes \underline{P}_2)(f) = \underline{P}_2(P_1(f)) ,$$

where $P_1(f)$ is the gamble on $\mathscr{X}_2$ defined by $P_1(f)(x_2) := P_1(f(\cdot, x_2))$ for all $x_2 \in \mathscr{X}_2$.

Proposition 13. *Let $\underline{P}_1^{A_1}$ be the vacuous lower prevision on $\mathscr{L}(\mathscr{X}_1)$ relative to the non-empty set $A_1 \subseteq \mathscr{X}_1$, and let $\underline{P}_2$ be any coherent lower prevision on $\mathscr{L}(\mathscr{X}_2)$. Then for all gambles f on $\mathscr{X}_1 \times \mathscr{X}_2$:*

$$(\underline{P}_1^{A_1} \times \underline{P}_2)(f) = (\underline{P}_1^{A_1} \otimes \underline{P}_2)(f) = \min_{x_1 \in A_1} \underline{P}_2(f(x_1, \cdot)) .$$

6 Factorisation and Independence

Since we know from Prop. 5 and Thm. 5 that both the strong product and the independent natural extension are strongly factorising, we wonder if we can use factorising lower previsions as many-to-one or many-to many independent products.

Theorem 6. *Consider an arbitrary coherent lower prevision $\underline{P}_N$ on $\mathscr{L}(\mathscr{X}_N)$. If it is factorising, then it is a many-to-one independent product.*

In the same vein, one could expect strong factorisation to be sufficient for being a many-to-many independent product. So far, we are only able to prove this for coherent lower previsions that satisfy an extra positivity property. It is still unclear whether we can extend the theorem below to general strongly factorising joints.

Theorem 7. *Let $\underline{P}_N$ be a strongly factorising coherent lower prevision on $\mathscr{L}(\mathscr{X}_N)$. If $\overline{P}_N(\{x_n\}) > 0$ for all $x_n \in \mathscr{X}_n$ and $n \in N$, then $\underline{P}_N$ is many-to-many independent.*

7 Conclusions

This paper is an attempt to lay down the foundations for a general notion of independence of finite-valued variables for imprecise probability models. We have taken the epistemic stance in that we regard a number of variables as independent when they are irrelevant to one another; and we have distinguished many-to-many from many-to-one independence based on whether the independence judgements affect sets of variables or single variables, respectively. This distinction turns out to vanish when we focus on least-committal models, as there is a unique smallest model for any (and therefore both) type of requirement: we have called it the independent natural extension. This generalises a proposal by Walley originally made for the case of two variables [7, Sec. 9.3]. Moreover, the independent natural extension satisfies a practically important strong factorisation property. This brings the independent natural extension closer to more traditional definitions of independence that are indeed based on factorisation, and it should make it easier to work with epistemic independence, since we can impose it through factorisation. Finally, other interesting contributions in this paper concern the relationship between epistemic independence and strong independence, and the proof of a number of their basic properties.

Acknowledgements. This work is supported by Swiss NSF grants n. 200020-116674/1 and 200020-121785/1, projects TIN2008-06796-C04-01 and MTM2007-61193, and SBO project 060043 of the IWT-Vlaanderen.

References

1. Cozman, F.G.: Constructing sets of probability measures through Kuznetsov's independence condition. In: de Cooman, G., Fine, T.L., Seidenfeld, T. (eds.) ISIPTA '01 – Proceedings of the Second International Symposium on Imprecise Probabilities and Their Applications, pp. 104–111. Shaker Publishing, Maastricht (2000)
2. de Cooman, G., Hermans, F., Antonucci, A., Zaffalon, M.: Epistemic irrelevance in credal nets: the case of imprecise Markov trees. International Journal of Approximate Reasoning (2009) (accepted for publication)
3. de Cooman, G., Miranda, E.: Weak and strong laws of large numbers for coherent lower previsions. Journal of Statistical Planning and Inference 138(8), 2409–2432 (2008)
4. Miranda, E.: A survey of the theory of coherent lower previsions. International Journal of Approximate Reasoning 48(2), 628–658 (2008)
5. Miranda, E.: Updating coherent lower previsions on finite spaces. Fuzzy Sets and Systems 160(9), 1286–1307 (2009)
6. Vicig, P.: Epistemic independence for imprecise probabilities. International Journal of Approximate Reasoning 24(3), 235–250 (2000)
7. Walley, P.: Statistical Reasoning with Imprecise Probabilities. Chapman and Hall, London (1991)

On Elementary Extensions in Fuzzy Predicate Logics

Pilar Dellunde[1,2] and Francesc Esteva[2]

[1] Universitat Autònoma de Barcelona
08193 Bellaterra, Spain
pilar.dellunde@uab.cat
[2] IIIA - CSIC
08193 Bellaterra, Spain
{pilar,esteva}@iiia.csic.es

Abstract. Our work is a contribution to the model-theoretic study of equality-free fuzzy predicate logics. We give a characterization of elementary equivalence in fuzzy predicate logics using elementary extensions and introduce an strengthening of this notion, the so-called *strong elementary equivalence*. Using the method of diagrams developed in [5] and elementary extensions we present a counterexample to Conjectures 1 and 2 of [8].

Keywords: Equality-free language, fuzzy predicate logic, model theory, elementary extensions, elementary equivalence.

1 Introduction

This work is a contribution to the model-theoretic study of equality-free fuzzy predicate logics. Model theory is the branch of mathematical logic that studies the construction and classification of structures. Construction means building structures or families of structures, which have some feature that interest us. Classifying a class of structures means grouping the structures into subclasses in a useful way, and then proving that every structure in the collection does belong in just one of the subclasses. The most basic classification in classical model theory is given by the relations of elementary equivalence and isomorphism. Our purpose in the present article is to investigate and characterize the relation of elementary equivalence between two structures in terms of elementary extensions. We introduce also an strengthening of this notion, the so-called *strong elementary equivalence*.

The basic notion of elementary equivalence between models is due to A. Tarski (see [11]) and the fundamental results on elementary extensions and elementary chains were introduced by A. Tarski and R. Vaught in [1]. In the context of fuzzy predicate logics, elementarily equivalent structures were defined in [8] (Definition 10), there the authors presented a characterization of conservative extension theories using the elementary equivalence relation (see Theorems 6 and 11 of [8]). A notion of elementary equivalent models *in a degree d* was presented in [10] (see Definition 4.33).

E. Hüllermeier, R. Kruse, and F. Hoffmann (Eds.): IPMU 2010, LNAI 6178, pp. 747–756, 2010.
© Springer-Verlag Berlin Heidelberg 2010

P. Hájek and P. Cintula proved in Theorem 6 of [8] that, in core fuzzy logics, a theory T_2 is a conservative extension of another theory T_1 if and only if each exhaustive model of T_1 can be elementarily embedded into some model of T_2. Then, they conjectured the same result to be true for arbitrary structures (Conjecture 2 of [8]). In this paper we present a counterexample to Conjecture 2, using the method of diagrams developed in [5] and elementary extensions.

The paper is structured as follows: Section 2 is devoted to preliminaries on fuzzy predicate logics. In Section 3 we introduce some known definitions and basic facts on canonical models (see section 4 and 5 of [8]) and of the method of diagrams for fuzzy predicate logics developed in [5]. Later on we prove some new propositions related to canonical models and diagrams. In Section 4 we present a counterexample to Conjectures 1 and 2 of [8], using the results of Section 3. Finally, in Section 5 we prove a characterization theorem of elementary equivalence in fuzzy predicate logics. We conclude the paper with a section of work in progress and future work.

2   Preliminaries

Our study of the model theory of fuzzy predicate logics is focused on the basic fuzzy predicate logic MTL$\forall$ and stronger t-norm based logics, the so-called *core fuzzy logics*. For a reference on the logic MTL see [6]. We start by introducing the notion of core fuzzy logic in the propositional case.

Definition 1. *A propositional logic L is a* core fuzzy logic *iff L satisfies:*

1. *For all formulas ϕ, φ, α, $\varphi \leftrightarrow \phi \vdash \alpha(\varphi) \leftrightarrow \alpha(\phi)$.*
2. *(LDT) Local Deduction Theorem: for each theory T and formulas ϕ, φ:*

$$T, \varphi \vdash \phi \text{ iff there is a natural number } n \text{ such that } T \vdash \varphi^n \to \phi.$$

3. *L expands MTL.*

For a thorough treatment of core fuzzy logics we refer to [8], [4] and [3]. A *predicate language* Γ is a triple $(\mathbf{P}, \mathbf{F}, \mathbf{A})$ where $\mathbf{P}$ is a non-empty set of predicate symbols, $\mathbf{F}$ is a set of function symbols and $\mathbf{A}$ is a mapping assigning to each predicate and function symbol a natural number called the *arity of the symbol*. Functions f for which $\mathbf{A}(f) = 0$ are called *object constants*. Formulas of the predicate language Γ are built up from the symbols in $(\mathbf{P}, \mathbf{F}, \mathbf{A})$, the connectives and constants of L, the logical symbols $\forall$ and $\exists$, variables and punctuation. Throughout the paper we consider the equality symbol as a binary predicate symbol not as a logical symbol, we work in equality-free fuzzy predicate logics. That is, the equality symbol is not necessarily present in all the languages and its interpretation is not fixed. Given a propositional core fuzzy logic L we denote by $L\forall$ the corresponding fuzzy predicate logic.

Let L be a fixed propositional core fuzzy logic and $\mathbf{B}$ an L-algebra, we introduce now the semantics for the fuzzy predicate logic $L\forall$. A $\mathbf{B}$-*structure* for predicate language Γ is a tuple $\mathbf{M} = (M, (P_{\mathbf{M}})_{P \in \Gamma}, (F_{\mathbf{M}})_{F \in \Gamma}, (c_{\mathbf{M}})_{c \in \Gamma})$ where:

1. M is a non-empty set.
2. For each n-ary predicate $P \in \Gamma$, $P_\mathbf{M}$ is a $\mathbf{B}$-fuzzy relation $P_\mathbf{M} : M^n \to \mathbf{B}$.
3. For each n-ary function symbol $F \in \Gamma$, $F_\mathbf{M} : M^n \to M$.
4. For each constant symbol $c \in \Gamma$, $c_\mathbf{M} \in M$.

Given a $\mathbf{B}$-structure $\mathbf{M}$, we define an $\mathbf{M}$-*evaluation* of the variables as a mapping v which assigns to each variable an element from M. By $\phi(x_1, \ldots, x_k)$ we mean that all the free variables of ϕ are among $x_1, \ldots, x_k$. Let v be an $\mathbf{M}$-evaluation, we denote by $v[x \to d]$ the $\mathbf{M}$-evaluation such that $v[x \to d](x) = d$ and for each variable y different from x, $v[x \to d](y) = v(y)$. Let $\mathbf{M}$ be a $\mathbf{B}$-structure and v an $\mathbf{M}$-evaluation, we define the values of the terms and *truth values* of the formulas as follows:

$$\|c\|^\mathbf{B}_{\mathbf{M},v} = c_\mathbf{M}, \ \|x\|^\mathbf{B}_{\mathbf{M},v} = v(x)$$

$$\|F(t_1, \ldots, t_n)\|^\mathbf{B}_{\mathbf{M},v} = F_\mathbf{M}(\|t_1\|^\mathbf{B}_{\mathbf{M},v}, \ldots, \|t_n\|^\mathbf{B}_{\mathbf{M},v})$$

for each variable x, each constant symbol $c \in \Gamma$, each n-ary function symbol $F \in \Gamma$ and Γ-terms $t_1, \ldots, t_n$, respectively.

$$\|P(t_1, \ldots, t_n)\|^\mathbf{B}_{\mathbf{M},v} = P_\mathbf{M}(\|t_1\|^\mathbf{B}_{\mathbf{M},v}, \ldots, \|t_n\|^\mathbf{B}_{\mathbf{M},v})$$

for each n-ary predicate $P \in \Gamma$,

$$\|\delta(\phi_1, \ldots, \phi_n)\|^\mathbf{B}_{\mathbf{M},v} = \delta_\mathbf{B}(\|\phi_1\|^\mathbf{B}_{\mathbf{M},v}, \ldots, \|\phi_n\|^\mathbf{B}_{\mathbf{M},v})$$

for each n-ary connective $\delta \in L$ and Γ-formulas $\phi_1, \ldots, \phi_n$. Finally, for the quantifiers,

$$\|\forall x\phi\|^\mathbf{B}_{\mathbf{M},v} = \inf\{\|\phi\|^\mathbf{B}_{\mathbf{M},v[x\to d]} : d \in M\}$$

$$\|\exists x\phi\|^\mathbf{B}_{\mathbf{M},v} = \sup\{\|\phi\|^\mathbf{B}_{\mathbf{M},v[x\to d]} : d \in M\}$$

Remark that, since the L-algebras we work with are not necessarily complete, the above suprema and infima could be not defined in some cases. It is said that a $\mathbf{B}$-structure is *safe* if such suprema and infima are always defined. From now on we assume that all our structures are safe. In particular, throughout the paper we will work only with $\mathbf{B}$-structures such that $\mathbf{B}$ is an L-chain.

If v is an evaluation such that for each $0 < i \leq n$, $v(x_i) = d_i$, and λ is either a Γ-term or a Γ-formula, we abbreviate by $\|\lambda(d_1, \ldots, d_n)\|^\mathbf{B}_\mathbf{M}$ the expression $\|\lambda(x_1, \ldots, x_n)\|^\mathbf{B}_{\mathbf{M},v}$. A Γ-sentence is a Γ-formula without free variables. Let ϕ be a Γ-sentence, given a $\mathbf{B}$-*structure* $\mathbf{M}$, for predicate language Γ, it is said that $\mathbf{M}$ is a *model* of ϕ iff $\|\phi\|^\mathbf{B}_\mathbf{M} = 1$. And that $\mathbf{M}$ is a model of a set of Γ-sentences Σ iff for all $\phi \in \Sigma$, $\mathbf{M}$ is a model of ϕ.

From now on, given an L-algebra $\mathbf{B}$, we say that $(\mathbf{M}, \mathbf{B})$ is a Γ-*structure* instead of saying that $\mathbf{M}$ is a $\mathbf{B}$-structure for predicate language Γ. Let $(\mathbf{M}, \mathbf{B})$ be a Γ-structure, by $Alg(\mathbf{M}, \mathbf{B})$ we denote the subalgebra of $\mathbf{B}$ whose domain is the set $\{\|\phi\|^\mathbf{B}_{\mathbf{M},v} : \phi, v\}$ of truth degrees of all Γ-formulas ϕ under all $\mathbf{M}$-evaluations v

of variables. Then, it is said that $(\mathbf{M}, \mathbf{B})$ is *exhaustive* iff $Alg(\mathbf{M}, \mathbf{B}) = \mathbf{B}$. Now let $(\mathbf{M}_1, \mathbf{B}_1)$ and $(\mathbf{M}_2, \mathbf{B}_2)$ be two Γ-structures, we denote by $(\mathbf{M}_1, \mathbf{B}_1) \equiv (\mathbf{M}_2, \mathbf{B}_2)$ the fact that $(\mathbf{M}_1, \mathbf{B}_1)$ and $(\mathbf{M}_2, \mathbf{B}_2)$ are *elementarily equivalent*, that is, that they are models of exactly the same Γ-sentences.

Finally we recall two notions of preserving mappings: elementary mapping and quantifier-free preserving mapping.

Definition 2. *Let $(\mathbf{M}_1, \mathbf{B}_1)$ and $(\mathbf{M}_2, \mathbf{B}_2)$ be Γ-structures. We say that the pair (f, g) is a* quantifier-free preserving mapping *iff*

1. $g : \mathbf{B}_1 \to \mathbf{B}_2$ *is an L-algebra homomorphism of $\mathbf{B}_1$ into $\mathbf{B}_2$.*
2. $f : M_1 \to M_2$ *is a mapping of M_1 into M_2.*
3. *For each quantifier-free Γ-formula $\phi(x_1, \ldots, x_n)$ and elements $d_1, \ldots, d_n \in M_1$, $g(\|\phi(d_1, \ldots, d_n)\|_{\mathbf{M}_1}^{\mathbf{B}_1}) = \|\phi(f(d_1), \ldots, f(d_n))\|_{\mathbf{M}_2}^{\mathbf{B}_2}$*

Moreover, if condition 3. holds for every Γ-formula, it is said that (f, g) is an elementary mapping. *And it is said that (f, g) is an* elementary embedding *when both f and g are one-to-one.*

We have presented so far only a few definitions and basic notation. A detailed introduction to the syntax and semantics of fuzzy predicate logics can be found in [7].

3   Diagrams and Canonical Models

In this section we recall first some definitions and basic facts on canonical models (see section 4 and 5 of [8]) and of the method of diagrams for fuzzy predicate logics developed in [5]. Later on we prove some new propositions related to canonical models and diagrams.

Definition 3. *Let $(\mathbf{M}, \mathbf{B})$ be a Γ-structure, we define:*

1. $Th(\mathbf{M}, \mathbf{B})$ *is the set of Γ-sentences true in the model $(\mathbf{M}, \mathbf{B})$.*
2. $\Gamma_{\mathbf{M}}$ *is the expansion of Γ by adding a constant symbol c_d, for each $d \in M$.*
3. $(\mathbf{M}', \mathbf{B})$ *is the expansion of $(\mathbf{M}, \mathbf{B})$ to the language $\Gamma_{\mathbf{M}}$, by interpreting for each $d \in M$, the constant c_d by d.*
4. *The* Elementary Diagram *of $(\mathbf{M}, \mathbf{B})$, denoted by $EDIAG(\mathbf{M}, \mathbf{B})$, is the set of all $\Gamma_{\mathbf{M}}$-sentences true in $(\mathbf{M}', \mathbf{B})$.*
5. *The* Complement of the Elementary Diagram *of $(\mathbf{M}, \mathbf{B})$, denoted by $\overline{EDIAG}(\mathbf{M}, \mathbf{B})$ is the set of all $\Gamma_{\mathbf{M}}$-sentences ϕ such that $\phi \notin EDIAG(\mathbf{M}, \mathbf{B})$.*

Definition 4. *Let $(\mathbf{M}, \mathbf{B})$ be a Γ-structure, we expand the language further adding new symbols to the predicate language $\Gamma_{\mathbf{M}}$ and we define:*

1. $\Gamma_{(\mathbf{M}, \mathbf{B})}$ *is the expansion of $\Gamma_{\mathbf{M}}$ by adding a nullary predicate symbol P_b, for each $b \in B$.*
2. $(\mathbf{M}^*, \mathbf{B})$ *is the expansion of $(\mathbf{M}', \mathbf{B})$ to the language $\Gamma_{(\mathbf{M}, \mathbf{B})}$, by interpreting for each $b \in B$, the nullary predicate symbol P_b by b.*

3. $EQ(\mathbf{B})$ *is the set of* $\Gamma_{(\mathbf{B},\mathbf{M})}$*-sentences of the form* $\delta(P_{b_1}, \ldots, P_{b_n}) \leftrightarrow \epsilon(P_{a_1}, \ldots, P_{a_k})$ *such that* $\mathbf{B} \models \delta(b_1, \ldots, b_n) = \epsilon(a_1, \ldots, a_k)$, *where* δ, ϵ *are L-terms and* $a_1, \ldots, a_k, b_1, \ldots, b_n \in B$

4. $NEQ(\mathbf{B})$ *is the set of* $\Gamma_{(\mathbf{B},\mathbf{M})}$*-sentences of the form* $\delta(P_{b_1}, \ldots, P_{b_n}) \leftrightarrow \epsilon(P_{a_1}, \ldots, P_{a_k})$ *such that* $\mathbf{B} \models \delta(b_1, \ldots, b_n) \neq \epsilon(a_1, \ldots, a_k)$, *where* δ, ϵ *are L-terms and* $a_1, \ldots, a_k, b_1, \ldots, b_n \in B$

5. *The Basic Full Elementary Diagram of* $(\mathbf{M}, \mathbf{B})$, *denoted by* $FEDIAG_0(\mathbf{M}, \mathbf{B})$, *is the set*

$$EDIAG(\mathbf{M}, \mathbf{B}) \cup EQ(\mathbf{B}) \cup \{\phi \leftrightarrow P_b : \phi \in \Gamma_{\mathbf{M}} \text{ and } \|\phi\|_{\mathbf{M}^*}^{\mathbf{B}} = b\}$$

6. *The Full Elementary Diagram of* $(\mathbf{M}, \mathbf{B})$, *denoted by* $FEDIAG(\mathbf{M}, \mathbf{B})$, *is the set of all* $\Gamma_{(\mathbf{M}, \mathbf{B})}$*-sentences true in* $(\mathbf{M}^*, \mathbf{B})$.

Proposition 5. [Proposition 32 of [5]] *Let* $(\mathbf{M}, \mathbf{B})$ *and* $(\mathbf{N}, \mathbf{A})$ *be two* Γ*-structures. The following are equivalent:*

1. *There is an expansion of* $(\mathbf{N}, \mathbf{A})$ *that is a model of* $FEDIAG_0(\mathbf{M}, \mathbf{B})$.
2. *There is an elementary mapping* (f, g) *from* $(\mathbf{M}, \mathbf{B})$ *into* $(\mathbf{N}, \mathbf{A})$.

Moreover, g *is one-to-one iff for every sentence* $\psi \in NEQ(\mathbf{B})$ *the expansion of* $(\mathbf{N}, \mathbf{A})$ *(defined in condition 1.) is not a model of* ψ.

Corollary 6. [Corollary 38 of [5]] *Let* $(\mathbf{M}, \mathbf{B})$ *and* $(\mathbf{N}, \mathbf{A})$ *two* Γ*-structures such that* $(\mathbf{M}, \mathbf{B})$ *is exhaustive. The following are equivalent:*

1. *There is an expansion of* $(\mathbf{N}, \mathbf{A})$ *that is a model of* $EDIAG(\mathbf{M}, \mathbf{B})$.
2. *There is an elementary mapping* (f, g) *from* $(\mathbf{M}, \mathbf{B})$ *into* $(\mathbf{N}, \mathbf{A})$.

Moreover, g *is one-to-one iff for every sentence of* $\Gamma_{\mathbf{M}}$, $\psi \in \overline{EDIAG}(\mathbf{M}, \mathbf{B})$, *the expansion of* $(\mathbf{N}, \mathbf{A})$ *(defined in condition 1.) is not a model of* ψ.

Remark that, as pointed out in [5], the mapping f of Proposition 5 and of Corollary 6 is not necessarily one-to-one, because we do not work with a crisp equality. Now we will see that, using canonical models, we can improve these results finding elementary expansions of a given model, in which f is one-to-one. We start by recalling some definitions from [4].

Definition 7. *A* Γ*-theory* T *is* linear *iff for each pair of* Γ*-sentences* $\phi, \psi \in \Gamma$, $T \vdash \phi \rightarrow \psi$ *or* $T \vdash \psi \rightarrow \phi$.

Definition 8. *A* Γ*-theory* Ψ *is* directed *iff for each pair of* Γ*-sentences* $\phi, \psi \in \Psi$, *there is a* Γ*-sentence* $\chi \in \Psi$ *such that both* $\phi \rightarrow \chi$ *and* $\psi \rightarrow \chi$ *are probable.*

Definition 9. *Let* Γ *and* Γ' *be predicate languages such that* $\Gamma \subseteq \Gamma'$ *and let* T *be a* Γ'*-theory. We say that* T *is* Γ*-Henkin if for each formula* $\psi(x) \in \Gamma$ *such that* $T \nvdash \forall x \psi$, *there is a constant* $c \in \Gamma'$ *such that* $T \nvdash \psi(c)$. *And we say that* T *is* $\exists$*-Γ–Henkin if for each formula* $\psi(x) \in \Gamma$ *such that* $T \vdash \exists x \psi$, *there is a constant* $c \in \Gamma'$ *such that* $T \vdash \psi(c)$. *Finally, a* Γ*-theory is called* doubly-Γ-Henkin *if it is both* Γ*-Henkin and* $\exists$*-Γ-Henkin. In case that* $\Gamma = \Gamma'$, *we say that* T *is* Henkin *($\exists$-Henkin, doubly Henkin, respectively).*

Theorem 10. [Theorem 2.20 of [4]] *Let T_0 be a Γ-theory and Ψ a directed set of Γ-sentences such that $T_0 \nvdash \Psi$. Then, there is a linear doubly Henkin theory $T \supseteq T_0$ in a predicate language $\Gamma' \supseteq \Gamma$ such that $T \nvdash \Psi$.*

Definition 11. *Let T be a Γ-theory. The* canonical model *of T, denoted by $(\mathbf{CM}(T), \mathbf{Lind}_T)$, where $\mathbf{Lind}_T$ is the Lindenbaum algebra of T (that is, the L-algebra of classes of T-equivalent Γ-sentences) is defined as follows: the domain of $\mathbf{CM}(T)$ is the set of closed Γ-terms, for every n-ary function symbol $F \in \Gamma$, $F_{(\mathbf{CM}(T), \mathbf{Lind}_T)}(t_1 \ldots t_n) = F(t_1 \ldots t_n)$ and for each n-ary predicate symbol $P \in \Gamma$, $P_{(\mathbf{CM}(T), \mathbf{Lind}_T)}(t_1 \ldots t_n) = [P(t_1 \ldots t_n)]_T$.*

From now on we write $\mathbf{CM}(T)$ instead of $(\mathbf{CM}(T), \mathbf{Lind}_T)$.

Lemma 12. [Lemma 2.24 of [4]] *Let T be a Henkin Γ-theory. Then,*

- $\mathbf{Lind}_T$ *is an L-chain iff T is linear*
- *For every sentence $\phi \in \Gamma$, $\|\phi\|_{\mathbf{CM}(T)}^{\mathbf{Lind}_T} = [\phi]_T$*
- *For every sentence $\phi \in \Gamma$, $T \vdash \phi$ iff $\mathbf{CM}(T) \models \phi$*
- $\mathbf{CM}(T)$ *is exhaustive*

Now we prove some new facts on diagrams and elementary extensions, using canonical models.

Proposition 13. *Let $(\mathbf{M}, \mathbf{B})$ be a Σ-structure and $T_0 \supseteq \mathrm{FEDIAG}_0(\mathbf{M}, \mathbf{B})$ a consistent theory in a predicate language $\Gamma \supseteq \Sigma$. If $\Psi \supseteq \mathrm{NEQ}(\mathbf{B})$ is a directed set of Γ-sentences such that $T_0 \nvdash \Psi$, then there is a linear doubly Henkin theory $T \supseteq T_0$ in a predicate language $\Gamma' \supseteq \Gamma$ such that $T \nvdash \Psi$ and an elementary mapping (f, g) from $(\mathbf{M}, \mathbf{B})$ into $\mathbf{CM}(T)$, with f and g one-to-one.*

Proof: By Theorem 10, there is a linear doubly Henkin theory $T \supseteq T_0$ in a predicate language $\Gamma' \supseteq \Gamma$ such that $T \nvdash \Psi$. By Lemma 12, $\mathbf{CM}(T)$ is a model of $\mathrm{FEDIAG}_0(\mathbf{M}, \mathbf{B})$. Then, by Proposition 5 (Proposition 32 of [5]), there is an elementary mapping (f, g) from $(\mathbf{M}, \mathbf{B})$ into $\mathbf{CM}(T)$, defined as follows: for each $d \in M$, $f(d) = c_d$ and for each $b \in B$, $g(b) = [P_b]_T$. Moreover, since $T \nvdash \mathrm{NEQ}(\mathbf{B})$, for every sentence $\psi \in \mathrm{NEQ}(\mathbf{B})$, $\mathbf{CM}(T)$ is not a model of ψ and thus, g is one-to-one: indeed, if $b \neq b'$, then $P_b \leftrightarrow P_{b'} \in \mathrm{NEQ}(\mathbf{B})$ and, by assumption, it is not true in $\mathbf{CM}(T)$ and consequently, $[P_b]_T \neq [P_{b'}]_T$ and thus $g(b) \neq g(b')$. Finally, by definition of $\mathbf{CM}(T)$, f is also one-to-one.   □

Now as a Corollary of Propositions 6 and 13 we obtain the following result for exhaustive structures:

Corollary 14. *Let $(\mathbf{M}, \mathbf{B})$ be an exhaustive Σ-structure and $T_0 \supseteq \mathrm{EDIAG}(\mathbf{M}, \mathbf{B})$ a consistent theory in a predicate language $\Gamma \supseteq \Sigma$. If $\Psi \supseteq \overline{\mathrm{EDIAG}}(\mathbf{M}, \mathbf{B})$ is a directed set of formulas of Γ such that $T_0 \nvdash \Psi$, then there is a linear doubly Henkin theory $T \supseteq T_0$ in a predicate language $\Gamma' \supseteq \Gamma$ such that $T \nvdash \Psi$ and an elementary mapping (f, g) from $(\mathbf{M}, \mathbf{B})$ into $\mathbf{CM}(T)$, with f and g one-to-one.*

Now we recall the notion of witnessed model and show a direct application of Proposition 13, giving a generalization of Lemma 5 of [8] for non-exhaustive models. Let $(\mathbf{M}, \mathbf{B})$ be a Γ-structure. We say that $(\mathbf{M}, \mathbf{B})$ is *witnessed* iff for each Γ-formula $\phi(y, x_1, \ldots, x_n)$ and for each $d_1, \ldots, d_n \in M$, there is an element $e \in M$ such that $\|\exists y \phi(d_1, \ldots, d_n)\|_{\mathbf{M}}^{\mathbf{B}} = \|\phi(e, d_1, \ldots, d_n)\|_{\mathbf{M}}^{\mathbf{B}}$, and similarly for the universal quantifier. In [8] the following axiom schemes, originally introduced by Baaz, are discussed: $(\mathrm{C}\forall)$ $\exists x(\phi(x) \to \forall y \phi(y))$ and $(\mathrm{C}\exists)$ $\exists x(\exists y \phi(y) \to \phi(x))$.

Proposition 15. *Let T be a Γ-theory and T' its extension with axioms $\mathrm{C}\forall$ and $\mathrm{C}\exists$. Then every Γ-structure model of T' can be elementarily embedded into a witnessed model of T.*

Proof: Let $(\mathbf{M}, \mathbf{B})$ be a Γ-structure model of T'. We consider the theory $T_0 = \mathrm{FEDIAG}(\mathbf{M}, \mathbf{B})$. Now let Ψ be the closure of $\mathrm{NEQ}(\mathbf{B})$ under disjunctions. Clearly Ψ is a directed set. We show that $T_0 \not\vdash \Psi$: it is enough to prove that for every $\alpha, \beta \in \mathrm{NEQ}(\mathbf{B})$, $T_0 \not\vdash \alpha \vee \beta$. Assume the contrary, since $\mathbf{B}$ is an L-chain, we have that either $\alpha \to \beta \in T_0$ or $\beta \to \alpha \in T_0$. Then, since L is a core fuzzy logic, we will have either that $T_0 \vdash \alpha$ or $T_0 \vdash \beta$, which is absurd, by the same definition of $\mathrm{NEQ}(\mathbf{B})$.

Then, by Proposition 13, since $T_0 \supseteq \mathrm{FEDIAG}_0(\mathbf{M}, \mathbf{B})$ and $\Psi \supseteq \mathrm{NEQ}(\mathbf{B})$, there is a linear doubly Henkin theory $T^* \supseteq T_0$ such that $T^* \not\vdash \Psi$ and $(\mathbf{M}, \mathbf{B})$ is elementarily embedded into $\mathbf{CM}(T^*)$. The rest of the proof follows the same lines that the corresponding part of the proof of Lemma 5 of [8].   □

4   Counterexample to Conjectures 1 and 2 of [8]

Given two theories $T_1 \subseteq T_2$ in the respective predicate languages $\Gamma_1 \subseteq \Gamma_2$, it is said that T_2 is a *conservative extension* of T_1 if and only if each Γ_1-formula provable in T_2 is also provable in T_1. P. Hájek and P. Cintula proved in Theorem 6 of [8] that, in core fuzzy logics, a theory T_2 is a conservative extension of another theory T_1 if and only if each exhaustive model of T_1 can be elementarily embedded into some model of T_2. In Theorem 7 of [8], they conjectured the same result to be true for arbitrary structures, showing that the following two conjectures were equivalent:

Conjecture 1 of [8]: Let P be a nullary predicate symbol and for $i \in \{1, 2\}$, T_i be a Γ_i-theory, and T_i^+ be a $\Gamma_i \cup \{P\}$-theory such that $T_i^+ = T_i$. If T_2 is a conservative extension of T_1, then T_2^+ is a conservative extension of T_1^+.
Conjecture 2 of [8]: A theory T_2 is a conservative extension of another theory T_1 if and only if each model of T_1 can be elementarily embedded into some model of T_2.

We present here a counterexample to Conjecture 2 (and thus to Conjecture 1) using the method of diagrams. Our example is based in one used by F. Montagna in the proof of Theorem 3.11 of [9]. Let L be the logic that has as equivalent algebraic semantics the variety generated by the union of the classes of Łukasiewicz and Product chains, for an axiomatization of this extension of BL we refer to [2] (in this article it is proved that the only chains of the variety are precisely the Łukasiewicz and Product chains). Let now $(\mathbf{M}, \{0, 1\})$ be a classical first-order structure in a predicate language Γ, and let $\mathbf{B}_1 = [0, 1]_\Pi$ and $\mathbf{B}_2 = [0, 1]_L$ be the canonical Product and Łukasiewicz chains, respectively.

Remark that the structure $(\mathbf{M}, \{0, 1\})$ can also be regarded as a Γ-structure over both $\mathbf{B}_1$ and $\mathbf{B}_2$ chains, since for every two-valued n-ary predicate $P_\mathbf{M}$: $M^n \to \{0, 1\}$, $P_\mathbf{M}$ is also a fuzzy relation $P_\mathbf{M} : M^n \to [0, 1]_\Pi$ and $P_\mathbf{M} : M^n \to [0, 1]_L$. Thus, we have $(\mathbf{M}, \mathbf{B}_1) \equiv (\mathbf{M}, \mathbf{B}_2)$ (in fact we have that $(\mathbf{M}'', \mathbf{B}_1) \equiv (\mathbf{M}'', \mathbf{B}_2)$, where $\mathbf{M}''$ is the structure of Definition 3).

Let $T_1 = \text{EDIAG}(\mathbf{M}, \mathbf{B}_1)$ and $T_2 = \text{FEDIAG}(\mathbf{M}, \mathbf{B}_2)$. We have that T_2 is a conservative extension of T_1: for every $\Gamma_\mathbf{M}$-formula ϕ, if $T_2 \vdash \phi$, then $\|\phi\|_{\mathbf{M}''}^{\mathbf{B}_2} = 1$ and since $(\mathbf{M}'', \mathbf{B}_1) \equiv (\mathbf{M}'', \mathbf{B}_2)$, $\phi \in T_1$. Now we show that there is a model of T_1 that can not be elementarily embedded into some model of T_2, this model is $(\mathbf{M}, [0, 1]_\Pi)$. Suppose, contrary to our claim, that there is a model of T_2, say $(\mathbf{N}, \mathbf{A})$, in which $(\mathbf{M}, [0, 1]_\Pi)$ is elementarily embedded. By Proposition 5, since $(\mathbf{N}, \mathbf{A})$ is a model of T_2, there is an elementary mapping from $(\mathbf{M}, [0, 1]_L)$ into $(\mathbf{N}, \mathbf{A})$. Consequently, there is an L-embedding k from $[0, 1]_\Pi$ into $\mathbf{A}$ and at the same time there is an L-homomorphism h from $[0, 1]_L$ into $\mathbf{A}$ (not necessarily one-to-one). If $\mathbf{A}$ is an L-chain, it is clear that this is not possible. We show now that, for any arbitrary L-algebra $\mathbf{A}$, this fact leads to a contradiction.

If such embeddings k and h exist, and c and b are the images of $1/2$ under h and k respectively, we have $b = \neg b$ (because h is an L-homomorphism), $c < 1$ and $\neg c = 0$ (because k is an L-embedding and the negation in $[0, 1]_\Pi$ is Gödel). If we decompose $\mathbf{A}$ as a subdirect product of an indexed family of subdirectly irreducible BL-chains, say $(\mathbf{A}_i : i \in I)$, every such $\mathbf{A}_i$ is either a Łukasiewicz, or a Product chain (for a reference see [7] and [2]). Therefore, if we take an index i such that the i-component, c_i, satisfies $0 < c_i < 1$, we will have at the same time $\neg c_i = 0$ and for the i-component b_i, $b_i = \neg b_i$, which is absurd, because $\mathbf{A}_i$ can not be, at the same time, a Łukasiewicz and a Product chain.

5   A Characterization Theorem of Elementary Equivalence

In this section we characterize when two exhaustive structures are elementarily equivalent in terms of elementary extensions. We provide an example showing that the result can not be extended to arbitrary models.

Theorem 16. *Let $(\mathbf{M}_1, \mathbf{B}_1)$ and $(\mathbf{M}_2, \mathbf{B}_2)$ be two exhaustive Γ-structures. The following are equivalent:*

1. *$(\mathbf{M}_1, \mathbf{B}_1) \equiv (\mathbf{M}_2, \mathbf{B}_2)$.*
2. *There is a Γ-structure $(\mathbf{N}, \mathbf{A})$, such that $(\mathbf{M}_1, \mathbf{B}_1)$ and $(\mathbf{M}_2, \mathbf{B}_2)$ are elementarily mapped into $(\mathbf{N}, \mathbf{A})$.*

Proof: 2. $\Rightarrow$ 1. is clear. 1. $\Rightarrow$ 2. First we expand the language introducing two disjoint sets of new constants, C_{M_1} and C_{M_2} for the elements of M_1 and M_2, respectively, that are not interpretations of the constant symbols in Γ.

Now consider the theory $T_0 = \text{EDIAG}(\mathbf{M}_1, \mathbf{B}_1) \cup \text{EDIAG}(\mathbf{M}_2, \mathbf{B}_2)$ in the language expanded with the set of constants C_{M_1} and C_{M_2} respectively. Let us show that T_0 is consistent: If $T_0 \vdash \bot$, since $\text{EDIAG}(\mathbf{M}_2, \mathbf{B}_2)$ is closed under conjunction and the proof is finitary, there is $\psi \in \text{EDIAG}(\mathbf{M}_2, \mathbf{B}_2)$ such that $\text{EDIAG}(\mathbf{M}_1, \mathbf{B}_1), \psi \vdash \bot$. Then, by the Local Deduction Theorem (see Definition 1), there is a natural number n such that $\text{EDIAG}(\mathbf{M}_1, \mathbf{B}_1) \vdash (\psi)^n \to \bot$. Let $\widehat{\psi}$ be the formula obtained by replacing each constant $c \in C_{M_2}$ by a new variable x. Thus we have $\text{EDIAG}(\mathbf{M}_1, \mathbf{B}_1) \vdash (\widehat{\psi})^n \to \bot$ and by generalization over the new variables we obtain $\text{EDIAG}(\mathbf{M}_1, \mathbf{B}_1) \vdash (\forall...)((\widehat{\psi})^n \to \bot)$, thus $(\forall...)((\widehat{\psi})^n \to \bot) \in Th(\mathbf{M}_1, \mathbf{B}_1) = Th(\mathbf{M}_2, \mathbf{B}_2)$ (because $(\mathbf{M}_1, \mathbf{B}_1) \equiv (\mathbf{M}_2, \mathbf{B}_2)$) and consequently, $\bot \in Th(\mathbf{M}_2, \mathbf{B}_2)$, which is absurd.

Now let $\Psi = \overline{\text{EDIAG}}(\mathbf{M}_1, \mathbf{B}_1)$. It is easy to check that Ψ is a directed set: given $\alpha, \beta \in \Psi$, we show that $\alpha \lor \beta \in \Psi$. If $\alpha \lor \beta \in \text{EDIAG}(\mathbf{M}_1, \mathbf{B}_1)$, using the fact that $\mathbf{B}_1$ is an L-chain, we have that either $\alpha \to \beta \in \text{EDIAG}(\mathbf{M}_1, \mathbf{B}_1)$ or $\beta \to \alpha \in \text{EDIAG}(\mathbf{M}_1, \mathbf{B}_1)$. Then, since L is a core fuzzy logic, we will have either that $\alpha \in \text{EDIAG}(\mathbf{M}_1, \mathbf{B}_1)$ or $\beta \in \text{EDIAG}(\mathbf{M}_1, \mathbf{B}_1)$ which is absurd because $\alpha, \beta \in \Psi$.

We show now that $T_0 \nvdash \Psi$. Otherwise, if for some $\alpha \in \Psi$, $T_0 \vdash \alpha$, since $\text{EDIAG}(\mathbf{M}_1, \mathbf{B}_1)$ is closed under conjunction and the proof is finitary, there is $\psi \in \text{EDIAG}(\mathbf{M}_1, \mathbf{B}_1)$ such that $\text{EDIAG}(\mathbf{M}_2, \mathbf{B}_2), \psi \vdash \alpha$. Then, by the same kind of argument we have used to show that T_0 is consistent, we would obtain that $\alpha \in \text{EDIAG}(\mathbf{M}_1, \mathbf{B}_1)$, which is absurd.

Then, by Corollary 14, there is a linear doubly Henkin theory $T \supseteq T_0$ in a predicate language $\Gamma' \supseteq \Gamma$ such that $T \nvdash \Psi$ and an elementary mapping (f, g) from $(\mathbf{M}_1, \mathbf{B}_1)$ into $\mathbf{CM}(T)$, with f and g one-to-one. Moreover, since $\mathbf{CM}(T)$ is also a model of $\text{EDIAG}(\mathbf{M}_2, \mathbf{B}_2)$, by Corollary 6, $(\mathbf{M}_2, \mathbf{B}_2)$ is elementarily mapped into $\mathbf{CM}(T)$. Finally, by Lemma 12, $\mathbf{Lind}_T$ is an L-chain. $\square$

Remark that Theorem 16 can not be generalized to arbitrary structures. If we take the structures of the counterexample to Conjectures 1 and 2 of Section 4, we have $(\mathbf{M}, [0,1]_\Pi) \equiv (\mathbf{M}, [0,1]_L)$, but there is not a Γ-structure $(\mathbf{N}, \mathbf{A})$ in which both are elementary mapped.

6 Future Work

When working with models over the same L-algebra, we can introduce a stronger notion of elementary equivalence. Given a Γ-structure $(\mathbf{M}, \mathbf{B})$ let $\Gamma_{\mathbf{B}}$ be the expansion of Γ by adding a nullary predicate symbol P_b for each $b \in B$. Let $(\mathbf{M}^\sharp, \mathbf{B})$ be the expansion of $(\mathbf{M}, \mathbf{B})$ to the language $\Gamma_{\mathbf{B}}$, by interpreting for each $b \in B$, the nullary predicate symbol P_b by b. Then we say that two Γ-structures, $(\mathbf{M}_1, \mathbf{B})$ and $(\mathbf{M}_2, \mathbf{B})$, are *strong elementarily equivalent* (denoted by $(\mathbf{M}_1, \mathbf{B}) \equiv_s (\mathbf{M}_2, \mathbf{B})$) if and only if $(\mathbf{M}_1^\sharp, \mathbf{B}) \equiv (\mathbf{M}_2^\sharp, \mathbf{B})$.

By an argument analogue to the one in Theorem 16 (but using Proposition 13 instead of Corollary 14), it is not difficult to check that two strong elementary equivalent structures (not necessarily exhaustive), over the same L-algebra, are elementary embedded in a third structure. Future work will be devoted to the study of the properties of this stronger notion of equivalence.

The work we have done so far can be extended to Δ-core fuzzy logics, by finding analogues to Theorem 10 and Proposition 13 for these logics. Work in progress includes characterizations of elementary equivalence for other expansions of MTL and the study of the relationship between elementarily embeddability and amalgamation properties.

Acknowledgment

Research partially funded by the spanish projects CONSOLIDER (CSD2007-0022), MULOG2 (TIN2007-68005-C04-01) and ARINF (TIN2009-14704-C03-03) by the ESF Eurocores-LogICCC/MICINN project FFI2008-03126- E/FILO and by the Generalitat de Catalunya under the grants 2009-SGR 1433 and 1434.

References

1. Baaz, M., Fermueller, C.G., Zach, R.: Arithmetical extensions of relational systems. Compositio Math. 13, 81–102 (1957)
2. Cignoli, R., Esteva, F., Godo, L., Torrens, A.: Basic fuzzy logic is the logic of continuous t-norms and their residua. Soft. Comput., 106–112 (2000)
3. Cintula, P., Esteva, F., Gispert, J., Godo, L., Montagna, F., Noguera, C.: Distinguished algebraic semantics for t-norm based fuzzy logics: Methods and algebraic equivalencies. Ann. Pure Appl. Logic 160(1), 53–81 (2009)
4. Cintula, P., Hájek, P.: Triangular norm based predicate fuzzy logics. Fuzzy Sets and Systems 161, 311–346 (2010)
5. Dellunde, P.: Preserving mappings in fuzzy predicate logics(2009) (submitted)
6. Esteva, F., Godo, L.: Monoidal t-norm based logic: towards a logic for left-continuous t-norms. Fuzzy Sets and Systems 124(3), 271–288 (2001)
7. Hájek, P.: Metamathematics of fuzzy logic. Trends in Logic-Studia Logica Library, vol. 4. Kluwer Academic Publishers, Dordrecht (1998)
8. Hájek, P., Cintula, P.: On theories and models in fuzzy predicate logics. The Journal of Symbolic Logic 71(3), 863–880 (2006)
9. Montagna, F.: Interpolation and beth's property in propositional many-valued logics: A semantic investigation. Ann. Pure Appl. Logic 141(1-2), 148–179 (2006)
10. Novák, V., Perfilieva, I., Močkoř, J.: Mathematical principles of fuzzy logic. The Kluwer International Series in Engineering and Computer Science, vol. 517. Kluwer Academic Publishers, Boston (1999)
11. Tarski, A.: Der wahrheitsbegriff in den formalisierten sprachen. Studia Philosophica 1, 261–405 (1935)

Logical Proportions – Typology and Roadmap

Henri Prade[1] and Gilles Richard[1,2]

[1] IRIT, Université Paul Sabatier, 31062 Toulouse Cedex 09, France
[2] British Institute of Technology and E-commerce, London, E7 9HZ, UK
prade@irit.fr, grichard@bite.ac.uk

Abstract. Given a 4-tuple of Boolean variables (a, b, c, d), logical proportions are modeled by a pair of equivalences relating similarity indicators $(a \wedge b$ and $\neg a \wedge \neg b)$, or dissimilarity indicators $(a \wedge \neg b$ and $\neg a \wedge b)$ pertaining to the pair (a, b) to the ones associated with the pair (c, d). There are 120 distinct logical proportions. One of them models analogical proportions which correspond to statements of the form "a is to b as c is to d". The paper inventories the whole set of logical proportions by dividing it into 5 subfamilies according to what their logical proportions express, and then identifies the proportions that satisfy noticeable properties such as full identity (the pair of equivalences defining the proportion hold as true for the 4-tuple (a, a, a, a)), symmetry (if the proportion holds for (a, b, c, d), it also holds for (c, d, a, b)), or code independency (if the proportion holds for (a, b, c, d), it also holds for $(\neg a, \neg b, \neg c, \neg d)$). Finally, the paper provides a discussion of the potential interest of logical proportions, which clearly have a cognitive appeal.

1 Introduction

In mathematics, a proportion is a statement of equality between two ratios, i.e., $a/b = c/d$. Thus, it amounts to a relative comparison between numbers, as a statement of equality between two differences, i.e., $a - b = c - d$, will do as well. Assuming that the fourth value, say d, is unknown, such statements are at the basis of reasoning procedures that enable us to "extrapolate" its value as $d = c \times b/a$ in the first case, which corresponds to the well-known rule of three, or as $d = c + (b - a)$ in the second case. Due to their structural similarity with the previous equations, statements of the form "a is to b as c is to d" are called *analogical proportions*, where a, b, c, d are no longer necessarily numbers, but may refer to situations described through words, equations, pictures, ... In this paper, we take the simple, but quite general view that such a situation is described as a vector of considered Boolean properties that are true, or false in this situation.

Starting from the pioneering works of [5], [11], [6] on the formal modeling of analogical proportions, a logical representation has been proposed for these proportions [7], which amounts to state that "a is to b as c is to d" is to be understood as "a differs from b as c differs from d, and b differs from a as d differs from c". This view has recently led the authors of this paper to introduce two

E. Hüllermeier, R. Kruse, and F. Hoffmann (Eds.): IPMU 2010, LNAI 6178, pp. 757–767, 2010.

other related proportions named *paralogy* and *reverse analogy* also expressed in terms of compared similarity /dissimilarity of the pairs (a, b) and (c, d) [9]. These three proportions can be expressed by equating the truth values of similarity indicators $(a \wedge b$ and $\neg a \wedge \neg b)$, or dissimilarity indicators $(a \wedge \neg b$ and $\neg a \wedge b)$ pertaining to the pair (a, b) together with the ones associated with the pair (c, d). These proportions can be applied component by component on the vectors describing four situations in order to extrapolate missing values in the fourth vector [8].

More recently, the authors [10] have identified and studied the properties and the inferential power of a larger family of 15 proportions that are also defined on the basis of the equivalence between similarity and dissimilarity indicators pertaining to two pairs of situations, and obey a "full identity" postulate requiring that the proportion holds between the particular pairs (a, a) and (a, a). The purpose of the present paper is to investigate the whole set of logical proportions (there are in fact 120 distinct proportions as we shall see), and to try to understand their role.

The paper is organized as follows. The next section, after providing the formal definition of a logical proportion, identifies 5 subfamilies of proportions, counts their members, and studies a transformation based on negation that preserves subfamilies or exchanges them. The first subfamily, which corresponds to proportions that are purely defined either in terms of similarity or in terms of dissimilarity, has four members, three already known: analogy, reverse analogy, paralogy, and a new one called *inverse paralogy*. Section 3 studies the truth tables of the proportions (which can be viewed as quaternary logical connectives), their semantic behavior with respect to requirements expressing symmetry, or independence w. r. t. the way the vectors describing the situations are encoded. Section 4 discusses the interest and the intended use of these proportions.

2   Syntactic View of Similarity/Dissimilarity-Based Proportions

When comparing situations, one determines what features make them similar and what features make them dissimilar. Let a and b be two Boolean variables describing the truth status of the same binary property for two situations. If $a \wedge b$ is true, the property is true in both situations, while it is false if $\neg a \wedge \neg b$ is true. The property is true in the first (resp. second) situation if $a \wedge \neg b$ (resp. $\neg a \wedge b$) is true. Proportions involve four items. Let c and d be two Boolean variables corresponding to the same property for a third and a fourth situation. We have again two similarity indicators, a positive one $c \wedge d$ and a negative one $\neg c \wedge \neg d$, and two dissimilarity indicators $c \wedge \neg d$ and $\neg c \wedge d$. Then the comparison of two pairs of situations can be only based on these indicators.

2.1   Definition

Let us introduce the following notations: $S_1 = a \wedge b$, $S_2 = \neg a \wedge \neg b$, $D_1 = a \wedge \neg b$, $D_2 = \neg a \wedge b$, $S'_1 = c \wedge d$, $S'_2 = \neg c \wedge \neg d$, $D'_1 = c \wedge \neg d$, and $D'_2 = \neg c \wedge d$ (letters with a ' will refer to the right hand side of equivalences). Then logical proportions are defined as:

Definition 1. *A logical proportion* $T(a, b, c, d)$ *is a logical expression of the form* $(X \equiv X') \wedge (Y \equiv Y')$, *where* $X, Y \in \{S_1, S_2, D_1, D_2\}$ *and* $X', Y' \in \{S'_1, S'_2, D'_1, D'_2\}$. *The cases* $X = Y$ *and* $X' = Y'$ *are forbidden.*

For instance, $(S_2 \equiv D'_1) \wedge (D_2 \equiv D'_2)$ defines the proportion whose logical expression is $((\neg a \wedge \neg b) \equiv (c \wedge \neg d)) \wedge ((\neg a \wedge b) \equiv (\neg c \wedge d))$. As can be seen, stating that the proportion $T(a, b, c, d)$ holds (i.e. is true) amounts to require that the truth values of the corresponding X and X' are equal and the truth values of Y and Y' are also equal.

Let us view the description of a situation $\mathcal{A}$ as a vector of Boolean values $(a_1, ..., a_i, ..., a_n)$ corresponding to the truth values of n properties ($a_i = 1$ if property i holds, and $a_i = 0$ otherwise). Then if the same proportion $T(a_i, b_i, c_i, d_i)$ holds for the n properties between four situations $\mathcal{A}, \mathcal{B}, \mathcal{C}, \mathcal{D}$, then the proportion translates into set-valued constraints $x = x'$ and $y = y'$ where $x, y \in \{A \cap B, \overline{A} \cap \overline{B}, A \cap \overline{B}, \overline{A} \cap B\}$ and $x', y' \in \{C \cap D, \overline{C} \cap \overline{D}, C \cap \overline{D}, \overline{C} \cap D\}$, where $\mathcal{A}$ (resp. $\overline{A}$) denotes the set of properties true (resp. false) in $\mathcal{A}$. Since there are 4 choices for choosing X and 4 choices for choosing Y, it makes 16 choices for $(X \equiv X')$, and similarly 16 choices for $(Y \equiv Y')$. Hence, there are $16 \times 16 = 256$ potential choices for $(X \equiv X') \wedge (Y \equiv Y')$ minus 16 choices corresponding to the forbidden cases $X = Y$ and $X' = Y'$, i.e., 240 cases which are to be divided by 2 since the ordering between $(X \equiv X')$ and $(Y \equiv Y')$ is not relevant. Thus,

Proposition 1. *There are 120 logical proportions that are syntactically different.*

2.2 Typology

Depending on the way X, X', Y, Y' are chosen, one may mix the similarity and the dissimilarity indicators differently in the definition of a proportion. This leads us to distinguish between 5 subfamilies. In the four first subfamilies it is required that both $X \neq X'$ and $Y \neq Y'$, while in the fifth subfamily of so-called *degenerated proportions*, one has $X = X'$ or $Y = Y'$ (but not both, which is forbidden). Let us identify the first four subfamilies first.

The homogeneous proportions. They involve similarity (or dissimilarity) indicators only. They are of the form $(S_i \equiv S'_j) \wedge (S_k \equiv S'_l)$, or $(D_i \equiv D'_j) \wedge (D_k \equiv D'_l)$ with $i \neq k$ and $j \neq l$, and $i, j, k, l \in \{1, 2\}$.

Thus, there are 4 homogeneous proportions:

- paralogy: $((a \wedge b) \equiv (c \wedge d)) \wedge ((\neg a \wedge \neg b) \equiv (\neg c \wedge \neg d))$, denoted $a; b :: c; d$
- inverse paralogy: $((a \wedge b) \equiv (\neg c \wedge \neg d)) \wedge ((\neg a \wedge \neg b) \equiv (c \wedge d))$, denoted $a \dagger b :: c \dagger d$
- analogy: $((a \wedge \neg b) \equiv (c \wedge \neg d)) \wedge ((\neg a \wedge b) \equiv (\neg c \wedge d))$, traditionally denoted $a : b :: c : d$
- reverse analogy: $((a \wedge \neg b) \equiv (\neg c \wedge d)) \wedge ((\neg a \wedge b) \equiv (c \wedge \neg d))$, denoted $a!b :: c!d$

Analogy already appeared under this form in [7]; paralogy and reverse analogy were first introduced in [9]. While the analogical proportion (analogy, for short) reads "a is to b as c is to d", reverse analogy reads "a is to b as d is to c", and paralogy reads "what a and b have in common, c and d have it also".[1] Thus, *inverse paralogy* reads "what a and b have in common, c and d miss it, and conversely". As can be seen, inverse paralogy expresses a form of antagonism between pair (a, b) and pair (c, d). Note that we use two different words, "inverse" and "reverse", since the changes between analogy and reverse analogy on the one hand, and paralogy and inverse paralogy on the other hand, are not of the same nature. The meanings of the four above proportions is perhaps still more easy to grasp when moving from Boolean variables, to situations described in terms of sets of properties. From now on, to alleviate the notations, let us agree to denote analogy with A, paralogy with P, reverse analogy with R, inverse analogy with I. When we need to denote any proportion, we will use the letter T.

The conditional proportions. Their expression is made of the conjunction of an equivalence between similarity indicators and of an equivalence between dissimilarity indicators. Thus, they are of the form $(S_i \equiv S'_j) \wedge (D_k \equiv D'_l)$, where $i, j, k, l \in \{1, 2\}$. There are 16 conditional proportions (4 choices per equivalence). Those with $i = j$ which do not mix positive and negative similarity are

- $((a \wedge b) \equiv (c \wedge d)) \wedge ((a \wedge \neg b) \equiv (c \wedge \neg d))$, denoted $b|a :: d|c$
- $((a \wedge b) \equiv (c \wedge d)) \wedge ((\neg a \wedge b) \equiv \neg c \wedge d))$, denoted $a|b :: c|d$
- $((\neg a \wedge \neg b) \equiv (\neg c \wedge \neg d)) \wedge ((\neg a \wedge b) \equiv (\neg c \wedge d))$, denoted $\neg b|\neg a :: \neg d|\neg c$
- $((\neg a \wedge \neg b) \equiv (\neg c \wedge \neg d)) \wedge ((a \wedge \neg b) \equiv (c \wedge \neg d))$, denoted $\neg a|\neg b :: \neg c|\neg d$

and as for reverse analogy, one may switch c and d, which yields:

- $((a \wedge b) \equiv (c \wedge d)) \wedge ((a \wedge \neg b) \equiv (\neg c \wedge d))$, denoted $b|a :: c|d$
- $((a \wedge b) \equiv (c \wedge d)) \wedge ((\neg a \wedge b) \equiv (c \wedge \neg d))$, denoted $a|b :: d|c$
- $((\neg a \wedge \neg b) \equiv (\neg c \wedge \neg d)) \wedge ((\neg a \wedge b) \equiv (c \wedge \neg d))$, denoted $\neg b|\neg a :: \neg c|\neg d$
- $((\neg a \wedge \neg b) \equiv (\neg c \wedge \neg d)) \wedge ((a \wedge \neg b) \equiv (\neg c \wedge d))$, denoted $\neg a|\neg b :: \neg d|\neg c$

Changing the first half of the above expressions into $((a \wedge b) \equiv (\neg c \wedge \neg d))$ and into $((\neg a \wedge \neg b) \equiv (c \wedge d))$ yield 8 new proportions (with $i \neq j$): $b|a :: \neg c|\neg d$, $a|b :: \neg d|\neg c$, $\neg b|\neg a :: c|d$, $\neg a|\neg b :: d|c$, $b|a :: \neg d|\neg c$, $a|b :: \neg c|\neg d$, $\neg b|\neg a :: d|c$, and $\neg a|\neg b :: c|d$. The first 8 proportions are considered in [10], but not the last 8, since they do not satisfy full identity as we shall see in the next section. We use the notation | for all of them, since the conditions that define them are reminiscent of the semantical equivalence between conditional objects. Indeed, it has been advocated in [3] that a rule "if a then b" is a three valued entity that is called 'conditional object' and denoted $b|a$ (true if $a \wedge b$ is true, false if $a \wedge \neg b$ is true, and not applicable if $\neg a$ is true), and where equivalence between two conditional objects $b|a$ and $d|c$ amounts to state that they have the same

---

[1] Although we have been using the term "paralogy" since we introduced this proportion in [9], "parallelogy" could be more accurate for expressing a logic of parallelism between situations (a, b) and (c, d).

examples, i.e. $(a \wedge b) \equiv (c \wedge d))$ and the same counter-examples $(a \wedge \neg b) \equiv (c \wedge \neg d)$. It is worth noticing that such proportions have equivalent forms, e.g.: $b|a :: d|c = \neg b|a :: \neg d|c$, which agrees with the above semantics, and more generally with the idea of conditioning. The next two subfamilies have not been considered before.

The hybrid proportions. They are characterized by equivalences between similarity and dissimilarity indicators in their definitions. They are of the form $(S_i \equiv D'_j) \wedge (S_k \equiv D'_l)$, or $(D_i \equiv S'_j) \wedge (D_k \equiv S'_l)$, or $(S_i \equiv D'_j) \wedge (D_k \equiv S'_l)$, with $i \neq k$ and $j \neq l$, and $i, j, k, l \in \{1, 2\}$.

There are 20 hybrid proportions (2 of the first kind, 2 of the second kind, 16 of the third kind: there are 4 choices for $S_i \equiv D'_j$, and 4 choices for $D_k \equiv S'_l$).

The semi-hybrid proportions. One half of their expressions involve indicators of the same kind, while the other half requires equivalence between indicators of opposite kinds. They are of the form $(S_i \equiv S'_j) \wedge (D_k \equiv S'_l)$ with $j \neq l$, or $(S_i \equiv S'_j) \wedge (S_k \equiv D'_l)$ with $i \neq k$, or $(D_i \equiv D'_j) \wedge (S_k \equiv D'_l)$ with $j \neq l$, or $(D_i \equiv D'_j) \wedge (D_k \equiv S'_l)$ with $i \neq k$, and $i, j, k, l \in \{1, 2\}$.

There are 32 semi-hybrid proportions (8 of each kind: 4 choices for the first equivalence, times 2 choices for the element that is not of the same type as the three others (D or S) in the second equivalence). Let us consider an example: $T(a, b, c, d) = ((a \wedge b) \equiv (c \wedge d)) \wedge ((\neg a \wedge \neg b) \equiv (\neg c \wedge d))$. It can be checked that $T(a, b, c, d)$ is true if and only if $d \equiv (a \equiv b)$ holds and ($c \equiv a$ or $c \equiv b$), due to $(a \equiv b) = (a \wedge b) \vee (\neg a \wedge \neg b)$. This suggests that the semi-hybrid proportions are already partially degenerated.

The degenerated proportions. In all the above categories, the 4 terms related by equivalence symbols should be all distinct. In degenerated proportions, they are only 3 different terms. So, they are of the form, for $i, j, k, l \in \{1, 2\}$,

- $(S_i \equiv S'_j) \wedge (S_i \equiv S'_l)$ with $j \neq l$, or $(S_i \equiv D'_j) \wedge (S_i \equiv D'_l)$ with $j \neq l$, or $(S_i \equiv S'_j) \wedge (S_i \equiv D'_l)$, or
- $(S_i \equiv S'_j) \wedge (S_k \equiv S'_j)$ with $i \neq k$, or $(D_i \equiv S'_j) \wedge (D_k \equiv S'_j)$ with $i \neq k$, or $(S_i \equiv S'_j) \wedge (D_k \equiv S'_j)$, or
- $(D_i \equiv D'_j) \wedge (D_i \equiv D'_l)$ with $j \neq l$, or $(D_i \equiv S'_j) \wedge (D_i \equiv S'_l)$ with $j \neq l$, or $(D_i \equiv D'_j) \wedge (D_i \equiv S'_l)$, or
- $(D_i \equiv D'_j) \wedge (D_k \equiv D'_j)$ with $i \neq k$, or $(S_i \equiv D'_j) \wedge (S_k \equiv D'_j)$ with $i \neq k$, or $(D_i \equiv D'_j) \wedge (S_k \equiv D'_j)$.

There are 48 degenerated proportions (there are 12 proportions for each of the four above dashes: 2 choices in each of the two first expressions, and 8 choices for the third one: 2 choices for the common indicator × 4 combinations for the two other indicators that should be of different types). Note that 8 degenerated proportions are homogeneous in the sense that they involve similarity (or dissimilarity) indicators only. Let us consider one expression of the first three types in the first "-". Their expressions are respectively

- $((a \wedge b) \equiv (c \wedge d)) \wedge ((a \wedge b) \equiv (\neg c \wedge \neg d))$, which is true if and only if $(a \wedge b) \equiv \bot$ and $((c \equiv \bot$ and $d \equiv \top)$ or $(c \equiv \top$ and $d \equiv \bot))$

- $((a \wedge b) \equiv (\neg c \wedge d)) \wedge ((a \wedge b) \equiv (c \wedge \neg d))$, which is true if and only if $(a \wedge b) \equiv \bot$ and $((c \equiv \bot \equiv d)$ or $(c \equiv \top \equiv d))$
- $((a \wedge b) \equiv (c \wedge d)) \wedge ((a \wedge b) \equiv (c \wedge \neg d))$, which is true if and only if $(a \wedge b) \equiv \bot$ and $c \equiv \bot$.

As can be seen, degenerated proportions correspond to mutual exclusiveness conditions between component(s) (and/or negation of component(s)) of one of the pairs (a, b) or (c, d).

2.3 Transformation: Negating One Term in a Proportion

Let us observe that negating anyone of the two terms of a dissimilarity indicator turns it into a similarity indicator, and conversely. From this observation, it follows that changing a into $\neg a$ (and $\neg a$ into a), or applying a similar transformation with respect to b, c, or d, turns

- a degenerated proportion into a degenerated proportion;
- a semi-hybrid proportion into a semi-hybrid proportion;
- an hybrid proportion into an homogeneous or a conditional proportion;
- an homogeneous or a conditional proportion into an hybrid proportion.

This indicates the close relationship of hybrid proportions with homogeneous and conditional proportions. In fact hybrid proportions can be written as homogeneous or as conditional proportions, e.g. $((\neg a \wedge b) \equiv (c \wedge d)) \wedge ((a \wedge b) \equiv (\neg c \wedge d))$ can be written as $\neg a | b :: c | d$.

3 Semantics: Truth Tables of Logical Proportions

It is now time to consider logical proportions from a semantic perspective. Since a, b, c, d are Boolean variables, proportions can be considered as Boolean operators whose semantics is given via their truth tables.

First of all, let us recall the truth table of the 4 core proportions A, P, R, I. It is an easy game to build up these tables that we exhibit in Table 1.

Table 1. Analogy, Reverse analogy, Paralogy, Inverse Paralogy truth tables

A	R	P	I
0 0 0 0	0 0 0 0	0 0 0 0	1 1 0 0
1 1 1 1	1 1 1 1	1 1 1 1	0 0 1 1
0 0 1 1	0 0 1 1	1 0 0 1	1 0 0 1
1 1 0 0	1 1 0 0	0 1 1 0	0 1 1 0
0 1 0 1	0 1 1 0	0 1 0 1	0 1 0 1
1 0 1 0	1 0 0 1	1 0 1 0	1 0 1 0

Note that there are only 8 distinct 4-tuples that appear in Table 1, which go by pairs where 0 and 1 are exchanged. There is one fact immediately appearing when building up these tables: only 6 lines among 16 in the tables have truth value 1, all the remaining lines (not shown here) lead to 0. It can be proved that this is a general result for all logical proportions:

Proposition 2. *The truth table of a logical proportion has 6 and only 6 lines with truth value 1.*

Proof (sketch): By considering patterns of the previous sections that satisfy this property, and then by permutation reasoning over the other ones.   □

Proposition 3. *The truth tables of the 120 proportions are all distinct.*

It appears that despite their similar structure, logical proportions are semantically distinct and then they cover distinct situations. This result may look all the more amazing as our proportions are rather rare. Indeed we know that we have $C_{16}^6 = 16 \times 15 \times 14 \times 13 \times 12 \times 11/6! = 5765760/720 = 8008$ tables with exactly 6 lines leading to 1 but only 120 of them are tables of logical proportions. It has been shown [9] that the three main proportions A, R, P are defined via a set of 3 axioms (see Table 2), describing their characteristic properties. Now, instead of having 3 proportions, we have 120 ones and it is legitimate to consider if they satisfy the A, R, P axioms, or if we have new properties to study.

Table 2. Axioms for Analogy, Reverse analogy and Paralogy

Analogy	Reverse analogy	Paralogy
$A(a,b,a,b)$ (or $A(a,a,b,b)$)	$R(a,b,b,a)$ (or $R(a,a,b,b)$)	$P(a,b,a,b)$ (or $P(a,b,b,a)$)
$A(a,b,c,d) \rightarrow A(a,c,b,d)$	$R(a,b,c,d) \rightarrow R(c,b,a,d)$	$P(a,b,c,d) \rightarrow P(b,a,c,d)$
$A(a,b,c,d) \rightarrow A(c,d,a,b)$	$R(a,b,c,d) \rightarrow R(c,d,a,b)$	$P(a,b,c,d) \rightarrow P(c,d,a,b)$

3.1   Full Identity Axiom

As can be seen in Table 2 A and P satisfy the following axiom: $T(a,b,a,b)$. Obviously, this is not the case for R which satisfies a dual axiom: $T(a,b,b,a)$. When it comes to I, none of these axioms is satisfied.

It appears that a minimal agreement between A, R, P i.e., a common axiom satisfied by these 3 proportions is $T(a,a,a,a)$. This property means that when a, b, c, d involves a unique value (i.e. $a, b, c, d = 1111$ or 0000), then the proportion is satisfied and thus has truth value 1. We call this axiom *full identity* . Obviously I does not satisfy this axiom because of the exchange of the negation operator between pairs (a, b) and (c, d) in the definition. Still this axiom can be considered as intuitively appealing, and it is interesting to identify the proportions that satisfy it. The following result can be established:

Proposition 4. *There are only 15 proportions satisfying full identity: 3 of them are homogeneous (they are A, R, and P), 8 of them are conditional proportions and the 4 remaining ones are degenerated.*

Table 3. The 15 proportions satisfying full identity axiom

$$
\begin{array}{c|c||c|c||c|c}
\bar{a}b \equiv \bar{c}d & a\bar{b} \equiv c\bar{d} & \bar{a}b \equiv c\bar{d} & a\bar{b} \equiv \bar{c}d & ab \equiv cd & \bar{a}\bar{b} \equiv \bar{c}\bar{d} \\
\bar{a}b \equiv \bar{c}d & a\bar{b} \equiv c\bar{d} & \bar{a}\bar{b} \equiv \bar{c}\bar{d} & a\bar{b} \equiv \bar{c}d & ab \equiv c\bar{d} & ab \equiv cd \\
\bar{a}b \equiv \bar{c}d & \bar{a}b \equiv \bar{c}d & \bar{a}b \equiv c\bar{d} & ab \equiv cd & \bar{a}\bar{b} \equiv \bar{c}d & ab \equiv cd \\
\bar{a}b \equiv \bar{c}d & \bar{a}b \equiv c\bar{d} & a\bar{b} \equiv \bar{c}d & ab \equiv cd & a\bar{b} \equiv \bar{c}d & \bar{a}\bar{b} \equiv \bar{c}\bar{d} \\
a\bar{b} \equiv \bar{c}d & a\bar{b} \equiv c\bar{d} & \bar{a}b \equiv c\bar{d} & a\bar{b} \equiv \bar{c}d & \bar{a}b \equiv \bar{c}d & \bar{a}b \equiv cd \\
\end{array}
$$

Table 3 shows these proportions ($\wedge$ are omitted, $\neg x$ is written $\bar{x}$ for a compact notation). A, R, P are on the first line, while degenerated ones are the last four.

Then a new question arises: Are there proportions satisfying only "half" of the full identity axiom, i.e., with truth value 1 for 1111 and 0 for 0000, or vice-versa? We have the following result:

Proposition 5. *There are 30 proportions satisfying 1111 but not 0000. Dually, there are also 30 proportions satisfying 0000 but not 1111.*

Each of the above two categories satisfying "half of full identity" contains 4 hybrid proportions, 12 semi-hybrid ones, and 14 degenerated ones. The four hybrid ones satisfying 1111 are defined by $a\bar{b} \equiv c\bar{d}$ and $\bar{a}b \equiv \bar{c}d$, $a\bar{b} \equiv c\bar{d}$ and $a\bar{b} \equiv \bar{c}d$, $\bar{a}b \equiv \bar{c}d$ and $\bar{a}b \equiv \bar{c}d$, $\bar{a}b \equiv \bar{c}d$ and $a\bar{b} \equiv \bar{c}d$. Thus they correspond to the conditionals $b|\bar{a} :: c|\bar{d}$, $a|\bar{b} :: c|\bar{d}$, $b|\bar{a} :: d|\bar{c}$, $a|\bar{b} :: d|\bar{c}$. The four hybrid ones satisfying 0000 correspond to $\bar{a}|b :: c|d$, $\bar{b}|a :: c|d$, $\bar{a}|b :: d|c$, $\bar{b}|a :: d|c$.

As a consequence of the previous results, there are 45 ($= 120 - 15 - 30 - 30$) proportions that are false for both 1111 and 0000. They include 1 homogeneous proportion (the inverse paralogy), 8 conditional ones, 12 hybrid ones, 8 semi-hybrid ones and 16 degenerated ones. Among hybrid ones, let us mention the presence of the proportions corresponding to analogy (or paralogy) where one literal is negated, such as $\bar{a} : b :: c : d = a ; b :: \bar{c} ; d$.

3.2 Symmetry Axiom

As seen in [9], there is a common axiom satisfied by P, A and R, the so-called *symmetry axiom*: $T(a,b,c,d) \rightarrow T(c,d,a,b)$. This axiom tells us that we can exchange the pair (a,b) with the pair (c,d) in these logical proportions. This is a required property for analogical proportion for instance since if *a is to b as c is to d*, we want to have also that *c is to d as a is to b*. This property holds as well for I, but symmetry is a quite rare property. Indeed, it can be checked that we have the following result:

Proposition 6. *There are only 12 proportions satisfying symmetry axiom. Apart from P, A, I, R (homogeneous proportions), there are 4 conditional proportions and 4 hybrid proportions.*

We exhibit the 4 conditional and the 4 hybrid proportions in Table 4.

This result points out that we have to be careful: despite the definitions of proportions are based on equality between 2 terms (involving negation and conjunction), the symmetrical nature of equality is not sufficient to ensure the symmetry of all logical proportions. Only few of them satisfy the symmetry axiom.

Table 4. The 4 conditional (1st line) and 4 hybrid proportions satisfying symmetry

$$ab = cd \mid \overline{a}b = \overline{c}d \parallel ab = cd \mid a\overline{b} = c\overline{d} \parallel \overline{a}b = \overline{c}d \mid \overline{a}b = \overline{c}d \parallel \overline{a}\overline{b} = \overline{c}\overline{d} \mid a\overline{b} = c\overline{d}$$
$$a\overline{b} = c\overline{d} \mid ab = c\overline{d} \parallel \overline{a}b = cd \mid ab = \overline{c}d \parallel \overline{a}b = \overline{c}d \mid \overline{a}b = \overline{c}d \parallel \overline{a}\overline{b} = c\overline{d} \mid a\overline{b} = \overline{c}d$$

3.3   Code Independency Axiom

Finally, we consider a very important property that we call *code independency*. The main idea underlying this axiom is the fact that, from a semantical viewpoint, a proportion should be independent from the coding convention, i.e., true represented by 1 and false by 0. That is why if we switch the values $(0, 1)$ in the coding of the 4 variables (a, b, c, d), the proportion should lead to the same result. This is formally expressed by the so-called *code independency axiom*:

$$T(a, b, c, d) \rightarrow T(\overline{a}, \overline{b}, \overline{c}, \overline{d})$$

When examining our proportions, we get the following result:

Proposition 7. *There are exactly 8 proportions satisfying the code independency axiom. Apart from the homogeneous proportions P, A, I, R, there are 4 hybrid proportions.*

We exhibit the 4 hybrid proportions in Table 5. It is remarkable that, apart from P, A, I, R which are homogeneous proportions, we get the hybrid proportions simply by adding a negation operator on the right hand-side of the equalities. For instance, the first hybrid one corresponds to the definition of $a \; ; b :: c \; ; \overline{d}$, the second to $a \; ; b :: \overline{c} \; ; d$, the third one to $a : b :: \overline{c} : d$, and the 4th one to $a : b :: c : \overline{d}$. It appears that the code independency property is the most effective "filter" for all the proportions. This results confirms the central role played by the proportions P, A, R and I as the most important ones, enjoying all the properties, and allowing here to simply generate the 4 hybrid proportions satisfying code independency. It remains to see how we could make an effective use of all these proportions. In the following section, we provide some hints on this issue.

Table 5. The 4 hybrid proportions satisfying code independency

$$ab = c\overline{d} \mid \overline{a}\overline{b} = \overline{c}d \parallel ab = \overline{c}d \mid \overline{a}\overline{b} = c\overline{d} \parallel \overline{a}b = cd \mid a\overline{b} = \overline{c}d \parallel a\overline{b} = cd \mid \overline{a}b = \overline{c}d$$

4   Intended Use

As said in the introduction, the idea of a proportion is closely related to the idea of extrapolation. Given an equation of the form $T(a, b, c, x) = 1$, for some logical proportion T, where a, b, c are binary truth values, and $x \in \{0, 1\}$ is unknown, two natural concerns are the existence and the unicity of solutions. First of all, it is easy to see that there are always cases where the equation has no solution. Indeed, the triple a, b, c may take $2^3 = 8$ values, while any proportion T is true only for 6 distinct triples (Proposition 2). For instance, for the analogy $a : b :: c : x$, the condition of existence is $(a \equiv b) \vee (a \equiv c) = 1$ [7], and the (unique) solution, already hinted in [4], is given by $c \equiv (a \equiv b)$.

Regarding the unicity of the solution when it exists, the solution will be always unique for proportions T such that each of the 6 lines of their truth tables starts with a different triple of values for a, b, c. There are 64 proportions that have this property, and 56 proportions for which the equation T(a,b,c,x)=1 may have 2 solutions for some entries. These 56 proportions divide into 8 conditional ones, 8 hybrid ones, 8 semi-hybrid ones, and 32 degenerated ones. Thus, homogeneous proportions P, A, R and I always lead to a unique solution when it exists. Remarkably enough, this is true for half of the conditional ones (e.g., $b|a :: \neg c|\neg d$, which is true for 1100, 1010, 0111, 0101, 0011, 0001), and false for the other half (e.g. $b|a :: d|c$, which is true for 1111, 1010, 0101, 0100, 0001, 0000). This suggests that these two kinds of conditional proportions play different roles, and this has to be further investigated.

Let us envisage now a practical context where we have a set S of data, represented as binary vectors. A new piece of data **d** is considered, but is incompletely specified, i.e., $\mathbf{d} = (0, 1, 1, 0, 1, x)$ and x is unknown. The problem is then to try to complete **d** in a way consistent with the previously observed data in S. The main principle is to consider that, if a proportion T holds for the known features of **d** with respect to completely known data **a**, **b**, **c**, then this proportion should hold for the unknown component of **d** as well. Then, by solving the logical equation, we find a solution for x (when it exists and is unique).

It has been shown in [1,6], that this kind of technique, using only the analogical proportion, can be successfully used for classification purpose. In that case, the missing information for the 4th item d is only its binary class: d is then classified according to analogical patterns extracted from the data at hand. This suggests that, when having more than one pattern available (as it is the case when we use A, P, R, I), alternative solutions may be found, helping to achieve a better accuracy.

5   Conclusion

Beyond our previous work [9,8] initially centered on 3 proportions that can be related to analogy proportion, and then expanded to the 15 proportions satisfying full identity [10], it has appeared that many other options are available for defining new proportions: we have called these proportions, defined via a pair of equivalences, *logical proportions*. These equivalences relate the basic similarity and dissimilarity indicators that can be considered when comparing two states of fact. In this paper, we have provided the first inventory of the 120 existing proportions both through a syntactic typology, and through a semantical classification based on expected properties. Despite the fact that numerous other proportions exhibit interesting properties, only our initial P, A, R proportions satisfy full identity, symmetry and code independency. When relaxing this trio of properties by removing full identity, a new remarkable proportion appears, namely I (for Inverse paralogy). Despite their obvious appeal, these proportions could not be the only ones to provide good induction power. Our 16 conditional proportions, allowing to model exceptions via conditional objects, could be of valuable help for real life induction-oriented applications. Then, it is clear that logical proportions, which apparently have never been considered before in spite of their conceptual simplicity, have to be further investigated. We have indicated that these proportions may be used to complete an existing pattern, taking into account some regularities with respect to an existing set of data, then paving the way to a machine learning technique, similar in nature to the well known k-nearest neighbor technique, but offering many more options. Finally, let us also mention another line of research worth investigating: one may think of associating measures to these proportions. First, for a systematic study of graded proportions based on similarity/dissimilarity indexes, such as the ones built from the contrast model proposed by Tversky [12] where the same similarity and dissimilarity indicators appear. Besides, we may also consider to associate uncertainty measures (such as possibility or probability) to the similarity and dissimilarity indexes involved in the equivalences defining the proportions [2].

References

1. Bayoudh, S., Miclet, L., Delhay, A.: Learning by analogy: A classification rule for binary and nominal data. In: Proc. IJCAI '07, pp. 678–683 (2007)
2. Dubois, D., Fargier, H., Prade, H.: Possibilistic likelihood relations. In: Proc. 7th IPMU'98, Paris, pp. 1196–1202 (1998)
3. Dubois, D., Prade, H.: Conditional objects as nonmonotonic consequence relationships. IEEE Trans. on Systems, Man and Cybernetics 24, 1724–1740 (1994)
4. Klein, S.: Culture, mysticism & social structure and the calculation of behavior. In: Proc. Europ. Conf. in Artificial Intelligence (ECAI), pp. 141–146 (1982)
5. Lepage, Y.: Analogy and formal languages. In: Proc. FG/MOL 2001, pp. 373–378 (2001) (in French), http://www.slt.atr.cos.jp/lepage/pdf/dhdryl.pdf.gz
6. Miclet, L., Bayoudh, S., Delhay, A.: Analogical dissimilarity: definition, algorithms and two experiments in machine learning. JAIR 32, 793–824 (2008)
7. Miclet, L., Prade, H.: Handling analogical proportions in classical logic and fuzzy logics settings. In: Sossai, C., Chemello, G. (eds.) ECSQARU 2009. LNCS, vol. 5590, pp. 638–650. Springer, Heidelberg (2009)
8. Prade, H., Richard, G.: Analogical proportions: another logical view. In: Nicholson, A., Li, X. (eds.) AI 2009. LNCS, vol. 5866, Springer, Heidelberg (2009)
9. Prade, H., Richard, G.: Analogy, paralogy and reverse analogy: Postulates and inferences. In: Mertsching, B., Hund, M., Aziz, Z. (eds.) KI 2009. LNCS (LNAI), vol. 5803, pp. 306–314. Springer, Heidelberg (2009)
10. Prade, H., Richard, G.: Reasoning with logical proportions. In: Proc. Int. Conf. on Principles of Knowledge Representation and Reasoning (KR'10), Toronto (2010)
11. Stroppa, N., Yvon, F.: Analogical learning and formal proportions: Definitions and methodological issues. ENST Paris report (2005)
12. Tversky, A.: Features of similarity. Psychological Review 84, 327–352 (1977)

Author Index

Printed in the United States
By Bookmasters